THE WPA GUIDE
TO CALIFORNIA

Also available from Pantheon Books

★

THE WPA GUIDE TO FLORIDA

With a New Introduction by John McCollum
0-394-72293-0   *$11.95 (paperback)*

★

THE WPA GUIDE TO ILLINOIS

*With a New Introduction by Neil Harris
and Michael Conzen*
0-394-72195-0   *$9.95 (paperback)*

★

THE WPA GUIDE TO MASSACHUSETTS

With a New Introduction by Jane Holtz Kay
0-394-71581-0   *$9.95 (paperback)*

★

THE WPA GUIDE TO NEW ORLEANS

*With a New Introduction by
the Historic New Orleans Collection*
0-394-71588-8   *$8.95 (paperback)*

★

THE WPA GUIDE TO NEW YORK

With a New Introduction by William H. Whyte
0-394-71215-3   *$8.95 (paperback)*

★

THE WPA GUIDE TO WASHINGTON, D.C.

With a New Introduction by Roger G. Kennedy
0-394-72192-6   *$8.95 (paperback)*

THE WPA GUIDE
TO CALIFORNIA

THE FEDERAL WRITERS' PROJECT
GUIDE TO 1930s CALIFORNIA

WITH A NEW INTRODUCTION
BY GWENDOLYN WRIGHT

*Written and compiled
by the Federal Writers' Project
of the Works Progress Administration
for the State of California*

PANTHEON BOOKS · NEW YORK

Introduction Copyright © 1984 by Gwendolyn Wright
Copyright 1939 by Mabel R. Gillis, California State Librarian

Library of Congress Cataloging in Publication Data

California.
The WPA guide to California.

Reprint. Originally published: California. New York:
Hastings House, 1939. (American guide series)
Bibliography: p.
Includes index.
1. California—Description and travel—1865-1950—
Guide-books. I. Federal Writers' Project. II. Title.
III. Title: The W.P.A. guide to California.
F859.3.C24 1984   917.94'0453   83-43163
ISBN 0-394-72290-6

Display design by Naomi Osnos

Manufactured in the United States of America

First Pantheon Paperback Edition

WORKS PROGRESS ADMINISTRATION

F. C. HARRINGTON, ADMINISTRATOR
FLORENCE S. KERR, ASSISTANT ADMINISTRATOR
HENRY G. ALSBERG, DIRECTOR OF THE FEDERAL WRITERS' PROJECT

Preface

California has so great a diversity of places and people and things that the problem of getting it between the covers of a single book seemed almost unsolvable. The final preparation of this guide has involved the difficult task of choosing between what to put in and what to leave out. The staff of the Federal Writers' Project in California knows that its own trials in gathering, checking and rechecking, assembling, and selecting the thousands of items that go into the making of a guide book have been shared by the editors of the forty-seven other State books in the American Guide Series. But in the course of eliminating more words than there are in these pages, the California staff has sometimes wished that its State were just a little smaller, so that it might be described in more detail.

And yet there is more in this book than the editors thought it could possibly include; for, although the distance between the borders of Oregon and Mexico is more miles than they like to think about, they have covered every mile. The book, moreover, has been written to be read, not only by those to whom California is still an unseen and fabulous land of sunshine and oranges, but also by those who will look in these pages for something new and little-known about the everyday California in which they live and work. For readers of both kinds, visitors and residents, the editors have tried to make this book a true mirror of the State and its people. Romance has been kept in its place —Joaquin Murrieta does not jump out from behind *every* tree or boulder in California to hold up travelers, and yet he does pop up often enough that the observant reader will have little trouble finding him.

The editors wish to acknowledge their indebtedness to the work of others who have preceded them in describing California, and especially to *California, an Intimate Guide* by Aubrey Drury, *Rider's California; A Guidebook for Travelers* by Fremont Rider, and *Historic Spots in California* by H. E. and E. G. Rensch and Mildred Brooke Hoover.

The California staff gratefully acknowledges the aid of Federal, State, and local governmental agencies, and of commercial and civic associations and automobile clubs. Particular appreciation is due the staffs of the Bancroft and State Libraries, for their cooperation.

v

Among the many individuals to whom the editors wish to express their gratitude for generous aid in special fields are: Herbert E. Bolton, Will G. Corlett, Richard Down, Alfred Frankenstein, Louis J. Gill, Florence Hagee, Norman E. A. Hinds, Paul Robinson Hunter, Rupert Hughes, Olaf Jenkins, William Templeton Johnson, Idwal Jones, William Knowles, R. B. Koeber, A. L. Kroeber, Grace L. McCann Morely, Richard S. Requa, C. J. Ryland, Carl Sauer, Windsor Soule, W. L. Stephenson, George R. Stewart, Jr., Hilmuth Ulmer, T. K. Whipple, Lloyd Yoder, and finally the sponsor, Mabel R. Gillis, State Librarian, for her interest and gracious advice.

Field supervision from the Washington office of the Federal Writers' Project was done by Clair Laning, Assistant National Director.

JAMES HOPPER, *State Director for Northern California*
LEON DORAIS, *State Director for Southern California*

Editorial Staff

FOR NORTHERN CALIFORNIA:

PAUL C. JOHNSON, *Assistant State Director*
WALTER McELROY, *State Editorial Supervisor*
MARGARET WILKINS, *State Editorial Supervisor*
MIRIAM ALLEN DEFORD   NAHUM SABSAY
S. S. GREENLEAF   AMY SCHECHTER
ROBIN KINKEAD   DOROTHY DONN WAGNER
CORA VERNON LEE   CARL WILHELMSON
KENNETH REXROTH   THEODORE BARON (*photographs*)

FOR SOUTHERN CALIFORNIA:

KENNETH BOLLEY, *Editorial Supervisor*
ROBERT C. BROWNELL, *Editorial Supervisor*
HARRY PARTCH   FRANCIS WOODWORTH

FOR THE FEDERAL ART PROJECT, NORTHERN CALIFORNIA:

SONYA SITOMER   CHARLES SURENDORF

Acknowledgments are also due to the many other persons on the Federal Writers' Project who faithfully aided in the gathering and preparation of material for this book.

Contents

Part I. California: From Past to Present

Part II. Signposts to City Scenes

Part III. Up and Down the State

Part IV. Appendices

Illustrations

Maps

Introduction by Gwendolyn Wright

The WPA Guide to California begins and ends with a vision of El Dorado. The first is the historical myth which lured the early Spanish explorers, that of an uncharted land rich with gold and exotic spices. This legend of a supremely bountiful natural setting has endured over the centuries, undergoing numerous transformations.

The concluding image is that of an urban El Dorado, captured in the 1939 Golden Gate Exposition in San Francisco. This "Magic City" commemorated the completion of the Bay Bridge (1936) and the Golden Gate Bridge (1937), at the time the two longest bridge spans in the world, linking San Francisco with the predominantly residential counties to the north and east. The exposition conjured up an urban splendor through its blend of stylized, pseudo-historical architecture from non-Western cultures, including Malayan, Incan, and Cambodian forms. Iridescent paints and thousands of floodlights accentuated the powerful shapes of the buildings, creating the illusion of a metropolis at once ancient and contemporary, diverse and unified. The "Jewel City" embodied an ideal of California's major cities that still endures: a sense of marvelous fantasy and excitement. This urban ideal, like that of the arcadian El Dorado, has helped draw tourists to the state, and those who believe they can indeed find something uniquely fulfilling in this magical place often choose to remain.

The myth that has symbolized America for the rest of the world has found its ultimate expression here. Americans consider this state a land of exceptional opportunities, both urban and rural, personal and social. A desire for dramatic change is at the heart of California's appeal. The California dream implies a break from the constraints of the East Coast, a divine inspiration from nature, and a willingness to be daringly innovative. Observers of the state—especially those who chose to stay—have seen limitless possibilities for individual expression and, in many cases, opportunities for social transformation.

Yet there is a darker side to this belief in redemption and fulfillment. The minority groups who have been branded as obstacles to this dream of perfection have repeatedly faced discrimination and even violence. *The WPA Guide*, with all of its appreciation for the lure of California, also describes anti-Chinese riots near Eureka's famous Carson House and vigilante attacks against mine workers seeking to unionize in Grass Valley and Nevada City, close to what was once the country's second largest gold mine.

One of the accomplishments of this Writers' Project guide is its balanced synthesis of the potentials and problems of California in the 1930s. The tone rings with great enthusiasm, yet there is a consistent recognition of those who have been left out or abused by the forces of progress. The guide makes an appeal for an even more generous vision of California, one that provides equally for all races and all classes of people.

Visiting California a few years after the guide was published, journalist Samuel Grafton noted the blend of idealism, industrial expansion, and political tensions wherever he traveled in the state. In Los Angeles he mused presciently upon:

> a hungry and questing crowd, strangely like California itself, which is a questing sort of state, ever on tip-toe to peep into the future. This great coast sees itself in the future as the trade corridor between East and West. It likes that grand vision. But at the same time a good many Californians have an unreasonable private wish for peace and quiet, for fewer invasions by either the farm-hungry people of Asia or job-hungry people of Oklahoma, Arkansas, and Texas.

The men and women working for the Writers' Project captured an extraordinary moment of self-consciousness about the state's past, its future, and its present—the California of the thirties, caught between the dilemmas of the Depression and the fear of war. They offer a potpourri of historical bravado and sociological data; they portray human diversity and rapacity, artistic creativity and industrial productivity—to which workers and businessmen, farmers and Indians, rich and poor, all contributed.

The need for a Federal Writers' Project emerged early in the Depression, when out-of-work poets, novelists, and journalists picketed to demand federal aid. Poet Marianne Moore had first suggested the preparation of guidebooks and state histories as possible Emergency Civil Works Administration jobs for unemployed writers. The automobile had created a demand for such books, she contended, and existing guides dealt only with major cities. The original plan, funded by the Works Progress Administration (WPA) in 1935, anticipated five regional guides, with an allotment of $6,288,000 for 6,500 staff people. This was quickly changed to a state-by-state series, in part to assure support from prominent state and local politicians.

Over the next seven years, the Writers' Project underwent frenetic changes. There were cutbacks, then increased subsidies; permissive recruiting policies followed by obligatory loyalty oaths when the Writers' Project was charged with harboring a predominantly Communist staff. Finally, in 1942, the "biggest literary project in history" was terminated, having spent a total of $27,189,370. The California staffs had produced a greater number of publications than any other state's, including separate book-length guides to San Francisco, Los Angeles, San Diego, Santa Barbara, the Monterey Peninsula, and Death Valley, as well as this volume, then called *Guide to the Golden State.*

The Federal Writers' Project, like the broader Works Progress Administration, acknowledged the fiscal and cultural needs of American artists and intellectuals, and recognized their value to the nation. Both the northern and the southern branches of the California Writers' Project employed a number of bright young writers who desperately needed an income: poets Kenneth Rexroth, Kenneth Patchen, Raymond Larsson, Madeline Gleason, and Harvey Breit; screenwriter Carl Foreman; and novelists Tillie Olsen, Leon Dorais, Nahum Sabsay (a Russian refugee), and Eluard Luchell McDaniel (a black writer who left the Project to join the Abraham Lincoln Brigade in Spain). Perhaps the most versatile writer was Miriam Allen de Ford, a San Francisco poet, novelist, labor journalist, and social historian.

This ambitious, non-exclusive enterprise employed talented professionals and non-professionals to produce a work that is still compelling and interesting. It is difficult to attribute particular sections to a given author, since WPA administrators insisted upon a general policy of anonymity. Nonetheless, there are individual voices and concerns expressed within the framework of this collective enterprise. They raise social and political issues that are still relevant, and they describe fascinating, little-known places throughout the state.

Opposition to the Project came mostly from the press and Congress, concerning the issue of Communists within the California staffs. A few party members did work in both the northern and southern California offices, but, rather than attacking the American way of life, the predominant tone of the writing evokes sympathy for the New Deal and for Roosevelt's "forgotten man."

In some cases the guide's commitment to egalitarianism came from the editorial staff in Washington, who insisted that all guides acknowledge historical and contemporary discrimination against racial and ethnic minorities. At Washington's direction, the guide discusses the vast Catholic church holdings worked by Indian converts during Spanish rule, and the 1910 bombing of the *Lost Angeles Times* building—an event that, the writers declare, certainly harmed the Socialist movement in the United States since it was unjustly held responsible. A few writers were particularly interested in these topics. Thus the guide includes selections from Tillie Olsen's life stories and folk songs of Mexicans, Filipinos, and Slavs, and Miriam de Ford's coverage of the rise of Harry Bridges and the 1937 longshoremen's strike on the San Francisco docks.

The focus of national administrators on the problematic present of each state, as well as its illustrious past, constituted a revolution in the field of guidebooks. While the maze of instructions emanating from Washington often annoyed the writers, these guidelines generally emphasized a "restrained and dignified" style, particularly in the index of hackneyed phrases and untenable attributions of local "firsts." The directors insisted on the value and diversity of American culture, and the California guide conveys this commitment remarkably well. When the guide discussed industrial growth, it described people at work. There are portraits of Japanese divers on the Monterey docks searching for abalone along the rocks, and of the artists of illusion in the prop and make-up sections of the early Hollywood studios.

Essays on art and architecture were featured as a way of awakening the American public to the merit of their indigenous architecture and local artists. Writers on architecture stressed plan, structure, and idea rather than the style of the façade; they juxtaposed Richard Neutra's experimental schools in Los Angeles or Timothy Pflueger's commercial buildings in San Francisco with vernacular architecture ranging from bridges and factories to bungalows and movie theaters.

The guide stressed the state's recurring explosions in population, a phenomenon that has continued to inform public policies and alter environments to this day. Periods defined by particularly promising or catastrophic events witnessed the most dramatic increases and the greatest changes. The earliest surge of American in-migration was the Gold Rush of 1849, when people from all parts of the country dropped their jobs and came west to try their luck. Fraternal lodges and Wells Fargo offices still survive in the towns of the Mother Lode along Route 49, described in Tour 4. The next surge came with the southern California real estate boom of the 1880s, when the orange groves and suburbs of Glendora, Monrovia, and Arcadia sprang up outside Los Angeles. Then the calamitous Dust Bowl of the 1930s brought cars and trains filled with desperate families who had lost their farms in Texas and Oklahoma. When the cities sought to outlaw these newcomers, they moved into the Central Valley towns to dry grapes on huge squares of brown paper in Selma or pick dates in Ceres. Details of their varied work and the communities they formed are brought to life in a tour through the center of the state.

Since the publication of the guide, migration from other parts of the country has continued to have an enormous impact on California. Each of the Pacific wars has increased the state's population. Just after World War II the Bureau of the Census reported with "a shock of recognition" that California had gained three million new residents between 1940 and 1947. The Korean War and the Vietnam War also added significant numbers to the census rolls. The World War I and II "Arsenals of Democracy" in Oakland, San Francisco, Richmond, and San Pedro continue to produce equipment and house military installations, now augmented by new installations in Long Beach, Los Angeles, and San Diego.

As weapons of warfare have grown more advanced, so has the training of the Californians who design and build them. During the twenty-five years following the end of World War II, the number of technical and professional workers has increased by over 200 percent, five times the rate on the East Coast. Specializing in the fast-growing fields of micro-electronics

and computers, these new technicians have helped develop modern equipment for domestic industry and aerospace, as well as military materiel.
While the rest of the country has grappled with a recession in recent times,
California has recorded banner years in these industries and in the state's
other major economic bases: entertainment, tourism, and agribusiness.

The fact that California, long the nation's top agricultural producer, is
now, in addition, its leading industrial power and entertainment center has
altered both the rural and urban landscapes, but many of the recent
changes and their economic causes were anticipated in the guide. San
Francisco's financial district offers a dense panorama of twentieth-century
documentation of this evolution. Looking from the old Ferry Building
(1906) to Pflueger's Telephone Building (1923) (both noted in the section
on that city) to Johnson/Burgee's multifaceted glass prism at 101 California
(a 1983 office building for Houston developer Gerald D. Hines), one sees
the shift from local entrepreneurs to corporate giants. Commercial interests
now wield power on a national and even international scale. This trend is
epitomized in the 52-story, granite-clad headquarters (built in 1971) of
what has been, since 1945, the country's largest commercial bank, the Bank
of America. Nearby are the offices of the nation's six largest savings and
loan associations and the headquarters of the largest construction engineering
firm in the world, the Bechtel Corporation.

Compared to the 1930s downtown described in these pages, there is a
decided paucity of public space in this architectural showcase of economic
power. Lotta's Fountain and several stately hotels remain, but the days of
workers' fairs and temporary housing for the homeless in now staid Union
Square have passed away. Unlike earlier monuments to commercial and cultural glory—structures like the Palace Hotel, the Montgomery Block, and
the Municipal Opera House (later the War Memorial) in the Civic Center
—most of the new office towers do not seek to represent the city as a whole;
they are individual symbols of corporate might, not of San Franciscans'
civic pride.

Southern California bears witness to the boom in the filmmaking and
recording industries, which were already thriving in the 1930s. As with the
earlier industrial growth in Los Angeles, the new industries are relatively
dispersed, although Hollywood still displays the greatest presence of icons
to stardom. The round Capital Records Tower of 1954 and ubiquitous
billboards promoting new record releases stand alongside the more fanciful
monuments of the film industry's first heydey in the 1920s. Grauman's
Chinese Theatre, the Egyptian Theatre, and the Brown Derby restaurant,
where stars and film moguls stood out against extravagantly fanciful architecture, are all described with wit and pride in this *WPA Guide*.

The principal expansion in the new high-tech industries has occurred outside the cities, where slick, well-landscaped, low-rise buildings for research
and production are just a short walk from the car and a short drive from
the house or apartment complex. Southern Orange County is now home of

the immense Fluor Corporation, housed in a futuristic building visible from the San Diego Freeway, on land that was once agricultural, bordering on national forests. Even more extensive is the Silicon Valley, between San Francisco and San Jose; in a few decades the lush farmland we read about here in the guide was transformed into a world center for electronics research.

Nearby Stanford University provides well-trained engineers for these industries. This business-university partnership became characteristic of California in the 1930s. The guide notes the trend, pointing in particular to research patterns at the California Institute of Technology in Pasadena, where geological and now aerodynamic research has strong corporate affiliations, and at the University of California at Berkeley, where strong governmental ties have resulted in three major nuclear laboratories.

The phenomenal growth of California's technological industries has helped change the character of the American newcomers to the state. Many of them are already wealthy, without the worries that troubled earlier groups. As often as not, they are transferred to California, rather than choosing to risk going on their own. It is surprising, then, that the latest flock exhibits many of the same preoccupations as its predecessors. The guide describes among the new Californians of the thirties a boundless enthusiasm for the outdoors, a fanaticism about personal health, and a fascination with technological innovation that sound altogether contemporary. While each wave of hopeful new Californians has come with a dream of individual economic success, it has also tended to share a common vision of the good society and a preoccupation with personal improvement.

California's growth has involved different races of immigrants in radically divergent ways, and the writers of the guide addressed the issues raised by prejudice. They wrote openly about attacks on Orientals brought over to build the railroads and about the extreme poverty of Mexican migrant laborers. The racial problems they described have by no means disappeared; in fact, the same pattern of ethnic neighborhoods and occupational stratification exists today for most minority groups, even as their numbers keep expanding. West Oakland and the Watts neighborhood of Los Angeles were then and are still the major black ghettos—typically California ghettos, distinct in appearance from those of East Coast cities. The railroads that once provided jobs for thousands of black workers have markedly declined, but the Victorian cottages and trim bungalows from those days—and the poverty of their inhabitants—are still present.

The Chinatowns and Japantowns depicted in the guide also remain. In fact, Asian immigration soared after 1965, when Congress lifted its quota system, which had been based on national origin. In an eighteen-block core area, San Francisco's Chinatown now houses 40,000 people, of whom 40 percent are estimated to be living in poverty. The guide devotes several pages to this area, including a discussion of the joss house and the Chinese Telephone Exchange on Washington Street—where the operators were required to know five dialects and to memorize the numbers of 2,300 subscribers, since most Chinese called by name and not by number.

The Mexican community is also poignantly described. The great migration from Mexico to the Southwest (after that of the seventeenth century) had begun in the 1920s, for the immigration laws, which then severely restricted entry for Orientals, placed no limits on Mexicans. In 1939, with a community of 103,000 Mexicans living in slums around the downtown Plaza, Los Angeles was already the fifth largest "Mexican city" in the world. Today Hispanics comprise almost half the population of that city.

Then as now, the greatest number of *braceros* ("strong-armed ones") crossed over the border legally or illegally to do manual labor in the agricultural valleys. In 1962, based in the San Joaquin Valley town of Delano, César Chávez organized the predominantly Mexican laborers into the National Farm Workers Association. Three years later, 500,000 Chicano farmworkers joined unionized Filipino grape pickers in a massive strike; the cries of *"Viva la Huelga!"* (long live the strike) gained support for a three-year national boycott against table grapes, eventually resulting in state legislation to protect the union and improve the lot of the migrant workers. Here, too, the guide points out important antecedents to contemporary events, describing a 1934 strike by 8,000 Mexican lettuce workers in El Centro. With support from urban unions and from national newspapers, as violence against them spread, they too won some concessions from the owners.

The plight of the migrant farmworkers represents but one aspect of a larger economic and political phenomenon, also noticed by the guide's authors: the growth of agribusiness. By 1959, 6 percent of all California farms controlled 75 percent of the land under cultivation, but the trend toward such concentrations had already become apparent in the giant farms of the 1930s. The increasingly corporate definition of the state, so evident in the cities, could also be seen in rural areas and in many small towns. Agribusiness shaped the model dairy and experimental fields at the Davis College of Agriculture, one of the small schools described in these pages. Today a branch of the University of California, Davis undertakes research projects to aid the state's agriculture interests, notably the development of mechanized tomato picking and hard, tasteless tomatoes.

Even more costly has been the ongoing investment in massive water projects to irrigate formerly parched farming areas. Most of California's water is located far from both its urban populations and its prime agricultural lands, and this has resulted in a history of water wars characterized by bribery, deception, and enormous profit. In an effort to promote small family farms, the Newlands Act of 1902 limited the amount of water one owner could obtain from federal reclamation projects; yet the gigantic agribusiness farms of the Central Valley and the southern Imperial Valley still receive cheap, publicly subsidized water without diminishing their holdings. As the guide points out, campaigns to bring water to the cities also led to inequities. The once fertile Owens River Valley was drained of its water, and thus its farming, in 1913, but the water never reached Los Angeles. Instead it stopped at the San Fernando Valley—vacant land that clever entrepreneurs annexed at just the right time so that they could turn around and sell it at $1,000 an acre. Behind all these stories lies the vast complex of dams, aqueducts, and pumping stations described in the guide. The authors who covered the back country recognized both the corruption and the technological splendor of the state's water system.

The Writers' Project presented an integrated portrait of the state in the late 1930s, tying north to south, urban metropolis to rural farmlands; linking architecture and town planning to economics and social history. The essays and the touring sections emphasize the interconnectedness of the state, not only for the traveler, but also for the businessman, the conservationist, and the labor union leader. The tours stress this statewide perspective by proceeding along cardinal axes from the borders inward, rather than emanating from the urban centers—an approach designed to favor the automobile tourist while giving all parts of the state equal time.

Staff writers were required to cover every mile of highway and foot trail in search of interesting material. And they found it. One learns that the northern fishing town of Pescadero, near Pigeon Point (an excellent source of oysters), became the whitest town in the state after its residents salvaged a huge cargo of white paint from an offshore wreck. Victorville, near the New Mexico border, was an old mining town with quaint, false-front frontier buildings that caught the attention of early moviemakers, who used the town and its "Wild West" back country as the locale for more than two hundred films between 1914 and 1937. Descriptions of hot mineral springs, fossils in Pleistocene caves, and lavender-and-gray desert landscapes complement accounts of simple white courthouses, bandstands, and West Hollywood bungalow courts. There is an appreciation of novelty and innovation: the Chicken Pharmacy in Petaluma, the town where artificial incubation was invented; the Sikh Temple in rural Stockton; Fresno's campaign to sell tiny packages of raisins to the Chinese, who, it was said, believed that eating raisins ensured the birth of male children. But most of all one finds a love for the California landscape in its many variations, for artichoke fields and pine forests, coastline and mountains, culminating in a special tour section devoted to the national parks as they were in the late 1930s, when it was possible to take a 25¢ taxi ride from the Yosemite ranger station or hotels to the start of the trails.

Poet Kenneth Rexroth's descriptions of the national parks—their forests, lakes, and deserts—are some of the most beautifully written passages in the guide. Detailed data about indigenous trees, mosses, wildflowers, and animals are interspersed with picturesque portraits of farm hamlets, fishing villages, and coastal promontories. The guide's authors were particularly concerned about natural conservation and expressed indignant anger over the ecological destruction brought about by water-relocation projects, mining, and residential overbuilding. The conflict between industrial and agribusiness interests on the one hand and conservationists on the other continues to rage today, for the loyalties divided between preserving and exploiting the state's superb natural resources run deep.

Much has changed since 1939, often for the worse. Monterey's Cannery Row has become a prettified tourist attraction rather than a viable fishery, and so has San Francisco's Fisherman's Wharf, where Italian fishermen wearing large gold earrings once mended their nets in their bright blue boats, or boiled crabs in huge iron cauldrons on the curbside. The hills above Daly City, just south of San Francisco, are no longer covered with fields of lettuce, artichokes, pansies, and violets, but now sprout rows of tract houses.

Yet many of contemporary California's idiosyncrasies were already present and recognized in 1939. The incidence of communes and religious cults, for example, is by no means a phenomenon limited to the 1960s. The guide describes Aimee Semple McPherson's Angelus Temple in Los Angeles, which opened in 1923. Her prayer tower beamed out continual radio messages on the "Four-Square Gospel" and patriotism, and the temple's domed auditorium accommodated 5,300 people. They listened to McPherson's dramatic sermons while sitting under an enormous mural depicting Christ's Second Coming—to America, that is, as evidenced by the gigantic American flag celebrating the event. There is an account of the Klamath Shakers, a group of Indians who performed a frenzied ghost dance in their barnlike church; and of the San Jose Rosicrucians, whose Egyptian Museum still provides an extraordinary collection of artifacts. The authors also describe the Kaweah Co-Operative Commonwealth, which sought to establish a collectivized lumber town in what was quickly made Sequoia National Park; this group vowed never to cut the giant trees, and named the outstanding ones after heroes of the Paris Commune and American socialism, honoring the largest as the Karl Marx Tree. In 1978, according to Mark Satin's *New Age Politics*, fully one-third of America's spiritual, political, and other "alternative" groups were concentrated in California. But, as the guide makes clear, the precedent extends back for generations.

Educational communities also began to expand dramatically in the 1930s, and campuses are a prominent feature of the guide. The year after its publication, the University of California at Berkeley became the nation's largest university. Freshmen then wore distinctive "beanies" and smoked only corncob pipes on campus, but many of the buildings where they attended class still remain, and the characteristically beautiful landscaping of the state univerities, state colleges, and various private colleges (University of the Redlands, Mills College, Whittier College) still merits the attention given it here. Since the guide's publication, the postwar construction boom in California higher education has produced impressive modern campuses—notably that of Santa Cruz, based on the models of an English college system and an

Italian hill town, set on a dramatic site along the Pacific coast. At private universities and colleges, state colleges, and junior colleges, a combination of luxuriant landscape and scholarship remains characteristic.

Education is a larger matter than universities, of course. The Los Angeles Public Library, with its "outdoor reading rooms" and WPA murals inside, achieved the largest circulation among American libraries in the 1930s. Scholars visited the Huntington Library in San Marino, mingling with visitors to its museum and magnificent gardens. In the generation since, the Salk Institute in La Jolla and the Stanford Research Institute in Palo Alto continue to provide specialized facilities in settings that combine beautiful sites with dramatic modern architecture.

Entertainment facilities have increased in size and in scale of fantasy since the 1930s, and the state's cultural life has shifted from San Francisco —still "the City" in 1939—to southern California. It is there one finds the Los Angeles County Museum of Art (1964) and the J. Paul Getty Museum (1974), the world's wealthiest cultural institution, housed in a replica of a Herculaneum villa near the surfers' paradise of Malibu.

Both northern and southern California have seized upon major-league sports as popular entertainment, building such giant stadiums as the Oakland Coliseum and Stadium (1964), San Francisco's chilly Candlestick Park (1960), and Dodger Stadium (1962) and the Forum (1967) in Los Angeles. These complexes suggest how much sports has changed since 1939, when the guide noted where to find public swimming pools, archery ranges, fishing piers, and playgrounds, and the spectator sports of interest were primarily wrestling, boxing, and neighborhood baseball. And all were rowdy events.

Accommodating the state's new residents and moving its tourists from one place to another has continually posed transportation problems. A year after the *WPA Guide* first appeared, the Arroyo Seco Parkway, now more commonly known as the Pasadena Freeway, inaugurated freeway driving. Since World War II, freeway construction has expanded throughout the state, particularly in and around Los Angeles. In addition, San Francisco installed its expensive public transportation system, BART (Bay Area Rapid Transit), in 1972. Since then it has resulted in some exceptionally handsome stations, and some exceptionally hostile commentary about poor service and private financial gain in the fourteen communities it now serves.

While the state gas tax has given us a pervasive network of freeways, and local bonds have built subterranean transit systems, the roads followed by the Writers' Project remain, and they are by far the most interesting routes for travel. The *Guide to the Golden State* was designed to encourage the exploration of California and to promote an appreciation of its natural beauty, its history, and its diversity. Reading through these pages and following the routes they describe reinforce the notion that California is simultaneously movement and reflection. It offers a perpetual combination of entertainment and education, natural beauty and varied architecture, a rich compost that continues to be the essence of the state.

General Information

Railroads: Southern Pacific Lines (SP), Western Pacific R.R. (Feather River Route), Northwestern Pacific R.R., Great Northern Ry., Atchison, Topeka & Santa Fe Ry. (Santa Fe), Sacramento Northern Ry., Union Pacific R.R. (overland Route).

Highways: Network of State highways and good country roads cover the State. Highway patrol to safeguard traffic and enforce regulations. Inspection at State Lines.

Bus Lines: Burlington Lines, Greyhound Lines, Santa Fe Trailways, Union Pacific Stages, Inland Stages, and Feather River Stages.

Air Lines: American Airlines, Inc., Pan American Airways Co., Transcontinental & Western Air Inc. (TWA), United Air Lines, Western Air Express. Los Angeles and San Francisco are terminals for transcontinental lines, San Francisco (Alameda Field) for the Pan American Airways service to Hawaii and the Philippines.

Waterways: Scheduled services to Alaska and Mexico, from San Francisco to Oregon and Washington, and from San Francisco to Sacramento.

Trails: The Pacific Crest Trail traverses the main divides of the highest mountain ranges in the three Pacific states. There are five sections of this trail in California: Lava Crest Trail, 330 miles; Tahoe Yosemite Trail, 260 miles; John Muir Trail, 185 miles; Sierra Trail, 160 miles; and Desert Crest Trail, 475 miles. All trails are open in July and Aug.; the southern trails from May through November. For information address Clinton C. Clark, President of the Pacific Crest Trail System Conference, 125 S. Grand Ave., Pasadena, Calif.

Traffic Regulations: Speed: 15 miles per hour at grade crossings, road intersections, and curves where the driver's view is obstructed; 15 miles per hour in passing schools where persons are entering or leaving; 20 miles per hour in business districts; 25 miles per hour in residential districts; 45 miles per hour under all other conditions.

Lights: Spotlights allowed. Headlights to be deflected or dimmed when passing other cars on the open road.

Licenses: Nonresidents must have operator's license from their home States and must obtain visitors' permits for their vehicles within 5 days. Licenses issued to adults, no fee; to minors 16 to 21 yrs. of age, with parental liability.
Required: Hand signals must be used. All accidents must be reported to some civic authority (police department in cities and towns). On narrow mountain roads the upgrade vehicle has the right-of-way. Prohibited: Coasting in neutral, parking on highways, passing streetcars on left (in cities and towns), passing on curves or at crests of hills.

Trailers: All highways in State suitable for house and camp trailers, except steep and unimproved mountain roads. State and National parks, and trailer parks in some towns, have special facilities for trailers. Trailers are licensed according to weight. (*For city ordinance governing trailers see Cities.*)

Border Rules (digest): All persons returning to the United States from Mexico must make a declaration to the customs officers covering all goods and merchandise purchased in Mexico. Articles for personal or household use, up to the value of $100, are exempt from import duty. Exemption is allowed each person not more often than every 30 days. Cigars, cigarettes, tobacco, and foodstuffs may be included in the exemption, but the quantities are limited. American citizens wishing to visit any place farther south than Ensenada, or in the interior of Mexico, must obtain a tourist card (*cost $1.01 in U. S. currency*) from the nearest Mexican consul, or from the Mexican Immigration Office at the port of entry.

Accommodations: State is well provided with hotels, lodges, motor courts, housekeeping cabins, and campgrounds, both public and private. Recreation areas have large resort hotels, swimming pools, golf courses, tennis courts, and well-equipped campgrounds. State and National park campgrounds are equipped with necessary conveniences.

Regulations in Parks and Monuments: U. S. Forest Service offices in the parks or in cities and towns furnish maps and special information.

Campfires, including fires in wood or oil stoves, are illegal without a permit, which will be issued free by the nearest forest officer. All camping parties in national forests must be equipped with a shovel (over-all length at least 26 in., head weight not less than 2 lbs.). During fire season (indicated by signposts) smoking is prohibited except in camps, at places of habitation, in special posted areas, and above 7,000 ft. elevation. Be careful to extinguish lighted matches, cigars, cigarettes, and pipe heels. Observe carefully all posted signs, particularly the "No Smoking" and the "Closed Area" signs. Build small fires. Clear an area of not less than 10 feet in diameter down to mineral soil, extinguish all fires with plenty of water. If garbage pits or incinerators are not provided, burn or bury all refuse. Do not pollute springs, streams, or lakes by unsanitary acts. Observe the fish and game laws. Drive carefully on mountain roads.

Wild Flower Regulations: No wild flowers may be picked at any time.

Hunting and Fishing: Because of the complexity of the State laws, it is advisable to write for the *Abstract of California Sporting Fish and Game Laws.* Detailed information may be secured by writing the State Division of Fish and Game.

Climate and Equipment: State has a mild climate with no snow in winter except at high altitudes. Visitors should be prepared for warm weather in summer, but carry sweaters or light coats for cool evenings and sudden changes in temperature. In general there is no rain during the three summer months. Special equipment for winter sports and mountain climbing may be rented in resort areas. Hikers and riders in high mountain regions should have hats with brims at least three inches wide, stout leakproof shoes or boots, woolen hose, denim jeans, warm sweater or jacket, and raincoat or poncho (preferably on U. S. Army pattern).

Poisonous Plants and Reptiles: Poison-oak grows throughout State except in higher altitudes. It has crinkly edged, shiny leaves; is found at the edge of highways, in wooded areas, and in fields. Rattlesnakes exist, but are not numerous, being found in rocky regions below the 3,000 ft. level; will not strike unless disturbed. Black widow spiders are rare.

Calendar of Events

Note: "nfd" means *no fixed date*

Jan.	1	Pasadena	Tournament of Roses
	1	Pasadena	Rose Bowl Football Game
	1	San Francisco	East-West Football Classic
	1st wk	San Diego	New Year Regatta
	4th wk	Yosemite	Invitational Figure-Skating Championships
	nfd	San Francisco	California Dog Show
Feb.	1st wk	Big Pines	Annual Snow Pageant
	3rd wk	San Bernardino	National Orange Show
	nfd	San Francisco and Los Angeles	Chinese New Year
Mar.	1st wk	Pasadena	Kennel Club Show
	1st wk	Pasadena	Spring Flower Show
	nfd	place chosen each year	California Ski Championship Meet
	nfd	place chosen each year	Pacific Coast Championship Polo Games
Apr.	1st wk	Oakland	Spring Garden Show
	3rd wk	Hemet	Ramona Pageant
	4th wk	San Francisco	Rowing Regatta
	nfd	Santa Clara	Mission Play
May	1st wk	Mendocino Coast	Rhododendron Festival
	2nd wk	Sonora	Mother Lode Rodeo
	3rd Sunday	Mt. Tamalpais	Mountain Theater Play
	nfd	Angels Camp	Jumping Frog Jubilee
	nfd	Los Angeles	Festival of Allied Arts
June	1st wk	Auburn	Auburn Fair and Gold Rush Festival
	3rd wk	San Juan Bautista	Mission Pageant
	nfd	Long Beach	Water Sports Carnival

July	4	Oakland	Motorboat Regatta
	1st wk	Santa Barbara	Semana Nautica (marine events)
July	4th wk	Santa Barbara	National Horse Show
	nfd	Carmel	Bach Festival
	nfd	Hollywood	Hollywood Bowl Symphony Season
	nfd	Hollywood	Pilgrimage Play
	nfd	Salinas	California Rodeo
Aug.	1st wk	Carmel	Serra Pageant
	2nd wk	Santa Barbara	Old Spanish Days
	3rd wk	Sutter Creek	Gold Rush Fete
	4th wk	Newport Beach	Race Week and Yachting Championships
	nfd	place chosen each year	California Amateur Golf Tournament
Sept.	1st wk	Sacramento	State Fair
	2nd wk	San Gabriel	Mission Festival
	nfd	Los Angeles	Pacific and Southwest Tennis Tournament
	nfd	Berkeley	Pacific Coast Tennis Championship
Oct.	1st wk	Bakersfield	Frontier Days
	4th wk	Mare Island, Vallejo, San Diego, San Pedro, San Francisco	Navy Day
Nov.	nfd	Berkeley or Palo Alto	University of California— Stanford University "Big Game"
Dec.	3rd wk	Los Angeles	Great Western Livestock and Poultry Show
	4th wk	Los Angeles	Book Fair

A Guide to Recreation

PLACES TO GO

Aquariums, Marine Museums, and Submarine Gardens: Submarine gardens, marine museum and aquarium at Avalon, Santa Catalina Island. Aquarium and marine museum, Scripps Institute of Oceanography at La Jolla. Submarine gardens, Municipal Museum, Hopkins Marine Biological Laboratory at Pacific Grove. Stillwater Cove submarine gardens at Pebble Beach. Steinhart Aquarium in Golden Gate Park at San Francisco, Cabrillo Beach Marine Museum at San Pedro. Aquarium at Venice.

Art Collections: Carmel Art Association at Carmel. The Artists' Barn at Fillmore. Laguna Beach Art Association at Laguna Beach. Los Angeles County Museum of History, Science and Art, Southwest Museum, and Los Angeles Art Association at Los Angeles. Keith Memorial Gallery in St. Mary's College at Moraga. Oakland Art Gallery and Mills College Art Gallery at Oakland. Museum of Fine Arts and Thomas Welton Stanford Art Gallery in Stanford University at Palo Alto. Pasadena Art Institute at Pasadena. Mission Inn at Riverside. E. B. Crocker Art Gallery at Sacramento. Fine Arts Gallery in Balboa Park at San Diego. San Francisco Museum of Art, San Francisco Art Association, California Palace of the Legion of Honor, and M. H. de Young Memorial Museum at San Francisco. Huntington Library and Art Gallery at San Marino. Faulkner Memorial Art Gallery at Santa Barbara. *Museo* (museum) in Mission Santa Ynez at Solvang. Louis Terah Haggin Memorial Galleries in Victory Park at Stockton.

Aviaries: Santa Catalina Island Aviaries at Avalon. Roeding Park at Fresno. Griffith Park Bird Sanctuary and Cawston Ostrich Farm at Los Angeles. Bird Shelter at Lake Merritt in Oakland. Balboa Park at San Diego. Golden Gate Park and Fleishhacker Playfield and Zoo at San Francisco.

Museums: Pony Express Museum at Arcadia. Herbarium and Museums of Anthropology, Geology, Paleontology, and Vertebrate Zool-

ogy, University of California at Berkeley. Naval Museum at Mare
Island. Los Angeles Museum of History, Science, and Art, and
Southwest Museum at Los Angeles. Municipal Museum and Snow
Museum at Oakland. Municipal Museum at Pacific Grove. Leland
Stanford Jr. Memorial Museum and Jordan Hall natural history
collections, Stanford University, at Palo Alto. Palace of Science,
Museum of Anthropology, and Natural History Museum in Balboa
Park and Junipero Serra Museum at San Diego. M. H. de Young
Memorial Museum and California Academy of Sciences Museum in
Golden Gate Park at San Francisco. Museum of Natural History
at Santa Barbara. Museum in Victory Park at Stockton. Collec-
tions of pioneer relics at Columbia; Downieville; Fort Humboldt,
Eureka; Independence; Customs House, and First Theater, Mon-
terey; William B. Ide Memorial Museum, Red Bluff; Mission Inn,
Riverside; State Capitol and Sutter's Fort, Sacramento; Estudillo
House, San Diego; Shasta; Mission San Francisco Solano and Vallejo
Home, Sonoma; and Ventura. Small natural history collections at
Mae Loomis Memorial Museum, Lassen Volcanic National Park;
Government Center and Mariposa Grove, Yosemite National Park.
Mineralogical collection at State Division of Mines museum, Ferry
Building, San Francisco.

National Parks and Monuments: Death Valley National Monument, Devil Postfile National Monument, General Grant National
Park, Joshua Tree National Monument, Lassen Volcanic National
Park, Lava Beds National Monument, Muir Woods National Monument, Palm Canyon National Monument, Pinnacles National Monument, Sequoia National Park, Yosemite National Park.

Observatories: Lick Observatory on Mount Hamilton near San Jose,
Mount Wilson Observatory near Pasadena, Chabot Observatory at
Oakland, California Institute of Technology Observatory on Palomar
Mountain (*under construction*). Planetarium at Griffith Park, Los
Angeles.

Zoological Gardens: Gay's Lion Farm at El Monte. Deer enclosure, aviary, and duck ponds in Roeding Park at Fresno. California Zoological Society Gardens, Cawston Ostrich Farm, and alligator farm near Lincoln Park, and Bird Sanctuary and Zoo in Griffith
Park at Los Angeles. Oakland Zoo in Sequoia Park at Oakland.
William Land Park Zoo at Sacramento. Zoological Society of San
Diego Gardens in Balboa Park at San Diego. Aviary, deer park, and
bison and elk paddocks in Golden Gate Park and Fleishhacker Playfield and Zoo at San Francisco.

SPORTS

Athletic Stadiums: California Memorial Stadium, University of California at Berkeley. Marine Stadium at Long Beach. Coliseum in Exposition Park at Los Angeles. Stanford University Stadium at Palo Alto. Rose Bowl at Pasadena. Balboa Park stadium at San Diego. Kezar Stadium in Golden Gate Park at San Francisco.

Baseball: Played year round throughout the State. Leading professional circuit, Pacific Coast League, has ball parks in Los Angeles, Oakland, Sacramento, San Diego, and San Francisco.

Football: Played during fall and winter months throughout State by teams from universities, colleges, high schools, and independent clubs. Chief intercollegiate games are New Year's Day East-West games at Rose Bowl in Pasadena and Kezar Stadium in San Francisco.

Golf: Played year round throughout State at more than 200 country club courses and many municipal links, including those in Griffith Park at Los Angeles, Lincoln and Harding Memorial Parks at San Francisco, and Balboa Park at San Diego.

Horse Racing: Continuous from fall until spring, with season divided among various tracks. Pari-mutuel betting at Bay Meadows and Tanforan, south of San Francisco; Santa Anita, near Arcadia; Hollywood Racetrack, Inglewood; and Del Mar, north of San Diego. Other tracks at Los Angeles County Fair Grounds in Pomona, State Fair Grounds in Sacramento, and various county fair grounds, operating during fairs.

Polo: Played chiefly during first four months of year at Coronado, Burlingame, Del Monte, Santa Barbara, San Mateo, and Santa Monica.

OUTDOOR RECREATION

Boating: Favorite yachting centers include San Francisco Bay, with yacht harbors at Black Point and San Francisco and clubhouses at Alameda, Alviso, Belvedere, Richmond, and Sausalito; Monterey Bay; Stillwater Cove yacht harbor at Pebble Beach; Santa Barbara yacht harbor in Santa Barbara; Terminal Island in Los Angeles Harbor; Alamitos Bay at Long Beach; Newport Bay; Coronado and San Diego. Accommodations for pleasure craft of other kinds at these and other seaside cities. Sailing in launches and sloops on lower Sacramento and San Joaquin and other rivers; canoeing, motor-boating, rowing on Russian River and other streams and lagoons. Boating of all kinds on Big Bear Lake, Clear Lake, Lake Arrowhead, and Lake Tahoe. Motorboat races on Lake Elsinore, Lake Merritt in Oakland, Alamitos Bay, Newport Bay, and Salton Sea.

Camping: Campgrounds, trailer camps, cabins, auto courts, "motels," and "tent cities" at mountain, forest, desert, lake, river, and seaside resorts throughout State. Summer homesites in National forests for rent from U. S. Forest Service at $5 per year up. Camping 50¢ per car per night in State parks.

Fishing: Trout fishing throughout the Sierra Nevada in Lake Tahoe, glacial lakes and their tributaries, and headwaters of Kern and Kings Rivers; in the north, upper Sacramento River and its tributaries, Klamath River, and streams of the Coast Range; in southern California, streams of the Sierra Madre and San Bernardino Mountains. Native varieties include rainbow (known as steelhead after going to sea), cutthroat, Dolly Varden, golden, and Tahoe; imported varieties, Loch Leven, Eastern brook, European brown. Lake shallows and riffles stocked with millions of trout fry from fish-hatcheries yearly. Other game fish imported from East include: black bass, found in Clear Lake, northern rivers, and lagoons south of Los Angeles; striped bass, in Suisun and San Pablo Bays; sunfish; and yellow perch. Giant king salmon caught in Monterey Bay in June, July, and August and in San Francisco Bay in August; quinnat and dog salmon caught off northern coast and during spawning season, in Klamath River and rivers of Coast Range. Best ocean fishing in Monterey Bay, where species from both northern and southern waters are found, and off southern California coast. South of Point Concepcion, most common ocean fish are albacore, barracuda, black sea bass, bonito, leaping tuna, sheepshead, swordfish, yellow-fin tuna; peculiar to southern California waters are corbina, croaker, flatfish, roncador and yellowfin. Piers for surf fishing at Long Beach, Ocean Park, Redondo, and Santa Monica. Best deep-sea fishing off Portuguese Bend, Redondo, and Coronado, Santa Catalina, San Clemente, and Santa Barbara Islands. Santa Catalina Island waters especially noted for sport with albacore, broadbill swordfish, dolphin, giant bass, leaping tuna, marlin swordfish, white sea bass, and yellowtail. Shellfish, especially abalone, clams, and mussels, are dug at many points along coast.

Hiking: Well-marked trails lead through national parks and forests and radiate from resorts in Sierra Nevada, Coast Range, and southern California ranges. Horses, pack animals, and guides available at mountain resorts throughout State. Camps and lodges make wilder mountainous regions accessible to skilled mountaineers. All trails open in July and August; southern trails from May to November. Easy trails lead into Sierra Madre Mountains from Big Pines, Camp Baldy, Crystal Lake, and Mount Wilson; into San Bernardino Mountains from Big Bear Lake and Lake Arrowhead; San Jacinto Mountains from Idyllwild and Kenn Camp; Santa Ynez Mountains from Santa Barbara; Mount Hamilton Range from Alum Rock Park near San Jose; Santa Cruz Mountains from California Redwoods State Park; Berkeley Hills from Berkeley; Mount Diablo Range from Danville or Walnut Creek; Mount Tamalpais region from Mill Valley; Bear Valley forest and Tomales Ridge from Inverness, Olema, or Point Reyes; Castle Crags State Park from Castella; and into redwood groves from resorts along Redwood Highway. Short trails to points of interest in General Grant, Lassen Volcanic, Sequoia, and Yosemite National Parks are well marked. Among peaks easily climbed by amateur hikers are Mount San Antonio, Mount Wilson, Mount Lowe, Mount Diablo, Mount Tamalpais, and Lassen Peak. Mount Shasta is climbed from late June until early October. Trails into Trinity-Salmon Alps lead from Cecilville and Trinity Center, into Marble Mountain primitive area from camps along State 96. For skilled mountaineers, trails radiate into High Sierra from Lake Tahoe, Tuolumne Meadows, Yosemite Valley, General Grant and Sequoia National Parks, Kings River Camp in Kings River Canyon, Huntington Lake, and Bishop, Lone Pine, and Independence in Owens Valley. Pacific Crest Trail, traversing main divides of highest ranges in Pacific Coast States, has five sections in California: Lava Crest Trail, 330 miles; Tahoe Yosemite Trail, 260 miles; John Muir Trail, 185 miles; Sierra Trail, 160 miles; and Desert Crest Trail, 475 miles. For information address Clinton C. Clark, President Pacific Crest Trail System Conference, 125 S. Grand Ave., Pasadena, California.

Hunting: Deer, most common large game animal, are of three varieties: blacktail, mule, and white-tail. Found in Sierra Nevada north of Lake Tahoe, in northeast above Alturas, and in coast Range from Oregon to Mexican border. Open season varies according to region, beginning August 1 in Coast Range and ending October 15 in Sierra Nevada. Bears hunted with aid of guides and trained dogs in Sierra Nevada, parts of Coast Range, and San Bernardino Mountains. Cougars, fair game at any season (bounty on scalps), hunted with dogs in regions where deer are found. Foxes common, especially in Coast Range; gray wolf and wildcat (red lynx) sometimes hunted. Smaller game animals include badgers, cottontails and jackrabbits, gray and Douglas squirrels, porcupines, raccoons, and woodchucks. Most hunted game fowl are wild ducks, including bluebill, canvasback, gadwall, mallard, ruddy, spoonbill, sprig (pintail), teal, and widgeon. Open season usually October 15 to January 31. Chief duck hunting grounds are Suisun marshes to north and Alviso marshes to south of San Francisco Bay; "tule lands" along Sacramento, San Joaquin, and other rivers of Central Valley; marshlands back of beaches at Alamitos Bay, Newport Bay, and lagoons in southern California; and scattered regions in Imperial Valley, around Monterey Bay, and in Klamath River country. Characteristic method is shooting in marshes from "tule splitter" boats, but bay blinds and baited ponds are also employed. Wild geese and brant are fair game in duck season. Also hunted in autumn and winter are mountain quail, chiefly in higher Sierra and counties north of San Francisco Bay, and valley quail, in lowlands and foothills. Blue grouse, sage-fowl, and Wilson snipe are hunted frequently; also avocet, band-tailed pigeon, golden and upland plover, ruffed grouse, sandhill crane, and wild dove.

Motoring: Among favorite scenic drives for automobilists are Redwood Highway through redwood groves of Humboldt County (*see Tour 1a*), Victory Highway over Donner Pass and down Yuba Bottoms (*see Tour 9a*), Feather River Highway through gorge of Feather River (*see Tour 6B*), Skyline Boulevard along crest of the Sierra Moreno south of San Francisco (*see Tour 1b*), Seventeen-Mile Drive around Monterey Peninsula (*see Tour 1c*), Carmel-San Simeon Highway along coast (*see Tour 1c*), and Rim-of-the-World Drive through San Bernardino Mountains (*see Tour 12b*). Good highways scale Sierra Nevada, Coast Range, and southern California Mountains. Among peaks climbed to summit by highways are Mount Wilson, from Pasadena; Mount Hamilton, from San Jose; Mount Diablo, from Danville; Mount Tamalpais, from Mill Valley.

Ocean Bathing: Sheltered bathing beaches along coast from Trinidad to San Diego and at Avalon, Santa Catalina Island. Among favored beaches in north are Neptune Beach at Alameda, Ocean Beach at San Francisco, and the beach at Santa Cruz; in south, beaches at Malibu, Santa Monica, Ocean Park, Venice, Redondo Beach, San Pedro, Long Beach, Seal Beach, Newport, and San Diego. Favorite season for bathing extends from June to September, but hardy swimmers take dips the year around. Amusement zones at Neptune Beach, Ocean Beach, Santa Cruz, Ocean Park, Venice, Redondo, Long Beach, and Seal Beach.

Riding: Scenic equestrian trails in foothill, mountain, and desert regions throughout State, especially in Griffith Park, Los Angeles, and Golden Gate Park, San Francisco; Del Monte Forest; and foothills back of Santa Barbara, Beverly Hills, and Pasadena. Horses trained for mountain trails available at most resorts in Sierra Nevada.

Winter Sports: Favorite spots for tobogganing, snowshoeing, ski-running, sleighing, and ice-skating include national parks; Mount Shasta; Quincy and Portola in Feather River Country; Downieville, Grass Valley and Nevada City, Placerville, and Longbarn above Sonora in Mother Lode country; Alta, Cisco, Emigrant Gap, Norden, Tahoe City, and Truckee in central Sierra; Huntington Lake and Shaver Lake Heights in southern Sierra; Big Pines, Camp Baldy, Mount Wilson, and Wrightwood in Sierra Madre Mountains; Big Bear Lake and Lake Arrowhead in San Bernardino Mountains; and resorts in San Jacinto Mountains.

PART I
California: From Past to Present

El Dorado Up to Date

THE FIRST to come were explorers by sea, venturing uneasily northward along the shores in pygmy galleons on the lookout for fabled El Dorado, a vaguely imagined treasure trove of gold and spices somewhere near the Indies. Finding no riches, they returned disappointed. But the legend of El Dorado lingered, even when men driving their cattle in the dusty march from the south searched in vain for hidden wealth. At least the new country was a land of rich soil and gentle climate, and the newcomers stayed to grow rich from the herds they pastured, the fields and orchards they planted. Who could foresee that the legend would prove to be true almost as soon as the province had passed into the hands of the next comers from the East? Once more the old fable illumined California, more refulgent than before, as gold-seekers thronged westward by land and sea, risking hardship in the hope of ease. After a few years it faded. And yet people still came, tempted by the picture of rich acres, unbelievably fertile. California became that legendary land of perpetual summer, of orange groves in sight of snowy peaks, of oil wells spouting wealth, of real estate promising fortunes, of cinema stars and bathing beauties. It seemed to promise a new start, a kinder providence, a rebirth of soul and body. The aura faded again, slowly. And yet people came —in rickety automobiles piled high with all their belongings, people asking nothing but a chance to work in a country where the weather might be gentle enough to let them live.

"All the passengers . . . thronged with shining eyes upon the platform," exulted Robert Louis Stevenson as the train that had carried

him across the continent headed down the western slope of the Sierra
Nevada. "At every turn we could look further into the land of our
happy future. At every turn the cocks were tossing their clear notes
into the golden air and crowing for the new day and the new country.
For this indeed was our destination—this was 'the good country' we
have been going to so long."

It required little literary artifice to spin legends of an earthly
Utopia so real that men would risk toil, hunger, and even death to
seek it in the West. The diarists of the early expeditions, the newly
settled immigrants who wrote back home, the enthusiastic globe-
trotters who recorded their travels—all extolled the virtues of El
Dorado, and after them a growing throng of professional boosters—
newspaper lyricists, real-estate promoters, chamber-of-commerce press
agents—swelled the chorus.

"I love you, California, you're the greatest State of all," begins
the semiofficial State song; it closes with the solemn declaration:

"And I know when I die I shall breathe my last sigh
For my sunny California."

When the first white men came by foot into California in 1769,
they failed to recognize the Bay of Monterey, so overenthusiastically
described by the chronicler of Sebastian Vizcaino's expedition, and
passed by. Since their time, similar panegyrics have misled others, for
California is both more and less than its eulogists have claimed it to
be. There is something more to it than sunshine and vineyards and
orange orchards, bathing beaches and redwood trees and movie studios
—more than the hurried visitor to a few chosen showplaces may glimpse.
For California, in more than one sense, is all things to all men. The
ballyhooers have called it a sun-kissed garden spot cooled by gentle
zephyrs from the sea. The description is appropriate enough for the
sloping valley plains along the coast. They might also call it a sun-
scorched waste of boulder-scarred mountains and desert plains, or a
rain-drenched highland of timbered gorges and snow-capped granite
peaks. Or they might describe the vast spreading plains of its Central
Valley, or the smooth-worn brown slopes of its undulating oak-dotted
foothills, or the lava crags and juniper forests of its volcanic plateaus.
Its seashore has stretches of smoothly curving sandy beach and of saw-
toothed, rock-strewn coast; its plains are checkered with fertile fields
and pastures, and desolate with crags and alkali; its rivers brim with
water between fringes of greenery and lose their flow underground in
sandy washes. California's contrasts are extreme. It has fierce heat
and bitter cold, some of the country's wettest regions and some of its
driest, the continent's lowest point and the country's second highest.
Its landscape is so variegated that when the Californian goes traveling,

he is apt to say to himself as he looks at parts of the rest of the country: "I have seen all this before."

The people are as diverse as their environment. The tide of newcomers who arrived on foot, in prairie schooners, on clipper ships when California became American territory were from every corner of the land: New England farm boys, Irish-Americans from the streets of New York, younger sons of southern slave-owning families, and midwesterners imitating their fathers' trek from still farther east. Before this onrush of men with the "California fever," the leisure-loving pastoral civilization of the Spanish-Californians was swept into oblivion. It disappeared as fast as the way of life of the short, dark aborigines had disappeared three-quarters of a century before. The Yankee conquerors, all citizens of the same Nation, were still "of every possible variety," as traveler Bayard Taylor wrote in 1849. They differed individually from each other almost as much as they differed collectively from their predecessors.

People from nearly every nation of the earth still mingle in a polyglot conglomeration. In the dark and grotesque alleyways of Chinatowns in San Francisco, Los Angeles, and smaller cities live the Chinese, descendants of pioneers who came in the Gold Rush. The Japanese are found in Los Angeles' "Little Tokyo," and in small towns and farms in southern California. In Imperial Valley, in Los Angeles and its suburbs thousands of Mexican field workers live in rude shacks. The short brown men of the Philippine Islands gather in employment agencies and shabby roominghouses of the big cities. The vineyards around Santa Rosa and Napa, the fishing fleets of the seaports, the shops of San Francisco's North Beach give employment to the Italians. On the dairy farms of Alameda County live the Portuguese; in the lumber towns of the northern coast, the Scandinavians. In the big cities are colonies of Russians, Germans, French, and people of every other nation in Europe. Negroes live in the Central Avenue District of Los Angeles and the West End of Oakland—railroad porters and waiters, domestics and bootblacks, entertainers, and businessmen.

The people differ in more than their place of origin. Their lives have been shaped by the parts of the State in which they have settled. The sawmill workers of the bleak mountain shack towns of Weed and Westwood are a world removed from the orange growers of garden-surrounded Whittier and Pomona. It is a far cry from the tough-skinned, wizened old-timers of the Mother Lode ghost towns to the comfortable, retired midwestern farmers and storekeepers of Long Beach and San Diego, and a farther cry from the cowboys and sheepherders of Susanville and Alturas to the cameramen and movie extras of Hollywood. The vineyardgrowers of the sun-warmed Napa and Sonoma valleys, the grease-stained oil workers of the torrid Kettleman

Hills, the wandering pea-and-cotton-pickers of the San Joaquin Valley's river-bottom camps—all are strangers to each other.

The Union's second largest State in area might well have been christened by its discoverers *Las Californias,* for there are several Californias. Of all the many rivalries that make the life of the State an exciting clash of opposites, the chief has always been the rivalry between San Francisco and its neighbor cities and Los Angeles and its neighbor cities. Northern California was peopled with Americans during the Gold Rush, four decades before real estate booms brought settlers to southern California. Los Angeles remained a lazy village long after San Francisco had grown into a thriving city. San Francisco, with its more deeply rooted population, has the charm and conservatism of an older town, holding still to some of the traditions of gold rush days. In the interior towns of the north, more characteristically rural than those of the south, are the old-fashioned houses and quiet, tree-lined streets of a country village "back East"—especially in the towns of the mining country, where descendants of forty-niners live in almost clannish isolation from the State's more up-and-coming sections. In rural southern California, on the other hand, the inhabitants are more likely to be recent immigrants from the Middle West, and their towns have the neon lights, the stucco "Spanish" bungalows, and the chromium-trimmed cocktail bars of their big-city neighbors. The southlanders, for the most part, have had only a short time to get used to what is still a strange wondrous land—which accounts, perhaps, for their famed susceptibility to unorthodox religions, architectures, and political movements frowned upon by northerners. The inter-sectional rivalry has often prompted demands for the division of the State; yet despite the geographical, temperamental and commercial differences, the sentiment for divorce has never grown very strong.

No matter how fervent his local patriotism, the Californian will stop arguing the claims of rival regions when faced with the challenge of an out-of-State visitor. At once he becomes a citizen of "the greatest State of all," just as the *caballeros* of pre-American days haughtily set themselves up as *Californios,* a race apart. Whether northerner or southerner, native son or transplanted Iowan, the true Californian develops a proprietary interest that prompts him to tell the world about his State. So fond is he of bragging about it that he is always ready to "sell" California to whoever will lend an ear. Few joys in life so please him as an opportunity to declare with pride—and perhaps even on occasion with justification—that it has the tallest trees, the highest mountains, the biggest bridges, the fastest-growing population—in fact, the best, the most, or the greatest of whatever is being discussed at the moment.

The Californian may possibly be pardoned his pride in the extension, by three or four generations of human effort, of the bounties of nature. The aggressive energy of the Yankees, against which the leisure-loving ways of the easy-going *Californios* could not prevail (with some few exceptions in the south) still moves a people who have built aqueducts from faraway mountains to reclaim whole deserts, strung power lines from mighty dams across inaccessible wilderness to distant cities, dredged one of the Nation's great harbors from mud flats and flung the world's biggest bridges across a bay. The wild wastes of a century ago are dotted now with lumber mills, mine shafts and smelters, power plants and factories. The valleys are squared off in grain field and pasture, vegetable patch, vineyard and fruit orchard, watered with a labyrinth of irrigation ditches and criss-crossed with highways and railroads. Mountain streams have been dammed for electric power; plains and slopes drilled for oil. Under the earth extends a network of pipelines for oil and natural gas and above it, a network of high-tension wires for electric current. The canneries and packing houses, oil refineries, aircraft factories and movie studios ship their products to every corner of the Nation and beyond. The Californian of today feels a personal pride in the State's gargantuan public works: highways, bridges, dams, and aqueducts. And most of all, of course, he exults in the region's "happy future."

The days when the American people finally reached land's end on the Pacific are almost within the memory of living men. If Californians seem to display the brash boastfulness of adolescents, perhaps they deserve charitable forgiveness; for after all, they are citizens of a young State. And boastfulness is not the only telltale sign of its youth. The restlessness of the men who made the westward trek persists in the unquenchable wanderlust with which their descendants have taken to the automobile, thronging the highways with never-ending streams of traffic bound for seashore, deserts, forests and mountains. And the sturdy instinct for independence that inspired the rough-and-ready democracy of the mining camps and towns has lasted too; quiescent at intervals, it has always revived in time to save Californians from unprotesting resignation to hardship. They hope, perhaps, that the stubborn search for a better land that brought their grandfathers here to the shores of the Pacific has not spent itself. They hope, in fact, that they can yet make of El Dorado the promised land that has fired men's imaginations for four hundred years.

Natural Setting and Conservation

"IF CALIFORNIA lies beyond those mountains we shall never be able to reach it," wrote John Bidwell, leader of the first overland emigrant train, in his journal on October 29, 1841. But on the next day he set down: "We had gone about three miles this morning, when lo! to our great delight we beheld a wide valley. . . . Rivers evidently meandered through it, for timber was seen in long extended lines as far as the eye could reach." The day after he continued: "Joyful sight to us poor, famished wretches! Hundreds of antelope in view! Elk tracks, thousands! The valley of the river was very fertile, and the young, tender grass covered it like a field of wheat in May."

Thousands of later emigrants who struggled to the crest of the Sierra Nevada, towering like a massive wall along the State's eastern border, were equally overjoyed at their first glimpse of El Dorado. As they stood at the summit, the dry wilderness of the Great Basin lay behind them. To north and south rose the rock-ribbed flanks of the huge Sierra Nevada, about 385 miles long and with an average width of about 80 miles. Westward they looked toward the Great Valley of California, a vast elliptical bowl averaging 50 miles in width and more than 400 miles long, larger in area than Vermont and New Hampshire combined. Beyond the valley stood the dim blue peaks of the Coast Range, skirting the ocean and parallel to the Sierra in chains from 20 to 40 miles wide and 500 miles long. Far to the north, beyond their vision, the rugged Cascade Range and Klamath Mountains closed in on the valley's northern rim; and far to the south, the Tehachapi Mountains thrust their barrier from east to west across its southern end.

California, with a total area of 158,297 square miles, is the Union's second largest State. In the language of the geographer, its latitude extends from 32° 30′ to 42° N., and its longitude from 114° to 124° 29′ W. Its medial line, from Oregon to the Mexican border, is 780 miles long. Its width varies from 150 to 350 miles. Its coastline is approximately 1,200 miles—somewhat less than one-tenth of the total coastline of the United States. So pronounced is the eastward curve of the State's southern coast that San Diego lies farther east than Reno in Nevada, although Eureka, a northern port, is the most westward city in the United States. On the east the State is bordered by Nevada and by the Colorado River, which separates its southeastern corner from Arizona.

Beyond each end of the mountain-walled Great Valley, which is California's most distinctive topographic feature, the terrain is broken and rugged. Northward lie the Siskiyou Mountains, a natural barrier between California and Oregon. In the northwest, wild timbered slopes reach to the Pacific; in the northeast, mountain spurs hem in barren lava-bed plateaus. South of the Tehachapis' dividing line lies southern California comprising one-third of the State's area. Here the complex network of the Sierra Madre, the San Bernardino, and other ranges separates the so-called Valley of Southern California, a broad strip of broken country near the coast, from the arid wastes of the Mojave and Colorado Deserts in the hinterland. From Point Concepcion, where the Coast Range breaks into numerous ridges and the coast swings in sharply to the east, the Valley of Southern California, which includes the V-shaped coastal plain of the Los Angeles Basin, stretches southward to the Mexican border.

These chief geographical districts—the Sierra and Coast Range regions and the Central (Sacramento-San Joaquin) Valley in the north, the coastal lowlands, the mountains, and the desert country in the south—present startling physiographic contrasts and extremes, from active volcano to glacier, from arctic flora on mountain tops to cotton plantations below sea level. From the peak of Mount Whitney, the highest point in the United States, it is but 60 miles to Death Valley, the continent's lowest area. Human activities range from fur-trapping in the snows of the Klamath region to prospecting for minerals in the furnace-like heat of the southeastern deserts.

California's contour is marked by lofty mountain peaks towering above precipitous gorges and canyons. Of the 41 peaks that exceed 10,000 feet in height, the tallest is Mount Whitney (14,496 alt.) in the southern Sierra. The Sierra's abrupt eastern slope has one of the steepest general gradients on the North American continent. Over a

160-mile stretch the lowest pass is at an altitude of 9,000 feet, while Kearsage, the most frequently used pack horse pass on this stretch, is 12,050 feet; in this area the peaks range from 13,000 to 14,000 feet in height.   Although there is a gradual decline in altitude to the north, other isolated peaks of the Sierra rise above 14,000 feet.   Northward the western slopes are gashed by river canyons sometimes half a mile deep.

The Sierra's sculptured splendor is in part the work of glaciers which carved deep valleys, expanses of polished rock, and towering granite walls over which roar great waterfalls, glacial lakes and meadows.   Most beautiful of the valleys is Yosemite, in the midsection of the Sierra; loveliest of the lakes is Tahoe (6,225 alt.), cupped between the main Sierra and the basin ranges at the angle of the Nevada-California boundary.   A few glaciers even now survive on the highest summits, the finest of them being a group of five supported by Mount Shasta (14,161 alt.).

Dominating the northern end of the Sacramento Valley is Mount Shasta, the most striking of the many extinct or dormant volcanoes in the northern California mountains.   Lassen Peak (10,435 alt.), 85 miles southeast of Mount Shasta, is a mildly active volcano—the only one in the United States that has had a generally observed eruption. Although traces of volcanic action are most abundant in the State's northeastern sector, where lava beds spread over vast tracts, there are also extinct or dormant volcanoes in Owens Valley and the Mojave Desert, and numerous hot springs in the Coast Range.

The Coast Range, more complex than the Sierra, includes numerous indistinct chains from 2,000 to 7,000 feet high.   Each chain is broken down into forested spurs and ridges enclosing small pleasant valleys and plains drained by rapid streams.

The Santa Ynez, San Barnardino, and San Gabriel Mountains bound the lowland of southern California on the north and northeast, and subdivide it into more or less distinct valleys or basins.   Farther south the coastal lowland is bounded by the Santa Ana and San Jacinto Ranges, an elevation that extends into Mexico.   The southern California ranges are marked by the lofty peaks (more than 10,000 feet high) of San Bernardino, San Jacinto, and San Antonio and by the well-defined passes of Soledad, Cajon, and San Gorgonio.

Among the mountain-walled valleys between the southern end of the Sierra and the border of Nevada is the long and narrow Owens Valley, bordered by granite walls.   About 40 miles east of dry Owens Lake, along the California-Nevada border, lies Death Valley, its lowest point 276 feet below sea level.   It stretches between the sheer rocky walls of the Panamint Range on the east and the Amargosa Range on the west—130 miles long and from 6 to 14 miles wide—a region of stark simplicity, majestic silence, and spectacular desolation.   South of Death Valley spread the Mojave and Colorado Deserts. The Mojave is an expanse of ancient dried lake bottoms, short rugged ranges, and immense sandy valleys. Parts of the Colorado Desert lie below sea level—250 feet below at its lowest point. In its southern end is the fertile Imperial Valley, largely reclaimed from the desert for agricultural use by irrigation, where the Salton Sea, formed when the Colorado River broke its banks in 1905, floods an ancient lake bottom.

In addition to the Great Valley in the north and the coastal district (including the rich Los Angeles Basin and Santa Clara and San Fernando Valleys) in the south, cultivated lowlands occur elsewhere in the State. Below San Francisco Bay stretches another Santa Clara Valley; and southeast of Monterey Bay, between the Santa Lucia and Gabilan Ranges, lies the long Salinas Valley. North of San Francisco in Sonoma, Mendocino, and Humboldt Counties are similar areas. The northeast corner of the State, hemmed in by steep ranges, is suitable for cattle raising and restricted agriculture despite its lava beds and sagebrush.

In the whole 400-mile length of the Great Valley there is only one break in the mountain walls through which the waters of the interior can escape to the sea. Behind the Golden Gate at San Francisco, cutting across the full width of the Coast Range, is a great gap through which passes almost the entire drainage of the Great Valley. Into Suisun Bay pour the waters of the Sacramento and San Joaquin Rivers; they empty through Carquinez Strait into San Pablo and San Francisco Bays, and through the Golden Gate into the Pacific Ocean.

The scantily forested eastern flanks of the Coast Range contribute no stream lasting enough to reach either the Sacramento or the San Joaquin in the dry season; but down the western slopes of the Sierra, tributaries pour through precipitous canyons to the great rivers at each end of the valley. Fed by Mount Shasta's melting snows, the Sacramento, California's largest river, is joined by the Pit, McCloud, Feather, Indian, Yuba, and American Rivers as it flows southward 350 miles to its confluence with the San Joaquin in the Delta region. The Sacramento's lower course is through a marshy plain partly inundated yearly. The San Joaquin, whose valley comprises more than three-fifths of the central basin, flows northward from its headwaters in the mountains of Fresno County. Into it drain the waters of the Fresno, Merced, Tuolumne, Stanislaus, Calaveras, Mokelumne, and Consumnes Rivers, together with many smaller streams.

The seaward slopes of the Coast Range are drained by the Klamath (joined by the Scott and Trinity), Mad, Eel, and Russian Rivers north of San Francisco, and south of it by the Salinas, Santa Maria, Santa Ynez, Santa Clara and other secondary rivers, many of them intermittently dry. Southern California's so-called rivers—the Ventura, Los

Angeles, San Gabriel, Santa Ana, San Luis Rey, Santa Margarita, and San Diego—are for the most part dry creek beds except during spring floods.

A peculiarity of the State's drainage system is its many river "sinks" where the waters either dry up from evaporation or, like the Amargosa River in Death Valley, disappear beneath the surface. Through Modoc and Lassen Counties, in the far northeast, stretches a chain of alkaline "lakes"—Goose, Upper and Middle, and Honey Lakes. They are all without drainage to the sea, and the spring run-off rapidly evaporates. In the Central Valley, south of the area drained by the San Joaquin, the Kings, Kaweah, and Kern Rivers, fed by the melting snows of the high Sierra, formerly emptied into shallow marsh-girt lakes. But with the impounding of water for irrigation these lakes have dried up, and the old lake beds have become farm lands. The Mojave Desert, in whose sandy wastes the Mojave River is swallowed up, is dotted with glistening alkaline-incrusted dry lake beds. In Riverside, San Diego, and Imperial Counties, many creeks (so-called rivers whose beds are normally dry) run toward the desert sink of the Salton Sea region.

California has two magnificent natural harbors, San Francisco and San Diego Bays, both landlocked; and one great artificially built harbor, the port of Los Angeles. San Francisco Bay, entered through the Golden Gate, is among the world's finest; here, besides the port of San Francisco itself, are those of Oakland, Alameda, and Richmond. San Diego Bay, safe at all seasons, is sheltered from ocean winds by Point Loma, a promontory seven miles in length. The Los Angeles harbor, fronting on open San Pedro Bay, 20 miles from the city, is protected by a breakwater. California's best minor harbors are those of Monterey and Santa Cruz, on Monterey Bay, and Eureka, on Humboldt Bay, some 280 miles north of San Francisco.

There are two groups of islands off the California coast. The Santa Barbara Islands, nine in number, lie between Point Concepcion and San Diego, 20 to 60 miles from the mainland. From San Miguel Island in the north to San Clemente Island in the south they are scattered over a distance of 155 miles. The best known island of the group is rugged Santa Catalina, 25 miles long with an average width of four miles, which stands 20 miles south of San Pedro. The Farallones, a group of six small rocky islands, lie about 28 miles west of the entrance to San Francisco Bay.

CLIMATE

The first American writer to describe California's natural features refrained from the rhapsody which has characterized most of the subsequent discussion of the State's far-famed weather. "The climate of

California," wrote Captain William Shaler, "generally is dry and temperate, and remarkably healthy; on the western coast the sky is generally obscured by fogs and haze, but on the opposite side it is constantly clear; not a cloud is to be seen, night or day. The northwest winds blow very strong eight months in the year, on the western coast, with very little interruption; the land breezes at that time are hardly perceptible; but in the winter months they are stronger and regular. In the months of January, February, and March there are at times very high gales from the southeast, which render most of the bays and harbours on the coast unsafe at that season."

California's climate is characterized by certain peculiar features: the temperature of the entire Pacific Coast is milder and more uniform than that of regions in corresponding latitudes east of the mountains; the year divides, in general, into two seasons—wet and dry—instead of into the usual four seasons; and where extreme summer heat occurs, its discomfort is lessened by the dryness of the air.

Despite these general characteristics the State is a place of many climates, due to distance from the ocean, situation in reference to mountains, and, above all, altitude. Thus there are sharp climatic contrasts within a single limited area. One may go sleighing within sight of blossoming orchards, or view snow-clad peaks while bathing in the sea. A winter traveler in the high Sierra will be reminded of the Alps, while anyone venturing into the scorching inland valleys in midsummer will conclude that whoever labeled California "semitropical" was a master of understatement.

The term, however, is applied with good reason to the strip of land between the coastal mountains and the ocean. For those who have never visited this area the most restrained account of its climate is likely to seem hyperbole. The year-round weather is more equable than that of any other part of the United States; and from San Francisco southward to Monterey, the difference between the average summer and winter temperatures is seldom more than 10 degrees. In this coastal region frost heavy enough to halt the greening of the hills under winter rains is as rare as thunder and lightning; and always some flowers are in bloom. Sea breezes and fogs tend to stabilize the temperature without extremes of heat or cold.

The annual mean temperature of San Francisco is 56°; the summer mean is less than 60°, the winter 51°, and the lowest recorded temperature 27°. In San Diego the winter mean temperature is 54°, the summer 68°. In Monterey the difference between January and August mean temperatures is from 10° to 14°; in Los Angeles 14° to 16°. Because of the California current and the marine air from the Pacific anticyclone, summer in San Francisco is actually cooler than fall. These same factors induce fogs, night and morning, in that region and all along the California coast during the greater part of the summer. So dense and persistent are these coastal fogs that great areas south of San Francisco devoted to truck gardening require no other moisture during the summer months. The Coast redwood, as well as the plants which grow beneath it, is watered by the fog that condenses on its foliage.

In the southern part of the Central Valley, temperatures are often very high. Although the annual mean temperature of the inland is 64°, in Fresno and Bakersfield the mercury occasionally soars above 110°. The desert temperatures are still higher, the summer mean in Fort Yuma being 92°. In Death Valley, the average daily minimum for July, the hottest month, is 87.6°. But on July 10, 1913, it reached 134°, only slightly less than the highest natural air temperature hitherto accurately measured. In the mountain regions, on the other hand, summer temperatures are much lower and the winters are very severe. At the top of Mount Lassen, in the winter of 1932-33, the mercury registered 56° below zero.

Annual rainfall in the State varies from about 80 inches at Crescent City in the extreme north to about 10 inches at San Diego in the extreme south. At San Francisco the annual average is about 22 inches; at Los Angeles, 16 inches. The northern half of the Sierra and the northwest counties are covered by a heavy rain belt. In the high mountains precipitation, almost entirely in the form of snow, provides most of the run-off which supplies water for the cities and for irrigation. In the high Sierra the average annual snowfall is from 300 to 400 inches. At Tamarack in Alpine County the snowfall during the winter of 1906-7 was 844 inches, the greatest ever recorded for a single season anywhere in the United States. The belt of heavy rain shades off to a region of lighter rainfall which covers all the rest of the State except Inyo, Kern, San Bernardino, and Imperial Counties, and the eastern portion of Riverside County. The limits of this third region may, in dry years, include all of the State below Fresno and the entire Central Valley.

In general, rains occur in California only in the months from October to May. Even during this rainy season, the valley districts usually have no more than from 25 to 35 rainy days. Throughout the rest of the year excursions may be planned everywhere, except in some parts of the mountains, with considerable confidence that no rain will dampen the occasion.

GEOLOGY AND PALEONTOLOGY

Every major division of geologic time is represented in California by marine sediments, and many of them by continental deposits as well.

As the Pacific Ocean on the west and the ancient Great Basin Sea on the east alternately encroached on the California region, each supplied that part of the record which the other omitted. In formations of the last two periods, the Tertiary and the Quaternary, California is particularly rich.

Structurally the Sierra Nevada is a single colossal block of earth's crust lifted along its eastern edge to a height of more than 11,000 feet above the adjoining blocks, and gently tilted westward. The oldest known rocks making up these mountains are intrusions of molten rock (magma) and limestones, cherts, shales, and sandstones, all sedimentary, and nearly all changed into their metamorphic equivalents in the process of mountain building. These older sedimentary rocks were deposited in ancient seas of shifting extent and depth, which during the second half of the Paleozoic and the first two periods of the Mesozoic era, covered now one part, now another, of the Pacific Coast. Toward the close of the Jurassic period, the lands that were eventually to become the ancestral Sierra Nevada, the Cascades, and the Klamath Mountains began to emerge from the sea.

During the Cretaceous period the Sierra's whole block tilted westward. This process of tilting and folding wrenched open leaves of slates, once shales; heated mineral-bearing solutions escaped from the magma that was cooling and solidifying below and filled the slate openings with gold-bearing quartz. The Eocene epoch of the Tertiary period was comparatively quiet. The Sierra slowly underwent additional elevations and subsidences accompanied by active erosion of the surface rocks. Meanwhile the rivers were cutting their channels down the western slope and carrying the products of erosion to the inland sea. There was further release of gold from the bedrock, and the formation of rich placers. In the Oligocene epoch following, there was volcanic activity, and the Sierra gold-bearing stream channels were dammed and filled with rhyolite ash.

Volcanic activity continued during the Miocene age, and in addition to lava there were extensive mud flows and tuffs. In the Pliocene epoch the volcanoes were far less active, and in the Pleistocene the volcanic cover was removed in part by erosion. The veins and buried stream channels were cut into, and gold-bearing gravels were washed from their ancient channels and redistributed along new streams. This is the origin of so-called free gold. The Sierra had been greatly worn down in late Tertiary times, but the Pleistocene epoch of the Quaternary period was an era of re-elevation. There was much faulting, and a new period of volcanic activity began which is not quite ended today.

In the early Tertiary period the Sierra slopes were luxuriant with vegetation, but toward the end of that period the climate became much cooler. The slopes and summits were encased in thick ice and snow, which kept them captive. The glacial periods of the Pleistocene were relieved by intervals during which the ice fields retreated toward the crests, yielding to climates even milder than that of California today. But when the ice of the last glacial age had finally retreated (traces of this epoch still linger in various glaciers such as those on Shasta), the Sierra crest stood stripped of vegetation and soil, exposing those bare expanses of whitish granites and schists that now give it its dazzling beauty. Yosemite and other extraordinary Sierra valleys and canyons are also glacial legacies, as are the numerous lakes in the high Sierra. Tahoe, lovely lake and the deepest in the United States, was made partially by glaciation and partly by faulting, erosion, and volcanic damming.

The volcanic activity of Miocene times was especially great in the Cascade Range, where a number of volcanic peaks rose in a comparatively short time. Mount Shasta was one; the still active Mount Lassen was another, and the volcanic range extends north into Oregon and Washington. Eastward from the range extends one of the largest lava fields in the world, covering 200,000 square miles to depths of from 200 to 2,000 feet. This lava plateau, generally decomposed on the surface, which stretches beyond California into Oregon and across into Idaho and Wyoming, did not for the most part erupt through typical volcanic vents, but flooded up through great cracks or fissures. The Pit River, flowing through the Cascades, has cut deep into the series of volcanic rocks (andesites) some 7,500 feet in thickness, and the thin but widespread basalts. Because of the depth of this covering, the pre-Miocene history of the region is uncertain.

The oldest of the accessible formations of the Klamath Mountains are pre-Cambrian metamorphic rocks including schists, quartzites, and crystalline limestones—the last named consisting partly of sedimentary, partly of igneous rocks, both metamorphosed. The first two periods of the Mesozoic are represented by smaller proportions of sedimentary rocks which are covered by remnants of once extensive beds of sandstones, shales, and conglomerates of the Cretaceous period. There were also periods when volcanoes were active, especially the early Devonian period and the greater part of the Mesozoic era. The mass had been uplifted during the Jurassic period, but erosion and subsidence brought the ancestral Klamath mountains to below sea level in the Cretaceous period. This oscillation continued more or less quietly, except for an outburst of great volcanic activity in the middle of the Miocene. The most recent re-elevation, like that of the Sierra, was at the beginning of the Quaternary period. At approximately the same time, gold-bearing gravels were carried down along the sides of many canyons by erosion.

There are no Paleozoic (old life) rocks in the northern Coast Range, but crystalline limestone and schist, probably of this age, are found in the Santa Cruz, Gabilan, and Santa Lucia Ranges. Of the next era, the Mesozoic, Triassic period remains are lacking, but from the Jurassic come most of that complex series of Coast Range rocks known as the Franciscan. These are sedimentary rocks of several types: conglomerate, sandstone, shale, variegated chert, and (rarely) limestone. With them is embedded a great series of volcanic and plutonic rocks of the same age.

Cretaceous rocks in the Coast Range are abundant. They make up considerable parts of the Santa Lucia, the Temblor, and Diablo Ranges, and they become even more widespread north of San Francisco. The rocks consist chiefly of shale, siltstone and sandstone, with some small streaks of coal, and—near Coalinga—shale, which is the source of the oil in overlying Tertiary beds. The Cretaceous sea covered considerable parts of what is now the north Coast Range, but the region that now comprises the Santa Lucia Range and the Salinas Valley was relatively higher than at present, and formed Salinia, a long narrow peninsula running out to the northwest. The Eocene strata are relatively uncommon except in the eastern foothills near Coalinga and in the Mount Diablo region. The rocks are similar to those of the Cretaceous. There are considerable beds of coal, but the latter is of poor quality. Salinia had become an island, and there was a similar island whose axis ran along what are now the Gabilan and Mount Hamilton Ranges northwest to Marin County.

The Oligocene formations in the Coast Range are chiefly of red sandstone; there are also certain organic shales, which seem to be the source rocks for the oil of Kettleman Hills. The seas had become less widespread. Salinia extended farther north and west, but the San Joaquin Valley still formed an arm of the sea into which drained the rivers of Mohavia—a name given to the region now covered by the Mojave Desert, Death Valley, and the Owens River Valley. In the early Miocene there was much volcanic activity in the Coast Range, and this ultimately cut off the sedimentary deposits from Mohavia and prevented their reaching the sea. There followed in the late Miocene another period of widespread shallow seas and many coastal islands. Much organic siliceous shale was laid down, and this is the source of the oil in the Santa Barbara and Ventura coast region as well as elsewhere. Of Pliocene origin are calcareous and feldspathic sandstones and thick beds of brown and blue sandy clay. As elsewhere in California, the climate became cooler. There was still a series of islands and peninsulas along the entire coast.

In the Pleistocene epoch most of the old interior seas and bays disappeared. This was a period of violent deformation of structure, with foldings and bendings of the strata and a series of faults. Of these latter, the San Andreas fault, which was responsible for the earthquake of 1906, extends from Tomales Bay, 40 miles north of San Francisco, to the Mojave Desert, 600 miles southeast. In contrast to the more common type of vertical movement, it has a horizontal drift. The extent of its movement during Tertiary times was at least 700 feet, and according to some estimates as much as 10 or 20 miles. The Hayward fault, which runs sub-parallel to the San Andreas across San Francisco Bay and through Berkeley, is also important; and the Coast Range is cut by several smaller faults.

The Great Valley is an immense trough formed late in the Jurassic period when the mountain ranges inclosing it began to rise from the water. Unlike most valleys in the United States, which were cut by streams, it came into being through the sinking of the earth's crust. From that time on it remained an inland basin. For long periods it was flooded with salt water, as the sea flowed in through gaps in its intermittently rising barriers. The upward thrust of the Coast Range in the middle of the Tertiary period made it a nearly landlocked and shallow inland sea. Finally, in early Pleistocene times, the streams of the Sierra and the Coast Range, steadily carrying down their loads of sediment, caused a recession of the sea and laid down the flat valley floor. Although the valley is probably still sinking, it has filled with alluvium as fast as it has sunk. In some places drillings to depths of more than 3,000 feet fail to reveal bedrock.

The Transverse Ranges, comprising the San Bernardino, San Gabriel, Santa Monica, Santa Inez, and Santa Susana Mountains, have a general east-west trend, but differ only slightly in their geology from the chains of the Coast Range. Some of their Tertiary sedimentary rocks are more than 30,000 feet thick, exceeding in thickness any other such rocks in North America. They are remarkably rich in fossils.

Extending southeast of the Los Angeles Basin to a point beyond the Mexican border, the Peninsular Ranges include the San Jacinto, Santa Ana, Santa Rosa, and Coyote Mountains, with plateaus and valleys in between. Their geology has been but little studied, but they seem to belong to the fault-block type of mountains. While the faults are branches of the San Andreas, their general geology is rather like that of the Sierra, the dominating rocks being granitic.

The Great Basin comprises all that part of California lying southeast of the Sierra and east of the Peninsular Ranges, including the Colorado Desert, the Mojave Desert, and the Basin Ranges. Except for the Imperial Valley and some smaller areas under irrigation, the section is today a complete desert. The Colorado Desert, in part 245 feet below sea level, is a depressed block between active branches of the alluvium covered San Andreas fault in the Peninsular Ranges and the Mojave Desert to the north and east. The Mojave Desert region has isolated mountain ranges rising abruptly from desert plains. Farther north the Basin Ranges, of typical fault-block structure, run roughly parallel from north to south and are separated by deep basins or troughs. Death Valley, the most famous of the basins, is the bed of a lake of Pleistocene times and shows distinct sets of shore lines. The Great Basin had a number of such lakes in recent geologic time, although the region as a whole has been a land area since Cretaceous times. In the Panamint and Amargosa Ranges, which fence in Death Valley on the east and west, are formations from as far back as the Paleozoic era, but the valley, as such, is recent. The Mojave Desert's many short mountain ranges of various trends are largely of ancient volcanic and metamorphosed Tertiary rocks. The rest of the Mojave is an expanse of great sandy valleys and of dry lakes holding deposits of dead seas—salt, gypsum, soda, and borax. The last named was formed when the red-hot lava streams flowed into the saline lakes. The Colorado Desert is underlaid with Tertiary volcanic flows and coarse conglomerates, above which lie Quaternary fresh-water silts and sandstones.

With the rise of the mountains to the north and west in the early Miocene epoch, the sea that covered them was cut off and inland drainage systems were created. Rainfall decreased and the region slowly dried up. However, lakes of considerable extent have existed in the basin of the Colorado River within the period of the occupation of the country by the Indians, whose old camps may still be found on the margins of what are now salt flats.

A number of regions in California, particularly in the Coast Range and the Los Angeles Basin, are rich in fossils. Numerous fossil radiolaria found in the Franciscan cherts show their marine origin, and the north Coast Ranges have yielded fossil ferns, cyads, and conifers, as well as several kinds of mollusks and smaller marine organisms of the Cretaceous period. The types of marine organism found in the Eocene rocks indicate a much warmer surface water than exists on the California coast at present, and consequently a warmer climate.

From the Sespe beds between Los Angeles and Ventura have come bones of a variety of mammals of Oligocene times: the rhinoceros, the oreodont, the miohippus, the camelid, primitive carnivores, rodents, and insectivores. At a number of places the remains of primitive horses, peccaries, and camels have been found in Miocene formations. In the Pliocene strata there are primitive horses close in form to the modern horse.

The best-known paleontological area in California, and one of the richest in the world, is La Brea Pits in Los Angeles County. Since Tertiary times the quaking and sticky area of the La Brea asphalt beds has been a death trap for unwary animals. Beneath it have been preserved the skeletons of a prehistoric menagerie, including the imperial elephants, largest of all land mammals, whose domain extended from eastern Nebraska to Mexico City, hideous great ground sloths and little ground sloths, sabre-tooth tigers, giant wolves, camels and horses, llamas, wide-front bison, and numerous smaller species such as turtles, snakes, beetles, and birds. Well-preserved forms of vegetation, which show the evolution of plant life, have also been unearthed here. Noteworthy among these is a complete eight-foot cypress of the McNab species, which was discovered standing upright, buttressed by bones. This species is now found only rarely on the dry hills and flats of the Coast Range in northern California.

The Mojave and Death Valley Deserts of southern California have yielded fossils of the Oligocene and Miocene epochs, deposited as long as 25,000,000 years ago. In a narrow canyon near Barstow, where layers of breccia in dazzling colors were thrust up by an ancient volcanic upheaval, scientists have discovered during the past twenty years the remains of three-toed horses, several varieties of camels, antelope, and smaller animals, and an animal almost identical with the desert coyote of today. The complete skeleton of an Ice Age elephant (terrabeladon), similar to fossils discovered in the Gobi Desert, was found in 1938 near Saltdale, Kern County, in the northern part of the Mojave Desert. Death Valley's Tertiary beds have yielded the remains—including a skull three feet long—of a titanotherium, a large mammal that somewhat resembled the rhinoceros, found in red sandstone formations of the Oligocene epoch near Leadfield.

The fossils of Inyo County's "oldest muds in the world" are so abundant that, in geologist G. D. Bailey's words, they "are hauled away by carloads to fill the museums of the East." In Fresno County, less rich paleontologically, submammalian fossils have been found near Coalinga, a Pliocene mastodon skull at the north end of the Kettleman Hills, and fossil mastodon bones near Fresno. A rare find, uncovered in the Coast Range west of Fresno in 1937, was a fossil of eight vertebrae of a mesasaurus, huge sea lizard of the upper Cretaceous epoch. Kern County has yielded fossil animal bones of Tertiary and earlier ages and exceptionally rich marine fossils of the mollusca phylum, among them some highly ornamented forms showing a considerable degree of advancement in racial development.

The first dinosaur remains ever uncovered on the west coast of America were found in 1936 in the hills west of Patterson, Stanislaus County, by a high school student. The remains consisted of the tail and one hind foot. In other mountain counties of northern California, ancient caves—including Hawver's Cave on the North Fork of the American River in Eldorado County, and Potter and Samwell Caves on the McCloud River in Shasta County—have proved to be veritable storehouses of the bones of mammals swept in by river floods in the remote past. Remains of the giant ground sloth (megalonyx) have turned up in the earth fan at the entrance to Mercer's, or Murphy's Cave in Calaveras County.

The State's most unexpected paleontological discovery was dredged from the mud of San Francisco Bay during construction of the island site of the 1939 Golden Gate International Exposition. From sandstone strata 45 feet below the bay level, a tooth and a section of the ivory tusk of a Columbian mammoth (*elephas Columbia*) of the middle Pleistocene epoch were scooped up and pumped through 17,000 feet of pipe line. On the Peninsula, near Menlo Park Station, San Mateo County, remains of a mastodon skeleton were found in June 1927, buried in the plain formed by the coalescent fans that fringe the Bay. The discovery included a molar tooth, preserved without even discoloration of the enamel, three sections of a tusk, and fragments of ribs and other bones.

The most complete quarry in California for specimens of the Tertiary period was discovered in 1926 near Moraga, Contra Costa County, on the site of an ancient fresh-water lake. The fossils so far recovered are not so well preserved as those of the La Brea Pits, but they are believed to be more complete and to predate the La Brea remains by about 9,000,000 years. A three-toed giant horse and a three-footed antelope, a camel much larger than any known today, and the most primitive dog of its type yet found are among the species. Other discoveries include fossils of mastodons, hyenalike dogs, sabretooth cats, oreodons, peccaries, and a host of smaller creatures. At Irvington, in Alameda County, remnants of a prehistoric horse, an antelope, a mammoth, and a horned toad—all more than 500,000 years old—were found in 1936 and turned over to the University of California department of paleontology, which discovered the beds.

PLANT AND ANIMAL LIFE

California's plant and animal life is as diverse as its environment. Since its climate ranges from subtropical to Arctic, its terrain from arid, below sea level deserts in the south to moist, forested mountains in the north and from icy Sierra ridges on the east to foggy coastal slopes on the west, the State embraces a wide variety of flora and fauna. All the life zones of North America, except the tropical, are represented, their distribution depending not so much on latitude, as in most regions, as on altitude. California's plant and animal life, virtually isolated from the rest of the continent, is frequently distinctive and sometimes unique. While some species have migrated into the mountain slopes and coastal fog belt of the north from Oregon, and into the semiarid deserts, plains, and mountains of the south from Mexico, only a few eastern species have had the hardihood to cross the inhospitable deserts of the Great Basin and scale the barrier of the Sierra. These have undergone striking transformation in their migration.

Botanically, California is notable in particular for the unusual number of its annuals, both species and individuals, and for its numerous rare species of the lily family. More evergreens, especially the conifers, and fewer deciduous trees are found here than in most other States. Notable also are the many species of trees surviving only in limited localities from past ages, of which the best known are the Monterey pine and Monterey cypress and the two Sequoias (the coast redwood and the "big tree"), representing a family extinct elsewhere since the Ice Age. Still another distinctive feature is the chaparral—extensive pigmy forests of shrubs, stunted trees, and associated herbaceous plants —which covers the hillsides of the Upper Sonoran zone in dense thickets. It remains dormant throughout the hot dry summer, but becomes active with the rains of late winter and early spring.

The eucalyptus and acacia of Australia, the pepper tree of Peru, and the palm tree of the tropics flourish in both rural and urban areas; the eucalyptus (*eucalyptus globulus*) especially has been so widely planted in groves and roadside lanes both along the coast and in the Great Valley as to seem like a native. The wild yellow mustard, that covers orchard lands and hillsides in season with a yellow-green tide, was planted by the earliest Spanish settlers, as was the wild radish. The geranium and fuchsia both grow to extraordinary size in all the coast counties, where there are no extremes of heat and cold. In a number of places in the Sierra foothills, Scotch broom (*cystisus scoparius*) more than holds its own as an "escape" in the chaparral; and a species of filarese (*erodium macrophyllum*), a valuable forage crop, has become widely distributed.

The animals of the State are also distinctive, though less conspicuously so than the vegetation. The birds as a whole tend to be grayer, paler, and of slighter build than their eastern relatives. There are fewer species of snakes and more of lizards. Except for several species of trout, few fresh-water fish are native to the State, although some interesting indigenous species are found among the fauna of the 'tidal strip.

The streams were once abundantly supplied with sturgeon, but this magnificent fish has practically disappeared save in the least accessible rivers of the State's northwest coast. The icy lakes and streams of the Sierra favor many species of native and introduced trout. The former include the rainbow trout, or steel head, the Tahoe trout, the golden, the cutthroat, and Dolly Varden. Salmon, migrating from the ocean to their upstream spawning beds, are found in the northern coastal rivers in the spring. Dog salmon and quinnat salmon frequent coastal waters and the great king salmon enters the Bay of Monterey during the summer months. Other deep-sea fishes are the black and white sea bass, the yellowtail, the sheepshead, the "tonno," the albacore, the leaping and the yellowfin tuna, the bonito (the *Sardo chilensis* of the Pacific), the voracious barracuda (*Sphyraena barracuda*), and the battling swordfish.

Marine life of every kind is prolific and variegated. The California lobster, though large, lacks the huge pinchers of his eastern cousin. The pilchard or sardine (*Sardinia caerulea*) is found in such numbers during its run as to comprise 20 percent of the annual value of the State's fisheries. Herds of sea lions roar from the rocks off San Francisco, and elsewhere the leopard seal is occasionally seen. The abalone, most noted of California's shellfish, is a table delicacy and its shell is of use in manufacture. Oysters are plentiful but smaller than eastern varieties.

California is divided by biologists into six life zones, in each of which the altitude and climatic conditions are roughly uniform throughout the zone (*see accompanying map*). These are designated the Lower Sonoran, Upper Sonoran, Transition, Canadian, Hudsonian, and Arctic zones. The first is the lowest in altitude, and the warmest; the last is the highest and coldest. The Lower Sonoran zone includes the larger part of the Great Valley from Red Bluff to Bakersfield, all of the great arid and desert regions southeast of the Sierra to the Nevada and Arizona lines, and several long narrow strips extending from the Salinas Valley south. The Upper Sonoran takes in all the foothill country of the Sierra Nevada, the lava plateaus of Modoc and Lassen Counties, the western slopes of the Sacramento Valley, the inner chains of the Coast Range and Valleys from Mendocino County to San Francisco Bay, and all of the coastal region south of San Francisco except the Santa Cruz Mountains and the higher elevations of the Santa Lucias. These latter belong to the Transition zone, which also includes all of the coast country north of San Francisco, the heavily watered northeastern counties and a long belt, between 2500 and 5000 feet high in the Sierra. The Canadian, Hudsonian, and Arctic zones lie in the higher elevations of the Siskiyous, the Trinity Mountains, the Sierra, the San Bernardino and San Jacinto ranges.

It is possible to mention here only a few of the commoner or more characteristic inhabitants of these biologic zones, as a brief indication of the extraordinary range and variety of California's plant and animal life.

In the Colorado Desert section of the Lower Sonoran zone are found the California fan palm; the cylindrical cacti, echinocactus, and bigelovia; the mesquite, screwbean, and palo verde; and in the rainy season, among other flowers, the dwarf desert poppy and several diminutive asters. The most famous of plants peculiar to the Mojave Desert is the Joshua tree (*Yucca arborescens*). Along the river bottoms of the Great Valley grow Fremont cottonwoods and valley oaks. The mammalian life, mostly nocturnal in its habits, includes jack rabbits, kit foxes, kangaroo rats, pocket mice, and white-footed mice. Few animals besides the various species of chipmunks and ground squirrels appear in the daytime. In recent years the San Joaquin and Tulare basins have been overrun by Texas opossum, all originating from imported animals which either escaped or were liberated. The birds of the Lower Sonoran include Texas nighthawks, mocking-birds, blue grosbeaks, road runners, phainopeplas, cactus wrens, hooded orioles, verdins, and LeConte thrashers. Because of the large number of rodents, hawks and owls are unusually common. The tule elk once roamed over the marshes and sloughs of the Tulare Basin and San Joaquin River; today the last herd can be seen at the State park west of Bakersfield. The reptiles include the sidewinder (a small rattlesnake), the desert tortoise, and the horned toad.

The Upper Sonoran zone includes the State's great chaparral belt. This was the home of the now extinct California grizzly; it is still the haunt of the rapidly disappearing California condor, largest flying bird of the northern hemisphere. Here are found Digger pines, blue and scrub oaks, California buckeyes, many species of manzanita and ceanothus, certain kinds of yucca, and a host of other shrubs. Some of its distinctive species of birds are the California jay, stellar jay, California thrasher, bush tit, Anna hummingbird, bell sparrow, house finch, dusky poorwill, valley quail, mourning dove, and yellow-billed magpie. Among the animals are the brown-footed woodrat, brush rabbit, antelope, and ring-tailed cat (a relative of the raccoon).

This is a region rich in flowers. Early travelers in the State were eloquent in their descriptions of the continuous garden that once blanketed the plains and lower slopes. At a later time John Muir wrote, "For a distance of four hundred miles, your foot crushed a hundred flowers at every step." Most of this land is under cultivation now, and much of the rest is heavily grazed; but on fallow lands, in spite of the ravages of careless tourists in well-traveled regions, wild flowers still flourish in surprising abundance and soon recapture abandoned fields and ranges. Among the most common genera are gilia, nemophila, mint, mimulus, godetia, phacelia, lupine, orthocarpus, castilleia, dodecathon, viola, and calochortus. The State flower, the California poppy, or eschscholtzia, is most abundant in this zone. In the spring it colors hills and fields and roadsides with great masses of brilliant orange. It acquired its generic name from Adelbert von Chamisso, a German poet and naturalist, who saw it in bloom at San Francisco in 1816 and named it for a college friend who accompanied him—the German naturalist Johann Friedrich Eschscholtz. Though the eschscholtzia is widely distributed, it is not found in the densely wooded regions or at high elevations. A plant that is common to all parts of California and that occurs in a greater number of species here than anywhere else in the world is the lupine. As herb or shrub it varies from dwarf kinds in the high Sierra to the arborescent varieties growing close to the ocean. The pea-shaped flowers are of many colors, ranging from white through pale yellow, pink, and lavender to deep blue and purple.

In the Transition zone, which includes most of the State's great forests and therefore supplies most of its commercially valuable timber, are the redwood (*Sequoia sempervirens*) forests of the Coast Range, extending from the Oregon border on the north to the coastal canyons below Monterey on the south and as far as the inner limit of the summer fogs on the east. The redwood is one of the tallest trees in the world, commonly growing more than 200 feet high, and sometimes more than 300 feet. Trunks are often 15 to 20 feet in diameter, and occasionally from 20 to 25 feet. One of the peculiarities of the redwood is its shallow root system, though the trunks are strongly buttressed at the base. Because of the spongy, fire-resistant bark, these trees survived the annual fires set by the Indians of the region to clear out the underbrush and make hunting easier. The gently tapering shafts are almost bare of branches for a hundred feet or more above the ground. The bark is a deep purplish red, massively fluted; the foliage is delicate and feathery. A virgin redwood forest, with the light filtering through the treetops and falling in diagonal beams between the great columns, is one of the most beautiful sights in the world.

Beneath the trees, watered by the fog which they have trapped and precipitated, is an extraordinarily luxuriant growth. Swordferns, woodwardia ferns, alumroot, fringecups, barrenwort, fetid adderstongue, erythronium and violas, trillium and fritillaria carpet the floor. In almost impenetrable thickets grow the huckleberry, Oregon grape, rhododendron, azalea, California buckthorn, salmonberry, elder, and wild currant. The trees most commonly found in association with the redwood are the broad-leaved maple, madroña, tanbark oak, California laurel, and (usually in separate stands) the somber Douglas fir. Of these Coast Range trees the most picturesque is the madroña, a species of arbutus, which moved Bret Harte to write:

Captain of the western wood
Thou that apest Robin Hood!
Green above thy scarlet hose,
How thy velvet mantle shows!
Never tree like thee arrayed,
O thou gallant of the glade!

The Transition zone is particularly rich in animal life. It is the home of the Columbian black-tailed deer, black bear, Pacific coon, marten, mink weasel, skunk, fox, packrat, and mountain beaver. The California ring-tailed cat, common in both the Upper Sonoran and the Transition zones, is one of the handsomest animals peculiar to the West; it is often tamed and kept as a pet. Cougars and bobcats are fairly common. A few small herds of Roosevelt elk survive in the extreme northwest. Of the few reptiles, gopher snakes, garter snakes, and the rattlers are commonest. Amphibia are numerous, as is to be expected in so moist a region. The streams abound in water-puppies, and the woods in big mottled redwood salamanders which thrive on the abundant yellow groundslugs. In the depths of the Transition zone forests the birds are neither very numerous nor very conspicuous. Kingfishers, chickadees, various warblers, towhees, varied and hermit thrushes, robins, juncos, mountain quail, and hummingbirds are the most common.

East of the redwood belt, on the slopes of the Klamaths, the Cascades, and the northern Sierra, is a mixed forest of coniferous and deciduous trees, with the former predominating. Yellow pine, Douglas fir, sugar pine, white fir, incense cedar, western yew, mountain birch, and white oak are the important trees of this region. The herbaceous flora resembles that of the southern Sierra and the drier portions of the redwood belt. This is the home of the white Washington lily, the orange *Lilium pardalinum,* the erythronium, western azaleas of white or pink, several lupines, and the curious darlingtonia, which traps unwary insects in its hoodlike leaves. The Klamath Mountains, marking the border line between the Oregonian and Californian floras, are of great interest to botanists. With the exception of the antelope of the Modoc lava beds, the mule deer, the eastern kingbird, and an occasional eastern bobolink, the fauna of this area is much like that of the coastal region.

South of Lake Tahoe lies the characteristic Sierran forest. Here at an average elevation of about 3,500 .feet is found the "big tree" (*Sequoia gigantea*). Unlike the redwood (*Sequoia sempervirens*), it does not form great belts of continuous forest but stands in about 35 isolated groves, scattered from the American River to the Tule. These trees are probably the oldest living things in the world—some of them have been shown by ring counts to be not less than 4,000 years old. In diameter they average from 15 to 20 feet; their average height is about 250 feet. The "big tree" is bulkier than the redwood, with cinnamon-colored bark and foliage similar to that of its coast cousin. The two Sequoias, with the ginkgo tree and the marestail, are survivals from a flora that was nearly destroyed in the glacial period. In Miocene times, Sequoias of various species were common over much of the northern hemisphere. In spite of their great age, both individually and as a species, the "big trees" are not dying out, but rather are increasing with the aid of the reforestation work of the United States Forest Service and office of National Parks. The "big tree" is found on the edge of the Transition and Canadian zones, usually close to stands of fir. Below it, in the Transition zone, stretch extensive forests of yellow and sugar pine, incense cedar, golden and black oak, California laurel, and broadleaved maple. In this Sierran forest, the most common wild flowers are pentstemons, gilias, mariposa tulips, pussypaws, mimulus, lappulas (wild forget-me-nots), collinsias, tiger and leopard lilies, buttercups, and the omnipresent lupines.

As one enters the Canadian zone, a change is immediately noticeable. The yellow pine gives way to the related Jeffrey pine. As one ascends, mountain pines and red firs and (higher still) lodgepole pines dominate the forest. Brushy areas are covered with dwarf manzanita and ceanothus. Under the firs grows some herbaceous vegetation, mostly living on the decayed wood common in fir forests. Notable in this vegetation are the brilliant snowplant, several species of corallorrhiza, and the cancerroot. This is also the home of the unique Sierra puffball. Some of the more conspicuous birds are the blue-fronted jay, Sierra junco, western chipping sparrow, Sierra hermit thrush, water ouzel, evening grosbeak, Sierra grouse, and Townsend solitaire. Among the animals are the mountain weasel, yellow-haired porcupine, snowshoe rabbit, golden-mantled ground squirrel, Sierra chickaree, and certain species of chipmunks.

The Hudsonian zone is the belt of forest immediately below timber line. With the Canadian zone it shares the lodgepole pine, which is here the dominant cover. Usually associated with, or above the level of, the lodgepole are the white bark, foxtail, and silver pines. These latter trees, with the mountain hemlock, form the stunted and twisted growth of the timber line. Birds become scarcer in this zone, though mammals remain plentiful; some of the species extend up from the zones below. The California pine grosbeak, mountain bluebird, white-crowned sparrow, alpine chipmunk, Sierra marmot, Sierra cony, pine marten, Sierra least weasel, and wolverine are typical of the region.

The Arctic-Alpine zone, the highest of all, is a treeless area stretching from an elevation of about 10,500 feet to the summits of the loftiest peaks. Here are found the Sierra primrose, the blue and fragrant polemonium, the yellow columbine, the alpine buttercup, the steershead, and the alpine shootingstar. Only one species of bird is native to the zone, the Sierra rosy finch; but many others visit it, notably flocks of migrating hummingbirds and, in the summer, gray and white Clark nutcrackers. The principal mammals are visitants from lower elevations; however, the Sierra cony is often found in these heights and the Sierra white-tailed jackrabbit makes its home here. The Sierra Nevada bighorn sheep are seen occasionally in the White Mountains east of Owens Valley and in some of the southeastern ranges. A small band remains in the Mount Whitney region, survivors of those described by John Muir, which in his day ranged along the Sierran crest to the vicinity of Sonora Pass.

Certain animals range through several zones, particularly the mule deer, the coyote, and the cougar or mountain lion; as do a number of birds notably the blue-fronted jay, the Sierra junco, the redshafted flicker, certain hawks, and some of the sparrows. The flowers and trees are generally confined within the limits of their native zones, although various similar forms, distinguishable only by botanists, occur at several elevations. Thus, the Jeffrey and western yellow pines can be differentiated with certainty only by a chemical analysis of their sap; while the Compositae generally, and particularly the asters, are the despair of all but highly trained specialists.

Gone now from most sections of the country is Nature's intricately organized population of bear, marten, beaver, otter, elk, deer, and badger. Tilled fields have replaced the natural haunts of fox, lynx, bobcat, and fisher. But in California these animals still possess the sunny chaparral and the green shade of forests. The United States Forest Service estimates that in the 18 national forests of California, covering nearly one-fifth of the State's area, there are 111,000 blacktail deer, 148,000 mule deer, 7,000 bear, 2,800 antelope, 24,000 foxes, and 1,230 mountain lions. Man's encroachments have not yet driven out all the mountain sheep, weasels, badgers, raccoons, muskrat, beaver, and otter. Over vast areas of the California wilderness, human footprints seldom obliterate the tracks of paw and hoof.

NATURAL RESOURCES AND THEIR CONSERVATION

Gold was the first natural resource—scarcely noticed by the Indians and Spanish-Californians—to be discovered in the land fronting the Pacific. Its discovery spelled the destruction of the simple economy of pre-Yankee California, attracted tens of thousands of fortune seekers, and radically affected the history of the State.

California's minerals, forests, soils, and water power, its scenery and climate, and its two great natural harbors, place it among the regions most richly endowed by nature. But its natural resources, originally so great as to seem inexhaustible, were thrown open to private exploitation without restriction. Gold miners, taking little thought of the future, despoiled forests, denuded land of its surface soil, and clogged rivers with debris. Cattlemen deliberately set fire to forests to increase their acreage of grazing lands; ranchers exhausted the soil by growing wheat year after year on the same areas. The inevitable consequences were floods, erosion, and soil depletion.

The land surface of the State comprises about 100,000,000 acres, of which approximately 30,000,000 acres are tillable. Since cultivation in many areas is dependent on irrigation, it is impossible to estimate the amount of tillable land with accuracy. About 500 variations in soil types have been listed by the U. S. Bureau of Chemistry and Soils; taken as a whole, they are uncommonly productive.

Ever since pioneer days, the State's forest lands have yielded vast quantities of lumber. Some 7,700,000 acres have been logged over, and 500,000 have been reclaimed for agricultural use. The commercial forests, mainly in the mountain sections, consist chiefly of coniferous trees: Ponderosa pine, sugar pine, and white and red fir in the Sierra; Douglas fir and the towering redwood in the northern coast counties of Del Norte, Humboldt, and Mendocino. Many stands in both regions are very heavy, capable of yielding as much as 100,000 board feet to the acre. The total bulk of old-growth timber in California is estimated at 213,500,000,000 board feet. The forest lands are divided almost equally between public and private ownership, but the heavier and more accessible stands are privately owned.

Legislative attempts early in the present century to conserve forest resources were mostly unsuccessful because of the opposition of corporate interests. In recent years the division of forestry of the State department of natural resources has done useful work, especially in fire and insect control.

Since 1892 the Federal Government has set apart as national forests 18 tracts along the headwaters of California streams, with a combined area of 19,216,332 acres—about one-fifth of the State's total acreage. These tracts have been "set aside to protect and maintain in a permanently productive and useful condition lands unsuited to agriculture but capable of yielding timber and other forest benefits, such as forage for livestock and water for irrigation, domestic use, and power." They are controlled and supervised by the Forest Service of the U. S. Department of Agriculture. Extensive forest tracts are also reserved as State parks. Artificial reforestation is done mostly in the redwood region, where the climate fosters the growth of seedlings. In the pine region, with its hot dry summers and cold winters, natural reforestation is usually more successful. Artificial reforestation is carried on by the U. S. Forest Service and a few county organizations, some 4,000 acres being planted annually.

Of the 58 counties, each has some of the State's mineral substances. The six most important products of 1936 (latest available figures), listed in order of financial value, are petroleum, gold, natural gas, stone, soda, and cement. California is rich in petroleum, which has replaced gold as its most important mineral. Its oil, which is in general distinguished by an asphaltum base, is found, along with great quantities of natural gas, on the coastal plain of southern California, in the San Joaquin Valley, and in scattered smaller areas elsewhere. California continues to outrank the rest of the United States, including Alaska, in the production of gold; its 1936 production topped any previous year in the history of the State. Quicksilver, copper, silver, lead, and zinc are found in substantial amounts, as are cement, clay products, stone, sand, and gravel. Most of the world's supply of borax comes from California. Platinum, tungsten, magnesite, chromite, pyrites, silica, diatomaceous earth, potash, sodium salts, and talc are also mined.

In the early 1870's, Sacramento Valley farmers organized anti-debris associations as a defense against the strongly intrenched mining interests, and in 1893 an act was passed by the State legislature to control hydraulic mining. Shortly after 1900, steps were taken for co-operative work between owners of land and the State and Federal governments to reclaim valuable swamp and overflow lands along the rivers. Not until 1911, however, did the State legislature create a conservation commission.

Since petroleum and natural gas are classed as minerals, their production is controlled by Federal laws; but under the California laws of 1911 and 1915 the State may regulate oil-drilling methods and prevent the waste of natural gas. Under the act of 1915, "to protect the natural resources of water, petroleum, and gas from damage, waste, and destruction," oil operators must use every effort to prevent contamination of fresh water suitable for irrigation or domestic use, to avoid the waste of natural gas, and to make regular reports of production to the State gas and oil supervisor. In 1919 several previously existing agricultural commissions were combined in a State department of agriculture, under the charge of a director of agriculture. The department is organized in several divisions, such as plant industry, animal industry, and agricultural chemistry. Its work is supplemented by that of the College of Agriculture of the University of California, with its central establishments at Berkeley and Davis. State conservation activities include restoration of soil fertility, control and exclusion of pests, and study of plant diseases.

The task of protecting wild life is divided between State and Federal agencies. The State maintains an effective patrol organization to enforce its regulations in this field. U. S. Forest Service officers help the State to enforce the fish and game laws, and aid in the restocking of streams and lakes with trout. Throughout the national forests, many areas have been set aside as State game refuges. California's lakes and streams are stocked annually with millions of fingerlings, under State and Federal conservation programs. The work of breeding the numerous game fishes is carried on at twenty State and two U. S. fish hatcheries, and distribution to the lakes and streams at higher elevations is effected through co-operation with the anglers' associations and the Sierra Club.

The future of California is closely linked with the future of its water supply. From the earliest days of the State, a popular movement for public ownership and distribution of irrigation water has struggled for domination over private ownership and sale. Californians have undertaken many comprehensive investigations of the problems of water control, pollution abatement, watershed protection, and beach erosion. In 1931 a complete water utilization plan, reported by the State division of water resources, outlined specific projects for the great agricultural districts. The reports of the California Basin Committees, drafted for the National Resources Committee (1937), recommended projects in flood control, irrigation, soil and wildlife conservation in the northern California-Klamath, Central Valley, central California coast, and southern California coastal drainage basins.

The project of making the desert blossom as a rose, or (more prosaically) of turning desert areas into productive farmland, has held the imagination of western settlers for more than half a century. The possibility of irrigating the Imperial Valley area through the diversion of the waters of the Colorado River was first considered in 1876. The Colorado Irrigation Company was formed in 1892 and constructed a canal in the vicinity of the Mexican border. The plan almost ended in disaster when the powerful Colorado River changed its course during a flood in 1905-6 and hurled its waters through Imperial Valley into the big inland sink since known as Salton Sea, threatening to make a clean sweep of the valley ranches and settlements. After the damage had finally been repaired at great cost, the problem of effectively regulating the Colorado River was repeatedly brought before Congress. The completion in 1936 of Boulder Dam, second in size only to Grand Coulee in the Northwest, finally solved the problem, assuring the future of Imperial Valley as one of the most important agricultural regions in the country. Boulder Dam will control the waterflow of the All-American Canal, opened in 1938, which will distribute irrigation water throughout the reclaimed desert region in the southeastern corner of the State.

Despite the extremely high productivity of Central Valley's alluvial soils, large parts of the valley have been threatened for years with reversion to desert through drought and salinity, largely caused by prodigal and unplanned use of water resources over a long period. In order to conserve and regulate the water resources of the valley, and to prevent the acute water shortage threatening over a million acres in the Sacramento and San Joaquin basins, the Bureau of Reclamation of the U. S. Department of the Interior has now under construction another great irrigation, flood control, and power project, known as the Central Valley Water Project. Its key unit, the Shasta Dam, above Redding, which will be the second largest concrete dam in the world, will back up the Sacramento, Pit, and McCloud Rivers for a distance of 35 miles, to create a storage reservoir with a capacity of nearly a billion gallons. The Central Valley project also includes the construction of the Friant Dam on the upper San Joaquin River east of Fresno, with a reservoir capacity of 147,000,000 gallons. Developed water power in the State is more than 2,000,000 horse-power, with large potential reserves still undeveloped.

The California Conservation Council, representing a number of national and State organizations, stresses the necessity for local initiative in conservation work and urges not only wise utilization of natural wealth but also cooperation with Federal, State, and county agencies, enforcement of protective laws, and nonpolitical administration of natural resources. Since 1935, the Council has annually sponsored a "Conservation Week."

One of the most forward-looking phases of Califorina's conservation program is that which has preserved and developed the beaches all along the coast as State parks. Numerous historic sites are protected as State monuments. The national conservation program in the State embraces three national parks—Lassen, Yosemite, and Sequoia—and the two great national monuments, Death Valley National Monument and Joshua Tree National Monument.

The First Californians

WHEN on June 17, 1579 "it pleased God" to send Francis Drake's *Golden Hind* into the "faire and good bay" north of the Golden Gate, he encountered "the people of the country, having their houses close by the water's edge." Overawed, they supposed the bearded, white-skinned sailors who bestowed on them "necessary things to cover their nakedness" to be gods and "would not be persuaded to the contrary." The men, their faces painted in all colors, left their bows behind on a hill and came down to the shore bearing presents of feathers and tobacco. The women remained on the hill, "tormenting themselves" in some sacrificial frenzy and "tearing the flesh from their cheeks." Their king, "clad with conie skins and other skins," arrived with a retinue of "tall and warlike men," bearing a sceptre. After much singing, dancing, and speech making, they begged Drake to "take their province and kingdom into his hand and become their king."

In the interior Drake's men found other villages. Up and down California, if they had traveled farther, they would have discovered others, for the Indians of California were widely but unevenly scattered over the State's fertile regions. The estimated native population of almost one inhabitant to each square mile was comparatively large; the Central Valley was probably more densely populated than any other part of North America at that time.

For an unknown age before the white man first stumbled upon them in the sixteenth century, the Indians of California had dwelt in their scattered bands, walled off from the rest of the aboriginal world by mountains and deserts. On the shores of San Francisco Bay, along the southern California and Humboldt Bay seacoasts and in the San Joaquin Valley, evidence has been unearthed from their shell mounds— huge kitchen middens of shell, ash, and earth, piled up layer by layer from the refuse of daily living over the centuries—indicating, a culture which remained almost unchanged over a period of perhaps three or four thousand years. It was probably the simplest culture in all aboriginal North America.

The scattered bands dwelt in isolation one from another, each fishing in its own creek, catching game in its own preserves, gathering nuts, seeds, and berries in its own forests. The village, composed of groups of kin and relatives by marriage, was the unit of society, its members holding rights in common to a specific tract of land; seldom was it united with other villages by tribal ties. Even among the semi-organized tribes of northern central California, the village was the real social unit. The Maidu of central California, although united in language and customs, distinguished their local groups into Hill Maidu, Valley Maidu, and Mountain Maidu. The only exceptions were the Mojave and Yuma in the far southeast, who displayed aggressive tribal unity against outsiders.

In customs and in culture the isolated villages varied widely, but in nothing so widely as in language. Over most of the State a villager needed to travel little more than 50 miles to encounter other Indians whose language he could not speak; in a 50-mile journey through many regions he might pass the boundaries of three or four distinct language groups. More than 100 dialects of 21 distinct language stocks were spoken. Of all the many language groups, only three larger language families from outside the State were represented in California: the Hupa and their neighbors in the far northwest belonged to the Athabascan; many groups in the south to the Shoshonean, and the Mojave and Yuma along the Colorado to the Yuman linguistic stock.

Drake's men discovered tribes living in conical, dome-shaped, or round huts. In the northwest part of the State they were covered with light planks or poles; towards the south with bark, brush, or thatch; in the Sacramento Valley, with sod. The ceremonial center for most villages was the *temescal* (sweat house), round and earth-covered, almost airtight. Confinement in its steam-vapored interior, followed by a plunge into icy water, was considered an effective remedy for illness and a pleasant cleanly habit.

California's great stands of oak provided the Indians with their staple food in most parts of the State. Acorns were dried, ground with pestles in stone or wooden mortars, and leached with repeated soakings in hot water to remove their tannic acid. This acorn meal, seasoned with salt or wood ashes, was eaten as it was, baked in unleavened cakes, or boiled in a gruel. In the southwestern desert country the Indians gathered mesquite beans and on the eastern Sierra slopes, piñon nuts; only near the Colorado River did they cultivate plants for food. Often they ground or roasted grass seeds, berries, roots, and nuts, and stored them in baskets. Lacking pottery, which only the Indians in the extreme southeast near the Colorado River knew how to make, most of the California natives boiled their food in close-woven baskets, into which they dropped hot stones. They hunted small game with snares, sticks and nets, or bows and arrows; larger game with the aid of pits and traps, and, in the north, dogs. Deer-hunters often donned deer-skins and stuffed deer's heads to approach their game. Grasshoppers and caterpillars were also eaten. Everywhere fish were caught with hook, net, or spear; by the seashore clams and mussels were gathered, and along the rivers of the north, salmon were speared during the spawning season.

The California Indians perfected basketry and thus supplied themselves with utensils for gathering and winnowing grain, cooking and storing water. Into their weaving went sedge, bulrush, redbud, willow, diggerpine, juniper, bracken, grape, or tule. With strands stained with vegetable dyes in clear blues, deep reds, warm yellows, and luminous pinks, the weavers worked fine geometric patterns. The Pomo families of Lake, Sonoma, and Mendocino Counties sometimes wove into their baskets the downy, many-colored feathers of birds.

The California Indian's other possessions were few and crude. Out of bone, shell, or stone he carved his arrowheads, awls, pestles and mortars, pots, charm stones, beads, and pendants. For money he used dentalium or clamshell disk beads, ground, bored, and strung, and valued according to size, thickness, and polish. His musical instruments were varied; most widespread was the rattle, made of split clap-sticks, gravel-filled cocoon bunches, bundles of deer hoofs, or turtle shells and gourds; in addition there were bone whistles, flutes, musical bows, and drums.

He built two kinds of vessels for navigation: the balsa, a raft or float made of tule rushes for use in quiet waters, sometimes replaced by huge woven baskets in which goods or human beings were ferried across streams; and the wooden canoe, hollowed out of a log, for use on the ocean. The Canalino Indians living along the Santa Barbara Channel made boats of lashed planks, craft found nowhere else in North America.

Most village groups were headed by a chief, who held the office more often by virtue of wealth than heredity; he was privileged only to advise, not to command. Within the village group, scarcely any distinctions, either of social status or vocation, were drawn, except in the northwest, where social classes based on the possession of wealth tended to form. In the absence of any coherent tribal organization warfare as practised in eastern North America was unknown, although sporadic feuds broke out between kin or local groups.

The only other tribal functionaries besides the chief were the shamans. The shaman might be either a man or a woman, who acquired supposedly supernatural powers through consultation with spirits in a dream. Sometimes he cured illness by "sucking the pain object" from the patient's body, sometimes by bringing back his wandering soul, sometimes by blowing tobacco smoke on the affected part, by chanting incantations, or by inducing a trance. Supposedly he could kill, as well as cure. Among these shamans were specialists, the rain, rattlesnake, and grizzly bear doctors. Most feared of all in northern California were the grizzly bear shamans, who either dressed in bearskin robes, or were credited with the power of turning themselves into ferocious grizzlies in order to destroy their enemies.

Birth, puberty, marriage, and death called for religious observances. In most localities the husband kept to his house for several days (usually four) after the birth of a child, abstaining with his wife from meat and salt. Among the Achomawi and Shasta in the northeast, boys at the age of puberty were initiated into the life of the group with simple ceremonies by fasting, whipping with a bowstring, and the piercing of their ears. The initiation of girls was more elaborate: hidden away, sometimes in a separate hut, they were instructed in womanly duties, meanwhile eating no meat, bathing frequently, and scratching themselves with special carved sticks (since scratching with the hands was taboo). Marriage was a somewhat loosely defined institution except in the northwest, where the bridegroom presented gifts in proportion to the social standing of his bride's family. In most parts of the State the dead were forgotten as soon as their bodies had been buried or cremated; to speak their names was commonly taboo. Among the southern California group, however, the chief public demonstrations were mourning ceremonies, celebrated at annual or semi-annual memorials by burning the piled-up effigies of all the recent deceased, to the accompaniment of sad wailing.

The only organized religious cults which gained a foothold in California were the *kuksu* (big-head) and *toloache* (Jimsonweed) cults. The *kuksu* rites, practised in the southern Sacramento Valley, were celebrated, almost always in winter, by dancers representing gods. Their faces painted and disguised by curtains of feathers, grass, or shredded rushes, they danced in earth-covered, dome-roofed dance houses to the accompaniment of stamping on a hollow-slab foot drum. The cult trained the adolescent boys and girls (initiating the boys with puberty rites), organized the male members of the community, and focused the activities of the shaman. The *toloache* cult, practised in the San Joaquin Valley and in southern California, centered about the taking of the narcotic Jimsonweed plant to induce hallucinations. Its practitioners used sand paintings to picture the cosmos. The *toloache*, like the *kuksu* cult, conducted puberty rites, some groups extending them to girls as well as boys, with the intention of making the initiate strong, fortunate, and successful. Some groups celebrated with ceremonial rites such events as the first fire-making or acorn-gathering of the new year or the first catch of salmon in the spawning season. In the northwest, the exhibition of prized possessions like prepared deerskins was celebrated by dancers decked out in all their valuable goods. The groups of the southeast and desert performed ritual dances to accompany song cycles in celebration of mythical events.

In 1769, nearly two centuries after Drake's brief visit, Franciscan friars trudged into the country to convert the "heathen." Cross or sword, the Indians had to choose. On several occasions bloody struggles broke out, in which the Indians were usually defeated. Only the groups in the mountains escaped missionary efforts: those who submitted were baptized. Almost all the natives in the coastal regions were brought to live in and around the 21 Franciscan missions, established from San Diego to Sonoma between 1769 and 1823. From 4,000 in 1783, the Mission Indian population was increased to 7,500 by 1790, to 13,500 by 1800, and to 20,355 by 1805. The monotonous round of work and prayer, the rigid moral regulations, the cramped and prisonlike housing made life unbearable for many. They ran away, although they faced whipping if caught, or they died.

The resentment against the missions flared several times into open rebellion. On November 4, 1775, some 800 rebels swept down from the hills and set fire to San Diego Mission. The year after, San Luis Obispo was burned. The Yumas in 1781 destroyed their mission and freed themselves, arousing the spirit of revolt among the Indians of San Diego and San Juan Capistrano. During the last two decades of the century there were conflicts at Santa Barbara, at most of the southern missions, and at San Juan Bautista. In February 1824 the neophytes at Purisima Concepcion, Santa Ines, and Santa Barbara revolted simultaneously, killing several people and burning the buildings at Santa Ines. In 1829 secular authorities waged a campaign against the forces of Chief Estanislao (for whom Stanislaus River and County are named). A fugitive from Misión San José, Estanislao led a band of other escaped neophytes and wild Indians of the San Joaquin Valley in an uprising that was crushed only by a force of 100 Spaniards with muskets and cannon.

When the Mexican Government broke the mission system's land monopoly with its secularization decrees of 1833-34, the Indians were suddenly freed. Well-meaning in their despotism as the mission fathers may have been, they had degraded their converts into dependent slaves, unable to shift for themselves. In theory, secularization was to grant rights of citizenship to the Indians and restore to them one-half of all mission land, livestock, and farm tools. In practice, the neophytes relapsed into helpless vagrancy, too demoralized to work their own lands, if indeed they had not been dispossessed of them by crooked administrators. The mission population fell off rapidly, decreasing from 24,634 in 1830 to 6,000 in 1840. The Indians took up their old life in the wilds, if luck was with them; if not, they fell into wretched peonage on the vast private ranchos.

On the ranchos the Indians were never paid, and in the small industrial establishments of the later Mexican period they were paid only with glass beads, parched corn, or homemade brandy. The raw, poisonous liquor, drunk with greediness, killed many of them; scarlet fever, smallpox, tuberculosis, and syphilis killed many more.

From an estimated total of 133,000 in 1770 the Indian population had already fallen by 1852 to 85,000, and continued to decline at an accelerated rate under the American regime. The drop in Indian population between 1849 and 1856 has been estimated at 50,000. One of John C. Frémont's men reported in 1847: "We killed plenty of game and an occasional Indian. We made it a rule to spare none of the bucks." As Americans acquired the Mexican grants, they drove the ranch Indians off; the squatters who staked off so-called Government lands pushed the aboriginal inhabitants back into the mountains and deserts. Their salmon waters muddied by mining operations, acorn groves cut down for firewood, hunting lands confiscated, the Indians were left to starve. In the towns and cities, where they were paid only half the wages of whites, they were cut down by disease and drink.

When the less submissive of the Indians resisted starvation by depredations on American property or livestock or retaliated for outrages by killing white men, they were massacred without mercy. For nearly three decades after American occupation of California, "Indian wars" continued—the Klamath War of 1851-52, Kern River War of 1856, Pit River massacres of 1867, and the Modoc War of 1873. During the campaign of 1855-59 in the north, soldiers killed more than 100 Indians, while settlers of the Mad and Eel River regions put at least 200 to death in a series of massacres. Up to December 1854 the State had spent $1,030,530 on Indian campaigns; during the next six years it spent twice that amount. The cattle raids and attacks on emigrant trains of the Yumas and Mojaves were answered in the Owens Lake incident of 1865, when the settlers drove 100 Indians to a terrible death in the corroding waters of an alkaline lake. The Pit River Valley massacre of 10 or 15 white men in 1867 was followed by the destruction of a whole village. During the troubles in the far north which eventually culminated in the last and bloodiest of the Indian "wars," the Modoc War of 1873, a company under Captain Ben Wright fell upon the Indians when they laid down their arms to make a treaty and murdered so many that Wright could boast of making a "permanent" treaty with at least 1,000 Indians.

The Indian, his affairs entrusted to special agents who seldom interfered in his behalf, had no spokesman before the Government of a people who wanted only to steal his land. The white man found it easy to support almost any charges against him. According to Helen Hunt Jackson, early champion of the Indian, " 'Papers from Washington' seemed to give the white man the right to deprive any Indian of the land of his forefathers—so the Indian gradually disappeared, 'hunted down, driven out.' The United States Government took over all the Indian holdings, and grants to white people could be obtained on application without any consideration for the right of occupancy by the Indian. To betray sympathy with the Indian was more than any man's 'political' head was worth."

As early as 1849 the Federal Government had commissioned agents to collect data on Indian rights and land titles. In the following year it appointed a commission of three which eventually succeeded in signing 18 treaties with chiefs of more than 100 groups, representing most of the State's Indian population. In return for their promise to recognize United States sovereignty, keep the peace, settle on reservations—18 in number, aggregating 7,500,000 acres—and cede their land rights to the Government; they were to receive farm implements and goods, instructors in blacksmithing, woodwork, and farming, and maintenance of permanent reservations. The treaties were transmitted to the Senate but never ratified; for over half a century they remained hidden in Senate archives. Meanwhile the Indians of California, having fulfilled their part of the bargain, remained uncompensated for their losses, seeing their promised 7,500,000 acres dwindle to 500,000.

Beginning in 1853, the Indians were gradually gathered together on reservations. The first one was established at Tejon; others were established later on the Klamath River south of Crescent City, at the mouth of the Noyo River on the Mendocino coast, and at Nome Lake in the Sacramento foothills. The results at first were far from happy, since bands of diverse origin and speech were lumped together indiscriminately. Under a system of education which forced the white man's ways upon the Indian, aboriginal culture disintegrated rapidly. As the natives ran away faster than they died, one reservation after another was abandoned. Little by little the reservations were robbed of their more valuable lands. The 32 which exist today, as well as the land allotments made to individuals, are located chiefly in unproductive hill country. Here the Indians, housed and clothed much like their white neighbors, practice farming, stockraising, and handicrafts, on some reservations under the guidance of Indian Bureau agents. The children attend either Indian schools, such as the Sherman Institute near Arlington, Riverside County, or public schools to which the Indian Bureau makes tuition payments.

For every seven or eight Indians living in California before the white man came to stay, only one remained 14 decades later. The Indian population, including half and mixed bloods (nearly 30 percent of the total), had fallen by 1910 to 16,371—a decline of about 90 percent. Since then the Indian population has increased to an estimated 24,000 in 1938.

There are Indians in every county in the State, but in only four— Humboldt, Mendocino, Riverside, and San Diego—are there more than 1,000. About three-fifths of the Indian population live on reservations; many of the remainder live on land allotments or homesteads. Indian ranch hands work at hop-picking, fruit gathering, sheep-shearing, and general ranching. In the larger urban centers, where they have doubled in number during the last three decades and total about 1,100 today, the women find employment as domestics, the men as mechanics, factory hands, or railroad workers.

Under the Indian Bureau's influence, native arts are now fostered, particularly at the Sherman Institute. The Luiseno and other groups are encouraged to stage their picturesque ceremonies at summer fiestas, ceremonies whose primitive origin is plainly apparent despite Christian transformations. Unfortunately, this policy of encouragement has succeeded that of persecution too late to save more than a tiny remnant of Indian culture.

California's Last Four Centuries

WITHIN the half century after Christopher Columbus discovered the new world, Europeans discovered and named California. In 1513 Vasco Núñez de Balboa reached the Pacific coast at Panama; twenty-two years later another Spaniard, Hernando Cortés, discovered a land he named California; and in 1542 Juan Rodríguez Cabrillo, a Portuguese navigator, rode at anchor in San Diego Bay, the first white man to see any part of the region now known as California.

The chain of events that led to California started with the search by Columbus in the Caribbean in 1493 for the island Mantinino, which he had been told "was peopled merely by women." Columbus thought this might be Marco Polo's Amazonian island "near the coast of Asia." He failed in his search, but the fabulous isle fascinated other navigators during the next decade. After Garcia Ordóñez de Montalvo published his romance *Las Sergas de Esplandián* in 1510, Spanish navigators were familiar with both the legend and with the name California. A passage reads: "Know that, on the right hand of the Indies, there is an island called California, very near to the Terrestrial Paradise, which was peopled with black women. . . . Their arms were all of gold."

Spain's dominion in the new world was extended to the western coast of Mexico by Cortés' conquest of the empire of Montezuma. In an attempt to push it farther west and north Cortés sent two ships commanded by his kinsman Diego Hurtado de Mendoza on a "voyage of discovery" in 1532. Mendoza got as far north into the Gulf of Cali-

41

fornia as 27° N. before a mutinous crew compelled him to send back one of the ships; of his own vessel, nothing but vague rumor was ever heard again.   Fortuno Ximenes, pilot of an expedition sent to search for Mendoza, anchored in a small bay "near the 23rd degree of latitude," landed, and was killed by natives, along with 20 of his men. The survivors reported the discovery of an island, said to "abound in the finest pearls."   On May 5, 1535, Cortés entered the little bay Ximenes had found (possibly the present La Paz) called it Santa Cruz, landed and named the supposed island California.   He was convinced that it lay "on the right side of the Indies," if not "near to the Terrestrial Paradise."

For more than a year Cortés stayed in the new land, a desolate sandy waste, while the mutinous soldiers cursed him, "his island, bay, and his discovery."   Clinging tenaciously to his search for the "seven cities of Cibola" in the north, he sent three ships, under command of Francisco de Ulloa, to begin a thorough survey of the coast line in 1539. Ulloa examined both shores of what he called "The Sea of Cortés," now known as the Gulf of California, discovered that Cortés' island was really a peninsula.   Later in the same year, it is said, he sailed around Cape San Lucas and surveyed the Pacific coast line of the peninsula, getting as far as the 28th degree—some say as far as "Cape Engano, near the 30th degree."   By this time, however, Cortés had gone back to Spain, never to return.

The new viceroy, Don Antonio de Mendoza sent Cabrillo, in command of the ships *San Salvador* and *La Victoria* "to examine the western side of California as far northward as possible, seeking particularly for rich countries and for passages leading towards the Atlantic." Cabrillo sailed from Navidad, a small port in Xalisco, on June 27, 1542. Slowed by adverse winds, he finally entered "a very good closed port" on September 28, which he named San Miguel—the bay of San Diego. He discovered Santa Monica Bay and the three large islands of the Santa Barbara group, rounded Cabo Galera (Point Concepcion) and Cabo de los Reyes (Point Reyes).   The ships passed the Golden Gate without seeing it.   On the way back they found the harbor in the island of the Santa Barbara group which they named *La Posesion*.   There Cabrillo, who had been suffering from a broken arm, died on January 3, 1543, and the command passed to his pilot, Bartolomé Ferrelo. Sailing north again, the ships reached a promontory on February 26, probably Cape Mendocino, which Ferrelo named Cabo de Fortunas (Cape of Perils or Stormy Cape).   Turning back, they eventually came into their home port, Navidad.

Disappointed by the reports of the expedition, Spanish officials became more and more convinced that north of Mexico the New World contained "neither wealthy nations, nor navigable passage . . . between the Atlantic and Pacific Oceans." Later, when the treasures of the Orient began to come into the port of Acapulco from the Philippines and from China, Spain found in the long continental mainland the best protection of its inland sea—the Pacific. England's sea rovers had no way into the Pacific except by rounding Cape Horn. This Francis Drake did in his 100-ton schooner, the *Golden Hinde;* he anchored on June 17, 1579, in what became Drake's Bay and named the region New Albion.

Drake's visit seems to have aroused Spain's dormant interest in California. In 1584 Francisco Gali made a much more thorough examination of the California coast than Cabrillo had done 42 years before, and 11 years later Sebastián Cermeno was directed, while returning from Manila to Acapulco, to examine the California coast, "in search of harbors in which galleons might take refuge." Losing his own ship, somewhere "near San Francisco Bay south of Cape Mendocino," he sailed southward along the coast in a small boat and sighted the Bay of Monterey, which he named "San Pedro Bay."

With three ships "well officered," Sebastián Vizcaíno made a second attempt in 1602 to explore the coast, sailing as far as Cape Mendocino, naming the first harbor he reached, "the best in all the South Sea," San Diego. On November 12, Carmelite friars of his party celebrated Holy Mass ashore—the first time in Upper California. Vizcaíno spent almost a year in the survey, but like Cabrillo he missed the Golden Gate. He renamed many places named in 1542 by Cabrillo, among them San Diego, Santa Catalina, Santa Barbara, Point Concepcion, the Carmel River, Point Reges, and Monterey Bay—in honor of the viceroy, Gasper de Zunigay Acebedo, who was the Count of Monterey.

After Vizcaíno's visit Spain's efforts were largely spent in attempts to colonize New Mexico rather than Upper California, though recurrent attempts were made to keep alive the pearl-fishing industry on the eastern coast of the Gulf of California. The most pretentious of these was in 1683, when Don Isidro de Atondo, placing settlers, soldiers and Jesuits at different points, planned a steady penetration of California. But the project lagged, and not until 1697 did Jesuits receive royal warrants to enter upon the reduction of California at their own expense. In that year the first permanent colony was planted in Baja California —at Loreto by Father Juan Maria Salvatierra. Father Kino, in 1701, crossed the Colorado near Yuma and entered Alta California, working among the Indians of "Pimeria Alta."

By 1734 Vitus Bering was pushing his exploration of Alaska, and Spain began to fear the colonizing activities of Russia along the Pacific coast. Twenty years later a new peril arose, when France was swept from sovereignty in America by Britain. Spain could put off no longer the settlement of Alta California.

A high officer of the Spanish "Council of the Indies," José de Gálvez, was sent to Mexico as *visitador-génerál* and arrived in Mexico City in 1766. Early in the following year Carlos III of Spain issued a decree banishing all Jesuits from Spanish territories. Franciscans were to take over the mission at Loreto, which was to be the base of the operations, both military and pastoral.

Captain Gaspar de Portolá was appointed Governor of Baja California and ordered to proceed to Loreto to superintend the transfer of mission property. He reached Loreto with an escort of fifty soldiers, accompanied by fifteen Franciscan monks, and was joined by Father Junípero Serra, who was made president of the missions in California, and Gálvez. The king had ordered Gálvez "to send an expedition by sea to rediscover and people the bays of San Diego and Monterey." Gálvez thought it would be well to send a land expedition also and Father Serra concurred with this plan. Three missions in Alta California—at San Diego, Monterey and at an intermediate point—were to be established, also two presidios or military posts.

On January 9, 1769, one of the ships, the *San Carlos,* left La Paz; two days later the *San Antonio* sailed from San Lucas, and the *Señor San José,* from Loreto soon after. The vessels were loaded with ornaments, sacred vases, church vestments, household utensils, field implements, seeds, and other settlement needs. The *San Antonio,* under Captain Juan Pérez, reached its destination, San Diego Bay, on April 11; the *San Carlos* on April 29. Scurvy had swept both vessels, but its ravages on the *San Carlos* had so prostrated the crew that not even a boat could be lowered. The *San Antonio's* boats carried the sick ashore, where they convalesced behind a temporary stockade.

The march by land was no less long and painful. The forces divided into two columns, one under an army captain, Fernando de Rivera, and the other under Portolá. With the latter went Father Serra. The columns took different routes, each driving a herd of cattle. Rivera's party reached San Diego on May 15; Portolá's route was more difficult and his party did not arrive until July 1.

The expedition lost no time in putting its plans into action. Misión San Diego de Alcalá was dedicated on July 16, two days after Portolá had led sixty-four members of the expedition away to the north to find the Bay of Monterey. Through country described by Portolá as "rocks, brushwood and rugged mountains" wound these newcomers—Spanish officers in brilliant uniforms, monks in gray-brown cowls, leather-clad soldiers, Indians on foot. On October 2 they reached Monterey, failed to recognize it, and pushed on. In Father Crespi's words: "The expedition strove to reach the Punta de los Reyes, but some immense arms of the sea which penetrate into the mainland in an extraordinary fashion would have made it necessary to take a long, circuitous detour." Those arms of the sea, first seen by Sergeant Ortega and his band of scouts, were the reaches of San Francisco Bay. Curiously inept at foraging for food, the company would have starved except for their pack animals. They ate twelve in as many days.

At last, on January 24, 1770, they returned to San Diego, "smelling frightfully of mules." At San Diego there was so much suffering from illness and hunger that Portolá decided to abandon the expedition and return to Baja California if help did not come from Gálvez by March 20. But at dusk on March 19 they sighted a sail on the horizon—and less than a month later were on their way back to Monterey.

This time they recognized the Bay, and on June 3, 1770, dedicated the sites of the mission and the presidio. Serra felt that they were dedicating themselves to the task of civilizing the natives and winning them for God. To Portolá, the planting of royal standards and crosses in the name of King Carlos III of Spain, signified the assertion of Spain's rights in California. During the next half century nineteen more missions were established, and near some of them presidios and pueblos. The last mission—San Francisco Solano—was founded north of San Francisco Bay on July 4, 1823.

The missions formed a chain of civilized outposts along the coast, spaced a day's journey apart. Each had its herd of cattle, its fields and vegetable gardens, tended by the Indian neophytes. The Indians were taught by the padres to build irrigation systems and they became weavers, masons, carpenters, and blacksmiths. Thus the missions could be nearly self-sustaining, though they did receive clothing, furniture, implements, and tools from New Spain, in exchange for their surplus of meal, wine, oil, hemp, hides, and tallow.

The work of the padres, measured by the number of Indians reclaimed from their free life in the wilderness and put to tilling fields, was for a time successful. But even in 1786—at a time when the future of the missions was most promising—a discerning French scientist, Jean François Galaup de la Pérouse, visited California and wrote that he was not impressed with what the padres were accomplishing. He doubted whether the mission system would ever develop self-reliance in the aborigines.

The presidios, with their small military staffs, were established to protect the missions from hostile natives and possible invaders. Their military equipment was meager and antiquated, but fortunately the soldiers had little use for it. They occupied themselves with explorations, bear hunts, capture of run-away neophytes, carrying of the mails, and providing their own food supply. Like the padres, the soldiers were supposed to receive regular wages from New Spain, but more often than not the money failed to come, and they were forced to become more self-reliant than most subjects of the paternal Spanish Government.

Gradually small towns began to grow. Some of them, like San Diego, San Francisco, Santa Barbara, and Monterey, spread around the edges of the presidios, and were at first under military rule. Others sprang up near the missions; among these were Sonoma, San Juan Bautista, San Juan Capistrano, and San Luis Obispo. Los Angeles and San José began as independent towns, with civic governments, and San Francisco, although an adjunct to the Presidio, was definitely planned by the Spanish authorities as a civic enterprise. Its first settlers were 240 immigrants brought from Sonoma, and Tubac, Mexico, by Juan Bautista de Anza. Leaving Tubac in October 1775, he led them over the present Arizona desert and the snows of the high Sierra, and arrived with his company, almost intact; only one person, a woman, died on the way, and eight children were born. (The Spanish Government had supplied every anticipated need.) On March 28, 1776, Anza located a presidio along the Golden Gate. The settlers, who had stopped in Monterey, arrived on June 27.

Although Portolá had hoped to establish the authority of Spain in California, his successors could not even repel the small company of Russian fur traders who landed in 1812 and boldly built a stockade, Fort Ross, in the Spanish province. The Spaniards made polite protests but the intruders stayed as long as was convenient to them. Because of their military weakness, the presidio commanders were also forced to receive respectfully the visits of British, French, South American, and *Yanqui* ships—all of which were technically forbidden to enter the California harbors. The captains of these vessels carried home eloquent reports of life in California . . . and it was inevitable that one or another covetous nation would snap the weakening Spanish rule.

After Mexico won its independence from Spain in 1821 and California settlers had their first taste of self-government, their dissatisfaction with the patriarchal mission authority crystallized. The Indians were virtual slaves—who could not be sold, but could be pursued if they left the mission grounds, brought back, whipped, and locked up, and when penitent allowed to go to work again. Though unhappy enough to plan two or three revolts—the worst occurring in 1824— the Indians were not very articulate about their plight, but the "young Californians"—a party of progressive Castilians—took up the Indians' cause. Their efforts, added to the republican sentiment in Mexico, resulted in a decree issued by the Mexican Congress in 1833 removing the missions from Franciscan management. California's Mexican Governor, José Figueroa, had made a careful plan for the secularization of the missions, but he died before it could be carried out and the impatient *Californios* made the change unwisely and with too much haste.

One-half of the mission land and livestock was to have been given to the Indian neophytes who had developed it and to whom it had belonged before the coming of the Spaniards. Since they had never been taught self-discipline, they were to be forbidden to sell or mortgage their holdings. But when the missions were finally dismembered colonists helped themselves to mission lands and the cattle. The Indians received little cash for what they were able to sell, and that little they quickly squandered.

The Good Life: A few years after Portolá's earnest little company struggled up from Baja California, there rode into the new province a new kind of Spanish immigrants. Travelers returning to New Spain had told how the mission herds were thriving on the virgin pastures of Alta California. Castilian colonists, attempting to raise their cattle on the stonier soil of Mexican ranchos, were tempted to move on up the coast. The viceroy encouraged them with generous land grants. Although mission authorities opposed such colonizing by individuals, in 1786 Lieutenant Colonel Fages, Governor of Alta California, was empowered to make private grants and to outfit each *ranchero* with a storehouse and at least 2,000 head of cattle. By 1824 the colonist was also guaranteed security of person and property and freedom from taxes for five years.

The ranch houses, built of sun-dried adobe brick were plain but comfortable. Fields, worked by Indian labor, surrounded the house and beyond these were the vast pasture lands for the family's herds. The *rancheros* and their wives worked from dawn to sunset as industriously as the people who labored for them. The individual ranchos had to be self-sustaining, for the arrival of the supply ship was uncertain. All visitors praised their hospitality. "If I must be cast in sickness or destitution on the care of the stranger," wrote Walter Colton, "let it be in California; but let it be before American avarice has hardened the heart and made a God of gold."

It was the younger sons of these families who led the progressive factions when the *Californios* were forced into politics. As long as Spain's American colonies remained loyal, even California, the remotest of them, looked to Madrid for guidance and assistance. The *Californios* took no part in the struggle to sever Spanish dominance in the New World but, when they learned early in 1822 that an independent government had been set up in Mexico City, they suddenly became conscious of their republican rights. On April 9, 1822, Governor Pablo Vicente de Sola and ten delegates—eight presidio *comandantes* and military officers and two priests—met at Monterey, recognized California "from this time . . . as a dependent alone of . . . the Empire of Mexico and independent of the dominion of Spain." On November 9, 1822, California set up her own legislative body, the *Diputación,* composed of six *vocales,* or representatives, one from each presidio and pueblo district. During this first brief period of independence, the province acted decisively. It declared the Indians free citizens, opened the ports to trade, levied import and export duties, and taxes on crops and cattle, and established a military force and militia, and a judiciary.

California in March 1825 formally became a Territory of the Republic of Mexico. Under the Republic, California government consisted of: a governor, appointed by the national government; a secretary; a territorial legislature; a superior court; a prefect and sub-prefect (sheriffs); district judges; *alcaldes* (minor judges); justices of the peace; and *ayuntamientos,* or town councils. The Territory of California could send one *diputado* to represent it in the Mexican Congress but had no vote.

In November 1825 Luís Antonio Arguello's provisional governorship (1822-25) was ended by the arrival of a Mexican governor, José Maria de Echeandía. Echeandía's troubles began at once. The soldiers struck and marched against some of his Mexican troops, when he was not immediately able to pay their wages. But as generally happened in the local rebellions of this period, no blood was spilled. Although Echeandía rescinded some of the measures put into effect during Arguello's term, on the whole he was liberal and just. But in March 1830 he was replaced by a dictatorial governor, Manuel Victoria, who did not, however, take office until February 1831. Victoria opposed secularization of the missions, ordered the death penalty for small misdemeanors, and refused to convoke the *Diputación* or to give the *Californios* more voice in their affairs, although urged to do so by prominent *diputados.* The *Californios,* led by Pío Pico, Juan Bandini, and José Carrillo, seized the presidio at San Diego and advanced towards Los Angeles. On December 5, 1831, they clashed with Government troops near Cahuenga Pass. The fight was not severe, for there was only one fatality, but Victoria was convinced that he probably could never subdue the independent spirit of these provincials, and he returned to Mexico.

Into the *rancheros'* lives of gentlemanly leisure had come a new sense of political responsibility. Although they had no heritage of democratic ideals, as a class the *caballeros* acquired quite suddenly a natural desire to take their own government into their own hands. This they did in 1836, revolting against Mexico to proclaim the "Free and Sovereign State of Alta California." But the Republic of Mexico made concessions which brought California back into the Union.

During this transitional period, 1830 to 1846, a number of "battles" were fought which usually settled the current controversy. But the *Californios* had such an aversion to shedding blood that the opposing forces generally were careful not to shoot if the enemy was within range of their guns. Most of the decisions were won by oratory and *pronunciamentos.* Some of the *Californios'* controversies were with the

Mexicans, some with each other.   When they had an unpopular Mexican governor to oust, they united fervently, but between times they indulged in just as violent local disputes.   Jealous from the beginning were Los Angeles and Monterey, each wanting to be the capital.   The balance of power between customhouse and legislature was never settled. One of the most bitter of the many individual rivalries involved two of California's respected citizens—Juan Bautista Alvarado, a spellbinding young leader who became civil governor at 27, and his uncle, Mariano Guadalupe Vallejo, Alvarado's co-ruler as military chief. Their disagreement brought down upon them Mexican authority, in the person of General Manuel Micheltorena who arrived with an army of convict soldiers in August 1842.   Micheltorena, the last of the Mexican governors, stayed in the province for three years.   He was driven out by the *Californios* under Castro and Alvarado in March 1845, 15 months before the Americans took command at Monterey.

Yankee Bargain: The tide of American pioneer families that flooded California in the 1840's was preceded a generation earlier by a smaller migration of skippers, traders, and trappers who came on brief commercial missions.   True to their reputation for driving a good bargain, they secured wives, estates, and finally control of the province and its gracious people.   The visitors were welcomed by the *Californios,* but not by their rulers in Mexico City or Madrid.   Even before 1800 the Spanish Court had instructed the colonists that no foreigners were to land at California's ports or cross its borders.

Since the Court had neglected, however, to send regular supply ships to the colonists, the *Californios* seldom turned away the *Yanqui* skippers when they arrived with shiploads of such essentials as skillets, needles, cotton cloth, and plows.   The captain of an American vessel wrote in 1817:   "We served to clothe the naked soldiers of the king, when for lack of raiment they could not attend mass, and when the most reverend fathers had neither vestments nor vessels fit for the church, nor implements wherewith to till the soil."   The first United States ship, the *Otter* of Boston, docked at Monterey in 1796.   In 1799 the *Eliza* stopped at San Francisco, and in 1800 the *Betsy* at San Diego.   In addition to the regular traders, storm-battered whalers bound home from the North Pacific stopped at California harbors for repairs and supplies, paying for them with household goods brought from New England.   Gradually, in spite of Spain's embargo, California hides and tallow began to find their way to Atlantic coast markets.

While Yankee skippers were breaking into the California ports, Yankee trappers climbed the barrier of the Sierra and descended the canyons into the Sacramento and San Joaquin Valleys.   They explored many parts of California the Spaniards had never reached and took away a fortune in furs. On the whole, since they offered the Spaniards little and threatened much, they were not received as well as were the sea-faring traders. But one trapper, James Ohio Pattie, assured himself a welcome by bringing smallpox vaccine.

Before foreigners settled among the *Californios* there had been little commercial enterprise in the province, but the newcomers immediately started to organize its business life. One ambitious firm, McCullough & Hartnell—called "Macala and Arnell" by the soft-spoken Spaniards —contracted to dispose of the entire mission output of hides for a yearly shipload of supplies. While the foreigners aided California financially in this period, they held it back politically; in most cases they supported the despotic Mexican governors against the rebellious *Californios* because they feared that revolution would endanger their commercial interests.

The influence of the Americans after the arrival of the first United States immigrant train, the Bidwell-Bartleson company, in 1841 rose steadily. They had not yet declared any intention of raising the United States flag over the presidios, pueblos, and ranchos, but that purpose was stirring in their minds, as the *Californios* must have realized after October 19, 1842. On that day two American vessels sailed into Monterey Bay and their commander, Commodore Thomas Ap Catesby Jones, ordered the port to surrender to the United States. Stationed at Peru, the Commodore had heard a rumor that the United States and Mexico were at war and had hurried north to annex California. When he learned that no war had been declared, he retired from Monterey on October 20 with elaborate apologies . . . leaving the *Californios* something to think about.

Quieter but more significant was the arrival of Captain John C. Frémont, the U. S. topographical engineer later honored as "The Pathfinder," who came to California in 1844 on a scientific expedition. The next year he came again, this time visiting Monterey for several weeks as the guest of the United States Consul, Thomas O. Larkin. José Castro, the prefect, met Frémont and entertained him—but in January 1846 Castro learned that Frémont, en route to Monterey, had left two detachments of soldiers behind him in the back country. Upon Frémont's assurance that his party were interested only in scientific data, Castro gave them permission to spend the winter in California, with the express provision that they remain away from the coast settlements. Frémont left Monterey to rejoin his soldiers. Six weeks later the prefect learned that Frémont's band were camped at his back door, in the Salinas Valley, and demanded that they leave California at once. Then Frémont, acting perhaps under secret orders from Washington (the whole question of Frémont's official instructions remains a controversy), fortified a little hill, Gabilan (Hawk's Peak), and raised the American flag. His force was so small that it seems fantastic to regard this gesture as the first maneuver in the annexation of a great territory—but so it was. It came to nothing. When General José Castro made some not very effective military advances, Frémont withdrew up the Sacramento Valley, and after spending a week at the fort of Johann August Sutter, the Swiss immigrant who welcomed overland caravans at his colony of New Helvetia on the Sacramento River, retreated northward toward Oregon.

The retreat was made without haste, however. On the shores of Klamath Lake, Frémont was overtaken by two men from Sutter's Fort with the message that Lieut. A. N. Gillespie was following his trail with dispatches for him from the United States Government. Frémont and his company broke camp and retraced their steps. When he had read Gillespie's dispatches, he knew, as he wrote later, "that at last the time had come when England must not get a foothold; that we *must be first.* I was to *act,* discreetly but positively." Soon afterwards all the American ranchers north of San Francisco Bay were informed by an anonymous paper that a band of Californians were on their way north to destroy the crops, cattle, and houses of the Americans. What followed remains largely conjecture, since Frémont withheld most of the story. Probably the Americans, when they reported to Frémont for aid, were advised to provoke the Californians into an act of overt hostility. At any rate, they struck first when a small band headed by Ezekiel Merritt captured 250 horses which a group of *vaqueros* were driving southward to Castro's camp in the Santa Clara Valley.

As dawn was breaking on June 14, 1846, in the pueblo of Sonoma, the northern frontier, a little band of Yankees who had surrounded the house of the comandante of the presidio, General Mariano G. Vallejo, seized him and the other officers. The presidio, ungarrisoned, was taken without a shot. The rebels, led by farmer William B. Ide, hauled down the Mexican flag and raised a new one of their own, fashioned of homespun with a strip of red flannel and decorated in brown paint with a star, the figure of a grizzly bear, and the words "California Republic." Although war had begun between the United States and Mexico on May 13, neither the rebels nor Frémont knew it. Despite the provocation of the Americans, the *Californios* remained strangely reluctant to make reprisals, even when the force at Sonoma grew to 130 and Frémont marched to join them at the head of 72 mounted riflemen.

Although the intentions of the Americans must have been thoroughly revealed to the *Californios,* by July 1, their two ranking officials, Governor Pio Pico in Los Angeles and General José Castro in Monterey, were so absorbed in a private dispute that they made no preparations to defend the province. While they were arguing with each other in Los Angeles, Commodore John D. Sloat sailed into Monterey Bay and on July 7, raised the American flag on the custom-house, and claimed California for the United States. Two days later the flag was flying over San Francisco and Sonoma.

In alarm, Castro and Pico combined at last to resist the invasion. Mustering a hundred men, they were ready when the American forces —350 strong—landed in San Pedro under Commodore Robert F. Stockton, who had arrived in Monterey on July 15 to succeed Commodore Sloat. But before a shot was fired, both Castro and Pico had fled to Mexico, and on August 13 Stockton entered Los Angeles. Leaving Capt. Archibald Gillespie in charge, he returned northward. On September 23 the *Californios* attacked the small garrison. John Brown (California's Paul Revere) carried an appeal for help to San Francisco on horseback, covering more than 500 miles in less than five days. But, by the time Captain Mervine had reached Los Angeles with reinforcements on the *Savannah,* Los Angeles had been recaptured. On October 6 the *Californios* met and defeated Mervine and his sailors in a battle at the Domingues Rancho and drove them back to their ship in San Pedro Bay. At Santa Barbara and at San Diego the American flags so recently raised were hauled down again.

Meanwhile the *Californios,* skirmishing with the Americans led by Frémont and Thomas O. Larkin in the Salinas Valley, seemed to be getting the better of it, until late in the fall assistance arrived for the Americans. An expeditionary force sent overland from Santa Fe by the War Department, under command of Colonel Stephen W. Kearny, arrived on December 5 and engaged with General Pico's forces the day following in an indecisive skirmish. Kearny's men, when combined with Stockton's and the resident Americans, now made an army of 600, equal to the *Californios'* forces. The two "armies" met in the battle of San Gabriel and of La Mesa on January 8 and 9, 1847. So decisive were the American victories, that the *Californios* surrendered. On January 10 General Kearny and Commander Stockton once more raised the American flag over Los Angeles, and on the 13th hostilities finally ended with the signing of articles of capitulation by General Andres Pico and Frémont at a ranch house near Cahuenga Pass. The incident was like the patching up of a quarrel by old friends, for the Americans required of the *Californios* only that they give up their artillery and pledge to obey the laws of the United States. On February 2, 1848, when the Treaty of Guadalupe Hidalgo was signed, California was formally relinquished by Mexico.

California's adopted sons had one more job to do. Although the United States now owned California, Congress made no satisfactory provision for its civil government because the Congressional slavery and anti-slavery factions could not come to an agreement on these questions. After a confused period in which military law, Spanish law, and American law were simultaneously administered in California, Brigadier-General Bennet Riley, U.S.A., military Governor, took official action on June 3, 1849, when he issued a proclamation "recommending the formation of a State constitution, or a plan for a Territorial government." When the convention met in Colton Hall, Monterey, on September 1, 48 delegates were admitted to seats. On October 10 they adopted a constitution, which was ratified by people on November 13, 1849. It remained in force until 1879.

On the day of ratification (as provided by the constitution) the people elected a Governor, Lieutenant Governor, 16 State senators, and 36 assemblymen. On December 15, 1849, the State legislature convened and on the 20th inaugurated Peter H. Burnett as Governor, and John McDougal as Lieutenant Governor. On the same day the legislature elected two United States Senators, John C. Frémont and William M. Gwin, and on December 22 most of the State officials and the supreme court judges.

On December 20, 1849, the military Governor, General Riley, issued a remarkable proclamation: "A new executive having been elected and installed into office in accordance with the provisions of the Constitution of the State, the undersigned hereby resigns his powers as Governor of California." The proclamation constituted a recognition by the highest United States agent in California that California had declared itself to be a State, although legally, of course, it had no right to do so without Federal permission. Its action precipitated an eight months' argument in Congress, prolonged by pro-slavery Congressmen who fought to prevent the admission of a new non-slavery State. Finally on September 9, 1850, California was admitted to the Union as a free State.

Flood Tide: Hundreds of reports describing California as "a perfect paradise, a perpetual spring" had started eastern families building prairie schooners several years before California became American territory. The first pioneer train, organized largely by John Bidwell, left Independence, Missouri, May 19, 1841 and reached the San Joaquin Valley on November 4. The first to travel in wagons, the Chiles-Walker Party, came in 1843. By 1846 thousands, including the tragic Donner party, almost half of whom died of exposure and starvation en route, were on the westward trails. It was in that year that immigrants also started to come around the Horn, one group of 200 Mormons arriving at San Francisco on the ship *Brooklyn* on July 31.

A member of one of the overland trains in 1845 was a young New Jersey wagon builder, James Wilson Marshall, who went to work for Sutter, building a saw mill on the south fork of the American River near the site of Coloma. While inspecting the tail race there, one morning late in January 1848, Marshall picked out of the water a piece of shining metal half the size of a pea. At first he thought it was iron pyrites, but when he pounded it between stones and found it soft, he knew that what he held in his hand was gold. Alone in the upland forest Marshall "sat down and began to think right hard," as he wrote in his diary. It is doubtful whether he guessed that his discovery would start the greatest mass movement of people since the Crusades.

Less than six months later Walter Colton, *alcalde* of Monterey, wrote: "The blacksmith dropped his hammer, the carpenter his plane, the mason his trowel, the farmer his sickle, the baker his loaf, and the tapster his bottle. All were off for the mines, some on horses, some on carts, and some on crutches, and one went in a litter." By June 1848 scarcely a male remained in Monterey, San Francisco, San Jose, or Santa Cruz. Soldiers deserted, and so did the detachments sent to capture them. Hundreds of ships lay at anchor in San Francisco Bay, their crews gone to the foothills. Fields of wheat went unharvested, homes and shops were abandoned, newspapers suspended publication, and city officials closed their desks.

The gold fever spread almost as quickly throughout the Nation and the world. At one time westbound wagon trains passed between Missouri and Fort Laramie in an unbroken stream for two months. By March 1849, 17,000 had embarked for California from eastern ports. Within its first 10 years as one of the United States, California became generously populated—not only with Americans, but with the adventurous of all nations. Between 1847 and 1850 the population of California increased from 15,000 to 92,497 and a decade later the Federal Census enumerated 379,994 persons in the State. Substantial pioneer families were among the Argonauts who danced and played games on the crowded little ships, while gales, scurvy, and starvation threatened them. Others trudged courageously over trails so bordered with the wreckage of previous parties that one immigrant, James Abbey, counted in 15 miles 362 abandoned wagons and the bleaching bones of 350 horses, 280 oxen, and 120 mules.

> Oh! Californy!
> That's the land for me!
> I'm bound for Sacramento
> With the washbowl on my knee.

In the boisterous shanty-towns of gold rush days—Git-up-and-git, Bogus Thunder, Angel's Camp, You Bet, Shinbone Creek, Red Dog, Lazy Man's Canyon—the average return was up to $50 a day, though many made much more. From one panful of dirt $1,500 was washed, and a trench 100 feet long yielded its two owners $17,000 in 7 days.

Sometimes gold was picked out of the rock "as fast as one can pick kernels out of a lot of well-cracked shell barks." Fully as much was made by those who served the miners. Many a tent-store took in $1,000 a day. Owners of river steamers and stage coaches, conveyors of water, innkeepers, entertainers gathered in copious wealth. They supplied the elementary needs; amenities were nonexistent. One of the "best hotels," described by Hinton R. Helper, was a canvas structure, floored with dirt. It consisted of an undivided room were guests ate, drank, and slept in tiered bunks. "When we creep into one of these nests it is optional with us whether we unboot or uncoat ourselves; but it would be looked upon as an act of ill-breeding to go to bed with one's hat on."

The colorful ruffians of the times have been so immortalized as to create the impression that the camps were lawless. As a matter of fact, the mining camps, in distinction to the cities, stand as one of the world's best examples of men's spontaneous ability to govern themselves. With no formal legal setup, the miners, extremely diverse in background and nationality, established a society with a high degree of justice and democracy—particularly in the early years. Later, when "loose fish" and "bad whites" came to California in increasing numbers, crime became more difficult to control, both in the camps and in the feeder-town, San Francisco.

Gold seekers, disembarked after a nine-month trip around the Horn or down from the camps with bags of gold, wanted the lustiest entertainment imagination could provide. They got it. Visitors gambled around the roulette tables—residents gambled in real estate, nails, cork, calico, rice, whatever commodities could be cornered—all gambled with their lives, for it is said that during the years from 1849 to 1856 more than a thousand murders were committed in San Francisco, with but a single execution. Of city government there was practically none. An alarmed official addressed his fellow citizens in 1849: "We are without a dollar in the public treasury. . . . You have neither an office for your magistrate, nor any other public edifice. You are without a single police officer or watchman, and have not the means of confining a prisoner for an hour." To remedy the situation the citizens formed the vigilance committees of 1851 and 1856. The former drove out the "Hounds," a gang that attacked various racial minorities, and the latter dispersed more "reputable" crooks in league with bankers and politicians. Both groups sprang from a widespread desire for democratic control, representing the community as a whole. Less clearly characterized by a sense of responsibility for its actions was the similar sort of spontaneous government that arose in Los Angeles, where voluntary citizens' committees broke up the bandit organizations of Salomon Pico, Juan Flores, and Pancho Daniel.

In 1854 the Great Bonanza suddenly slackened. Fortunes large and small collapsed. Disillusioned miners drifted up and down the State. Added to their numbers were the wagon trains and boatloads of immigrants arriving, now, to homestead on Uncle Sam's new fertile acres. They came not realizing that most of this vast land had been apportioned long before to the *Californios,* who had been guaranteed their property rights at the end of the Mexican war. The Americans simply moved onto the ranchos and dared the owners to put them off. What to do with these squatters became the question of the hour. Unfortunately the boundaries of the ranchos had never been fixed exactly. "Professional squatters" were hired by land-grabbing corporations. Unscrupulous legislators defended the squatters in order to court their votes. When at last riots and bloodshed forced the Federal Government to take action, a survey of the State was ordered and a land commission formed to adjust disputes. In the end many of the Spanish families were reduced to comparative poverty. They were remarkably patient. General Vallejo, one of them, wrote, "The inhabitants of California have no reason to complain of the change of government, for if the rich have lost thousands of horses and cattle, the poor have been bettered in condition."

The admission of California into the Union had not satisfied all Californians. In 1850 Walter Colton had predicted that an independent nation would spring up on the Pacific unless Congress built a railroad to the Coast, for without it, California would easily have become self-sufficient. The cry for independence was soon taken up by southern sympathizers, the followers of pro-slavery Senator William S. Gwin, who overran southern California, especially San Bernardino County. The Democratic Party, which controlled the State legislature in every session but one from 1851 to 1860, was torn by the struggle between the Gwin faction and the anti-slavery faction headed by David C. Broderick, who was elected to the Senate in 1857. When Broderick was slain in a duel by Gwin's henchman, David S. Terry, in September 1859, his successor in the Senate, Milton S. Latham, joined Gwin in the demand for a republic on the Pacific. He declared in 1860 that if civil war should break out, California would declare its independence. In 1860 the pro-slavery Democrats had gained overwhelming strength in both houses of the legislature, but in the year following they split, and Abraham Lincoln carried the State—by less than a thousand votes. In the nick of time a plot to seize Federal strongholds in California and raise Confederate forces was frustrated. When news of the fall of Fort Sumter came on May 17, California pledged its loyalty to the Union, and in the next session of the legislature Republicans controlled the assembly. Gold from California s mines began traveling eastward to help win the war for the North.

Steel Rails to Sunny Shores: When the first transcontinental railroad was completed in May 1869, new multitudes of pioneers traveled westward. Although two decades had passed since the first Argonauts set out across the plains, California had still not absorbed its surplus population. The new pioneers found their promised land in a state of poverty and strife—wages low and unemployment widespread, capital scarce and interest rates prohibitive, land titles uncertain, freight rates exorbitant, and water rights held by monopolies. They found the labor movement restless, anti-Chinese agitation rampant, and the whole people in an uproar against a government corrupted by railroad control.

Following collapse of a wild frenzy of speculation in wildcat mining and oil company stocks in the 1860's had come an even wilder boom in Nevada silver mining stocks, set off by exploitation of the Comstock Lode's Bonanza mines in 1872. The California Stock Exchange Board, organized in that year, became the scene of such violent excitement that the flush days of forty-nine paled in comparison. Throughout the State people invested in stocks every cent they could borrow, beg, or steal. A few made millions; most lost all they had. For on August 27, 1875, the Bank of California crashed—and California was shaken to its foundations.

The hard times that followed the bank panic bore down on people in town and country alike. The farmers of the interior valleys, already oppressed by inequable mortgage and taxation laws, the railroad's high freight rates, monopoly of land and water rights by the railroad and land companies, and finally by the ravages of a severe drought in 1876, took with ill grace the added burdens of an economic depression. In the cities wages fell and breadlines grew as thousands were thrown out of work—and hungry men walking the streets began to resent the Bonanza kings' ostentatious display of their newly found wealth.

Meanwhile the long-smouldering hostility against the Chinese, who had been thronging in since 1848 as miners, truck gardeners, laundrymen, fishermen, and workers on the railroad, had begun to break out in flames. It was incited by politicians, among them Governor Henry Haight, who had said in December 1869: "The Chinese are a stream of filth and prostitution pouring in from Asia, whose servile competition tends to cheapen and degrade labor." As workingmen, under artful urging, began to blame the Chinese for all their wrongs, the anti-Chinese feeling spread throughout the State. In 1871 a lawless gang looted and pillaged Los Angeles' Chinatown and lynched nineteen Chinese. The labor movement took up the cry: "The Chinese must go!" On July 23-24, 1877, several thousand rioters burned and sacked Chinese laundries in San Francisco and fired the Pacific Mail Steamship docks where Chinese immigrants landed. Elsewhere there were sporadic outbreaks of violence.

Despairing of redress for their difficulties from the railroad controlled State government, city and farm workers, and even some small businessmen and small landholders organized the Workingmen's Party of California, promptly nicknamed the Sand-Lot Party for its Sunday afternoon meetings on San Francisco's vacant sand lots harangued by the Irish spellbinder, Dennis Kearney. The party vowed "to wrest the government from the hands of the rich and place it in those of the people, where it properly belongs; to rid the country of cheap Chinese labor as soon as possible; to destroy the great money power of the rich . . . to destroy land monopoly in our state by a system of taxation that will make great wealth impossible in the future."

For a solution to their problems, the people looked to the legislature. The authors of California's first constitution, framed in the idealistic days of the Gold Rush, had given the legislators sweeping powers—to levy taxes, make appropriations, grant franchises, and give away public lands—of which the legislators of the seventies took full advantage. By 1878 the Workingmen's Party had grown so strong that it forced the legislature to adopt an act calling a constitutional convention. Of the 152 members of the convention who came together on September 28, 1878, 51 were members of the Workingmen's Party and 78 were nonpartisan; they included mechanics, miners, farmers, and even a cook, as well as lawyers, doctors, journalists, and teachers.

The constitution which they adopted was ratified by the voters May 7, 1879. It was termed reactionary by some, radical by others. It remodeled the judiciary department, improved prison regulations and prohibited convict labor, and passed a law instituting the eight-hour working day. In general, it differed little from the organic law common in most States of the Union, but when compared with the constitution of 1849, it marked a distinct advance toward popular control. The power of the legislature was everywhere curtailed. "Lobbying" was made a felony. Provisions to tax and control common carriers and corporations, and to regulate public utilities and services were inserted. A two-thirds vote in both houses and ratification by the people were required to pass a constitutional amendment. Suffrage was extended to "every male citizen," 21 years or more old who had lived in California for a year, "provided *no native of China*," and no idiot, lunatic, convicted criminal, or illiterate "shall ever exercise the privileges of an elector." The legislature was to consist of 40 senators and 80 assemblymen, meeting biennially. The Governor, Lieutenant Governor, secretary of state, controller, treasurer, attorney general and surveyor general were to be elected by the people for four-year terms. A two-thirds vote of each house could overcome the Governor's veto. Judicial powers were confined to a supreme court (a chief justice and six associate justices), three district courts of appeal, a superior court for each county, and also minor courts (as amended Nov. 8, 1904).

The Workingmen's Party was driven out of existence in 1880 by a fusion of Democrats and Republicans—but not before its anti-Chinese agitation had led to a vote by the people of the State (154,638 to 883) against further immigration from China. On March 20, 1879, the national Congress passed an exclusion bill, killed by the veto of President Rutherford B. Hayes. Two years later a treaty with China giving the United States the power to "regulate, limit, or suspend" Chinese immigration was ratified by the Senate.

Although the State's population had increased 54 percent during the 1870's, its professional boosters—fast becoming a familiar type—discovered soon after 1880 that promotion would bring still more new settlers. For the first time California went afield to bid for immigrants with advertisements, books, magazine and newspaper articles telling about the extraordinary climate and resources of "the Coast." Typical was this from B. F. Taylor's *Between the Gates:* "Whoever asks where Los Angeles is, to him I shall say: across a desert without wearying, beyond a mountain without climbing . . . where the flowers catch fire with beauty . . . where the pomegranates wear calyx crowns . . . where the bananas of Honolulu are blossoming; where the chestnuts of Italy are dropping; where Sicilian lemons are ripening; where the almond trees are shining . . . in the midst of a garden of thirty-six square miles—there is Los Angeles." The inducements were so convincing that by 1884 the Southern Pacific was doing a rushing passenger business at fares of $125 from the Midwest to Los Angeles. When the Santa Fe was completed the following year, the two roads entered on a rate war that reduced fares to $5 and even, at one time, to $1. Multitudes climbed on the trains and started West, savings in their pockets, bound as they thought for a sort of South Sea paradise.

A real estate boom began, legitimate enough in that it originated in a sudden influx of buyers. But the shrewd encouragement of swindlers led most of the citizens to believe that the 1885 boom was only the prelude to another that was to "outclass the present activity as thunder to the crack of a hickory-nut." Prices of Los Angeles lots rose from $500 to $5,000 within a year. Truck gardens and outlying vineyards worth $350 an acre were squared off into lots and sold for $10,000 an acre. Networks of sidewalks ran mile after mile out into the sagebrush. Elaborate hotels were built on desert tracts—and never occupied except on the opening day.

The newcomers, many of them unsophisticated farmers and small tradespeople from the Middle West, grew hysterical when the boom got really under way. The wealthier among them paid $20,000 to $50,000 for waterfront lots on a lonely stretch of shore, "Redondo-by-the-Sea," because "engineers" had declared that a submarine oil well off Redondo kept the water smooth and made an ideal harbor. Smaller savings were invested in Widneyville-by-the-Desert, a wasteland covered with Joshua trees, spiny and tortuous. Since the grotesque trees failed to give the site a homelike atmosphere, the promoters stuck oranges on the spines—and sold a citrus grove! To Widneyville, as to the other boom towns, prospective buyers were carried in tallyhoes and stages, accompanied with bands, to be greeted on the grounds by the smoothest of high-pressure salesmen and plied with free chicken dinners and all the liquor they could drink. "Millionaires of a day," to quote Theodore C. Van Dyke, "went about sunning their teeth with checkbooks in their outside pockets."

In 1887 many of those millionaires were suicides, as syndicates collapsed, banks closed, individuals and business firms went bankrupt, and the bands, the tallyhoes, and the oratory disappeared from the sunny scene. Once more the bubble had burst. The hard times of the early 1890's lay ahead, breadlines once more lengthened, unemployed men mustered to join Coxey's Army in a hunger march on Washington, and the cities put their jobless thousands to work on public works projects. The influx of new settlers dwindled.

Twentieth Century: But the tide of immigration once more rose and new multitudes flocked in, swelling the population by 60 percent in the decade from 1900 to 1910. "A new century—a new order" became the slogan. The new century began with prosperity, marked by rising wages and industrial expansion, the development of the petroleum and hydroelectric industries, and of intensive fruit growing on a big scale. But the newcomers, mostly people from the Midwest who brought with them a long tradition of active participation in community affairs, found much in California to challenge—corruption in municipal politics, machine control of government by corporations, industrial strife, and anti-Oriental agitation.

For once more the outcry against the "yellow peril" had broken out. The Japanese, imported in increasing numbers by large agriculturists to take the place of the Chinese as farm workers, had begun to settle as farmers and tradesmen, managing their small holdings so thriftily that soon they were displacing white workers and farmers. Although they numbered but 14,243 in 1906—and for many years had been excluded along with other Orientals from the privilege of naturalization—military and patriotic groups, merchants' associations, and labor organizations combined to raise the cry: "California shall not become the Caucasian graveyard." In 1906 the San Francisco Board of Education passed an order segregating the 93 Japanese pupils in the city schools in an Oriental public school. When Japan protested that the action was a violation of her treaty with the United States, the

Federal Government persuaded the board to rescind its order. The result of the diplomatic controversy was the "Gentlemen's Agreement" of 1907, by which the United States agreed to admit Japanese children below the age of 16 to the regular public schools, while Japan contracted to prevent the emigration of laborers to the United States. But anti-Japanese feeling persisted and grew in California.

One of the first evils that challenged the attention of California's civic-minded newcomers in the early years of the century was corruption in city politics. The prosecution of San Francisco's "City Hall graft ring" led the way in a series of exposures of municipal scandals that introduced the muckraking era in California. From 1906 to 1908 the whole State followed with eager interest the prosecutions of political boss Abraham Ruef, Mayor Eugene Schmitz, and Patrick Calhoun, United Railroads head, pushed by Fremont Older, Rudolph Spreckels, and James D. Phelan; attorneys Francis J. Heney and Hiram Johnson; and detective William Burns. In Los Angeles the reform movement was taken up in 1909 when the editor of the *Herald,* T. R. Gibbon, accused Mayor A. C. Harper and his associates of enriching themselves through forcing owners of vice dens to buy stock in fictitious sugar companies by promising police protection. The municipal clean-up campaign, soon joined by the editors of the *Evening Express* and various citizens' committees, succeeded in defeating Harper in the next election.

In State politics the battle against control by corporation lobbyists, fought so ardently in the 1870's, was still to be won. As early as 1905-06, resolutions demanding Government ownership of railroads were passed at Bakersfield and Fresno, aimed against the Southern Pacific. The demand for public ownership was linked with demands for other reforms. The Independence League, a group of liberal Democrats meeting in Oakland in September 1906, came out for equal suffrage, the eight-hour working day, and State arbitration of industrial disputes, as well as for public ownership. At the same time a demand for direct primary legislation to reform the election laws was arising out of charges of fraud at the State party conventions. When a new economic depression shook the whole financial and business structure of the State in 1907, the reform movement gathered sudden strength.

The outcome was a political revolt which took form in a coalition of liberal Republicans, organized in Oakland in August 1907 as the Lincoln-Roosevelt League. It proposed to give the people of the State a direct voice in government by freeing the Republican Party from domination by "Vested Interests." Its platform included such planks as the direct primary, popular election of Senators, and institution of the initiative, referendum, and recall. It promised to elect "a free, honest, and capable legislature, truly representative of the common interests of the people of California." As leading newspapers throughout the State swung to the support of the Lincoln-Roosevelt League, it rallied enough votes in 1908 to elect a legislature which passed a direct primary law, soon ratified by the people. When it gained control of the Republican Party in 1910 by electing its candidates to nearly every State and Congressional office, the State was shaken by a political upheaval.

The Lincoln-Roosevelt League's candidate for Governor, Hiram Johnson, took office in 1911. The new legislature which convened at the same time fulfilled its platform promises by approving a long series of legislative reforms. The 22 amendments to the Constitution of 1879, which it adopted and the people ratified, included provisions for woman suffrage, a new railroad commission, the initiative, referendum, and recall, and workingmen's compensation for industrial accidents. Theodore Roosevelt called its enactments "the most comprehensive programme of constructive legislation ever passed at a single session of an American legislature." When the Roosevelt Republicans bolted the Republican National Convention of 1912, they nominated Hiram Johnson as Theodore Roosevelt's running mate on the progressive "Bull Moose" ticket, which carried the State in the national elections.

A concession to anti-Japanese agitation was the 1911 legislature's alien land law. It was supplemented in 1913 by the Webb Act, forbidding aliens ineligible to citizenship to own agricultural land in the State, which the legislature passed over President Woodrow Wilson's protests. The Japanese evaded its operation by forming land corporations or by transferring ownership to their American-born children, but the hue and cry forced enactment in 1920 of the Asiatic Land Law, forbidding such evasions. Despite Japan's protests, the United States Supreme Court upheld in 1923 the constitutionality of the Webb Act. And in 1924 Congress revised the immigration law to exclude Japanese.

The reform wave continued into the early years of the World War. In December 1913 the Republican State Central Committee, announcing that it foresaw no hope of progress within the Republican Party, recommended the formation of the Progressive Party. The new party, formally launched on December 6 of that year, attracted a mass of former Republican voters. In the elections of November 1914, when Hiram Johnson was returned to office, the Progressives won more decisively than in any previous election. But in 1916, the year in which Johnson was elected to the Senate, the bitter feud between Republicans and Progressives gave California to Woodrow Wilson by the narrow—and history-making—margin of 3,773 votes.

Already California had embarked on the feverish expansionist period of the World War boom years, as wages, industrial output, and

Agriculture

VINEYARD, LIVERMORE VALLEY

ORANGE GROVE LOS ANGELES COUNTY

DATE PALMS, NEAR INDIO

ORCHARD SCENE IN NAPA COUNTY

FIGS IN THE DRY YARD

HARVESTING TOMATOES IN SACRAMENTO VALLEY

MIGRATORY WORKERS WEIGHING PEAS

YOUNG COTTON PICKER

BED OF THE ALL-AMERICAN CANAL

CONSTRUCTION WORK ON IMPERIAL DAM

MURAL IN POST OFFICE, WHITTIER

WINE STORED FOR AGING, NAPA COUNTY

EARLY SPANISH WATER WHEEL, NEAR LONE PINE

DROUGHT REFUGEES FROM TEXAS ENCAMPED NEAR EXETER

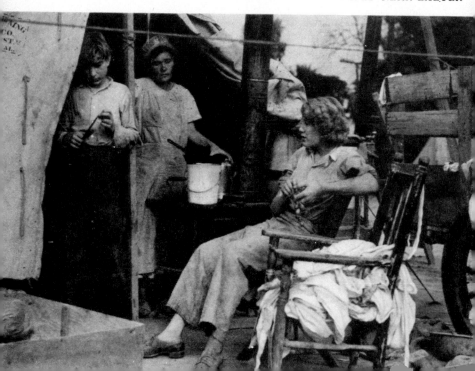

the number of wage earners and industrial plants soared dizzily. Between 1910 and 1920 the assessed value of real and personal property doubled. The opening of the Panama Canal in 1914, celebrated the following year by the Panama-California Exposition at San Diego and the Panama-Pacific International Exposition at San Francisco, seemed to promise unlimited growth of California's maritime trade. The reform movement was soon forgotten. In southern California the unexpected plea of guilty by J. B. and J. J. McNamara, on trial in 1911 for the dynamiting of the Times building, had crushed the labor movement and turned the tide of a municipal election against the socialist candidate. When the bombing of San Francisco's Preparedness Day parade July 22, 1916, was followed by the swift arrest of labor organizers Thomas Mooney and Warren K. Billings, the voices raised in protest were drowned out by the clamor of war-era patriots. The period of repression continued into early post-war years, when the newly passed criminal syndicalism law was invoked against members of the I. W. W. and other nonconformists.

The westward moving hordes of forty-nine were as nothing to the new influx of settlers whom California welcomed in the 1920's, as prosperity, unrestrained, reached giddy heights. The high-pressure efforts of boosters and promoters were devoted to making prosperity and California synonymous in the public mind. Its harbors, its oil wells and factories, its movie studios, its orange groves and irrigation projects, its booming real estate subdivisions all helped to renew its association in people's thoughts with the El Dorado of the Argonauts. The cities around San Francisco Bay advanced as maritime and manufacturing centers and the new metropolis of the south, Los Angeles, surrounded by fast expanding suburbs, as a manufacturing, oil-refining, fruit-shipping, and movie-making center. By 1930 the population of California had grown to 5,677,251—an increase of 65 per cent in 10 years, greater than in any other State in the Union during the same period. The increase gave it sixth place among the States in population.

And again the bubble burst. The newcomers who had thronged in by the hundreds of thousands—the wage earners and farmers, the small investors and businessmen, the elderly retired people—found themselves in the same situation as those who had come before them: jobless, their savings exhausted, their businesses bankrupt, their farms foreclosed, or their investments wiped out.

As they had done in the 1900's and earlier still in the 1870's, the people turned to politics. Of the State-wide political movements that began to follow close on one another throughout the 1930's, the first was the EPIC movement, which rallied around the "End Poverty in California" (EPIC) plan presented by Upton Sinclair when he consented in August 1933 to run for the gubernatorial nomination on the

Democratic ticket. Sinclair's plan called for the establishment of self-sustaining State land colonies and the opening of idle factories, both to be operated on "production for use" principles for the benefit of the unemployed and to be financed by State-issued scrip. The plan called also for repeal of the State sales tax, exemption of small homes and ranches from taxation, and for levying of graduated taxes on incomes, inheritances, corporations, and unused lands and buildings. Another plank in the EPIC platform was pensions for the aged, the physically incapacitated, and widows with dependent children. After the hottest election campaign hitherto waged in the State, Sinclair was defeated for the governorship by a narrow margin, although EPIC candidates were elected to city and Congressional offices.

The people turned to other movements which seemed to promise a way out, some of which, like the EPIC movement, spread into other States. A short-lived one that swept southern California was the Utopian Society, which employed semi-dramatic rites to educate its members in social and economic affairs. The Townsend Plan, devised by an elderly Long Beach physician, Dr. Francis E. Townsend, enlisted the support of large numbers of the State's more elderly citizens with its proposal to promote business recovery by paying $200 per month to each person over 60 years of age. In 1938 another project for economic recovery, the so-called "Thirty Dollars Every Thursday" or "Ham-and-Eggs" plan, rose to prominence, promising to pay aged persons $30 weekly in State warrants, financed by a 2¢ tax on all sales.

California Bound—1939: On the highways leading into California there appeared in the late 1930's, among the long lines of streamlined automobiles, more antiquated vehicles. Like the covered wagons of earlier days they carried all their owners' worldly goods: those elemental necessities that change but little in 80 years—pots, pans, bedding, basins, washtubs. These latter-day prairie schooners, like their predecessors, stopped for the night at wayside camps, where the informality of hardships loosened tongues. Once again campfires burned along western trails—but the stories told around them resembled not at all the stories of the earlier pioneers. "The dust was drifted high as the window sills." "The cattle died a-lookin' at you." "Wouldn't a blade of grass grow anywhere in the valley."

Over the spirits of the starving migrants the desolation they had seen lay heavy—until they remembered that they were going to California. That horizon was a bright one, for they were sure that in a State which supplies nearly half the Nation's fresh fruit and a third of its truck crops there would be a place for them among the pickers. What few of them had learned was that earlier immigrants—Japanese, Mexicans, Filipinos—had swarmed so thickly over the fertile acres that wages never rose above the standard accepted by coolie and peon labor. Or that they would have to make their homes in districts like the one where in 1934 the National Labor Relations Board found "filth, squalor, an entire absence of sanitation, and a crowding of human beings into totally inadequate tents or crude structures built of boards, weeds, and anything that was found at hand to give a pitiful semblance of a home at its worst." For these workers the workmen's compensation law failed to operate, the State's minimum wage law for women and minors was ignored, medical aid was denied unless death was imminent, and labor contractors took an exorbitant percentage of wages—wages which averaged, in 1935, but $289 per family, including the income of all its members. Such were the conditions that awaited 97,642 Dust Bowl migrants in 1936 and 104,976 in the following year. In 1938 they were arriving at the rate of 10,000 a month. Their coming served to bring to people's consciousness the long unsolved problem of how to feed, clothe, and shelter the hundreds of thousands of homeless farm workers who follow the crops over the State.

When the people of California went to the polls in November 1938, the surge of protest and demands for reform that had swept the State throughout the 1930's came to a climax. They elected a new Governor, Culbert L. Olson—the first Democrat to hold the office since the Republican Party had captured it 43 years before. During those four decades, California's period of expansion had run its course. At the end of the 1930's, Californians could look forward neither to the opening up of new lands nor, probably, to the discovery of new resources. The dramatic influx of fortune seekers, following in successive waves as boom succeeded boom, has subsided. What lies ahead is an intensive struggle to solve the social and economic problems which are the inevitable heritage of California's four centuries of development.

Riches From the Soil

WITHIN the rock wall formed by California's two great mountain ranges lies the long level stretch of the Sacramento-San Joaquin or Central Valley—the "Long Valley," as John Steinbeck has named it—called the world's most fertile growing region, which contains about two-thirds of the State's 30,000,000 acres of agricultural lands. Other major growing areas are the coastal valleys, the intensely developed farm area south of the Tehachapis, center of the citrus industry, and the arid but potentially highly productive desert region in the southeastern corner of the State, which includes Imperial Valley.

The wide range of topography, soil, and climate makes it possible to produce every species of temperate zone and subtropical fruit, vegetable, and field crop within the limits of the State. Pears grow on the cool mountain slopes to the north; asparagus, celery, beans, onions, and rice in the black soil of the Sacramento-San Joaquin delta area; lettuce in Salinas Valley, called "the Valley of Green Gold"; grapes for dry wines on the sunny foothills of Napa and Sonoma Counties; prunes —most of America's supply—in the sheltered orchards of Santa Clara Valley; table, wine and raisin grapes, peaches, apricots, plums, olives, and a fabulous yield of cotton in the brown silted loam of San Joaquin Valley; oranges, lemons, limes, pomegranates, figs, avocados, loquats, guavas, almonds, and walnuts to the south; dates far out in the desert to the southeast beyond Indio.

The State is ideally adapted to the modern, industrialized, mass-production type of specialized intensive farming. The dominant unit in the agricultural pattern is the large-scale, mechanized, irrigated "ranch," operated with the precision of a Ford factory, employing hundreds of workers and turning out specialized crops for eastern and foreign markets or for California's $174,000,000 fruit and vegetable canning and preserving industry.

A typical large-scale fruit ranch in the extreme southern end of San Joaquin Valley—6,000 acres devoted exclusively to the production of "green" or fresh fruit—ships more than two dozen carloads of peaches, plums, and grapes daily at the peak season and employs 2,500 men and women in orchards, vineyards, and packing sheds. Hidden by the gentle, scarcely perceptible swell of the plain is the heart of the ranch: the cluster of administrative buildings, the white staff bungalows on a miniature Main Street with gay little gardens and tennis courts, the packing-sheds and refrigeration plant and railroad siding, the schoolhouse and store. Beyond lie the separate labor camps for American, Mexican, Filipino and Japanese workers.

The elaborate irrigation system is equipped with 18 pumps, run by 125- to 250-horsepower deepwell turbines. They draw the ranch's water supply from subterranean springs, fed by melting snow in the mountains. Farm machinery includes 15 caterpillar tractors, 43 trucks and trailers, over 50 company-owned automobiles, and 22 mules—apparently still indispensable to farming even in this ultra-modern form. The carpenter shop puts together a reserve supply of 300,000 crates before the season opens; 60,000 crates can be stored in the refrigerating plant when they are packed with fruit.

Ranch personnel includes the ranch manager, his assistants and office staff, a physician, an electrician, a blacksmith and five assistants, a cook and 11 assistants for the single men's cook houses. The labor force of men and women engaged in irrigating, tractor driving, and picking, packing, and shipping fruit ranges from 700 at the lowest point in December to 2,500 at the highest in the summer, averaging 2,200 from April through December. At peak season, in the packing sheds alone, 450 workers pack plums and about 325 pack grapes. The conveyor system is used from the time the crated fruit is brought in on trucks for sorting and packing until the finished, boxed, scientifically pre-cooled product glides out on the belt to the refrigerator cars, waiting on the siding of the ranch's special branch line.

Agriculture is the basic industry of the State, occupying a key position in its economic structure. Its income far outstrips the combined income of oil and mining, and its production cost more than triples that of the motion picture industry. In addition, more than a fourth of the total value of products from manufacturing industries is in industries directly allied to agriculture, such as milling, canning, packing, and preserving. In 1937, California was second only to Texas in gross farm income. It produces nearly one-half of the country's fresh fruit output, about 95 percent of its dried fruit, a third of its truck crops, and nearly a third of its canned fruits and vegetables. California holds first place in many of the country's most important fruit and truck crops and some field crops. In many crops, such as lemons, dates, figs, and olives, the State has a monopoly of commercial production.

Farm production in California rose over 120 percent in the period 1909 to 1936. This expansion has been accomplished, with practically no accompanying expansion in acreage for the last 50 years, by intensive cultivation. Since about 1885, the tendency has been to concentrate on increasing output, with an accompanying expenditure of money and labor per acre which today has reached a point probably unequalled anywhere else in the world. The huge outlays for power, irrigation, water rights, fertilizer, machinery, labor, and transportation have necessarily developed California's intensive agriculture into an extremely complex industrial and commercial enterprise, far removed from the simplicities of farming in the familiar sense of the word.

The old family-size farm, run by the farmer and his family and a few hired hands, is steadily declining in importance and in number. Those that remain are increasingly operated, not as self-sufficing family units, but as commercial enterprises, imitating on a miniature scale the big "outdoor factories." Many are direct adjuncts of fruit and vegetable packing corporations, for which they produce selected crops according to company specifications under supervision of the company's fieldmen and, in many cases, with funds advanced by the company.

Among the small submarginal farm units are the tens of thousands of little farms, often worked on a part-time basis, which are as characteristic a feature of the California scene as the great thousand-acre ranches, especially in the south around Los Angeles. Many of these are run by retired business and professional men, or midwestern farmers attracted to California from more austere territory.

Two percent of California farms control one-fourth of the acreage, nearly one-third of the crop value, and pay more than one-third of the bill for hired labor. "Of all farms in the United States whose product is valued at $30,000 or above," according to Paul Taylor, University of California authority, "nearly 37 percent are found in our own state. California has within its borders 30 percent of the large-scale cotton farms of the country, 41 percent of the large-scale dairy farms, 44 percent of the large-scale general farms, 53 percent of the large-scale poultry farms, 60 percent of the large-scale fruit farms of the United States."

The growth of the two extremes, very large and very small farms, progressively eliminating the middle farmer, has been promoted by the high and steadily rising value of land to over twice the United States average. Other major factors are the high costs of land development and labor in intensive cultivation of fruit and truck crops.

The bulk of farm work in California today is performed, not by the independent farmer, but by a vast army of some 200,000 wage earners, most of them migrant laborers. According to a recent study, three-fifths of those engaged in agriculture in 1936 were wage-earners, as against less than half in 1920. The big landowners, following the railroads in scouring the world for sources of cheap labor, imported in succession Chinese, Japanese, Hindus, Mexicans, and Filipinos to do field work. Today the ranks of migratory workers also include refugees from Dust Bowl areas.

This great mass of landless field and shed workers constitutes a major social problem in the State. Under the system of intense crop specialization steady employment for most of the year is an impossibility; labor requirements fall from an estimated peak of 198,349 in September to 46,448 in January. Since huge areas are devoted to a single crop, employment begins and ceases simultaneously throughout the whole region. Migrants stream up and down the valleys, covering hundreds of miles from Imperial Valley to the coast valleys, to San Joaquin Valley and the Sacramento-San Joaquin delta, and back to Imperial Valley— homeless, cut off from stable rural communities, existing continuously near the hunger line.

An effective approach to the migrant problem is now being made, for the first time in California history, by the Federal Government. Its Farm Security Administration is aiding the Dust Bowl exiles through the series of camps extending from Brawley, in the Imperial Valley, to Marysville, in the Sacramento Valley, through food grants made to workers in danger of starvation between crops; and through the recently organized Agricultural Workers Health and Medical Association, which utilizes existing medical apparatus in agricultural counties.

Friars as Farmers: The large-scale pattern for agriculture was set in the opening days of California agriculture by the Spanish-Mexican mission and rancho. The mission padres used their Indian neophytes to cultivate large tracts of desert land, and experimented boldly with a variety of vegetables and fruits. Today mission olives and grapes, planted 150 years ago by the Spanish padres, are still among the most favored varieties of these fruits. From the end of the eighteenth century until the secularization of the missions (1834-37), mission agriculture developed with amazing rapidity. A maximum Indian labor force of 20,000 to 30,000 was said to have been reached in 1804. In 1834, according to the historian, Duflot de Mofras, the 21 missions existing in California territory had under cultivation a total of 70,000 hectares (a hectare equals 2.471 acres) of wheat, corn, barley, and beans and possessed 242,000 cattle, 65,000 horses, and 321,500 sheep.

When the Spanish monarchy under King Carlos III occupied Alta California in 1769, only usufructuary title of various grades was granted to individuals, since absolute title in all lands was vested in the king. Theoretically the Indians were recognized as natural owners of lands sufficient for their subsistence, and the missions, therefore, held the vast grants ceded them in trust for their Indian wards. Few large grants were made under the Spanish regime except to missions, for the padres strenuously opposed secular grants. When Mexico proclaimed her independence from Spain in 1823, only 20 secular grants existed in California. Ten years later the number increased to about 50 and by 1845, to 700 or 800.

The padres' bitter opposition to Mexican secession from Spain rose to a climax when the Mexican Congress issued its decree of August 17, 1833, ordering the division of mission properties in Alta California. With the Indians deprived of most of the land that was theirs, the *rancheros* assumed prominence in the State's agricultural development.

Cattle on the Range: The era of the Spanish-Mexican land grant was a purely pastoral period. The cattle ranch with its tens of thousands of acres of wild range land was the dominant form, farming being conducted only to raise sufficient produce for the immediate needs of the individual ranch. Cattle were raised largely for their hides and tallow, the principal export articles, which the *rancheros* exchanged with the Yankee traders for flour and various luxury and other manufactured articles. For half a century California was considered a major source of tallow and hides.

The bigger *rancheros* lived like feudal lords with scores of retainers and servants. Their vast herds, roaming the valleys and foothills, were rounded up yearly at rodeo season and driven into home pastures. Don Manuel Nieto, recipient in 1784 of the second grant given in California, sixteen square leagues (71,016 acres) including the site of Long Beach, ran 100,000 head of cattle on his tract. Don José Domingo Peralta, owner of the Rancho Cañada del Corte de Madera, in Santa Clara Valley, had his private embarcadero, chapel, bull ring, and fleet of boats to transport his hides and tallow. On a *rancho* in the San Luis Obispo district, there was said to be a room filled with baskets of silver and gold and huge chests brought by galleon from China stuffed with rare silken shawls, satins, laces, embroideries, and jewels.

The American conquest opened a new market for agricultural products even before the discovery of gold. The period is graphically described in the diary of John Sutter, the great adventurer-agriculturist and first white man to settle the interior, who combined a longing to live in the grand style with an intensely practical passion for farming. In California Sutter achieved all his dreams, raising fine crops and cattle on the immense grant he received from Governor Alvarado—22 square leagues (97,648 acres) including the present site of Sacramento. He ruled his domain, called New Helvetia for his native Switzerland, in the manner of an independent fortified kingdom "with 24 pieces of ordnance available," until the discovery of gold on his land ruined instead of enriched him.

"I found a good market for my products among the new-comers and the people in the Bay district" Sutter wrote of the period immediately following the American occupation. "Agriculture increased until I had several hundred men working in the harvest fields, and to feed them I had to kill four or sometimes five oxen daily. I could raise 40,000 bushels of wheat without trouble, reap the crops with sickles, thrash it with bones, and winnow it in the wind. There were thirty plows running with fresh oxen every morning. The Russians were the chief customers for my agricultural products. I had at the time twelve thousand head of cattle, two thousand horses and mules, between ten and fifteen thousand sheep, and a thousand hogs. My best days were just before the discovery of gold."

The wave of wild speculation, rising in the wake of discovery of gold in 1849, affected agriculture along with every other phase of California life. A huge new population had to be fed—93,000 in 1850 as against 15,000 in 1848. Gold was plentiful, meat and vegetables scarce. Prices reached astronomical heights. The return from 150 acres planted to onions, tomatoes, and potatoes near San Jose is said to have been $200,000 in one season. Near Sacramento four men made $40,000 from 16 acres of potatoes. The price of cattle rose from $6 a head in 1846 to $300 a head by the close of 1849, with sales as high as $500 a head recorded in Sacramento. Stock raising, like every other phase of activity in California, went through an artificial forced growth.

When the gold rush passed its crest, agriculture began to take over the dominant role in the economic life of the State as thousands of ex-miners settled on the land or went to work on the big cattle or wheat ranches. The number of miners in the State rose from 57,797 to 82,573 in the fifties; the number of farmers rose from 1,486 to 20,836.

The stock raising industry advanced rapidly as measures were taken to improve the breed of cattle, previously bred for hide and tallow, in order to suit them for eating and dairy purposes. Spanish cattle were interbred with American stock which settlers drove hundreds of miles across the plains. Stock raising had reached its highest point when the great drought of 1862 hit the "cow country" that stretched from the Monterey area to San Diego, burning up thousands of acres of range land, killing over a million cattle and horses, ruining and driving off the land thousands of ranchers. The drought delivered the death blow to the Mexican cattlemen, whose California grants, already insecure, now passed almost entirely into the hands of Americans, largely land speculators.

The forced sales of those years, when land prices fell to from 25 to 50 cents an acre, precipitated the first genuine California land boom. A syndicate of San Francisco financiers, incorporated as the Los Angeles and San Bernardino Land Company, bought up Don Abel Stearn's *rancho* of 200,000 acres south of the Tehachapis, placed it on the market in 1868 in tracts of 40 acres and up, and put on a high-pressure advertising campaign that brought in a flood of buyers from the East and the North. As land values rose, the syndicate cleaned up a $2,000,000 profit. In the late sixties and the seventies the railroads received immense land grants from the Government—the Central Pacific alone received 1,349,000 acres—and brought in settlers by the thousand with similar boom methods.

The public domain in California was rapidly disappearing. The *Pacific Rural Press* showed in 1875 that 45 men held 4,000,000 acres of land. The struggle against absentee ownership and the evils of landlordism became a major political concern, and the Constitutional Convention of 1879 stressed the need for legislation curbing the great land companies and railroads. The California State Grange, today an important organization of the family-farm type of farmer, was formed as a protective organization against the big interests that were becoming the decisive influence in agriculture. In the seventies, at the peak of its early growth, the Grange demanded a Government curb on grain speculation; taxation of uncultivated land held for speculation at the same rate as cultivated land; Government control of irrigation, then in its beginnings; and railroad freight rates.

The Epoch of Wheat: In the 1870's California became the second wheat State in the Union. In addition to the sudden decline in stock raising, after the great drought, there were other basic causes for the rapid rise of wheat. Rates for shipment by water were low. Wheat was a staple commodity in international trade, and it could be shipped long distances without deterioration. The huge bonanza wheat farms, celebrated by Frank Norris in *The Octopus,* became the outstanding feature of the eighties. The Central Valley became a world granary. On these wheat ranches the process of mechanization, which has played such an important role in California's trend towards large-scale farming, was first developed.

This era was short-lived, however. Although wheat, barley, and other extensive crops continued increasing in value up to 1919, fruit, vegetables, and other intensive crops had begun to supplant them in importance by the turn of the century. The exorbitant railroad freight rates which raised land prices and cut wheat profits, the competition of new grain fields in the Mississippi Valley and Russia, and the rapid growth of population were factors in forcing all farmers to raise crops promising higher returns from a given area. The development of irrigation projects, begun in 1872 along the San Joaquin and Kings Rivers and rapidly pushed after 1885, spurred the change from extensive farming. Meanwhile the construction of new railroad lines and introduction of the refrigerator car facilitated transportation of fruit and vegetables.

Mass Production in the Orchard: Although the accomplishments of mission agriculture had pointed the way, the real development of present-day California farming began with the conscious efforts of the "fruit pioneers" of the early American period. Many of the early settlers who sailed around the Horn or toiled across the plains showed their deep faith in the brave new land by bringing along seeds and slips and even trees from their former homes. In more recent years the United States Department of Agriculture has sent its men to scour four continents in search of valuable fruits and plants adapted to growing conditions in the State.

The work of Luther Burbank contributed materially to the agricultural pre-eminence of intensive fruit growing in the State. When as a young man Burbank arrived in 1875 from Worcester, Massachusetts, to carry on his experimental work in California, he wrote of the Sonoma Valley: "I firmly believe from what I have seen that it is the chosen spot of all this earth as far as nature is concerned. . . . I cannot describe it! I almost have to cry for joy when I look upon the lovely valley from the hillsides." Among the new plant varieties which he originated were 60 varieties of plums and prunes, the result of 40 years of experimentation. He also introduced important varieties of peaches, nectarines, quinces, and apples, and his experimentation with berries resulted in the origination and introduction of 10 new varieties. In addition to the famous Burbank potato, he introduced varieties of asparagus, tomato, squash, and corn.

The establishment of orange growing on a commercial basis drew the attention of farmers all over the country to the financial possibilities of irrigated intensive fruit growing in California. The exotic picture of orange groves set in hot valleys surrounded by snow-capped mountains, of trees with their glossy green foliage hung heavily with golden globes, fitted into the California legend, caught men's imaginations almost as strongly as the gold of '49, and brought California before the Nation as an agricultural Eldorado.

The first orange grove was set out at the San Gabriel Mission near Los Angeles in 1804, although the orange had been introduced into California about 1770 and was reported as flourishing at Mission Buena Ventura in 1792. The first commercial grove was planted in 1841 by the Kentucky trapper, William Wolfskill, with trees from the

San Gabriel Mission; his success stimulated a number of other farmers to experiment with the friut. The present great citrus industry was mainly developed from two seedless orange trees, sent to the pioneer Eliza C. Tibbetts at the newly established Riverside farming colony, by the U. S. Department of Agriculture in 1873. The trees belonged to the "Washington Navel" variety, originally imported from Bahia in Brazil. The introduction of the navel orange by the U. S. Department of Agriculture initiated an industry which today has about 250,000 acres planted with 20,000,000 bearing trees, netting the greatest income of any one crop in the State (*see TOUR 2d*). Lemon growing, too, was gradually developed to a point where it could meet European competition; today the lemon crop is fifth among all crops in farm value.

As completion of railroad connections opened eastern markets, feverish agriculturists pulled up flourishing and highly profitable orchards and vineyards and planted expensive orange trees in their stead. Speculators preyed on inexperienced and unorganized growers with disastrous results, which soon pointed to the urgent necessity of some type of regulative action. The first significant step towards the organization of packing, shipping, and marketing cooperatives was made in Los Angeles in 1893; two years later it was succeeded by the Southern California Fruit Exchange. This organization, broadened in 1905 to include the whole State, was the forerunner of the widespread network of marketing cooperatives today covering most major branches of agriculture.

Californians not only drink a lot of wine—almost seven times as much per capita as other people in the United States—they also produce 58 percent of the wine consumed in the country and 93 percent of the Nation's grapes—$43,108,000 worth, covering a half-million acres. Viticulture is second only to orange growing in the State's agricultural economy. The wine industry of the State, including the grape-growing and wine-making divisions, has an investment of some $420,000,000 in vineyards, plant, building, and wine inventories and is estimated to employ, directly and indirectly, 125,000 persons.

The Franciscans set out the first California vineyard at Misión San Diego de Alcalá about 1770. Each of the missions had its vineyard and its winery. The industry in its later developments was pioneered by vineyardists and wine producers from France, Italy, Hungary, and Germany. The noted Hungarian viticulturist, Agoston Haraszthy, brought cuttings of the Muscat Alexandria grape in 1851, founded California's huge raisin-growing industry, introduced the Zinfandel red wine grape, and later imported 200,000 vine cuttings including all the most important European varieties. The finest dry wines come from the coast area, especially Sonoma, Napa, and Alameda Counties: the Pinot of Burgundy, Cabernet of Gironde, Riesling and Traminer of the Rhine and Moselle. Sweet fortified wines come from great vine-yards of the Lodi area, from the Fresno area, and from San Bernardino County, where the 500-acre Guasti vineyard, largest in the western world, is planted on land reclaimed from the desert. The Fresno grape-growing region has a combined area of almost 250,000 acres planted in raisin, table, and wine grapes; about 160,000 acres are in raisins alone.

Peaches had grown in California from early mission days, but it was the trees, seeds, and seedlings brought in by settlers from the East that laid the basis for the present great industry which today supplies 98 percent of the country's canned peach crop, all of its dried peaches, and a fresh fruit crop exceeded only by Georgia. Although peaches are produced on uplands and plains in most parts of the State, the most concentrated production is in the "peach bowl" of San Joaquin Valley, which accounts for 36 percent of the entire crop.

Santa Clara County is the largest dried fruit packing and fruit canning center of the world. The Santa Clara Valley grows 70,000 acres of prunes, producing over 40 percent of California's total crop, and 20,000 acres of apricots. Fifty percent of California's fancy canned fruit is packed in the valley, and 30 percent of its general canned fruit, amounting to over 72,000,000 quart cans.

Among California's more exotic products are olives, dates, and avocados—all, except avocados, monopoly crops. The gray-green olive groves are scattered over the State from the Mexican border almost up to Mount Shasta in the north. Among leading varieties are the Mission from Mexico, the large Manzillo and Sevillano from Spain, the Ascalano from Italy. The production of dates, practically all grown within a 25-mile radius from Indio, where the California Date Growers Association processes most of the crop, was 3,580 short tons in 1937 valued at $430,000. In order to find the best varieties of avocado for commercial cultivation in California and Florida, the Office for Foreign Plant Introduction of the U. S. Department of Agriculture spent nine years exploring the avocado districts of Mexico and South and Central America. In 1927 California had 690 bearing acres; in 1935, 8,564 acres.

Walnuts, leading nut crop, occupied 134,638 acres in 1937 and produced a crop valued at $9,975,000. Two-thirds of the State acreage is in southern California. The California Walnut Growers Association, to which 90 percent of the growers belong, has central warehouses where the nuts are scientifically treated, handled, and marketed.

Field, Farm, and Vegetable Garden: California typically combines age-old methods of cultivating its "stoop" crops—as fieldhands classify truck and field crops that need intensive hand cultivation—with the most modern machine farming technique. The airplane seeding of rice fields was first tried in the Sacramento area, where over 90 percent of the California crop is raised. Pilots flying within 25 feet of the ground, plant in 5 minutes eight 100-pound sacks of rice. From 30 to 40 acres can be planted in an hour. Before seeding in early spring, tractor-drawn fleets of giant gang plows and scrapers construct the levees around the rice fields. For five months after seeding, levees are used to maintain water on the field at a level of 6 inches in depth. Nine gallons of water per minute must be pumped to each acre. In October big threshers harvest the crop.

The development of California's extensive dairy industry has been largely dependent on the State's high production of tame hay. The value of the tame hay crop in 1937 was $53,112,000, topped only by the value of the orange crop. This figure includes $39,351,000 for alfalfa, which flourishes even in semi-arid districts. In the areas where alfalfa is grown as an irrigated crop, it yields up to seven and eight cuttings a year; sometimes there is a new crop every 30 days. In the old days, settlers coming around the Horn found the dark green alfalfa fields of Chile so attractive that they took along cargoes of hay and seed. Henry Miller, landowner and cattle rancher, who is said to have boasted that he could drive his herds from Oregon to Mexico on his own land, initiated California's commercial production of alfalfa in the San Joaquin Valley, sending to Chile in the seventies for shipments of the seed. His alfalfa holdings became the largest in the United States.

Cotton in this State, largely a speculative crop, has been subject to booms like those that formerly plagued the citrus industry. The 1937 crop was the largest in California history—738,000 bales valued at almost $32,000,000. The average yield was 570 pounds per acre, as against the United States average for the same year of 266.9 pounds per acre. Cotton became an important crop in 1917, when representatives of the Department of Agriculture were sent to California to experiment in production of the tough-fibred type of cotton urgently needed for tire fabric and airplane wing coverings. The State's cotton production is only about two percent of the national total, but the crop is significant for its concentration on a single quality variety, Alcalá, rare and in great demand in this country.

The development of the "lettuce bowls" in the Imperial Valley and Salinas-Watsonville areas has come almost entirely since the World War. Effective advertising, new health and diet concepts stimulated the demand, and the rise of lettuce from a small truck crop to a mass-produced commodity within the past few years has been spectacular. A large part of the lettuce crop is produced by "migratory" farming. In 1937, 102,500 acres produced lettuce valued at $23,230,000, highest of any truck crop. It is exceeded in acreage among truck crops only by tomatoes.

Big capital investment also has gone into asparagus growing, centering in the delta area, which has always been cultivated largely by Oriental contract labor. While the fertile peat soil produces rich crops, the cost of reclaiming the land and maintaining levees and drainage systems is too large for the average farmer to bear. A number of the great holdings, sometimes including whole islands, have remained undivided from early days. Asparagus in 1937 was third among truck crops in size of acreage (67,260 acres) and farm value ($9,146,000).

The harvesting of peas, done entirely by hand, employs big labor forces—20,000 pickers at peak season. California has over a half of the country's pea acreage and has led in carload shipments since 1927. California is exceeded only by Colorado in sugar beet production and exceeds it in production per acre. The 1936 acreage—140,000 acres— almost tripled the 1929 acreage. Beet farming, an adjunct of the sugar factories, is usualy carried on near the plants, because the bulkiness of the beets involves high costs in transportation. It requires an exceptionally large amount of hand labor, most of which is done by Mexicans and Filipinos, at Government-fixed wage standards under the sugar beet program. Artichokes, introduced into the United States by the Italians of California and the French of Louisiana, are grown today in the fog-moistened coastal strip extending from Marina on the north to San Luis Obispo on the south.

Although the days when stock raising was the heart of California's life have long since passed, great flocks and herds still roam the foothills of the Coast Range and the Sierra Nevada, high mountain valleys in the north, and the range land in the far south. The value of the annual cattle, sheep, and hog production runs into impressive figures— about $135,000,000, or roughly $45,000,000 more than the total truck crop. In 1937 California had 2,298,000 cattle, 820,000 hogs, and 3,600,000 sheep and lambs. It was third among the States in wool production with 28,901,000 pounds shorn. In poultry it ranked sixth (June 1938) in total numbers and seventh in value of products; in egg production it ranked second.

Growers' Organizations: Farm organizations formed by California growers, stockraisers, and dairymen fall into three main categories, overlapping in function and membership. The first includes organizations such as the Grange, the Farm Bureau Federation, the Farmers Educational and Cooperative Union, and Associated Farmers, Inc., embracing growers engaged in all branches of agriculture in one organization; the second, the marketing cooperatives such as the Citrus Growers Exchange, and the Prune and Apricot Growers Association, and the California Walnut Growers Association; and the third, organizations such as the Wool Growers and Cattlemen's Association, organized on the basis of a single industry.

The California Farm Bureau, organized in 1913, has done effective work in advising growers on technical questions involved in farming—fertilizers, soil, irrigation, and stockbreeding; it collaborates with the Agricultural Adjustment Administration and other governmental agencies. The Farm Bureau also concerns itself with labor relations in agriculture and carries on legislative activities on a State and national scale. Membership in the State is about 25,000 in 43 counties.

The Farmers Educational and Cooperative Union, powerful in the middle west, is comparatively small in this State, centering around Santa Clara County. The Grange—or, to give its full title, The Patrons of Husbandry—tends to represent family rather than commercial farming in this State. A fraternal and social organization with ties to the consumers' cooperative movement, it admits farmers' wives and children to membership. It has played an important historical role in California in pushing through measures of benefit to the rural population.

The marketing cooperatives, of which California has about 450 with a membership of some 80,000, are primarily business organizations seeking efficient control of produce, closely allied in their functioning to the State agricultural prorate commissions. With main emphasis on price, shipping and marketing problems, they also operate processing plants for their members, maintain purchasing services, and carry on scientific research to improve quality of production. The California Fruit Growers Exchange, oldest of the cooperatives and typical of them all, has about 13,500 members, comprising about 210 local packing associations grouped in 26 district exchanges. It handles over 75 percent of the State's citrus crop, selling 75,000 to 100,000 cars of fruit in a normal crop year for about $125,000,000. In addition, it manufactures by-products such as citric acid and pectin, purchases supplies in volume for its membership, supplies lumber for crates from its own lumber properties, provides growers with the latest technical information on citrus culture, enforces grade regulations in shipping fruit, using X-ray machines to inspect the crated product. It is responsible for the Nation-wide advertising campaigns which have attempted to make the California orange—more than gold, or oil, or movies—register unmistakably as the State's own peculiar symbol.

Industry and Finance

FOR HALF a century the first outposts of Spanish rule, the missions, were the centers of economic life in California's shut-in feudal world. They grew into industrial institutions, each with its weaving room, blacksmith shop, tannery, wine press, and warehouses. The Indian neophytes, held in subjection by the energetic, practical Franciscan friars, learned to tan leather, weave coarse cloth, bake bricks and pottery, make soap and candles, and grind corn. When the missions were secularized (1834-37), however, their industrial activities disappeared rapidly as the skilled neophytes, now free but most of them robbed of their land rights, either worked on the ranchos or took to the wilds.

Hardly had secularization been accomplished when the 1840's heralded an economic revolution. Canny, ambitious foreigners, most of them Americans, pushed into the sleepy province. They harnessed the streams to run the wheels of gristmills and sawmills that soon supplanted the household *metates* (mortars) and the crude mule- and ox-power mills of the Californians. In 1843 an American trapper, Stephen Smith, set up California's first steam gristmill and sawmill at Bodega. John Augustus Sutter, a Swiss emigrant, built a flour mill, set up a distillery, and began the weaving of coarse woolen blankets at his colony of New Helvetia (now Sacramento). On the eve of the American conquest, according to Thomas O. Larkin, United States Consul, California was exporting enormous amounts of lumber, soap and brandy.

The treaty of Guadalupe Hidalgo, recognizing the American conquest, had not yet been signed when gold was discovered in the tail-race of Sutter's sawmill at Coloma. Although a small scale gold rush had sprung up in the San Fernando Hills back of Los Angeles six years earlier, the enormous riches of the California Hills had remained unsuspected. Virtually every enterprise but mining now stopped. Larkin later wrote: "Every blacksmith, carpenter, and lawyer is leaving; brick-yards, saw-mills, and ranches are left perfectly alone." Another writer reported: "Every bowl, warming pan, and piggin has gone to the mines. Everything in short that has a scoop in it that will hold sand and water. All the iron has been worked up into crowbars, pick axes and spades."

During the first three years of the rush, placer miners took out the surface "pay dirt" from the "diggin's" with pick, shovel, crowbar, and tin pan. Other contrivances replaced the pan: the washing rocker or "cradle," a criblike wooden box mounted on rockers, with a "riddle" or sieve; the "Long Tom," a wooden trough with a riddle at one end over a riffle box; and the "board-sluice," a long open flume with riffle-bars across the bottom. Even with such primitive tools as these, fabulous amounts of gold were mined—in 1849, approximately $10,-000,000 worth; in 1850, more than $41,000,000; and in 1852, the year of largest production, more than $81,000,000.

The demand for money far outstripped the supply. Californians scorned paper money. Gold dust, a "pinch" to the dollar, substituted for currency. Silver coins of many nations crept into circulation: Mexican dollars, German marks, French 5-franc pieces. Private assayers coined gold pieces of widely varying denominations for profit. Not until April 1854, when the new San Francisco mint began operations, did Government minted coins circulate in needed quantities.

Merchants received gold dust and specie for safe-keeping in their vaults; soon they were buying and selling gold, loaning funds, dealing in exchange. Stephen A. Wright opened his "Miners' Bank" in San Francisco late in 1848, Naglee and Sinton their "Exchange and Deposit Office," and the Rothschilds of London their San Francisco branch early in 1849. The Wells Fargo Bank and Union Trust Company of today, founded as an express company, entered banking in 1852. By the close of 1853, San Francisco had nineteen banks, carrying on business in cramped offices and shacks. Few of these, however, survived the depression following the bank panic of Black Friday, February 23, 1855. For nearly a decade afterwards, banking continued to be marked by instability.

As the "flush days" of mining drew to a close, machines began to replace men. In 1851 the first mill for crushing quartz was erected ir Grass Valley, Yuba County; by 1857, more than 150 quartz mills had been built for working the lode. In 1852 placer mining was revolutionized when hydraulic methods were introduced at American Hill in Nevada County. By the seventies, millions of tons of gold bearing sand had been washed down under powerful jets of water and flushed into the Yuba and Feather Rivers. The destruction of valley farm lands by the debris precipitated a struggle between farmers and miners which finally led to prohibition of hydraulic mining by injunction in 1880.

Mining remained the chief industry throughout the first decade of the American regime, absorbing almost 60 percent of the inhabitants. After 1859, however, the annual output of gold began to decrease, falling to $18,000,000 by 1870. Meanwhile, a population increase from 92,597 in 1850 to 379,994 a decade later, gave manufacturing its first great impetus.

By the winter of 1849-50 San Francisco had grown into a lively manufacturing center of shipbuilding yards, foundries, flour mills, and workshops. To supply tools and machinery for the mines, Donahue Brothers established their foundry (later the Union Iron Works) in 1849; other foundries were soon opened. The wool of California's sheep was utilized in the weaving of cloth; the hides of its cattle in the tanning of leather. A sugar refinery, using raw sugar from the Hawaiian Islands, was established on the Bay in 1860. In that year there were close to a hundred gristmills throughout the State, while about three times as many sawmills were making lumber of its ponderosa pine, its redwood, and Douglas fir. The gold mines still held first place in 1860, with a $45,000,000 production, but manufactures assumed growing importance, with an output valued at $24,000,000.

During the middle 1860's a prospecting mania swept the State, recalling the feverish "flush days." Prospectors wandered into California's most isolated regions, hunting for gold, copper, silver, quicksilver. So many amazing discoveries were reported that a thousand new companies began to peddle mining stock. Frenzied financiers extended their efforts to a new field, oil wells. From Humboldt County to San Diego, wildcat wells were drilled as more than 60 companies entered the field. The San Francisco *Bulletin* reported that from 40,000 to 50,000 gallons of oil had been produced in 1865. But the bubble soon burst. The wildcat mining companies began to collapse and by the end of the decade the oil companies, too, wound up in practical failure when their product was pronounced of no value.

None the less, the growth of industry continued. When the Civil War interrupted normal communications, goods once imported from the Atlantic Seaboard, shoes and clothing, chemicals and drugs, furniture, iron and steel, distilled liquors, soaps and candles, and tobacco were produced within the State. As cities grew, gas plants, planing mills, foundries, brick and pottery works were built, and banking institutions sprang up. Four years after the legislature had provided for incorporation of Savings and Loan Societies in 1862, there were five savings banks with total deposits of $8,650,000. In southern California, remote from the gold fields of the populous north, I. W. Hellman in 1865 hung up his sign, "I. W. Hellman, Banker"; three years later Alvinza Hayward and Company opened, with a capitalization of $100,000.

Even after two decades of industrial development, California was not yet a manufacturing State in 1870. Industry still labored under some of its original handicaps: lack of fuel for power, of facilities for transporting goods to markets, of an adequate banking and credit system. A further setback was the financial panic of 1875, which followed the eastern panic of two years before, and was itself aggravated by the collapse of wild speculation in mining stocks. It broke with startling suddenness when the Bank of California, a financial power since 1864, closed its doors because of the speculations of its president, William C. Ralston. Banks collapsed throughout the State; in Los Angeles all closed, two permanently.

A widespread demand for Government regulation of banking forced the legislature in 1878 to pass the Banking Act, under which "a board of three bank commissioners was appointed with power to call for statements from the banks, make examinations of their affairs, regulate the conduct of their business, and to close insolvent concerns." Of the 84 banks then in existence, five were forced into liquidation. In spite of this temporary slump, bank deposits by 1890 had grown to $230,-000,000, representing an 88 percent increase in 10 years, while the number of banks increased from 120 to 232.

Industrial expansion kept pace with banking. The growth of agriculture called for farm implement and wagon factories and for mills and factories to process its goods for market. The influx of inhabitants during the Great Boom of 1887-88 widened the local market, furnished needed capital, and increased the labor supply. By 1890 the number of manufacturing establishments was nearly twice that of 1870, the value of manufactured products more than three times as great, and the capital invested nearly four times as great.

The Nation-wide panic of 1893 rocked industry and banking to their foundations once more. On June 14, the Riverside Banking Company crashed. Two banks closed in San Francisco, four in Los Angeles, and several others throughout the State. After 1898, as the business trend turned upward again, banking resources were more than doubled. But again in 1907, as another national depression hit California, bank failures shook the State. One consequence was the Bank

Act of 1909, imposing more stringent regulations, which brought greater stability to California banking.

Industrial production, meanwhile, had risen. By 1899 California had 4,997 manufacturing establishments, representing an estimated capital investment of $175,000,000, which produced goods valued at $257,000,000. The chief industries were, in the order of their importance, sugar and molasses refineries, meat-packing plants, lumber mills and brickyards, flour and gristmills, fruit and vegetable canneries, foundries and machine shops. Manufacturing had far outgrown mining, which produced $29,313,460 of mineral products in 1899. Handicapped by lack of fuel, it was still little more than an adjunct to agriculture. But by this time manufacturing had begun to draw upon new resources of power—petroleum and hydroelectric energy.

In 1893 E. L. Doheny and C. A. Canfield sank a shaft with pick, shovel and windlass on a plot of ground at the corner of Patton and West State Streets in Los Angeles. A little oil oozed up, the first trickle from a vast reservoir which numberless derricks in the Los Angeles field would soon begin to drain. Years before, the early Spanish settlers, whose cattle sometimes got mired in surface oil pools, had plastered the sticky *brea* (Sp., tar) on the roofs of their adobe houses. As early as 1855 or 1856, Andres Pico had distilled small quantities of oil for use at Mission San Fernando. Wildcat companies were drilling wells throughout the State in the 1860's. In 1874 the California Star Oil Company established the first refinery near Newhall. During the next decade fields were being worked in the Puente Hills, Whittier, Summerland, Newhall, Ventura, and Los Gatos districts. By 1888 annual production had risen to 690,000 barrels. The Coalinga, McKittrick, and Midway-Sunset fields in the San Joaquin Basin were producing by 1890 or 1891, the Los Angeles-Salt Lake field by 1893. Production had risen in 1900 to 4,319,950 barrels and this was but a fraction of the yearly output to follow.

In 1882 George Chaffey began to operate a small power plant near Etiwanda. When the San Antonio Light and Power Company was formed, just a decade later, to transmit electricity from its power station in San Antonio Canyon near Pomona, only two other commercial plants, one in Oregon and the other in Colorado, were producing hydroelectric power. A year later the Redlands Electric and Power Company was operating its plant on Mill Creek in the San Bernardino Mountains. By 1900 the hydroelectric industry, grown to a producing capacity of 30,500 kilowatt hours, was developing speedily to meet the demands for electricity of railroad, mine, factory, home, and farm.

The new century saw a marked increase in the industrial development of the State. The value of manufactured products increased nearly tenfold in the first quarter of the century, from the $257,000,000 of 1899 to $2,443,000,000 in 1925. During the World War period of forced expansion, industrial output rose 170 percent in value and after the abrupt decline of post-war deflation, industrial growth continued rapidly. From 1919 to 1925 the increase in value of manufactured products was 1.5 percent for the country as a whole but 28 percent for California. Industry, as it expanded, became more evenly distributed. Los Angeles, like San Francisco, became a foremost manufacturing center; Oakland, Richmond, San Jose, Berkeley, and Fresno outstripped Sacramento, their former leader.

The State's industrial output soared to a total value of more than three billion dollars in 1929. After an abrupt drop to less than two billion in the following two-year period, it has risen somewhat, though not to its 1929 level. If the cost of motion picture production (prior to 1933 included in computations of the total value of industrial output) is added to the value of other manufactured products for 1935, the total is very close to that of a decade earlier. It should be noted, however, that because films are rented, not sold, production costs are not a measure of the value of output. With a production of $265,-385,925 in 1935, petroleum refining stood at the top of eighteen manufacturing industries whose products were valued at more than $25,000,000. Fruit and vegetable processing totaled $174,011,865 for that year and both meat packing and the automotive industry, more than $120,000,000.

Oil production has been first among the State's industries since 1919. The era of greatest productivity began in 1920, with the opening of such fields as Huntington Beach, Santa Fe Springs, and Signal Hill. From 1920 to 1926 California produced 1,300,000,000 barrels, more oil than in all its previous history. During this boom period the industry had more than its share of unscrupulous promoters and in 1927, the year of the startling Julian Petroleum Corporation scandal in Los Angeles, the department of natural resources took over State regulation of oil production. Today in the oil fields that dot Los Angeles, Ventura, Kern, Fresno, Orange, and Santa Barbara Counties, the passerby may see enormous forests of oil derricks sucking black gold from the earth night and day. In 1937 production was 238,521,000 barrels. In the same year production of natural gas, in daily consumption of which the State leads the nation, was 357,420,000,000 cubic feet.

Second in value of production among California's industries are its fruit and vegetable canneries, which in 1937 produced a fruit and vegetable pack of almost 60,000,000 cases, thirty percent of the Nation's total output. To supply its demands, the manufacture of tin cans and tinware has itself risen to seventh place among the State's industries. An important branch of fruit and vegetable processing is the dried fruit business, largely conducted by co-operative organizations whose advertising efforts have made California brands familiar throughout the world. The sea food canning industry, centered chiefly in Monterey, San Diego, and Los Angeles, leads the world in commercial production of tuna fish. Another industry, wine making, representing an estimated investment of $350,000,000, shipped nearly 60,000,000 gallons in 1937. The meat-packing industry utilizes shipments from other States as well as California's supply of livestock.

California's importance as an automobile market (in 1937 there were 2,484,653 automobiles registered) has influenced eastern manufacturers in opening branch factories within the State. A flourishing allied industry, motor vehicle bodies and parts, was responsible for an output valued at $19,155,337 in 1935, while manufacture of rubber tires and inner tubes took tenth place among all industries. In aircraft manufacture the output for 1935 was valued at $15,883,918; by the end of 1937 a single manufacturer reported net sales in excess of $20,000,000.

Metal products and machine production have become increasingly important in the industrial life of the State. Pig iron from Utah has largely supplanted scrap and pig iron from England or Belgium as raw material. Southern California's iron deposits, smelted with coke from Utah and Colorado, promise to furnish another source of supply.

Except for redwood, production of lumber is far less than that needed. Much of the material imported (in 1937 a billion feet) is timber which California mills convert into lumber. The total output of the lumber products industries, including saw- and planing-mills, box factories and furniture plants, was valued at $97,386,559 in 1935.

Before the turn of the century mining had fallen behind manufactures in value of output, though it continued to be an important factor in the State's economic life. The value of mineral output for 1936 (excluding petroleum) was $227,539,942. In gold output the State still leads the Nation. A total of 1,174,578 ounces of gold were mined in 1937, the greatest amount since 1861. Between 1900 and 1915 dredging displaced other methods in placer mining. Huge chain-bucket dredgers worked their way down the shallow rivers, creating their own channels as they went. The gravel was scooped from the river bed to the deck of the dredger, washed in revolving screens, and the gold particles captured on gold saving tables supplied with riffles, or in short sluices. Since the World War machine worked quartz mines have been a chief source of supply; the gold is reclaimed by amalgamation or by cyaniding. Forty counties produce gold, 60 percent from lode mines, 40 percent from placers, but the Grass Valley and Nevada City district is by far the outstanding center of production.

Of the State's 58 commercial minerals, silver is next in importance to gold; 2,103,799 fine ounces, valued at $1,629,392 were produced in 1936. Copper production, centering in Trinity County, was 10,-502,000 pounds, valued at $1,270,742; lead production, centering in Inyo County, was 2,372,000 pounds, valued at $139,948. Most of the borax mined in the United States comes from Inyo, Kern, and San Bernardino Counties, and the greatest United States production of sodium bicarbonate is from Searles Lake in San Bernardino County. The State's producing quicksilver mines, numbering 54 in 1937, provide a large portion of the world supply. Tungsten is produced at Atolia in San Bernardino County; magnesite, in Stanislaus and Santa Clara Counties. Building materials account for approximately $50,-000,000 of the total value of mineral output.

California today ranks third among the States in the production of electricity. The hydroelectric industry generated 30,500 kilowatt hours in 1900 and 8,365,205,000 in 1937. Steam heat and internal combustion added 1,266,974,000 kilowatt hours to the total production within the State for that year. California also consumes electricity generated at Boulder Dam, carried by high-power transmission lines operating at 287,500 volts over a distance of 266 miles.

From 1900 to 1917 the State's banking resources accumulated steadily, advancing from $384,785,000 to $1,682,000,000, while the number of banks increased from 269 to 718. The post-war era witnessed the emergence of powerful financial institutions through bank mergers, the establishment of branch banking on a wide scale, and the importation of capital from the East. In 1927 banking resources were $3,833,957,000, an increase of 128 percent for the decade following 1917. In 1928 the Bank of Italy (now the bank of America) had become the fifth largest in the country, with 279 branches throughout the State. The growth of the banking system was paralleled by the growth of banking and loan companies, whose assets increased 100 percent from 1895 to 1920 and 400 percent from 1920 to 1927. California shared with other States the debacle of bank failures that came with the depression. The banks recovered gradually from this setback until in 1937 their resources were greater than they had been a decade earlier.

Following 1929, California's industrial graph, here as elsewhere in the Nation, fell in a dizzy curve. After an upturn from 1935 to 1937, during which period the losses of 1930-1935 were partially offset, the trend headed downward during the latter part of 1937. Agriculture remains (1939) the dominant factor in the economy of the State, but manufacturing runs a close second, and far outdistances mining; it contributes one-third to the State's yearly income. Despite all reverses, California still holds its position of eighth manufacturing State in the Union.

From Clipper Ship to Clipper Plane

"TOO SWIFT arrives as tardy as too slow" might have been the motto in Spanish California. The pack mules of the padres ambled from one mission to another. The horses of the rancheros might gallop fast enough in a round-up, but not in going from ranch to town. There was no reason for speed nor was speed possible in a *carreta* (cart), squeaking with its ponderous wheels of solid oak over roads little more than trails. Soldier-couriers carried the mail along the *Camino Real* (king's highway) from San Francisco to San Diego and continued along their slow, hot, dry way to Loreto in Lower California, whence letters went across the gulf of San Blas and on to Mexico City.

Trade was no less leisurely. Although the Spanish government prohibited trade with other than Spanish ships, American and British ships successfully smuggled their goods into California long before the Mexican government removed this restriction. Californians needed too many products to resist the temptation of dealing with smugglers, while the profits which awaited the Yankee sea captains from trading their manufactured wares for seal and sea otter pelts, hides, tallow, and lumber were enough to induce them to risk capture of their ships and confiscation of their cargoes. Their illicit trade grew to the point where a hide came to be called a "California bank note," substituting for money as the common medium of exchange.

When gold was discovered in 1848 the sudden mass movement taxed intercoastal transportation facilities to the utmost. By March 1849, 17,000 persons had sailed from Atlantic and Gulf coast cities for

California; in the same year fully 35,000 traveled the tortuous overland routes. With such mushroom growth came an extraordinary demand for goods, so that freight rates rose to $50 and even $60 a ton. The Pacific Mail Steamship Company, established when the gold rush began, speeded construction of its three 1,000-ton steamers for the New York-to-San Francisco run. The first of these, the *California,* arrived at San Francisco February 28, 1849, laden to the water's edge with 400 Argonauts taken aboard at Panama. The company rapidly built up a combined Atlantic and Pacific fleet of 29 steamships. Aided by the Panama Railroad and a government subsidy for carrying mail, it did an enormous business, bringing some 175,000 passengers to California and taking back $200,000,000 in gold within ten years.

The New England shipbuilders, too, rose to the emergency. Soon that most beautiful of sailing ships, "the knife-edged clipper with her ruffled spar," was cutting the sailing time around the Horn to little more than three months. The *Flying Cloud* and the *Andrew Jackson* made the trip in 89 days. All this record-breaking bustle meant enormous profits to the owners. In one passage the *Samuel Russell,* carrying a 1200-ton cargo, earned a gross revenue of $72,000, or more than the cost of building the ship.

From San Francisco, travelers continued by horseback or steamer to the mines. The first river steamer to make regular runs from San Francisco to Sacramento was a little launch named the *Pioneer,* imported in sections on the deck of a sailing ship, which began puffing and blowing up the river in the summer of 1849. A number of other vessels of not too great draft were pressed into service on the Sacramento and San Joaquin, where rivalry for speed led sometimes to forcing of the boilers and terrific explosions. Since there were not enough steamers of light draft to handle the traffic, the high fares—2 ounces of gold or its cash equivalent—and the freight rates of $50 per ton from San Francisco to Sacramento led the owners of medium-sized sailing vessels to attempt the trip. Once the master had got his craft out of the tangle of shipping in the harbor of San Francisco, the bay breezes made the passage up through San Pablo and Suisun Bays easy enough. If his destination was Stockton, he could still count on a little breeze, his chief trouble being to keep to the main channel through a circuitous course in the San Joaquin delta. But if he began to sail up the Sacramento, his troubles were manifold, as Captain Coffin of the *Sophronia* complained in his account of "fifteen days' labour, boiling and roasting" en route to Sacramento. The river banks were "so overgrown with oaks and sycamores that we lay becalmed. . . . The only way to advance was to warp and tie." Before a year was out, however, several steamers suitable for the river run had made the trip around the Horn or through the Straits of Magellan. The most famous of these was the *Senator,* of which it was later said that she carried enough gold to sink her had it been carried all in one load.

From Stockton, Sacramento and Marysville, focal points on the river routes, *carreta,* calash, and spring wagon carried men and supplies to an ever growing number of new mining camps. Driven by Mexican *arrieros* (mule drivers), each animal with a load of 300 pounds, mule teams set out not only with bacon and beans and shovels, but with plows, barrels of whisky, pianos, and printing presses. Later, as roads took the place of trails, the stage coach and the heavy freighter were pressed into service. The first Concord Coach reached California in 1850. With its steer-hide springs, its stout ash spokes, its landscaped panels, and damask-lined curtains, it was, by comparison with the *carreta,* a model of beauty and comfort.

In June 1851 there were but 34 post offices in all California. With gold or high wages beckoning, no one would carry the mail at Government pay; hence the rise of the expressman who carried mail independently from San Francisco, Sacramento, or Stockton, charging at first the fantastic price of $4 a letter. If the post rider was shrewd, he presently became a treasure carrier, or even a banker—if he could get hold of a safe. Within another year the business of carrying gold from the mines had attracted a number of far-sighted Easterners. The Adams Express Company established itself, and in May 1852, Wells, Fargo and Company announced, "We are now prepared to forward gold dust, bullion, specie, packages, parcels, and freight to and from New York and San Francisco, thence to Sacramento, Marysville, Nevada, Shasta, Stockton, Sonora, and all the principal towns of California and Oregon."

In 1858 Congress gave the Butterfield Overland Mail an annual subsidy of $600,000. Their stages went across the old Santa Fe Trail from San Francisco to St. Joseph in 23 days. When the Civil War interrupted service on the Butterfield line, the stages used the middle or California trail route via Colfax and Truckee, across the Nevada desert to Salt Lake City. Stages also ran north to the mines in Trinity and Shasta Counties and across the Siskiyous into Oregon. In 1862 the discovery of the rich Comstock silver mines in Nevada brought about a kind of reversal of the emigrant trail. As a rival to the California Route, a toll road was built from Placerville over the summit of the Sierra Nevada down the steep drop to Tahoe Valley and thence into Nevada. Over it ran the stages of the Pioneer Line.

Far swifter than the best stages were the riders of the Pony Express, who for a brief period carried a fast mail service from Missouri to California each week. Riding a horse bred for the race track, carrying no arms, even wearing clothes and boots as light as possible, the rider sped across some 1,900 miles in eight days. With the opening of telegraph service across the continent in 1861, the Pony Express was discontinued, but it had already blazed the way for the first trans‑continental railroad.

In striking contrast was another brief experiment. In 1852 Jefferson Davis urged, in Congress, the use of the camel on the Great American Desert. The California press became naively eloquent. Why not "a dromedary express to carry the fast mail"? Congress made a small appropriation and two caravans of camels were shipped to Texas. Some of these or their offspring eventually reached California and the Army used them between Fort Tejon and Los Angeles. Unfortunately the camels frightened horses and mules. The teamsters and mule skinners and *vaqueros* swore in two languages that they would have no trek with these strange beasts. The Army drivers could not pack or manage the camels properly and were unwilling to learn. In the end the camels were auctioned off: some to end their days in circuses, others to carry salt to the Comstock mines, still others to be set adrift on the desert.

California's first railroad was the modest little Sacramento Valley line which in 1856 began running east 22 miles from the capital to Folsom, reducing considerably the time to the mines. It had a wood‑burning locomotive, as did the line which joined San Francisco and San Jose in 1864. In Southern California, over a line from Los Angeles to Wilmington, ran a vainglorious black and gold locomotive called the *San Gabriel,* alongside of which the *vaqueros* used to race, shouting at it derisively and profanely in Spanish.

As early as 1836 there had been talk of a transcontinental railroad, but partisan rivalry over the slavery question between North and South held up action by Congress until 1862. In that year Theodore Judah, who had been chief engineer for the Sacramento Valley Railroad and agent of the Pacific Railroad Convention in Washington, returned to California to announce that he had found a practicable railway route across the Sierra Nevada. His enthusiasm and vision were such that he was able to fire the imaginations of four wealthy, hard-headed Sacramento merchants: Leland Stanford, a grocer, Charles Crocker, a dry-goods man, and Collis Huntington and Mark Hopkins, partners in a hardware establishment. These became the "Big Four."

In 1863 the Union Pacific began to build west from Omaha, the Central Pacific east from Sacramento. Men were scarce; money was short; labor troubles halted construction until Crocker imported Chinese coolies. There were no power tools in the 1860's and no explosives but black powder. With pick and shovel, steel and jack, the crews dug and blasted through the granite of the Sierras. It became a race with the Union Pacific which ended in May 1869 at Promontory, in

Utah, where Stanford drove in the golden spike. The Southern Pacific completed its line to Los Angeles in 1876 and a year later to Texas tidewater, connecting southern California directly with the South and East.

The first coach trains to cross the continent, for all their red plush and polished brass, were none too comfortable. In winter a stove at one end of the coach gave very uneven heat, and in summer there was no ventilation without dust and cinders. However, the coaches were palaces on wheels compared to the emigrant trains that brought to the west the hopeful tide of Europe's poor. The discomfort and squalor of these trains was described in detail by Robert Louis Stevenson in *The Amateur Emigrant*. Provisions for sanitation were quite inadequate; the journey long. "Haste," we learn from this account, "is not a foible of the emigrant train. It gets through on suffrance, running the gauntlet among its more considerable brethren."

The enthusiasm which had greeted the Southern Pacific in 1869 fell to a low ebb in the eighties, when this railroad and the Santa Fe entered into an agreement with the Pacific Mail Steamship Company and formed the Transcontinental Association with the purpose of keeping up freight rates. The farmers and businessmen in the interior of the State complained bitterly at paying rates which were not only high but also fluctuating. The board of railroad commissioners, controlled by the railways, refused relief; it permitted tariffs which were grossly discriminative. The struggle between the Southern Pacific and the farmers was long and bitter, leading even to bloodshed in Tulare County.

Also chafing under the burden of the freight rates charged by the Transcontinental Association, San Francisco merchants in 1891 organized the Atlantic and Pacific Steamship Line with six steamers designed to compete with the Pacific Mail. In the same period businessmen of the interior towns and cities joined San Franciscans in forming the Merchants' Traffic Association. The new organization, besides sponsoring the new Atlantic and Pacific Steamship Line, enabled the Panama Railway Company to establish a competitive line between New York and San Francisco via the Isthmus of Panama. It was chiefly responsible for the building in 1895-6 of the San Francisco and San Joaquin Valley Railroad from Stockton to Bakersfield.

On the coast line from San Francisco to Los Angeles, the Southern Pacific did not complete the section between Lompoc and Santa Barbara until 1901, and the Northwestern Pacific road to Eureka was not completed until 1914. Even with these lines constructed there were (and still are) a number of fair sized towns which have never been served by any railroad. In addition to these, many places popular for vacations—the Geysers, Tassajara Springs, even Yosemite until 1907—could be reached only by coach and six.

The coast country, inaccessible by both sea and land, has remained largely cut off from the rest of the State. Santa Monica, Santa Barbara, Port San Luis, Monterey, Drake's Bay, Fort Bragg—none of these has deep water facilities or even very safe anchorage in stormy weather. Indeed, apart from the superb bay of San Francisco, only San Diego and Eureka have good natural harbors. To overcome the lack of safe anchorages along the rocky coast, shippers have resorted to the ingenious device of the "high line," lowering their goods with block and tackle over hawsers strung from the cliffs to waiting vessels offshore. Up and down the northern coast are lumber towns where lumber has been shipped in this fashion since the 1870's.

For years Los Angeles was handicapped by the lack of an adequate harbor. The final selection of San Pedro ended the long "Free Harbor Fight" between the people of Los Angeles and the Southern Pacific, which had greatly favored the plan for a harbor at Santa Monica. The choice also greatly benefited the new San Pedro, Los Angeles and Salt Lake Railroad, which followed the old Mormon trail across southern Nevada to its western terminus at San Pedro. San Pedro's open bay, protected only on the west by a headland, seemed not too promising until the completion in 1910 of an 11,000-foot breakwater protecting the outer harbor and the excavation of a spacious inner harbor from shallow tidal areas. In 1937 it was the terminal for 165 steamship lines and three transcontinental railroads reaching coastwise, intercoastal, and foreign markets.

Since the opening of the Panama Canal, intercoastal vessels, tramp steamers, naval craft, luxury liners in round-the-world service—all have made California harbors regular ports of call. Today the flags of every maritime nation flutter in the winds. During the first quarter of the century San Francisco's foreign commerce increased fourfold, while traffic in cargo destined to the region west of the Rockies, for which both San Francisco and Oakland harbors are particularly designed, swelled the volume of trade. During the 1920's, growing fleets of lumber freighters and oil tankers passed in and out of Los Angeles harbor until it became one of the greatest lumber-importing and oil-exporting harbors. In 1937 the Los Angeles-Long Beach tonnage was 21,208,681, valued at $925,451,543; the San Francisco tonnage 28,812,967, valued at $1,209,641,226.

The Sacramento and San Joaquin Rivers were almost ruined for navigation by silting up with the debris from hydraulic mining along their tributaries until legislation halted the destruction. Only by persistent dredging were they kept open for small steamboats. Though floods still fill these rivers with silt, much of the fruit and vegetables shipped from the interior goes by water from Sacramento and Stockton. The Stockton harbor has been deepened sufficiently to accommodate the largest ocean-going freighters. Today California's river-borne commerce reaches an annual total of over 2,000,000 tons of freight, exceeded in value only by the trade on the Mississippi, Columbia, and Hudson River systems. The Shasta Dam, now (1939) under construction near Kennet in Shasta County, will keep the flow of the Sacramento relatively uniform throughout the year, once more permitting navigation to Red Bluff as in the steamboating days of the 1850's.

The ferryboats which for so many years have been as much a feature of San Francisco Bay as the islands of Yerba Buena, Angel, and Alcatraz, had as their forerunner a whale boat named by some flight of the imagination the *Pirouette*. In 1851 she began running as a ferry to San Antonio (now East Oakland) with a tariff of $1 per person, $3 per horse, $3 per wagon, $5 per two-horse wagon, $3 per head of meat cattle, $1 per sheep, and $1 per hog. The appearance of competitors cut these rates in half within a few years. The ferries, which eventually achieved the luxurious air of great floating palaces, continued to serve the Bay until completion of the San Francisco-Oakland Bay Bridge in November 1936 and the Golden Gate Bridge in May 1937. As traffic poured across the two bridges, the ferry lines, one by one, began gradually to suspend service. A few are still running.

The development of urban and interurban street railways began in 1861, when San Francisco acquired its first street cars, drawn by horses whose hoofs clattered loudly over the basalt paving blocks of the streets. In one street they continued their anachronistic clatter until 1913. When people began to build homes on the steep hills, up which the streets of San Francisco climb without compromise, a transportation problem arose. It was ingeniously solved by Andrew Halladie, who in 1873 produced the first cable-drawn street cars in the world. The cable car has continued to accommodate the people of San Francisco, arousing mingled delight and distrust in the hearts of visitors.

In 1863 trains ran from the ferry wharf into the center of Oakland. Now an electric interurban system, utilizing the San Francisco-Oakland Bay Bridge, connects San Francisco with Oakland, Alameda, and Berkeley. An extensive network of urban and interurban lines dispatches 3,700 trains daily in and out of Los Angeles over 1,200 miles of track, serving 45 cities and towns.

In California, as elsewhere, the automobile led to improvement in roads. The counties had for many years kept up a few good macadamized roads but the general condition of roads was lamentable until the legislature created, in 1909, the California Highway Commission with full authority over the construction of a great system of highways. In adopting both the motor bus and the motor truck California was a pioneer State, since many communities had either not been reached at all or had been inadequately served by the railroads. By 1915 trucking had become one of the important means of transportation, particularly of farm and dairy produce. Its growth created a further demand for better roads which the State met. At present (1939) trucks carry 70 percent of the total intrastate business. In November 1937 California had some 40,000 freight trucks in operation. They ranged from old Fords carrying supplies into the Sierra Nevada camps to 10-ton tractors and trailers costing over $10,000.

The considerable distance from San Francisco and Los Angeles to other centers of population has made California an important State in the short but dramatic history of the airplane. In 1883 John J. Montgomery, professor of physics at the University of Santa Clara, built a glider which soared some 600 feet, but this was only one of many abortive attempts to fly in heavier-than-air craft. Among the memorable pioneer flights with which California has been associated were Silas Christofferson's first non-stop flight from San Francisco to Los Angeles in 1914; Lindbergh's preliminary flight from San Diego to New York in 1927; the first non-stop flight over the Pacific to Hawaii by Lts. Maitland and Hegenberger in 1927; and the 7,800-mile flight from Oakland to Australia by way of Hawaii and the Pacific Islands of Kingsford-Smith, Ulm, and Lyon in 1928. From the California shore the Pacific was first bridged commercially by air. Climaxing six years of intensive preparation by the Pan-American Airway system, the world's first trans-Pacific commercial service opened in October 1936, when the "China Clipper" made a round-trip passenger flight between San Francisco and Manila. In July 1937 the "Philippine Clipper," arriving at Cavite Bay, Manila, completed the first 1,000,000 miles of commercial flight over the big water. At the end of 1937 California had 72 airports and 133 landing fields. The airplane has come to be taken as much for granted as were the pack mule, the ox-cart, the stage coach, and the wood-burning locomotive in their day.

Workingmen

"THERE is no state in the Union, no place on earth, where labor is so honored and so well rewarded," David C. Broderick told the United States Senate in his maiden speech in 1858, "no time and place since the Almighty doomed the sons of Adam to toil, where the curse, if it be a curse, rests so lightly as now upon the people of California."

The vigorous independence of the pioneer has persisted until present times as a characteristic of the State's labor movement. Of the men who had the hardihood to make the long westward trek in Gold Rush days, many were skilled workingmen from trades in which unions were being organized. Among the European-born immigrants were English Chartists, Irish nationalists, French and German political exiles of 1848—men schooled in the labor movement, in struggles for national independence, or for democratic liberties. In the new-born camps and towns of California, they found no feudal tradition to influence social relationships. To people who saw men in overalls win or lose fortunes overnight, there was no place for concepts of the superiority or special privileges of the wealthy.

The State's labor movement began in its first big city, San Francisco, since early days the trade-union center of California and, until later years, of the whole region west of the Rocky Mountains. The second great metropolitan center, Los Angeles, remained an open-shop stronghold for half a century, the lower labor standards of its competing industries threatening the gains won by labor in the north. But, as Los Angeles outstripped San Francisco in population, the disparity between labor conditions in the two cities began to diminish, for San Francisco trade unionists came to realize that labor in the north could hold its gains only with the aid of labor in the south. During the 1930's the organized labor movements of both cities began to pool their strength in an effort to overcome the sharp contrast between urban and rural working conditions and attempted to organize the vast numbers of underprivileged migratory workers in the State's dominant industry, agriculture.

The swift tempo of San Francisco's growth from village to metropolis characterized the development of its labor movement. The printers organized in 1850; teamsters, draymen, lightermen, riggers and stevedores in 1851; bakers and bricklayers in 1852; calkers, carpenters, plasterers, brickmasons, blacksmiths, and shipwrights in 1853; and musicians in 1856. Although most of these organizations had to make several starts before they achieved stability, they gained better working conditions for their members, kept wages balanced with the wildly rocketing cost of living, and launched the movement for progressive labor legislation. Of the labor laws pushed through in two decades, 1850-70, by these infant labor unions, the most important were provisions for payment of wages, a mechanics' lien, and an eight-hour day. In no other city in the country, it is said, did so many workers enjoy the eight-hour day as in San Francisco during these years.

The outstanding labor struggle of the 1860's, the molders' and boilermakers' strike of 1864, was conducted along lines typical of those spacious days. The strikers were opposed by a newly formed ironworks employers' association, which threatened to levy a fine of $1,000 on the first employer to grant the strikers' demands. The association wired Portland, New York, Boston, and Providence for strikebreakers and paid their fare West. When the strikebreakers arrived at Panama, however, they were greeted by a delegation of representatives from the striking unions and the San Francisco Trades Union, the city's first central labor body. All arrived at San Francisco on friendly terms as fellow union members.

The organization of the first effective State federated labor body, the Mechanics' State Council, was the labor movement's defense against employers' opposition to the eight-hour day. Forming the "Ten Hour League" (1867) to counter labor's "Eight Hour League," the employers, following the shipowners' action in discharging all who worked on the eight-hour basis on the chief steamship lines, pledged themselves to hire no one for less than a ten-hour day. "By so doing," they stated, "we believe that we are working for the best interest of the journeymen mechanics as well as for the best interests of the city and state at large." The Mechanics' State Council, organized in the Los Angeles as well as the San Francisco area, responded by affiliating with the National Labor Union, America's first great national labor federation.

An era of comparative protection for labor came abruptly to its end with completion of the first transcontinental railroad in 1869. Labor, hard hit by the falling wages and the rising unemployment of the depression-ridden decade that followed, began to lay the blame for its misfortunes on the thousands of Chinese coolie railroad workers suddenly turned loose on the labor market. For the next two decades the campaign against the use of Chinese labor, pushed to the limit by politicians and demagogues, diverted the energies of the trade union movement. But labor's fear of being reduced to servitude was well founded. Still fresh in men's minds was the struggle against the efforts of pro-slavery officials and landowners to introduce slavery to California; this had first been brought to the fore in 1852 when railroad and landowning interests were prevented, by protest meetings of miners and city workers, from forcing a law permitting importation of contract labor through the legislature. The anti-Chinese movement, although accompanied by racial discrimination which gave rise to outbreaks of brutal violence, was primarily based on economic interest. In ever greater numbers the Chinese were taking over work in the fields, in the service trades, in the light manufacturing industries—until by 1872 they comprised half of all the factory workers in San Francisco. The wages paid them were far below wages of American workers. And when Americans refused to have their wages lowered to the pay levels of the Chinese, employers threatened to hire Chinese workers instead. On the other hand, the builders of the Central Pacific had threatened to hire American workers when Chinese construction hands struck against $30 monthly for a 12-hour day (1867).

"The Chinese Must Go!" was the slogan that carried Dennis Kearney, one of the most widely known figures in the early California labor movement, to prominence. Until he appeared on the scene in 1877 as a saviour of the masses, he had been vociferously anti-labor. Joining the "law and order" group formed by nervous businessmen in July 1877 when rioters roamed the city denouncing Chinese and capitalists, he suddenly left it to lead the rioters. Refused admission to the Workingmen's Party of the United States, he set up in October 1877 a rival organization, the Workingmen's Party of California. At Sunday afternoon meetings of workers and unemployed on vacant sand lots, where he delivered incendiary speeches, his favorite pose was with a noosed rope in his hand. This he declared was his platform. He was jailed for advising every man "to own a musket and a hundred rounds of ammunition" but was soon released. Eventually, as opposition arose within the Workingmen's Party, an investigating committee charged him with being a "dictator . . . more than suspected of selling out to the enemy"—the enemy in this case being railroad and banking interests. Discredited, Kearney went back to the draying business he had left and devoted himself to getting rich.

The man who headed the opposition to Kearney, Frank Roney, remained an outstanding figure in the State's labor movement long after Kearney's retirement. Active as a young man in the movement for Irish independence, he had emigrated to the United States to become a national figure in the iron molder's union. He arrived in San Francisco in 1875, wrote the constitution and platform of the Workingmen's Party, and soon took his place as a leader in the labor organization drive of the 1880's. Following the disappearance of the Workingmen's Party from the political scene, he was elected president of the Federated Trades and Labor Unions of the Pacific Coast, later the San Francisco Central Labor Council. To Roney was entrusted the job of organizing the seamen of the port of San Francisco, twice previously attempted with no more than short-lived success.

In what was known as the world's worst shanghaiing port, the Seamen's Protective Association, headed by Roney as president, took up the fight against wages so low and shipboard conditions so brutal that crews could be filled only by kidnapping. The association faced the opposition of shipowners, crimps, and underworld elements who preyed on sailors. During one meeting held in 1880, according to the union's minute book, "there were constant interruptions by the boarding-house sharks and their whiskey-brought bummers, going even so far as to throw valuable eggs, that did not have time to get the proper age and odor, at the agitators; but they made a bad failure, for the superior intelligence and calmness of the speakers entirely discomforted their enemies." The union fought for seamen's civil rights by preferring charges against brutal ships' officers in Federal courts. It won the backing of progressive San Franciscans, chief among them Henry George, single-tax proponent, editor of the San Francisco *Post,* and a consistent supporter of the labor movement. The fight to improve seamen's working conditions was extended into the legislative field when Roney drew up and presented to Congress two laws, one embodying the union's demand for punishment of brutal officers and the other specifying that two-thirds of the crew of every American vessel should be American citizens. The legislative struggle was later taken up and carried on for some thirty years by Andrew Furuseth, as secretary of the Sailors' Union of the Pacific and (from 1908) of the International Seamen's Union of America.

As a result of the struggle against a sharp wage cut in 1885 a stable organization, the Coast Seamen's Union, was at last set up with the aid of officers of the Knights of Labor, then at the peak of its growth in California, and Socialists from the International Workingmen's Association, of whom five served on the union's original advisory committee. The union halted the drive for wage cuts, organized branches at leading ports up and down the Pacific Coast, and launched (1887) the *Coast Seamen's Journal,* for years the Coast's most important labor paper. In 1891 the Coast Seamen's Union and the deep-sea steamship sailors' union dropped their jurisdictional differences and merged as the present Sailors' Union of the Pacific.

Following organization of the seamen, the waterfront unions became an important factor in San Francisco's labor movement, for longshoremen, ship calkers, pile drivers, and other waterfront workers had already been organized for a period of years. Feeling a bond of common interest, the maritime unions made repeated efforts to achieve joint organization. The Wharf and Wave Federation (1888), the City Front Labor Council (1891), and the Waterfront Federation (1914-1923) were predecessors of the present Maritime Federation of the Pacific.

The City Front Federation of 1901, reputed to have been the strongest trade federation in the country at the time, grew out of the intense organizational drive in all crafts that accompanied the great industrial boom at the turn of the century. During the two decades that followed its organization, the trade union movement grew at such a pace that San Francisco took first place among the unionized cities of the United States. But labor's gains were not achieved without opposition. To meet what they considered the threat of union domination, employers organized on a broader and more effective basis than in the past. A complicated and tense situation developed, which culminated in the building trades strike of 1900 and the City Front Federation strike of 1901. The successful conclusion of the building trades strike was followed by organization of the Building Trades Council, which became the most powerful factor in the labor movement. The City Front Federation strike, in which the waterfront unions went out in support of locked-out teamsters, was bitterly fought because both labor and employers knew that the question of establishing the open shop in San Francisco was at stake. Although the unions partially lost the strike, they checked the open-shop drive and survived.

Out of the City Front Federation strike grew the Union Labor Party, supported by the San Francisco Central Labor Council because of its resentment over Mayor James D. Phelan's use of police to protect strikebreakers brought into the city. The Union Labor Party's candidate for mayor, Eugene Schmitz, was elected in 1902 to succeed Phelan. The story of how an alleged alliance of politicians, utilities, and vice interests won control of the party has been told by Fremont Older, editor of the San Francisco *Bulletin,* who helped lead the reform movement that culminated in the graft prosecutions initiated against Schmitz, Abraham Ruef, and a long list of municipal office-holders in 1906. Older's story deals, too, with the activities of Patrick Calhoun, political boss and United Railroads head, who, it is said, pre-cipitated the 1907 traction strike in an effort to halt the prosecution, by diverting public attention. Having aroused public indignation against labor, on the ground that the strike was holding up reconstruction of the earthquake-wrecked city, Calhoun melodramatically broke the strike. Those in control of the Union Labor Party had by this time been denounced by the San Francisco Central Labor Council in an emphatic statement published May 30, 1906, which said, in part: "We declare every corruptionist, briber and bribed, should be prosecuted and punished according to law and hereby pledge our cooperation to that end." In the end Calhoun was brought to trial, but acquitted.

Despite the rapid growth of the labor movement in San Francisco, Los Angeles remained largely a non-union town. The employers of San Francisco had stated flatly that unless the unions acted to level competition with the south by organizing Los Angeles they would begin a new drive for open-shop conditions in the Bay area. Taking up the challenge, labor sent a corps of organizers south in June 1910. In Los Angeles the Founders and Employers Association was refusing to meet with union representatives of some 1,200 workers idle in a metal-trades lockout covering all plants in the city. The International Molders Union sent its national organizer, George Gunray, to aid the Los Angeles drive. As the organizing drive got underway, the pub-lic began to develop a sympathetic attitude toward unionism.

And then occurred the disaster that for many years was to delay labor organization in Los Angeles. At one o'clock in the morning of October 1, 1910, an explosion shattered the plant of the Los Angeles *Times,* owned by General Gray Otis, leader of the city's anti-union forces. Twenty-one of the workers in the building were killed and many injured.

Intense excitement followed and while the Labor Council, investi-gating, announced that the explosion had been a gas explosion, the police, the grand jury, the Mayor's committee, civic bodies, the City Council, also investigating, declared that the explosion had been caused by dynamite. Otis offered a reward of $300,000 for the finding of those responsible. Three groups of detectives began the search.

On April 14, 1911, James B. McNamara and Ortie McManigal were arrested in Detroit by the detective William J. Burns. Ortie McManigal in a confession implicated, among others, James Mc-Namara's brother John J. McNamara, Secretary of the International Association of Bridge and Structural Iron Workers' Union. J. J. McNamara was arrested on April 22 in Indianapolis. The Mc-

Namaras were taken to the Los Angeles jail and held; McManigal was taken along as prosecution witness.

Labor, convinced of the innocence of the McNamaras, rose to their defense. According to Perlman and Taft (*History of Labor in the United States 1896-1932,* Volume IV) "Los Angeles was at the time the battlefield of several simultaneous labor wars. . . . The explosion in the morning of October 1, 1910 . . . came as a climax in these hard fought battles." The American Federation of Labor raised a quarter of a million dollar fund, and the famous advocate, Clarence Darrow, was retained to defend the men.

The trial dragged on slowly with labor—still certain of the men's innocence—engaged in a veritable crusade. But Clarence Darrow apparently became convinced of the great strength of the State's case. Through the journalist Lincoln Steffens, he began to negotiate with the authorities. In retrospect, Steffens wrote in his autobiography that his newspaper report of the case "began by saying that both capital and labor had pleaded guilty, and showed that the McNamaras had made no confession which involved other persons but had entered into an agreement by which, without force, the labor problem was to be reconsidered in the most anti-labor city in America."

The details of the agreement made with the prosecution have remained a source of argument. According to Perlman and Taft, "The agreement with the prosecution stipulated that both brothers would plead guilty, and that J. B. McNamara would receive life imprisonment but John J. McNamara a less severe sentence, and that all other prosecutions would be dropped." Influential people of Los Angeles and the court officers were won over, and so finally were the McNamaras. On December 1, 1911, Attorney Darrow rose in court and stated that his clients wished to change their plea from "not guilty" to "guilty as charged." Four days later James B. McNamara was sentenced to life imprisonment and John J. McNamara to a term of 15 years. In passing sentence the judge verbally castigated the men: which action, it is alleged, was against the agreement. Later that part of the stipulation concerned with the prosecution of others was also disregarded.

The decade that followed saw a rapid growth in the influence on California's labor movement of the Industrial Workers of the World, central organizing agency in Northwest logging camps and Midwest wheat fields, as it began extending its work to the mines, lumber camps, ports, and agricultural areas of the State. It came into prominence in California at the time of the Wheatland hop field riots of 1913, which brought before the Nation for the first time the intolerable conditions of field labor in the State and prompted an investigation leading to the first Government action in cleaning up these conditions. The

situation that prompted the riots at the Wheatland hop ranch, said
to belong to the State's largest single employer of field labor at the
time, was later described by Carleton W. Parker, executive secretary
of the State Commission of Immigration and Housing: "Twenty-eight
hundred pickers were camped on a .treeless hill . . . Some were in
tents, some in topless squares of sacking . . . there was no provision
for sanitation, no garbage disposal. The temperature during the week
of the riot remained near 105 degrees, and though the wells were a
mile from where the men, women and children were picking . . . no
water was sent into the fields . . . It developed in the state investigation that the owner of the ranch received half of the net profit earned
by an alleged independent grocery store, which had been given the
grocery concession and was located in the center of the camp grounds."
The overcrowding of the camp was found to have been aggravated by
the fact that the ranch owner had followed the common practice of
advertising for twice the necessary number of pickers in order to keep
down wage levels. In the rioting that began when a sheriff's posse
broke up a protest meeting, four were killed. A week after the riot,
the first act regulating California labor camps went into effect.

The I. W. W. continued to play an important part in the labor
movement until the early post-war period. Among the causes contributing to its decline were the anti-union drive and the prosecution
of many of its members under the State's newly passed criminal syndicalism laws. Its last important appearance in the State was in the
1923 seamen's strike at San Pedro, when Upton Sinclair was arrested
for publicly reading the Declaration of Independence.

A prominent defender of the two I. W. W. leaders, Richard Ford
and Herman Suhr, who were arrested in the Wheatland disturbance
and convicted after a long-fought trial, was a young Irish member of
the molders' union, Thomas Mooney. The leading part that he played
in the electrical workers' strike of 1913 and in the attempted organization of United Railroads workers in 1916 also brought him to the
fore in northern California as an aggressive trade unionist. He was
a leading member of the group that began preparing a new organizational drive in southern California to counter a new open-shop campaign
in the north organized by employers. As such he came particularly to
the attention of the "law and order" committee formed by the San
Francisco Chamber of Commerce to promote adoption of an anti-
picketing ordinance.

The newspaper files of the period reveal the combination of anti-
union and wartime preparedness propaganda in an attempt to label as
disloyal labor's determination to maintain its organizational lines. In
the tense atmosphere of the growing struggle a bomb exploded, killing
ten persons, on the route of the Preparedness Day parade staged in San

Francisco July 22, 1916. Among those arrested were Mooney, his wife Rena, and his friend, Warren K. Billings. Found guilty, Mooney was sentenced to be hanged and Billings to life imprisonment. After world-wide protests, Governor William D. Stephens, at the behest of President Woodrow Wilson, commuted Mooney's sentence to life imprisonment in November 1918.

The case soon became one of the most celebrated labor controversies of modern times. In the course of repeated State hearings and Federal inquiries, a picture of corruption was revealed that strengthened the conviction held by many people that the case had been a frame-up. On the basis of new evidence soon uncovered, and of confessions and other evidence exposing the perjury of key prosecution witnesses, the jurors who found Mooney guilty and the judge who sentenced him publicly reversed their positions. As the years went by, more and more evidence indicating Mooney's innocence came to light. In August 1928 every living person connected with the prosecution, except District Attorney Charles Fickert and an assistant, recommended Mooney's pardon. The trial judge, Judge Griffin, declared in a public address in February 1929: "The Mooney case is one of the dirtiest jobs ever put over and I resent the fact that my court was used for such a contemptible piece of work." But for 22 years, Mooney remained in San Quentin penitentiary while successive Governors resisted appeals for a pardon. Throughout these years the case was carried through State and Federal Courts as Mooney's defense attorneys asked for a review of new evidence and opening of a new trial. Finally in October 1938, after lengthy hearings in San Francisco before a referee, the United States Supreme Court, passing on the case a second time, found itself compelled on legal grounds to deny a requested review of the case. A month later Culbert L. Olson, who had expressed his firm belief in Mooney's innocence while still a State senator, was elected Governor of California. One of his first steps on taking office in January 1939 was to issue an unconditional pardon.

In the meantime the wartime anti-union campaign had driven ahead to success, initiating a period of open-shop domination that lasted throughout the 1920's. It reached its climax in 1921, when the newly formed Industrial Association of San Francisco raised a war chest of $1,250,000 to break the building trades strike of that year. With the collapse of the building trades unions, too weakened to resist when the Industrial Association's wage board cut wages twice within a year, the strongest single force in the labor movement of that period was rendered helpless. At about the same time, the Metal Trades Council was defeated, losing agreements it had held with the employers since 1907. The seamen's unions, too, went down to defeat in 1921. The loss of the dock strike of 1919, called in protest against alleged endangerment of life and limb by speed-up and excessive loads, had already caused the collapse of the riggers' and stevedores' union. In the succeeding decade, the "American Plan," substituting individual for collective bargaining, prevailed throughout the State.

The resurgence of the labor movement following enactment of the National Industrial Recovery Act in 1933 was marked especially by the outburst of latent protest against long-standing grievances on San Francisco's waterfront. The conditions that prompted the 1919 strike had continued under the agreement signed in December 1919 between the Waterfront Employers' Association and the Longshoremen's Association of the Pacific, organized by longshore gang bosses, which longshoremen designated a "company" union, calling it the Blue Book Union (for the color of the membership book); the agreement made every dock worker who refused to join ineligible for employment. Another basic grievance was the "shape-up" system of hiring from the docks, which longshoremen claimed forced them to wait without compensation for hours at a time, fostered corrupt control of employment by hiring agents from whom men had to buy their jobs, and resulted in some men working 24 and 36 hours and longer without sleep, while others starved for lack of work. As a leader in protests against abuses, the lanky young Australian, Harry Bridges, who had been working on the docks ever since he had come ashore as a sailor 12 years before, was coming to the fore; among longshoremen he was known as "Limo Harry," a first-class winch driver and a man who stood up for his rights. Within a few weeks after a charter had been secured from the International Longshoremen's Association in September 1933, about 90 per cent of the men on the front had joined the new union. At a coastwise convention held in the spring of 1934, the longshoremen formulated demands to correct the abuses on the docks. When hearings led to no definite result, they took a strike vote on March 7. The seamen's unions, likewise showing a new vitality, had also been refused when they presented demands to the shipowners. On May 15, 1934, they voted to join the strike; and the ship clerks and licensed officers' organizations followed suit.

The killing of two waterfront picketers and the clubbing and gassing of a hundred others by police on Thursday, July 5, 1934—afterwards known as "Bloody Thursday"—was the incident that swept nearly every union in the Bay area into the second important general strike up to that time in the Nation's history. From July 17 to July 19 stores closed, shops and factories shut down, and trucks and street cars stopped running in San Francisco as 127,000 workers left their jobs. The strike aroused the emphatically expressed opposition of many newspapers, individuals, and organizations throughout the Nation. The NRA Administrator, General Hugh S. Johnson, appeared on the scene to denounce it in a public address. On July 20 the strikers began returning to their jobs. The waterfront unions, however, after mediation of the dispute, won agreements with the shipowners which still serve as the basis of labor relations in the maritime industry. They were enabled to organize in 1935 the Maritime Federation of the Pacific, first attempt to apply the principle of joint organization on a coastwise basis. It now has 28,000 members, drawn from A. F. of L. and C. I. O. unions, and from unions in Canada and the Hawaiian Islands. The strong public feeling aroused by the general strike soon subsided, but not the opposition to one of its leaders, Bridges, longshoremen's president and later C. I .O. Pacific Coast director. It was still being expressed four years later in a controversy involving the United States Secretary of Labor over his right (since he had not yet been naturalized) to remain in the country.

As the labor movement began to advance again after its long period of decline, the unions weakened in 1919-21 gained renewed strength, while new unions staged intensive drives in industries never before organized. San Francisco and Oakland recovered more than their old union strength; organization extended into Los Angeles from its port at San Pedro; it reached even into the inland valleys where the labor movement had never before made headway. Throughout the 1930's the labor movement has continued to make steady gains.

In union-minded San Francisco, more than 120,000 of whose inhabitants belong to labor unions, the principle of collective bargaining has come to be accepted as a matter of fact. In the neighborhood of the port, where the outward signs of the labor movement's flourishing condition are most apparent, longshoremen swing along the streets with union buttons conspicuously displayed on their white (union-made) caps. Big Irish teamsters driving their trucks down to the docks wear union buttons; so do the Italian fishermen, the taxi drivers, streetcar conductors and motormen, newsboys and bootblacks. Almost every restaurant, bar, barber shop, drug store, and laundry displays a union sign. The A. F. of L. unions are strong among teamsters, streetcar employees, and workers in the building trades and service industries, including retail store clerks, hotel employees, and others; the C. I. O. unions, among longshoremen, warehousemen, newspapermen, and smelter and tunnel workers. In recognition of labor's strength, employers have organized in distributors', waterfront employers', hotel owners', and other associations covering all the major industries. A San Francisco Employer's Council, organized in 1938, announced a desire for more cooperative relations with labor. A development of the same year, tried out with much success during a warehousemen's lockout, was the town meeting, at which employers and union leaders presented their respective sides of the dispute before a public audience.

As against 30,000 trade union members in 1933-34, Los Angeles today has 200,000. The trade union movement had advanced despite the continued open-shop stand of employers, who in 1938 pushed through a drastic anti-picketing ordinance. Although a number of industries remain largely unorganized, the disparity between labor conditions in the State's two larger cities no longer exists. A basic factor in bringing about this change was the rapid growth of unionization in such mass production industries as aircraft, auto, rubber, and oil. Intensive organizational drives have been staged among musicians, teamsters, workers in the building trades, and in the motion-picture and other industries. The almost complete organization of all trades in the harbor district, San Pedro, has given the city's growing labor movement solid backing. A force to be reckoned with has been the rise of unions in the motion-picture industry, which number (1939) some 12,000 members. To the surprise of many who believed that movie people would never step out of their make-believe world, screen actors, writers, and directors have come forward as topnotch trade union members.

The most important downward pull on California's labor standards is exerted today by the rural areas, where some 200,000 almost completely unorganized agricultural workers, mostly homeless migrants, live and work under conditions generally recognized as sub-standard. Of these nomadic workers, the majority are refugees from the Dust Bowl area, although Mexicans work in the citrus groves of the south and the sugar-beet fields of the north and Filipinos and Japanese in the asparagus and celery fields of the Sacramento-San Joaquin delta region. Just as labor's weakness in the south once threatened its gains in the north, so now its weakness in the rural areas threatens its gains in the cities. The sharp divergence between urban and rural labor standards has begun to worry city unionists especially because of the dominant position in the State's economy of its highly mechanized agriculture, which provides most of the freight handled by both rail and water and a large proportion of the raw material processed by manufacturing plants.

The sharpest conflicts since the revival of the West Coast labor movement in 1933-34 have developed out of what employers have termed the "inland march" of city trade unions. To meet it, the forces opposing unionism have systematized and extended their organization. Led by the Associated Farmers, Inc., representing the corporative farm interests of the State, they have induced a number of the valley towns to adopt anti-picketing ordinances. The Farmers' Transportation Association of Southern California, organized in 1938 in nine southern counties under the auspices of the Associated Farmers, has announced its intention to maintain "the right of every man to work without being coerced into joining or not joining a union"; it issues licenses to truck drivers, after questioning them on union affiliation, only when they have pledged to pick up and deliver cargoes under all circumstances except when prevented by "acts of God."

Labor's "inland march" has been blocked increasingly often during the last decade, in rural and company towns where trade unions lack the support of public opinion which they have won in the cities, by the activities of vigilante organizations that have helped themselves to the name of groups organized for different purposes in the pioneer period. In the 1933-34 wave of agricultural strikes, vigilante methods were invoked to break the Imperial Valley lettuce strike and the San Joaquin Valley cotton strike, largest strike of field workers in California history. In the 1936 Salinas lettuce strike, vigilantism attained proportions that shocked public opinion in the State and Nation. Again in the spring of 1937 vigilante methods were used to break the Stockton cannery strike. In April 1938 about 300 men, women, and children (members of the International Mine, Mill, and Smelter Workers Union) were driven by vigilante raids from their homes in Grass Valley and Nevada City, site of the country's second largest gold mine. Under police escort they returned to their homes, reopened their union hall, and carried on.

When anti-union forces undertook an intensive campaign to secure adoption of a State-wide anti-picketing law at the polls in 1938, labor unions—both A. F. of L. and C. I. O.—saw their common danger, recognizing the campaign as the prelude to a general open-shop drive, and united to defeat it. The proposed law, known as Proposition No. One, was considered by many groups to be more stringent than any similar act since the anti-conspiracy laws of Colonial days. Commented the official publication of the California State Grange: "Said by its proponents to be needed legislation for industrial peace, this initiative proposition would really take away the constitutional rights of labor; it is dangerous because the layman does not recognize the fascistic provisions hidden within the proposal." Proposition No. One became the central issue in the campaign preceding the November elections. A. F. of L. and C. I. O. unions, central labor bodies, maritime workers, teamsters, steelworkers, newspapermen, carpenters, tunnel miners, movie stars, railwaymen, and clergymen joined in a successful counter-campaign which defeated the measure.

Out of the cooperation of A. F. of L. and C. I. O. unions in this campaign, strengthened by the victory in the elections of candidates for public office endorsed by both, grew a movement for unity of the labor movement's two wings. In Stockton and in Sacramento, joint labor committees formed by A. F. of L. and C. I. O. locals continued to function.

Another influence promoting the unification of the labor movement has been the gradual disappearance of the racial discrimination that once characterized it. The anti-Chinese and anti-Japanese agitation that kept American and Oriental workers apart has largely vanished. Today the International Ladies Garment Workers Union, the retail clerks', culinary, and other A. F. of L. unions, and all the C. I. O. unions admit Chinese, Japanese, and Filipino workers to membership with full rights, including eligibility to hold office. The hostility once directed against Chinese, Japanese, or Mexican workers is more apt to be directed now against native-born Dust Bowl refugees when attempts are made to use their labor at wage rates that endanger general California standards.

Organized labor in California shows a growing tendency to welcome the help of technical experts in dealing with the complex problems of negotiation with employers, arbitration cases, and presenting the union point of view to the public. Notable in this field is the work of the Pacific Coast Labor Bureau, a non-profit service organization specializing in economic counsel to labor unions. It has headquarters in San Francisco and branches in other West Coast cities. The bureau represents A. F. of L., C. I. O., Railroad Brotherhood, and bona fide independent unions.

The extension of labor's activities to the political field has enabled it to report many legislative gains. California has an old-age assistance law, an unemployment compensation act, a 48-hour maximum work week law for women workers, and an apprentice law (recently passed). The State protects workmen suffering from occupational diseases. In order to protect and supplement such legislation, unions have begun to participate in politics to an increasing extent.

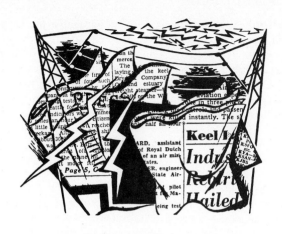

Press and Radio

"TRUE with his rifle, ready with his pen, and quick at the type case"—thus Walter Colton, American *alcalde* at Monterey, described California's pioneer journalist, Dr. Robert Semple, a buckskin-clad Kentucky emigrant, who stood 6 feet 8 inches in his stockings. On August 15, 1846, only a month after the American flag was raised at Monterey, Semple and Colton printed news of the United States' declaration of war on Mexico in the *Californian,* the first newspaper published within the State. "A crowd was waiting when the first sheet was thrown from the press," wrote Colton. "Never was a bank run upon harder; not, however, by people with paper to get specie, but exactly the reverse." For twelve and a half cents the customers got a single sheet a little larger than foolscap, printed half in English and half in Spanish.

A wooden, hand-operated Ramage press ran off this first issue. It had been manufactured in New York about 1800, shipped to Mexico City for use in the Mexican government printing office, and packed on mule-back to Monterey about 1834. Colton described the equipment as "old enough to be preserved as a curiosity; the mice had burrowed in the balls, there were no rules, no leads, and the types were rusty and all in pie." When he and Semple had cleaned the type, cut rules and leads out of a sheet of tin with a jack-knife, and hunted up part of a keg of ink, they were still faced by their worst problem— lack of paper. All that could be found was a small supply of the coarse stuff used to wrap cigarettes on board a coastwise sailing ship. It had to serve.

The *Californian,* after appearing intermittently for nearly a year, was moved, old press and all, to San Francisco. There, on May 22, 1847, the paper reappeared in competition with San Francisco's first journal, the weekly *California Star,* which the Mormon pioneer, Samuel Brannan, had established on January 9 of the same year.

Neither paper displayed any interest in what was perhaps the biggest news story in California history—James Marshall's discovery of gold at Coloma. "Great chances here for scientific capitalists," wrote Dr. Robert Semple in the *Californian* of March 15, 1848, seven weeks after the event, in a 67-word paragraph which chilled any possible excitement. Although the rival *Star* occasionally devoted its columns to unenthusiastic and somewhat technical discussions of gold during the next few weeks, it was word-of-mouth rumors of prospectors having "struck it rich" that convinced San Francisco's unscientific non-capitalists that Marshall's discovery might concern them too.

"All sham—a superb (*sic*) take-in, as was ever got up to guzzle the gullible," wrote the *Star's* acting editor, E. C. Kemble, on his return from a trip to the mines in April. Unluckily for Kemble, his boss, Sam Brannon, who had also gone out to investigate, appeared one day on Portsmouth Square flourishing a whisky flask full of gold dust and shouting, "Gold! Gold from the American Fork!" Even the most apathetic citizens were so fired by Brannan's dramatic proclamation that hundreds followed him back to the mine.

Before the stampede of readers—and even printers—San Francisco's two infant newspapers were helpless. The *Californian* suspended publication May 29. Two days earlier the *Star* had urged its readers: "Pay up before you go—everybody knows where. Papers can be forwarded to Sutter's Fort with all regularity. But pay the printer, if you please, all you in arrears." On June 4 it, too, ceased publication, and again California was without a single newspaper.

The gold rush, however, far from stifling journalism, fostered its growth. By August 1848 the *Californian* had resumed its career. It was bought the following month, together with the *Star,* by Kemble, who merged the two papers into one which he introduced November 18, 1848, as the *Star and Californian,* soon to be renamed the *Alta Californian.* So rapid was its growth that two years later it became a daily, and soon its publishers were printing it on a steam press. Enlisting the services of Mark Twain as a contributor and Bret Harte as an editor, it became—and for more than a generation continued to be—one of California's leading papers.

Meanwhile the creaking old Ramage press which had printed the original *Californian* had continued on its travels. Together with an assortment of old type and a lot of Spanish foolscap, it was shipped by Kemble up the Sacramento River to the settlement of New Helvetia (now Sacramento). It was set up in a makeshift office of adobe, wood, and cotton cloth, and on April 28, 1849 ran off the first weekly issue of the *Placer Times,* the Sacramento Valley's pioneer paper. Kemble soon lost his monopoly of the Sacramento news market, for on April 1, 1850 the Sacramento *Transcript* appeared and on August 3 of the same year the *Settler's and Miner's Tribune.* After a two-months championship of the Squatter's Association, however, the *Tribune* was buried in Sacramento's newspaper graveyard, the first of some 70 or 80 short-lived papers which started and discontinued publication during a period of 30 years.

Still farther into the interior, the pioneer Ramage press was packed to continue its newspaper-founding exploits. On July 4, 1850 it printed the Mother Lode's first paper, the Sonora *Herald.* It went on running off news of fights and gold until the fall of 1851, when it was moved to Columbia to print the Columbia *Star.* In most of the larger mining towns, newspapers were soon flourishing. Within ten years after the discovery of gold, Jackson and Marysville each had seven papers; Columbia, five; and Sonora, Mariposa, and San Andreas, three. Nor did all these die with the gold rush. Auburn's *Placer Herald* has been issued ever since 1852, and Downieville's *Mountain Messenger* since 1853.

Even in the sun-baked adobe village of Los Angeles, newspapers were making a place for themselves. The first paper was run off May 17, 1851 on a hand press brought around the Horn in a windjammer. This was the Los Angeles *Star* or *La Estrella de Los Angeles,* a four-page weekly, printed half in Spanish and half in English. So isolated was the sleepy pueblo that the *Star's* news, which often appeared as late as six weeks after the event, was news to nobody when it finally saw print. The uncertainties of waiting for the mail—once delivered as late as 52 days after leaving San Francisco—so disgusted the editor that eventually he gave up his job. The publishers of the *Southern Californian,* founded July 20, 1854, inherited an old font of Spanish type. They struggled along with it, substituting two "V's" for the missing letter "W" until a sailor who had heard of their hardships strolled in one day with news of a fine font of English type which he had seen in the Sandwich Islands (Hawaiian Islands). Overjoyed, they solved their difficulties by sending for it. An all-Spanish paper, *El Clamor Público,* began competing for the Spanish-speaking readers in June 1855.

San Diego, too, was by this time reading its pioneer paper, the *Herald,* established in May 1851. Many a chuckle must have escaped its subscribers when they read the writings of "John Phoenix," as the irrepressible wag and practical joker, Lieut. George H. Derby, called himself. This young Army officer, assigned to the job of diverting the San Diego River, which was silting up the bay, found San Diego such a dreary hamlet that he began writing for the *Herald* to relieve his boredom. Derby perpetrated his most famous exploit when the paper's editor, confident of the victory of the Democratic ticket he had been supporting, entrusted Derby with the management of the paper while he spent a fortnight in San Francisco. "John Phoenix" promptly reversed the *Herald's* politics. Not content with attacking all the candidates his editor had been boosting, he eloquently sang the virtues of the rival Whigs. His counter-campaign was so effective that the Whigs carried the election in San Diego County by a four-to-three majority—although the Democrats managed to carry the State.

Within eight years of the *Californian's* first appearance, 57 newspapers and periodicals within the State were serving an average total of 290,000 readers. The dreams of sudden riches, with which the gold rush had fired men's minds everywhere had transformed California into one of the most important news markets of the world. Now, as the scramble to lay hands on her wealth bred graft and political skulduggery, many of California's newly-born papers became the mouthpieces of the law-and-order citizenry and took the lead in crusades against corruption. Their editors needed courage, for in those turbulent days the Colt revolver was deemed mightier than the pen.

Into the turmoil of San Francisco's early political strife stepped the most influential of the fighting editors, James King of William, who used that signature to distinguish himself from another James King. On October 8, 1855, he published the first number of his *Daily Evening Bulletin*. He found much to attack, for San Francisco, after the spasmodic outburst of indignation which brought into being the Viligance Committee of 1851, had slipped back into lawlessness. King's editorials slashed mercilessly at the unholy coalition of grafting officials, financial magnates, and gang leaders who were swindling the people through political power. These were the forces, as King soon pointed out in his stinging attacks, that maintained a reign of terror, encouraging robbery and murder, in order to continue stuffing ballot boxes, fixing the courts, and plundering the treasury. Not hesitating to print names, King boldly exposed a rogue's gallery of public enemies in high places. Within a year the *Bulletin* had out-stripped all other papers in the city, winning recognition as the foremost champion of the people's right.

The *Bulletin* charged, on May 14, 1856, that political boss James P. Casey was an ex-inmate of Sing Sing prison who "had stuffed himself through the ballot box . . . to the board of supervisors." On the afternoon of the same day, Casey shot and mortally wounded King. Without hesitation Casey gave himself up at the police station, confident that his friends would protect him. As King lingered between life and death, a second Vigilance Committee, led by some of the active members of the original committee of 1851, was formed. When King died on May 20, the vigilantes brought both Cora, a notorious character, and Casey before them for trial, found them guilty, and hanged them both at "Fort Gunnybags," the vigilantes' headquarters. Two days later King's funeral procession marched by the spot where the bodies were hanging.

San Francisco's other papers were forced to take their stand on the most burning issue of the day. The *Alta Californian's* owners tossed a half-dollar to decide whether or not to support the Vigilance Committee of 1856. The committee won. When the *Herald* decided to oppose the vigilantes, the merchants boycotted it and switched their advertisements to the *Alta Californian*. As a result, the *Herald* dwindled and died. A new paper which stood for the people's rights took over some of its readers—the *Morning Call,* first published December 1, 1856, by the Associated Practical Printers, a craftsmen's co-operative. Of all the San Francisco papers then published, the *Call-Bulletin,* a merger of the *Call* and James King of William's *Bulletin,* is the only one still appearing.

As vigilante activity in the north steadily drove gangsters and political crooks southward, Los Angeles editors soon found themselves confronted with problems long familiar to their San Francisco colleagues. In the face of the most gruesome local disorders, the Los Angeles newspapermen displayed an astonishing air of sang-froid. The Los Angeles *Star* in 1855 even published an account of a lynching before the lynching happened. Because he wanted to put the paper aboard the San Francisco steamer at 10 a.m., hours before the affair was scheduled, a young printer-reporter proceeded to write up a first-class lynching—even including the condemned man's "confession" on the gallows.

Since there were 40 "legal" hangings and 37 impromptu ones in Los Angeles between 1850 and 1870, newspapers became adept at handling crime news. The following is typical of their reporting style: "With the exception of a little legitimate shooting affair last Saturday night, by which some fellow had well-nigh the top of his head knocked off, and one or two knock-downs and drag-outs, we have had a very peaceful week indeed. Nothing has occurred to disturb the even tenor of our way, and our good people seem to be given up to the quiet enjoyment of delicious fruits and our unequalled climate,— each one literally under his own vine and fig tree, reveling in fancy's flights, or luxuriating among the good things he finds temptingly at hand."

While metropolitan editors were dealing with lawlessness and corruption in the cities, one of California's best known papers was leading the struggles of the Sacramento Valley farmers. The Sacramento *Bee,* founded February 3, 1857, took up the cudgels against land monopoly under the editorship of James McClatchy. When the cattle interests were still powerful, the *Bee* began agitating for legislation to protect farms against injury from cattle—and it won the fight. Though it seemed hopeless to oppose the rich and influential mining interests, the *Bee* began educating the people of the Sacramento Valley to fight for defense of the farming lands against threatened ruin by hydraulic mining debris, a struggle that ended with victory for the farmers in the courts.

Of the important metropolitan dailies published in California today, most were founded in the two decades beginning with the Civil War era. The pro-Confederate *Democratic Press* of San Francisco, established in 1863, was so violently "secesh" in its sentiments that indignant Unionists wrecked its plant and threw its type out the window following the assassination of President Lincoln. In order to resume publication with safety on June 12, 1865, it had to change its name to the *Daily Examiner.* The first paper in San Francisco to publish the news of the assassination had made its debut only three months earlier as a small sheet called the *Dramatic Chronicle,* "A Daily Record of Affairs Local, Critical and Theatrical," written, printed, and distributed by two youths of 19 and 17, Charles and M. H. de Young. Soon shedding the word "Dramatic," the *Chronicle* appeared as a daily after 1868.

Los Angeles' oldest newspaper in point of continuous publication made its first appearance in 1871, when a group of five printers founded the *Evening Express.* Four years later it passed into the hands of the pioneer publisher, Colonel James M. Ayers, one of the founders of the *Calaveras Chronicle.* The rival *Daily and Weekly Herald,* now combined with the *Express* as the *Herald-Express,* appeared in 1872; and this was followed in 1873 by the four-page *Weekly Mirror,* which was distributed free. The *Daily Times* made its first appearance in 1881, and within a month was taken over by the *Mirror's* publishers, who printed it on a ramshackle press run by water power from the city *zanja* (ditch). Whenever the pipes became clogged by fish, as occasionally happened, the press had to be stopped. In August 1882 a newcomer to Los Angeles, Colonel (later General) Harrison Gray Otis, ex-editor of the *Grand Army Journal,* took over the management of both the *Mirror* and the *Times,* put his wife to work as a reporter and his daughters as clerks in the business office, and soon afterward merged the two papers to found the Los Angeles *Times.* The day after his arrival in Los Angeles in 1884, Charles F. Lummis, who had made a 3,507-mile walking trip from Cincinnati in 143 days, contributing breezy letters to the *Times* en route, was appointed city editor.

The era of modern journalism in California was inaugurated in

1887 when young William Randolph Hearst took over his father's chaste and ultra-conservative San Francisco *Daily Examiner,* installed some of his college classmates on the staff, and began to publish California's first eight-page daily. Introducing to the Pacific Coast the "human interest" style popularized by Joseph Pulitzer's *World,* the *Examiner* provided its readers with sensational news of strikes, legislative scandal, hospital abuses, jury briberies. Its reporters were assigned to such spectacular stunts as testing the ferryboats' life-saving devices; one of them "fell" overboard, while others stood by with stop watches to time the rescue. Circulation boomed, and the *Examiner* became the nucleus of a Nation-wide chain, which today includes in California the San Francisco *Call-Bulletin,* the Los Angeles *Examiner* and *Herald-Express,* and the Oakland *Post-Enquirer.*

The fighting traditions of James King of William seemed to be reviving when Fremont Older, whom Oswald Garrison Villard called "one of the two first-rate journalists of the Pacific Slope," became editor of the San Francisco *Bulletin* in 1895. Entering vigorously into the struggle to oust the all-powerful Southern Pacific Railroad Co. from political control of the State, Older became one of the star figures —along with his famous fellow-Californian, Lincoln Steffens—of the muckraking era. In 1906 he joined the campaign to expose the graft ring headed by Mayor Eugene E. Schmitz and political boss Abraham Ruef which ruled from the City Hall. At the height of the campaign, when most of the other newspapers were attacking the graft prosecution with bitter invective, Older waged his fight so aggressively in the *Bulletin* that his enemies kidnaped him and carried him to Santa Barbara. A decade later, when he became convinced that District Attorney Fickert had used perjured evidence to convict Thomas J. Mooney and Warren K. Billings of the Preparedness Day bombing in 1916, Older published an extra edition of the *Bulletin* with the headline: "FICKERT FRAMED THE MOONEY CASE." This was the first time that the charge had been made by any disinterested person.

In 1909 the Los Angeles *Herald* began a reform crusade with a series of red-bordered articles entitled "Is Vice Protected in Los Angeles?" The movement thus initiated, which was soon joined by the Los Angeles *Evening Express,* the Fresno *Republican,* the Sacramento *Bee,* and the Oakland *Tribune,* strengthened a political revolt leading to formation of the anti-monopolist Lincoln-Roosevelt League. But in Los Angeles the crusade was suddenly swept into the background by the dynamiting of the *Times* building, on October 1, 1910. J. B. McNamara, secretary of the Structural Bridge and Iron Workers, and his brother were arrested and tried in a long-drawn-out court case which ended in the McNamaras' sudden and unexpected plea of guilty.

Although labor disavowed violence, Governor James N. Gillett said, "Whether guilty or not, labor unionists will have to be blamed for the crime until it is shown they are not guilty." The San Francisco *Daily News* vehemently sprang to the defense of the unions. This little four-page penny paper was started in 1903 in a shabby wooden house "south of the slot." The equipment was of the humblest—a few old chairs and tables, a decrepit linotype machine, and a press purchased from a Chinese newspaper. From the start it was a working-man's paper, costing but 25 cents a month. The guiding principle of the editor, William Wasson, to "cut every item to the bone but increase the number of items," made the writing admirably succinct. Greatly expanded, it became in 1921 a part of the Scripps-Howard national chain, and is now called the *News.* The Scripps-Howard group in California also includes the San Diego *Sun.*

Since the appearance of the *News,* most California papers have tended towards increasing conservatism in editorial policy. The *People's World,* youngest of California's 141 English-language dailies, alone carries on the militant traditions in editorial policy once followed by such papers as the San Francisco *Bulletin* and *News* and the Sacramento *Bee.* It was founded in San Francisco on January 1, 1938, and at the end of its first year it was reaching some 15,000 subscribers. The first left-wing daily newspaper to be published in the West, it bears on its masthead the slogan: "For Security, Democracy, Peace."

Since the earliest days of statehood, many of California's racial minorities have published their own papers. The oldest Negro newspaper still published in the State, the *California Eagle,* has been appearing in Los Angeles since 1879: there are at present eight other Negro papers. The first French journals, the *Californien* (1850) and the *Gazette Républicaine* (1850), were followed by the *Courrier du Pacifique* (1852), which is still published today. Both the first German and the first Italian paper, the *California Demokrat* (1852) and the *Voce del Popolo* (1859), were founded in San Francisco and are still appearing. San Francisco's Chinese published the first of many newspapers, the *Gold Hills News,* in 1854; today (1939) they are publishing five. California's foreign-language journals of today, of which 15 are dailies, include publications in Spanish, Japanese, Swedish, Russian, Greek, and other languages.

RADIO

The first California radio station to broadcast the human voice, KQW of San Jose, was pioneering for the world, as well as for California, when it initiated in 1912 regular broadcasts of speech and music. KQW, operated by the Herrold Wireless Laboratories, had begun its experiments in 1909, broadcasting from a "carpet" antenna —11,000 feet of wire strung between two seven-story office buildings—connected with a crude arc transmitter. Three years later it again took the lead in the use of radio as an entertainment medium, when it began sending out the songs and ukelele tunes of two high school boys, Al and Clarence Pearce. The Government license granted KQW in 1912 was reputedly the first to be issued for actual radio telephony. More than a quarter of a century later, in 1938, the station was still on the air—as was one of its first "stars," Al Pearce.

KQW was also a pioneer in developing the mechanics of radio. Dr. Charles D. Herrold's arc transmitter, the first improvement made on Marconi's equipment, was too high-powered for any microphone then in use; so Herrold constructed a microphone by hooking six telephone transmitter units to a single diaphragm. Using the antenna at Mare Island near San Francisco, Herrold's transmitter established in 1913 what was at the time a world's record for long-distance radio transmission, when its broadcast was tuned in by the army transport *Sherman,* 950 miles at sea. In the same year two-way communication over a distance of 250 miles was established between Mare Island and Point Arguello. Visitors to the Panama-Pacific Exposition at San Francisco in 1915 were thrilled at listening through ear phones to music broadcast by KQW from San Jose. Soon afterward, this station established two-way communication with KDN in San Francisco and opened a studio for the reception of daily concerts broadcast from the Fairmont Hotel—the first such receiving studio in the world.

Californians have been contributing their share of radio inventions ever since the days when crystal detectors and loose-coupler tuners comprised radio receiving equipment. The so-called "Father of Radio," Dr. Lee de Forest, began experimenting in 1912, at his laboratory in Palo Alto, with Audion tube "cascade" amplifiers. His success in amplifying signal strength led to perfection of the amplifying systems used in present-day transmission and reception. Ten years later the Magnavox loudspeaker, developed in Oakland, introduced for the first time the dynamic principle (moving coil in a magnetic field) which loudspeakers on modern receiving sets still use.

By the early 1920's these inventions and others, freeing radio from the crudeness that drew ridicule from early critics, had won for program producers an untold number of ardent listeners. New stations began competing with KQW and KDN—KUO (1922), KPO (1923), and KJBS (1925) in San Francisco; KLX (1922) and KGO (1924), said to be the "world's largest radio transmitter" at the time, in Oakland; KFI (1922), KHJ (1922), KMTR (1924), and KNX (1924) in Los Angeles. During these first years a typical broadcast schedule for the day began with a weather report, followed by recorded music alternating with more weather reports, and ended with a final announcement about the weather.

Since 1922 many of radio's most popular forms of entertainment have been developed in California. The earliest "audience show" was KFRC's *Blue Monday Jamboree,* presented as an experiment to determine how the song-and-patter show could be given appeal for an air audience; its variety technique is still considered to have a more predictable popularity than any other type of radio entertainment. *One Man's Family,* inaugurated on KGO in 1932 and still broadcast, was the first program to adapt radio's particularly intimate facilities to drama by using casual dialogue, unhurriedly delivered, to lend verisimilitude to the characters. One of the earliest of the hillbilly folk programs, *Mac's Haywire Orchestry,* was put together by a California cowboy, "Mac" McClintick, who assembled a quartet of guitar, harmonica, fiddle, and banjo ukelele. The latter was played by San Francisco's now famous critic, Joseph Henry Jackson, whose program of book reviews, began in 1922, is the oldest sustaining program heard transcontinentally. The first broadcast from an airplane was made in a Martin bomber, loaned by the U. S. Army, over Crissey Field, San Francisco. In July 1925, KJBS pioneered mobile short-wave radiophone transmission by relaying the band music of California's Diamond Jubilee celebration. Broadcasts from the *Malolo* in 1931 were the first regularly scheduled programs from a ship at sea.

Since 1933 radio has leaned more and more heavily on motion picture personalities, a change that has emphasized the star system in radio entertainment and caused a westward shift in production. The shift began in 1933, when Rudy Vallee broadcast from an improvised studio on the RKO lot between scenes in his first motion picture. Commercial shows, though often financed, planned, and written in the East, are staged more and more frequently in California—to the discomfort of directors needing authorization for changes in the last few frenzied moments of rehearsals. The cost of talent and production in Hollywood is high, but many sponsors have found that the extra expense is justified by the prestige of a Hollywood "date-line." The ultra-modern studios of Columbia and NBC in Hollywood, where these shows are staged, are among the few places where tourists may see motion picture stars in person.

Radio has been used more and more as a medium by religious groups in California, several organizations having their own broadcasting stations. Of importance to the State's agriculture is the broadcasting of frost warnings and the agricultural programs sponsored by governmental agencies. Possibly the most important practical application of the radio in California is as an aid to air navigation. A coast visited by frequent dense fogs, and mountains subject to violent storms constitute hazards to air travel that the radio has helped to lessen.

In 1938 broadcasts were transmitted from 54 California stations, 10 of which are affiliated with NBC networks, 4 with CBS, 11 with Mutual-Don Lee, and 2 with Hearst. Also within the State are the short-wave stations that handle all the Nation's transpacific broadcasts to and from Hawaii and the Far East; the 750-acre Bolinas station, with its 46 transmitting antennas; and the 1500-acre Point Reyes station, with its 21 directive receiving antenna units.

The Movies

IT all began so suddenly—decorous suburban Hollywood must have felt that a strange new race had descended from the sky. One actress did alight from on high, unintentionally. She was Pearl White, heroine of thriller serials, who had been performing in a "prop" balloon before the cameras when it broke its moorings. She was rapidly drifting seaward until she pulled the rope that deflated it, landing herself—and so demonstrating the resourcefulness demanded of movie actresses in 1912.

Hazardous though life might be for performers in the "flickers," the trek to Hollywood had started. Any girl could get a job if she would ride along in the cab of a runaway locomotive—any man if he could shoot a rabbit from the back of a galloping horse. The next best thing, in 1912, was to be very tall or short or weigh 300 pounds or 30 or, at the very least, to resemble a tramp or a colonel or a duchess. The thrillers of those hectic days told their stories in the main titles: *The Outlaw and the Child, True Love Never Dies, Mary's Stratagem, A Good Turn, Her First False Step.* Most of them were advertised as having "a strong moral tone." They were expected to have, as well, plenty of excitement. As a director of the time expressed it: "Never mind the acting—we want *action!*"

The producers, working at the same speed as the characters in their dramas, never stopped to build a stage if they could rent a barn, or a dressing room if they could buy a tent. Behind the flimsy walls of the mushroom studios, Tom Mix and his director were vying with each other to invent stunts dangerous enough for their thrill-fed fans.

Custard pies were flying between Mack Sennett and Ford Sterling. Mae Marsh, in a voluminous grass skirt, was tempting Bobby Herron. Hollywood in 1912—a small town carnival!

A decade and a half before, the cinema industry had got under way on the other side of the continent in New York, where Thomas Alva Edison's kinetoscope made its first appearance on April 14, 1894. The spectators dropped a nickel in the slot and peeped into a cabinet. Two years later the first modern screen projector, Thomas Armat's vitascope, liberating the moving images from Edison's peepshow, began its commercial career at Koster & Bial's music hall in New York. To curious spectators the vitascope showed picture sequences of simple incidents: a snowstorm raging through a city, a policeman chasing a hapless tramp, a fire engine racing to a midnight alarm. Its audiences were amused, but as soon as the novelty wore off, they dropped away.

An Edison cameraman, Edwin S. Porter, had an idea: the motion picture should tell a story. The overwhelming success of his first film, *The Life of an American Fireman,* encouraged him to make others, of which *The Great Train Robbery,* released in 1903, was the classic. At first the films were exhibited by itinerant showmen on portable projectors, but on Thanksgiving Day, 1905, the first theater devoted exclusively to the showing of motion pictures opened in a Pittsburgh storeroom. The price of admission for the 15-minute program was a nickel, which gave rise to the name "nickelodeon." Soon scores of Bijoux, White Ways, Fairylands, and Lyrics appeared in eastern cities.

As the "flickers" grew in popularity the chief producers found it necessary to safeguard their claims to the promised profits. Since 1897 Edison had been suing them for pirating his patents. In defense they formed, in January 1909, the Motion Picture Patents Company, soon widely known as the "movie trust." Their airtight monopoly was threatened, however, by the small producers, exhibitors, and exchanges excluded from the trust, who began importing bootleg equipment and filming their pictures in obscure hide-outs. Against them the trust launched a battle of suits and injunctions, raids and riots. They fled—from one loft to another, to Florida, to Cuba, and finally, to California.

California had been claimed for the movies when William Selig, one of the "patent pirates" fought by Edison, skipped to Los Angeles in 1908 to complete a film began in his Chicago studio. His picture, *The Count of Monte Cristo,* was the first commercial film produced in the State. Two years passed before another picture was made in the West. By that time, the patents group were hounding the independent New York Motion Picture Company. The flight of this company to Los Angeles began a westward movement of independents and, eventually, of the trust companies themselves. They opened their studios in Los Angeles, Santa Monica, Glendale, and, finally, in Hollywood—where

David Horseley's Nestor Film Company of New Jersey settled in the autumn of 1911 to make Hollywood's first movie in a studio at Sunset Boulevard and Gower Street.

The arrival of the trust companies on the Coast brought the war with the independents to a new battleground—where the independents found two weapons which won them victory. The first was the "feature" picture; the second was the "star" system.

The "feature" picture—a film of more than one or two reels—was revolutionary in 1912. While France, Italy, and Germany were experimenting with the long film, the monopolistic Motion Picture Patents Company, controlled by financiers, had limited American pictures to two-reel elementary treatments of elementary concepts. There was no room in this production scheme for artistic experimentation. The independents, on the other hand—many of whom had been old-clothing, jewelry, and junk dealers—proved to be better showmen.

Adolph Zukor imported the first multi-reel picture, *Queen Elizabeth,* made in France in 1911 by Louis Mercanton with Sarah Bernhardt and Lou Tellegen. The enthusiasm of American audiences proved that they were ready for picture drama in the grand style. While other European features were being imported, American producers began getting their own long films ready for the market. The first gallant attempts included James Young's *Cardinal Wolsey* with Clara Kimball Young, and D. W. Griffith's *Judith of Bethulia* with Blanche Sweet. Within six years appeared other films that critics still remember with respect: Griffith's *The Birth of a Nation, Broken Blossoms,* and *Intolerance;* Sennett's *Tillie's Punctured Romance;* Lubitsch's *Carmen* starring Pola Negri; *The Squawman;* and Chaplin's *A Dog's Life.* In *The Birth of a Nation*—America's first super-feature—Griffith revolutionized production technique, creating a picture which attracted the attention of the intelligentsia to the cinema for the first time in this country. The picture rolled up an astounding box-office record; though the validity of its characterization has since been questioned, it still plays occasionally in the world's out-of-the-way places. During this period the trust, persisting on the whole with mass-produced short films, languished.

As Zukor, onetime furrier, introduced the full length picture, so Carl Laemmle, onetime clothing dealer, introduced the star system. The patents trust, pursuing a mass production policy, had paid the screen player very low wages, assuming that the public would let him remain as anonymous as a bookkeeper. But Carl Laemmle, one of the trust's shrewdest foes, noted that patrons were asking at the box office when "the cute little girl with the curls" would appear again; and so he hired the cute little girl from Biograph at double her former salary. She was Gladys Smith—better known by the name of the character she had played in Biograph pictures, "Little Mary." As Mary Pickford, she was presently receiving $10,000 a week in salary and half the profits on her pictures.

At about the time the little girl with the curls was attracting notice, a young player deserted an English music hall company to work in Mack Sennett's Keystone Comedies at $150 a week. His shoes and small moustache, his talent for getting into pathetically funny situations, and his genius for expressing himself through simple gestures soon made Charlie Chaplin a universally beloved character. Producers scrambled for him, the successful bidder paying him $150,000 for signing a contract which guaranteed him $10,000 a week.

Now picture patrons were demanding not only feature pictures, but "stars." The names of Marguerite Clarke, Blanche Sweet, Pauline Frederick, Theda Bara, William Farnum, Tom Mix, Anita Stewart, Alice Joyce, Earle Williams, William S. Hart, Norma and Constance Talmadge, Lillian and Dorothy Gish, Mae Marsh, Harold Lockwood, and May Allison went up in marquee lights. Many of these players came to the films from the shipping rooms and offices of large cities, others from small town beauty contests and midwestern farms. Many had no previous dramatic training of any sort, and some never found it necessary to acquire any. Some built hillside mansions with swimming pools, and Japanese gardens; hired armies of servants, agents, and secretaries; gave parties which lasted for days, stirring the talk of the Nation. Some saved their money, helped their relatives, and retired wealthy and happy; others died early of drink and drugs; others faded back into obscurity. All of them in their hour of glory were sent fan mail by the carload and mobbed by hysterical crowds at docks and railroad stations.

The introduction of movie cycles accompanied the rise of movie stars. *Traffic in Souls* inspired a series of "daring" exposés; *The Miracle Man* was responsible for a cycle of heavily moralistic pictures; *The Spoilers,* for two-fisted Northwesterns; *Passion,* for costume films. *Over the Hill* started a race for the profits to be made on mother love. While critics pleaded for originality—and continued pleading for two decades—successive themes were milked: desert love, crime, war, aeronautics, exploration, the private lives of royalty and geniuses, the gaiety of the nineties. The 1930's brought in cycles of adaptations of Victorian novels, Shakespearean dramas, musical farces, and comedies.

The years from 1912 to 1920 passed without radical improvements in mechanical methods—although cameramen perfected the dissolve, the fade, double exposure, and the close-up—but not without an important change in the industry's financial structure. The World War had ended the competition of European film companies, leaving the huge and growing market to the American producers. The conservative patents trust let this opportunity escape, and the independents through superior showmanship won by 1930 control of the industry—an industry of world-wide proportions which had grown in a single decade into one of the United States' ten largest.

The independent producers began at once to exhibit imagination and initiative—as well as partiality for the grandiloquent. They enlarged the studios and gave them ornate facades. Dozens of new stages were constructed, many vast enough to house skating rinks in one end and ballrooms in the other. Outgrowing the informality of the early years—when householders were generally glad to lend their fishponds for the swimming party in Mabel Normand's latest farce—they built their own sets. One producer erected a range of lath-and-plaster mountains, and another, a canvas desert diorama half-a-mile in length, while Paramount built a full-size steamship to lie forever at anchor on the lot. Million-dollar "prop" and wardrobe departments were organized. Every studio amassed its library. One acquired a zoo. And each opened a laboratory for developing a new art—that of illusion. Here ingenious craftsmen built miniature models of clippers and cathedrals, painted foregrounds on glass, engineered filming of underwater scenes on dry land through a thin tank of moving water, and discovered an effective imitation fog in sprayed mineral oil. Studio staffs were augmented by architects, decorators, gag men, publicity writers, script girls, couturiers, research directors, and technical experts.

As expansion of the industry attracted new thousands to Hollywood, until the crowds outside the casting offices overflowed the streets and "still pictures" overflowed the files inside, the studios formed the Central Casting Bureau. Within a short time 10,000 would-be stars had applied. A clearing house for extras, "Central Casting" began filling the studios' daily talent needs. For each registered applicant was assembled a record of physical characteristics—height, weight, color and type of hair, color of eyes, and health; abilities—driving a car, swimming, diving, dancing, riding; history—former residence, marital status, court record (if any), income from other sources. A complete inventory of the applicant's wardrobe with the interviewer's critical comments went into the file, and finally the answer to the question: Can the applicant act? Only a few dozen were able to make an adequate living. In 1928 and 1929, with production at its height, but 194 registered extras worked two days or more a week. Fifty-four of these were women, whose incomes averaged $14.25 weekly. The men earned $14.52 weekly.

Meanwhile the industry's expenditures, if not the wages paid the extras, were mounting dizzily. Salaries kept pace with expansion as studio executives paid themselves up to $500,000 a year and their top flight stars even more. If Hollywood in 1912 was a carnival, by 1925

Education

UNIVERSITY OF CALIFORNIA, BERKELEY

CLASS IN GARDENING, LOS ANGELES PUBLIC SCHOOL

HIGH SCHOOL STUDENTS, LOS ANGELES

DOHENY LIBRARY, UNIVERSITY OF SOUTHERN
CALIFORNIA, LOS ANGELES

AVIATION STUDENTS, LOS ANGELES

LICK OBSERVATORY, NEAR SAN JOS

MT. WILSON OBSERVATORY

o

HENRY E. HUNTINGTON LIBRARY, PADADENA

ARCADES, STANFORD UNIVERSITY, PALO ALTO

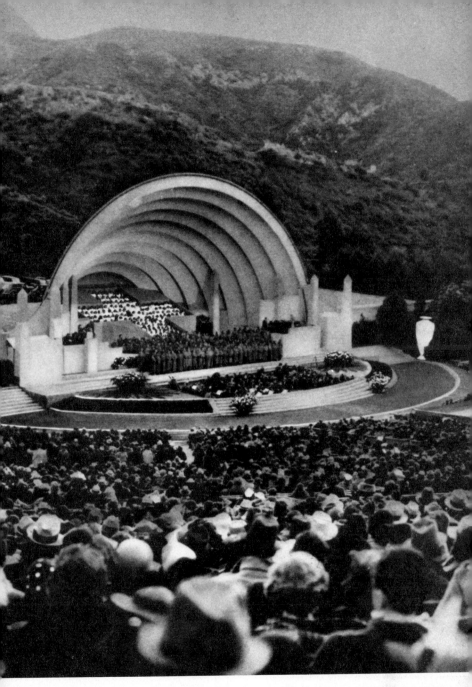

EASTER SUNRISE SERVICE, HOLLYWOOD BOWL

RACE TRACK, SANTA ANITA

ALONG THE BEACH, SANTA CATALINA

it resembled an extravaganza, mad and merry. In one picture the star wore a $30,000 chinchilla coat; since it could never be used again, of course, the fur was cut up and sewed on bathing suits. Greta Garbo was reported to be getting 90,000 fan letters every month.

Lavish too were the pictures of this decade in conception, plot, and background. In 1920 audiences were impressed by *Way Down East* and in 1921 by *The Three Musketeers*. In the five years following they were successively staggered by *Robin Hood, The Covered Wagon, Scaramouche, The Hunchback of Notre Dame, The Iron Horse, The Ten Commandments, The Merry Widow, Beau Geste,* and by *Ben Hur,* which took three years to film and cost more than $4,000,000. Producers hoped the public would be staggered. Actually, there were dawning signs of boredom. The public was giving unanimous approval to an unpretentious little film called *Nanook of the North,* to the slow-paced, realistic *A Woman of Paris,* and—strangest of all—to the German film *The Last Laugh,* a simple story about the heartbreak of a doorman.

During these years the producers were expanding in still another direction, the ownership of theaters. Chains were organized and battles fought for the control of first-run houses. In an effort to eliminate all competition, the producers bought hundreds of legitimate theaters and either dismantled them or remodeled them for screen showings. A public that had been devoted to its stock, its big and small time vaudeville, and its weekly visits from touring companies began making its choice in theatrical entertainment among the productions of Universal, Paramount, Fox, Warner Brothers, Metro-Goldwyn-Mayer.

The general extravagance required money, money required bankers, bankers demanded boards of hard-headed directors. And so it happened that the one-time independents, grown powerful (Adolph Zukor, Carl Laemmle, William Fox, Sam Goldwyn, and others), now found themselves taking orders from Wall Street. Under banker control began an effort to wed efficiency and showmanship. Stage producers had always recognized it as the very essence of harlequinade to be spontaneous, unpredictable—but now Pierrot was regimented. Sharp eyes in New York grew very sharp indeed when they read that Erich von Stroheim kept 5,000 extras waiting all day in a square while he rehearsed an actress in the grand manner of royalty descending from a coach. Over the stages hung the smoke of the battle between showmen and efficiency experts.

In this decade it was a mechanical invention that caused the inevitable upheaval. Agents of the Bell laboratories were knocking on producers' doors in 1925 with a device for synchronizing the images of the projector with the sounds of a talking machine, but with box office returns bad and getting worse, the picture executives shook their heads.

Finally the salesmen took their device to Warner Brothers, a second-string studio which had fallen behind in the theater-building race. The Warners were desperately interested and, after a demonstration, hopeful. In April 1926 they formed the Vitaphone Corporation for sound experimentation and production. *Don Juan,* their first full-length picture with recorded musical accompaniment, caused a stir. Soon after the release in 1927 of *The Jazz Singer,* starring Al Jolson, the public began to demand sound films.

By autumn of 1929 the talkie trend had become a stampede. In the scramble to revamp production methods, First National was absorbed by Warner Brothers, and William Fox—himself a pioneer in the talkie field—was forced into retirement. Other major producers survived, but not all their studio personnel. Writers and directors of "silent days" were scrapped along with equipment and techniques, while strange new faces—song writers and musicians hustled out from New York's Tin Pan Alley—began appearing on the lots. Old acting favorites who lacked the pleasing voice which talkies demanded quietly disappeared, and new stars rose in their places.

From the talkie revolution the movie industry went into the depression of the 1930's, a crisis that affected mechanical techniques, production methods, financial structures, and even the type of entertainment.

In the effort to attract depression audiences, perfection of the color process was speeded. *The Toll of the Sea,* one of the early experiments in color, was filmed in 1921, though not very satisfactorily, since the blues failed to register. Later Jack Warner had experimented with color somewhat more successfully in *The Desert Song* and *On With the Show. Becky Sharp,* produced by an affiliate of the Technicolor Corporation, demonstrated the possibilities in color movies but was itself a failure. Use of color is still limited because of its extremely high cost. The Technicolor Corporation, which has a virtual monopoly on patents, controls use of the color process by leasing the $15,000 color cameras and selling, developing, and printing color film. Production of color films is complicated by the necessity of shooting them on three negatives. Besides the color cameras, a staff of experts is required to harmonize settings and costumes and plan lighting. Actors must be found who are handsome even without hair dye, grease paint, eye shadow, and mascara, because the increased intensity of light used reveals any camouflage in make-up.

Walt Disney, the most outstanding figure in the development of the animated cartoon, contracted with the corporation in 1934 to make his Mickey Mouse and Silly Symphonies cartoon films in color. He began work the same year on the first feature-length animated cartoon, *Snow White and the Seven Dwarfs.* A new type $75,000 camera was employed to lend a three-dimensional illusion to the 250,000 separate paintings which went into the making of the film. Three years later, when *Snow White* was released, audiences delighted in the large surfaces of rich, clear color. In no previous cartoon film had there been such successful treatment of running water, clouds, dust, steam, and the glint of sunlight on a steel blade. The success of *Snow White* and such feature films as *A Star Is Born* indicates the tremendous strides made in the color medium during recent years.

The end of the fourth decade finds the industry's use of illusion developed to extraordinary lengths. Window glass is generally made of rock candy; stones of tar paper, balsa wood, and cork; snow of gypsum and bleached corn flakes; icicles of fibre hair dipped in plaster of Paris. Strawberry gelatine is the usual substitute for blood. Since about 80 percent of all pictures are shot indoors on the studio stages, the prop shop must stock many sorts of artificial flowers and trees. (One studio has enough daisies to cover a ranch meadow and apple blossoms for 28 trees.) Each studio has a library of at least 10,000 sound effects and the equipment for producing them. An important member of the sound staff is the scream expert.

During the 1930's, bankers have tended more and more to leave production details in the hands of professional showmen. Nevertheless financial control has left its mark on Hollywood. Even the producers of "Poverty Row" have junked the helter-skelter production in which carpenters doubled as gladiators, leading ladies made their own costumes, and one man might finance, write, direct, cut, and sell a motion picture film. The movies that reach the first-run houses today are produced by a streamlined system in which all efforts are organized and specialized.

Before a film is shipped away in its round tin cans, it passes through approximately 25 studio departments. First a staff writer takes the story—usually a purchased magazine story, novel, or play—and tailors it to fit the stars assigned to the leading roles. After one or many "adaptations" have been made, a continuity writer breaks down the story into scenes, a gag man may insert funny business, and a dialogue expert snaps up the actors' lines. Working closely with the writers are the director and a corps of research workers who answer such questions as: what kind of calling cards did women use at the period of the story, what sort of buttons did men wear on their coats, what did the streetcar transfer of the time look like?

Talent scouts now assist the casting office in the search for actors. Location scouts select settings for the outdoor scenes, which may be found 50 miles away or 5,000. The music director prepares his score, costume designers make sketches for the dressmakers, set designers fabricate miniature sets for the draftsmen and carpenters. The prop department, too, has its scouts, whose task is to produce such unlikely merchandise as nineteenth-century velocipedes, authentic duplicates of the Lichtenstein crown jewels, Cleopatra's tablewear, or a live boa constrictor. The make-up department is studying the proposed lighting effects, the production department is making innumerable charts: costume charts, weather charts, charts to indicate set and shooting schedules from the first day to the last. Meanwhile the director, besides consulting with all these assisting departments, is studying the hundreds of scenes in the final script and creating in his mind each bit of action.

The average picture is "shot" in about six weeks. During this time a new crew of workers joins the staff—cameramen, electricians, sound men, "grips," script girl, cutter, and technicians who produce mechanical effects. The picture is photographed not in its proper sequence but in whatever order is best adapted to the actors and sets involved. Each day's "takes" are developed in the laboratory and run through the projection machine at the close of the day for supervisor, director, cutter, and assistants who pick the most effective. As shooting progresses, the cutter patches together the chosen "takes," gradually fitting in the missing scenes. Upon his work, seemingly mechanical but actually creative, largely depends the picture's "pace."

When the cutter's work is finished and approved, a print of the picture is taken into a suburban theater for a "sneak preview." Members of the production staff clock laughs, yawns, fidgeting, and other audience reactions, from which the director decides whether to add or delete. Finally, from the miles of exposed negative, two master negatives are put together—one for domestic and one for foreign showings. The prints shipped to the theaters are made from these.

The studio lots of today combine the efficiency of the factory with the irrationality of the theater. A small town in itself, each studio has its network of paved streets, lined with stucco buildings that house the various departments—the huge stages, the prop warehouses, the carpenter and machine shops. In the shadow of a planing mill may stand a star's "quaint" dressing room, and behind the barnlike structure that houses the wardrobe, a piece of Venice, complete with canal, gondolas, and flower-strewn balconies.

Perfection of mechanical technique and streamlining of picture production are two of the industry's answers to depression problems. Another answer has been the general improvement in the quality of entertainment.

Some producers, believing that audiences wanted to forget their troubles, gave them farces; others became aware of a plea, grown more insistent, for realism. "Authentic," "natural," "unexaggerated"—during the thirties these adjectives were heard, almost for the first time, at studio conferences. As a result, fans have had the pleasure of giving box-office laurels to such lifelike films as *I Am a Fugitive from a Chain*

Gang, Of Human Bondage, The Informer, Dead End, and *It Happened One Night.* And even the romantic films have achieved greater fidelity to essential truth and significance of theme.

Important in raising the standards of motion picture writing, directing, and acting have been the annual awards of the Academy of Moving Picture Arts and Sciences, first bestowed in 1927-1928. Actors and actresses so honored include Emil Jannings, Janet Gaynor, Warner Baxter, Mary Pickford, George Arliss, Norma Shearer, Lionel Barrymore, Marie Dressler, Frederic March, Helen Hayes, Charles Laughton, Katharine Hepburn, Clark Gable, Claudette Colbert, Victor McLaglen, Bette Davis, Paul Muni, Louise Rainer (twice), and Spencer Tracy. Among directors and writers to receive two awards have been directors Franz Borzage, Frank Lloyd, Frank Capra, and writers Ben Hecht and Frances Marion. The list of films selected by the Academy for distinction includes *All Quiet on the Western Front, Cavalcade, Grand Hotel, Mutiny on the Bounty, The Life of Louis Pasteur,* and *The Life of Emil Zola.*

The social and artistic significance of motion pictures has increasingly concerned educators, church groups, women's clubs, and critics of American life. Because the average weekly attendance of 75,000,000 gives the movies an influence equalled only by newspapers and radio, the Payne Fund, in 1929, financed several surveys to estimate what that influence might be. The 115 films examined were found to portray a world where 33 percent of the heroines, 34 percent of the villains, and 63 percent of the sirens and villainesses were either wealthy or millionaires—only 5 percent of the characters were poor. If the population of the United States were arranged as indicated in these films, "there would be no farming, no manufacturing, almost no industry, no vital statistics (except murders), no economic problems and no economics," wrote Mr. Henry James Forman, analyzing the survey. It was pointed out that pictures of the type studied portray a world unreal in fundamentals, yet so like the world outside the theater in superficial details that movie-goers fail to distinguish clearly between the two and carry home a sense of grievance at their similar but much more dreary lot.

The artists—directors, writers, actors—whose creative efforts go into picture making have long felt hampered by the fact that, as Walter Wanger said, "any minority group, any individual, any rag, any nation could dictate to us." In July 1938, a distributors' boycott of *Blockade* crystallized their discontent. At a meeting of 300 delegates, representing 150,000 members of motion picture unions, guilds, and other organizations, these artists demanded that "gag rule" be removed from the industry, so that motion pictures may become, as they rightfully should be, "a very important pillar in the democratic structure."

The newest "independents" are the group of scenarists and cameramen who recently organized the non-profit Frontier Films. Other groups whose aim is to revitalize the content of the motion picture include Triple-A (*One-Third of a Nation*) in the East and in Hollywood the George Randol Productions, the latter a unit interested solely in producing Negro films. Since there are more than 600 theaters in the country that cater largely to Negro audiences, the significance of pioneering attempts in the field, such as *Spirit of Youth* featuring Joe Louis, may be readily appreciated.

In dodging realism American film producers have also avoided censorship to some extent. A clamor for laws to regulate the subject matter of films arose, following the white slave pictures and the sex and crime films of the 1920's. Formation of the Motion Picture Producers and Distributors of America, Inc., headed by Will Hays, was the industry's effort to police itself. Ten years later, under the pressure of various groups, the Hays organization imposed further taboos. The distributors' export departments added their prohibitions: there must be no American flag-waving, no propaganda for peace which might offend warrior nations, and no villains of foreign nationality except Russian. (Soviet Russia imports few American films.)

Many an endeavor is indebted to the motion picture art, or craft. Schools use motion pictures in visual education, sports for the recording of finishes, science in a multitude of ways. Movies are taken of the heavens and of babies learning to walk. X-ray movies are made of ailing human beings, microscopic and color movies of almost every sort of living organism. Metallurgists, experts in acoustics, and specialists in other applied sciences have benefited—as well as the thousands of amateur photographers who have acquired a hobby.

Education

FRANCISCAN friars, the first white settlers who plodded northward into California, came with books in their hands, for the
purpose of their pilgrimage was to educate the heathen Indians.
Their pioneer successors—fur trappers and gold miners—were often
men of action rather than learning, but they had an extraordinary
respect for the wealth bound between the covers of books. With
first-hand knowledge of the many miles from California to the older
institutions of learning in New England and Europe, they voted generous expenditures for schools.

For California's native Indians, five decades of rigorous training—
planned to make them civilized tax-paying subjects of the Spanish
king—were in store when the Franciscan missionaries arrived in the
spring of 1769. Beyond manual and religious training they did not
aspire, however. Mission authorities feared the growth of learning
among the Spanish, as well as the Indian population, claiming that
education had no purpose but to breed discontent in the common people.
They excommunicated two of the province's most illustrious citizens,
Juan Bautista Alvarado and Mariano G. Vallejo, for reading Jean
Jacques Rousseau.

The first efforts to found secular schools were made by the Spanish
Governor, Diego de Borica (1794-1800). During his administration,
schoolmasters—mostly retired soldiers who could wield the *disciplinas*
(cat-o'-nine-tails) began teaching reading, writing, and figuring in
one-room schools at San Jose, Santa Barbara, San Francisco, San Diego,
and Monterey. No sooner had Borica left the territory, however, than

his educational system collapsed. The schools established during the next thirty years were also short-lived.

Governor José Figueroa (1833-1835) reported, soon after his arrival, that only three schools were in existence, taught by incompetent and ill-paid teachers; he established six more schools and ordered higher salaries for the teachers. Juan Bautista Alvarado (1836-1842) imported teachers from Mexico to give instruction in reading, writing, arithmetic, and the catechism; girls were also taught needlework and boys typesetting and printing. Attendance was compulsory for children between the ages of six and eleven. The schools were handicapped by their lack of funds and equipment. Despite the meager opportunities and the opposition of most of the clergy, some of the more ambitious sons of the land-owning families acquired a fair classical education, but only with the private tutoring of educated military officers, foreigners, or priests.

The American immigrants of the 1840's followed eastern and midwestern rather than Californian precedents in education. In December 1864 California's first American school was founded—in a dilapidated structure, once a stable, on the grounds of Mission Santa Clara. Here an overland immigrant, Mrs. Olive Mann Isbell, taught two dozen pupils, sitting on boxes around a fire in the center of the earthen floor. In the following year a schoolroom was equipped with desks and benches in the Monterey customhouse, and Mrs. Isbell tried to teach 56 scholars, although she could speak no Spanish and they no English. San Francisco's first American school was opened April 3, 1848 in a redwood schoolhouse on Portsmouth Square. The building was also used for town hall, court house, church and jail. The schoolmaster, Thomas Douglass, a Yale graduate, began with a class of six pupils which soon increased to 38, but six weeks later the gold rush excitement swept him off to the mines. On April 8, 1850 the first free public schools were established by an ordinance of the city council in San Francisco. This was California's first public school ordinance.

The educational needs of children in mining towns, lumber camps, ports, and rural villages were recognized by the State when California's first constitution provided, that a school "be kept up in every school district at least three months in every year." Fabulous revenues were expected from the sale of Federal Government land grants, "inviolably appropriated to the support of the common schools"; but since the total proceeds from grants of 500,000 acres were only about $250,000, that early ambition had to be curtailed. Gradually State school legislation was extended until by 1860 it provided for levying of city and school district taxes, appointment or election of county and city school superintendents and city boards of education, and authorization of boards of examination to grant teachers' certificates. Finally, in 1866, California's legislators adopted the Revised School Law, drafted by the far-seeing superintendent of public instruction, John Swett, which fixed State and county school taxes at adequate levels and established district school libraries, county teachers' institutes, and city boards of examination. For the first time in the State's history, public schools—in rural as well as urban areas—were free for every child.

The State's first colleges were established almost as early as its first public schools. Santa Clara College (now the University of Santa Clara), founded by Jesuit Fathers Giovanni Noboli and Michele Accolti, and California Wesleyan College (now the College of the Pacific at Stockton), founded by the Reverend Isaac Owen of the Methodist Episcopal Church, were both opened at Santa Clara in 1851. A year later the town of Benicia welcomed girls, who came to attend opening classes of the Young Ladies' Seminary. Southern California's first institution of higher learning, St. Vincent's College (now Loyola University), was opened in Don Vincente Lugo's adobe home on the Los Angeles Plaza in 1865 by Fathers of the St. Vincent de Paul Mission.

The first State constitution called for establishment of a State university to promote "literature, the arts, and sciences." But the nucleus of the University of California was a private institution, known at first as Contra Costa Academy and later as the College of California. Opened by the Reverend Henry Durant at Oakland in 1853, it began collegiate instruction in 1860. On March 23, 1868, Governor Henry H. Haight signed the legislative act creating the University of California. The institution was formally opened September 23 of the next year on the College of California's campus. In 1873, the year in which the first 12 graduates ("the twelve disciples") received their diplomas, the university moved to its present site on the slopes of the Berkeley hills.

Although the first public high school was opened in San Francisco in 1856, the legislature declined to support secondary institutions for more than half a century. The more thickly settled communities were obliged to conduct high schools at their own expense. In 1884 the University of California inaugurated the "accrediting system," which admits pupils with excellent high school records to the university without examination. The result of university supervision under this system was to raise secondary school standards to a uniformly high level. Finally, in 1903, the legislature amended the school law by passage of an act providing for State support of high schools.

The legislature in 1907 authorized high school boards to prescribe postgraduate courses of study. First to take advantage of the new regulation was Fresno, followed soon by Los Angeles and Santa Barbara. By 1910 the number of these "upward extensions of high schools" had grown to ten. A law enacted in 1917 recognized junior colleges as an integral part of the State's secondary school system. Today California has 42 such institutions.

Colleges as well as high schools multiplied in the late nineteenth century. The University of Southern California, founded under the auspices of the Methodist Episcopal Church in 1880, has grown into an institution with a faculty of 1,000. Other colleges established in Southern California were Pomona College (now a unit of Claremont Colleges, Inc.), Occidental College, Whittier College, the University of Redlands, and the California Institute of Technology. Leland Stanford Junior University, wealthiest privately endowed university in the West, and now the State's second largest institution of higher learning, was opened at Palo Alto in 1891. Public normal schools were established—the first at San Francisco in 1862 (moved in 1870 to San Jose), and others at San Francisco, San Diego, Chico, Fresno, Santa Barbara, and Arcata. By legislative enactment these became in 1921 State teachers' colleges.

Today citizens of all ages find in California's educational system every sort of practical and theoretical training. In the 6,500 public schools, with their more than 1,000,000 pupils, $135,000,000 is spent yearly. The University of California registered 25,806 full-time resident students in 1938. This institution includes universities in Berkeley and Los Angeles, the agricultural colleges at Davis and Riverside, colleges of oceanography at La Jolla and of astronomy at Mount Hamilton, and affiliated colleges of law, medicine, pharmacy, and art. By the expansion of its facilities to include study centers, lecture courses, traveling libraries, correspondence study, and scientific and technical instruction at various points throughout the State, the university is extending the advantages of higher education to many who have hitherto been denied college training.

In addition to the State university, 7 State colleges, and 42 junior colleges, California today has 7 schools rated as junior colleges, and 23 publicly or privately endowed universities and colleges—including three noted women's colleges: Mills College in Oakland, Scripps College in Claremont, and Dominican College in San Rafael.

California's educators have faced the problem, common to educators everywhere, of adapting traditional schoolroom methods to a swiftly changing social structure. A State curriculum study, made in 1925, led two years later to formation of a permanent curriculum commission to evaluate school study courses and recommend minimum standards. In a detailed *Teachers' Guide to Child Development,* the commission expounded the philosophy and methods of the new education used in California's more progressive schools. The publication of the guide gave a strong impetus to the modernizing of California's entire school system. Progressive communities began to eliminate the old, formal, coercive teaching of subjects, and to substitute activity programs.

Under the new methods the class is no longer treated as a group of artificially isolated units, but rather as a world in miniature, where enterprises are undertaken by children and teacher, all working together. The requirement that a child shall behave co-operatively is accented in order to check the tendency toward "self-expression of all types, at all times, in all places," favored by some of the earlier progressive educators. The Sequoia Union High School at Redwood City and the Alexandria Demonstration School at Los Angeles are progressive schools in which standards formulated in the *Teachers' Guide* are being realized.

As soon as California's schools were conspicuously committed to a changed procedure, the public, as well as teachers and administrators, began to question and appraise. In 1930 the California Commission for the Study of Education Problems, composed of nine lay citizens, reported on a year's study and a post-card survey of public opinion. The activity type of program was criticized as failing to train pupils in the use of the "tools" of learning—spelling, arithmetic, punctuation, sentence and paragraph structure, and penmanship—and in habits of precision and promptness. On the other hand, young people educated under the newer methods were found to excel former generations in intelligence, initiative, and physical fitness.

In accepting and applying the newer conceptions of education, California has kept pace with the rest of the country and in some respects stepped ahead. Even in early days, the California high school teacher of mathematics was likely to stress the value of original demonstrations, while California high schools led from the beginning in adoption of laboratory methods in teaching natural sciences. Today California's public schools teach scientific subjects integrated into the social studies unit in the elementary grades. Los Angeles high school students have built and are operating a seismological station, school weather stations, astronomical observatories, amateur radio stations, and sound-recording studios.

The general tendency to emphasize functional knowledge has been marked in the State. The department of education's commission for vocational education directs an extensive vocational training program in agriculture, business, homemaking, trade and industry, and vocational rehabilitation. Its bureau of agricultural education, in 1935-36, was supervising 137 vocational agricultural departments in the schools and a teacher-training course. The bureau of business education oversees courses of training adjusted to the needs of merchants and businessmen, in which specially selected students are taught. All except 13 of the State's 519 high schools conduct classes in homemaking, a third for boys as well as girls, under supervision of the bureau of homemaking education. The bureau of trade and industrial education supervises apprentice training programs, organizes trade advisory committees of employer, employee, and public school representatives in many communities, and conducts State-wide conferences of foremen, personnel managers, salesmanagers, and other executives.

In the California Polytechnical Institute at San Luis Obispo, established in 1901, agriculture students conduct their own farm enterprises and aeronautics students operate a Government-approved commercial airplane repair station. The California Nautical School, conducted on board the U.S.S. *California State* with Tiburon as its home port, trains personnel for the coast's merchant marine. Three months nautical courses are given on three-masted, square-rigged ships, the *Tusitala* and the *Joseph Conrad,* sailing from Government Island off Alameda.

In carrying out the new curriculum, California schools have taken advantage of the State's many opportunities for outdoor play to stress their physical training and recreation programs. During the four depression years, 1932-1936, more gymnasiums, tennis courts, playgrounds, and swimming pools were constructed than in any previous four-year period. The recreation program is supplemented in many schools by health supervision. Both the construction and the recreation programs were conducted largely with the aid of the Works Progress Administration.

The Co-ordinating Council has been operating in California cities for more than 15 years. Originating with Virgil E. Dickson, now superintendent of schools in Berkeley, the plan sets up a voluntary board of members from school, police, health, and recreation departments, welfare societies, and research and guidance bureaus, to pool ideas, information, and mutual support in all matters pertaining to the welfare of youth. Not only are problem children given understanding aid, but also the gifted are sought out and provided with special opportunities. The work of California's co-ordinating councils, particularly those in Berkeley, San Francisco, and Los Angeles, has so materially decreased juvenile delinquency that scores of communities in other States have organized similar bodies. In 1933 the National Committee on Crime Prevention reported: "Your Committee believes that there is no other single step that could be put into operation that would be as far-reaching and as quickly beneficial as the widespread use of the co-ordinating council."

The handicapped child in California, if completely disabled, is taught at home or in a hospital or preventorium; if crippled, he is transported to special classes; if handicapped by vision, hearing, or speech defects he receives remedial instruction. California is the only State that carries on a program of speech correction with adequate

State aid.   Classes have been established in 54 cities, with more than 14,000 students and 150 speech-correction teachers. The State's method of training mentally subnormal children may be seen applied in San Francisco's Ungraded School.   When the handicapped child is 16 years of age, responsibility for his further instruction is transferred to the bureau of vocational rehabilitation.

Rural school children in California enjoy special attention, thanks to general recognition of the concept that "a child in the rural district is worth as much to the future of a state as one in the city." Constitutional amendment No. 16 (passed in 1920) provides for collection of school money where the wealth is and expenditure of it where the pupils are. The task of instructional supervisors, working from the county superintendent's office, is to weld the isolated rural schools into one closely co-ordinated county school system. Their "supervision," as the department of education likes to call it, does as much for the rural school as the automobile and radio do for the rural home. They are aided by the periodicals issued by the department of education's division of textbooks and publications: the *Science Guide,* the monthly *California Schools,* the quarterly *California Journal of Elementary Education,* and the bi-monthly children's magazine, *The California Nugget.* Another aid to rural pupil and teacher alike is the county library system, established in 1911, under which county libraries in 46 of the State's 58 counties bring to the children of 2,313 rural districts collections of the best modern books and classics, as well as phonograph records, motion picture films, prints, globes, maps, and exhibits. Acting as advisor to the libraries of the entire State is the State Library at Sacramento, with its nearly 500,000 volumes. Rural children are also given the benefits of health education. Most counties employ traveling health nurses to examine children, remedy defects, advise in nutritional problems, and conduct health clinics. The children travel to and from school by means of tax-supported school transportation systems in most rural districts.

California was one of the first States to set up a division of adult education and to finance adult classes from its public education fund. In 1938 enrollment in adult classes equalled more than a tenth of the State's total population. So complete is the curriculum that entrants may study even the chemistry of lubrication or the Cantonese language. Among the most popular of many vocational training courses are the San Francisco classes in aeronautics, which are attended by about half as many women as men; these classes own two planes and study navigation, theory of flight, meteorology, air law, and solo flying. Courses in homemaking and consumer education are always in demand. But most popular of all are the classes in sociology, economics, and public affairs, conducted in accord with the department of education's belief that "if this civilization survives it will do so because of the wisdom expressed in adult activities. If it disintegrates, adult incompetence will have to carry the onus."

A modern school system calls for well-trained teachers as well as a modern curriculum. California elementary school teachers, certified by county examinations, are now decreasing in numbers, and those certified by the State—which require a four year university or college course, including practice in directed teaching—are increasing. Unique in California is the requirement that high school teachers be university graduates with at least one additional year of graduate study.

The planners of California's activity program believe that an eager exploring spirit is stifled by the old-type schoolroom, with its desks nailed in stiff rows and its walls covered with black slate. The State division of schoolhouse planning finds architects whose inspiration coincides with its own. The educators and architects of this division have worked out a one-story functional plan in which each schoolroom has an activity alcove and an outdoor terrace for class sessions on pleasant days. The old desks have been replaced by movable chairs and tables, the "blackboards" by light-colored slate. Flowers, pictures, and curtains give charm to the room. In the activity alcove are a workbench, tools, a gas plate, a sink, and built-in cupboards for raw materials. Assembly rooms in these new schoolhouses have level floors so that they can be used as playrooms in rainy weather. In the two years from 1934 to 1936 more than 500 sets of plans for new and remodeled school buildings were submitted by school districts to the State division of schoolhouse planning; and as finally approved, 75 per cent of the elementary classrooms provided a proper setting for activity programs. The men and women who guide the development of California children believe, that "the chief purpose in organizing a school is not to obtain economy in effort; it is to give to each little child within its doors as nearly as possible the best environment in which to grow."

The Arts

I LEARNED that there were a number of artists in the city who had sought to try Dame Fortune in the gold-fields, but with such scant success that they returned to the harbor . . . to seek patrons in . . . gilded temples of chance," wrote Prince Paul of Wurttemberg in his unpublished account (in the Stuttgart Archives) of his visit to the gambling halls of brawling, new-grown San Francisco in 1850. "Here we were regaled with very good music," he wrote. "In order to allure the public the owners of these gambling places employed musicians, among these many real orchestral artists and singers." He found the walls covered with a "great number of copper prints and oil paintings." And through the open doorways of saloons and public houses he saw "Mexicans dancing old California steps to the tunes of their national airs. The dancers carried out many very different movements and steps, and all with a certain haunting charm of grace and rhythm. . . ."

An earlier visitor to California would have gone to the mission churches to satisfy an interest in the arts, for the mission fathers were the first art patrons, decorating their chapels with paintings, instructing their Indian neophytes in music and church drama, and writing accounts of their missionary labors. But in 1850, Prince Paul mapped the best itinerary for the art lover when he visited San Francisco's "gilded temples of chance." If he had come later, he might have visited the cramped newspaper and magazine offices where Bret Harte and Mark Twain worked or the crude gas-lit theaters where Lotta Crabtree and Lola Montez performed. Later still, he might have paid calls to the art galleries and grand opera houses founded and endowed by the millionaire "bonanza kings." Today the arts flourish in so many places throughout California—in seaside artists' colonies, in big city garrets and studios, "little" theaters and concert halls, and in the sound-proofed stages of Hollywood lots—that Prince Paul, if he were visiting California now, would find it much more difficult to decide where to go. Perhaps he would find it more difficult still to understand how all the many activities of California's artists, musicians, painters, and writers arose from humble beginnings in gambling halls only ninety years ago.

LITERATURE

The history of California letters begins long before the gold rush and Bret Harte and Mark Twain. During the Spanish and Mexican periods a number of able men, to whom authorship was but one of many tasks, were recording their experiences and observations, with little reward in money or fame. Their writing consists mostly of diaries and reports, with detailed descriptions of the country; but much of it bears the impress of unconscious artistry.

When in 1542 Juan Rodríguez Cabrillo explored the coast of California, one of the members of his expedition, Juan Paez, wrote a *Relación* or narrative of the voyage. Later in the same century, Chaplain Francis Fletcher and others accompanying Francis Drake, the dashing English buccaneer, wrote of the northwest coast of California and its red-skinned inhabitants near whose primitive villages Drake anchored his ship, the *Golden Hind*. These accounts were included in *The World Encompassed* (1628), compiled by Drake's nephew. The expeditions organized by Sebastián Vizcaíno in 1602 were described in journals kept by Father Antonio de la Ascensión and an unknown scrivener. From these journals the history of the Vizcaíno expeditions was retold by Father Juan de Torquemada in his *Monarquía indiana* (1615) and later by Martín Fernández de Navarrete and Jerónimo Martín Palacios in their collected accounts of voyages of discovery, published a few years later.

The true father of California literature, however, did not appear until after the middle of the eighteenth century. Junípero Serra was then president of the new missions in upper California, and Francisco

Palóu was his most highly-valued associate. Out of devotion to the Father President, Palóu wrote the memorable *Life and Apostolic Labors of the Venerable Father Junípero Serra* (1787); and during his ten years at Mission Carmel and Mission Dolores, he wrote his *Historical Memoirs of New California* (1857), recording the work of the Franciscans in the new province and describing with dramatic power the gradual conquest of a wild land.

The expeditions of Juan Bautista de Anza, trail-maker and the founder of San Francisco, had several chroniclers, foremost of whom was Father Pedro Font, astronomer with the expedition of 1775-76. Font's complete diary, which he compiled at leisure from notes written during his laborious 3,000-mile journey from Mexico to Monterey and to the site of present San Francisco, was published in 1930 in an English translation by Herbert Eugene Bolton. The journals of Juan Crespi and Pedro Fages also depict faithfully the new land as it appeared in the latter half of the eighteenth century.

In 1798 two books containing descriptions of California during the mission period were published in London—*A Voyage Round the World,* from the French of Jean François de Galup, Comte de la Pérouse, the distinguished navigator, and *A Voyage of Discovery,* by Capt. George Vancouver, the English explorer. Other seafaring travelers who wrote on Spanish California were George von Langsdorff and Otto von Kotzebue, who came on behalf of the Russian Government. When Kotzebue visited San Francisco in 1816, he was accompanied by the German poet and naturalist, Adelbert von Chamisso, who wrote a curiously gloomy description of the presidio.

California's first printing press was brought to Monterey by Governor José Figueroa in 1833 and taken over by Augustin V. Zamorano, California's first printer, who in 1834 issued the *Reglamento provincial.* The 55 separate items published by this press were mostly Hispano-Californian official documents, but they also included proclamations of the United States officials, a commercial paper, and at least two catechisms.

Several accounts of the province were written by foreigners during the Mexican period. The *History of Upper and Lower California* (1839) by Alexander Forbes, a British merchant in Mexico, was the first book in English dealing exclusively with California. *Explorations du territoire de l'Oregon, des Californies, etc.* (1844) by Duflot de Mofras reflects much enjoyment found in the province by a young French traveler. Alfred Robinson, an American trader who arrived in California in 1829 and married into the aristocratic De la Guerra family, wrote *Life in California* (1846), a pleasant and informative work. Richard Henry Dana, then a young sailor on the *Alert,* was in Santa Barbara at the time of Robinson's marriage, and he described the wedding in his famous *Two Years Before the Mast* (1840), other parts of which throw a vivid light on contemporary Monterey, San Francisco, and San Diego.

Of all early American accounts of the region during this period the journal of the indefatigable explorer and fur scout, Jedediah Strang Smith, is the most entertaining. His journeys through California in 1826 and 1828 were faithfully recorded in sketches and diaries, thought to have been burned in San Francisco until they were discovered, edited by Maurice Sullivan, and published in 1934.

Sixty Years in California (1889) by William Heath Davis, another Yankee who married into an important California family, is an excellent account of experiences in the new country before and after the gold rush. Other books by early American arrivals in the territory are James O. Pattie's *A Personal Narrative* (1833) and David H. Coyner's *The Lost Trappers* (1847). John Charles Frémont, who played such a conspicuous role in the American occupation of California, wrote several books dealing in part with the late pastoral era, which ended with the discovery of gold.

Most of the chronicles written in California during the Spanish and Mexican periods remain unpublished; many of the manuscripts, however, survive in various collections—notably the Bancroft Library at the University of California, which contains the lengthy *Historias* of Antonio Mario Osio, Juan Bautista Alvarado, and Gen. Mariano Guadalupe Vallejo, the *Memorías* of José María Amador, and the *Reminiscencías* of Estevan de la Torre.

Within the new society created by the gold rush, journalists, story writers, and verse makers soon began to flourish. Among the many enthusiastic commentators of this period was Bayard Taylor, poet and globe-trotter, whose California ballads and high-flown prose work, *Eldorado, or Adventures in the Path of Empire* (1850), gave easterners an idealized picture of life in the gold fields.

Meanwhile the grotesque humor peculiar to the West was making its appearance in southern California, where Lieutenant (later Colonel) George H. Derby, writing in the San Diego *Herald,* spun his webs of satirical nonsense under the pen names of "John P. Squibob" and "John Phoenix." Derby's hilarious and often vitriolic commentaries, some of which were later compiled in the two volumes, *Phoenixiana* (1856) and *The Squibob Papers* (1859), have remained dear to the hearts of many Californians to this day.

But the literature of American California did not begin officially, so to speak, until 1852. In that year J. Macdonough Foard and Rollin M. Daggett founded the *Golden Era,* a journal devoted to mining, commerce, education, agriculture, local and foreign news, fine arts, and literature. It attained a large circulation not only in San Francisco, its place of publication, but also throughout the mining districts, and acquired many contributors who later became famous. The *Pioneer,* established in the same city two years later, was more strictly a literary magazine, but it lasted only two years, while the *Golden Era* survived until 1882. The *Pioneer* is remembered for the brilliant series of papers contributed to it by Colonel Derby and for the letters of "Shirley" (Mrs. Laura A. K. Clapp). The *Illustrated California Magazine* and the *Hesperian* were other short-lived periodicals established in the 1850's.

In 1857 the *Golden Era* printed a few verses signed "Bret"; and three years later their author, Francis Bret Harte, a young man from Albany, New York, found a badly needed job in the *Era's* composing room. Many of his early sketches were published in the journal. Another contributor to the *Era* was Samuel L. Clemens, a young eagle-eyed Missourian with a skeptical drawl, who had recently quitted Nevada to become a reporter on the San Francisco *Call.* In 1864 Clemens met Bret Harte, by this time a clerk in the local United States Branch Mint and star contributor to a new literary magazine, the *Californian.* A little later, when Harte was temporarily in editorial charge of the *Californian,* he engaged his new acquaintance as a regular contributor. Clemens' first sketch for the magazine was "A Notable Conundrum," signed with his usual pen-name of "Mark Twain." It was through Harte's influence and encouragement that Mark Twain, according to his own testimony, was changed "from an awkward utterer of coarse grotesqueries to a writer of paragraphs and chapters that have found a certain favor." Besides these two, the *Californian* numbered among its contributors Charles Warren Stoddard and Ina D. Coolbrith, both destined to more than local literary fame.

Mark Twain's first book, *The Celebrated Jumping Frog of Calaveras County and Other Sketches,* published in 1867, marked the true beginning of the California school. Twain soon became known outside the borders of the State. He visited the Sandwich Islands and then made a journey to Europe and the Holy Land, which he described in 50 letters to the *Alta Californian,* one of the oldest of San Francisco newspapers. These letters later became *Innocents Abroad,* which together with *Roughing It* (based upon his experiences in Nevada) established his reputation throughout the English-speaking world.

In 1868 Bret Harte became the editor of the *Overland Monthly,* which had just been established in San Francisco. In the second issue he published, after considerable hesitation, "The Luck of Roaring Camp." With the exception of "The Work on Red Mountain" (later rewritten and called "M'liss"), which lay forgotten in the *Golden Era,* the fastidious Harte had previously ignored the mining camps as background for his fiction. Many Californians now derided the story as unworthy of the author and of their home State. But when the comments of the eastern critics began to arrive, Harte knew that, like some of his miners and gamblers, he had struck it rich. This, with such subsequent stories as "The Outcasts of Poker Flat" and "Tennessee's Partner," made Bret Harte and the *Overland Monthly* household words among readers at home and abroad. Harte was embarrassed by the fame of his "Heathen Chinee" and other humorous verse, but gratified by the success of his stories. He left the Coast in a blaze of glory, never to return. His later years were spent abroad, chiefly in England.

Before Harte's arrival in London, another California writer, "Joaquin" (Cincinnatus Heine) Miller, had created a sensation there, both as a poet and as a picturesque personality, addicted to high top-boots and long flowing hair. Born in Indiana, Miller had been an Oregon editor and judge and a gold-miner before becoming a poet. The poems that brought him fame were written mostly on the Pacific Coast and published in England in 1871. After extensive wanderings abroad, he settled down in Oakland in 1885 and died there in 1913. His *Songs of the Sierras* (1871) and *Songs of the Sunlands* (1873) deal for the most part with the turbulent exploits of pioneers, outlaws, and Indians, and with the scenic marvels of the West.

Henry George came to California in 1858, and for more than two decades made a precarious living through his work for Sacramento and San Francisco newspapers. Here he wrote his famous treatise on the single tax, *Progress and Poverty* (1879). Other, though less distinguished, California authors of the same general period were Prentice Mulford, the humorist; Noah Brooks, journalist, historian, and writer of books for boys; and John Vance Cheney, poet and essayist.

None of the outstanding writers of the pioneering days was born in the State; few of them became permanent residents there. Reflecting the excitement and shifting character of the period, much of their fiction and poetry consists of broad caricature and sentimental melodrama; but the regionalism expressed in their work was complete, self-contained, and solidly founded. Their humor, irreverent and lusty, was characteristically American.

On the cover of Harte's *Overland Monthly* a grizzly bear stands on a railroad track, apparently defying an approaching train. But the strongest grizzly is no match for a locomotive; neither could the sectional character of California's culture long resist the influences that came with the completion of the railroad. Nevertheless, in the closing decades of the nineteenth century, California literature partly retained its regional character. A new literary magazine, the *Argonaut,* established in 1877 by Frank M. Pixley, had numerous able contributors and long maintained high standards. Many literary works produced in the State still dealt with the local scene. Helen Hunt Jackson's well-known romance of southern California, *Ramona* (1884), presented a touching picture of the interrelations of the whites and the Indians. Gertrude Atherton, who was born in San Francisco in 1857 and began her literary career in the late 1880's, gathered material for her early novels by visiting old towns and talking to the descendants of old Spanish settlers. In *The Doomswoman* (1892), *The Californians* (1898), *The Splendid Idle Forties* (1902), and *Rezanov* (1906), she embodied her knowledge of the Spanish era. Her *California—an Intimate History* (1914) is an unconventional treatment of the subject.

Ina Coolbrith, still retaining the lyrical fervor that had impressed Bret Harte, published *A Perfect Day and Other Poems* (1884), *The Singer of the Sea* (1894), and *Songs of the Golden Gate* (1895), all three full of local color. *The Mountains of California* (1894), the first book to appear from the pen of John Muir, scientist and prose poet, was permeated by a deep love for nature in the spectacular aspects that she displays in California. A less gifted nature-lover, George Wharton James, published his *Picturesque Southern California* and *Nature Sermons.*

Southern California and its Spanish and Indian backgrounds was the *milieu* of Charles Fletcher Lummis, who died in 1928. Author of such charming studies as *The Enchanted Burro, The Land of Poco Tiempo,* and the collected *Spanish Songs of Old California,* he is lovingly remembered for his long editorship of the California magazine *Out West.*

But the work of Ambrose Bierce, acknowledged leader of California letters during this period, is in no sense regional. His stories deal with the corpse-strewn battlefields of the Civil War, the nameless places of morbid fancy. They are meticulously finished; and in them, as in his other writings, his satire stings like the scorpion. In connection with the brilliant tales collected in *Black Beetles in Amber* (1892), *Can Such Things Be!* (1893), and *In the Midst of Life* (1898), Gertrude Atherton said that Bierce had "the best brutal imagination of any man in the English-speaking race." Through his columns in the *Wasp,* the *Argonaut,* and the San Francisco *Examiner,* Bierce became a power in California journalism. Some of his stories are still reprinted, while his invective has by no means lost its biting force. The strange disappearance of Bierce in Mexico, just before the World War, lent a dramatic touch to his career.

Charles Warren Stoddard, continuing the literary labors begun in company with Bret Harte, Mark Twain, and Ina Coolbrith for the *Californian,* added the Pacific and the South Seas to his domain. One of his last books deals with the California missions. Edward Rowland Sill, author of *The Hermitage* (1868) and other volumes of verse, taught for a number of years at the University of California. His "Opportunity" and "The Fool's Prayer" are still often reprinted.

Gelett Burgess, that friendly humorist, lived in California for several years before and after the turn of the century.   In 1895-97 he edited *The Lark* for a San Francisco publisher, gaining renown that was later to embarrass him with his "Purple Cow":

> I never saw a PURPLE COW,
> I never hope to see one;
> But I can tell you, anyhow,
> I'd rather SEE than BE one!

Hubert Howe Bancroft collected a library of 60,000 books, maps, and manuscripts (now lodged in the Bancroft Library of the University of California), and working with a large corps of assistants produced in 30 years nearly 40 volumes of history, biography, and essays, including a *History of the Pacific States of North America* (1882-90) in 28 volumes.   Bancroft has been accused of "factory" methods in writing history and of perpetrating many errors as a result, yet some authorities consider the *History of the Pacific States* to be the greatest feat of historiography in modern times.   No serious student of Western history can wisely ignore it, and many general readers find it enjoyable.   The four-volume *History of California* (1885-97) by Theodore Hittell, however, holds a greater fascination for the lay reader.

Notable in the literary annals of California was the visit in 1879-80 of Robert Louis Stevenson, then on the threshold of his literary career. He lived for a while in Monterey and later in San Francisco, where his marriage to Mrs. Osbourne took place.   *The Silverado Squatters* (1883), *The Wrecker* (1892), *The Amateur Emigrant* (1894), and many of his published letters have to do in whole or part with the California scene.   Ten years later a young British journalist named Rudyard Kipling paid a brief visit to San Francisco, and endeavored without success to sell some of his writings to the editors of that city.

With the beginning of the present century came a third period in California literature.   Increased facility of communication and increased centralization of cultural activities on the eastern seaboard had finally broken down the old regionalism.   The local scene was no longer the chief source of inspiration.   Many young Westerners, dreaming of a career in literature, yearned to reverse Horace Greeley's dictum and go East in search of fame and fortune.   The work of some of these writers bespoke an awakening social consciousness.   Edwin Markham, a fervent champion of democracy, stands at the threshold of the new era.   "The Man with the Hoe," a poem published in a San Francisco newspaper near the turn of the century, made Markham famous in a single day.

Of principal importance in this pre-war period were Frank Norris and Jack London and the literary colony founded at Carmel by the poet George Sterling in 1905.   Norris, leaving the University of California, had studied art in Paris and there had fallen under the influence of Zola and the naturalistic school. Abandoning the brush for the pen and returning to California, he began to write novels conceived on a gigantic scale. The unforgettable *McTeague* (1899) was followed by *The Octopus* (1901) and *The Pit* (1903)—the first two volumes of a trilogy the "epic of wheat." Norris died at the age of 32, with the trilogy unfinished; but in *McTeague* and *The Octopus* he left two pioneering books that, despite their extravagance of expression, remain distinguished landmarks in American fiction.

In the Carmel group, besides George Sterling, were: James Hopper, a short-story writer of distinction; Mary Austin, author of *The Land of Little Rain* (1903) and several other notable books; Nora May French, a young lyric poet; and Frederick R. Bechdoldt, a writer of western stories. Jack London and Herman Scheffauer were regular visitors. Sinclair Lewis came a little later and with William Rose Benet spent a year there, as did Upton Sinclair. Michael Williams, author of *The Book of the High Romance* (1918), lived at Carmel for several years; and Harry Leon Wilson, who wrote his *Ruggles of Red Gap* (1915), is still a resident.

Rupert Hughes, popular author and playwright, lives in Los Angeles. Both Will and Wallace Irwin studied at Stanford, were editors in San Francisco, and celebrated before-the-fire Chinatown, Wallace in *Chinatown Ballads* (1905) and Will in *Old Chinatown* (1908). Stewart Edward White is known in California chiefly for his *Story of California* (a trilogy, 1927) and for his novels of the gold rush and vigilante days, *The Gray Dawn* (1915) and *The Forty Niners* (1928).

But the most spectacular literary figure of the time and the most widely read of California authors was Jack London, born at San Francisco in 1876. An "oyster pirate" and longshoreman, he turned to literature in his teens. After an arduous apprenticeship, he began to produce short stories, novels, autobiographical and sociological works that were enthusiastically received throughout the western world. As a fiction writer he glorified the elemental in men; as a socialist he foresaw a merciless "war of the classes." Supermen and superwomen stalk through his stories, many of which are based upon his own experience, interpreted through an intensely romantic imagination. London's peregrinations took him to many places, and even on his great ranch in Sonoma County he managed to live dramatically, with an air of grandeur. His fight with alcohol, as described in *John Barleycorn* (1913), was in itself a desperate adventure. The doctrine of crude force and the purely materialistic philosophy that he expounded have fallen into disfavor, his stories of blond primitive brutes now find fewer readers (though *The Call of the Wild, The Sea Wolf,* and many of his short stories still remain popular, especially in Europe); but as adventurer and storyteller, as a powerful and unique voice of his time and his region, Jack London will long be remembered.

George Sterling was a poet whose brilliant imagination and poignant sense of beauty were held tightly within classic forms. His poetic dramas, odes, and sonnets are now somewhat at variance with the prevailing taste. But *The Testimony of the Suns* (1903), several of the sonnets, and certain shorter poems such as "Autumn in Carmel," possess enduring beauty. Sterling, for many years well known in Carmel and San Francisco, has become an almost legendary figure since his death in 1927. Herman Scheffauer, like Sterling a disciple of Ambrose Bierce, was another lyric poet of similar talent and expression; and Clark Ashton Smith, younger in years than either Sterling or Scheffauer, is nevertheless akin to them in his search for verbal beauty and his aloofness from the modern scene.

The era of disillusionment following the World War has been a period of change and experiment. Cross-currents and divergent tendencies make it impossible any longer to divide California writers into definite groups. Today the State has no literary magazine of importance (although the *Overland Monthly* and the *Argonaut* still exist in name), and no group of contemporary authors constitutes a distinctive California school.

Nevertheless, many prominent writers of the post-war era are Californians by birth or residence. Gertrude Atherton, who has continued to write fiction, published in 1932 her autobiographical *Adventures of a Novelist*. Kathleen Norris, prolific chronicler of middle-class family life, is a Californian; as is her husband, Charles Norris (a brother of Frank Norris), who writes realistic problem novels. Charles Caldwell Dobie has skilfully depicted San Francisco and its people in his short stories and in *San Francisco: A Pageant* (1933). Gertrude Stein spent her early girlhood in the Bay region. Robert Frost, the New England poet, is a Californian by birth. Lincoln Steffens, journalist of the muckraking era and author of *The Shame of the Cities* (1904), was born in Sacramento; he left California soon after graduating from the State University, but came back to it ten years before his death to write his now famed autobiography.

Upton Sinclair, socialist and reformer, wrote *The Jungle* (1906) before he came West to settle in Pasadena. Of his many later books, some have been printed and published, as well as written in that city. Such novels as *Oil* (1927), *Boston* (1928) and *Mountain City* (1930), though they lack the youthful fire evident in *The Jungle,* are shot through with fierce indignation against various industrial and political evils. Sinclair's controversial and somewhat raucous sociological treatises, such as *The Brass Check* (1919), *The Goose-Step* (1923), and *The Goslings* (1924), criticizing the nation's newspapers and schools, have had reverberations far beyond the Pacific Coast. In *Mammonart* (1925) and *Money Writes!* (1927) he maintains that in the present social system writers in general, especially the most successful, are directly or indirectly subservient to those who control the important publishing outlets. Southern California and its Spanish and Indian backgrounds was the *milieu* of Charles Fletcher Lummis, who died in 1928. Author of such charming studies as *The Enchanted Burro, The Land of Poco Tiempo,* and the collected *Spanish Songs of Old California,* he is lovingly remembered for his long editorship of the California magazine *Out West.*

Although several authors and artists still live in Carmel, that community is now famous chiefly because of Robinson Jeffers and the stone tower that he built there. Jeffers' first book to gain wide notice was *Roan Stallion* (1925). Since then he has published several other narrative poems of similar provocative and startling intensity, leaving little serious doubt that as a poet he stands considerably above all his California predecessors. He perceives the non-human world to be inherently noble and sees great beauty in the sea, the mountains, and the hawks and eagles soaring above them. But man's place in this beauty is always unsure and often "curiously ignoble or curiously vile." Much of Jeffers' poetic appeal lies in the intensity of his feeling for dramatic conflict, for the terrible and the unusual, and for the Carmel coast region whose beauty and grandeur permeate virtually all his writing.

Among other present-day poets deserving of mention is Yvor Winters of Stanford University, who for a time edited a now defunct literary periodical called *The Gyroscope.* The lyrics of Hildegarde Flanner, Marie de L. Welch, and Helen Hoyt are well known to readers of contemporary anthologies. Sara Bard Field is the author of *Barabbas* (1932) and other volumes of verse. Charles Scott Erskine Wood, who came to California from Portland, Oregon, is known for his *Heavenly Discourse* (1927) and *Earthly Discourse* (1937).

Within the walls of San Quentin penitentiary there has been for years a group of convict writers, at least two of whom (both now out of prison) have gained national recognition. They are Ernest Booth, author of *Stealing through Life* (1929), and Robert Tasker, who wrote *Grimhaven* (1928). It was in San Quentin, too, that David Lamson went through the ordeal that resulted in his noted book, *We Who Are about to Die* (1935).

John Steinbeck, a native of Pacific Grove on Monterey Bay, writes of the common people of the State. His *Tortilla Flat* (1935) tells of life and death among light-hearted Monterey panhandlers, members of a California racial group called *paisanos* because of their mixed Indian and Spanish origin. *In Dubious Battle* (1936) is a novel of agricultural workers on strike. *Of Mice and Men* (1937) is a brief and tragic tale of two homeless laborers, wandering up and down the rich central California farming district.   William Saroyan, born of Armenian parents in the San Joaquin Valley, is the author of a large number of discursive, almost plotless, short stories, some hilarious and others sad, which have appeared in book form under the titles of *The Daring Young Man on the Flying Trapeze* (1934), *Inhale and Exhale* (1936), and *Little Children* (1937).   Robin Lampson, grandson of a pioneer couple, wrote *Laughter out of the Ground* (1935), a long novel in verse, giving the life story of a typical forty-niner who remained to found a family in the State.   In recent years many prominent writers have made their homes more or less permanently in the State.   Among these are the novelist, Hamlin Garland; Max Miller, author of *I Cover the Waterfront;* and Jim Tully, the blunt-spoken author of autobiographical and documentary fiction such as *Beggars of Life, Jarnegan, Circus Parade,* and *Blood on the Moon.*

The present is too much a time of transition to justify any dogmatic predictions about the future of literature in California.   Many extraneous traditions and influences are at work.   Although the State has more than its share of poetasters, local orators, businesslike students of short-story manuals, manipulators of plot machines, and members of amateur literary clubs, it has also many writers of distinction, both native Californians and immigrants from the East and Middle West. Their work, only a small part of which has been mentioned here, cannot entirely fail to uphold the State's literary reputation, originally created, under conditions much less complex than those existing today, in the pages of the *Golden Era* and Harte's *Overland Monthly.*

MUSIC

Centuries ago California Indians were acting out primitive music drama—celebrating triumph over enemies, invoking rain and plentiful harvest, dramatizing deeds of wonder.   Drums of different timbre, flutes, rattles made from gourds to turtle shells, and bone whistles from the forelegs of deer were among their important instruments.   Their ritual chants dealt with birth and death, the succession of the seasons, cursing enemies, instructing young boys, invoking the spirits. The Luiseno and Diegueno of San Diego and the Cahuilla of Riverside County still observe annual fiestas.

With the coming of the Franciscan friars in 1769, the Indians heard a new kind of music—the thousand-year-old music of the Roman Catholic mass. A great illuminated vellum volume of Gregorian chants, brought from Spain, may still be seen at the Mission of San Juan Bautista. The notes for the tenor, bass, and baritone were written in different colored inks in some of the scores, to help the natives distinguish their parts. Patiently the California Indians were taught to sing the sacred melodies. When Robert Louis Stevenson was living in Monterey, toward the end of the nineteenth century, he went to the annual festival in honor of San Carlos, held in the ruins of the Mission San Carlos Borromeo, and heard aged Indians, who had come many miles to attend the ceremony, sing the Latin words and music with good accent. Even today some Indians in San Diego County assist in church services by chanting medieval Latin hymns.

The appearance of Spanish-Mexican folk music in California brought to pueblo and rancho the passionate rhythms of the fandango, piquant serenades, amorous Andalusian ditties, and grim and tragic ballads of wandering singers. At the dwelling houses on the great ranchos, the strains of the *jarabe,* the fandango, the *zorrita,* the *contradanza,* or any of a dozen other excitingly lively dances were heard. Great lovers of color and rhythm, the Spanish colonists were forever, it seems, dancing, singing, and improvising ballads on their guitars, which were as much a part of their costume as their sombreros and serapes. Troubadours from Monterey and Santa Barbara used to wander northward to visit the great hospitable ranchos around the village of Yerba Buena. Their songs were long popular, and their descendants today in many places still delight in the tradition. The picturesque fiestas held annually in Santa Barbara, Los Angeles, Monterey, and other towns are popular reminders of this period.

No sooner had American conquest put an end to the slow, feudal life of the ranchos than the forty-niners began swarming into the new El Dorado from all over the world. On the long journey overland across the plains or by sea around the Horn, they whiled the time away with song and dance. The chorus of "Oh! Susanna!" sung on the way, runs:

> "I'm going to California,
> With my banjo on my knee!"

In the "diggin's," around the camp fire at night, the miners sang pre-Civil War songs—"Ben Bolt," "The Last Rose of Summer," "Pop Goes the Weasel"—often improvising new words for the old airs, or making up new melodies. A stick beat out the accompaniment on a tin wash-pan. A universal favorite was the picturesque ballad celebrating the exploits of Joe Bowers, a Ulysses among the adventurous riffraff of the "diggin's." Two of its printable stanzas read:

> "There's New York Jake a butcher boy
> That was always gettin' tight;
> Whenever Jake got on a spree,
> He was spoilin' for a fight.
>
> One day he ran against a knife
> In the hands of old Bob Cline—
> So over Jake we held a wake
> In the days of Forty-nine!"

The folk music of the 1850's included old English and Scotch ballads, fiddle tunes, singing games and play-party songs from the Atlantic seaboard and the Appalachians, native American hymns, ballads and love ditties, Cornish miners' chants and old Irish airs. Sailors sang their chanteys, or "shanties" as the old salts call them, and according to Joseph Conrad the best chanteys in the world came from San Francisco. Immigrants from all over the world brought their own songs with them: Basque shepherds' tunes and German stein songs, Hindu *ragas* and Hawaiian melodies, Tagalog chants, and Sicilian pastoral airs. *Put's Original California Songster* (1854), which ran into five editions and sold 25,000 copies, was the forerunner of a flood of similar collections. Many of them have a distinctly Californian flavor, suggesting contemporary incidents when feeling ran high regarding navigation on the Sacramento, stage-coach bandits, the California Legislature, the miner's hard lot, living conditions in San Francisco, or John Chinaman. In later years the armies of migratory workers, who still wander up and down the inland valleys of California and pitch their wretched camps to harvest the seasonal crops, sang Joe Hill's songs, the famous parody on Casey Jones, and other ballads, which spread all over the country. The little red I. W. W. songbooks that many of them carried, once passports to jail, have since become collectors' items.

Opera—French, German, and Italian—made its appearance in California almost as early as the forty-niners. Regular performances were given in San Francisco in 1851. In Los Angeles traveling companies that wandered up from Mexico gave performances. Often these companies came to grief, leaving their stranded artists to settle where luck had left them. The famous old Tivoli Opera House was a result of their congregating in San Francisco. Starting as a public beer garden in 1877, where citizens drank to the strains of the Vienna Ladies' Orchestra, the establishment decided to put on Gilbert and Sullivan's *H.M.S. Pinafore* in 1879. The Tivoli continued until 1906 with an unbroken run of comic and grand opera, directed by impresario "Doc" Leahy. With its low prices—25 to 50 cents—and its democratic atmosphere, the Tivoli did more perhaps to popularize opera than almost any other American theater. Its contemporary, the Grand Opera House, was built in 1876 as "a new and elegant temple of the drama" seating over 3,000, with a handsome proscenium and mezzanine boxes. Here a long line of famous singers appeared in an operatic career culminating in a brilliant performance of *Carmen* with Sembrich and Fremstad, Scotti and Caruso, on the night before that memorable date in the history of San Francisco, April 18, 1906. Among the singers who began their careers in California were Emma Nevada, Luisa Tetrazzini, and Lawrence Tibbett.

Opera is still popular in California—kept alive by the San Francisco Opera Association under the direction of Gaetano Merola—though the season lasts only a few weeks. Here the Nation's only municipal opera house, completed in 1932, offers a standard operatic repertoire. The Federal Music Project, established in 1935, has presented such classics as *Hansel and Gretel, Faust, Aida,* and *Lohengrin* in Los Angeles, Santa Barbara, San Diego, and San Francisco. Operas, operettas and musical satires by modern composers, some of whom are connected with the project, have also been given.

Because of the mildness of the seasons, al fresco music has become an integral part of California culture. In the Hollywood Bowl, audiences of 25,000 people listen to a six-weeks' summer series of symphonies under the stars. Its establishment in 1921 was chiefly due to the efforts of Artie Mason Carter, unpaid enthusiast who built the Bowl on the nickels of the people when the rich failed to grasp the significance of her vision. Audiences are never lacking at the Woodland Theater in Hillsborough, the Dominican College performances at San Rafael, the Greek Theater in Berkeley, and the Ford Bowl in San Diego.

San Francisco, which heard its first symphony concert in 1865, now subsidizes its symphony orchestra. The Los Angeles Philharmonic, founded in 1919, has become an outstanding orchestra thanks to the generosity of the late W. A. Clark. To the development of California's metropolitan symphony orchestras, conductors Walter Henry Rothwell, Alfred Hertz, Issay Dobrowen, Artur Rodzinski, Pierre Monteux, and Otto Klemperer, among others, have contributed much. In Stockton, San Jose, Sacramento, Santa Rosa, San Bernardino, and Pasadena, smaller orchestras perform symphony music.

Since pioneer days, there have been choral societies in California cities and towns. The choir of Trinity Church in San Francisco sang most of the standard oratorios over a period of many years, but there was no large municipal chorus in San Francisco until the coming of Dr. Hans Leschke, whose success with the choral works of Bach, Beethoven, Brahms, Handel, and Stravinski has amply justified his labors. Through the annual November Bach festival, inaugurated by Director John

Smallman in 1934, the First Congregational Church Choir has established a notable place for itself in the Los Angeles musical season. The Negro choral group conducted by Hall Johnson has won an important place in the State's musical life. Sacramento, Glendale, Santa Barbara, and San Diego all have well-supported choruses. The Federal Music Project gives California audiences an opportunity to enjoy many rare, new, or seldom heard choral compositions.

When celluloid became audible in Hollywood, Tin-pan Alley began to move West. Theme song inventors, "hot" jazz arrangers, and modernistic orchestrators were at a premium. The early history of jazz—or ragtime, to use the term that came into vogue about 1910—had been closely connected with San Francisco. "They've got a dance out there, they call the grizzly bear"—so went the lyric. One of the original popularizers of the jazz tempo was Art Hickman, whose first contact with ragtime had been on the Barbary Coast. But Hollywood was destined to become the jazz center as musicians, emulating the prospectors of '49, began their trek to California. In the early days of the talkies most musical scores were patchworks of themes from familiar classics. Then Hollywood began importing the better composers of popular songs—men like Irving Berlin and George Gershwin—to write melodies which were inserted with infinite labor into film drama plots.

Only recently have American producers begun to follow the example of their European confrères by commissioning serious composers to write synchronized musical scores. Today composers of reputation, such as Werner Janssen, George Antheil, Ferde Grofe, Jerome Kern, and Erich Korngold, have begun writing directly for the screen. Kurt Weill's score for *You and Me,* George Antheil's for *The Buccaneer,* and Werner Janssen's for *The General Died at Dawn* and *Blockade* have enhanced the artistic quality of the films. Conductors and performers as well as composers of international prestige have been summoned to Hollywood, as producers have lavished greater and greater sums on their music budgets.

California composers include Ernst Bacon, whose *Symphony in D Minor* won the 1932 Pulitzer Prize; Charles Wakefield Cadman, noted for his use of Indian themes, and William Grant Still, well-known Negro composer and conductor. Henry Hadley, for some years conductor of the San Francisco Symphony, did much of his work in the State; Ernest Bloch wrote his symphonic suite *America* in the hills of Marin County; and Arnold Schoenberg, in exile from Germany, is chairman of the department of music at the University of California at Los Angeles. Among the moderns are Gerald Strang, Roy Harris, Frederick Jacobi, and Henry Cowell, leader of an experimental school of composition.

PAINTING AND SCULPTURE

In the days before the Civil War, the Rocky Mountains were a favored subject among American landscape painters. The artists who came to the Western territories were stirred by the magnificence, grandeur, and sheer size of the new country. To them, as to the gold seekers, America had suddenly opened extravagant possibilities. Here was a land of prodigies: mountains, precipices, cataracts, dead craters, snowy ascents, vertiginous cliffs. It seemed to the pioneer artists that this wild country was prepared to yield limitless esthetic rewards.

California art of this period succeeded in exciting eastern imaginations and in disclosing the scenic marvels of the virgin territory. Artistically, however, it overshot its mark in attempting to reproduce in pictorial terms the gigantic proportions of the mountains, canyons, and forests of the West. Many of the huge canvases of that time, technically weak and devoid of emotional content, today seem of dubious value.

The painters of spectacular scenery were not, however, the first artists to reach California. Before their arrival, a unique artistic development had taken place in connection with the Spanish Missions which administered California territory for the larger part of a century. The Indians whom the padres found in the locality had practiced handicrafts and pictorial art according to traditions extending back to prehistoric times—the "rock paintings" discovered in California mountains and caves are evidence of this early skill. The missions, which exploited the labor of the natives, brought them under the influence of Spanish teachings in religion and the crafts. The indigenous art, with its motifs and symbols representing the sun, men, animals, and nature mysteries, thus became oddly intermingled with the old World tradition. For example, in the "Stations of the Cross" series painted on sail-cloth at the San Gabriel Mission before 1779, Indian neophytes working under direction of their Spanish masters repeated a centuries-old Christian theme. Most of the early mission murals were later covered with whitewash and plaster; they are being reclaimed today, chiefly through the efforts of the Index of American Design division of the Federal Art Project. Indian craftsmen, and on occasion the padres themselves, also produced carved and painted statues and figurines, plaques, iron grille work, church implements, costumes, stamped and colored leatherwork, textiles, metalwork, and embroideries. An exceptionally rich and varied "folk art" was thus contributed to early California.

During this era numerous paintings and sculptures were brought into California from Spain and Mexico, and wandering artists from those countries painted panels and altarpieces and portraits of the Spanish gentry. While somewhat primitive technically, the unsigned portraits, a few of which are still owned by descendants of the haciendados and by California museums, are often charming and esthetically satisfying in their direct, literal treatment.

By the end of the eighteenth century books of travel and exploration began to include illustrations of California. Perhaps the first of these is Vancouver's *A Voyage of Discovery,* published in London in 1798, which contains two sketches of mission and presidio buildings "taken on the spot" by J. Sykes. Interesting aquatints of California scenes are to be found in other volumes of the first half of the nineteenth century. The first painter to remain and practice in California, whose name is known, is W. S. Jewett. Early in 1850 he executed a large oil, which, according to the first issue of the famous *Overland Monthly,* July 1868, "properly ought to begin the record of California art production." The painting represents a newly arrived immigrant family on a summit of the Sierra Nevada.

The discovery of gold brought, along with members of the other professions, a few painters, and for some 30 years their chief aim was to reproduce the California scene. One of the most successful was Charles C. Nahl, born in Germany of a family of accomplished artists. His work, little known outside of California, shows a familiarity with European traditions. His *The Fandango* and *Sunday in the Mines* are excellent pictorial documents.

Of the school of heroic landscape, Albert Bierstadt (1830-1902), Thomas Hill (1829-1913) and Thomas Moran (1837-1926) achieved the widest popularity both at home and abroad. Bierstadt, born in Düsseldorf, was brought to America as a child. His *Landers' Peak,* drew an enthusiastic response from his contemporaries. Bierstadt spent much time in California among the natural wonders of the Yosemite Valley, the Sierra, and the great valleys of the Sacramento and San Joaquin.

Thomas Hill started his career as a coach painter. His canvases, like those of Bierstadt, were enormous panoramic views of mountain ranges, which seemed in their day to express the "magnificent scenery of that marvelous region, where the roar of the whirlwind and the roll of thunder reverberate like the tread of countless millions who evermore march westward." Later generations, however, have found less substance in Hill's paintings.

Thomas Moran, a man of extraordinary versatility, had profited from study abroad. The influence of Turner enriched his canvases, and though in his own time he was less eagerly acclaimed than Bierstadt or

Hill, his solid talent has since given him a higher rank. Like others of the California group, Moran devoted much of his work to the dramatic scenery of the West; he also was considered one of the best etchers of his day. Moran painted with ease and fluency, and his composition was masterly; yet, on the whole, his work lacks subtlety of handling and is too solid and inert for modern taste.

Notable among the many lesser painters who followed Bierstadt, Hill, and Moran, are Raymond A. Yelland, marine painter and art educator; Jules Tavernier, whose work includes numerous paintings of Indian life as well as many landscapes; Thaddeus Welch, painter of the Mount Tamalpais region; and Charles D. Robinson, who celebrated the scenic marvels of the Yosemite Valley.

Of special distinction among California landscapists was William Keith (1838-1911), who came to California in 1859. Like the painters of the French Barbizon school and his friend George Inness, Keith sought subjective harmony and poetic mood in his painting. He avoided the grandiose, and in his work the theatrical naturalism of Moran and Bierstadt gave way to brooding and tranquil scenes—serene groves of live oak, clearings in the interior of woods, hillsides, brooks—remarkable for their play of light and shade. Toby Edward Rosenthal (1848-1917), a native of Connecticut, was brought as a child to San Francisco, where he studied under the Mexican painter, Fortunato Arriola. Rosenthal spent much time in Europe, maintaining a studio in Munich. In its literary themes and scrupulous craftsmanship, his work reflected the styles of the Munich and older Düsseldorf schools. His method was laborious and scholarly; it was not exceptional for him to spend three years in research, travel, and sketching, to produce a single canvas like *The Trial of Constance of Beverley*, now owned by Stanford University. Rosenthal's documentary paintings brought to his studio many admirers and buyers, while lithographers bid against one another for permission to reproduce them, even before they were dry.

With the decline of the heroic school new influences from the East and from abroad began to affect California painting and sculpture. In the last quarter of the nineteenth century, the currents of impressionism, Munich genre painting, eclecticism, and French romanticism mingled with the local development. Public interest in art during this period was stimulated by the organization of the San Francisco Institute of Arts in 1874; the founding of the E. B. Crocker Art Gallery in Sacramento in 1884; the exhibition of 60 local artists at the World's Columbian Exposition in Chicago in 1893; the establishment of the M. H. de Young Memorial Museum in San Francisco in 1895, and of the Southwest Museum in Los Angeles in 1903.

The Bohemian Club of San Francisco, founded in 1872, reflected the diversity of interests animating the newer art. Among its members during the decades that followed were Arthur Matthews, painter, architect, and decorator, examples of whose works may be seen on the walls of many public buildings in the State; Bruce Porter who executed stained glass and mural paintings for California churches and public buildings; Gottardo Piazzoni, landscapist, who contributed the murals at the San Francisco Public Library; Xavier Martinez, born in Mexico, who has lived for many years in the Bay region, where many of his works are in the possession of the Oakland Art Gallery; Charles Dickman, painter of landscapes and marines; and Henry Joseph Breuer, landscapist. Arthur Atkins, who despite his early death left a number of excellent landscapes, was close to the Bohemian Club.

Having moved to Monterey in 1895 Francis McComas, Bohemian Club painter of oils, water colors, and murals, became one of the Monterey-Carmel group which included Charles Rollo Peters, widely known as the painter of the "nocturnal witchery and glamour of California," and Armin Hansen, colorist and etcher. William Ritschel painted many landscapes of the Monterey-Carmel coast line.

By the turn of the century notable artists were working in Los Angeles, where the painting of William Wendt exerted an early influence. The hills of this region, drenched in sunlight for the greater part of the year, furnish the subject matter of most Southern California landscapists. Soon Los Angeles was no longer the only Southern California art center: groups were formed in Santa Barbara, Laguna Beach, San Diego, La Jolla, and other localities.

California's first eminent sculptor was Douglas Tilden, born in 1860. He received his early education at Berkeley and later studied sculpture in Paris. Among his best known works are *The Football Players* in Berkeley and the *Mechanics' Fountain* in San Francisco. Robert I. Aitken, whose many monuments in the State have received high praise, was one of Tilden's pupils. Edgar Walter and Earl Cummings were also influenced by Tilden. Other California sculptors of the period are Roger Noble Burnham, Frank Happersburger, Marion F. Wells, Chester Beach, and Haig Patigian. The figures of wild life executed by Arthur Putnam, who died in 1930, received wide appreciation.

The San Francisco Exposition of 1915 brought the work of the French moderns to the attention of a considerable number of Californians. As elsewhere, the immediate response to this new art was mainly one of bewilderment and irritation. In the next decades, however, the aims of Cezanne, Van Gogh, Seurat, Gaugin, and their twentieth century followers gradually became more intelligible both to California artists and to the public. Modern influences entered the California School of Fine Arts, founded in 1874, through courses by Arnold Blanch and Maurice Sterne. New decorative and experimental techniques began to be applied by an increasing number of local artists. Abstract and surrealist art, regionalism, and social realism became major trends. The Mexicans, Rivera, Orozco, and Siqueiros, inspired in many artists of the San Francisco and Los Angeles areas a new interest in the problems of mural painting.

Today there are so many artists in California, working in such a profusion of styles and aims, that the State has become one of the leading centers of art activity in the Nation. It is, unfortunately, impossible to describe here the scores of personalities and accomplishments that merit attention.

In sculpture, too, new possibilities were explored: the massive figures of workmen produced by the social realists; the archaic formalism favored in architectural ornament; the suggestive shapes of the abstractionists; and the controversial experiments of the pioneers of new media.

Important museums and galleries have appeared in California since the beginning of the twentieth century. Among these are: the Los Angeles Museum of History, Science and Art, founded in 1913; the Los Angeles Art Association, organized in 1925; the Fine Arts Society of San Diego, 1925; the Henry E. Huntington Art Gallery at San Marino, opened in 1928; the Louis Terah Haggin Memorial Galleries at Stockton, 1928.

The Federal Arts Projects of the WPA have developed an extensive program for bringing art and the general public into closer relation. Murals, sculpture, easel painting, and graphic work executed under its auspices have been allocated to public buildings throughout the State. Its Index of Design Division and art teaching staffs have performed broad services in popular education. Another Federal Agency, the Treasury Department Art Project, has commissioned murals for government buildings on a competitive basis.

The plan of the 1939 Golden Gate International Exposition includes a comprehensive art program which may have important effects upon the local development of art. California painters and sculptors, including representatives of the newer styles, are reaching a larger public with murals and sculptures for the fair grounds. The vast exhibition of old masters assembled at the Palace of Fine Arts will make available for study examples of the Italian, Flemish, Dutch and English schools; various governments are loaning to this exhibition masterpieces never before seen on this continent. The Exposition's decorative arts and crafts exhibit, comprising work from many countries and periods, will endeavor to show the parts played by machine and handmade products in daily life.

Art in California today, attentive to new creative impulses from every part of the world, is striving to overcome passive imitation and to make a contribution of its own to the progress of art. Whether it will be possible, or even desirable, to distinguish in the future a distinct "California style" no one can state with assurance. In the meantime, art in the State has discovered in such essentially public genres as mural painting and reliefs, sculptured monuments, and government-sponsored exhibitions a deeper orientation with respect to the social life of the community.

THE THEATER

The fiesta, the pageant, and the outdoor theater were natural developments in California, where people have always spent much of their time in the open. When Americans first came to California, they found a people who amused themselves with singing and dancing, and on fiesta days watched the fandango danced to the accompaniment of choruses. This essentially Mediterranean type of entertainment has survived in such diverse forms as the Ramona Pageant, La Fiesta de Los Angeles, the Bohemian Club's "high jinks" and the Mt. Tamalpais Mountain Play. But for fifty years after the influx of Americans California was, in general, not very conscious of its Spanish heritage, and the theater as elsewhere in the United States, followed the British and French tradition.

In 1846 the wing of an adobe house in Monterey, surviving today as the oldest theater in California, became an amusement hall for Stevenson's New York Regiment. Minstrel shows, old English farces, and even Shakespearean plays were produced. American soldiers at the Sonoma garrison played Benjamin Webster's *The Golden Farmer* in an improvised theater for four months in the following year, and minstrel shows were given by the American soldiers in Santa Barbara.

The forty niners—most of them without families—were enthusiastic and generous patrons of any kind of entertainment. The gold rush brought actors from the Mississippi showboats; from the theaters of New Orleans, Galveston, Mobile, and New York; from Europe and Australia. Dramatic actors, "Ethiopian serenaders," minstrels, circus clowns, acrobats, performed in tents and crudely contrived temporary halls, or in the gambling rooms of the hotels and saloons, surrounded by French mirrors, French pictures, and blazing chandeliers, while faro, monte, rouge et noir, vingt-et-un, ronda, and roulette games went on night and day. Female performers, who were extremely rare at first,

met with sure success. Home melodies sung by women had a powerful
effect on the miners, who frequently showered the performer with
nuggets and small pouches of gold dust.

In Sacramento *The Bandit Chief* was performed by professionals
at the Eagle Theater, the first building erected in California especially
for theatrical performances. It was a wooden frame with canvas walls
and a roof of tin and sheet iron. Estimates of its cost ranged from
$30,000 to $85,000. It was formally opened October 18, 1849, although the "Stockton Minstrels" had played in it to a full house the
month before.

Driven from Sacramento by floods, the Eagle Theater Company
went to San Francisco in January 1850, and in a second-floor hall
performed *The Wife,* a touching tale in blank verse. San Francisco
had already, on June 22, 1849, witnessed its first theatrical performance. In a rickety schoolroom, crowded to suffocation, Stephen C.
Massett, a stout, red-faced little Englishman, with a great mop of curls,
sang original ditties and burlesqued famous singers of the day. The
front seats were reserved for ladies, of whom there were four present.
Rowe's Olympic Circus and several minstrel companies appeared during
the same year. Most of the halls erected in San Francisco were destroyed by the fires of 1850 and 1851, but new theaters were rapidly
built, including the Museum and the famous Jenny Lind. The Museum's first play, *Seeing the Elephant,* ridiculed the gold rush, and, in
general, performances at this theater had local flavor. The Jenny Lind,
twice burned to the ground and rebuilt by Tom Maguire, was more
ambitious and gave many Shakespearean plays. In 1853 there were
seven theaters in San Francisco, among them the American, the Adelphi
(built by the French), and the costly and massive Metropolitan.

Junius Brutus Booth, the elder, came to San Francisco with his
19-year-old son, Edwin, in 1852; on the death of his father young
Edwin remained for a while in California laying a firm foundation for
his later fame. Kate Hayes, "the willowy swan of Erin," arrived in
the same year, "fresh from triumphs at the Covent Garden." Other
actors came—James Stark, Anna Thillon, Signora Elise Biscaccianti—
and many more. Shortly afterwards Lotta Crabtree, aged nine, made
her first dramatic appearance, in Petaluma as Gertrude in *A Loan of a
Lover.* Breaking into an occasional jig and roll in the midst of the
performance, she won her audience; thereafter, whether playing her
banjo, dancing, and making merry, or acting scenes of overwhelming
pathos as "Little Nell," Lotta could do no wrong. She attained extraordinary popularity throughout northern California,

"Because in Lotta we can see
Artistic concentration
Of sweetness, strength and piquancy,
A pungent combination."

and to many Californians her legend remains alive to this day. The celebrated Lola Montez, favorite of kings, made her home for a time at Grass Valley, and danced there and at other camps and slumgullion centers.

In San Francisco the opening of the California Theater in 1869, under the joint direction of the two great actors, Lawrence Barrett and John McCullough, dimmed the glory of the Metropolitan. The first plays were Bulwer-Lytton's *Money,* followed by *Marie Antoinette* and *Richelieu.* In 1877 Hélène Modjeska, the Polish actress, came from the southern California bee ranch where she and her husband had spent several months in political exile, and appeared at the California in *Adrienne Lecouvreur,* the first of her successes on the English-speaking stage. The California, rebuilt in 1888, remained a popular playhouse until destroyed by the fire in 1906. Among its competitors was the Baldwin Theater, for a time managed by young David Belasco, later to become a world-famous actor-manager and producer. His direction, at the Grand Opera House in 1878, of *The Story of the Passion,* based on the birth of Christianity, aroused a storm of controversy.

Although minstrel companies and circuses frequently went to Southern California, Los Angeles did not see its first complete troupe until November 1860, when the Stark and Ryer Company played to enthusiastic audiences in a ramshackle hall called the Temple Theater. San Diego was visited by a professional troupe as early as 1868 and plays were performed in both Spanish and English. The leading actors usually came from the north and more than one performance was delayed when a steamer from San Francisco failed to arrive on time. In Los Angeles the Merced was opened in the late sixties, but the first theaters of consequence—Child's Opera House, Tivoli Opera House, and the Burbank Theater—were not built until the great real estate boom in the 1880's. It long remained difficult to engage the best road companies for southern California, and Los Angeles did not become a good theater town until after 1900.

By the turn of the century the management of most theaters was in the hands of national syndicates. San Francisco was an important theatrical center, with many road attractions, frequent productions of new plays, opera, and large spectacles. At the Alcazar, which had housed Belasco's famous company after the Baldwin Theater burned down, and at the Savoy, Henry Duffy's stock companies played for many years in spite of the growing pressure of the movies. During the decade preceding the World War, the professional theater in Los Angeles largely centered on three houses managed by the Morosco-Blackwood Company. The new plays produced in Los Angeles during this period included Richard Walton Tully's *The Bird of Paradise,* and *Kindling,* with Margaret Illington in the lead. Henry Duffy's chain of theaters later extended to Los Angeles. Linden E. Behymer, Simeon Gest, and Ellis Reid opened theaters where good plays were acted by movie professionals "at liberty." There is no independent professional theatrical activity, though many Broadway importations reach the city.

While accepting the Broadway diet, Californians can boast of the stars who began their careers in the old Coast theaters. The roll includes—in addition to those already mentioned—the names of Nance O'Neill, Maude Allan, Isadora Duncan, Minnie Maddern Fiske, Maude Adams, Marjorie Rambeau, Holbrook Blinn, Blanche Bates, Pauline Lord, and Edna Wallace Hopper. Mary Anderson was a native of Sacramento; Frank Mayo made his debut in San Francisco; David Warfield once worked as an usher in a San Francisco theater. Like Belasco, William A. Brady, the eminent producer, was born in California and had his first professional experience in San Francisco, while Morris Mayerfeld, who built the Orpheum circuit, was prominent in the rapid development of vaudeville entertainment.

At about the turn of the century, California rediscovered its Spanish heritage of outdoor drama. San Francisco's Bohemian Club presented the first of its annual plays in 1902 in its private redwood grove near Monte Rio. Usually poetic in form with musical accompaniment, the play is written, staged, and acted by club members. About the same time the Forest Theater in the Carmel artists' colony began to give plays. Typical of the many mission spectacles was the *San Gabriel Mission Play,* given annually for about two decades after 1912, which interspersed historical episodes with dances, songs, and ceremonies. The *Ramona Pageant,* presented in April and May in the Ramona Bowl, near Hemet, is a dramatization of Helen Hunt Jackson's *Ramona;* the cast is made up of local people, many of whom are Spanish Californians. *Tahquitz,* dealing with the traditions of the Coahuila Indians, the *Pilgrimage Play,* at Hollywood, and *La Fiesta de Los Angeles* are among the many pageants now given annually in natural amphitheaters.

California also has several outdoor theaters, modeled on Greek or Roman forms. The best known is the Greek Theater of the University of California in Berkeley. Many celebrities have appeared here, including Sarah Bernhardt in Racine's *Phedre,* Maude Adams as Rosalind in *As You Like It,* and Margaret Anglin, who in 1910-15 revived Sophocles' *Antigone,* and *Electra,* and Euripedes' *Medea.* Sam Hume and later Irving Pichel directed the Greek Theater and gave notable productions. There are other Greek Theaters in Los Angeles, Bakersfield, and Pomona College, and many garden theaters, modeled after the Italian and German types, throughout the State.

The little theater movement in California, as elsewhere in America, developed in the second decade of the present century, when road companies ceased to be commercially profitable. Small local theaters were built in many places; elsewhere performances were given in private homes, school auditoriums, halls of fraternal lodges, and converted barns. Little theaters have a large following in the State, community drama associations flourish, and high school and college students take active interest in the stage.

In 1916 Gilmor Brown, director of a financially unsuccessful road company, induced a number of Pasadena citizens to support a local theater. In 1918 the Pasadena Community Playhouse Association was organized on a non-profit basis, with Brown as manager and director. One of the theater's most spectacular productions was Eugene O'Neill's *Lazarus Laughed.* The performance of this religious drama required over 350 masks (designed and made by college students in Los Angeles), 350 costumes, and 6 sets. The present building of the Pasadena Playhouse was opened in 1925. In 1937 the house was drawing its performers, aside from occasional well-known stars, from a list of 1,000 players and had a school of dramatics with 200 students.

The Lobero Theater in Santa Barbara was founded in 1872 by the popular Jose Lobero, an Italian saloonkeeper and musician, whose fling at the production of grand opera proved financially calamitous; rebuilt in 1924, and now controlled by the Community Arts Association, the theater houses community drama, road shows, and concerts.

Sacramento, Palo Alto, Laguna Beach, and Escondido, and other California towns have well-organized groups of community players. Oakland, in 1934, had more than 60 separate producing organizations. Among the San Francisco groups are the Players Club, the Wayfarers, the Golden Bough, and Theater Union. At the Gaité Française, André Ferrier carries on the long tradition of French theaters in the city.

In Los Angeles professional players take part in little theater activities, while waiting for their chance in the movies, or between jobs. The Cordova Playhouse, the Beverly Hills Community Players, the Little Theater of Beverly Hills, the Contemporary Theater, and the Spotlight Theater Club are semi-professional community theaters. A group of Mexican players has recently organized the Padua Hills Theater in Claremont, Los Angeles County.

The University of California Little Theater in Berkeley, directed by Edwin Duerr, gave the first performance of Robinson Jeffer's *Tower Beyond Tragedy* and the American première of *Intermezzo* by Jean Giradoux. At Stanford several noteworthy productions have been given, including that of T. S. Eliot's *Murder in the Cathedral,* elaborately staged late in 1937. Students at the University of California at Los Angeles co-operate with the Pasadena Community Playhouse in designing scenery and costumes for many productions. Several of the little theater groups have laid stress on encouraging local playwrights.

The Federal Theater Project of the Works Progress Administration has acting groups in many cities and towns in the State. One of their first ventures was *Follow the Parade,* a semitopical revue, which in 1936 ran six months in Los Angeles. Later came such plays as *It Can't Happen Here, Chalk Dust, Battle Hymn, Class of '29,* and *Triple A Plowed Under.* The Negro group has produced *Black Empire, Macbeth, Androcles and the Lion,* and *Run Li'l Chillun.* The project at its peak has employed approximately 2,000 persons in the State, and has played to an aggregate audience of 2,000,000.

ORIENTAL THEATERS: There were enough Chinese in California in the 1850's to support a company of 123 actors, which opened at a San Francisco theater in October, 1852. At one time as many as six companies were playing in San Francisco, though at present (1939) only one, the Mandarin Theater, presents legitimate drama; the Great China Theater is devoted to the Chinese motion picture. Almost without exception Chinese drama in America is Cantonese; but occasionally an example of the North China, or Mandarin, drama is presented when an artist such as Mei Lan-fang makes a tour. The plots are generally stories from the Chinese classics well known to the average auditor.

Each Chinese play, though complete in itself, is only a fragment of the total story, and usually a cycle of plays is closely knit around one legend. The average play lasts five hours, and the bulk of the audience arrives for the third and fourth hour. They come for the high spots of the particular play—much as the cultured Westerner would go to the Metropolitan in time to hear Lily Pons sing the mad scene from *Lucia.* The first hour of the play, given over to explanations which connect it with the cycle, is considered unimportant by the authors. Another factor which accounts for the empty theater during the first hour is that the highest admission prices prevail at the opening, and each hour thereafter they are reduced. The Chinese who cannot afford 75¢ or $1 at the beginning, can usually afford 25¢ after 10 o'clock.

The Westerner who goes to a Chinese theater unprepared may well believe that pandemonium has broken loose. But a definite pattern lies back of the seemingly endless blare of gongs, one-stringed fiddles, snakeskin drums, and wailing woodwinds. It would seem that the actor in superb bejeweled silken costumes—is it a man or a woman?—screams, or whines more or less in company with the orchestra. In the front of the house the audience sits stolidly watching the stage. In the rear, small groups cluster together, eating and gossiping, but they rarely miss an important moment in the play. The food stall in the foyer does a brisk business in candies, oranges, pickled duck feet, ice cream, lichee nuts, and the ever-present watermelon seeds—the cracking of which adds an interesting counterpoint to the opera's music. Children, who are always admitted free, scurry up and down the aisles, dash between seats, and generally add to the hurly-burly of the stage, yet appear to disturb no one.

Unbelievably, the full five-hour performance is produced without a rehearsal. Because the actor begins his profession at about the age of ten and plays and replays the classics for many years, he needs very little time to brush up in any part. Furthermore, the actor must be rigidly word-perfect only in the high spots of the play. The balance follows a pattern which is loose enough to allow extemporaneous speeches, and an actor's ability is judged by his facility in improvising. But woe betide the actor who falls down on a set aria; the audience becomes hawk-like in its attention during the classic moments.

Since 1912 women have been allowed to act—a thing forbidden throughout the Manchu rule—and in recent years stage properties such as back drops, curtains, and realistic props have replaced the former pantomime and imaginative handling of stage accessories. Yet the magnificent costumes, many of which cost more than a thousand dollars, the grotesque facial makeup for traditional characters, the intricate sword dances continue despite changes, and even the uninitiated Westerner is fascinated by this art, centuries older than his own civilization.

Prominent actors from Japan occasionally visit the principal California cities and towns, and with local help present some of the favored *Kabuki* and *Ken-Geki* plays, founded on the epic legends of feudalism and involving traditionally set roles and action. These events take place in local Japanese meeting halls, also used for amateur dramatics, dances, and funerals. In Los Angeles there is a Japanese theater that occasionally gives performances with imported Japanese companies, and a motion picture house that shows imported Japanese films.

Architecture

THE EARLIEST architecture in California was that of the Spanish Franciscans. These missionary friars, led by Fra Junípero Serra, founded 21 missions along the coastwise *Camino Real* between 1769 and 1823—the first at San Diego, the last at Sonoma. It has been said that the poverty to which the Franciscan monks were pledged is the virtue of their mission churches. In comparison with eighteenth century Spanish Colonial architecture in Mexico and the Southwest, they exhibit simplicity of form and humility in treatment. The relative austerity of the missions was due mainly to the limited resources in materials and skilled labor.

There are three general types of plans in mission churches: those having only a simple nave without side aisles, as San Miguel and Dolores; those of rectangular plan with a single bell tower on the front, as San Buenaventura and San Luís Rey de Francia; and those with two belfried towers, as admirably exemplified by Mission Santa Barbara. Typically, the missions were planned around a patio quadrangle, usually enclosed by the church and minor buildings—the cells of the friars, quarters for the Indian workmen, servants and soldiers, guest rooms, work shops, refectory, kitchen, and convent for young Indian women. These minor buildings were arranged in two and sometimes three rows of chambers with arcaded cloisters fronting the patio and sometimes the outer plaza. The arches were carried on heavy piers rather than columns.

The missions were constructed of stone and adobe, finished inside and out with mud plaster and frequently strengthened on the outside with heavy buttresses. The whitewashed exterior walls, with their simple architectural adornments and deeply recessed wall openings, are in striking contrast to contemporary Churrigueresque style of vice-regal Mexico. They were relieved only by the typical grouping of detail around the doors and windows—pilasters, classic trim, paneling, and an occasional iron or wooden grille. The most characteristic features, however, are the pitched roofs of hewn timber covered with red tile; the square towers with their domed and arched belfries, usually in two stages; and the curvilinear gables rising above the peak of the roof to give a more elaborate silhouette and added height to the facade. Frequently the gable ends were adorned with a niched figure of a saint or pierced with arched belfries, as at Mission San Gabriel. Occasionally they were designed in the form of a classic pediment. Perhaps the most notable mission church in California is Santa Barbara. The design of its strictly classic facade with columns and pediments, based upon a drawing in the Spanish edition of Vitruvius, is entirely in keeping with the earliest phase of the Spanish Renaissance. The restored San Juan Capistrano Mission with its ruined sanctuary and cloistered arcades is architecturally one of the most pretentious of the chain. Other notable missions in California are San Carlos de Borromeo at Carmel, San Gabriel Arcangel near Los Angeles, San Diego Alcalá in San Diego, and San Antonio de Padua near Jolon.

Generally free of the emotionalism and excesses of the Spanish baroque, the interiors of the missions reflect the simple taste of the Franciscan order. They are characterized by long narrow naves with whitewashed walls and painted ornaments, low dados, slender pilasters naively rendered in imitation of marble, occasional festoons and draperies, and timber ceilings with dark hand-carved, stenciled beams supported at the walls by scrolled brackets. Forming the focal point at one end is the sanctuary with its high altar, decorative reredos and wine glass pulpit. The altar and reredos were often freely embellished with colorful paintings, draped figures and gilded carvings executed by the padres and Indian craftsmen in the manner of both the Plateresque and Churrigueresque Spanish tradition. The fine detail of the facade of San Carlos near Monterey, the delicately carved reredos of San Juan Capistrano and the ornate retable of the mortuary chapel of San Luís Rey de Francia are striking but not isolated examples of Franciscan decoration. The monks also acquired ornate and gilded furnishings from Mexico and Spain and enriched their walls with paintings, as exemplified by the elaborate reredos of the Mission Dolores and the murals at San Miguel.

Within a few years of the coming of the Franciscans the Spanish Government made vast grants of land, where the Spanish and Mexican *rancheros* built their homes and established themselves with their families, their *vaqueros,* and their herds. Like the builders of the missions they used adobe, but whereas the monks wished to put up churches as nearly as possible in a style traditionally ecclesiastical, the Spanish dons were concerned only with comfort and convenience. The charm of these adobe houses lies in their simplicity, their admirable proportions, and their fitness with the landscape.

Many Spanish Colonial houses are still standing. In southern California they are usually one story in height and rectangular in plan, occasionally with a wing forming an "L." Their timber roofs, covered with hand-riven shingles or tile, frequently extend over a long veranda supported by wooden posts along one or sometimes three sides of the house. The interiors are planned with and without corridors; circulation from one room to another in the case of the latter is provided by way of the veranda. The thick adobe walls are covered with white-washed mud plaster and pierced with small double-hung windows, set flush with the outside wall surface and frequently protected by simple iron or wooden grilles. The interiors, also finished in plaster, have tile and wooden floors, ceilings with exposed hewn beams of pine or redwood, and deep splayed and paneled windows, often having seats and inner shutters.

Farther north the houses are frequently two stories in height with massive first story walls, three feet thick, and thinner second-story walls generally offset from the inside. The two-story dwellings have balconies at the front and rear, occasionally extending around the entire house. The balconies are generally of two types: two storied, with posts extending from ground to roof of upper gallery; and cantilevered, with posts at the second story supporting an overhanging roof. Due to the weight of tile roofing, the balconies are frequently covered with wood shakes or hand-split shingles.

Numerous adobe structures erected by the Spanish dons during the prosperous 1830's and 1840's are still found along the streets of small coast towns, in the old sections of the large cities, and scattered over the valleys and plains. By far the greatest number are in Monterey. Among the most notable of these Colonial structures in this historic town are the Larkin house, the Old Customs House, the Pacific Building (one of the early hotels), the Eldorado House, the Escolas House, and the Old Whaling Station. Perhaps one of the most picturesque ranch houses is the Olivos House near Ventura with its two-story porch, outer stairway and belfried gate. Other notable examples are found in the Paseo de la Guerra in Santa Barbara, on Olvera Street in Los Angeles, and along the picturesque streets of Old Town in San Diego.

Many of the first American settlers were from New England and they brought with them the stern architectural traditions of that region. Even before 1850 an architectural fusion had begun. The Americans combined their sound workmanship and feeling for good design with the traditions of Spanish California. In the coast counties already settled by the Spanish, they frequently used adobe, but added early nineteenth-century American detail in the form of clapboard siding, green blinds and double-hung windows and paneled doors flanked by small side lights. Some of the intrepid pioneers from the East dismantled the homes they had occupied, brought the material with them around the Horn, and reconstructed their dwellings in California. One of these structures, erected in 1852, is on the Sherwood ranch near Salinas.

During the eighteen thirties and eighteen forties, while the first overland immigrants were arriving in the Sacramento Valley, Russian pioneers were also attempting to establish a permanent settlement in Sonoma County. Little remains of the pioneer structures of these two groups except the quaint timbered Russian church at Fort Ross with its two silo-like cupolas and adjoining stockade, and the Old Bale Mill in Napa County, built in 1846. The latter, covered with narrow clapboards, is a notable example of American pioneer architecture with its high "false front" and huge mill wheel.

With the discovery of gold in 1848 and the mushroom growth of the older cities (especially in the north) and of the mining towns, the orderly development of the Spanish-American style of architecture was pushed into the background. The older inhabitants in the south and in the rural districts continued to build in the traditional manner, sometimes crudely imitated by the newcomers. But most of the buildings of the mining towns in Sierra, Amador, El Dorado, and Tuolumne Counties, many of which are still in use today, frankly record the restless and temporary aspects of the era. Here are found numerous dilapidated structures of frame, brick, and stone, one and two stories in height; some with steep gable roofs and overhanging eaves, others with front porches with rickety plank floors, slender wood posts and sagging shed roofs, while many are characterized by their "false fronts" with straight and saw-tooth silhouettes. Answering the needs of these mushroom towns countless general stores, makeshift hotels, rooming houses, banks, and saloons were erected. Many of these buildings may be seen in the vicinity of Downieville, El Dorado, Columbia, Knight's Ferry, and Weaverville. With their iron doors and window shutters, they still stand—sometimes gutted with fire as at El Dorado; sometimes deserted as in the ghost towns of Old Shasta or Hornitos; but sometimes, as at Sonora or Angels Camp, they continue to serve the purposes for which they were built.

Until the building of the transcontinental railroad in 1869, new fashions in architecture, as in other spheres, came slowly across the plains or around the Horn. The railroad was not an unmixed blessing, architecturally, for not only did it bring the lumber mill closer to every town, it brought the silver of the fabulous Comstock Lode, which meant wealth—and wealth meant ever larger buildings with more and more fantastic architectural elements. An epidemic of the Victorian pestilence in aggravated form seized California. Whether it was the American version of Victorian Gothic with its pointed arches, battlements, and crestings or the vagaries of the French style of Napoleon III with its mansard roofs and cupolas, bracketed pediments, iron crestings, and the addition of interminable jigsaw work, the results were lamentable and are obvious enough in all the older towns and cities. In San Francisco thousands of Victorian horrors were destroyed in the earthquake of 1906; but many remain, their lines sometimes a little softened by shrubs and vines, sometimes stark and bare in their shabby decay. The architecture of San Francisco, prior to the great fire and earthquake, was predominantly a product of this period and taste. Notable among the city's remaining mid-nineteenth century buildings are the Octagon House near the corner of Union and Gough Streets, the Hoataling Store on Jackson Street, standing among a number of earlier structures, and Fort Winfield Scott in the Presidio. Other examples of this era are the old schoolhouse at Almaden; a quaint hillside house with a broad veranda adorned with jigsaw ornaments, at the corner of Dodge and Stuart Streets in Sonora; and the pretentious gabled and bracketed Carson House, built by a wealthy lumberman in Eureka.

During the late nineties a number of buildings were erected along more academic lines: the State Capitol in Sacramento with its Italian Renaissance dome and Corinthian porticos, the Fresno County Courthouse, and the Ferry Terminal Building in San Francisco, with its slender tower pleasantly recalling the Giralda in Seville. At this time the architecture of California was influenced in a relatively minor way by the Romanesque Revival of H. H. Richardson. At Palo Alto the buildings for Stanford University afforded a group of his followers a fine opportunity to adapt the massive stonework, arcades, and mosaics of the Romanesque style to the design of the Memorial Church and the adjoining quadrangle. Other examples of this stylistic phase are the Mills Building in San Francisco, designed by Daniel Burnham, and the old Santa Fe Station in Los Angeles.

At the turn of the century an improved but somewhat eclectic taste became manifest in California as elsewhere. The Neoclassic and Italian Renaissance styles, popularized in the East by McKim, Mead and White and by the grandiose buildings of the Chicago World's Fair in 1893, were freely adapted to the designs of monumental public buildings. In 1915 the buildings of the Panama Pacific Exposition in San

Francisco contributed a lasting impetus to these traditional and stylistic trends. The Palace of Fine Arts, with its monumental colonnades and great rotunda, still standing on a lagoon in the old exposition grounds, admirably illustrates the academic formula of the Neoclassic style. And so, also, does a charming circular water temple at Sunol.

More recent adaptations of classic architecture are the buildings of the formal civic group in San Francisco: the Renaissance City Hall by Bakewell and Brown, the Opera House, and the War Memorial Building. The Neoclassic California Palace of the Legion of Honor, by George Applegarth and H. Guillaume, is another example of formal design in this city. The Public Library, the State Building and the new Federal Building, with its long colonnade leading up to the plaza, all show the academic training of their architects in the Beaux-Arts tradition. In Berkeley the buildings of the University of California are of white granite in the Neoclassic style. Correct and academic, they indicate a high order of talent, but perhaps only the tall campanile and the highly stylized Life Sciences Building by Arthur Brown show a touch of genius. The United States Post Office at Sacramento, enriched by a fine Doric colonnade, follows the classic tradition with a rugged modern simplicity. At San Marino is the Huntington Library, by Myron Hunt, suggesting a more feminine rendering with coupled Ionic columns, and enhanced by formal landscaping. Perhaps the most modern adaptations of the Neoclassic style in civic buildings are the massive new Civic Center in San Diego, and the lofty Los Angeles City Hall, by Parkinson, Martin, and Austin, with its skyscraper tower and crowning pyramidal roof.

Bertram Goodhue's California Building erected in San Diego (1915) displays a masterly handling of the highly ornate Spanish Churrigueresque style of old Mexico and has been a guiding influence in the development of the modern California Mission style. Of the modern Spanish Colonial buildings, many are frankly reminiscent, direct copies or close modifications of existing Spanish or Mexican structures, while others show considerable change and development. One of the most consistent examples of the former is the palatial City Hall of Santa Barbara, the work of Thomas Mooser, Jr. Other instances are to be found in the numerous buildings of Morgan, Walls and Clements. Although there exists no rule or ordinance governing architectural design in the city of Santa Barbara, the art commission and the county regional planning board have encouraged and regulated the use of Spanish designs throughout the city. Various college buildings, including those at Occidental, Mills, and Scripps, display an admirable use of Spanish forms. The buildings making up the Pasadena Civic Center, the most notable of which is the library by Myron Hunt, are grouped about a terraced square. Their style is a formal expression of the Spanish Renaissance, florid in its detail but admirable in its unity and mass. The individual buildings, held together by a consistent handling of the architectural elements, are dominated by the reddish gold dome of the City Hall. Several buildings of the California Institute of Technology in Pasadena, the Henry Data House and the Country Club in Montecito, the W. K. Kellogg Ranch buildings near Pomona, and in San Diego the Serra Museum, the permanent buildings of the Panama-California Exposition, the U. S. Marine Corps Base, and the U. S. Naval Air Station demonstrate the validity of the style to all but extremists.

In recent years a number of outstanding works have been designed in a more modern version of the Romanesque style than that of H. H. Richardson. The University of California at Los Angeles has a fine group of buildings designed in this manner. Smaller but no less admirable Romanesque designs are seen in the junior college building and Sacred Heart Church in Sacramento, the Church of the Precious Blood and St. John's Church in Los Angeles, and, surprisingly enough, in the tower of a wholesale coffee establishment near the San Francisco waterfront. Splendid examples of the ecclesiastical Gothic tradition, all adapted with a freshness and vigor of style, are St. Dominic's in San Francisco, the First Presbyterian Church in Oakland, Emanuel Presbyterian Church in Los Angeles, and the unfinished Grace Cathedral in San Francisco. There are also occasional examples of the more colorful Byzantine style in such buildings as the Temple Emanuel in San Francisco and the B'nai B'rith Temple in Los Angeles.

Since the beginning of the twentieth century one of the chief developments in California domestic architecture has been the bungalow, which derives its name, and, rather remotely, its structure from the domestic architecture of the white population of southeast Asia. The bungalow was first developed in southern California, where its wide overhanging eaves, flat pitched roof extending over broad porches, and low windows were admirably adapted to the climate. Cheap and easy to build, the type soon swept the State and later the country. Well-to-do clients demanded two- and even three-story bungalows, and these buildings are often handsome as well as homelike. Berkeley and the residential areas of Los Angeles, which were most fashionable prior to the World War, contain many fine examples.

The truly encouraging element in contemporary domestic architecture is the return to a simple interpretation of the Spanish Colonial type of house. The fusion of the Spanish adobe with the early eighteenth and nineteenth century traditional American wooden types with the addition of such modern features as corner windows, has come to be called the "Monterey" style. It is admirably suited to modest living and today, for the first time since 1870, great numbers of well-designed houses are being erected in this manner. The David Selznick House in Beverly Hills and the Edward Heath House in San Marino, both by Roland E. Coate, and the Gregory Farm, near Santa Cruz, by William W. Wurster, are excellent examples of this modification of a traditional style.

The development of modern domestic architecture in California stems from the International Style, established immediately after the World War in France, Holland, and Germany by such men as Le Corbusier, Gropius, Van der Rohe, and Oud, as well as from the highly radical innovations of Frank Lloyd Wright. The international phase has been enthusiastically adapted in California by Richard Neutra, William Lescaze, R. M. Schindler and others. Independently, both Wright and Neutra follow the dictum, "Form follows function." Both have envisaged a new architecture designed to conform with twentieth century industrial society. Following the epigram of Le Corbusier, "A house is a machine for living," the work of the ultra-modern practitioners demands the use of both modern building materials and engineering methods: the use of synthetic plastics, ferro-concrete, cantilevers; the blending of interior and exterior construction, and, subsequently, built-in furniture; and finally the complete lack of applied ornament and decoration.

Wright, however, developed from the earlier Chicago School of Louis Sullivan in a direction of his own. His work, recognized in Europe before it was widely accepted at home, is romantic, full of imaginative flights, very daring structurally, and highly personal. Among his finest homes in California are the Freeman House in Los Angeles, and the home of George Millard in Pasadena, both with low massive exterior walls constructed of decorated blocks; the Aline Barnsdall House in Hollywood, with its tapering walls and its geometric ornaments suggesting an Aztec or Mayan temple; and the Dr. Paul Hanna House at Stanford.

Perhaps no one has been more courageous in carrying the principles of functionalism to their final conclusions than Richard Neutra. His earlier work in Los Angeles, including his Garden Apartments, the Lovell House, the All-Plywood House, and his own Research House has been the subject of wide discussion. Because of his rigorous engineering training and his awareness of social issues, he has stressed the use of prefabricated building materials, engineering devices derived from utilitarian structures, economy and efficiency of construction, and constant emphasis on the relation of the house to the movement of its occupants. He has dealt admirably with the problems of mass housing and community planning. R. M. Schindler, another exponent of this modern school, has designed many "outdoor" houses of prefabricated materials, revealing the mingling of interior and exterior in his "garden with walls and roof," his use of disjunct planes, sun walls, and open areas. The beach house of Professor Alexander Kaun at Richmond and the V. McAlmon House on Waverly Drive, Los Angeles, are notable examples of his domestic work.

No survey of the contemporary architectural scene is complete without mention of the steady growth and improvement of commercial buildings. The office building exhibits a development from the steel skeleton structure embellished with various stylistic forms (as exemplified by the Mills Building and Hunter-Dulin Building, both in San Francisco) to the modern version of the skyscraper, with its simple mass and emphasis upon vertical and horizontal lines. Splendid examples of the latter are Timothy Fleuger's Four-Fifty Sutter, the Russ Building, and the Empire Hotel, originally built to house the Temple Methodist Episcopal Church and the William Taylor Hotel, in San Francisco. Excellent if less soaring are the Oakland Courthouse, fronting Lake Merritt, and the Times Building in Los Angeles. The United States Post Office in Stockton, the Los Angeles County Hospital and the new San Francisco Mint are both modern and monumental. The Los Angeles Public Library by Goodhue—a towering buttressed structure of modern design, set in a beautifully landscaped tract—is a noteworthy example of highly stylized traditional architecture.

Business has made further use of the modern formula. The dispensers of oil and gasoline are taking advantage of its possibilities, while many industrial plants, such as the Chrysler Motors of California and the United Aircraft Corporation in Los Angeles, have housed themselves in buildings that are modern in the best sense. Even bankers have discovered that a bank need not resemble a Greek temple or a Roman bath. Shops, bars, cocktail lounges, and theaters have all too frequently become ready outlets for the more tasteless examples of the modern mode. As elsewhere fashionable shopping districts have been remodeled with polished steel, chromium, glass bricks, and synthetic onyx. Hollywood and Wilshire Boulevards in Los Angeles, despite these modern innovations, are somewhat depressing. Better examples of modern commercial architecture are the Columbia Broadcasting System Center in Hollywood, by Howe and Lescaze, and the expansive but somewhat too colorful National Broadcasting Company Studios nearby.

Following the earthquake in 1934, which revealed the poor construction of many public schools in southern California, the State embarked on an extensive program of construction and remodeling of its public schools. The trim, rambling, well-lighted experimental schools in Santa Monica and Los Angeles, with their outdoor classrooms and ample play areas, ably illustrate the principles of modern planning. Other notable examples of efficient and economical planning are the Emerson junior and the Corona senior high schools in Los Angeles, by

Richard Neutra, and the John Adams junior high school in Santa Monica, by Marsh, Smith and Powell.

The mild climate of southern California affords unusual opportunities for the construction of numerous outdoor theaters and stadia. Among the most notable of these are the huge Hollywood Bowl, the Spreckels outdoor organ and amphitheater in Balboa Park at San Diego, the Los Angeles Memorial Coliseum, and the celebrated Rose Bowl in Pasadena.

The opening of the San Francisco-Oakland Bay Bridge, designed by C. H. Purcell of the State Department of Public Works, and the Golden Gate Bridge, by Joseph B. Strauss, mark the completion of outstanding engineering projects of modern times. The Bay Bridge is over eight miles long, with carefully planned approaches, two decks of traffic and an island tunnel; the Golden Gate Bridge, with its 6-lane roadway suspended from giant cables strung between two lofty steel towers, is the longest single-span suspension bridge in the world.

The 1939 Golden Gate International Exposition on Treasure Island in San Francisco Bay is a compelling example of architectural phantasy. Compared to the World's Fair in New York its architectural and decorative scheme is imaginative rather than realistic. The general scheme, not unlike that of the San Francisco Fair of 1915, is highly concentrated; it consists of long ranges of monumental buildings surrounding broad open areas and courts. The principal element is T-shaped with minor adjoining exhibits of the Pacific countries, and amusement areas, each designed with the same symmetry, formality and focalization of interest as the principal group. The architectural theme of the Exposition is drawn principally from the Far East. The design of the buildings with their log walls and pinnacles encrusted with elaborate sculpture, the massive pylons and gates and finally a massive spired tower forming the lofty climax of the group, is at once playful and impressive.

PART II
Signposts to City Scenes

Berkeley

Railroad Stations: University Ave. and 3rd St. for Southern Pacific Lines; University Ave. and West St. for Atchison, Topeka & Santa Fe Ry.
Interurban Stations: Shattuck Sq. for Interurban Electric Ry. transbay service; Bancroft and Telegraph Ave., main Berkeley station for Key System. All trains make frequent stops throughout the city; fare to San Francisco, 21¢.
Bus Station: University and San Pablo Aves. for Pacific Greyhound Lines, and National Trailways.
Airport: Berkeley Airport, Harrison and 4th Sts., no scheduled service.
Bridge: San Francisco-Oakland Bay Bridge approach, Ashby Ave. and East Shore Highway, toll 50¢, 1 to 5 passengers.
Streetcars: Within Berkeley and Oakland, fare 10¢ or one token, 7 tokens for 50¢; free transfers.
Taxis: 20¢ first ¼ m., 10¢ each ⅖ m. thereafter, 10¢ each 2 minutes waiting.

Accommodations: Eleven hotels.

Information Service: Chamber of Commerce, American Trust Bldg., Shattuck Ave. and Center St.; Berkeley Travel Bureau, 81 Shattuck Sq.; University general office, U. C. campus.

Radio Station: KRE (1370 kc.).
Theaters and Motion Picture Houses: Campus Little Theater, 2440 Bancroft Way; Women's City Club Little Theater, 3315 Durant Ave.; eight motion picture houses.
Golf: Tilden Park in Wildcat Canyon, Grizzly Peak Blvd. and Shasta Rd. 18 holes, greens fee $1.
Tennis: Sixteen public courts, at Grove, Garfield, Cordonices, Live Oak, James Kenney, and San Pablo playgrounds.
Swimming: Aquatic Park, Eastshore Highway, between University and Ashby Aves., swimming and boating facilities.
Boating: Berkeley municipal yacht harbor, W. end of University Ave., rowboats 30¢ per hour, sail and power boats $1 per hour.
Fishing: Shore line of San Francisco Bay, and yacht harbor wharf, bass and smelt; license required for adults; information and licenses at sporting goods stores.

Annual Events: Night Tennis Tournament, August, Live Oak Park; California-Stanford football game on even-numbered years.

BERKELEY (0-1,300 alt., 82,109 pop.), on a wide plain that stretches gently upward to a low range of hills, borders on the east shore of San Francisco Bay, facing the Golden Gate. At the upper edge of the city, against protective hills and wooded canyons, stand the buildings of the University of California. Viewed from the bay, the city seems to radiate from the white campus buildings.

Berkeley, however, is more than a college town. It is an industrial center, a business city, a suburban home for thousands of workers. Upward from the industrial waterfront extend myriads of small homes occupied by those who man the factories in East Bay cities and San Francisco. Office workers whose jobs are in San Francisco reside chiefly in north and southeast Berkeley. According to a 1937 survey, Berkeley has 11,000 residents who commute daily to San Francisco.

The two main shopping districts exemplify characteristic differences between the two parts of town. The Shattuck Avenue district, just west of the university campus, bears all the signs of ordinary commercial development. The Telegraph Avenue shopping area, extending southward from the main campus entrance, is full of young people and of shops reflecting their needs and interests.

South of the campus is a residential section with old homes of an architecture peculiar to Berkeley. The early inhabitants, aware of the corrosive effect of sea air on paint, utilized pitched roofs, walls of unpainted shingles, and vines to cover them, and built rustic houses that blended with a background of hills overgrown with oak, boxwood, manzanita, and bay. Bordering the campus on three sides are fraternity and sorority houses, some in the old tradition of Berkeley architecture, some designed in modern fashion. Vying with them in importance as student dwellings are modern stucco apartment buildings and old-fashioned boarding houses. On steep hills to the north, rising above the campus, cling those homes which have given Berkeley the right to be compared to Amalfi and Naples. Here every residence has a prospect of the bay, and some have canyon views as well; gardens hang to the edge of rock banks or trail in terraces down the hillside.

Along the waterfront, from Emeryville on the south to Albany on the north, is Berkeley's factory district where industrial plants produce $50,000,000 worth of commodities yearly, employ approximately 5,000 persons, and have an annual payroll of $5,000,000.

Berkeley took its name from George Berkeley, Bishop of Cloyne (1685-1753), the Irish philosopher who crossed the Atlantic to found an institution for evangelizing and educating the Indians, and who wrote "Westward, the course of empire takes it way." Henry Durant, one of the trustees of the College of California, hailed the words as prophetic. Bishop Berkeley's ideals were thought so proper for a young college town that the trustees adopted his name.

Originally, Berkeley was part of the 46,800-acre Rancho San Antonio granted to the Peralta family in 1820 by the Spanish Governor de Sola. American squatters had a false survey made in the 1850's, cutting off 7,000 acres of redwood timber and all the waterfront. They drove off

Peralta cattle, and had José Domingo Peralta jailed for trying to eject them from his land. In 1853, title to what is now Berkeley was purchased by American speculators for $82,000. The first American building in Berkeley was a roadhouse erected in 1853 near San Pablo Avenue and Delaware Street.

Foundation of the university gave impetus to Berkeley's growth, but other factors contributed. In 1874 there were only a few residences south of the campus, and two years later the population was only 948. Following 1884, however, when a large reservoir was built and water pipes were laid, growth was rapid. By 1906 streets were paved and huge residential tracts had been opened; the Santa Fe built a station, and the Key Route established 38-minute service to San Francisco, opening the way for large scale commuting. A determined effort failed to make Berkeley the State capital, but attracted notice to the town. Following the San Francisco earthquake and fire in 1906, many refugees moved permanently to Berkeley. In 1905 the population was 23,378; in 1907 it was 38,117.

A fire, starting in the hills and fanned by a strong wind, destroyed most of the city north of the campus in September, 1923. The disaster resulted in the creation of one of the most efficient fire-prevention systems in the United States and in a Disaster-Preparedness Plan. A deputy fire warden is on duty day and night in a Berkeley hills tower to insure against a repetition of the fire.

Berkeley's civic pride expresses itself in municipal administration, law enforcement, and education. In 1923 the city adopted the council-manager form of government and since has been regarded as a model in municipal administration. August Vollmer, Professor of Police Administration in the Department of Political Science at the University of California, as head of the police department, brought Berkeley national notice for his effective law enforcement. The department has established an unusually amicable relationship between citizenry and police, who are locally known as "Ph.D. policemen" or "supercops."

In addition to its other institutions, Berkeley has State schools for the deaf and blind.

THE UNIVERSITY OF CALIFORNIA

The 530-acre University of California campus extends across Berkeley from Oxford St. east to the hills and from Hearst Ave. south to Bancroft Way, on rising land that affords a splendid view of San Francisco Bay. The campus, originally a plain of oaks cut through by Strawberry Canyon, is now a beautifully landscaped park, with spacious white buildings, groves of eucalyptus, oak, and pine, lawns planted with shrubs and flowering trees, and brilliant gardens. Against the hills stand the Big C and the Campanile, visible for miles.

In 1896 Mrs. Phoebe Apperson Hearst financed an international competition for a comprehensive university building plan. The winning plan by Emile Benard was subsequently modified by himself and by

John Galen Howard, brought from New York as university architect. The Hellenic style of architecture and the main lines and vistas, with modifications, were determined by the original plan. Gaunt old South Hall, the first campus building, and sturdy old Bacon, once the library and art gallery, were built before the plan.

The State constitution of 1849 provided for the university, but it owes its inception largely to the efforts of two zealous educators and clergymen. The founding of the university was delayed for two decades by legislative disagreement, but Henry Durant and Samuel Hopkins Willey prepared privately for its coming. In 1853 Mr. Durant opened the Contra Costa Academy in Oakland, grandparent of the unborn institution; in 1860 the academy became the College of California under Mr. Willey's leadership; and finally in 1869 the college became the nucleus of the new university.

A charter was granted in 1868, but the College of California carried on instruction for 18 months until the work of organization was complete. By that time a faculty of 10 was ready to serve 40 students entering the new university. Registration and public interest increased in 1870 when a co-education plan was adopted.

In 1937-38 there were 14,672 students registered at Berkeley and 8,238 at the University of California at Los Angeles and at the branches. The principal branches are the Agricultural School at Davis, Lick Observatory, the Affiliated Colleges (medical and dental) in San Francisco, Scripps Institution of Biology at La Jolla, and Hastings College of the Law in San Francisco. There are also large graduate schools in Berkeley and Los Angeles, and a far-spread extension division. There was in the same year a faculty of 1,132 members. A home of celebrated scholars and a brilliant center of research, California has never, in recent qualitative ratings of American universities, ranked lower than fourth. Fifteen of its present faculty (1939) are listed in *American Men of Science.*

The Associated Students of the University of California, a nonprofit organization, is responsible for extracurricular activities on the campus. It operates a store and restaurant in Stephens Union, the students' building. It arranges intercollegiate athletic contests, using the funds to support debating, dramatics, sport, student publications, and many other activities. The A.S.U.C. building contains offices for the athletic coaches and student executives and clubrooms for the students.

The University of California has its student customs and traditions. The freshman wears his "beanie" and smokes only a corncob pipe on the campus. The other classes give wide berth to sophomore lawn, and none but a senior may sit in peace on senior bench. Each year three large rallies are held in the Greek Theater around a bonfire for which freshmen haul wood all day. Close to the fire in the diasome (the section around the pit) the men students sit by classes, the sophomores and seniors opposite the freshmen and juniors. A sophomore vigilance committee sees that all the men are with their classes. Those caught above, among the women and visitors, are tossed down to their places.

Among its graduates noted businessmen, educators, and scientists seem to be in greatest abundance, although many gifted writers, engineers, and public servants have studied at California. Among Alumni rising to the highest places are many from Latin America and the Orient. President Madero of Mexico, President Capina of Colombia, World Court Judge and Premier Wang Chung-Hui of China, and Sun Fo, Chinese Minister of Communications and son of Dr. Sun Yat-Sen, were all students at the university. Notable in America are former Secretary of the Interior Franklin K. Lane, former U. S. Commissioner of National Parks Stephen Mather, former Director of the U. S. Bureau of Mines Frederick Cottrell, and several U. S. Senators and California Governors. Novelists Irving Stone and Charles Norris, playwrights Richard Tully and Sidney Howard, cartoonist Rube Goldberg, and composer John Seymour are University of California alumni, and the names of others appear on Broadway and on the motion picture screen.

LOWER CAMPUS

(Buildings are open during class hours unless otherwise indicated; see map for location of points of interest.)

1. SATHER GATE, built of bronze and concrete above a bridge and roadway was erected with funds provided by Jane K. Sather in memory of Peder Sather. College meetings and rallies are often held here.
2. WHEELER HALL, housing classrooms and auditorium of the College of Arts and Sciences, is a neo-classic structure of white granite, adorned with Ionic colonnades, built in 1917 and named for Benjamin Ide Wheeler, university president from 1899 to 1919.
3. The LIFE SCIENCE BUILDING, a majestic neo-Classic structure with rusticated base, modified Corinthian columns, high attic story and fine bronze grilles, was completed in 1930 under the supervision of Arthur Brown. In addition to the life sciences and their allied departments, it contains the MUSEUM OF VERTEBRATE ZOOLOGY (*open to students only*), the Institute of Experimental Biology, the Laboratory of the State Board of Health, and the HERBARIUM (*open 8:30-12, 1-5 Mon.-Fri.; 8:30-12 Sat.*)
4. The AGRICULTURE GROUP consists of Hilgard Hall, Giannini Hall, and Agriculture Hall, all of modified Italian Renaissance design, with corner quoins and tile roofs. In the greenhouses (*not open*) nearby experiments are conducted in plant breeding.
5. The PRESIDENT'S HOUSE (*private*), completed in 1911, is constructed of grayish tan sandstone in Italian Renaissance design. Two marble lions guard the entrance, which is in the form of an arcaded loggia. It contains rare old tapestries, among which is a Beauvais dating from the sixteenth century. *Portrait of a Man,* by Lawrence, is also in this building.

6. HAVILAND HALL, the School of Education, contains the Alexis F. Lange Educational Library and an exhibition of photography, handicraft, and etchings.

7. The STUDENTS' OBSERVATORY (*open 8-10 p.m. first Sat. each month*) is a group of domed buildings completely equipped for the study of astronomy. It contains 5- and 8-inch refracting telescopes. The university's main astronomical work, however, is done at Lick Observatory (*see TOUR 2b*).

8. The SCHOOL OF ARCHITECTURE BUILDING, a rambling shingled structure with a fireproof library wing, contains laboratories, drawing and modeling rooms, and architectural exhibition rooms.

9. The ENGINEERING GROUP comprises the Engineering Laboratory, the Engineering Design Building, Hesse Hall, and the Mechanics' Building. In the Engineering Laboratory is one of the world's largest testing machines (capacity 4,000,000 pounds) for trial of structural members. Materials for Boulder Dam, the San Francisco-Oakland Bay Bridge, and other important public projects were tested here.

10. LAWSON ADIT, extending under Charter Hill, a shaft constructed by students of mining engineering, is a laboratory for mine-fire and mine-rescue work, and for actual mining experience.

11. The HEARST MEMORIAL MINING BUILDING, of Italian Renaissance design, was given in 1907 by Phoebe Apperson Hearst in memory of her husband, Senator George Hearst. It has classrooms for mining engineering students, the Pacific Coast Experiment Station of the United States Bureau of Mines, and the MUSEUM OF PALEONTOLOGY (*open 8-5 Mon. and Fri., 9-12 Sat.*), which contains the largest paleontological collection on the Pacific Coast.

12. The ANTHROPOLOGY MUSEUM, houses an extensive anthropological exhibit.

13. BACON HALL, a red brick structure, is headquarters of the department of geological sciences and the division of seismology. Its GEOLOGICAL SCIENCES EXHIBIT is *open to the public 8:30-12 and 1-5 Mon. and Fri.; 8:30-12 Sat.*

14. The CHEMISTRY GROUP includes Gilman Hall, built in 1918 and named for Daniel Coit Gilman, the university's second president, who organized the chemistry department in 1872.

15. The HYDRAULIC TIDAL MODEL TESTING BASIN was built by the U. S. War Department for investigation of problems of erosion and deposition in the rivers and harbors and on the shore line of the Pacific Coast.

16. The CHARLES FRANKLIN DOE MEMORIAL LIBRARY (*open during regular terms 8 a.m.-10 p.m. Mon.-Fri., 8-6 Sat., 1-10 Sun.*) has a collection of more than 900,000 volumes and more than 16,000 serial publications. The original collection was made early in university history from the Michael Reese fund of $50,000; since then the library has acquired the Henry Douglas Bacon Art and Library Collections; the Library of French Thought; the Alexander F. Morrison Library for recreational reading; and the Bancroft Library with its

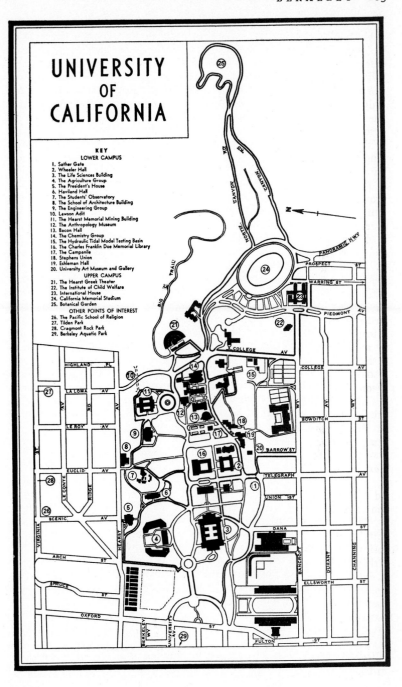

UNIVERSITY
OF
CALIFORNIA

KEY
LOWER CAMPUS
1. Sather Gate
2. Wheeler Hall
3. The Life Sciences Building
4. The Agriculture Group
5. The President's House
6. Haviland Hall
7. The Students' Observatory
8. The School of Architecture Building
9. The Engineering Group
10. Lawson Adit
11. The Hearst Memorial Mining Building
12. The Anthropology Museum
13. Bacon Hall
14. The Chemistry Group
15. The Hydraulic Tidal Model Testing Basin
16. The Charles Franklin Doe Memorial Library
17. The Campanile
18. Stephens Union
19. Eshleman Hall
20. University Art Museum and Gallery
UPPER CAMPUS
21. The Hearst Greek Theater
22. The Institute of Child Welfare
23. International House
24. California Memorial Stadium
25. Botanical Garden
OTHER POINTS OF INTEREST
26. The Pacific School of Religion
27. Tilden Park
28. Cragmont Rock Park
29. Berkeley Aquatic Park

75,000 volumes and manuscripts relating to Spanish-American and western American history. The neoclassic building, constructed in 1911, is adorned with Corinthian pilasters which rise in support of a heavy modillioned cornice. The School of Librarianship and the Bureau of Public Administration are in this building.

17. The CAMPANILE (*elevator service 9-5 daily, fee 10¢*), designed by John Galen Howard, was built in 1914 through a bequest by Jane K. Sather. Designed in the Italian Renaissance style, with pyramidal roof, belfry, and pinnacles, it recalls the lofty campanile in St. Marco square in Venice. It is constructed of granite, 397 feet high, 36 feet square, with a clock on its four sides, and an observation platform at the top. The belfry contains 12 bells, cast in England. A Gutzon Borglum bust of Lincoln stands at the south base.

18. STEPHENS UNION is of Tudor Gothic design with turrets, buttresses, leaded casements and oriel bays. Dedicated in 1923 to the late Henry Morse Stephens, professor of history at the university, it is the center of student social life and extra-curricular activities.

19. ESHLEMAN HALL is the headquarters of student publications, including the *Daily Californian,* the *Blue and Gold,* the *Pelican,* and the *Occident.* It was built in 1930 and dedicated to John Martin Eshleman, an alumnus and former Lieutenant Governor of California.

20. UNIVERSITY ART MUSEUM AND GALLERY (*open 10-5 weekdays, subject to change*), is a low brick structure adorned with exterior frescoes and two Chinese lions guarding the entrance. Among its permanent exhibits are a portion of the Albert Bender collection of Chinese art and a collection of Russian icons.

Other buildings on the lower campus include California Hall, containing the administrative office; Le Conte Hall, housing the departments of physics and optometry; Bowles Hall, the only dormitory on the campus; Boalt Hall of Law; and South Hall, a notable example of the architecture of the elegant eighties.

UPPER CAMPUS

21. The HEARST GREEK THEATER is designed in the manner of an ancient amphitheater. Built of concrete, it has a semicircular auditorium seating 7,154 persons, and a stage adorned with Doric columns and pilasters. The theater, which is the center of university musical and dramatic activities, was presented by William Randolph Hearst in 1903. Classic dramas are occasionally given.

22. The INSTITUTE OF CHILD WELFARE, 2739 Bancroft Way, an off-campus university institution organized through the Laura Spellman Rockefeller Memorial Foundation, carries on a series of long-time research projects in the psychological development of children. A nursery school serves as a basis for these studies.

23. INTERNATIONAL HOUSE (*open by arrangement*), Bancroft Way and Piedmont Ave., is a gift of John D. Rockefeller, Jr., and was completed in 1930 as a residence for foreign students, of whom 450,

Cities I

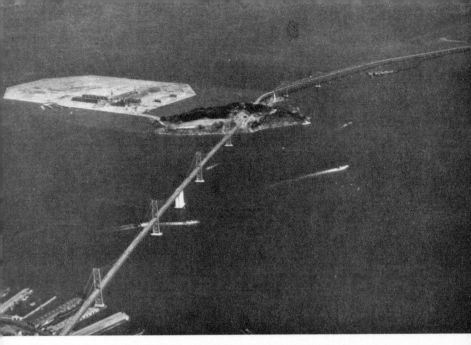

SAN FRANCISCO-OAKLAND BAY BRIDGE

GOLDEN GATE BRIDGE

SAN FRANCISCO SKYLINE

IN THE HARBOR, SAN FRANCISCO

DEVASTATED AREA. SAN FRANCISCO FIRE AND EARTHQUAKE (1906)

CALIFORNIA STREET FROM NOB HILL (1900) SAN FRANCISCO

ELEPHANT TOWERS AND TOWER OF THE SUN

GOLDEN GATE INTERNATIONAL EXPOSITION

COURT OF PACIFICA

CALIFORNIA STATE AND SAN FRANCISCO BUILDINGS

GOLDEN GATE INTERNATIONAL EXPOSITION

Bufano

DR. SUN YAT SEN MEMORIAL

CHINESE QUARTER

SAN FRANCISCO

THE CAPITOL, SACRAMENTO

SUTTER'S FORT SACRAMENTO

RESIDENTIAL SECTION, FRESNO

OLD WHALING STATION, MONTEREY

representing 30 nationalities, live here. Of modified Spanish-Moorish design it is distinguished by its deep arcades, tile roofs and lofty domed towers. Lectures and concerts are given in the auditorium.

24. CALIFORNIA MEMORIAL STADIUM, seating capacity 78,-000, was built in 1923 at a cost of $1,750,000, in memory of students who died in the World War. Football, soccer, and rugby games, and commencement exercises are held here.

25. BOTANICAL GARDEN (*open 9-4 daily*), in Strawberry Canyon above the Memorial Stadium, is a 35-acre tract devoted to plant culture. The collection includes 5,000 rare rhododendrons, and 2,000 cacti and succulents, growing in natural settings of sand and stone. There is an open-air theater, a memorial to Stephen Mather, first director of the National Park Service, in a five-acre tract of pine and redwood.

OTHER POINTS OF INTEREST

26. The PACIFIC SCHOOL OF RELIGION (*open by appointments, guides*), 1798 Scenic Ave., is a graduate theological school, interdenominational and co-educational. An A.B. degree is a prerequisite for entrance, and the school trains for all branches of religious work. There are three buildings, the Administration Building of Gothic architecture in gray cut stone; the gray stucco Dormitory, of Tudor design; and the HOLBROOK MEMORIAL LIBRARY (*open 8-6 Mon.; 7-6 Tues.-Fri., 9-12 Sat.*), the twin of the Administration Building in structure. The library houses a collection of 30,000 volumes, including a "Breeches" Bible, Geneva, 1560; Babylonian cuneiform tablets; fourth century Biblical inscriptions on papyrus; and an extremely rare copy of the inscription on the Nestorian Monument in China. An archeological exhibit has relics dating from 3500 B.C. to the beginning of the Christian era.

27. TILDEN PARK, in Wildcat Canyon over the hills from Berkeley, is a part of the 10,000-acre East Bay Regional Park. Lately a rough, hilly country of manzanita and scrub oaks, and abounding in birds and small mammals, the park, improved with WPA labor, includes a golf course, scenic drives, and three camp districts.

28. CRAGMONT ROCK PARK, Regal Rd. and Hillside Ave., a neatly landscaped four-acre plot, rises from the lawns around it to the abrupt outcropping of rock that gives the park its name, and at 800 feet altitude has a lookout station with a fine view of San Francisco Bay, the bridges, and Golden Gate directly opposite.

29. BERKELEY AQUATIC PARK, flanked for more than a mile by the Berkeley bayshore and US 40, is built in the bay, and is composed largely of the lagoon thus formed. Water depth ranges from 3 to 15 feet and is controlled by floodgates. Small boats can be rented at the boathouse, there are facilities for model yacht racing, and the lagoon is a wildfowl sanctuary.

Fresno

Railroad Stations: Mariposa and H Sts. for Southern Pacific Lines; Tulare and Q Sts. for Atchison, Topeka and Santa Fe Ry.
Bus Stations: Mariposa and H Sts. for Pacific Greyhound, Huntington State Lines, Moyer Stages; Mariposa St. and Broadway for Santa Fe Trailways.
Airport: Chandler Municipal Airport, 1.5 m. W. on Kearney Blvd. for United Air Lines, Transcontinental & Western Air; taxi 50¢.
Taxis: 25¢ for first ½ m., 10¢ for each additional ¼ m.; no charge for extra passengers.
City Busses: Basic fare 7¢, "short haul" fare 5¢ in business district, tokens, 3 for 20¢, free transfers.

Accommodations: Fifty-nine hotels, six tourist camps.

Information Service: San Joaquin Valley Tourist & Travel Assn., 1044 Fulton St.; California State Automobile Assn. (AAA), 660 Van Ness Ave.; National Auto Club, 1252 Broadway; Fresno County Chamber of Commerce, 2345 Fresno St.; California State Chamber of Commerce, Fulton and Tulare Sts.; Central California Tourist Assn., T. W. Patterson Bldg.

Radio Stations: KMJ (580 kc.); KARM (1310 kc.).
Theaters and Motion Picture Houses: White Theater, 1300 Broadway, stock and road shows; University Street Playhouse, 1000 University Ave., college plays; 8 motion picture houses.
Swimming: Frank H. Ball Playground pool, Mayor Ave. and Inyo St., 10¢, children 5¢; Crown Plunge, 1730 H St., 25¢, children 15¢; De Vaux's Del Mar Rose Pool, Moroa and Rialto St., 25¢, children 15¢; Prescott's Swimming Pool, California St., 20¢, children 10¢; Weymouth's Swimming Pool, White Bridge Rd., 25¢, children 15¢.
Golf: Fort Washington Golf Club, Blackstone Ave. and Friant Rd., 18 holes, $1 weekdays, $2 Sat., Sun., and holidays, monthly tickets, $10; Fresno municipal Golf Course, Herndon Ave., ½ m. S. on US 99, 18 holes, 50¢ weekdays, 75¢ Sat., Sun., and holidays, monthly tickets, $4.50.
Tennis: Roeding Park, Belmont and Thorne Aves., free, four lighted courts 25¢ a half hour. Courts at Fresno State College open to public when not in use by students.
Annual Events: Raisin Day, second Sat. in May; West Coast Relays, same day, at Fresno State College; Fresno District Fair, Sept.; Fresno Junior Tennis tourney, about Oct. 1.

FRESNO (292 alt., 52,513 pop.), world's "raisin center" and principal marketing, shipping and purchasing point for the fertile San Joaquin Valley, is almost in the geographical center of the State.

Tall modern buildings rise abruptly from the flat valley floor, surrounded by residential sections planted with trees to provide shade in the sweltering heat of summer. The business district, in the central and oldest part of town, grew around the railroad station, with the streets parallel to the tracks and diagonal to the cardinal points. Later streets were squared with the compass, and a set of 45-degree intersections resulted, all around the original square. Residential preference has extended the city mainly to the northward and eastward, where homes are set back from the street along broad avenues lined with eucalyptus and palm trees.

From the city limits the vineyards radiate in seemingly endless rows, set exactly 10 feet apart. The grapes ripen in August, September, and October, and are placed on trays to dry in the sun. With these agricultural environs, and with the country's largest fig gardens only four miles away, Fresno naturally is predominantly a farming community, despite its skyscrapers, neon lights, modern store fronts, and busy traffic. Farm markets are held on Fresno Street alongside Courthouse Park on Tuesdays, Thursdays, and Saturdays, and fresh vegetables, fruits, and flowers are sold direct to the consumer. Farm workers and growers throng the streets on Saturday nights, and the Fresno District Fair in September is an event of major local importance

Across the Southern Pacific tracks, opposite the business district, is the foreign section where curious articles of food are displayed in shop windows, Spanish motion pictures and Japanese plays are advertised, and men of many nations idle on the sidewalks. Armenians outnumber all others in the 15 percent of Fresno's population that is of foreign extraction. Forced out of Armenia by hardships and persecution, they found the Fresno area similar in soil and crops to that of their homeland, and settled here in numbers. There are two Armenian restaurants specializing in native dishes, three Armenian weekly newspapers, and many small retail businesses are Armenian-owned.

Fresno, unlike many California cities, is purely an American growth. Spanish and Mexican expeditions passed up the site as desolate and barren. Indian troubles scared away settlers of the period preceding the gold rush, and the Forty-niners, bound for the Sierra foothills, hurried across the valley to the diggings. After the gold rush, the Americans turned to stock raising, and the site of Fresno supported thousands of cattle.

The first permanent settlement on this site is supposed to have been made in the 1860's by A. J. Manssen, a Hollander, who sank a well, built a watering trough, and put up this sign:

HORSE RESTAURANT
Bring Your Horse in
One Horse by Fresh Water One Bet
One Day Hay Water 3 Bet

By "bet" he meant twelve and a half cents, a "bit."

A few families joined Manssen, but the place remained "the sorriest and most woe-begone little settlement on the map" until 1872, when it became a station on the Central Pacific Railroad, which pushed through the valley that year. The railroad builders staked out a town, which they called Fresno (Sp., ash tree) Station, for the name of the county. The ash trees were in the foothills, and not near the embryo town.

In 1874 Millerton, the only important settlement in the area, voted to relinquish the county seat to Fresno Station; and soon after, practically the whole population of Millerton moved to the new county seat in order to be on the railroad line. In those days Fresno's main street was "a rough depression, billowy, dusty in dry weather and in winter a mudhole for its three blocks to the railroad station." The countryside was so bare that boys had to play hide-and-seek in the graveyard. Cows, horses, dogs, and pigs wandered about in the streets, and flocks of sheep were driven through the town.

With the spread of controlled irrigation and the realization that the soil was extremely fertile, new crops were developed and the town grew fast. Partly through the efforts of Agoston Haraszthy, Hungarian financier and investor, grape raising was popularized in California (*see AGRICULTURE*). Americans planted vines in their wheat fields. Italians, French, and Swiss started growing grapes on 20-acre parcels acquired for that purpose.

The dry white wine made by foreign growers was of indifferent quality, but the continuous sunlight led naturally, after about 1874, to the preparation of raisins. An output of 103,000,000 pounds in 1894 overloaded the market, and the price dropped to two cents a pound. The Raisin Growers Association, a co-operative group organized in 1898 for the protection and efficient handling of the raisin industry, still controls the bulk of the crop. During the World War profits were large because raisins were a convenient food to pack and ship. When it was discovered that raisins are rich in iron, an advertising campaign was launched with the slogan "Have you had your iron today?" and raisins sold in five-cent packages at candy counters. Today 60 per cent of the United States raisin production comes from the Fresno district.

In 1886, Frank Roeding and his son had begun experiments with Smyrna fig culture at their own expense and in the face of open ridicule from other horticulturists. In June, 1889, they learned the secret of caprification (cross-fertilization of the Smyrna fig by the fig wasp), and the industry was at last able to compete with foreign importations.

With a population of 12,470 in 1900, Fresno adopted its first city charter. Agriculture progressed rapidly in the next ten years. Cotton growing was introduced in the valley and cotton is now a leading product. Manufacture of sweet wines supplanted that of the dry wines.

Manufacturing kept pace with agricultural growth, and Fresno now ranks fifth among California cities as an industrial center. It has 370 manufacturing establishments including flour and lumber mills, machine shops and foundries, potteries, brickwork, and soap factories.

POINTS OF INTEREST

COURTHOUSE SQUARE, Van Ness Ave. at Mariposa St., a central park two blocks square, is dominated by the neo-Classic FRESNO COUNTY COURTHOUSE, a symmetrical three-story edifice with flat balustraded roof, pedimented Corinthian entrance portico, and a dome and cupola. A fountain, the BOY WITH THE LEAKING BOOT, the figure of a lad holding a worn shoe with water coming out a hole in the toe, was presented by the Salvation Army in 1895. The STATUE OF DR. CHESTER ROWELL, by Haig Patigian, shows the doctor at a patient's bedside. Dr. Rowell (1844-1912) was an early mayor of Fresno, builder of the city's first skyscraper, and a State senator. There is also a bandstand where weekly concerts are held in summer.

The FRESNO MEMORIAL AUDITORIUM, 2435 Fresno St., erected by the city in 1932 in honor of the war dead, is a massive concrete structure in modern classic style, used for civic gatherings, concerts, and dances. On the balcony is the FRESNO COUNTY HISTORICAL MUSEUM (*open 3-5 weekdays*), containing firearms, gold-mining equipment, and articles used by early settlers.

FRESNO STATE COLLEGE, 1101 University Ave., an institution for the training of teachers, has a student body of about 2,000. Most of the buildings on the 27-acre campus are modern two-story concrete structures with red tile roofs, designed in the Spanish mission tradition with arched windows and arcades. The REFERENCE LIBRARY (*open 8-5 Mon.-Fri.*) in the main group of buildings has 32,000 volumes. The college was organized in 1921 through union of the local junior college and the normal school. Summer school is held at Huntington Lake (*see TOUR 3b*).

ROEDING PARK, Belmont and Thorne Aves., 157 acres in area, is planted with 650 species of trees and shrubs, through which guinea hens and peafowl wander. The ZOO (*open 9-5 daily*) has about 90 animals and 170 wildfowl.

The JAPANESE BUDDHIST TEMPLE (*open 9-8 daily*), 1340 Kern St., erected in 1902, is a three-story building with stucco finish, scrolled tile roof, and an ornamental carved entrance of white wood with swastikas set into the portico. Some of the sacred ashes of Buddha, brought from India, are guarded in the temple. The congregation of 700 is served by two Japanese priests. Services are held Sunday evenings at 8 o'clock before an altar finished in gold leaf. Special services in April celebrate the birth of Buddha.

The SUN MAID RAISIN PLANT (*open 8:30-4:30 weekdays, July-Jan.; guides*), Butler Ave. and Hazlewood Blvd., the largest raisin-packing plant in the world, occupies many-windowed gray concrete buildings that cover several acres. Trucks deliver sun-dried grapes from the vineyards. The grapes are run through a series of machines that grade, stem, seed, and process them, after which they are packaged for the trade. Tiny packages, 15 or 20 raisins in each, are prepared for sale in China, where it is believed that eating raisins insures the birth of male children. The seeds are bricked for fuel, and the stems are sold for cattle feed.

POINTS OF INTEREST IN ENVIRONS

General Grant National Park, 60 *m.*; Sequoia National Park, 73.5 *m.* (*see SEQUOIA AND GENERAL GRANT NATIONAL PARKS*); Yosemite National Park, 75.8 *m.* (*see YOSEMITE NATIONAL PARK*).

Hollywood

Bus Stations: Union Bus Terminal, 1625 N. Cahuenga Blvd. for Greyhound Lines, Inland Stages, Pacific Electric Motor Coach; Pasadena-Ocean Park Stage Line, Inc., 1646 N. Cahuenga Blvd., for Union Pacific busses.
Airports: Union Air Terminal, 2627 N. Hollywood Way, Burbank, 9 m. N., for Transcontinental & Western Air, Inc., United Air Lines, and Western Air Express; Grand Central Air Terminal, 1224 Airway, Glendale, 6 m. NE. for American Airlines and Pan-American Airways; taxi to both airports, $1.50-$2.
Taxis: 20¢ first ¼ mile, 10¢ each additional ½ mile.
Streetcars and Busses: Fare 6¢ (streetcars only) and 10¢; 20¢ to Santa Monica.

Accommodations: 21 hotels.

Information Service: Automobile Club of Southern California, 6902 Sunset Blvd.; Hollywood Chamber of Commerce, 6520 Sunset Blvd.

Radio Stations: KNX (1050 kc.); KFWB (950 kc.); KMTR (570 kc.); KFI (640 kc.); KECA (1430 kc.).
Theaters and Motion Picture Houses: Hollywood Bowl, Bolton Road 1 block S. of junction Highland Ave. and Cahuenga Blvd.; Pilgrimage Play Amphitheater, 2580 N. Highland Ave.; El Capitán Theater, 6838 Hollywood Blvd.; Hollytown Playhouse, 1743 New Hampshire Ave.; Ben Bard Playhouse, Wilshire Blvd. and Fairfax Ave.; road shows. Hollywood Playhouse, 1735 N. Vine St., Federal Theater shows. Columbia Square Playhouse, Sunset Blvd. and Gower St.; CBS broadcasts; National Broadcasting Co. studios, Sunset Blvd. and Vine St., daily broadcast programs. Twenty motion picture houses.
Boxing and Wrestling: Hollywood Legion Stadium, 1628 N. El Centro St.
Tennis: Poinsettia Playground, 7431 Willoughby Ave., day and night play, free.
Sightseeing Tours of Motion Picture Studios: Tanner Gray Line Motor Tours, (enter only Warner Bros.-First National Studios, Burbank), leave Biltmore Hotel, 5th and Olive Sts., on weekdays, $4.50 per person; busses pass all other major studios, but do not enter. Clifton Motor Tours, Inc. leave from 618 S. Olive St. daily, $1.50 per person; busses pass all major studios, but do not enter.

Annual Events: Easter Sunrise Services, Hollywood Bowl; "Symphonies under the Stars," Hollywood Bowl, summer, several times weekly; Pilgrimage Play, in Amphitheater, July and August.

HOLLYWOOD (385 alt., 153,294 pop.), motion picture center of the world and as such the focal point of a billion-dollar industry, is popularly regarded as a separate entity but is officially the Hollywood District of Los Angeles. Shaped roughly like the state of New York, it fits into the parent city like a piece of a jigsaw puzzle, occupying the same alluvial plain as Los Angeles, and lying eight miles west of the city's center and twelve miles from the Pacific Ocean. The northern half of the Hollywood District spreads upward in a network of winding roads, into the tawny foothills of the Santa Monica Mountains (known locally as the Hollywood Hills), which constitute a natural boundary in that direction.   Hyperion Avenue and Riverside Drive, along the Los Angeles River, mark the eastern limits.   To the south, at Melrose Avenue, Hollywood merges into Los Angeles; to the west it is' linked to Beverly Hills.

Hollywood Boulevard, running due east and west, is the main thoroughfare.   Known simply as "the Boulevard," it is a clue to Hollywood's character: a contrast in sophisticated luxury and small-town naivete.   Shops, office buildings, movie houses, and skyscrapers make it the central business and amusement district; yet it is also a promenade where people saunter along to look at one another and at window displays.   Costumes worn on the Boulevard, as elsewhere in Hollywood, are informal and colorful.   There are men in polo shirts and sports jackets; women in a variety of costumes, slacks and dark glasses predominating.   White is popular from spring to fall.   At night thousands of names and slogans are outlined in neon, and searchlight beams often pierce the sky, perhaps announcing a motion picture premiere, perhaps the opening of a new hamburger stand.

The business district centers at Hollywood Boulevard and Vine Street, a corner made famous by Hollywood columnists and magazine writers.   Just south of the Boulevard, on the east side of Vine Street, is the Hollywood Brown Derby restaurant, where movie fans swarm at the entrance with autograph books in hand, waiting for celebrities.

South of the Boulevard are other principal thoroughfares, laid out according to the cardinal points of the compass.   Most of them are lined with green parkways, pepper trees and palms—familiar sights to those who remember the chase scenes in old two-reel comedies.   Between Sunset and Santa Monica Boulevards and Hollywood Boulevard is an agglomeration of stores, taverns, small hotels, bungalow courts, drive-in markets, apartment houses, and small homes.

Some of the houses on side streets are small-town style frame dwellings with lawns, hedges, and flower gardens.   The prevailing type, however, is the one-story stucco bungalow: white, green, yellow, pink, red, or blue, roofed in red tile, with lawn and gardens front and rear and a driveway leading back to a two-car garage.   A palm may grow on the lawn and perhaps a pepper tree in the strip between sidewalk and curb.   Sprinklers water the grass and flowers in late afternoons and early evenings during the rainless summer months.

In contrast to this suburban aspect of Hollywood are the small independent studios on Sunset Boulevard near Gower Street, which grind out features, westerns, comedies, and "quickies."   Cowboys in chaps and sombreros and extra girls in the traditional slacks and dark glasses, bright kerchiefs protecting their freshly waved hair, lunch at corner hot dog stands or gossip and talk shop.   Even "featured" players in make-up often cross Sunset to a line of hamburger stands for snacks between shots.

Farther west on Sunset Boulevard, toward Beverly Hills, is a section popularly known as "the Strip."   Here are the Trocadero and other movie colony night spots, high-priced antique shops, salons, gift shops, restaurants hung with Venetian blinds, *couturiers* and *modistes,* theatrical agencies; most of them white-painted modified Georgian-Colonial buildings with green shutters.

Motion picture influence is visible in another purely Hollywood contribution: drive-in barbecue stands, restaurants, and bars, built of papier-mache to represent fairy-story castles, tumble-down houses, gargantuan fish, ice cream cones, and lop-eared puppies. Each stands on a large parking area, and waitresses in slacks and brass-buttoned jackets hook trays over open car windows to serve the customers in their automobiles.

Hollywood probably attracts more types and nationalities than any city of its size in the world. Here are the nobility, ex-nobility, and pseudo-nobility of a dozen countries; the artistically inclined from every corner of the world who aspire to movie jobs; and average Americans who live here because they like the climate, or were born here. Precocious children from all over the country are brought to Hollywood in hope of breaking into motion pictures. Dozens of dance studios and dramatic schools attempt to train children and adults for screen careers. About 75 percent of the population is connected in some way with the motion picture industry.

Many actors and extras still live in Hollywood, but most of the stars prefer Beverly Hills, Bel Air, Brentwood, and ranches in the San Fernando Valley. In the first flush of cinema prosperity Hollywood society went in for extravagance and informality, evidenced by carefree parties and sporty cars. Now top-flight movie society affects white ties and evening gowns, with the accent on dignity and position, but the yardstick of eminence is still the number of digits in the salary.

The first habitation on the site of Hollywood was an adobe dwelling built by Don Tomás Urquidez in 1853. In the sixties and early seventies much of the valley was laid out in 160-acre farms, and families of immigrants from all over the world settled here. The present name dates from the boom of 1887 when Horace H. Wilcox opened a real estate subdivision, which his wife christened Hollywood.

In 1896, the year T. L. Tally opened his "Phonograph and Vitascope Parlor" in Los Angeles, with four peep holes for spectators, Hollywood was still a crossroads where the arrival of the Toluca stage to San Fernando Valley was the event of the day. Open country separated it from Los Angeles. One of the first ordinances of the village government, incorporated in 1903 by vote of the 177 male inhabitants, made it a misdemeanor to drive bands of more than 2,000 sheep through the streets.

In 1910, when it had a population of 4,000, Hollywood traded its civic independence for a share in Los Angeles' water supply, but held tenaciously to its identity, choosing to appeal as a home-owning center and emphasizing its schools and churches, frostless citrus groves, winter flower and vegetable gardens.

At about this time an ironic fate selected this ultra-respectable, church-going village as headquarters for a new form of amusement: the motion picture. Independent film companies, trying to escape a monopoly in the East, took refuge in Hollywood and under its almost continuous sun began shooting scenes in orange grove and canyon, ranch house and barn.

The Horsley brothers, operating under the name of the Nestor Company, were the first producers to settle in Hollywood; they leased the old Blondeau Tavern and barn at Sunset Boulevard and Gower Street in October, 1911, converted it into a studio, and made the first Hollywood picture, *The Law of the Range*. Wilcox had opened the original subdivision as a temperance colony, and the sudden appearance of boisterous show people and cowboys parading the hitherto quiet streets in the best wild-west fashion came as a rude shock to the inhabitants. The villagers at first considered the "fillums" and those who made them disreputable and somewhat sinful, and resented their intrusion. But the pioneers were followed by other independents, and eventually members of the eastern producers' trust took advantage of the climate and low rents in Hollywood. When Cecil B. De Mille moved his troupe west, he is said to have had tickets for Flagstaff, Arizona. Deciding that Flagstaff didn't "look western enough" he too went on to Hollywood.

The town boomed. In the 1920's motion pictures became a billion dollar industry. Sound films necessitated better writing, direction, acting, and management. There was an increasing trek westward from Broadway and other centers. While "Hollywood" is commonly used to designate the motion picture industry as a whole, most of the major producing units are not in the Hollywood District, but are scattered through the outlying areas.

In 1935 the motion picture industry in the United States averaged more than $20,000,000 a week income from attendance; its financial center is Wall Street, but its workshops and factory is Hollywood (*see THE MOVIES*). Because of locally available talent, Hollywood is also an important broadcasting center. Major companies have large local studios in which many Nation-wide broadcasts originate.

Other industries have grown up in connection with motion pictures. Two international film companies manufacture hundreds of thousands of feet of "celluloid." The make-up business, founded to supply studios with grease paint and powder, outgrew its origin when the appeal of goods stamped "Hollywood" was felt. Lipsticks, rouges, creams, powders, unguents, and lotions are now turned out on a mass production basis for Nation-wide distribution.

POINTS OF INTEREST

HOLLYWOOD BOWL (*always open; adm. prices vary during season*) end of Bolton Rd., 1 block S. of Highland Ave. and Cahuenga Blvd. intersection, is a 60-acre natural amphitheater framed by chaparral-covered hills. The white-walled platform is surmounted by a removable sounding shell, designed by Lloyd Wright, and the acoustics are such that an unaided voice on the stage can be heard in the back row. "Symphonies under the Stars," held yearly since 1922, grand opera, and the Easter Sunrise Service are presented here. The bowl has more than 20,000 seats, and the sloping runways provide standing room for 10,000. Near the entrance is a large bowl for voluntary contributions. The top is covered with wire netting and the accumulated coins are removed only at the end of the season. No one has ever tampered with the netting to pilfer the heap of silver and copper.

The PILGRIMAGE PLAY AMPHITHEATER (*open during performances; adm. 50¢-$1.50*), 2580 Highland Ave., is a natural amphitheater where a play based on the life of Christ is enacted nightly during July and August. The Pilgrimage Play was written by Mrs. Christine Wetherill Stevenson in collaboration with H. Ellis Reed, and first produced in 1920. A large wooden cross on the hillside, lighted at night, is a guidepost to the theater.

The JAPANESE GARDENS (*open 10-6 daily; adm. 25¢, children with adults free*), Orchid and N. Sycamore Aves. (also known as the California Scenic Gardens and Home), were built and decorated at a cost of $2,000,000 by Adolph and Eugene Bernheimer in 1913. The elaborately landscaped hillside estate contains more than 30,000 trees, many rare tropical shrubs, several goldfish pools, and a Japanese shrine. Overlooking the Japanese terraces is the 14-room Yama Shiro, (castle on the hill), designed in the manner of a Buddhist Temple of the ancient Shoguns. It is filled with rare objects of Japanese and Buddhist art. There is also a miniature garden with dwarf trees, canals, waterfalls and reproductions of ancient dwellings.

GRAUMAN'S CHINESE THEATER, 6925 Hollywood Blvd., a spectacular adaptation of the Chinese style of architecture, designed by Meyer and Haller, is the scene of Hollywood's super premieres, where stars and film moguls attend opening performances of new films with the ballyhoo of searchlights, floodlights, microphones and loudspeakers, and roped-off aisles covered with carpet.

The facade, in the form of a U-shaped forecourt with a Chinese gate, set between terminal piers, suggests the approach to an ancient temple garden. Four large obelisks, embellished with oriental decorations, surmount the two colossal piers. In the forecourt is a grove of palm trees and other shrubs, and concrete slabs bearing the hand and foot prints of stars and their messages of congratulation. At the end of the forecourt a colorful pagoda forms the entrance to the theater, roofed in bronze aged to the color of jade green, and supported by two coral-red octagonal columns mounted with wrought-iron masks. Under the curved roof, and deeply set between the flanking piers, is a great stone dragon, modeled in relief on a slab 30 feet high.

The EGYPTIAN THEATER, 6712 Hollywood Blvd., now a second-run movie house, is the spot where the Hollywood premieres originated as a scintillating social event, with the showing of *Robin Hood* in 1922. An Egyptian god in the forecourt bears out the motif of the building.

The CROSSROADS OF THE WORLD, 6673 Sunset Blvd., is a shopping area in which most of the stores and cafes represent foreign countries architecturally and in their wares. The shops face wide foot lanes radiating from a central patio; above them is a large, slowly revolving terrestrial globe.

DE LONGPRE PARK, De Longpre and Cherokee Aves., with landscaped lawns, bamboo, and palms, is named for the celebrated French painter, long a Hollywood resident. In the center of the park is a bronze statue *Aspiration,* a nude male surmounting a globe, by Roger Noble Burnham, erected as a memorial to Rudolph Valentino, super-lover of the silent screen, who died in 1926.

The NATIONAL BROADCASTING COMPANY STUDIOS (*open 10-10 daily; studio tour 40¢, guides*), Sunset Blvd. and Vine St., occupy a three-story concrete building, designed in the modern "International" style, forming a composition of low horizontal lines and masses relieved by a higher corner pavilion with deep vertical fenestration. The outer walls are a light shade of blue-green. The building, designed by the Austin Company of Los Angeles, was opened in 1938, and contains eight studios, four of which are built as individual sound stages after the motion picture plan, and seat 350 persons each.

COLUMBIA SQUARE PLAYHOUSE (*open 10-10 daily; studio tour 40¢, guides*), Sunset Blvd. and Gower St., opened in 1938, is the Hollywood headquarters of the Columbia Broadcasting System. The work of William Lescaze, the building is entirely modern in design. It has a five-story central unit of concrete and glass, with long horizontal lines and corner fenestrations, and lower, outflung studio sections. Visitors can watch rehearsals and some of the 14 weekly broadcasts that originate in the seven "streamlined" studios, peer behind the scenes at the master control, and see the laboratory for the development of special sound effects.

HOLLYWOOD CEMETERY, 6076 Santa Monica Blvd., is the flower-bordered and elaborately landscaped resting place of many Hollywood notables, including Rudolph Valentino, John Gilbert, and William Desmond Taylor. Harrison Gray Otis, long-time publisher of the Los Angeles *Times,* and William Andrews Clark, Jr., multimillionaire patron of the Los Angeles Philharmonic Orchestra, are also buried here. As a publicity stunt, a veiled woman was supposed to decorate Valentino's grave on each anniversary of his death. More and more veiled ladies appeared each year, and the whole thing was finally called off.

In the CENTRAL CASTING OFFICE, 5504 Hollywood Blvd., 20,000 actors, bit players, and extras are registered. On short notice it can supply types of actors ranging from Siberian Samoyeds to British Members of Parliament.

BARNSDALL PARK, Hollywood Blvd. and Vermont Ave., with an area of 10 acres, has a wading pool for children, picnic tables, and cooking conveniences. The donor, Miss Alice Barnsdall, retains an encircling strip of land valued at $2,000,000, where she advertises her social and political views on signboards.

The CALIFORNIA ART CLUB (*open 2-5 daily; adm. 25¢, free Thurs.*), 1645 N. Vermont Ave., is a white arcaded granite building designed by Frank Lloyd Wright in a modified Aztec style and erected in 1915 as Miss Barnsdall's family house. It is considered a good example of Wright's "organic" architecture, its low mass designed to blend into the setting. The guest house, a smaller residence on the west side of the park, has a first story designed by Wright, and the second story closely follows Wright's basic idea. The Art Club has a permanent exhibit of handicraft and California relics, and occasionally exhibits the work of contemporary artists.

MOTION PICTURE STUDIOS

(*Studios are not open to the public.*)

HOLLYWOOD: Paramount Pictures, Inc., 5451 Marathon St.; RKO Studios, Inc., 780 N. Gower St.

LOS ANGELES: Charlie Chaplin Studios, 1416 N. La Brea Ave.; Walt Disney Studios, 2719 Hyperion Ave.; Samuel Goldwyn, Inc. of California, 1041 N. Formosa Ave.; United Artists Studio Corp., 1041 N. Formosa Ave.; Grand National Studios, Inc., 7250 Santa Monica Blvd.; Schulberg Studios, Inc., 650 N. Bronson Ave.

UNIVERSAL CITY: Universal Pictures Co., Inc., Lankershim Blvd.

CULVER CITY: General Pictures, 9499 Washington Blvd.; Metro-Goldwyn-Mayer Studios, 10202 Washington Blvd.; Hal Roach Studios, 8822 Washington Blvd.; Selznick International Pictures, Inc., 9336 Washington Blvd.

BURBANK: Warner Bros. First National Studios, 4000 S. Olive Ave.

NORTH HOLLYWOOD: Republic Productions, Inc., 4024 Radford Ave.

HOMES OF MOVIE STARS

All homes are of course private, but viewing them from the outside is a popular tourist diversion. Sightseeing busses leave downtown Hollywood for tours of these and other homes.

IN BEVERLY HILLS

RICHARD BARTHELMESS ESTATE, 501 Sunset Blvd., is a two-story English type dwelling in landscaped grounds surrounded by a brick wall.

GROUCHO MARX'S HOME, 710 N. Hillcrest Road, a Monterey style house of whitewashed brick.

HOME OF JOAN BLONDELL AND DICK POWELL, 711 N. Maple Drive, is a massive two-story building, antique in appearance, fronted by a neat lawn.

HOME OF GEORGE BURNS AND GRACIE ALLEN, 720 N. Maple Drive, is a two-story white frame and brick structure partly covered with vines, with formal garden, swimming pool, and playground for the Burns children. Gracie's dressing room, according to Paramount, contains hundreds of bottles of rare perfumes.

WALLACE BEERY'S HOME, 816 N. Alpine Drive, is of modified Norman-Colonial style. Flower pots under the windows add bright spots of color. A game room houses Beery's hunting trophies.

EDWARD G. ROBINSON'S HOME, 910 N. Rexford Drive, a two-story English type white brick house surrounded by low walls, contains the owner's collection of modern French paintings and his comprehensive musical library.

JOE E. BROWN'S HOME, 707 N. Walden Drive, is a two-story stucco Spanish dwelling. Brown has a special room for hundreds of autographed baseballs, "big game" footballs, and trunks and boxing gloves of champions, from Jim Corbett to Gene Tunney.

LIONEL BARRYMORE'S HOME, 802 N. Roxbury Drive, a white stucco Spanish type dwelling, is without front windows, to insure privacy.

MARION DAVIES' HOME, 1700 Lexington Road, one of the star's three palatial residences, is a rambling brick and stucco house on a tree-studded knoll.

CHARLIE CHAPLIN'S HOME, 1085 Summit Drive, a tile-roofed three-story yellow stucco house, is screened from view by towering trees.

FRED ASTAIRE'S HOME, 1121 Summit Drive, a two-story white stucco Monterey style house, has landscaped gardens and a fine tennis court.

PICKFAIR, a 20-acre landscaped estate, formerly the home of Mary Pickford and Douglas Fairbanks, is occupied by Miss Pickford and Buddy Rogers. The three-story white stucco and frame house was formerly a hunting lodge.

HAROLD LLOYD'S ESTATE, Green Acres, 1225 Benedict Canyon, second largest in southern California, includes a 25-room house with 27 telephones, canoe stream and waterfall, private 9-hole golf course, handball court, swimming pool, and a four-room playhouse for the Lloyd children. Mr. Lloyd breeds great Danes and St. Bernards.

ROBERT MONTGOMERY'S HOME, 144 Monovale Drive, a two-story white frame building of New England design, is perched on a hill and surrounded by a rustic rock garden and sloping lawn.

FREDERIC MARCH AND FLORENCE ELDRIDGE'S HOME, 1026 Ridgedale Drive, is a three-story French-Norman house with a swimming pool in the rear.

CONSTANCE BENNETT'S HOME, 280 Carolwood Drive, is a white-washed brick house with shuttered windows, reached by a winding driveway.

GINGER ROGER'S HOME, 1605 Gilcrest Drive, a one-story house of irregular field stone and frame, is on the highest point in Beverly Hills. There is a shining, well-stocked soda fountain in the house, to fulfill a childhood dream.

IN BRENTWOOD HEIGHTS

GRETA GARBO'S HOME, 350 N. Cliffwood Ave., is a one-story Spanish-style stucco house with blue awnings and flower urns. A five-foot white brick wall insures privacy.

JOAN CRAWFORD'S HOME, 426 N. Bristol Ave., is a two-story white stucco house of modified Colonial design, set in landscaped grounds. In the right wing is a private motion picture theater.

ZASU PITTS' HOME, 241 N. Rockingham Ave., is a two-story white stucco building fronted by a landscaped lawn.

SHIRLEY TEMPLE'S HOME, 227 Rockingham Road, is a two-story house in the English country style, surrounded by a stone wall with an iron gate.

IN BEL AIR, WESTWOOD

CLAUDETTE COLBERT'S HOME, 615 N. Faring Road, is a two-story white stucco building, fronted by a lawn with a single live oak.

JOAN BENNETT'S HOME, 515 S. Mapleton Drive, is a two-story white painted brick mansion of Norman design, surmounted by two large chimneys.

CAROLE LOMBARD'S HOME, 609 St. Cloud Road, called "The Farm," is a two-story brick building, painted white, almost hidden by trees and shrubs.

JEANNETTE MacDONALD AND GENE RAYMOND'S HOME, 783 Bel Air Road, is a two-story English country style house, of white stucco and irregular field stones, with many gables and imitation-thatched roof that give it a fairy-tale appearance.

LORETTA YOUNG'S HOME, 10539 Sunset Blvd., is a two-story brick and frame structure, painted white with green shutters, and built on a knoll.

W. C. FIELD'S HOME, 655 Funchall Road, a mission style white stucco residence, is at the end of a winding road.

HOME OF JANE WITHERS, 10731 Sunset Blvd., a one-story white frame building with blue window shutters is somewhat reminiscent of a doll's house. On the grounds is a two-story playhouse containing a soda fountain, 800 dolls, a motion picture theater, and guest rooms. In the rear of the house is a miniature zoo.

FREDDIE BARTHOLOMEW'S HOME, 226 Tilden Ave., is a two-story white stucco and frame house on a quiet residential street, lined with silk oak trees.

Long Beach

Bus Stations: 221 E. First St. for Greyhound Lines, Motor Transit and Motor Coach; 49 American Ave. for Union Pacific System, Chicago and Northwestern Stage Lines, and Interstate Transit Line; 56 American Ave. for Santa Fe Trailways.
Airport: Long Beach Municipal Airport, Spring and Cherry Ave., 4.5 m. NE.; no scheduled service.
Taxis: Zone system, fares 15¢-25¢, additional passenger 10¢-15¢; also meter cabs. Flat rate, municipal Navy landing to central points, 10¢.
Streetcars and Busses: Streetcars 7¢, busses 5¢.
Traffic Regulations: Parking meters in business district, 5¢ per hour.

Accommodations: 88 hotels, 11 tourist camps; Long Beach Municipal Trailer camp on beach.

Information Service: Chamber of Commerce, 109 American Ave.

Radio Stations: KFOX (1250 kc.); KGER (1360 kc.).
Theaters and Motion Picture Houses: Municipal Auditorium, S. end of American Ave., concerts; 21 motion picture houses.
Golf: Municipal course in Recreation Park, E. 7th St. at West Blvd., 18 holes, 75¢; 9 holes, 50¢; $1 Sun. and holidays. Monthly tickets, $3.50 to $5.
Tennis: Public courts in Recreation Park, E. 10th St. at West Blvd., free.
Swimming: Surf on ocean beach; still-water in Alamitos Bay and at S. end of American Ave.; still-water and salt-water plunge, Marine Stadium, Recreation Park.
Boating: Rowboats and canoes, Alamitos Bay, 25¢ to 50¢ per hour, $1 to $2 per day.
Fishing: Fishing boats, $2 and $3 per day, leave frequently between 2 and 7:30 a.m. from Pier B, S. end of Santa Clara Ave. Barges, $1 per day, reached by boat from Belmont Pier at S. end of 39th Pl.; departures at 1-½ hr. intervals, 8 a.m.-3 p.m.; prices include bait and tackle. Surf and pier fishing.

Annual Events: New Year's Eve Penny Scramble, in which $100 in pennies is scattered; Twins' Convention, May; Baby Parade, Sept. Bonfire and Costume Parade, Oct.

LONG BEACH (47 alt., 142,032 pop.), California's fifth largest city, spreads over a level plain to the edge of sandy bluffs overlooking the 8½-mile-long, crescent-shaped beach of San Pedro Bay. From the shore it stretches north, laid out as evenly as a checkerboard, to the diagonal spur of low, barren knolls dominated by Signal Hill on the northeast, palisaded with oil derricks and dotted with tanks and stucco bungalows, and spills over the slopes to the level plain beyond. On the east Long Beach extends over rolling slopes to the edge of vacant fields; on the west, to the mills and warehouses along levee-embanked Los Angeles River (now a flood control channel). At its southeast tip are the winding lagoons of Alamitos Bay; to the southwest are the channels and breakwaters of Long Beach Harbor.

Against the wide expanse of San Pedro Bay are silhouetted tall office buildings, beach clubs, and hotels. Along the bluffs, from Long Beach Harbor on the west to Alamitos Bay on the east, curves broad Ocean Boulevard, skirting first the shops, hotels and theaters of the business district, then the tree-shaded mansions, lawns, and gardens of the residential section. From the garish seaside amusement zone below the bluffs, the business and shopping district extends northward along Pine and parallel streets. The rest of the city, laid out following the cardinal points of the compasses, extends west, north, and east—its chief boulevards lined with cafes, markets, garages, used-car lots; its residence streets bordered with frame and stucco bungalows in the shade of palms and peppertrees. In the east end, on sandy slopes overlooking the ocean, on lagoons and winding canals around Alamitos Bay, perch the white stucco houses of the newer Belmont Shore and Naples districts.

Long Beach is several towns in one—a seaside resort, a haven for elderly retired persons, and an industrial center drawing its income from oil, shipping, and manufacturing. Its population is correspondingly diverse—including amusement zone barkers, sailors and Naval officers and their families, oil and factory workers, retired farmers and tradesmen from the Middle West. Eighty-nine percent of the people are native-born whites. Although great numbers of the inhabitants depend on the city's industrial payroll for their living, they are outnumbered by the preponderance of elderly emigrés from the Middle West, attracted here by the sunny climate, the seaside location, and the low cost of living. It was in Long Beach that Dr. Francis Townsend, a local physician, first won support for his old-age pension movement.

The strip of mud and sand on which Long Beach was built, long the bartering place of Indians from Santa Catalina Island and the mainland, was part of the vast 200,000-acre tract granted in 1784 by the King of Spain to Manuel Nieto in payment for his services in the royal army. Divided into Rancho los Alamitos (little cottonwoods) and Rancho los Cerritos (little hills), it passed in 1840, after Nieto's death, into the hands of John Temple and Abel Stearns, both Massachusetts Yankees who married into Spanish families, and became Mexican citizens and wealthy landowners. Around their homes centered the social life of the region, marked by bull fights, horse races, and rodeos in which the two families and their servants carried on a friendly rivalry, the winner sponsoring a celebration at which casks of wine were opened, an ox was barbecued, and dancing and merrymaking lasted far into the night. The drought of 1863-64 killed off so many of their sheep, cattle, and horses that the owners lost their land through foreclosures. It was bought by Llewellyn Bixby and Benjamin and Dr. Thomas Flint.

Home owners were first attracted in 1881 when W. E. Willmore subdivided 10,000 acres of barley field and sold it for $12.50 to $25 an acre, naming his community Willmore City. The only connection with the outside world was a horse and buggy and later a four-horse stage coach to Wilmington, until a wooden car track was laid for a horse-car line known as the "Get Off and Push Railroad" because the passengers had to supply locomotive power when the horses balked. When Willmore City went bankrupt in 1888, it was re-named Long Beach—just in time to advertise itself as a seaside resort to the throngs of new settlers attracted by the southern California real estate boom of the same year. Its later growth was slower and steadier. The development of the surrounding territory (54 towns, including Los Angeles) led to the establishment of small industries supplying the increasing demand for manufactured articles. Not until discovery of the Signal Hill oil field in 1921, however, did Long Beach acquire large industries. The oil boom, opening the region to frenzied speculation, brought an influx of men and money that transformed it almost overnight into a rapidly growing city.

After the gradual subsidence of the oil boom, Long Beach continued to grow slowly and peacefully, its serenity seldom disturbed—except when the run-off from winter rains forced inhabitants in low-lying sections to take to rowboats—until the earthquake of March 1933. The shock leveled buildings throughout the city, including most of the Long Beach schools, killed 120 persons and destroyed property valued at $40,000,000. The extent of the destruction was attributed largely to lax building standards. A widespread rebuilding program was immediately undertaken under more rigid restrictions.

The oil industry still plays the dominant role in the Long Beach industrial scene. Second in importance is fish canning, carried on by eight large canneries which pack tons of tuna and mackerel. The three largest manufacturing plants produce motor cars, soap, and vegetable oil. The shipping industry accounts for a growing share of the city's income. And, like most southern California cities, Long Beach relies on the tourist trade as an important factor in its economic well-being.

POINTS OF INTEREST

The CIVIC CENTER, Broadway between Pacific and Cedar Aves., consists of the City Hall, the Municipal Utilities Building, and the Veterans' Memorial Building—all modern reinforced concrete structures. The Veterans' Building is notable for the restrained and effective sculpture on its facade.

LINCOLN PARK, Ocean Blvd. between Pacific and Cedar Aves., is a 5-acre tract, green with lawns and shade trees, where idlers pitch horseshoes or sun themselves on benches.

The CENTRAL PUBLIC LIBRARY (*open 9-9 weekdays*), in the center of the park, erected 1936-37 to replace the library destroyed in the 1933 earthquake, is built of earthquake-proof reinforced concrete. It is cruciform in plan, designed in formal modern style. The flat roofline is unbroken, except by the pediment of the facade, surmounting the vertical lines of the main entrance and second-story trio of windows. The two unified groups of window channels running up the face of the building on either side of the main entrance accent the vertical treatment. In the first floor hall is a mural, a series of scenes from English and American literature, by Suzanne Miller of the Federal Art Project. The library has 148,365 volumes.

The MUNICIPAL MARKET (*open 7-12 m. Tues., Thurs., Sat.*), a public food bazaar of temporary canvas booths set up along the sidewalk on the north and west sides of the park, provides a colorful display of fruit and garden produce, seafoods, honey, nuts, homemade bakery goods, and home-cured meats and fish. In about 150 stalls, members of 16 racial groups sell their goods under rigid municipal inspection.

The PIKE, or Amusement Zone, S. end of Pacific Ave., is flanked by theaters, reptile exhibits, dance pavilions, side shows, curiosity shops, shooting galleries, "oriental stores," penny arcades, and cafes. Here, against a flamboyant background of flags and posters, side-show barkers spiel incessantly. The attractions include an underground imitation of Los Angeles' Olvera Street, with "Mexican" and "Indian" stands, the "Million-Dollar Bathhouse," and the Silver Spray Pier with its roller coaster and amusement concessions extending into the ocean.

The MUNICIPAL AUDITORIUM, S. end of American Ave., stands on a landscaped square of filled-in land in the placid 32-acre lagoon sheltered from the ocean by the horseshoe-shaped rock embankment of RAINBOW PIER. The 3800-foot pier has a motor driveway and pedestrian promenade. A massive neo-classic structure, nine stories in height, with a two-story arcaded gallery in the rear suggesting the Coliseum in Rome, the auditorium contains three assembly halls, the largest of which seats 4,875. On its facade is an immense tile mosaic mural, the work of the Federal Art Project. The Long Beach Municipal Band presents its concerts here (*3:30 and 7:30 Tues., Sat., 2:30 Sun.*). The lagoon is the scene of year-round bathing and boating, of water carnivals and fireworks displays on festive occasions.

The WAYSIDE ART COLONY, 74 Atlantic Ave., covering about half a city block, consists largely of art shops, studios, and a private art school. Activities of the artists or "crafters," include needlework, weaving, wood and metal working, painting, music, and dancing. The colony sponsors many exhibitions of the work of Long Beach artists. The brown, shingle-roofed buildings of the colony are designed in rustic cottage style to convey an "old world art colony atmosphere."

BIXBY PARK, Ocean Blvd. and Cherry Ave., 10 acres in area, is primarily a picnic park, noted as the site of State society picnics. Wide, slightly rolling lawns, shaded by groups of oak, pine, cypress, sycamore, and palms, overlook the boulevard and ocean. The Federation of State Societies estimates that 100,000 people attended the Iowa picnic in this park in 1937.

ALAMITOS BAY, S.E. end of Second St., has a popular beach for still-water swimming, boating, and water sports. From the bay a labyrinth of canals branch into the residential section of Naples and a long arm runs inland to Recreation Park. ALAMITOS STATE PARK, at the tip of the peninsula sheltering Alamitos Bay from the ocean, is a 34-acre recreation park with facilities for picnicking and swimming (*overnight camping prohibited*). On the bay side is a sandy beach protected from high tides by a rubble wall.

RECREATION PARK, entrance 7th St. and West Blvd., has picnic facilities, playgrounds, a salt-water swimming pool, an artificial lagoon, and the MARINE STADIUM, which was constructed for the rowing races of the 1932 Olympiad. The stadium, bordered by public beaches, is the scene of national inter-collegiate regattas. The park also has workshops where children learn to build toy boats.

SIGNAL HILL, climbed by Panorama Dr., overlooks the spreading city blocks of Long Beach, the curving shoreline, and the ocean. On its slopes is the independent community of SIGNAL HILL (2,932 pop.), an island of tanks, steel and wooden oil derricks, and stucco bungalows shaded by pepper-trees. The town government levies taxes only on oil wells. The hill, once an Indian signal post and later a lookout point for signaling incoming ships, was sold by "Don Juan" Temple in 1866 for 74¢ an acre. It was a quiet residential suburb when discovery of oil in 1921 transformed it into a booming oil field that reached a maximum production of 268,000 barrels per day. In the vicinity now (1939) are some 1,400 oil derricks.

The LONG BEACH MUNICIPAL AIRPORT, Cherry Ave. and Spring St., was the starting point for Douglas Corrigan's "wrong-way" flight to New York and back by way of Ireland in 1938. A bronze plaque commemorates the flight.

The PROCTOR AND GAMBLE PLANT (*tours 9:30, 10:30, 2 and 3 Mon.-Fri.*), 1601 W. 7th St., covers 15 acres. Visitors can see the process of soap manufacture from vegetable oils (principally cocoanut, cottonseed, and linseed) in all its stages.

LONG BEACH HARBOR, at the city's southwest tip, approached by Ocean Blvd. or 7th St., consists of inner harbor channels dredged from tidal flats and an outer harbor sheltered by three great breakwaters. Pipelines radiate from the 28 miles of waterfront to adjacent oil fields. Boats can be rented for a cruise through Cerritos Channel into the Los Angeles Inner Harbor and back through the outer harbor.

POINTS OF INTEREST IN ENVIRONS

Santa Catalina Island, 25 m. (*see TOUR 2C*).

Los Angeles

Railroad Stations: Central Station, Central Ave. at E. 5th St. for Southern Pacific Lines and Union Pacific R.R.; Santa Fe Station, Santa Fe Ave. at E. 1st St. for Atchison, Topeka & Santa Fe Ry.; new Union Station, Alameda Blvd. between Aliso and Macy Sts., in use after March 1939 (estimated) for Union Pacific R.R., Southern Pacific Lines, and Atchison, Topeka & Santa Fe Ry.; Pacific Electric Ry., 610 S. Main St. and 423 S. Hill St. (interurban).
Bus Stations: Motor Transit Lines, 560 S. Los Angeles St. and Union Stage Depot, 202 E. 5th St.; Pacific Electric Ry., 423 S. Hill St.; Pasadena Ocean Park Stage Line, Inc. (Hollywood to Pasadena only), 1625 N. Cahuenga Blvd. (all interurban). Central Bus Depot, 603 S. Main St. for Santa Fe Trailways, Burlington Trailways (Nat'l. Trailways System), and Airline Bus Co.; Union Pacific Stage Depot, 451 S. Main St. for Union Pacific-Chicago and North-western Stages, and Inter-State Transit Lines; Union Stage Depot; 202 E. 5th St. for Original Stage Lines, Mount Wilson Stages, and Inland Stages; Grey-hound Terminal, 560 S. Los Angeles St. for Pacific Greyhound and Inland Stages; Independent Bus Depot, 218 E. 7th St. for Dollar Lines and Independent Stages; All American Bus Depot, 629 S. Main St. for All American Bus Lines and Overland Stages; 809 E. 5th St. for Los Angeles-Trona Stages.
Sightseeing Tours: Rosslyn Hotel, 5th and Main Sts. and depot at 544 S. Hill St. for Tanner-Gray Line (city and Southern Calif.); Pacific Electric Bldg., 6th and Main Sts., and Biltmore Hotel, 5th and Olive Sts., for California Parlor Car Tours, Inc. (Los Angeles to San Francisco, and to Yosemite).
Streetcars and Busses: Los Angeles Ry. (yellow cars, local), fare 7¢, four tokens for 25¢, weekly pass $1; (yellow busses, local), fare 10¢, weekly combination pass (also good on P.E. local cars) $1.50; Pacific Electric Ry. (red cars, local), fare 6¢ local zone, 10¢ additional zone, and up; Los Angeles Motor Coach Co. (yellow and red busses, local), fare 10¢ local zone, 15¢ additional zone, and up.
Airports: Grand Central Air Terminal, 1224 Airway, Glendale, for American Airlines and Pan American Airways, taxi 75¢, time 45 minutes; Union Air Terminal, 2627 Hollywood Way, Burbank, for United Airlines, TWA, and Western Air Express, taxi $1, time 55 minutes; Catalina Airport, Wilmington, near Catalina Terminal, to Catalina only (Avalon) fare by P.E. 44¢ to Wilmington, free fare to airport, time 46 minutes via P.E., 5 minutes to airport.
Taxis: Fare 20¢ first ¼ mile, 10¢ each additional ½ mile, 1 to 5 passengers.
Piers: Ships berth in Los Angeles Harbor, San Pedro, Wilmington, West Basin, and at Terminal Island. Coastwise passage on occasional freighters only. For travel to East Coast, outlying possessions, and foreign countries consult telephone directory or travel bureaus.
Boats for Santa Catalina Island: Leave Catalina Terminal (berths 184-185) foot of Avalon Blvd., Wilmington, 10 a.m. daily; round trip, $3, children $1.50, automobile storage at pier, 50¢. Boat train leaves Pacific Electric Station, Los Angeles, daily, 9 a.m.
Traffic Regulations: Speed limit 20 m. in business districts, 25 m. in residential districts. Right turn against red from right hand lane after full stop, but pedestrians and vehicles proceeding with signal have right of way. No parking along red or yellow curb; 3 min. limit at white curb; 15 min. limit at green curb; otherwise 45 min. parking in Central Traffic District 7-4:30; no parking 4:30-6 p.m. Unlimited parking 6 p.m.-2 a.m.; 30 min. limit 2-4 a.m.; unlimited 4-7 a.m.

Information Service: All-Year Club, 505 W. 6th St.; Chamber of Commerce, Broadway at 12th St.; Automobile Club of Southern California, 2601 S. Figueroa St.; Pacific Electric Co. Information Bureau, 610 S. Main St.; Times Information Bureau, 1st and Spring Sts.

Street Order and Numbering: Numbered streets run approximately E. and W., and are divided by Main St. North and south streets are divided by First St. Houses are numbered E. and W. from Main St., and N. and S. from 1st St.

Accommodations: 860 hotels; 48 trailer camp sites; licensed by City Planning Commission; auto camps numerous on major highways approaching the city.

Radio Stations: KMTR (570 kc.); KFI (640 kc.); KEHE (780 kc.); KHJ (900 kc.); KFWB (950 kc.); KFVD (1000 kc.); KNX (1050 kc.); KRKD and KFSG (1120 kc.); KGFJ (1200 kc.); KFOX (1250 kc.); KFAC (1300 kc.); KGER (1360 kc.); KECA (1430 kc.).

Theaters, Concert Halls and Motion Picture Houses: Belasco, 1050 S. Hill St., Biltmore, 530 W. 5th St., Mayan, 1040 S. Hill St., Theatre Mart, 605 N. Juanita Ave., road shows; Philharmonic Auditorium, 427 W. 5th St., Shrine Civic Auditorium, 665 W. Jefferson Blvd., Trinity Auditorium, 847 S. Grand Ave., concerts; Greek Theater, N. end of Vermont Ave., Griffith Park; 181 motion picture houses.

Beaches: Venice, Playa del Rey, El Segundo, and Cabrillo beaches; lifeguards.

Archery: Public ranges at Griffith Park, Glendale Blvd. at Los Angeles River, and Banning Playground (Wilmington).

Baseball: Wrigley Field, 435 E. 42nd Place.

Boating and Yachting: Boating at Echo Park, 1732 Echo Park Ave.; Hollenbeck Park, Cummings, 4th, and St. Louis Sts. and Boyer Ave.; Lincoln Park, 3600 N. Mission Road; Westlake Park, Alvorado St. and Wilshire Blvd.; average charge 1 to 2 persons, 30¢-40¢; 3 to 6 persons, 40¢-60¢. Yacht Clubs, Balboa Yacht Club, 1806 S. Bay Front, Balboa Island; Los Angeles Yacht Club, foot of Terminal Way, San Pedro; California Yacht Club (San Pedro), Wilmington Yacht Anchorage (Wilmington), Main Street Yacht Landing (Wilmington).

Boxing: Olympic Stadium, 1801 S. Grand Ave.

Fishing: Boats for ocean fishing at San Pedro or Los Angeles Harbor. Prices on boats accommodating 16 to 40 persons average $1 to $2 per day per person; charter boats $25 to $50 per day. Game fish licenses, $2 resident, $3 nonresident. Surf or still fishing from piers and at beaches.

Football: Los Angeles Memorial Coliseum, 3911 S. Figueroa St., Pacific Coast Conference games. Gilmore Stadium, 100 N. Fairfax Ave., Loyola University and professional games, October to January.

Golf: Griffith Park, Glendale Ave. at Los Angeles River, two 18-hole courses, greens fee 75¢ first round, 35¢ each additional round, 50¢ for 2½ hours before sunset, $1 Sat. after 11 a.m., Sun., holidays, with 50¢ each additional round, $5 for monthly permit; 9-hole course, greens fee 40¢; Holmby Park, Beverly Glen Blvd. and Comstock Ave., Westwood, 18-hole pony course, 15¢.

Horse Racing: Hollywood Park, Inglewood, summer racing, mutuels. Santa Anita, Arcadia, winter racing, mutuels.

Ice Skating: Pan Pacific Ice Arena, Beverly Blvd. between La Brea and Fairfax Aves., early winter to late spring; Polar Ice Palace, 615 N. Van Ness, September to May; Tropical Ice Gardens, end of Weyburn Ave. just off Westwood Blvd., 365-day season, open all day.

Midget Auto Racing: Atlantic Stadium, Atlantic and Bandini Blvds., Tues. nights April or May to October; Gilmore Stadium, 100 N. Fairfax Ave., from April to Thanksgiving.

Polo: Riviera Country Club Field, Sunset Blvd. and Capri Drive; Will Rogers Memorial Field, Sunset Blvd. and Chautauqua Drive. Games nearly every Sun., 2:30.

Riding: Numerous riding academies; bridle paths in Arroyo Seco Parks, Pearl

St. to Ave. 57 and California St. between Crescent, Ferrara, and Bredwell Sts., and in Griffith Park.

Swimming: 16 municipal swimming pools; admission generally 5¢ for children under 16, 10¢ for children 16 to 20, 20¢ for adults; outdoor pools open during summer months.

Tennis: Municipal courts at 33 recreation centers; free in daytime; 25¢ per half hour for floodlighted courts at night. Among them are: Echo (5) 2 lighted, 1632 Bellevue; El Sereno (2), 2501 Eastern Ave.; Exposition (8) 5 lighted, 3981 S. Hoover St.; Griffith (28) 6 lighted, 3401 Riverside Drive; Harvard (8) 4 lighted, 6120 Denker Ave.; Manchester (4) 2 lighted, 8800 S. Hoover St.; North Hollywood (5) 3 lighted, 5301 Tujunga Blvd.; Poinsettia (8) 6 lighted, 7341 Willoughby Ave.; Rancho Playground (12) 4834 Exposition Blvd.; Arroyo Seco Park (5) San Pascual Ave.; Hollenbeck Park (2) Boyle and St. Louis Sts.; Peck Park (4) Summerland Ave., San Pedro.

Wrestling: Olympic Stadium, 1801 S. Grand Ave.; Eastside Arena Club, 3400 E. Pico St.; Huntington Park Coliseum, 2010 E. Gage Ave.

Annual Events: Los Angeles Open Golf Tournament, Griffith Park, Jan.; International Polo Matches, Feb.-Mar.; International Tennis Matches, National A.A.U. six-day bicycle race, Mar.; Easter Sunrise Services; Los Angeles Yacht Club Gold Cup Races, Harbor, Japanese Spring Festival, Greek Theater, Apr.; Southern California Festival of Allied Arts, Carnival Mascaras (Mexican), Cinco de Mayo Fete (Mexican), Kennel Club Show, Ambassador Hotel, May; Ocean Swim Meet, Ocean Park-Venice, June; Nordlinger Trophy Race, Los Angeles Harbor, July; Nisei Festival (Japanese), Western Golf Assn. Amateur Championship Matches, Aug.; Founding of Los Angeles Pageant, Mexican Independence Day Celebration, Annual California Yacht Club Race, Harbor, Pacific Southwest Tennis Matches, Sept.; Great Western Livestock Show and Rodeo, San Francisco Opera Company (week long), Nov.; Pacific Coast Intra-circuit Polo Championship, Dec.; Philharmonic Orchestra Season, Nov.-Mar.

LOS ANGELES (286 alt., 1,238,048 pop.), known to the ends of the earth as the mother of Hollywood, that dazzling daughter still sheltered under the family roof, has other liens on fame and fortune. The country's fifth largest city, in area the nation's largest municipality, Los Angeles extends one thin arm to embrace the harbors of San Pedro and Wilmington, and with the other reaches past the Santa Monica to the San Gabriel Mountains.

For the most part, its 451 square miles of territory are level, sloping gently from the brush- and pine-clad mountains to the sandy Pacific shore, but on the northern limits the city spills over into canyons and climbs fire-scarred foothills. Amoeba-like, it has grown out and around many independent communities: among others, Beverly Hills, Santa Monica, Culver City, Universal City, Inglewood, each with its own business district and enterprises. On all sides it is fringed with other cities, towns, villages, and subdivisions—so numerous that wits never tire of describing the scene as "nineteen suburbs in search of a city."

In more than one sense Los Angeles is many cities. To some it is a slightly unreal stage set, some elaborate artifice on a movie lot, as they catch a first glimpse of its new white buildings gleaming in the sun between the cobalt sea and the purple hills. To others it is a comfortable cottage on a quiet street, with flowers in bloom about it the year round, a haven of rest and retirement after years of back-breaking work on a midwestern farm. Some know it for its ubiquitous signboards advertising everything from the doctrine of the latest sect to a sandy bluff offered cheap as a "Choice Site for a Lawyer." To still others it is a fashionable cafe, a luxurious hotel, a boulevard on which to stroll and see and be seen by the great and the near-great, a paradise for the collector of autographs and the hunter of social lions.

But to most Angelenos it is, like any other city, a place to work. The fifth largest industrial center of the country in 1935, it cans fruit, fish, and vegetables; manufactures long ribbons of "celluloid" on which to film miles and miles of movies; packs meat and fashions clothing, from blue jeans to today's creations of the reigning movie queens; fabricates tires, tubes, and airplanes; builds furniture and assembles automobiles. It is an oil town, the production and refining center of one of the greatest of our petroleum fields. It is a farm town, the trading and banking center of one of the world's richest ranch and orchard areas, producing great quantities of berries, winter vegetables, and citrus fruits. It is a busy seaport, shipping and receiving cargoes from all quarters of the globe. And there is, of course, its tourist trade, a major "industry." Visitors each year outnumber settled residents, in 1937 they accounted for more than 20 percent of all retail sales.

Reflecting its rapid expansion, the city's population is largely a transplanted one. From census to census a steady flow of newcomers has created virtually a new city; in only one decade since 1870 has Los Angeles failed at least to double its population. Many of the recent arrivals are from the Middle West and the East, elderly folk who have retired on a moderate income. Others have been drawn by the business opportunities offered by a growing community. Others, driven from their homes by depression, droughts and dust storms, have come seeking a new start in the City of the Angels.

Several large racial and language groups add contrast and color to the vast mosaic of the city. With a community of 103,000 Mexicans brought in to work on farms and in canneries, most of whom live north and east of the Plaza in some of the worst local slums, Los Angeles is the fifth largest Mexican city in the world. Living almost wholly to themselves, many of them speak only their mother tongue. Negroes comprise the next largest group, numbering 38,000, most of whom are employed as unskilled or semiskilled laborers, although a few are to be found in almost every business and professional field. At night, along Central Avenue between E. 28th and E. 53rd Streets, their night clubs and dance spots get "hot," as the young and not-so-young "swing it."

The 21,000 Japanese, many of them American citizens, have their own shops, restaurants, native-language schools and newspapers, chamber of commerce, and American Legion post, in the district centering on E. First Street, between Los Angeles Street and Central Avenue. Many of the Japanese are engaged in trade, particularly in the fruit and vegetable markets. A part of old Chinatown along Alameda Street near the Union Passenger Terminal remains, but the 3,000 local Chinese are building and rapidly moving to New Chinatown, north of Main

Street. The Filipino colony, approximately equal in number to the Chinese, is almost entirely male, employed for the most part as domestic servants.

The growth of the modern city dates roughly from 1880, almost precisely a century after its founding. In 1769 a party of explorers and missionaries under Capt. Gaspar de Portolá discovered an Indian village named Yang-na here, and impressed with the fertile river valley, named the spot Porciuncula for a chapel in Italy beloved by St. Francis. When Franciscan padres returned two years later, they selected a site nine miles northeast on which to build San Gabriel Mission and begin their work of converting the Indians and cultivating farms, orchards, and vineyards, but settlement did not really begin for another decade. On September 4, 1781, as the American Revolution was drawing to a close on the other side of the continent, Don Felipe de Neve, Governor of California, marched from San Gabriel with a handful of soldiers and eleven families from Mexico, chiefly Indians, Negroes, and mulattoes. A few priests from San Gabriel Mission assisted him as with solemn rites and ceremonies he founded El Pueblo de Nuestra Señora la Reina de Los Angeles de Porciuncula (The Town of Our Lady the Queen of the Angels of Porciuncula).

Each of the First Families of Los Angeles was given a plot to cultivate and a lot facing the Plaza, the large square that for a century remained the hub of community life. It took three years for the straggling village to acquire a small adobe church on the Plaza. For seven years the reins of government were in the hands of a corporal, Vicente Felix, a Spaniard in command of an "army" of four or five Mexican soldiers. Discharged soldiers and colonists from Mexico drifted in from time to time; by 1800 the settlement numbered 70 families, living in some 30 adobe dwellings and engaged chiefly in raising grain and cattle.

The old pueblo was an ugly town, with crooked and ungraded streets, down which caballeros galloped trailing clouds of dust. Lawns, sidewalks, and shade trees were unknown. Each family did its own butchering. Huge flocks of crows acted as "white wings," removing garbage set out for their convenience on the roofs. Only after the "Plague of the Crows" was an effort made to exterminate them. During epidemics such as smallpox the people were ordered to stay locked up at home, to keep out all strangers, and "to refrain from eating red peppers, spices, and unripe fruit, and to cleanse themselves with a good bath every eight days; and to burn sulphur in the houses."

Intruders from the outside world were rare. In 1805 the *Lelia Byrd* touched at San Pedro, the first American vessel to anchor here in defiance of the Spanish law prohibiting trade with foreign ships. The master of the ship carried back to the United States along with a cargo of hogs and sheep, a glowing account of the wealth of California, a report that brought an increasing number of American ships to these shores in the next few years. Captured as a "pirate" in 1818, Joseph (rebaptized José) Chapman became the first English-speaking settler.

Held prisoner for a time, he was set to work, being a skilled carpenter, and later erected the church, since remodeled, that still stands facing the Plaza; he capped his career by marrying into one of the pioneer families. After the secularization of the missions (1834-1837), more American traders, miners, and adventurers drifted in, embraced the Roman Catholic religion, married Mexican heiresses and became Yankee dons. During the storied rancho period all of southern California was held under the virtual feudal sway of a handful of Mexican cattle barons—Pico, Figueroa, Sepulveda, Bandini, and others, whose wealth and power are still recalled by the streets and places that bear their names.

In 1846, at the outbreak of the Mexican War, the sleepy pueblo was a nondescript village of less than 3,000, but with the seizure of California by the United States it suddenly became a rip-roaring frontier town. Times were good after 1849 when the rush of gold-hunters into the country to the north created an insatiable market for southern California cattle. Los Angeles' reputation for violence was almost unmatched even in those rough-and-ready days; its lawlessness was such that many referred to it as Los Diablos (the devils). Violence increased in 1854 to a murder a day, some accounts said. A contemporary account states that "criminals, murderers, bandits and thieves were hung in accordance with the law or without the law, whichever was most convenient or expedient for the good of the town." The town's civic conscience fell so low that the editor of the *Star* despairingly complained that "her bowels are absolute strangers to sympathy, when called upon to practically demonstrate it." Finally in 1871, as the result of the accidental killing of a white man by a Chinese, a mob attacked Chinatown, and slaughtered 19 Chinese. For the first time Los Angeles was front-page news. The town was shocked into sudden sobriety.

The Southern Pacific Railroad reached Los Angeles in 1876 and the Santa Fe in 1885. Immediately one of the bitterest railroad rate wars in history broke out. The Santa Fe reduced the fare from the Mississippi Valley from $100 to $95; the Southern Pacific reduced it to $90. Passengers scurried from one railroad office to the other to obtain the latest bargain. At the height of hostilities the fare dropped to $15, then to $5, and for one day in the spring of 1886 the Santa Fe advertised "Kansas City to Los Angeles for a dollar!" Train after train rumbled into Los Angeles, packed to the doors, and the first and gaudiest of its real estate booms was under way.

Within little more than two years the population swelled from 12,000 to 50,000. Many swept in on the tidal wave were homeseekers, but most came to make a fortune in real estate, and to make it quick. At first the little town scarcely knew what was happening. Buildings went up overnight. Land speculation reached fantastic proportions. Lots around the Plaza sold at $1,000 a front foot; subdivisions were laid out from Santa Monica to San Bernardino, a distance of 70 miles; promoters paid cash in advance for full-page advertisements to spur the dilatory:

HE OR SHE
That hesitates is lost
An axiom that holds good in real estate, as well
as in affairs of the heart.
Selah!

Los Angeles, said the *Times,* is no place for "dudes, loafers, paupers; those who expect to astonish the natives, those afraid to pull off their coats, cheap politicians, business scrubs, impecunious clerks, lawyers, and doctors." Money talked, and talked loudly, until 1887 when the banks suddenly refused to loan on real estate except at pre-boom value. The bubble burst, scores of paper "millionaires" found themselves penniless. Salvaging what they could, people fled the city at the rate of 3,000 a month. "Heroic measures" were necessary. Businessmen united with the railroads to form the Los Angeles Chamber of Commerce, which opened in Chicago an exhibit of local produce and sales literature. The whole middle western farm belt was bombarded with advertising that sang of sunshine, oranges, cheap land, easy profits. By 1892 the population had again reached the boom-time figure of 50,000, having doubled within two years.

And already, the year before, a prospecting well drilled in the front yard of a private home by E. L. Doheny and C. A. Canfield had struck oil. Soon the city was dotted with 1,400 derricks, in chicken yards, back gardens, and front lawns. Children of a generation ago rode up and down on the slow-moving walking beams, as on a teeter-totter. The wells within the city were gradually depleted, but oil production in the vicinity jumped to new heights with the discovery in 1921 of the huge Signal field at Long Beach.

Meanwhile Los Angeles businessmen were agitating for the development of an adequate harbor at San Pedro, but not without bitter opposition. Ocean frontage at Santa Monica was controlled by Collis P. Huntington, president of the Southern Pacific, who sought to have Congress appropriate $4,000,000 to build a breakwater and harbor there. The Santa Fe Railway, a majority of the Chamber of Commerce, and other business groups sent lobbyists to Congress, which in the end selected San Pedro and appropriated $2,900,000 to start the work that has since created the huge artificial harbor.

The want of an adequate water supply, always a vital need in this land of much sunshine and little rain, inspired a gigantic project to pipe in the entire flow of the Owens River, 238 miles distant in the High Sierra. A $22,500,000 bond issue to finance construction was proposed; as part of the campaign, the existing supply of water was reduced by running it into sewers; strict prohibitions were issued against watering lawns and gardens; with the hot sun burning and baking the ground, the vote on the bond issue was a foregone conclusion. In 1913 the Owens River was on its way to Los Angeles, but it did not arrive. The enormous pipeline had been built only as far as the arid San Fernando Valley, which, it transpired, had been taken over by a small group, who meanwhile had persuaded the city to annex its 108,000 desert acres. The bond issue had stipulated that the water be brought to the city; the stipulation was ingeniously met by extending Los Angeles to the water, to the great profit of those who then subdivided and sold the new annex to the city for as much as $1,000 an acre. With the diversion of the river, the once fertile and prosperous Owens Valley became, in Will Rogers' phrase, "a valley of desolation."

In the face of bitter opposition from open-shop industrial interests organized into the powerful Merchants and Manufacturers Association, led by Gen. Harrison Gray Otis, publisher of the *Times,* labor unions had long struggled to gain a foothold in Los Angeles. A feud of twenty years standing had been precipitated when Otis locked out the paper's typographers in 1890. The climax came early in the morning of October 1, 1910, when an explosion wrecked the *Times* building, killing 20 men (*see WORKINGMEN*).

During the now fabulous 1920's the city's population of approximately 600,000 more than doubled; a phenomenal building boom resulted, with contractors working vainly to meet the great need of housing. Subdivisions sprang up like mushrooms all over the metropolitan area; office buildings, apartment houses, and theaters were rapidly erected until the sole reminders of the town of Spanish and early American days were a few adobe houses and buildings tucked away here and there.

Architecturally, modern Los Angeles is a potpourri of styles, reflecting its different periods of almost convulsive growth. There are many survivors of the post-Civil War area, with their cupolas and curlicues; many brownstones of the 1880's, with elaborate ornament and great bay windows with colored glass; a large number of frame bungalows and box-like office structures of the first two decades of the century. The booming 1920's contributed the stucco dwellings and apartment houses, many pseudo-Spanish in style, as well as the skyscrapers, the movie "cathedrals," and the restaurants of bizarre design—one like a hat, another like a rabbit, a third like an old shoe, another a fish. In striking contrast with all of these are the extremely modern houses and buildings of concrete, steel, and glass. Prominent also on the landscape are huge gas tanks, gaunt and grimy oil derricks, and silvery power lines.

Socially, too, Los Angeles is a medley of many philosophies and ways of life. To the newcomer southern California is a curiously exciting combination of massive mountains, blue sea, Spanish romance, and Hollywood glamor, offering many of them a welcome change from the stereotyped patterns of the old home town. Here is a spirit of live and let live that encourages the transplanted Iowan or Bostonian to experiment with the unconventional in dress, houses, ideas, and religions. Countless movements flourish in Los Angeles, from the crusades of such religious sects as the Rosicrucians, the "Mighty I Am Presence," and Aimee Semple McPherson's Church of the Four-square Gospel, to groups organized to promote a score of economic and political doctrines. If Los Angeles has been called "the capitol of crackpots" and "the metropolis of isms," the native Angeleno can not fairly attribute all of the city's idiosyncrasies to the newcomer—at least not so long as he consults the crystal ball for guidance in his business dealings and his wife goes shopping downtown in beach pajamas. His, too, are many of the notions given form in grotesque architectural effects, and he is frequently of the crowd that rushes movie stars on their appearance in theater lobbies for gala premières. Yet it is true that most people in Los Angeles, like American city-dwellers everywhere, live in the usual apartments and suburban houses, work in stores, offices, and factories by day, and spend their evenings quietly at home listening to the radio, playing bridge, or reading the popular magazines.

Another Los Angeles is steadily coming to the fore—the Los Angeles of libraries, art galleries, concerts, museums, universities, educational and scientific institutions of all kinds. In the city is concentrated a large number of gifted writers, composers, singers, actors, playwrights, painters, cameramen, and other workers in the arts, attracted by the motion picture studios. Although their work has founded no native "school," it exercises a worldwide influence through radio and movies.

The crash of 1929 and the subsequent depression sharply reduced or entirely destroyed the incomes of many in the city, working hardship especially on the elderly people who had retired to live on their small investments. Many lost their homes for which they had saved a lifetime; one reason for the strong appeal of the Townsend Plan here. Much southern California real estate passed into the hands of the banks where a large part of it remains. After a period of relative stagnation new enterprises have been started and old ones resumed. The city's congenital optimism has not been destroyed, and it finds solid ground for its hopes as homeseekers and tourists increasingly turn their eyes once again to the City of Angels.

POINTS OF INTEREST

(*Plaza and Civic Center*)

1. The PLAZA, bounded by Main, Los Angeles, and Marchessault Sts. and Ferguson Alley, lies southeast of the first plaza, laid out in 1781 by Gov. Felipe de Neve, founder of the city, whose statue stands on the circular fountain in the center of the park. Long ago floods forced the abandonment of the original adobe houses clustered about the first square. Around the present plaza laid out between 1800 and 1812, the pueblo's aristocracy built their homes. Under the American regime the square was transformed into a round park with paths radiating from the center, occupied until 1873 by a water tank. The Plaza is today the scene of many labor demonstrations.

2. The PLAZA CHURCH (*always open*), 100 Sunset Blvd., also known as the Church of Our Lady the Queen of the Angels, the oldest in the city, was constructed in 1818-22 under the supervision of José Chapman, California's first Yankee. The mission padres at San Gabriel

donated several barrels of brandy to raise the funds. Its historic bronze bells in the squat corner tower still chime the Angelus above the noise of the city streets, as they did over a century ago.

3. OLVERA STREET (El Paseo de los Angeles; Sp., the walk of the angels), a brick-paved lane running from Marchessault St. north to Macy St., named for Don Agustin Olvera, who fought against Frémont, has been restored in the manner of an old Mexican street. Work began in 1929, with prison labor, and the street was dedicated in 1930.

A carved wooden cross at the entrance commemorates the founding of the pueblo of Los Angeles in 1781. On the street are 70 shops; a line of stalls runs down the center. The street is at its best in the evening, when cafes are gay with music, and colored lanterns light the shops. Every year from December 16 to 24 the colorful ceremony of Los Posados (the lodgings), telling the story of Mary's journey to Bethlehem in search of a birthplace for Jesus, is enacted. Another rite, on the Saturday before Ash Wednesday, is the Blessing of the Animals, when a varied assortment of beasts is led through the street to receive a priest's blessing.

The AVILA ADOBE (*open 9 a.m.-11 p.m. daily; adm. 10¢*), 14 Olvera St., now a private museum, was the home of Don Francisco Avila, *alcalde* of the pueblo in the early nineteenth century. After Avila's death in 1831, it passed into the hands of his widow, Doña Encarnación. Occupied by Commodore Robert F. Stockton in 1847, it was damaged by an earthquake in 1857 and restored along with Olvera Street in 1929. Today, only one wing remains of the L-shaped 18-room mansion.

LA GOLONDRINA, 35 Olvera Street, a two-story brick house, was built before 1865, when Antonio Pelanconi purchased it for use as a winery, one of the first in Los Angeles. Only the hand-grooved balcony, the beams, and the fireplace of the original structure remain.

LA ZANJA MADRE FOUNTAIN (the mother ditch), opposite 35 Olvera St., is an unpretentious stucco monument commemorating the great open ditch that in early days supplied the pueblo with water from the Los Angeles River. A diagonal band of brick in the paving of Olvera Street marks the line of the ancient canal.

4. The LUGO HOUSE, 516-22 N. Los Angeles St., one of the first two-story adobe buildings in the city, and the only one remaining, was built in 1840 by Don Vicente Lugo. In 1865 it housed St. Vincent's College, the first college in southern California, now Loyola University. The building with its hip roof, dormers, and frame siding retains little of its original appearance, and is now occupied by a Chinese curio shop.

5. The OLD PICO HOUSE, 430 N. Main St., a hotel built in 1869 by Pío Pico, who was the last Mexican Governor of the State, became the rendezvous of the elite of the Southwest because it had bathtubs and gaslight. Both the corner restaurant and the poolroom on Plaza Street lead to a small patio.

6. The BAKER BUILDING, N. Main and Arcadia Sts., a broad three-story structure, designed in the manner of the French second Empire, with classic arcades, central tower, and corner turrets, mansard roof and large dormers, was built in the late nineteenth century by Col. R. S. Baker.

7. The KONG CHEW CHINESE TEMPLE (*usually open until 5 p.m.*), 215½ Ferguson Alley, is one flight above the street. Inside are intricately wrought wood carvings bright with gold tinsel, large umbrellas carried by priests during street ceremonies, and two Oriental gods.

8. The LOS ANGELES UNION PASSENGER TERMINAL, N. Alameda St. between Aliso and Macy Sts., designed under the supervision of Donald B. Parkinson, is a T-shaped group of 30 low, white-stucco, red-tile-roofed buildings of modified mission architecture, topped with a 135-foot clock tower. The terminal of the Southern Pacific, Union Pacific, and Santa Fe railroads; the large main structure and the smaller buildings are separated by narrow areas designed to absorb earthquake shock. The plan of the main building includes a vestibule, a concourse, a large arcade, and a waiting room. Flanking the waiting room are two large patios; east of the south patio is the reception hall adjoining the departure and arrival lobby. Leading from this lobby is a passenger tunnel with ramps giving access to eight platforms and sixteen tracks.

9. In the JAPANESE THEATER (*admission varying, sometimes free*), 323 Jackson St., the colony's residents gather for funerals, dances, and occasional performances by imported Japanese actors. A three-story brick building, it houses stores and offices on the ground floor. The theater on the second floor seats 1,300.

10. The JAPANESE TEMPLE (*open 10-9 daily, Japanese services 7 p.m. Sun.; English services 7 p.m. Wed.; admittance through office at 119 S. Central Ave. when temple proper is closed*), E. 1st St. and Central Ave., was built in 1925. The temple, a three-story brick building, is reached by stairs leading to the second floor. The temple altar is intricately carved and covered with gold leaf.

11. CATHEDRAL OF ST. VIBIANA (*open 6 a.m.-8 p.m.*), 2nd and Main Sts., was Los Angeles' first Roman Catholic cathedral, opened in 1876. It was made the seat of the Archdiocese of Southern California in the fall of 1936. Cruciform in plan, the design of the classic edifice is based upon that of the church of San Miguel del Puerto, Barcelona, Spain. A relic of St. Vibiana, the child saint, allegedly recovered from the Roman catacombs, reposes in its original brass-bound casket in a niche in the upper part of the main altar.

12. COURT FLIGHT (*round trip fare 5¢*), 151 S. Broadway, built in 1903, is the smaller of the city's two cable railways. The lumbering wooden cars pass each other along rows of palm trees, traveling with occasional short jerks from top to bottom, but have never had a serious accident.

13. The LOS ANGELES TIMES BUILDING (*conducted tours 3 p.m. weekdays, 2:30 p.m. Sat.; reservations 2 days in advance; free*), 202 W. First St., designed by Gordon B. Kaufman, is the new home of The Los Angeles' *Times,* one of the city's three morning newspapers. The modern setback structure (1935) has a lofty central section flanked with massive buttress piers and low four-story wings. On a base of polished black granite rises pinkish granite to the second floor, above which the walls are of cream-colored limestone, with dark metal window frames. On the face of the towering section is a large clock, illuminated with red and blue neon lights, and surmounting the roof is the bronze eagle that survived the dynamiting of the old First-and-Broadway plant in 1910.

The entrance of polished red granite opens into a rotunda, in which is a large aluminum globe, set in a bronze standard and revolving within a bronze band showing the twelve signs of the zodiac. The floor and walls of the rotunda are finished in colorful mosaic and marble. Above the base are rust-colored murals, executed by Hugo Ballin, depicting various phases of newspaper production. A private power plant drives the great Hoe presses, capable of printing 320,000 thirty-two-page papers an hour. On the fifth floor are remote-control broadcasting studios and an auditorium seating 2,000.

14. The CIVIC CENTER (*all buildings open 8-5 weekdays*) is bounded by Main St. on the east, Broadway on the west, 1st St. on the south, and Temple St. on the north.

The CITY HALL (*top-floor observation balcony open 9-3; guides, free*), 200 N. Spring St., the city's tallest building, rising from its block-square grounds to a height of 464 feet, is visible for miles around. Designed by Parkins, Martin, and Austin, it is dominated by a buttressed skyscraper tower, capped with a stepped pyramid dome resting on a square colonnaded base. The Lindbergh airplane beacon is at the apex. The central tower soars above a four-story base and flanking wings. The exterior is finished in granite and glazed terra cotta. Notable among its rooms are the basillica type city council chamber, with beamed ceiling and Italian marble columns; the session room of the board of public works, with blue, green, and gold arcades at each end; and the mayor's reception room, with teakwood floor and redwood ceiling, adorned with coats of arms.

U. S. POST OFFICE AND COURT HOUSE, 312 N. Spring St., designed by G. Stanley Underwood, is an 18-story structure of neo-Classic design, opened in January 1939. The building houses the main post office, some 60 United States Government departments and bureaus, and Federal courts.

The exterior, finished in white ceramics with a granite base, is entirely without embellishment. The central section rises above a broad three- and four-story base. Its dark metal windows and white piers emphasize the vertical lines of the exterior. On either side of both the Main and Spring Street entrances are two flagpoles with bronze bases and four Doric columns. Ceramic medallions adorned with eagles flank the doors, and between the columns are aluminum grills bearing the seals of various Federal departments. Walls of the public lobbies are lined with rose marble and sienna travertine.

The LOS ANGELES COUNTY HALL OF JUSTICE, Temple St. between Broadway and Spring Sts., occupying a city block and rising 14 stories in height is a massive limestone and granite structure. The building erected in 1925 is designed in the Italian Renaissance style with rusticated stonework, heavy cornices, and crowning two-story colonnade. The building houses the County Jail in its five upper stories.

The HALL OF RECORDS between First and Court Sts., the oldest of Los Angeles County public buildings, was erected in 1909. A gray sandstone and marble structure, 11 stories high, it is topped with corner turrets and dormers. Here are the offices of the county government divisions, and more than 100,000 volumes in the County Law Library. In the office of the Board of Supervisors on the 11th floor are old prints picturing Los Angeles as it was in 1854, in 1857, and later.

The modern steel and concrete STATE BUILDING, 1st and Spring Sts., consists of a massive main section, rising above two nine-story wings. The interior is finished with gleaming marble.

(Downtown)

15. ANGEL'S FLIGHT *(open 6 a.m.-12 p.m. daily; round trip fare 5¢)*, 3rd and Hill Sts., built in 1901 by Col. J. W. Eddy, is a commercially operated miniature cable railway transporting passengers up and down the steep slope of Bunker Hill, between Hill and Olive Streets. The line climbs 315 feet up the 33 1/3 percent gradient from its starting point just south of the entrance to the Third Street Tunnel. An observation tower rises 100 feet above the tunnel mouth, and commands a view of the distant San Gabriel Mountains.

16. PERSHING SQUARE, bounded by 5th, 6th, Hill and Olive Sts., Los Angeles' best-known downtown park, has walks lined with coco palms; the central plaza with its ornamental fountain is surrounded with clusters of banana trees. In the park, renamed for General Pershing in 1918, are a Spanish War Monument, a statue of Beethoven, a World War Memorial, a bronze Napoleonic cannon, and an iron cannon from the U. S. S. *Constitution*.

17. The BILTMORE HOTEL, 5th and Olive Sts., opened in 1923 and the city's largest hostelry, is an E-shaped, stone and brick, 12-story structure of modified Italian Renaissance style. In the *Galería Real,* extending the full length of the hotel from the 5th Street entrance, is the BILTMORE ART SALON *(open 10-9 weekdays)*, in which exhibitions of oils and etchings from the fifteenth century to the present day are changed monthly.

18. The EDISON BUILDING *(open 8-5 Mon.-Fri.)*, 5th St. and Grand Ave., 13-story home of the Southern California Electric Power combine, designed by Allison and Allison, is in the setback style, with offsets at the third, fourth, twelfth and thirteenth floors. It is constructed of granite, limestone, and terra cotta in harmonizing cream-colored hues, with delicate terra cotta ornamentations of modern design. After dark the central tower is brightly illuminated, its crown of neon lights standing out sharply against the skyline. A corner octagonal entrance pavilion, embellished with sculptures, leads to the huge marble lobby with Hugo Ballin's allegorical mural, *Power*.

19. The LOS ANGELES PUBLIC LIBRARY *(open 9-9 weekdays; readingroom only open 1-9 p.m. Sun. and holidays)*, 5th St. between Flower St. and Grand Ave., rises from the crest of a low hill

beyond cypress-fringed flights of steps and tile-inlaid lily ponds. Massed shrubbery and trees dot its rolling lawns used in summertime as "outdoor reading rooms." Of buff-colored stucco, the low buttressed structure is capped with a 188-foot square tower, topped with a mosaic pyramid. Surmounting the pyramid is a sculptured hand bearing a torch. The structure is the work of Bertram Goodhue.

The interior of the building is decorated with many sculptures, murals, and frescoes. The theme of the sculptural decorations, executed by Lee Lawrie, is centered in the illuminated book, symbolized by the torch of knowledge which is handed down from age to age by the great literary figures of all time. The murals in the History Room, by Albert Herter, depict dramatic episodes in California history, while those by Dean Cornwell, in the rotunda, are designed in the manner of a fifteenth century tapestry, suggesting rather than portraying epoch-making events. The interior is further enriched with frescoes painted by artists on the Public Works Art Project.

The Central Library, completed in 1926, is the main unit of the municipal library system.

20. The SUNKIST BUILDING (*open 9-5 weekdays*), 705 W. 5th St., standing on the flank of steep Bunker Hill, is headquarters of the California Fruit Growers Exchange. The U-shaped structure, with roof garden, was designed by Walker and Eisen in the modern manner with emphasis on simple mass and vertical lines. It is constructed of reinforced concrete, with a marble and aluminum entrance opening into a lobby adorned with colorfully decorated ceiling beams.

21. The RICHFIELD BUILDING (*open 8-5 Mon.-Fri.*), NW. corner 6th and Flower Sts., designed by Morgan-Walls and Clemens, is particularly striking in its black masonry and gold terra cotta trim symbolizing the "black gold" of the oil industry. One of Los Angeles' few set-back skyscrapers (371 feet), the massive exterior is lined with narrow vertical piers. Above the main entrance are heroic figures in gold by Haig Patigian, representing Aviation, Postal Service, Industry, and Commerce. The building is surmounted with a metal tower.

22. The LOS ANGELES STOCK EXCHANGE (*open 7-11 a.m. by invitation of members only*), 618 S. Spring St., is a squarely built modern 12-story structure. The granite facade, with its fluted pylons and bronze reliefs, is windowless, except for two narrow grilled apertures at the second floor. Completed in 1930, the structure also houses the Stock Exchange Club and the Stock Exchange Institute. The boardroom of the Stock Exchange is the largest outside of New York City, and the Stock Exchange floor is modeled after that of the New York Exchange.

(North and East)

23. ELYSIAN PARK (*open 6 a.m.-8 p.m. daily*), entrance N. Broadway and Los Angeles River, is a 600-acre municipal park, with

seven miles of paved roads twisting in hairpin curves through arroyo-gashed hills, a matted tangle of wild roses, creepers, blue gum eucalyptus trees, drooping pepper trees, and gnarled live oaks. Ten miles of foot trails lead through canyons and up steep hills. From Point Grand View, a rustic lookout, is a view of the city and mountains beyond. In Memorial Grove are trees with bronze tablets in memory of the World War dead. The park has a recreation lodge, and picnic grounds, with free firewood and water. Elysian Park has been so popular that much land has been added to the original 500-acre park established in 1886. A landslide in 1938 revealed a forgotten tunnel that provided an auxiliary water supply for the city in the 1870's. The PORTOLA-CRESPI MONUMENT, left of the park entrance, is a granite boulder. Here, on August 2, 1769, Don Gaspar de Portolá and Padre Juan Crespi, leading the first overland exploration of California, pitched camp on the site of the future city.

24. EL ALISAL (*open on application at Southwest Museum*), a large house on the west side of the Arroyo Seco at Avenue 43, is named for the giant sycamore tree around which it was built and which still towers from the patio high above the Spanish roof of the very un-Spanish stone building. Charles F. ("Don Carlos") Lummis, who arrived in Los Angeles in the 1880's after a 3,507-mile marathon hike, built the house with his own hands, aided only by a young Indian boy. He is remembered not only for his Promethean cultural activities but for his prolific publicity of the region.

25. SYCAMORE GROVE, N. Figueroa St. and Sycamore Park Dr., is a 15-acre plot of lawns studded with giant sycamores. Since its establishment as a park in 1905, it has been used frequently for those State picnics so typical of Los Angeles, at which the city's adopted citizens congregate to reminisce about days "back home." The park provides free stoves, firewood, tables, tennis courts, and playground equipment for children.

26. CASA DE ADOBE (*open 2-5 Wed., Sun.*), 4605 N. Figueroa St., built by the Southwest Museum, is a replica of a typical California dwelling of the early nineteenth century. One room contains a display of numerous household articles; the others are arranged and furnished in keeping with the period. Walks shaded with grapevines divide the gardens, which contain many varieties of cactus.

27. The SOUTHWEST MUSEUM (*open 1 p.m.-5 p.m. daily except Mon., Christmas, Independence Day, and during Aug.*), Marmion Way and Museum Drive, overlooks the Arroyo Seco and Sycamore Grove. Opened in 1914, the white concrete building, without ornamentation, has a tile-roofed tower at one end and a high square tower at the other. The museum contains relics and art of the primitive peoples of Western America, collected by the Southwest Society of the Archeological Society of America, founded in 1903.

A bright MAYAN PORTAL, designed in the manner of the portal of the House of Nuns at Chichen Itza, in Yucatan, forms the entrance to a 260-foot tunnel leading into the base of the hill on which the

LOS ANGELES 221

building stands. Dioramas on the sides of the tunnel depict the history of the primitive Asian men who settled the Western American coast.

An elevator runs to the LOWER LOBBY, 108 feet above, containing American Indian exhibits. In the south wing is the SOUTHWESTERN INDIANS ROOM, with relics and modern handicraft of the "sky-dwelling" Pueblos, and of the nomadic Navajo and Mojave. In the NORTH-WESTERN INDIANS ROOM, directly north are displays of Alaska and British Columbia Indians' handicraft—carved ivory, blankets, and elaborately carved and stained totem poles.

From the lower lobby the center stairway leads to the PLAINS INDIAN ROOM, displaying a tepee of tanned skins, clothing and weapons of Blackfeet, Cheyenne, Crow and Arapaho. The adjoining room on the north is the PREHISTORIC PUEBLO INDIANS TOWER, containing relics from Southwestern cliff dwellings—fabrics woven from yucca and turkey feathers, and colored with brilliant vegetable dyes.

In the south wing of the same floor is the AUDITORIUM (*lectures on Indians and Southwestern history, travel and exploration, at 3 p.m. Sun., Nov.-Mar.; free*). West of the Auditorium is the TORRANCE TOWER (*open by special permission*) which contains the Library of the Southwest, a collection of works on archeology, ethnology, and primitive art of the Southwest and Spanish-America.

The HOPI TRAIL, resembling the stone trails of the Hopi "sky cities" in northern Arizona, leads from the lower lobby to the base of the hill.

28. OCCIDENTAL COLLEGE, 1600 Campus Rd., is housed in a group of modified Spanish Renaissance buildings in a spacious and eucalyptus-planted campus of 95 acres. On the slope of a low range of hills, Occidental has frequently been the setting of "college" movies.

The present nonsectarian, co-educational college was founded in 1888 by a group of Presbyterian ministers and laymen. First situated on Boyle Heights, it was removed to Highland Park after fire destroyed it in 1896. In 1910 the college became nonsectarian, and in 1914 acquired the present campus.

Approximately 750 students here study liberal arts and natural sciences under a faculty of 70 members; a graduate school grants the Master of Arts degree. Notable alumni include Dr. Arthur Young, financial adviser to the Chinese Government, Robinson Jeffers, the widely known poet, and Raymond Leslie Buell, director of the Foreign Policy Association. There are 14 major buildings, most of them donated by alumni and friends; an athletic field, gymnasiums, a swimming pool, tennis courts, the outdoor Hillside Theater seating 5,000 persons, a 50,000-volume library, and a large concrete auditorium.

29. ARROYO SECO PARK (dry creek), entrance Avenue 60 and Arroyo Drive, a 276-acre plot of decorative greenery planted in the dry gully and on the surrounding irregular hills of the seasonally torrential Arroyo Seco, has four bowling greens, two baseball diamonds, five tennis courts, bridle and hiking paths, a maypole, picnic grounds, and children's play apparatus.

30. ZOO PARK (*open 9-5 daily; adults 35¢, children 10¢*), 3800 Mission Road, is one of the largest zoos in California, with more than 600 animals, some of them trained. They are fed at 2:30 and put through their paces at 3 p.m. The zoo, now controlled by the California Zoological Society, occupies the site of the old Selig Motion Picture Studios.

31. The ALLIGATOR FARM (*open 9-6 daily; adults 25¢, children 10¢*), 3627 Mission Road, contains 1,000 alligators, some as small as lizards; others of immense size are reputedly 500 years old. Visitors can watch the reptiles slide down chutes and see their eggs in incubators.

32. The LOS ANGELES OSTRICH FARM (*open 9-6 daily; adults 25¢, children 10¢*), 3609 Mission Road, has 30 or more full-grown birds.

33. LINCOLN PARK, bounded by Mission Road and Alhambra Ave., containing eucalyptus-shaded picnic grounds and a six-acre lake for boating, has two tennis courts, a merry-go-round, children's play apparatus, four horseshoe courts, and a conservatory of rare tropical plants.

34. COUNTY HOSPITAL (*visiting hours 7-8 p.m. weekdays, 2-4 p.m. Sun.; tours with guide 2-3 p.m. Fri.*), 1200 N. State St., occupies 123 structures on a 56-acre site. The ACUTE UNIT, the main building, is a massive, set-back structure with soaring vertical lines rising 20 stories from a slight eminence. It is visible from most of the hilly eastern section of the city. The building is constructed of steel and reinforced concrete with ample fenestration, 31 acres of floor space, a large kitchen, 75 wards, 16 major surgeries and 4 maternity delivery suites. The unit, designed by 60 local architects, was completed in 1932.

Among the other hospital units, on the western section of the grounds, are the OSTEOPATHIC BUILDING, the PSYCHOPATHIC BUILD-ING, the COMMUNICABLE DISEASES BUILDING, and the INTERNES' HOME. The hospital's capacity is 3,600 patients, the average daily patient load about 2,500. Full-time physicians number 237, attending physicians 525, and nurses 1,200.

The institution was founded in an adobe house on North Main Street in 1858 and operated by the Sisters of Charity. A two-story frame hospital was erected on the present site in 1878.

35. CHURCH OF OUR LADY OF LOURDES (*open all hours*), 3772 E. 3rd St., designed by L. G. Scherer in the form of a Spanish mission church but highly stylized in its modern treatment of traditional architecture, is dominated by a lofty corner tower. The building is notable for its fine metal and stone grills and the gleaming metal cap of the tower. The traditional beamed ceiling of the nave contrasts with the modern peaked arches bordering the side aisles and the stepped silhouette of the chancel arch. Over the altar is a slender baldachino.

(Wilshire and Northwest)

36. ECHO PARK, a 31-acre tract extending from Temple St. to Park Ave., encloses a willow-fringed lake that up to 1891 furnished power for an early woolen mill. In the park are a community building, four-and-one-half-acre playground along Bellevue Avenue, two outdoor gymnasiums, and a wading pool for children.

37. ANGELUS TEMPLE (*open 9:30-4:30; daily services 10 a.m., 1 p.m., 2:30 p.m., 7:30 p.m.; guides*), 1100 Glendale Blvd., a' huge rotund edifice, bustles with the energetic evangelism of its moving spirit, Mrs. Aimee Semple McPherson. Some 4,000 sightseers are conducted through this Church of the Four-square Gospel each month to gaze on the domed auditorium seating 5,300 persons; the stage on which sermons are dramatized; the organ that can simulate the tones of 40 different instruments; the stained-glass windows depicting the life of Christ (one presented by Gypsies); and the mural depicting the return of Christ under an enormous American flag. Then there is the prayer tower, in which prayer has been continuously said in two-hour shifts since the building was opened in 1923; the control room of the temple's radio station, KFSG; and the communion service set of 5,300 cups. Adjoining the temple is the ministerial training school, known as the Lighthouse of International Four-square Evangelism. In the children's church youngsters conduct as well as attend services. Additional religious facilities include a music conservatory, a kindergarten, a charity commissary, a free employment bureau, a salvage department, a printing plant, and Mrs. McPherson's home, with a roof garden above the temple book store.

38. GRIFFITH PARK (*open 6 a.m.-8 p.m. daily*), at Griffith Park Drive and Riverside Drive, is a 3,761-acre slice of the easternmost of the Santa Monica Mountains. A highway runs through valleys and rises in tortuous curves through the sere hills, offering a panorama of the mountains to the west and the ocean on clear days. The park has been left largely in its original state. Originally part of Rancho Los Feliz, it was donated to the city March 5, 1898, by the last owner, Col. Griffith J. Griffith.

GRIFFITH PARK ZOO (*open 8-5 daily*) is impressive for its rugged mountain setting. The cages and pens are scattered along the top of the low hills of the zoo grounds.

The GREEK THEATER (*admission varying with performance*), sheltered in Vermont Canyon, is an amphitheater of simple Doric design. The three-story stage was erected in 1930, and serves for memorial services, conventions, concerts, ballets, and drama. The open-air tiers of seats accommodate more than 4,000 persons.

The BIRD SANCTUARY (*open 8-5 daily*), at the head of Vermont Canyon, was dedicated in 1925 by the Audubon Society. A high metal fence around the confine protects the birds against natural enemies, and the 30 to 50 varieties disport themselves in utmost confidence against molestation; they are fed once a day.

The OBSERVATORY AND PLANETARIUM (*open 11-11 weekdays, 2-11 Sun.; free; planetarium demonstrations 3 and 8:30 p.m. daily; adm.*

25¢), designed by John C. Austin, is built on a spur of foothills. Before the entrance is a dedicatory obelisk, designed by Archibald Garner, bearing the names and dates of the world's great astronomers. Surmounting the shaft is the early astronomical instrument, the astrolabe. Inside the building are observatory exhibits, and a large model of the moon; a creeping light is thrown on it to represent the sun and reveal the changing shadows, mountains, craters, as they would appear from a distance of 500 miles. Other exhibits cover the fields of electricity, optics, spectroscopy, electronics, geology, and chemistry. At night the 12-inch refractor telescopes allow visitors a view of the celestial bodies.

39. WESTLAKE PARK, entrance Wilshire Blvd. and Alvarado St., is cut in two by the Wilshire Boulevard viaduct. This 32-acre park in the heart of one of Los Angeles' most densely populated sections is shady and landscaped, and fringes a small artificial lake. Free band concerts are given on Sunday afternoons. On the eastern shore of the lake is a cream-colored stucco boathouse. The park contains a sculptured figure of Prometheus giving fire to the world, and a bronze statue of Gen. Harrison Gray Otis, for years editor and publisher of the Los Angeles *Times*.

40. OTIS ART INSTITUTE (*open 3-4 weekdays; guides*), Wilshire Blvd. and Park View St., is a two-story stucco building of Mission architecture, with Corinthian columns at its portal. In the side yard, visible from the boulevard, is a stone miniature of the old Los Angeles *Times* building, dynamited in 1910 as the climax to a savage war waged by that paper against organized labor. Formerly the home of General Otis, the Institute is now an adjunct to the Los Angeles County Museum of History, Science, and Art.

41. IMMANUEL PRESBYTERIAN CHURCH (*admission by application at office*), Wilshire Blvd. and Berendo St., designed with the Germanic serenity of a northern Gothic cathedral, has a 207-foot tower. Five lancet windows rise to the immense rose window portraying the Nativity in stained glass. Within, the Gothic hammer-beam trusses of the ceiling, columns and arches, oak furnishings, and huge Gothic chandeliers harmonize with the massive dignity of the exterior.

42. The AMBASSADOR HOTEL, 3400 Wilshire Blvd., a vast rambling structure with spreading tile-roofed wings, sits far back from the street in a huge expanse of lawn. The hotel has its own swimming pool, playground, shopping center, and movie theater.

43. The WILSHIRE BOULEVARD CHRISTIAN CHURCH (*admission by application at office*), Wilshire Blvd. and Normandie Ave., designed by Robert H. Orr, is distinguished by its west facade cartwheel window, based upon that of the Rheims Cathedral in France. Romanesque in style, with basilica type auditorium and soaring campanile, the church recalls the churches of northern Italy.

44. B'NAI B'RITH TEMPLE (*open for services 8 p.m. Fri., 10:30 a.m. Sat.*), Wilshire and Hobart Blvds., is the city's largest Jewish temple. Dominating the temple is an immense 135-foot dome, inlaid with mosaic, surrounded with the minaretlike pinnacles of the octagonal main auditorium. Broad stone steps lead to three arched

entrances, above which is a huge rose window. Within, Byzantine columns of black Belgian marble rise to the majestic domed ceiling, finished in dull gold, from which hang chandeliers of bronze. The altar, ark, and choir screen are of carved, inlaid, dark walnut, and framed in marble and mosaic. The walls are enriched by Hugo Ballin's Warner Memorial paintings, depicting Biblical and post-Biblical themes.

45. The WILSHIRE METHODIST EPISCOPAL CHURCH (*admission by application at office*), Wilshire and Plymouth Blvds., is of modified Spanish Romanesque architecture. The design of the interior is dominated by a large rose window and a tall corner tower with buttressed and pinnacled belfry.

46. HANCOCK PARK, entrance Wilshire Blvd. and Curson Ave., a 32-acre preserve, is known chiefly for the LA BREA PITS, near the center of the park. They are ugly bogs with subterranean oil and tar bubbling slowly to the surface. A film of water camouflages the sticky quagmire, forming a trap for the unwary, as it did in ages past when prehistoric animals gathered here to drink and were caught in the preservative tar. Birds of prey and carrion-eaters fed on the sinking animals and were themselves caught in the pitch. The pits are the richest source of Pleistocene or Ice Age remains in the world. Skeletal remains of the only American peacock ever found, of sabre-tooth tigers, Imperial elephants, woolly mammoths, giant ground sloths, small early camels, condors, Great American lions, and other prehistoric species have been removed from the pits. There is an exhibit of La Brea fossils at the Los Angeles Museum of Science, History and Art in Exposition Park. A restoration of Ice Age animals floundering in the tar, by Charles R. Knight, hangs in the Field Museum, Chicago.

The Indians used the pitch to waterproof their baskets and canoes. When Governor Portolá came to this region from Mexico in 1769, he wrote, "We came to swamps of a certain material like pitch, or bitumen. We debated whether this substance which flows melted from underneath the earth could occasion so many earthquakes as we noted during our sojourn here." Father Serra noted in his journal, "This black oily pitch evidently came from a volcano in the nearby mountains."

Early settlers used the tar to cover their adobe houses, and when it was granted to Antonio Rocha in 1828 as part of Rancho La Brea (tar), José Antonio Carillo, local alcade, stipulated that the brea pits be reserved for the use of the people. The first discovery of prehistoric remains was in 1906, when the skeleton of a giant bear was found. Since then many college and research groups have explored the pits and made important finds. The pits are in a productive oil area, from which great quantities of petroleum have been taken. The last private owner of La Brea, G. Allen Hancock, donated the park to the city in 1916.

47. The CARTHAY CIRCLE THEATER, 6316 W. San Vicente Blvd., designed by Dwight Gibbs in early Spanish style, dominated by a high tower illuminated at night, is now used exclusively for important motion picture premières. *Snow White and the Seven Dwarfs* and *Hurricane* had their first showing here. Representative

scenes of early California provide the decorative motif. In the first floor lobby is a painting, *California's First Theater,* by Frank Tenney Johnson, picturing the Eagle Theater built in Sacramento in 1849. Another in the main lobby mezzanine, *Jedediah Smith at San Gabriel,* by Alson Clark, portrays the arrival of the renowned scout at San Gabriel Mission on November 27, 1826, the first white visitor from across the continent. The drop curtain depicts *An Emigrant Train at Donner Lake,* also by Frank Tenney Johnson, a tribute to the survivors of the ill-fated Donner Party. As part of the fountain in front of the theater, stands Henry Lion's PIONEER, a typical forty-niner of gold rush days. Beside the theater stands a Chinese peach tree, with a plaque recording that Yi Seng Kiang, Chinese consul, presented it to commemorate the world première of the motion picture, *The Good Earth.*

Carthay Center bears a corruption of the name of Daniel O. McCarthy, pioneer of '49, whose San Francisco paper, the *American Flag,* helped keep California within the Union at the outbreak of the Civil War. The McCARTHY MEMORIAL FOUNTAIN, Vista and San Vicente Blvd., a bronze basin surmounted with the figure of a miner panning the gold, bears a tablet inscribed to "The Gallant Pioneers of '49." Nearby is a stump from the Petrified Forest north of San Francisco, dedicated by the Native Sons of the Golden West to Galen Clark's discovery of the Mariposa Big Trees. At the end of the parkway, across Commodore Sloat Drive, is a boulder inscribed to the memory of "Snowshoe" Thompson, pioneer hero, who for twenty years carried the mails over California's mountains and rescued lost travelers.

48. The UNIVERSITY OF CALIFORNIA AT LOS ANGELES, campus entrance at Westwood Blvd. and Le Conte Ave., occupies a 334-acre grassy campus on a terraced knoll overlooking valleys, plains, and rolling hills. On a low hilltop, approached by a monumental bridge from the east entrance on Hilgard Avenue, stand the university's terra cotta, brick and tile central buildings of Lombardic Romanesque design, grouped about a central esplanade. On the north side of the esplanade is JOSIAH ROYCE HALL, housing the auditorium, classrooms, and faculty offices, named for the eminent American philosopher, a graduate of the university. Across the green on the south side is the large red brick LIBRARY BUILDING dominated by its enormous arcaded octagonal tower. It is designed in the early Italian Romanesque style with rich brick and stone ornamentations of Byzantine Romanesque design. Especially notable are the canopied entrance, the striped coursing of the lower story, and the arched loggia above the portal. Both Royce Hall and the Library were designed by George W. Kelham.

Simpler in detail and more modern in treatment are the lesser buildings grouped to the east and south: the Chemistry-Geology, Physics-Biology, Administration, and Education Buildings. Westward from the esplanade, an imposing brick stairway with terra cotta balustrades descends the hill to the men's and women's Gymnasium Buildings, that repeat the Romanesque motif. Set apart from the main group southwest of the Education Building is KERCKHOFF HALL, social center for students and faculty, of Tudor-Gothic design with graceful pinnacled tower, oriel bays, and leaded windows. Overlooking the campus from the north is the Provost's Residence. Near the south entrance on Westwood Boulevard are a Mechanic Arts Building, shops, and an outdoor amphitheater seating 12,000.

An integral part of the University of California, the University of California at Los Angeles grew out of the old Los Angeles State Normal School, founded in 1881. In 1919 the institution became the University of California, Southern Branch, and in 1927 the University of California at Los Angeles. It outgrew its original campus and in 1925 a new site in Westwood Hills was presented to the Regents by the cities of Los Angeles, Santa Monica, Venice, and Beverly Hills. The new campus was dedicated in September 1929.

With a faculty of more than 300, the university offers courses in the humanities, sciences, business administration, education and agriculture, to a student body of more than 7,000. The University Library has a collection of 260,000 volumes and 2,200 current periodicals.

49. The U. S. SOLDIERS' HOME (*open 3-4 daily*), entrance Wilshire Blvd. and Veteran Ave., provides free hospitalization for veterans of the Civil, Spanish-American, and World Wars. On the rolling, wooded, 700-acre estate are almost 170 buildings. Modern buildings are being erected (1939) to replace the old rambling wooden structures dating back to the late 1880's when the home was established on land donated to the Government.

(Southwest)

50. ST. VINCENT DE PAUL ROMAN CATHOLIC CHURCH (*always open*), Figueroa St. and W. Adams Blvd., designed by Albert C. Martin, is an imposing white edifice in the Churrigueresque style, embellished with a wealth of exterior carvings and statuary in Indiana limestone. Its ornate façade is topped with a 125-foot corner tower, and a tile-inlaid dome, rising majestically from the crossing. The interior is lavishly embellished with murals, polychromed carving, marble, and bronze. The high altar is set against a retablo of morocco red marble with a high-relief carving of the Last Supper; above the altar is a tabernacle of gilded bronze, and behind it a great reredos of carved and gilded wood in Spanish baroque style. The marble pulpit is approached by a bronze staircase and sheltered by a carved walnut canopy. St. Vincent's was opened in 1925, the gift of the late Edward L. Doheny, multimillionaire oil magnate, and his wife.

51. ST. JOHN'S EPISCOPAL CHURCH (*open 7-5 daily*), 514 W. Adams Blvd., recalls the eleventh century church at Toscanella, Italy. The interior is distinguished by its elaborate beamed ceiling, copied from that of the Church of San Minato in Florence.

52. CHESTER PLACE, extending north from West Adams Blvd. to 23d St. (*speed limit 10 m.p.h.*), has been for 40 years the habitat of the wealthy. An arched iron gateway opens into this two-block-wide

private residential park, the seat of baronial mansions. A short block westward, behind a high brick wall, stand the shabby structures of St. James Place, forming two sides of half-acre St. James. Park.

53. The FIGUEROA ADOBE (*open on application*), 3404 S. Figueroa St., built in 1846 by Ramon Figueroa, brother of the Mexican governor of California in the 1830's, stands well back in a small copse of pepper and palm trees. The original adobe section is comparatively well preserved, but the unsightly frame additions in the rear add an incongruous note. The house is occupied by a great-granddaughter of a Spanish soldier who accompanied Gov. Felipe de Neve on the march from San Gabriel Mission to found Los Angeles in 1781.

54. The UNIVERSITY OF SOUTHERN CALIFORNIA, University Ave., between 34th St. and Exposition Blvd., spreads over a 45-acre campus. Ten new buildings have been erected since 1921. The university was founded in 1876 by the Southern California Conference of the Methodist Episcopal Church, which is still represented on its board. Now, nonsectarian and coeducational, it has a faculty of 820 and an enrollment of approximately 16,000.

The GEORGE FINLEY BOVARD ADMINISTRATION BUILDING, University Ave. at 36th St., commemorates the university's second president. Designed in the early Italian Renaissance style, it is built of red brick, with a red tile roof. The massive square central tower is buttressed at each corner by eight heroic statues, the work of Caspar Gruenfeld. Before the main entrance is an 8-foot statue of an armed Trojan warrior, the university's symbol, mounted on a 10-foot pedestal, designed by Roger Noble Burnham.

Across University Ave. from the Administration Building is the EDWARD L. DOHENY, JR., MEMORIAL LIBRARY, the outstanding building on the campus, erected in 1932, a gift of the late Edward L. Doheny. It is designed in a modified Italian Romanesque style.

The STUDENT UNION BUILDING, SW. corner 36th St. and University Ave., designed in the manner of an Italian Renaissance *palazzo,* is the social and recreational center of the University. Adjoining, are the Science Building and Pharmacy Hall; and across the street, the Law School and Bridge Hall, housing the School of Engineering.

Southernmost of the west side of University Ave. is the COL. SEELEY WINTERSMITH MUDD MEMORIAL BUILDING containing the Hall of Philosophy. Surrounding a central courtyard are separate wings for administration offices, classrooms, and the general library. Above it rises a clock tower with chimes. Across the front of the court extends an open cloister forming a quadrangle. The style of its architecture is based upon Byzantine and Lombardic Romanesque traditions.

55. EXPOSITION PARK, bounded by Figueroa St., Menlo Ave., Exposition Blvd., and South Park Drive, known in early days as Agricultural Park, was the scene of Los Angeles' first agricultural fairs. The 114-acre tract acquired by city, county, and State near the turn of the century, was improved and opened as Exposition Park in 1910.

On the Exposition Boulevard side is the MEMORIAL GATEWAY, flanked by massive pylons commemorating the Tenth International Olympiad of 1932, held in the park's Memorial Coliseum. Broad bench-lined walks lead to the seven-acre SUNKEN GARDEN, planted with 15,000 rose bushes of 118 different varieties, and marked at each corner by white marble statuettes. Paralleling the Sunken Garden on the east is the red brick Armory, headquarters and training barracks for the 160th Infantry, California National Guard.

The STATE EXPOSITION BUILDING (*open 10-5 daily except Wed., Sun., holidays; 10-12 m. Wed.; 2-5 p.m. Sun. and holidays*), an E-shaped edifice in Spanish mission style with walls of brick and terra cotta, designed by Nathan Elery, houses a permanent exhibition of the resources and industries of California. The main entrance leads to a two-story rotunda lighted by stained glass windows, which picture scenes in the annals of Los Angeles. In the rotunda are huge relief maps of California, San Francisco Bay, and Los Angeles Harbor. In the great West Wing are the horticultural and agricultural exhibits. A series of alcove exhibits in the Hall of Animal Industries contain miniatures of all types of ranches. The California fish and game exhibits, classified by counties, display series of habitat groups. Among the mining exhibits are accurately scaled models of coal mines, oil wells, gold development properties, and lumber camps.

The LOS ANGELES COUNTY MUSEUM OF HISTORY, SCIENCE, AND ART (*open 10-4 weekdays, 2-5 Sun. and holidays*), west side of Sunken Garden, is a repository of art objects, scientific exhibitions, and relics. The original T-shaped, glass-domed building of red brick was formerly opened Nov. 6, 1913. Two units of a new building have been added, one in 1925, the other in 1929. With their completion, the original structure became a subordinate unit and a new main entrance, adorned with Doric columns, was erected on the south facade of the new building, facing the Coliseum.

The museum has one of the world's largest and best-preserved assemblages of Pleistocene mammal remains, dug from the celebrated La Brea Pits in Hancock Park.

The Natural History Wing was especially designed for the display of animal habitat groups. The bison and waterhole groups dominate the American and African Big Game Halls; in all, the division contains 37 exhibits of wild animal life.

Of note among the special permanent collections are the Harrison Collection of Contemporary American and Contemporary French Paintings, the Reagan Collection of Rembrandt etchings, the Coronel Collection of early Los Angeles relics, and the Otis Collection of weapons. The museum maintains a library for research in history, science, and art.

The LOS ANGELES MEMORIAL COLISEUM, designed by John and Donald Parkinson, is at the end of The Mall, a 1,065-foot oblong stretch of green bordered by young deodars. A huge peristyle with a 400-foot arcade and a 70-foot central arch, topped with a pedestaled urn, forms the main gateway. Within, rising in vast tiers above the circular field of turf, are 79 rows of seats accommodating 105,000 people. A fifth of a mile long and three-fifths of a mile in circumference, the stadium covers 17 acres; its walls, 106 feet high, enclose a five-acre playing field, the scene of major football games, track meets, rodeos, pageants, religious ceremonies, and civic gatherings. The opening and closing ceremonies and the track and field events of the Tenth International Olympiad were held here in 1932.

POINTS OF INTEREST IN ENVIRONS

Santa Catalina Island, 46.7 *m.* (*see TOUR 2C*); Los Angeles Aqueduct, longest in the world, 25.1 *m.* (*see TOUR 3c*); Gay's Lion Farm, 15.2 *m.*, Kellogg Institute of Animal Husbandry, blooded Arabian horses, 27.9 *m.*, Guasti Vineyard, largest in U.S., 38.7 *m.* (*see TOUR 3d*).

Monterey

Railroad Stations: N. end of Adams St. for Southern Pacific Lines.
Bus Stations: Franklin and Pacific Sts. for Pacific Greyhound Lines; 216 Del Monte Ave. for Burlington Trailways.
Airport: Community Airport, 3 m. E., off Monterey-Salinas Highway, taxi $1, time 15 min.; special week-end service to San Francisco.
Taxis: 15¢ first ¼ m., 10¢ each additional ⅓ m.
Busses: To Oak Grove 5¢, Del Monte 5¢, Asilomar 10¢, Pacific Grove 10¢, Carmel 25¢.
Traffic Regulations: Pedestrians have right-of-way at all street crossings.

Accommodations: 13 hotels.

Information Service: Hotel Del Monte; Chamber of Commerce, 585 Munras St.; California State Auto Assn., 520 Fremont St.

Radio Stations: KDON (1210 kc.).

Theaters and Motion Picture Houses: First Theater, Scott and Pacific Sts., occasional plays; two motion picture houses.
Tennis: Monterey High School courts, S. end of Larkin St., open to public.
Swimming: Surf swimming at beaches in environs; Monterey High School pool, S. end of Larkin St., free.
Riding: 10 miles of beach; 200 miles of forest trails near Monterey, rates from $1 per hour.
Hunting: Los Padres National Forest, 32.2 m., deer, boar, rabbit, quail, dove, and pigeon; Forest Service regulations.
Fishing: Fresh water fishing in nearby rivers; surf fishing: Monterey Bay, Pacific Grove, Carmel Bay and below Carmel; deep sea: boat rentals at Fisherman's Wharf, N. end of Main St., 50¢ per hour and up.

Annual Events: Birthday Party, commemorative pageants, June 3; Flower Show, June; County Fair, Sept.; Blessing of the Fleet, Sept.

MONTEREY (0–600 alt., 9,141 pop.), lies on sloping shores at the southern end of Monterey Bay, within the northward curve of Point Pinos, which protects the harbor from heavy seas and high winds.

Richard Henry Dana, arriving at Monterey on the brig *Pilgrim* in 1834, thought the town made a "very pretty appearance" with its red-roofed, white stucco houses, the white sand beach, green pines, and deep blue bay. The city gives the same impression today.

To the north the shore sweeps in a curving line toward Santa Cruz. To the east are the convolutions of the Santa Lucia Range, covered with oak and pine, beyond which rise the bare heights of the Gabilan Range. The near hills and pines of Point Pinos block the view to the south, where the coast abruptly changes to stone crags topped with weirdly-shaped trees, and small deep coves and sheltered beaches. Monterey cypress along the shoreline and Monterey pine, both named for the city, are indigenous to a limited area in the vicinity.

In 1890 Monterey still looked like a Mexican town; adobe buildings with red tile roofs were numerous. The march of commerce removed many of these, and the adobe structures standing today are the result of a tardily awakened interest in the city's colorful past. Some of them have been preserved by descendants of the original builders; some were bought by appreciative "Americanos"; a few have been made State monuments.

Alvarado Street, running north and south, is the town's main artery. Starting from the weather-beaten Fisherman's Wharf that puts out into the bay, passing the Old Customhouse, flanked at first by stores selling fishermen's supplies and small restaurants specializing in sea food and Mexican dishes, it crosses the center of the town with its more choice shops, banks, hotels, office buildings, and finally comes to an end at the old Cooper mansion. To the west of Alvarado the business district soon yields to a residential section, which climbs steep hills block after block to wooded heights where its gardens mingle with a semi-wilderness of trees and shrubs high above the port.

At the northern limits of the city is the Presidio of Monterey, the United States Army post. Its rolling 396 acres cover territory reaching from the bay to the hills; here the old Spanish works once put up a show of protecting California with eight or ten cannon, even then obsolete. Stretching along the shore below is the row of fish canneries representing Monterey's chief industry, and moored to the wharves or anchored off shore are the brightly painted boats of the fishing fleet.

The bulk of Monterey's population is native-born American, some of whom are descendants of old Spanish families. Mexicans, Italians, Portuguese, Chinese, and Japanese give a foreign flavor to the street scene. The first fishermen to troll the bay were Chinese, then Portuguese whalemen came from the Azores, but Italians, who live in old frame houses near the wharf, man most of the boats today. Japanese control the abalone fishing, going down in diving suits and picking the univalves from submarine rocks. The Japanese quarter is in the southern section of town near the railroad tracks.

On Saturdays the main street is wide awake. Ranchers and cowboys in blue jeans and high-heeled boots drive in to buy supplies and go to movies; housewives from outlying ranches and truck farms do their week's shopping; tourists and weekenders wander about looking at old adobes, snapping pictures of the fishing fleet, and buying abalone shells; cavalrymen from the post search for amusement; music blares from a few beerhalls; diners in white ties and evening dress sip wine in a resort lodge.

Monterey can be called the kernel of California history. Founded by the Spanish Crown, it was the capital of old California for most of the time between 1775 and the American occupation, and for all that time the social, military and political center.

Cabrillo, exploring the unknown coast in 1542, saw Point Pinos. Sebastian Vizcaíno, merchant-explorer, sailing into the bay in 1602, named it Monterey for the Count of Monte-Rey, Viceroy of Mexico, and described it in such superlatives that those who came after him could not recognize it for 167 years. Gaspar de Portolá's "sacred expedition" of 1769 worked its way overland to find and settle it, twice camped near without recognizing it, passed by, discovered San Francisco Bay, returned, and only on another expedition in the spring of 1770 realized that they were on the stubbornly sought spot. Father Crespi and Father Junípero Serra took formal possession of the land, established the Presidio, and founded the Mission San Carlos de Monterey. In 1775 the King of Spain formally recognized Monterey as the capital of California.

From that time until 1822, when, through the Mexican revolution, California became part of the Mexican republic, Monterey had five different governors. They tried, without much success, to develop Alta California and to pour gold into the coffers of Spain (*see CALIFOR-NIA'S FIRST FOUR CENTURIES*). In 1818 Hypolite Bouchard, the French pirate, raided the town, chased the residents inland, and pillaged for a week before sailing south. After the revolution, the first legislature met in Monterey to draw up California's first constitution. Meanwhile Yankees were learning of tremendous profits to be made in sea otter and whales. Their ships anchored off the Old Customhouse and the town traded for silks, shoes, spices, mirrors, and cartwheels.

Under the Mexican flag there were endless squabbles and bickering, and Monterey was the seat of intrigue and plotting even up to the time Commodore Sloat raised the American flag over the Customhouse in 1846. In 1836 Juan Bautista Alvarado, assisted by Isaac Graham, an American trapper, attacked Monterey. Governor Gutiérrez fled to Mexico after the insurgents landed one cannon ball near his house. A subsequent compromise made Alvarado governor, with headquarters at Monterey. The population of Monterey increased slowly under governors with such resonant names as Figueroa, Arguello, Micheltorena, Castro, Pío Pico. Secularization of the missions in the 1830's increased the number of rancheros and Monterey achieved an impressive social life.

In 1849 Bayard Taylor visited Monterey to observe the last of the old Spanish mode of life, and found that "the native population possesses a natural refinement of manner which would grace the most polished society." William H. Brewer in 1861 found Monterey Bay "a great place for whale hunting," and saw that the beach was white with whale bones; "hundreds of carcasses there decayed, fattening clouds of vultures."

Monterey began to lose its drowsy Mexican ways as specialized agriculture began to supplant cattle raising, and as the fisheries and the allied canning industry developed. Its natural beauty drew artists and writers: Robert Louis Stevenson passed some time here; Charles Warren Stoddard retired and died here; and by the late 1800's many landscape painters had settled in Monterey.

The leading industry of the city today is fishing. Monterey Bay abounds in sardines (the principal catch), mackerel, sole, bass, shrimp, squid, crabs, lobsters and other sea food. Albacore run offshore in spring and late summer, and farther out tuna are caught. Important by-products are fish meal, fish fertilizer, and fish oils. "Del Monte white sand" is shipped from here for building, sand blasting, children's sand boxes, and traps on golf courses.

POINTS OF INTEREST

There are 55 points of interest in Monterey worthy of notice. These all lie along a "historic route" charted by the city and marked by a red and orange checkered line in the middle of the street. This route starts at the Royal Presidio Chapel and loops through the city back to its starting point. Each historic building and site has an explanatory sign. Good maps are available locally. The following list includes outstanding points along the route.

ROYAL PRESIDIO CHAPEL (*open 9-12, 1-5:30 Mon.-Fri.; 9-12, 1-4 Sat.; 1-5 Sun.; ring for guide, adm. 25¢*), Church St. between Camino El Estero and Figueroa St., founded in 1770 by Father Junípero Serra, was the second in the California system of missions. To keep his acolytes away from the soldiers of the presidio, Father Serra moved the mission in 1771 to the Carmel Valley, where its church stands today (*see TOUR 1C*). The Monterey building remained as the presidio chapel. Damaged by fire in 1789, it was reconstructed and dedicated in 1795. It has been in continuous use since, and is the only presidio chapel remaining in California.

The facade, perhaps the most ornate among California missions, rises higher than the roof of the church in the form of a carved gable, and is covered with cream-colored stucco. The arched entrance with its heavy paneled doors is flanked by Doric pilasters and topped with a classic entablature. In the upper gable is a shell-headed niche bearing a statue of Our Lady of Guadalupe. A wide square tower and belfry, roofed in red tile, rises at the left of the facade. In it are two old bells. There are fine vestments, holy vessels, and ornaments in the building.

Every September fishermen of Neapolitan and Sicilian origin celebrate the Festival of Santa Rosalia at the Chapel. The statue of the Saint is carried down to the harbor in religious procession to bless the fishing fleet.

CASA ABREGO (*private*), 592 Abrego St., built by Don José Abrego in the late 1830's, is a long one-story white adobe building with a narrow porch. The walls of the upper gables are of vertical boards. Abrego brought the first full-length mirror to California. When his daughter saw her reflection in it she asked her husband, "Who is that very lovely girl?"

ROBERT LOUIS STEVENSON HOUSE, Houston St., between Webster and Pearl Sts., now an interior decorating shop, is a two-story house with adobe walls, white plaster finish, and shingle roof. Stevenson lived here for three months in 1879 while working on *Amateur Immigrant* and *Vendetta of the West*.

GENERAL JOSE CASTRO'S HEADQUARTERS (*private*), NW. corner Pearl and Tyler Sts., houses a Spanish handcraft forge and cabinet-making shop. On the west side is another adobe occupied by a leather craftsman.

The COOPER HOUSE (*private*), 508 Munras Ave., a long two-story adobe finished in pinkish plaster, was built by Capt. John Bautista Rogers Cooper in 1829. In its day it was a *casa grande*, or "big house," bespeaking its owner's wealth and importance.

CASA AMESTI (*private*), 516 Polk St., a two-story, white-plastered adobe with a balcony, was built in the 1830's by José Amesti as a gift for his daughter.

The STOKES HOUSE (*private*), 500 Hartnell St., built by Dr. James Stokes in the 1840's, is a two-story white-plastered adobe structure with two-story porches, front and rear. A well-preserved pottery kiln is in the back courtyard.

HOUSE OF THE FOUR WINDS (*private*), Main St. between Jefferson and Maddison Sts., is a small, white-plastered adobe, built in the late 1830's by Thomas O. Larkin. Its windows and doors are painted green, and just under the roof a hand-hewn beam can be seen. The building was named for a weather vane on the roof.

SHERMAN'S QUARTERS (*closed*), Main St. between Jefferson and Maddison Sts., is a one-story house, roofed in red tile, its peeling plaster showing the adobe brick beneath. William Tecumseh Sherman lived here from 1847 to 1849.

The LARKIN HOUSE (*private*), 462 Main St., was built in 1835 by Thomas Oliver Larkin, first and only United States consul to California, and used as a consulate from 1844 to 1846. It is a two-story hip-roofed house of adobe construction, finished in soft pink plaster, with a two-story gallery running around the front and two sides. Larkin was a tactful diplomat who smoothed political upheavals of the day, encouraged trade with his native country, and finally helped in the American conquest.

FRIENDLY PLAZA, Pacific St. between Jefferson and Maddison Sts., Civic Center of Monterey, covers two blocks.

COLTON HALL (*open 9-5 weekdays*), west side of Friendly Plaza, is a two-story stone building finished in plaster, designed in the New England post-Colonial style by the Rev. Walter Colton, Yankee alcalde (mayor) from 1846 to 1849.

MONTEREY JAIL, flanking Colton Hall on the south, a one-story buff sandstone building erected in 1854, is still in use, but rarely holds a criminal so desperate as some of the past: Tiburcio Vásquez, the gentleman bandit who could kill with a smile; Anastacia García, the killer who "went to God on a rope" pulled by his friends; Matt Tarpey, taken from his cell by vigilantes and strung up for the murder of a woman; and highwaymen of stage-coach days.

FEW MEMORIAL CITY HALL, Friendly Plaza, S. of the jail, is a one-story, L-shaped structure built in 1934. The foot of the "L" incorporates an adobe house, built in 1843.

CASA VASQUEZ (*private*), Dutra St., between Maddison and Jefferson Sts., is a white adobe half hidden by shrubbery and a large Monterey cypress, and set behind a cactus hedge and picket fence. It is said to be the birthplace and home of the bandit, Tiburcio Vásquez.

CASA ALVARADO (*private*), 510 Dutra St., a long, low adobe with a red brick front porch, was the home of Juan Bautista Alvarado, revolutionist, patriot, and governor of California from 1836 to 1842. He was so busy with politics that he could not attend his own wedding; a friend stood proxy at the ceremony in Mission Santa Clara and brought the bride home.

FIRST AMERICAN THEATER IN CALIFORNIA (*open 1-5 weekdays*), SW. corner Pacific and Scott Sts., a long, rectangular adobe with a frame shack at one end, was built in 1843 as a boarding house and saloon. In 1847 members of Stevenson's regiment produced *Putnam or the Lion Son of '76* and packed the house—at $5.00 a seat. A large wooden door, raised like the lid of a box, served as curtain. Footlights were candles and whale oil lamps. There is an exhibit of early theatrical programs and historical relics in the wooden shack.

The FIRST BRICK HOUSE IN CALIFORNIA, 351 Decatur St., a small two-story house, now a restaurant, was built by the Dickinson family in 1847 of red brick kilned in Monterey.

The OLD WHALING STATION (*private*), 391 Decatur St., is a restored two-story adobe structure, with a shingle roof and a second story balcony across the front. A white-washed frame lean-to extends across the rear in the manner of a New England "salt box." It was built for Portuguese whalers in 1855 when there were 500 whaling vessels in Pacific waters, most of them out of the Sandwich Islands. The diamond-patterned walk and the patio are paved with whale vertebrae.

The PRESIDIO OF MONTEREY, entrance Pacific St. N. of Decatur St., covers 360 acres, running from the shore back into the pine-covered hills. The garrison consists of the 11th U. S. Cavalry, and the 2nd Battalion, 76th Field Artillery. The post has a polo field, drill ground, theater, swimming pool, tennis courts, and recreation hall. On a hill above the entrance is a STATUE OF FATHER SERRA, a life-size figure standing in a boat, a gift of Jane L. Stanford, 1901. Viscaíno landed here in 1602, and Father Serra said mass on the same spot in 1770. Near the entrance is a STATUE OF JOHN DRAKE SLOAT, commander of the American forces that took Monterey. The Presidio was developed in 1902, as a cantonment for troops returning from the Spanish-American War.

OLD CUSTOMHOUSE (*open 1-5 daily*), N. end of Alvarado St., consists of a low central section of plastered adobe and frame built by the Spanish in 1814 and higher additions at each end, built later. On the front of the building, facing the bay, runs a full-length porch covered by the sloping tile roof. The end sections have second-story galleries. Low walls enclose a garden with two old cypress trees and smaller pepper trees.

A STATE MUSEUM in the building preserves a $1,000 Parisian lace dress worn by Doña Escolástica de Dye, a famous beauty of the time. Other historic exhibits include a burro cart with solid wood wheels, and a woman's wedding dress of the Mexican period. Upstairs is the BOHEMIAN MEMORY ROOM, containing the Albert W. Bender collection of original letters and manuscripts of Robert Louis Stevenson, Ambrose Bierce, and George Sterling.

FISHERMEN'S WHARF, N. end of Main St., is a collection of weather-beaten wooden sheds and buildings built on a complicated pattern of piers. Seafood restaurants and fresh fish shops line the first pier. There is always noisy activity on the wharf: the foreign tones of Italian and Japanese fishermen, the creak of the wooden piles as heavy trucks pull out loaded with fish, the shouts of skippers docking their boats; the croaking of sea gulls. Inside the sheds lie great piles of fish. Japanese abalone divers hang their rubber suits out to dry, and Japanese girls prepare abalone steaks for shipment. When the albacore run, there is real excitement on the wharf. Boats go out empty and come back loaded to the gunwales with the game fish, each one caught by a hook and lure. The fish are cleaned and packed on the wharf.

The SANCHEZ ADOBE, 412 Alvarado St., built by Gil Sánchez in 1829 and now housing shops and a bar, is the only house on the street with a balcony.

Oakland

Railroad Stations: W. end of 16th St., and Broadway at 1st St. for Southern Pacific lines; San Pablo Ave. and 40th St. for Atchison, Topeka & Santa Fe Ry.; Washington and 3rd Sts. for Western Pacific R.R.; Shafter Ave. and 40th St. for Sacramento Northern Ry.

Bus Stations: Union Stage Depot, 2047 San Pablo Ave. for Greyhound and Peerless Lines; 1801 Telegraph Ave. for Santa Fe and Burlington Trailways; 1901 San Pablo Ave. for all American Line.

Airports: Oakland Municipal Airport, Bay Farm Island, via Alameda, for Transcontinental & Western Air, Inc., and United Airlines; taxi, $1.80, time 25 min.; Alameda Airport, Alameda via Posey Tube, for Pan-American Airways; taxi $1.60, time 15 min.

Taxis: Average rate 20¢ first quarter mile, 10¢ each additional half-mile, 1 to 5 passengers.

Streetcars: Fare 10¢, 7 tokens for 50¢, no extra fare to adjoining cities; interurban to San Francisco, 21¢.

Ferry: W. end of 7th St., for Southern Pacific ferry to San Francisco, fare 30¢, round trip 50¢, 1 to 5 passengers. (Autos only, no foot passengers.)

Bridge: San Francisco-Oakland Bay Bridge approach, 38th and Market Sts.; 8th and Cypress Sts. from business district; toll 50¢, 1 to 5 passengers.

Traffic Regulations: 25 m.p.h. in residential areas, 20 m.p.h. in business districts, 15 m.p.h. at intersections; 40-min. parking limit in business district, all-night parking prohibited in all areas.

Accommodations: 102 hotels; tourist and trailer camps mostly in East Oakland.

Information Service: Oakland *Tribune* Information Bureau, 13th and Franklin Sts.; Chamber of Commerce, 14th and Franklin Sts.; Dept. of Motor Vehicles, 1107 Jackson St.; California State Automobile Association, 399 Grand Ave.

Radio Stations: KLX (880 kc.); KLS (1280 kc.); KROW (930 kc.).

Theaters and Motion Picture Houses: Municipal Theater, 12th and Fallon Sts., for opera productions and road shows; 36 motion picture houses.

Baseball: Oakland Baseball Park, San Pablo Ave. and Park St., Emeryville; Pacific Coast League.

Golf: Oakland Municipal Golf Course, E. end of Golf Links Road, 18 holes, greens fees 50¢ weekdays, 75¢ Sun. and holidays.

Tennis: 31 municipal courts; lighted, 25¢ per half hour; Athol Plaza, Lakeshore Blvd. and Athol Ave.; Bella Vista, 10th Ave. and E. 28th St.; Brookdale Plaza, High St. and Brookdale Ave.; Dimond Park, Fruitvale Ave. and Lyman Road; Mosswood, Moss Ave. and Webster St.

Swimming: Lions Pool, Dimond Park, Fruitvale Ave. and Lyman Road, children 15¢, adults 25¢, daytime only, no suits or towels furnished; Neptune Beach (and pool), Alameda, children 20¢, adults 35¢, including suits, towels, lockers.

Riding: Bridle paths in hills; horse rental $1 per hour up.

Boating: Lake Merritt, boathouse at E. end of 14th St.; rowboats, canoes 30¢ to 50¢ per hour, motorboats $1 per hour. Around-the-lake water tour, 10¢, children 5¢.

Annual Events: California Spring Garden Show, Exposition Bldg., 10th and Fallon Sts., April; I.A.A. Sports Carnival, Municipal Auditorium, 12th and

Fallon Sts., Winter and Spring; Mills College Horse Show, May; Festival of the Holy Ghost (Portuguese), Pentecostal week, Exposition Bldg., 10th and Fallon Sts.; East Bay Gladiolus Society Exhibition, June; Boys' Smelt Derby, Lake Merritt, July; Bowling Green Contests, Lakeside Park, Sept.; Outboard Motorboat Races, Lake Merritt, Sept.; Columbus Day Celebration, Lakeside Park; Christmas Pageant, Municipal Auditorium, 12th and Fallon Sts.

OAKLAND (0–1,600 alt., 284,063 pop.) is the metropolis of the industrial and residential East Bay municipal area, in which approximately half a million people reside in seven abutting cities. Third in the State in population, the city has outgrown the idea that it is merely "San Francisco's bedroom."

Oakland and its sister communities, Berkeley, San Leandro, Hayward, Emeryville, Piedmont, and Alameda, are framed by the relatively low Berkeley Hills (up to 1,200 feet), which parallel the shoreline of the Bay. Eastward beyond these wooded slopes appear the higher elevations of the Contra Costa Hills, culminating in Mount Diablo (3,800 feet) some 30 miles east of the city. Southward the hills drop to the level East Bay shore permitting the city to expand without hindrance in that direction. Five miles to the west, across the bay, is San Francisco. Of the 30,000 passengers transported daily between the cities, the majority are Oakland commuters.

The port of Oakland has facilities to accommodate any vessel in the Pacific trade. The Oakland Estuary, formerly a shallow slough, is called the inner harbor, and the open bay portion to the north is the outer harbor. Three transcontinental railroads enter the city.

Along the ridge of the Berkeley Hills winds the Skyline Boulevard, offering a view to the east of the dry, tawny hills of Contra Costa; to the west spreads the thickly settled marginal plain and the glowing bay, rimmed by the jagged silhouette of San Francisco. Below is the metropolitan cluster of downtown Oakland, dominated by the 17-story city hall.

Residential areas surround the business district and run up the foothills to the ridge. The modern Oakland home is of light stucco, tile-roofed, studio-windowed, with arches and patios. Built on hillsides, flats, and knolls, these houses show, in construction and landscaping, the benefits of a mild climate. Here and there, however, are sharp-gabled, high-ceilinged, full-basemented, weathertight houses built by pioneers who did not realize they had come to a moderate climate. City parks and private gardens contain many varieties of semitropical trees—camphor, acacia, pepper, dracena, and several species of eucalyptus and palm. Citrus fruits and figs ripen in Oakland yards.

Lake Merritt, a salt-water lake, is a few blocks from the Oakland business district. Until 1898 it was an unsightly tidal basin fed by waters from the Estuary; today it is a 155-acre, Y-shaped lake with grassy banks, the water level controlled by hydraulic gates. Encircling the lake are a hiking path, a park strip, and a high-speed boulevard, and in the crotch of the "Y" is 53-acre Lakeside Park. At the base of the "Y" is Peralta Park (reclaimed from the mud flats).

Of Oakland's ethnic groups the most numerous is the Negro community, concentrated in West Oakland near the railroad shops and yards, which provide their chief employment. On the outskirts of the city live many of the Portuguese dairy farmers who have settled in great numbers in Alameda County. Other minor groups are Italians, Chinese, Japanese, Filipino, and Mexicans.

The first white men to see what is now Oakland were Spaniards— Lieutenant Fages and Father Crespi, who headed an expedition in 1772. The expedition pushed as far north as Antioch, and active developments took place across the Bay, but it was nearly half a century before the site of Oakland was colonized.

Cavalry Sergt. Luís María Peralta, as a worthy soldier of the royal Spanish army, received title in 1820 to a 48,000-acre domain, named it Rancho San Antonio, added "Don" to his name, and lived as befitted a gentleman of leisure. His grant included the entire East Bay area.

For twenty years Rancho San Antonio played an important part in the commercial, religious, and social life of California. In 1842, the sergeant divided the ranch among his four sons, and Vincente Peralta was given the area where Oakland now stands. They owned great herds of cattle, maintained a large retinue of *vaqueros* (cowboys), and pursued the Spanish life of "fiesta and siesta." The American victory over Mexico in 1848 ended the era of the Spanish landowner in California, and the discovery of gold in the same year hastened the rout. Mobs of gold seekers came to the flourishing town of San Francisco, many of whom tramped to the diggings through the Peralta holdings. Some of them visualized greater riches from these acres than from the Mother Lode. They squatted on the rancho, built shacks and fences, and ran off cattle, and resisted every effort of the owners to evict them.

Moses Chase, however, who came to Oakland in 1849, was of a more ethical turn of mind. He became associated with the three Patten brothers in a lease of 460 acres from Antonio Peralta. They were the first farmers of the district, raising good crops of grain and hay. The early town of Clinton took form on their acreage. The Patten brothers soon entered the lumbering business in the Peralta Redwoods, a stand of giant trees that extended from the top of the range midway to the Oakland estuary. In the middle 1850's more than 400 men were employed in the mills, cutting lumber for the building of San Francisco, Oakland and their environs.

In 1851, the Rancho San Antonio was well spotted with squatters and purchasers, and in that year there appeared a man who gave the Latin owners, and the Americanos, a lesson in plain and fancy financing. Horace W. Carpentier had a degree from an eastern university, a keen sense of values, and more than one man's share of vision. He acquired a townsite in the present downtown Oakland, imported a few "residents" from the redwoods, and in 1852 incorporated the Town of Oakland, with himself in the mayor's chair. The name he selected from the numerous stands of *encinas* (evergreen oaks) that dotted the landscape. Two years later Mr. Carpentier incorporated the town as a city, and by that time had acquired the entire Oakland waterfront in exchange for building three tiny wharves and a frame schoolhouse. Thus began the "battle of the waterfront," which was terminated in 1910 when the assigns of Carpentier agreed with the city to waive title to their properties in exchange for long term leases.

The first ferry across the bay began operating in 1850; first train chugged through Oakland in 1863; and overland service was established in 1869. In 1906, when San Francisco fell victim to earthquake and fire, 50,000 refugees moved to Oakland. There was a building boom to provide housing for refugees who became permanent East Bay residents. The city annexed all hamlets and towns to the southeast and in 1907 the population reached 147,000. The industrial stimulation that followed this influx moved Oakland into third place among California manufacturing cities as early as 1910, and by 1920 its population increased to 216,000. During the World War four large shipbuilding plants were operating under forced draft, and following that period the city production increased in automobiles, lumber and allied products, electrical machinery, canning, and cereal products. The aggregate value of Oakland's industrial output was multiplied five times between 1914 and 1927. In 1936, Oakland celebrated with San Francisco the opening of the San Francisco-Oakland Bay Bridge (*see SAN FRANCISCO*).

POINTS OF INTEREST

1. OAKLAND CITY HALL, Washington St. between 14th and 15th Sts., designed by Palmer, Hornbostle and Jones, and completed in 1914, is the highest building in the city, its 17 floors rising 360 feet and towering in three set-back sections embellished with classic colonnades and arches and topped with a baroque cupola.

2. The SNOW MUSEUM (*open 10-5 weekdays, 1-5 Sun. and holidays*), 247 19th St., a white frame structure with a columned portico, contains stuffed Arctic, African, and American mammals, collected by the explorers, Henry A. Snow and his son, Sidney, in 1919-21. They made a motion picture, *Big Game Hunting in Africa,* the first of its kind released by a major Hollywood studio. In 1922 the Snow specimens were donated to the City of Oakland, which purchased a site for their exhibition.

3. LAKESIDE PARK, irregularly bordering the N. shore of Lake Merritt, threaded by Bellevue Ave., has facilities for tennis, bowling-on-the-green, and horseshoe pitching, and a municipal bandstand where free outdoor concerts are given on Sundays, August to October, 2-4 p.m.

4. LAKE MERRITT WILDFOWL SANCTUARY is a game refuge administered by the United States Biological Survey, which maintains a banding station near the Canoe House. Ducks and other wildfowl, which make their headquarters here from November to March, are fed at 10 a.m. and 3:30 p.m.

5. The EMBARCADERO (landing place), on the NE. tip of Lake Merritt, is a horseshoe-shaped walk bordered by concrete columns.

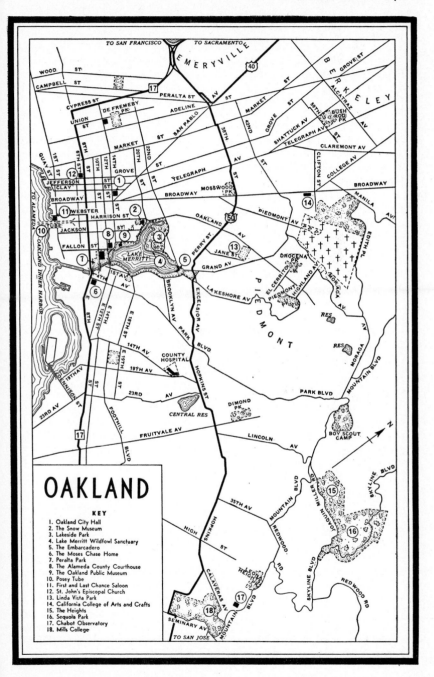

TO SAN FRANCISCO   TO SACRAMENTO
EMERYVILLE
BERKELEY

WOOD ST
CAMPBELL ST
CYPRESS ST
PERALTA ST
DE FREMERY PK
ADELINE ST
UNION ST
MARKET ST
GROVE ST
SAN PABLO AV
BROADWAY
MOSSWOOD PK
TELEGRAPH
JEFFERSON
CLAY
BROADWAY
WEBSTER
HARRISON ST
JACKSON ST
FALLON ST
LAKE MERRITT
OAKLAND INNER HARBOR
TO ALAMEDA
TUBE
SHATTUCK AV
TELEGRAPH AV
CLAREMONT AV
CLIFTON ST
COLLEGE AV
BROADWAY
MANILA AV
PIEDMONT AV
BUSH ROD PK
GROVE ST
ALCATRAZ AV
PERALTA ST
MARKET ST
GROVE
PIEDMONT
EL CERRITO AV
MORAGA AV
MOUNTAIN BLVD
EDITH PL
HIGHLAND
DROCENA
PERRY ST
JANE ST
GRAND AV
LAKESHORE AV
EXCELSIOR AV
PARK BLVD
BROOKLYN AV
OAKLAND AV
RES
RES
MORAGA
COUNTY HOSPITAL
14TH AV
19TH AV
23RD AV
CENTRAL RES
DIMOND PK
PARK BLVD
BOY SCOUT CAMP
FRUITVALE AV
LINCOLN AV
DENNISON ST
23RD AV
FOOTHILL BLVD
35TH AV
HOPKINS ST
MOUNTAIN BLVD
REDWOOD RD
JOAQUIN MILLER RD
SKYLINE BLVD
REDWOOD RD
HIGH ST
LINCOLN
CALAVERAS AV
LEONA HEIGHTS
MOUNTAIN BLVD
SEMINARY AV
TO SAN JOSE

OAKLAND

KEY

1. Oakland City Hall
2. The Snow Museum
3. Lakeside Park
4. Lake Merritt Wildfowl Sanctuary
5. The Embarcadero
6. The Moses Chase Home
7. Peralta Park
8. The Alameda County Courthouse
9. The Oakland Public Museum
10. Posey Tube
11. First and Last Chance Saloon
12. St. John's Episcopal Church
13. Linda Vista Park
14. California College of Arts and Crafts
15. The Heights
16. Sequoia Park
17. Chabot Observatory
18. Mills College

The Spaniards shipped hides and tallow from here in flat-bottomed barges.

6. The OAKLAND PUBLIC MUSEUM (*open 10-5 weekdays, 1-5 Sun. and holidays*), 1426 Oak St., is a two-story brown frame house containing exhibits in natural science, ethnology, and history. In the Natural Science Section are birds, mammals, insects, and butterflies; the Ethnology Department displays artifacts of Alaska, British Columbia, California, and Pacific Islands. The History Section contains relics of the War of 1812, Civil War, Spanish-American War, and the World War; the California Room has relics of Indian, Spanish and pioneer days. In the two Colonial Rooms are reproductions, including a "whatnot" once the property of Abraham Lincoln. The museum also houses displays of old coins, firearms, medals, and currency.

7. The MOSES CHASE HOME (*private*), NE. corner 4th Ave. and E. 8th St., the oldest dwelling in Oakland, was built about 1850. The four original rooms are still intact, and serve as a nucleus for the white-painted 14-room house with its gable roof and green shutters, and its porch extending across the front. Chase was Oakland's first American settler, arriving via Cape Horn from Massachusetts in 1849.

8. PERALTA PARK is a landscaped tract on the S. shore of Lake Merritt between 8th and 12th Sts. The MUNICIPAL AUDITORIUM, 10th and Fallon Sts., is of concrete finished in California granite, and divided into the Arena, the Theater, and the Art Gallery. Conventions and boxing and wrestling matches are held in the Arena; opera, road shows, and lectures are given in the Theater; the Art Gallery (*open 1-5 daily*) houses a permanent collection of painting, sculpture, and prints, and conducts annual exhibitions. The EXPOSITION BUILDING, Fallon St. between 9th and 10th Sts., similar in design to the Auditorium, is used for athletic and civic events.

9. The ALAMEDA COUNTY COURTHOUSE, Fallon St. between 12th and 13th Sts., a concrete building of neo-classic design, with terra cotta and granite trim, was completed by PWA in 1936 at a cost of $2,000,000. The HALL OF RECORDS is on the general floor. The COUNTY FREE LIBRARY (*open 9-5 Mon.-Fri., 9-12 Sat.*), and mosquito control exhibit are in the basement.

10. POSEY TUBE, entrance Harrison and 6th Sts., a $4,500,000 subway, 4,436 feet long, under the estuary connecting Oakland with Alameda, was opened to traffic in 1928. Its lighting, ventilation, drainage, fire protection, and traffic control systems have brought it to the attention of engineers the world over. The inside diameter of the tube is 32 feet, the walls are 2½ feet thick, and it is claimed to be earthquake-proof. The tube is named for George A. Posey, its designer and builder.

11. FIRST AND LAST CHANCE SALOON, 50 Webster St., an unpainted wooden shack, is noted as the place where Jack London, in his ambitious early days, studied and wrote through the kindness of the barkeeper. The saloon, built about 1880, retains an early western atmosphere, with its battered bar, its wall plastered with pictures of forgotten celebrities, its decrepit card tables, and its brass spittoons.

12. ST. JOHN'S EPISCOPAL CHURCH, SW. corner Grove and 8th Sts., a shingled building with a square Gothic tower, built in 1860, is the oldest Episcopal church in Oakland. Hand-carved plaques adorn the walls.

13. LINDA VISTA PARK, Oakland and Olive Aves., is a landscaped area containing the eight-acre MUNICIPAL ROSE GARDENS. Some of the 100,000 rose bushes of more than 3,000 varieties are in bloom continuously.

14. CALIFORNIA COLLEGE OF ARTS AND CRAFTS, 5212 Broadway, a coeducational institution founded in 1907, is set on a high hill, behind an ivy-clad red stone wall. The landscaped four-acre campus with 12 buildings of wood and stucco includes two fine specimens of *Sequoia gigantea* (big tree). The institution presents a full course in the various branches of the arts and crafts, leading to bachelor's degrees in Arts.

15. THE HIGHTS (JOAQUIN MILLER PARK), NE. on Joaquin Miller Road, so spelled by Miller, was the home of the "Poet of the Sierras," where he and his friends planted 75,000 eucalypti, pines, cypresses, and acacias. The city bought the tract in 1917, granting a life tenure in it to the poet's widow and daughter, each of whom occupies a cottage on the grounds. The ABBEY (*open by appointment*), built in 1886, where the poet lived until his death in 1913, consists of three one-room frame structures connected to form a single unit, each room roofed by a shingled peak. Here he wrote "Columbus" and other poems. The poet claimed he could not write without rain on the roof; he had pipes installed to sprinkle water on the roof when he wanted inspiration. On the eminence to the north he built a stone foundation intended as his funeral pyre (never used); native rock towers dedicated to Gen. John C. Frémont and Robert Browning; and a pyramid to Moses.

16. In SEQUOIA PARK, adjoining The Hights to the E., a wooded area of 182 acres, is the OAKLAND ZOO (*always open*), Robinson Drive and Joaquin Miller Road, housing 30 specimens.

17. CHABOT OBSERVATORY, 4917 Mountain Blvd. (*open 1-4 p.m. and 7-10 p.m. Tues.-Sat., except during school holidays and vacations*), a two-story stucco building with a dome at either end, occupies 12 acres on a landscaped hill and contains 8- and 20-inch refracting telescopes.

18. MILLS COLLEGE, Trenor St. and Seminary Ave., oldest college in the West exclusively for women, was founded in 1852, in Benicia, as the Young Ladies' Seminary. It reached full collegiate standing and became known as Mills College in 1885. The college is nonsectarian and has about 550 students; it confers bachelor and master degrees in arts and sciences, and is particularly distinguished in music and art. The more modern buildings on the campus are designed in the Mediterranean style of architecture. The CAMPANILE, in mission style, has ten bells, originally cast for the World's Fair in Chicago in 1893. The design of the MUSIC BUILDING is based upon the church

architecture of the Spanish Renaissance, with an elaborate arch-canopy doorway embellished with twisted columns, decorative finials and a sculptured lunette. It contains nearly 60 soundproof practice rooms. ETHEL MOORE HALL, one of the six residence halls, is built on 16 different levels, with five patios. The ART GALLERY (*open 2-5 Wed., Fri., Sun.; group visits by arrangement other days*) contains a permanent American collection of painting, sculpture, and art objects, including a group of Chinese paintings, an extensive art library, and a notable collection of the works of Robert Browning. Student painting and sculpture is exhibited in May and June. The LIBRARY (*private*) has a large collection of early western literature and books by California writers.

SKYLINE BOULEVARD—north approach from Berkeley, south approach from Foothill Boulevard, Oakland—from the tourists' standpoint the most distinctive feature of Oakland, is a winding road high above the city, which affords a magnificent panorama of the East Bay, the harbor, and San Francisco and Marin County across the bay. By means of a tunnel through the Berkeley Hills into Contra Costa County (and by a low-level tunnel at the head of Broadway) the driver from Oakland can pass from a temperature of 65 degrees to one of 100 degrees or more; from lush greenery to the golden brown of sundrenched Contra Costa hills; from a busy urban area to one of dreamy open spaces.

POINTS OF INTEREST IN ENVIRONS

Mount Diablo, 38.5 *m.* (*see TOUR 9A*); University of California, 6 *m.* (*see BERKELEY*).

Pasadena

Railroad Stations: 222 S. Raymond Ave. for Atchison, Topeka & Santa Fe R.R.; 148 E. Colorado Blvd. for Southern Pacific Lines, and Pacific Electric Ry. (interurban).
Bus Stations: Union Bus Terminal, 48 S. Marengo Ave., for motor transit lines, and Pasadena-Ocean Park Line, and Mt. Wilson Stage Line.
Taxis: 10¢ for first passenger mile, 5¢ per mile for additional passengers, 20¢ per mile after 5 miles.
Streetcars: Zone system, fare 6¢ and 12¢; four tokens for 25¢; free transfers.
Traffic Regulations: All parking prohibited 1-6 a.m.; right turns against signal after full stop.

Accommodations: 25 hotels; tourist camps; rates slightly higher in winter season.

Information Service: Chamber of Commerce, N. Garfield Ave. and Union St.; information booth, City Hall, 100 N. Garfield Ave.

Radio Station: KPPC (1210 kc.).
Theaters and Motion Picture Houses: Pasadena Community Playhouse, 39 El Molino Ave., local productions; Civic Auditorium, Civic Center at Green St., lectures, opera, music, community dances; Gold Shell, Memorial Park, N. Raymond Ave. and Union St., concerts, occasional light opera, drama, pageants; 11 motion picture houses.
Baseball: Brookside Park, 1645 Arroyo Blvd., spring training grounds for Chicago White Sox, occasional exhibition games.
Golf: Brookside Park, 18-hole course, 50¢, $1 all day; 9-hole course, 35¢, 50¢ all day; locker fee 50¢ per month, 30 tickets for $5, 30 tickets for man and wife, $7.50, not good Sat. afternoon or Sun.; Altadena Municipal course, 2492 Country Club Dr., 18 holes, 40¢, monthly tickets $5.
Tennis: Besse Playgrounds, 3303 E. Colorado St.; La Pintoresca, N. Fair Oaks Ave. and Washington St.; Washington Park, N. El Molino Ave. and Washington St.; Brookside Park; all lighted, meter charge 25¢ for 40 min.
Swimming: Brookside Park, 2 pools open Apr. 1-Oct. 1, adults 25¢, with suit and towel 25¢; children under 12, 10¢, with suit and towel 15¢; children 12-18 years, 15¢, with suit and towel 20¢.
Riding: In Arroyo Seco, and other parks, mountain trails N. and E. of Pasadena. Horses, $1 per hour average.

Annual Events: Pasadena Rose Tournament Jan. 1; football game between eastern and western collegiate teams, Jan. 1, Rose Bowl; Pasadena Flower Show, Busch Gardens, 3 days in April and Oct.; Pasadena Kennel Club Show, Civic Auditorium, Feb. and July.

PASADENA (800–1,200 alt., 76,086 pop.), lies in the foothills of the Sierra Madre Mountains, overlooking the San Gabriel Valley. Behind it, to the north, are suburban Altadena and the pine-clad heights of Mount Wilson and Mount Lowe. Its southern limits are separated from Los Angeles by the small communities of South Pasadena and Alhambra. On the east, it stretches for several miles along broad

Colorado Street, and ends abruptly in the west along the curving Arroyo Seco (dry watercourse).

From a vantage point in the hills, the city looks like a lumpy sea of green trees, from which rise church spires, the boxlike procession of business buildings along Colorado Street, and the massive resort hotels. An air of prosperity—the unhurried tenor of a Sunday afternoon— is engendered by the substantial buildings, the pretentious homes, generous foliage, and the winding, flower-edged streets. The center of the small business district is the intersection of Colorado Street and Fair Oak Avenue. Here the streets are lined with smart shops, lighted at night with a restrained display of neon lights. There is no large-scale industry in Pasadena; business is mostly restricted to retail trade and stores that supply the wants of good living.

In the residential section, surrounding the business district, are homes in carefully tended gardens, mansions in estates with sunken gardens, swimming pools, and tennis courts. Resort hotels spread their wings and terraces over grounds well back from the street, their lawns spotted with gay garden furniture. Near the western margin of the city is a remnant of the architectural glory of the 1890's—Orange Grove Avenue, known as "Millionaires' Row," a street of mansions in massive style set behind well-manicured lawns.

On Christmas Tree Lane (Santa Rosa Avenue, Altadena), giant deodars, planted as seedlings from the Himalayas in the 1890's, have stretched their branches across the street and almost conceal the houses. Each Christmas the trees are festooned with thousands of colored lights, creating a festive effect that attracts thousands of visitors.

On New Year's Day the city stages the Tournament of Roses, inspired by the flower fetes in Nice, and introduced in 1890 as a simple village festival to celebrate the midwinter flowering season. Residents decked their buggies with roses, went picnicking, sent pictures back home, and connected roses with New Year's Day so effectively that Pasadena has been called "the town that roses built."

On this day young girls elected for their beauty are carried through the streets in floats of elaborate design, where they sit pelting the crowds with flowers. Citizens forget their dignity to join in a battle of blossoms. Floats represent every prominent city in California and even other States and foreign countries. The floral decorations follow a single theme, and floats bearing 100,000 to 300,000 fresh flowers are not uncommon. The holiday became more elaborate each season; for twelve years the climaxing feature of the day was a thundering, ripsnorting chariot race, finally displaced in 1916 by the football game between picked eastern and western teams in the Rose Bowl.

Pasadena is staid—a city with an unusual number of churches for its size—but it supports an excellent small theater and several art and music associations. The Pasadena Community Playhouse is one of the leading little theaters in the country; its productions have originality and a professional finish. The city's educational institutions are relatively long established and rank high. The California Institute of

Technology, with Dr. Robert Millikan, the physicist, as president, has made important contributions to scientific theory, notably Millikan's study of cosmic rays and researches into the nature of the electron. The Institute has also aided in advancing aeronautics, and by virtue of several foundations has carried forward cancer and other medical research.

The site of Pasadena, once part of the lands of the San Gabriel Mission, has changed owners with perplexing frequency. The Rancho San Pasqual was first granted by the mission fathers to an aged mission housekeeper in 1826, and passed from her hands when she married at nearly 100 years of age. Her stepson sold his interest in 1839 to two dons who later abandoned the property.

Governor Micheltorena, looking about for a suitable present in 1843, granted the land to Don Manuel Garfías, a Mexican army officer. Garfías had his title validated by the United States Land Commission in 1854 and was sent a patent signed by Lincoln in 1863. Meanwhile Garfías sold his interest to Benjamin D. Wilson, a Yankee, who has given his name to a mountain, a canyon, a lake, a trail, an avenue, and a school. Wilson and his associates swapped, traded, and borrowed from each other, with the land as security, until in 1873 the land was divided between Wilson and Dr. John S. Griffin, who came to California as chief medical officer with the American Army. Griffin's share was approximately 4,000 acres and included the original site of Pasadena.

The story now moves East. The winter of 1872-73 was cold in Indiana. Dr. Thomas B. Elliott, of Indianapolis, and his friends "to get where life was easy," formed the "California Colony of Indiana," and sent a scouting committee to spy out the promised land. It looked as if it would be easy. The colony bought Griffin's land for $25,000, and that was the beginning of the exodus of wealthy men from the Middle West and East that resulted in the present millionaires' retreat.

The city was incorporated in 1886, and chartered by the State in 1901. By this time Pasadena had begun to take on definite character. It was settling in the mold of a dignified, permanent community, and began to support more vigorously its educational institutions. Throop University, ancestor of the California Institute of Technology, had been founded by Amos G. ("Father") Throop, in 1891, as a polytechnic school; Mt. Wilson Observatory was established in 1904; and Pasadena gradually became a recognized center of learning.

The richest city per capita in America, Pasadena is something of a paradox. Situated in the heart of open-shop southern California, it has been friendly to organized labor since the time of the McNamara case. The neighboring Los Angeles *Citizen,* published during that time, received the bulk of its advertising from Pasadena merchants.

So far, with the conservative wealthy in control, the city has maintained its lovely appearance against any encroachments of factories or large-scale business enterprises.

POINTS OF INTEREST

The CIVIC CENTER, Garfield Ave., between Walnut and Green Sts., is a harmonious group of modified Spanish and Italian Renaissance buildings, dominated by the CITY HALL, 100 N. Garfield Ave., an impressive domed three-story concrete structure occupying an entire block. The large red- and gold-topped dome rises above the entrance pavilion on an arcaded and pinnacled drum, the lower stage of which is adorned with Ionic columns. At the upper end of the Civic Center is the PUBLIC LIBRARY (*open 9-9 Mon.-Sat.*), 285 E. Walnut St., a rambling buff stucco building with walled forecourt, low tiled roof and projecting wings. The forecourt is planted with stately rows of palms. The library has more than 200,000 volumes. The circulation hall, in the main section of the building, is decorated with a coffered ceiling and oak paneling; the children's room in the left wing and the periodical room in the right wing have outdoor reading rooms in frescoed cloisters that flank the forecourt. At the lower end of the Civic Center is the CIVIC AUDITORIUM (*open 2-4 Wed.*), 300 E. Green St., that seats 3,000.

BROOKSIDE PARK, Arroyo Blvd. between Holly St. and Devil's Gate Dam, is a city recreational preserve of more than 500 acres, with a picnic and playground section, swimming pool, and municipal golf course. Trails and bridle paths run through forests of oak and pine. Within its grounds is the ROSE BOWL (*open free, except during performances*), Arroyo Blvd. at Salvia Canyon Rd., a concrete stadium of elliptical shape, seating some 85,000. It is used for other football games besides the annual Rose Bowl game, and for political rallies and civic festivities.

The MILLARD HOUSE, 645 Prospect Crescent, is a studio-residence built by Frank Lloyd Wright for Mrs. George M. Millard in 1923. Framed by eucalyptus trees, at the end of a ravine, its two-story facade is reflected in a pool of the sunken gardens. The double walls of concrete blocks are stamped with a radical cross design. Also forming a part of the house plan are the garage with its tall castle-like doors and the Little Museum of the Book designed by Mr. Wright's son.

The BUSCH GARDENS (*open 9-5 daily; admission free*), Arroyo Blvd. at Madeline Dr., is named for the St. Louis brewer. Its landscaped 75 acres contain formal gardens, natural woodlands, and miles of mazelike paths. Scattered about the grounds are groups of terracotta gnomes and fairies in scenes from the tales of the Brothers Grimm and Hans Andersen. The Gardens are part of the Busch estate.

The CALIFORNIA INSTITUTE OF TECHNOLOGY (*not open to public*), 1201 E. California St., is a scientific institution of international repute. White buildings of modified Spanish design occupy the 22-acre campus—laboratories, classrooms, dormitories, and the Athenaeum, which houses visiting foreign scientists and scholars. The Daniel Guggenheim Aeronautical Laboratory, the Norman Bridge Laboratory of Physics, and the W. K. Kellogg Laboratory of Radiation (for cancer research) are maintained here. Dr. Robert A. Millikan of cosmic-ray fame has long been president of the Institute, the faculty of which includes several other Nobel prize winners. Prof. Albert Einstein worked here for some time after fleeing Germany. The 200-inch telescope lens for the Palomar Mountain Observatory—largest in the world—was ground in the laboratories here.

The FLORES ADOBE (*private*), Garfield Ave. and Foothill St., was built in 1839 for Doña Eulalia Perez de Guillen, original owner of the Rancho San Pasqual. The house, greatly restored, has reddish plaster walls and red tile roofs. The original beams of rough-hewn timber still protrude beneath the eaves. After the battle of La Mesa in January, 1847, the decisive fight in the conquest of California, Gen. José Mariá Flores, defeated commander of the Californian lancers, took refuge here (*see CALIFORNIA'S LAST FOUR CENTURIES*).

The PASADENA COMMUNITY PLAYHOUSE, 39 El Molino Ave. (*open 9-4 daily, except during Sat. matinees; theater usually dark in Sept.*), a U-shaped group of two-story, white-plastered Spanish Colonial buildings surrounding a rough-flagged forecourt, is one of the few nationally known little theaters. In the right wing is the School of the Theater, and the Laboratory Theater, a workshop in which the plays of new authors are given test productions. The theater was built in 1925, and seats 820. Since its organization in 1916 by the present director (1939), Gilmor Brown, the playhouse has produced 80 national and world premieres, and most of Shakespeare's plays.

MEMORIAL FLAGPOLE, at Colorado St. and Orange Grove Ave., is a lofty pole with a bronze sculptured base, designed by Bertram Goodhue and Lee Lawrie, and dedicated in 1927 as a memorial to Pasadena men who fell in the World War.

POINTS OF INTEREST IN ENVIRONS

Huntington Library and Art Gallery, San Marino, 11.5 *m.;* Mount Wilson Observatory, 25.7 *m.* (*see TOUR 12c*).

Sacramento

Railroad Stations: 4th and I Sts. for Southern Pacific Lines; 19th and J Sts. for Western Pacific R.R.; Union Station, 11th and I Sts., for Sacramento Northern Ry.

Bus Stations: 7th and L Sts. for Greyhound and Pierce Arrow Lines; 913 5th St. for River Auto Stages; 1127 9th St. for Burlington Trailways.

Airports: Municipal Airport, 5 m. S. on Freeport Blvd., for United Airlines; taxi 75¢ for passengers; time 15 min.

Taxis: Zone fares 25¢ to $1.50, usual charge, 5¢ for each additional passenger; hourly rate $2 to $2.50.

Streetcars: Fare 5¢ and 7¢.

Piers: M St. Wharf, River Lines to San Francisco, 6 p.m. daily.

Accommodations: 109 hotels; 13 tourist and trailer camps.

Information Service: California State Automobile Association, 1700 L St.; Tourist Association, 1724 L St.; Consolidated Travel Bureau, 1128 10th St.; Chamber of Commerce, 917 7th St.

Radio Stations: KFBK (1490 kc.); KROY (1210 kc.).

Theaters and Motion Picture Houses: Tuesday Clubhouse, 2722 L St., amateur plays; Memorial Auditorium, 16th and J Sts., symphony and choral concerts; 15 motion picture houses.

Baseball: Cardinal Field, 11th and Broadway, Pacific Coast League.

Golf: Sacramento municipal golf course, Auburn Blvd., 18 holes, 25¢ for 9 holes, monthly tickets $2.50 (for weekdays); William Land Park municipal golf course, Freeport Blvd. and 13th Ave., 9 holes, 25¢, monthly tickets $2.50 (for weekdays).

Tennis: McKinley Park, Alhambra Blvd. and H St.; McClatchy Park, 35th St. and 5th Ave.; Roosevelt Park, 10th and P Sts.; Southside Park, 7th and T Sts.; all free.

Swimming: Clunie Memorial Pool, McKinley Park, Alhambra Blvd. and H St., 25¢, children 10¢; James McClatchy Pool, 35th St. and 5th Ave., 25¢, children 10¢; suits and towels included; Riverside Baths, 3540 Riverside Blvd., 25¢, children 10¢.

Riding: Bridle paths in William Land Park, Freeport Blvd. and Sutterville Rd., horses 75¢ to $1 an hour.

Boating: Southside Park Lake, 7th and T Sts., free mornings, 25¢ 1-8 p.m.

Fishing: Catfish, salmon, striped bass, in Sacramento River; rowboats 25¢ per hour, $1 per day; motorboats 50¢ and $2.

Annual Events: Rodeo, State Fair Grounds, 5th Ave. and Stockton Blvd., Apr.; California State Fair, 10 days, early Sept.

SACRAMENTO (30 alt., 93,750 pop.), capital of California, lying in a loop of the Sacramento River at its confluence with the American River, is a calm city of trees, green lawns, and governmental buildings. Along the bank of the river is the oldest part of town, red brick buildings, with tall narrow windows, and tin-roofed awnings projecting over the sidewalk. Curbstones are high, recalling the times when the river flooded its banks.

Back from the river older buildings gradually give way to the concrete and stone of the business section. In summer the policemen on traffic duty wear white helmets, like African explorers, for there are three-day cycles of heat when the sun is intense and soft drink consumption reaches incredible figures. During these spells, Capitol Park, with its 40 acres of tree-shaded lawns, attracts hundreds of steaming citizens.

The wide shady streets of the residential sections and the masses of flowers and shrubbery on the lawns give the city something of the appearance of a Southern river town. In the older districts most of the houses are of brick, although ungainly frame houses with scrollwork twisting from eaves and cornices, are left from the effulgent period of the seventies and eighties. The newer homes reflect wide differences in architectural taste, from simple stucco bungalows to old English, Moorish, Spanish, and California mission styles.

The domed capitol dominates the city. The legislature meets biennially in odd years, holding two sessions broken by a recess. Epic struggles have been waged here, among others the long fight against the railroad stranglehold on the valley, ending in the reforms under Governor Hiram Johnson; and the bitter contest over Japanese immigration, which ended with exclusion.

Mexicans, Italians, Chinese, Japanese, and Filipinos are generously represented in the city's population, especially among agricultural workers. Germans and German Swiss were among pioneer settlers. Migratory farm workers, dust bowl refugees, and itinerants "lay up" in Sacramento between harvests.

Flat stretches of unclaimed land, the navigable river, which was named Sacramento in honor of the sacrament, by Jose Moraga, comandante of the presidio of San Jose, and tractable Indians for workers drew the attention of Capt. John Augustus Sutter, the pioneer settler, in 1839. The Swiss ex-army officer took up a 50,000-acre grant by swearing allegiance to the Mexican flag, and built a principality named "New Helvetia" in memory of the old country. He ruled in baronial splendor, with Indians as his subjects, and a fort of timber and adobe brick as his castle, with twelve guns mounted on the ramparts. Sutter built forges and shops, grazed herds on his lands, trapped for furs, and carried on a lively trade. The spot was a haven for settlers in the tide of overland emigration in the early 1840's. In 1848 the town of Sacramento was laid out on Sutter's farm, and the first lots were sold in January, 1849.

It was Sutter's boss carpenter, James W. Marshall, who, on January 24, 1848, found the first gold flake while building a mill for Sutter near Coloma (see *TOUR 4a*) on the South Fork of the American River, which resulted in the great gold rush of 1849 and the 1850's and in California's admission to the Union as a State. It also led to Sutter's ruin. Trampling hordes from the East overran his hospitable fort, stole his cattle, drove off his Indians, disputed his rights to the land. His white retainers deserted for the mines. Meantime, millions of dollars in gold dust passed over Sutter's landing. He moved to Pennsylvania in 1873, with only a small pension from California, and died at Washington, D.C., in 1880, after vainly beseeching Congress for the restoration of his property.

The settlement became the supply center for the northern mines of the mother lode. Thousands of gold-hungry men came pouring in to outfit for the diggings. The 1850 census showed 6,820, and the population soon jumped to 10,000, with gold seekers camped along the river bank in tents, frame houses, and even under trees—a packing box or a strip of canvas was considered good housing. Bearded men from the mines flashed pokes of gold dust with assumed indifference, and spent grandly in saloons, fandango halls, and gambling houses. The most profitable mining was done by entrepreneurs, who took it out of the miners' pockets. Bitter struggles took place between squatters and men who claimed titles to farmlands.

Three disastrous floods came between 1849 and 1853, and in 1852 a fire wiped out two-thirds of the town. In 1849 Sacramento had offered $1,000,000 for the honor of being the State capital. The Legislature met in 1852, sitting on hot ashes, and when it officially became the capital in 1854, flood debris was still in evidence. The floods caused epidemics, and corpses were shoved into the swollen river to drift away. Levees were finally built, and the town pulled itself up out of the foot-deep dust of summer and the hub-deep mire of the rainy season. For many years the water remained unpalatable for those who had the temerity to drink it. Few did.

In 1856 Sacramento was the terminus of the first railroad in California, built as a short line to Folsom by Theodore Dehone Judah, the young engineer who planned the first transcontinental railroad through the passes of the Sierra Nevada. Four years later came the Pony Express, which ran until 1861, when the transcontinental telegraph went through.

The Central Pacific Railroad joined East and West in 1869. Judah's financial sponsors were all Sacramento storekeepers: Collis P. Huntington, Mark Hopkins, Charles Crocker, and Leland Stanford, the "Big Four." The Central Pacific branched out and became the Southern Pacific, the "octopus" of Frank Norris' novel, which for 40 years practically controlled the State. Large-scale wheat growing and cattle raising soon after lost their lead to more lucrative fields of fruit, vineyards, cotton, and vegetables. Land prices rose, and Sacramento's prosperity with them.

Sacramento's position as the capital was challenged by Berkeley in 1907, and more recently by San Jose and Monterey, but with little effect. The river channel was dredged in 1911, and seagoing vessels could reach the city when the river stage was high. The early years of depression saw several State hunger marches, and in 1938 refugees from the labor troubles in Nevada City camped for a week outside the fairgrounds.

Some of the earliest unions in California were formed in Sacramento, which was rated a "good town" for labor. Industry got a start with the gold rush, and soon boiler plants, farm machine factories, breweries, carriage shops, and processing plants were humming.

Today 18 percent of all vegetables and fruits in California is grown and canned in this district. A can-manufacturing plant has a daily output of a million and a half cans. Every month some crop is harvested or processed in and around Sacramento. River shipments approximate a half-million tons of freight a year, ranking high in value per ton. The city is also a railroad center, its large shops employing 5,000 men.

POINTS OF INTEREST

1. CAPITOL PARK, L St. between 10th and 15th Sts., and extending to N St., is a 40-acre plot with more than 1,000 varieties of trees and shrubs from all over the world, including the Cedar of Lebanon, camphor tree, gingko, Guadalupe cypress, and the Australian bunya-bunya. Three acres are planted exclusively with California flora. A central plot of half an acre contains trees from Civil War battlefields. The CAPITOL BUILDING is on a gently sloping terrace, approached by short flights of stone steps. Begun in 1860, it was dedicated with the laying of the cornerstone May 15, 1861, and was completed 13 years later. The building, designed by F. M. Butler and completed under the supervision of Reuben Clark, G. P. Cummings and A. A. Bennett, is E-shaped, with four stories and a basement. It is of Roman-Classic architecture adorned with Corinthian columns and pilasters. The wing is semicircular on the east facade. In the center of the plan is a rotunda topped with the great gold dome. The ball surmounting the lantern above the dome is 237 feet from the ground. The basement and first story are of California granite, while the remainder of the structure is of brick, painted white. The main west entrance is protected by a pedimented Corinthian portico. The entrance vestibule is finished in white sandstone, trimmed with onyx and marble. On the floor of each of the entrances is the Great Seal of California in colored mosaic. On the walls of the rotunda are 12 murals by Arthur F. Mathews, a California artist, each depicting a historical period in the State. In the center of the rotunda stands a heroic statue, *Columbus before Isabella,* by Larkin G. Mead, presented to the State by Darius Ogden Mills, a pioneer banker.

On the first floor are the offices of the Governor, the secretary of State, and the State treasurer. The legislative chambers are on the second floor, the Senate to the south and the Assembly to the north. On the third floor are the entrances to the galleries, open to visitors when the legislature is in session. Committee rooms occupy the fourth floor.

There is an excellent view of the city and surrounding country from the second balcony of the dome (*take south elevator to fourth floor*). No children are allowed in the dome without parent or guardian.

2. The STATE OFFICE BUILDING and the STATE LIBRARY AND COURTS BUILDING (*open 9-5 Mon.-Fri., 9-12 Sat.; 8-4 July and Aug.*), 10th St. between L and N Sts., extending to 9th St., are twin five story buildings of neo-classic design, adorned with Ionic porticoes and colonnades, completed in 1928. The State Building houses State government departments; the library, across a terraced garden, contains 800,000 volumes, including many rare items of Californiana, 65,000 volumes of law, and the only Braille library in California. The library was begun in 1850 with a collection of books donated by John C. Frémont. GILLIS HALL, at the entrance to the reference room, contains murals by Maynard Dixon depicting a Spanish-Mexican and an American migration pageant. The octagonal APPELLATE COURT ROOM, also in this building, is finished in Roman Corinthian style. The room has gilded walls and columns, bronze-embedded windows, purple velour upholstery, and a gold and alabaster chandelier.

3. The MEMORIAL AUDITORIUM, 15th St. between J and I Sts., and extending to 16th St., of Italian Romanesque design, is a massive dark red brick building with colonnaded loggia and stone trim. It was completed in 1927, as a memorial to World War veterans. The main auditorium seats 3,200; the Little Theater in one wing seats 300, and the Memorial Hall in the other wing 200. The auditorium contains a huge stage, a movable floor and a $35,000 organ. Chimes above the building strike each quarter hour, and every evening at 6 o'clock play "The Star Spangled Banner."

4. The CITY PLAZA, SE. corner 9th and I Sts., was given to the city by Sutter in 1849. On the south side of the park, facing J Street, is a statue by Albert Weiner, erected "by his co-workers" in 1899 to A. J. Stevens, "a friend of labor," and a prominent railroad man of the 1870's. A fountain in modernist style by Ralph Stackpole is a memorial to W. T. Coleman, a pioneer real estate man.

5. The SACRAMENTO CITY LIBRARY (*open 9-9 weekdays*), SW. corner 9th and I Sts., dates from 1857, when the Sacramento Library Association was formed, among its founders being the railroad "Big Four," then all young men. The three-story building in Florentine Renaissance style, was erected in 1918, partly with Carnegie funds. It contains 350,000 volumes, and has a valuable file of government documents.

6. The GOLDEN EAGLE HOTEL, 627 K St., was the first headquarters of the Republican party in California. Just across the street, where a department store now stands, was the headquarters of the Democratic party. In the 1860's and 1870's there were pitched battles between the two, marked occasionally by showers of rotten eggs.

7. The SOUTHERN PACIFIC RAILROAD STATION, 4th and I Sts., has a monument to Theodore D. Judah at the main entrance, erected by employees of the railroad in 1930. It is a massive stone structure adorned with a bas-relief of Judah, below which is inserted a wooden tie from the old Central Pacific Railroad. On the east wall

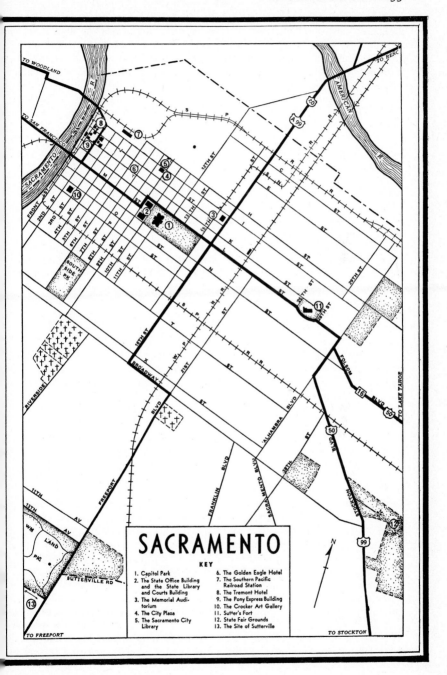

SACRAMENTO

KEY

1. Capitol Park
2. The State Office Building and the State Library and Courts Building
3. The Memorial Auditorium
4. The City Plaza
5. The Sacramento City Library
6. The Golden Eagle Hotel
7. The Southern Pacific Railroad Station
8. The Tremont Hotel
9. The Pony Express Building
10. The Crocker Art Gallery
11. Sutter's Fort
12. State Fair Grounds
13. The Site of Sutterville

of the waiting room is a mural by Arthur McQuarry depicting the breaking of ground for the first transcontinental railroad in 1863.

8. The TREMONT HOTEL, 112 J St., one of Sacramento's first "luxury hotels," was built in the early 1850's. It is of brick, three stories in height, with tall, old-fashioned windows and a wooden awning over the sidewalk. It had one of the largest gambling rooms in the West, where an ante of $1,000 was required in poker games, and as much as $500,000 in gold dust or nuggets sometimes changed hands in a single game.

9. The PONY EXPRESS MUSEUM (*open 10-4 daily*), 1015 2nd St., a two-story brick structure with cement facing erected in 1860, was for eight months in 1860 and 1861 the office and relay station of the celebrated Pony Express from Sacramento to St. Joseph, Missouri. With the passing of the Pony Express, the building was bought by the Alta California Telegraph Company (later merged with the Western Union), which established the first link of the transcontinental telegraph lines.

10. The CROCKER ART GALLERY (*open 10-5 daily in summer, 10-4 daily in winter*), SW. corner 2nd and O Sts., consists of two large Victorian buildings in landscaped grounds. The gallery, which mingles once fashionable mediocre canvases with genuine masterpieces, was donated to the city in 1885 by the widow of Judge E. B. Crocker, brother of Charles Crocker of the "Big Four." Its collection includes studies by Leonardo da Vinci, Michelangelo, and Rembrandt. In the late 1930's priceless drawings by Holbein, Dürer, Watteau, and other masters were found in the basement. Among the noted paintings in the gallery are Dürer's *St. Joseph and the Virgin Mary,* Van Dyck's *Christ Healing the Blind,* Rubens' *Portrait,* Murillo's *Gypsy,* a Claude Lorraine Landscape, and Guido Reni's *Entombment of Christ,* cut from its frame and stolen in 1923, but returned by mail ten days later to a San Francisco newspaper. Crocker built the gallery as a separate building. The California Museum Association later bought the Crocker home next door and connected the two buildings.

11. SUTTER'S FORT (*open 8-4 weekdays, 10-4 Sun.*), 26th and L Sts., is a complete restoration on the original site of Captain Sutter's ranch house, workshops, home, and fort, erected in 1839. Ivy-covered concrete walls, 18 feet high, surround the fort. Immediately inside the gate is the bell of Young America Engine Company No. 6, which rang for Lincoln's election and tolled for his assassination. Near the bell are the cannon that guarded the fort when it was first erected.

The buildings are in a hollow square, one story high; the central museum, which was Sutter's quarters, is raised to two stories by a low raftered basement. The original adobe bricks are protected by stucco, but the covering is removed in places so they can be seen. The original pine door frames were from Fort Ross, which Sutter bought from the Russians when they left California in 1841; they were brought from Norway around the Horn. The basement and main floor are filled with relics of early California days—furniture, clothes, printing presses, guns, letters from gold seekers to their families back home, mining pans and rockers, and saddles and spurs of Pony Express riders.

On the low doors of the barrack-like side buildings are signs showing their original use—granary, blacksmith shop, wine cellar, quarters of the Indian guard, and bunkrooms where immigrants were housed. In open sheds are prairie schooners, old fire engines, millstones, stagecoaches, and other reminders of the past.

The Indian Museum, formerly in the capitol, is being removed to a building just outside Sutter's Fort. It contains some 40,000 articles illustrative of the life and crafts of California Indians.

12. STATE FAIR GROUNDS, 2nd Ave. and Stockton Blvd., are the scene of the California's State Fair. The extensive grounds include a race track, where running and trotting races and livestock shows are held, pavilions, and free picnic grounds.

The centrally placed HORTICULTURAL HALL, a buff brick, tile-roofed structure of modified Italian Renaissance design with a flat central dome, is used to display California fruits, grains, and other products.

13. The site of SUTTERVILLE, the town first projected by Captain Sutter in 1844, is S. of William Land Park, across Sutterville Rd. The first brick house in California was built here in 1847. All that remains is the old Sutterville brewery, built in 1853, a square, two-story structure made of brick dug and baked in the immediate neighborhood. Here the first steam beer in Sacramento was made. The building was a place of refuge from floods before levees were built.

San Diego

Railroad Stations: Union Depot, Broadway and Kettner Blvd., for Atchison, Topeka & Santa Fe Ry., and San Diego and Arizona Eastern Ry.
Bus Stations: 120 W. Broadway for Greyhound, Inland Stages, and All American Lines; 137 E. Broadway for National Trailways; 232 E. Broadway for Interstate Transit Lines and Union Pacific Stages.
Airport: Lindbergh Field, Pacific Hwy. and Laurel St., 1.7 m., for United Air Lines and Western Air Express; taxi 35¢ for passengers.
Taxis: 20¢ first ⅔ m., 10¢ each additional ⅔ m.; one to five passengers.
Streetcars: Zone system, fare 5¢ and 10¢; four 10¢ tokens for 30¢; interurban to La Jolla, 50¢ round trip, 35¢ one way. Weekly urban and interurban passes $1 to $1.75.
Ferry: Coronado Ferry Slip, S. end of Pacific Blvd.; 20¢ for automobile, 5¢ per passenger.
Piers: Bay tours covering harbor, Star & Crescent Pier, W. end of Broadway, 10 and 2 daily, $1, children 50¢. Short bay trips from United Water Taxi Pier, 1050 Harbor St., 6 a.m.-12 p.m. daily, every 20 min., 25¢. To visit naval vessels in harbor, take United Water Taxi, 25¢, or ships' shore boats, free; visiting days 1-4 Sun. and holidays.

Accommodations: 148 hotels, rates higher in winter and spring; auto camps and trailer courts in environs.

Information Service: Chamber of Commerce, 499 W. Broadway; Plaza Information Booth, 3rd and Broadway.

Radio Stations: KFSD (600 kc.), KGB (1330 kc.).
Theaters and Motion Picture Houses: Savoy Theater, 236 C St., road shows; Ford Music Bowl, E. and W. Palisades Drives, Balboa Park, concerts; 20 motion picture houses.
Golf: Municipal Golf Course, Pershing Drive, Balboa Park, 18 holes, 50¢ weekdays, 75¢ Sat. afternoon and Sun.; 9-hole course, 25¢ per round.
Tennis: Municipal courts, Balboa Park, 10 courts, free, several lighted; Memorial Park, 28th St. and Logan Ave., 4 courts; North Park, Idaho St. and Lincoln Ave., 4 courts, lighted, free.
Swimming: Municipal pool, Balboa Park, open 10-10 daily, May 15-Sept. 15, 25¢, suit and towels 10¢, children under 18, 10¢. Ocean Beach, open year round, 10-10 Mon.-Fri., 10-6 Sat., lifeguards; 25¢, suit and towels 10¢, children 15¢, adults in bathing suits 15¢. Mission Beach Natatorium, Mission Beach, open daily 10-10, Fourth of July to Labor Day, lifeguards; 35¢, with suit and towels 50¢, children 15¢; Pacific Beach, La Jolla; Tent City Beach, Coronado.
Riding: Bridle trails in Balboa Park; Silver Strand, Coronado; and Point Loma. Horse hire 75¢-$1.50 an hour.
Boating: Power boats, W. end of Broadway, $2 an hour up; 30-passenger boats $5 an hour. Sailboats and rowboats, Mission Bay, 25¢ an hour up; Coronado Boathouse, Glorietta Bay, 75¢-$1 an hour.
Fishing: Surf, pier, and barge; deep-sea; fresh-water, lakes in back country, May 1-Oct. 31.

For further information regarding this city, see SAN DIEGO: A CALIFORNIA CITY, another of the American Guide Series, published 1937 by the San Diego Historical Society.

SAN DIEGO (0-822 alt., 147,995 pop.), the oldest Spanish settlement in California, is in the extreme lower left-hand corner of the United States. Although only 16 miles north of the Mexican boundary, it is completely American. Its landlocked natural harbor is headquarters for the Eleventh Naval District, for marine and coast guard bases, and home port for a fleet of tuna clippers and fishing smacks manned by Portuguese and Italian fishermen.

The city has much of the easygoing spirit of Spanish days, and people dress and live for comfort. Life moves at a modulated pace, particularly because of the large number of retired and elderly persons. The downtown area, dominated by a group of tall buildings, is small for a city of this size; Broadway, the main artery, runs from the waterfront due east and divides the city into distinct sections. Although liners no longer call at the port Max Miller wrote of in *I Cover the Waterfront,* freighters and tramp steamers dock here regularly. Tuna clippers bring in big hauls of huge fish, and sport fishing parties return with catches of yellowtail, barracuda, and swordfish. Navy shoreboats run between ships at anchor and the piers.

South of Broadway many plain buildings of the 1870's and gingerbread structures of the 1890's are still in use. Markets and grocery stores along Twelfth Avenue display fruit and vegetables in pyramids and cascades. Third, Fourth, and Fifth Avenues have taverns with three-piece jazz bands, shooting galleries, inexpensive movies, hamburger stands, pawn shops, and small hotels.

Balboa Park's giant green square begins just north of the business district. North and northwest of the park are the newer residential districts, and to the west is Middletown, a narrow segment extending from the bay to the low hills, occupied by Italian fishermen and airplane factory employees. Old Town, site of the original Spanish settlement, is northwest of Middletown. It has some fine adobe buildings, fringed with rose bushes and flowers, but most of the land is occupied by small houses and auto courts.

Most of San Diego's inhabitants, apart from the shifting Navy personnel, are immigrants or descendants of immigrants from the East and Middle West. Many are retired; ten percent of all retired U. S. Navy officers live in San Diego.

In the Logan Heights district, south and east of downtown along the curved southern shore, sprawl San Diego's Mexican and Negro communities, with Mexican restaurants vending tamales and tacos, and with chicken palaces and big ovens where Negroes barbecue meat. About 10,000 Mexicans, most of them clinging to their own language and customs, live in this district; they are employed mainly as day laborers and cannery workers. The 4,500 Negroes are mostly manual or domestic workers. The Japanese colony, of about 1,000 persons, is in this area also; some in huts on stilts over the water. About 5,000 Portuguese fisherman, who live on the bay side of Point Loma, form a distinct group preserving its own customs. Italian fishermen mingle more generally with the community.

The site of San Diego was visited in 1539 by Father Marcos and his followers, from the desert side, in their search for the "Seven Cities of Cibola"; in 1542 by Juan Rodriguez Cabrillo, a Portuguese explorer in the service of Spain, who spent six days in the harbor; and sixty years later by Sebastian Vizaíno, merchant navigator charting the coast for Spain.

In 1769 Governor Portola, with Franciscan friars and soldiers, established a mission and presidio here. The English sloop *Discovery,* engaged in scientific research, visited San Diego in 1793, and in 1803 the Yankee-owned *Lelia Byrd,* caught while smuggling otter skins, fought a cannon duel with the battery of Ballast Point. San Diego became the center of the coastal hide trade, and was organized in 1834 as a pueblo. By 1838 the population had decreased and San Diego became a department of Los Angeles.

During the Mexican regime, San Diego took on more color. "The beautiful señoritas danced their picturesque dances at the balls which followed bull-fights and cock-fights." Many Spanish families, on bad terms with the Mexican governor, assisted the Americans in their conquest. After the Treaty of Guadalupe Hidalgo, the town came peacefully under American rule.

In 1850 the present Old Town was incorporated as a city. The site of the present city was called New Town, or "Davis's Folly" for William Heath Davis, who first built there. Alonzo E. Horton, for whom New Town was named "Horton's Addition," profited more than he. From 1867 to 1872 New Town grew steadily; then a fire wiped out Old Town's business district, and New Town became the city's center.

In 1885 the Santa Fe Railroad laid tracks into San Diego and made it a transcontinental terminus. Two years later it had 40,000 residents, but the boom collapsed, and by 1890 there were only 17,000. Since 1910 its population has doubled about every decade.

San Diego's 335 factories are mostly small enterprises; Consolidated Aircraft is the only large-scale industrial plant. Fishing and canning are basic sources of income. A large lumber mill handles timber rafted in from the Northwest.

San Diego was an open-shop city until the strong wave of unionization in the early thirties; during the bitter "Free Speech Fight" of 1912 radical headquarters were raided and radicals ordered out of town.

Depressions have touched lightly on San Diego. Establishment of Army and Navy bases during the World War, completion of the San Diego and Arizona Eastern Railway in 1919, and the expositions of

1915-16 and 1935-36 have contributed to its prosperity. The outdoors, however, is San Diego's chief commodity, and tourists are its best customers.

Music is enthusiastically supported by local citizens. Performances by the San Diego Civic Symphony Orchestra and the Federal Music Project are well attended, and the service bands conduct free weekly programs. The San Diego open forum is well known on the West Coast.

POINTS OF INTEREST

1. BALBOA PARK, entrance Laurel St. and Sixth Ave., 1,400 acres in area, is the cultural and recreational center of San Diego. El Prado (the public walk), a continuation of Laurel Street, runs west to east through the landscaped area and is lined with palaces of two expositions, galleries, museums, and gardens.

The eastern section of the park, cut by canyons and covered with chaparral, contains the municipal swimming pool, tennis courts, golf course, Naval Hospital, city stadium, and San Diego High School.

(See map for location of lettered points of interest.)

A. CABRILLO BRIDGE, over Cabrillo Canyon, 450 feet long and 110 feet high, is a concrete cantilever type span, with seven graceful arches.

B. The CALIFORNIA BUILDING (*open 10-4:30 Tues.-Sat., 1-4:30 Sun.*), a cream colored concrete structure designed by Bertram Goodhue in the form of a Greek cross, is richly ornamented in the Spanish Churrigueresque style, and houses the San Diego Museum and Archaeological Institute, the Hall of Anthropology, scientific library, the Chapel of St. Francis, and the California Tower. The Quadrangle Building, with an ornamented octagonal dome, is adorned with figures of Spanish explorers and Franciscan monks. The Mayan, Aztec, and Indian exhibits in the Museum include plaster casts, weapons, and handicrafts. The Hall of Anthropology has a permanent exhibit of sculptures illustrating the racial history of mankind.

C. The ALCAZAR GARDEN, built for the fair of 1915, has Moorish fountains in blue, green, and yellow tile, and an ornamental gateway.

A graveled path leads across Palm Canyon to other exposition buildings in Spanish and Mayan styles. The PACIFIC RELATIONS GROUP (*open Sun.*) is a cluster of small Spanish style houses around a pond, in which 13 national groups display furnishings and handicrafts.

D. The FORD BUILDING (*not open*), a modern structure designed by Walter Teague, is to be a permanent museum of mechanical development.

The FEDERAL BUILDING (*not open*), E. Palisades Drive, a huge windowless concrete structure, will be used as a city auditorium.

E. The SPRECKELS ORGAN PAVILION (*open: organ recitals four variable days a week, 2 p.m.*), is an open-air amphitheater, having one of the world's largest outdoor organs.

F. The FINE ARTS GALLERY OF SAN DIEGO (*open 10-4 weekdays, 1-5 Sun.; free except Mon. adm. 25¢*), a Spanish Renaissance building erected in 1925, has paintings valued at more than $1,000,000. Notable exhibits include laces, ceramics, Oriental costumes, and ivories. Among the art treasures are four rare Flemish Renaissance tapestries, a Spanish altarpiece of St. John, El Greco's *St. Francis,* and canvases by Murillo, Sorolla, Rubens, Goya, Zurbaran, Corot, and Zuloaga. Among the moderns are Matisse, Henri, and Bellows.

ZOOLOGICAL GARDEN (*open 8-5 daily; adults 25¢, children under 16 free*), Avenida de España, has the first two mountain gorillas in cap-

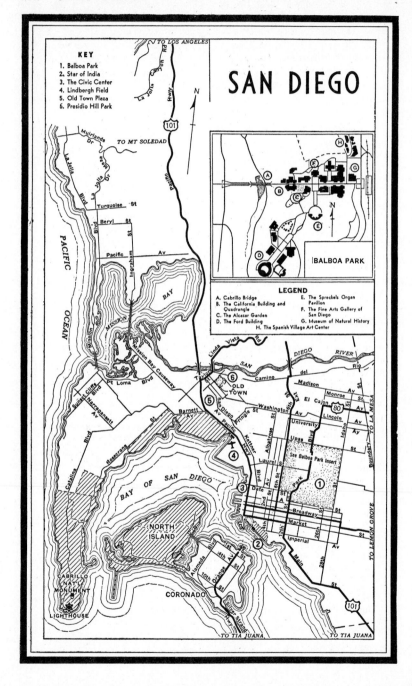

KEY
1. Balboa Park
2. Star of India
3. The Civic Center
4. Lindbergh Field
5. Old Town Plaza
6. Presidio Hill Park

SAN DIEGO

BALBOA PARK

LEGEND
A. Cabrillo Bridge
B. The California Building and Quadrangle
C. The Alcazar Garden
D. The Ford Building
E. The Spreckels Organ Pavilion
F. The Fine Arts Gallery of San Diego
G. Museum of Natural History
H. The Spanish Village Art Center

tivity (gifts of Martin and Osa Johnson). Snakes are kept in an arcaded open-air house, and trained seals are shown in an amphitheater.

G. MUSEUM OF NATURAL HISTORY (*open 9-5 daily*) is designed in the Spanish Renaissance style. On the ground floor are exhibits of dinosaur fossils, minerals, reptiles, and fish. The Stephens collection of mounted birds and mammals, and the Ingersoll collection of birds' nests and eggs are on the second floor. The top floor has exhibits of fossils, seashells, corals, insects, and 1,200 water colors of flowers.

H. THE SPANISH VILLAGE ART CENTER (*open 9-4 daily*), contains workshops of artists in Spanish colonial cottages. Art work is for sale, and there is a puppet show and a cafe.

2. STAR OF INDIA (*opens 8-5 daily, adm. 10¢*), foot of Second Ave., a full-rigged ship, is a maritime museum. The vessel, built on the Isle of Man in 1863, carried emigrants between England and New Zealand for 30 years.

3. The CIVIC CENTER, Pacific Highway between Ash and Grape Sts., overlooking the bay, is a modern office building with a four-story central section and set-back tower. It was completed in 1938 and houses municipal offices.

4. LINDBERGH FIELD, Pacific Highway between Laurel and Sassafras Sts., is a 287-acre airport dredged from the bay, with six hangars and an administration building. It was named to commemorate Lindbergh's flight to Paris in a San Diego-made plane—the *Spirit of St. Louis,* though he actually took off for the East from North Island.

5. OLD TOWN PLAZA, Calhoun and Wallace Sts., original center of town, retains some of its early Spanish flavor, and around it are several houses of interest.

CASA DE CARRILLO (*open 8-5:30 daily*), 4136 Wallace St., is a restored box-like adobe, built about 1820.

CASA DE BANDINI (*private*), 2660 Calhoun St., is a two-story adobe with an overhanging balcony. Originally one story, it was built in 1829 by Juan Bandini and enlarged in 1869. Bandini's daughters made the American flag that Lt. Stephen C. Rowan raised on the plaza in 1846. Commodore Robert Stockton made his headquarters here in 1846-47, and Kit Carson brought news to this house of Gen. Stephen W. Kearny's plight at the battle of San Pasqual.

CASA DE ESTUDILLO (*open 8:30-5:30 daily, adm. 10¢*), Mason St. between Calhoun St. and San Diego Ave., is known as Ramona's Marriage Place. Built about 1825 and restored in 1910, it is now a museum of Spanish-California days. Helen Hunt Jackson used this house as a background in her novel, *Ramona,* though it had no connection with the prototypes of her hero and heroine.

The WHALEY HOUSE (*private*), NE. corner San Diego Ave. and Harney St., was built in 1856 by Thomas Whaley, of bricks he himself manufactured and of plaster from seashells.

ADOBE CHAPEL, Conde St. between San Diego Ave. and Congress St., a restored light yellow adobe building with low lean-to wings forming a cruciform plan, was the original Church of the Immaculate Conception. Built about 1850, it was consecrated in 1858.

6. PRESIDIO HILL PARK, Presidio. FORT STOCKTON, beyond the park entrance, was named for Commodore Stockton, who occupied it

in 1846.   The SERRA MUSEUM (*open 10-5 Tues.-Sat., 2-5 Sun.*),
2727 Presidio Drive, of Spanish mission architecture, exhibits local historical relics.   On the river flats below the hill stands the SERRA PALM,
supposedly planted in 1769.   EL PRESIDIO REAL (the royal garrison),
bisected by Presidio Drive, the area of the original settlement in 1769,
is the oldest part of San Diego.

POINTS OF INTEREST IN ENVIRONS

Torrey Pines Mesa, rare trees, 15.9 *m.;* Mission San Luis Rey, 41.1 *m.;*
(*see TOUR 2d*).   Palomar Observatory, 200-inch telescope, 41.7 *m.* (*see TOUR 6e*).   Mount Helix, 12.8 *m.* (*see TOUR 14b*).

San Francisco

Railroad Stations: 3rd and Townsend Sts. and Ferry Bldg., foot of Market St., for Southern Pacific R.R.; by bus from 44 4th St. for Atchison, Topeka and Santa Fe Ry.; Ferry Bldg. for Pacific R.R. and Northwestern Pacific R.R.; Bay Bridge Terminal, 1st and Mission Sts., for Sacramento Northern R.R.
Bus Stations: 75 Fifth St. for Pacific Greyhound Lines; 44 Fourth St. for Santa Fe and Burlington Trailways, Napa Valley Bus Co., Sacramento Northern, Key System, and River Auto Stages; 781 Market St. for Dollar Stages and the Gray Line; 40 Eddy St. for all American Bus Lines and Airline Bus Co.
Airport: San Francisco Municipal Airport (Mills Field) 13 m. S. on US 101, for United Airlines, Transcontinental & Western Air, Inc.; Treasure Island for Pan American Airways; taxi to San Francisco Airport, flat rate from downtown business district, $3 one way, $5 round trip, time 25 min.
Taxis: 25¢ first ⅓ m., 10¢ each additional ⅖ m.
Streetcars and Busses: Fares 5¢ and 7¢, free transfers; cable railroad fare 5¢, free transfers; interurban cars serving Peninsula to San Mateo, fare 27¢, round trip 47¢; interurban cars serving Eastbay, fare 21¢, round trip 42¢.
Ferries: Ferry Bldg., foot of Market St. for Southern Pacific ferries to Eastbay, pedestrians 21¢, automobiles 30¢ one way, round trip 50¢ (1 to 5 passengers); for Key Route System ferries to Treasure Island, pedestrians only, 10¢; for Northwestern Pacific ferries to Sausalito, pedestrians only, 15¢, round trip 25¢.
Bridges: San Francisco-Oakland Bay Bridge approaches: 5th and Bryant Sts., and Fremont and Harrison Sts.; toll 50¢ (1 to 5 passengers), 5¢ for each additional passenger. Golden Gate Bridge approaches: Marina Blvd. and Baker St., and Lombard and Broderick Sts.; toll 50¢ (1 to 5 passengers), 5¢ for each additional passenger; pedestrians 10¢ within turnstiles.
Piers: Embarcadero, foot of Market St. Coastwise passage in occasional freighters only. For travel to East Coast, outlying possessions, and foreign countries consult telephone directory or travel bureaus.
Traffic Regulations: 20 m.p.h. in business district; 25 m.p.h. in residential district; no U-turn in business district; right turn on red when not interfering with pedestrians, except in business district. No daytime parking on Market St.

Accommodations: 1,439 hotels, auto and trailer camps in environs.

Information Service: California State Chamber of Commerce, 356 Bush St.; California Automobile Association (A.A.A.), 150 Van Ness Ave.; San Francisco Chamber of Commerce, 333 Pine St.; National Auto Club, 228 Pine St., U.S. Forest Service, 760 Market St.

Radio Stations: KSFO (560 kc.), KFRC (610 kc.), KPO (680 kc.), KGO (790 kc.), KROW (930 kc.), KJBS (1070 kc.), KYA (1230 kc.), KSAN (1420 kc.).
Theaters and Motion Picture Houses: Three legitimate theaters regularly showing; numerous little theaters; 80 motion picture houses.
Concert Halls: War Memorial Opera House, Van Ness Ave. and Grove St.; Veterans' Auditorium, Van Ness Ave. and McAllister St.; Civic Auditorium, Grove St. between Polk and Larkin Sts.; Scottish Rite Auditorium, Van Ness Ave. and Sutter St.; Community Playhouse, 609 Sutter St.; Dreamland Auditorium, Steiner and Post Sts.

Athletics: Kezar Stadium, Frederick St. between Willard St. and Arguello Blvd.; Kezar Pavilion, Stanyan St., near Frederick (SE. corner of Golden Gate Park); Ewing Field, Masonic Ave. between Geary and Turk Sts.; Roberts Field, 15th and Valencia Sts.; Seals' Stadium, 16th and Bryant Sts. (Pacific Coast League baseball).

Golf: Harding Park Municipal Golf Course, 36th Ave. at Sunset Blvd., 18 holes, 75¢ weekdays, $1 Sat., Sun., holidays; monthly ticket $3, also 6-hole practice course. Lincoln Park Municipal Golf Links, 33rd Ave. and Clement St., 18 holes, 50¢ weekdays, 75¢ Sat., Sun., holidays; monthly ticket $2. Ingleside Public Golf Course, Junipero Serra Blvd. and 19th Ave., 18 holes, 75¢ weekdays, $1.25 Sat., Sun., holidays, except Sat. before 11, 75¢, after 4, 50¢; monthly $3.

Tennis: Municipal courts at 44 recreation centers. Among them are: Golden Gate Park Courts (21) free. Excelsior Courts (1), Russian and Madrid Sts.; Folsom Courts (2), 21st and Folsom Sts.; Margaret S. Hayward Courts (4), Golden Gate Ave. and Laguna St.; North Beach Courts (2), Lombard and Mason Sts., all lighted, free. Palace of Fine Arts Courts (18), foot of Lyon St., lighted, $1 per hour per court.

Swimming: Fleishhacker Pool, Sloat Blvd. and Great Highway, heated outdoor pool open 8-5, Apr. 1-Nov. 15, children 15¢, adults 25¢ (including locker, suit, towel), private dressing rooms 40¢. Mission Pool, 19th and Angelica Sts., municipal outdoor pool for children 18 years and under, open 10-4, adm. 5¢ (including suit, towel); girls Mon., Wed., Fri.; boys Tues., Thurs., Sat., Sun.; North Beach Pool, Lombard and Mason Sts., municipal outdoor pool for children 18 years and under, open 10-4, adm. 5¢ (including suit, towel); girls Tues., Thurs., Sat.; boys Mon., Wed., Fri., Sun.

Riding: Fourteen miles of bridle paths in Golden Gate Park; 25 miles of paths along Funston Ave., in the Presidio, and along beach. Average charge for horses $1.50 first hour, 75¢ each additional hour.

Horse Racing: Golden Gate Park Stadium (opposite 36th Ave.), occasional harness races on ¾ mile track.

Polo: Golden Gate Park Stadium, games nearly every Sun. in fall and spring.

Yachting: Municipal Yacht Harbor, Marina Blvd. between Scott and Baker Sts.; Aquatic Park Harbor, foot of Polk St.

Fishing: Municipal Pier at Aquatic Park, N. end of Van Ness Ave.; free. Lake Merced; free.

Annual Events: Shrine East-West football game, Kezar Stadium, Jan. 1; Chinese New Year celebration, one week between Jan. 20–Feb. 20; Parilia Artists' ball, Feb.; National Open Matchplay golf championship, Feb.–Mar.; Army Day, Apr. 2; Livestock and Baby Beef Show, first and second weeks in Apr.; California Spring Blossom and Wildflower Show, Apr.; Spring Yachting Regatta, fourth week in Apr.; Children's Festival, Golden Gate Park, May 1; Rowing Regatta, July 4; Harbor Day, third week in Aug.; Dahlia Show, Aug.; Columbus Day Festival, Oct. 12; International Livestock Exposition, fourth week in Oct.; Pacific Auto Show, Civic Auditorium, Oct. 30–Nov. 6; Opera Season, War Memorial Opera House, Nov.-Dec.; Grand National Livestock Exposition, Nov. 27–Dec. 5; Symphony Season, War Memorial Opera House, Dec.–May.

SAN FRANCISCO (6 to 956 alt., 634,394 pop.), born of the meeting of sea captains and gold seekers, spills over its many hills—three times Rome's seven—at the tip of a peninsula that walls the narrow channel of the Golden Gate through which the tides of the Pacific pour into San Francisco Bay. The far-flung causeways of the San Francisco-Oakland Bay Bridge and the Golden Gate Bridge across the strait link it with the mainlands opposite. Behind the city the San Bruno Hills roll away to the south.

Once a barren stretch of sand dunes and rocky hills, covered with brush, broken here and there by wooded valleys, dotted with swamps and lagoons, the site of the present city is in large part man-made. Smaller hills have been leveled; valleys, tidal marshes, and lagoons have been filled in. Mission Swamp was drained to provide industrial sites. Only the line of cliffs along the Pacific, frequented by sea gulls and sea lions, remains almost as it was.

Approached from the bay, San Francisco appears as a serried skyline of hills and tall buildings. In the foreground is the sweeping arc of the waterfront, with piers jutting out from the Embarcadero like cogs on a giant wheel. High above the broad Embarcadero rises the clock tower of the Ferry Building, from which Market Street runs diagonally southwest, cutting the city in half. A street of large department stores, banks, public buildings, and business houses; of pageants and parades; of bustling activity, hurrying throngs, and the traffic din of automobiles and streetcars on four sets of tracks—Market Street is at once San Francisco's Broadway and Fifth Avenue. On both sides rise clusters of skyscrapers, built back from the bay on steep slopes—office buildings, hotels, apartment houses, at night alive with sparkling lights.

In downtown San Francisco, compact and accessible, the shopping district centers on Union Square, surrounded by department stores, smart women's shops, furriers, fine book stores, theaters, hotels, and specialty shops. Here are many of the better apartment houses in this city of apartment houses, whole blocks consisting of unbroken rows of these super-tenements. Along the sidewalks downtown are numerous flower stalls at which the passerby can inexpensively have his choice of carnations, chrysanthemums, roses, and a wide variety of blossoms every month in the year.

Of the city's many hills three of the highest are in the northeastern section. Telegraph Hill rises abruptly from the bay shore to a height of 300 feet; overlooking the bay, the Golden Gate, and farther stretches of water, it was long used as a signal tower to inform the town of approaching ships. Just westward is Russian Hill, near the crest of which in early days was a burying ground for Russian sailors. The hills are now covered with residences, apartment houses, and studios. Many of the city's artists and writers live in this section. Dropping off to the south of Russian Hill is Nob Hill, now clotted with towering hotels and apartment houses, once resplendent with the marble and stone castles of the Comstock millionaires, derisively titled "Nabobs" by the townsfolk; hence the name of the hill.

The city's hills account for the continued use of cable cars, which, as they slowly crawl up and down the heights, amaze and amuse the newcomer. At their terminals some of the cars are turned around by hand on a turntable for their return trip. Many San Franciscans depend on these little old-fashioned cars every day, and while they are long since used to them, delight in them quite as much as the stranger.

South of Market ("south of the slot," as the phrase went when cable cars were still plying Market Street) is the Mission district, one of the oldest and most densely populated in the city. With a main street of the same name, it is almost a city in itself, homogeneous in appearance and tone, with marked characteristics of its own; its residents, so some say, can be identified by their slightly different accent. Between the Mission and the bay lies the old Potrero district, now largely industrial; to the south stretch more miles of residential streets.

The geographical center of San Francisco is Twin Peaks, two hills of nearly equal height, offering one of the best views of the city, bay, and surrounding country. Southwest is Mount Davidson, the highest elevation in San Francisco. The city's westward expansion has resulted in new residential developments in this section; even the smaller houses here are set in lawns or colorful gardens. Along the slopes of Mount Davidson, and in such rolling areas as St. Francis Wood and Ingleside Terrace, are many more palatial residences on landscaped grounds.

Golden Gate Park, three quarters of a mile wide, extends four miles to the ocean, dividing the two largest residential sections of the city: the Richmond district to the north, the newer Sunset-Parkside district to the south, not many years ago a waste of sand dunes, now almost solidly built up. The street pattern of short blocks east and west and long blocks north and south has stimulated the building of almost identical houses in long rows; the houses built wall to wall, with a raised basement story and garage at the street level, crowd the sidewalk.

From the days of '49 San Francisco has been a great banking center, the largest west of Chicago. But since the first white man came, the city's prosperity has been founded on its maritime trade. San Francisco, a port of entry since 1849, possesses one of the finest land-locked harbors in the world, 3 to 12 miles wide, with 50 miles of frontage and 15 miles of wharfage. It pulsates with activity as ships from the Orient and the South Seas disgorge pungent and aromatic cargoes, and freighters from the East Coast creakily unload steel and heavy crates of machinery. A luxury liner disembarks her fashionable cargo as a tramp steams west through the Golden Gate, bound for strange places on the seven seas. Small but self-assertive tugs toot their shrill whistles as they run in and out among the ferries plying to Oakland and other cities; occasionally a gray man-of-war rides lazily at anchor in the blue bay.

Naturally, this direct and continuous contact with the world has created a cosmopolitan city. Foreign sailors deserting ship during the gold rush, the influx of Orientals, successive waves of European immigration, have made San Francisco a city of many races and tongues.

The Chinese are the predominant minority group, although more than fifty percent of them are native-born. In San Francisco's Chinatown, the largest Chinese settlement outside the Orient, pagoda roofs and iron-grilled balconies appear side by side with American tin roofs and straight fronts; a Chinese graduate of an American medical school practices modern surgery in competition with a native herb doctor; men and women in the dress of old China rub elbows with those frantically following the latest occidental fashions. The old Chinatown of brothels, opium dens, gambling houses, and slums was destroyed by the great fire of 1906. Today, it is an orderly section, where old men quietly read the latest news bulletins, laboriously printed by hand in Chinese word-signs. It is a section of restaurants catering to those who know and enjoy Chinese cuisine; of shops and bazaars selling porcelains, lacquer-work, silks, jewelry, and trinkets of every kind; of Chinese theaters and joss-houses, or temples, in which the Chinese worship as their ancestors have for thousands of years. Chinatown is at its best during the Chinese New Year's celebration; the streets are lined with flower stands, the shrines in every shop are lavishly decorated, and a spirit of goodwill and revelry prevails.

The Latin Quarter, a densely populated area around Telegraph Hill, is a gourmet's paradise. Of the many nationalities in the district the Italians are the most numerous, although there is a generous sprinkling of French, Spanish, and Portuguese. In some blocks not a single sign is written or printed in English. To this section, dotted with restaurants, San Franciscans turn for a variety of foods, for embedded in the local *mores* is the custom of dining out. In one cafe Italian *ravioli* and *fritto misto* are served; in another, Mexican *chile con carne* and *chile rellena;* in a third, French *bouillabaisse* and *escargots.* The food, as a rule, is well cooked, and except for a few more elaborate cafes and hotels, inexpensive.

The San Francisco of the old vice-ridden Barbary Coast days is gone, but the traditions established by hordes of happy-go-lucky's miners, gamblers, adventurers of all kinds, epicures, and others of the city's first American population have not been entirely obliterated. Those were the days of laissez-faire, of easy-come-easy-go, of good-natured tolerance, not unnatural in a city where fortunes were made and lost overnight, where a bartender one day was a nabob the next, where today's bonanza king was tomorrow's roustabout. Here, as in few cities, side streets downtown were named for reigning belles among the *filles de joie.* San Francisco has always cherished its eccentrics; it has been inclined to regard graft with a tolerant eye; it has always prided itself on the international flavor of its food and drink, and its cosmopolitan tastes in feminine beauty; it has always been a "good" town for the actor and the musician.

The first men known to have visited the site of San Francisco were Tamal Indians from present Marin County, north of the Gate, who braved treacherous bay tides in frail canoes to obtain salt in the marshes here. For years the Spanish sought to find a good harbor in this region to serve as a stop on the long voyage from Mexico to the Philippines, but three expeditions between 1542 and 1602 failed of their purpose. A century and a half passed before the great harbor here was discovered, quite by accident, and not by sea but by land, when in 1769 an expedition was led northward from San Diego by Don Gaspar de Portolá. A reconnoitering party was detached under the command of

Sgt. José Ortega, who with his handful of men reached the shores of San Francisco Bay in November, 1769.

Settlement began seven years later when Don Juan Bautista de Anza, with his "army" of 30 soldiers and their families, marched some 200 colonists overland to the tip of the peninsula, where they began erecting shelters in 1776. A presidio and a mission were immediately laid out; the latter was established by Father Junípero Serra and named San Francisco de Asís, later known as Mission Dolores.

For seventy years the new colony of Yerba Buena was no more than an isolated outpost, occupied largely by the military. Its few civilians and priests carried on sporadic trade in tallow and hides, sea otter and seal pelts. For the most part they lived in tents and adobe huts. The first house, it appears, was erected in 1835 by an Englishman, Capt. William A. Richardson, for whom Richardson's Bay was named. Jacob Primer Leese, an American, opened the first store in the following year; Jean Vioget, a Swiss, made the first attempt to lay out streets in the straggling settlement, which had been named Yerba Buena (good herb), for a grass that grew thickly on the sand dunes.

By 1840 the Spanish-Americans of Yerba Buena were threatened with foreign invasion by Anglo-Americans from the East. In July, 1846, within three months of the outbreak of the Mexican War, Capt. John B. Montgomery landed marines from the *Portsmouth* on the plaza, hoisted the Stars and Stripes, and took possession of the town in the name of the United States. Soon the plaza was Portsmouth Square; the street passing along it was rechristened in honor of Captain Montgomery; and Yerba Buena became San Francisco.

Some 20 nationalities and races were represented in the population of the settlement when, in 1846, a group of thrifty and energetic Mormon artisans arrived under the leadership of Samuel Brannan, who had tried unsuccessfully to induce Brigham Young to abandon Utah and settle in California. For twenty years Brannan was a powerful figure in San Francisco; in January, 1847, he established its first newspaper, the *California Star,* and later was the principal organizer of the first vigilantes. Brannan and Brigham Young continually bickered over the disposition of tithes collected by Brannan from the Mormons in California; on several occasions Young sent his Destroying Angels to seize them by force, but they were never successful. Although he amassed a fortune, Brannan became a drunkard and died in poverty.

When news reached San Francisco that on January 24, 1848, James W. Marshall had picked up a gold nugget on the South Fork of the American River, its first effect was to depopulate the town. Almost every able-bodied man hurried off to the diggings. Ships lay abandoned in the harbor as crews and, in some cases, their officers turned from the sea to dig feverishly for gold. Communications were slow, and it was autumn before the East had first account of the discovery. The news trickled north, south, and into the Middle West, setting thousands of fortune-seekers in motion toward the Golden Gate, augmented by throngs from Central and South American countries. By 1850 the city had a more or less settled population of almost 25,000, of every race, creed, and color. Those that remained in San Francisco probably profited more than miners at the diggings. Lodgings were scarce; rooms rented from $200 to $300 a month; washing cost $20 for a dozen pieces; an apple brought $5, an egg $1, a loaf of bread 75¢. Many huge fortunes had their inception in San Francisco during this era of profiteering. In the last nine months of 1849, 549 vessels dropped anchor.

Portsmouth Square became the city's amusement center. In the streets spreading fanwise from it, dozens of gambling houses opened, some in lean-tos or tents. In the early days of the rush women were so few that the passage of one down the street emptied the ubiquitous saloons and gambling dens. Theatrical performances and other amusements were rare; gambling and drinking were the sole diversions left to the miners.

Six great fires devastated the town within four years; one in 1850 consumed 18 blocks of frame houses in 10 hours. Necessity directed attention to fireproofing of buildings and paving of streets, for in the rainy season the latter were quagmires into which horses, wagons—and fire engines—sank.

After the fires came the days of vice and extensive gambling. Dozens of saloons studded Portsmouth Square and environs, each a gambling hall and a recruiting station for the brothels of the world-notorious Barbary Coast on Pacific Street, from Sansome Street to Grant Avenue. This area was closed in 1917, but many of the old frame buildings still bear signs of their boisterous heyday—"Spider Kelly Presents Texas Tommy"—"Purcell's Liveliest Colored Show in Town"—"No Minors Allowed." In dark corners of the city were hideouts of such vicious gangs as "The Hounds" and "The Sydney Ducks," the latter composed largely of escaped convicts from Botany Bay, Australia. These gangs preyed on other thugs and respectable citizens without discrimination, entering business places and helping themselves, invading the Chinese and foreign sections and clubbing the residents unmercifully. Their leaders were allied with powerful politicians, and they generally escaped punishment.

The city might smile at the gambling and the Barbary Coast, but it could not condone gangsterism married to crooked politics. The first Vigilance Committee was formed in June, 1851, an organization that at the height of its influence had several thousand members, who took the law into their hands, hanged the worst offenders, and inspired a general exodus among the others. A grand jury indicted nine of the vigilantes, but they stood high among the "respectables" and the serious charges against them were dropped. During the relatively peaceful years between 1852 and 1854 the Committee disbanded.

By the summer of 1855 the city was again swarming with swindlers, thieves, highwaymen, and thugs. A few months later U. S. Marshal George W. H. Richardson was shot and killed by Charles Cora, an Italian gambler, with powerful political supporters. A demand for his immediate trial and conviction was led by thundering editorials in the

Bulletin, established in October, 1855, under the editorship of James King of William, who signed his name thus to distinguish himself from other James Kings.   He was bitterly opposed by James Casey, rival editor and local politician, who, exhausting his verbal weapons, shot King down as he emerged from the office of the *Bulletin* in May, 1856. Confident of protection, Casey immediately gave himself up to the authorities.

A crowd began to collect at the police station, summoned by the tolling of a fire bell.   As it grew, confederates rushed Casey to the county jail, where a large force of armed deputies and militia was mustered to defend him from the mob.   Before nightfall a new Vigilance Committee was begun, and during the night it enrolled some 2,000 members, all sworn to absolute secrecy, under the leadership of William T. Coleman and other members of the Vigilance Committee of 1851. An executive committee of thirty-three was formed; all vigilantes, soon numbering almost 10,000, were equipped with arms and organized into military companies; headquarters were established in a mercantile building on Sacramento Street, which was fortified with cannon as "Fort Gunnybags."   Unlike its predecessor, the committee of 1856 was a deliberately planned and well-knit organization.

Four days after the shooting of King, the vigilantes surrounded the jail and demanded Casey and Cora, both of whom were surrendered without a struggle.   They were tried, found guilty, and hanged from a window in Fort Gunnybags on May 22, two days after the death of King, whose large funeral procession was directed down Sacramento Street past the dangling bodies.   A cleansing and reform of the local government was instituted, with salutary effects for years to come, and the Vigilance Committee disbanded in August, 1856.   San Francisco continued to be a lively and lighthearted city, but with less physical and moral violence.

An era of expansion followed, broken by brief excitement during the Civil War, when California heatedly debated whether to support the Union cause or set itself up independently as the Pacific Republic. Oratory waxed loud and feeling ran high in the city until the State legislature voted against secession.   During these years Bret Harte contributed to the *Golden Era* and in 1864 became secretary of the U. S. branch mint; Mark Twain paused momentarily, one jump ahead of his creditors; a dozen newspapers were established, and as many weeklies, some of which are still extant.   From the fabulous Comstock and Mother lodes, from the Central Pacific Railroad, came the vast fortunes that Leland Stanford, Charles Crocker, Collis P. Huntington, Mark Hopkins, James Flood, William S. O'Brien, John W. Mackay, James G. Fair, William C. Ralston, "Lucky" Baldwin, and others spent on ornate Victorian palaces on Nob Hill, Lucullan banquets, enameled carriages with liveried footmen, great country estates, and on the fabrication and lubrication of political machines as relentless as steam rollers. There were frequent scandals and occasional duels.   Dennis Kearney addressed large crowds of workers on the sand lots; the base of San

Francisco's development as a union town had been laid previously with the formation of the Working Men's Trade and Labor Union.

In 1873 the lumbering horsecars and the unique round "balloon cars" were supplemented with and later superseded by Andrew Hallidies' cable cars. The city's population doubled in two decades, and San Francisco celebrated in 1894, with the Midwinter Exposition, its first great carnival, in "Opal City," Golden Gate Park. Weathering the depression of 1893-96 and its attendant strikes, it became increasingly the railroad and maritime center of the Pacific Coast. In those days a traveler from any point along the coast between the Mexican and Canadian borders simply asked for a ticket to "the City" with complete assurance that he would be routed to San Francisco. Although Seattle profited most, the Klondike gold strike brought new wealth and residents; by 1903 the city had a population of 425,000, and plans were laid for immediate improvements and future expansion.

Steps were being taken for rezoning, for the creation of additional public parks, for the elimination of slum areas, when at 5:16 o'clock on the morning of April 18, 1906, the great San Andreas fault, extending up and down the coast, settled violently. The greatest earthquake ever to strike California shook San Francisco to its foundations. With the breaking of gas and water mains, fire broke out and for three days roared through the city unchecked; it was finally brought under control by dynamiting buildings along Van Ness Avenue. An early edition of a Los Angeles newspaper, so it is said, carried a huge headline, "San Francisco Punished!" In New York, Will Irwin, an adopted son, sat down and wrote sadly of "the city that was."

But the city's decease, like Mark Twain's, was greatly exaggerated, although it had suffered a staggering blow. Casualties included 500 dead and missing; four square miles, including virtually all of the business district, were destroyed—an area of 497 blocks, some 30,000 buildings. Damage was estimated at 500 million dollars, of which 200 millions remained a net loss after payment of insurance. Food and clothing for the thousands of homeless were rushed from all parts of the United States; Europe and Asia contributed millions to relieve suffering.

The ruins were still smoking when plans for reconstruction were started. The first contract for a new building was signed six days after the disaster. "Don't talk earthquake, talk business," read placards on the streets. New building and fire laws insured that no catastrophe of such proportions could occur again. Within three years, in spite of graft scandals and civic turbulence, 20,000 new buildings had been constructed. Within seven, a new City Hall and a new Public Library were under way, and electric tramways had replaced the cable lines except on the hills.

For four years before the fire the government of San Francisco had been dominated by the notorious Ruef-Schmitz machine. Masquerading as the Union Labor Party, the ring was financed by gambling houses, saloons, the brothels of the Barbary Coast—but principally by the city's traction and utility corporations. The attack on the machine was launched by Hearst and followed up by Fremont Older of the San Francisco *Bulletin,* Rudolph Spreckels, and James D. Phelan. The newspaper campaign was interrupted by the earthquake and fire, but shortly after was resumed and the charges against Ruef and Schmitz led to their indictment. Other figures prominent in promoting public utilities were named codefendants. Francis J. Heney was appointed special prosecutor and detective William Burns was retained. The trials dragged on for two years amidst considerable violence, in the course of which Older was kidnapped, Heney was shot (to be replaced by Hiram Johnson), and the residence of an important witness was dynamited. The trials ended with the conviction of Ruef, and the cases against his codefendants, the utility promoters, were not pressed.

In 1914 the city acquired control of the Hetch Hetchy watershed, near Yosemite, ultimately to supply 400,000,000 gallons of water daily. The opening of the Panama Canal on August 15, 1914, was of immense benefit to the city's maritime trade. In 1915 the Panama-Pacific International Exposition at "Rainbow City," built beside the Presidio on the Marina was inaugurated. At its close, the exposition presented the city with funds to build the Municipal Auditorium.

The history of the years from 1915 to the building of the bridges and the planning of the Golden Gate International Exposition for 1939, has been in part a story of labor unrest, particularly during the World War and the depression of the 1930's (*see LABOR*).

The bombing of the Preparedness Day Parade made the year 1916 a black one. The conviction of Tom Mooney and Warren K. Billings for the bombing on questionable evidence inspired a world-wide protest that was not allayed until 1939, when Governor Olson unconditionally pardoned Mooney. On the following day Mooney led a large parade up Market Street, lined for miles on both sides with cheering crowds. Above the cheers screamed the siren on the Ferry Building, opened full blast, as it had been to announce the bombing 23 years before.

In 1936 the Pan-American Airways initiated weekly passenger service from San Francisco to the Orient by means of giant flying "clipper ships," but the crowning accomplishment of 1936 and 1937 was the completion of the two great bridges—the San Francisco-Oakland Bay Bridge in November, 1936; the Golden Gate Bridge in May, 1937. The site of the Golden Gate International Exposition of 1939 is Treasure Island, created by dredging the bay near Yerba Buena Island (*see GOLDEN GATE INTERNATIONAL EXPOSITION*).

San Francisco has been associated in larger or smaller measure with the careers of many who have made names for themselves in the arts, notably, Jack London; Isadora Duncan, the dancer; George Sterling, the poet; Bret Harte; Henry George, founder of the single tax movement and at one time managing editor of the local *Times.* It has been the subject of innumerable stories, novels, and non-fiction works. First described as an unlovely Spanish settlement by Richard Henry Dana in *Two Years Before the Mast,* the city has been pictured in Frank

Norris' *McTeague*, Gertrude Atherton's *Rezanov*, Stewart Edward White's *The Rose Dawn* (vigilante days), Dashiell Hammett's *The Maltese Falcon*, and William Saroyan's stories. From the days when audiences showered gold nuggets and pouches of gold dust at a popular performer's feet, when a theater was built and given to Edwin Booth to keep him from deserting his public, when "road shows" skipped from Chicago to Salt Lake City and San Francisco and back East again without a stop, the city has been stage-struck and music-mad. It has a club founded by artists and art lovers, which has grown and prospered until it possesses massive quarters on a downtown street, and holds an annual musical festival in its own private forest.

Perhaps some of San Francisco's glamor has been drowned under a flood of neon lights; skycrapers have replaced some of the rambling buildings mellowed by time and weather; and old-timers lament the happy-go-lucky days "before the fire." But it is still a gay city, convivial and dignified, for its gayety has always worn a silk hat; and it heatedly objects to the nickname " 'Frisco," used by unsuspecting outsiders. San Francisco has granite qualities as well; fogs cannot dampen its ardor; earthquakes, political scandals, and labor wars have failed to shake its confidence in itself and the future; it has remained unmistakably itself. It is still "the City."

POINTS OF INTEREST

(See San Francisco Map for Nos. 1-3, 41-76; see San Francisco Downtown Map for Nos. 4-40.)

(Market Street and Downtown)

1. The FERRY BUILDING, foot of Market St., completed in 1903, has a 240-foot central tower topped with a four-faced clock and a set-back "belfry" and cupola in four stages. Each dial of the clock is 22 feet in diameter, with numerals 3 feet long. The clock was stopped at 5:16 a.m., April 18, 1906, by the earthquake, and remained so for more than a year until repairs were completed. The first ferry sheds, erected in 1877, succeeded a wharf built here as early as 1850. The State Division of Mines has a GEOLOGICAL MUSEUM (*open 9-5 Mon.-Fri., 9-12 m. Sat.; July and Aug. 8-4 Mon.-Fri., 8-12 m. Sat.*) Along the entire second floor corridor is a huge relief map of California, broken only by entrances to the upper decks of ferry boats.

The EMBARCADERO, formerly called East St., is a crescent-shaped street lined with piers and wharves paralleling the bay shore for three and one-half miles. The west side is largely given over to stores and lodging houses frequented by sailors and longshoremen. During the maritime strike of 1934 the Embarcadero was the scene of numerous battles between police and strikers.

2. The SITE OF THE PREPAREDNESS DAY PARADE BOMBING (1916), SW. corner Steuart and Market Sts., is unmarked but has been kept continually in the public mind by unremitting

efforts to establish the innocence and obtain the release of Tom Mooney and Warren K. Billings from prison. Mooney was pardoned by Governor Olson on January 7, 1939. The Southern Pacific Building now covers this site.

3. The SAN FRANCISCO-OAKLAND BAY BRIDGE, San Francisco approach from Bryant and 5th Sts., completed in 1937, was designed and constructed by the Department of Public Works of the State of California. Spanning the broad waters of the East and West Bay, this magnificent steel and concrete bridge serves as a giant traffic artery between San Francisco and the neighboring towns in Alameda County. It stretches its lofty spans from the anchorage in San Francisco to Yerba Buena Island, and continues at an oblique angle to the eastern approaches of Berkeley and Oakland. The bridge proper, including the island crossing, is approximately 4.5 miles long, and more than 8 miles in length from the ends of the east and west approaches.

The bridge is a double-deck structure, with six traffic lanes for automobiles on the upper level, and three truck lanes and two interurban tracks on the deck below. The western section of the bridge, 216 feet above the water, consists of two suspension spans, fastened midway between San Francisco and Yerba Buena to a steel and concrete anchorage, the latter rising 502 feet from the rock floor of the bay. The two center spans on each side of the anchorage are 2,310 feet in length. The bridge is illuminated at night with strings of yellow sodium vapor lights, the brilliant rays of which can penetrate the thickest fog.

DOWNTOWN SAN FRANCISCO. Points of Interest

1, 2, 3.—See San Francisco map.
4. San Francisco Terminal
5. Donahue Monument
6. Nevada Bank Building
7. Lotta's Fountain
8. Palace Hotel
9. Telephone Building
10. San Francisco Stock Exchange
11. Russ Building
12. St. Patrick's Church
13. The Turntable
14. Native Sons Monument
15. Union Square
16. St. Francis Hotel
17. 450 Sutter Building
18. Native Sons Building
19. Olympic Club
20. Bohemian Club
21. Mark Hopkins Hotel
22. Fairmont Hotel
23. Pacific Union Club
24. Grace Cathedral
25. Kong Chow Temple
26. Mandarin Theatre
27. Chinese Hospital
28. Chinese Telephone Exchange
29. Tin How Temple
30. Old St. Mary's Church
31. St. Mary's Square
32. Portsmouth Square
33. Montgomery Block
34. "Golden Era"
35. Hotaling Building
36. Stevenson and Booth Houses
37. Pioneer Park
38. SS. Peter & Paul Church
39. California School of Fine Arts
40. Fishermen's Wharf

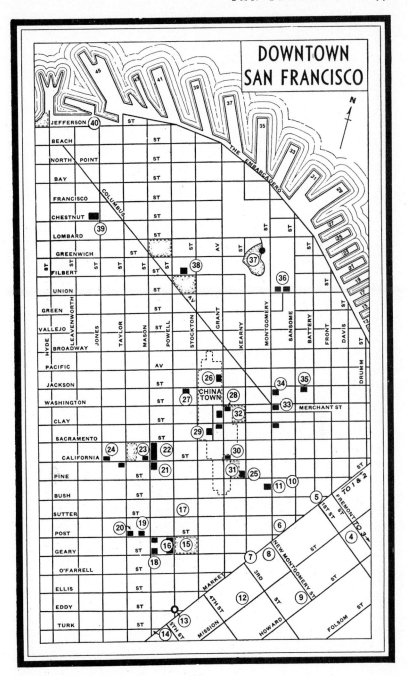

DOWNTOWN SAN FRANCISCO

At YERBA BUENA ISLAND (formerly called Goat Island) midway between San Francisco and Oakland, a 300-acre Government reservation (*open only with written pass, obtainable at 100 Harrison St.*), the roadway passes through a double-deck tunnel, 76 feet wide by 50 feet high, the largest bore tunnel in the world, and emerges on the East Bay sector of the bridge. The main cantilever span of 1400 feet has 510-foot anchor arms. East of this span are five truss spans, each 509 feet in length, and 14 truss spans, 291 feet long.

The east or Alameda County approaches, each accommodating two-way traffic, are on Ashley Avenue in Berkeley, and on 38th and 37th Streets, at Market and Cypress, and at Cypress and Seventh Streets, in Oakland.

The west approaches in San Francisco are in the form of long overhead runways with a system of branching loops to minimize the intersection of incoming and outgoing traffic lines.

4. The SAN FRANCISCO TERMINAL BUILDING, 1st and Mission Sts., completed in 1939, the final unit of the Bay Bridge Electric Railway facilities, was constructed under the jurisdiction of the California Toll Bridge Authority by the State department of public works.

This modern building is virtually an enclosed system of ramps and stairs connecting the elevated tracks of the Interurban Electric (S.P.), the Key System, and the Sacramento-Northern Railways, which enter the terminal over a looping viaduct from the bridge to the streetcar concourse and the street. There are six railway tracks on the upper level, arranged in pairs, with long 700-foot platforms between. The tracks and platforms are 164 feet wide, roofed over with large skylights. From these platforms spacious ramps and stairs lead to a mezzanine concourse half way between the upper level and the street, with access to an outer streetcar platform at the same level, and to the main passenger entrance on Mission Street.

5. The DONAHUE MONUMENT, intersection Market, Bush, and Battery Sts., locally known as the "Mechanics' Monument," is the work of Douglas Tilden, noted deaf-mute sculptor. Executed in bronze and dedicated to Peter Donahue, founder of one of the city's first iron works, it consists of a fountain surmounted with a group of three artisans struggling to force the blade of an enormous mechanical punch through plate metal. A tablet set in the pavement at the foot of the monument marks the shoreline of Yerba Buena (San Francisco) in 1848.

6. In the NEVADA BANK BUILDING, NE. corner Market and Montgomery Sts., 10th floor, is a MUSEUM (*open 9-5 Mon.-Fri., 9-12 Sat.*) of California history. Among the Wells-Fargo relics here are a stagecoach shipped around the Horn in the 1850's; the massive scales used in the Wells-Fargo office at Columbia, Tuolumne County, and said to have weighed 55 of the 87 million dollars worth of gold mined in the Mother Lode; the mining tools used by James W. Marshall, discoverer of the gold; and a priceless collection of nuggets loaned by

the Menendez estate.   Another exhibit contains a large collection of
Colt firearms.

7. LOTTA'S FOUNTAIN, intersection of Market, Kearny, and
Geary Sts., transformed from a watering trough for horses to a drinking fountain for humans, is of bronze, in the ornate style of the 1870's.
It was presented to the city in 1875 by Lotta Crabtree, the beloved
actress of gold rush days.   Here on Christmas Eve, 1910, Luisa Tetrazzini, who won her first acclaim in San Francisco, sang carols to great
throngs in the streets.

8. The PALACE HOTEL, SW. corner Market and New Mont-
gomery Sts., is a seven-story, yellow brick structure erected in 1910 by
Trowbridge and Livingston of Boston on the framework of the early
hostelry gutted by the fire of 1906.   Its main attraction was the driveway extending into the huge Palm Court, enabling guests to alight from
their carriages at the desk.   Within the walls of these successive buildings a king and a president have died—King Kalakaua of Hawaii
in the old, President Warren G. Harding in the new.   In the Pied
Piper Buffet is a Maxfield Parrish mural depicting the legend, and
many caricatures of local and national celebrities by Antonio Soto-
mayer.

9. The TELEPHONE BUILDING, 140 New Montgomery St.,
designed by Miller, Pflueger and Cantin, is a modern setback skyscraper
erected in 1923, one of the first in San Francisco.   It rises twenty-six
stories on a steel frame faced with off-white terra cotta tile.   Pilasters
capped by a cluster of stylized flowers.   The setbacks are adorned with
pilasters, and a row of eagles crowns the towers.   As the official storm-
warning station in the city, the building has a high flagpole flying storm
and hurricane flags by day and supporting three great electric lanterns
at night.

10. The SAN FRANCISCO STOCK EXCHANGE, SW. corner
Pine and Sansome Sts., consists of a one-story structure, housing the
trading room, and an adjoining ten-story office building, both designed
in the neo-classic style.   Flanking the Doric entrance loggia of the trading room are heroic sculptures by Ralph Stackpole.   Above the entrance
to the office on Sansome St. is a bas-relief figure by the same sculptor.
The interior of the trading room is adorned with concrete bas-reliefs by
Robert Boardman Howard, while in the luncheon club room are frescoes by Diego Rivera, representing the growth of California's agriculture, mining, and industry.

11. The RUSS BUILDING, Montgomery St. between Bush and
Pine Sts., is an imposing 31-story skyscraper of stone and terra cotta
facing, with modified Gothic detail.   Before the fire of 1906 this site
was occupied by the Russ House, once San Francisco's finest hostelry,
built by Christian Russ, a pioneer of 1847 and proprietor of an immensely popular beer garden and concert hall in the early days.   The
building was designed by George Kelham.

12. ST. PATRICK'S CHURCH, Mission St. between 3rd and 4th
Sts., is sometimes called "the most Irish church on this continent."

Constructed of brick, with a slender tower and steeple, it is the fourth building and the third site of this parish, established in 1851 by Father Maginnis, then the only English-speaking priest in San Francisco. The interior of the church is finished in green translucent Connemara marble and Caen stone, for which the late pastor, Father Rogers, searched Ireland. On the floor is a mosaic, *The River of Life.* The crucifix and vestments are by Mia Cranwill, Irish artist, after designs of the sixth and eighth centuries.

13. On the TURNTABLE, Powell and Market Sts., the southern terminus of the Powell Street cable line, the cars are turned around bodily by the crew before starting the journey up the hill again.

14. The NATIVE SONS MONUMENT, intersection of Market, Turk and Mason Sts., by Douglas Tilden, is a tall granite shaft surmounted by a bronze figure holding an open book inscribed "September 9, 1850," the date of California's admission to the Union; below stands a male figure holding a flag with a new star for California. The column was presented to the city in 1897 by Sen. James D. Phelan, then mayor.

15. UNION SQUARE, Post St. between Stockton and Powell Sts., extending to Geary St., originally a huge sandbank known as O'Farrell Mountain, was presented to the city in 1850 by John W. Geary, first mayor of the American City. The plot, leveled and landscaped, was given its present name because of pro-Union meetings held here before and during the Civil War. In 1864 the Mechanics' Institute held a fair in the pavilion on the square; after the 1906 disaster the square was dubbed "Little St. Francis" because of the temporary building erected here to house guests of the St. Francis Hotel. In the center of the square is the VICTORY MONUMENT, by Robert Ingersoll Aitken, commemorating Dewey's victory in Manila Bay, a 96-foot granite shaft topped with a bronze figure symbolizing naval conquest.

16. The ST. FRANCIS HOTEL, SW. corner Post and Powell Sts., a gray stone structure, is one of San Francisco's largest and best-known hotels. Almost destroyed by the 1906 fire, its walls were scarcely cold when a banquet was held in the White and Gold Room to celebrate the beginning of reconstruction. The rebuilt hotel has a Borgia Room, a replica of the room of that name in the Vatican at Rome. A large painting of Mount Tamalpais by Jules Mersfelder hangs over the desk in the main lobby.

17. The 450 SUTTER BUILDING, 450 Sutter St., is a modern 25-story skyscraper of steel, glass, and terra cotta, designed by Miller and Pflueger. Light buff in color, it has windows set flush with the outside walls, accentuating the vertical mass. Ancient Mayan hieroglyphs and stylized ornament carry out the decorative motif in both exterior and interior detail.

18. The NATIVE SONS BUILDING, 414 Mason St., a red brick building with terra cotta facing, is the headquarters of the Native Sons of the Golden West, an organization of native-born Californians. Around the two entrances are tile plaques representing California ex-

Cities II

CITY HALL, LOS ANGELES

WILSHIRE BOULEVARD, LOS ANGELES

AIRVIEW, LONG BEACH

OLD SPANISH LIGHTHOUSE, SAN DIEGO

COURT HOUSE, SANTA BARBARA

CABRILLO BEACH, SAN PEDRO

ROSE BOWL, PASADENA

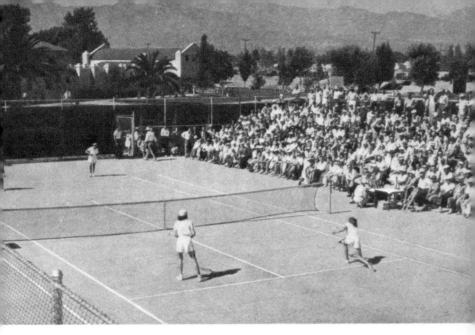

LOS ANGELES TENNIS CLUB

TOURNAMENT OF ROSES, PASADENA

REAL ESTATE OFFICE   RESTAURANT

LOS ANGELES

ANGELUS TEMPLE, LOS ANGELES

YACHT RACE IN ALAMITOS BAY, LONG BEACH

GRAUMAN'S CHINESE THEATER, HOLLYWOOD

TORTILLA MAKER, OLVERA STREET, LOS ANGELES

plorers and pioneers. The building has an auditorium seating 1,300, frequently used for lectures.

19. The OLYMPIC CLUB (*private*), 524 Post St., is a buff brick building with the club's "winged O" symbol carved over the white stone entrance. The club was organized in 1860 and claims to be the oldest amateur athletic club in existence. In the club is a large swimming pool supplied with salt water directly from the Pacific Ocean. Annually on New Year's Day it holds a modified beach marathon along the ocean shore, after which participants take their first plunge of the new year.

20. The BOHEMIAN CLUB (*private*), NE. corner Post and Taylor Sts., a massive dark red brick building, houses one of San Francisco's best known artistic organizations. Originally, its membership was limited to distinguished artists and writers, but others interested in the arts are now permitted to join. Every January the club sponsors a free exhibition of paintings by its members, one of the rare occasions when women are admitted to any part of the building, and during its "Mid-summer Jinks" at Bohemian Grove on the Russian River (*see TOUR 2a*) holds an annual Grove Play, with text, music, and performance members. On the Post Street facade is a bronze bas-relief memorial to Bret Harte, the work of Jo Mora.

21. The MARK HOPKINS HOTEL, SE. corner California and Mason Sts., a buff brick skyscraper, combines baronial French and Spanish Renaissance styles. The hotel, perpetuating the name of Mark Hopkins, one of the railroad "big four," occupies the site of the old Hopkins residence, a "magnificent monstrosity" destroyed in 1906. The Room of the Dons contains murals of early California history by Maynard Dixon and Frank van Sloun. The Peacock Court has a lunette of *Leda and the Swan,* by Ray Boynton, done by the ancient method of encaustic painting, in which hot wax and color are applied directly to the wall.

22. The FAIRMONT HOTEL, NE. corner California and Mason Sts., was built in 1906, by Mrs. Herman Oelrichs, daughter of James G. Fair, one of the bonanza kings of the Comstock Lode. In this massive granite hostelry are the TERRACE PLUNGE (*open 10 a.m.-10 p.m. daily*); the CIRCUS ROOM, with murals by Esther Bruton; and two rare sixteenth century Florentine mirrors, the only examples of this type in America, brought from the Castello de Vincigliata, Florence, by Mrs. Oelrichs. The hotel contains a theater seating 200.

23. The PACIFIC UNION CLUB, NW. corner California and Mason Sts., the only one of the brownstone Nob Hill mansions little damaged by the great fire, was formerly the home of James C. Flood, bonanza king who began his career as a saloonkeeper.

24. GRACE CATHEDRAL, NE. corner California and Jones Sts., is an uncompleted gray stone building of modified Gothic design, the work of Lewis P. Hobart. The spire will rise 500 feet above sea level, and in size its nave will exceed that of any English cathedral. The Chapel of Grace, the apse, and half of the nave are finished (1939); the

carillon, donated by Dr. N. T. Coulson, will be used in the Golden Gate International Exposition before being installed in the bell tower. Off the south nave, the Chapel of Grace, a delicate structure in Gothic style and the gift of Ethel Sperry Crocker, contains a tenth century stone altar from Brittany and a fourteenth century carved stone table used as a credence table. The cathedral stands on the site of homes built by Charles Crocker, the "hurry-up man" and hard driver of the "big four," and his son, William H. Crocker, a banker. Heirs of the family donated the land to the Protestant Episcopal Diocese of California in 1910.

(*Chinatown and Old San Francisco*)

25. The KONG CHOW TEMPLE (*open 10 a.m.-1 a.m. daily; voluntary offering*), 520 Pine St., is the largest Chinese joss house in America and is one of two in San Francisco open to the white public. Dedicated to the hero Quan Dai, it has two altars; before one tea is served every morning; on the other are paper and pencil for recording worshipers' requests. On the balcony, overlooking the courtyard, is the "prayer tree" in which written prayers may be placed.

26. The MANDARIN THEATER (*open 7:30-12 p.m. daily, adm. 25¢-50¢, 25¢ after 9 p.m. patrons may enter at any time*), 1021 Grant Ave., is at the northern end of Chinatown, where it merges with "Little Italy." The uninitiated Occidental is apt to be amazed at the performance, which lasts from 7:30 p.m. to midnight. The stage is devoid of curtains or scenery, and "props" are brought on and removed throughout the performance by nonchalant stagehands; there are no actresses, for all female roles are played by males; the musicians, when not playing, sit on the side of the stage and sip tea; meanwhile, the audience comes and goes, interrupts the players at will, and chews watermelon seeds continuously. The Chinese theater in the United States originated at the Mandarin, although another on Jackson Street occasionally presents Chinese operas (*see the THEATER*).

27. The CHINESE HOSPITAL, Jackson St. between Stockton and Powell Sts., a four-story stone building, is the only one in the United States. It is completely modern in equipment and procedure and largely staffed by Chinese doctors and nurses. There are 57 beds, including a small maternity ward. White patients are welcome.

28. CHINESE TELEPHONE EXCHANGE (*open 8 a.m.-9 p.m. daily*), 743 Washington St., a building of Chinese architecture, is a branch of the Pacific Telephone and Telegraph Company, being the only completely Chinese exchange outside of China. The operators are Chinese girls who are required to know, in addition to English, five Chinese dialects, and to memorize the numbers of 2,300 subscribers, for most Chinese call by name and not by number.

29. The TIN HOW TEMPLE (*open 10 a.m.-1 a.m.; voluntary offering*), 125 Waverly Pl., the oldest Chinese joss house in San Francisco, is situated on the fourth floor of the building (*ring for priest or*

assistant), because no human creation but a roof is allowed to stand above the gods. This joss house was established by Day Ju, one of the first three Chinese to arrive in San Francisco. The altar to Tin How, Queen of the Heavens and Goddess of the Seven Seas, was installed on their ship for daily worship and later removed to the temple. The present main altar, covered with gold leaf and intricate carvings representing the life of Confucius, is many centuries old. In the temple are ceremonial wands resembling ancient battle-axes; massive bronze urns containing prayer sticks; and Yuen Bo Pon, a fireplace in which written messages to the gods can be burned and thus recorded in the ether.

30. OLD ST. MARY'S CHURCH, NE. corner Grant Ave. and California St., in the heart of Chinatown, is a red brick structure of Victorian Gothic design. Material for the structure was brought both from China and around the Horn; in 1855 bells arrived, were hung, and blessed. The church, the main part of which was built by Archbishop Alemany in 1854, later became the Roman Catholic Cathedral, and in 1894 was transferred to the Paulist Fathers. The congregation is still white although there is a Chinese branch of the church at Stockton and Clay Streets. The clock in the California Street tower bears the inscription, "Son, observe the time and flee from evil."

31. ST. MARY'S SQUARE, opposite Old St. Mary's Church, formerly explained the inscription on the church tower, for it was once St. Mary's Alley, a part of the old red-light district. This grass-covered municipal square is a favorite romping place for Chinese children. In the center is a stainless steel and concrete STATUE OF SUN YAT SEN by Beniamino Bufano.

32. PORTSMOUTH SQUARE, Kearny St. between Washington and Clay Sts., the birthplace of San Francisco, was Candelario Miramontes' potato patch in 1833; then it became the Spanish and Mexican Plaza. A plaque in the NW. corner commemorates Montgomery's raising of the American flag here in 1846. In the square also is a BRONZE GALLEON, mounted on granite, "to remember Robert Louis Stevenson," who frequented the park and its environs for local color.

33. The MONTGOMERY BLOCK, 628 Montgomery St., built in 1853 by Gen. H. W. Halleck with bricks and cement brought in clipper ships from England and France, is the oldest of San Francisco's "fireproof" buildings. Once the home of the Stock Exchange, the rambling structure, affectionately nicknamed the "Monkey Block," is now the heart of the city's Bohemia; many artists and writers have had studios in the building. During the fire of 1906 it narrowly escaped dynamiting by the Army.

In 1938 the revived "Order of E Clampus Vitus," the gold miners' burlesque fraternity, placed a commemorative plaque on the site of Parker's Bank Exchange Saloon, at the Washington Street corner of the block, where Duncan Nichol invented the celebrated drink, Pisco Punch. This saloon was frequented by the mad "Emperor" Norton and the reform editor, James King of William, who was brought here after being shot by Casey.

Joshua A. Norton, the "Emperor," was born in England in 1819. At the age of 30 he arrived in San Francisco with $40,000, which he pyramided to a quarter of a million. Attempting to corner the rice market, he and his colleagues lost their fortunes. Norton went into seclusion for several years; when he reappeared, his mind was unbalanced, and he soon became the favorite ward of the city. Clad in an old uniform and military cap, with a small sword dangling at his side and a stick or umbrella in his hand, trailed always by two mongrel dogs, Bummer and Lazarus, he was a familiar figure on the downtown streets. Norton declared himself Emperor of the United States and Protector of Mexico: one of his frequent proclamations dissolved the Democratic and Republican parties in the interests of peace; another dissolved a steamship company because a purser, violating imperial privilege, had summarily put him ashore; a third called the public's attention to the duty of replenishing his wardrobe. He was the first to "propose" a bridge across the bay. He was permitted to eat, drink, and amuse himself gratis, and to draw checks up to 50 cents on San Francisco banks. These checks were always honored, and Norton added to his cash by selling 50-cent bonds and by collecting "taxes." He dropped dead on the street in 1880 and was given an elaborate funeral by the city.

34. The "GOLDEN ERA," 718-20 Montgomery St., an old red brick building now used as a plumbing shop and Chinese laundry, is the last of San Francisco's noted ship buildings. These odd structures were built around abandoned ships drawn up and fastened at what was then the waterfront. In the interior the tapered woodwork on the forecastle leads to a forepeak. It was here that Bret Harte worked as a compositor on the *Golden Era* and wrote his earliest works.

35. The HOTALING BUILDING, 451 Jackson St., a three-story stone and brick building designed in the style of the French Second Empire, has been continuously occupied since 1866 by a wholesale liquor company. Some of the original furniture is still in use—desks, chairs, and bookcases of beautiful hardwood in excellent condition. Prints of early San Francisco hang on the walls. After the earthquake and fire of 1906, a popular ditty by Charles K. Field ran:

If, as they say, God spanked the town
For being over-frisky,
Why did He burn all the churches down
And spare Hotaling's Whiskey?

36. The STEVENSON AND BOOTH HOUSES, 287 and 289 Union St. between Sansome and Montgomery Sts. (*accessible only on foot*), are pointed out as the former homes of the author and the actor. Actually, the decrepit little frame house at 287, with steeply pitched roof and gingerbread trim, was the home of Edwin Booth's hostler (Booth himself lived on Pine Street), and the modernized stucco studio building next door was Booth's stable. Robert Louis Stevenson, however, did live at 289 during the early 1870's.

37. In PIONEER PARK, on the crest of Telegraph Hill, stands the COIT MEMORIAL TOWER (*elevator service 9-4 daily; adm. 25¢*), erected in 1933 with a legacy left by Mrs. Lillie Hitchcock Coit. It is a cylindrical concrete structure 210 feet high, affording a fine view of the city and bay. The frescoes on the walls of the ground floor, depicting life and labor in California, are by the Public Works Art Project. A plaque at the main entrance marks the site of "the inner signal station—1849, and the first Western Telegraph Station—1853."

38. SS. PETER AND PAUL CHURCH, 650 Filbert St., facing Washington Square, is of Romanesque design, with two 191-foot turreted towers of terra cotta. It was built in 1924 by Charles Fantoni. Two mosaics are in preparation (1939) for the front entrance, depicting Columbus disembarking on American soil and Dante at work on the "Paradiso." In the heart of San Francisco's Italian section, this church is known locally as the "Church of the Ten Commandments," because part of the motion picture of that name was filmed here. Shortly after the construction of the church it was bombed three times by an unknown fanatic but was not seriously damaged.

39. The CALIFORNIA SCHOOL OF FINE ARTS, Chestnut and Jones Sts., of modified Italian Renaissance design, is constructed of unpolished concrete, with a campanile. In one of the exhibition rooms a huge fresco by Diego Rivera in seven sections illustrates the painting of a fresco, and shows a startling rear view of the Mexican artist himself. The Anne Bremer Memorial Library, one of the best art libraries in America, has received numerous donations from the well-known collector, Albert Bender.

The school was started in 1874 and is still maintained by the San Francisco Art Association. In 1893 the Mark Hopkins residence was deeded in trust to the University of California for the Art Association, and under the name of the Mark Hopkins Institute of Art it became well known. The catastrophe of 1906 left it a heap of ruins, but the school carried on in temporary buildings until the site was sold in 1923, and the present building was erected on the top of Russian Hill, affording matchless views of the Bay. The college gives fine and applied arts courses, a special four-year normal school course for art teachers, and courses in commercial art and design. In 1938 it had an enrollment of 600.

40. FISHERMAN'S WHARF, Taylor St. at the Embarcadero, is the embarking and landing point for the city's many Italian fishermen. Brightly painted fishing boats, mostly in blue, the Virgin's color, lazily tug at their anchors or mooring lines as weather-beaten old men, wearing large gold earrings, mend nets with wooden needles on the wharf. When vessels arrive with their day's catch, the wharf seethes with activity as dealers and fishermen haggle over prices. Along Taylor Street are sidewalk stands displaying shellfish, and at the curb big iron cauldrons boil large freshly caught crabs to be eaten there or carried away by the purchaser. In the neighboring sea-food restaurants, the diner has the assurance that his favorite dish was swimming in the Pacific only a few short hours before.

(Marina and Presidio)

41. ST. BRIGID'S CHURCH, SW. corner Van Ness Ave. and Broadway, probably the only church in the world built of old paving blocks, is constructed of slabs of hewn granite that served as pedestrian crossings in the days of cobblestone streets. It is of Romanesque design, with a terra cotta entrance carved with liturgical symbols. Henry A. Minton was the architect.

42. The OCTAGONAL HOUSE (*private*), 2618 Gough St., a two-story adobe structure covered with frame, was built in 1864 for Mrs. Harriet Sober McElroy, a pioneer. This house with a small cupola has eight sets of double windows on each floor. The rooms are square, with the angles taken up by closets. In front of the house are three California live oaks.

43. AQUATIC PARK (*open daily*), foot of Polk Street and Van Ness Ave., San Francisco's newest recreation center, was built by the WPA and opened in January, 1939. The landscaped park spreads along a semicircle of beach on a cove in the lee of Black Point. The municipal pier, circular in shape, encloses a half-mile stretch of water for swimming, boating, and racing. Inland rises the white Casino, four stories high toward the sea, with ends rounded like a ship's stern, and stories, or decks, semielliptical in shape. Its seaward face is almost entirely of glass. On the lowest floor are bathing facilities to accommodate several thousand persons a day. In the Polk Street entrance is a large slate sculpture executed by the Federal Art Project; the central lounge room on the second floor is decorated with murals by the Federal Art Project, picturing marine and undersea life; elsewhere are statues of St. Francis and Sun Yat Sen. Opening from the main lounge is a glass-enclosed dining salon in yacht club motif. Above, on the smaller floors or decks, are other lounges and dining rooms, with windows like portholes on the land side, and wide expanses of glass toward the sea. On each side of the Casino are stone bleachers and a promenade running the length of the beach. At the eastern and western extremities of the playground are 50-foot towers in modernistic style, containing loudspeakers to broadcast sporting events and music.

44. FORT MASON, Van Ness Ave. and Bay St., is an Army Supply Depot and contains the residences of the commanding general and ranking staff officers of the Ninth Corps Area. This 67-acre reservation was once the home of John C. Frémont, who built a house here in 1853, since occupied by 36 commanding officers.

THE ARMY TRANSPORT DOCKS, northwest shore of the reservation, are three in number, one 500 feet long, the others 650 feet; each year they receive and ship to and from Pacific and Far East posts about 45,000 officers and enlisted men.

45. YACHT HARBOR, Divisadero St. and Marina Blvd., is protected on the north by a narrow spit, Marina State Park. Hundreds of pleasure craft are berthed here, from small speedboats and sailboats to palatial private yachts. The ST. FRANCIS YACHT CLUB (*private*)

is on the eastern tip of Marina State Park. To the south of the harbor is MARINA PARK, fronting the bay, a long grass-covered strip, popular on Sundays with promenaders.

46. The PALACE OF FINE ARTS, Baker St. between Jefferson and Bay Sts., is the last surviving building of the Panama-Pacific International Exposition of 1915. This neo-classic structure, built on land reclaimed from the bay, is of brown stucco with a Roman rotunda and Corinthian peristyle. Once an art gallery, it is now used for indoor tennis. Two ornamental gondolas float on the lagoon before the Palace entrance.

47. The PRESIDIO (*open: night parking prohibited*), entrance gate at Baker and Lombard Sts., once the garrison of Spanish soldiers protecting the mission, is a U. S. military reservation of 1,542 acres, and the headquarters of the Ninth Corps Area. Within the reservation is the LETTERMAN HOSPITAL for service men and their families. One block to the west is the old STATION HOSPITAL, built in 1854 and still in use. Its brick foundations and pine and hemlock girders were shipped around the Horn. The CEMETERY, largest national cemetery in the United States with the exception of Arlington, contains the graves of more than 15,000 veterans and their wives. One woman interred here is not a veteran's wife—Pauline Cushman Tyler, a young actress, who was a Union spy during the Civil War and later commissioned an honorary officer of the Army. At the southern anchorage of the Golden Gate Bridge stands FORT WINFIELD SCOTT, on a site fortified since 1776, but from which a hostile shot has never been fired. It was originally known as the Castillo de San Joaquin. In 1846 Frémont stole over from the Sausalito and spiked its guns, and the American flag was hoisted over the Presidio on July 9 of that year. In 1854, the bluff at Fort Point was graded to the water's edge, and the present fort, somewhat similar to Fort Sumter, was completed in 1860. The old fort is now dismantled, but plans are under way to restore it as a historical monument, with old artillery pieces remounted and their muzzles pointing out over the Golden Gate. The OFFICERS' CLUB, once the Spanish comandante's headquarters and the oldest building standing in San Francisco, is a long low adobe structure built about 1776; the Presidio MARKER nearby records its history. In front of the marker stand two old Spanish guns, named "Poder" and "San Pedro," bearing the Spanish coat-of-arms and inscribed, "Lima, Peru—1673."

On August 27, 1915, in a destructive fire at the Presidio, the wife and three daughters of Gen. John Pershing lost their lives.

48. The GOLDEN GATE BRIDGE, main San Francisco approach from the Presidio, was designed by Joseph B. Strauss, and completed in May 1937 at a cost of $35,500,000. The huge web-like span, illuminated at night with strings of yellow sodium vapor lights, suspended high above the water, links northern California to the peninsula of San Francisco. Two enormous steel towers, erected on concrete piers, act as props and hold up the giant "clothes line" cables from which the bridge is hung. The massive steel framework of these towers consists

of two soaring steel legs which rise in five tapering stages, with heavy diagonal and horizontal cross braces or struts to the cable saddles at the top. The legs of the tower, each 32 feet by 53 feet, rise 746 feet above the water (the height of a 65-story building). The skeleton super-structure of the towers, together with the steel framework of the bridge floor and the sweeping cables, forms an impressive silhouette.

The main central span, 4,200 feet in length, is the longest single span in the world. The minor spans at either end are each 1,125 feet in length. Above are the two sagging cables, each more than a yard in diameter and fastened at both shores to huge concrete anchorages. The suspended floor structure is 90 feet wide and 25 feet deep, and supports a reinforced concrete six-lane roadway and sidewalks. The center of the span clears the water by 220 feet.

At the south end of the bridge proper are a large steel arch passing over Fort Winfield Scott, four 125-foot truss spans, and finally the Toll Plaza, from which lead two roads, one to the northeastern section of San Francisco and the other southward. The Marin County end of the bridge has five 175-foot truss spans and is in Fort Baker, a U. S. Army reservation.

49. TEMPLE EMANU-EL, Arguello Blvd. (1st Ave.) between Lake and Clay Sts., erected in 1925, is a huge, cream-colored concrete edifice of modified Byzantine design with a red tile dome. Standing in the Pacific Heights residential district, this temple is the home of the largest Jewish congregation in San Francisco.

(Midtown)

50. The UNITED STATES POST OFFICE, NE. corner 7th and Mission Sts., one of the few public buildings to withstand the fire of 1906, is Italian Renaissance in design. Constructed of granite, it was built in 1905 under the direction of James Knox Taylor, then super-vising architect of the Treasury Department. The first floor corridors, decorated by skilled artisans brought from Italy, are of Pavonezza marble trimmed with glass mosaic; the floors and ceiling are of mosaic tile.

51. The CIVIC CENTER, just off Market St., roughly bounded by McAllister, Franklin, Hayes, and Leavenworth Sts., has a number of municipal and Federal buildings designed in Italian Renaissance style grouped about it.

The FEDERAL OFFICE BUILDING, McAllister St. between Leaven-worth and Hyde Sts., extending to Fulton St., is a five-story colonnaded structure built around a central court, with entrances at the north and south ends. The building, newest of the Civic Center group, was erected in 1936 and houses practically all the Federal offices of San Francisco except the Post Office, and those in the Appraisers Building.

The SAN FRANCISCO PUBLIC LIBRARY (*open 9 a.m.-10 p.m. week-days; 1:30-5 Sun.*), SE. corner McAllister and Larkin Sts., is on the site of the old City Hall and Public Library destroyed in the 1906 fire. De-signed by George Kelham, the new granite structure was completed in

1917, the Carnegie Foundation donating a third of the cost. The principal facade is designed with a colonnaded loggia at the second story, adorned with coupled Ionic columns and sculpture. The entrance hall and staircase, and the main delivery room on the second floor are finished in travertine marble. Along the second floor corridor are low-toned murals of California scenery by Gottardo Piazzoni; in the reference and reading rooms are murals by Frank Vincent DuMond, depicting various phases of the State's history. The library has an excellent music department, with a piano for the use of patrons wishing to try out selections. The main stack room accommodates 500,000 volumes, 40,000 by foreign writers; on exhibition and in the library are the Max John Kuhl collection of fine printing and binding, and the James D. Phelan Memorial, a collection of manuscripts and first editions of the works of California writers.

The STATE BUILDING, McAllister St. between Larkin and Polk Sts., is a five-story granite structure of neo-Classic design, housing the San Francisco offices of the State government, chambers of the California Supreme Court, and the Hastings College of Law of the University of California. The LAW LIBRARY (*open only to students and alumni, 9-1, 2-5 daily*) contains about 46,000 volumes.

The CIVIC AUDITORIUM (also called Municipal Auditorium and Exposition Auditorium), facing Grove St. between Polk and Larkin Sts., is a heritage from the Panama-Pacific International Exposition of 1915. Constructed of granite, and designed in the Italian Renaissance style, with a triple-arched central section, flanking wings and low octagonal dome, the auditorium was designed by Arthur Brown, Jr. and cost $2,000,000. The main auditorium has an elaborate canopied ceiling and seats more than 10,000 persons; there are 11 smaller halls. The building contains one of the largest pipe organs ever constructed. The 1920 national convention of the Democratic Party was held here.

MARSHALL SQUARE, Hyde St. from Fulton to Grove Sts. and extending to Larkin St., used frequently for open-air meetings, is the city's nearest approach to a "Hyde Park." The PIONEER MONUMENT, at the southeastern corner, was donated in 1894 by James Lick, founder of the Lick Observatory. The work of Frank Happersberger, it is really a group of five monuments, the central figure representing California and the others characterizing significant periods in the State's history.

The PUBLIC HEALTH BUILDING, SW. corner Polk and Grove Sts., constructed of granite and marble, is designed in harmony with the civic group and contains the Central Emergency Hospital, a detention hospital, and the offices of the city health department.

The War Memorial Group, facing Van Ness Ave., consists of twin buildings erected as a unit in 1932—the MUNICIPAL OPERA HOUSE, the only one in the United States, and the VETERANS WAR MEMORIAL BUILDING—both constructed of granite, and designed in modified Italian Renaissance style, with arched and rusticated first story walls, Doric colonnaded loggias and ribbed metal roofs. The Opera House seats 3,000 and possesses the most modern equipment. The basement has an emergency hospital and a buffet. The War Memorial Building, commemorating San Franciscans killed in the World War, is headquarters for almost 150 veterans' organizations. In the SOUVENIR AND TROPHY GALLERY (*open 9-9 daily*) on the first floor stands a granite shaft with sod from a soldier's grave inside it and a perpetual light burning over it. The gallery contains relics of the Civil, Spanish-American and World Wars. The fourth floor of the building is occupied by the GALLERIES OF THE SAN FRANCISCO ART ASSOCIATION (*open 1-10 daily*), in which permanent and traveling exhibitions of all schools and periods are presented.

The CITY HALL, facing Polk St. between McAllister and Grove Sts., is modeled after the U. S. Capitol, its dome being 13½ feet higher. Designed by Bakewell and Brown in the Italian Renaissance style, it is constructed of granite; the interior is finished with carved sandstone and marble. Its two main facades have central Doric pedimented pavilions, flanked by long two-story colonnades. The high drum of the central dome is adorned with a colonnade of the same order, and topped with an elaborate cupola. In the interior, winding stairs lead up from the center of a vast rotunda, with balconies on the four upper floors looking down into the lobby. Facing the building is a formal French garden with flower beds, fountains, tiled walks, and flocks of pigeons. Left of the Polk Street entrance is a bronze STATUE OF LINCOLN by Haig Patigian, while at the McAllister Street side is a MONUMENT TO HALL MCALLISTER, a distinguished lawyer of early days; it is the work of Robert Aitken.

52. The LIBRARY OF THE CALIFORNIA HISTORICAL SOCIETY (*open 10-4 Mon.-Fri., 10-12 Sat.*), 456 McAllister St., opened in 1938 and conducted in conjunction with the Society of California Pioneers, contains rare prints and other material illustrating the State's history, including "State documents" by "Emperor" Norton, a notice of an exhibit of "the head of the renowned bandit, Joaquin Murrieta, and the hand of three-fingered Jack, notorious robber and murderer"; solid ivory poker chips used by the bonanza kings in their $75,000 games at the old Palace Hotel; the watch of Luis Antonio Arguello, first Mexican governor of California; and the whisky flask that Jack London carried on his celebrated voyage on the *Snark*.

53. ST. MARY'S CATHEDRAL, NW. corner Van Ness Ave. and O'Farrell St., a brick building of Victorian Gothic design, dates from 1891 and is the seat of the Roman Catholic diocese of San Francisco. The church narrowly escaped destruction in 1906 when flying brands ignited the belfry. Two priests climbed to the roof and extinguished the blaze by means of buckets and a garden hose.

54. In LAUREL HILL CEMETERY, entrance Bush St. and Presidio Ave., dating back to 1854, are the graves of Senator David C. Broderick, William C. Ralston, James King of William, Senator James G. Fair, Senator William Sharon, and many other pioneers and mining kings. Samuel Woodworth, author of "The Old Oaken Bucket," has a tombstone here, although his body has been removed. On the tombstone of Judge Sanderson, an early jurist, is the inscription, "Final Decree."

55. The MEMORIAL COLUMBARIUM (*open 9-5, daily*), entrance, 1 Loraine Court, is a cream-colored building constructed entirely of stone, metal, and glass. The structure has a metal dome and is adorned with mosaic ornaments and stained glass windows. The only columbarium in San Francisco, its niches contain the ashes of more than 25,000 persons.

56. The SAN FRANCISCO COLLEGE FOR WOMEN, Turk St. between Parker and Masonic Aves., opened in 1932, is a Roman Catholic institution offering a four-year arts course to girls of any denomination. The buildings, of Gothic design, are finished in pale pink stucco, and the campus occupies the whole arc of Lone Mountain, one of the city's major hills.

57. The UNIVERSITY OF SAN FRANCISCO, Fulton St. between Clayton St. and Parker Ave., founded as St. Ignatius College in

1855, was granted a State charter in 1859. In 1930, on the 75th anniversary of the founding, the name was changed to the University of San Francisco. After the acquisition of the present 20-acre campus, the cornerstone of the first of its pinkish concrete buildings was laid in 1920. The university, coeducational and with an average enrollment of about 1,000, consists of a day school for men, and a law school and night school for both men and women. Although the institution is controlled by the Jesuits, its faculty and student body are nonsectarian.

58. ALAMO SQUARE, Fulton St. between Steiner and Scott Sts., and extending to Hayes St., was part of the squatter's stronghold held by Charles and Jack Duane in the 1850's. Charles P. (Dutch Charlie) Duane, a lieutenant in the political army of Senator Broderick and chief engineer of the fire department, narrowly escaped hanging by the vigilantes in 1851 after he shot and killed a theater manager who had refused him free admission. The second Vigilance Committee "deported" him from the city, and the municipality finally gained possession of the property in 1877 after nine separate suits.

59. SAN FRANCISCO STATE COLLEGE, 124 Buchanan St., is still in process of rehabilitation (1939). A few of the old wooden buildings erected when the college was founded in 1899 still remain, but they are being superseded by one-story buff colored concrete buildings of Mediterranean style. On the campus are tennis and basketball courts, and the Roberts Stadium. This was originally a teachers' college, being distinguished in the field by the pioneer work of Dr. Frederick Burk; authorized in 1937 to offer a B.Ed. degree, it has a faculty of 81 and 1,970 students.

60. The UNITED STATES MINT, NW. corner Duboce Ave. and Buchanan St., completed in 1937, replaced the old mint at 5th and Mission Streets, where Bret Harte once worked. The present structure, designed by Gilbert Stanley Underwood, Treasury Department architect, was built at a cost of $1,500,000. Three stories high in the rear and five in front, it has heavy exterior walls of reinforced concrete and granite. The severity of the walls is relieved by a row of medallions below the fourth floor, representing all coins issued by the United States. Precautions against robbery include electrically controlled doors, a gun tower, and tear gas lines. The Mint stands on a 100-foot cliff, with foundations set deep into solid rock, and was considered impregnable until January 1939, when two schoolboys by daylight scaled a wall by means of a drain pipe, slipped through a window opened for ventilation, and threw out a copper plate, "just to see if it could be done."

61. The SPANISH WAR MONUMENT, just below Market St. in the parkway that intersects Dolores St., a Tilden sculpture, erected in honor of California's volunteers in the Spanish-American War, represents an equestrian Victory of heroic size, with a young soldier marching beside her.

62. The MISSION DOLORES (*open 9-5 daily, May-Sept.; 9:30-4:30, Oct.-Apr.*), Dolores St. between 16th and 17th Sts., was founded in 1776 by Father Junípero Serra. First named in honor of St. Francis

of Assisi, common usage soon gave it the name of Misión de los Dolores from a nearby marsh known as Laguna de Nuestra Señora de los Dolores (Lagoon of Our Lady of Sorrows). The first mass was sung five days before the Declaration of Independence was signed at Philadelphia. The adobe building was begun in 1782 and is an unusual example of Spanish mission architecture. Due to the angle of the coping line on the façade, the original roof line is believed to have been changed. The rectangular structure is constructed of stone covered with plaster. The façade is designed with a simple arched entrance and a superimposed surface colonnade of crudely shaped Doric columns. A thin iron railing once extended along the cornice above the doorway. The side and rear walls have been covered with clapboards. No nails were used in its construction; the wooden beams of the arched roof were tied with leather thongs by Indian workmen. The Indians painted the interior walls with vegetable colors that are still bright after more than 150 years. The high hand-carved altar covered with gold leaf was brought from Mexico in 1870. The earthquake of 1906 damaged the building, but failed to raze it.

Behind the mission in the high-walled, flower-covered GRAVEYARD are buried many of the famous dead of San Francisco's early days, including Don Luís Argüello, a native San Franciscan and the first governor of California under Mexican rule. Argüello was a brother to Concepción Argüello, famed in California legend and stories because of a romantic love affair with Rezanov, the Russian plenipotentiary. The graves of Casey and Cora, hanged by the vigilantes in 1856, are a reminder of lawless days. Many of the graves are unmarked.

63. MOUNT OLYMPUS, 17th and Clayton Sts., is crowned with the LIBERTY MONUMENT, the work of the Belgian sculptor, Antoine Wiertz, and a gift of Adolph Sutro in 1887. Sometimes called "The Triumph of Light," it portrays a woman symbolizing Liberty, with a male figure, representing Despotism, cowering at her feet. The figure's torch and sword, it is said, were removed by ship masters because the statue threw them off their course to the Golden Gate.

64. TWIN PEAKS (910 alt.), Twin Peaks Blvd., appear in legends of the Tamal Indians, and were called by the Spanish Los Pechos de la Choca (the breasts of the Indian maiden). The figure-eight drive around the peaks affords a wide view from all vantage points. At night the lights of the city twinkle far below. The long tunnel constructed under Twin Peaks by the Municipal Railway, leading from Market Street to the St. Francis Wood and Ingleside districts, stimulated the development of these residential districts. On Twin Peaks will be erected Beniamino Bufano's 180-foot stainless steel statue of St. Francis, storm center of a spirited controversy.

65. The AFFILIATED COLLEGES OF THE UNIVERSITY OF CALIFORNIA, Parnassus Ave. between Arguello Blvd. and 4th Ave., consist of the Hooper Foundation for Medical Research, the University of California Hospital, and the Schools of Medicine and Dentistry of the University of California. The Hooper Foundation

and the Medical Research Library (*private*) are housed in a single brown brick building; the Dental School in another. The Hospital, the Medical School, and the Experimental Research Laboratory are in new buildings of concrete and white stone. The Hooper Foundation conducts experiments in hygiene, surgery, and preventive medicine, and has accomplished important work in botulism, infantile paralysis, sleeping sickness, and undulant fever.

66. SUTRO FOREST, a large tract northwest of Twin Peaks and through which paved roads have been constructed, is dark with cypress and eucalyptus trees, and alive with small animals and birds. The forest was planted by Adolph Sutro in the 1870's and has been enlarged by additional plantings by school children. Mount Sutro, 909 feet high, occupies the center of the area; this originally barren hill was part of San Miguel Rancho.

(*Along the Ocean*)

67. LINCOLN PARK, entrance 33rd Ave. and Clement St., extends northwest almost to the ocean. A flagpole in the park marks the western terminus of the Lincoln Highway (US 30-40). Here at one time were the city's cemeteries, each segregated according to nationality. The old Chinese Cemetery is now the Municipal Golf Links, on which the first hazard is the sacrifice stone, a stone oven used for roasting pigs to propitiate the gods. Near the 15th green is a 25-foot bronze monument to Mrs. Rebecca H. Lambert, founder of the Ladies' Seamen's Friend Society.

The PALACE OF THE LEGION OF HONOR (*open 10-5 daily; free organ recitals 3-4, Sat. and Sun.*), adjacent to the golf links, is designed in the manner of the Legion of Honor Palace in Paris. The entrance to the classic U-shaped building is through an impressive forecourt in form of an Ionic peristyle with a massive central arch. It was constructed as an art museum and presented to San Francisco in 1924 by Mr. and Mrs. Adolph B. Spreckels as a memorial to the California soldiers who lost their lives in the World War. The palace has 19 galleries exhibiting permanent and loan collections of paintings, sculpture, porcelain, tapestry, antique furniture and prints; it also has a little theater, two enclosed gardens, and a pipe organ used for recitals.

68. LAND'S END, a precipitous promontory reached by a path leading northeast from Lincoln Park along the route of the former "Scenic Route" streetcar line, has long been a favorite haunt of lovers of the sea. From here is a fine view of Mile Rock Lighthouse, a few hundred feet offshore, which can be reached by boat (*by arrangement with U. S. Lighthouse Service at Customs-house*). Beyond Mile Rock, toward the Marin shore, is an area of ocean known as the Potato Patch, usually covered with whitecaps, which mark a navigable channel through the dangerous shoals near Golden Gate.

69. SUTRO HEIGHTS (*house private; visitors on foot permitted in garden*), Point Lobos Ave. and Great Highway, was the home of Adolph Sutro, Nevada capitalist and former mayor of San Francisco.

The house, built in 1879, is surrounded by a 20-acre garden donated to the city by Sutro's daughter, Dr. Emma Sutro Merritt; the shrubbery is dotted with marble statues from Belgium, carried to San Francisco in ships as ballast.

70. CLIFF HOUSE, Great Highway opposite Sutro Heights, has been a noted restaurant since the first house of that name was built in 1858. The original Cliff House, bought by Adolph Sutro in 1883, was destroyed by fire in 1894, and its successor likewise in 1907. The present house, erected in 1907, was remodeled and reopened after being vacant a number of years. The building has a dining room overlooking the ocean, and a redwood cocktail bar. From the lookout platform by the Cliff House is a view offshore of the sharply pointed SEAL ROCKS, on which hundreds of "seals" (actually California sea lions) disport themselves, being protected by State law. Binoculars can be rented for a close-up view. On clear days the Farallon Islands are visible.

OCEAN BEACH, extending from the Cliff House to Golden Gate Park, is not much used for bathing at this end because of a strong undertow, but the Esplanade flanking the beach affords a broad view of the Pacific Ocean and is crowded with sun bathers on warm days. On the east side of the Great Highway below Sutro Heights is a miniature Coney Island, with restaurants and the usual attractions.

71. The FLEISHHACKER POOL (*open 8-5 daily*), PLAYGROUND (*open 9-5 daily*), and ZOO (*open 10-5 daily*), Great Highway and Sloat Blvd., occupy a 128-acre tract. The open-air pool is 1,000 by 100 feet, with a 150-foot offset in the center for races, and contains 6,500,000 gallons of water. It has locker accommodations for 5,000, and 20 lifeguards are on duty.

On the Playground are tennis courts, a baseball field, sand boxes, a miniature steam railway, and a wading pool.

The Zoo is being remodeled (1939) by the Works Progress Administration on the cageless plan, under which the animals will live in a reproduction of their natural environment with deep moats between them and the public. The zoo has 900 specimens, including a notable collection of members of the cat family.

72. MOUNT DAVIDSON (956 alt.), in Mount Davidson Park and accessible only on foot, is the highest point in the city. On the summit stands the Easter Cross of concrete and steel, 103-feet high, before which Easter sunrise services are held, attended by 60,000 persons and broadcast from coast to coast. During Easter Week floodlights illuminate the cross. At its base is a crypt containing relics from Palestine; the crypt is sealed with concrete mixed with water from the Holy Land. The present permanent cross is the fifth on the site.

(*Golden Gate Park*)

73. GOLDEN GATE PARK, Stanyan St. between Fulton St. and Lincoln Way, extending to the ocean, contains 1,013 acres. A half mile wide and more than four miles long with its "Panhandle" to the

east, the park was created from bare sand dunes in the 1870's by John McLaren, a Scotsman, who is still superintendent (1939) in spite of his 90-odd years. The park is noted for its rhododendrons; the Midwinter Fair of 1894 was held here.

KEZAR STADIUM, Frederick St. between Stanyan St. and Arguello Blvd., is a concrete bowl accommodating 60,000 spectators. Municipally owned, it is the scene of the annual All-Star East and West football game on New Year's Day sponsored by the Shrine. During football season the stadium is used by college teams that are not members of the Coast League.

The CONSERVATORY has a collection of rare orchids and begonias, and many varieties of ferns. In front of the Conservatory is a large flower bed on which various messages adapted to the season or special events are spelled out with flowers. The building, similar to the conservatory in Kew Gardens, London, was bought by popular subscription.

The DEYOUNG MEMORIAL MUSEUM (*open 10-5 weekdays; 1-5 Sun.; closed holidays*) houses a broad art and historical collection, much of which has never been catalogued. The museum is especially rich in Aztec, Mayan, Incan, and pre-Columbian American Indian art. The original building was a gift of M. H. deYoung in 1919; in 1920 a new wing, designed by Louis C. Mullgardt in the Spanish Renaissance style with elaborate bas-relief frieze and cresting, was added, with sculptures by Haig Patigian. This wing includes 56 galleries and a sunken court. Near the museum, among other statues, are the ROBERT BURNS STATUE, by Earl Cummings, the JUNIPERO SERRA MONUMENT, by Douglas Tilden, and the CERVANTES MONUMENT by Jo Mora, depicting Don Quixote and Sancho Panza kneeling before their creator.

A stone BANDSTAND, the gift of Claus Spreckels, is an open-air shell in the Music Concourse; the Municipal Band presents concerts here every Sunday afternoon.

The JAPANESE TEA GARDEN, an authentic reproduction of an original in Nippon, includes a *zashiki*, or Japanese home; a granite shrine with an altar; and an arched bridge built in the shape of a drum. In and around the thatched tea houses, rice cakes and tea are sold by girls dressed in native costume.

The NATURAL HISTORY MUSEUM (*open 10-4 weekdays; 10-5 Sun. and holidays*), together with the Steinhart Aquarium and the Simson African Hall, is conducted by the California Academy of Sciences. The museum contains departments of ornithology, herpetology, and paleontology, but the half million persons who visit it annually are mainly attracted by its mammal groups, mounted animals in social or family assemblage against natural backgrounds. Other exhibits include flowers, semiprecious stones, butterflies, herbariums, and Indian baskets. Set in the pavement at the main entrance of the academy building are four old millstones, the oldest of which was brought around the Horn for use in a local flour mill in 1851.

SIMSON AFRICAN HALL (*open 1-5 Sun., 1-4 Wed.*), was built in 1932 to house a number of habitat groups of African mammals collected by Leslie Simson and mounted by Frank Tose, who spent many years in Africa. In the basement is an exhibit of fish, and on the second floor one of insects, neither of which is specifically African.

The STEINHART AQUARIUM (*open 10-5 daily, 1-4 in winter*), approached through an open court in which are five large pools, was named for Ignatz Steinhart, who donated $240,000 for its foundation. The large reinforced concrete aquarium contains one of the most colorful collections of live fish in the world, including many Hawaiian and Oriental specimens. Outside the aquarium is a tank in which California sea lions swim and sun themselves on artificial rocks.

The SHAKESPEARE GARDEN, suggested in 1923 by Miss Alice Eastwood of the Academy of Sciences, contains every flower mentioned in Shakespeare's plays. The only duplicate of the bust of Shakespeare in the Stratford (England) church was presented to the city by Sir Archibald Flower, mayor of Stratford-on-Avon. This bust is preserved, and a bronze reproduction is displayed in the garden.

STOW LAKE, the largest of the park's ponds, all of which are artificial, holds 25,000,000 gallons of water and is densely populated with waterfowl, from mud hens to swans. The San Francisco Fly Casting Club, with headquarters here, holds contests every Saturday and Sunday from March to November.

The PRAYER BOOK CROSS, a gift of George W. Childs, Philadelphia publisher, is an Iona cross of Colusa marble, 57 feet high, designed by Ernest Coxhead and erected under the auspices of the Protestant Episcopal Diocese of Northern California. It commemorates the first Christian service held in English on the Pacific Coast, in 1579, by Sir Francis Drake's chaplain on the shore of Drake's Bay (*see TOUR 1a*).

On Lloyd Lake, beyond Lindley Meadow, is the celebrated PORTAL OF THE PAST, a classic marble doorway from the A. N. Towne home destroyed in the fire of 1906. The doorway, flanked by Irish yews, bears an inscription relating its history.

SPRECKELS LAKE is the scene of miniature yacht races every Sunday. The owners of the model yachts, built to scale, complete in detail, and not more than three feet long, are members of a model yacht association and hold occasional regattas. Beyond Spreckels Lake is the Chain of Lakes, a "waterscaped" series of artificial lakelets with artificial islands and banks of waterlilies.

The DUTCH WINDMILLS, facing the ocean, at the northwestern and southwestern corners of the park, are operated by electric pumps. The water enters a reservoir two miles away to feed the park lakes. To the left of the northern windmill is the ship *GJOA* (pronounced Yoah), presented to the city by the late Roald Amundsen, the Norwegian explorer. This tiny vessel was the first craft to navigate the Northwest Passage, the objective of many of the early voyages to the New World.

ELK GLEN is a fenced enclosure containing several varieties of elk, so tame that they accept leaves and grass from visitors' hands.

Beyond the ARBORETUM, which includes trees from many parts of the world, the southeastern section of the park is devoted to recreation, with a baseball park, handball courts, bowling greens, and a children's playground. To the north is DELAVEAGA DELL, with its rhododendrons and bear pits.

(Islands)

74. ALCATRAZ ISLAND (Sp., pelican), in the bay between San Francisco and Sausalito, is one of the world's most feared and widely publicized penal institutions, the Federal prison for incorrigibles (*visitors by warden's permission only*). Alcatraz, known colloquially as "The Rock," a 12-acre island, was fortified by the Spanish prior to American occupation. From 1859 it was used as a military prison and a United States Army disciplinary barracks; during and after the World War many conscientious objectors were removed here from Fort Leavenworth. Alcatraz was made a Federal penitentiary in 1933, to house unruly prisoners from other Federal institutions. The rigid discipline, its elaborate barriers to prevent escape, including the "electric eye" to detect the presence of metal on a prisoner, and the names of its notorious inmates have combined to make thousands of newspaper headlines. Swift currents flowing around "The Rock" make escape by water

practically impossible. Two prisoners made the attempt in 1938, but their ultimate success or failure is unknown.

75. ANGEL ISLAND (*Government boats make free trips from Fort Mason and Pier 5, Ferry Building, daily, 7 a.m.-12 p.m.*), N. of Alcatraz and the largest island in the bay, is the district headquarters and detention barracks of the Immigration and Naturalization Service; here immigrants arriving via the Pacific are received, and deportees to the Orient and the Antipodes are shipped out. It is also the quarantine station of the Public Health Service, and an overseas replacement depot for the U. S. Army.

The first white visitor to the island was Juan Manuel de Ayala, who came in 1775 and gave the island its name. In 1851 a prison brig was anchored near it, but escape proved too easy and the prisoners were removed to San Quentin, which was completed in 1854. Angel Island was the scene of many duels, the most famous being the Johnston-Ferguson encounter in 1858, over the slavery question. Senator William I. Ferguson was killed, and his antagonist, George P. Johnston, clerk of the U. S. Circuit Court, was tried and acquitted. In 1853 Johnston, then an assemblyman, had advocated severer punishment for dueling.

76. The FARALLON ISLANDS (*closed*) consist of three groups of small islands in the Pacific, 26 miles west of the mainland, and visible on clear days from the Cliff House and other points. They are a constituent part of San Francisco, yet no county or city official may set foot on them without the permission of the lighthouse superintendent. The bare waterless islands are inhabited by four lighthouse keepers, seven Navy men in charge of the Radio Beam Compass Station, and their families. The light, one of the most powerful on the coast, stands 358 feet above water at high tide. The islands are a bird refuge; only Italian fishermen visit the Farallon Banks regularly.

San Jose

Railroad Stations: 65 Cahill St. for Southern Pacific Lines.
Bus Stations: Union Bus Station, 25 S. Market St., for Pacific Greyhound and Peerless Stages; San Jose Travel Bureau, 44 W. San Carlos St., for Airline Bus Line and Dollar Line.
Airport: San Jose Airport, 4.2 m. NW. of business district; taxi 60¢ to 85¢; no scheduled service.
Taxis: Meter system, 15¢ first half-mile, 10¢ each additional half-mile, no charge for extra passengers; zone system, 10¢ to 25¢, 10¢ for each additional passenger.
City Busses: Fare 7¢, 4 tokens for 25¢.
Traffic Regulations: Pedestrians have right-of-way except at controlled crossings.

Accommodations: 33 hotels; nine auto trailer camps.

Information Service: Chamber of Commerce, Civic Auditorium, San Carlos and S. Market Sts.; American Automobile Assn., 926 The Alameda; California State Auto Assn., 1024 The Alameda.

Radio Station: KQW (1010 kc.).
Theaters and Motion Picture Houses: Main Theater and Dunn Little Theater in Civic Auditorium, San Carlos and S. Market Sts., road shows and concerts; 10 motion picture houses.
Golf: Hillview Public Golf Course, Tully Rd. and Swift Lane, 18 holes, greens fee 50¢ weekdays, 75¢ Sat., $1 Sun. and holidays.
Tennis: San Jose Tennis Courts, 7th and E. Humboldt Sts., lighted; Backesto Park, 13th and Jackson Sts., 12 courts; City Playfield, Home St. and Delmas Ave., 4 courts.
Swimming: Alum Rock Park, 7 m. NE. on Alum Rock Ave. (pool open Mar.-Nov.), adm. 50¢, includes suit and towel, children, 25¢; Roosevelt Junior High School pool (open to public during evenings in summer), 17th and Santa Clara Sts., adm. 35¢, includes suit and towel.
Riding: Twenty-five miles of bridle paths in Alum Rock Park, 7 m. NE. on Alum Rock Ave.; $1 first hour, 75¢ each hour thereafter.

Annual Events: Maximum bloom of 100,000 roses in Municipal Rose Garden, Naglee and Dana Aves., early May; Fiesta de las Rosas Golf Tournament, Hillview Public Golf Course, Sept.

SAN JOSE (pronounced San Ho-say'; 100 alt., 57,651 pop.) is built on the flat alluvial soil of the Santa Clara Valley at the southern and shallow end of San Francisco Bay, 50 miles south of San Francisco. The city itself is eight miles from the waters of the bay, separated by low ground and marshlands. Mountains are visible from almost any point in the city: brown, bare foothills merge into the peaks of the Mount Hamilton Range to the east and to the west is the green and thickly wooded Coast Range. These mountains trap rains and fogs generated over the ocean and give San Jose a semi-arid climate with no rain at all during the summer months. The Guadalupe and Coyote Rivers run through the city, but water flows in their channels only in early spring.

San Jose's business district, compact and busy, particularly during the packing season, is roughly in the form of a cross, with its arms running north and south and east and west. Office buildings, department stores, hotels, theaters, and shops are grouped along First and Santa Clara Streets. The geographical center of town is the crossing of these two streets. West of First Street, business buildings merge into an industrial district of shops, warehouses, garages, and factories.

East of First Street is the older residential district, its streets running at right angles, landscaped with lawns, gardens, and rows of palms, oaks, and willows. The older houses are of frame construction, built of local redwood; newer residences are stucco. North of the business district on First Street is another of the older residential sections—frame mansions built during the 1870's and 1880's. These sedate homes give way farther out to bungalows and more pretentious houses in the Spanish-Colonial style. Fringing the city limits are new residential sections.

Santa Clara (*see TOUR 2b*) is a separate city northwest of San Jose, but connected with it by solid blocks of houses and stores. The main artery between the two cities is The Alameda, a broad avenue lined with willow trees originally planted as windbreaks and for protection against wild cattle. Along The Alameda are some fine examples of the gingerbread school of architecture: large Victorian frame mansions with tall windows, towers and turrets, stained glass, intricate fretwork decorations, built by wealthier citizens during the city's first agricultural prosperity; they are being gradually replaced by modern houses.

San Jose was California's first town, as distinguished from forts and missions, and was the first capital of the State following American occupation. It is the seat of Santa Clara County, and has a State College, which was the first and for many years the only normal school in California.

First known inhabitants of this section were the Olhone Indians, who painted themselves with cinnabar ore from New Almaden and worshiped the sun. Mission life and white men's diseases and ways gradually exterminated them. An anthropologist in San Jose has a standing offer of $500 to anyone who will bring him a full-blooded Olhone.

The population now includes a few descendants of early Spanish settlers, such as the Bernals, Ortegas, Peraltas, and Berryessas; a solid core of "old families" descended from Americans who settled after 1840; farmers, workers, business and professional men, students, and teachers, all largely of native American stock; and groups of Italians, Mexicans, Portuguese, Slavs, and a few Negroes, attracted by farming and industry. These groups retain only a few of their folk ways, chiefly manifested in religious festivals.

On November 29, 1777, in response to orders from the viceroy of Mexico, nine soldiers, five *pobladores* (settlers) with their families, and one cowboy, were detailed to found the Pueblo de San José de Guadalupe, named in honor of St. Joseph. This was the first of a series of towns established in Alta California to foster agriculture and handicraft and make the territory self-supporting. Each man was allotted two cows, two oxen, two mules, two sheep, two goats, seed, necessary implements for cultivation of the soil, and was promised monthly stipends of about $10 during his first years. The missions were not pleased by this encroachment, but could do nothing about it. The first settlers built their small huts about a mile north of the present business section. In later years the town was moved to higher ground because of seasonal floods from the Guadalupe River.

Mexico broke from the Spanish Crown in 1821, and the Mexican flag was raised over Monterey, the capital, the next April (1822); but it was not until May 10, 1825, that San Jose got around to acknowledging Mexican rule. Then there was a three-day public celebration, complete with music and dancing.

In 1831 the town had only 524 residents (Indians were not counted). The chief industry was stock raising; only enough crops were grown to satisfy local needs. The main interest of the young bloods was the bull and bear fights; bears were lassoed in the foothills and brought back to town in a bullock cart. The bear and bull were tied together and the fight continued—one bear usually being good for three or four bulls—until a fresh bull finally gored the tired bear to death.

In the 1840's, with the beginning of mass emigration from the East on the overland route, San Jose began to grow. Descendants of such noted expeditions as the Bidwell-Bartleson, the Donner, and the Murphy parties still live in San Jose, some of them grown rich through mining and real estate operations.

When Capt. Thomas Fallon, with 19 men, entered San Jose on July 14, 1846 and raised the United States flag over the town hall, he found a sleepy pueblo, its population composed mostly of Mexicans, Peruvians, Chileans, Spanish Californians, and Indians. The gold rush changed all that. San Jose became one of the supply cities for men on their way to and from the mines in the Sierra foothills. It grew so fast that in 1849 it was the logical choice for State capital.

The first California Legislature convened in San Jose on Dec. 15, 1849. It was known as "the legislature of a thousand drinks." Because of the shortage of local women, the countryside was "raked for señoritas," who, at the appointed time, made their appearance at the Assembly Hall and danced and imbibed with the solons of the region. "The legislators were good drinkers—they drank like men. If they could not *stand* the ceremony on any particular occasion, they would *lie* down to it with a becoming grace." Drinking and gaiety did not end with the first grand ball. A fandango usually cheered the weary legislators each evening after strenuous hours of deliberation. But accommodations were poor in San Jose and in Feb. 1851, the capital was moved to Benicia.

Meanwhile the city was incorporated in 1850, with a population of 3,000. Stage and boat connections were established with San Francisco, but were discontinued in 1864 when the first railroad came through. In the 1880's the steady growth of the city was stimulated by a real estate boom which came to a climax in August 1887. Land sales zoomed to a high of $2,000,000 a day, and then collapsed. After the Civil War, when the gold fever had run its course, experiments in prune and apricot growing were made in the fertile regions around the city. Growth of apricots, prunes, and grapes promised to be profitable. Ranch land rose in value, and San Jose, with its rail connections, became the region's logical shipping center.

San Jose is today the largest canning and dried-fruit packing center in the world, and a distributing point for the prune and apricot industry. There are 18 canneries, 13 dried-fruit packing houses, and 12 fresh-fruit and vegetable shipping firms. It was one of the first California cities to develop industries for making all the mechanical equipment for specialized farming—or ranching, as it is called in the West. There are also pottery works, meat-packing houses, lumber and boatbuilding yards, and breweries.

POINTS OF INTEREST

CITY HALL PARK, a double landscaping of S. Market St. between San Carlos and W. San Fernando Sts., is the civic center of San Jose. The CIVIC AUDITORIUM, San Carlos and S. Market Sts., is a one-and-a-half-story, yellow concrete building, erected in 1936. Besides offices, it contains the Main and Little (Dunn) Theaters. CITY HALL, at the south end of the park, a four-story red brick building, contains city offices. North of City Hall is a plaque commemorating the site of California's first State capitol. The actual site is at San Antonio and South Market Streets.

ST. JAMES PARK, N. 1st St. between St. John and St. James Sts., is planted with shrubs and flowers and is distinguished for its tall palms and elm trees. In 1933 two men accused of kidnapping and murdering the son of a wealthy merchant were dragged from jail and hanged to trees in the park. The country rang with details of the lynching, and James Rolph, Jr., then Governor, caused further reverberations by approving the mob's action. The trees, stripped of bark and twigs by souvenir hunters, had to be cut down.

COUNTY COURT HOUSE, on 1st St. facing the park, of classic design with a wide portico supported by Corinthian columns and surmounted by a dome, was built in 1866-68.

SAN JOSE STATE COLLEGE, main entrance S. 4th and San Antonio Sts., in the center of Washington Park, is the oldest State-owned public educational institution in California. It was opened on this site in 1862. The original building, a towering frame structure built of California redwood, burned in the seventies and was replaced by a four-story brick building, fronted by a wide lawn. In the early 1900's the campus was enlarged to 26 acres, and the older buildings were erected at this time. New groups of California mission style buildings have been added, with red tile roofs and arched windows. The student body numbers 2,600.

The EDWIN MARKHAM HOME, 430 S. 8th St., is a simple three-story redwood building with a wide front porch—a typical family home of the period. The poet lived here between 1857 and 1899; in the last year of his residence here he wrote "The Man with the Hoe." The building is now the infirmary, or Health Home, of the San Jose State College, from which Markham was graduated.

The SOUTHERN PACIFIC STATION, main entrance on The Alameda at Stockton Ave., built in 1935, is of glazed brick in yellow and dull red shades. It is designed in a modified mission style, modernized by bronze doors and window frames. In the waiting room is a mural by J. MacQuarrie depicting an early California scene, with skyscrapers and a railroad train in the background.

ROSICRUCIAN PARK AND HEADQUARTERS, 1342 Naglee Ave., is the center of the Ancient and Mystical Order of the Rosy Cross (AMORC) for the Western Hemisphere. This fraternal order claims to be the only genuine representative of the ancient Rosicrucian Order, and states that it is neither a school, a forum, nor a religious body. The buildings are all of stone and concrete in the Egyptian style of architecture.

In the EGYPTIAN TEMPLE AND ORIENTAL MUSEUM (*open 9-5 Mon.-Fri., 7:30-9 Mon., 9-1 Sat., 12-5 Sun.; guide*) the walls, painted in the ancient Egyptian manner, are hung with gold and bronze plaques and with tapestries said to be from temples in Cairo and Luxor. The interior is lighted by artificial moonlight. The Museum contains a full-size reproduction of an Egyptian rock tomb of the seventeenth or eighteenth dynasty.

The PLANETARIUM (*open 3:45-5 and 7:30-9 Sun., free; lecture and demonstration 4 and 8 p.m. Sun., adm. 25¢, children 15¢*) is one of the few in the United States and the only one in northern California.

The AMENHOTEP SHRINE, a stone pylon in the center of the park, bears a descriptive tablet. The other buildings include the Francis Bacon Auditorium and Convention Hall, the Science Lecture Hall and Laboratories (for classes and correspondence courses in "esoteric science"), and the General Administration Building and Library.

The SAN JOSE MUNICIPAL ROSE GARDEN (*open daily*), Naglee and Dana Aves., of five-and-a-half acres, was opened in 1931. The finest collection of roses in the United States has been built up by donations from private sources. Mrs. Fremont Older gave bushes from 18 of the 21 California mission gardens. Besides 1,686 varieties of old-fashioned climbing and hedge roses, there are 42 species, 2,451 varieties of show roses, two of which have never been on the market. Choice items are the red and white Lancaster-York rose, symbolizing the peace that ended the English War of the Roses; the Damascene rose of the

Crusaders; and the Viridifolia, a Chinese rose with green petals. In the center of the garden is a reflecting pool, bordered by copper-colored and yellow roses. The garden is at its best early in May, when 100,000 are in bloom, but there are always blossoms.

POINTS OF INTEREST IN ENVIRONS

Winchester Mystery House, externalization of a psychopathic mind, 4 *m.;* Alum Rock Park, 8.5 *m.;* New Almaden Village and Quicksilver Mines, worked since 1844, 12.3 *m.;* Lick Observatory, 18.8 *m.* (*see TOUR 2b*).

Santa Barbara

Railroad Stations: State and Montecito Sts. for Southern Pacific Lines.
Bus Station: 29 W. Carrillo St. for Greyhound Lines.
Airport: Municipal at Goleta, 8 miles N. on US 101, for United Air Lines;
taxi $1, time 20 min.
Taxis: 15¢ first ⅓ m., 10¢ each additional ½ m.; five passengers permitted
for one fare.
Busses: 5¢ and 10¢ fare zones.
Traffic Regulations: Pedestrians have right-of-way at all street crossings.

Accommodations: 18 hotels; auto courts.

Information Service: Chamber of Commerce, 14 E. Carrillo St.; Community
Center, Carrillo and De la Vina Sts.

Radio Station: KDB (1500 kc.), KTMS (1220 kc.).
Theaters and Motion Picture Houses: Lobero Theater, 33 E. Canon Perdido
St., commercial and community productions; four motion picture houses.
Golf: Montecito Country Club, Summit Road, Montecito, 3.7 m., 18 holes, guest
cards available through Santa Barbara Golfers' Association; greens fee $1
weekdays, $1.50 Sun. and holidays; club rental, 75¢ per set. La Cumbre Golf
and Country Club, Modoc Road (Hope Ranch), 4 m., fee $1.50 per day, short-
time memberships available.
Tennis: Oak Park, W. Junipero St. at Mission Creek; Plaza del Mar, W.
Cabrillo Blvd. and Castillo St., meter lights; Biltmore Hotel courts, Channel
Drive and Olive Mill Rd., Montecito, free; Stadium Tennis Courts, US 101,
opposite Bird Refuge, 9 courts, 4 meter lighted. Shower and lockers free in
daytime.
Swimming: West Beach, 320 W. Cabrillo Blvd., still water and surf, public
dressing rooms, 20¢ up; East Beach, E. Cabrillo Blvd. and Por la Mar Drive,
surf, dressing rooms, May to Sept., 20¢; wading pool for children.
Riding: 30 miles of bridle paths in foothills, 20 on beaches; rates usually $1
per hour.
Polo: Fleischmann Field, Serena, 8 miles E. on US 101, Dec.-Apr., free weekdays, 50¢ Sun.; July-Sept., 50¢ daily.
Fishing: Surf fishing off breakwater and Stearns Wharf, S. end of State St.
Deep-sea and channel fishing for halibut, tuna, marlin, swordfish, mackerel, cod,
and black sea bass; boats for rent at Stearns Wharf.

Annual Events: Garden Tours, from Recreation Center, 110 E. Carrillo St.,
spring and summer; Old Spanish Days, 3 days full moon of each Aug.; horse
and dog show in summer; Semana Nautica, marine celebration, July 4; Artists'
Street Fair, July.

SANTA BARBARA (37 alt., 33,613 pop.) lies on a coastal shelf
that rises from a curving beach into the southern slopes of the Santa
Ynez Mountains. With its extensive landscaped estates, and the predominant Spanish flavor of its architecture, Santa Barbara has long
maintained a reputation of ease and leisure, principally because of its

large proportion of wealthy residents. The earthquake of 1925 created the opportunity to condense within a few years the rebuilding of a city in harmony with the dominant architectural motif. As a result, it has an air of spaciousness and quiet comfort; even the railroad roundhouse is disguised, and looks like a Spanish bull ring.

During the 1870's the city overcame a temptation to number and letter its streets, which commemorate ancient Spanish families (De la Guerra, Carrillo), the Indians (Yanonali), and even an outlaw (Valerio). Canon Perdido (lost cannon), Salsipuedes (get out if you can), and Indio Muerto (dead Indian) all refer to episodes in Santa Barbara's history.

Santa Barbara has carefully preserved the beauty of its waterfront. From the foot of State Street a broad strand stretches for several miles to the east, a large section of it operated by the city as a public bathing beach. The paralleling highway is landscaped, and an area of marshland near the beach's eastern extremity has been converted into a bird refuge.

The city is bisected by its main thoroughfare, State Street, which carries a steady stream of coastwise motor traffic. It is flanked by residential sections, the more restricted areas being to the north. Upper State Street is lined with swanky shops and motion picture theaters; the lower end is a district of second-hand stores, "second-run" movie houses, drinking places, and a small Mexican quarter. A few hundred Negroes also live in this area, and there is a small group of Chinese, Japanese, and Filipinos near the old presidio area. In outlying districts meandering streets and roads conform to the rolling and hilly terrain.

For three days during the full moon in August the city returns to its past in "Old Spanish Days," a fiesta inaugurated in 1924. It commences with a reception and pageant held on the steps of the old Mission, where Franciscan padres welcome the participants beneath chiming ancient bells. The following afternoon thousands line the main streets for the parade, depicting the city's past from Indian times to the arrival of American troops. Squealing *carretas* (carts) carry old Spanish families, and scores of fine horses mounted by distinguished visitors pass between red and gold banners along the line of march. Gaily caparisoned serenaders stroll the streets singing songs of Spanish days, and descendants of pioneer families dance the folk dances of their forefathers. There is a pageant on the site of a Canalino village, street dances every night, and a variety of free entertainment.

In 1542, when the navigator Cabrillo came up the coast, he was met in the channel by a fleet of Canalino (channel) Indians, who greeted him from great canoes. Cabrillo's account states that "most of the Indian chiefs were men, but the ruler of one of the villages was a very wrinkled old woman, which seemed very queer to us." Cabrillo was fatally injured in a perilous landing and lies in an undiscovered grave on one of the Channel Islands. Vizcaíno entered the channel on Saint Barbara's Day, December 4, 1603, and named the region Santa Barbara.

In 1768, rumor reached Spain that Russia intended to explore and claim the territory south of Alaska, and King Charles III ordered the Viceroy of Mexico to establish presidios and missions in California. Spanish colonization had already begun when Capt. José Francísco Ortega, accompanied by Governor Neve, Father Junípero Serra, and fifty men, entered Santa Barbara on April 21, 1782, and founded the presidio.

Indians, paid in food and clothing, brought fish and game and assisted in hewing timbers and making adobe bricks for the fort. After their conversion to the Catholic faith, they were set to work, under supervision of the padres, constructing dwellings, building the mission, cultivating large acreages, and raising cattle. After secularization of the Missions in 1834 the presidio officers became barons of wide estates and prolific herds, and the Indian population waned. (The last survivor of the Canalino tribe died in 1930.) The presidio "dons" were of a proud heritage, many bearing noble names, and they indulged their traditions of urbanity and social grace. Mexico shook off the yoke of Spain in 1821, Yankee trade developed, and the exchange of New England wealth for hides and tallow greatly enriched them.

The Barbareños enjoyed this productive economy for three decades. "My house is your own, Señor," was the greeting, and *mañana* was the philosophy. An occasional revolution was staged, bloodless and courteous as a tennis match.

But the influx of the Yankees foretold a change. The serene existence of the Californios had led many a Yankee sea captain to desert his calling for marriage with a wealthy señorita; American trappers had been drawn by the rich hauls of seal and otter at the Channel Islands. Commodore Stockton landed in Santa Barbara Bay in August 1846, ran up the American flag, and left a small garrison. Several weeks later the garrison was attacked, and given the choice of surrender or flight. It fled, but in Christmas week of the same year Lt. Col. John C. Frémont, after dodging an ambush in Gaviota Pass, re-entered Santa Barbara and held it. Three weeks later California was ceded to the United States.

Under the new American regime the town prospered. Great herds of cattle were driven north to feed the miners. "Every bullock was a skinful of silver and his marrow as fine as gold." Luxurious furnishings filled adobe dwellings, and fine silks trailed on clay floors. The civilization of the dons reached its apex, with gay Castillian cavalcades, the gallantries of caballeros and fan-wielding señoritas, cock-fighting and gambling.

The decay of all this glory began with a drought in 1864. There were 200,000 cattle in the county in 1863; only 5,000 gaunt creatures were alive the following year. A primitive wharf built two years later put an end to landings in small boats through the surf such as those described in *Two Years Before the Mast*. In 1872 a more elaborate wharf was completed to which ships and side-wheel steamers could tie. The real estate boom of the early 1870's collapsed in 1877 because of another drought, and Santa Barbara dozed in gentle dignity until the Southern Pacific Railroad entered the city from the south in 1887. In 1901 the line was extended to San Francisco; Santa Barbara took its place on the tourist map and began its metamorphosis into a wealthy residential community.

There are oil wells on the mesa south of the city, and some commercial fishing, but industry is almost nonexistent. Cattle raising and agriculture are important in surrounding areas.

POINTS OF INTEREST

The SANTA BARBARA COUNTY COURTHOUSE, Anapamu and Anacapa Sts., is a rambling, white stucco structure with wide arches and towers, resembling the palace of a Spanish prelate. The assembly room (*open 9-5 weekdays*) on the second floor has murals by Dan Sayre Groesbeck portraying the arrival of Cabrillo, the building of the mission, and the coming of the American troops.

The MUSEUM OF THE SANTA BARBARA HISTORICAL SOCIETY (*open 2-4 Mon.*), at the top of the circular staircase, contains Indian relics, saddles, branding irons, and the like, and the *cañón perdido* (lost cannon), which was cast ashore on the wreckage of the American brig *Elizabeth,* lost off the coast of Santa Barbara during the winter of 1847-48. The 12-pound brass cannon was found by a group of native Californians, who hid it in the vicinity of the present Canon Perdido Street. Fearing that the natives might use the gun against the Americans, Governor Mason levied a fine of $500 on the town of Santa Barbara, and sent soldiers from Los Angeles to collect it. Tradition relates that the State returned the money to the town to build a jail. Local officials, dissatified with the amount, sought to increase it to $1,000 by staking it in a game of Yankee poker. They lost the whole $500, and shamefacedly gave up their plan for a jailhouse.

The CARRILLO ADOBE, 15 E. Carrillo St., the old Joaquín Carrillo House, is occupied by the Santa Barbara Foundation and an antique shop. Little of the original structure remains, but the restored patio is notable. This house belonged a century ago to one of the most illustrious families of the region. Leo Carrillo, actor of Spanish and Mexican roles in motion pictures, is a descendant.

LOBERO THEATER, 33 E. Canon Perdido St., a commercial playhouse presenting foreign films, legitimate drama and concerts, occasionally stages amateur community plays, as it did exclusively before 1937. The original Lobero Theater was built in 1872 by José Lobero, an Italian who opened a saloon in Santa Barbara in the sixties and made the fortune he later lost in sponsoring local-talent orchestras and grand operas. In 1924 the original adobe buildings were torn down and the present structure erected by the Community Arts Association.

EL PASEO DE LA GUERRA, 15 E. De la Guerra St., called the historical center of Santa Barbara, is built around the house of Don José de la Guerra, comandante of the presidio a century ago. Courtyards and passageways simulating streets in old Spain, with small shops and a restaurant opening into them, have been built around the original adobe. Another notable house on this street is 29 E. de la Guerra.

The COVARRUBIAS ADOBE, 715 Santa Barbara St., built about 1817, and still in excellent repair, is a notable example of Spanish-Colonial architecture.

The YACHT HARBOR, bordering W. Cabrillo Blvd. SW. from the foot of State St., is a placid 92-acre shelter for transient and resident craft, protected by an L-shaped breakwater 2,364 feet long. The municipal West Beach, also protected by the breakwater, attracts summer bathers to its restrained surf.

ANDREE CLARK BIRD REFUGE (*open 9-5 weekdays*), E. end of E. Cabrillo Blvd., is a landscaped preserve of 49½ acres with an island-dotted lake in the center, where geese, swan, and other wild fowl live; the land was reclaimed from a swamp and is maintained by the city. There are bridle paths among the trees, and a large parking space on the east shore.

SANTA BARBARA COUNTY BOWL, E. end of E. Anapamu St., completed in 1937, is a 4,000-seat amphitheater where a historical play is produced annually as part of the city's "Old Spanish Days" festival. Its large revolving stage—75 by 40 feet—holds two sets at once. Cut stone seats follow the natural contour of the canyon in which the bowl is built. The bowl is also used for concerts and other programs.

SANTA BARBARA STATE COLLEGE, 1920 Lasuen Rd., a small group of concrete buildings of Eastern Mediterranean architecture standing on an 18-acre hillside campus overlooking the city and the sea, has a four-year teacher training course and uses the city schools as a laboratory for directed teaching. A new 66-acre site on Cliff Drive along the mesa is being developed as the future home of the college.

It was founded in 1909 by Ednah Rich Morse as a State normal school of manual arts and home economics. The LIBRARY of 30,000 volumes contains the 7,000-volume William Wyles collection of Lincolniana and Civil War and Reconstruction treatises.

SANTA BARBARA MISSION (*open 8-5 weekdays, 11-5 Sun.*), Los Olivos St. between Garden and Laguna Sts., called Queen of the Missions in the days when it was rich and powerful, is the best preserved and architecturally one of the finest missions. A blending of old Spanish and Moorish architecture, it was constructed in 1815 by the padres, using Canalino Indian labor, to replace the building destroyed in the 1812 earthquake. The original mission chapel was made of boughs in 1786. Damage to mission buildings by the 1925 earthquake was promptly repaired.

The church, designed by Padre Riptoll, is constructed of native sandstone, painted ivory. It is rectangular in plan with massive square front towers of solid masonry and arcaded and domed belfries. The towers are flanked by heavy buttresses. The design of the classic facade, with its engaged columns of modified Ionic order, its dentiled cornice and frieze adorned with a heavy fret motif and its crowning pediment, is based upon the detail of a plate of the classic orders, appearing in a Spanish volume of Vitruvius, still in the Mission library. In the tympanum of the pediment is a niched figure of Saint Barbara. Surmounting the pediment are three seated figures and a stepped gable cresting topped with a cross.

Across the entire width of the facade is a traditional broad-stepped platform. The deeply recessed arched entrance with its simple classic trim has double paneled doors. Above the entrance is a circular "rose" window with deep splayed reveal. At the left is the long, low arcaded mission house with red-tile roof, enclosing one side of the rear patio.

The interior of the long narrow nave is lighted by small splayed windows in the side walls. It is finished in plaster with Ionic pilasters painted in imitation of veined marble rising in support of a painted dentil cornice and has a flat wooden ceiling, embellished with painted and carved rosettes. The structural roof timbers are concealed.

At the left of the entrance is a door leading to the Mission House and a spiral stairway in the left tower. The walls of the nave are flanked by side altars with religious paintings above. In the first bay, left and right, are chapels, recessed in the deep side walls. The main altar is screened by a painted and paneled reredos, adorned with Roman Doric columns, painted floral festoons and figures. On the Epistle side of the main altar is the tomb of Father Francisco García Diego y Moreno, first Bishop of California, flanked by Ionic columns and topped with a pediment. A doorway to the left of the sanctuary leads to the sacristy and the choir room. The stations of the cross were brought from Mexico in 1797.

Two small side doors near the center of the nave lead to the patio or Monks Garden, on the left, and the Mission Cemetery on the right. The patio is landscaped with trees, flower beds, and radiating walks around a central well. Two sides are enclosed by the rooms and arcaded corridors of the Mission House. Especially notable are the deeply recessed windows with their turned wooden grilles and the unstilted arches of the arcades, supported by heavy square piers.

This is the only California mission in which the altar light has not been extinguished since the founding. Bodies of Franciscan friars are interred in crypts set in the thick walls of the building, and 4,000 Indians are buried in trenches across the garden. Art and relics of the Canalino tribe are exhibited in the curio rooms. The mission has old paintings, creased in their journey from Spain and the pack-trip across Mexico, and a copy of Murillo's *Assumption of the Virgin,* which research may prove an original.

The MUSEUM OF NATURAL HISTORY (*open 9-5 weekdays, 10-5 Sun.*), Puesta del Sol Road and Mission Creek, its one-story stucco Spanish-Colonial type buildings grouped upon two acres of sycamore and live-oak studded grounds, has pavilions with permanent exhibitions of the flora and fauna of the region, natural habitat groups of animals from all parts of the world, artifacts of the Hunting People and the Oak Grove and Canalino Indians, and a library on natural science. Lectures and motion pictures on natural science are presented in a 410-seat auditorium.

The museum, maintained by gifts, endowments and memberships, publishes pamphlets on natural history and geology, gives special classes four afternoons a week and broadcasts over KTMS on Friday afternoons during the winter.

BLAKSLEY BOTANIC GARDEN (*open 9-5 weekdays, 10-5 Sun.*), 1289 Mission Canyon Rd., is a 30-acre creekside tract planted with trees, shrubs and flowers indigenous to California. Specimens are labeled and arranged in ten sections to show characteristic flora of the desert, foothill, canyon, waterside and other plant associations. Literature on plants and birds in the garden is available near the entrance. Experimental culture here has added to existing knowledge on the habits of native plants and their adaptability to home-gardening.

POINTS OF INTEREST IN ENVIRONS

Mission San Buenaventura, 27.9 *m.;* Mission Santa Ynez, 45 *m.* (*see TOUR 2c*).

Stockton

Railroad Stations: E. Weber Ave. and Sacramento St. for Southern Pacific R.R.; San Joaquin and Taylor Sts. for Santa Fe R.R.; Main and Union Sts. for Western Pacific R.R.

Bus Stations: 227 N. Hunter St. for Pacific Greyhound; 27 E. Weber Ave. for Byron and Brentwood; 245 N. Hunter St. for River Auto Stages.

Airport: Stockton Airport, 5 m. SE. on Sharp's Lane, private planes only.

Streetcars: Fare 7¢, 4 tokens for 25¢; free transfers.

Accommodations: 88 hotels; 4 tourist camps.

Information Service: California State Auto Assn. (AAA), 929 N. El Dorado St.; Chamber of Commerce, 234 N. El Dorado St.

Radio Stations: KGDM (1100 kc.); KWG (1200 kc.).

Motion Picture Houses: Seven.

Golf: Stockton Municipal Golf Course, 7th St. and Sharp Lane. 9 holes; 50¢, 75¢ Sat. and Sun.; monthly tickets $3; children 25¢ weekdays.

Tennis: 10 municipal courts, Oak Park, Victory Park, Municipal Baths, Arbor Park; all free.

Swimming Pools: Stockton Municipal Baths, S. end of S. San Joaquin St.; open 9-5, 20¢, children 10¢, suit and towel 10¢; American Legion Park Lake, 1400 N. Baker St., free; lifeguards in summer.

Riding: Bridle paths around Municipal Golf Course and in Louis Park; horses 75¢ an hour.

Annual Events: Concerts by Stockton Symphony Orchestra, winter; Port Stockton Regatta and Water Carnival, May 30 and 31; San Joaquin County Fair, last full week of Aug.

STOCKTON (23 alt., 47,963 pop.), at the head of tidewaters on the San Joaquin River, has something of the appearance of a coastal city. Its northernmost section, campus of the College of the Pacific, borders the Calaveras River, which flows into the San Joaquin on the west. The Stockton Channel extends eastward from the San Joaquin, cutting through the city and stopping at its center. Other waterways wind in and around the city, among them the Mormon Channel, through the southern part of Stockton.

The 32-foot Stockton Channel—nucleus of the Port of Stockton—is the shipping point for agricultural products of the fertile San Joaquin Valley. A flotilla of barges and launches, the "Mosquito Fleet," goes out from here, carrying to market the rich produce of the netherlands farms; huge ocean-going freighters ply the river from Stockton to San Francisco. The Port is the outstanding commercial feature of the city, and warehouses, factories, and mills line the Channel.

The business district radiates from Courthouse Plaza, Weber Avenue and Hunter Street. The tall office buildings, modern shops, metropolitan stores, and Civic Center reflect the new Stockton, starting point for trips to such places as the Bret Harte country, Lake Tahoe, and Yosemite Valley, while only a few blocks west, along Main and El Dorado Streets, stand the aged landmarks of the pioneer days, when Stockton was a wide-open gold rush town, the jumping off place for the Mother Lode country. Twenty-six tracts are set aside as parks, playgrounds, and squares, including Victory Park, a 27½-acre landscaped area in the heart of the northwest residence district.

Ten per cent of Stockton's population is Mexican. It is also a center for Basque sheepherders. There are many Basque restaurants, where wine is poured Basque fashion in a stream from the leather flask into the drinker's open mouth. There was at one time a considerable number of Hindus in California's Central Valley, brought into the State for their knowledge of irrigation; in recent years many of them have returned to India with money they managed to accumulate. Bearded, turbanned Sikhs, grave and dignified, may still, however, occasionally be seen in the streets of Stockton.

Capt. Charles M. Weber, a native of Germany who came to California with the Bidwell-Bartellson party in 1841, is generally recognized as the founder of Stockton. Weber first settled in San Jose, where he met William Gulnac, a naturalized Mexican citizen. The two men formed a partnership to establish a colony in the San Joaquin Valley: and to this end Gulnac obtained a tract from the Mexican government, about 50,000 acres, including the site of Stockton. Gulnac led the first group of settlers to the area, which they called El Campo de los Francesces (Sp. French Camp), but in 1845 he became discouraged and sold out to Weber for a $60 grocery bill.

Weber remained in San Jose, though in 1847 he founded the town of Tuleburg on the site of the present levee of that name. He built corrals, planted wheat, and set up houses for ranchers. After discovery of gold in 1848, Weber moved to Tuleburg, which he planned to promote as a supply post for miners. He surveyed the town in 1849, renaming it Stockton for his friend Commodore Robert Stockton.

The Gold Rush took Stockton by storm. Bayard Taylor, noted author and traveler, found it in 1849 "a canvas town of a thousand inhabitants, and a port with twenty-five vessels at anchor! The mingled noises of labor around—the click of hammers and the grating of saws —the shouts of mule drivers—the jingling of spurs—the jar and jostle of wares in the tents—almost cheated me into the belief that it was some old commercial mart. . . . Four months had sufficed to make the place what it was." One of a dozen new wholesale firms already had done $100,000 worth of business. A lot 80 by 100 feet sold for $6,000; a common, one-story clapboard house cost $15,000 to build.

In 1850 Stockton became the county seat, and within three years the population grew from a few hundred to 5,000. Between the time he became an outlaw in 1851 and his death in 1853, the Mexican bandit Joaquin Murrieta ranged as far north as Stockton. On one occasion he rode into town, noticed a sign offering a reward for his capture, wrote underneath it "I will give $10,000—Joaquin!" then galloped off through the crowd, unmolested. An incendiary fire in 1851 destroyed many structures, as a result of which Stockton has few historic landmarks.

The settlers of Stockton built churches and schools as early as 1850, despite the gold rush. The introduction of irrigation after the 1860's and the decline of the gold mines turned attention once again towards agriculture. Grain poured into the city's warehouses to await shipment by the railroad which first reached the city in 1869. This increased the demand for farm implements, and Stockton began production of tractors, harvesters, and other farm machinery. The caterpillar tractor, first machine to use the track-laying traction principle, originated in Stockton; the device employed in these tractors was later applied in the development of the military tank, first used in the World War.

The Deep Water Project, an $8,000,000 harbor development, begun in 1928, has provided 18 miles of water front, with 24 miles of undeveloped frontage along the various side channels. The channel is now navigable for 90 per cent of all ocean-going vessels, permitting the shipment of Stockton's wide variety of manufactures—paper and cedar products, motorboats, road-building and farm machinery, canned goods, flour and feeds, and bricks.

In June 1934 the last of the Pony Express riders, William Campbell, died at Stockton. He was on the 95-mile run from Fort Kearney to Fort McPherson. Chased once for miles by a pack of wolves, on his return he left a poisoned ox on the trail for their benefit. His reward was a dozen dead wolves whose hides brought $50.

POINTS OF INTEREST

SAN JOAQUIN COUNTY COURTHOUSE, Main and Hunter Sts., designed in 1890 by E. E. Myers & Son of Detroit, is built in classic style, with a lofty, gilded dome bearing a figure of justice.

The two-story brick SIKH TEMPLE (*open*), 1930 S. Grant St., is said to be the only temple of this sect in the United States. The building has high stained-glass windows and an ornate mosaic entrance framed by a horseshoe of electric lights. The first floor contains a library and a meeting room. Visitors must take off their shoes and leave them on the veranda before entering the temple proper, which occupies the entire second floor. There are no chairs, and the floor is carpeted with green velvet. Among its possessions is a fine portrait of Guru Nanak, born in 1469, founder of the Sikh religion, a dissenting sect from Brahmanical Hinduism. The Guru Sacred Book (*Granth Sahib*) is covered with rich silk draperies from India. Sikhism combines the teachings of Hinduism and the Persian Sufis; it rejects caste and practices purity of life and toleration.

The FORTY-NINE DRUGSTORE, Main and El Dorado Sts., a two-story building of gray stone with gingerbread trim, has been

used continuously for the same purpose since 1850, when E. S. Holden
built it and opened Stockton's first pharmacy. The main room, with
its vaulted ceilings, is the same one in which bearded miners of the boom
days purchased their medicines.

Another landmark of the middle 1850's is the ODD FELLOWS
HALL, 17 El Dorado St., a two-story brick building, once fraternal
headquarters for lusty miners on holiday from the gold fields. It now
has a fish market on the lower floor, and a twenty-cents-a-night hotel
on the second.

The SITE OF WEBER'S HOUSE is on the S. side of the Channel at Center St. Weber first lived in an adobe hut surrounded by
a stockade and a ditch. In 1850 or 1851, he brought his bride to
Tuleburg, and built a two-story frame house adjacent to his adobe.
The house, constructed of lumber shipped around the Horn, and surrounded by spacious gardens, was destroyed by fire shortly after Weber's
death in 1881.

CITY HALL, El Dorado and Lindsay Sts., is a stone structure of
modern design. This site is called Lindsay's Point for Thomas Lindsay,
one of the company that came here in 1844 under the leadership of
Gulnac. The tule hut Lindsay erected on the point just back of the
City Hall was the first house built by a white man within the city
limits. A smallpox scare drove out most of the settlers soon after their
arrival, and in the spring of 1845 a band of Indians killed Lindsay,
set fire to his hut, and drove off the cattle. He is buried on the Point.

The HAGGIN MEMORIAL GALLERY AND PIONEER
HISTORICAL MUSEUM (*open 1:30-5 daily except Mon.; free*),
Magnolia St. and Pershing Ave., was given to the city by Louis Terah
Haggin, who had immense holdings of land and dominated stock raising in pioneer days. Haggin, of Turkish descent, was an art collector
and his collection of 300 nineteenth century European and American
paintings forms the nucleus of the gallery. There are also on exhibit
numerous relics of early California, among them the weapons of a party
that came over the Oregon Trail, old wagons, fire engines, porcelains
and silverware.

The COLLEGE OF THE PACIFIC, Pacific Ave. and Stadium
Drive, oldest incorporated educational institution in California, is conducted by the Methodist Church on an interdenominational basis. The
school has a student body of about 450. The 11 buildings on the
50-acre campus are in English Gothic style, of red brick with light stone
trim. WEBER MEMORIAL HALL, honoring the founder of Stockton,
stands near the Pacific Avenue entrance to the campus. It houses the
school auditorium and the College of Pacific Little Theater. For its
first 20 years (1851-1871) the college was in Santa Clara, having been
founded there by Isaac Owen, the first Methodist minister in California.
It was moved to San Jose in the 1870's, and since 1924 has been in
Stockton.

PART III
Up and Down the State

Tour 1

Westport—Fort Bragg—Point Arena—San Francisco—Santa Cruz—
Monterey—Carmel—San Simeon—Morro Bay—San Luis Obispo—
Las Cruces; 554.5 *m.* State 1.

Roadbed paved except for stretches between Pismo Beach and Las Cruces,
winding continuously, with frequent sharp turns; occasional slides during rainy
season.
Southern Pacific Lines parallel route between Davenport and Pacific Grove.
Accommodations limited except in larger towns.

State 1 skirts closely the waters of the Pacific. It swings outward
around headlands and inland past sandy-edged coves in a succession of
hairpin curves; it climbs barren slopes and dips into brush-choked
ravines. At times it edges along sheer bluffs high above the surf. Eastward, wind-swept hills, wooded only in patches, rise to the timbered
crests of the Coast Range. After the first rains these hills are briefly
green; at other times their slopes are brown with dried grass, close-
cropped by grazing sheep.

Walled off by mountains, the narrow coastal shelf is sparsely settled
except around San Francisco and Monterey Bays. The half-primitive
ways of the seventies and eighties, when lumbering, fishing, and sheep
raising flourished, linger on in the isolated villages and farms. The
region now affords only a meager living to its hard-working inhabitants.
Along the northern section, where redwoods grow down to the sea in
forest-choked ravines, the lumber towns at the mouths of rivers, once
shipping points for logs hauled by narrow-gage railways from the forested hinterland, are sinking into decay beside abandoned mills.

Fishing is still a gainful pursuit at such points as Noyo, Tomales
Bay, Monterey, and Half Moon Bay. Flocks of sheep roam over the

317

hills up and down the coast and great herds of dairy cattle over the knolls and hollows around Tomales Bay. Berries and peas are grown around Fort Bragg; brussels sprouts and artichokes, in the foggy strip near Half Moon Bay; and apples in the Pajaro Valley; but most of the country is too rough, too bleak for farming. The occasional weather-beaten farm buildings huddle behind ragged, protective files of wind-battered cypress or eucalyptus trees.

The coastal strip between the mouth of the Russian River and Big Sur attracts increasing numbers of vacationers every year. It is a picturesque stretch, indented with rocky, islet-studded coves where crescent-shaped beaches of white sand lie between bold promontories. Along the highway in this area are a succession of resort towns and camps that offer bathing and fishing in the surf, clam and abalone hunting along the shore, and riding and hiking in the forested hinterland.

Section a. WESTPORT to SAN FRANCISCO; 205.4 m.

On the maps the northern end of State 1 is extended to a junction with US 101 not far south of Eureka, with feeders from US 101 north of Westport; but these connections are barely passable even in good weather.

WESTPORT, 0 m. (50 alt., 200 pop.), a rambling settlement of frame houses with rickety picket fences, perched on bare bluffs. First named Beal's Landing for Lloyd Beal, who arrived in 1864, the town was renamed Westport at the instigation of James T. Rogers, a native of Eastport, Maine. After construction of two wharves in 1878, it became for a while an important lumber-shipping point.

> North from Westport on a poor road (the sketchy continuation of State 1), past ROCKPORT, 11.5 m., a small lumber camp with bleak, weather-beaten shacks, to the junction with a narrow, ungraded dirt road, 14.5 m. Right here, up a long, steep forested grade to a summit, 25.5 m., then downward to a junction with US 101, 30.1 m. (see TOUR 2a).

South of Westport State 1 winds over close-cropped pasture lands sloping to the sea. Crossing the marshy bottoms of sluggish Ten Mile River, 7.8 m., it strikes through an eerie wilderness of storm-blasted pine and cypress groves, edged at intervals by sand dunes. Patches of farm land and orchard, crisscrossed by files of cypress windbreaks, hedge the road.

FORT BRAGG, 16.2 m. (60 alt., 3,022 pop.), spreads over a sloping coastal shelf to the edge of a wild and rocky coast line. A settlement of wooden buildings—false-front stores, steepled churches, and gabled frame houses in fenced yards—it has a weather-worn, settled air. Fort Bragg's chief stock in trade is lumber, but it also ships farm and truck-garden crops (especially berries), poultry and dairy products, and fish. Its racial make-up is mixed: Finns and Swedes predominate; after them, Germans and Italians.

In June 1857 Lt. Horatio Gates Gibson was ordered to establish a military post within the boundaries of the Mendocino Indian Reservation. The fort he set up here and named for Gen. Braxton Bragg of Mexican War fame covered a 10-acre clearing. The land was thrown open for purchase in 1867, when the reservation was abandoned, and a lumber town grew up. It was damaged by the earthquake of April 18, 1906, but rebuilt at once.

The heart of the town's industrial life is the UNION LUMBER COMPANY PLANT, a large redwood sawmill with a capacity of 350,000 to 400,000 board feet a day. Its red-painted mill buildings, lumberyards, and log pond lie along the railroad yards at the edge of the rocky bluffs. The UNION LUMBER COMPANY REFORESTATION AND ORNAMENTAL NURSERY (*open workdays 8-5*), on Main Street (R) near the southern outskirts, established in 1922, raises redwood and other seedlings for systematic reforestation of cutover lands.

NOYO (*boats for ocean fishing rented*), 17.9 *m.* (sea level, 93 pop.), lies at the mouth of placid, winding Noyo River, crowded with small fishing craft tied up alongside tumble-down warehouses. Noyo was the name given by Northern Pomo Indians to their village at the river's mouth. The village escaped the fate of most former lumber towns along the Mendocino coast by turning to fishing for a living. Settled largely by Italian fishermen, it is now the center of the area's commercial fishing industry. It has fish-canning and drying plants and a deep-water harbor protected by a breakwater.

CASPAR, 22.3 *m.* (52 alt., 250 pop.), on the edge of high bluffs at the mouth of Caspar Creek, is a collection of old frame houses amid weed-grown vacant spaces, dirt paths, and picket fences. The lumber mill beside the log pond and chute, occasionally operated, was built in 1861.

At 25.2 *m.* is the junction with a dirt road.

Right on this road 0.3 *m.* to RUSSIAN GULCH STATE PARK HEADQUARTERS (*camping 50¢ per car a day, picnicking 25¢ per car a day*). The park contains more than 1,000 acres of second-growth redwood. Along the fern-banked canyon bottom, deep among redwoods, alders, and Douglas fir, are scattered camp sites and picnic grounds.

MENDOCINO, 27.3 *m.* (41 alt., 500 pop.), ranges over the northern shore of a half-moon-shaped bay at the mouth of Big River—a jumble of weathered, gabled wooden buildings fronting dirt streets, edged by the gloomy pine woods of encircling hills. It was named for Cape Mendocino, which Juan Rodríguez Cabrillo discovered in 1542 and named for Don Antonio de Mendoza, first viceroy of New Spain (Mexico).

Intermittent lumbering provides Mendocino's main support. A party sent out from Bodega in 1851 to salvage tea and silk from a vessel wrecked nearby carried back information of the country's rich timber resources to Alderman Harry Meiggs of San Francisco, lumberman and mill owner. On July 19, 1852, the brig *Ontario,* chartered by Meiggs, arrived with sawmill machinery imported from the East. Meiggs, finding that one William Kasten had staked out a claim to the

water-front, purchased the claim with the first lumber from his sawmill
—the first on the Mendocino coast—as part payment.

The architecture of Mendocino's well-preserved buildings (there has
been only one serious fire) reflects the New England origin of most of
its early settlers.   Notable remnant of a bygone era is the MASONIC
HALL (R), on Main Street.   A buff-colored, gable-roofed structure,
the hall bears on its cupola a piece of sculpture carved from a single
block of redwood.   It represents the Masonic emblem and the symbolic
figures of Masonic lore: the broken pillar, the maiden beside it with
a sprig in her hand, and Father Time dallying with her wavy locks.

At 30.1 *m.* is the junction with a graveled road.

> Right on this road 0.3 *m.* to VAN DAMME BEACH STATE PARK
> HEADQUARTERS (*camping and picnicking fees as at Russian Gulch*).
> This 1,800-acre tract fronting a lagoon with a sloping bathing beach
> stretches 4 miles up the forested canyon of the Little River.   The chief
> attraction for visitors is the fishing: trout are caught in the Little River;
> red, blue, and China cod in the surf; leaf cod and salmon in the bay.

ALBION, 34.3 *m.* (37 alt., 75 pop.), a village of brightly painted,
shingle-roofed cottages, overlooks the cove at the mouth of the Albion
River, where an abandoned lumber mill decays amid half-ruined company shacks.   A sawmill was erected here in 1852-53 and operated until
1928.   Today the inhabitants subsist chiefly by fishing and berry picking.

At 38.6 *m.,* in a deep valley where the broad Navarro River winds
over marshy bottoms and through a sand bar into the sea, is the junction
with paved State 28.

> Left on State 28, which runs along the riverbank, shadowed by a forest
> of second-growth redwood, 8.4 *m.* to DIMMICK MEMORIAL PARK (*pic-
> nicking*), a 12-acre reserve.   The Navarro River offers fine swimming, and
> is one of the best trout and bass streams in the State.
> On State 28 at 14.8 *m.* is NAVARRO.   Many of its gray, weathered
> houses stand empty, reminders of its lively past as a lumber town.
> The road enters Anderson Valley, a fertile basin given over to apple
> growing, and reaches BOONVILLE, 30.2 *m.* (pop. 315).   Named in 1868
> for an early settler, W. W. Boon, the settlement today furnishes supplies
> to ranchers and travelers.   It celebrates an annual County Fair and Apple
> Show in October.
> Southwest of Boonville the highway climbs over a succession of hills,
> winds past rolling sheep pasturage, and joins US 101 (*see TOUR 2a*) at
> 57.5 *m.*

ELK, 44.6 *m.* (200 pop.), also known as Greenwood, lying along
the highway skirting the very edge of steep bluffs—is a string of
frame store buildings, most of them left to sag and gather cobwebs since
lumbering operations stopped in 1931.   In its heyday, when two or
three boats anchored offshore every week to load lumber brought from
inland by railroad, Elk had nearly a dozen saloons and half as many
hotels.   The loading trestle remains, flung from the edge of the bluffs
to a jagged islet in the surf.   In the debris-littered gravel bottoms just
south of town lie the remains of the mill, rusted and rotting.

State 1 winds between fences over sheep ranges and strips of farm land that roll upward from the narrow coastal shelf to forest-fringed hills. A vast sweep of surf-scalloped shore line appears at intervals, curving off in the long promontory of Point Arena (*see below*). A far stretch of rolling country sweeps to timbered hills (L) as the highway strikes inland from the shore.

MANCHESTER, 58.8 *m.* (300 pop.), a handful of buildings widely scattered among farms and pastures, lies in a farming, dairying, and sheep- and cattle-raising region, one of the few sections along the northern coast level enough to permit extensive farming.

At 62.6 *m.* is the junction with a paved road.

> Right on this road 2.5 *m.* to POINT ARENA LIGHT STATION (*visitors 1-3 Mon., Wed., Fri.*), where gray, red-roofed frame houses cluster around the tall cylindrical white light tower. On November 10, 1792, Capt. George Vancouver spent the night off this promontory in his ship *Discovery,* en route from Nootka to San Francisco. He named it Punta Barro de Arena (Sp., point sand bar). A brick light station erected here in 1870 was replaced, after its destruction in the 1906 earthquake, by the present 115-foot tower, which has a light of 380,000 candle power.

POINT ARENA, 64.5 *m.* (39 alt., 385 pop.), has scattered cottages in cypress-sheltered gardens and trim, stuccoed business buildings, churches, and schools. It traces its history to the opening of a store here in 1859. Although it was said to be the most thriving town between San Francisco and Eureka at the height of lumbering operations, it was not incorporated until 1908. Today it is a trading center for a dairying region.

South of Point Arena State 1 again skirts the coast, running through dense patches of dwarf-pines and dipping into gulches choked with undergrowth.

GUALALA, 79.6 *m.* (sea level, 15 pop.), is on a curving beach at the mouth of the broad, forest-bordered Gualala River. Its name (pron. Wah-lá-la), is probably the Spanish spelling of the Pomo Indians' "wala'li" or "wa'lali," meaning a meeting place of waters. Gualala had its lumbering boom in the 1860's and 1870's—although its sawmill, abandoned now at the river's mouth, was operated until 1920. Its life centers today around the two-story, white frame GUALALA HOTEL (1903), with veranda and balcony. The fishing season attracts many visitors.

STEWART'S POINT, 91.3 *m.* (20 alt., 30 pop.), named for a pioneer lumberman and settler, is a handful of frame houses around a general store. On the rocky point at the edge of the cove, hidden by trees, are the abandoned sheds and trestle from which lumber was once shipped.

As State 1 winds southward, through rolling stretches thickly wooded with dwarf pines and littered with boulders, the coast becomes more and more rugged—saw-toothed with jutting promontories and rocky inlets where the surf crashes on kelp-strewn crags. The route makes a short swing inland through the KRUSE RHODODENDRON RESERVE, 99.3 *m.,* maintained in its natural state, where the rhododendrons, growing 20 to 30 feet high, blossom in late May and early June.

FORT ROSS, 107 m. (100 alt.), once chief outpost of Russian civilization in California, stands on a high shelf sloping from wooded hills to the edge of the cove. At this place, in the spring of 1812, the Russian-American Fur Company's vessel, the *Chirikov,* deposited a party of fur traders and Aleut hunters under command of Ivan Alexander Kuskof. Since 1806, when the Tsar's chamberlain, Nikolai Rezanof, had visited the San Francisco Presidio (*see SAN FRANCISCO*) in quest of food for the starving Russian settlement at Sitka, Alaska, the Russian-American Company had planned to establish settlements in California as sources of food supply for its fur-trading posts in the north. On May 15, 1812, Kuskof's party began building a fortress; three months later, on August 30, they dedicated it with ceremony, naming it Rossiya (Russia).

The settlement, laid out in a rectangle, was enclosed by a 14-foot stockade of hewn timbers and guarded by two-story blockhouses with portholes for cannon at the north and south corners. There were 59 buildings. Inside the enclosure were the chapel, the commandant's house, barracks, two warehouses, blacksmith and other shops, and a jail. Outside clustered the redwood huts of the Aleut hunters, a windmill, several farm buildings, and a tannery. At the foot of the steep bluffs were a small wharf, a workshop for shipbuilding, a blacksmith shop, a bathhouse, and sheds for the bidarkas (skin boats) of the Aleuts and for storing lumber.

Despite the efforts of apprehensive Spanish officials to check the growth of La Fuerte de los Rusos (the fort of the Russians), the colonists began a thriving trade with the San Francisco Presidio and mission, exchanging tobacco, sugar, kitchen utensils, iron, cloth, and wax candles for grain, peas, meat, tallow, flour, and hides. When Missions San Rafael and San Francisco Solano (*see TOUR 2a*) were founded to halt Russian expansion southward the Russians extended their trade to the missions themselves.

The Russian settlement began to face economic difficulties, however, when the revenue from sea-otter hunting diminished with the rapid extermination of the otter along the coast. Unable to make a living from farming, the colonists turned to shipbuilding; they used the green timber of oak to construct four vessels, two of 160 and two of 200 tons, between 1819 and 1824; but the timber decayed so rapidly that this activity was abandoned. The settlement was in the end a failure. Restrained from expanding southward by the Spanish, Russia agreed in 1824 to limit its future settlements to Alaska.

The man into whose hands Fort Ross finally passed, when in 1841 the Tsar ordered withdrawal of his subjects, was Johann August Sutter, founder of New Helvetia (Sacramento). The price agreed on for the entire property—buildings, chattels, livestock, and even the 20-ton schooner *Constantine*—was $30,000; of this Sutter agreed to pay $2,000 in cash and the rest in yearly installments of produce, chiefly wheat. Sutter dismantled fort and buildings and shipped everything he could carry on his schooner to New Helvetia. The transferred property included 1,700 head of cattle, 940 horses and mules, 9,000 sheep, agricultural implements and industrial machinery, and an arsenal, including brass pieces, cannon, and muskets—all French weapons picked up in 1813 in the path of Napoleon's retreat through the snow from Moscow. Even a 20-foot-square conservatory, with glass windows and doors, was removed in sections to Sacramento; Madame Rotchev, the Russian governor's wife, had begged Sutter (he wrote) "not to destroy the garden house which she had built and in which she had spent so many happy hours. . . . However . . . my men . . . could not put it together because they did not understand the workmanship of the Russian carpenters . . ."

The few remaining buildings were neglected until in 1906, after damage by the earthquake, the State began restoration. The only part of the original stockade left is a heap of rotting redwood logs—the remains of the heptagonal blockhouse that stood at the north corner. At the eastern corner is the partly restored GREEK ORTHODOX CHAPEL (*open 8-5 except Tues.*), a crude structure 20 feet wide and 25 long, with a squat, dull yellow belfry and dome on its weather-worn red-gabled roof. Exhibited in its two rough-boarded rooms are Russian, Spanish, and Indian relics. The RUSSIAN COMMANDANT'S HOUSE, a spacious edifice with a shingled roof sloping over a wide veranda, preserves remnants of the original structure—including the fireplace and the log finish between the doors and windows of the facade—reinforced by later additions.

South of Fort Ross State 1 winds tortuously around brush-grown, rocky hillsides and through twisting ravines, on a narrow ledge overhanging the boiling surf. At 118.8 *m.* it swings up the broad valley of the Russian River (*see TOUR 2a*), which finds its way to the ocean through a narrow strait in the great sand bar that holds back its waters in a wide, placid lagoon.

JENNER-BY-THE-SEA, 119.7 *m.* (0 alt., 160 pop.), is a resort with peak-roofed white and green cottages hugging the steep slopes above the river.

At 120.8 *m.,* where State 1 crosses Russian River on a giant concrete and steel bridge, is the junction with paved State 12 (*see TOUR 2a*).

At 121.7 *m.* is the junction with a dirt road.

Right on this road 0.2 *m.* to BODEGA-SONOMA COAST STATE PARK, which stretches along 5 miles of picturesque ocean shore from the mouth of the Russian River to Bodega Bay. The shore waters abound with shellfish and abalones and the surf with fish that can be caught by line from the rocks or by net in the breakers.

At 122.9 *m.* on State 1 is the junction with an oiled road.

Right on this road 0.2 *m.* to SHELL BEACH in Bodega-Sonoma Coast State Park.

WRIGHT'S BEACH is at 124.3 *m.* and ARCH ROCK BEACH at 127 *m.* Both are wide sandy strands sheltered in rocky coves in the State park.

SALMON CREEK BEACH, 128.5 *m.,* rimmed by great sand dunes, lies at the mouth of Salmon Creek, where a sand bar impounds a lagoon below scattered cottages.

BAY, 130.4 *m.,* a string of frame houses sheltered by a lane of eucalyptus trees overlooking a row of small wharves where fishing smacks are moored, lies along the curving shore of BODEGA BAY.

Bodega Bay is now a shallow, sand-choked inlet, rimmed by mud flats at low tide; its egress to the sea on the south is blocked, except for a narrow strait, by a sandspit stretching from the mainland on the east to Bodega Head at the tip of the long promontory on the west. The bay was named for its discoverer, Lieut. Juan Francisco de la Bodéga y Cuadra, who anchored his schooner, the *Sonora,* off Bodega Head October 3, 1775. In 1809 the Russian-American Fur Company's agent, Ivan Kuskof, landed with a party from Sitka. They sowed wheat, and in August, with the harvested grain and a catch of 2,000 sea-otter skins, returned to Alaska. In 1811 the Russians returned to found the settlements of Port Roumiantzoff on the bay and Bodega (*see below*) and Kuskof in the hinterland. They cultivated land toward the tip of the Bodega peninsula and erected two warehouses.

First Yankee settlers at Bodega Bay were three sailors. In 1835 Gen. Mariano G. Vallejo gave them large land grants on condition that they settle at the border of the Russian claims to check Russian expansion. In 1843 Capt. Stephen Smith was granted the land formerly occupied by the Russians. Five years later he erected a small warehouse and in 1852 a hotel. By 1860 the port was alive with people and business, its harbor crowded with sails. The warehouses lining the shore overflowed with potatoes—a variety known as Bodega Reds for the bright maroon coat beneath their rough skins—raised on great ranches roundabout. Regular freight and passenger boats from San Francisco anchored in the open roadstead outside the sandspit, where they were loaded from small lighters. In the 1870's the bay began to fill with sand. In time, potato raising was supplanted by dairying, the chief industry of the region ever since. Vessels no longer call here—nor have they for a generation past.

State 1 winds inland over rolling farm lands where cattle graze in fenced pastures, bordered by lanes of eucalyptus trees and patches of orchards.

BODEGA, 136.4 *m.* (40 alt., 100 pop.), clusters amid cypress patches around a red-roofed schoolhouse and two white-spired churches.

Beside the road (R) at 138.4 *m.* stands the WATSON DISTRICT SCHOOL, built in 1856, a white clapboarded building with a bell tower jutting from its peaked red roof. It was named for James Watson, an immigrant of 1853, who acquired so many thousand acres of land from the yield of bumper crops of the high-priced Bodega Reds that he became a land baron, entertaining the whole countryside with horse racing at his private course.

VALLEY FORD, 142.3 *m.* (45 alt., 200 pop.), with old brick and frame stores, is among gently rolling pasture lands dotted with gracious white farmhouses, roomy barns, and corrals. It lies at the head of tidewater on the Estero Americano (American Creek), which empties into Bodega Bay; it was named for the "valley ford," where an ancient Indian and Spanish trail crossed the Estero. This is a dairying town: when the bank was organized in 1893, it was called The Dairymans Bank.

TOMALES, 149.3 *m.* (75 alt., 450 pop.), a trim looking town, rambles over the slopes of a hollow. The countryside is noted for its butter, cheese, and milk. Tomales' first house was built in 1850 by John Keyes, who operated a small schooner between Bodega Bay and San Francisco and opened a trading post here in the spring of 1854.

State 1 winds through the shallow gully of San Antonio Creek to its mouth in a delta of mud flats at TOMALES BAY, 151.9 *m.,* and then runs for 13 miles along the shore. (Tomales is a Spanish corruption of the Coast Miwok Indian word *tamal,* bay.) The bay is a long, narrow, fingerlike inlet, resembling a firth in the Scottish Highlands. On the east bare brown hills slope down to the shore; on the west, low, tumbled peaks densely forested with green. In the shallow water offshore, oyster beds are fenced in by a long file of slender stakes.

At NICK'S COVE (*boats for hire*), 153.2 *m.,* cottages cluster around the store and the wharf, where small dories bob up and down with the lapping tide.

The lower end of Tomales Bay is a dank expanse of mud flats.

POINT REYES STATION, 166.4 *m.* (31 alt., 143 pop.), named for nearby Point Reyes (*see below*), faces an abandoned railroad station. The town and surrounding region have had one product—butter—since the 1850's, when a 57,066-acre tract was acquired by three men and leased to dairy farmers who began to ship their butter to San Francisco by schooner.

At 166.7 *m.* is the junction with a paved road.

Right on this road, which runs northeastward along the western shore of Tomales Bay, to the junction with a dirt road, 1.5 *m.;* L. here 0.2 *m.* to the MARIN COUNTY FISH HATCHERY, a large plant for hatching rainbow trout.

The main side route continues to INVERNESS, 3.8 *m.* (sea level, 200 pop.), a summer colony, deep among greenery at the edge of a 6-mile sandy beach. James Black, a native of Inverness, Scotland, settled here in 1832, but the town was not founded until 1908. The Inverness Yacht Club is a center for yachting on Tomales Bay.

West of Inverness the road, paved for 0.7 miles beyond the town, winds over the thickly wooded hilltops of the ridge paralleling Tomales Bay to the headwaters of Drake's Estero (creek).

At 9.8 *m.* is the junction with a dirt road; R. here 0.1 *m.* to the RADIO CORPORATION OF AMERICA STATION (*open by arrangement at 28 Geary St., San Francisco*), the receiving station for RCA's San Francisco radiotelegraph terminal. The 1,500-acre station has 21 short-wave directive receiving antenna units, which tune in signals from Japan, China, the

Dutch East Indies, French Indo-China, the Philippine Islands, and Hawaii. The Beverage diversity system for receiving short-wave signals, in operation here, utilizes a bank of three antennae spaced approximately 1,000 feet apart. Each antenna is connected by a separate receiver to a specially built combining unit. Besides radio telegrams, the station receives occasional trans-Pacific programs from the Far East for rebroadcasting in America.

Southeast of this point the main side route follows the bleak, wind-swept slopes of POINT REYES. The half-mile distant wide beach (R) extends north in an unbroken straight line toward the hazy bluffs of Tomales Point and Bodega Head. The low-growing vegetation on the hill slopes is brightened in spring with myriads of tiny red, yellow, and purple flowers.

At 11 *m.* is the junction with a dirt road; R. here 0.7 *m.* to the UNITED STATES RADIO COMPASS STATION, which broadcasts compass bearings to ships at sea.

At 15 *m.* on the main side route, south of a barnyard gate near a farmhouse, is the junction with a dirt road; L. here 1.3 *m.* to the UNITED STATES COAST GUARD LIFE-SAVING STATION, facing DRAKE'S BAY from a cove in the lee of Point Reyes. The white-faced bluffs fringing the bay in an immense crescent-shaped sweep suggested the white cliffs of the English coast near Dover to Sir Francis Drake on June 17, 1579, when he took refuge here in the *Golden Hinde.* The Drake company, in the last of the five vessels with which it had sailed from England nearly two years earlier, was searching southward along the coast for a haven from the wind, the fog, and the bitter cold that had plagued them for weeks. In this sheltered bay, its waters as smooth as a mill pond, they found a "convenient and fit harborough." For nearly six weeks Drake and his men remained, reconditioning their boats and causing wonderment among awe-struck Indian visitors from villages for miles around (*see INDIANS*).

A small party led by Drake made a journey inland, where they found, as chaplain Francis Fletcher wrote, "a goodly country and fruitful soyle, stored with many blessings fit for the use of man." Drake named it Nova Albion (Lat., New England). On July 23, after religious ceremonies, they set sail again while Indians watched from the hilltops. But before "we went from thence," wrote Fletcher, "our generall caused to be set up a monument of our being there, as also of her maiesties and successors right and title to that Kingdom; namely, a plate of brasse, fast nailed to a greate and firme post, whereon is engrauen her graces name, and the day and yeare of our arrival there, and of the free giving up of the province and Kingdom, both by King and people, into her maiesties hands; together with her highnesses picture and armes, in a piece of sixpence current English monie, shewing itself by a hole made of purpose through the plate . . ."

Late in 1933 a chauffeur, on a hunting expedition with his employer at the Laguna Ranch, just east of Drake's Bay, picked up a slab of blackened metal near the roadside and wiping it off, uncovered in one corner what looked like the word "Drak." He placed the metal in the side pocket of the car.

A week later, as he drove past a point near the mouth of Corte Madera Creek, where the southern shore of Point San Quentin reaches away from the mainland (*see TOUR 2a*), he threw the plate away. On April 6, 1937, a motorist, stopped by a flat tire, picked up the plate near the highway. For months it lay unnoticed among his effects until one day, using it to tinker with his automobile, he noticed its crude engraving and took it to the head of the University of California history department.

Carefully cleaned, the plate revealed the inscription:

Bee It Knowne Vnto All Men By These Presents
Ivne 17 1579
By The Grace Of God And In The Name Of Herr
Maiesty Queen Elizabeth Of England And Herr
Successors Forever I Take Possesson Of This
Kingdome Whose King And People Freely Resigne
Their Right And Title In The Whole Land Vnto Herr
Maiesties Keepeing Now Named By Me And To Bee
Knowne Vnto All Men As Nova Albion
Francis Drake

After exhaustive investigation by metallurgists, chemists, museum cura-
tors, archeologists, and geologists, the plate was finally accepted in America
as the real "plate of brasse" left by Drake, though British scientists still
question the authenticity.

The main side route turns westward to POINT REYES LIGHTHOUSE (*open*),
19.9 *m.*, at the verge of a cliff on the tip of a knifelike headland, one of
the windiest points on the coast. The light was established in 1870. Its
white pyramidal tower is 294 feet above water. Throughout the summer,
when dense fog blankets the coast, the fog signal blasts almost constantly.
Back of the lighthouse are a storm-warning display and telegraph station.
So many ships have piled up on the treacherous rocks off Point Reyes that
the San Francisco newspapers are said to keep set up the headline, "Ship
Aground at Point Reyes." At dawn of November 29, 1938, a Seattle-
Oakland airliner off its course and hours overdue, landed on the water
1,000 yards offshore and was battered on the rocks by crashing surf, with
the loss of 5 lives.

OLEMA (Ind., Olemaloke: coyote valley), 168.8 *m.* (67 alt., 150
pop.), consists of three or four old frame buildings gathered around an
old-fashioned two-story frame hotel and a little steepled white church.

The moss-grown, masonry RUINS OF A LIME KILN occupy a
ravine near the roadside (R) at 172.8 *m.,* where lime from an outcrop
on Olema Creek was fired in the early 1850's. Against a cut in the
slope of the ravine tower the kiln's three chimneys—two of them still
standing and a third in ruins—resembling giant beehives in shape.

State 1 runs southeast to the junction, at 177.5 *m.,* with a paved
road.

Right on this road, along the western shore of a landlocked lagoon, to
the head of crescent-shaped Bolinas Bay, in the lee of cliff-edged Bolinas
Point, probably named for Francisco Bolaños, pilot of the Vizcaino expedition in 1602. The SITE OF THE BOLINAS LIGHTER WHARF (L), 0.4 *m.,* is
marked by a few piles. During the 1850's ox-drawn wagons with wooden
wheels—crosscut sections of huge tree trunks—hauled lumber to the wharf.
From this point their loads were carried by flat-bottomed lighters to cargo
vessels anchored in the bay.
At 1.7 *m.* is the junction with a paved road; R. here 2.6 *m.* to the RADIO
CORPORATION OF AMERICA STATION on a 1,500-acre tract on the western
shore of the Bolinas peninsula. RCA's San Francisco radio-telegraph
terminal has its sending station here for transmitting short-wave messages
across the Pacific. The transmitting equipment includes 46 antennae—
about half of them of the high-power short-wave directive type.
BOLINAS, 2.1 *m.* (10 alt., 125 pop.), circles the base of the headland.
A miniature church, parsonage, and houses built a half century ago are
neighbors of the shingled summer homes of San Franciscans. Low tide
brings out dozens of rubber-booted clam diggers. First settler here was
Gregorio Briones, owner of the 8,911-acre cattle domain of Baulinas Rancho,

whose daughter Maria's marriage to Francisco Sebrean, celebrated May 20, 1850, with feasting on a barbecued fat bullock and dancing on a floor of whip-sawed lumber, was Bolinas' first.

At Bolinas is a UNITED STATES COAST GUARD LIFE-SAVING STATION. The jagged rocks of Duxbury Reef, stretching seaward about 100 feet below the cliff-edged tableland of Duxbury Point, west of the town, have been the grave-yard of many ships. The Panama-San Francisco propeller steamer *Lewis* was battered to pieces here April 9, 1853, with the loss of all its freight and baggage and the narrow escape of 400 passengers.

STINSON BEACH (*accommodations; boats, tackle, and bait for surf fishing*), 182.1 *m.* (sea level, 130 pop.), a family resort thronged on holidays by vacationers, fronts a 3-mile white sand beach curving around Bolinas Bay; the surf is warm enough for bathing all year. The winters are so mild that swarms of big brown Monarch butterflies immigrate from the high Sierra. The settlement has evolved from a campground beside a grove of willows and alders near the beach at the end of the Dipsea (Lone Tree) Trail ("Dipsea" is an Indian corruption of "deep sea"); from the slopes of Mount Tamalpais (*see TOUR 2a*) to the beach, the trail is followed every year by cross-country hikers in the Dipsea Trail Race from Mill Valley (*see TOUR 2a*).

At 182.4 *m.* is the junction with the dirt Mount Tamalpais Road (*see TOUR 2a*).

State 1 twists upward, high above the crashing breakers. At 187.1 *m.* it winds along the crest of a knifelike ridge overlooking the timbered hollows of Muir Woods (*see TOUR 2a*) on one hand and ocean expanses on the other.

At 188.6 *m.* is the junction with the Muir Woods Road (*see TOUR 2a*).

At 188.8 *m.* is the junction with a dirt road.

> Right on this road 0.7 *m.* to MUIR BEACH (*swimming and fishing*), a sandy strip curving around the shores of Big Lagoon.

At 194.6 *m.* is the junction with US 101 (*see TOUR 2a*), with which State 1 unites into SAN FRANCISCO, 205.4 *m.* (18 alt., 634,-394 pop.) (*see SAN FRANCISCO*).

Section b. SAN FRANCISCO to MONTEREY; 133.1 m. State 1

The rugged flanks of the Peninsula ridge south of San Francisco crowd State 1 to the edge of blunt-faced mesas battered by the waves. The highway dips to wide, sandy beaches and climbs to tumbled heights above the surf. Swinging inland around the great curve of Monterey Bay, it crosses the fertile Pajaro Valley's apple orchards. Its way back to the shore leads through low, rolling land, fringed with sand dunes. Along the whole route the countryside—early, but thinly, settled—has a look of age about it, except where seaside resorts have replaced the whaling stations, the old fishing villages, the abandoned schooner land-ings.

Along this forbidding coast line in the autumn of 1769 struggled the

first white men to come by land into California—"that small company
of persons, or rather say skeletons, who had been spared by scurvy,
hunger and thirst," as their commander, Don Gaspar de Portolá, described them. They were searching for the "fine harbor sheltered from
all winds" of Monterey, over enthusiastically and misleadingly described
by Sebastián Vizcaíno in 1602—there to found a military port and a
mission.   The expedition included Portolá's aides, Capt. Don Fernando
de Rivera y Moncada, Lt. Don Pedro Fages, and army engineer Ensign
Miguel Constanso; the two Franciscan friars, Fray Juan Crespi and
Fray Francisco Gómez; Sgt. José Francisco de Ortega, with his 27
soldiers; and a troop of servants and Christian Indians from Lower
California.   The soldiers wore leather jackets fashioned of seven thick-
nesses of deerskin and carried bullhide shields, lances and broad-swords,
and short muskets.   At the head of the expedition, with its four pack-
train divisions of mules each, rode Portolá; at the rear, behind the
spare horses and mules and their guard, Rivera.

On September 30, two and a half months after leaving San Diego,
they came to the coast at the mouth of the Salinas River on Monterey
Bay.   The open gulf so little resembled the "fine harbor sheltered from
all winds" for which they were looking that they went on—now with
17 men on the sick list, 11 so ill that they had to be carried on litters
fastened with long poles to the mules.   As they continued northward
in 5- and 10-mile stages, toiling up steep grades and across deep arroyos,
often cutting their way through brush, they had to ration their rapidly
diminishing store of food.   Finally on October 31 they climbed to the
heights above San Pedro Point and saw the Gulf of the Farallones and
Point Reyes far to the north.   Forced to the unhappy conclusion that
they had overshot their mark, they turned eastward and then southward
down the Peninsula—having in the meantime discovered San Francisco Bay—and retraced their steps to Monterey Bay.   Once more failing to recognize the object of their search, they went on south to San
Diego, where Portolá reported his expedition a failure.

West from Van Ness Ave. in SAN FRANCISCO, 0 m., on Hayes
St. to Franklin St.; R. to Fulton St.; L. to Funston (13th) Ave.; L.
through Golden Gate Park into Nineteenth Ave. and south into Junipero Serra Blvd.

At 6.1 m. is the junction with Sloat Blvd.

Right on Sloat Blvd. to the junction with Sunset Blvd., 6.7 m. and L.
around Lake Merced to the SITE OF THE TERRY-BRODERICK DUEL, 9.6 m.,
at the southern tip of the lake, marked by two granite shafts, one bearing
the name "Broderick" and the other "Terry" in bronze letters. At dawn on
September 13, 1859, a United States Senator and a California Supreme
Court Chief Justice took their positions here with duelling pistols, 30
paces apart. They represented opposing factions in the struggle on the
issue of slavery which was tearing the Democratic Party in California
apart—Broderick the anti- and Terry the pro-slavery side. Broderick was
the son of an Irish stone mason, schooled in politics by Tammany Hall;
Terry, a Kentucky-born aristocrat, aligned with the "Chivalry" Democrats.
Terry had publicly attacked Broderick and the Douglas Democrats for
sailing under "the banner of the black Douglass, whose name is Frederick,

not Stephen." When Broderick replied in kind, Terry resigned from the bench and demanded a retraction; Broderick refused. Broderick was no match for his opponent; his shot, fired first, entered the ground only 9 feet from where he stood. Terry's shot entered his breast. He died three days later. A crowd of 30,000 people gathered at Portsmouth Square in San Francisco to hear the funeral oration.

State 1 turns southwest on Alemany Boulevard through neat truck gardens toward the ocean.

At 9.8 *m.* is the junction with Skyline Boulevard (State 5).

Left on Skyline Boulevard, up from gently rolling hill country to the crest of the forested Sierra Morena and down the ridge of the Peninsula. The highway skirts the western shore of long, narrow, fingerlike SAN ANDREAS LAKE, 10.3 *m.,* and CRYSTAL SPRINGS LAKE, 14 *m.,* along which the Portolá expedition traveled November 4 and 5, 1769 on their way southward.

Near the northern end of Crystal Springs Lake is the JEPSON LAUREL, 55 feet high and 22 feet 4 inches in circumference. It is called the Deathshead Tree because of the skull and crossbones carved in its fork in the days when the Spanish held barbecues beneath its branches.

State 5 crosses SKYLINE DAM, 15.4 *m.,* at the head of San Mateo Creek, and strikes westward from Crystal Springs Lake.

At 25 *m.* is the junction with King's Mountain Road; L. here 5 *m.* to the WOODSIDE STORE, the first opened between San Francisco and Santa Clara. It was built in 1854 by Dr. R. O. Tripp. It is a two-story structure with a peaked, shingled roof; the posts upholding the wide veranda, where horses were once hitched, are well-worn. The wooden sign over the porch was put up before the Civil War. Inside are the post office pigeon-holes, the old-fashioned counters, the oil lamps with their tin reflectors, the tin signs advertising plug chewing tobacco. As many as a thousand lumberjacks from the dense redwood forests roundabout—where 15 sawmills operated in a radius of 5 miles—called here for mail, food, and liquor.

Skyline Boulevard continues to the SKYLINE METHUSELAH REDWOOD (L), 26.2 *m.,* a lone giant dominating the countryside. More than 1,500 years old, it measures 55 feet in circumference. Its trunk is blackened by the repeated fires that long since felled its neighbors.

At 31.1 *m.* is the junction with the paved La Honda (the deep) Canyon road; R. on this road that winds down the slopes in a flicker of sun and shadow through clumps of redwoods and madrones 7 *m.* to LA HONDA (403 alt., 150 pop.), a mountain resort center (*cabins, campgrounds*) in the La Honda Grove of redwoods. In the winter of 1861-62, John L. Sears settled here and built the LA HONDA STORE, employing two newcomers to the vicinity, Jim and Bob Younger. Their stay was brief, for they left suddenly to rejoin the James gang in the Midwest for a bank robbery at Northfield, Minnesota, that landed them in the penitentiary.

Left from La Honda on a paved road 1 *m.* to the junction with a paved road; R. here 5 *m.* to the SAN MATEO COUNTY MEMORIAL RED-WOOD PARK, a 310-acre grove.

At 38.4 *m.* on State 5 is the junction with a dirt road; R. here 4 *m.* and L. to ISLAM SHRINE PARK, 7 *m.,* a 1,400-acre redwood grove.

State 5 continues down the east slope of the Sierra Morena to its junction with State 9 (*see TOUR 2b*) 45 *m.*

State 1 skirts hills velvety with matted chaparral that slope steeply to the water's edge, where flocks of sea birds perch on the crags.

SHARP PARK, 14.7 *m.,* a resort hamlet facing a wide, sandy beach, clusters near the northern edge of SHARP PARK MUNICIPAL

GOLF COURSE, 15.2 *m.*, part of the 480-acre park given the city of San Francisco by Mrs. Honora Sharp. The smooth green links on either side of the highway are indented (R) by tule-grown Laguna Salada.

ROCKAWAY BEACH, 16.4 *m.* (50 alt.), lies at the edge of a hill-sheltered cove.

The road cuts across the mouth of Pedro Valley to SAN PEDRO CREEK, 17.8 *m.*, guarded by lofty SAN PEDRO POINT. Near the mouth of the creek, by an Indian village, the Portolá expedition camped on October 31, 1769 and feasted on mussels pried from the rocks. After mass the next morning, Portolá sent Sgt. José Francisco de Ortega with a party to scout eastward. As they climbed to the top of the ridge, the vast expanse of San Francisco Bay, never before seen by white men, appeared in the distance. Before they could report their discovery, however, another party that went out November 2 to hunt and returned before nightfall had brought tidings of the "great arm of the sea, extending to the southeast farther than the eye could reach." On the morning of November 4, the expedition broke camp. Abandoning their trek in search of Monterey Bay, they climbed the ridge to the east, looking for the "port and a ship therein" only two days distant of which Indians had told Ortega.

The ragged leaves and green globes of row on row of silvery-green artichoke plants carpet fertile Pedro Valley, thriving here—and near Half Moon Bay—as nowhere else. Much of the United States supply of artichokes is grown in this fog-moistened coastal strip, where the first commercial planting was made in 1900. The plants are trimmed to the ground in the spring and watered and cultivated in summer to force the buds to mature in the fall and winter, although they mature naturally in June and July. The harvest season, beginning in August or September, reaches its peak in February, March, and April. About half the crop is hauled to market in California by truck and the rest shipped to the East in refrigerator cars. The plants, spaced four to six feet apart in rows, produce from three to four dozen buds apiece by the end of their third year, and up to twice that number in succeeding years, until their sixth year, when they are usually replaced.

On the south bank of San Pedro Creek is the junction with a graded road.

> Left on this road 1.3 *m.* to the decaying old two-story SANCHEZ ADOBE, the balconied ranchhouse of Rancho San Pedro, built by Don Francisco Sánchez in 1842. It stands on the site of an older house, which is said to have been rebuilt in 1817 with timbers from a ship wrecked on San Pedro Point.

State 1 climbs over the hump of MONTARA MOUNTAIN; on the summit above San Pedro Point, Portolá's men at noon of October 31, 1769, sick and hungry and exhausted from the tortuous climb through matted brush up the southern slope, looked out over a vast sweep of sea and land—Twin Peaks and Mount Tamalpais rising to the north, Point Reyes curving out to sea far beyond, and the rocky Farallon Islands jutting from the misty horizon. The road dips to the spot where the Portolá party stopped the night of October 30, 1769, in despair, their way northward blocked by the steep slopes.

The rolling land east of MONTARA, 22 m. (300 pop.), is checkered with fields that supply large quantities of everlasting-flowers. The blossoms are cut from their stems, mounted on fine wire, and dried for about 36 hours. The industry, begun in 1925, has achieved a production of 20,000,000 or more blossoms in recent years.

As State 1 continues past plots of artichokes and brussels sprouts, the stout tower of POINT MONTARA LIGHT and the wire-webbed steel masts of a UNITED STATES NAVAL RADIO COMPASS STATION appear (R) at 22.7 m. on Point Montara, near a half-submerged circle of upstanding rocks.

MOSS BEACH, 23.3 m. (75 alt., 300 pop.), is a tiny cluster of weather-beaten houses sheltered by wind-battered cypresses. From the rocks along the shore delicate sea mosses can be gathered. The strangely beautiful marine gardens offshore are famous for their flora.

The highway rounds gently curving HALF MOON BAY, 25.5 m., whose blue waters stretch southward, breaking in hissing foam on a long white beach guarded by the rocky headland of PILLAR POINT, which navigator Francisco de Gali sighted from his galleon in 1585. He reported: ". . . we passed by a very high and fair land with many trees, wholly without snow; there likewise we found great store of seals; whereby it is to be presumed and certainly to be believed, that there are many rivers, bays and havens along by those coasts . . ." The harbor, protected by a submerged reef off the point, became a port of call for whalers and traders—and, more recently, for rum runners.

The town of HALF MOON BAY, 30.3 m. (10 alt., 1,000 pop.), now populated largely by Italians and Portuguese, is a quiet farm village surrounded by neatly laid out fields of artichokes and brussels sprouts. The weary men of the Portolá expedition pitched camp near the mouth of Pilarcitos Creek, at the northern edge of town, on the rainy night of October 28, 1769, and spent a wet and miserable weekend—their medicine gone and their food running low—before they could gather enough strength to move on. The creek, extending up Pilarcitos Valley, was later the boundary between Tiburcio Vásquez' (no relative of the bandit) part of Rancho El Corral de Tierra (the enclosure of earth) and Candelario Miramontes' Rancho Miramontes. The two *rancheros* built their low-roofed, rambling adobe houses on opposite banks of the creek in the 1840's, affording each other company at a time when the region was a wilderness roamed by grizzly bears. Around their houses grew up a settlement that went by the name Spanishtown for 40 years or more after it was platted in 1863.

State 1 continues past small farms where large whitewashed barns and small weather-beaten farmhouses are sheltered from the wind by lines of dark, ragged cypresses. The rising hills curve gently, splotched in the hollows with dusky chaparral.

The village of PURISIMA (purest), 34.5 m. (46 alt.), once a lively town on José María Alviso's Rancho Cañada de Verde y Arroyo

de la Purísima, is ghostly and deserted now. Its weathered gray buildings stand among mosshung cypresses and eucalyptus trees, their windows broken, their stairs falling in, their facades rudely stuck with gay
circus posters.

From a VIEWPOINT at 38.6 m., tawny bluffs bordered by surf
stretch south. The highway descends to the beach at TUNITAS
GLEN, 38.8 m. (25¢ a car for camping).

The farm hamlet of SAN GREGORIO (St. Gregory), 42.1 m.
(100 alt., 107 pop.), in a valley where suave hills sweep up to the
Sierra Morena crest, is near the mouth of San Gregorio Creek. The
place so enchanted Fray Crespi of the Portolá expedition that he proposed it for a mission site, naming it Santo Domingo—but others called
it the Valley of the Curses of the Soldiers, for "they were sick and tired
and hungry," as diarist Miguel Costanso wrote. They stayed two days
to rest.

Although PESCADERO (fishing place), 49.5 m. (56 alt., 979
pop.), was named for Pescadero Creek's once plentiful supply of speckled trout, the town's predominantly Portuguese inhabitants neither
catch nor sell fish. Pescadero's cluster of prim white buildings give it
the appearance of a New England village. It was long the whitest
town in the State; when the S.S. Columbia was wrecked near Pigeon
Point, most of her cargo of white paint drifted ashore and, salvaged
by the inhabitants, was used lavishly.

At 50.5 m. is the junction with a dirt road.

> Right here 2 m. to PEBBLE BEACH, famous for its polished pebbles—
> small agates, jaspers, opals, moonstones, moss agates, and water-drops
> (white pebbles with drops of water in their centers).

South of Pescadero State 1 crosses low mesas that break off abruptly
in bluffs, jagged with deep caves and gulches created by the waves.
The PIGEON POINT LIGHTHOUSE, 55.8 m. (open 2-4 Tues., Fri., Sat.),
overlooks a rock-bound coast, on whose headland the Boston clipper
Carrier Pigeon was wrecked May 6, 1853. The tower was built in
1872. The powerful lens was used first on the New England and later
on the South Atlantic coast, where it was buried in the sand during the
Civil War—according to one story, to keep it from falling into Confederate hands.

The road curves inland from PUNTA DEL ANO NUEVO
(New Year's Point), stretching out to sea at 63.5 m., the NEW YEAR'S
POINT LIGHTHOUSE at its tip. This was the first important spot
sighted by Sebastián Vizcaíno's crew when they sailed from Monterey
January 3, 1602; they named it for the season of the year.

The pine-forested mountainsides slope steeply to the sea, crowding
the highway to the edge of a narrow bench. Then State 1 drops to a
cove to travel along a roadway carved from the cliffs. The wide beach
here, where the long rollers arch in transparent blue-green hues and
crash in a welter of foam, was once the greatest hazard on the Santa
Cruz to Pescadero stage line. Since the coaches could travel along

the hard-packed, sandy strip only at low tide, a delay in schedule was apt to prove disastrous. The more adventurous drivers enjoyed timing the trip down to the last second so that they could race the tide to safety, much to the consternation of their passengers.

At the mouth of Waddell Creek, 65.5 *m.*, "a very deep stream that flowed out from between very high hills of the mountain chain," the Portolá expedition camped for three nights, beginning October 20, 1769. On October 22 "the day dawned, overcast and gloomy; the men were wet and wearied for want of sleep, as they had no tents, and it was necessary to let them rest. . . . What excited our wonder on this occasion was that all the sick, for whom we feared the wetting might prove exceedingly harmful, suddenly found their pains very much relieved. This was the reason for giving the canyon the name of La Salud" (health).

The highway swings inland, climbing in hairpin twists up a mountain spur, with excellent views of the coast to north and south. From the heights it descends to a forested canyon, traverses a narrow, logged-over valley, reaches seaside terraces once more, and cuts through alternating dairy farms and fields of artichokes and brussels sprouts.

The countryside around DAVENPORT, 75.5 *m.* (90 alt., 600 pop.), a company town near a large cement plant, is liberally powdered with lime dust. In the 1850's Davenport Landing was the site of whaling operations, directed by Capt. John P. Davenport, who devised a stay-at-home method of hunting. The whalers lived in cabins on the shore, from which they sallied forth in whaling boats when a whale was sighted. They towed their catch to the beach and there tried the blubber in huge pots. The Portuguese who came from the Azores to settle hereabout built lookouts with bells and stationed watchmen there to sound a warning when they sighted whales to summon the others from their farms to their boats. The heyday of whaling lasted until the 1880's, when the mammals began to disappear.

State 1 continues along the coast, crossing the mouths of one stream-hollowed gully after another, which the Portolá expedition crossed with infinite difficulty in October, 1769. At the mouth of Coja Creek, 79 *m.*, their camp site on the 18th, they had to build a bridge of poles and earth. The next day they encountered seven ravines in all, clambering down one side and up another. One had such steep sides that the mule bearing the olla (cooking pot) fell to the bottom.

SANTA CRUZ, 86.8 *m.* (15 alt., 14,395 pop.), faces south across Monterey Bay from its perch beside a broad, curving beach at the edge of the timbered Santa Cruz Mountains. When the Portolá party planted a cross on the bank of the river which they named the San Lorenzo, on October 17, 1769, they noticed redwoods and "roses of Castille" but—to Fray Crespí's disappointment—no Indians. Only 22 years later, however, a fellow Franciscan, Fray Fermín Francisco de Lasuen, said mass in the presence of a great gathering of Indians and raised another cross to consecrate the site of a mission. Misión la Exaltación de la Santa Cruz (the elevation of the holy cross) was formally founded two months later, September 25, 1791, when Don Hermenegildo Sal, *comandante* of the Presidio of San Francisco, took the name of King Carlos IV. Fathers Alonzo Salazar and Baldomero López began their work, equipped with an image of Our Father Saint Francis, a painting of Our Lady of Sorrows, and gifts from nearby missions—including barley for seed, cows, sheep, oxen, horses and mules. For more than two years they baptized the heathen without even the roof of a church above their heads, for the first church was not completed and dedicated until March 10, 1794.

On May 12, 1797, the schooner *Concepción* anchored in the bay with a boatload of colonists for the Villa de Branciforte, the Spanish Government's third, last, and least successful experiment in pueblo founding. The instructions of Governor Diego de Borica for the pueblo, named in honor of the Mexican Viceroy, the Marquis de Branciforte, had been sensible and to the point: "An adobe house to be built for each settler so that the prevalent state of things at San Jose and Los Angeles, where the settlers still live in tule huts, being unable to build better buildings without neglecting their fields, may be avoided; the houses not to cost over $200." The government had promised each colonist a musket, a plow, a few animals, and a loan of 116 pesos. Unfortunately, the farmers, mechanics, artisans, and sailors for whom Borica had called proved to be a tatterdemalion crew of vagabonds and ex-convicts. Futhermore, none of the houses was ready when they arrived. Don Alberto Córdoba, a Spanish Army engineer, arrived in August to supervise digging an irrigation canal, erecting public buildings, and building houses—all according to plans laid out in Mexico— but he got little further than submitting estimates for the work, since funds failed to arrive.

The model village across the river was a sore trial for the mission padres, who regarded it with suspicious anxiety—justifiably, as it turned out. When the Buenos Aires privateersman Hippolyte de Bouchard sacked Monterey in November, 1818, the padres retired in haste to Mission Santa Clara, leaving the mission in the hands of Branciforte's inhabitants for safekeeping. The protectors found the stock of aguardiente in the padres' cellar pleasantly useful for bolstering their morale. The damage to the church and its furnishings was considerable. Unfortunately, since Bouchard never appeared for his scheduled raid, they could not blame him for the depredations as they had planned.

The mission, secularized in 1834, fell into decay, while Branciforte survived. By 1840, when twenty ranchos had been granted in the vicinity, whalers were finding it a good place to buy fresh vegetables for scurvy-ridden crews. A new town grew up around the mission plaza, borrowing the mission's name. Under the Yankee regime it developed a fine trade, shipping lumber from the redwood-forested hinterland. One of its first industrial plants was Elihu Anthony's foundry, which in 1848 was turning out light-weight iron picks for the mines and cast-iron plows, the first made in California. In 1866 the city of Santa Cruz was granted a charter by the State. Meanwhile neighboring Branciforte preserved the easy-going ways of old. As late as July, 1867, the bull ring was gay with red flags and noisy with firecrackers on bull fight days—"Admission and seats—$1.00. Standing room on the sunny side—50 cents." Finally in 1907 Branciforte, now a mere suburb of its former rival, was incorporated in Santa Cruz.

A reproduction of MISSION SANTA CRUZ (*adm. 25¢*), on Emmet St. facing the Upper Plaza, was built in 1931 about 75 yards from the old site. The original structure built in 1793 suddenly collapsed with a loud crash a month after an earthquake had weakened its walls on January 9, 1857. About one-half the size of the original but identical in proportions, the mission has a square bell-tower topped with a dome, overlooking one-story porticoed living quarters at one side and a rear garden court. It houses old relics—richly ornamented vestments, a candle chandelier, and a statue of Our Lady of Sorrows brought from Monterey on muleback. The brick CHURCH OF THE HOLY CROSS, facing the Plaza, was built in 1858 and rebuilt in 1889. Back of the mission, on the brow of the hill, the ancient headstones of the eucalyptus-shaded graveyard are half hidden by tangled myrtles. The adobe NEARY HOUSE, R. from the mission on School St., was formerly the headquarters of the corporal of the mission guard. The adobe RODRIGUEZ HOUSE, joined to it by a 5-foot adobe wall, has been in the possession of descendants of José Antonio Rodríguez ever since 1838.

The SANTA CRUZ MUNICIPAL PIER, at the foot of Pacific Ave., projects into the surf from the half-mile strip of smooth white sand bordering the bay. At the western end of the boardwalk is the Casino, and nearby are a bathing pavilion and pleasure pier.

Right from Pacific Ave. into 2.8-mile West Cliff Dr. On the drive are the SANTA CRUZ LIGHT STATION (*open 2-4 Tues., Thurs.*); the 565-acre expanse of the municipal recreation ground, LAVEAGA PARK, still in its natural state; and SWANTON NATURAL BRIDGES BEACH STATE PARK, in a sandy, cliff-edged cove where jutting rocks have been carved into natural bridges by the waves.

Santa Cruz is at the junctions with State 9 (*see TOUR 2b*) and State 17 (*see TOUR 2b*).

East of Santa Cruz State 1 passes through farms and nurseries to SOQUEL, 91.1 *m.*, in a canyon on Soquel Creek, now among bulb gardens, orchards, and vineyards, but a booming lumber town in the days when the hills roundabout were forested with redwoods. Marching toward Soquel Creek October 10, 1769, Portolá and his men saw "low hills well forested with high trees of a red color, not known to us. They have a very different leaf from cedars, and although the wood resembles cedar somewhat in color, it is very different, and has not the same odor; moreover, the wood of the trees that we found is very brittle. In this region there is a great abundance of these trees and because none of the expedition recognizes them, they are named redwoods from their color." Awe-struck Pedro Fages wrote: "Here are trees of girth so great that eight men placed side by side with extended arms are unable to embrace them."

Right from Soquel on a paved road to CAPITOLA, 1.5 *m.*, a long-established resort facing NEW BRIGHTON BEACH STATE PARK in sheltered Soquel Cove.

Over the route of State 1 on their way to Santa Cruz by way of San Juan (*see TOUR 2b*) ran the mail stages from San Jose. The most daring driver on the line in the 1860's was swaggering "Cock-eyed Charley" Parkhurst, outstanding even among teamsters for his profanity. A naturally truculent expression, enhanced by a black patch over a missing eye and tobacco-juice stains on mouth and chin, made Charley the toughest looking fellow in the region. Not until Charley's death in 1879 was it discovered that "he" was a woman. Born Charlotte Parkhurst in New Hampshire in 1806, "Charley" had turned up in California in 1848. More than 50 years before introduction of woman suffrage, this enterprising Amazon had voted, "his" name appearing on the Santa Cruz Great Register for 1866.

At 94.2 *m.* on State 1 is the junction with a paved road.

Right on this road 0.5 *m.* to SEACLIFF STATE PARK, where the beach affords fine surf bathing and clamming. At the end of a pier stands an old hulk, one of the concrete ships built during the World War, anchored here by an enterprising night club owner as a dance hall. Although a large crack yawns in the hull—and signs reading "DANGER" are numerous—fishermen cast their lines from the prow (*10¢ charge*) in serene indifference.

APTOS (Ind., the meeting of the streams), 94.6 *m.* (100 pop.), at the base of oak- and chaparral-clad hills, was, long a fashionable resort, but its OCEAN VIEW HOTEL (L) is deserted today. Late in the nineteenth century Claus Spreckels, founder of the State's first sugar dynasty, who built a great sugar beet refinery near Watsonville, bought up most of Don Rafael Castro's Rancho Aptos. His estate—with its race track and its mansion containing an elevator, the first south of San Francisco—became the wonder of the countryside, especially when Spreckels welcomed as a visitor the King of the Hawaiian Islands.

From the hill country east of Aptos, State 1 descends across the broad, level Pajaro Valley, watered by the river that the Portolá expedition named the Río del Pájaro (river of the bird) because they found on its banks a great eagle stuffed with straw by the Indians. The Pajaro Valley is a vast sweep of apple orchards—in springtime snowy with blossoms, whose petals eddy in fragrant showers on the breeze. In the summer, when the orchards are luxuriantly green, the trees—bellflowers and pippins—drooping under their burden of fruit, are propped up to prevent their branches breaking. Along the way are stands selling cold cider.

The orchard hamlet of FREEDOM, 104.4 *m.* (115 alt., 350 pop.), went by the name of Whiskey Hill—up until the era of sobriety inaugurated by prohibition.

The brisk modern trade center of the apple country, WATSON-VILLE, 106.4 *m.* (25 alt., 8,344 pop.), on both sides of the Pajaro River (which has often overflowed its banks and flooded the town), was laid out in 1852 by Judge John H. Watson and D. S. Gregory on land purchased from Don Sebastián Rodríguez' Rancho Bolsa del Pájaro. Many other settlers dispensed with the formality of purchase, squatting on the rest of Rodríguez' land before his numerous heirs could claim it after his death in 1855. Jesse D. Carr's success with his apple orchard in 1853 led others to plant trees. Today Watsonville ships as many as 6,500,000 boxes of apples in a year—as well as vast quantities of strawberries, apricots, lettuce, and garden crops. The town has more than 75 packing houses and numerous evaporating plants, canneries, and cider and vinegar factories.

Watsonville's Plaza in the center of town was the scene of bull and bear fights and horse races were held on its main street in the days when the townsmen spent their Sundays—after dutiful attendance at early mass—gambling, dancing, and racing. The small cannon in the square is the one fired from the Pacific Mail steamship *Oregon* as it steamed into San Francisco Bay in October, 1850, announcing California's admission into the Union.

Watsonville is at the junction with State 152 (*see TOUR 2b*).

Right from Watsonville on paved Beach Road 5 *m.* to SUNSET BEACH STATE PARK, a broad sandy strip bordering Monterey Bay.

At the foot of the hill on the stretch of road south of Watsonville the stages from Natividad and Monterey used to meet and race into town—the drivers hunched forward, whipping their four-horse teams to a gallop, the lumbering coaches swaying and careening while the cheering male passengers made bets and the ladies fainted quietly away.

On the edge of a bluff overlooking the Pajaro Valley (R), 109.3 *m.,* stands the rapidly disintegrating HOUSE OF GLASS, the Casa Materna (mother house) of the history-making Vallejo family, once the wonder and envy of the countryside because of its glass windows. The mansion was built, supposedly about 1824, by Don Ignacio Vincente Ferrer Vallejo, on the Rancho Bolsa de San Cayetano (pocket of St. Gaetan). The two-story structure has walls 20 inches thick, joists and window frames of hewn redwood, and a shingle roof upheld by a single beam; the floor of its two downstairs rooms is of hard-packed earth. According to legend, the upper veranda was glassed-in—at a time when glass windows were all but unknown in California—because Vallejo received a shipment of twelve dozen windows instead of the one dozen he had ordered. The Vallejo family consisted of eight daughters and five sons—of whom the most distinguished was Mariano, the founder of Sonoma.

From the Vallejo ranch the young rebels, Juan Bautista Alvarado and José Castro, led an army of 75 armed with antiquated muskets on Monterey in November, 1835, bound to overthrow Gov. Nicolás Gutiérrez and proclaim the "free and sovereign State" of Alta California. The army set out to the martial strains of a fife and drum corps recruited from San Juan. On the way they were joined by 50 daredevil Yankee riflemen, led by the reckless Tennesseean, Isaac Graham, who had turned from trapping and hunting to the more profitable business of operating a whisky distillery in the Pajaro Valley. A single shot was enough to capture Monterey—one cannon ball, fired by a lawyer who had to consult a book to learn how to fire it; it struck the Governor's house, reducing him to such abject terror that he surrendered forthwith. Young Alvarado wrote to Vallejo: "It is wonderful, Uncle, with what order our expedition has been conducted. Everybody shouts *vivas,* for California is free."

The rancho of 1847 was described by young Lt. William T. Sherman, who called early one morning on one of the sons, Juan Antonio: "It was on a high point of the plateau, overlooking the plain of the Pajaro, on which were grazing numbers of horses and cattle. The house was of adobe, with a long range of adobe huts occupied by semicivilized Indians, who at that time did all the labor of a ranch, the herding and marking of cattle, the breaking of horses, and cultivating the little patches of wheat and vegetables which constituted all the farming of that day. Everything about the house looked deserted, and, seeing a small Indian boy leaning up against a post, I approached him and asked him in Spanish, 'Where is the master?' 'Gone to the Presidio.' 'Is anybody in the house?' 'No.' 'Is it locked up?' 'Yes.' 'Is no one about who can get in?' 'No.' 'Have you any meat?' 'No.' 'Any flour or grain?' 'No.' 'Any chickens?' 'No.' 'Any eggs?' 'No.' 'What do you live on?' "Nada' (nothing)."

As the forested hills retreat to the foot of distant mountains, the way lies through rolling fields and pastures where white-faced cattle graze.

The warm-colored marsh grasses of ELKHORN SLOUGH, 114.6 *m.,* crossed by a concrete bridge usually lined with fishermen (*tackle, bait, boats for rent*), are the haunt of wild fowl. A peculiar form of marine algae colors the water red.

At 115.1 *m.* is the junction with an oiled road.

Right on this road is MOSS LANDING, 0.1 *m.* (10 alt., 100 pop.), a whaling station and schooner landing established about 1865 by Capt. Charles Moss. So large was its shipping business that at times wagons from the Salinas Valley farms were lined up for 5 miles, waiting their turn to' unload. Up until 1920 as many as five whales a week were handled here, despite the complaints of inhabitants for miles around when the wind blew its odors inland; the Board of Health finally declared it a public menace. The fish reduction plant that took its place was scarcely an improvement in an olfactory sense.

CASTROVILLE, 117.7 *m.* (819 pop.), was founded in 1864 by Juan B. Castro on his father's rancho, which bore the curious name of Bolsa Nueva y Morro Coyo (new pocket and lame Moor)—in reference, according to one conjecture, to a lame black horse, and according to another, to the black soil (since the Spaniards used the word *morro* to mean anything black). Once predominantly Portuguese in population, it is today mostly Swiss-Italian.

State 1, turning seaward, crosses the SALINAS RIVER, 120.7 *m.,* which the Portolá expedition followed to the coast in its search for

Monterey Bay.   Arriving near its mouth on September 30, the men
spent a week exploring the shores of the bay, but—as Sgt. Ortega wrote
—"not finding the shelter and protection ascribed . . . to the port
caused us doubt, since we saw a gulf . . . large enough to hold thousands of vessels, but with little protection from some winds." After
consultation, they resumed their weary journey northward.   As the
highway skirts sand dunes along the shore, the hazy blue Santa Lucia
Mountains loom ahead above Monterey on its curved sweep of bay,
gleaming in the sun.

The entrance to HOTEL DEL MONTE, 132.1 *m.*, leads to a woodland
maze of terraces, courts, gardens, promenades and road ways, surrounding the large white hostelry.   The hotel is faintly reminiscent of the
Spanish Colonial regime.   It is California's oldest large resort hotel;
it plays such a part in the life of the region that it has come to be
regarded almost as a public institution.   Its prestige value makes it
particularly popular with honeymooners who yearn to have a glimpse
of the haute monde.   It is also popular with businessmen who like to
temper the rigor of their conventions with luxurious comfort.   In the
surrounding forest are bridle trails, a racetrack, steeplechasing and cross-
country racing courses, skeet and trapshooting grounds, archery and
badminton courts, and swimming pools, golf courses, and polo fields
where championship matches are played.   The first hotel was erected
in 1880; the second in 1887; the present one in 1924.   The Art Gallery (*open 2-5*) exhibits works of local artists.

MONTEREY, 133.1 *m.* (0-600 alt., 9,141 pop.) (*see MON-
TEREY*).

Section c. MONTEREY to LAS CRUCES, 217 m. State 1.

In 1897 young Dr. John Roberts tended the sick on the isolated
ranches south of Monterey, riding long, slow miles on horseback over
the narrow wagon road that twisted in and out of the foothills and
canyons of the Santa Lucia Range.   Later he traveled along the coast
from San Luis Obispo to Monterey on foot, sketching—planning the
road in which he tried for years to arouse interest.   Roberts estimated
that $50,000 would pay for its construction.   When he could raise
only half that sum, he carried his fight to the State Legislature.   One
ardent legislator—Senator James Rigdon—was largely responsible for
the passage of the bill in 1919 that authorized construction of the road.
In 1920 the first surveys were made and the work was begun.   Hundreds of men—free and convict—labored for 18 years; not $50,000 but
$10,000,000 was spent; lives and equipment were lost in the sea; and
in June 1937, the section of State 1, known as the Carmel-San Simeon
Highway, was opened to the public.

In MONTEREY, 0 *m.* is the junction of Del Monte Avenue and
Washington St.

Right from Monterey on Washington St.; R. on Lighthouse Avenue; R.
on First Street; and L. on Ocean View Avenue along the shore to HOPKINS

MARINE STATION OF STANFORD UNIVERSITY (R), 1.7 *m.*, on Cabrillo Point, founded by Timothy Hopkins in 1892. Its studies of oceanic biology include a hydrobiological survey of Monterey Bay. It has a collection of marine life for the observation of students and visitors.

In a pine forest by Monterey Bay is PACIFIC GROVE, 2.3 *m.* (47 alt., 5,558 pop.), a family recreation and residential community. The site of the first Chautauqua in the West, it was founded by Methodist Episcopal Church members in 1874, as a center for conferences, meetings, and outings; it still, by deed restriction, forbids the sale of liquor within its boundaries. The MUNICIPAL MUSEUM (*open 2-5 daily except Mon.; free*), on Forest Ave., displays collections of California butterflies and Monterey Bay marine life among other exhibits. The salt-water MUNICIPAL PLUNGE (*adm. children 15¢, adults 30¢; suit rental 15¢*) is near the bathing beach, fishing pier, and bath house. Glass-bottom boats (*10-4 daily; fare 25¢*) afford a view of underwater plant and animal life in the MARINE GARDENS offshore.

Left from Pacific Grove on Asilomar Boulevard 0.5 *m.* to the BUTTERFLY TREES, two pines that serve as the refuge every fall for thousands of huge brown, red, and white butterflies (*amosiae plexippus*) from east of the Rocky Mountains. One year they settle on one tree, the next year on the other—to the amazement of scientists.

As the road continues westward round POINT PINOS at the southwestern extremity of Monterey Bay, the rocky coastline, lashed by foaming breakers, grows more and more rugged.

At 3.5 *m.* is the junction with a paved road; L. here 0.3 *m.* to POINT PINOS LIGHTHOUSE (*open 1-4 Tues., Thurs.*), built in 1872, which guards the coast with a white oscillating light and an electric fog siren.

The snowy crests of sand dunes fringe the beach at ASILOMAR (Ind., a place of retreat), 6.2 *m.*, the 60-acre resort opened by the Young Women's Christian Association when the growth of Pacific Grove crowded religious conventions out of the city.

The toll gate to the Seventeen-Mile Drive, 6.4 *m.* (*50¢ per car*) opens on a dirt road winding through Monterey pines and scrub oaks, their branches hung with long streamers of Spanish moss. In a filled-in lake bed (R) at 6.9 *m.* is the SAND PLANT of the Del Monte Properties Company, only one of its kind on the Pacific Coast, which washes and dries sand for bathing beaches. The Seventeen-Mile Drive skirts MOSS BEACH, running along a wide mesa between dazzling white sand dunes, to POINT JOE 8.6 *m.*, named for a Japanese squatter who lived here many years. It overlooks the surging deep indigo currents of the RESTLESS SEA, where three large vessels have foundered.

At 11.5 *m.* is the junction with a paved road; R. 0.1 *m.* to CYPRESS POINT, commanding crescent-shaped CARMEL BAY. Along the cliffs grow Monterey cypresses. Once widely distributed over this section of the coast, they now make their last stand in the limited area between Cypress Point and Point Lobos (*see below*). Robert Louis Stevenson compared them to "ghosts fleeing before the wind." Clutching at precarious footholds in the face of ocean gales, they lift their gnarled and twisted branches, hung with rags of yellow moss, in grotesque postures.

A lone cypress, the most painted and photographed in the forest, crowns MIDWAY POINT (R), 12.4 *m.* The strangely contorted GHOST TREE, 13.1 *m.*, worn white by spray and wind, appears as the road rounds PESCADERO POINT.

The Seventeen-Mile Drive curves through the spacious homes and gardens of PEBBLE BEACH, 13.8 *m.*, a socially exclusive playground with its Del Monte Lodge, sport field, and golf course.

At 14 *m.* is the junction with a paved road; R. 0.3 *m.* to STILLWATER COVE, with its arch rock offshore, its fishing club and bathing beach, yacht harbor and marine gardens (*glass-bottom boats, 50¢*).

At 15.9 *m.* is the junction with a paved road; L. here, past the forest sheltered homes of CARMEL WOODS, to another toll gate at the junction with State 1, 17.4 *m.*

From Del Monte Ave. and Washington St. in Monterey, 0 *m.,* State 1 follows Washington St., turns L. on Abrego St., and cuts across the Monterey Peninsula to the junction with Seventeen-Mile Drive (*see above*), 2.3 *m.* At 2.8 *m.* is the junction with Carmel Road.

Right on Carmel Rd. is CARMEL, 1 *m.* (220 alt., 3,000 pop.), art center of the Monterey Peninsula, affectionately termed "The Village," facing the dazzling white beach of Carmel Bay from pine- and oak-forested slopes. The village dates from about 1904, when Mary Austin, James Hopper, George Sterling and other young writers and artists built small shacks in the woods. Determined to keep out modern inventions, they fought introduction of paved streets, gas and electricity, and jails. As dilettantes, charlatans, and idlers flocked in after them, the town grew. The divergence of point of view between artists and non-artists led to sharp local battles. By and large the "artists" have won, for Carmel still has no public utilities of its own, no house numbers, no mail delivery; and it forbids cutting down of trees without a police permit. The business buildings bordering the main street with its pine-dotted parkway and the dwellings along the residence streets meandering through untidy flower patches are a weird conglomerate of Spanish, Italian, French, and English styles, built according to the individual taste of each owner. The community supports a little theater, a small art gallery, a forum for visiting lecturers, a music society that presents winter concerts and an annual Bach festival. Among the better-known residents have been the scientist David Starr Jordan; photographers Arnold Genthe and Edward Weston; artists Maynard Dixon, Jo Mora, Armin Hansen, Rollo Peters, William Ritchel; writers Ambrose Bierce, Don Blanding, Martin Flavin, Lincoln Steffens, Jesse Lynch Williams, Rhys Williams, and Harry Leon Wilson. The FOREST THEATER, in a grove of trees on Mountain View Ave., founded in 1919, is said to have been California's first open-air community theater. A village showplace is TOR HOUSE with its tower rising from Carmel Point, the home and workshop of the poet Robinson Jeffers, built by his own hand from natural rock.

At 4.2 *m.* on State 1 is the junction with an oiled road.

Left on this road through the farms, orchards and pastures of CARMEL VALLEY, along the Carmel River between the chaparral-clad Santa Lucia Mountains. The valley was the setting for Mary Austin's *Ysidro,* an idyll of mission days. Beyond the SAN CLEMENTE DAM (R), 15.5 *m.,* built (1921) to impound the Carmel River, the road climbs through lonely cattle ranches into more rugged country.

At 24 *m.* is the junction with a dirt road; R. on this road is JAMESBURG, 27.1 *m.* (*cabins available*), founded in 1867 by John James, but now little more than a country store.

The road climbs up jagged forested mountain slopes to MADRONE FLATS, 31 *m.,* which provides a splendid view. It drops sharply downward through chaparral dotted with yucca trees, sycamores, and maples.

In a heavily wooded canyon is TASSAJARA (Ind., meat curing place) SPRINGS, 41.3 *m.* (1,700 alt.), hot mineral springs (160° F) flowing from boulders beside a rushing stream. Under one of the present bath houses is a crude tub hollowed out of a large rock by Indians, who believed the waters to have magic qualities. The resort has a large hotel, built in the 1890's of sandstone quarried nearby; two large sanitary bath houses, 14 private bathrooms, tubs and showers, and natural vapor baths; two plunges, a swimming pool, an outdoor dance floor, and stables.

At 4.5 *m.* on State 1 is the junction with an oiled road.

Right on this road 0.6 *m.* to MISIÓN SAN CARLOS BORROMEO DEL RIO CARMELO (Mission St. Charles Borromeo of the Carmel River), on the cypress-dotted slopes overlooking Carmel Bay. To the three Carmelite priests of Sebastián Vizcaíno's expedition who visited the site in 1602, it so closely resembled the landscape around Mount Carmel in Palestine that they named it for the birthplace of their order. The mission, second in California, was founded in 1770 by Junípero Serra at Monterey and moved to its present site the following year. It remained the home of Serra, who was buried here beside his devoted co-worker, Padre Juan Crespi, at his death in 1784. The present church was founded July 7, 1793 by Serra's successor as *Padre-presidente* of the missions, Fermin Francisco de Lasuen. The mission reached the height of its prosperity in 1794, when its Indian population numbered 927. After its secularization it fell rapidly into ruin, overrun by birds and squirrels. The restoration of the mission was begun in the 1880's, when the ruins of the fallen roof were cleared off the graves of Serra and Crespi. The roof, shingled at that time, was later replaced by one of tile. The walls of the church, five feet thick, built of sandstone blocks cemented with lime made by the Indians from abalone shells, remain standing on their granite foundation; they curve in a parabolic arch to the ceiling, which is supported by stone and wooden pillars. To the left of the main entrance are the baptistry and font, carved by neophytes, and the modern mortuary chapel (1924) with its beams and murals reproducing the original decorations and its monument to Serra (Jo Mora, sculptor). To the right of the entrance, hollowed sandstone steps lead to the balcony, lighted by an irregular star-shaped window. The interior has many of its original paintings and statues. In the sanctuary are buried Serra, Crespi, Lasuen, and López. Serra's grave is marked by the simple wooden cross placed on it at the time of his death by an Indian convert. The mission is the setting today of the annual Serra Pageant in August.

From its crossing of the CARMEL RIVER, 5.1 *m.*, State 1 climbs out of the valley, past the CARMELITE MONASTERY (L), 6.2 *m.*, where the Discalced Nuns of Our Lady and Saint Therese live in absolute seclusion.

Just beyond the boundary of POINT LOBOS STATE PARK is the entrance (R) to POINT LOBOS RESERVE, 7 *m.* (*adm. 50¢ per car; picnicking, no camping*), a wildly rocky promontory fringed with wind-blown trees. The sea lions that congregate on the rocks gave rise to the Spanish name, Punta de los Lobos Marinos (point of the sea wolves). The point is the northernmost habitat of the brown pelican and the southernmost of the Monterey Cypress. The visits of Robert Louis Stevenson in 1879 have given rise to the legend that Point Lobos was the inspiration for Spyglass Hill in *Treasure Island.* The somber battle of the elements waged here inspired Robinson Jeffers to make it the setting for his poem *Tamar.*

State 1 follows the coast, alternately dipping to the mouths of creeks and climbing over promontory ridges, to the ruins of NOTLEY'S LANDING (R), 16.2 *m.*, where timber and tanbark brought by muleback from the canyons were once loaded by cable on waiting vessels.

Above the surf-beaten cove at the mouth of Bixby Creek arches the single concrete span of RAINBOW BRIDGE, 17.8 *m.*, 718 feet long and 260 feet high. On the cliff edge (R) are the ruins of BIXBY'S LANDING, the setting for Robinson Jeffer's poem *Thurso's Landing,* where

in the early 1900's lime from inland quarries was carried in great
buckets over a 3-mile aerial tramway down the canyon to the pier.
At 23.1 *m.* is the junction with a narrow, winding road.

> Right on this road 0.5 *m.*, scaling a great rock, to the POINT SUR LIGHT-
> HOUSE (*open 1-4 Mon., Wed., Fri.*), perched 270 feet above the surf at
> the tip of POINT SUR. When the S. S. *Los Angeles* ran aground here
> in 1873, young Dr. John Roberts rode the 30 miles from Monterey in 3½
> hours to find 150 victims, alive and dead, clinging to the shore or washed
> up on the beach. From miles around came the ranchers in 1879, when
> the *Ventura* went down, to salvage its cargo of fine linens and knock-
> down wagons. Old men on the lonely ranches still boast to their grand-
> children of having helped build in 1889 the lighthouse and its buildings,
> the former stairway with its 395 wooden steps, and the water system.
> When the light intended for Pigeon Point, brought from France and
> shipped around the Horn, was delivered here instead, there was mighty
> rejoicing among the mountain folk. Only dissenter was old Choppy Casuse,
> who commented: "Good light, but she no work. Go all the time sad,
> 'Boo-Boo,' but the fog, she creep in just the same." Off Point Sur in
> 1935 the United States Navy dirigible *Macon* went down in a dense fog,
> with the loss of two lives.

State 1 turns inland up the valley of the BIG SUR RIVER, past
the white buildings and orchards of Rancho El Sur (R), 26.3 *m.*,
claimed in 1852 by the region's first settler, sea captain Juan Bautista
Roger Cooper, a Yankee trader who had been in the habit of landing
cargoes here to evade customs duties at Monterey. The bleak Big Sur
Country provided a meager living to the homesteaders who settled it
in the 1870's. The few who have remained live far off the road in
isolated ranches. The inbreeding, passion, moroseness, and suspicion
engendered by their primitive, lonely lives have been well interpreted
by Robinson Jeffers, who has made this country the background of many
of his poems.

The highway continues along the river bank, fringed with oaks,
sycamores, and young redwoods, into PFEIFFER REDWOOD
STATE PARK, 30 *m.* (*picnic grounds, swimming pools*), a resort
where CCC boys have constructed an outdoor theater and winding
lagoons. It is named for Michael Pfeiffer, who settled here in November, 1869, and brought up a family whose descendants homesteaded
roundabout. In the park is BIG SUR, 30.5 *m.* (*post office, cabins,
lodge, restaurant; saddle horses*).

Climbing abruptly from the canyon, State 1 emerges on high bluffs
above the ocean at 32.9 *m.* Soon it gains spectacular heights, cut from
sheer cliffs. Ahead rise hills, rumpled and scarred—some smooth and
brown, some mantled in green, some mottled with the hues of red clay
and white granite. The road twists in around creek mouths, out
around headlands, rising and falling. The almost ever-present fog
drifts in and out, drawn up the funnel-like canyons, swept back to reveal
long vistas of coastline. Off-shore the crags are girdled by floating
forests of seaweed, greenish-brown, red-purple, and black.

ANDERSON'S CANYON, 41.7 *m.*, is the site of the road-con-
struction convict camp maintained here (1932-37) with few safeguards

against the escape of prisoners beyond the offer of a $200 reward, chargeable against the wages of the convicts, for the capture of a runaway. One of many stories about the convicts tells how, one winter night when slides had blocked the road, the word spread that the wife of a man in the freemen's camp, about to give birth to a child, needed a doctor; of their own free will, men from both camps poured out to work in pouring rain and pitch darkness, blasting open with dynamite a road to the Community Hospital.

The DOLAN CREEK BRIDGE, 45.8 m., largest timber-arch bridge in the State, carries the highway 150 feet above the canyon. Its carefully fitted redwood sections are held together by hinges.

At wide intervals are schoolhouses, small farm clearings, or the buildings of cattle ranches, isolated in the midst of almost unsettled wastes. The one-building hamlet of LUCIA, 54 m. (*hotel, restaurant, gasoline*) is the first place south of Big Sur where gasoline is available. The mountainsides are too steep in most places for human habitations —so steep at some spots, in fact, that it was literally necessary to move mountains to make room for the road. At the curve around LIME KILN POINT, 56 m., 163,000 yards of solid rock had to be excavated in 1,000 feet; one blast of 70,000 pounds of dynamite moved 95,000 yards, blowing 75,000 yards into the sea 300 feet below. Southward State 1 continues over a cliff-edged tableland to the house and gas station comprising GORDA, 66.8 m. The canyon below SALMON CREEK BRIDGE, 74.7 m., which affords a glimpse of a waterfall (L), is the southernmost stand of the redwood tree.

From sharp windings high above the sea, the highway descends to SAN CARPOJO CREEK, 79.8 m., where the mountains retreat inland from meadows dotted with grazing cattle. Over a difficult trail up the creek, Gaspar de Portolá and his expedition (*see TOUR 1b*) turned inland on their march north September 16, 1769, when they found the way up the coast blocked by precipices. Southward State 1 skirts Rancho Piedra Blanca (Sp., white rock), first of the three ranchos that comprise William Randolph Hearst's 240,000-acre San Simeon Ranch, stretching for 50 miles southward. Rancho Piedra Blanca, nucleus of the estate, was acquired by his father, Senator George Hearst, for 70¢ an acre and stocked with prize cattle.

At 87.1 m. is the junction with a dirt road.

Right on this road 0.2 m. to the PIEDRAS BLANCAS LIGHTHOUSE (*open 2-4 Mon., Wed., Fri.*), rising from a low point guarded by two large white rocks offshore, its conical tower and white, red-roofed buildings neatly silhouetted against the sea.

At 92.8 m. is the junction with a dirt road.

1. Right on this road is the village of SAN SIMEON, 2 m. (20 alt., 50 pop.), overlooking a wide bay from San Simeon Point, where Portuguese whalers made their home between 1865 and 1890. A handful of the old frame buildings remain. Back of the town Senator George Hearst built his great frame ranch house. His son now owns all but two lots in the village, where several large warehouses are crammed with still-unpacked art treasures from all over the world.

2. Left on this road (*private*) about 6 *m.* to the WILLIAM RANDOLPH HEARST "CASTLE" (*no admission*) on the summit of La Cuesta Encantada (Sp., the enchanted hill), resembling as closely as possible a castle dominating a fortified hilltop village (although the big house, La Casa Grande, has also been compared to a Spanish mission and the four guest houses to French chateaux). The estate has its own flying field, tennis courts, and swimming pool. The zoo is stocked with whole herds of bison, giraffes, kangaroos and with other more exotic beasts; the house with paintings, statuary, and other treasures of antiquity. Entire shiploads of castle ruins from abroad have been delivered here and reassembled. The guests at the estate, sometimes brought from Los Angeles in the owner's private plane, are said to be bound by four rules: they are obliged to come to the great hall of La Casa Grande every evening and to attend the nightly moving picture performance in the private theater, and they are forbidden to drink liquor in the guests' suites or to mention the word "death" in the presence of their host.

From the moss-draped pine forest surrounding the resort of CAMBRIA PINES, 100.2 *m.,* State 1 turns inland through dairy farm pastures to CAMBRIA, 101.2 *m.* (59 alt., 500 pop.), a farming and dairying center, continues down a narrow valley edged by brown hills, past HARMONY, 106.3 *m.* (180 alt., 75 pop.), another dairy center, and returns to the coast.

Sprawling along ESTEROS BAY is the weatherbeaten fishing village of CAYUCOS, 115.9 *m.* (34 alt., 260 pop.), named for the canoes paddled by the Indians who dwelt here when Juan Rodríguez Cabrillo named the bay in 1542. A small pleasure pier replaces the wharf built in 1870 by James Cass, who laid out the town in 1875.

At 120.4 *m.* is the junction with US 466 (*see TOUR 12b*).

On a bluff commanding land-locked MORRO BAY are the summer cottages of MORRO, 122.4 *m.* (72 alt., 800 pop.), named for immense MORRO (Sp., headland) ROCK, sometimes called the "Gibraltar of the Pacific," which rises 576 feet above a shallow lagoon impounded by sand dunes. From the rock, a great pile of trachyte (volcanic rock) covering 40 acres, thousands of tons of building material have been blasted.

Right from Morro on an oiled road 1.5 *m.* to MORRO BEACH STATE PARK (*adm. 50¢ per car for camping, 25¢ for picknicking; clubhouse, tennis, golf*), bordering Morro Bay.

State 1 turns sharply inland, passing (R) the chain of volcanic cones to which Morro Rock belongs—CERRO ALTO (1,415 alt.), CERRO ROMUALDO (1,310 alt.), and BISHOPS PEAK (1,510 alt.), for which San Luis Obispo is named.

SAN LUIS OBISPO (*see TOUR 2b*), 135.8 *m.,* is at the junction with US 101 (*see TOUR 2b*), with which State 1 is united southward for 12.2 miles.

Branching southward from US 101 at PISMO BEACH (*see TOUR 2b*), 148 *m.* State 1 crosses vegetable and flower-seed farms to their shipping center, OCEANO, 151.6 *m.* (19 alt., 600 pop.). Its beach, fringed by sand dunes, invites vacationers with a preference for seclusion. The dunes, piling up to surprising heights, are at their best in the late afternoon when the sun casts long shadows accenting their undulating lines. Here at one time was a group of shacks and tents inhabited by artists and others escaping high rents. When the tide is out, the sandy beach in this region is hard-packed, a natural race track often used by automobiles.

Across a broad mesa checkered with fields and flower beds, State 1 continues to GUADALUPE, 163.8 m. (80 alt., 1,250 pop.), an ancient community whose population is as jumbled as its streets and houses. The inhabitants are a conglomerate mixture of Japanese, Chinese, Filipinos and Mexicans, a few Swiss, and a sprinkling of native-born whites—mainly farm and dairy hands employed on the ranches for which Guadalupe serves as shipping center. The two-story AREL-LANTES ADOBE and the one-story OLIVERA ADOBE, Third St. near State 1, built in 1843 by the grantees of 30,048-acre Rancho Guadalupe, Teodoro Arellantes and Diego Olivera, now house Mexican workers and their families.

At 164.9 m. is the junction with a hard-surfaced road.

Left on this road to the junction with a hard-surfaced road, 1 m.; R. here and L. at 2.7 m. to BETTERAVIA, 5 m. (185 alt., 125 pop.), a settlement dominated by the 7-acre, sprawling, red-brick plant of the Union Sugar refinery. In 1938, 16,000 acres of surrounding beet field contributed the raw material for 512,000 hundred-pound bags of sugar produced here.

ORCUTT, 173.4 m. (314 alt., 500 pop.), born with the discovery of oil in the hills (R) in 1900, is still exclusively a petroleum producing and shipping point.

Through rolling hills State 1 winds erratically southward into broad LOMPOC VALLEY, 184.5 m., said by local boosters to be the world's largest commercial flower seed-growing center. Among fields of mustard, beets, beans, and potatoes are interspersed beds of nasturtium, delphinium, larkspur, poppy, and marigold, in summer time vividly ablaze with color.

The bustling, modern valley trade center of LOMPOC (Ind., shell mounds), 194.9 m. (95 alt., 2,845 pop.), originated as California's first successful land colonization project in October, 1874, when the California Immigrant Union purchased and subdivided Ranchos Lompoc and Misión Vieja. So successful was the venture that one week's sale of land aggregated $700,000, including $70,000 in town lots. The deeds of sale, forbidding sale of liquor on the land, lend documentary support to Lompoc's claim of pioneering prohibition in California. In the 1880's, irate citizens destroyed every bottle and keg of liquor in the drugstore of a would-be violator. The store of another violator blew up one night in an explosion which the next day's newspaper reported as an earthquake that had conveniently spared every other building in town.

At 196.1 m. on State 1 is the junction with a paved road.

Left on this road 2.6 m. to MISION LA PURISIMA CONCEPCION (Sp., the immaculate conception), eleventh of the 21 missions, founded December 8,

1787 by Padre Fermín de Lasuen. Following destruction of the first church by earthquake in 1812, the present one was built. Between 1815 and 1823 it was the seat of mission government in California. In 1824 the Indian neophytes seized the mission and held it for nearly a month before soldiers came to disperse them. La Purísima, with all its lands and buildings, was sold in 1845, 11 years after its secularization, to Don Juan Temple for $1,100. Acquired by an oil company in 1903, it was donated to Santa Barbara County. The present buildings, with their mellow cream-colored walls and red-tile roofs, have been restored by the Civilian Conservation Corps under direction of the National Park Service. The RESIDENCE BUILD-ING, 318 feet long and 65 feet wide, with walls 4½ feet thick, has a cloister with a colonnade of 20 fluted columns, notable for their design, supporting a low, red-tile roof. The church, yet to be restored (1939), which was once connected to the Residence Building by work rooms and neophytes' quarters, still has part of its original tile flooring. Under the floor, before the altar, is the grave of Padre Mariano Payeras, under whose direction it was built. The CAMPANARIO (Sp., bell tower) at its southeast corner is also to be restored, under present plans (1939).

State 1 winds upward through foothills of the Santa Ynez Mountains, a sparsely settled region ranged by great herds of cattle, to its junction with US 101 (*see TOUR 2c*) at LAS CRUCES (*see TOUR 2c*), 217 *m*.

Tour 2

(Brookings, Ore.)—Crescent City—Eureka—Santa Rosa—San Francisco—San Jose—Santa Barbara—Los Angeles—San Diego—San Ysidro (Mexican border); US 101.
Oregon Line to Mexican Border, 980.8 *m*.

Paved roadbed throughout; open all seasons; small landslides during heavy rains; snow in higher elevations during winter months.
Excellent route for trailers.
Route paralleled by Northwestern Pacific R.R. between Eureka and Sausalito, by Southern Pacific between San Francisco and Los Angeles, and by Santa Fe between Los Angeles and San Diego.
Accommodations plentiful; many camps and resort hotels.

Section a. *OREGON LINE to SAN FRANCISCO; 392.5 m.*
US 101.

This section of US 101 in natural beauty is one of the most diversified routes in the State. In the north, where it parallels the Pacific Ocean, the highway traverses farm and forest, climbing from surf-bordered meadows to skirt high crags overlooking the sea. South of Crescent City the road is called the Redwood Highway, taking its name from the giant redwoods through which it passes. It gradually ascends to a high plateau cut by numerous fertile valleys; descending, it traverses a wine-grape and orchard area—a region converted each spring into a wonderland of white blossoms. Nearing sea level once more, the road reaches into the heart of the State's poultry-raising district; but even here fringes of the blue Coast Range are always in sight.

US 101 crosses the State Line, 0 m., 6.5 miles south of Brookings, Ore., and follows the coast of Pelican Bay to PARADISE VALLEY, 1 m., where sheep and cattle graze on broad terraced meadows that slope from forested hills to foam-bathed rocky promontories. Isolated farm buildings and an occasional white-steepled country schoolhouse blend into the farmland and forest.

SMITH RIVER, 7.6 m. (50 alt., 300 pop.), on Rowdy Creek, is a trading center for a small dairying country and headquarters for sportsmen during the fishing and hunting season (*auto and trailer camps*).

Salmon and steelhead trout are plentiful in the wide, green waters of SMITH RIVER, 11 m., named for Jedediah Smith, adventurer and trapper, who explored the region in 1828.

South of FORT DICK, 13 m. (46 alt., 75 pop.), the broad grazing lands are interspersed increasingly with wooded areas, until at 13.4 m. the highway enters the WEBBER GROVE, northernmost of the redwood groves. Here, on a thick carpet of green clover and luxuriant fern, these coast redwoods (*Sequoia sempervirens*) stand straight and tall, dwarfing the lesser trees that grow beneath their heavy shade.

At 21.4 m. is the junction with US 199.

> Left on US 199 to HIOUCHI STATE PARK (*picnic facilities*), 8 m., a redwood forest. The highway continues through undeveloped country and crosses the Oregon Line, 43.6 m., at a point 35 miles south of Grants Pass, Ore.

CRESCENT CITY, 21.9 m. (7-35 alt., 1,720 pop.), seat of Del Norte County, facing a shallow harbor edged by arc-shaped Crescent Beach, ships lumber and shingles, dairy products, and fish by boat and truck. It was laid out in 1852, the year after discovery of the harbor by a party of treasure-seekers hunting gold hidden by a legendary prospector. A town of 800, with its own newspaper by 1854, it grew so fast that by 1856 it was enjoying its first drama—a presentation of *The Toodles* and *Paddy Miles, the Limerick Boy* by the Crescentonian Club. Crescent City was at first the seat of the former Klamath County, and so jealous were Crescentonians of the honor, that when the seat was moved to Orleans Bar, they angrily forced formation of a new county, Del Norte, in order to make their city its seat. Before construction of the pier in the 1860's, passengers arriving on the *Oregon* were transferred to surf boats and then to horse-drawn carts—to be hauled ashore over the shallow tidal flats—for a $2 fee.

Just north of the beach is POINT ST. GEORGE, which protects the city from heavy north winds. It was on St. George Reef that the sidewheeler, *Brother Jonathan,* was wrecked in the 1860's. A LIGHT-

HOUSE and RADIO STATION are maintained on BATTERY POINT, on the north arm of the bay. A light and fog signal station, SEAL ROCK LIGHT, on a small reef about 7 miles off-shore, was completed in 1891 after four years of labor.

At 24.1 *m.* is a junction with a narrow road.

> Left on this road into the HIOUCHI REDWOOD STATE PARK (141 acres), 0.3 *m.*, to the FRANK A. STOUT MEMORIAL GROVE of 44 acres, 8 *m.* Here giant Woodwardia ferns grow shoulder high, and in the spring scores of vivid-hued flowers enhance the loveliness of the rich vegetation.

US 101 begins the slow ascent of low foothills, 26 *m.*, to climb high above the sea. There is evidence of the work of lumber companies that chose only the best of the trees and burned off the rest; denuded, blackened hillsides alternate with thinly wooded slopes. The road follows a high ridge, through whose trees the ocean (R) intermittently appears in the distance. To the left are miles of blue-green treetops, a section of DEL NORTE COAST PARK. From KNAPP POINT, 35 *m.*, overlooking the Pacific, the highway descends almost to the surf, shortly to enter another of the small valleys whose meadows stretch from forest to sea.

At 41 *m.* is a junction with a graded dirt road.

> Right on this road is REQUA (Ind., rek-woi: mouth of the river), 0.5 *m.* (sea level, 108 pop.), on the north bank of KLAMATH RIVER, near its mouth, where a schooner arrived in 1851 with prospectors who founded Klamath City. The camp grew rapidly. Frames of houses, ready to assemble, arrived in sailing vessels from San Francisco, and a small iron building was erected, probably as a guard house for gold and protection against Indians. But the town declined as rapidly as it had grown; the men left to explore up river, and the iron house was shipped back to San Francisco. When Requa was on the old route of US 101, travelers crossed the Klamath by ferry, a motor-driven barge attached trolley fashion to a cable, but in 1925 the construction of a bridge upstream eliminated the crude ferry service and isolated the town. A law enacted in 1934 prohibited commercial fishing in the tidewater, and the population declined. Near Requa's large modern inn are the scattered, vine-covered shacks of Klamath Indians who compose the bulk of the population. The cannery at the water's edge is now used only during the fishing season, when sportsmen's catches are tinned and labeled by the Indians.
>
> The word Klamath is thought to be a derivation from *maklaks* (Lutuami Ind., people), translated as "the encamped." According to Indian tradition, the river once met the sea at Wilson Creek, about 6 miles north, where it was kept in its course by high parallel bluffs. When Po-lick-o-quare-ick (the Wise One)—the Indian equivalent to Christ—had completed his mission on earth, he gathered his possessions and prepared to depart. His grieving people watched him paddle toward the mouth of the river and began to follow him seaward, whereupon the Wise One commanded the bluffs to separate, forming a breach through which the river could flow quickly to the ocean. When the followers reached the shore they glimpsed the Wise One fading into the setting sun. Since then the Klamath has followed that course.
>
> Close to the river mouth, on the northern bank, stands a Family House of weather-beaten planks, said to be at least 150 years old. The house sheltered only the women and children of a family; the men and boys slept in the underground chambers used as sweathouses. Built without nails or

pegs, the walls were adjustable to permit smoke from the open fire to be carried out by the breeze.

KLAMATH, 43 *m.* (40 alt., 75 pop.), on the site called Hah-Paew by the Indians, is at the northern end of the DOUGLAS MEMORIAL BRIDGE over Klamath River. During August and September, when the town's hotels and camps are crowded, the river is so densely dotted with fishing craft that one can cross the stream by leaping from boat to boat. But the townspeople themselves, many of whom are Indians, are forbidden to earn their livelihood by fishing. Klamath folk blame mining companies operating on the upper Klamath and Trinity Rivers for the anti-fishing laws. It is said that when commercial fishermen objected to pollution of the stream by debris from hydraulic mining, mining interests retaliated by obtaining the support of sportsmen anglers for a law designating Klamath River as a recreational stream, on the premise that commercial fishing would deplete the supply of fish. Mining operations proceed unchallenged except during the sportsmen's fishing season.

The SHAKERS' CHURCH is a small, unpainted, barnlike structure (L) at the southern end of town. The congregation is composed of Indians, whose services consist mainly of violent shaking and shouting; their sect has no relation to that founded by Mother Ann Lee. On evenings when "the Shakers are at it" the townspeople are kept awake late by the clamor attending the devotions. The ghost dance, a principal rite of the sect, is a whirling performed before the congregation by one or two persons. The sect was brought to Klamath from the State of Washington by a local Indian, Jimmie Jacks. The medicine man, Smohalla, chief of the Columbia River Indians, founded the religion. When his tribe was crushed by the whites, Smohalla became a wanderer, his travels taking him as far south as Mexico. In 1860, he devised a religious ceremony showing the influence of his observation of Roman Catholic, Mormon, and Protestant rituals.

A sudden turn in the road, 47.4 *m.,* reveals a wide sweep of surf in the distance below, and the highway climbs high above the shore into PRAIRIE CREEK STATE PARK (*fishing, swimming, horseback riding, camping*), 50.9 *m.,* a reserve of 6,467 acres. At the park's lower end are the last surviving herd of Roosevelt elk in California, about 150 in number. These elk, a rich dark brown in color, are larger than other animals of the species.

ORICK, 63 *m.* (75 alt., 250 pop.), trade center of a prosperous dairy region, has a milk products plant.

LOOKOUT POINT, 65.4 *m.,* affords a view of the ocean in three directions. At the foot of the cliff is FRESHWATER LAGOON, separated from the Pacific by a narrow sand bar; its waters, always fresh, are believed to be fed by an underground stream. STONE LAGOON, 68.2 *m.,* and BIG LAGOON, 72.2 *m.,* overflow into the ocean during the winter when rainfall is heavy, permitting steelhead and salmon to enter both lagoons to spawn. In the vicinity of BIG LAGOON PARK (*motorboat regattas in summer*), 77.3 *m.,* are many small summer cabins. (*Warning: dangerous, powerful undercurrent.*)

In TRINIDAD, 83 *m.* (200 alt., 107 pop.), scattered business buildings offer little reminder of the town of 3,000 of 1851-52, when the settlement was the distribution point for the Trinity County mines. Small straggling houses, windows broken and boarded, fringe the empty offices, refineries, and vats of the California Sea Products Company, a whaling firm.

> Right from Trinidad on a narrow graveled road to TRINIDAD HEAD, 1.7 *m.*, a large promontory. The white granite memorial cross at the summit replaces the Spanish cross of pine erected there June 11, 1775, by Capt. Bruno Heceta and Lt. Juan Francisco Bodéga y Cuadra. The original wooden marker bore the inscription "Carolus III Dei G. Hyspaniarum Rex," signifying that the explorers took possession of the territory in the name of Charles III of Spain. The Spaniards named the region Trinidad because they took possession on the day following the feast of the Holy Trinity.

At the mouth of LITTLE RIVER, 86 *m.*, northern boundary of LITTLE RIVER BEACH STATE PARK, an exploration party of nine men headed by Dr. Josiah Gregg reached the coast in December, 1849, after weeks of hardship. They had left Weaverville, about 100 miles inland, the month before, in search of a harbor described by the Indians as "a large bay with fertile land and tall trees, eight suns to the west." Their supplies gave out, and before they reached the coast, they were near starvation.

CLAM BEACH (*auto camps nearby*), 87.9 *m.*, is a popular clam-digging and picnicking spot.

At 95.7 *m.* is the junction with US 299 (*see TOUR 8b*).

ARCATA (Ind., where boats land), 100 *m.* (100 alt., 1,709 pop.), on the western shore of Humboldt Bay, is built around a plaza. Many of the dwellings on the town's wide streets have broad lawns and flower gardens. Lumber, shingles, wool, and milk compose the bulk of exported products. Uniontown—as the place was named by its founders April 10, 1850—was a shipping point and until 1856 the seat of Humboldt County. Bret Harte is said to have written his first newspaper story here, while working as compositor and assistant to S. G. Whipple, editor of the *Northern California,* as well as agent for Wells, Fargo & Co., from 1857 to 1859. On the crest of a hill are the cream-colored stucco buildings of the HUMBOLDT STATE TEACHERS COLLEGE, established 1913.

> Right from Arcata on a paved road that traverses a narrow, sandy peninsula to SAMOA (97 alt., 600 pop.), 5 *m.*, a company town around an extensive redwood mill (*open to visitors*). The ocean lies just beyond the sand dunes behind the town. About one mile south is the HULK OF THE U.S.S. MILWAUKEE, grounded in 1917 while attempting to free a submarine that had run aground. Bids had been submitted to haul the submarine to land and to refloat it, but they were rejected as too high. The Navy Department then sent the cruiser *Milwaukee* from San Francisco to rescue the submarine. After the *Milwaukee* grounded, one of the original bids was accepted.

US 101 curves around the southern shore of HUMBOLDT BAY, a landlocked inlet so well guarded from the sea by its two narrow peninsulas of sand that it eluded discovery until Capt. Jonathan Winship, hunting seals and sea otter along the coast for the Russian-American Fur Company in 1806, steered the *O'Cain* through the narrow entrance. The search for a safe harbor along the northern coast prompted its rediscovery on December 20, 1849 by the Josiah Gregg party of Government-employed traders and explorers. On April 9 of the following year the United States revenue cutter *Laura Virginia* sailed into the bay, which the expedition's second officer, Capt. Hans Buhne, named for the German naturalist, Baron Alexander von Humboldt. The harbor's usefulness has been menaced, ever since its discovery, by the shifting sand bars at its mouth. To keep the channel open, construction of rock jetties and constant dredging have been required.

EUREKA, 105.7 *m.* (30 alt., 15,752 pop.), seat of Humboldt County, on the shore of Humboldt Bay, owes its name—as well as the surveying of its first town lots in 1850—to James Ryan, who drove his vessel onto the mud flats, shouting jubilantly "Eureka!" (Gr., I have found it!). The largest California town north of Sacramento, Eureka spreads in checkerboard fashion over an area large enough to accommodate a population several times its present size. Its solitary houses are scattered over vast stretches of vacant, weed-grown lots. Along the waterfront are the saloons, cheap hotels, and poolrooms of the late nineteenth century—relics of the days when the tough, flamboyant life of the lonely, frontier settlement centered here. Today, as in the beginning, when woodsmen and seafarers from New England and Nova Scotia settled here, the great redwood mills along the bay shore dominate the life of the community.

On a high plateau overlooking the bay near the southern city limits is FORT HUMBOLDT, where troops were garrisoned for protection against Indians between 1853 and 1865. Ulysses S. Grant was stationed here in 1854 as captain of the Fourth United States Infantry. The life of the lonely post was so dreary that, according to legend, he spent much of his time drinking in Ryan's saloon at Eureka. In the end he resigned from the army out of sheer discouragement. Of the string of offices and barracks that lined the parade ground on three sides, only one, the headquarters of the commissary department, remains today. Restored and repainted, it stands in a landscaped plot enclosed by a white picket fence; inside is a collection of relics, stuffed birds, odd bits of furniture, and yellowing photographs of Grant.

Most violent episode of the Indian warfare that prompted establishment of Fort Humboldt was the massacre of a band of Indians by whites, on INDIAN ISLAND, largest of several small isles in the bay near the waterfront. The remnants of two or three tribes were encamped on the island. On the night of February 25, 1860, when the warriors were away hunting and fishing, white settlers killed all the women and children, the old and infirm. The husbands, fathers, and brothers returning to burned homes and mutilated dead, swore vengeance; and months of bitter warfare followed. When Bret Harte, temporarily in charge of the Uniontown paper, denounced the outrage, he was compelled to return to San Francisco because of threats against his life. The island—also called Gunther's Island for the man who later settled on it—was thereafter protected from salt water by dikes and turned into farmland. Gunther deeded it to someone, then changed his mind and demolished the dikes by night, allowing the water of the bay to pour over the island and swamp the fields.

Eureka's Chinese, like its Indians, were hounded out of town. In 1885 Eureka's Chinatown housed several hundred; as in most small California towns, anti-Chinese prejudice was strong. When, on the evening of February 6, 1885, a Eureka councilman was killed by a stray bullet during an outbreak between warring tongs, feeling was inflamed to the point of mob violence. Cooler heads among the whites assumed command, and at a meeting held in Centennial Hall a committee was appointed to order members of the Chinese colony to leave the county within 24 hours. A scaffold was erected on Fourth Street, and a hangman's noose warned of the intention of the citizens, should their order be disregarded. When rough weather delayed the sailing of ships chartered to take the Chinese to San Francisco, the whites took advantage of the delay to go through the county and issue the same command to the entire oriental population. The Chinese properties were appropriated by Eurekans. A suit was subsequently brought against the city of Eureka for $132,820 but the case never went to trial. Today Humboldt County is one of the few California counties that have no oriental residents. When vessels with Chinese crews dock at Eureka, the sailors do not attempt to go ashore.

The CARSON HOUSE, 2nd and M Sts., is a startling architectural monument. The lumber magnate who built it next door to his lumber yards imported most of the General Grant ornamentation from eastern mills. It stands, carefully preserved, amid sprucely tended grounds. Its jagged roof line, visible from almost any quarter of the city, the tortured ornamentation, and the trim paint give it the air of a prop for a Silly Symphony. The STUMP HOUSE, on Broadway (US 101), an edifice built of the log and stump of a giant redwood, is likewise a monument to Eureka's chief industry; it houses a collection of articles fashioned from redwood burl and grotesque formations found in redwood forests. In the midst of a redwood grove inside the city is SEQUOIA PARK (*picnic tables, playgrounds*), surrounding a small lake, which has a zoo with deer and elk paddocks.

LOLETA, 119.7 *m.* (50 alt., 400 pop.), first named Swauger for a settler and renamed when it became a shipping point for a prosperous dairying region, has a milk condensing plant. Many of the dairymen are Portuguese who came here as milkers and later bought farms.

Right from Loleta on a paved road to the TABLE BLUFF RADIO STATION and LIGHTHOUSE, 5 *m.* The radio station, co-operating with the Coast Guard, has been instrumental in saving many ships.

Along the valley of the EEL RIVER, visible (R) at 120.8 *m.,*
the highway winds through pastures, where toward evening automobiles
may be delayed by unhurried cows being driven to the barn for milking.
It was discovered by the Gregg party, which came upon a small band
of Indians laden with eels from the river and named the stream accordingly. At this point the party divided. Gregg and three others followed the coast south, and the other four, led by L. K. Wood, returned
inland by way of Eel River. Both parties met disaster. Doctor Gregg
died of starvation, falling from his horse while still attempting to travel,
and Wood was mangled by bears that he and his men were forced to
attack. He begged his companions to shoot him and go on, but they
made a litter and carried him to a ranch.

FERNBRIDGE, 121.7 *m.* (35 alt., 51 pop.), is a settlement at
the approach to FERN BRIDGE, a graceful concrete span over Eel River
in a region notable for its luxuriant ferns.

FORTUNA, 124.7 *m.* (53 alt., 1,239 pop.), was first called
Springville because of the numerous nearby springs. The name was
changed to Slide, and then to Fortuna by a landowner who hoped to
attract home hunters.

CANYON PARK, 130.5 *m.* (*adm. 25¢ per automobile*), is noted
for its many varieties of ferns and moss.

Another Eel River bridge carries US 101 into SCOTIA, 136.2 *m.*
(101 alt., 2,000 pop.), named by its settlers, woodsmen from Nova
Scotia, called "Blue Noses." Here is the large PACIFIC LUMBER COM-
PANY REDWOOD LUMBER MILL (*visitors admitted*) established in 1886.
The company owns every foot of land and every building in the town,
renting the small houses on the side streets to those among its 1,600
employees with families. Furniture, household goods, and groceries
are sold at the company store for company scrip. It is said that many
employees do not handle legal tender for months at a time. The sawmill covers more than 400 acres; it produces 1,500 kinds of wooden
articles, besides lumber. For 2 miles stretch yards filled with cut
lumber, each pile stacked precisely to facilitate curing, which requires
three years. The wood of the *sempervirens* is light and surprisingly
straight-grained, has almost no resin, and shrinks or warps very slightly
after seasoning.

DYERVILLE, 152.3 *m.* (100 alt., 38 pop.), named for pioneer
"Dad" Dyer, has a post office, district school, and a State Park Headquarters. South of Dyerville is HUMBOLDT STATE PARK,
northernmost of the long chain of memorial groves and State parks
lining the highway for many miles. FOUNDERS' GROVE, 152.5
m., contains the WORLD'S TALLEST TREE, a redwood 364 feet in height
and 47 feet in circumference at the base. Its estimated timber-mill
cut is 125,000 feet—sufficient to build a dozen average-sized houses.
These groves have been preserved through the efforts of the Save-the-
Redwoods League, which in 1927 played an important part in the formation of the present State park system.

The redwood belt extends from extreme southwestern Oregon to the Santa Lucia Mountains over an area 450 miles long and from 1 to 40 miles wide. The *Sequoia sempervirens,* the earth's tallest trees, are exceeded in girth only by the *Sequoia gigantea* of the Sierra Nevada. The trees were named for the Cherokee chief, Se-quo-yah, who perfected a phonetic alphabet of 86 symbols for his tribe. The *sempervirens* are between 500 and 1,300 years old and the *gigantea* between 900 and 2,100. The two varieties of redwood are similar in appearance; the bole of each tapers gently from a heavily buttressed base, free of branches for a full third of the height. The branches are short, and the evergreen foliage, of small, stiff, sharp-pointed leaves, is usually a deep but brilliant yellow green. The thick, cinnamon-brown bark is deeply furrowed, giving the tree a sharply ribbed appearance. The redwood matures at a height exceeding 200 feet, when about 10 feet in diameter, and it may grow half again as high. Although a remarkable feature of the redwood is its resistance to disease and fire—because of the thick bark, the small amount of resin, and the soft spongelike quality of the wood, which absorbs water easily—fires occur almost every year in the scrub areas and in deforested sections among fallen logs, dead trees, and waste from cuttings. During the fall a heavy pall of blue-gray smoke often hangs over the entire region.

South of Dyerville the groves are increasingly dense and the under-foliage more luxuriant. Heavy carpets of fern and clover in season are embroidered with delicately colored trillium and other blossoms; at intervals vivid yellow moss outlines the forms of fallen trees.

From WEOTT, 154.5 *m.* (168 alt., 150 pop.), among the redwood stands, the road climbs to skirt the sheer bluffs of the narrow gorge (R) of the south fork of Eel River, occasionally glimpsed below. South of MIRANDA, 165 *m.* (187 alt., 44 pop.), where the woods are interspersed with small clearings in which sheep graze, the highway closely follows the bank of the river.

The country around GARBERVILLE, 181.9 *m.* (225 alt., 361 pop.), on a high, terraced bluff overlooking Eel River, was chosen by pioneer J. C. Garber as a potential stock-raising area. The Iowan's foresight was good, for this town is a shipping point for sheep ranches.

At BENBOW, 185 *m.,* summer homes are scattered near a resort hotel in lush green mountain meadows where the waters of the Eel River, flowing here around two great bends, are backed up in a placid lake by a "summer dam."

Below RICHARDSON GROVE STATE PARK, 190.6 *m.* (*cabins, campgrounds, swimming pool, dance floor*), US 101 climbs the high rim of a narrow canyon. Lilley Redwood Park (*private*), 198.3 *m.,* is the home of the Quadruped Tree, called by Robert L. Ripley "the tallest one-room house in the world." This hollow 250-foot tree, used as a shop for redwood novelties, has a ground circumference of 101 feet. Four openings have been made, one in each of the huge, footlike roots. It has been used as a barn, a blacksmith shop, and, during the construction of the highway, as sleeping quarters for 32 convicts. US 101 descends from the high rim of the gorge among redwoods interspersed with Douglas and lowland fir, alder, madroña, coast hemlock, and tanoak—the latter festooned with yellow-green elk moss.

At COOLIDGE REDWOOD PARK, 206.4 *m.*, southernmost of the State redwood parks, an archway has been cut in one of the redwoods through which an automobile can pass (*25¢ per car*).

From a small, broad valley, US 101 now climbs rugged mountains where seemingly illimitable miles of blue-green forest reach in every direction.

LAYTONVILLE, 229.1 *m.* (1,600 alt., 116 pop.), is the trading center for cattle and sheep ranches.

> Left from Laytonville on a narrow dirt road to DOS RIOS (Sp., two rivers), 11.8 *m.* (924 alt., 20 pop.), a resort at the junction of the Middle and South Forks of the Eel River. COVELO, 27.8 *m.* (1,397 alt., 600 pop.), in the ROUND VALLEY INDIAN RESERVATION, is a trading center for the valley and an outfitting point for sportsmen and vacationists. The reservation's productive farming land is coveted by white farmers who have encroached steadily on it. The Indians here, excellent farmers, choose to live in brush huts rather than wooden houses.

The former lumber community of WILLITS, 254 *m.* (1,360 alt., 1,424 pop.), a division point on the Northwestern Pacific R.R., was once Willitsville, so named for the Indiana immigrant, Hiram Willits, who purchased the store opened here in 1865. The center of a hay, stock, and poultry raising region, it pays homage to the past at its yearly Frontier Days Celebration.

BLACK BART ROCK, 265.2 *m.*, commanding a clear view of southbound traffic from a slight incline (R), is so-named for the robbery of a mail stage here by the elusive road agent, "Black Bart," a lone highwayman, traveling on foot, who robbed 27 coaches in the Sierra and Coast Range mountain country between 1875 and 1883. Always polite, fastidiously dressed in a linen duster and mask, he used to leave behind facetious rhymes signed "Black Bart, Po—8," in mail and express boxes after he had finished rifling them. A laundry mark on a handkerchief dropped near the scene of one robbery in Calaveras County eventually led pursuers to San Francisco, where "Black Bart" was discovered to be the highly respectable Mr. Charles C. Bolton, ostensibly a mining engineer who frequently made trips to the mines. A stay in San Quentin from 1883 to 1885 cut short his career.

The highway descends to CALPELLA, 271 *m.* (623 alt., 300 pop.), named for an Indian chief whose name meant "Shell Bearer," a slow-moving country town in the center of an area producing large, black grapes that make an excellent dry wine. There are three wineries (*open to visitors*), with a combined annual capacity of 200,000 gallons, one of them very old, and built of heavy stones that keep the interior cool and dark. Laid out in 1858, Calpella in 1873 rivaled Ukiah in importance, but as the latter town grew it fell into decay.

US 101 cuts through vineyards to a junction with State 20 (*see TOUR 2A*) at 274.1 *m.*

UKIAH (Ind., Yo-Ka-Ya, deep valley), 276 *m.* (650 alt., 3,124 pop.), seat of Mendocino County, is in long, narrow, mountain-flanked Ukiah Valley, where pears, prunes, grapes, and hops flourish. Ukiah celebrates the valley's important occupation of stock raising at its yearly rodeo in June. The first settler was Samuel Lowry, who built a log cabin here in 1856. Although Mendocino County was one of the 27 counties created in 1850, so few people lived in it that neighboring Sonoma County administered its affairs until a county seat was established here in 1859; and—as a recent historian has said—it "did not receive recognition at the hands of capitalists until about 1910."

Ukiah's INTERNATIONAL LATITUDE OBSERVATORY (*open in daytime*), near US 101 (R) at the end of town, is one of five in the world, widely distributed in longitude but all situated on the same parallel of latitude (39° 8' north). They were established by the International Geodetic Association, beginning in 1898, to derive from observation of selected stars the harmonic analysis of the latitudes, which are shifting constantly, as is the North Pole. The other observatories are situated in Gaithersburg, Maryland, Sardinia, Russian Turkestan, and Japan.

1. Left from Ukiah on an oiled road, which becomes a dirt road, 3.9 *m.* to VICHY SPRINGS, a resort noted for its "champagne baths."

2. Left from Ukiah on a graveled road 8 *m.* to THE TERRACES, mountainside gardens of Carl Purdy, who in 1900 started a project for propagation of native western bulbs, shrubs, wild flowers, and trees. Although not the first to gather native seeds and flowers—the Royal Horticultural Society of London had sent David Douglas to California for the purpose as early as 1830—Purdy was the first to start many California wild flowers on foreign migrations. Besides gathering native plants—which he collects at elevations up to 10,000 feet—he acclimatizes in his mountain garden many foreign species—from Morocco morning-glories to Scotch harebells.

The trellised green tendrils of hop vines shade the fertile fields around HOPLAND, 290 *m.* (488 alt., 860 pop.), center of the Sanel Valley's rich farmlands along the upper reaches of the Russian River. The village that grew up here around the adobe ranch house of the Mexican Fernando Felix stands on the site of a populous Indian settlement, called "Sanel" by the aborigines. The first hops were planted in 1858 by Stephen Warren Knowles, who sold his first crop, dried in the loft of his barn, for 30¢ a pound. During the growing season, the hop vines—burgeoning at the rate of 10 or 12 inches a day—are trained along strings until they cover the fields with leafy, tent-like bowers. The migratory hop pickers, arriving at harvest time in their dilapidated autos piled high with dogs, babies, pots, pans, and bedding, camp in the fields round about. The fresh-picked hops are hauled in trucks to the weather-stained drying kilns that dot the countryside—odd-looking shingled, peak-roofed structures with chimney-shaped wooden towers. The hops are dumped into the dryers and dried out by means of wood-and-sulphur fires built under each kiln.

At 302.6 *m.* is the junction with a narrow graveled road.

Left on this road to THE GEYSERS, 14.5 *m.* (1,500 alt.), where, in a small canyon, jets of steam shoot high in the air from hissing fumaroles and 35 mineral springs, no two of them alike, bubble from the earth. The Devil's Inkstand emits a black water which can be used for writing purposes. The springs early acquired fame for therapeutic qualities, and in 1851 a hotel was built.

At 303.2 *m.* is the junction with State 28 (*see TOUR 1a*).

CLOVERDALE, 304.8 *m.* (318 alt., 759 pop.), has a residential area with wide streets shaded by maple and eucalyptus trees; picket fences and well-tended lawns front neat frame houses. The town lies in an orange grove belt at the head of Santa Rosa Valley; it celebrates an annual citrus fair.

ASTI, 309.3 *m.* (264 alt., 100 pop.), is the home of an Italian-Swiss colony established in 1881 by a group of San Francisco Italians as a commercial venture to employ Italians and Swiss of that city. Today Italian-Swiss Colony wines are nationally known. Beside the highway (L) is the CHURCH OF OUR LADY OF MOUNT CARMEL, built by the vineyardists in the shape of half an enormous wine barrel. For miles vineyards stretch along the highway, dotted with old stone wineries, in one of which is a large winevat with a capacity of 500,000 gallons, cut out of solid rock and lined with a special glass-surfaced cement. Wine is shipped from this area in tank cars.

In the spring the region south of Asti is one of exquisite beauty. Yellow mustard and golden poppies brighten a countryside of hundreds of acres of plum and pear trees, whose soft blossoms form a sea of white reaching to green foothills.

GEYSERVILLE, 314.8 *m.* (250 alt., 629 pop.), a shipping point for great quantities of apples, pears, and plums, was settled in 1852.

Right from Geyserville on a paved road to SKAGGS SPRINGS, 9 *m.* (800 alt., 30 pop.), a resort town, where Samuel Brannan attempted to settle Mormons in 1847.

HEALDSBURG, 323.3 *m.* (101 alt., 2,296 pop.), a trade center, was founded by Harmon G. Heald in 1852 as a trading post. Many of its inhabitants are Italian grape-growers.

At 334.5 *m.* is a junction with an oiled road (*see TOUR 2A*).

SANTA ROSA, 338.7 *m.* (150 alt., 10,636 pop.), seat of Sonoma County, is said to owe its name to Padre Juan Amarosa of Mission San Rafael, who baptized an Indian girl of the region in 1829, calling her Rosa because it was the feast day of St. Rose of Lima. The main distributing center for the ranches of Sonoma Valley, it has enough industrial activity to provide an annual payroll of $450,000.

The rich soil and gentle climate of the Santa Rosa Valley so delighted Luther Burbank (1849-1926) that he chose this as the best place for his experiments in plant breeding. For half a century he worked here, experimenting with thousands of kinds of plants, developing a long series of what he called "new creations." Uninterested in proving special scientific theories, Burbank aimed solely to produce more and better varieties of cultivated plants. Among his achievements were the Burbank potato; thornless cactus; edible cactus; the Santa Rosa, climax, Wickson, apple, gold, and other plums; a new fruit, the plumcot; the giant, sugar, and stoneless prunes; the Burbank cherry; the Burbank, Santa Rosa, and peachblow roses; Shasta daisies; giant and fragrant callas; and many other new flowers, fruits, vegetables, ferns, grasses, trees, and nuts. He lies buried under a tall deodar, a few steps from his charming greenhouse, where his tools are still stacked against the wall. The LUTHER BURBANK. HOUSE AND GARDENS (*open*), Santa Rosa Ave. at Tupper St., were given by his widow to the Santa Rosa Junior College botanical department.

Recently a mob said to be organized by local businessmen, invaded the homes of three men accused of radicalism, took them to a warehouse, and beat, tarred, and feathered them. The affair aroused Nation-wide attention; widespread protest resulted in the arrest and trial of a number of suspects. Most of the defendants were excused, and the few who were tried were acquitted. The three victims received no redress.

1. Right from Santa Rosa on State 12 is SEBASTOPOL, 4.2 *m.* (68 alt., 1,762 pop.), trade center for vineyard- and orchard-growers, lying in the heart of an area known as the Gold Ridge which is famous for its early Gravenstein apples. It derived its name from a fight between two men in 1855; when one barricaded himself inside Dougherty's store, besieged by the other, onlookers dubbed the store Hibbs' Sebastopol, in reference to the Crimean War siege then taking place. The town helped itself to the name. On the outskirts is the LUTHER BURBANK EXPERIMENTAL GARDEN, established here in 1885 when Burbank's 4-acre garden in Santa Rosa proved too small. Not a show garden, the tract has none of the formal air of a landscaped plot about it; it was planted for working purposes.

State 12 cuts across vineyards and orchards to the RUSSIAN RIVER, which once drained into San Francisco Bay, until geological changes forced it to seek a new channel through the Coast Range to the sea. The river, which the Indians called Shabaikai or Misallaako (Ind., long snake) and the Russians, Slavianka (Russ., charming little one), is named for the Russian occupation (1812-1841). Capt. L. A. Hagermeister, writing to the Russian-American Fur Company in 1817, praised the fertile fields along the river, protected from wind and fog, as being suitable for wheat growing and cattle raising, but the Russians never settled there. The Russian River today is a famous fishing stream; in its fresh-water pools, small-mouth black bass abound, and in the lower river near the sea, striped bass. During the winter steelhead and salmon are caught in great numbers. For nearly 25 miles inland from its mouth, the river is bordered by an almost unbroken line of summer resorts, where from 100,000 to 150,000 people spend their vacations.

State 12 crosses the river to GUERNEVILLE, 18.2 *m.* (52 alt., 800 pop.), trade center of a dairying, fruit growing and lumbering region, especially noted for its apples. Its population expands in summer to about 10 times its winter size. The environs are thronged with tent colonies and camping grounds by the river's brink. The town is named for George Guerne, its founder, who built a large mill here in 1865.

Right from Guerneville on a paved road 2.8 *m.* to ARMSTRONG WOODS, a 400-acre grove of virgin redwoods, where outdoor plays and festivals are presented during the summer in rustic ARMSTRONG FOREST THEATER, seating 1,000.

At 23.1 *m.* on State 12 is the junction with a paved road; L. on this road, which bridges the river, to MONTE RIO, 0.2 *m.* (41 alt., 320 pop.), a summer resort by the river where redwoods shadow a thicket of rock maples and wild grapevines.

Right from Monte Rio 0.9 *m.* to BOHEMIAN GROVE, a 2,437-acre grove of virgin redwoods extending from the river bank. The grove, owned by the Bohemian Club of San Francisco, is open to members only; it contains a large outdoor theater seating 1,200 with seats of bark-covered logs and a bark-covered cement structure housing a pipe organ. At the annual two-week summer encampment of the club, celebrations called High Jinks have been presented ever since 1878.

At 26.1 *m.* is the junction with a paved road; R. on this road, 6.4 *m.* through a redwood belt, thick with summer camps and cabins, to CAZA-DERO (87 alt., 300 pop.), a resort center in a dairying district.

State 12 continues to DUNCAN MILLS, 28.1 *m.* (26 alt., 37 pop.), a summer resort in the center of a small dairying region along the banks of the Russian River.

At 32 *m.* is the junction with State 1 (*see TOUR 1a*).

2. Left from Santa Rosa on State 12 around the northern end of a foot-hill spur and southeastward down long, narrow Sonoma Valley between wooded hills. The name Sonoma is probably of Indian origin, derived from the words *tso* (earth) and *noma* (village) of the Yukian Wappo dialect, although Jack London popularized the fanciful translation "Valley of the Moon" in his novel of that name. Sun-drenched for long months—but cooled by ocean fogs in summer—the vineyard-mantled slopes grow some of the State's best wine grapes.

At 14.6 *m.* is the junction with the Valley of the Moon Highway; R. on this road 1 *m.* to GLEN ELLEN (131 alt., 100 pop.), in the shade of ancient oaks and maples.

Right from Glen Ellen on an oil surfaced road 0.4 *m.* to the entrance to the JACK LONDON RANCH, overlooking the valley from orchard-clad knolls, where the author of *The Call of the Wild* spent his last years in a fling at running an experimental model farm which his widow operates as a "dude" ranch. During London's life on the ranch, his daily schedule began with a gallop around the estate; after lunch, having finished his 1,000-word writing stint for the day, he spent the afternoons supervising ranch operations from horseback. In the white ranch house where the Londons lived, his library is preserved. All that remains of the costly Wolf House, which London built but never lived in, are its bare stone walls; the unfinished building was razed by fire, supposedly set by an incendiary. Only a short time later London died at the ranch on November 22, 1916—by his own hand, according to his latest biographer. On "Little Hill" near the ruins of his unfinished house, a rough boulder, unmarked, shelters his ashes.

South of Glen Ellen, the Valley of the Moon Highway follows Sonoma Creek, through a quiet countryside fragrant in season with acacia blossoms and new-mown hay, to the SONOMA STATE HOME, 2 *m.,* a group of red-roofed buildings on extensive lawns, established in the late 1880's. Al-though it is one of the largest hospitals for the mentally deficient in the State, it was badly overcrowded until additions were built in 1939.

The once-thriving farm and poultry center of EL VERANO (Sp., the summer), 6.2 *m.* (103 alt., 200 pop.), suffered a sharp decline when the railroad discontinued service to its station here, as a huge, empty hotel, windowless stores and homes, and rusting railway tracks attest.

At 7.2 *m.* the Valley of the Moon Highway rejoins State 12.

South of its northern junction with the Valley of the Moon Highway, State 12 continues through AGUA CALIENTE, 18.3 *m.* (75 alt., 150 pop.), FETTERS SPRINGS, 18.7 *m.,* and BOYES SPRINGS, 19.4 *m.* (129 alt., 400 pop.)—all resorts with cabins, hotels and swimming pools around hot mineral springs.

SONOMA, 21.9 *m.* (97 alt., 980 pop.), sprawls over the flat valley floor, with low-lying frame and adobe buildings, typically Californian in their second-story Spanish balconies, along wide streets around a plaza. Established as a frontier post, Sonoma has survived threatened invasion by Russians from the north, raids by horse thieves, and rebellion by *Americanos,* and still pursues its leisurely ways, untroubled by bustle and scurry, amid pleasant acres of farm, vineyard, and cattle land.

The straggling Russian settlements along the northern coast (*see TOUR 1a*) worried Gov. Luís Argüello so much that he urged Padre José Altimira to move Missions San Francisco de Asís and San Rafael Arcángel northward without delay. Too impatient to wait for the sanction of church authorities, the young priest set out in June 1823 to find a site. On July 4, 1823, he dedicated his chosen spot with rites before a cross of tree limbs and an altar of woven willow twigs and named it Misión San Francisco Solano for the saint known as the Apostle to the Indies. The mission authorities were so outraged by Padre Altimira's precipitous action that at first they forbade him to continue. By April 24, 1824, however, this, the last and most northerly of the missions, had been finished and dedicated —a crude structure of whitewashed boards—and by the end of the year a long, low tile-roofed adobe with overhanging eaves, a priest's house and guards' houses, and a granary had been added. During the 11 years before it was secularized in 1834, the mission grew rich from its vineyards, orchards, and herds of stock.

Still plagued by the Russian menace, Gov. José Figueroa ordered the commissioner for the mission, young Alferez Mariano Vallejo, Comandante of the Line of the North, to found a pueblo on the northern frontier. In 1835, having failed to establish successful colonies at Santa Rosa and Petaluma because of the hostility of the Indians, he laid out the Pueblo de Sonoma around a plaza—the largest in all California—and built his own two-story *palacio* on the northern side. As other adobe dwellings— including those of his brother Salvador on the northern side and his brother-in-law, Jacob P. Leese, at the southwestern corner—were erected, the pueblo took on the shape of a quadrangle bordered with backyard gardens. By 1839, the population included more than 25 families, over whom Vallejo reigned like a feudal baron. In the plaza he drilled his Mexican soldiers, augmented by Indians paid out of his own pocket. From the four-story watch tower of his *palacio* he used field glasses to survey his lands, ranged by vast herds of cattle and horses. To guarantee the security of his domain—and of the northern frontier—he formed an alliance with the chief of the Suisun, Sem-Yet-Ho (Mighty Arm), baptised Solano, through whose powerful friendship he won the allegiance of Indian groups whom the missions had never touched.

The drowsy pueblo was awakened to sudden life before dawn of June 14, 1846, by a villainous-looking band of three dozen armed gringoes. A rapid "change in the political affairs of Sonoma" took place, as one of the gringo leaders, William B. Ide, put it. The invaders were Yankee trappers and settlers, led by rough, rawboned Ezekiel Merritt; they were acting on orders from Capt. John C. Frémont, encamped nearby with his purported scientific expedition. Uneasy at the threat of expulsion from the province by the Mexican authorities, they were ready to begin a struggle to bring California under the American flag—unaware that the United States had already declared war against Mexico. As Ide told the story in a letter to Commodore Robert Stockton: ". . . we charged upon the Fortress of General Guadaloupe Vallejo, and captured eighteen prisoners (among whom were three of the highest officers in the Californian Government and all the military officers who reside in Sonoma) eight field-pieces, two hundred stand of arms, a great quantity of cannon, canister, and grape-shot, and a little less than one hundred pounds of powder (quite too little to sustain us against an attack by the use of cannon) . . . the soldiers were set at liberty, and the said officers were escorted by ten armed men to an asylum under the generous protection of Captain Frémont. This day we proclaim California a Republic, and our pledge of honor that private property shall be protected . . . Destined as we are to certain destruction should we prove unsuccessful, we have the honor to be your *Fellow Countrymen* . . ." He signed himself "Commander-in-chief at the Fortress of Sonoma," having been elected president of the new "California Republic."

A flag was hastily improvised from a yard-wide strip of unbleached homespun and a 4-inch strip of red flannel. With brown paint William L. Todd, Mrs. Abraham Lincoln's nephew, painted a star in one corner—in memory of the Lone Star Republic of Texas—a grizzly bear, and the words "California Republic." Said Benjamin Dewell, one of the revolutionaries: "A bear stands his ground always, and as long as the stars shine we stand for the cause." The bear, however, was so fat and clumsily drawn that the Sonomans laughed and called it a pig. The flag was run up the high flag pole in the plaza, where it fluttered until the flag of the United States replaced it on July 9.

After the Yankee occupation, when a military garrison was stationed here, Sonoma grew into a prosperous town, with Vallejo, who soon adjusted himself to American rule, as one of its leading citizens. In 1856 the Hungarian nobleman Col. Agaston Haraszthy, called the father of wine making in California, purchased land east of town. By 1858 he had planted 85,556 vines in his Buena Vista Vineyard. When he wrote an article on viticulture and wine making in the latter year, Sonoma was deluged with a flood of inquiries; overnight it became the State's chief center for distribution of viticultural knowledge and nursery cuttings of foreign vines. From Col. Haraszthy's vineyard, cuttings of the Zinfandel, Flame Tokay, Black Morocco, Seedless Sultana, and Muscat of Alexandria were distributed throughout the State.

Sonoma's plaza, once a dusty square carelessly littered with the skeletons of slaughtered beeves, is green with lawns and shrubs today. It surrounds the stone COURTHOUSE AND CITY HALL, dedicated in 1908. At the northeastern corner is the BEAR FLAG MONUMENT, a bronze figure (John Mac-Quarrie, sculptor) of a pioneer waving the Bear Flag from a 40-ton granite chunk; it was unveiled on the sixty-ninth anniversary of the Bear Flag Revolution.

MISSION SAN FRANCISCO DE SOLANO, at the northeastern corner of the plaza, now a State Museum (*open 10-4*), was restored in 1910-14, after the chapel had served since 1880 as storehouse for cattle feed and the cloisters as wine cellars. The chapel (1824) and a tile-roofed one-story wing belong to the early days. The original mission bell, green with age, hangs near the door. In the cool, dim interior, old heavy unpainted beams support an adobe ceiling. One room houses pioneer relics, and another, examples of Indian handicraft.

The BLUE WING INN, 217 Spain St. East, a long, shabby, shingle-roofed adobe building with a balcony, was reputedly the first hotel north of San Francisco at the time of its erection in the early 1840's. It houses an old music box that still tinkles when fed coins, and Sonoma's first fire engine, decorated with faded birds and flowers. The SONOMA BARRACKS, Spain St. East and First St. East, a two-story adobe with a balcony (1836), has served as headquarters for Mexican troops, for the Bear Flag rebels, and for U. S. Army officers. The VALLEJO HOME, next door, the two-story adobe Palacio where Sonoma's overlord ruled his little principality, is still in use, although the tall tower from which he surveyed his holdings has disappeared. The two-story HOTEL EL DORADO, Spain St. West and First St. West, with balconies across the front of two long wings, consists of a first story of adobe—which in 1848-49 housed a noted hostelry—and a second story of wood, added in the 1860's. Vallejo's brother-in-law, Jacob P. Leese, erected the FITCH HOUSE, southwest corner of the plaza; both it and the RAY HOUSE, Main St. West and Second St. West, a two-story frame and adobe house with an overhanging roof, sheltered U. S. Army officers.

Left from Sonoma on paved Third St. West into a tree-lined avenue leading 0.5 *m.* to the VALLEJO HOME HISTORICAL STATE MONUMENT in a tree-shaded 17-acre tract. The two-story, ten-room frame mansion with its white fret-work dripping from the eaves was built by Vallejo in 1851 in the gabled and bracketed vogue of the period. In the front and back yards are white cast-iron fountains—one fashioned in the likeness of a fat swan with raised neck and open red bill spouting water. Vallejo called his place Lachryma Montis (Lat., tears of the mountain) because its first water supply came from a mountain spring. Near the house is the Swiss chalet, now the VALLEJO MUSEUM (*open 10-4*), a long, narrow edifice with a second-story overhang, built in 1850 of buff-colored brick and timbers supposed to have been brought around the Horn in sailing ships as ballast. Among the exhibits are the general's Spanish-embroidered christening robe, his derby and silk top hat, and his wife's enamel and silk jewel case.

South of Sonoma, State 12 continues to its junction with State 37 at SHELLVILLE, 25.5 *m.* (10 alt., 84 pop.) ; R. from Shellville on State 37 to the junction with US 101, 41.5 *m.*

COTATI, 346 *m.* (113 alt., 1,000 pop.), trade center of a poultry and farming area, is within the bounds of the former Rancho Cotati.

The roads leading into PETALUMA (Ind., beautiful view), 354.7 *m.* (100 alt., 8,245 pop.), which calls itself "The World's Egg Basket" —and has been called "Chickaluma"—are often clogged by trucks heavily loaded with crates of eggs and white leghorns. The slopes around town echo with the cackle of hundreds of thousands of chickens, for Petaluma produces eggs on a mass scale. Although the Mexican colony here dated from 1833 and the Yankee settlement from 1852, Petaluma rose to prominence only with the founding of its major commercial activity by a young Canadian, Lyman Ryce, who decided in 1878 that the region was adapted to poultry raising and sent to Canada for some white leghorns. Conceiving the idea of artificial incubation, he lived to see his incubators and brooders used throughout the world.

In Petaluma's scientific chicken yards, hens have outgrown the habits of their barnyard ancestors—scratching for worms, "setting," strutting about with their chicks. Petaluma eggs are hatched in mechanical incubators that even turn the eggs, a trayful at a time; Petaluma chicks are nurtured in heated brooders—the largest of which has a yearly output of 1,800,000 fledglings. One of the world's biggest incubator factories is here, producing machines that are widely distributed. Petaluma even has a CHICKEN PHARMACY, on the main street, devoted exclusively to the sale of remedies for ailing chickens.

Left from Petaluma on an oiled road 1.5 *m.* to the junction with a dirt road; L. here 1.8 *m.* to brown-roofed CASA GRANDE (*caretaker*), largest adobe structure in northern California, standing in wide, level fields. Gen. Mariano Vallejo in 1833-34 built the casa as headquarters of his 75,000-acre Rancho Petaluma. Here he farmed successfully with the aid of his Indian laborers—probably for several years before the land was formally granted to him in 1834. The adobe walls of the massive, fort-like structure are 4 feet thick. The heavy beams used in its framework—hewn from trees brought by ox-cart from Mendocino County—are bound

with tough rawhide thongs. Wide, second-story balconies run the length
of the three facades, enclosing the rear patio.

NOVATO, 365 *m.* (12 alt., 700 pop.), is a trade center of a fruit-
raising and dairying region.

At 368.5 *m.* is the junction with State 37 (*see above*).

At 370.5 *m.* is a junction with a paved road.

Left here to HAMILTON FIELD (*open 10-5*), 0.5 *m.*, 928-acre Army air
base, built at a cost of $5,000,000. Approximately 900 men, 125 officers,
and 60 planes are stationed here.

SAN RAFAEL, 376.3 *m.* (10 alt., 8,022 pop.), largely populated
by commuters to San Francisco, is the seat of Marin County, named for
a Lacatuit Indian chief. It grew up around the MISSION SAN RAFAEL
ARCANGEL, twentieth in the chain of California missions, founded by
Father Ventura Fortuni September 18, 1817. The present buildings
are restorations. In 1834 the mission had 1,250 Indians (Jouskionme),
3,000 head of cattle, 500 horses, 4,500 sheep, goats, and hogs, and a
harvest of 1,500 bushels of grain. In 1842, 8 years after the decree
secularizing all the missions, only 20 Indians remained.

At 720 Fourth St. is the ANGELOTTI HOUSE; built by prison labor
for the pioneer family, it stands as when it was constructed. A restaurant at 1339 Fourth St., built in 1886, was long a training place for
pugilists, among them James J. Corbett, Joe Gans, Jimmie Britt,
Battling Nelson, and Young Corbett. Another restaurant, at 603 Lincoln Ave., was the HOUSE OF PETER DONAHUE, early railroad builder
and capitalist; the spacious halls bear the murals and gold leaf that
decorated some dwellings of the wealthy in the late nineteenth century.

Left from San Rafael on a paved road to POINT SAN PEDRO, 5.9 *m.*,
where three Spaniards—Francisco and Ramón de Haro of San Francisco,
and José de los Reyes Berryessa, an aged rancher from Santa Clara—were
shot and killed by Kit Carson on June 28, 1846, during the Bear Flag
revolt, while Capt. John C. Frémont was temporarily in possession of
Mission San Rafael. Seeing a boat approaching from San Pablo, Frémont,
it is said, ordered Carson to intercept the passengers. The three men
disembarked at the point. A witness, Jasper O'Farrell, said that Carson
asked Frémont whether he should make prisoners of the strangers, and
that the general waved his hand and replied, "I have no room for
prisoners."

At GREENBRAE, 379 *m.* (32 alt., 100 pop.), where houseboats
are anchored along Corte Madera Creek, is a junction with a paved
road.

Left here, to the tip of Point San Quentin reaching eastward into San
Francisco Bay, to SAN QUENTIN PRISON, 2.5 *m.* (*relatives and persons with
legitimate reasons to see prisoners admitted weekdays 9-2:30*). The approach to San Quentin is barred by gates; only automobiles of prison
officials are permitted to pass. Within the gates, a concrete walk leads
past guards' cottages and the prison fire department (of which Norman
Selby—"Kid McCoy"—was once a member) to the prison wall. Construction of San Quentin, one of the largest and most overcrowded State prisons,

was started in 1852, and parts of the original cell blocks are still in use. With accommodations for about 3,500 prisoners, it now (1939) holds 5,200. The four principal cell units of the prison are of modern construction but cells built to house one man now accommodate two. About 1935 the dungeons, in use since 1852 as prison disciplinary quarters, were abolished; now transgression of prison rules results in confinement in "solitary," where the prisoner is fed only one meal each day and loses his privileges (visitors, tobacco, mail, or reading matter). Execution for capital offenses committed since August 1937 is by lethal gas.

New prisoners usually work in the jute mill, where grain sacks are made, for a year before being assigned to other duties. The prison manufactures furniture for use in State schools and offices. Its other industries supply its own needs. The inmates publish a *Sports News,* which has replaced the monthly *San Quentin Bulletin.* Prison dahlias win prizes regularly at the San Francisco Dahlia Show. San Quentin's most famous prisoner was Thomas J. Mooney, sent here to be hanged for the Preparedness Day explosion in San Francisco in 1917; his sentence was commuted to life imprisonment, and he was pardoned by Gov. Culbert Olson in January 1939. In the days following the World War, there were more than 100 prisoners at a time here under the criminal syndicalism act, most of them members of the I.W.W.

At 380.8 *m.* is a junction with a paved road.

Right on this road to MILL VALLEY, 2.1 *m.* (57 alt., 4,164 pop.), a residential community at the base of MOUNT TAMALPAIS (Ind., bay mountain country). The land on which the town stands was once part of the Rancho Saucelito (little willow). A mortgage on the property was foreclosed in 1891, and the land auctioned off in lots to form the town named for the sawmill built here by Juan Read in 1834. The heavy redwood frame of the mill stands in OLD MILL PARK, on Throckmorton Ave., on the bank of the stream that formed the boundary between the Rancho Saucelito and Read's Rancho Corte Madera del Presidio (cut wood for the army post). The latter grant was named from the fact that timber cut from the land went into the construction of the presidio at Yerba Buena (San Francisco).

The route continues L. from Throckmorton Ave. in Mill Valley on Cascade Ave. and climbs to a junction with paved Muir Woods Road, 4.6 *m.;* L. here 1.6 *m.* to an entrance (R) to MUIR WOODS NATIONAL MONUMENT (*picnicking facilities*), a 427-acre grove of redwoods in Redwood Canyon. The grove, named in honor of John Muir, the naturalist, contains redwoods as much as 2,000 years old and as tall as 250 feet, frequently growing in great circles around the fire-blackened stumps of trees burned in the remote past. An unusual feature of the grove is the albino redwood sapling, about 6 feet tall; containing no chlorophyll, it cannot manufacture its own food and therefore depends on the root of the nearby parent tree for sustenance. Among the other trees found in the woods are California laurel, tan-bark oak, Douglas fir, alder, madrone, nutmeg, and buckeye. Ferns and wild flowers grow in abundance. The park owes its existence to William Kent, an ardent conservationist, who purchased the nucleus—295 acres—and donated it to the Government in 1907 to save the grove from destruction by a water company which had filed condemnation proceedings to secure Redwood Canyon for a reservoir. The grove became a National Monument in 1908. South of the entrance the side road traverses Frank Valley and joins State 1 (*see TOUR 1a*) at 5.7 *m.*

From the junction with Muir Woods Road the main side route swings sharply R.; at 6.4 *m.* it crosses a trestle built over the abandoned road-bed of the old Mount Tamalpais and Muir Woods Railway, a steam-operated road known as "The Crookedest Railroad in the World," constructed in

1896. The line had 281 curves. The chief engineering feature was the Double Bow Knot, where the track negotiated a 100-foot rise by paralleling itself five times within 2,000 feet.

At PANORAMA GATE, 9.4 *m.,* the route turns R. on a toll road (*toll 50¢*).

Left from Panorama Gate on West Point Road 3.5 *m.* to the junction with State 1 (*see TOUR 1a*).

At 10.3 *m.* on the toll road is the MOUNTAIN THEATER, a natural amphitheater with terraced stone seats on the lower western side of Mount Tamalpais, more than 2,000 feet above sea level in a forest of redwoods, madrones, and mountain oaks. The backdrop of the natural stage is a sweeping stretch of San Francisco Bay and the Pacific Ocean. Since its inception in 1913, the Mountain Play Association has presented a play here annually on the third Sunday in May (*adm. 50¢*). Past presentations have included *Rip Van Winkle, The Pied Piper, Robin Hood, As You Like It, Peer Gynt,* and *Androcles and the Lion.*

The toll road winds along the slopes of Mount Tamalpais' three crests— West Peak (2,605 alt.), Middle Peak (2,570 alt.), and East Peak (2,586 alt.)—to the MOUNT TAMALPAIS TAVERN, 12.4 *m.* From the tavern's broad windows is a far view on clear days. Mount Tamalpais appears much higher than it is because it rises almost from sea level. Myriads of ferns and wild flowers grow in the forest shade. The entire mountain is a game refuge, with hundreds of deer grazing on its slopes.

IN RICHARDSON BAY, bridged by US 101 at 383.1 *m.* appear the faded hulks and naked masts of a few German sailing vessels seized during the World War, so rotted as to be worth nothing in salvage. In the distance is the graceful San Francisco-Oakland Bay Bridge.

At 383.2 *m.* is a junction with State 1 (*see TOUR 1a*), which unites with US 101 into San Francisco.

At 383.7 *m.* is a junction with a paved road.

Left on this road to SAUSALITO, 1 *m.* (8 alt., 3,667 pop.), whose first permanent English-speaking settler was Captain William Richardson, a shrewd and active business man, who although as a foreigner he had no such rights, engaged quite openly as a pilot for trading and whaling ships anchoring off the Marin shore and appropriated the fees for his services; he claimed this as his privilege, since he officially represented the Mexican Government on the San Francisco shore. Sausalito (corruption of Sp. *salcedo,* willow) was so named because of the abundance of willows in early times growing about its spring, from which in early days, all the fresh water used in San Francisco was transported in barrels on rafts. The place is a strange combination of fishing village, residential suburb, and literary art colony, with a polyglot population. It is divided into Old Town and New Town; local humor divides the residents into "Wharf Rats" and "Hill Snobs." The vicinity of the SAUSALITO YACHT HARBOR in Old Town is called Hurricane Gulch despite the attempts of realtors to rename it Shelter Cove; it is a natural funnel through which strong winds blow from the hills. Whalers first began to use the cove around 1800 and later came here in large numbers. On the western shore is FORT BAKER, with high batteries. Still farther south near POINT BONITA is FORT BARRY.

South of the Sausalito junction US 101 climbs through low, windswept hills, in sight of numerous craft on the broad bay.

The 3.6 mile Golden Gate Bridge (*see SAN FRANCISCO*), 386.1 *m.,* spans the entrance to San Francisco Bay. From the toll house

(*toll 50¢* per car), 389 *m.,* the island site of Alcatraz Penitentiary (L) is visible.
SAN FRANCISCO, 392.5 *m.* (18 alt., 634,394 pop.) (*see SAN FRANCISCO*).

Section *b.* SAN FRANCISCO *to* SAN LUIS OBISPO, *243.3 m.*

US *101*

South of San Francisco US 101 follows California's oldest road—El Camino Real (the king's highway), the life line that linked Spanish California's 21 missions, her straggling pueblos, and isolated presidios. In the days when it was just wide enough for an oxcart, it was used by the soldiers of the Spanish king, clad in leather cuirasses and helmets and armed with swords and smoothbore muskets. Brown-robed Franciscans plodded along it on their way between the missions, spaced a day's journey apart.

"Down the peninsula"—as local inhabitants say—the way is now a tree-lined boulevard in a country-club domain populated largely by San Francisco commuters. Here latter-day millionaires following in the steps of the mid-Victorian "bonanza kings" have laid out estates, golf links, racetracks, and polo fields. US 101 cuts across saucer-like Santa Clara Valley's prune and apricot orchards—in early spring a fragrant sea of white blossoms—dotted with fruit canneries and packing plants. It winds into Salinas Valley, a narrow trough checkered with lettuce fields and orchards and dairy farm alfalfa patches, stretching southeastward a hundred miles between bare rolling hills where cattle have ranged since the Mexican rancho era. From the southern tip of the valley the highway crosses the oak-dappled Santa Lucia Mountains.

Van Ness Ave. and Fell St., 0 *m.,* in SAN FRANCISCO, is the junction with US 101-Alt.

East from Van Ness Ave. on Fell St., which curves (R) into Tenth St.; R. on Potrero Ave. and L. on Bayshore Highway (US 101-Alt.), a speed road skirting the marshy flats along San Francisco Bay.

The LIVESTOCK PAVILION of Agricultural District No. 1-A, 8 *m.*—in local parlance the "Cow Palace"—stands (R) in a 15-acre tract beside a trotting track and grandstand. The vast rounded roof rests on rockers greased every ten days so that it can be moved back.

At the southern edge of hills that wall San Francisco's outskirts is SOUTH SAN FRANCISCO, 10.5 *m.* (11 alt., 6,166 pop.), "The Industrial City," as it calls itself, a closely built conglomeration of steel mills, foundries, smelters and refineries, machine shops and lumber yards, stockyards and packing plants.

On the Bay shore (L) is MILLS FIELD, 13 *m.,* San Francisco's municipal airport.

Overlooking the water is a PACIFIC PORTLAND CEMENT PLANT, 25 *m.,* that converts oyster shells dredged from the Bay bottom into cement. The industry took over holdings of the unsuccessful Morgan Oyster Company, formed in 1887 to grow transplanted Washington oysters in the Bay. The oyster shells are unloaded by crane from barges, pulverized in steel cylinders partly filled with steel balls, and subjected to heat above temperatures required to melt steel.

MOFFETT FIELD, 36 *m.* (*visitors 7-5*), a U. S. Army aviation base (acquired from the Navy in 1935 in exchange for three Army air fields), has a dirigible hangar almost a quarter of a mile long that housed the ill-fated *Macon,* a mooring mast, helium tank, airplane runway, barracks, and shops. In SAN JOSE (*see below*), 46.9 *m.* US 101-Alt. rejoins US 101.

South of Van Ness Ave. and Fell St., 0 *m.,* in San Francisco, US 101 follows Van Ness Ave. into Mission St.

From the hills around DALY CITY, 5.6 *m.* (190 alt., 7,838 pop.), named for dairyman John D. Daly and expanded in 1936 to include the former town of Colma, hundreds of people from the Peninsula watched San Francisco burn in 1906. When speculators who bought up the land here attempted in 1859 to drive settlers off the site, the squatters built a fort and armed themselves with muskets and a cannon loaded with grapeshot. Chased away by pluguglies, they went to court and recovered their land in 1866, when the Supreme Court upheld their rights. The fields and slopes are covered with fields of lettuce, artichokes, brussels sprouts, pansies, marigolds, and violets.

Smooth green burial grounds dotted with marble headstones comprise LAWNDALE, 8.1 *m.* (113 alt., 369 pop.), a town populated with cemetery employees. Nurseries, florists' establishments, marbleworks, and tombstone shops border the highway. Lawndale has placed an arbitrary value on its land—$60,000 an acre—in order to exclude unallied enterprises.

The soldiers of the San Francisco Presidio once pastured their cattle on the site of TANFORAN RACE TRACK (L), 11.7 *m.* (*gen. adm. 40¢; fall and spring seasons*), oldest commercial track in the State. Named for the Mexican rancher, Torbirio Tanforan, it was opened by the San Francisco Jockey Club in the late '90's; but racing scandals involving jockeys, trainers, and owners evoked so much hue and cry that betting was made illegal in 1912, forcing it to close. The track was the scene of a race between an automobile and a Wright pusher biplane in aviation's pioneer period The pilot, Lincoln Beachey, was the victor, thrilling watchers by scraping the earth with wingtips as he cut corners and narrowly cleared his rival's head as he swooped over the automobile. One of his stunts—seldom attempted even today—was to fly between two trees, where the opening was narrower than his wingspread, by tilting his plane. Beachey was killed soon afterward while stunting at the Panama-Pacific Exposition (1915). The track was reopened when betting was legalized in 1933.

On the site of SAN BRUNO, 12.7 *m.* (20 alt., 3,610 pop.), a community shipping vegetables and poultry, was a roadhouse where travelers by stagecoach down the Peninsula used to change horses and young bloods from San Francisco practiced target shooting.

The tree-shaded avenues of MILLBRAE, 14.6 *m.* (8 alt., 1,500 pop.), a nursery and dairy trade center, extend toward the bay shore over the former estate of Darius Ogden Mills. His was one of the baronial country retreats where San Francisco's "bonanza kings" set themselves up as country gentlemen. The great two-story, mansard-roofed MILLS HOUSE, built in 1866, stands in the shade of Himalayan cedars on lawns where cast-iron shepherd-maids pose with flower baskets. The garish iron and wooden grillwork that once festooned the exterior is gone—but not the carved grandfather clock, the chandeliers and the full-length mirrors, the marble mantlepieces and the red plush canopies over walnut bedsteads that graced the interior. On the oak-dotted acres sloping toward the bay, reclaimed with levees built by Chinese coolies in 1872, Mills pastured dairy cattle, built an up-to-the-minute dairy and a glass-domed conservatory with a white marble fountain. The fortune that he poured into the estate had begun accumulating in 1850, when he made his stake with a cargo of miners' supplies sold in Stockton; it had grown rapidly after he opened a bank at Columbia, a Sacramento merchandising house, and eventually—with William C. Ralston—the Bank of California. It grew even more rapidly as he acquired vast holdings in the Comstock mines. The fortune passed to his son, Ogden L. Mills, Secretary of the Treasury under President Hoover.

Ragged eucalypti—grown from seed brought from Australia by Mills—interlace in a green arch high overhead for 3 miles south of Millbrae. In the summer the trees give forth a pungent scent as the sun draws out the resinous sap; in autumn bonfires of the fallen branches and peeling bark fill the air with a spicy tang and bluish haze.

The first center of country-club life in the West was BURLINGAME, 17.3 m. (30 alt., 14,800 pop.), a spacious town laid out with long avenues running from the hills to the bay shore. The pseudo-Spanish stucco villas of commuters and the great rambling mansions of the rich stand in the shade of eucalypti, pepper-trees, and oaks among golf links and polo fields. Burlingame was the product of banker William C. Ralston's ambitious dream of a colony where—as Gertrude Atherton later wrote—". . . San Franciscans could have charming summer homes not too far apart for social gatherings; with small grounds, but houses spacious enough for entertaining . . . In those days everybody in society was more or less intimate, and of course no outsider would be able to buy an acre in this sacrosanct colony." The dream had already prompted Ralston to buy the site when "His Excellency, the Honourable Anson Burlingame, High Minister Plenipotentiary and Envoy Extraordinary to the Court of Pekin," came to Ralston's estate with members of the Chinese Imperial Embassy to be wined and dined. Full of enthusiasm for his project, Ralston drove his visitor, an imposing gentleman with luxuriant Dundreary whiskers, to the tract and christened it in his honor. Ralston cut his land into 5-acre lots, built roads and planted trees, drilled wells and installed water mains—and sold the plots for exorbitant prices. But the colony grew slowly; not till after establishment (1893) of the BURLINGAME COUNTRY CLUB, first in the State, did it become the city of "charming summer homes" that he had envisioned.

The millionaires' community of HILLSBOROUGH (40-700 alt., 1,891 pop.), southwest of Burlingame, climbing hills that command sweeping views, now contests Burlingame's long-unchallenged social supremacy. Its founders decreed that it should have no post office, no telegraph or express office, no stores, saloons, hotels, boarding houses, newspapers—and no sidewalks. In summer Hillsborough's WOODLAND THEATER is the scene of Sunday afternoon symphony concerts.

SAN MATEO, 19.2 *m.* (22 alt., 13,444 pop.), is a bustling sub-urban town, still shaded by live oaks that stood on the rolling acres of Cayetano Arenas' Rancho San Mateo. The region looked like a "noble-man's park" to officers of the British naval vessel *Blossom,* on their way to Monterey in 1827; "herds of cattle and horses were grazing upon the rich pasture, and numerous fallow deer, startled at the approach of strangers bounded off to seek protection among the hills." But they could trace the resemblance no further. "Instead of a noble mansion in character with so fine a country," they found on the banks of San Mateo Creek "a miserable hut dwelling before the door of which a number of half naked Indians were basking in the sun," surrounded with litter that "sadly disgraced the park-like scenery." The building, a long, low adobe, was a hospice where friars, officials, and soldiers broke their journey between Mission Dolores and Mission Santa Clara. The roof tiles, all that remained after the earthquake of 1868, were used on the Burlingame railroad station.

The first San Mateo settler, John B. Cooper, a deserter from the British Navy in 1833, took up his abode in 1851 in a brush booth beneath an oak. The town, platted in 1863, was eventually encom-passed by the estates of San Francisco rich men—W. D. M. Howard and Frederick Macondray, the merchants; John Parrott, shipping and financial magnate; and Alvinza Hayward, mine operator and financier. All that remains of the HAYWARD ESTATE is the white-painted stable (now a garage), between Rosewood Dr. and South B St. near Ninth St.; it housed Hayward's horses in rosewood and mahogany stalls and stood in the midst of a park where Hayward's own deer browsed under oaks. At the SAN MATEO POLO CLUB FIELD, near the southern city limit (R), high-goal players from California, the East, England, and Argentina perform before "society"-crowded galleries.

The stands of BAY MEADOWS RACE TRACK (L), 20.7 *m.* (*gen. adm. 40¢*), are filled with 25,000 horse fans during the winter racing season.

The wooded hills sloping steeply to BELMONT, 23 *m.* (32 alt., 984 pop.), delighted Capt. George Vancouver's appreciative eye when he paused here for lunch November 20, 1792, on his way to Mission Santa Clara with a military escort from the anchorage near the San Francisco Presidio of the British warship *Discovery,* first non-Spanish vessel to enter the Bay. On "a very pleasant enchanting lawn situated amidst a grove of trees at the foot of a small hill, by which flowed a stream of most excellent water," the party had their noontime refresh-ments "with some grog we had brought from the ship, spirits and wine being scarce articles in this country." For Vancouver, the countryside could properly be described only with eighteenth-century grandiloquence: "The stately lords of the forest were in complete possession of the soil, covered with luxuriant herbage and beautifully diversified with pleasing eminences and valleys; which, with the range of lofty, rugged mountains that bounded the prospect, required only to be adorned with the neat habitations of an industrious people to produce a scene not inferior to the most studied effects of taste in the disposal of the grounds."

Only "the most studied effects of taste" would do for William Chapman Ralston—the gambling financial genius of the Bank of California who poured his Comstock mining millions into countless enterprises—when he purchased Count Lussetti Cipriani's modest hillside villa in the Cañada del Diablo at Belmont and began transforming it into the Peninsula's most extravagant showplace. Architects, artisans, and gardeners changed the villa into what Gertrude Atherton called "an immense, rambling, French-looking structure," thrusting out guest wings in all directions. By 1867 it had accommodations for 30 guests; by 1868, for 120. The floors were of parquetry, the walls panelled with mirrors, the ceiling hung with chandeliers. Europe and the Orient were plundered for rugs, hangings, vases, furniture, glassware and napery to furnish the spacious, high-ceilinged chambers. Outside the mansion were brick-and-glass greenhouses; a bowling alley and gymnasium with a Turkish bath; a "Little Belmont" for the Chinese servants, the grooms and hostlers; and stables with walls of redwood outside and carved mahogany inlaid with mother-of-pearl inside, and with a glass-enclosed harness room having solid silver pegs for the silver-monogrammed trappings of Ralston's thoroughbreds. To illuminate his country seat, Ralston erected a gas-works; to irrigate his far-reaching gardens, he built a dam and reservoir in the hills.

At the great white mansion's long porte-cochère an almost continuous stream of carriages began discharging actresses, ambassadors, generals, and statesmen, the great and near-great from Mark Twain to Baron Ikakuri of the first Japanese delegation to visit America. One of the sights of the time was Ralston's four-in-hand, crowded with guests and drawn by spirited steeds, with Ralston himself cracking the whip. He usually managed to arrive with new guests just after dark when the house was a blaze of light against the black of the canyon. Often Ralston used to sit in his royal box, watching his guests dance in the dazzling chandelier-lighted ballroom, reflected in its great mirrors. As many as a hundred dinner guests used to be escorted to the library, there to wait until suddenly "the opposite wall gave a sort of shiver, then rose slowly like the curtain of a theatre, revealing an immense banqueting-hall laden with the most splendid plate, china and glass that had been imported to California at that period . . . As motionless as an army about to salute stood the pigtailed Chinese servants . . ." The San Francisco *Call* once described what appeared on the table before them: "Glorious was the grand salmon stuffed with brook trout and baked in rose leaves . . . the pyramid of skewered frogs *a la mode* Huguenots . . . But these were as nothing beside the grand course

. . . humming-bird filled with baked almonds, surrounded by a Spring linnet, which, in turn, was enveloped by an English snipe. These the carcass of a stuffed goose surrounded, covering which were two canvas-back ducks . . . the whole placed within the bosom of a Chicago goose. Soaked in raisin wine for six days, then larded, and smoked three weeks over burning sandalwood, it was at last placed on the spit and roasted with pig-pork drippings."

The day after Ralston's Bank of California closed its doors on clamoring investors, August 26, 1875, in a financial scandal that rocked the State, Ralston's body was found floating in the Bay. The estate passed to his partner, William Sharon, whose daughter's marriage was the last of Belmont's social flings. The great mansion became successively a young ladies' seminary, a private insane asylum, and finally, the college and convent of the Sisters of Notre Dame, who converted the ballroom into a chapel.

SAN CARLOS, 24.2 m. (21 alt., 1,132 pop.), a town of homes among oaks, named for Lt. Juan Manuel de Ayala's *San Carlos,* first vessel to enter the Golden Gate, was the seat of Rancho Las Pulgas (the fleas). "The ranch had been well-named by the matter-of-fact Spanish," wrote Gertrude Atherton in later years. "I may add that it was no breach of decorum to speak of fleas in California, nor even to scratch."

The flower beds in the neighborhood supply eastern markets with carloads of chrysanthemums, asters, roses, violets, lilies, irises, anemones, gardenias, acacia, heather, and peach blossoms.

REDWOOD CITY, 26.2 m. (10 alt., 8,962 pop.), seat of San Mateo County, spreads over land some miles eastward from the docks and ,piers, canneries, and salt works of its deep-water bay frontage. Redwood Slough once extended inland to the mouth of Redwood Creek, now the center of town, where the Mexican rancheros shipped from the Embarcadero de las Pulgas. As shipment of redwood lumber hauled from the forested ridges to the west began in 1850, Embarcadero became a busy shipbuilding, wagonmaking, and blacksmithing center. Each time that San Francisco burned to the ground the demand for lumber swelled. The redwood business prompted the renaming of the town in 1858, despite founder S. M. Mezies' attempts to substitute his own name for the more euphonious Embarcadero.

The country estates of ATHERTON, 28.7 m. (52 alt., 1,324 pop.), are so heavily wooded that little of the town beyond its shady lanes winding under great liveoaks can be seen from the highway. Besides its mansions, it has the old railroad station where the Peninsula's first steam carriages stopped, a handful of nurseries engaged in orchid cultivation—but no stores, and no sidewalks.

The first estate here was Faxon Dean Atherton's mile-square Valparaiso Park, laid out in 1860. The family mansion (no longer standing) was later described by his daughter-in-law, Gertrude, as "a large comfortable house with two bath rooms—few houses boasted more than one —and a wing for the servants . . . About the house was a continuous bed of Parma violets whose fragrance greeted one when passing the deer park. (The deer generally died, homesick for their forests on the mountains.)" Faxon Atherton, "in his early youth, had adventured as far as Chile in search of his fortune. He made it in hardware. Not long after his arrival he married Dominga de Goni . . ." Mrs. Atherton, her daughter-in-law wrote, "had hopes of making a true Atherton out of me, and I sometimes wonder she did not . . . 'Ladies in Spain do not write,' she said to me when I began to betray symptoms; and it was quite twelve years after I published my first novel before the painful subject that I wrote at all was mentioned by any of the family in my presence . . ." Life in Valparaiso Park for Gertrude Atherton seemed to be a long series of summer afternoons spent with neighbors "on the wide verandah, sewing, embroidering, exchanging recipes, gossiping. I often wondered if life anywhere else in the whole wide world were as dull."

When James L. Flood, the former San Francisco saloonkeeper who rose to sudden riches by speculation in Virginia City mines, began in 1878 to build the scrollwork-festooned extravaganza of gables, cupolas, and porticos that he called Linden Towers, "the impertinent invasion of . . . the Bonanza millionaires" threw the country aristocracy into a furore, and "for weeks the leading topic on the verandah was whether or not the Floods should be called upon when they moved in." The "colossal white house . . . looked more like a house on a wedding cake than something to live in." In the end, "for business reasons, impressed upon them by their husbands, the women did call." When the Floods returned the call at Valparaiso Park—Mrs. Flood wearing "a flowing dark blue silk wrapper, discreetly ruffled, and 'Miss Jennie' a confection of tourquoise-green flannel trimmed with deep flounces of Valenciennes lace!"—Gertrude Atherton fancied "they went away . . . with the pleasant feeling of superiority that only multi-millions can give." The trappings of Linden Towers—the sterling silver soap dishes initialed J.F., the statues and tapestries, the marble fireplaces and carved rosewood panels—went on the auction block in 1934 when the mansion was torn down; all that remains of the JAMES L. FLOOD ESTATE on Middlefield Rd. today are the lodge, the massive iron gateways, and the brick wall that enclosed the grounds.

The neighboring country home center of MENLO PARK, 29.9 m. (63 alt., 2,254 pop.), which grew up with the advent of the railroad in 1863 around an estate named by two Irishmen for their home in Ireland, was chosen in 1871 by Milton S. Latham, Governor and U. S. Senator, for his stately, pillared mansion. When the Duke of Manchester passed through on his way around the world, he was escorted here by train to meet the country fashionables. The company was gathered in the drawing room—the women in their Paris gowns and the men in their evening best eagerly awaiting their first sight of a real duke when the English butler announced him. "And then," as Gertrude Atherton told the story, "the duke strode in, and they nearly fainted. He wore boots that reached his thighs and a red flannel shirt! . . .

History

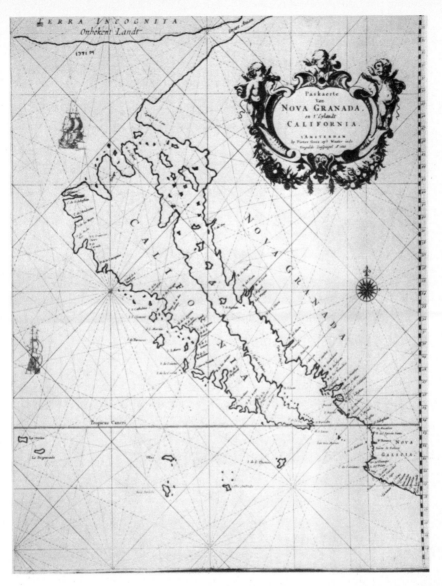

MAP OF CALIFORNIA, DRAWN IN 1666

A VIEW OF SUTTER'S MILL AND CULLOMA VALLEY

WORKING AT SUTTER'S MILL (1850), TWENTY-FIVE
FEET FROM WHERE GOLD WAS DISCOVERED

RUSSIAN CHURCH, FORT ROSS (1812)

HORNITOS

SAN FRANCISCO IN 1849

PRAIRIE SCHOONER, BROUGHT TO YOLO COUNTY
BY JOHN BEMMERLY FROM OHIO IN 1849

ON TO THE GOLD FIELDS

LYNCH LAW (1856)

STAGE COACH AND TRAIN, CISCO (1869)

PONY EXPRESS. HIGHWAYMEN IN PURSUIT

Poor man, he was terribly mortified, and explained to his suave and smiling host that all he knew of California he had gleaned from the stories of Bret Harte, and had provided himself with what he believed to be the regulation Western costume . . ." The MILTON S. LATHAM HOUSE, damaged in the 1906 earthquake and never repaired, stands among gardens, fountains, stables, and carriage houses on Ravenswood Avenue.

Visible above liveoaks and eucalypti for miles is the PALO ALTO (tall tree), 30.6 *m.*, whose branches shaded the camp of the Gaspar de Portolá expedition, November 6-11, 1769. The "barbarous heathen" of the region whom the chronicler, Fray Crespi, described as "very affable, mild, and docile, and very generous" believed that the Great Spirit dwelt in the tree and held their councils beneath it. When the expedition led by Don Fernando de Rivera y Moncada to hunt for a mission site on the Bay passed by five years later, Fray Palou marked the spot as suitable; and the Juan Bautista de Anza Party, bound for San Francisco in March 1776, found the cross he had erected. The tree in those days was double-trunked, but one of the trunks fell across the creek in the late 1890's. A reproduction of it appears on the seal of Leland Stanford Jr. University. Before the World War, Stanford students used to mount guard over the tree nightly just before their annual "Big Game" with the University of California, to prevent raiding parties of California students from cutting it down.

PALO ALTO, 31.1 *m.* (63 alt., 13,652 pop.), is a college town with lawns and flower gardens along avenues lined with liveoaks and pepper-trees. It owes its community theater, its advanced schools, and its distinguished residents to the influence of Leland Stanford Jr. University. Palo Alto is the home of cartoonist James Swinnerton, radio engineer Frederick Kolster, university president Ray Lyman Wilbur— and of Herbert Clark Hoover, the thirty-first President of the United States (1929-1932). The HOOVER HOUSE, 623 Miranda Rd., is on the heights of the university campus.

When the university was opened in 1891, Timothy Hopkins was still raising hay on the town site; he gave up his land in 1894 with the proviso that if liquor were ever sold on it, the land would revert to its original owners. To quench their thirst, early Stanford students traveled southward to the village of Mayfield (now part of Palo Alto), so named allegedly, because a recorder's office clerk mistook the first letter of Hayfield for an "M"; there they found no less than 27 saloons along the noisy main street in which to roar their drinking songs.

Right from Palo Alto on wide, palm-bordered Palm Drive (University Ave.) to the sandstone pillars guarding the entrance to the 9,000-acre campus of STANFORD UNIVERSITY (formerly Leland Stanford Jr. University). The campus, nicknamed The Farm, covers the former Palo Alto Stock Farm where Leland Stanford (one of the "Big Four," early railroad builders and financiers), who became Governor (1861-62) and U. S. Senator (1885-93), raised thoroughbred horses. Construction of the university buildings was begun in May, 1887, with a $30,000,000 endowment fund established by Stanford and his wife as a memorial to their only child, who had died at the age of 16. The university was opened to students in 1891. The institution had more women students than men until Mrs. Stanford limited the number of women to 500 (whereupon Stanford co-eds were dubbed the "500") ; but women now comprise about 1,000 of the 3,000 or 4,000 students.

At 0.5 m. is the junction with a paved road; R. here 0.1 m. to the marble STANFORD MAUSOLEUM among trees. A white marble statue, the weeping ANGEL OF MERCY, is a memorial to the Stanfords' son. Just beyond are the CACTUS GARDENS.

On Palm Dr. at 0.7 m. is the junction with paved Lomita Dr.

1. R. here 0.2 m. to the LELAND STANFORD JUNIOR MUSEUM (open 10-5, adm. 25¢), a reproduction in concrete of the museum at Athens, with mosaic panels and bronze entrance doors added. The south wing is devoted to anthropological, archeological, and paleontological exhibits; notable are the prehistoric Indian artifacts, baskets of the Klamath, Haida carvings in soft slate, and the David Starr Jordan drawings of fish of the Miocene period. Also in the south wing are the Timothy Hopkins Korean Collection, including costumes, household goods, screens, and carved furniture; the Di Cesnola Collection of Greek and Roman pottery and glass, excavated at Cyprus in 1865-76; and copies of Baron Rothschild's Tanagra figurines. The west wing houses the Ikeda Collection of Japanese and Chinese ceramics and bronzes, including an old peachblow vase, and an Imperial yellow Chinese vase. The north wing has a collection of early Californiana, including the first passenger locomotive used in California (1864), and the "last spike" of the Central Pacific Railroad, driven by Governor Stanford. Also here are early California tools and arms, Moro and Igorote weapons from the Philippines, and Chinese robes and ceramics. On the second floor is the Stanford collection of guns, jewelry, clothing, and toys.

2. Left from Lomita Dr., 0.3 m. to the OUTDOOR AUDITORIUM landscaped with trees and shrubs to make it look as natural as possible. The STANFORD STADIUM, 0.6 m., a great pit, holds more than 90,000 spectators. On alternate years the Big Game—between Stanford and the University of California—is held here, jamming the countryside with parked cars and traffic.

At the end of Palm Dr. is the UNIVERSITY QUADRANGLE, 1 m. The 15 buildings of the outer quadrangle and the 12 buildings of the inner quadrangle, built of buff sandstone and red tile are connected by long colonnades enclosing green lawns. The MEMORIAL CHURCH, built in 1900 by Mrs. Stanford in memory of her husband, is a buff sandstone edifice of cruciform shape in modified Moorish Romanesque design. The mosaic of the facade is a duplicate of one imported from Italy but destroyed in the 1906 earthquake. The brilliant stained glass windows depict Biblical incidents. Marble columns support the dome. The reredos is a mosaic reproduction of Da Vinci's *Last Supper*. JORDAN HALL, NW. corner of the Quadrangle, has among natural history exhibits an unusual collection of fishes. On Lasuen St., NE. corner of the Quadrangle, is the THOMAS WELTON STANFORD ART GALLERY, the gift of Thomas Welton Stanford, the university founder's brother; it houses a collection of paintings and reproductions of classic statuary and holds frequent temporary exhibits; the most costly painting is a portrait by Sir Joshua Reynolds. The STANFORD LIBRARY, on Lasuen St. facing the Quadrangle, is an adaptation of the mission type of architecture with red tile roofs and many windows. It contains more than 600,000 volumes, with specialized departments and a rare book section.

The HOOVER LIBRARY ON WAR, REVOLUTION, AND PEACE (open to specialists), 5,000,000 documents, books, and secret reports of the World War period (formerly housed in the library) is to be transferred to its own high tower. Compilation of the archives was begun during the war years when Herbert Hoover was first engaged in distributing relief supplies among the peoples of the European Allies; later, American Relief Admin-

istration employees collected cases full of the records of tumbling governments. Forty governments cooperated to build up the collection. Some
of the documents were deposited on the condition that they be kept sealed
for 20 years. The documents considered dangerous to persons now alive
are sealed in concrete vaults.

Beyond the Quadrangle, along Lasuen St., is The Row, lined with
fraternity and sorority houses and the homes of faculty members. All day
and all evening convertible coupes dash in and out of the circular drive-
ways; men pass footballs on the yards of fraternity houses, or sit on the
steps watching other students go by. On Saturday nights there are dances
in the fraternity and sorority houses, formal and informal—possibly "barnyard frolics" where couples dressed in overalls and gingham dance among
bales of hay and other bucolic decorations.

Right from the Quad on Serra St. to Lomita Dr.; L. on Lomita Dr.
(bordering the Quad on the west) to the junction with Searsville Rd.,
1.2 *m*. Right on Searsville Rd. about 0.3 *m* to the FOOD RESEARCH INSTITUTE,
organized under a Carnegie Corporation grant, which studies the production, distribution, and consumption of food. A well-equipped laboratory
facilitates the primary job of research and the secondary one of teaching.
Among the subjects being analyzed in 1939 were the world wheat situation,
fats and oils of animal and vegetable origin, and the agricultural situation
and policy at home and abroad.

On Lomita Dr. is (L) the STANFORD UNIVERSITY PRESS, 1.4 *m*., a printing
and publishing establishment.

At 1.6 *m*. is the junction with Lagunita Dr.; R. here on a footpath about
200 feet to LAGUNITA, a shallow lake, dry except in the spring, when it is
used for water sports.

At 2 *m*. is Mayfield Ave.; L. here 1 *m*. to the HARRIS J. RYAN HIGH
VOLTAGE LABORATORY, near the foot of Stanford Ave., which has electrical
transformers with a capacity of more than 2,000,000 volts.

Stanford graduates include many noted figures. Among the first were
Herbert Hoover and Ray Lyman Wilbur, later a member of President
Hoover's cabinet and now the university president. Although the children
of these men and other well-known personages have attended Stanford,
Senator Stanford's original purpose of starting a university for boys of
inadequate means still holds. More than half the students are fully or
partly self-supporting.

One of Stanford's unusual students in 1899 was hunch-backed Homer Lea,
a redoubtable poker player and a student of military history, whose favorite
diversion was wandering in the hills back of the campus while he plotted
military strategy. Told after a dangerous illness that he had only three
months to live he decided to end his life in a burst of glory. He went to
China, where he met Sun Yat Sen. As general of 60,000 Chinese soldiers,
he established a drastic regime; any officer found false to him was
beheaded. His own staff was seized by his enemies and given the same
treatment. By appealing for funds to San Francisco's Chinese, he was able
to return to the United States. As "Lieutenant General Homer Lea of the
Chinese Army in command of the Second Division," he drilled Chinese on
vacant lots in San Francisco and Los Angeles. On parade he wore a blue
uniform of his own design, complete with epaulets, gold braid, brass buttons, and a row of medals. When the Chinese revolution broke out in
1911, Lea rejoined Sun Yat Sen. He died in 1912.

On the rolling hills of the campus' southeastern outskirts is (R),
32.6 *m*., an abandoned tunnel, a round red-brick tower, and an arched
bridge in a tangle of weeds. An almost legendary figure—"The
Frenchman," Peter Coutts, had his Matadero (slaughterhouse) Ranch
here in 1874, with a race track, orchards, vineyards, a cottage, dovecotes, thoroughbred horses, and Ayrshire cattle. When he began de-

veloping a shrubbery-fringed lake with green islands connected by bridges, neighbors wondered what he was doing; and when he began digging tunnels into the hills, their speculations grew into wild rumors. Coutts was a fugitive, people said, and he was building a tunnel to flood the countryside from his lake in case his enemies found him. Suddenly in 1880 he disappeared. Although many of his neighbors never knew it, he had merely returned to France to resume his life as Paulin Caperon, Parisian banker and publisher, interrupted nine years earlier when he had been forced to flee to Switzerland because of his newspaper's opposition to Napoleon III's policy in the Franco-Prussian War.

US 101 cuts now through the fruit trees that sweep in row on row across SANTA CLARA VALLEY. The broad plain was so thickly studded with great oaks that to Capt. George Vancouver in 1792, it looked like "a park which had originally been planted with true old English oak." Now in the spring, from the foothills of its mountain walls—the Mount Hamilton Range on the east and the Santa Cruz Mountains on the west—it looks more like an expanse of snowdrifts because of the orchards white with blossoms. The almonds flower first, in late February, and following them in succession until early April, the peaches, cherries, pears, apricots, prunes and apples. In summer an army of wandering fruit pickers invades the valley—an army as large as the host of visitors in blossom time. The trays of prunes and apricots drying in the hot sun cover acres. The millions of prune trees stem from the tiny orchard of prune trees of the French type, *le petit pruneau d'Agen,* planted here in 1856 by Louis Pellier.

At 35.1 *m.* is the junction with a paved road.

Right on this road is LOS ALTOS, 2 *m.* (200 alt., 2,000 pop.), noted for its gardens and country club, where houses among oaks overlook the valley orchards.

The box-cars on the sidings at MOUNTAIN VIEW, 37 *m.* (76 alt., 3,308 pop.), are loaded with the produce of the town's pre-cooling plant, packing houses, and canneries, where the pick of surrounding orchards and berry patches is brought for processing. Before the railroad arrived in 1864, the Mountain View House with its wide verandah where men sat in tilted chairs with their feet on the railing, chewing tobacco and arguing, was a main stop for the four-horse Concord coaches on the San Francisco-San Jose line.

At 40.6 *m.* is the junction with State 9, paved.

1. Left on State 9 is SUNNYVALE, 0.4 *m.* (95 alt., 3,094 pop.), a quiet ranchers' trade center, once the seat of the tract purchased by Martin Murphy Jr. from Rancho Pastoría de las Borregas (shepherds of the lambs). Among fig trees grown from mission cuttings stands the two-story white MARTIN MURPHY JR. HOUSE, framed in Boston and shipped round the Horn when the Murphy family settled here in 1849. A room with an altar was set aside for mass, marriages, and christenings, celebrated by priests from Mission Santa Clara.

2. Right on State 9 is CUPERTINO, 3 *m.* (2,500 pop.), a crossroads town in flat orchard lands, settled in the 1850's by squatters who banded together when the owners of Rancho Quito tried to chase them off. In the 1880's several sea captains retired and built prim New England cottages here.

From the foothills, SARATOGA, 7.5 *m.* (100-800 alt., 1,191 pop.), looks down on orchards; its annual Blossom Festival draws throngs. It began life as McCarthysville, laid out by Martin McCarthy at the foot of the mountain toll road. It was rechristened Saratoga in 1863 because, like the New York watering place of that name, it was near springs. Among the noted residents are novelists Kathleen and Charles Norris.

The last flair of open-house hospitality in the bonanza tradition took place at Senator James Duval Phelan's VILLA MONTALVO, on the Saratoga-Los Gatos Highway at the eastern edge of Saratoga. The great tile-roofed two-story California-Spanish villa overlooks terraces approached by a long driveway and mounted by marble steps leading to a wide veranda. Roundabout are a guest house, a 20-car garage, an oval pool reflecting wistaria-draped pergolas, an amphitheater, and a fountain dedicated to Ordanez de Montalvo, who in 1620 was the first to use the name California. The doors were opened to guests in 1914. Phelan entertained legislators, opera stars, and the literary elite with luncheons on the terraces, open-air banquets at barbecue pits, and dinners in the patio where screaming macaws vied with a string orchestra in the balcony. After his death in 1930 the villa was bequeathed to the San Francisco Art Association "for the development of art, literature, music, and architecture in promising students." Only a caretaker disturbs the quiet today.

State 9 winds into the Santa Cruz Mountains to CONGRESS SPRINGS, 8.5 *m.,* in a wooded canyon, where capitalists who wanted to make the spot a private vacation place for themselves opened Congress Hall in 1866.

From the summit (2,650 alt.) of Castle Rock Ridge, at the junction with State 5 (*see TOUR 1b*), 14.4 *m.,* the highway descends in curves to the entrance of CALIFORNIA STATE REDWOOD PARK, 26.8 *m.* (*lodge, campground*) in Big Basin, a 10,028-acre reserve of massive, cinnamon-brown redwoods lifting spire-shaped green crests as high as 300 feet. In the shadowy depths, tangled with Ceanothus, madrone, oak, toyon, and Tumion, the floor is carpeted with ferns and shrubs. The park was the first set aside for preservation of the redwoods. Its formation in 1901 followed a long campaign carried on in the editorial columns of the Redwood City *Times and Gazette* by Ralph Smith and continued after his death in 1887 by Andrew P. Hill, early photographer of the redwoods.

GOVERNOR'S CAMP, 28.7 *m.* (*post office, inn and cottages, store*), so named in remembrance of visits by two Governors of California and a Governor of Utah in 1901 and 1902, is the starting point for the Redwood Trail, looping through the park past trees of curious formation. One of the tallest is the ANIMAL TREE, deformed by burls at its base. Even taller are the FATHER OF THE FOREST and the MOTHER OF THE FOREST, which towers 320 feet, although its top is broken off.

State 9 follows Boulder Creek to its confluence with Bear Creek and the San Lorenzo River at the settlement of BOULDER CREEK, 37.9 (500 pop.), a colony of summer homes that began as a redwood lumber camp.

The way leads down the valley to BEN LOMOND, 41.8 *m.* (458 pop.), which grew up in the 1880's at the base of Ben Lomond Mountain, named by a Scottish immigrant.

FELTON, 44.9 *m.* (350 pop.), stands within Rancho Zayante, which Isaac Graham bought in 1841—allegedly with the $36,000 indemnity he got for the outrage of having been arrested at Monterey as a dangerous foreigner and shipped to Mexico.

Left from Felton 1 *m.* crossing a COVERED BRIDGE (1892) to MOUNT HERMON, a mountain resort. At 4 *m.* is the junction with State 17 (*see below*).

State 9 continues to the junction with a dirt road, 46.5 *m.; L. here 0.5 *m.*

380 CALIFORNIA

to the BIG TREES, a county park of Sequoia sempervirens. The GIANT (306 feet), the JUMBO (250 feet), and the CATHEDRAL GROUP are among the tallest. The cavernous opening of the hollow FRÉMONT TREE (285 feet), large enough to hold 50 people, is persistently reported to have sheltered Capt. John C. Frémont and his aides in 1846. Frémont's comment, when he visited the grove in later years, was: "It is a good story, let it stand."

State 9 skirts the bank of the San Lorenzo River to its junction with State 1 (see TOUR 1b), 51.7 m., on the edge of Santa Cruz (see TOUR 1b).

Under the branches of the ARMISTICE OAK (R), 42.6 m., Santa Clara Valley's last anti-Yankee uprising ended January 8, 1847, when Francisco Sánchez and his men gave up their arms to the gringos. The armistice followed a skirmish nearby on January 2—the "Battle of the Mustard Stalks," later dignified as the Battle of Santa Clara—from which the Californians withdrew into the hills with four wounded and four dead. They had taken up arms, wrote Rev. Walter Colton, the Yankee alcalde at Monterey, "not to make war on the American flag, but to protect themselves from the depredations of those who, under color of that flag, were plundering them of their cattle, horses, and grain . . ." Colton could find no excuse for plundering "the Californian to procure the means of fighting him . . . Let foreigners land on our own coast, and do among us what Americans have done here, and every farmer, in the absence of a musket, would shoulder his pitchfork and flail."

SANTA CLARA, 45.9 m. (83 alt., 6,303 pop.), settled by miners who invested their stakes in the valley's fertile farmlands, has gleaned more wealth from its orchards than the richest "diggin's" yielded. From its canneries and packing houses go carload lots of canned and dried fruit. The first orchards in the neighborhood were set out by the padres of Mission Santa Clara de Asís, founded January 12, 1777 by the Río Guadalupe. Padre Palou wrote: "Besides an abundance of water in the river, there are several springs which fill the ditches made to carry the water to the fields for irrigation." The "abundance of water" proved the mission's undoing, for the river overflowed into it. On higher ground the padres built a new church (1781-84), only to have it come crashing about their heads in the earthquakes of 1812 and 1818. The third church was dedicated in 1822.

On March 19, 1851, Father John Noboli, S.J., began adapting the mission to the requirements of Santa Clara College (chartered 1855), now the UNIVERSITY OF SANTA CLARA. The church, which became the college chapel, was so badly damaged by the earthquakes of 1865 and 1868 that it finally had to be demolished. When the frame church that replaced it burned in 1926, a fifth church reproducing in concrete the adobe third was built to house relics rescued from the ashes. Among its most sacred mementoes is the memorial to Fray Maguín de Catala, "The Holy Man of Santa Clara," reputed to have prophesied the conquest of California by the United States, the discovery of gold, and the destruction of San Francisco by earthquake. All that remains of the third MISSION SANTA CLARA is a remnant of the adobe cloisters in the olive-shaded rear garden. The three bells, dated 1789, 1799, and 1805, were replaced by a new set through a gift from Alphonso XIII of Spain.

The Spanish-style buildings of the University form a series of quadrangles. The UNIVERSITY LIBRARY exhibits old missals, vestments, breviaries, paintings, and chairs, rescued from the various churches. In the THEATER, students enact a Passion Play every fifth year. The University of Santa Clara is best known for the meteorological and astronomical observations of its scientists. Weather predictions of the late Father Ricard, called "The Padre of the Rains," were so nearly infallible that farmers used to telephone each evening for the next day's forecast.

Along the Alameda (tree-lined road) now followed by US 101, once stretched three lanes of willow trees with dovecotes in their branches. On festival days the doves were unloosed with trailing ribbons fastened to their feet to fly in front of little girls scattering wild flowers.

At SAN JOSE, 49.6 m. (85 alt., 57,651 pop.) (see SAN JOSE), is the junction with US 101-Alt. (see above).

1. Left from San Jose on E. Santa Clara St., which becomes Alum Rock Ave., to the junction with Mount Hamilton Rd., 6.5 m.; L. here on Alum Rock Ave. 2 m. to ALUM ROCK PARK (picnicking, swimming, dancing, and other facilities), San Jose's 629-acre park, spreading up oak-studded Penitencia Creek canyon, with footpaths and bridle trails. The park, named for an "alum rock" in the lower canyon, is known for its 27 mineral springs.

Right from Alum Rock Ave. on Mount Hamilton Rd. and up the mountainside, making 365 turns in 5 miles. In January and February, when the first flowers are blooming in the valley, the peak is often still snow-capped, dazzlingly white against a blue sky. The summit of MOUNT HAMILTON, 18.8 m. (4,029 alt.), a mile-long ridge, commands far reaching views.

On the western peak rise the domes of LICK OBSERVATORY (guides; visitors permitted to look through large telescope on clear Sat. nights, 8-10), founded with a $700,000 endowment a year before his death in 1876 by James Lick, eccentric millionaire real estate speculator, whose body lies under one of the telescope's supporting pillars. Before the county built the road that Lick demanded as a condition in making his endowment, equipment and supplies had to be freighted up in a rough trip requiring five days. The observatory, costing $610,000, was completed in 1888. It has a 36-inch equatorial refractor with a photographic attachment, a 12-inch equatorial refractor, a 6.5-inch meridian circle instrument, a 36.25-inch reflecting telescope, a 37.25-inch Cassegrain reflecting telescope, a 6.5-inch comet seeker, and other instruments, including seismographs, spectroscopes, and photometers. A Carnegie Foundation gift has made possible construction of a 20-inch astrographic telescope of 12-foot focal length. A movable floor in the main dome, 60 feet in diameter, has a rise of 16.5 feet. One of the observatory's most dramatic discoveries, made in 1892 with the 36-inch reflecting telescope, was the fifth satellite of Jupiter—the first discovered since Galileo's time; since then watchers have discovered five more. Lick astronomers took the first really successful photographs of comets and the Milky Way. The modern study of nebulae was begun here in 1898. More than 33 comets and 4,800 double stars have been discovered and charted.

2. Right from San Jose on State 17 (San Carlos St.) 2 *m.* to the junction with San Jose-Los Gatos Rd. Straight ahead here on Stevens Creek Rd. 2 *m.* to the WINCHESTER MYSTERY HOUSE (*adm. 50¢*), a crazy-quilt, 6-acre, 160-room mansion resembling a small city more than a house. It was the home of Mrs. Sarah L. Winchester, widow of a son of the firearms manufacturer. Arriving in California in the 1880's she bought the 17-room mansion, then under construction, and assumed command of a corps of 16 or more carpenters and artisans. It was destined never to be finished, for Mrs. Winchester, who had become a spiritualist (following the death of her husband and two children within a short space of time), was informed by a medium's message that as long as she kept on building, death would never overtake her. As the rambling mansion began to take on gargantuan proportions, she bought more land to accommodate it. Every weekday for 38 years the structure resounded with the noise of hammering and sawing, as she poured the Winchester fortune into operations that finally reached a cost of more than $5,000,000. But in 1922, death overtook Mrs. Winchester and the hammering and sawing stopped.

The mansion stands in parklike grounds, hidden from prying eyes by dense hedges, an unscalable fence, and grim iron gates. The reception room scintillates with thousands of prisms amid silver and gold leaf. The ballroom is a vast maple-paneled chamber equipped with a pipe organ and fireproof vaults—but no ball has ever been held in it. The "white satin chamber," its walls, ceiling, and floor covered with the sumptuous fabric, was entered by no one but Mrs. Winchester, who shut herself up in it for hours at a time to commune with her departed mate. When the oldest part of the house was shattered by the 1906 earthquake, Mrs. Winchester, convinced that malign spirits were warning her to abandon these rooms, had them padlocked. The embossed plaster still hangs by shreds, the beveled windows are still broken, the inlaid floors lie thick under dust.

So labyrinthine are the miles of corridors that a stranger is in danger of losing himself completely. The mansion is a fantastic patchwork of trapdoors, crooked halls, steps leading nowhere, doors opening into space. Forty stairways twist in and out, up and down; 2,000 doors open at unexpected places, some of them on blank walls, into cellars, or into space from upper stories; 10,000 windows of almost as many varieties appear in walls, floors, ceilings, and chimneys, hundreds of them looking out on blank partitions. Electric push buttons, gongs, and switches form an electrical network impossible to trace. Rare polished woods and stained glass gleam beside rough screen doors and strips of bare lath and plaster.

State 17 turns L. from the junction with Stevens Creek Rd. on San Jose-Los Gatos Rd. to LOS GATOS, 10 *m.* (412 alt., 3,168 pop.), spilling over sheltered foothills at the mouth of a forest-choked canyon within the confines of the former Rancho Rinconada de los Gatos (little corner of the cats). The heights above were formerly infested with mountain lions and wildcats.

As State 17 rises through the canyon past pleasant foothill homes, it passes the cloistered Jesuit SACRED HEART NOVITIATE (L), rising like a medieval monastery from terraced St. Joseph's Hill. From the summit of the range at INSPIRATION POINT (1,600 alt.), the road drops down the western slopes to the junction with State 1 (*see TOUR 1b*), 32.8 *m.*, at the northern edge of SANTA CRUZ (*see TOUR 1b*).

At 51.5 *m.* on US 101 is the junction with asphalt-paved Almaden Rd.

Right on Almaden Rd. along the windings of the Arroyo de los Alamitos to NEW ALMADEN, 12.3 *m.* (473 alt.), a long-abandoned mining town. The reddish hillsides are scarred with abandoned shafts, flumes, and chimneys, for New Almaden in its day produced more quicksilver than any other place in America. As early as 1824, the Robles brothers,

Secundino and Teodoro, and Antonio Sunol had followed the Indian trail to the hill of cinnabar here where the short, dark Olhones of the Santa Clara Valley delighted to smear themselves with the powdered red pigment; but finding neither gold nor silver, they traded their claim for a rancho. A shrewd Mexican engineer, Andrés Castillero, gained title to the deposits in 1845 and began recovering mercury with whalers' try-pots for retorts. When gold miners found a sudden need for quicksilver to use in gold recovery processes after 1848, long pack mule trains loaded with heavy flasks of mercury began following the trail from New Almaden to the port of Alviso on San Francisco Bay. The 20-room CASA GRANDE of the mine superintendent, at the head of the street (L), with wide balconies, two-foot-thick walls, and hand-carved, inlaid fireplaces, was one of the great mansions of its time. The mines were worked until after the turn of the century, when the price of mercury fell. New Almaden's peace was undisturbed until its revival as a week-end resort in the late 1920's.

As US 101 crosses lower Santa Clara Valley's orchard stretches, passing through a string of fruit-shipping centers—COYOTE, 60.8 *m.* (253 alt., 100 pop.), MADRONE, 66.7 *m.* (344 alt., 37 pop.), MORGAN HILL, 68.7 *m.* (348 alt., 908 pop.), and SAN MARTIN, 72.4 *m.* (287 alt., 375 pop.)—it cuts across the vast domain of the Murphy family. Head of the Murphy dynasty was Irish immigrant Martin Murphy, Sr., who in 1844 led his sons and daughters and grandchildren with their household goods over the mountains to California with the first party to cross the Sierra Nevada through Truckee Pass. Murphy bought 8,927-acre Rancho Ojo de Agua de la Coche (sight of water from the coach) and built the adobe family headquarters at the foot of Murphy's Peak (officially Nob Hill) overlooking the settlement of Morgan Hill. Around the chapel that he built on his sons' neighboring rancho grew the village of San Martin. The sons and daughters went on acquiring more and more land until in 1883 their holdings totaled 3,000,000 acres in California, Nevada, and Arizona.

GILROY, 78.6 *m.* (190 alt., 3,502 pop.), is headquarters for ranchers of the lower Santa Clara Valley's truck garden and berry patches, prune and apricot orchards, dairy, hog, and poultry farms. It celebrates its cattle-raising industry with an annual gymkhana, a display of bronco busting, cattle roping, and trick riding that recalls Mexican days when the whole countryside turned out for fiestas and rodeos. Gilroy owes its name to California's first English-speaking settler, the Scotchman, John Cameron, who took the name Gilroy when he jumped ship at Monterey in 1814, ill of scurvy; he settled here, acquiring Rancho San Ysidro by marrying Ygnacio Ortega's daughter, but before his death in 1869 he had lost his cattle and land and had to live on charity.

At Gilroy is the junction with State 152.

Right from Gilroy on paved State 152, up the slopes of the Santa Cruz Mountains to the junction with a winding dirt road, 8.5 *m.*; R. here 3 *m.* to MOUNT MADONNA COUNTY PARK on the summit of MOUNT MADONNA (1,897 alt.); the terraces, fountains, and trees, around the mansion built here by the cattle king Henry Miller are being overrun by a wilderness of fern, madrone, manzanita, and live-oak. Henry Miller was born Heinrich Kreiser in Germany; in 1858—the year in which he formed a partnership with Charles Lux—he took the name of a chance acquaintance whose ticket he had used on the voyage to California. For 58 years the partners went on acquiring lands and cattle until the "Kingdom of Miller and Lux" included more than 1,000,000 acres, in California, Oregon, Nevada and Arizona. The vast herds—all marked with the Miller and Lux Double-H brand—were driven all the way to market in San Francisco from one feeding and resting place on the firm's property to another.

From the summit of Hecker Pass (1,300 alt.), 11 *m.*, State 152 descends the western slopes to WATSONVILLE (*see TOUR 1b*), 17 *m.*, at the junction with State 1 (*see TOUR 1b*).

At 86.5 *m.* is the junction with a narrow paved road.

Left on this road is SAN JUAN, 3.7 *m.* (200 alt., 772 pop.), a ranching community with galleried adobe dwellings along tree-arched sandy streets at the base of the Gabilan Range. The gnarled trees of its plaza still have the hitching rings that once tethered the horses of caballeros. Every year during the St. John's Day weekend the inhabitants don Spanish costumes for a two-day fiesta with a barbecue, a parade, dancing, and pageantry in the OPEN-AIR THEATER to commemorate the founding on St. John's Day, 1797, and the completion on the same day 15 years later of MISSION SAN JUAN BAUTISTA, fifteenth and largest of the California missions.

The mission church, cruciform in shape, with a squat corner belfry, stands beside a low quadrangle with a sweeping red tile roof, facing the Plaza. The massive walls are of adobe up to the 20-foot level and of brick above. In the interior, designed with unusual restraint, the murals have disappeared beneath coats of whitewash. On the floor are the original clay tiles, worn smooth. The ceiling is modern, but the heavy beams are those that Indian laborers set in place and bound with rawhide thongs. Beside the old high altar, fashioned of redwood and painted with vegetable dyes by Indian artisans, are chairs, candelabra, an altar rail and figures of saints brought from Mexico. The niched reredos in back was carved by Thomas Doak, California's first Yankee settler, in return for board and lodging. A little rear room contains two baptismal fonts carved in 1797 from limestone. In other rooms are embroidered ceremonial robes, old books, tools, religious paraphernalia, and hand-inscribed music on parchment. The old music box, said to have been given by Capt. George Vancouver, was carried to Indian encampments by Padre Felipe Arroyo on muleback in an effort to tempt erring converts back to the mission with its tinkling eighteenth-century tunes. Behind the mission, under gnarled olive trees that date from the mission's founding, more than 4,000 Indian victims of the white man's diseases lie buried in a big trench.

San Juan's oldest building, now protected along with others as part of the San Juan Bautista State Monument, is the PLAZA HOTEL, W. side of the Plaza, probably built about 1792 as a one-story, tiled adobe and enlarged with a second story of wood in 1856 when Angelo Zanetta opened it as a hotel. A stopping place for as many as 11 stage lines on the San Francisco–Los Angeles route, it made a name for its wines and cuisine. The CASTRO HOUSE next door, a typical two-story tile-roofed early California mansion with an overhanging balcony around its upper floor, was built in 1825 by Gen. Jose Castro, afterwards acting governor (1835) and *comandante general* of the northern California forces (1846). In 1849 it was purchased by Patrick Breen, a Donner Party survivor, and used as an inn. As a guest here in later years, Helen Hunt Jackson began to write *Ramona* —until the Breens' house manager discovered she was not a Catholic and put her out. On the south side of the Plaza is the ZANETTA HOUSE, a two-story edifice with the usual second-floor balcony, where gay balls were held in the sixty's and seventy's when its owner was Angelo Zanetta.

Above San Juan on PAGAN HILL a gigantic cross of concrete marks the site of a great wooden cross erected by the mission fathers to ward off evil when they discovered their Indian neophytes secretly practicing pagan religious rites on the spot. Above it rises GABILAN PEAK (3,169 alt.), highest in the range, now part of FRÉMONT PEAK STATE PARK, where Lt. Col. John C. Frémont retreated with his forces March 6, 1846, defying orders by Mexican officials to leave the country. For three days the flag of the United States flew over the log fort he erected, while Gen. Jose Castro gathered forces in San Juan to dislodge him. Castro's proclamation against Frémont's "band of robbers" read: ". . . we will prepare to lance the ulcer which (should it not be done) would destroy our liberty and independence . . ." Since Castro's men soon outnumbered his by five to one, Frémont withdrew, retreating northward to Sutter's Fort.

The main side route turns R. from Hollister on State 25 down the San Benito Valley to TRES PINOS, 19.1 m., among hay, grain and thorough-bred stock ranches. A ranch in the neighborhood, where Frank Norris spent two months studying large-scale wheat-farming, provided local color for *The Octopus*.

The Rancho Ciénega de los Paicines of which PAICINES, 24.1 m., is headquarters, is still intact; on its thousands of acres are alfalfa patches, prune orchards, and herds of pure-bred, short-horn cattle. The rugged fastnesses of the badlands roundabout were long the haunt of the bandit gang led by Tiburcio Vásquez, and here at Paicines' crossroads store Vásquez, second only to Joaquin Murrieta in the annals of California out-lawry, made his last robbery. Vásquez' career had begun in 1854, when as a youth of 15 he stabbed a constable during a quarrel at a Monterey fandango and escaping into the hills joined a band of horse thieves. Mounted on a beautiful cream-white horse, he was soon leading his own company in a daring succession of rapes, pillages, robberies, and murders. For years, sheriffs' posses and vigilantes were unable to bring him to jus-tice, hindered somewhat in their efforts by the aid rendered to him from a disgruntled peasantry. According to modern standards, however, his monetary rewards were trifling, for his men never divided more than $2,000 among themselves. The robbery at Paicines in August 1873 was his undoing; he left three dead men behind—a deaf man who had not heard his orders, a Portuguese who had not understood the language he was speaking, and a hotel keeper who had stood in the way of a bullet sent through his door when he refused to open it. When the neighbors became angry the gang fled south, trailed by sheriffs. A colleague cuckolded by Vásquez betrayed his hideout. Brought back to Hollister in May 1874, he was tried and hanged at San Jose March 19, 1875. The calm and dignity that he showed before witnesses of the hanging bore out his proudest boast—that he was "muy caballero."

At 43.3 m. is the junction with an improved road; R. here 5 m. to the eastern entrance of PINNACLES NATIONAL MONUMENT (*guides, cabins, campgrounds*), 10,000 acres of crags, rocks, pinnacles, and forests among the Chalones peaks of the Gabilan Range. The weird, theatrically colored rock formations of dark red conglomerate found nowhere else in North America, have been carved into long twisting caverns, narrow gorges between precipitous walls with spire-like abutments, and great terraced domes fluted with vertical grooves. The spires rise from 600 to 1,000 feet. The walls of the BRIDAL CHAMBER, a semi-circular amphi-theater overgrown with thickets of live-oak and wild cherry, rise a sheer 500 feet.

State 25 continues southward to the junction with a paved road, 54.8 m.; R. here to KING CITY (*see below*), 69.8 m., on US 101.

US 101 twists over the slopes of a low divide and across the broad plains near the mouth of the Salinas Valley, so named for the Salinas

River's salt pools along its lower course. The sandy river bed, virtually dry in summer when the river flows partly underground, stretches southeastward a hundred miles between the Santa Lucia Range on the west and the Gabilan and Diablo Ranges on the east. In the early days, wild oats and yellow mustard grew so tall on the Salinas Plain that horsemen traveling across it had to stand on their saddles to see ahead. Over the valley bottoms and foothill slopes roved the herds of a long string of ranchos. The valley is still cattle country—although most of the bottom land is covered now with rows of lettuces and sugar beets, grain and alfalfa fields, berry patches and orchards—and many of the ways of the rancho era linger on.

California's biggest rodeo, held every July in the SALINAS RODEO FIELD (L), 104.6 m., keeps alive a tradition dating from pre-American times, when the rodeo held first place among the events that enlivened the dull everyday routine. Once a year the whole countryside joined in rounding up the range cattle into corrals, where they were slaughtered —not for meat, because there was no way of shipping it, but for hides and tallow. After the work was done, there were horse races, bull and bear fights, and singing and dancing. The trick-riding exhibitions of today's rodeos would have provided few thrills for the men of those days, who grew up on their horses. One of their stunts was to pick up a coin from the ground while riding at a dead run; another was to snatch off the head of a chicken, buried up to its neck in the ground, while galloping past; and another, to carry a trayful of brimming glasses at a gallop and deliver it without spilling a drop.

SALINAS, 105.6 m. (44 alt., 10,263 pop.), seat of Monterey County, is still a cattle-raising center, as it was in the days when nothing stood here but the buildings of one of the Ranchos del Rey, where the stock of the mission at Carmel and of the presidio at Monterey were pastured. The town dates from 1856, when Deacon Elias Howe erected the Half-Way House, an inn, store, and county meeting hall. In 1869 Salinas had a population of 600—including 10 Chinese, 3 Negroes, and 50 Mexicans—and the first newspaper in the section, the Salinas *Standard,* then a year old. Today its bustling modern business district is the market center for dairy farms, truck gardens, and lettuce fields.

The Salinas area has more than 50,000 acres in lettuce. In and about the town cluster the ice-making plants and packing sheds that prepare the crop for shipment to eastern markets. More than 2,000 field workers move in to plant, cultivate, and harvest the spring, summer, and fall crops. In 1936, when lettuce workers struck for higher wages and better working conditions, Salinas burst into the Nation's headlines as the scene of tear-gas battles between State Highway Patrol officers and strikers. Highlight of this strike was the mobilization which followed a report to the Highway Patrol that a Communist advance on Salinas was under way. Red flags proving the statement were taken from the highway and rushed to Sacramento. Airplanes were sent up to reconnoiter. Embattled growers prepared to defend life and property. In the meantime, an indignant highway commission requested that the flags placed as markers on roadsides by its workmen be returned to serve their purpose of warning motorists.

An unusual Salinas industry is the AMERICAN RUBBER PRODUCERS GUAYULE PLANT, opened in 1931 with a daily production capacity of 15,000 pounds, which manufactures rubber for automobile tires from the Mexican guayule shrub. It was established here after 14 years of experimentation had determined that the valley offered proper conditions for raising the plant. Since 1926, 15,000 acres have been planted with guayule. After four years' growth the plant is harvested and its trunk and roots are cleaned, chopped, and ground into fine particles. The rubber is skimmed from the fiber, refined, then dried and compressed.

Left from Salinas on a paved road is NATIVIDAD, 5.7 *m.* (161 alt.), a bustling station on the Coast Stage Line in the fifty's now falling into ruin since the railroad and the highway were laid out to the west. The two-story adobe CASA DE JOAQUIN GOMEZ overlooks it from the Gabilan foothills. Here one winter night in 1847 young William T. Sherman and a companion from Monterey hitched their horses "and went in just as Gómez was about to sit down to a tempting supper of stewed hare and tortillas . . . The allowance, though ample for one, was rather short for three," wrote Sherman, "and I thought the Spanish grandiloquent politeness of Gómez, who was fat and old, was not over-cordial . . . I was helped to a dish of rabbit, with what I thought to be an abundant sauce of tomato. Taking a good mouthful, I felt as though I had taken liquid fire; the tomato was *chile colorado,* or red pepper, of the purest kind. It nearly killed me, and I saw Gómez' eyes twinkle for he saw that his share of supper was increased."

The chile was perhaps Gómez' way of retaliating for the losses suffered by his fellow countrymen in the Battle of Natividad, fought here November 16, 1846, when 150 Californians mustered to attack 60 or 70 Yankees on their way with 300 horses to join Frémont at Monterey. A scouting party sent ahead by the Yankees was ambushed and several of the men were wounded or killed; one of its members, a Delaware Indian, who brought news of the battle to Alcalde Walter Colton at Monterey, "was attacked by three Californians—one of whom he shot with his rifle, another he killed with his tomahawk, and the third fled." In the sharp skirmish that followed when the main detachment of Americans came up, the Californians inflicted rather serious damage on their opponents before retiring. The Americans saved their horses, but at the cost of four or five wounded and as many killed.

At 108 *m.* on US 101 is the junction with a paved road.

Right on this road to SPRECKELS, 2 *m.,* a company town around a large sugar beet factory (*visitors 9:30-1:30; guides; plant closed Dec.-July*). The factory's slicing capacity is 4,800 tons a day. It was built in 1899 by Claus Spreckels.

As US 101 cuts southeast in an arrow-straight line through trim rows of yellow-green lettuce heads, blue-green alfalfa patches, carrot fields and flower-seed farms, the valley begins to narrow. The pepper-tree-shaded village of CHUALAR (a place abounding in wild pig-weed), 116.2 *m.,* stands among lettuce fields. GONZALES, 122.4 *m.* (127 alt., 910 pop.), is a dairy center; thousands of cows in surrounding pastures supply its milk-condensing plant. SOLEDAD (Sp., solitude), 130.2 *m.* (189 alt., 594 pop.), is a farming and stock-raising center.

At 132.3 *m.* is the junction with a paved road.

Right on this road 1 *m.* to the junction with a paved road; R. here 2 *m.* to the crumbling, roofless mud walls in vacant lonely fields of MISIÓN DE NUESTRA SENORA DE LA SOLEDAD (Our Lady of Solitude), whose founders named it more fittingly than they knew. The thirteenth of the missions, it was founded October 9, 1791, by Fray Fermín Francisco de Lasuen; the thatched adobe chapel was finished in 1797. It was so impoverished after its secularization in 1835 that Padre Vincente Sarria, who refused to leave, died on the altar steps before mass one Sunday morning of starvation.

The main side route continues on a graveled road to PARAISO HOT SPRINGS, 5.8 *m.* (1,160 alt.), a resort in the Santa Lucia Mountains, where the mission padres used to come to drink the sparkling mineral waters. "Eternal Paradise" was the name they gave a 20-acre tract here, granted to them in 1791.

US 101 parallels the sandy river bed of the Salinas River, choked with cottonwoods and willows. The jagged peaks of the Pinnacles National Monument (*see above*) appear (L), in sharp contrast to the rounded brown Gabilan Mountains. Long files of eucalypti, planted as windbreaks, crisscross the fields.

Around GREENFIELD, 139.6 *m.* (287 alt., 150 pop.), stretch the alfalfa fields, green the year round, for which it is named, and seed farms, gooseberry patches, and orchards.

At 150.6 *m.* is the junction with an oiled road.

Right on this road through rolling grain and cattle country, where the hot summer sun bakes out a pungent smell of dry grass, tarweed, and dust, to the summit of Jolon Grade, 10.3 *m.* (1,343 alt.), and down into sequestered Jolon Valley. Over the rough route in a rattling spring wagon came George Atherton and his wife Gertrude with their child and its nurse and their Chinese cook in the eighty's sent here by George's father, Faxon Dean Atherton, to evict squatters from his 43,000-acre Rancho Milpitas. At JOLON, 17.4 *m.* (978 alt.), "a straggling village on the edge of a ranch," as Gertrude wrote—now a mere remnant of a town with little left but a country store, church, and school—they stayed in a room that had neither a fireplace nor a window at the two-story ADOBE HOTEL, built in 1870 to house stagecoach travelers. (It is still standing, its upper balcony shaded by an ancient grapevine.) The next morning, "armed to the teeth," George set out with two sheriffs to evict the squatters.

Right from Jolon on a dirt road 6.5 *m.* to MISIÓN SAN ANTONIO DE PADUA, where "the squatters had herded their families and livestock . . . while they went off to seek a warmer hospitality elsewhere" when Gertrude Atherton visited the place several days later. "It was a strange sight. The church and yard were crowded with women, children, sheep, and goats. Winter was approaching and it was already very cold, but the immensely fat Mexican women wore but a single calico garment. The brown children, playing with the goats, were stark naked. It was no warmer in the tottering church and the first rain would add to their miseries."

When Fray Junípero Serra founded San Antonio de Padua, third of the missions, July 14, 1771, in an oak-dotted glen, he began ringing the bells hung from an oak branch, crying: "Hear, O Gentiles! Come! Oh come to the holy Church of God! Come, Oh come, and receive the Faith of Christ!" A lone Indian appeared to watch him celebrate mass at the rustic altar. The mission grew rapidly in wealth, until its fine horses, its 50,000 cattle and 50,000 sheep began to tempt horse and cattle thieves; a stone mill, operated with water brought for miles through a stone zanja, was built to grind its wheat. All that remains today is the crumbling brick-faced church (1810-21) with its arched portals and bell opening flanked by low bell towers and the crumbling colonnade with clinging rose vines stretching off to two burnt-brick wine presses above a wine cellar. A modern shingle roof protects the interior, where benches, an altar and organ, and some old wooden statues have been placed. Every year St. Anthony's Day, June 13, is celebrated with masses and a fiesta.

A long bridge carries US 101 across the sandy wash of the Salinas River to KING CITY, 152.4 m. (338 alt., 1,483 pop.), chief marketing center of the southern Salinas Valley, lying at the edge of barren, wind-swept hills. Along the sidewalks are still a few old hitching posts, used occasionally by cowboys in from the ranges. King City, named for one of its first settlers, was founded in 1868. Its surrounding farms produce pink beans, fruit, grain, and cattle. At King City is a junction with the paved road leading to Pinnacles National Monument (*see above*).

As US 101 crosses the Salinas Valley's lower reaches, the blue and purple of the Santa Lucia Mountains dominate the landscape. Since Mexican days SAN LUCAS, 161.7 m. (408 alt., 75 pop.), has had a tradition of raising fine thoroughbred horses. As the highway continues through cattle ranges between low, bare hills, the valley narrows. SAN ARDO, 172.2 m. (458 alt., 111 pop.), lies among rolling acres of wheat field and pasture. Along the river bank through low hills US 101 continues to BRADLEY, 187.4 m. (552 alt., 110 pop.), which ships diatomaceous earth.

The village of SAN MIGUEL, 198.3 m. (615 alt., 300 pop.), surrounded by almond orchards, clusters near MISIÓN SAN MIGUEL ARCANGEL, sixteenth of the missions and probably the most unspoiled, founded July 25, 1797, on St. James Day but dedicated to St. Michael because another mission had already been named for St. James. The mission buildings include the church (1816-18) and a row of low buildings all opening on a court bordered by a corridor with arches of varying shape and size. The inside walls of the chapel are decorated with simple designs—fret borders, painted columns and a low dado, in imitation of marble, the work of Indians under the direction of a Spanish artist, Murros. Especially notable are the beamed ceiling, the choir gallery above the entrance and the pulpit with its old sounding board, decorated in soft purples, blues and greens. Over the altar is a statue of St. Michael the Archangel. In the adjoining quarters Indian relics and implements are displayed.

The rolling land around PASO ROBLES, 207.2 m. (721 alt., 2,573 pop.), is still dotted with the great spreading oaks that led the first Spanish explorers to name the place El Paso de los Robles. Its almond trees are more famous now than its oaks, for Paso Robles is surrounded by a large almond acreage; the trees blossom in February, turning the countryside into one of those scenes so often photographed for State advertising literature. Long before Paso Robles was a town the spot was known for its hot springs, by which the padres of Mission San Miguel placed a wall of rude logs to impound a pool. Even grizzly bears are said to have resorted to its warm waters for bathing; old-timers told of a grizzly who made regular nocturnal trips to cure a lame leg, grasping with forepaws an overhanging limb while he dipped his posterior with evident enjoyment. The MUNICIPAL BATH HOUSE is built over the main sulphur spring and the hotel mud-bath house and hot sulphur pool over the original lithia springs.

ATASCADERO (Sp., bog), 218.3 m. (849 alt., 932 pop.), rimmed by a semi-circle of wooded hills, was conceived in 1913 as a model community, designed on paper to conform to uniform architectural standards and laid out on a scale large enough to accommodate a metropolis—so large that its scattered residences could never get close enough together to compose a town in the usual sense. Following the failure of the enterprise, its grandiose rococo civic center was converted into a school, and its small-scale farms went to seed, until eventually the town found its salvation in chicken and turkey raising.

Atascadero is the junction with US 466 (see TOUR 11b).

On a knoll near the cattle-shipping center of SANTA MAR-GARITA, 225.8 m. (998 alt., 211 pop.), is the ASISTENCIA OF SANTA MARGARITA, an outpost of Mission San Luís Obispo, of which Capt. Alfred Robinson wrote in 1831: "It was divided into store rooms for different kinds of grain, and apartments for the accommodation of the mayordomo, servants, and wayfarers. At one end was a chapel, and snug lodging-rooms for the priest . . . and the holy friars of the two missions occasionally met there to acknowledge to each other their sins." The massive stone doorway, several arched windows, and the side and end walls remain, patched together now in a ranch barn.

> Left from Santa Margarita on State 178, paved, up Pozo Valley, through the fruit and dairy centers of POZO, 18.5 m. (264 pop.), and LA PANZA, 34.3 m. (16 pop.), and across the high plateau of Carisa Plain (1,400 alt.). In the southwestern part of the plain rises a lonely sandstone butte enclosing a great oval cavity with overhanging walls, entered by a narrow opening on the east, which Spanish settlers called the PAINTED ROCK. Along the walls for a length of 60 feet are a number of rude aboriginal paintings in bright red, white, and black lines, representing men, birds, suns, and other indecipherable figures. The place, believed to have been an ancient temple, has been used as a cattle corral.

US 101 twists up the wild, wooded slopes of the Santa Lucia Mountains to CUESTA PASS (1,570 alt.), 125.7 m., in sharp hairpin curves. Over this pass, in November 1846, John C. Frémont led his small army at night in a pelting rain to attack the town of San Luis Obispo, believing it to be heavily garrisoned. Only the sleeping villagers were there when the gallant Frémont rode down the main street and made them prisoners. Frémont reported that he had "brilliantly captured San Luis Obispo without bloodshed." A historian reviewing the incident remarked: "It detracted somewhat from its brilliancy that there was nothing to surrender, and nobody authorized to do it if there had been, and the army was uncomfortably wet."

In a bowl-shaped valley at the southern base of the Santa Lucia Mountains is SAN LUIS OBISPO, 243.3 *m.* (201 alt., 8,276 pop.), seat of San Luis Obispo County. The town grew up around MISIÓN SAN LUIS OBISPO DE TOLOSA (St. Louis, Bishop of Toulouse), Chorro and Montgomery Sts., which is said to have been so named because two of the pyramidal volcanic peaks in the neighborhood suggested a bishop's mitre. When Fray Junípero Serra established the mission, fifth of the chain, September 1, 1772, he found the Indians of the place friendly because soldiers of the Gaspar de Portolá expedition three years before had killed with their carbines and spears several of the great bears that were terrorizing the Indian rancherías. Padre José Cavaller began his work with four soldiers and two Lower California Indians for company, his provisions limited to 50 pounds of flour, three pecks of wheat, and one barrel of brown sugar. The burning of the tule-thatched mission roofs three times in a row led the friars to experiment with making tiles, which proved so sucessful that they became the fashion after 1784 for all California missions. Most noted of Padre Cavaller's successors was the rugged individualist, Fray Antonio Martínez who, in 1818, drilled and equipped Indian troops to help fight the pirate, Hippolyte de Bouchard, and got up out of a sick-bed to lead them. Later Fray Martínez grew friendly with Yankee skippers engaged in smuggling goods into California, often entertaining them with his best wines. The mission was formed in 1844 into a pueblo that was incorporated in 1856 as a city, but the settlement kept the attributes of a sleepy Mexican village until 1894, when the railroad pierced the mountains from Santa Margarita. Many of its streets still follow the winding trails beaten by Spanish horsemen.

The church of Mission San Luís Obispo (1793) has been so hemmed in by modern buildings and so disfigured by its protective sheathing of white-painted boards and the addition of a shingled roof and a steeple that none of its original grace remains. Among its relics are a wooden statue of its patron St. Louis wearing his mitre, a cope and stole of Fray Serra's, an ancient cross said to have been used at the first mass, and a collection of paintings, images, hand-wrought silver, vestments and altar-cloths.

At San Luis Obispo is the junction with State 1 (*see TOUR 1c*).

Section c. SAN LUIS OBISPO to LOS ANGELES; 203.6 m. US 101

This section of US 101, heavily traveled both by private motor cars and by trucks, swings briefly to the coast south of San Luis Obispo and then weaves inland across a broad river valley and into typical barren hills. Returning to the shore of the Pacific, which it follows for many miles, it swings inland again over low hills and descends to the San Fernando Valley. Its way into Los Angeles is disfigured with roadside stands and advertisements.

Southwest of SAN LUIS OBISPO, 0 *m.,* US 101 passes through a small valley and reaches the Pacific, where it skirts the beach of San Luis Obispo Bay for several miles.

PISMO BEACH, 12.2 *m.* (35 alt., 600 pop.), well advertised by posters and banners, is a busy seaside resort during the summer, popular for its Pismo clams. This variety is seldom found elsewhere to any extent, and unrestricted digging had made them almost extinct until State regulations conserved them.

US 101 leaves the sea and runs through Arroyo Grande Valley, where much of the once rich topsoil, improperly cultivated, has been washed away. In October, 1934, CCC workers began erecting check dams and contour ditches to catch the silt and restore fertility to 7,000 acres. Banks were seeded with a grass mixture, mostly red barley, to hold the soil. Thousands of trees and shrubs were planted.

ARROYO GRANDE, 16.2 *m.* (114 alt., 892 pop.), once merely a stagecoach station, sprang into life in 1877 because of a land rush. Surrounding it are cattle and grain ranches.

NIPOMO, 24.6 *m.* (114 alt., 750 pop.), is on one of the few early land grants that have remained in the hands of one family.

SANTA MARIA, 32.6 *m.* (204 alt., 7,057 pop.), is the market center for ranchers in Santa Maria Valley. Grain, beans, and seed are the leading crops. Trees and shrubs line most of the town's streets, though until the late 1860's the area was so desolate that adjoining ranchos scorned the sandy flats. The first building, erected in 1871, was a small general store to accommodate farmers who had begun irrigating the land. Santa Maria owes much of its more recent development to large oil districts nearby. The town has notably wide streets because four pioneer farmers, laying out the townsite, wanted plenty of space to turn their eight-mule teams.

For miles the countryside along US 101 is planted with beans. The lanes of eucalypti along the road lead to LOS ALAMOS, 49.4 *m.* (569 alt., 600 pop.).

BUELLTON, 66.4 *m.* (490 alt., 107 pop.), is called the Mission Cross Roads because it lies on the route between two missions.

> Left from Buellton on a paved road to the MISSION SANTA YNEZ, 4 *m.,* on the outskirts of the hamlet of SOLVANG. The nineteenth mission, established September 17, 1804, by Fra Estevan Tapis and three other brothers, its prosperity reached a peak in 1820, when it owned 12,000 head of stock. After 1850 the buildings began to crumble. They are of adobe, low, painted white, and roofed with red tile, with an arched colonnade in front. The walls are five or six feet thick, to support the big, hand-hewn beams of the roof. In the mission are vessels of beaten copper, parchment volumes of church music, bound mission records, and carved wooden crucifixes.

US 101 crosses the Santa Ynez River, 66.9 *m.,* and winds through heavily wooded country to Nojugui Pass (900 alt.) in the Santa Ynez Mountains. At places the hills are almost solid rock with massive blocks towering over the highway. Sycamores with mottled gray trunks grow along creek beds.

LAS CRUCES, 75.9 *m.* (339 alt.), at a junction with State 1 (*see TOUR 1c*) is a postoffice for numerous farmers.

The lovely GAVIOTA (seagull) PASS (200 alt.), between Las Cruces and the ocean, was named by the Gaspar de Portolá expedition when one of his soldiers shot a seagull here in 1769. The shore at the lower end was once a favorite spot for the landing of goods smuggled in to evade the high tariffs imposed by the Mexican Government. Yankee ships anchored in the small coves and sent their cargoes inland for sale to missions and landholders.

US 101 runs on a narrow shelf above the sea to GOLETA, 102.4 *m.* (50 alt., 519 pop.), named for a schooner built by Captain William G. Dana of Nipomo in 1828.

Passing between small farms, the highway is lined for several miles with poplars and bordered at intervals by walnut orchards. In the purplish blue Santa Ynez Mountains (L), the peak of La Cumbre (3,985 alt.) stands out.

SANTA BARBARA, 108.4 *m.* (37 alt., 33,613 pop.) (*see SANTA BARBARA*).

US 101 follows narrow and unattractive streets. An alternate route follows broad palm-lined Cabrillo Boulevard, skirting the bay, passing the yacht harbor and the bird refuge lagoon, and connecting with US 101 at the eastern city limits.

In the low wooded hills to the south is the millionaire colony of MONTECITO, 112.6 *m.* (250 alt., 3,500 pop.). Signs marked "Private" bar the paved roads leading to the estates of such living trademarks as Stetson, Fleischmann, Armstrong, Pillsbury, and Du Pont. (*Adm. to many estates on special tours conducted periodically by Santa Barbara Garden Club.*) The four-lane highway is divided by a parkway overgrown with iceplant, a flat-leaved plant (*genus Mesembryanthemum*), found along the southern coast from Marin County to the Mexican Border, with stout stems and large leaves encrusted by shining beads of a gummy substance that glistens like frost in the sunlight.

The transition from the ornate houses near Santa Barbara to the old frame ones of SUMMERLAND, 114.9 *m.* (32 alt., 300 pop.), comes suddenly. The colony was founded by spiritualists but soon became an oil town, with a cluster of derricks rising from the water.

Near the ocean just east of CARPINTERIA, 118.4 *m.* (12 alt., 1,000 pop.), are several pits of asphalt, used by the natives to waterproof their houses and canoes. A spreading Torrey pine (L), some 60 feet high, was transplanted from the island of Santa Cruz about 1900.

Right from Carpinteria on Linden Avenue into the CARPINTERIA STATE BEACH PARK, 0.5 *m.* Under a roof about 300 yards (L) is the dead trunk of a grapevine, planted in 1846. Before the vine died, in 1916, the circumference of its trunk measured nine feet; it covered a quarter of an acre and yielded eight tons of grapes each year.

Leaving the flat plains, US 101 mounts the narrow pass of RINCON CAPE, 121.4 *m.* In 1838, would-be Governor Alvarado sent out a hundred men with three cannons against the slightly larger army of Governor Carrillo, Mexican appointee, who was advancing from Mission San Buenaventura to the south. After an opera bouffe rattle of musketry and booming of cannon around the escarpments of the pass, Carrillo and his men fled to the mission. Alvarado's cannon balls bounced off the adobe walls for two days, before the enemy escaped under cover of night. The sole casualty of this typical early California battle was one besieger, killed by a sniper hiding in the mission belfry, and the sole upshot was a new governor: Alvarado.

Skirting small bays, US 101 passes beach houses, and concrete balustrades that protect the roadway from the ocean. In former days El Camino Real ran along the tide flats beneath the mountains, a space so narrow that the clumsy ox-drawn carretas were forced to synchronize their schedules with the ebb of the tide.

VENTURA, 135 m. (48 alt., 11,603 pop.), is a busy oil and lima bean exporting point. Thoroughly up-to-date, the city retains little of the atmosphere of an old mission town. Poinsettias grow profusely along the streets and in the private yards.

Two Norfolk pines towering above the belfry mark MISSION SAN BUENAVENTURA (25¢ fee), Main and Figueroa Streets. This outpost, ninth of the California missions, was the last founded by Father Serra, leader of the California missionary campaign, who planted his huge cross on the hill to the rear and consecrated the ground in 1782. The mission was twice damaged by fire in 1791-92, and by earthquake in 1812; little of the original structure remains. The low tile roofed structure with its heavy buttresses and large corner tower is largely a restoration. In keeping with Franciscan simplicity the facade has little ornamental detail. The tower with its double, arcaded belfry is topped with a stripe-ribbed dome. Perhaps the most distinguishing feature of the structure is its bold and simple mass. Mission relics are shown in a small building opening onto the patio, in which is an ancient stone olive-crusher. The wooden bells that once hung in the belfry are now in the museum. Each is made of a single block of wood with metal plates inside, against which the wooden clappers struck. Such bells are common in certain parts of Mexico.

The PIONEER MUSEUM (free), in the VENTURA COUNTY COURTHOUSE, N. California and Poli Streets, has a collection including feather flowers made by elderly women in Vermont, a small scale model of the mission, Eskimo harpoons, model of South Sea Island canoes, and stone bowls of the Canalinos. A suspiciously modern appearing revolver is reputed to be that of Tiburcio Vásquez, the bandit (see TOUR 2b). In front of the Courthouse is a large cement STATUE OF JUNIPERO SERRA, erected by the Federal Art Project.

US 101 passes over the Ventura River delta, a district of walnut trees and orange groves blocked by long windbreaks of tamarisk, eucalyptus, and other evergreens. The windbreaks are favorite nesting spots of western mocking-birds, slim and graceful, with slaty black wings and tail, and a prominent white wing patch.

At 137.6 m. is the junction with State 126, paved.

Left on State 126 through Santa Clara Valley, a fertile strip of fields and citrus orchards along the Santa Clara River, sheltered between the San Rafael Range on the north and the Sierra San Fernando on the south. The valley is dotted with oil wells, still pumping oil from the oldest field in California; from 1866 until discovery of the Puente Hills district in 1880, it yielded nearly all the oil produced in the State.

At 5.8 *m.* is the junction with a paved road; R. on this road to the farmers' village of SATICOY (Ind., I have found it), 1 *m.* (149 alt., 400 pop.), founded in 1861 at SATICOY SPRINGS, where a number of Chumash Indians headed by the chieftainess Pomposa were living as late as 1870. The springs were their traditional gathering place for ceremonials at which—according to a gory legend—they made human sacrifices.

State 126 continues through oil fields and lemon orchards to SANTA PAULA, 13.2 *m.* (288 alt., 7,452 pop.). Laid out in 1875, it boomed rapidly with the oil industry. From refineries here, the oil was carried by pipeline to the coast for shipment. The nearby lemon orchard of the Limoneria Rancho is one of the largest ever planted.

The countryside around FILLMORE, 24.3 *m.* (460 alt., 2,893 pop.), produces oil, lemons, and oranges. The town lies at the mouth of wooded Sespe Canyon, a favorite resort for trout fishermen and quail and deer hunters.

The home place of Helen Hunt Jackson's *Ramona* was CAMÚLOS RANCHO, 33.7 *m.*, the Moreno Rancho of the novel, which Mrs. Jackson observed with such an eye for detail during a two-hour visit in 1882 that she was able to describe it later with complete fidelity. It remains as it was when she saw it, "one of the best specimens to be found in California of the representative house of the half-barbaric, half-elegant, wholly-generous, and free-handed life led by the Mexican men and women of degree in the early part of this century. . . ." Camúlos Rancho was the heart of the 2,000-acre Rancho San Francisco granted in 1839 to St. Antonio del Valle, on which the first California gold was discovered—March 9, 1842. The rancho passed to his son, Don Ygnacio del Valle, whose wife, Señora Doña Ysabel, was the original of *Ramona's* Señora Morena, although Mrs. Jackson never saw her, and to his grandson, Reginald F. del Valle, the original of the boy Felipe. The severely simple whitewashed adobe house (1852) encloses on three sides a patio with graveled walks between flower beds, rose and cypress hedges, and a fountain, overlooked by wide verandas. The oldest part of the house is the front wing, containing the chief apartments, where Mrs. Jackson placed the rooms of Ramona and Father Salvierderra in the novel; the wing on the west and the *cocina* (kitchen) on the north were added ten years later. The "greater part of the family life went on" on the verandas, wrote Mrs. Jackson. "All the kitchen work, except the actual cooking, was done here, in front of the kitchen doors and windows. Babies slept, were washed, sat in the dirt, and played on the veranda. The women said their prayers, took their naps, and wove their lace there. . . . The herdsmen and shepherds smoked there, lounged there, trained their dogs there." The family chapel, near the house, is a tiny frame structure with an altar containing *santas* (saints) brought from Spain. Nearby are an orange grove with an old fountain, two ancient bells hanging from a wooden frame, a brick winery and a grape-arbor, and an olive-mill. In the family graveyard, a square white vault contains the grave of Ygnacio del Valle.

At 43.6 *m.* is the junction with US 99 (*see TOUR 3d*).

At 139.1 *m.* is a junction with Mulligan Alley, a dirt road.

Right here to the OLIVAS ADOBE, 1.4 *m.*, once the dwelling of Don Raymundo Olivas, who took a leading part in suppressing a native uprising. The house is now the Old Adobe Gun Club.

South of MONTALVO, 140.7 *m.* (93 alt., 215 pop.), a lonely railroad station and cluster of seedy frame buildings that ships large quantities of walnuts, US 101 crosses the Santa Clara River, in the willows of which Tiburcio Vásquez is said to have hidden while evading, in accredited will-o'-the-wisp fashion, the punitive efforts of the combined constabulary of five counties.

At EL RIO, 143.2 *m.*, a few frame houses squatting around a store in the midst of fields and orchards, is the junction with US 101-Alt. (*see TOUR 2B*). The general store of its founder is still standing (L), with the black letters on its brick wall reading "New Jerusalem—Simon Cohn, Proprietor."

Tree-shaded CAMARILLO, 151.4 *m.* (150 alt., 300 pop.), was named for an early ranchero.

> Right from Camarillo, a paved road leads to CAMARILLO STATE HOSPITAL, 4.6 *m.*, a large group of white buildings in California-Spanish style. The hospital's normal capacity is 1,925, although at present (1939) it houses 2,094 persons.

US 101 continues inland, following the old Camino Real into the higher inland valleys, cultivated, irrigated, hemmed by mountains, and cut by streams. From the summit of Conejo Grade (778 alt.) is a view of the patterned mountains and valley drained by the Santa Clara River.

At 157.5 *m.* is the junction with a paved road.

> Right on this road to HIDDEN VALLEY, 5.5 *m.*, a mountain-hemmed district of grazing lands approached through walnut groves and a narrow pass.
> SHERWOOD FOREST, 9 *m.*, takes its name from the scattered clusters of oaks on the northern shore of SHERWOOD LAKE. Large houses cling to the steep hillsides, including the palatial home of the movie czar, Will Hays. The signs, "Private Road," forbid circling the lake, but the view from the hillside reveals the body of water below. This was the location for parts of the movies *Robin Hood* and *Tarzan of the Apes.* East of the lake settlement is the dam that creates the lake and a slight divide from which the road turns L. into Potrero Rd. and to a junction with US 101 at 13 *m.*

The two-story white clapboarded house (R) with green jalousies, in NEWBURY PARK, 158.4 *m.* (700 alt., 135 pop.), was once a stage coach station.

THOUSAND OAKS, 161.9 *m.* (250 pop.), is a gathering of tourist accommodations around the GOEBEL LION FARM (*adm. 25¢*), which supplies many animals used by movie studios. In the afternoon between 3:30 and 5 the trainer sometimes obliges spectators by putting his head into a lion's mouth.

US 101 continues through huge oak trees, whose acorns supplied the Oak Grove Indians with their chief foodstuff—acorn meal. Since these trees took root two centuries ago, the water level has dropped to such an extent that no young growth can take hold.

At 164.9 *m.* is the junction with Potrero Road (*see above*) and at 168.9 *m.* is the junction with a paved road.

Right on this second road to PARAMOUNT MOTION PICTURE SETS, 1 *m.*, make-believe western cow town, Spanish haciendas, African native huts, and Colonial villages sprawling in false-front arrays in the valley below the road.

MALIBU LAKE, 3 *m.*, small, irregular, and deep in the crotch of steep and grotesquely-shaped mountains, is surrounded with homes and gardens. The MALIBU MOUNTAIN CLUB (R) is a favored resort of the cinema world.

East of the CALABASAS POST OFFICE, 174.9 *m.*, is the LOS ANGELES PET CEMETERY, approached by a private gravel road up a gentle slope of the Simi Hills. Visible from US 101 are a small white mausoleum and the name in huge recumbent cement letters. At this point is a view of the San Fernando Valley, a fertile farming area approximately 25 miles long. It is entirely encompassed by the low but impressive Santa Susana and San Gabriel Mountains, the Verdugo Hills, the Santa Monica Mountains, and the Simi Hills.

CALABASAS, 177.1 *m.* (928 alt., 150 pop.), is now a collection of tourist facilities but once was southern California's tough town. On the outskirts, in an area of orange and walnut groves, US 101 crosses the extraordinary city limits of Los Angeles.

TARZANA, 182.4 *m.*, is a copyrighted name used by permission of Edgar Rice Burroughs, the author, on whose estate the town grew. East of Tarzana are the semiurban skirtings of Hollywood and Los Angeles, a region of heavy traffic, small gardens and subdivisions, markets, oil stations, and various small businesses that continues for some 30 miles.

At the intersection of Radford Avenue, 191.1 *m.*, is the REPUBLIC STUDIO (L), with a large tile-roofed headquarters with large white barn-like structures behind it. Many Westerns and other "B" movies are made here.

At 193 *m.* is a junction with Lankershim Boulevard.

Left on Lankershim Boulevard is UNIVERSAL CITY, 0.5 *m.* (550 alt., 2,500 pop.), an independent municipality of 235 acres around the UNIVERSAL PICTURES CORPORATION STUDIO. Universal, like most large companies, maintains everything from its own fire department to a school for child actors. In the grounds and studios—the heart of an organization with 72 international branches—more than 9,000 pictures have been shot, among them *The Hunchback of Notre Dame, Dracula, Frankenstein, The Phantom of the Opera, All Quiet on the Western Front, Back Street,* and *Imitation of Life.*

South of the junction US 101 follows Cahuenga Boulevard and descends through Cahuenga Pass to HOLLYWOOD, 195.5 *m.* (400 alt., 153,294 pop.) (*see HOLLYWOOD*). Hollywood is at a junction with US 66 (*see TOUR 12c*).

LOS ANGELES, 203.6 *m.* (250 alt., 1,238,048 pop.) (*see LOS ANGELES*).

Section d.   LOS ANGELES to MEXICAN BORDER; 141.4 m.
US 101

Leaving Los Angeles' outskirts, this section of US 101 passes through oil fields, truck gardens, and miles of the most extensive citrus groves in California.   It returns to the sea at Doheny Park and skirts a barren coastline edged by brush-clad hills, passing occasional resort towns, south to San Diego and the Mexican border.

US 101 follows N. Spring St. in the center of LOS ANGELES, 0 m., then, after several turns follows Whittier Blvd. to MONTE-BELLO, 8.9 m. (600 alt., 5,498 pop.), surrounded by an incongruous mixture of flower gardens and oil fields.   It has fifty-two nurseries engaged in the wholesale ornamental shrub and flower business, and holds the annual State Flower and Horticultural Show.   Nine thousand barrels of oil are pumped daily from wells in the vicinity.

> Right from Montebello on First Street, which becomes Bluff Road, to the SITE OF THE BATTLE OF SAN GABRIEL, 1 m., where on January 8, 1847, the decisive engagement in the conquest of California by the Yankees was fought.   Gen. Stephen W. Kearny and Commodore Robert F. Stockton, with a company of 600, engaged a band of several hundred Californians under Gen. José Flores.   Typical of the skirmishes throughout the United States conquest of California, this battle lasted less than an hour, and the total number killed on each side was two, the number injured, eight.   The occupation of Los Angeles followed the engagement.

At 9.3 m. on US 101 is the junction with Rosemead Boulevard.

> Left on Rosemead Boulevard to San Gabriel Boulevard; L. on San Gabriel to the FIRST SITE OF MISSION SAN GABRIEL, 1.5 m., established in 1771 by two padres from Mission San Diego but in 1776 moved five miles north.

US 101 runs eastward across the San Gabriel River, passing the PIO PICO MANSION, 11.9 m. (R), a State monument identified by two markers.   Tall trees hide the two-story adobe from the road.   The house was built in the 1860's by Pío Pico, last Mexican Governor of California.

At 12.2 m. is the junction with Norwalk Boulevard.

> Right here to the DOWNEY HOME, 1847 Norwalk Boulevard, with white vine-covered arches along the one-story front.   The adobe house was built to serve as a fortress, with thick walls, barred windows, and huge locks on the door.   John Gately Downey, California's seventh Yankee governor (1860-62), lived in this house, which is hidden behind Monterey pine, cypress, pepper trees, and palm.
> LOS NIETOS, 2.5 m. (159 alt., 1,240 pop.), sprawls in the midst of orchards, fields, and truck gardens.   Three-fifths of the residents are of Spanish or Mexican descent.
> A thick forest of derricks identifies SANTA FE SPRINGS, 3.6 m. (147 alt.) one of the most productive oil fields in California.   The Santa Fe Railroad purchased the newly platted town of Fulton Sulphur Springs in 1886 and renamed it.   The Los Angeles Pioneer Oil Company abandoned its lease when experimental wells here failed to produce, unaware that

a billion-dollar pool waited tapping. Lots that had sold for $200 in the 1880's soared to dizzy figures in the 1920's after the drilling of spectacular gushers.

The NORWALK STATE HOSPITAL (L), 4.6 *m.*, a group of two-story tile-roofed buildings, was opened in 1916. After this site had been selected, one of the considered sites, Signal Hill, was discovered rich in oil. Had the hospital been built on the latter, oil proceeds would have paid for almost all State hospitals.

WHITTIER (L), 12.4 *m.* (246 alt., 14,822 pop.), is a wealthy residential city in a citrus, avocado, and walnut district named for John Greenleaf Whittier, the Quaker poet, by Friends who founded it in 1881. WHITTIER COLLEGE, with more than 700 students, is a co-educational institution of liberal arts.

Near US 101 is (R) the WHITTIER STATE SCHOOL for delinquent boys, a group of two-story Normandy-style buildings, cottages, a library, gymnasium, and athletic field, surrounded by lawns and gardens. The boys are taught the rudiments of agriculture and raise sufficient vegetables for the school's needs.

US 101 runs through the rolling Puente Hills, covered with groves of avocados (alligator pears). This fruit, sensitive to the sun and dry winds, grows in a humid atmosphere without intense heat or cold. Latticed windbreaks and sun shades must often be erected to protect the trees. Avocados do not soften on the trees but even though picked when quite hard, great care must be exercised in harvesting as the slightest bruise will spread rapidly and cause complete rot. Indigenous from Mexico to South America, the fruit attracted little attention in southern California until the 1890's, when trees were imported by amateurs. About 1900 emphasis was first given to commercial development, and in 1910 growers organized the present marketing group, the Calavo association.

From LA HABRA, 17.9 *m.* (325 alt., 2,273 pop.), the derricks of an oil field can be seen to the south. The active wells pump their output into twelve big tanks that feed a pipe line extending southwest to San Pedro.

US 101, in a region of low hills, passes through part of the 5,000-acre BASTANCHURY RANCH, now covered chiefly with orange groves.

At 21.2 *m.* is a junction with Cedar Street (Imperial Highway).

Left on Imperial Highway is BREA, 2 *m.* (363 alt., 2,435 pop.), trade center of the oil industry in Orange County.

FULLERTON, 25.9 *m.* (161 alt., 10,860 pop.), is the second largest oil-producing center in Orange County. Citrus fruits, walnuts, persimmons, avocados, and a variety of field crops are grown in the vicinity.

Fullerton has 22 industrial and citrus-packing plants. Manufactured products include machinery used for refrigeration and in petroleum production, and plate glass used in industrial construction.

HILLCREST PARK, eight blocks left of the business center, covers 40 acres and has an open-air theater. COMMONWEALTH PARK, three blocks left of the center, contains a ball park, a children's pool, and playground.

ANAHEIM, 27.9 *m.* (165 alt., 10,995 pop.), is the second oldest California town founded as an experiment in communal living. German settlers arrived in 1857. The name is a union of "Ana," from Santa Ana River, with the German word for home. In the CITY PARK, bounded by Lemon, Palm Cypress, and Sycamore Streets, is a Greek theater.

Left from Anaheim on Center Street to the RANCHO SANTA ANA BOTANICAL GARDENS, 9 *m.* (*adm. by card from Mrs. Susanna Bryant, Los Angeles*). Founded in 1926, the gardens contain plants indigenous to California. The characteristics of more than 40,000 now growing on the tract have been studied and recorded.

On US 101 is the junction with Chapman Avenue, 30.9 *m.*

Left on Chapman Avenue to ORANGE, 1.8 *m.* (176 alt., 8,066 pop.), a city depending almost wholly on the great orange industry. It was founded as Richland in 1868 by A. B. Chapman on land he had accepted in settlement of attorney's fees from Abel Stearns, of Los Angeles. In 1875 Chapman determined to change the name. Undecided between a choice of Orange, Lemon, Olive, or Almond, he played a poker game with three associates, and the orange, appropriately, won.

Two varieties of orange—the navel and the Valencia—which ensure fruit ripening throughout the year, are grown to the virtual exclusion of the few other existing varieties. The Valencia, production of which is favored over the navel, is a summer-ripening variety grown in the cooler coastal regions; it hangs in full color on the tree in spring along with the new blossoms. The navel is a winter-ripening fruit grown in the warmer inland areas. It is seedless, more highly colored than the Valencia, and is distinguished from all other varieties by the navel formation of the skin at the blossom end, which gives the fruit its name.

The orange, introduced into Spain from China, was brought into the State from Lower California by the Franciscan padres. The first orchard of any size was planted at San Gabriel Mission near Los Angeles about 1805. In 1873 two small navel orange trees were planted at Riverside (*see TOUR 13b*). In 1876, when the first Valencia seedlings arrived from London, the citrus industry was already established. Today it is one of California's most important resources.

Citrus growing in California is probably the most intensively developed crop-culture in the world. Every tree in the important groves of the State is of pedigreed stock. Careful records of the performance of each tree are kept, and only those known to produce high quality fruit in quantity are used as parent trees. When a tree, or even a single limb, has been found inferior, it is removed or cut back and re-budded with grafts from good parent trees. There are several strains of each variety of orange, but only one or two strains of each are considered fit for propagation. When tangerines—a small, thin-skinned, heavily-seeded, highly-colored variety of orange—were first grown in the orchards, the other orange trees in their vicinity became cross-pollinated with tangerine and the fruit produced was off-type. Growers learned to cover the offending plants with great cheesecloth tents that lessened the cross-pollinization hazard.

Seed for the root stock is selected from some hardy, strong-rooted, disease-resisting variety—usually the sour-orange—and planted in lathhouse beds. (Sweet orange rootstock has been found best for lemons.) The rootstock seedling tree is removed from the seed-bed after a year or more of growth, when it is about twelve inches high, and replanted in an outdoor nursery, where it grows a year or two longer before being budded. In this operation, a twig bearing a healthy bud is cut from a heavy-yielding parent tree that is an inherent bearer of a stable type and inserted in a slit made in the bark of the young seedling about four inches above the ground. When the grafted bud has grown into a branch, the seedling's own top is cut off, and the grafted branch is trained to form another top for the tree, which is ready for transplanting in the orchard the following year. It grows another three years before it is ready to bear commercially, making a minimum of six years from the sprouting of the sour-orange seed. Meanwhile control of the tree's shape is continued by pruning. Bearing commercially in its sixth year, an orange tree does not reach full bearing age until its tenth year. It continues to increase in size and yield for fifty or more years if well cared for.

The war against citrus pests is costly and difficult, since the use of tree medicines varies according to the soil, tree, and climatic types and conditions. Citrus red spider, most destructive and hardest to control, and the various types of scale insects are the commonest pests. About once a year the orchard trees are covered with a canvas tarpaulin and fumigated to kill scale. Insecticides of various types are sprayed upon the trees to eliminate other pests.

On every cold night in winter the grower must be ready with his orchard heaters. The heaters in commonest use (1939) are oil-burning stack pots, which are placed between the tree rows, one to a tree. With the broadcast of a frost warning the watchman in charge of an orchard stays up all night, keeping crews ready to light the heaters with gasoline torches resembling an engineer's long-spouted oil-can. The burners must be watched and regulated at intervals. Where the smudge-pot heating method is used, a thick blanket of black smoke produced by the fuel protects the trees from frost. Threat of frost is greatest about an hour before sunrise. During a cold period everything within miles—clothing, furniture, faces—is covered with the greasy soot.

During southern California's rainless summers the orchards must receive a 48-hour irrigation at three to five week intervals, depending upon the type of soil and the climate. Orchard lysimeters are used for frequent tests of the soil to measure the percolation of water through it, for the crop is as easily ruined by too much water as by too little. Water is usually carried to the edge of the orchards by an underground iron or concrete conduit, and brought above ground from this by a concrete stand pipe that empties directly into the rows of furrows passing between the trees.

Fertilization of the orchard is another problem thoroughly studied by citrus experts. The growing of a "cover crop," such as vetch or clover, which is plowed under in the spring, adds nitrogen to the soil. Stable manure and various other organic fertilizers are used. Inorganic fertilizers are necessary in some soils to add minerals or to counteract soil acidity. As in the base of insecticides, unless orchard conditions are correctly diagnosed and the proper materials, quantities, and methods used, harm to tree or fruit or both results.

Finally, the trees in windy areas must be protected by the planting of orchard-bordering rows of tall-growing evergreens. The eucalyptus is commonly used because it grows rapidly, resists disease, and is adapted to the climate, but it is a heavy surface feeder, retarding the growth of nearby orchard trees; the Monterey cypress grows less rapidly, but is also less injurious to adjacent orchard growth; the athel is even more injurious to the grove than the eucalyptus, but because of its excessively rapid growth it is used as a preliminary windbreak while slower-growing trees are maturing.

As picking time approaches a few typical fruits from the trees are tested and analyzed as to sugar content, and the time of picking determined thereby. Nearly every California citrus orchardist belongs to a growers' cooperative association (most of them to the giant California Fruit Growers' Exchange), and the fruit of these orchard owners is harvested by specially-trained picking-crews sent out by the association's nearest packing house. As in the growing of the orange, the utmost care is used in its handling from the moment it is cut from the tree until it reaches its market. The skin of the orange, although it is a perfect seal for the fruit, is very easily harmed by scratching or bruising, and blue mold may set in before the market is reached, or even before the fruit can be packed. Therefore, the orange "picker"—who does no actual picking but nips the stem with a pair of clippers close enough to the fruit that no sharp protrusion is left to scratch against other oranges—wears soft gloves and has a sack specially designed with a buttoned flap that releases the fruit from the bottom into the field box. (In gathering lemons, the picker also carries a ring and cuts only the fruit which is too large to pass through it; lemons are thus picked by size every month while still a dark green color.)

After being picked, oranges are allowed to stand a day or two at the packing house. During this time some of the moisture in the rind evaporates, making the skin less liable to injury in handling. The fruit is soaked in deep trays of warm water, then passed through long rows of revolving brushes that wash away traces of dirt, then rinsed in cold water, and finally passed over rollers or more brushes under a blast of air that dries them for the grading table. As they roll on canvas belts past the trained operators (usually women), they are sorted into grades according to certain standards of quality and appearance. Many packing houses now employ a recently invented citrus fluoroscope, with which frost damage, granulation and other internal imperfections are detected by X-ray. The size or the condition of the skin of an orange does not determine the inner quality of the fruit. Often, in the season when Valencias are on the market, oranges with a greenish tinge on the rind are mistaken for immature fruit. Actually, fruit in this condition is in its maximum stage of maturity.

After citrus fruits have been graded, stamped in vegetable dye with the name of the grade, and separated according to size and grade, they are wrapped in tissue paper and packed in boxes in a symmetrical pattern that allows a certain number of oranges of a certain size to be packed in each box. There are ten principal sizes of oranges: 100's, packed 100 to a box, are the largest; 344's, packed 344 to a box, are the smallest. In the bigger packing houses, the crates are thoroughly cooled before shipment in cars that are iced in summer and sometimes heated in winter. In recent years the large growers' cooperative associations have begun to use cull—below merchantable grade—fruit in various by-products, such as canned juice, juice concentrate, orange oils and acids, citrate of lime, lemon oil, and citrus pectin. Research laboratories conducted by the associations are studying methods of putting the citrus fruits to other uses.

The non-profit growers' cooperatives have contributed considerably to the reduction of the high cost of orange growing in California by facilitating picking, hauling, packing, and marketing and standardizing costs all along the line. The fruit of the grower-members is sold in a pool and the proceeds are divided among the orchardists on the basis of the quality, quantity, and grades of fruit each has put into the pool.

EL MODENA, 4.5 m. (250 alt., 510 pop.), is a small trading center on the outskirts of Orange.

East of El Modena, Chapman Avenue becomes County Park Road, which with its various continuations rises into the cactus-covered foothills of the Santa Ana Mountains. From this road other roads follow canyons into recreational areas.

At 7.8 m. is a junction with Santiago Canyon Road; L. (straight ahead) 1 m. to IRVINE PARK, a recreational area with oak-shaded picnicking and camping facilities. SANTIAGO RESERVOIR AND DAM, 3 m. (700 alt.), 160 feet high and 1,400 feet long, is a private reserve for irrigation purposes, Orange County's largest water conservation structure.

The main side route continues southeastward on Santiago Canyon Road to a junction with Silverado Canyon Road, 14.3 *m.* Left (straight ahead) to ROME SHADY BROOK, 3.5 *m.* (*accommodations, and small swimming pool*). Numerous summer homes line the canyon and hiking and horseback trails run through the surrounding CLEVELAND NATIONAL FOREST, a reserve of 815,000 acres formed in 1910 to insure watershed protection; millions of gallons of water are piped from its springs and rivers to supply the surrounding country.

Santiago Canyon Road, the main side road, continues southeastward to a junction with Modjeska Grade Rode, 18.9 *m.*; L. here 0.7 *m.* to the FOREST OF ARDEN, once the home of Mme. Helene Modjeska, the Polish actress. The large white house across the creek is well hidden among high trees and other greenery. In 1876 Modjeska came here with a group of refugee Polish artists. The colony failed. Modjeska learned English in a few months, turned to the American stage and began a new career that carried her to her greatest triumphs. Named for a scene in a favorite play, her home became a Mecca for well-known artists and actors. Shortly before her death in 1909, she moved to Modjeska Island.

On the main side route, surrounded by fields of black-eyed peas, is EL TORO (the bull), 27.8 *m.* (144 alt., 108 pop.), a ranch and farming village founded in 1891 by twelve English families.

At 29 *m.* is the junction of the main side route with US 101.

SANTA ANA, 34.9 *m.* (133 alt., 30,322 pop.), founded in 1869 and the seat of Orange County, contains 44 manufacturing plants, employing 1,200 workers, including one of the largest sugar-beet refineries in southern California. Carloads of canned chile peppers and pimentos are packed here, and walnuts are shipped to many markets.

The business section is for the most part modern, since much of it was rebuilt following a severe earthquake in 1933. SANTA ANA JUNIOR COLLEGE, N. Main at Tenth Street, conducts the Fine Arts Press. BOWERS MUSEUM, N. Main at Twentieth Street, houses a comprehensive exhibit of early California relics. The four-story, sandstone COURTHOUSE, 6th and Broadway, was a southern California Gretna Green prior to the enactment (1927) of the marriage law requiring a three-day interval between the issuance of the license and the performance of the ceremony. The old courthouse was the scene of many runaway marriages, a number of them couples from the motion picture colony, performed by Santa Ana's expeditious and obliging "marrying parsons."

On the main route are a number of houses designed and decorated in the Victorian manner. Suburban sections of the city have more modern houses in the California-Spanish style, with tropical and subtropical trees and shrubbery in front of them.

Large pepper trees line the main street of TUSTIN, 37.9 *m.* (122 alt., 926 pop.), which rivaled Santa Ana before the extension of the railroad to the latter city.

South of Tustin is RED HILL (325 alt.), known to the Spanish pioneers as Cerrito de las Ranas (hill of the frogs). It was a landmark to Indians, missionaries, and Spanish and Mexican rancheros; and served as a direction finder for early map makers. The twin peaks of MODJESKA (5,481 alt.), and SANTIAGO (5,680 alt.), on the eastern horizon, are the highest in the Santa Ana Mountains.

At 48.9 *m.* is the junction with the paved El Toro Rd. (*see above*).

SAN JUAN CAPISTRANO, 57.9 *m.* (103 alt., 1,200 pop.), grew up around Mission San Juan Capistrano, and is populated with the descendants of early Mexican settlers.   The village declared war on Mexico, during the early mission days, because of harsh treatment inflicted upon the Indians by Mexican officials.

The much-pictured ruins of MISSION SAN JUAN CAPISTRANO (*adm. 25¢*) are dear to the hearts of California mission romanticists. The church is in much the same condition to which the 1812 and 1918 earthquakes reduced it; few of the subsidiary structures have been restored.   The mission was formally dedicated on Nov. 1, 1776, by Father Junípero Serra, and named for St. John of Capistrano, the Crusader. Construction was begun in 1797 and completed in 1806.   The church was built in the form of a cross, 180 feet long and 90 feet wide; in its day it was one of the most beautiful of the California missions, with an arched roof, seven domes, and a tall campanario (belfry) that could be seen for 10 miles.   An official record says that a Mexican sculptor was sent by the Franciscans to carve the stone arches, cornices, and doorways.

The church was occupied only six years and three months.   In 1812 an earthquake wrecked the roof, the cloisters, the nave, five of the domes, and leveled the tall campanario, killing 29 persons.   Enforcement of the Secularization Act severed the Indians from the mission settlements.   In 1865 a rebuilding of the walls with adobe bricks was followed by a heavy rainstorm that reduced the building to mud.

The mission is widely known for the "Capistrano swallows" that have built their homes in the ruins from Spanish Colonial times.   It is said that for nearly a century the swallows have left the mission on St. John's Day, October 23, and returned again in the spring on St. Joseph's Day, March 19.   Only once have they been late, delayed by storm at sea, but they arrived only four hours behind their schedule. In the fall of 1936 elaborate preparations were made by the National Broadcasting Company to give listeners-in the fluttering sounds of their departure, but the birds muffed the chance, disappearing before necessary connections could be made.

Melodramatic tales of the supernatural woven about Capistrano are too well patterned to do the relic justice.   These generally involve a dark-robed and rope-girdled Franciscan ghost that reputedly walks, then melts into the garden twilight, and of bells that once rang in the mission campanario despite the motionless bell ropes, coiled as usual on their pegs.   The climax—recited *con agitato*—came with the discovery that a young Indian girl, a neophyte, had expired at the very moment of the reverberations of the self-tolling bells.

Within the entrance to the mission enclosure is a small garden beside the ruins of the church.   The curious diamond-shaped tiles on the floor of the sanctuary were made on the hillside north of the mission. Opening on the garden is a museum with old Spanish vestments, sheepskin and parchment bound manuscripts, Mexican and Spanish paintings and statues, an ancient confessional, Indian frescoes, and a golden altar.

Left from San Juan Capistrano on State 74 to SAN JUAN HOT SPRINGS, 12.4 *m.,* a spot of green in a narrow canyon formed by pre-cipitous chaparral-covered mountains. Steaming sulphur waters pour into various-sized baths and concrete pools belonging to a resort.

State 74 continues to the Olympic Fields Nudist Colony, 27 *m.* (*see TOUR 6e*).

The thick-walled adobe CAPISTRANO MISSION TRADING POST, 60.4 *m.,* overlooking the ocean was built in 1820. It was headquarters for an extensive trade in hides and other commodities between the mis-sion and the Yankee clippers.

At DOHENY PARK, 60.9 *m.* (15 alt., 549 pop.), is the junction with US 101 Alt. (*see TOUR 2B*). Doheny Palisades (L), high above the surf-level road, was developed as a restricted residential area by E. L. Doheny, the oil magnate. The precipitous sea cliffs are attractively landscaped, terraced with ice plant and bougainvillea.

SAN CLEMENTE (St. Clement), 64.4 m. (5 alt., 667 pop.), sometimes referred to as the "Spanish Village," was founded in 1925 by a Los Angeles realtor. The unvarying white stucco of all buildings and houses in this model village is surmounted by equally unvarying red tile roofs. A resident finds relief from this regimentation of color in the marine views, since streets conform to natural contours and each house is so placed that it is in sight of the sea. Strict building codes permit only replicas of Spanish dwellings—as a modern realtor conceives them—within the city.

A pueblo-style gateway leads into SAN CLEMENTE STATE PARK, 66.3 *m.* (*camping, picnicking facilities*) on the cliffs overlook-ing the Pacific, and a broad beach.

A tiny hexagonal toolhouse (L) marks LAS FLORES, 78.4 *m.,* a station of the Atchison, Topeka & Santa Fe Railroad serving the Santa Margarita Rancho. The stockyards and chute for loading cattle into railroad cars have almost become a landmark of the past, for trucks are now the favored method of transporting cattle.

At 86.4 *m.* is the junction with a private dirt road.

Left here through a wire gate to the headquarters of the RANCHO SANTA MARGARITA, 9.5 *m:,* in an adobe hacienda erected by Pío Pico in 1837, now a ranch office and residence. The large one-story house, with a wide porch on two sides, stands on a slight knoll near the Santa Margarita River. After numerous divisions and sales, the rancho still contains 132,310 acres in San Diego County and 51,000 acres in Orange County. The present owner, a corporation, engages in diversified farming and ranching. Con-trolled by Mission San Luis Rey, the rancho was returned to the Indians in 1835. In the same year, through political manipulations, the influential Picos acquired the property. Here they lived until 1862, when Andrés sold his share, 66,500 acres, to his brother Pío for $1,000 plus a San Diego residence. Pío—according to the story—shortly afterward acquired the adjoining 44,000-acre Las Flores Rancho from its Indian owners and added it to his extensive holdings. Last of the Mexican governors of California, Pío Pico was an inveterate gambler. It is said that when he rode to the races he was followed by a mule loaded with silver coin to be used on bets. The fluctuations of gambling eventually led to the sale of Rancho Santa Margarita. John Forster, who had assumed the more Spanish name of Don Juan Forster and had married Ysidora, sister of Pío, paid $14,000 for the rancho. (In 1931 its value was $6,800,000.) Forster and his family lived on the Santa Margarita for more than 30 years. Here he reigned in baronial style, surrounded by a host of vaqueros and Indian domestics. He allowed only Spanish to be spoken at the hacienda.

OCEANSIDE, 87.4 *m.* (45 alt., 3,508 pop.), is a residential town, beach resort, and agricultural produce distributing point. Its early inhabitants were composed largely of a group of English gentry who had first settled in the San Luis Rey Valley four miles inland.

Left from Oceanside on paved Second St., to MOUNT ECCLESIA, 1.3 *m.*, headquarters of the Rosicrucian Fellowship, landscaped grounds with white buildings, easily identified by the startling pale heliotrope and jade green coloring of the roofs. This organization is not affiliated with the Rosicrucian Order but is a group originated by Max Heindel in 1911. The Fellowship differs from the other group in that it is a religious organization instead of a secret fraternal order. A healing temple is maintained at Oceanside; lectures are open to the general public; astrological theories are taught; and the majority of its members are gained and instructed through correspondence. Mrs. Max Heindel has headed the organization since the death of her husband in 1919.

The white campanario of MISSION SAN LUIS REY, 4.7 *m.*, is a pleasing part of the landscape of the hilly valley and fixes the position of the church in the cloistered establishment. The mission was founded in 1798, completed in 1802, and dedicated to San Luís, Rey de Francia. It was designed to serve a tribe of the Shoshone later known as the Luiseno.

Architecturally, San Luís Rey is regarded as one of the most impressive of all the California missions. Its style was a composite of Spanish-Moorish and Mexican, built of adobe faced with brick. The brick-red delineaments of the facade and belfry and the cloisters of the long monastery running west of the church form a well proportioned whole. Farther west are remains of cloisters—rows of plaster-chipped arches high above the spread of the valley. Remains of the extensive adobe wall that once surrounded the mission are near the highway.

The church has been partly restored. The murals on the interior columns and beams are not vivid in color, but rich with small detail and paganistic patterning. The emblem of the Third Order of St. Francis, a cross and the stigmata (five wounds of Christ), is over the arched entrance to the Mortuary Chapel (R).

At 10.3 *m.* is a junction of the main side road with US 395 (*see TOUR 6e*).

CARLSBAD, 90.4 *m.* (42 alt., 2,600 pop.), in a winter vegetable growing district, ships green vegetables, flowers, and bulbs. CARLSBAD BEACH STATE PARK, immediately south of town, possesses a bathing beach, picnic grounds, and campsites.

South of Carlsbad the highway passes between ocean and lagoon, surf and cliff, and for approximately a mile the four lanes are divided and lined by three rows of large eucalypti.

At 97.3 *m.* is the junction with a paved road.

Left on this road; across the railroad tracks is a large yellow sign pointing to PAXTON'S PAPAYA CONSERVATORIES, 0.5 *m.;* containing 600 papaya trees under three-quarters of an acre of glass. A truly tropical fruit, the "tree melons" will ripen outdoors in the more favorable sections of California but require artificial heat for commercial production.

ENCINITAS, 99.4 *m.* (85 alt., 500 pop.), produces large quantities of blossoms and bulbs that are shipped east in refrigerator cars. The National Midwinter Flower Show is held here in March. Encinitas was settled in 1854 by a group of Germans from Chicago, Ill.

SOLANA BEACH, 103.4 *m.* (65 alt., 259 pop.), is in a small-farm area growing citrus fruits, avocados, flowers, and bulbs.

DEL MAR, 105.9 *m.* (100 alt., 430 pop.), is a shore line residential town and the scene of the annual San Diego County Fair, usually held in August.

> Left from Del Mar to the SAN DIEGO COUNTY FAIRGROUNDS AND RACE TRACK, 0.6 *m.* Horse racing is conducted by the Del Mar Turf Club, with Bing Crosby, film and radio star, as president.
> Eucalypti, date palms and peppertrees almost completely hide the SECOND OSUNA ADOBE (L), 4.8 *m.*, built in the 1830's and now part of the country home of Bing Crosby. The white posts of the porch and the low reveals of the regularly-placed windows disclose the California-Mexican origin of the reconstructed house. It was a California headquarters in the war with Mexico (1846), and its owner, who was the first alcalde of San Diego under Mexican rule, fought in the Battle of San Pasqual.
> The RANCHO SANTA FE CIVIC CENTER, 6.5 *m.*, is a block-long landscaped business district with one-story mission-type buildings and many eucalyptus trees to alleviate the commercial character of the spot. Rancho Santa Fe is the home of wealthy ranchers, among them Douglas Fairbanks, Sr., whose 3,000-acre tract contains 300 acres of Valencia oranges irrigated by an expensive overhead sprinkling system.
> Multiple-arch HODGES DAM, 11.7 *m.*, creates LAKE HODGES, a unit in the San Diego city water system. East of the dam the road passes high above the lake and a cluster of cottages, and enters a region of reddish soil and orange groves.
> ESCONDIDO, 18 *m.* (650 alt., 3,400 pop.), (*see TOUR 6e*), is at the junction with US 395 (*see TOUR 6e*).

At 107.9 *m.*, US 101 climbs a bluff to TORREY PINES MESA, part of which has been preserved as a park. Unlike most pines the branches of the Torrey pine spread, creating a tree of a rangy irregular shape. The needles are exceptionally long, ranging between five to seven inches, and grow in clusters of five.

At 109.3 *m.*, is a junction with several roads.

> 1. Left here to the UNITED STATES MARINE RIFLE RANGE, 0.3 *m.*, in Rose Canyon, where recruits are given an intensive 6-weeks training in the use of small arms. A large group of green barracks surrounds the central quadrangle.
> At 7 *m.*, is CAMP KEARNY, used during the World War as a training camp for recruits, and at 7.5 *m.*, is a junction with US 395 (*see TOUR 6e*).

> 2. Right from US 101 on a concrete road 1.7 *m.*, down hairpin curves to SCRIPPS INSTITUTION OF OCEANOGRAPHY, containing a museum and aquarium (*open 8 to 5*). The establishment is under the supervision of the University of California.
> The beach below the institution and the rocky stretch to the north harbor most of the marine life characteristic of this section. Perhaps the most common fish seen along shore is the wriggling, fast-swimming tidepool fish or sculpin, which darts about in rocky pools. The sting ray or stingaree, a flat fish with a long, whiplike tail, is occasionally encountered in quiet

water at very low tide, particularly on muddy bottoms. Its sharp, barbed spine can inflict a painful wound.

The beach south of the institution is a favorite spawning ground of grunion, a small, slender smelt that comes up on the sandy shore to lay its eggs a few minutes after the high tides of March, April, May, and June. On the second, third, and fourth nights after the full of the moon during these months, the female grunion rides in on the advancing wave, and then squirms and flops back into the wash of the next wave. In the brief time she is out of the water—about 30 seconds—the grunion digs tail first into the sand for about half the depth of her body and deposits her eggs. Two weeks later, at the time of the next high tide, the waves loosen the ripened eggs from the sand. As the eggs are freed the baby grunion hatch and are washed back into the sea.

The spawning habits of this striped smelt provide a popular southern California sport. About a quarter of an hour after high tide on the nights the grunion run, the long sandy beaches are crowded with people gathering the fish by moonlight, bonfires, and flashlights. Some nights, during the height of the season, thousands of grunion are visible at one time. No license is required, but the fish must be taken by hand in the brief seconds it is out of the water.

LA JOLLA, 3.9 *m.* (90 to 800 alt., 5,000 pop.), occupies a small rocky promontory popular with easterners who have built lovely homes and gardens on top of its sheer cliffs overlooking the sea. The name is variously explained as a corruption of *la joya* (the jewel), and *la hoya* (the hollow). The seven LA JOLLA CAVES, now accessible from Coast Blvd. (*adm. 25¢*), were formerly visited only by boat. In the contrast of light and darkness from within the caves the openings to the sea show strange and distinct forms, sometimes human in aspect.

La Jolla's most popular spot is the cove, with a small beach beneath the cliffs and a miniature marine garden off the rocks.

Prominent in the town's development was Ellen Browning Scripps, who endowed the Scripps Institution of Oceanography and several other institutions.

PACIFIC BEACH, 7.4 *m.* (65 alt., 1,626 pop.), is a small farming district and resort suburb. A section of its beach is exclusively for Negroes. MISSION BEACH, 8.9 *m.* (25 alt., 1,092 pop.), a narrow strand between Mission Bay and the ocean is popular for paddle-boarding. OCEAN BEACH, 10.4 *m.* (20 alt., 4,012 pop.), is a residential and resort area that has an indoor salt water plunge. A State fish and game refuge is on the northern edge of town, along Mission Bay.

The route winds back to a junction with US 101 (Pacific Highway) at 13.5 *m.*

US 101 continues south to SAN DIEGO, 123.8 *m.* (687 alt., 147,995 pop.) (*see SAN DIEGO*) at junctions with US 395 (*see TOUR 6e*) and US 80 (*see TOUR 14b*).

Right (straight ahead) from San Diego on Pacific Blvd. to the CORONADO FERRY (*25¢ per auto*), 0.1 *m.*, and across San Diego Bay (0.7 *m.*) to CORONADO, 1.5 *m.* (25 alt., 5,412 pop.), a residential and resort community named for the Coronado Islands. The town's most notable feature is the HOTEL DEL CORONADO, a well-maintained but rambling-towered and ornate building designed by Stanford White. It is noted for the beauty of its patio with the immense flame-colored bougainvillea vine.

From the beach part of the CORONADO ISLANDS are seen, some 20 miles to the south in Mexican territory. This group of three is the southernmost of the California Channel Islands, all rough, barren, and without fresh water. They had no permanent Indian population and are at present uninhabited, though sportsmen frequently visit them for the excellent big-game fishing. Discovered by the Cabrillo expedition in 1542, the islands are named for the Spanish explorer Coronado.

South of Coronado on State 75 is "Tent City," conspicuously lacking in tents, but having an abundance of straight-row frame shacks; and the SILVER STRAND, a narrow bar of sand and sand growth, some 8 miles long and in places less than half a city block wide over which the highway leads to Mexico.

SILVER STRAND STATE PARK, 5.8 *m.*, has campgrounds and picnic tables. At the south end of the strand is IMPERIAL BEACH, 9.3 *m.*, a resort.

At 12.9 *m.* State 75 meets US 101.

South of San Diego US 101 runs through a dismal stretch of factories, ancient frame buildings and tide flats, and passes among orange and lemon groves and fields of celery. The celery farms in southern California, ranging from 1 to 80 acres, are operated almost exclusively by Japanese. Seed, fertilizer, and water are expensive and the inherent thrift and industry of the Japanese farmer is an absolute necessity for successful celery cultivation. Japanese orderliness is clearly evidenced in the clean look of the farms. Celery seed is usually planted in greenhouses but when started outside, cheesecloth must occasionally be used to protect the young plants from the cold. In either case, from five to seven weeks growth is necessary before it is transplanted. Some areas along the coast harvest throughout the year, with the principal harvest between December and April.

CHULA VISTA, 133.9 *m.* (74 alt., 3,869 pop.), is in an agricultural district called the South Bay Region. Flowers and bulbs are raised here commercially and an annual flower show is held.

At 137.5 *m.* is the junction with State 75 (*see above*).

The southern boundary of SAN YSIDRO, 140.9 *m.* (70 alt., 1,368 pop.), one of the principal ports of entry from Mexico, is the INTERNATIONAL BOUNDARY, 141.4 *m.,* between the United States and Mexico.

Tour 2A

Junction with US 101—Lakeport—Middletown—Calistoga—St. Helena —Napa—Vallejo—Junction with US 40; 124.9 *m.* State 20 and State 29.

Roadbed partly oil surfaced, partly paved; easy grades.
Accommodations adequate.

Into the wooded glens of hermit-like Lake County—never penetrated by a railroad—lead State 20 and 29. From the rocky hillsides gush mineral springs, and in the sheltered, oak-dappled valleys, clearings are green with bean vines on poles, pear and walnut orchards. The road hugs the shore of hill-encompassed Clear Lake, largest sheet of fresh water lying wholly within the State. From narrow defiles it climbs over the slopes of soaring Mount St. Helena. The vineyard-mantled slopes of widening Napa Valley border it as it continues to the mouth of the Napa River on San Pablo Bay.

State 20 branches eastward from US 101 (*see TOUR 2a*), 0 *m.*, at a point 2 miles north of Ukiah, along the course of upper tributaries of the Russian River through rising foothills. It skirts twin BLUE LAKES, 14.5 *m.*, (*summer resorts*) whose deep blue waters mirror steep-walled wooded heights. At the trading and resort village of UPPER LAKE, 22.9 *m.* (1,350 alt., 400 pop.), the route turns R. from State 20 on State 29.

The placid reaches of CLEAR LAKE are embraced by undulating, oak-forested hill slopes. The Pomo Indians who dwelt on the islands, ferrying across on tule *balsas* (rafts), had a legend about the region that told how the mighty chief Konochti was so angry when his enemy, the chief Kahbel, asked for his daughter Lupiyomi in marriage that he took up his stand at the Narrows—where a long tongue of land almost cuts the lake in two—to do battle. Across the water the two chiefs hurled at each other the huge boulders that strew the mountainside until Kahbel lay dead and Konochti, dying, sank back to form great MOUNT KONOCHTI (4,200 alt.), which towers between the two arms of the lake east of the Narrows. The Pomos dwelt here undisturbed, chipping their spearheads out of black obsidian and weaving the plumes of the blue quail into their baskets, until white men came, trappers and cattle herders, in the 1840's. Before the end of the decade they had run afoul of the white man's justice when United States soldiers, to punish them for slaying two of their fellow countrymen, surrounded them on an island and shot them down. They forgave the white man, however, and signed a Treaty of Peace and Friendship with him in August 1851 —a treaty giving up their lands, for which they received a gift of "Ten head of beef cattle, three sacks of bread and sundry clothing."

The resort and farming center of LAKEPORT, 31.1 *m.* (1,350 alt., 1,318 pop.), seat of Lake County, once known as Forbestown for William Forbes, who deeded 40 acres of his land for a county seat in 1861, looks over the great expanse of the upper lake toward the hazy hills of the far shore.

Hidden from the lake by Mount Konochti's orchard-mantled slopes is KELSEYVILLE, 39 *m.* (1,500 alt., 200 pop.), called Peartown by its boosters, where Salvador and Antonio Vallejo built a log cabin for the mayordomo and the ten vaqueros who herded the cattle of their Rancho Laguna de Lu-Pi-Yo-Mi over the ranges. In 1847 they drove their cattle away and sold their land to Benjamin Kelsey, a man named Stone, and others. When Kelsey and Stone had an adobe built here, they earned the enmity of their Indian laborers by their unkindness, and in revenge the Indians killed them both in 1849.

At **44.1** *m.* is the junction with a paved road.

> Left on this road to the farming center of LOWER LAKE, 9.3 *m.* (1,350 alt., 870 pop.), dating from 1858, and L. from Lower Lake on State 53, 0.8 *m.*, to CACHE CREEK, near the outlet to the lake, where a dam built in 1866 by the Clear Lake Water Company raised the lake level until it flooded houses, farm lands and orchards. When repeated appeals for redress went unheeded, the farmers on Sunday morning, November 15, 1868, after a prayer service led by their pastor, began to destroy the dam—a job that required two days and two nights. It was never rebuilt.

State 29 continues through narrow, twisting valleys past hot springs resorts to MIDDLETOWN, 64.2 *m.* (1,300 alt., 450 pop.), serving the farming, dairying, and poultry-raising region of the Loconomi Valley. It was named Middletown because it lies exactly midway between Lower Lake and Calistoga (*see below*).

Along St. Helena Creek State 29 winds up a long grade at the base of MOUNT ST. HELENA (4,343 alt.), which Robert Louis Stevenson called "the Mont Blanc of the Coast Range." At the summit of the grade (2,960 alt.), 73.2 *m.,* is the ROBERT LOUIS STEVENSON MONUMENT (R), a pillar on a rock base holding an open book carved from Scotch granite. It stands on the site of the bunk-house where Stevenson spent his honeymoon with his bride, Fannie Van de Grift Osbourne, in the summer of 1880. "The mountain," Stevenson observed in the notes for *The Silverado Squatters* which he wrote here, ". . . feeds in the springtime many splashing brooks. From its summit you must have an excellent lesson in geography. . . . Three counties, Napa, Lake, and Sonoma, march across its cliffy shoulders. Its naked peak stands nearly 4,500 feet above the sea. Its sides are fringed with forest, and the soil, where it is bare, glows warm with cinnabar."

At the head of upper Napa Valley's vineyard stretches is its trading center, CALISTOGA, 82.2 *m.* (365 alt., 1,000 pop.), the watering place laid out by the enterprising Mormon, Samuel Brannan, in 1859, on the site which the Indians called Colaynomo (oven place), knowing that underground heat warmed its hot springs. Planning a popular spa, he built a hotel and 20 cottages and christened his development Calistoga—a compound from the names California and Saratoga. It was Brannan who first cultivated the surrounding hillsides, the terraced, vine-covered slopes whose grapes provide such excellent dry wines today.

> Right from Calistoga on State 28, 0.9 *m.* to the junction with a paved road; L. here to the PETRIFIED FOREST, 5 *m.*, a tract one mile long and one-quarter mile wide covered mostly by silicified and opalized redwoods. The trees lie in two tiers with their tops pointing away from Mount St. Helena, indicating that lava from that mountain killed them and preserved them in stone form. The conversion from wood to stone was so perfect that the texture and fiber are completely preserved. Most of the trees are broken but the pieces retain their relative positions. Many are of great size, the largest having been uncovered in 1919 at a depth of 90 feet. The Queen of the Forest is 80 feet long and 12 feet in mean diameter; The Monarch, 126 feet long and 8 feet in mean diameter.

State 29 continues southeastward past hillside meadows where sheep and cattle graze.

At 86.7 *m*. the highway passes the field (L) in which stands the old BALE MILL built in 1846 by the English settler Dr. Edward Bale, nephew-in-law of Gen. Mariano Vallejo and owner of the Carne Humana (Sp., human flesh) Rancho. The vine-covered water wheel, 40 feet in diameter, dwarfs the weatherbeaten mill—a small, two-story, gabled-roofed frame building, dignified by the false front typical of its era. The mill was restored in 1925 by the Native Sons of Napa County.

ST. HELENA, 90.2 *m*. (299 alt., 1,582 pop.), is proud of the great quantity of rich wine-grapes grown in the district it serves and of its many old wine cellars. Many of the inhabitants of St. Helena and its environs are Swiss, Germans, and Italians from vineyard sections of Europe. Here as abroad they hold their new-wine festivals each fall— with certain American additions in the form of floats with figures of Bacchus and his followers. Beside State 29 on the northern outskirts is the BERINGER BROTHERS WINERY (*open*), in whose underground storage cellars, hewn a half century ago from solid limestone in the hillside, hundreds of thousands of gallons of wine are aging in great casks.

> Left from St. Helena on a paved road 7.3 *m*. to the PACIFIC UNION COLLEGE, conducted by the Seventh Day Adventist Conference, which trains about 500 ministers, doctors, nurses, and teachers on the crater of an extinct volcano. The mountain has been drilled to a depth of 600 feet, where water at a temperature of 97° was tapped.

Southeast of St. Helena the highway skirts walnut, fig, and olive groves; apricot, cherry, plum, pear, peach, and prune orchards, and innumerable extensive vineyards; it then passes RUTHERFORD, 94.2 *m*. (183 alt., 350 pop.), and OAKVILLE, 96.2 *m*. (153 alt., 219 pop.), small wine-producing centers.

YOUNTVILLE, 99.6 *m*. (150 alt., 360 pop.), stands on what was once the southern section of the 11,814-acre Rancho Caymus, granted in 1836 to George C. Yount, who came to California from North Carolina with the Wolfskill party. Two miles north of here, Yount built the first white habitation in Napa Valley. Yount's Kentucky log blockhouse was unquestionably the first in California. In the walls of the 18-foot square lower room portholes were placed for defense. A year later Yount replaced the blockhouse with a narrow adobe structure, 100 feet long; the walls of this, too, he pierced with portholes.

> Left from Yountville, 3.1 *m*., to the junction with a dirt road; L. 0.1 *m*. to the STATE GAME FARM, where 15,000 pheasants are hatched and released annually.

War veterans have been cared for in the VETERANS HOME (R) on the southern outskirts of Yountville since 1881. Opened for disabled veterans of the Mexican War and the Grand Army of the Republic, the institution was privately operated until taken over by the State in 1897.

NAPA, 108.6 *m.* (20 alt., 6,437 pop.), seat of Napa County, serves the ranchers and grape-growers of the valley, tans leather and manufactures leather goods, ships valley products by barge down the Napa River. In spite of its bustling air, its neon lights, and automobiles, Napa has an old, settled air, emphasized by venerable shade trees and buildings of another era. Its courthouse square is an oasis of peace. Napa's history goes back to 1832, when the first settlers arrived, though the town did not come into existence until 1848, when Nathan Coombs erected its first building, a saloon.

Napa is at a junction with State 12 (*see TOUR 2a*), which unites with State 29 to a junction at 114.4 *m.,* where it branches east 6.2 *m.* to a junction with US 40 (*see TOUR 9b*).

The land east of Napa belonged to the Rancho Tulucay, where Cayetano Juarez stocked his herds in 1837 and built the first of the two JUAREZ ADOBES (L), 110 *m.,* in 1840. The second and larger one was built in 1845. During the Bear Flag Rebellion at Sonoma (*see TOUR 2b*) of which he was alcalde at the time, Juarez distinguished himself by swimming nine miles to escape capture.

The NAPA STATE HOSPITAL FOR THE INSANE, 110.7 *m.,* occupies a 1,900-acre tract of tree-shaded lawns dotted with buildings in a weird confusion of architectural styles. The first building (1875) is a jumble of gingerbread gables, turrets, and cupolas, embodying the architectural extravagances of its age. The institution, housing more than 3,000 patients, is considered a model asylum. A 250-acre farm, tended by male patients, produces much of the hospital's food supply. As occupational therapy plays an important part in the treatment, the male inmates engage also in dairying, hog- and poultry-raising, shoe- and brush-making; the female patients, in painting, sketching, and allied activities.

State 29 continues southward to VALLEJO, 123 *m.* (10 alt., 14,-476 pop.), situated at the point where the Napa River flows into San Pablo Bay. The town is built on low hillsides, its streets reaching down to the water's edge. Far-seeing Gen. Mariano G. Vallejo, undertaking a pilgrimage with his young bride in the late 1830's across the 99,000-acre domain of his Rancho Suscol (inhabited in those days only by Indians and wild beasts), declared that here he would found a city to bear his name. When the Yankee conquerors set up their State of California in 1850, Vallejo welcomed the new régime with an offer of 156 acres for a State capital. Here he proposed to endow a university, erect a museum, churches, schools, and asylums, and lay out public parks. Since his was the highest bid, the new government accepted it, and a town was laid out. But Vallejo's ambitions had proved too great a strain for his purse. When the State Legislature assembled on Jan. 5, 1852, they found their promised State building still unfinished. Disgruntled at being compelled to sit on boxes and barrels and to spend the night on the river steamer *Empire,* they moved away precipitately on January 12 to Sacramento, only to leave there with equal haste when a flood sent them scuttling. Vallejo finally was inaugurated as the seat of government with an elaborate Christmas ball, and in January 1853, the peripatetic government returned; but on February 4, it left for good, first going to Benicia and finally to Sacramento. Vallejo himself, giving up his cherished project as a bad job, petitioned to be released from his obligation. In spite of these initial handicaps, the town grew and flourished, because of the purchase in 1853 of nearby Mare Island for a United States navy yard (*see below*).

> Right from Tennessee and Wilson Sts., in Vallejo, 1 *m.*, over a great, million-dollar causeway to MARE ISLAND NAVY YARD, which covers the narrow, 876-acre spit of land between the Napa River channel and San Pablo Bay. The *San Carlos*, first Spanish ship to sail through the Golden Gate, sighted the low-lying island, and Capt. Don Juan Pérez de Ayala christened it Isla Plana (flat island). Later the crude cattle ferry that plied across Carquinez (Ind., great serpent) Strait was caught in a squall and overturned by the stampeding animals; some of them swam ashore, among them General Vallejo's prized white mare, which he found a few days later, peacefully grazing on the island. Overjoyed, he named the place La Isla de la Yegua (the island of the mare). So fond was Vallejo's young wife of the view from the island shore that she once said she wished it were hers. "My dear, it is yours," replied the General; and it was acknowledged as her property. The island was sold for $7,000 in 1850, and a year later for $17,000.
>
> Since 1869 Mare Island Navy Yard has built 86 ships; today repair and maintenance of Navy vessels is its chief function, requiring the labor of 5,000 employees. Along the waterfront rise giant cranes, drydocks, and shipbuilding ways, warehouses, and stone quays; the foundry, riggers' lobby, power plant, and the great shops of the industrial plant—electrical, sheet metal, pattern, paint, pipe and copper, structural, and boat. Irwin Park, the central esplanade, runs near naval officers' residences, the Marine Barracks, and the Naval Hospital. On Navy Day (October 27) the ships and government buildings, including the OLD MARINE BARRACKS, 12th Ave. and Cedar St., are open to visitors.

At 124.8 *m.* on State 29 is the junction with a narrow paved road.

Right on this road 0.3 *m.* to MORROW COVE (*fishing, swimming, boating facilities; moderate rates*), a grassy hollow framed by tall eucalypti, facing Carquinez Strait and the rugged Contra Costa (Sp., opposite coast) County Hills beyond. The hulls of old ships form a breakwater for the bathing beach, among them the *Contra Costa* (one of the twin Southern Pacific ferries that carried whole trains across the strait) and a small masted sailing vessel salvaged from the Alaska fishing fleet, one of the so-called "Bangor ships" that came from the Maine port's shipbuilding yards.

State 29 terminates at the junction with US 40 (*see TOUR 9b*), 124.9 *m.*

≪≪≪≪≪≪≪≪≪≪≪≪≪≪≪≪≪≪≪≪≪≪≪≪≪≪≪≪≪≪≪≪≪≪≪≪≪≫≫≫≫≫≫≫≫≫≫≫≫≫≫≫≫≫≫≫≫≫≫≫≫≫≫≫≫≫

Tour 2B

Junction with US 101—Oxnard—Santa Monica—Long Beach—Doheny Park; 113.6 *m.* US 101-Alt.

Paved roadbed.
All types of accommodations.

Branching southward from US 101 just south of the Santa Clara River crossing, US 101A leaves the bean and beet fields, orange groves and walnut orchards of the river delta and swings out to the shore of the Pacific. As the route continues along the smooth, curving beach, a rampart of rain-cut cliffs on the inland side hides the brush-covered Santa Monica Mountains paralleling the coast. The highway swings around Santa Monica Bay, cuts across the neck of the Palos Verdes peninsula, and continues down the coast, passing a long string of seaside resorts.

South of a junction with US 101, 0 *m.*, at a point 7 miles south of Ventura, US 101A leads through walnut groves to OXNARD, 2.9 *m.* (48 alt., 6,285 pop.), a town of wide streets, founded in 1898 with the establishment of the American Beet Sugar Company's converting plant and named for the company's owners. Beet sugar is still the town's principal product; next in importance is lima beans. Dairy farms provide orchard growers with a ready fertilizer source and the sugar factory with a market for dried beet-pulp.

> Right from Oxnard on Fifth Ave. to Ventura Rd., 1 *m.;* L. on Ventura Rd. to Hueneme Rd., 3 *m.;* R. on Hueneme Rd. to HUENEME (Ind., place of security), 4 *m.,* a seaport settlement by a natural harbor with a large citrus packing plant and a fish cannery. On Point Hueneme is a lighthouse.
> SILVER STRAND and HOLLYWOOD-BY-THE-SEA, 5.5 *m.,* and HOLLYWOOD BEACH, 6 *m.,* are seaside resorts at the end of sand dunes still pointed out as a film "location" for Rudolph Valentino's *The Sheik.*

Across lagoon lands, scarred with white patches of alkali and planted here and there with oats, US 101A travels seaward. From the beetling bluffs of Point Mugu it winds above breakers, on a ledge cut from rocky cliffs so steep that road surveyors had to be lowered by ropes in places.

MALIBU (Ind., deer), 36.8 *m.,* favorite beach-spot of cinema celebrities, is well-protected against sight-seers and autograph hunters by uniformed guards stationed at all entrances. Its dwellings, some of elaborate scale, sit facing the beach with their backs turned aloofly to the highway.

South of Malibu, on a promontory a mile from the road, is (L) the great white RINDGE MANSION, of the California Spanish type. It was never completed by its builder—wealthy, eccentric May K. Rindge. The 16,350-acre Rindge estate, Rancho Malibu, was purchased in 1892 by Fred H. Rindge, son of a Massachusetts manufacturer, and pastured with great herds and flocks. In 1905, before he could realize his dream of building a California Riviera here, he died, leaving the estate to his wife and three children. His widow began a 30-year series of bitter lawsuits, violence, and strategy to prevent the building of railroads and highways on her vast property. She hired armed, mounted guards to patrol her boundaries, built high wire fences with barred and chained gates, plowed county-built highways under, turned droves of hogs upon cuts for new roads or planted them with alfalfa; and during 1915-17, when her gates were systematically smashed and her guards overpowered every week by crowds of farmers and travelers trying to get through to Santa Monica, she dynamited her roads. She brought suits to oust squatters and to punish trespass, libel, and defamation of character. Her battle with the State against its plan to run the coast highway through her beach land was carried to the Supreme Court, where she lost. Her son brought her into court with the charge that her fights were dissipating the estate at the rate of more than $1,000,000 a year. When in 1929, four years after leasing the land that is now Malibu, she started building her mansion, she soon found herself without cash. In 1938 the Federal District Court awarded control of the estate to a trustee-corporation authorized to bring order to its chaotic financial condition. The estate is now rented to cattle ranchers and its Malibu beach lots are being sold.

South of MALIBU PIER, 37.9 *m.* (*pier-fishing 25¢, all day boat fishing trips $2*), is a mile-long stretch of expensive beach homes and cottages, ranging in architectural types from trim shingle-roofed New England cottages to ingeniously elaborate French châteaux. Many of the dwellings were built by motion-picture celebrities when the seaside film colony began to develop but sold when Malibu proved more fashionable.

At 41.9 *m.* is the junction with paved State 27.

> Left here through TOPANGA CANYON, a deep gorge in the Santa Monica Mountains, where a four-day brush fire in 1938 burned many of the old sycamores, and scores of mountain cabins. At TOPANGA SPRINGS, 7.7 *m.*, are picnic grounds. TOPANGA SUMMIT (1,560 alt.), 9.7 *m.*, is a splendid viewpoint at the edge of a sheer precipice (*telescopes, 10¢*).
> At 13 *m.* is the junction with US 101 (*see TOUR 2c*).

At 42.5 *m.* is one of the signs marking the city limits of Los Angeles which from time to time pranksters carry off and plant in remote spots as a jest at the city's widespread incorporated area; one has even been found in the wastes of Alaska.

The route proceeds past elaborate cliffside homes and strips of cottage-dotted beach protected from tides by long rock-and-pile piers.

At 53.2 *m.* is the junction with Sunset Blvd.

Left on Sunset Blvd. 1 *m.* to the BERNHEIMER ORIENTAL GARDENS (*grounds open 8-5:30; adm. 10¢; house open Sat. and Sun. 12:30-5:30; adm. 25¢*), 16980 Sunset Blvd., a seven-acre showplace landscaped with shrubs, trees and flowers and ornamented with waterfalls, artificial lakes, miniature models of eastern temples and dwellings, and bronze figures brought from China and Japan. Adolph Bernheimer's frame hilltop house, a double unit of oriental design with a central courtyard, is decorated with embroidered panels, handpainted screens, tapestries, and art objects.

Facing Santa Monica Bay from a high mesa is SANTA MONICA, 48.5 *m.* (100 alt., 37,146 pop.), a residential-resort city with a substantial business center, whose summer visitors swell the population figure to more than 100,000. Along the edge of the bluffs for 3 miles stretches green, tree-shaded PALISADES PARK. The half-moon-shaped ocean front, city-owned since 1917, faces a yacht harbor and breakwater.

The land here was once part of two ranchos, "the place called San Vicente," and "the place called Santa Monica," over whose boundaries the Sepulveda, Reyes and Marquez families quarreled for many years. In the 1860's people of Los Angeles began making buggy excursions to the beach for swimming, beach bonfires, and Saturday dances in a big tent. Across the plain where the town now stands, ox-teams hauled *brea* (tar) from La Brea tar pits to a little wharf for loading on San Francisco-bound steamers. In 1872, Col. R. S. Baker, a wool grower, bought the property and stocked it with sheep; and when two years later wealthy Senator John P. Jones bought a three-fourths interest, the two planned construction of a railroad, a wharf, and a town. An advertising campaign drew real-estate buyers from as far as San Francisco; within nine months the town had 1,000 residents and 160 houses. A bitter fight was waged in the 1890's between the Southern Pacific Railroad and the city of Los Angeles over the choice of a seaport, the railroad insisting on Santa Monica, the city preferring San Pedro. With premature conviction that its choice would hold, the Southern Pacific started construction of a million-dollar, mile-long pier here; today it is only a 50-foot jetty with a few sections of rusty railroad track running along the cliff-base.

Santa Monica is at the junction with US 66 (*see TOUR 12c*). US 101A leaves the ocean and turns R. on Lincoln Blvd.

At 49.8 *m.* is the junction with Ocean Park Blvd.

Left on Ocean Park Blvd. to the DOUGLAS AIRCRAFT FACTORY (*closed to public*), 1.6 *m.*, adjoining an airport and testing ground on Clover Field (*open to visitors*). Clover Field was the starting and finishing place of the U. S. Army "'round the world" flight in 1929.

At 52.1 *m.* is the junction with Venice Blvd.

Right here to VENICE, 0.7 *m.* (20 alt., 19,260 pop.), an ocean-front pleasure town with an elaborate amusement section on the beach and pier. A flying circus, giant dipper, bamboo slide, and rolling barrels are among the devices that have given Venice its title "Coney Island of the West." In the early 1900's Abbott Kinney, a middle-west manufacturer, set about creating a Venice on the tidal flats. He built 15 miles of concrete canals radiating from a central artery and planned to line their banks with Italian Renaissance houses. A few such structures were built, gondolas with singing gondoliers were trolled about the waterways, and lectures, "art" exhibits, and Chautauqua meetings were held in an attempt to make the town the western cultural center. Kinney provided transportation to bring prospective lot-buyers from Los Angeles and other places. They came in large numbers, but unfortunately they preferred the bathing beach to the lecture hall. In a final desperate effort Kinney brought in the divine Sarah Bernhardt to play *Camille* in an auditorium at the end of a pier. When that, too, failed, he quietly surrendered and imported sideshow freaks, tentshows, and flip-flop entertainment devices. And the boom began. By 1930, when the town had been part of Los Angeles for five years, an effort was made to fill in the smelly, fungus-covered ditches. A few remain, spanned here and there by ornately coy bridges.

US 101A climbs into the Del Rey Hills to the junction with 83rd St., 54.7 *m.*

Left here to LOYOLA UNIVERSITY, 1 *m.,* a group of handsome buildings on a large hillside campus, operated by the Jesuit order.

At 55 *m.* is the junction with Manchester Ave.

Left on Manchester Ave. to INGLEWOOD, 3 *m.* (140 alt., 19,480 pop.), a shopping center and an industrial town on the site of the Rancho Aguaje de la Centinela (spring of the sentinel), granted in 1844 to Ignacio Machado, who prized it so little that he traded it for a Los Angeles adobe and threw in two barrels of wine to make it a bargain. The land, passing into the hands of Yankees in 1857, was acquired in 1873 by Daniel Freeman, who laid out a town and sold lots. Although the ADOBE DEL RANCHO AGUAJE DE LA CENTINELA, a simple house of sun-dried clay with deeply-recessed windows and vine-clad corridors, is all that remains of Inglewood's Spanish past, the town celebrates "Centinela Days" with pageantry every August.
CENTINELA PARK, E. Redondo Blvd. between Centinela Ave. and West Blvd., is a green, pleasantly landscaped spot of 40 acres where city dwellers dip in a pool, picnic, and play bowls and tennis.
HOLLYWOOD PARK (*racing daily except Sun. and Mon. June 1-July 31; adm. clubhouse $2.75, grandstand $1.10, parking 25¢*), bounded by Century, Crenshaw, and Manchester Blvds. and Prairie Ave., is the $2,500,000 ultramodern home of southern California's mid-summer racing season. The 315-acre plant includes a one-mile oval track; a white concrete-and-steel double-decked grandstand seating 12,000 people; a clubhouse with terraces, lounges, and boxes for 8,000; an enclosed paddock equipped with indirect lighting; and a projection screen that flashes pictures of photographic finishes. The stables have 1,200 stalls and 300 tack- and feed-rooms. Within the 3,700-acre infield are three lakes, covering 10 acres, stocked with ducks, geese, and swans. Opened in June 1938, the track is owned and operated by the Hollywood Turf Club, which in turn is owned by a group of motion picture celebrities.

The mile-square LOS ANGELES MUNICIPAL AIRPORT (L), 57.1 *m.,* with five huge hangars and a five-story administration building, is used extensively for pilot training and plane testing. The two airplane manufacturing plants adjoining, the North American Aviation, Inc. and the Northrup Company, each employ more than 1,000 workers.
At 58.3 *m.* is the junction with paved El Segundo Blvd.

Right on El Segundo Blvd. is EL SEGUNDO, 1.3 *m.* (35 alt., 3,503 pop.), surrounded by huge black oil tanks, concrete reservoirs, and steel-mast lightning rods, which grew up around the Standard Oil Company's second (*segundo*) California refinery; its beach and surf are spoiled for bathing by oil scum.

At 60.2 *m.* is the junction with Manhattan Beach Blvd.

Right on Manhattan Beach Blvd. is MANHATTAN BEACH, 0.7 *m.* (46 alt., 1,891 pop.), a family seaside resort (*bath-houses and fishing tackle*) near the sandy strand of MANHATTAN BEACH STATE PARK, municipal regulations forbid establishment of the less sedate kinds of amusement facilities.

HERMOSA (Sp. beautiful) BEACH, 61.1 *m.* (43 alt., 4,796 pop.), is a quiet town of frame bungalows and seaside cottages on sandy hills, uncluttered by amusement concessions, facing a broad beach where the surf is free from undertow.

Over wide seaside terraces sprawls REDONDO BEACH, 62.6 *m.* (16 alt., 9,347 pop.), its handsome palm-bordered Esplanade lined with decrepit mansions. The now somnolent town began in 1905 with a frenzied boom when rumors spread that railroad tycoon Henry E. Huntington would pour millions into improvements; for five days hundreds of people jammed into real estate offices, bidding for lots—and then the boom collapsed. Today Redondo Beach's weatherbeaten cavernous stucco pavilion, crescent-shaped fishing pier, and salt-water plunge are hemmed by garish amusement concessions. Along the bluffs, riotous with green and reddish-purple ice plant, stretches the MUNICIPAL PARK.

Left from Redondo Beach on Torrance Blvd. is TORRANCE, 4.1 *m.* (75 alt., 7,271 pop.), founded in 1911 by Jared Sidney Torrance, wealthy Pasadena utilities magnate, who studied the best city plans in many parts of the world before he laid out his industrial-residential community. The oil fields, machine and tool shops, steel plant, and other factories are in a section apart from the quiet tree-shaded streets lined with houses. On Torrance Blvd. at Arlington Rd. is the large COLUMBIA STEEL PLANT, with bending and rolling mills, electric foundry, sheet-mill, and four open-hearth furnaces having a production capacity of 15,000 tons per month.

At 64.7 *m.* on US 101A is the junction with Palos Verdes Dr.

Right here to PALOS VERDES, 0.6 *m.* (200 alt., 750 pop.), a restricted residential district conceived in 1922 and developed ambitiously by its promoter, E. J. Lewis.
Right from Palos Verdes on Palos Verdes Drive West, winding around the rain-eroded San Pedro Hills along the curling cliff brim, to the junction with a dirt road, 2 *m.*; here 0.1 *m.* to the slim white tower of POINT VICENTE LIGHTHOUSE (*open 2-4 Tues. and Thurs.*).
Palos Verdes Dr. continues, skirting wide views of the Pacific, to the junction with Twenty-fifth St. 2 *m.*; straight ahead on Twenty-fifth St. to the junction with Paseo del Mar, 0.6 *m.*
Right on Paseo del Mar is FORT MCARTHUR UPPER RESERVATION, 0.9 *m.*, its great guns hidden from sight, guarding the approach to Los Angeles Harbor from the edge of ocean bluffs.
Crossing the ubiquitous Los Angeles city limits, Twenty-fifth St. continues to the junction with Pacific St. in SAN PEDRO (*see below*), 0.8 *m.*

US 101A cuts across the neck of the Palos Verdes peninsula to the junction with Gaffey St., 70.4 *m.*

Right on Gaffey St. 2.6 *m.* to the junction with Pacific Ave.; L. on Pacific Ave. to SAN PEDRO, 3.7 *m.* (o–100 alt., 36,000 pop.), the city created by inland Los Angeles' passion for calling itself a port, facing the western rim of San Pedro Bay from the edge of the San Pedro Hills. When the first Yankee ship, Capt. William Shaler's *Lelia Byrd,* anchored here in 1805—nearly three centuries after the bay's discovery by Juan Rodríguez Cabrillo—the place was an open roadstead bordered by mud flats, serving Mission San Gabriel for an embarcadero. Although foreign trade was forbidden by law, settlers—and the padres—were quite willing to barter their hides and tallow for contraband manufactured goods. Even after San Pedro was officially recognized as a port in 1826, smuggling was continued to evade custom duties. In 1852 the harbor became a port of call for its first boat line, when the *Sea Bird* began scheduled trips to and from San Francisco. When Richard Henry Dana returned here a quarter century after the visit described in *Two Years Before the Mast,* however, freight was still lightered "up the creek" from the bay through a winding channel past Deadman's Island at this "most desolate place on the California Coast."

The first Government harbor improvement, made in 1877, was the deepening of the channel to a depth of 16 feet. In 1892 began the Free Harbor fight, carried on for nearly a decade between Los Angeles business interests and the Southern Pacific Railroad Company, who agreed in demanding that Congress should appropriate money for harbor development but disagreed in their choice of a harbor, the former favoring San Pedro and the latter Santa Monica. The former won. In 1899 began the titanic job of creating a man-made harbor which by 1939 had cost the City of Los Angeles and the Federal Government a total of nearly $60,000,000.

The GOVERNMENT BREAKWATER, extending 2.11 miles from the tip of Point Fermin to a concrete lighthouse, built 1899-1910 of sandstone and granite blocks, protects the OUTER HARBOR, home base of 14 battleships, two aircraft carriers, 14 heavy cruisers, and auxiliary vessels of the Pacific Fleet (*open to visitors Sun. and holidays 1-5; free transportation from East Channel Landing*). As incoming vessels round the breakwater, they are piloted up the deep-dredged, 1,000-foot-wide channel that forms the tail of the Y-shaped 804-acre INNER HARBOR to the 1,600-foot-wide TURNING BASIN and there maneuvered into position for entrance into the subsidiary channels, slips, and docks that sawtooth the waterfront. The FORT MCARTHUR LOWER RESERVATION (*open except during artillery practice*), at the southern end of Pacific Ave., headquarters of the 3rd and 63rd Coast Artillery, guards the West Channel from the edge of steep bluffs, bristling with anti-aircraft service guns, railroad guns with 40-foot barrels, and the derricks that feed them heavy shells. Behind the piers and warehouses along the docks is a belt of fish canneries and industrial plants.

The city, State, and Federal buildings of the SAN PEDRO CIVIC CENTER, bounded by Harbor Blvd., Beacon, 6th, and 9th Sts., stand along a palm-lined parkway on a low bluff near the center of the business district. Over the foothill slopes, rising above, ramble the homes of the residence area. At the landward end of the breakwater is CABRILLO BEACH PARK, end of Stephen M. White Dr. (*open 6 a.m.-12 p.m.*), created by pumping sand dredged from the harbor over the rocky shore; the beach, with a bath house (*adm. 10¢ to 25¢*) and boat house (*boats 25¢ to 35¢ an hour*), lying on both sides of the breakwater, affords fine surf bathing. The CABRILLO BEACH MUSEUM (*open 9-5*) has a large aquarium and collection of native and foreign shells and mounted fish. POINT FERMIN PARK, on Paseo del Mar at the tip of the Peninsula (*picnicking*), is a 27-acre expanse of trees and lawns with winding flower-bordered footpaths on the bluffs overlooking the Pacific. In the park is the POINT FERMIN LIGHTHOUSE, built in 1876.

WILMINGTON, 72.6 *m.* (13 alt., 15,468 pop.), with its business streets, warehouses, and shipping offices lies on the flat ground facing Terminal Island across the San Pedro Inner Harbor. When the harbor and island were just a slough and a sand bar, this was marshy land, with the fish-smelling huts of an Indian village squatting on the mud. In 1857 Phineas Banning bought a 2400-acre parcel of old Rancho San Pedro, laid out a town called New San Pedro (now Wilmington) and began development of the harbor, and ran stages here to meet weekly steamers from San Francisco, Los Angeles' first landing-place for ocean-going freight. Wilmington grew with the building of a railroad, linking city with port, in 1869. A few years later the Southern Pacific Railroad built across the mud flats to deep water at San Pedro. In 1906 Los Angeles inched up to the harbor by annexing a "shoestring strip" to the very gates of Wilmington, and in 1909 she swallowed both Wilmington and San Pedro in her corporate embrace.

BANNING PARK (*free*), E. M St. and Banning Blvd., is a 20-acre tract, once the heart of the Phineas Banning estate, landscaped with a quiet, old-fashioned charm. A circular walk, lined with a white picket fence and rows of eucalyptus trees, leads to the old BANNING HOUSE (*not open*), a large house with a two-story pillared porch. The white frame stable and carriage house houses surreys and carriages and an old stagecoach.

DRUMM BARRACKS, 1031 Cary Ave., is now just another house on a residential street, a two-story white frame structure with green shutters and an unkempt hedge around its small yard. Built in 1861, it was a troop barracks and part of a supply depot for the U. S. Army of the Southwest.

The SANTA CATALINA ISLAND TERMINAL, at the foot of Avalon Blvd., is the embarcadero for Santa Catalina Island (*see TOUR 2c*). The CALIFORNIA YACHT CLUB, on Yacht St., is a white frame building topped by a tower resembling a lighthouse.

Wilmington is at the junction with US 6 (*see TOUR 7b*), which unites with US 101A to Long Beach.

Right from Wilmington to Henry Ford Ave., across a vascule drawbridge, 2 *m.*, to TERMINAL ISLAND, nearly one-half man made, which protects Wilmington from the sea. When Phineas Banning began his harbor developments, it was a sand bar named Rattlesnake Island. During the period of red plush sofas and stereopticons, it was popular as a beach resort for bathers in ankle-length bathing suits.
Near the western end of the island is the JAPANESE FISHING VILLAGE, the home of Portuguese and Italian, as well as Japanese fishermen. A babble of many tongues is heard on the streets. Along the waterfront and in the cottage yards men, women, and sometimes children squat, mending big fishing nets, some of them 2,000 feet long and valued at several thousand dollars. Along Tuna St. are little old-world shops, indifferent to tourist trade, and small restaurants with menus in foreign tongues that serve excellent fish and native dishes.
South of the village is FISH HARBOR, a small artificial basin protected by a sea wall. It is headquarters for 2,300 fishermen who put out to sea each day in 1,200 vessels, returning in the evening with their catch which, if luck is good, loads the vessels almost gunwales down. Big boats—such as

the tuna clippers—travel in fleets, some going as far as Panama or the Galapagos Islands. Sardine fishers go out on moonless nights and, finding schools of fish by their phosphorescent glow, haul them in by net. About Fish Harbor are eight large plants, where fancy tuna, mackerel and sardines are canned and fish oil, fish meal, fertilizer, and pet foods are manufactured.

LONG BEACH, 77.5 *m.* (47 alt., 142,032 pop.), (*see LONG BEACH*).

At 84.1 *m.* is the junction with a paved road.

Left on this road is SEAL BEACH, 0.5 *m.* (9 alt., 1,156 pop.), a resort town with a fishing pier hemmed in by power plants and gas storage tanks.

US 101 crosses two of the shallow inlets of Anaheim Bay to a straight stretch down a long low-lying tongue of land between a winding lagoon (L) and the surf (R), bordered by beach cabins that string north and south from SUNSET BEACH, 78.7 *m.* (10 alt., 150 pop.). The lower end of the lagoon is placid BOLSA BAY, 79 *m.,* (*speedboats, rowboats, canoes available*) fringed by tule-grown marshes where sportsmen come for duck-hunting.

Along the water's edge around HUNTINGTON BEACH, 90.8 *m.* (20 alt., 2,690 pop.), rise bleak oil derricks. Before oil was discovered here after 1920, the town had developed as a minor recreational resort, but local residents profited little, having sold most of their holdings before the discovery was known. The buying campaign had gone on so quietly that few were aware of the unusual number of sales. The tide lands here have remained State property but oil operators have developed a new technique of drilling to meet the situation; from their land, the former town lots, they drill on a bias to tap the pools under the tidelands. The practice has stirred up one of the State's bitterest controversies; Culbert L. Olson, Governor of California (1939), as a State senator, endeavored to put through a bill that would end the practice and enable the State to exploit the reservoirs for the benefit of the public.

At 96.4 *m.* is the junction with State 55, paved.

Right on State 55 over an inlet of landlocked NEWPORT BAY and along the low spit across its mouth to NEWPORT BEACH, 1 *m.* (2,203 pop.), and its suburb, BALBOA, 2 *m.* (810 pop.), facing the sail-dotted lagoon-like bay with its islands—Lido, Bay, Harbor, and Balboa Islands— where California-Riviera type stucco villas look down on yachts and pleasure craft at their moorings. Around the bay shore cluster the seaside cottages of neighboring resorts. The harbor, where Yankee smugglers once hid out, rose to brief prominence as a commercial port when a dock and warehouse were built here in 1872 but fell behind San Pedro after 1898. The Santa Ana River had carried so much silt into the bay by 1915 that it had to be diverted into a new channel directly to the sea; the bay has since been dredged to a depth of 10 feet at low water. The pleasure boat fleet is now one of the largest on the Pacific Coast. In spring the Pacific Coast Yacht Regatta is staged and in summer a spectacular water carnival, the "Tournament of Lights."

The crag-bound coves and headlands around LAGUNA BEACH, 104.9 *m.* (17 alt., 1,981 pop.), have served as inspiration for uncounted landscape painters. The cultivated quaintness of Laguna Beach's rustic dwellings and shops, sprawling over seaside slopes, is due to the influence of its sprinkling of artists—as are its studios, its "little" theater, and the LAGUNA BEACH ART ASSOCIATION GALLERY (*adm. 10¢*).

From the bluffs at THREE ARCHES, 110.4 *m.* (300 pop.), tile-roofed stucco houses, noticeably new, overlook spray-drenched crags—and the arch rocks to which the settlement owes its name.

Overlooking DANA COVE is the residential hamlet of DANA POINT, 112.4 *m.* (175 alt., 120 pop.). The cliffs rose "twice as high as our royal-mast-head," observed Richard Henry Dana when the *Pilgrim* anchored here in 1835. "The shore is rocky, and directly exposed to the southeast, so that vessels are obliged to slip and run for their lives on the first sign of the gale." The descent down the cliffs was so perilous that when Boston hide-traders anchored here to load, the hides were thrown to the beach from above.

DOHENY PARK (*see TOUR 2d*), 113.6 *m.* (549 pop.), is at the junction with US 101 (*see TOUR 2d*).

<<<<<<<<<<<<<<<<<<<<<<<<<<<<<<<<<<<<<<<<<<<<<<<<<<<<<<<<<>>

Tour 2C

Wilmington to Avalon, Santa Catalina Island, 27 *m.* by boat.

Transportation to island from Berths 184-185, Wilmington. Round trip $3; children $1.50; by air plane, $5 one way. Automobile storage at pier 50¢ a day. Rates vary somewhat with the seasons.
Accommodations range from camps to luxury hotels. Private automobiles prohibited. Year-round resort; summer months most popular.

Twenty-seven miles southwest of Los Angeles Harbor in the rolling wastes of the Pacific Ocean rise the mist-blown peaks of Santa Catalina Island. Twenty-two miles long and from one-half to eight miles wide, the island looks from the mainland as if a section of the Coast Range had been transplanted to the open ocean. In its numerous valleys the foliage is luxuriant; the rugged higher slopes are covered with chaparral. The beaches are narrow and pebbly, but the calm, clear waters of the many bays and coves make them popular for swimming and yachting. Abounding with tuna, swordfish, yellowtail, white sea bass, rock bass, barracuda, mackerel, bonita, whitefish, and sheepshead, the waters about the island are popular with sport fisherman.

Santa Catalina Island has one incorporated city, a $2,000,000 casino, a network of roads and trails, a $1,000,000 water system, a small industrial center, and numerous highly commercialized tourist attractions.

The island was discovered by Juan Rodríguez Cabrillo, Portuguese navigator who, seeking the mythical Strait of Anian under orders from the Spanish Crown, put into the small, placid bay now called Avalon on October 7, 1542. He named the island San Salvador, for his flagship. On November 28, 1602, the islanders saw the Spanish King's next emissary, Sebastián Viscaíno, enter the harbor with his three white-winged ships. He gave the island its present name in honor of St. Catherine. In 1811 a Russian vessel, seeking the prized sea otters, landed in the bay and slaughtered many of the Indians. Until 1821, when Mexico freed herself from Spain and lifted the Spanish ban on foreign trade in California, Santa Catalina was the base for unlawful trading operations with the mainland.

Although gold had been discovered on Santa Catalina in 1834, it was not until 1863 that several prospectors "struck it rich," starting a gold rush; some 100,000 feet of claims were staked and filed in the Los Angeles County Recorder's office, and indefatigable prospectors even ran their mine tunnels under the ocean floor. The boom was cut short by three developments: a new island owner, José María Covarrubias, bought the property in 1855 and vociferously objected to the freebooting activities of the prospectors; a pirate scare frightened the Federal Government; and last but not least the gold ran out.

The Government became worried when it was learned that Confederate sympathizers were planning to use Santa Catalina as a base for pirating the gold-carrying ships in the coastal trade, and Northern troops were hurriedly sent in with orders to evacuate all private citizens by February 1, 1864.

From then until 1919, when William Wrigley, Jr., bought the property, the various owners attempted subdivisions, promotion of pleasure resorts, and a silver mining venture. But it was Wrigley who had the formula needed to make the island a commercial success and who had the millions to create a romantic, palm-studded town on the beautiful bay, to construct the luxurious casino and other improvements; and to put on one of the most extensive and far-flung publicity campaigns ever staged in publicity-conscious California.

Boats for Santa Catalina leave from the CATALINA TERMINAL, foot of Avalon Blvd., Wilmington.

AVALON, 27 m. (0 alt., 2,200 pop.), the main settlement and center of resort and sports activities of SANTA CATALINA ISLAND, lies at the mouth of a large canyon along the crescent-shaped shore of Avalon Bay on the northwestern side of the island. The buildings are the usual miscellaneous collection of stucco-covered and frame structures in the Californian version of what Spanish design should be. Crescent Avenue, the principal street, follows the curve of the bay, widening in the downtown area to the size of a plaza. Palm and olive trees, set in stone boxes in the center of the street, shade low settees and stone benches; grassy squares and sparkling fountains, strolling señoritas in spangled skirts and strumming troubadours in velvet costumes, round out the scene. There are three hotels operated by the Santa Catalina Island Company, and 30 privately operated hotels, apartment houses, and bungalow courts.

Most of the island's tourist attractions are in Avalon or near it. Regularly scheduled boat and motorcar trips to the remoter points of interest leave from Avalon, as do the various speedboat, glass-bottom boat, and flying fish trips (*see below*).

The AVALON BOARDWALK skirts the harbor from Pebbly Beach. With many of the island's major attractions fronting on it, it is the principal recreation center.

EL ENCANTO, in the heart of Avalon, is a plaza surrounded by small shops and cafés.

The AVALON CASINO (*open 2-4 p.m. daily*), on the boardwalk, rises from the northwest promontory of Avalon Bay. The $2,000,000 white, circular building is styled in an adaptation of Moorish design. On the lower floor is a large motion picture theater. Five ramps give access to the second-story ballroom. A cocktail lounge with a 100-foot-long bar has walls covered with fantastic fish murals.

The SANTA CATALINA AIRPORT lies at the head of a deep canyon at HAMILTON BEACH, northwest of Avalon. Twice daily or oftener amphibian planes land on the water here, taxi up a ramp to a turntable, are then about-faced for the return trip.

The AVALON GREEK THEATER, east end of Crescent Ave., is used chiefly by civic and fraternal organizations.

The SANTA CATALINA ISLAND VISITORS' COUNTRY CLUB (*greens fee $1*), Sumner Ave. and Fremont St., is a rambling stucco clubhouse crowning a knoll and surrounded by an 18-hole golf course. There are also tennis courts and a 9-hole pitch-and-put course.

The CATALINA BASEBALL PARK, Fremont St. and Avalon Blvd., is the spring-training headquarters of the Wrigley-owned National League Chicago Cubs (*exhibition games 12 m. daily Feb. 12-March 15*).

The AVALON BIRD PARK (*open 8-6*), in Avalon Canyon (*reached only by bus, leaving corner Crescent and Metropole Aves. every one-half hr. from 7-7*), is a 20-acre home for more than 8,000 birds of 650 varieties, mostly from foreign countries.

The GLIDDEN INDIAN MUSEUM (*open 9-5; adm. 25¢*), on the hill over-looking Avalon, is a one-story yellow and tan frame structure exhibiting Indian artifacts and skeletons found on the island.

PEBBLY BEACH, at end of the Boardwalk, 1.5 miles east of Avalon, is an industrial district; here are a large pottery plant, a furniture factory, and a stone quarry. Mexican employees live in a small village near the shore.

EAGLES NEST LODGE, 10 miles from Avalon on the Avalon-Isthmus motor road (*on the Isthmus Auto Tour; see below*), is headquarters for goat, boar, and quail hunters, and an overnight stop for hikers and riding parties. The one-story rustic wooden lodge is named for nearby

EAGLE MOUNTAIN, on whose 1,000-foot pinnacle scores of eagles nest. All hunting on the Island is conducted on supervised trips (*$10 a person each day, including guide and transportation; license at Avalon Pier*). Boar and goats are hunted the year round from horseback with deer rifles. Large numbers of wild mountain goats roam the island interior. Some historians credit Cabrillo with having abandoned some goats on the island in 1542; others contend that they were left by Father Torquemada of the Viscaíno expedition of 1602.

The ISTHMUS lies in the northwestern section of Santa Catalina Island, 14 miles by water, 22 miles by motor road, from Avalon (*reached on the 'Round the Island Cruise and Isthmus Auto Tour; see below*), at a point where the island was almost cut in two when the land sagged during some cataclysm in the distant past. The terrain here is a flat mesa between bordering mountains. Fronting PAPEETE BEACH and ISTHMUS COVE is a settlement of one-story, thatched bungalettes for accommodation of a fluctuating summer population. The South Sea Island effect has been sought for all structures, including the store. Various abandoned movie sets are here, most noteworthy of which are the thatched ROUND HOUSE used in the silent picture *Rain,* and the CONTINENTAL HOTEL SET from the film *Sadie Thompson,* a remake of *Rain* in sound. Midway between Isthmus Cove and Catalina Harbor stands the former UNITED STATES GOVERNMENT BARRACKS, now living quarters for employees of the island operating company; it was built to house Union troops.

CONDUCTED TOURS

(All boats leave from Avalon Pier; auto trips from Avalon Plaza)

1. The GLASS BOTTOM BOAT TRIP (*fare 75¢, children 40¢*), visits the marine gardens that extend 17 miles along the protected north shore.

2. The SEAL ROCK TRIP (*fare 50¢, children 25¢*), is a one and one-half hour, 11-mile cruise in a 60-foot boat along the jagged lee shore to a sunny, wave-lashed cluster of rocks just off NORTHEAST POINT, where several hundred sea lions live.

3. The EVENING FLYING FISH TRIP (*April to Oct.; fare 75¢, children 40¢*), is a 40-minute, wave-bouncing, spume-dashed night ride behind a 45-million candlepower searchlight, into the beam of which glide thousands of flying fishes, their highly colored "wings" (fins) iridescent in the glare.

4. The AVALON SPEEDBOAT TRIP (*fare 75¢, children 50¢*) is a 50-mile-an-hour dash from Avalon to a point about 1 mile beyond the Santa Catalina Airport and return.

5. The ISTHMUS BOAT TRIP (*May to Oct.; fare $1, children 50¢, with return trip by auto, $2.50, half fare $1.50*) is a 3-hour 28-mile round trip cruise from Avalon Bay to Isthmus Cove along the northern coast. A 1-hour stop for lunch and sightseeing is made at the Isthmus.

6. The 'ROUND THE ISLAND CRUISE (*10:30 a.m. Sun. only, April to Oct.; fare $1, half fare 50¢*).

7. The ISTHMUS AUTO TOUR (*round trip $3, children $2*) follows the Old Stage Road over the Summit (1,520 alt.), past Middle Ranch Valley, and Eagles Nest Lodge, to the Isthmus.

8. The STARLIGHT DRIVE (*April to Oct.; fare 50¢, children 25¢*) is

a 55-minute 7-mile evening trip in an open bus. The sights are set to music by a Spanish-costumed guitar player who goes along.

9. The SKYLINE DRIVE (*fare 50¢, children 25¢*) is a 30-minute 5-mile motor trip similar to the Starlight Drive, but by daylight, and without the guitar player.

Tour 3

(Ashland, Ore.) — Yreka — Redding — Red Bluff — Sacramento — Stockton — Fresno — Bakersfield — Los Angeles — Ontario — Redlands — Coachella — Brawley — Calexico — (Mexicali, Mexico); US 99 and 99 W.

Oregon Line to Mexican Border, 880.6 *m.*

Paved roadbed throughout, open all season.
Southern Pacific R.R. parallels route between Oregon Line and Bakersfield, Saugus and Los Angeles, Banning and Mecca, Brawley and Calexico; Santa Fe Ry. parallels route between Oakland and Bakersfield.
Accommodations plentiful; numerous camping sites in northern counties.

US 99 presents a complete cross section of California. From the rugged wall of the Siskiyous on the north, it winds down barren river canyons, round Mount Shasta, and along the twisting Sacramento River between steep, evergreen-forested slopes.   Southward it parallels the two great rivers, the Sacramento and the San Joaquin, that drain the far-reaching plains of the Central Valley, stretching for 750 miles in an unbroken sweep.   From the valley's southern end it climbs the arid, brush-clad Tehachapi Mountains and descends to the fertile Southern California valleys where citrus groves and truck gardens extend for mile on mile.   Its course then turns southeast through the sagebrush reaches of a desert trough between the San Jacinto and San Bernardino Mountains, past the Salton Sea, into irrigated farmlands of the sun-scorched Imperial Valley.   The highway passes smoking lumber mills among bare, stump-dotted slopes; mines and quarries on scarred mountain sides and dredges scooping river gravel; herds cropping broad pastures and far-spreading acres of hay and grain; fruit-laden orchards around packing houses, truck garden plots, and groves of date palms.   The climate varies sharply, from the bracing cold of mountain highlands to the sultry heat of Imperial Valley below sea level.

Section a.   OREGON LINE to SACRAMENTO; 298.7 m.
US 99-99 W.

Northern California's oldest road in continuous use—the Oregon-California Trail—roughly paralleled today's concrete roadbed.   Starting as a faint pathway blazed through the wilderness by venturesome scouts and trappers from 1827 on, it was followed in the 1840's by early immigrants with their ox-drawn wagons, driving their cattle before them. It became a well-defined pack trail in the next decade, thronged with gold seekers, mule trains, ox-teams and covered wagons. In the late 1850's, the first turnpike between Portland and Sacramento was opened, and as the tide of travel mounted, outposts of civilization sprang up along the way. On the campsites where fur hunters had stopped for rest, inns were built. As freighters and stagecoaches supplanted mule trains, stage stations were opened; in 1886-87, when the Southern Pacific pushed its tracks from Redding to Oregon along the route, these became railroad stations and, finally, villages and towns.

South of the Oregon Line, 0 *m.*, crossed 22.8 miles south of Ashland, Oregon, stretch the wild slopes of the Siskiyou Mountains. As the highway descends, the lava mass of BLACK MOUNTAIN (5,270 alt.) looms up (L). Above it towers snow-crowned Mount Shasta (*see below*), seen for nearly 100 miles southward at intervals.

HORNBROOK, 8.2 *m.* (2,115 alt., 300 pop.), lies (L) downhill across Cottonwood Creek, its old brick business structures, store buildings with wooden awnings, and handful of shanties shadowed by shaggy black walnut trees.

To CAMP LOWE, 10.4 *m.*, where the rippling Klamath River (L) swings in to the highway, come anglers for the fine steelhead trout and salmon fishing.

At 14.7 *m.* is the junction with State 96, paved for 21 miles westward.

> Right on State 96, along the canyon of the lower Klamath, winding through one of California's most primitive regions. Until 1850, when a party of miners followed the river from the ocean, panning for gold at every bar, its course—variously known as Clamitte, Klamet, Indian Scalp, and Smith River—was unknown and incorrectly shown on the maps.
>
> At 2 *m.* is a boundary of Klamath National Forest, an area of 1,500,831 acres, crisscrossed by pine-clad ridges and cut by deep canyons. Almost untouched by logging operations, the reserve guards about 15 billion feet of sugar and ponderosa pine and Douglas fir. It is dotted with hydraulic and drift mines, dredges, wing dams, and stamp mills.
>
> BROWN'S RESORT, 16 *m.*, is a stopping place for fishermen and hunters.
>
> At 33 *m.* is the junction with a dirt road; L. here 3 *m.* to SCOTT BAR (1,687 alt.), in the deep gorge of Scott River, a ghost town of dilapidated buildings where prospectors led by John Scott panned for gold in 1850. Driven out by Indians, they spread news of a rich strike that brought miners flocking in. By 1863 William H. Brewer found the placers worked out, the population departed, and half the houses empty.
>
> The road winds on a ledge cut from steep canyon sides to SPRING FLAT, 16 *m.* (Forest Service Camp). Here trails start into the MARBLE MOUNTAIN PRIMITIVE AREA, a wildly picturesque 237,527-acre tract, culminating in castellated Marble Mountain, a monumental pile (8,925 alt.) of limestone and marble streaked with a vein of glistening white. Of the other peaks, Red Mountain (8,317 alt.) is the highest. Near their summits are about 50 small crystal-clear lakes, stocked with trout, and a dozen or more streams with 250 miles of fishing waters. Deer, bear, and mountain lion roam the region. The Forest Service maintains five camps:

Paradise Lake, Marble Valley, Sky High Valley, Spirit Lake, and Upper Cabin.

On State 96 is HAMBURG, 35 *m.* (1,580 alt., 70 pop.), with a general store and tourist cottages. A bustling mining town up to 1861, it had disappeared two years later, its buildings swept away by a flood.

At SEIAD VALLEY (*cabins; restaurant*), 45 *m.* (1,383 alt., 50 pop.), on a fertile little flat, which Brewer found to be "a delightful spot . . . an oasis in the desert," a New York farmer settled in 1854 and amassed a fortune raising potatoes that he sold for 15¢ a pound to the swarming miners.

HAPPY CAMP, 65 *m.* (1,088 alt., 566 pop.), a popular place for year-round fishing and a point of departure for trails into the wilderness (*guides, packers, and pack trip supplies*), is the District Forest Supervisor's Headquarters.

The road continues through wild country unsettled except for a few scattered ranches and small Indian villages.

At PICK-AW-ISH CAMP, 74 *m.*, Indians gather yearly in the dark of the August moon for a three-day festival. Among the ceremonies are the Brush, Deerskin, and Coyote Dances and one called The Working of the Earth, which has as its purpose the propitiation of the spirits of earth and forest to avert landslides, earthquakes, forest fires, and droughts.

SOMES BAR, 106 *m.* (580 alt., 50 pop.), where the Salmon River joins the Klamath, began as a mining town. It is a favorite spot for year-round fishing for king salmon and steelhead trout and a starting point for trails into the western part of the Marble Mountain Primitive Area.

ORLEANS, 114 *m.* (393 alt., 75 pop.) (*good accommodations*), lies below ORLEANS MOUNTAIN (6,184 alt.), a look-out point commanding a magnificent view.

At BLUFF CREEK, 124 *m.*, the Forest Service maintains a camp.

WEITCHPEC, 130 *m.* (367 alt., 64 pop.), is at the confluence of the Trinity River and the Klamath on the northern boundary of the HOOPA INDIAN RESERVATION, which occupies approximately 100 square miles of the Hoopa, or Trinity, Valley. The reservation was established in 1865, following a treaty of peace (1864) that ended 12 years of bitter warfare between the Hoopas (Hupalos) and white settlers. Soldiers were stationed at the reservation until 1892. About 500 Indians, many of mixed blood, support themselves here by farming, stock raising, and occasional work outside the reservation.

At HOOPA, 141.4 *m.* (100 pop.), only town on the reservation, are stores, administrative offices, and elementary and high schools.

State 96 crosses the reservation's southern boundary at 144.8 *m.* to the junction with US 299 (*see TOUR 8b*), 153.4 *m.*

At the southern end of KLAMATH BRIDGE, 14.8 *m.*, a graceful concrete span, the Shasta River, foaming over its stony bed far below (R), joins the Klamath. The highway twists through the tortuous gorge of the Shasta on a ledge blasted from the craggy walls, bridging the river three times more within the next three miles. Highest of the spans is steel and concrete PIONEER BRIDGE, 16.7 *m.*, arching the canyon 252 feet above the river.

At 21 *m.* is the junction with a dirt road.

Right on this road is HAWKINSVILLE, 0.3 *m.*, with its red church steeple rising above a handful of weather-beaten shanties. In 1851 it was a flourishing center of trade. Here began a string of miners' cabins that followed Yreka Creek southward for 3 miles.

The road winds on to HUMBUG CREEK, 5.6 *m.*, supposedly so named because a company of prospectors on the way there in 1851 met others returning who insisted that the rumors of gold were "all humbug" but paying no heed, pushed on and made a rich strike. Joaquin Miller, who, as a youth, had a cabin on the creek bank, drew a gloomy picture of the region: "It lay west of the city (Yreka), a day's ride down in a deep, densely timbered cañon, out of sight of Mount Shasta, out of sight of everything—even the sun . . ."

Beyond Humbug Creek is the junction with a dirt road; L. here 1.4 *m.* to the SITE OF HUMBUG CITY, chief of the mining camps. A wild place it was, "a sort of Hades," said Miller, "a savage Eden, with many Adams walking up and down and plucking of every tree, nothing forbidden here; for here, so far as it would seem, are neither laws of God nor man." The principal saloon was the Howlin' Wilderness, an immense log cabin with a log fire always burning in the huge fireplace, where so many fights broke out that the common saying was, "We will have a man for breakfast tomorrow."

YREKA, 23.1 *m.* (2,624 alt., 2,126 pop.), seat of Siskiyou County, is rimmed by sheltering slopes. Surrounding the compact business district along Miner Street are blocks of gracious old white houses on streets shaded by locust trees. After Abraham Thompson in March, 1851, struck it rich at Black Gulch Camp, 2,000 men flocked in within less than six weeks. The place was known as Thompson's Dry Diggings; then, when a town was laid out in May, as Shasta Butte City; and finally, in 1852, as Yreka, which is thought to be a corruption of Wai-ri-ka (Ind., mountain). It had its share of the early Indian troubles, once barely escaping massacre when an Indian woman, Klamath Peggy, traveled 20 miles of rough mountains to warn the citizens of an impending attack. Approaching along devious trails over the brush-covered hills, the Klamath warriors found Yreka strongly guarded by sentries and withdrew. For years Klamath Peggy lived in Yreka, fearing the vengeance of her kinsmen; finally Yreka's people pensioned her.

In Yreka's HALL OF RECORDS, of painted stucco (in a locust-shaded square at Fourth and Lane Sts.), is the SISKIYOU COUNTY GOLD EXHIBIT of ores and nuggets, a small fraction of the millions that the region has yielded. At the KLAMATH NATIONAL FOREST SUPERVISOR'S HEADQUARTERS (*open 8:30-4:30*), Broadway and Miner St., is a huge relief map of Klamath National Forest.

At 25.1 *m.* is the junction with a paved road.

Right here 0.1 *m.* to the SITE OF GREENHORN, marked today by a nondescript cluster of frame structures. In the early 1850's, a company of miners had failed to find gold here, and when a greenhorn asked where to mine, they directed him to their abandoned claim; the joke turned on them when he made a rich strike. Here was the battlefield of the "Greenhorn War" of 1855, which broke out when the Greenhorn men, angered over diversion of the water for their claims from Greenhorn Creek, cut the Yreka Flats Ditch. A Yreka court promptly issued an injunction. They defied it. When Yreka officers countered by arresting one of them, the Greenhorn men marched on Yreka and freed him. But the court decision stood, and the Yreka Flats Ditch Association continued using water from Greenhorn Creek.

Along Yreka Creek the road runs over rugged slopes to the summit of FOREST HOUSE MOUNTAIN (4,159 alt.), and along Moffett Creek into lovely SCOTT VALLEY, named for John Scott, who discovered gold at Scott's Bar.

At 15.3 *m.* is the junction with a dirt road; R. here 7.6 *m.*, along Mc-Adams Creek to its confluence with Deadwood and Cherry Creeks, to the SITE OF DEADWOOD, second only to Yreka among the region's mining centers in 1854-55. Here Joaquin Miller wrote his first poem, an epithalamium for the marriage of Deadwood's cook to a Yreka lady; he recited it at the reception for the pair.

FORT JONES, 17 *m.*, on the main side road (2,747 alt., 302 pop.), once known by a variety of names: Wheelock, for the man who built a hotel here in the 1850's; Scottsburg, for the surrounding Scott Valley; and Ottiewa, for a group of the Shasta Indians, acquired its present name from the camp the First United States Dragoons maintained here between 1852 and 1858 for protection against Indian raids.

GREENVIEW, 22 *m.* (2,812 alt., 94 pop.), is a starting point for hiking and horseback trips west into the valleys of the Salmon Mountains, where gold mining began in the 1850's.

ETNA, 29 *m.* (2,941 alt., 379 pop.), in the heart of rich farm lands, grew up about a flour mill, named the Rough and Ready, which began competition in 1856 with the neighboring Etna Mills, built two years earlier. As settlements sprang up about the two mills, rivalry waxed hot between them; but in 1863 the older fell behind when its post office was shifted to its neighbor. Rough and Ready Mills even took over the loser's name, giving up its own, since the town Rough and Ready in Nevada County had prior claims.

Southwest of Etna the road, now unpaved, climbs a 15 percent grade to the summit of SALMON MOUNTAIN (5,969 alt.), which affords a panorama of the Scott River Valley. Down another 15 percent grade it winds along North Russian Creek to FINLEY CAMP, 48 *m.* (2,600 alt.), on the North Fork of the Salmon River.

SAWYER'S BAR, 54 *m.* (2,171 alt., 100 pop.), began as a mining camp. It has a Roman Catholic Church built in the early days of whip-sawed lumber.

Left from Sawyer's Bar 5 *m.* on a dirt road with a 20 percent grade to the junction with a dirt road.

(1) Right here 0.5 *m.* to BLACK BEAR MINE, where quartz has been extracted since the days when mill machinery had to be carried over the mountains on muleback or on ox-drawn sleds.

(2) Left here on a narrow mountain road is CECILVILLE, 20 *m.* (2,350 alt., 20 pop.), an Indian village. This is a point of entry to the SALMON-TRINITY ALPS PRIMITIVE REGION (*see TOUR 8b*). A Forest Service trail (R) follows the South Fork of the Salmon River into the wilderness.

West of Sawyer's Bar the main side road continues along the North Fork of Salmon River. At its confluence with the South Fork is FORKS OF SALMON, 70 *m.* (1,242 alt., 100 pop.), where in June 1850 the first prospectors, pushing into the Salmon Mountains along the South Fork, found rich diggings. From Forks of Salmon, the gold-seekers spread along the North Fork and over the divide into Scott Valley, until the river was dotted with camps.

At 87 *m.* is the junction with State 96 (*see above*).

Through the narrow neck of the valley US 99 veers (L) between low undulating hills.

At 32.3 *m.* is the junction with a dirt road.

Left on this road, which runs through fields of blue-green alfalfa, dotted with trim, freshly painted farmhouses and barns amid clumps of trees, is

GRENADA, 1 *m.* (2,561 alt., 300 pop.), center of a prosperous farming and dairying district.

Here the highway swerves to cut in a straight line across the Shasta Valley's level, monotonous sweep of hayfield and grazing land with scattered farmhouses half-hidden among bunched trees.

Along the roadside (L) are low, smoothly rounded, conical hills of volcanic origin, visible throughout the length of Shasta Valley. Indian legend tells how the Great Spirit whose dwelling place was Mount Shasta, wanting a home close to his own for his only daughter, set the Indians to work building Shastina, the smaller peak that juts up from the western slope below the main crater. They carried dirt and rock in great baskets until one morning the Great Spirit saw that his daughter's dwelling place, already larger than he had planned, would soon be as great as his own. Instantly he commanded the Indians to stop work. Each emptied the dirt from his basket wherever he stood; and there, for each basketful of earth, was left a little, moundlike hill.

Around GAZELLE, 41.5 *m.* (2,758 alt., 116 pop.), a handful of frame houses, weather-beaten barns, and white-painted business buildings among bushy black walnut trees, stretch grazing lands.

At 48.9 *m.* is the junction with a paved road.

Left on this road is EDGEWOOD, 1.3 *m.* (2,953 alt., 250 pop.), a dairying center on the site picked by the first travelers on the California-Oregon trail for a stopping place, where William and Jackson Brown built a log cabin in 1851.

WEED, 52.1 *m.* (3,466 alt., 4,000 pop.), at the junction with US 97 (*see TOUR 3A*), is a lumber town, bleak and raw looking, in a hill-rimmed hollow. From the logged-over slopes, dotted with scrubby timber and blackened stumps, the brush sweeps down to encroach on weather-beaten houses and rickety fences. Along the railroad sidings (L) beyond the grimy business district, spread great lumber mills with vast rows of stacked pine boards. In clearings at the edge of the brush huddle desolate, unpainted company shacks, barracklike rooming houses, and company stores.

South of Weed US 99 winds over rounded hills through a wasteland of brush sparsely dotted with pines. The dense forests of pine, spruce, and fir that clothed these lower slopes of Shasta before 1880 were recklessly denuded. The lumber companies, when they had cut the most accessible timber, burned off the land to destroy the slash and debris, killing the young trees and seedlings.

The highway cuts around the eastern flanks of BLACK BUTTE (6,344 alt.), a volcanic cone that lifts its triple-crested peak 3,000 feet above the plain, reaching an elevation of 3,937 feet at 58 *m.*

MOUNT SHASTA CITY, 61.3 *m.* (3,554 alt., 1,009 pop.), was settled in the 1850's, near the base of the immense, snow-swept peak for which it was named. Roundabout spread the lush green meadows of Strawberry Valley, sweeping up the slopes to the belt of dark green conifers at the edge of the snowfields. To early travelers it was Sisson's, in honor of J. H. Sisson, pioneer postmaster and hotel keeper, who guided parties up Shasta's slopes. Only in 1924, as the tide of tourist travel grew, did the town become Mount Shasta City. The SHASTA NATIONAL FOREST SUPERVISOR'S HEADQUARTERS, one block R. of US 99, administers a reserve of 1,656,477 acres extending over the mountainous region east and west of US 99 for 60 miles.

1. Left from Mount Shasta City on Alma St. to the Shasta Trail, 3 m., where the trip can be continued by foot or, in part, on horseback. (*Season: July-Sept. For amateurs, round trip from lodge to summit requires 8 to 10 hours; record is 2 hours 24 minutes. Climbers should wear calked shoes, heavy clothing, colored glasses and carry food for three meals and water, an alpenstock, and a gunnysack or piece of carpet for sliding the mountain in descent.*) The trail, narrow, rough, and dusty, but compensating for its discomforts by ever changing vistas, winds through stretches of chaparral, in springtime fragrant with wildflowers. Then it ascends through stands of sugar and yellow pine and, at higher elevations, through whitebark pine and Shasta fir. On the edge of the Fir Zone, is the SHASTA ALPINE LODGE (7,992 alt.), 8 m., a stone rest house built at Horse Camp by the Sierra Club. (*Wood for fireplace and blankets from caretaker.*) A start from the lodge at 2 a.m. allows time to reach THUMB ROCK to watch the sunrise. The trail continues from the edge of the Alpine Zone's belt of storm-beaten dwarf pines at 9,000 feet and over stretches of bare, rough, brown lava to the snowfields and ice of the summit, 12 m., of MOUNT SHASTA, where a vast panorama of tumbled mountains and valleys spreads on every side.

"Lonely as God and white as a winter moon," wrote Joaquin Miller, "Mount Shasta starts up sudden and solitary from the heart of the great black forest . . ." Sixth highest mountain in California, it is more impressive than the highest, Mount Whitney. The Indians looked upon it with awe, believing it to be the abode of the Great Spirit. Even among whites a latter-day legend persists—that high within the snow-mantled crater dwells an ancient white-robed brotherhood, descendants of the Lemurians, inhabitants of a vast mid-Pacific continent, all of which but a small strip forming part of the California coast foundered beneath ocean water 400,000 years ago.

From the higher crevices, steam hisses, and nearby, molten sulphur bubbles out: "last feeble expression," wrote Muir, "of the mighty power that lifted the entire mass of the mountain from the volcanic depths far below the surface of the plain." He went on: "Shasta is a fire mountain, an old volcano, gradually accumulated and built up . . . by successive eruptions of ashes and molten lava which . . . grew outward and upward like the trunk of a knotty, bulging tree." The material came from two craters, that of Shasta itself and a smaller one, Shastina, on the western slope. Then came the glacial winter and with it "a down-crawling mantle of ice upon a fountain of smouldering fire, crushing and grinding its brown, flinty lavas . . ." The tremendous burden of ice shattered the summit and ground deep grooves in the slopes. Then, as the glacial period drew to an end, the ice melted and broke up, leaving tumbled heaps and rings of moraine on the mountainsides. Even today, the great downspreading ice streams of five glaciers—Hotlum, Bolam, Whitney, Wintun, and Konwakiton—grip the eastern and northeastern flanks above the 10,000-foot level, feeding numberless creeks.

Although it dominates the landscape for a hundred miles, Shasta was unknown to white men until Peter Skene Ogden discovered it February 14, 1827. Credit for the first ascent goes to Capt. E. D. Pearce, a merchant of Yreka, who made the climb alone in September 1854. The first ascent by scientists was made in September 1862, when the California State Geological Survey party, led by Josiah Dwight Whitney, followed today's trail to the top and made observations. They discovered that others had preceded them, for at the summit, said Prof. William H. Brewer, Whitney's assistant, "was a liberal distribution of 'California conglomerate,' a mixture of tin cans and broken bottles, a newspaper, a Methodist hymn book, a pack of cards, an empty bottle, and other evidences of a bygone civilization." Near the summit a blizzard trapped John Muir and his companion, Jerome Fay, in April 1875; finding refuge in the hot spring, they were forced to lie for 13 hours—scalded on one side, all but frozen on the other.

2. Right from Mount Shasta City on Alma Street to the STATE FISH HATCHERY (*feeding time 1:30-2:30 p.m.*), 1 *m.* Here, in 17-acre landscaped grounds, shaded by elms, cedars, and cottonwoods, are 50 rearing ponds. In the clear depths gleam the silvery blue-gray trout: Loch Leven, Eastern Brook, Mackinaw, and Rainbow. In five trim white buildings are rows of wooden hatching troughs, where young fish dart back and forth. The plant is capable of hatching 8,000,000 annually.

3. Right from Mount Shasta on Ream Avenue, which soon becomes a dirt road winding up scenic mountain slopes to CASTLE LAKE (*camping*), 10 *m.,* a little forest-girt body of water, more than a mile above sea level, hidden among the recesses back of Castle Crags (*see below*).

US 99 runs past lumber mills, lumberyards, and log ponds. From the green meadows of Strawberry Valley it climbs into sparsely forested rolling country.

At 63.7 *m.* is the junction with State 89 (*see TOUR 5a*).

The highway crosses a high tableland bordered by mountain ridges and descends a long grade to a junction at 67.5 *m.* with a paved road.

Right here to SHASTA SPRINGS, 0.2 *m.* (2,556 alt., 7 pop.). Above the narrow canyon of the Sacramento, on a little plateau carpeted with green lawns, stand trim green and white cottages. Here bubbling Shasta water is bottled and shipped all over the country.
Left 0.3 *m.* from Shasta Springs to MOSS BRAE FALLS. Fairylike falls differing from all others in California, they spill in feathery sprays over banks green with ferns and moss.

At 69 *m.* is the junction with a paved road.

Right on this road beyond a stone gateway to SHASTA RETREAT, 0.3 *m.* (2,554 alt.), where neat cottages cluster in a thicket of pines and California black oaks.

A high arching concrete span carries US 99 above the Sacramento River into DUNSMUIR, 70.1 *m.* (2,308 alt., 2,610 pop.). Hemmed by mountains, the little city perches on a narrow shelf along the winding canyon bed, its business buildings lining the highway for a mile and a half. Up the side streets, climbing steeply, frame houses cling to pine-forested slopes. Through the heart of town and southward stretch railroad shops and yards of a Southern Pacific division point. Thronged in season by hunters and fishermen, Dunsmuir is the supply center for a region abounding with fish and game.

The entrance (L) to CASTLE CRAGS STATE PARK PICNIC AREA, 74.7 *m.,* is at the northern end of CASTLE CRAGS STATE PARK, 50 square miles of wilderness surrounding the jagged ridge of

silver-gray granite that lifts crags (R) above the brow of the wooded
hill.   Among stately pines are camp sites by stocked streams and lakes.

Left from the entrance to the Picnic Area on a dirt road, across the
Sacramento River to the railroad station of CASTLE CRAGS, 0.4 *m.*, the
site of Lower Soda Springs in the green meadows at the mouth of Soda
Creek.   On his way south from the Rogue River in 1843, Lansford Hastings
once camped here with 16 others and built, it was said, the old fort of
pine logs, Hastings' Barracks.   First permanent settler was "Mountain
Joe" Doblondy, a guide of Frémont's; he tilled the soil, built houses, kept
a hotel, guided travelers up the California-Oregon Trail past Shasta, and
fought the Indians.   Mountain Joe's fabulous tales lured miners in the
spring of 1855, but they were unwarranted.   In anger the miners left—only
after they had killed or driven away the fish and game on which the
Indians lived.   Modoc warriors swooped down on the little settlement and
burned it in reprisal.   They were pursued into Castle Crags and, after
a battle, driven out.

At 76.3 *m.* is a junction with a dirt road.

Right on this road, along the bank of Castle Creek, to the base of
CASTLE CRAGS, 3.5 *m.*   This gigantic pile of gray-white granite, frequently tinged with pale rose, rears its jagged spires a sheer 6,000 feet
above forested slopes.   The crags were first called Castillo del Diablo.
Here, on June 26, 1855, settlers of the region fought the battle with the
Modoc who had burned the settlement at Lower Soda Springs.   Joaquin
Miller's version of it, garnished with boasts of his own exploits, is a
colorful if not an eyewitness account; the testimony, all except his own,
indicates that he was still a schoolboy in Oregon at the time it occurred.
As Miller tells it, the Indians were traced to their hiding place by the
flour they had spilled along the way as they made off with their loot.
Mountain Joe gathered a company with recruits from the mining camps
at Portuguese Flat and Dog Creek.   Its leader, Judge R. R. Gibson, who
had married the daughter of the Shasta chief, won over the Shasta as
allies.   Under the highest crag in the northwest corner of BATTLE ROCK,
most prominent of the spires, the 29 whites, with Shasta allies of about
the same number, fought face to face with the Modoc until they forced
them to withdraw, leaving many of their warriors dead.   Miller's fanciful
tale of his own exploits tells how he was carried, wounded, down the
mountainside in a big buckskin bag tied to the back of a wrinkled squaw,
and how Mountain Joe cared for his wounds in a camp by the riverbank.

CASTELLA, 76.5 *m.* (1,947 alt., 500 pop.), spreads its straggling
outskirts along the highway, but the town itself stands (L) on a paved
road that winds down to the pleasant green meadows along the rocky
river bed.

The highway winds along the deep canyon of the Sacramento, the
roadside edged with pines and glossy yellow-green black oaks in vivid
contrast.   At 81.2 *m.* begins the climb into the lofty mountainous region
that stretches ahead for 35 miles.

SHI-LO-AH MINERAL SPRINGS, (*cabins, trailer-camp, store*),
85.5 *m.,* cascade down the slope into a rough stone basin.   The water,
rich in sodium compounds and sulphureted hydrogen, lathers without
soap, and three times daily changes in color from clear to yellow to deep
green.

Along the winding gorge between steep, thick-forested slopes the highway twists to DOG CREEK, 95.7 *m.*, where the canyon opens out (R) to reveal magnificent vistas of rugged mountainsides. From POLLOCK, 103.8 *m.* (950 alt.), (*post office, gas station, auto camp*), the highway swings away from the river gorge to curve over tumbled slopes, luxuriantly green. Climbing easily, it winds along the slopes of huge, granite-ridged peaks to the summit, 110.2 *m.,* and then downward.

BAIRD (*garage, café, cabins*), 112.9 *m.* (856 alt.), perches high above the deep, wooded canyon of the McCLOUD RIVER, which twists through rough country inaccessible except on foot or horseback. Along its course, a number of Pleistocene caverns have yielded fossil remains of long extinct mammals.

Left from Baird on a dirt road 0.2 *m.* to the UNITED STATES FISH HATCHERY, where salmon are propagated in the California Caves on the banks of the river.

From its crossing of the Pit River, US 99 winds past the massive bulk (R) of BASS MOUNTAIN (2,778 alt.), 117 *m.,* through gradually thinning woods to the junction with a dirt road, 121.7 *m.*

Right on this road is KENNET, 8 *m.* (670 alt., 124 pop.), center of a region where copper mining was begun in 1896. The fumes from the great smelters killed vegetation for miles around. Near Kennet will rise gigantic SHASTA DAM, chief unit of the $170,000,000 Central Valley Irrigation Project. Thirty-seven miles of railroad track will be rerouted along US 99 to make way for a great lake impounded behind a dam 560 feet high and 3,500 feet long. Planned for 20 years, the project—a self-financing irrigation, power, and water conservation undertaking—will dwarf in size the Boulder Dam and Bonneville projects.

At 126.9 *m.* is the junction (L) with US 299 (*see TOUR 8a*), which unites with US 99 between this point and Redding. For 160 miles southward to Carquinez Straits the Sacramento Valley plain extends between sheltering mountain ridges.

On a flat half encircled by the swirling Sacramento River is REDDING, 129 *m.* (557 alt., 4,188 pop.), seat of Shasta County since 1888, a bustling town, dotted with hotels and small industrial plants, at the northern end of the Sacramento Valley. Although it stands within Pierson B. Reading's Rancho Buena Ventura, northernmost Mexican land grant, it owes its name not to Reading but to B. B. Redding, Central Pacific R.R. land agent. The town is a shipping point for the vast fruit-growing, farming, and mining district roundabout. Through it pour sportsmen and pleasure seekers bound for hunting and fishing grounds to the north.

Redding is at the southern junction with US 299 (*see TOUR 8b*).

Right from Redding on an unpaved highway to IGO, 12 *m.* (1,081 alt., 40 pop.), and ONO, 17 *m.* (900 alt., 17 pop.), twin mining camps. A miner known as McPherson, one of the first to build a substantial house here, had a small son who would put on his hat whenever his father started for the mines and say, "I go." "Oh, no," was always the answer. When one camp acquired the name Igo, its neighbor consequently was called Ono.

At 134.5 *m.,* on the southern bank of Clear Creek, is a junction with a dirt road.

> Right on this road to READING'S BAR, 11 *m.,* where in March 1848, only three months after Marshall's discovery at Coloma, Pierson Reading and his Indians found the first gold in Shasta County. By October 1849, 400 men were here digging. When a prospector who had arrived with one pack horse built a hotel, the settlement became One Horse Town, and, as time passed, simply Horsetown. It grew to a village of 1,000 inhabitants, with stores, hotels, 14 saloons, a Roman Catholic Church—even a newspaper, the *Northern Argus,* established in 1857. But fire leveled the town in 1868, and it never rose again.

ANDERSON, 140.3 *m.* (433 alt., 1,445 pop.), sprawls over weed-grown fields among clumps of oaks and willows, its dingy business blocks facing each other across the highway and railroad tracks. Growing up on the American Ranch, bought in 1856 by Elias Anderson, the settlement soon became a stop for travelers and the starting point of a trail to the Trinity mines.

In the fifties COTTONWOOD, 145.3 *m.* (435 alt., 150 pop.), now a scattered village of rutted winding streets, frame shanties, and red brick and frame false-front stores with wooden awnings, was a miners' trade center.

> Left from Cottonwood on the main street, which becomes a bumpy, gravel-strewn road as it winds off into fields and pastures, to the junction with a dirt road, 3.2 *m.;* R. here to the junction with a second dirt road, 3.7 *m.;* L. through a gate to a fork in the road, 4.2 *m.;* L. here, through another gate at 4.7 *m.;* and over stretches of cattle land to the READING ADOBE, 5.7 *m.,* a one-story oblong structure with crumbling walls of reddish adobe brick propped by boards and a brick chimney rising from a peaked, shingled roof. Built in 1846, this was the bunkhouse of ,Pierson Barton Reading's buckaroos. Here too stood a smokehouse, a barn, and Reading's two-story mansion where the pioneers of northern California—Sutter, Bidwell, Lassen, and Frémont—often gathered. Reading's 26,000-acre Rancho Buena Ventura, northernmost Mexican grant in California, stretched along the Sacramento; he took possession in 1845. When Shasta County was organized in 1850, the county seat was fixed here, where it remained till its removal to Shasta the next year. Here were grown the first cotton in the State and the first olives in northern California. Reading died in 1868; his grave is on a slight rise nearby.

At 159.5 *m.* on US 99 is a junction with a paved road.

> Left on this road to the ADOBE HOUSE OF GEN. WILLIAM B. IDE, 0.9 *m.,* still in use. Built by the first and only president of the short-lived Bear Flag Republic in 1849, the house stands sheltered by ancient oaks in a hedged garden overlooking the Sacramento. Here Ide established a ferry, which continued in operation until the 1870's. A small one-story structure, whose adobe bricks show through peeling whitewash, the house has been enlarged with a frame addition and lean-to porch. Across the north wall, beneath low eaves, are portholes for use in defense during Indian raids.

RED BLUFF, 160.6 *m.* (309 alt., 3,517 pop.), seat of Tehama County, spreads along low bluffs above the Sacramento, not far from the cliff of reddish sand and gravel for which Ide's Rancho de la Barranca Colorado (red bluff ranch) was named. Red Bluff's settlers, who first called their town Leodocia, never found the gold for which they were looking, although it was discovered in adjoining sections. Their wealth came from wheatfields and vineyards. A neat little town of quiet, tree-lined streets, with old brick business buildings, Red Bluff is the chief trading center for the upper Sacramento Valley.

In the 1850's the Sacramento, flowing past Red Bluff between tree-bordered banks, was churned into foam by the paddle wheels of steamers puffing up from Sacramento. By wagon and pack train their cargoes went westward to the Trinity mines and the Coast Range diggings. In those days the saloons, taverns, and corrals were alive with hordes of boatmen, packers, gamblers, and miners. As the great valley plains were ploughed and the river water diverted into irrigation ditches, the Sacramento dwindled. It is no longer the State's mightiest avenue of traffic, although it is still navigable for 225 miles at high water, and even now, with the San Joaquin River, forms an inland waterway that ranks high in tonnage of water-borne commerce. Its seasonal variation helped ruin river transportation, but Red Bluff may again hear steamboat whistles when Shasta Dam harnesses the temperamental waters in an even flow.

Of Red Bluff's former river traffic, the only remaining evidence is a neglected cluster of one-story false-front buildings, once shipping offices, overlooking the river. The WILLIAM B. IDE MEMORIAL MUSEUM, in the old two-story red brick CITY HALL, at Pine and Washington Sts., exhibits a collection of articles picked up along the Lassen Trail, relics of early settlers—firearms, riding gear, tools, and household treasures—and Indian and Chinese relics. Opposite the museum in a green square bordered by Pine and Washington Sts. is the modern TEHAMA COUNTY COURTHOUSE. The JOHN BROWN FAMILY HOUSE, at 135 Main St., is an undistinguished little clapboarded cottage with shingled roof and porch. In 1864 Red Bluff's citizens, ardent admirers of the abolitionist crusader, raised money to aid John Brown's widow and three daughters, who lived here until 1870.

Red Bluff is at the junctions with US 99E (*see TOUR 3B*) and State 36 (*see TOUR 6A*). South of Red Bluff the route follows US 99W.

South of Red Bluff the level plains of the Sacramento Valley spread like the prairie of the Midwest, rimmed by distant foothills. The route runs through grazing lands dotted with oaks and through great grainfields crisscrossed by miles of fences. At intervals are the little towns, half hidden in clumps of trees.

CORNING, 178.6 *m.* (277 alt., 1,377 pop.), stands in a belt of olive groves. The Sevillano olive, grown here in huge quantities, is one of the largest and best varieties; olive oil refining and olive canning are the chief industrial activities. The scattered frame houses are shaded by umbrella trees and long files of shaggy palms.

US 99 crosses an irrigation canal into ORLAND, 192.1 *m.* (259 alt., 1,195 pop.), where modern schools and business buildings are shaded by umbrella and black walnut trees. The Reclamation Service

Orland Irrigation Project was the first organized in the State after the passage of the Wright Irrigation Act in 1887.

Below Orland stretch grainfields where wheat and barley were first grown on a large scale in the late 1850's. As thousands of acres of virgin land were sown, California's output of wheat became as valuable as her gold. By 1872 the Glenn-Colusa area produced 1,000,000 sacks of grain yearly. Overlord of the region was Dr. Hugh J. Glenn, who in 1867 purchased the 7,000-acre Rancho Jacinto and added to it until his holdings totaled 55,000 acres, of which 45,000 were in wheat. To put in the crop, 108 mule teams were required; they were accompanied by cook houses and feed and water wagons. From 1874 until his death in 1883, Glenn was the leading grain farmer in the United States. Afterwards poor crops and low prices led to the subdivision of the ranch. During the early 1890's, as wheat yield decreased throughout the region, grain farming was linked with stock raising and the big ranches were broken up into small tracts.

WILLOWS, 208.6 m. (139 alt., 2,024 pop.), seat of Glenn County, was so named because the clump of willows bordering the creek was once the only landmark between the river and the foothill settlements. The first store here was known as "the store at the willows." The Sacramento Valley Irrigation Company, one of the largest privately owned irrigation systems in the West, pumps water from the Sacramento River into a great ditch and distributes it over 60,000 surrounding acres.

US 99 cuts into the heart of a great rice-growing belt. At harvest time the lush, water-soaked fields are a yellow-green sea of bending, plumed stalks. Rice was first grown in Colusa County in 1911, when W. K. Brown planted 75 acres.

At MAXWELL, 224.6 m. (95 alt., 506 pop.), ramshackle frame and brick buildings face the warehouses bordering the railroad tracks.

Right from Maxwell on a paved road, past prune and lemon groves covering low hills, to the junction with a dirt road; 6.1 m.; L. here 0.2 m. past a decrepit farmhouse and around the base of a craggy hill to an old STONE CORRAL, an enclosure of rough stone. Concrete pillars at the entrance bear the inscriptions: "Erected by John W. Steele 1855." Here were rounded up the herds of Granville P. Swift that grazed throughout the valley tended by Indian vaqueros. Swift, a tall Kentuckian, came to California in 1844 with the Kelsey party, first band of settlers to come directly overland; a leader in every important controversy between Yankees and Californians, he headed one of the three companies in the Bear Flag Revolt and served as Captain of Company C of the California Battalion under Frémont. After the Mexican War he became a miner and then a stock raiser.

Amid far-spreading rice fields is WILLIAMS, 233.8 m. (84 alt., 851 pop.), laid out by W. H. Williams in 1876, today a supply and shipping point. In 1914 when a band of about 50 I. W. W.'s created much excitement and hostility by marching through the county, the town of Williams calmly provided them with breakfast and gave them $60 for cleaning up its cemetery.

Left from Williams on State 20 is COLUSA, 9.8 *m.* (58 alt., 2,116 pop.), seat of Colusa County. The name comes from Ko-ru (scratcher), head village of the Ko-ru-si tribe, on whose ruins Colusa stands; among these Indians it was the privilege of a bride to begin her honeymoon by scratching her husband's face. Colusa was founded soon after Col. Charles D. Semple purchased two square leagues of land here from John Bidwell. Although snags, sandbars, and sharp turns made the river dangerous, he persisted in his efforts to develop river commerce until Colusa was connected with Sacramento and San Francisco by regular steamboat service. Up the Old River Road, which followed the west bank of the river from Colusa to Shasta City, ran stage coaches and freight wagons. River traffic continued until a railroad was built in 1876. After that a line of barges that towed wood to Sacramento was the only important river line until 1901, when the Farmers' Transportation Company established regular service with boats once a week. Notable for its dignified simplicity is the COLUSA COUNTY COURTHOUSE, a tall white edifice with huge pillars flanking the entrance.

ARBUCKLE, 244.6 *m.* (139 alt., 1,000 pop.), is a trade town. C. H. Locke, observing that oak trees here grew immense crops of acorns, planted 21 acres of almonds in 1892. Today more than 7,000 acres of almond orchards surround the town.

At 268.7 *m.* on US 99 is the junction with a paved road.

Left on this road is YOLO (Ind., place of rushes), 0.4 *m.* (78 alt., 296 pop.), an old-fashioned town with rutted streets and old houses, picket fences, and many walnut trees. From 1857 to 1861 it was the seat of Yolo County.

WOODLAND, 274.2 *m.* (63 alt., 5,542 pop.), trade center of a productive area, has its compact central business district of modern shops, bustling with traffic. Woodland's first settler arrived in 1853; two years later a blacksmith shop was set up, about which soon clustered stores and saloons. Experiments in irrigation were begun in the vicinity with the diversion of Cache Creek in 1856. First named Yolo City and nicknamed "By Hell" for an early saloonkeeper's favorite oath, Woodland acquired its present name—suggested by the grove of huge oaks in which it stood—when the post office was opened in 1859. The large, handsome, two-story YOLO COUNTY COURTHOUSE, its central portico with Corinthian columns and a balustraded cornice, stands in a landscaped square between Second and Third Streets.

At 283.8 *m.* is the western junction with US 40 (*see TOUR 9b*), which unites eastward with US 99 (*see TOUR 9b*).

SACRAMENTO, 298.7 *m.* (30 alt., 93,750 pop.) (*see SACRAMENTO*).

At Sacramento is the eastern junction with US 40 (*see TOUR 9a*) and the northern junction with US 50 (*see TOUR 10a*)

Section b.   SACRAMENTO to BAKERSFIELD; 265.5 m. US 99

This section of US 99 runs through the heart of the great Central Valley, a desert of almost unbelievable fertility under irrigation. But irrigation demands unremitting toil; the omission of a single quarterly watering throughout might kill every tree and cultivated plant on the vast valley floor. Farming here is not farming as Easterners know it; most of the ranches are food factories, with superintendents and foremen, administrative headquarters and machine sheds. Even the owners of small ranches usually concentrate on a single crop; and they must send to the store if they want as much as one egg. In addition to the permanent employees the valley uses a great deal of seasonal labor that forms a constant problem. The migratory worker, constantly on the move to catch the harvest seasons of one crop after the other—peaches, walnuts, apricots, grapes, celery—never stays long enough in any area to establish himself as a citizen. He lives apart from other residents, occasionally in barracks behind the fields and orchards, more often in crude shelters of his own devising along the river bottoms. Because there are too many who want work, the migrant cannot command an adequate return for his labor. The inhabitants of the towns do not know him and his family and local governments feel no responsibility for him. No one knows how to help him with his problems and no one knows how to get along without his help.

South of SACRAMENTO, 0 *m.,* US 99, which is united with US 50 to Stockton, runs between orchards, vineyards, and dairy farms.

OLD ELK GROVE, 16 *m.* now a scattering of houses and an old cemetery, was founded in 1850 by James Hall, who built a hotel that burned in 1857.

Left here on a dirt road to modern ELK GROVE, 1 *m.* (49 alt., 895 pop.), which sprang up after the burning of the hotel. The town lies in the midst of a Tokay grape district with one of the oldest wineries in California.

The area around GALT, 23 *m.* (46 alt., 700 pop.), which was laid out in 1869, produces poultry and dairy products, figs and grain.

No one knows how LODI, 30 *m.* (51 alt., 6,788 pop.), northernmost town in the San Joaquin Valley got its name. It is a typical valley town: the streets almost all wide, straight, and lined with trees that give a deceptive promise of protection from the intense heat in summer. Proud of its vineyards, it holds a Grape and Wine Festival in September.

STOCKTON, 43 *m.* (23 alt., 47,963 pop.), (*see STOCKTON*) is at the junction with US 50 (*see TOUR 10b*).

US 99 moves south across a flat expanse covered with great walnut orchards, truck farms, melon tracts, vineyards, and pastures.

MANTECA (Sp., *mantequilla,* butter), 56.2 *m.* (40 alt., 1,614 pop.), began in 1870 as Cowell's Station, a stop on the new Central Pacific Railroad. Its subsequent development as the shipping center for great quantities of dairy products led to the adoption of its present name. Grapes and sugar beets are also grown nearby.

Left from Manteca on State 120 to OAKDALE, 21.2 *m.* (150 alt., 3,112 pop.), a dairying center set on a plateau above the Stanislaus River overlooking irrigated valley land. Dairying is the principal industry, supplemented by diversified horticulture and almond growing. An annual Almond Blossom Festival is held in the spring. In the robust 1870's and 1880's Oakdale, on the road to the mines, was raucous at times. It takes its name from the live oaks that surrounded the site when the town was founded in 1871.

At 33.2 *m.* is the junction with an oiled road; L. on this road 0.8 *m.* to KNIGHT'S FERRY (200 alt., 80 pop.), through whose mud-bogged streets Mark Twain and Bret Harte trudged in the days when they were nobodies. In the early 1850's Knight's Ferry was temporarily renamed Dentville, for Lewis and John Dent, brothers-in-law of Ulysses S. Grant. One of the town's cherished landmarks is an old-fashioned COVERED BRIDGE over the Stanislaus River reputedly designed by Grant in 1854 while visiting them. Lewis Dent became Grant's aide-de-camp during the Civil War and Minister to Chile during his presidency. Among the buildings dating from the gold rush days are the MASONIC TEMPLE, the FIRE HOUSE with its dilapidated hosecart, and the adobe ruins of the COURT HOUSE, built in 1861 as a hotel, which served as a court house during the town's reign (1862-72) as seat of Stanislaus County.

At 48.2 *m.* is the junction with State 49-108 (*see TOUR 4b*) which unites with State 120 between this point and a junction at 55.1 *m.* (*see TOUR 4b*).

At PRIEST'S STATION, 64.9 *m.* (2,500 alt.), a busy supply depot for early gold miners, the old Priest Hotel was a stopping point on the route to the upper reaches of the Stanislaus River. The dances held in its 50-foot ballroom were gala events of the region.

BIG OAK FLAT, 66 *m.* (2,950 alt., 317 pop.), was founded as Savage Diggings by James Savage, who settled here with his five Indian wives and a retinue of red-skinned servants in 1850. The present name was derived from an oak, 11 feet in diameter at the base, that stood in the center of town until it was felled for the gold that clung to its roots; an arch, with remnants of the tree embedded in its framework, marks the site. Several pioneer structures remain, including the ODD FELLOWS HALL.

GROVELAND, 67.9 *m.* (2,850 alt., 300 pop.), once known as First Garrote for an execution by that method carried out here during the gold rush, is an attractive rural village. Reminders of the past are the iron doors and stone walls of the WELLS FARGO OFFICE and the GROVELAND HOTEL with its second-story balconies.

SECOND GARROTE, 69.9 *m.*, took its name from the HANGMAN TREE, still standing (L), from whose branches criminals of mining days are said to have been hanged. Although historians find no evidence that Bret Harte ever saw this region, two old prospectors, Chaffee and Chamberlain, who lived in the BRET HARTE CABIN (R), are locally claimed to be the originals of his *Tennessee's Partner*.

State 120 continues to rise into the mountains to the junction with a paved road, 85.9 *m.* (*see YOSEMITE PARK TOUR 3*).

Around RIPON, 62.5 *m.* (68 alt., 1,100 pop.), radiate large vineyards. Chief industrial plant in the district is the SCHENLEY DISTILLERY (R). A large roadsign proclaims the sprawling, white, peaked-roof building as the "World's Largest Exclusive Brandy Distillery."

Ripon also claims "The World's Largest Out-door Rummy Game," sponsored by the American Legion post; the first out-door game was held in 1932, with 600 rummy, whist and bridge players, surrounded by as many onlookers, seated at tables set up in the town's main street. The 1938 card party, which attracted 900 participants, was staged in PORTUGUESE GROVE. Players and spectators alike pay $1 admission. The proceeds, minus the prize money, go to charities.

US 99 crosses the STANISLAUS RIVER, 63.2 *m.,* one of the fabulous streams of the gold rush era, whose pastoral beauty in this region was described by Bret Harte in his *Down on the Stanislaus.*

SALIDA, 65.5 *m.* (70 alt., 600 pop.), a fruit, alfalfa, and grain shipping point, is a center for dove and quail hunting.

MODESTO (Sp., modest), 71.9 *m.* (86 alt., 13,842 pop.), seat of Stanislaus County, is on the banks of the Tuolumne River, here a muddy trickle because its waters have been impounded in the foothills behind 200-feet high Don Pedro Dam to provide waters for the Modesto and Turlock Irrigation Districts. Modesto was laid out by the Southern Pacific in 1870 after an older settlement nearby had bickered over concessions; the railroad company proposed naming it for W. C. Ralston, the San Francisco banker, but when he declined the honor some official turned a neat compliment to his modesty by bestowing the present name. The railroad company showed foresight in the town planning; the streets, crossing at right angles, run northeast, southwest, northwest and southeast to give the maximum of shade during the days of intense heat. Modesto has canneries, dairies, packing plants, and warehouses to care for the agricultural products of the prolific area for which it is a trade and shipping center.

In the neighborhood of CERES, 76 *m.* (88 alt., 981 pop.), checkered with vineyards and fig, peach, apricot, and pear orchards, the date gardens are of particular interest—new groves with low feathery palms as well as older ones whose trees are so tall that adjustable platforms, resembling painters' scaffolds, are fastened around them to facilitate the picking and pollinating. The latter process, which is always done by hand (late March or April), affects the size of the seed, the size of the fruit, and even the time of its ripening. Experiments in which pollen from different varieties of male palms was applied to separate strands of inflorescence on the same female palm (by means of glassine bags) demonstrated that by selection of the male pollen, the growers could control the ripening time of their fruit by as much as twenty to thirty days.

US 99 crosses and recrosses a network of canals on its way to TURLOCK, 84.6 *m.* (101 alt., 4,276 pop.), in the midst of hundreds of small farms—all depending upon the vast Turlock Irrigation District launched in 1887. The farms produce dairy and poultry products and a variety of crops: alfalfa, sweet potatoes, watermelons, peaches, apricots, grapes, and grain. The town celebrates its watermelon crop at an August melon carnival.

US 99 crosses the MERCED RIVER, 92.8 *m.,* which rises in Lakes Merced and Tenaya in Yosemite National Park. The stream was named by Lieut. Gabriel Moraga, a Spanish army officer, who explored the valley in 1813. Weakened by thirst, the party drank greedily of the waters; in gratitude they named it River of Our Lady of Mercy (*de las Mercedes*).

LIVINGSTON, 94.4 *m.* (131 alt., 803 pop.), trade center of a sweet potato belt, also ships raisins, grapes, peaches, and alfalfa.

Left from Livingston 4 *m.* to the 1,100-acre VALLEY AGRICULTURAL COR-
PORATION VINEYARD, producing Thompson seedless grapes. The vineyards
are enclosed by a rabbit-proof fence.

ATWATER, 100.9 *m.* (153 alt., 319 pop.), styles itself the "Home
of the Merced Sweet Potato."

BUHACH, 102.4 *m.* (155 alt., 100 pop.), is the trading center for
a district of Portuguese farmers who specialize in growing pyrethrum
(feverfew), the powdered blossoms of which are used in certain insecticides.

MERCED, 108.3 *m.* (167 alt., 7,006 pop.), seat of Merced County,
is the principal rail and motor gateway to Yosemite National Park. It
is in a grazing and hay and cotton-producing area and has a cotton gin,
cement factories and potteries. A rodeo is held in June and a District
Fair in October.

Left from Merced on G St., which becomes State 140; at 0.5 *m.* is the
junction with Snelling Rd.; L. here to a junction at 6 *m.;* R. 1.5 *m.* to
700-acre LAKE YOSEMITE, a summer resort. On Snelling Rd. is
SNELLING, 19 *m.* (252 alt., 324 pop.), once a mining town and until 1872
the seat of Merced County.
On State 140 is PLANADA, 10 *m.* (167 alt., 350 pop.), called Geneva
when platted in 1912 as a model town.
State 140 ascends 1,900 feet in 27 miles through the foothills of the
Sierra.
Since 1854 MARIPOSA (butterfly), 80 *m.* (1,962 alt., 383 pop.), has been
the seat of Mariposa County. In summer the town does a brisk tourist
business as Yosemite-bound traffic roars past its mellow frame buildings
with sidewalk roofs. The COURTHOUSE, a two-story, square, white-frame
building, topped by a slender, square clock tower, is the oldest in California; it was built in 1854, fastened together with wooden pegs. The
MARIPOSA GAZETTE OFFICE (1854) has yellowed newspaper files that hold
much of California's early history as one of the United States.
Mariposa is at the junction with State 49 (*see TOUR 4b*).
West of Mariposa State 140 mounts steadily, passing camps and resorts
to EL PORTAL, 72 *m.,* the railroad entrance to Yosemite National Park
(*see YOSEMITE TOUR 1*).

CHOWCHILLA, 125.2 *m.* (240 alt., 847 pop.), is in a district of
dairying, hog and poultry raising, cotton, fruit, and grain growing. In
the city are cotton gins, creameries, concrete pipe factories, and a cottonseed oil mill. The Chowchilla River is referred to locally as the region's
Mason and Dixon Line; legend has it that Union soldiers marching
south from Stockton during the Civil War were ordered to load their
guns when they reached it.

US 99 passes through olive groves and apricot orchards to
BERENDA, 133.6 *m.* (255 alt.), a small collection of frame dwellings
grouped about the characteristically tan-gray frame Southern Pacific
railroad station. Beyond the MADERA COUNTY FAIRGROUNDS AND
RACE TRACK (R) 139.4 *m.,* it spans the Fresno River.

MADERA, 140.4 *m.* (272 alt., 4,655 pop.), seat of Madera
County, was laid out in 1876 by the California Lumber Company.
Besides lumber, it produces great quantities of sweet wine. In October
Maderans celebrate Old Timers' Day.

South of Madera the grape vineyards are displaced by cotton fields and orchards. The small cluster of frame houses in HERNDON, 152 *m.* (296 alt., 60 pop.), is bowered in fig orchards, which press to the edges of the highway and railroad tracks.

FRESNO, 161 *m.* (287 alt., 52,513 pop.) (*see* FRESNO).

1. Left from Fresno on Kearney Blvd., to KEARNEY PARK, 7 *m.,* an experimental farm and park operated by the University of California. Five thousand acres are devoted to experimental work; the picturesque 240-acre park in the center of the tract is a recreational area.

2. Left from Fresno on State 180 (Ventura Ave.), to a junction at 13.2 *m.*; R. here 2 *m.* to SANGER (370 alt., 2,967 pop.), trade center of a region producing semi-tropical fruits, grapes, plums, and various field crops.

State 180 continues eastward, crosses the fertile Kings River Valley, and begins to rise into the Sierra foothills. The highway passes through GENERAL GRANT NATIONAL PARK, with Administrative headquarters at 62 *m.* (*see SEQUOIA AND GENERAL GRANT NATIONAL PARKS*), where guides and packhorses are available for trips into adjacent areas. The highway, winding in a generally northward direction through the park, bends abruptly R. when it reaches the canyon of the South Fork of Kings River, 76 *m.* The road is being pushed on up the canyon year by year over what is now merely a pack trail. Connoisseurs of mountain scenery have long exalted this route as one of the most beautiful in the world. Everything that the Sierra can offer in the way of breath-taking contrast and dramatic beauty is here—tiny peaceful meadows below towering polished domes, dozens of cascades, any one of which would be considered a crowning glory in an Eastern State, and multi-colored crags against skies unbelievably blue.

3. Left from Fresno on State 168 (Fresno St.), paved in the lower regions, oiled in the mountains, is CLOVIS, 11 *m.* (360 alt., 1,310 pop.), the trade center for a wine-producing, lumbering, and dairying hinterland. ACADEMY, 22 *m.* (580 alt., 45 pop) has granite quarries. State 168 mounts rapidly to TOLLHOUSE, 32 *m.,* at the upper end of the circuitous Tollhouse Road. SHAVER LAKE (5,200 alt.), 48 *m.,* lies star-shaped in a pine-rimmed depression of the Sierras; in its waters are lake, rainbow, Lochleve, big mouth, black bass, and blue gills. HUNTINGTON LAKE 70 *m.* (7,000 alt.), 7 miles long, is fed by melting snows from the 14,000-foot peaks that rise from its shores. One of California's foremost summer and winter mountain resorts, the lake is also part of a gigantic hydro-electric project. From Florence Lake, formed by a great multiple-arch dam across the South Fork of the San Joaquin River 14 miles northeast, water is diverted through a tunnel carved through solid rock to Huntington Lake, where it is held by three concrete dams, each about 1,000 feet long and 200 feet high. From here the water shoots 2,000 feet down a 45-degree incline to the turbines of the Big Creek power house. Along the lake are various bathing beaches and at the tiny resort centers on the shores guides and horses are available for trips into the High Sierra. The highway continues further into the mountains to various summer camps.

South of Fresno trim vineyards border US 99 for unbroken miles.

MALAGA, 166.3 *m.* (293 alt., 125 pop.), is a wine center specializing in muscat grapes, a species imported from Malaga, Spain, in 1852. Sheep raising is the next most important activity of the area.

FOWLER, 170.3 *m.* (290 alt., 1,166 pop.), is an important horse and mule market. It has several whisky warehouses, grape processing plants, and fruit packing houses.

SELMA, 176.3 *m.* (305 alt., 3,047 pop.), is another packing center in the muscat grape belt. Some of the grapes are converted into muscatel wine; some are seeded and dried to become raisins; others—those that come from the vine in large, full clusters—are dried on the stem for the fancy Christmas trade. Although considered by some of better flavor than the Thompson Seedless, the muscat is second in commercial importance because an extra seeding process is required. Most of the drying is done in September; the muscats are spread on large squares of brown paper to stand in the sun for 2 or 3 days.

In the foothills around KINGSBURG, 181 *m.* (300 alt., 1,321 pop.), are many peach orchards, vineyards, and orange groves. The population, still 90 per cent Swedish in descent, is made up of the children and grandchildren of a colony of Michigan Swedes that settled here in the 1870's.

KINGS RIVER, crossed at 182.8 *m.*, was discovered in 1805 by Spaniards who piously named it El Rio de los Santos Reyes (River of the Holy Kings).

At GOSHEN JUNCTION, 196.3 *m.*, is the junction with State 198, paved.

1. Right on this road to HANFORD, 13.2 *m.* (246 alt., 7,028 pop.), seat of Kings County and the trade center of ranchers who specialize in stock-raising and dairying. Around the 50-year-old, two-story tan-brick courthouse, and the squat, granite-block jail an ambitious Civic Center is being built. The new reinforced-concrete Community Auditorium is the first unit.

The Mussell Slough feud, upon which Frank Norris based his novel, *The Octopus,* came to a climax here. A group of angry ranchers had organized as the Settlers' League to fight the Southern Pacific Railroad, which under an Act of Congress was taking possession of every odd-numbered section of land along its newly built line. In May 1880 they did battle with the sheriff's forces here. Five ranchers and two deputies were killed, and 17 league members went to jail—the same rock-walled jail that stands next to the courthouse.

ARMONA, 18.2 *m.* (239 alt., 250 pop.), is a shipping point for spinach, grapes, and other fruit. LEMOORE, 23 *m.* (226 alt., 1,399 pop.), is a dairying and fruit growing trade center.

COALINGA, 55 *m.* (162 alt., 2,851 pop.) is a supply point for oil fields. In 1928 rich new sources were discovered in the nearby Kettleman Hills.

PRIEST VALLEY (2,373 alt., 67 pop.), 46 *m.*, near the crest of the Coast Range, was first explored by old Ben Williams, the trapper, in 1849. Not long after that William Galman and Captain Walker came upon a priest and 100 Indians resting here after rounding up wild horses. The valley was named because of this encounter, but it is better known as the place where Joaquin Murrieta, California's most notorious bandit, was killed in 1853. The spot where Murrieta made his last stand is said to be the Arroya Cantova, at the head of a small nearby canyon.

Unjust and brutal treatment at the hands of some Yankee miners started Murrieta on a career that terrorized the mining regions and stage routes. He began by fighting invaders of his native land but soon became a bandit. He was reputed to have killed every man of the group that originally mistreated him. The State offered $5,000 reward for his capture in 1852. In July 1853, Capt. Harry Love of Santa Clara, with a posse of 20 State Rangers, left San Jose to find him. La Molinera, Murrieta's former wife, told Captain Love that he would probably be hiding here. To mislead spies, Love and his squad pretended they were on their way to Los

Angeles, but at night doubled back to the arroyo, where they surprised Murrieta and his gang. Three-Fingered Jack, Murrieta's lieutenant, scrambled away through the underbrush with Love in chase. Love shot him between the eyes. Murrieta jump'ed on an unsaddled horse. Henderson, one of the Rangers, followed and shot the horse. Murrieta, stunned, began stumbling away on foot. One shot from Henderson's pistol brought him to one knee, another killed him. A man named Bill Byrnes, who had once been Murrieta's partner in a monte game, cut off his head, which was packed in salt and taken back to San Jose to prove that the bandit was dead. This head and the hand of Three-Fingered Jack were put in jars of alcohol and exhibited all over the State. They disappeared during the San Francisco earthquake and fire of 1906. Murrieta's exploits were celebrated in the picture *Robin Hood of El Dorado,* in which Warner Baxter played the title role.

SAN LUCAS, 71 *m.* (*see TOUR 2b*) is at a junction with US 101 (*see TOUR 2b*).

2. Left from Goshen Junction on State 198 to VISALIA, 6.4 *m.* (333 alt., 7,263 pop.), seat of Tulare County, founded in 1852 by Nathaniel Vice, a bear hunter, who combined his own surname with his wife's given name, Sallie, to form Visalia. Modern Visalia, with its eight blocks of stores, restaurants, cocktail bars, and filling stations, is quite unlike the town of the 1870's and 1880's, chiefly interested in the cattle business and noted for the skill of its saddlemakers. It was particularly sympathetic to the enraged immigrants who were living on the sections of land given by Congress to the Southern Pacific Railroad. Towns like Visalia, where the inhabitants' interests were tied up with those of the ranchers rather than the railroad, gave encouragement to the revolt and refuge to hunted rebels. The lines of warfare became very ragged as rebels held up trains and looted mail cars and passengers to bring the railroad company to terms —and bandits in the guise of rebels did the same. In 1892 three leaders, John and George Sontag and Chris Evans, were captured; Evans and John Sontag escaped. George was sentenced to life imprisonment at Folsom. Nearly a year later the two who had escaped were surprised at a place a few miles northeast of Visalia. Sontag was fatally wounded but Evans, with one arm shattered and one eye gouged out, again escaped, only to be captured on the following day.

Under the branches of the ELECTION TREE (R), 14 *m.,* a party under the command of Maj. James D. Savage held an election on July 19, 1852, by which Tulare County was formed. The oak was actually the county seat until Visalia was founded.

The KAWEAH RIVER comes into view at 20 *m.* and parallels the road for 19 miles eastward. Its North and South Forks unite at THREE RIVERS, 28.7 *m.* (825 alt., 18 pop.).

At 29.9 *m.* is the junction with a graveled road; L. here 1 *m.* to KAWEAH, now little but a name. It was founded in 1891 by former members of the International Workingmen's Association who, in 1885, had made plans for a socialistic community. The members had shocked the countryside by filing individual claims to what was Sequoia National Park a few years later (*see SEQUOIA AND GENERAL GRANT NATIONAL PARKS*). The group, which formally took the name of Kaweah Co-operative Commonwealth Colony in 1886, had ambitious plans that included the founding of a town to be called Avalon. Their difficulties over land claims were but the beginning of their troubles, however, and the plan was finally abandoned.

At 33.9 *m.* is the junction with another dirt road; R. here 25.5 *m.,* cutting across part of Sequoia National Park, to MINERAL KING (*summer lodge*). This tiny settlement (7,831 alt.), at the base of SAWTOOTH PEAK (12,340 alt.), was founded in 1873 by three spiritualists; here they staked the White Chief Lode silver claim, named in honor of the Indian spirit control who they said had guided them to it. By 1875 they had interested enough capital to enable them to build a toll road to the claim. There was a brief inrush of miners but the silver could not be recovered in paying quantities and in 1888 a snowslide destroyed much of the property.

At 37.5 *m.* on State 198 is the Ash Mountain entrance to Sequoia National Park (*see SEQUOIA PARK TOUR*).

The 7,000-acre TAGUS RANCH, 199.7 *m.*, advertises itself as the "World's Largest Peach, Apricot, and Nectarine Orchard." In a two-story, white-colonial building (L) 200.8 *m.* are the administrative offices. The fruit warehouses, cotton gins, and loading platforms piled high with cotton range along the railroad sidings.

TULARE, 205.2 *m.* (287 alt., 6,207 pop.), has been a hard-luck town. Founded in 1872 as division headquarters and a railroad repair center by the Southern Pacific, it was just beginning to get on its feet in 1883 when a fire destroyed a large part of it. Rebuilt by 1886, it was mowed down again by fire. For 19 years the Southern Pacific pay train rolled in regularly to distribute $40,000 in $20 gold pieces. Then in 1891 a double blow was dealt: the railroad shops were moved to Bakersfield, division headquarters to Fresno. When the pay train stopped rolling the citizens had to turn to the land and develop the orchards and vineyards that make it an important shipping center.

The WHILTON MUSEUM, in the Hotel Tulare, has more than 1,000 mounted native birds and mammals, and an extensive collection of California wild flowers.

>Left from Tulare on Tulare St. to LINDSAY, 15.5 *m.* (380 alt., 3,878 pop.), a foot-hill town in a citrus and olive growing belt. The vast acres keep busy several citrus-packing houses, two olive canneries, and two plants making olive oil. The area is at its loveliest in blossom time, and then particularly on moonlight nights.

Fields of cotton, white-tufted in the fall, border US 99 on its way to TIPTON, 215.5 *m.* (272 alt., 414 pop.), a shipping point for cotton, milk, and poultry. PIXLEY, 221.5 *m.* (270 alt., 350 pop.), dating from the railroad building era, was named for Frank Pixley, founder and fiery editor of the early San Francisco weekly, *The Argonaut*. At EARLIMART, 227 *m.* (300 alt., 225 pop.), the one-story frame-brick buildings are dwarfed by the huge cotton-oil plant, the great cotton gin, and the long sheep and wool loading sheds (R) along the railroad.

DELANO, 234.9 *m.* (319 alt., 2,632 pop.), is a grain and fruit shipping point.

McFARLAND, 241 *m.* (350 alt., 400 pop.), with five operating gins, is the chief cotton ginning point in the State. Founded in 1877, it drew for its first settlers people opposed to the whisky drinking tolerated in nearby Delano and Famosa. All land deeds contained a clause prohibiting the selling of liquor. Test cases carried to the higher courts nullified the clause in 1933-1934; today McFarland's bartenders do a lusty, legal business.

South of FAMOSA, 246.3 *m.* (423 alt., 110 pop.), shipping point for cotton, corn and dairy products, US 99 unites with US 466 (*see TOUR 11b*), for 19 miles.

The massed rigs of the Kern Front oil field stand (L), 261 *m.*, beyond a strip of fruit orchards; farther on its derricks merge with those of the Round Mountain and Kern River fields.

BAKERSFIELD, 265.5 *m.* (420 alt., 26,015 pop.), seat of Kern County, spreads along the south bank of the Kern River in the narrow southern end of the San Joaquin Valley. From the foothills that string out on both sides comes the petroleum that has made Bakersfield an important oil-producing and refining center, and an important oil-tool manufacturing point. The West-side oil fields—the Midway-Sunset, Elk Hills, Maricopa and Belridge districts—have produced more than 800,000,000 barrels of the Kern County production of 1,400,000,000 barrels.

Between the various oil fields spread the ranches for which the town is a trade and shipping center—a checkerboard of cotton and alfalfa, pastures, vineyards, orchards, and apiaries. Bakersfield was named for Col. Thomas Baker, who arrived in 1862 to direct a reclamation project and remained to lay out the townsite in 1869. At that time the mining town of Havilah was the county seat, but after the enterprising new community organized a Bakersfield Club, an Agricultural Society, and a Cotton Growers' Association, the business men of Havilah began moving in. The editor of the Havilah *Courier,* leading newspaper in Kern County in the 1870's, followed his advertisers with type and press. In 1873, when Bakersfield became the county seat, most of the other citizens of Havilah came in too. That year one Alex Mills was elected town marshal. He constituted himself private censor of the citizenry; he knew the history, sometimes unsavory, of everyone in town, and he had a fondness for relating it. Repenting its choice, Bakersfield speedily incorporated when it learned it could thus legally oust the marshal. That accomplished, the citizens found no further advantage in incorporation of their settlement and therefore disincorporated it. Not until 1898, when the town had become a sedate agricultural trade center, did it reincorporate.

The discovery of gold in Kern River Canyon in 1885 invested Bakersfield with the color and vigor of the earlier Mother Lode boom towns. It assumed all the roughness and toughness of the camps of the unrestricted 1850's; its streets were filled with swaggering miners and gamblers, the sound of gunshots was frequently heard. In 1889 fire destroyed most of the old buildings; rebuilding resulted in modernization. Then came the discovery of oil in the Kern River fields in 1899, and Bakersfield again saw rough and tumble boom days. Today the downtown district (R. of US 99) is metropolitan in its variety of shops, cafés, department stores, theaters, and office buildings. In its streets great motor vans of potatoes, lettuce, and grapes are as familiar a sight as trucks loaded with oil well casing, drilling equipment, and derrick parts.

Bakersfield is at the junction with US 466 (*see TOUR 11b*).

Left in Bakersfield on State 178 (Nile St.) 7.5 *m.*, to a junction with Alfred Harrell Blvd.; L. here 6.5 m. to KERN RIVER COUNTY PARK, a 345-acre recreational reserve on high bluffs overlooking the Kern River. The moonlight view from these bluffs is regarded as exceptionally beautiful, even in this region where scenic grandeur is expected of the surroundings. The park has a small zoo and a pheasant and quail breeding farm for stocking the hunting areas.

At 11 *m.* on State 178 the route enters KERN RIVER CANYON, a gorge walled by steep cliffs; at their base the Kern River (L) tumbles, twisting and cascading, to the valley floor.

DEMOCRAT HOT SPRINGS, 28 *m.*, is a health resort centering about hot sulphur springs.

BODFISH, 38 *m.* (2,500 alt.), a ghost town of tumble-down, deserted shacks, was a mining camp during the Kern River Canyon gold boom in the 1880's.

Right from Bodfish 8.1 *m.* on Caliente Rd. to HAVILAH, 8.1 *m.* the ghost town that was once Kern County seat.

On State 178 is ISABELLA, 43 *m.* (2,525 alt., 50 pop.), another of the old mining towns, saved only from ghosthood by its position on a tourist route.

Left from Isabella 4 *m.* on a hard-surfaced road to KERNVILLE, (2,569 alt., 175 pop.), which came to life as Whiskey Flat during the 1885 gold rush, when a man named Hamilton opened a saloon, Kernville's first "building," which was merely a plank laid across two whisky barrels. When Whiskey Flat became a prosperous mining center in its own right it took its present name. That it was a camp of quick action and nervous trigger fingers is evidenced by the name of the old cemetery south of the town, still called Gunmen's Row, because so many local men who died with their boots on are buried in it. Kernville, still engaged in mining, is also the trade center for cattle raisers, and an outfitting point for hunters and fishermen. The characteristically "western" or "frontier" appearance of its streets has attracted many a motion picture company on location.

State 198 continues upward through magnificently beautiful country along the south fork of Kern River, following the route blazed by Joseph Walker in 1834. Walker, attached to the party of Captain Bonneville, who was looking over the Oregon country, had been detailed to lead an expedition to explore the country around and beyond the Great Salt Lake; this party, the first to cross the Sierra, spent the winter around San Francisco, then turned south through the San Joaquin Valley and up along Kern River, under guidance of two Indians. They crossed what is now called WALKER PASS (5,248 alt.), 76.6 *m.*, and descended into Indian Wells Valley, where State 178 meets State 7. Left here 11 *m.* to BROWN, on US 395 (*see TOUR 6c*).

Section c. BAKERSFIELD to LOS ANGELES; 109.5 m. US 99

US 99 shoots south across the floor of the San Joaquin Valley in a course that bends only once. Reaching the towering Tehachapi Mountains, it rises swiftly through a jagged canyon into a lofty, mountainous country. From the mountains it descends into the sheltered Santa Clara Valley, climbs into wooded hills and descends again to San Fernando Valley.

South of BAKERSFIELD, 0 *m.*, US 99, bordered by great ash trees and ragged palms, cuts through a cotton- and oil-producing region. In the fall, the distant oil derricks form a strange background for large fields of cotton, white with bursting bolls. Far ahead the road's straight strip is visible to the foot of the range. Grazing lands, dotted with wandering cattle and bands of sheep, stretch away on both sides, with patches of wild flowers in untilled fields. From February to May, this valley and the canyons leading out of it comprise an immense wild-flower garden. In summer, the blooms appear at higher altitudes.

On rain-eroded heights (R) perch oil derricks as a 5-mile grade begins the winding ascent of GRAPEVINE CANYON, deep fissure in the TEHACHAPI RANGE, once the home of Yokut and Shoshone. Through this gap in 1772 came Don Pedro Fages, *comandante militar* of Alta California, in search of two deserters. Descending through the canyon, Fages caught his deserters—the first known explorers of the valley. From GRAPEVINE, 31 *m.* (1,700 alt., 15 pop.) (*fuel, restaurant, and cabin accommodations*), is an excellent view of both the canyon and the San Joaquin Valley. A telescope offers a better view—for 5¢ or 10¢, depending upon the length of the peep. Rising steadily, US 99 reaches the summit of the grade, 35.1 *m.*

At 35.2 *m.* is a junction with a dirt road.

Right on this road to FORT TEJON (*adm. 10¢*), 0.2 *m.*, a once flourishing Army outpost. On August 10, 1854, Lt. Col. E. F. Beale established this fort in the wilderness as protection for travelers over the mountain trail and as an administrative post for regulating affairs of the surrounding Indians. Ten years after its establishment, on September 11, 1864, it officially expired. In 1858 a strange procession wound into the clearing of Fort Tejon—a camel train imported from the Near East in an attempt to provide the Army with transportation in the deserts of the South and West—and a year later part of the train returned. The camels were of little use, since on long marches they foundered because their tender feet were not adapted to the rocky soil. In 1864 all that remained in California were auctioned off at Benicia. Some entered the circus, some packed freight, and some, turned loose, frightened the wits out of desert prospectors for many years. Another event of 1858 was the arrival of the first stagecoach of the Butterfield Overland Mail on its way to San Francisco.

On the trunk of an oak tree, 200 feet north of the fort, a Bakersfield party on an outing late in the last century discovered carved on the tree the words:

PETER LEBECK
KILLED
BY
A X BEAR
OCTr. 17
1837

Digging at the base of the tree, they disinterred the skeleton of Peter Lebecque, young voyageur of the Hudson Bay Company. On his way south through this wild land with one or two companions, he had sighted and shot a grizzly as it stood beneath this tree. Believing the animal dead and approaching to obtain the pelt, he was caught by the reviving animal, clawed, and crushed to death.

US 99 climbs through a wooded valley to LEBEC, 38.5 *m.* (3,575 alt., 30 pop.), where shimmering CASTAIC LAKE is visible (L). Ever since an earthquake in 1924, the lake has been a mineral-laden puddle of alkaline water only a few feet deep. There is a tale that white men drowned the inhabitants of a small Indian village in its waters, and that years later the mineralized bodies of men, women, and children bobbed back to the surface. The Indians had been suspected of murdering a cook and a boy at Fort Tejon.

South of CHANDLERS, 40.5 *m.* (*gas station and garage*), US 99 ascends to the summit of TEJON PASS, 41.3 *m.* (4,182 alt.).

GORMAN, 42.7 *m.* (3,774 alt., 68 pop.), was named for Private Gorman of Fort Tejon who, on his discharge from service in 1864, was one of three soldiers to take up homesteads in this region.

US 99 intersects the Grapevine grade, 42.8 *m.,* its former route, considered the final word in road building at the time of its construction in 1919. The Ridge Route, completed in October 1933, follows the course used by the early stagecoaches. An engineering achievement, it cut 9.6 miles from the earlier corkscrew road; but even the new route is not without hazards, for its smooth surface and long downgrades tempt motorists to excessive speed, particularly hazardous because of the crawling lines of diesel-powered trucks.

CASTAIC, 69.7 *m.* (1,008 alt., 61 pop.), is in the fork of US 99 and the old Grapevine road. US 99, winding through the narrow Castaic Valley, emerges into the Santa Clara Valley.

A spindling steel bridge crosses SAN FRANCISQUITO CREEK, 74 *m.,* a sleepy trickle of water that once went on one brief and murderous rampage. On the night of March 13, 1928, the St. Francis Dam far up the San Francisquito Canyon broke without warning. Down the canyon roared billions of gallons of Los Angeles' water supply, crushing houses and drowning 600 persons. The rushing mass of water destroyed ten bridges, several miles of highway, part of the Los Angeles Aqueduct, one power plant, several hundred homes, and more than 10,000 acres of crops. Immense chunks of the dam, some as big as houses, are still seen, scattered up and down the canyon.

US 99 rises into the foothills of the SANTA SUSANA MOUNTAINS (R).

At 78.4 *m.* is a junction with a road, oiled for 1 mile.

> Right on this road at 2.6 *m.* is a one-way private lane, leading to the FIRST OIL WELL IN CALIFORNIA, 4.6 *m.* Here as early as 1835 vaqueros found cattle from the San Fernando Mission bogged down in beds of pitch. In 1875 a well drilled by manpower to a depth of 30 feet brought to the surface oil subsequently piped to the Newhall Refinery six miles distant. The well is still producing.

US 99 crosses high, grassy hills into San Fernando Valley.

The black trunk of the LOS ANGELES AQUEDUCT, 84.4 *m.,* snakes down the slope alongside an open spillway near the highway (L). The 233-mile aqueduct, built at a cost of $23,000,000, converted the parched San Fernando Valley into the rich "market basket of Los Angeles," but it also ruthlessly turned towns and farms of fertile Owens River Valley high in the Sierra to semidesert.

SYLMAR, 86.1 *m.,* is a Southern Pacific loading station for an olive-packing plant.

At 86.3 *m.* is a junction with a paved road.

Left on this road to the OLIVE VIEW SANATORIUM, 1.5 *m.,* a tuberculosis hospital supported jointly by Los Angeles County and the State. Behind a front of modern Spanish buildings, a series of neat but barracks-like structures houses a thousand tubercular patients.

The VETERANS' ADMINISTRATION FACILITY, 4 *m.,* is a hospital for tubercular ex-service men. Its sand-colored, red-roofed buildings along the base of the foothills spread over 632 acres of landscaped grounds.

SAN FERNANDO, 88 *m.* (1,066 alt., 7,567 pop.), maintains its independence of Los Angeles, whose territory entirely surrounds it, by means of a municipally owned water system supplied by deep artesian wells. The town prospers from reclaimed acres covered with citrus orchards.

Right from San Fernando on State 118 to MISIÓN SAN FERNANDO REY DE ESPANA, 1.6 *m.* (*adm. 25¢*). The Franciscans' seventeenth mission in order of time, it was established Sept. 8, 1797, by Fathers Fermín Lasuen and Francisco Dumetz on a site selected primarily for its natural advantages. By December 1806, the first chapel was completed. Before secularization took place in 1835, Mission San Fernando had become one of the most prosperous in California. Today a crumbling pile of adobe stretches from the restored adobe CONVENTO to the falling adobe CHURCH. The convento has an arcade of 19 semicircular arches along its main facade; its easternmost room has been remodeled into a chapel in which several old paintings and relics are kept.

MEMORY GARDEN in BRAND PARK (*playgrounds*), directly opposite the convent, is one of the few restored mission gardens. Pergolas and quiet, flagged walks surround garden plots. In one section of the park is the mission's fountain, built in 1812-14 in imitation of one in Cordova, Spain.

BURBANK, 96.5 *m.* (560 alt., 16,622 pop.), is a city of small residences and shaded streets, built on land purchased from the immense Rancho la Providencia for 37½¢ an acre. In 1887, during a Los Angeles real estate boom, the next purchaser, Dr. David Burbank, gave his name to the small ranch settlement.

1. Right from Burbank on Empire Ave. to UNION AIR TERMINAL, 0.5 *m.* (*open*), which serves three transport lines—United Airlines, Western Air Express, and Transcontinental and Western. Beyond the terminal building great cement runways spread in five directions. Sixteen transports land here daily. Immense hangars fringe a field ablaze at night with strong floodlights.

2. Right from Burbank on Olive Ave. to WARNER BROS. FIRST NATIONAL STUDIOS, 2.8 *m.,* the main plant of one of the largest producers in the motion picture industry. This 108-acre "lot," beautifully landscaped and gardened, contains several miles of paved streets and more than 65 buildings, including 18 sound stages covering more than 1,000,000 square feet of space under roof. Other buildings include four theaters for previewing pictures, a restaurant with three dining rooms, an electric power plant, greenhouses, a school for children who work in pictures, and massage parlors, barber shops, steam baths, dressing rooms. The "back lot" is used for exterior sets. The streets of many cities are represented here, and nearby are the straw huts of a hula land and the log cabins of the Canadian woods. In another corner is a huge man-made lake, around which are reproductions of a dozen water fronts, including those of San Francisco, New York, Shanghai, and Venice. Adjoining the studio is an 11-acre enclosed ranch, where exterior scenes on the grand scale are made.

GLENDALE, 99.7 *m.* (573 alt., 62,736 pop.), primarily a residential suburb of Los Angeles, grew rapidly as the population wave from the Middle West inundated southern California. A modern city with wide, well-paved streets and boulevards, its recently erected stucco houses convey an impression of impermanence to visitors from older communities. The site of Glendale is a part of the former Rancho San Rafael, first (1784) Spanish land grant in California. Sharp Yankee traders, who invaded the region following annexation by the United States, deviously secured possession of most of the rancho. The townsite was plotted in 1886-87. The town languished until 1902. Its reawakening brought the Pacific Electric Railroad from Los Angeles. Glendale has a high percentage of elderly persons in comfortable circumstances with leisure to encourage cultural groups, which include a symphony orchestra and several music and art associations.

FOREST LAWN MEMORIAL PARK, Forest and Glendale Aves. (*open 9 a.m. to 5 p.m.*), described by Bruce Barton as "above the level of this world, a first step toward Heaven," is a 200-acre graveyard—one of the most elaborate in the world and one of the most important commercially. Those who own burial plots here must be content with flat inconspicuous markers for their dead, though they may erect costly memorials of a type that the management approves for the embellishment of the park. The park's statuary ranges from reproductions of the works of Michelangelo—Forest Lawn is "the only place in the world where all Michelangelo's great works are gathered in one place" —to the Duck Baby, the Spirit of Forest Lawn. There are two churches in the park: the older one, the LITTLE CHURCH OF THE FLOWERS, which has a Bride's Room, a carved oak contribution box, a framed tribute from Barton, and alcoves where, according to the management, "songbirds trill the melody of love," became so popular for weddings that a second church had to be constructed to avoid embarrassing traffic tangles. The WEE KIRK O' THE HEATHER is a copy of the church where Annie Laurie worshipped; near it is the ANNIE LAURIE WISHING CHAIR, constructed with stones obtained from the old church in Scotland; tradition, says the advertising literature, has it that the fairies have blessed these stones and that fortune will forever smile on the bridal pair that sits in this seat on the wedding day.

CASA ADOBE DE SAN RAFAEL, 1340 Dorothy Dr., stands in a two-acre city park. The building was erected between 1864 and 1872 by the one-time sheriff of Los Angeles County, Tomas Sánchez, whose wife, María Sepulveda, inherited part of the vast Rancho San Rafael. Married at the age of 13, she bore 21 children in this house. Cooking utensils of her time are preserved within, together with other relics. The park is planted with orange, fig, lemon, avocado, tangerine, and eucalyptus trees. LA CASA DE CATALINA VERDUGO was the last of five adobes built on Rancho San Rafael. Across the road is a huge oak beneath which Gen. Andrés Pico made his last camp before surrendering to Gen. John C. Frémont on Jan. 13, 1847.

Glendale's Grand Central Airport, 1224 Airway, serves American Airlines and the Mexican Aviation Company.

LOS ANGELES, 109.5 *m.* (250 alt., 1,238,048 pop.), (*see LOS ANGELES*).

At Los Angeles is the junction with US 60-70 (*see TOUR 13b*) with which US 99 is united eastward to Ontario.

Section d. POMONA to BEAUMONT; 59.4 m.   US 99-70

The wide concrete roadbed of US 99-70 in this section runs smoothly over miles of flatland, bordered by far-stretching orange groves and acres and acres of close-cropped grape vines.

US 99-70 branches south from US 60 (*see TOUR 13b*) at Pomona (*see TOUR 13b*), 0 *m.*

ONTARIO, 6.2 *m.* (980 alt., 13,583 pop.), at the junction with US 60 (*see TOUR 13b*), is surrounded by orange groves and small ranches; primarily a residential town, it has citrus by-product factories and other industrial plants. The main street, Euclid Avenue, is distinguished by its broad central strip of green lawn bordered with double rows of pepper trees, formerly the route of a mule-drawn carline; the mules, after pulling up-grade to the summit of the line in the foothills to the north, were there prodded aboard the car platform to ride back down the incline. Founded by Canadians in 1882, Ontario was named for their home province. De Anza Park, at S. Euclid Ave. and Dessau St., is supposed to have been the campground of Juan Bautista de Anza on his first expedition into California.

The 5,000-acre Guasti Vineyard, 2.2 *m.* (*open 9-5 workdays*), extends from the foothills of the San Gabriel Mountains deep into the valley floor. For five miles the highway runs between rows of vines stretching far away between furrows of sandy loam. Here are more than 500 varieties of grapes, 25 of which are raised on commercial scale. The annual crop is slightly more than 20,000 tons. The large, modern winery produces both dry and sweet wines and one of the few California "champagne" wines. During harvesting season, from August to December, an average of 400 tones of grapes are stemmed and crushed daily. The stems are returned to the soil of the vineyards in the form of fertilizers. The fermenting plant's 200 tanks have a capacity of a million gallons. In 1904 the U. S. Department of Agriculture leased 20 acres of the vineyard and planted 500 varieties of grapes to study their quality and their suitability to the soil. Just previous to the passage of the Eighteenth Amendment, 3,000,000 gallons of wine were being manufactured each year.

GUASTI, 9.7 *m.* (952 alt., 600 pop.), at the center of the Guasti vineyards, is recognizable (R) by the long, reddish-colored administration building and the corrugated iron and brick distillery with smokestacks showing above the trees. The small community bears the name of the Italian immigrant, Secundo Guasti, who in 1902 set out the first grapevines here in an almost desolate waste of sand.

Steep MOUNT SLOVER, 24.1 *m.,* with craggy rock outcroppings, juts up sharply in a white mist of smoke and dust. Here the corrugated iron roofs and smokestacks of a large cement plant climb the hillsides. The whole hill is gradually being carted away and ground up.

COLTON, 27 *m.* (847 alt., 8,014 pop.), is an industrial and railroad center not far from the site of Rancho Jumuba, a Mission San Gabriel stock ranch established before 1819. About a mile away José María Lugo built a house in 1842, when he, his brothers, and Diego Sepulveda were granted the valley. It was on Jumuba that Fort Benson was erected in the late 1850's by Jerome Benson, who raised earthworks and loaded a cannon with rocks to protect his land against seizure by the Mormons who dominated the region. Here, on the trail from Santa Fe, calvacades of pack mules and horses stopped on their journey to the coast. In 1875 Colton was a Southern Pacific Railroad terminus, but freight charges were so high that farmers of the region organized a mule line from San Pedro, threatening to put the railroad out of business unless the rates were lowered.

Colton is at the junction with US 395 (*see TOUR 6e*), which unites with US 99-70 eastward.

From the SANTA ANA RIVER, 28.1 *m.,* a winding trickle in a broad, brush-grown bed, the highway strikes through a jungle of auto courts, roadside cafés, and fruit and vegetable stands; through fields with scattered trees and ranch houses where cattle graze; past barns, fenceposts, and windmills. Orange trees reappear, clustering thick and leafy along the route.

REDLANDS, 32.9 *m.* (1,351 alt., 14,177 pop.), deriving its name from the red soil of the region, is an attractive residential community. Lying at the eastern boundary of the southern citrus belt, it is the packing and distributing point for more than 15,000 acres of citrus fruits, yielding annually 5,000 to 6,500 carloads of produce, and for many varieties of deciduous fruits, poultry, vegetables, and dairy products. Despite the activity of its many packing houses during the picking season, Redlands is quiet, with broad, tree-lined streets and a profusion of flower gardens and green lawns. Its cultural character, influenced by the University of Redlands, is exemplified by free community concerts in the Redlands Bowl and a public library circulation list including three-quarters of the population.

SMILEY HEIGHTS, Cajon and Cypress Sts., is a magnificent formal garden of 400 acres with trees and shrubs from all the world, including rubber, banana, and Persian flowering peach trees, kurrajongs and deodars from Hindustan, and cedars of Lebanon. Established by A. K. Smiley, the garden is now a public park.

The UNIVERSITY OF REDLANDS, on University Hill, E. Colton Ave. and University St., occupies 15 buildings on a verdant 100-acre campus. Founded in 1907 by the Southern California Baptist Convention, it had in 1938 some 750 students and a faculty of 50. In the GREEK THEATER, students hold their annual Zanja Fiesta, named for the old water ditch of mission days, that now carries a stream between the audience and the actors. A 725-acre tract owned by the university in the nearby San Bernardino Mountains is used as a geological station and as a retreat for students.

The WATCHORN LINCOLN MEMORIAL, an octagonal granite building on the grounds of the A. K. SMILEY PUBLIC LIBRARY, Fourth St., was given to the city by Robert Watchorn in memory of a son who was killed in the World War. Abraham Lincoln relics are on exhibit with books, newspapers, and letters; interior murals by Dean Cornwell show scenes from Lincoln's life.

The REDLANDS BOWL, in SMILEY PARK, Eureka Ave. between Parkwood and Brookside Sts., is an outdoor theater under tall palm trees where public concerts are presented by the Community Music Association.

The SAN BERNARDINO ASISTENCIA (Sp., chapel), Barton Rd. and Mountain View Ave., is the reproduction of an outpost of San Gabriel Mission that served as both a chapel for the Indians and headquarters for Rancho San Bernardino. As early as 1819 the padres of San Gabriel had built an adobe station at Guachama, the Indian village at this spot. Abandoned after secularization of the missions, it remained virtually deserted until 1842, when the Mexican Government granted a large part of the rancho, including the chapel, to the Lugo family of Los Angeles. In 1852 the Lugos sold the entire 37,000 acres to a colony of Mormons, who used the station as a tithing house until 1857. It was razed to make way for orange trees; oranges have never grown well on this spot—according to legend because an Indian medicine man put a curse on the land. The present *asistencia* was built by the San Bernardino Historical Society, which brought an expert adobe brick- and tile-maker from Mexico to mold the materials as they were fashioned in mission days.

US 99 winds past hedges of roses through Reservoir Canyon. Small green orchards of walnut, pecan, and cashew trees alternate with hayfields. The crest of the San Bernardino Mountains (L) rises above in the distance. Over creek beds and past small farms, the route leads across the flat floor of valley land surrounded by rolling shrub-covered hills.

BEAUMONT, 59.4 m. (2,559 alt., 2,314 pop.) (see TOUR 13b), is at the junction with US 60 (see TOUR 13b), with which US 99 is united for 52.1 miles.

Section e. INDIO to MEXICAN BORDER; 95.4 m. US 99

US 99 in this section traverses a region of sharp contrasts. Its northern end lies through the Coachella Valley, an intensely cultivated area; it cuts through a long, desolate stretch of desert in the region of the Salton Sea; and then it returns to rich farm land as it passes through the Imperial Valley (see TOUR 14a).

US 99 branches south from its junction with US 60-70 (see TOUR 13a), 0 m. at a point 2 miles south of Indio.

COACHELLA, 1.5 *m.* (— 72 alt., 1,100 pop.), is a sprawling village in the heart of the Coachella Valley, which extends from San Gorgonio Pass to the northern shores of the Salton Sea between the Little San Bernardino Mountains (L) and the San Jacinto and Santa Rosa Mountains (R). The valley produces dates, grapefruit, cotton, alfalfa, fruit, and vegetables, irrigated by water from deep wells. Like many of the valley towns, Coachella has its Mexican section of ramshackle houses, fronting dust-covered side roads, and inhabited by agricultural workers (*see TOUR 14a*).

Left from Coachella on State 111, the North Shore road, which runs below sea level for its entire length; it is noted for its desert scenery and geological curiosities. The region is at its best in the early winter mornings, when mirages are most common, or in late afternoon when the coloring is most pronounced. In summer the temperature often rises to 125° F.

THERMAL, 3 *m.* (—127 alt., 400 pop.), in a grape and date producing area, is well named, for the days are hot almost all the year, though evenings are fairly comfortable.

MECCA, 10.9 *m.* (—197 alt., 800 pop.), a town of date gardens shimmering in the heat, was named because of its association with dates and desert.

Left from Mecca on Shaver's Canyon Road 3 *m.* to the junction with Painted Canyon Road; L. here 3.5 *m.* through PAINTED CANYON (*no water*) in the vivid Mecca Hills. At 3 *m.* on Shaver's Canyon Road is the junction with a foot trail; straight ahead on this trail 2 *m.* to PAINTED CANYON PICNIC GROUND, where the steep 500-foot walls are a multicolored blend of ochres, reds, lavenders, purples, ashy dark green, and brilliant scarlet. At 4 *m.* on Shaver's Canyon Road is a junction with Dos Palmas Spring Road; R. here 4 *m.* to a junction with a spur road; L. again 4 *m.* to HIDDEN SPRINGS, an oasis in the OROCOPIA (Sp., plenty of gold) MOUNTAINS. Here the Cahuilla Indians once gathered and held powwows.

On State 111 is CALEB'S SIDING, 15.4 *m.,* a railroad loading point. Right here 1 *m.* on a dirt road to the TORRES MARTINEZ RESERVATION, the home of 215 Indians.

South of Caleb's Siding the highway swings toward the Orocopia Mountains and the shore of Salton Sea (*see main route*). In the desert (L) bordering the Salton Sea a few smoke trees are visible. From a distance the slate-gray branches of these trees, which become 10 to 15 feet in height, resemble the long narrow pillar of smoke made by an Indian campfire. When the trees bloom in June their large, powder-blue blossoms give the appearance of the cloud of smoke made by a bonfire.

DATE PALM BEACH, 20.1 *m.,* and SALTON BEACH, 24.1 *m.* (—22 alt.), are small resorts on the shore of the Salton Sea (*camping, swimming, boating*). Some mullet can be caught in the very salty sea, but little else. There is little vegetation besides the olive and buff mesquite and creosote bushes, which cover the desert as it stretches eastward to the gully-slashed slopes of the CHOCOLATE MOUNTAINS.

A solitary CAHUILLA INDIAN ROCK MOUND is visible at 29.1 *m.,* rising out of the desert (L) a mile from the road. On its surface are many petroglyphs. Cut in the solid rock is the likeness of an Indian head. Travertine, or petrified scale (calcium carbonate), clinging to the flat surface of the rocks, shows that it was once below the water line of prehistoric Lake Cahuilla.

South of BOMBAY BEACH, 35.8 *m.,* another small resort, the route swings out into the desert around the southern end of the sea, crossing many little gullies.

NILAND, 53.8 *m.* (— 30 alt., 1,815 pop.), is at the northern end of Imperial Valley (*see TOUR 14a*), surrounded by some of the largest ranches in the valley; on one ranch alone are 4,000 grapefruit, 17,000 orange, 6,000 lemon, and 2,000 tangerine trees.

At 56.8 *m.* is the junction with a dirt road; R. here 3.8 *m.* to a D<small>RY</small> I<small>CE</small> P<small>LANT</small>, where dry ice is manufactured from the carbon dioxide gas obtained from wells in the nearby Mud Pots area. The MUD POTS, 5 *m.*, 20 acres of boiling mud craters, geysers, and mineral springs, bubble up from the depths of the earth into small basins, shooting out jets of steam and sulphurous gases. As the hot grayish mud spouts out, it builds a rim around the edge of each geyser and slowly builds up the edge of the basin. The pots are believed to be caused by water seepage from the Salton Sea coming into contact with underground beds of hot rock. The wrinkled grayish-white craters, pitted with crevices, ranging in height from 1 to 7 feet, closely resemble a series of miniature mountain ranges.

In MULLET ISLAND, at the northern end of this geyser area, is the DAVIS MUSEUM (*adm. 25¢*), containing fossils, sharks' teeth, and similar remains from ancient Lake Cahuilla, as well as old Indian pottery.

A short distance by foot trail southwest of the Mud Pots are the INDIAN PAINT POTS, where water from oxide springs has formed motley incrustations.

CALIPATRIA, 60.1 *m.* (—183 alt., 1,554 pop.), is the center of an area where green peas are the principal crop. Alfalfa is also important. A local mill grinds the alfalfa into meal for cattle fodder.

Near Calipatria are several duck preserves and gun clubs. Best duck hunting is found on the southern shores of the Salton Sea in the tule marshes between the New and Alamo Rivers (*blinds and boats available*).

The highway crosses NEW RIVER, 65.8 *m.*, a channel marked by high, reddish bluffs, slashed in the loose alluvial soil of the Imperial Valley in 1905-1907 when the Colorado River broke loose on its last rampage. The break occurred when the irrigation engineers opened a breach in the river wall in 1905 just south of the Mexican boundary, in order to supply valley canals with the water held back by an accumulation of silt. The gap was cut far enough ahead of flood time for safety, but before gates could be installed a premature flood raced down the river. Rebuffed by a natural levee at the tip of the Gulf, it backed through the new opening into the Salton Sink. Within two years the lake covered an area extending from Mecca to Niland, reached a length of 45 miles and a maximum width of 17 miles. The railroad company had to shift 67 miles of track to a higher level. Just as the railroad was rolling down its sleeves, the river again broke its banks and poured disastrous quantities of water into the basin. The company again set to work, built a 90-foot trestle across the break, commandeered equipment from 1,200 miles of track, and dumped 3,000 carloads of rock into the opening. Finally, in February 1907, the break was plugged, and the railroad's ledgers showed another $1,000,000 in the red. Suit was filed against the Federal Government for the $3,000,000 spent, and in 1930 the company received a check for $1,012,665.

South of New River, State 111 is bordered by the emerald green of alfalfa fields, alternating with pasture lands, corn and melon patches, and fruit groves. At intervals the route is lined with eucalyptus trees, planted as windbreaks.

BRAWLEY, 73.8 *m.* (—115 alt., 10,439 pop.), (*see below*), is at the junction with US 99.

At 9.5 *m.* on US 99 is the junction with a dirt road.

Right on this road, crossing the All-American Canal to the F<small>ISH</small> T<small>RAPS</small>, 2.5 *m.*, piles of rock two or three feet high. The handiwork of the ancient Mountain Cahuilla, they were devised in the remote period when a great Indian village stood on the shores of the prehistoric Lake Cahuilla.

They are easily discerned among the boulders and consist of circular walls of rock with cleverly arranged openings.

The SALTON SEA, (L), 14 *m.* (— 244 alt. at surface), a gourd-shaped body of water 30 miles long and from 8 to 14 miles wide, was only a vast, sandy depression when discovered in 1853 by Professor W. P. Blake, who made the first governmental survey of Imperial Valley. In 1905 the Colorado River overflowed into the Imperial Valley (*see above*) and poured into the Salton Sink, filling it to a depth of 83 feet and a length of 45 miles. When this flood was checked in 1907, it left the lowest area still filled with the present Salton Sea—a lake with no outlets. The present depth of the sea is kept approximately constant, despite evaporation, by waters draining from the irrigation ditches into the New and Alamo Rivers, which empty into the southern end of the sea.

The lake replaces the final remnant of prehistoric Lake Cahuilla, created when the silt from the Colorado River dammed back the waters at the head of the Gulf of California. The old lake dried up gradually, leaving behind in the San Jacinto Mountains, 1,000 feet above the level of the Salton Sea, enormous beds of fossil sharks' teeth and oyster shells. Bits of fragile conch shell today glisten everywhere in the desert sands of this region. A printer's error in setting *conchilla* (Sp., small sea shell) gave Coachella Valley its unusual name.

OASIS, 17.5 *m.* (— 198 alt.), is not a town but a series of large date orchards and a few orange groves on the line of the All-American Canal.

Beyond the vineyards lining the highway south of Oasis, the petrified coral scale of the ANCIENT BEACH LINE (R), thin and sharp as a knife edge from this distance, cuts an even whitish stripe along the sides of the Santa Rosa Mountains. Despite the heat, pink and white oleanders flourish along the highway and the green (in winter) or gold (in summer) strands of dodder industriously ensnare occasional trees.

TRAVERTINE ROCK, (R), 23.4 *m.,* a geological relic of Lake Cahuilla, rises from the desert a few score yards from the highway. The once submerged lower half of this great mound of rocks is covered with a layer of travertine (calcium carbonate), a scaly, petrified shell formation; the upper part, of travertine rock, shows its core of dark granite and many petroglyphs, or rock carvings, incised ages ago by the ancestors of the Mission Indians. From the highway, the curved and twisted patterns of rock composing the mound resemble plant cells under a microscope.

At 25.3 *m.* is the junction with a dirt road.

Left on this road to a privately owned camp (*rates reasonable*), 0.7 *m.,* at the rim of the Salton Sea in a grove of tamarack trees. Here are motor courts and a swimming pool with mineral water at a constant temperature of 112° F. Stands of cattails and bamboo grass near the seashore offer blinds for duck shooting in the fall.

At 47.3 *m.* is the junction with State 78 (*see TOUR 6C*).

KANE SPRINGS, 48.8 *m.* (— 150 alt.), is the oldest known water hole on the Colorado Desert (*service station, restaurant*), long a camping ground of desert explorers and Indians. One of the most prevalent of local myths concerns a Spanish galleon that sailed into the northernmost arm of the prehistoric Gulf of California, to be abandoned there with its fabulous cargo of gold. As the sea dried up, the hapless ship sank beneath shifting dunes. In 1890 an oldtimer appeared at Kane Springs asserting he had seen the ancient ship nearby almost covered by a ·dune. Searchers, however, failed to find it. The probable inspiration for the legend was a boat built in 1862 by a Colorado River mining company, transported part way across the desert by ox team, and then abandoned because of the difficulty of the journey from San Gorgonio Pass to the Colorado River.

South of Kane Springs a long sand mound, or desert wall (R), protects the highway from floods during the rare but sudden thunderstorms. As the road turns abruptly east, sagebrush, creosote, and the grayish green greasewood give way to trees and bamboo grass.

WESTMORELAND, 62.3 *m.* (— 150 alt., 1,300 pop.), founded in 1910, boasts of having the widest main street in the valley and no cemetery. In the community live Yankees, Negroes, Indians (Asiatic), Mexicans, Chinese, and Japanese. As in other valley towns, the population is swelled during the harvest season by itinerant agricultural workers, frequently referred to as "fruit tramps," who, with their families, follow the ripening crops in a great nomadic trek, living in makeshift huts and "jungles" (*see EL CENTRO, TOUR 14a*).

Through fields of grain, vegetables, and cotton, vast melon patches, and endless rows of winter lettuce, runs a network of irrigation canals. Long lines of sugarcane stand in green files along the edges of ditches. Dates, grapes, grapefruit, and oranges grow now, where only a quarter of a century ago the bleached bones of travelers lay in the burning sand.

Intense heat prevails in this region through the summer months, with temperatures ranging up to 125°, but the torrid heat is made tolerable by the extreme dryness of the desert air. In winter the temperature varies as much as 60° between day and night.

BRAWLEY, 70.2 *m.* (— 115 alt., 10,439 pop.), is the largest town in Imperial Valley and one of its two largest shipping centers. It is a well-planned community with wide streets and cool greenery in its several public parks. The long, one-story building housing the city offices and public library, a good example of modern adobe construction with its 3-foot outer walls and low, timbered ceilings, stands in a plaza filled with tropical trees, flowers, and plants. More Mexican laborers live here than anywhere else in the valley; their efforts to raise their standard of living have made the town the most conspicuous center of labor unrest among valley towns.

South of Brawley US 99 cuts through one of the valley's most productive areas. Here grow the best cantaloupes, white head lettuce, and alfalfa. Contrary to usual dairying methods, cows are milked in the open and their fodder—baled hay—remains stacked and uncovered in the fields.

IMPERIAL, 79.9 *m.* (— 67 alt., 1,943 pop.), is the oldest town in the valley. A common sight along the highway are signs announcing "Cotton Pickers Wanted." Shacks occupied by the migrant workers straggle along the irrigation ditches whose line can be easily traced by sugarcane on the embankments.

The IMPERIAL COUNTY AIRPORT, 80.4 *m.,* is a flagstop for transcontinental airlines; opposite it are the IMPERIAL COUNTY FAIR GROUNDS.

EL CENTRO, 84.4 *m.* (— 52 alt., 8,500 pop.) (*see TOUR 14a*), is at the junction with US 80 (*see TOUR 14a*).

South of El Centro, blue-green fields of alfalfa—which here yield five or six crops a year—and eucalyptus trees line the highway.

HEBER, 90.4 *m.* (— 9 alt., 991 pop.), is a shopping and shipping point for the southern valley. Founded in 1901 by the Imperial Land Company some distance eastward and named Paringa, the town was moved two years later following completion of the Southern Pacific Railroad survey and renamed for a president of the California Development Company.

CALEXICO, 95.4 *m.* (5 alt., 6,232 pop.), a border town, is a port of entry to the United States. Here Mexican travel permits are available (*no permit necessary if visitor returns same day he leaves*). Calexico is on a former 160-acre tract owned by George Chaffey, one of the promoters of the first irrigation projects in the valley. The tent city of the Imperial Land Company was the first Calexico. A press agent of this company is said to have coined the names of the twin cities of Calexico and Mexicali (just over the border) by combining syllables from the words California and Mexico. Before the repeal of the Volstead Act, Calexico was chiefly a week-end town visited by Imperial Valley workers in pursuit of the bright lights, dance halls, and saloons of the adjacent Mexican town. In recent years Calexico has thrown off its tawdry border aspect and carried out civic improvements, and Mexicali's bars and cantinas have lost the lure they once held for pleasure-bent valley inhabitants.

ROCKWOOD HALL, on the International Boundary Line, is an old adobe building, amid date palms, once used by Charles R. Rockwood, the man most closely associated with the development of Imperial Valley. The structure, restored in 1932, contains two assembly halls.

Tour 3A

(Klamath Falls, Ore.)—Dorris—Macdoel—Weed; US 97
Oregon Line to Weed, 57.4 *m.*

Paved roadbed throughout.
Accommodations limited.

US 97 follows a southwesterly course through the central section of northern California, a thinly populated country, high, rugged, and semiarid. The northern section of the route runs through a high mountain valley, walled by the Siskiyou Range. South of the valley the course swings more sharply westward and follows the foothills at the northwestern base of Mount Shasta through rough, lava-scarred country. The region, one of farming, lumbering, and stock raising, was settled late, after the advent of roads and railroad. Lumbering is the major source of income. Here, as throughout most of Siskiyou County, are stands of yellow and sugar pine, red fir, and cedar. This section has recently become popular for hunting and fishing.

US 97 crosses the Oregon Line, 0 *m.,* 21 miles southwest of Klamath Falls, Ore., and runs through Butte Valley. The valley, 17 miles in length and approximately 10 miles wide, once cradled a great lake, long since dried up. When the Southern Pacific Railroad was built through this region, a colony of Dunkards settled here. Coming from Iowa and states further east, they were unacquainted with the principles of dry farming, and their first crops failed. In time, however, they learned to irrigate from the water sources that underlie the valley.

DORRIS, 3.5 *m.* (4,238 alt., 762 pop.), a trade center for farmers and vacationists who visit the area, was one of the Dunkard colonies. East of the town lies dry Lower Klamath Lake.

US 97 continues southwestward. To the west is the basin known as Meiss, or Butte Lake, in ancient times part of the lake that covered the valley.

MACDOEL, 14.5 *m.* (4,258 alt., 150 pop.), also a Dunkard colony, is now a business center for the Butte Valley Irrigation District. The whine of saw mills and the ring of sharp-bitted loggers' axes resound in the high clear air.

US 97 was rerouted south of Macdoel late in 1938 to skirt, rather than cross, DEER MOUNTAIN (5,380 alt.), whose height (L) is unimpressive. For several miles the highway traverses a desolate, sagebrush-covered region.

US 97 enters the rugged, lava-strewn region that fans out from the base (L) of snow-covered Mount Shasta (*see TOUR 3a*).

At 45.6 *m.* is the junction with a rough dirt road.

> Right on this road, through pine- and juniper-forested wastes, 2.3 *m.* to the junction with a dirt road; R. here 2 *m.* to the base of SHEEP ROCK (5,500 alt.), a forbidding pile of weather-scarred crags resembling battlements. In early days, several square miles of level surface nearby, dotted with patches of grass, was a winter pasture for thousands of wild Mount Shasta sheep. From the higher ridges they came down to the warm lava crags and plateaus. Naturalist John Muir marveled when he heard how they were seen leaping from an almost perpendicular lava headland 150 feet high ". . . without evincing any extraordinary concern, hugging the rock closely and controlling the velocity of their . . . movements by striking at short intervals and holding back with their cushioned, rubber feet . . ." Long hunted by tribesmen, the sheep disappeared altogether after wanton slaughter by white settlers.
>
> The main side road continues to a junction with a narrow dirt road, 3.3 *m.*; L. here 0.3 *m.* to the end of the road, where a faintly discernible foot trail marked by paint-daubed rocks leads 0.3 *m.* through junipers and over hummocks of lava to a great hole walled with lava crags—the entrance to PLUTO'S CAVE. The trail descends to a great archway that leads into a high-ceilinged cavern. Opposite (R), through another arch is another great well. The rough floor slopes down to the opening of an enormous tunnel, roofed by a jagged ceiling that arches 50 to 60 feet above a floor piled high with tumbled rocks. A short distance beyond the opening is a third large well; beyond another vast arched gateway the cave winds into the depths of the earth,—for nearly a mile it is 30 to 40 feet wide and 50 to 60 feet high. Within its black depths early explorers found owls and bats, the bones and horns of wild sheep, and blackened ashes of fires.

US 97 swings round the reddish brown, craggy hump of YELLOW BUTTE (R), dips to the valley floor, and climbs again into rubble-scarred foothills at the base of Mount Shasta. At 51.9 *m.* there is a view (R) of Little Shasta Valley. The route crosses rolling hills where stands of pine and cedar grow amid stretches of cutover land, and reaches WEED, 57.4 *m.* (3,466 alt., 4,000 pop.) (*see TOUR 3a*), at the junction with US 99 (*see TOUR 3a*).

Tour 3B

Red Bluff—Marysville—Roseville; 123.4 *m.* US 99E

Southern Pacific R.R. parallels route between Marysville and Los Molinos; Sacramento Northern R.R. between Marysville and Chico. Accommodations plentiful; hotels and auto camps in larger towns. Paved highways throughout; open all seasons.

US 99E runs between the river and the highlands through the great plains of the eastern Sacramento Valley. Far eastward, paralleling the route, the land slopes upward to the dim blue foothills of the Sierra Nevada. Level grainfields—green with young wheat and barley in season, or yellow with stubble—and gently rolling stretches of grazing land, dotted with groves of oaks, spread on either side. In the valley lands, where water is plentiful, orchards fringe the highway for miles, white and pink with blossoms in spring. Many of the quiet valley towns, half buried among trees, preserve traces of their mid-nineteenth century origin.

Branching east from US 99, 0 *m.* (*see TOUR 3a*) in RED BLUFF, US 99E crosses the tree-fringed bed of the placid Sacramento River. Beyond orchards and fields, far in the east above the foothills, towers Lassen Peaks (*see TOUR 5a*).

At 2.6 *m.* is the junction with State 36 (*see TOUR 6A*).

At 14.8 *m.* is the junction with a paved road.

> Right on this road crossing the Sacramento River to TEHAMA, 1.3 *m.* (218 alt., 190 pop.), until 1857 the seat of Tehama County, a quiet village of dusty, tree-shaded byways, surrounding a frame steepled church and false-front buildings with wooden awnings. Settled in 1847 when Robert H. Thomas built an adobe here on his Rancho de los Saucos (ranch of the elder trees), Tehama became a busy freighting and trading center and the chief ferry crossing between Marysville and Shasta until Red Bluff outrivaled it as a river town.

LOS MOLINOS (the mills), 15.3 *m.* (211 alt., 200 pop.), is headquarters for small dairy, poultry, and orchard tracts.

The SITE OF BENTON CITY, 21.3 *m.,* is marked by a concrete monument and a dugout, formerly a cellar. Peter Lassen laid out a town here in 1847 on his 26,000-acre Rancho Bosquejo. To round up settlers Lassen went to Missouri, in honor of whose expansionist senator, Thomas H. Benton, he named the place. He returned in the summer of 1848 with the first group to come overland to settle in the upper Sacramento Valley. With him he brought a charter, granted by the Grand Lodge of Missouri, for the first Masonic Lodge in California, Western Star Lodge, No. 2. But the discovery of gold depopulated Lassen's embryo city and the lodge was moved to Shasta in 1851.

At 22 *m.* is the junction with a paved road.

> Right on this road is VINA, 0.8 *m.* (206 alt., 300 pop.), center of Senator Leland Stanford's former 55,000-acre grape-producing Vina Ranch, established in 1881. Given to Stanford University on his death in 1892, the ranch has been subdivided into fruit, nut, and garden tracts.

US 99E continues through far-stretching grainfields and farmlands. At 37.9 *m.* is the junction with a paved road.

> Left here to RICHARDSON SPRINGS, 9.6 *m.* (*hotel and cottages*), an all-year resort in the foothills near mineral waters.

CHICO (Sp., little), 40.8 *m.* (193 alt., 7,961 pop.), a trade center since Gen. John Bidwell planted his orchards here, stands in a farm belt producing fruit, grain, and almonds. In the late 1840's John Bidwell, a member of the first overland party to cross the Sierra Nevada, combined the Rancho Arroyo Chico and Rancho de Farwell into the Rancho Chico which became renowned for its great and varied productivity and its miles of tree-arched avenues. Bidwell maintained an experimental orchard of 1,800 acres, which at the time of his death contained 400 varieties of fruit. A pioneer in raisin growing and olive oil manufacture, he began wine making in 1864 or 1865, but after two years plowed up his vineyards. He later ran for President of the United States on the Prohibition Party ticket. When in 1860 he laid out the town of Chico, he offered free lots to any who would build on his townsite. Before the end of a decade Chico was a city of 2,000, boasting hotels and churches—and even saloons and gambling houses, despite Bidwell's advocacy of temperance.

A memorial to Chico's founder is the granite monument on the SITE OF THE BIDWELL ADOBE, built for him by the Maidu Indians in 1852. Beyond, in a parklike preserve, is the two-story, stone BIDWELL MANSION with its broad verandas and huge central tower. The mansion is now the girls' dormitory of the CHICO STATE COLLEGE, whose tile-roofed Romanesque buildings are grouped among trees about broad green lawns. Construction of the college was begun in 1887 on a 10-acre plot donated by Bidwell.

The INDIAN VILLAGE, where lived the Maidu (known as the Bidwell Indians), extends along Sacramento Avenue (R) on the northwest outskirts of town. When Bidwell arrived in the late 1840's, the Maidu were wild as deer, the men going about wholly naked, the women clad only in skirts of grass. Under the régime of Bidwell, who built houses, a school and a church for them, they worked as ranch hands on the property that had belonged to their ancestors. Their village today is a desolate, weed-grown tract of weather-beaten shanties about a crumbling little belfried church.

Donated by Bidwell's widow, 2,400-acre BIDWELL PARK (*picnicking and other facilities*), at the east end of Fourth St., winds for 10 miles along Big Chico Creek, a narrow strip luxuriantly green with vines, oaks, and sycamores, which served as the Sherwood Forest of *The Adventures of Robin Hood,* filmed here in 1937. The HOOKER OAK, approached by South Drive, was named for the British botanist, Sir Joseph Hooker, who in 1877 adjudged it the world's largest oak tree; it has been estimated to be 1,000 years old, and rises 101 feet. From its massive trunk, 28 feet in circumference, giant branches spread over an area 147 feet in diameter.

At 42.5 *m.* is the junction with a paved road.

Left here to the UNITED STATES PLANT INTRODUCTION STATION, 2 *m.*, (159 alt.) a 240-acre farm where plants brought from many parts of the world are studied, acclimated and, if possible, developed into proved species for American soils.

The highway cuts through plum and almond orchards to the roadside hamlet of DURHAM, 47.7 *m.* (159 alt., 1,500 pop.). A tract of 6,300 acres here, purchased by the State, was subdivided in 1918 and sold to settlers, many of them war veterans, under supervision of the State Land Settlement Board.

NELSON, 54.4 *m.* (121 alt., 200 pop.), in the midst of a grain-growing area where the first wheat was planted in the early 1850's is named for Capt. A. D. Nelson, early wheat grower.

RICHVALE, 58.4 *m.* (121 alt., 100 pop.), has grown up in the heart of California's leading rice-growing region, where the U. S. Department of Agriculture established in 1908 a rice-experiment station that tested 275 varieties. In 1912, 1,000 acres about Richvale were planted. The rice thrived and spread throughout the region. The side-roads westward run through swampy fields covered with the rippling green of top-heavy rice plants. Low irrigation dikes weave through them in intricate patterns.

At 61.5 *m.* is the junction with a paved highway.

Left here to OROVILLE, 7.9 *m.* (205 alt., 3,698 pop.) (*see TOUR 6B*), at the junction with State 24 (*see TOUR 6B*).

Deep among peach trees is·LIVE OAK, 76.9 *m.* (74 alt., 800 pop.).

Right from Live Oak on a paved road to the base of SUTTER BUTTES, 7 *m.,* jutting up from the flat valley floor. Of the four jagged peaks, SOUTH BUTTE (2,132 alt.) is the highest. The buttes are the eroded remains of an ancient crater that formerly rose twice their present height. The Indians hereabouts were driven from their homelands by horse and cattle thieves who found hiding places in the buttes. Just before the Bear Flag Revolt, (*see TOUR 2A*) Capt. John C. Frémont and his expedition camped here.

The road continues around the base of the buttes.

YUBA CITY, 87.5 *m.* (50 alt., 3,605 pop.), seat of Sutter County, a pleasantly shaded town by the Yuba River, is the center of a vast peach-growing region. One tale relates that Yuba is a corruption of Uva (grape), the name given the river in 1824 by Spanish explorers who found its banks overgrown with wild grapes; another, that a branch of the Maidu tribe in the neighborhood was called the Yu-ba. Laid out in July 1849 by Samuel Brannan, Pierson B. Reading, and Henry Cheever, Yuba City stands on the site of an Indian village whose round earthen huts overlooked the river. Opposite the old-fashioned HALL OF RECORDS in its tree-shaded square, 229 B Street, a giant walnut tree planted about 1878, rises 100 feet, its branches spreading over a 104-foot area from a trunk 15½ feet in circumference at the 4-foot level.

Yuba City is at the junction with State 24 (*see TOUR 6B*).

US 99E crosses the Feather River to MARYSVILLE, 88.6 *m.* (61 alt., 5,763 pop.), seat of Yuba County, at the confluence of the Feather and the Yuba Rivers. Here in 1842 Theodore Cordua built a trading post that became a way station on the Oregon-California Trail. In the winter of 1848-49 Cordua sold out to men who opened a general store and laid out a townsite. Moving spirit behind the town's early growth was Stephen J. Field, later appointed by Lincoln to the United States Supreme Court, who arrived in 1849 and three days later was elected mayor, chiefly because he had bought 200 lots for $16,250. The night of his election the town was named Marysville for Mary Murphy Covillaud, a survivor of the Donner party and wife of one of the owners of the townsite. Field straightened out the legal tangle on the land ownership, drove off squatters and organized posses to clear out cattle thieves. Within two years Marysville was a town of 5,000, third largest in the State, with an iron foundry, a theater, a jail, two banks, and several churches. Stores, saloons, gambling houses, and hotels of lumber and canvas crowded around the plaza above the river, where barges and river boats tied up—for Marysville overnight became the head of Feather River navigation. Freight and passengers went on by wagon, pack train, saddle horse, or on foot to the Yuba and Feather River diggings; by 1854 twenty freighting companies were operating out of here, with 400 wagons and 4,000 mules.

Marysville is no longer a river town. Hydraulic mining changed the face of the countryside, burying farms and villages under débris, choking river bottoms with silt. Its bed raised 70 feet or more, the Yuba, on which Marysville looked down, is now above the city streets behind great earthen dikes, eight to 74 feet wide at the crown, constructed after 1875. A brisk little city of wide streets and shady parks, Marysville lives now on trade with the farmers and orchardists of this region where the Thompson seedless grape and the Phillip cling peach originated.

Reminders of the past are the many old brick buildings that line the tree-arched streets. The YUBA COUNTY COURTHOUSE, Sixth and D Sts., with three towers looming castlelike above brick walls, and the CITY HALL and fire house, Fourth between B and C Sts., were built in 1855-56. Three brick churches date back to the 1850's: the Episcopal, Fifth and E Sts., designed in Norman style; St. Joseph's Roman Catholic (1855), Seventh and C Sts.; and the Presbyterian (1860), Fifth and D Sts. The brick STEPHEN J. FIELD MANSION, 630 D St., was built by Marysville's first mayor. The RAMIREZ HOUSE, 220-222 Fifth St., former home of José M. Ramírez, built in the 1850's, is a rambling, vine-shrouded edifice with a first story of gray stone blocks and a second of wood, with outside stairways and Gothic windows.

US 99E crosses the wide, sandy bottoms of shallow, winding Yuba River and runs through peach orchards to the junction with a paved road, 90.4 m.

Left on this road is HAMMONTON, 9.8 m. (135 alt., 836 pop.), which sprang up in 1905 when the Yuba Consolidated Goldfields began dredging in the Yuba River bottoms; it was named for the company's W. P. Hammon, builder of the first successful dredge. As many as seven giant dredges, costing from $1,000,000 to $3,000,000 each, operated here in landlocked artificial basins, scooping up earth in front, washing out the gold, and moving on, trailed by piles of sand, rock, and gravel.

WHEATLAND, 101.6 m. (90 alt., 479 pop.), is a village of weather-beaten tree-shaded houses among hop fields. During the picking season, thousands of migratory workers camp on the fringes of the

Industry, Commerce and Transportation

MINERAL SODA WORKS, INDEPENDENCE

WARNER BROS. STUDIOS, BURBANK

CHINA CLIPPER PASSING SAN FRANCISCO

PLANES ON ASSEMBLY LINE, SANTA MONICA

UNLOADING STEEL FOR BAY BRIDGES, SAN FRANCISCO

MODERN STUDIO SET DURING FILMING

CATERPILLAR TRUCK WITH WHEELER

GRAPES INTO WINE

INSPECTING PEACHES AT CANNERY

OIL WELLS ALONG HUNTINGTON BEACH

OIL TANKS

fields, one of which employs as many as 4,000; the Wheatland hop pickers' "riot" of 1913 (*see THE LABOR MOVEMENT*), California's first important strike by field workers, grew out of their protest against miserable living conditions. William Johnson's ranch here, settled in 1844-5, was the first settlement reached by the Argonauts who crossed the Sierra over the Donner's Pass branch of the California trail; in the winter of 1846-47 seven of the Donner party came here to seek help for those still snowbound at Donner Lake (*see TOUR 9A*).

SHERIDAN, 104.9 *m.* (116 alt., 198 pop.), a desolate village of ramshackle frame houses in the midst of an unshaded plain, was first called Union Shed, because of a great shed built in 1857 to shelter freight teams from summer heat and winter rains.

LINCOLN, 112.8 *m.* (163 alt., 2,094 pop.), a trading point for a wide grain- and fruit-growing area, since the 1870's has made pottery. The smokestacks and many-windowed, iron-roofed buildings of the huge pottery and terra cotta works are near the western edge of town. Deposits of glass sand and a lignite coal mine have been discovered nearby.

Softly undulating land, patched with clumps of oaks, sweeps away from the highway as it continues to ROSEVILLE, 123.4 *m.* (6 alt., 6,425 pop.), which clusters about the extensive Southern Pacific shops and yards, its shady side streets of frame dwellings lined with olive, maple, and fig trees. Roseville ships plums, berries, almonds, and grapes chilled in its huge icing plants, in large quantities.

Roseville is at the junction with US 40 (*see TOUR 9A*).

Tour 3C

Greenfield—Taft—Maricopa—Ojai—Ventura; 121.5 *m.,* US 399
Route paralleled between Ojai and Ventura by Southern Pacific R.R.

Accommodations plentiful except in mountains.
Paved roadbed. Care should be taken in slide areas, particularly during and after rains.

US 399 crosses the flat, torrid floor of the San Joaquin Valley, leaving broad farming and grazing lands for a forest of oilwell derricks. Ascending the Coast Range, the highway twists for almost 70 miles through mountain heights and descends into peaceful Ojai Valley.

West of GREENFIELD, 0 *m.,* at a junction with US 99 (*see TOUR 3C*), is PANAMA, 3.2 *m.,* dependent on dairying.

US 399 follows a straight course through a land devoted to cattle raising. In the summer, it seems to dance in the shimmering heat waves.

At 17.3 *m.* is a junction with a dirt road.

Right on this dirt road to the STATE ZOOLOGICAL PARK, 3.1 *m.*, where herds of elk are occasionally seen grazing from beyond the boundaries.

Passing the Elk Hills (R), dotted with the derricks of the ELK HILLS NAVAL OIL RESERVE, US 399 enters barren Buena Vista Valley, 22.1 *m.* Southwest of the bleached Buena Vista Hills, 27.4 *m.*, is Midway Valley, black with oil derricks that rise above a land the hue of wood ashes. This valuable West Side Oil Field (also called the Midway Sunset Field), dating from 1899, was the homeland of what was probably the most poverty-stricken race on the North American continent. The wealth is far from exhausted, partly because the four companies—Standard, Union, Associated, and General Petroleum—by mutual agreement and their monopoly of pipe lines—control both the spacing of wells and the production rate of the other 200 producing companies in the field.

FORD CITY, 29.6 *m.* (1,000 alt., 2,900 pop.), has a bleak and treeless business street. Adding to the importance and size of the business section, is Standard Oil's CAMP 11C (1,200 pop.), lying west of the community. In the boom days of the field, Ford City was an unnamed tent city; its plethora of Model-T Fords led to the name.

TAFT, 30.3 *m.* (1,000 alt., 3,442 pop.), the metropolis of the West Side Oil Field, is bleakly typical of the oil fields. The town has three men to each woman among the inhabitants, a very busy Supply Row for field equipment, and a monthly population turnover of transient labor that frequently amounts to 25 per cent of the total population. Although most of Taft's 20 bars operate all night because of the three shifts in the fields, life is otherwise quiet. The town has several civic, social, and religious organizations, and in a region where early settlers purchased water by the quart, school facilities have recently been improved by a $50,000 plunge for children.

Only the early history of Taft is spectacular. In 1908 the Southern Pacific and Santa Fe decided to operate a joint line—the Sunset (now owned by the Southern Pacific)—to carry prospective investors to and from a settlement camp in the expanding field. When this camp burned down, a battle started between the Southern Pacific, which owned land north of the tracks, and J. S. Jameson, who owned land to the south. The Southern Pacific erected a town, Moron, and Jameson pushed a rival community, Jameson. At the height of the rivalry, when the outcome of the battle hung upon the location of a proposed post office, a fire obliged the Southern Pacific by destroying Jameson. Moron was chosen as the site of the post office, its name changed to honor President Taft. Later Taft was incorporated and rebuilt Jameson became South Taft.

US 399 follows Kern St. through the residential areas of SOUTH TAFT and TAFT HEIGHTS into an arid, derrick-sentineled countryside. Gradually, the highway rounds the outflanking Temblor Range.

MARICOPA, 38 *m.* (850 alt., 1,071 pop.), is another bleak and dreary product of the oil fields, a community of treeless streets and sun-baked houses.

US 399 ascends GROCER GRADE of the Temblor Range, where blanched desert land is replaced by the browns and blacks of mountain rock and the green of chaparral.

STUBBLEFIELD GULCH, 49 *m.,* widens into the oak-decked floor of Cuyama Valley, a green region of isolated farms. Cuyama River runs along the highway through the narrowing, southern section of the valley, between hills increasingly rugged.

A boundary of the SANTA BARBARA NATIONAL FOREST is crossed at 60.5 *m.* Only 80,000 of the 1,772,555 acres are strictly timberland; the reserve is primarily for protection of the watershed. Fishing and hunting in this unfrequented region are excellent. Streams here are kept well stocked with trout; deer, quail, wild pigeon, fox, and even mountain lion are among the game.

Continuing upward through slashed, oak-grown hills past CUY-AMA PEAK (5,880 alt.), US 399 loses the accompanying murmur of the Cuyama River and begins a steep and twisted ascent to Pine Mountain Crest, 75.8 *m.* (5,300 alt.). Visible (L) is REYES PEAK (7,488 alt.). Behind is a tumultuous terrain of rugged green hills; ahead, scarred country. The highway reaches a trough cut in the mountains by Sespe Creek and follows the course of the trout-stocked waters as its banks narrow and heighten. Oaks lean from precipitous gorge sides.

Crossing a last summit (3,700 alt.), 91.8 *m.,* the highway follows an erratic course, sweeping through the three WHEELER GORGE TUN-NELS, 100.8 *m.,* concrete-lined burrowings, through solid mountain sides.

The pleasant countryside is characterized by its many vacation resorts. Bridle trails mark the hillsides. Hot and cold mineral springs and plunges and rustic resort cabins are passed. MATILIJA CANYON, 104.1 *m.,* is abloom through the summer with the lovely matilija-poppies. These flowers, 4 and 5 inches in diameter, whose white petals and yellow centers appear to have been cut from crepe paper, blossom from bushes that reach heights of 5 and 6 feet.

Ojai Valley, 106.1 *m.,* 12 miles long and 3 miles wide, is a rolling, fertile land protected from inclemencies of weather by the Topatopa Mountains on the north and the Sulphur Mountains on the south. It is dotted with luxuriant oaks and sycamores and checkered with fruit orchards.

At 108.3 *m.* is a junction with a paved road.

Left on this road is OJAI, 1 *m.* (743 alt., 1,468 pop.), the residential heart of the valley. Originally, this affluent municipality was called Nordhoff in honor of Charles Nordhoff, whose column in the New York *Herald* in the 1870's and booster book aided the California real estate boom that created the town. (Charles Nordhoff is grandfather of the co-author of the *Bounty* series.) Although in 1888 two Yale men, S. D. and W. L. Thacher, established nearby an expensive preparatory school for the sons of the wealthy, Nordhoff remained primarily a rustic village until

1916. In that year, however, great changes occurred. E. D. Libbey, whose 500-acre estate and Spanish-style castle adjoined the village, persuaded the residents to remodel structures in Spanish style and to change the name of the community. The climate was advertised; resort hotels sprang up; retired men of means came here and took up ranching; ranchers took up culture; businessmen took up tourists; and architectural development was rapid.

The conductor, Leopold Stokowski, has a home here, as has J. Krishnamurti, Hindu poet and mystic. The valley population of about 3,500 is swelled during winter and spring months by an influx of tourists and vacationists. Culture is encouraged by art classes every Thursday evening, Sanskrit instruction every afternoon, and open forums maintained by the University of California. Supplementing these activities are those of numerous organizations—choral, histrionic, terpsichorean, orchestral, and others. The Rosicrucians and the adherents of the American Inner School (headquarters of the Theosophist Society) on Krotona Hill form one social group; the memberships of the Jack Boyd Club and the Ojai Valley Country Club form others. The Ojai Valley Tennis Club in the last week of April conducts a State-wide tennis tournament, during which even the schools are closed. So constant are Ojai activities that the city has earned the title, "a miniature Santa Barbara."

South of the Ojai junction, US 399 sweeps between ARBOLADA (R), the former Libbey estate—now a residential subdivision—and the OJAI VALLEY COUNTRY CLUB and GOLF COURSE (L), built with its prize-winning architectural design at an expense of $250,000 and given to the club by Mr. Libbey.

South of MIRROR LAKE (R), 110.4 m., a marshy abode of wild ducks, US 399 leaves Ojai Valley behind. Oak-covered hills again close in upon the highway and the accompanying Ventura River spread.

FRESNO CANYON, 115.8 m., permits a view of FOSTER PARK (L), a wooded mountain side improved by a great, outdoor, concrete AUDITORIUM, the gift of the region's wealthy citizens. South of the derricks of the VENTURA OIL FIELD, 118.8 m., the highway crosses the broadening Ventura River Valley to the junction with US 101 in VENTURA, 121.5 m. (see TOUR 2C).

Tour 4

Junction with State 24—Sierraville—Sierra City—Auburn—Placerville —Sonora—Mariposa; 301.8 m. State 49.

Roadbed narrow and unpaved between State 24 and Sierraville, sometimes impassable in winter; paved elsewhere.
Hotels in larger towns; camping grounds plentiful.

When James Wilson Marshall found a few flakes of gold on January 24, 1848, in the tailrace of a mill he was building on the American River, he started a mass movement into California. More than 100,000 gold seekers poured into El Dorado within the next two years in a feverish search for riches, half depopulating some eastern villages and causing a labor shortage. Some men made a comfortable stake but more were constantly on the move in an effort to find richer strikes—and in the end had nothing to show for their frantic activities. Even though they panned as much as $100 worth of gold a day for a time, they spent it all in gambling or for food, drink, and shelter, retailed at fantastic prices. Sooner or later perhaps half of the gold hunters went back to their eastern homes; some remained to hunt ceaselessly for the fabulous strike that was never made; others moved on to Nevada, Oregon, Idaho, Colorado, and other places where gold and silver were found in the next decades; and a considerable number settled down in California, speculating in land, founding towns, and establishing businesses of one kind and another. A few moved to high positions in the new State.

State 49 runs through the very heart of the California gold country —including the Mother Lode. Within a decade millions of dollars' worth of gold were taken out of the streams and hills, the bulk of it going to comparatively few men. In this brief span, during which mining camps mushroomed on every river bar and wandering prospectors swarmed the hills by the thousands, a civilization sprang up overnight, endured briefly, and fell in ruins—the full-blown but short-lived civilization of the wide-open, riproaring gold towns. After its decade of glory, as placer mines gave out and placer miners wandered away, the gold region lost its fine flush of feverish enthusiasm. Gone was the day of the roving prospector on muleback, whose stock in trade was a pick and a pan. To unlock the riches in the years that followed, tremendous labors were required and millions in capital. The giant mining companies with their vast and elaborate equipment, sank shafts deep to underlying quartz, built networks of tunnels, stamp mills to crush the ore, wing dams, and ditches, lifted rivers from their beds, and brought in hydraulic monitors that washed whole mountains away.

Along State 49 are strewn the relics of these labors and of the men who performed them; decaying shanties of the "pick and pan" men, abandoned hillside shafts of the quartz mines, high-piled débris of the hydraulic workings. Some of the gold rush towns have disappeared completely, others are mere heaps of rubbish. Even in his day Mark Twain could write of ghost towns: "You will find it hard to believe that here stood at one time a fiercely flourishing little city, of 2,000 or 3,000 souls, with its newspaper, fire company, brass band, volunteer militia, bank, hotels, noisy Fourth of July processions and speeches, gambling-halls crammed with tobacco smoke, profanity, and rough-bearded men of all nations and colors, with tables heaped with gold dust—streets crowded and rife with business—town lots worth $400 a front foot—labor, laughter, music, swearing, fighting, shooting, stabbing —a bloody inquest and a man for breakfast every morning—and now nothing but lifeless, homeless solitude. In no other land, in modern times, have towns so absolutely died and disappeared, as in the old mining regions of California."

A few towns, kept alive by continuing or sporadic operations, remain to delight those who take pleasure in pioneer relics. Three or four of them nurture their picturesque aspects for the benefit of visitors, even to the point of encouraging some "quaint character" who can grind out the tales to enchant the antiquarian. The surviving settlements are more or less alike. Each grew up along a road or a stream; hence few have even a single straight street. In each the building that has best weathered the years is usually the office of the Wells Fargo Company, which shipped out the gold; it had to be sturdy to survive attack from the considerable number of gold seekers who preferred others to do the backbreaking digging and panning for them. It also had to be reasonably fireproof because of the frequent fires resulting from the careless, rough and tumble life. In many towns some old stores remain because they, too, were strongly built; like the express offices they handled gold and were subject to attack by bandits, as well as by hilarious, devil-may-care celebrants. A characteristic of the buildings erected with the need of defense in mind is the iron shutters—heavy, full length iron doors that protected all openings, windows and entrances alike. These doors were usually brightly painted; the blues, reds, and greens are now faded pastels. Symbol of aristocracy is the "ancient" building constructed of lumber "brought round the Horn"—the number is smaller than local pride admits. These stand behind ailanthus and locust trees, sometimes in good condition. Another survivor in some places is the fraternal association hall; fittingly, the Independent Order of Odd Fellows was particularly strong in the gold country.

The region still yields gold; in the Mother Lode region alone 175 lode mines and 130 placer mines were active in 1937. Smoke began to rise from old stacks of hillside workings after the 1933 rise in the price of gold again made operations profitable. The 1930's also brought thousands of unemployed men flocking in to try their luck, as did the forty-niners fleeing the economic collapse of the 1840's. Along State 49, near the ruins of crude cabins built by the men who first panned the creeks are the shacks and tents of "snipers," who work the river gravels for what little gold they can find, which is rarely more than enough to keep them in coffee and beans. Even the more experienced miners average only $1.53 a day, and the creeks can be worked only for an average of 86 days a year.

Near State 49 between Auburn and Mariposa runs the Mother Lode itself, but the whole region covered by this route claims the name. Geologically, the Mother Lode is a long narrow strip in the Sierra foothills, a mile wide and 120 miles long. Great masses of quartz crop out at intervals, seamed and laced with gold—precious yellow metal inlaid in rock. Because of the more or less continuous deposits, there was a belief in the fifties that this was an unbroken ribbon, set with gold, like a chain of massive nuggets. The streams in the region and the ancient river beds were filled with auriferous gravel, the first gold taken by the early miners.

In the region pierced by this route young Bret Harte (*see LITER-*

ATURE) picked up the material that helped set the pattern for what Stanley Vestal has called "the histrionic West." Westerns—novels, magazines, and movies—maintain the sentimental tradition first accepted and given prestige by New England Brahmin literary patronage of such stories as *Outcasts of Poker Flat*.

Section a.   *JUNCTION WITH STATE 24 to EL DORADO;*
168.4 m.   State 49.

State 49 branches southwest from State 24 (*see TOUR 6B*), 0 *m.,* 1 mile west of Chilcoot, across the level mountain-hemmed Sierra Valley.

LOYALTON, 11.5 *m.* (4,949 alt., 837 pop.), named during the Civil War by mountaineers who were loyal Union men, is a lumbering center. An ordinance unusual in an early Western town forbade the sale of liquor within the "city limits," with the result that Loyalton became California's second largest city; its incorporators spread the town as widely as possible to discourage lumberjacks from walking beyond the city limits for a drink.

SIERRAVILLE, 24.5 *m.* (4,950 alt., 180 pop.), at the junction with State 89 (*see TOUR 5b*), a crossroads center where four stage lines once met, lies in the Sierra Valley, where farming began in 1853. In 1881 a fire swept and destroyed practically the entire business section, which, however, was soon rebuilt.

West of Sierraville on State 49 is SATTLEY, 28.5 *m.* (4,992 alt., 30 pop.), at the foot of the steep and winding climb over the mountain through YUBA PASS (6,700 alt.), through which winter storms occasionally sweep, marooning travelers as they did the Duchess and John Oakhurst in Bret Harte's tale of the outcasts.

At 42.5 *m.* is a junction with a dirt road.

> Right here into a rugged wilderness, where resorts and camps cluster along almost two score trout-stocked lakes fed by melting snows, to GOLD LAKE, 6.9 *m.* In 1850 one Stoddard led a group of miners here in search of a lake whose shores, he asserted, were covered with pure gold. When they found no nuggets lying about, the miners almost lynched Stoddard on the spot. The expedition, however, led to discovery of the rich Plumas County deposits. At LONG LAKE, 10.4 *m.,* is ELWELL PUBLIC CAMP, starting point for the climb to MOUNT ELWELL (7,846 alt.), which offers fine views of the mountains.

By the North Fork of the Yuba River lies SIERRA CITY, 46.8 *m.* (4,100 alt., 250 pop.), where in 1850 settlers panned the river gravel for gold. From the jagged SIERRA BUTTES (8,600 alt.), rising sheer above it, an avalanche roared down to destroy the first town of shacks and tents; but Sierra City lived to make its fortune from the buttes. Honeycombed with the tunnels of quartz mines by 1852, they yielded gold through the 1850's and 1860's. Among the richest claims was the Monumental Mine, where a 100-pound gold nugget valued at $25,000 was found August 18, 1860. Still producing is the Buttes

Mine, opened in 1850; others, such as the Young America, Colombo, and Gold Point, have taken a new lease on life since 1933.

But the distant clangor of the stamp mills fails to offset the ghostly air of the deserted buildings along the main street. At its head (L) stands an empty frame hotel, built of "resawn" lumber, with broken windowpanes and sagging beams. At the far end is another old hotel where old-timers tell their tales; and opposite it is a butcher shop with the sign: "Fresh Meat Tuesdays, Thursdays and Saturdays." In the FIRE HOUSE (R) is a two-wheeled cart, brought round the Horn in the 1850's.

An imposing structure (R) is the BUSCH BUILDING (1871), which has two stories of brick and a balcony and third story of wood. Over one of the doorways are the initials "E.C.V.," standing for "E. Clampus Vitus," the hilarious "Incomparable Confraternity" that swept through the mining country. It was organized in Pennsylvania in 1847 and transplanted to California before 1853. The organization was one of the biggest hoaxes of a country where hoaxes were the order of the day. The initiations were masterpieces of ingenious and humorous torture, and only those who survived them understood what E.C.V. stood for. So powerful was the sway of the mysterious brotherhood as developed by the miners that newcomers found they could not conduct business in mining towns until they had joined it. When Lord Sholto Douglas brought his theatrical group to Marysville, he found the first night audience too small to pay for the rent of the theater. Enlightened by a friendly miner, he applied for membership, and thereafter the miners flocked to his company's presentations.

State 49 runs westward along the North Fork of the Yuba River, where slopes rise abruptly, scarred by the streams of the hydraulic giants that tore away earth and gravel.

DOWNIEVILLE, 59.4 m. (3,000 alt., 640 pop.), seat of Sierra County, is in a little basin walled by sheer mountainsides. At the western end, State 49 runs through JERSEY FLAT, with cottages—some of them built in the 1860's—in bright gardens. Across the river is narrow, locust-bordered Main Street where on Saturday nights, when Downieville had a population of 5,000, rows of horses were tethered to the posts that held up the wooden awnings and men thronged the boardwalks lighted only by the rays of kerosene lamps shining through saloon windows. During the week, heavily loaded pack trains and lumbering stagecoaches choked the dusty street, while miners crowded the stores to buy grub at fabulous prices. The first Yankee woman to arrive in town was escorted through Main Street by most of the male citizens; Signora Elise Biscaccianti, famous pianist of her day, was carried in on men's shoulders, as was her piano.

In September 1849, Frank Anderson arrived, the first man to pan gravel here, and in November, Major William Downie and his motley band—a Kanaka by the name of Jim Crow, an Irishman, an Indian, and 10 Negro sailors. Downie found the river filmed with ice the first morning he went out to pan, but the gravel was so rich in gold that he put up crude cabins and set his men to sifting the snow-covered bars. When provisions began to run low, he sent nine of the men, including Jim Crow, with newly dug gold to buy food and supplies in the lower country. Only Jim Crow came back, and he not till spring, when he found Downie and his companions on the verge of starvation. A crowd of would-be miners followed the Kanaka back to The Forks. Camps sprang up on every bar and flat. At one of them, Tin Cup Diggings, each of three owners filled a tin cup with gold dust every day. There is a story that Jim Crow, boiling a 14-pound salmon, found flakes of gold at the bottom of the pot. Gold continued to turn up in surprising places. A woman who kept a tent restaurant, sweeping her dirt floor one day, saw yellow particles and investigated, then folded her tent, for it was pitched over a gold mine. On Durgan's Flat, across the river, $80,000 worth of gold was taken out during the first half of 1850; in 11 days Frank Anderson and three companions took $12,900 worth from a claim 60 feet square. Still enough remained to make it worthwhile for the Chinese, who came in later years, patiently to lift the heavy stones by hand, clearing out the bed of the North Yuba.

The SIERRA COUNTY COURTHOUSE was erected in 1855 on Durgan's Flat; it has 12-paned windows, lofty ceilings, and an old-time courtroom. In its yard is an arrastre, or mill wheel, used by pioneers to crush gold quartz. Behind it, at the base of PIETY HILL (nearly every mining town had its Piety Hill) is the GALLOWS that served for executions after 1857. The wooden building (1864) in front of the courthouse houses the Downieville *Mountain Messenger,* whose first issue (1853) came off the old Washington hand press now in the basement. Where Downieville's movie house stands today was the theater in which Edwin Booth, Lola Montez, Lotta Crabtree, and other famous troopers played to entertainment-starved audiences who showered them with coins and gold dust pokes worth more than a king's gift after a command performance. Relics of the days when gold dust served for currency are preserved in the MEROUX MUSEUM (*open Sun. and holidays; keys with storekeeper weekdays*) on Main St., typical of the earliest substantial mining camp construction, with walls of flat stones laid horizontally. In the COSTA STORE (L), on Main St., built in 1853 of uncemented shale with walls 4 feet thick at the base and 27 inches at the top, are glass-enclosed scales that still weigh gold dust and nuggets. During the summer the store buys from $50 to $60 worth a day from "snipers." Under the overhanging roof of the ST. CHARLES HOTEL (L), are benches and chairs polished smooth by countless pairs of blue jeans. Except for a row of locust trees in the front of it, the St. Charles, with a balcony running the length of the upper story, looks much as it did when James McNulty built it in 1853.

Superb mountain peaks look down on old GOODYEAR'S BAR, 63.3 *m.,* where the tumbling, ice-cold waters of Goodyear's Creek join the North Yuba. Miles and Andrew Goodyear arrived here in the summer of 1849 and built the solidest cabin in the region. Miles Goodyear had come west in 1836 as a stripling in the little missionary party led by Dr. Marcus Whitman on his way to establish a mission along the Columbia River; when the missionary stubbornly insisted on taking a wagon through from Fort Hall, young Goodyear issued his ultimatum. If the cart went on, he would leave. The cart continued, and Goodyear went off into the wilderness alone. In time he took an Indian wife and started farming near the Great Salt Lake—the first white settler in the region. When the Mormons arrived in 1847, Miles cleared out for another wilderness in California. When he died in the fall of 1849 his brother buried him in a gold rocker until he could take the bones down to Benicia.

Lively camps sprang up nearby: Ranse Doddler, Hoodoo, St. Joe's and Cutthroat Bars, Nigger Slide, and Kennedy's Ranch. During the early 1850's the North Yuba was diverted from its channel so that gold in the bedrock could be taken out; and each summer, after winter floods had washed out the makeshift dams of the preceding season, the tremendous labor of rebuilding them was repeated.

At this point is a junction with an improved mountain road.

Left on this road, which follows the route of the stage road built from Marysville in the early 1860's, to the present-day GOODYEAR'S BAR, 0.2 m. (3,200 alt., 60 pop.), a handful of scattered houses. Through pine and cedar, the road climbs to MOUNTAIN HOUSE, 5.9 m. (5,641 alt.), where a splendid panorama of wooded mountains and deeply chiseled canyons, with glimpses of the river far below, opens out northward. The inn that stood here was a stopping place as early as 1850, when 2,500 mules carried supplies in pack trains over narrow and precipitous trails to Downieville.

At FOREST CITY, 8.7 m. (4,500 alt., 343 pop.), high-gabled houses cling to the walls of the ravine up which climbs the main street. Here in the summer of 1852, a company of sailors found gold. Brownsville they called the thriving town that grew up, but the name was not good enough. Some favored the poetic Yomana, Indian name for a nearby bluff; others, the more practical Forks of Oregon Creek. The final decision was to name the town for the first woman to reside there; but it was neither the first, nor yet the second, who appropriated the honors, but the third, Mrs. Forest Mooney, aggressive feminine journalist.

On a series of terraces connected by winding streets perches ALLE-GHANY, 12 m. (4,500 alt., 519 pop.), where all the citizens depend on gold mining for a living. Gold was discovered on the creek below in May, 1850, by one of several parties of Hawaiians (Kanakas sent out by a certain Captain Ross, reputed son of King Kamehameha). At the lower end of Alleghany is the BRADBURY HOUSE, where lived Thomas J. Bradbury. Working the nearby Sixteen-to-One Mine, which he discovered in 1908, he found 20 years later that the neighboring Tightner Mine was tapping the same vein, which had its apex in his own backyard. The two mines, together with the nearby Twenty-one, were consolidated as the Original Sixteen-to-One Mine, which still produces.

State 49 winds along the North Yuba, where tributary creeks spill down precipitous ravines. Ahead the way leads up GOLD RIDGE, whose slopes are luxuriantly green with yellow pine, fir, oak, and madrone. A lone cemetery, all but obliterated by the returning forest, a desolate cabin, or an ancient apple tree, mark the sites of once thriving gold camps: Galena, Young's, Railroad, Depot, and Hell's Hills,

Celestial and Oak Valleys, Dad's Gulch, Indian Springs, and Pike City.

At DEPOT HILL, 76.1 *m.,* is the JOUBERT HYDRAULIC MINE (L), which has produced $1,850,000 in its 82 years of continuous operation by one family and still operates during the rainy season. A gashed hill, a metal pipe line, and hydraulic monitor (or long nozzle), long sluice boxes, a muddy stream red with detritus from the mine are the signs of its activities.

At 81 *m.* is a junction with a mountain road.

> Left on this road, which runs between picket fences enclosing weather-worn clapboarded houses, to CAMPTONVILLE, 0.3 *m.* (2,900 alt., 75 pop.), a hamlet whose spreading elms and old-fashioned flower gardens emphasize its Yankee origin. Though the town was moved twice to make way for hydraulic operations and several times almost destroyed by fire, the old houses behind picket fences on the outskirts escaped its vicissitudes; most of the other buildings were restored along the old lines after the fire of 1907. At the western end of town stands the PELTON MONUMENT (R), with a model of the Pelton Water Wheel surmounting a pedestal; Lester A. Pelton's invention of the wheel here in 1878 was an important step in the development of hydroelectric power.

At 82.6 *m.* on State 49 is a junction with an improved road.

> Right here to BULLARD'S BAR DAM, 7.6 *m.* (1,500 alt.), which impounds the North Yuba's waters to operate generators in the power-house at its base. The bar was named for a Dr. Bullard, who wandered into town after a shipwreck off the California coast on his way from Brooklyn to the Sandwich Islands. Nothing but names remain as memorials of nearby camps: Foster's Ferry, Stoney, Rock Island, Succor, Slate Range, Cut-eye Foster's, Kanaka, Winslow, Negro, Missouri, Condemned, Frenchmen's, and others.

NORTH SAN JUAN, 90.6 *m.* (1,900 alt., 135 pop.), in spite of its name, was as much a Yankee settlement as any other town along the Mother Lode. The most likely explanation of the Spanish name is that Christian Kientz, a Mexican War veteran, saw a resemblance to San Juan de Ulloa in Mexico in the hill (L) where he discovered gold in 1853, and named it accordingly. A population of 10,000 gathered here when the town was headquarters for the rich hydraulic workings on San Juan Ridge. Here was the main office of the first long distance telephone line in the West, strung up in 1878 for 60 miles, between Milton and French Corral, to connect the hydraulic mining centers.

Along Main Street, bordered with poplars, walnut trees, and locusts, stand decaying, red brick business houses and frame buildings with shake roofs. The two-story brick ODD FELLOWS HALL (L) was dedicated in 1860. In the old frame NATIONAL HOTEL (R), silk-hatted mining company officials from San Francisco discussed gold production with superintendents of the nearby hydraulic mines. Next door (R) is the TOWN HALL, with arched doorway, massive iron doors and shutters, and fine cornice work; from its second-story iron balcony, the town band used to give concerts. An old brick store (L), operating now with electric refrigerators and cash registers, preserves the primitive register in which steel balls, placed in the groove corresponding to the amount of purchase, rolled down, rang a bell, and caused a marker to spring up.

At 93.1 *m.* is the junction with a graveled road.

Right here to FRENCH CORRAL, 4.5 *m.* (1,700 alt., 138 pop.), where a Frenchman built a corral for his mules in 1849; it is the oldest town in San Juan Ridge. The school house (L) was a hotel in the 1850's. Behind the solid brick walls and iron doors and shutters of the WELLS FARGO EXPRESS OFFICE (R) millions in gold were guarded. The MILTON MINING AND WATER COMPANY OFFICE, now a grocery store, was the lower terminus of the Ridge telephone line. One of the Edison instruments, made in Boston in 1876, is preserved here.

At 94.2 *m.* is a junction with a mountain road.

Left here up SAN JUAN RIDGE, where the rich quartz veins of the mountain peaks, during an age long process of erosion, were washed into a preglacial river bed, which geologic upheavals lifted high and dry above today's drainage system. Nowhere in California was hydraulic mining undertaken on so vast and spectacular a scale as here. The network of flumes and canals, more than 300 miles in length, cost not less than $5,000,000. The ridge is almost deserted today. The Sawyer Decision of Jan. 23, 1884, following passage of the Federal Anti-Debris Act the year before, closed all the hydraulic mines in the State, ending a long and bitter warfare by farmers of the valley lowlands against the inundation of their fields by the thousands of tons of silt the rivers carried down from the mines.

TYLER, 5.6 *m.* (2,550 alt.), called Cherokee in the 1850's, has a handful of weathered houses, a church, a school house, and the inevitable "diggin's."

At NORTH COLUMBIA, 9.1 *m.* (3,000 alt., 156 pop.), many of the old homes are still occupied, although the superintendent's office across the mining ditch, the pretentious Eureka Lake and Yuba Canal Company office building, the machine shop where gold was once retorted, and the blacksmith shop, have long been deserted.

A picture of decay is LAKE CITY, 12.5 *m.* (3,300 alt.), where two or three decrepit houses and a forlorn hotel (1855), its balcony sagging drunkenly, huddle by the grassy depression in the pasture which was once the "lake."

Neat gardens still bloom at the doors of the old homes in NORTH BLOOMFIELD, 15.5 *m.* (3,200 alt., 90 pop.), along the broad, locust-lined main street. In the MALAKOFF MINE OFFICE gold was reduced to bars for transportation to the San Francisco Mint. The largest single bar weighed a quarter of a ton and was valued at $114,000. At the edge of town (L) rise the exquisitely molded pinnacles and minarets, "touched with vivid colors like a place enchanted," of the MALAKOFF MINE, most colossal hydraulic excavation on San Juan Ridge.

The name of SNOW TENT, 19.5 *m.* (4,250 alt.), recalls some canvas station—snow-bound in winter—along the old stage route.

Mail is brought into GRANITEVILLE, 28 *m.* (4,900 alt., 150 pop.), by sleigh or on snowshoes in winter. Some deep quartz mines are still worked here.

At BOWMAN LAKE, 34.4 *m.* (5,500 alt.), a massive dam of granite, part of the Nevada Irrigation District system, stands today where a dam was first built in 1868 and twice razed, in 1872 and 1876.

NEVADA (Sp., snowy) CITY, 106 *m.* (2,450 alt., 1,701 pop.), seat of Nevada County, has always drawn its wealth from gold mines

—the rich placer diggings of the 1850's and 1860's, the hydraulic excavations of the 1870's, and the deep quartz mines of today. James W. Marshall, the man who started the gold rush with his chance discovery at Coloma, found gold at Deer Creek in the summer of 1848 but moved on, searching for richer fields. Within two years 10,000 miners were working every foot of ground within a radius of three miles. Near the rich gravel beds of the LOST HILL section (L), uncovered early in 1850, a mushroom town, Coyoteville, sprang up, named for the coyote or tunnel method of mining; during the two years it lasted, the gravel banks are said to have yielded $8,000,000 in gold dust and nuggets. Forerunner of Nevada City was Beer Creek Diggings or Caldwell's Upper Store—so called for a log cabin store kept by Dr. A. B. Caldwell.

On the main thoroughfare, Broad Street, a prominent land mark is the three-story NATIONAL HOTEL (R), an important stopping place in the 1860's and 1870's, when five or six stagecoaches daily lumbered down the street, to stop with a jolt in front of it. Inside, at the long bar over which $1,000 is said to have passed every day, travelers washed the dust out of their throats with a Pisco punch made from Peruvian brandy, a bonanza cocktail, or the miner's standby, Bourbon whisky. On Commercial Street, the UNION HOTEL (R) stands on a site occupied continuously by a hostelry ever since the spring of 1850, when Madam Penn built the first boarding house in town; this industrious lady often took her turn at the gold rocker in the ravine beyond Coyote Street where the Stampses, first family in town, settled in October 1849. The ASSAYER'S OFFICE (R), with its original furniture and iron safe, is run by the son of the original owner. Although $27,-000,000 in gold is said to have passed through the office, it was never held up or robbed. Here the first samples of ore from the Comstock Lode in Nevada were assayed in 1858.

State 49 strikes southward through green meadows and gardens and over gentle hills. In the meadows where GRASS VALLEY, 110.3 m. (2,400 alt., 3,817 pop.), was to spring up, an immigrant party of 1849 found their half-starved cattle, which had strayed from camp on the heights, feasting on the green grass. In August 1849 a band of 20 men, led by a Dr. Saunders, built and wintered in the first cabin on BADGER HILL (L), where homes and gardens spread today. The rich quartz mines which were to make Grass Valley one of the outstanding gold towns were not tapped until 1850. On pine- and fir-clad GOLD HILL, at the eastern outskirts of town (R), stands the KNIGHT MONUMENT, commemorating the first discovery of gold-bearing quartz in California. George Knight's find of 1850 initiated an industry that still produces wealth long after the depletion of the placers and the close of hydraulic operations. Between 1850 and 1857 the GOLD HILL MINE alone produced $4,000,000. The EMPIRE MINE on Ophir Hill, opened in 1850, and the NORTH STAR MINE on Lafayette Hill, opened in 1851, have yielded $80,000,000 worth of gold. Others still in operation are the GOLDEN CENTER and the

IDAHO-MARYLAND, opened in 1863. An immense outlay of capital and labor is represented in the stamp mills, cyanide tanks, and shafts. The quartz veins, one nearly two miles long, are honeycombed with mine workings. The Empire mine is worked to the 7,000 level, 3,620 feet wholly below the shaft collar at 928 feet below sea level. The deepest mine in the district is the North Star, where the 9,800 feet level is 1,600 feet below sea level.

Grass Valley's wide, paved Main Street with its sidewalks, filling stations, and neon signs, has a modern prosperous air. But wooden awnings over the sidewalks remain, and the old buildings, some with new fronts, retain unchanged interiors. More redolent of old times are the side streets, where the homes of two famous early day residents stand. At the corner of Mill and Walsh Sts. is the HOME OF LOLA MONTEZ, to which the famous beauty, who was born María Dolores Porris Gilbert and lived to become Countess of Lansfeld, returned from her triumphs in Europe and America. Here she lived in retirement from 1852 to 1854, with a pet bear, some dogs, and a husband. The husband she later divorced because he killed her bear when it clawed and bit him. The beautiful and daring Lola brought with her a reputation that made her the talk of two continents, fame for public performances of the Spider Dance, and friendships with the great. In her modest cottage—since altered by the addition of a second story— she entertained at soirees, held mainly for the benefit of the younger miners, that became the talk of the Mother Lode.

Nearby is the childhood HOME OF LOTTA CRABTREE (*see THE THEATER*), Lola's protégée. Here, in the two-story house at 220 Mill St., where her mother boarded miners, Lotta met La Montez. The days she spent with the glamorous Lola, learning dance steps, and ballads and riding horseback through the woods, turned her into a dancer and actress. Beginning her career as a child entertainer, she traveled from camp to camp with her mother. At the age of 16 she scored a triumph in San Francisco, and, traveling to the Atlantic Coast, repeated it.

Right from Grass Valley on State 20 to ROUGH AND READY, 4.4 *m.* (1,900 alt., 145 pop.). Here gold was discovered by a group of Wisconsin men who arrived in September, 1849, in a dozen covered wagons that bore the name of the town-to-be painted on their canvas sides. The leader of the group was Captain Townsend, who had served under Gen. Zachary Taylor, old "Rough and Ready" of Mexican War fame. Popular legend says it was the distaste of the Wisconsin men for newcomers from New England that prompted them, at a mass meeting called by E. F. Brundage in 1850, to organize the independent State of Rough and Ready, adopt a constitution, and announce their secession from the Union; thus they would have more freedom to deal with New Englanders as they felt they should be dealt with. A more likely explanation, however, is their rebellious objection to the Federal taxes on miners. Today the Rough and Ready diggin's are half hidden by chaparral; up to the edge of town, where aged apple trees shade weather beaten houses, stretches a green meadow. The white painted frame ROUGH AND READY HOTEL (L), part of which dates from 1853, is now the store and post office.

AUBURN, 134.6 *m.* (1,360 alt., 2,661 pop.), spills over hill and hollow, encircled by orchard-covered knolls. Its winding streets, where old-fashioned white houses sit back among maples and walnuts, are dappled with a leafy lacework of sun and shadow. Long before the orchards were planted, this was a mining camp, for Claude Chana and his Indians mined gold here in May 1848. First called Wood's Dry Diggings, the camp was renamed a year later by miners who had come from Auburn, N. Y., with Stevenson's Volunteer Regiment. Prospectors poured in during 1849, until a network of trails radiated to camps in the hills and ravines; these became turnpikes choked with stagecoaches, mule teams, and freight wagons, where highwaymen often lay in wait for hold-ups. The gold gave out, but Auburn's decline was circumvented by the advent of the railroad in 1865, and by the planting, in the 1880's and 1890's, of the foothill orchards. The flavor of gold days lingers in Old Town, which lies in a hollow at the head of Auburn Ravine, overlooked by the arcaded dome of the handsome, tan brick PLACER COUNTY COURTHOUSE. Here narrow streets twist uphill under wide-branching trees, past crumbling brick buildings with sagging iron doors and shutters and over-hanging balconies. Still open for business are the I. O. O. F. HALL and the PLACER COUNTY BANK. The Auburn *Herald* has been published continuously since 1852.

At Auburn is a junction with US 40 (*see TOUR 9a*).

South of Auburn the rolling countryside gives way to deep-cut gorges twisting between mountain ridges. The highway, wide and well-paved, twists in and out through rough countryside conveying some idea of the hardships its early prospectors endured.

At 138 *m.* is a junction with an improved road.

Left here, over the route of the old turnpike up FOREST HILL DIVIDE, over which in the 1850's a constant stream of traffic poured. An arrow on a marker at 3.5 *m.* points to LIME ROCK (R) across the canyon of the North Fork, where a woman confederate used to signal to highwaymen lying in wait for approaching stages.

At intervals are the sites of the early stage stations: GRIZZLY BEAR HOUSE, 4.5 *m.* (1,600 alt.), BUTCHER'S RANCH, 6.5 *m.*, SHERIDAN'S, 7 *m.*, MILE HILL TOLL HOUSE, 9.3 *m.*, and SPRING GARDEN, 11.2 *m.* (2,400 alt.), where fresh vegetables were served as a luxury.

FOREST HILL, 18.5 *m.* (3,200 alt., 200 pop.), is in one of the State's most productive cement tunnel-mining districts. The FOREST HOUSE (L), which replaced the first store, a brush shanty of 1850, and two brick stores with iron doors and shutters of the gold-rush period, still serve men from the mines. Into the mountain to depths of from 200 to 5,000 feet penetrate the shafts of big mines, among them the Dardanelles, the Rough and Ready, and the Jenny Lind.

Left from Forest Hill 3 *m.* to YANKEE JIM'S (2,650 alt., 16 pop.), where only a cluster of cottages and the acres laid waste by hydraulic mining remain as evidence of the days when this was the trading center for camps in the neighboring canyons. Just north is SHIRT TAIL CAN-YON, which acquired its name in the summer of 1849, when a miner was discovered busily panning the stream clad in nothing but his shirt. Tributary to Shirt Tail are other canyons, cutting across the rough highland country that might have become Donner County, if a movement of 1869 had succeeded. The proposed new county would have included such settlements as Ground Hog's Glory, Hell's Delight, Miller's Defeat, Ladies' Canyon, Devil's Basin, Hell's Half-acre, and Bogus Thunder.

On the main side road is MICHIGAN BLUFF, 25.6 *m.* (3,500 alt., 39 pop.), on the brink of a ridge 2,000 feet above the Middle Fork of the American River. Here Leland Stanford, who became one of the "Big Four" of railroad fame, kept a store from 1853 to 1855. Most of the frame and brick buildings that lined the locust- and poplar-bordered street are ruins.

Crossing the North Fork of the American River at LYON'S BRIDGE (650 alt.), State 49 winds nearly 1,000 feet up the east side of the canyon to the diminutive settlement of COOL, 141.8 *m.* (1,525 alt., 10 pop.).

> Left from Cool on an improved road is GREENWOOD, 7.5 *m.* (1,650 alt., 385 pop.), where the Greenwoods, a father and two sons, found gold and built their cabin in the spring of 1848. Discovering that hunting was more profitable than mining, they gave up their claims to supply prospectors with venison.
>
> On Oregon Creek, where a group of Oregonians discovered gold in 1849, is GEORGETOWN, 13 *m.* (2,275 alt., 679 pop.), at the northern end of the true Mother Lode. Growlersburg, it was called in 1850, when George Phipps led a company of sailors in; in honor of him the present title was adopted two years later. In its prime Georgetown was the trading center of 10,000 miners from almost a hundred camps, among them Mamaluke Hill, Sailors' Slide, Divine Gulch, Spanish Dry Diggings, and Volcanoville. The main street, with locust trees, uneven boardwalks, stone and brick buildings—built soon after a fire in 1856—remains much as it was.

A monument to Alexander Bayley's blasted dreams is the BAYLEY HOUSE (R), 145 *m.,* built as an inn. Bayley lavished $20,000 on this three-story brick mansion with its Colonial porticoes and terraced garden. He opened the house with a grand ball on May 15, 1862. Today it stands a wilderness because Bayley guessed wrong; he thought the overland railroad would be carried through here.

In COLOMA, 155 *m.* (850 alt., 85 pop.), at a spot by the river that the Indians called Culloomah, is a monument of stones (L) marking the SITE OF SUTTER'S SAWMILL (*see SACRAMENTO*), where on Jan. 24, 1848, James W. Marshall, while shutting off the water, happened to notice flakes of gold. Marshall's discovery was not the first in California—six years earlier gold deposits had been found and worked in Placerita Canyon near Los Angeles—but his was the discovery that spread the gold lust over the world. From every town and rancho in California men swarmed in until by summer almost every foot of ground had been staked out. With the influx of fresh thousands from the East, the gold hunters began to push out north and south.

Marshall's discovery won him little but hard luck. When he took his samples of gold to Sacramento to be tested, he was laughed at. It remained for another man, Sam Brannan, a San Francisco publisher, to tell the world, and for yet others to claim the profits. They swarmed in to prospect Marshall's claims and posted armed guards to keep him off them. When he appealed to the courts, friends of the trespassers sat as judge and jury; even his attorneys sold him out and joined the opposition. For ten years Marshall was spied upon, threatened, swindled—and all this time hated so violently that he could scarcely earn a living. Turning to the lecture platform, he spread his story throughout the country; but by the time he returned to California, twenty years after his discovery, it was too late. Larger interests had consolidated all the richer veins of gold, and California justice was confirming them in the ownership of lands, forests, and mines squeezed from the early settlers. In 1872 public opinion forced from the Legislature an appropriation of $200 a month for two years for Marshall, but at the next session this was cut in half. Marshall died in abject poverty on Aug. 10, 1885, and was buried within sight of the spot where he made his find.

Little is left today of the Coloma the forty-niners knew—only a few houses, fallen stone walls, and the ever present locust trees. Half hidden by matted vines and Chinese heaven trees are the CHINA STORE and the JAIL (R), both built of stone and both guarded by iron doors and shutters.

Right from Coloma on a road that leads uphill to the MARSHALL MONU-MENT, 0.5 m., a State park of 18 acres. The bronze MARSHALL STATUE, high on a granite pedestal, was erected by the Native Sons of the Golden West in 1890 over Marshall's grave. The MARSHALL CABIN, where he lived from 1848 to 1868, has been restored.

South of Coloma, State 49 passes through fruit orchards. So scarce was fruit in the early 1850's that $800 was once bid for one small plot containing four apple trees. The lack of fruit, green vegetables, and fresh meat in the miners' diet often threatened them with scurvy. Only their strenuous physical work enabled them to digest their steady fare of beans, sowbelly (salt pork), doughy saleratus bread—or sometimes, by way of variety, flapjacks—and coffee brewed from beans crushed in a sack between two stones and used over and over again. Real bread sold for a dollar a slice in hotels, and butter for one slice cost a dollar extra. Potatoes, when they first appeared in the camps, sometimes brought a dollar apiece. Only after 1855, when men began to bring their wives to the camps, did greens become plentiful, for the women planted small kitchen gardens.

PLACERVILLE, 163.3 m. (1,848 alt., 2,322 pop.), seat of El Dorado County, was born when men who found the land about Coloma well occupied plodded on to virgin territory. In July 1848, after a tour of the new mines in the Sierra Nevada foothills, Gov. Richard B. Mason reported to Washington, D. C., that William Daylor and Perry McCoon, ranchers from the Sacramento Valley, with their Indian retainers, had struck it rich at a place called "Old Dry Diggin's"; they had taken $17,000 from one small ravine in a week's time. Soon thousands were swarming up and down the gulches around what became known as the Ravine City. The lure of easy wealth brought not only miners but a small army of plundering outlaws known as the Owls.

One night three of them held up a Frenchman named Cailloux at the point of a knife, ransacked his cabin, and stole 50 ounces of gold dust. Captured the next morning, the three culprits were speedily tried and hanged from the great oak, known thereafter as the hang tree, which stood at the corner of Main and Coloma Sts. Punishment for later malefactors was as swift. The street became the alcalde's courtroom, and the crowd the jury for such men as "Irish Dick" Crone, Bill Brown, and others who were summarily hanged. Thus Hangtown acquired the name by which it has been known (unofficially) ever since.

From the first a strategic point on the overland trail and the Coloma Road, Placerville had boomed into a town of 2,000 people by 1850. By 1854 it was a serious contender with San Francisco and Sacramento in wealth and population, surpassed by them only in number of votes. Disastrous fires that swept most of the town—three times in 1856 and again in 1864 and 1865—were only temporary setbacks; its importance as a stopping place on a transcontinental route assured its prosperity. Through Placerville passed the Overland Mail, the Pony Express, and the overland telegraph. When the rush to the Comstock Lode in Nevada broke, Placerville became the chief station on the way from the west. Through it poured a stream of ponderous wagons drawn by six-mule teams, bearing merchandise and provisions to the Washoe mines. During these turbulent days men who were later to become industrial giants began their careers here: Mark Hopkins, later a railroad magnate, who set up shop on the muddy main street with a wagonload of groceries from Sacramento; Philip D. Armour of meatpacking fame, who ran a small butcher shop in the center of town; and John Studebaker, who laid the foundation for a great automobile industry by his success in building miners' wheelbarrows.

Along the winding banks of rock-lined Hangtown Creek, where the first comers settled, twists Placerville's Main Street from which scores of narrow lanes and crooked side streets lead up the ravines and hillsides past neat clapboarded cottages in tangled old gardens. Now a hotel is the IVY HOUSE (L), a rambling three-story brick edifice with wide two-story verandas; it housed the Placerville Academy from 1861 to the 1890's. Also of brick and ivy clad is the METHODIST CHURCH, on a corner of Main St. and Cedar Ravine, dedicated Sept. 8, 1861, during the pastorate of Adam Bland. At the lower end of Main St. is the OLD HANGTOWN BELL, which hung for years in the Plaza, where it was rung to summon the vigilantes or sound fire alarms. At ST. PATRICK'S CHURCH (L), near the edge of town, an old silver bell, the gift of the miners, still calls the faithful to worship; built in 1865, the church stands on the site of the frame structure built in 1852.

Placerville is at a junction with US 50 (see TOUR 10a), with which it unites southward to El Dorado.

South of Placerville, State 49 heads into variegated country, climbing up steep slopes, coasting along high ridges where rivers hundreds of feet below churn over sands once rich in gold and shoots down into valleys.   In places it winds through rolling hills, green in spring, burned almost white by the sun in summer.

By WEBER'S CREEK, 165.2 *m.* (1,550 alt.), is the SITE OF WEBERVILLE, where in 1848 Capt. Charles M. Weber, founder of Stockton, mined with the help of the Indian chief, José Jesús, and his twenty-five retainers.   Setting up his store at this spot, Weber exchanged beads and cloth for the gold brought by the Indians, who found they were on the losing end of the bargain only after he had built up a respectable fortune.

DIAMOND SPRINGS, 176.3 *m.* (1,791 alt., 860 pop.), now a supply center for lumbering interests, was in 1849 a camp on the Carson Pass Emigrant Trail and remained so until the placer and quartz mines in the outlying hills had been worked out.   One of the many sandstone buildings that lined the main street is the GOLDEN WEST HOTEL (L), recently gutted by fire, which dates from 1856.   At about the same time, the lumber for the CALIFORNIA HOTEL (L) was brought round the Horn.

EL DORADO (Sp., the golden), 168.4 *m.* (1,610 alt., 417 pop.), began life with the less romantic name of Mud Springs, inspired by the nearby watering place, which the cattle of immigrants had trampled into a boggy quagmire.   The frame HILL HOTEL (R), built in 1852, still holds together, but the UNION CHURCH on the hill (L) is only a restored version of the structure of 1853.   The roofless shells and rusted iron shutters of three old business buildings, stand (L), overgrown by ailanthus trees.

At El Dorado is the western junction with US 50 (*see TOUR 10a*).

Section b.   EL DORADO to MARIPOSA; 133.4 m. State 49.

South of EL DORADO, 0 *m.,* State 49 continues through the Mother Lode country.

On the SITE OF LOGTOWN, 2.5 *m.,* once a humming camp, are the ruins of a stamp mill, where quartz was crushed to extract the gold. At 7.3 *m.* is the MONTEZUMA MINE, from which probably about $1,000,000 in gold was taken.

Between El Dorado and HUSE BRIDGE over the Cosumnes River, 10.1 *m.,* once stretched a continuous line of stamp mills.   Exploring miners went on digging up every foot of ground for gold, until not one of the buildings was left standing.

PLYMOUTH, 14.6 *m.* (900 alt., 343 pop.), amid rolling oak-dotted fields, preserves little evidence of its former wealth.   The PLYMOUTH CONSOLIDATED includes all the deep mines in this country, which produced about $15,000,000 worth of gold.

Left from Plymouth on an improved road to FIDDLETOWN, 6.4 *m.* (1,700 alt., 250 pop.), settled by Missourians in 1849.   "They are always fiddling.   Call it Fiddletown," said one Missouri patriarch; and so the name, which Bret Harte memorialized in *An Episode of Fiddletown,* was chosen.   A certain Judge Purinton, whose home, the PURINTON HOUSE, is a local landmark, was so embarrassed at being known as "the man from Fiddletown" in the business circles of Sacramento and San Francisco, that he had the name changed to Oleta in 1878. In later years, however, the pride of the townspeople in the original name revived and it has been officially restored.

On Dry Creek is DRYTOWN, 18.1 *m.* (700 alt., 150 pop.), which, far from being dry, had 26 saloons in its day. In the surrounding gulches—Blood, Murderer's, and Rattlesnake—as much as $100 was sometimes washed out of a single pan. Some of the inhabitants were as wild and woolly as the names of the gulches indicate. The recent re-opening of some of the quartz mines—the AMADOR MOTHER LODE and the FREMONT—keeps 80 to 90 men employed. Closed since 1926, the EXCHANGE HOTEL (R), with its old pump and watering trough, is plastered with posters advertising chewing tobacco, circuses, and an Italian fiesta. The restored TOWN HALL on the hill (L), having served at various times as a church, dance hall, and a residence, is now (1939) a community center.

AMADOR CITY, 21 *m.* (1,100 alt., 171 pop.), at the bottom of a gulch on Amador Creek, was a camp in 1849. Here, on the south side of the creek, was the Ministers' Claim, where in 1851 the Rev. Mr. Davidson and three other preachers made the first quartz discovery in the region. The three reverend gentlemen made quite a good thing out of their claim on weekdays, and preached for the good of the miners' souls on Sundays. Quartz mines, such as the famous KEYSTONE (L) —adjoining the original Amador—yielded fortunes; in 1869, when the Bonanza vein was discovered, the first month's crushing paid $40,000. Rows of decaying frame, brick, and stone buildings line the main street, but prospectors still haunt the neighborhood, for millions in gold may yet be taken from the ledge—they hope.

In SUTTER CREEK, 23.2 *m.* (1,200 alt., 1,013 pop.), which Gen. John Augustus Sutter, in search of a site for his sawmill, passed up in favor of Coloma, many miners decided to settle down after the first gold fever had died. Its main street meanders past neat little cottages among lawns, flowers, and trees and the scattered dumps of quartz mines. Among the older brick buildings, besides MASONIC HALL and the KEYES BUILDING, is the HAYWARD OFFICE, headquarters of Alvinza Hayward, who went broke many times trying to make the quartz finds of 1851 pay. Shafts and tunnels had to be bored through solid rock, the art of timbering mastered to prevent cave-ins, and equipment shipped in at high rates from the East—it all required hundreds of thousands of dollars. Many men in the district were ruined financially, but Hayward kept on developing his mines until he had an income of $50,000 a month. One of his holdings, the CENTRAL EUREKA MINE, opened in 1869, is still the best producer in the neighborhood. Between 1859 and 1872 Leland Stanford, too, had to pour so much cash into his holding, the LINCOLN MINE, formerly the Union, that he once offered to sell for $5,000. Dissuaded by his superintendent, Robert Downs, he held it, made a fortune out of it, and sold it for $400,000.   The money went into building the Central Pacific Railroad, from which venture Stanford garnered part of the millions that later endowed Stanford University.

At MARTEL, 25.8 *m.* (1,500 alt., 150 pop.), is a junction with an oiled road.

> Right on this road is IONE, 9.4 *m.* (300 alt., 950 pop.), a camp that the first miners called Bedbug and Freeze Out. Later, when churches, homes, schools, and stores replaced the miners' tents, the citizens decided that neither term would do for a post office address. They chose the present name in honor of one of the ladies in Edward Bulwer-Lytton's *The Last Days of Pompeii.* The PRESTON INDUSTRIAL SCHOOL, established here in 1889, is a State reform school for boys.

JACKSON, 28.6 *m.* (1,250 alt., 2,000 pop.), seat of Amador County, boasts of having some of the deepest mines on the North American continent.   No ghost town, Jackson is full of life and bustle, its main street crowded with stores, cafés, bars, and movie houses, for the big quartz mines on the northern outskirts, which have been the town's mainstay for 80 years, are still active.   The ARGONAUT and the KENNEDY mines, whose deepest shafts strike a mile below the surface, have produced since the early 1850's.   Up to 1931 the Argonaut had yielded $17,391,409 worth of gold.

From 1848 to 1851 Jackson was important as a stopping point on the branch of the Carson Pass Emigrant Trail, which met roads here from Sacramento and Stockton. At a spring on the banks of Jackson Creek, teamsters hauling freight between Drytown, and Mokelumne Hill, below, and miners on their way through the Mother Lode used to break their journeys.   So convivial were these overnight stops that piles of bottles collected and gave the town its first name, Bottileas. In 1850, having grown to respectable size, it borrowed the name of an energetic citizen, Colonel Jackson; but the rough-and-ready habits of its unruly infancy persisted.   More than 10 men were strung up from a great oak that stood on Main Street.   As impatient with the formalities of government as it was with those of the courts, Jackson made itself county seat in characteristically aggressive style.   With plenty of gold in their pouches, a group of Jacksonians called at Double Springs, the county seat in 1851, and invited all the county officers to refreshments at the local saloon.   During the festivities, a pair of Jackson men loaded all of the county archives, seals, and paraphernalia into a buggy and whisked them off to Jackson.   Despite the subsequent fury of the county clerk, Jackson remained the county seat.   Not Jackson, however, but Mokelumne Hill enjoyed the last laugh; in 1852 the citizens of that town won the seat from Jackson.   The overwhelming number of ballots cast in the election—several times as many as there were county residents—was due to unusual industry; mounted men rode all over the county, voting at every camp and town.   A decade later Jackson again won the county seat.

Jackson's Main Street, narrow and winding, passes between rows of iron-shuttered stone buildings with overhanging balconies.   On

Courthouse Hill stands the brick AMADOR COUNTY COURTHOUSE of
the 1850's. Opposite is the WOMAN'S CLUBHOUSE with its Native
Daughters' Room, where the Native Daughters of the Golden West
organized in 1886. Through a residence section with schools and
churches, the road winds down to the little GREEK ORTHODOX
CHURCH 'midst tombstones and cypress trees.

At Jackson is a junction with State 8 (*see TOUR 10a*).

State 49 continues south over open, rolling hills. The GINOCCHIO
STORE (L), 30.4 *m.*, a roofless shell with stone walls and iron shutters,
is all that remains of BUTTE CITY (1,100 alt.), a mining town in
the 1850's. Forgotten miners lie in a forlorn graveyard on a hill (R).
Nearby towers the conical bulk of JACKSON BUTTE (2,348 alt.),
an isolated volcanic peak.

BIG BAR BRIDGE, 31.8 *m.*, spans the Mokelumne River, where in
the fall of 1848 Col. J. D. Stevenson and men of his discharged regiment mined gold. Soon camps were on every bar and flat along the
stream. Because the miners were an unruly bunch, prone to brandish
their Colts at the least dispute, Colonel Stevenson drew up what was
probably the first code of miners' laws in California. Here in 1850
the crude Whale Boat Ferry carried passengers across the river; it
was replaced by a bridge that yielded as much in tolls as did many a
mine. The old GARDELLA INN, at the northern end, and KELTON's,
at the southern end of the bridge are now dwellings. Under water
lie the sites of former camps, inundated by PARDEE RESERVOIR, visible
in the distance (R), which supplies the cities on the eastern shore of
San Francisco Bay, 150 miles away, with water.

High on the divide between the Mokelumne and Calaveras Rivers
perches MOKELUMNE HILL, 38.4 *m.* (1,500 alt., 595 pop.), over
river beds that yielded rich gold-bearing gravels. Settled in 1848,
"Mok Hill," or "The Hill," grew into one of the Mother Lode's
biggest and liveliest towns. It is said that at one time one man was
killed each week-end for 17 weeks, and at another, five men in one
week. From 1857 to 1866 Mokelumne Hill was the seat of Calaveras
County. Nearby is FRENCH HILL, scene of the "French War"
skirmishes of 1851, in which American miners drove off Frenchmen
and appropriated their claims. Here too is NIGGER HILL, named for
the Negro who drifted into town one day in the 1850's and asked the
miners what they did for a living. All he had to do, they told him,
was dig holes in the ground and lift out nuggets. For a joke, they
sent him to a hilltop that had been prospected unsuccessfully many
times. Within two days he returned, casually exhibiting a poke of
gold dust and some nuggets; the jokers promptly dropped whatever
they were doing and ran to stake out claims on the hill.

State 49 passes the walls of a gray ruin roofed only by the green
of ailanthus trees, and climbs the hill to the I.O.O.F. HALL (L), one
of California's first three-story buildings. Next door are the GOLDEN
EAGLE HOTEL and STURGES STORE, both built in 1854. On the SITE
OF CHINATOWN (R), long ago destroyed by fire, a thousand Chinese

once burned punk in their joss houses, bought rice in their shanty stores, and—according to old-timers—sold Chinese slave girls.

On a vacant lot (L) between a garage and barber shop is the SITE OF THE ZUMWALT SALOON, where, according to legend, the desperado, Joaquín Murrieta, sat one evening playing cards, unrecognized. The talk got round to him, as it often did. Flushed with courage and Bourbon, a young miner named Jack slapped a sack of gold on the table and cried, "Here's $500 which says that I can kill that —— —— Murrieta, if I ever come face to face with him!" Onto the table leaped Murrieta, a pistol in each hand, "I am Murrieta. Now is your chance!" No one made a move. The man with a price on his head calmly strode out of the saloon and rode away.

A large ailanthus casts its shadow over the balconies of two stone buildings (L)—the LEDGER HOTEL and the FORMER CALAVERAS COURTHOUSE, now the hotel annex. Built in 1856 as the Hotel de l'Europe, the Ledger has been renovated, but still has its original stone facade and windows, black walnut bar and balustraded staircase. Dating from the early 1850's is a little white church (R), built with gold collected by a godly and determined lady who stopped the men as they came back from the mines at night, holding out a miner's pan for contributions of gold dust and nuggets. From Stockton Hill on the southern outskirts of town rise the ruins of the great three-story HEM-MINGHOFFEN-SUESDORF BREWERY, like some ancient abbey, with crumbling, roofless walls, shattered archways, and great vaults choked with fallen stone blocks.

1. Right from Mokelumne Hill on an oiled road is FOSTERIA, 5.3 m. (1,500 alt.), at the head of Rich Gulch, where Senator William M. Gwin once operated the famous GWIN MINE.
To CAMPO SECO, 11.9 m. (700 alt., 216 pop.), the Penn Copper Mine brought wealth in the 1860's. Ruined stone buildings, a two-story clapboard house, and a cemetery are relics of the past.

2. Left from Mokelumne Hill on a graveled road to a junction at 1.3 m.; R. here to the sites of two old mining camps: JESÚS MARÍA, 3.7 m. (1,500 alt.), where an old adobe dwelling built by Mexican miners is now a granary; and WHISKEY SLIDE, 7.4 m., where the ruined JOHN NOCE HOUSE of the 1850's exhibits a stone chimney, still intact.

South of Mokelumne Hill, State 49 runs through CHILE GULCH, where American and Chilean miners fought the "Chilean War" in December 1849. The Chileans' practice of acquiring claims in the names of their peons so angered the Yankees that they passed laws against it. In resistance to the law the Chileans, led by a certain Dr. Concha, drove the Americans out of the gulch. The incident embroiled the United States in a diplomatic dispute with Chile, which was settled in favor of the Americans. But the gulch remained the scene of violence; a monument in an old graveyard keeps alive the memory of two young Massachusetts men who "were Cruelly Murdered at the Chilean Gulch, July 18, 1851 by three Mexican assassins for the sake of Gold."

The highway crosses the NORTH FORK OF THE CALA-
VERAS RIVER, 41.5 *m.*, so-called because Spanish explorers found
Indian skulls (*calaveras*) along the banks of its lower course.

SAN ANDREAS, 44 *m.* (1,000 alt., 1,082 pop.), seat of Calaveras
County, was first a Mexican town, as a few scattered adobe dwellings
built in 1848 indicate. Along the main street—thinly disguised in
their modern dress of paint, stucco, chromium, and plate glass—are
the buildings of the early Yankee era. Documents dating back to 1866
are preserved in the courthouse; relics and historic records, among
them a red sash of Joaquín Murrieta's, in the CALAVERAS CHAMBER
OF COMMERCE MUSEUM (L) at the north end of town. San Andreans
assert that here in the barroom of the Metropolitan Hotel—which
burned down in 1926—occurred the event memorialized in Mark
Twain's *The Jumping Frog.* They also assert—and so does many
another gold country town—that here Joaquín Murrieta began his
career of murder and banditry.

South of San Andreas the long ridge of BEAR MOUNTAIN
(2,831 alt.), rises (R) as State 49 winds through dry meadows overgrown with clusters of oaks.

At SAN ANTONIO CREEK, 49.4 *m.*, the few decaying buildings
that remain of FOURTH CROSSING, a stop-over point of stagecoaches appears (R). The tallest of them is the HERRICK HOUSE,
once a hotel; next to it are the REDDICK HOUSE and the remains of
an old stable. Across the street is the dance hall.

ALTAVILLE, 55.2 *m.* (1,525 alt., 320 pop.), where the old inn
(L) and the PRINCE STORE (R) date from the 1850's, was known as
Cherokee Flat when Bret Harte made it the setting of his poem, "To
the Pliocene Skull." Here in February 1866, 130 feet down in the
shaft of the Mattison Mine, on the slopes of nearby Bald Hill, was
unearthed the Calaveras skull. A storm of controversy arose. Unquestionably Pliocene, declared the geologists, were the mud, gravel,
and sand of the stratum in which it had turned up; but the anthro-
pologists, threatened with the upset of every theory about the age of
man on earth, were not so sure. Amused at the discomfiture of J. D.
Whitney, State geologist, the public hailed the affair as a huge hoax,
perpetrated by enemies he had made when he interfered with plans
of local financiers for selling wild-cat stocks. Nevertheless, Whitney,
in a final summary that appeared 13 years later, maintained the skull's
authenticity; the last official word on the subject declared the skull
to be prehistoric, if not Pliocene. Old-timers still insist, however,
that the affair was a practical joke—that at about the time it was found,
Dr. Kelly, the Angels Camp dentist, discovered that the skull of an old
skeleton he kept in his office was missing.

ANGELS CAMP, 56.2 *m.* (1,500 alt., 915 pop.), was named not
for the heavenly host but for one of Col. J. D. Stevenson's very earthly
volunteers, a man called Angel, who found gold on the creek running
through town, in the summer of 1848. The man who made Angels
Camp famous was Mark Twain. Local people insist that it was in

their HOTEL ANGELS barroom that Twain one winter's night heard the story on which he based *The Jumping Frog*. Every year in May, Angels Camp holds a Jumping Frog Jubilee. In the main event frogs, after rigid inspection to prevent loading with buckshot as in Twain's tale, compete for a first prize of $500. Models of frogs appear in the windows of stores and hotels. One restaurant advertises a jumping frog pie—made of prunes and raisins; and local businessmen have organized a Frog Boosting Club.

Angels Camp was also the locale of Bret Harte's story, *Mrs. Skaggs' Husbands*. And here, in a little theater since burned down, appeared Edwin Booth. Here, too, gold was reputedly discovered by Bennager Raspberry, whose name is honored by Raspberry Lane; while hunting, he jammed the ramrod in his gun, and when he shot it out to dislodge it, it stuck in the earth at the roots of a manzanita bush; pulling it out, he found a piece of glittering quartz in a rich vein, from which he took $7,700 in the first three days. Relics of mining days survive on the main street, despite such evidence of progress as neon signs and Venetian blinds. The STICKLE STORE (L), now a five-and-ten, was built in 1857 and the CALAVERAS HOTEL (R) at about the same time. At the southern city limits (L) is a model of the UNDERSHOT WATER WHEEL used to operate an *arrastre* (mill) for crushing gold ore.

Left from Angels Camp on State 4, a paved road, is VALLICITO (Sp., little valley), 4.8 *m.* (1,800 alt., 160 pop.). Mounted on the branches of a big oak tree (R) is an old bell—brought around the Horn—that used to summon the miners of this once lively camp to Sunday services.

DOUGLAS FLAT, 7.3 *m.* (2,000 alt., 85 pop.), once produced enough gold to make hundreds rich for a brief period. A bank as well as a store was the well-preserved stone-walled, iron-shuttered GILLEADO BUILDING (L).

At MURPHYS, 9.1 *m.* (2,200 alt., 600 pop.), the brothers Murphy, John and Daniel, were the first to discover gold. The town has the usual Joaquín Murrieta legend: here the ubiquitous bad man is said to have been a three-card monte dealer in 1851 and to have begun his bloody career when his brother, unjustly accused of horse stealing, was hanged, and he himself flogged. Outwardly much as they were in the 1850's, Murphys' store, saloons, and business houses sprawl along the main street in the shade of elms and Chinese heaven trees. In front of them in the evenings, their chairs tilted back against the walls, loll men in blue jeans and broad felt hats.

The MITCHLER HOTEL (L) was built in 1856 by John L. Sperry to accommodate important visitors when Murphys became the gateway to the Calaveras Big Tree Grove. Inside and out, the Mitchler—which Bret Harte is said to have described in *A Night in Wingdam*—remains just as it was. At the windows hang the old iron shutters; along the second-story balcony runs a fine iron railing. Embedded in the trunks of the heaven trees that shade the front are bits of the wire cable once used for hitching horses, and in the doorway are the bullet marks left from the time when a stranger shot the town's current bad man. Inside, horsehair sofas and red plush furnish the best suite. The iron safe standing behind the bar preserves old ledgers with the names of such notables as Horatio Alger, Jr., Charles E. Bolton (Black Bart), Thomas Lipton, Ulysses S. Grant, Henry Ward Beecher, John Jacob Astor, Jr., John Pierpont Morgan, and Will Rogers, who made a movie here in 1934.

Right from Murphys 1.1 *m.* on a paved road to MERCER'S CAVE, a series of 20 caverns filled with stalactite and stalagmite formations. SHEEP

RANCH, 8.6 *m.* (2,400 alt., 75 pop.), was a quartz mining camp where George Hearst, father of newspaper magnate William Randolph Hearst, laid the foundations for his fortune. An old frame hotel with double balconies still stands.

State 4 continues northwestward through rolling mountain country, cut by gorges. The CALAVERAS BIG TREES, 24.9 *m.,* the first grove of *Sequoia gigantea* discovered, were found by a hunter who was stalking deer for a mining camp in 1854. He hurried back and told of seeing trees taller than the masts of clipper ships and thicker than houses.

The road mounts higher into the Sierra through BIG MEADOWS, 41.7 *m.* (6,600 alt.), and crosses the crest of the Sierra Range at EBBETS PASS, 67.2 *m.* (8,800 alt.), discovered in the 1840's. State 4 comes to a junction with State 89 at 77.9 *m.*; L. here on State 89. MARKLEEVILLE, 81.9 *m.* (5,500 alt., 469 pop.), in a high mountain valley on an early immigrant route, was settled in the 1850's. It later furnished timber for the mines of the Comstock Lode.

At 88.5 *m.* is a junction with State 8; R. on State 8, 8.1 *m.* to cross the Nevada Line at a point 21.2 miles south of Carson City, Nev.

The main route turns L. on State 89-8 to a point at 95 *m.* where State 8 swings sharply L. and State 89 goes R. (*for both routes, see TOUR 10a*).

By State 49 on ALBANY FLAT, 58.5 *m.,* stands the half-ruined ROMAGGI BUILDING, a store, saloon, and hotel patronized by travelers on the road to the wild camp, a favorite haunt of Joaquín Murrieta and his gang, on the Arroyo de los Muertos (creek of the dead). A sprawling, two-story edifice, with an outside stairway, cellars, and courtyard walls, it was built of rock and adobe in 1852.

The somnolent, half-deserted village of CARSON HILL, 60.1 *m.* (1,400 alt., 50 pop.), looks like a ghost of the old days. CARSON HILL, rising (L) above the village, was the richest diggings in the whole Mother Lode. In Carson Creek James H. Carson, led to the spot by friendly Indians, found gold in August 1848. The 180 ounces of gold that he panned in 10 days were the first of more than $20,000,000 worth that diggings here have produced. A great gash in the hillside shows the position of the MORGAN MINE, where 15 miles of tunnels pierce the hill and one shaft bores 3,500 feet below sea level. Here the largest nugget ever found in the United States, a solid mass of gold weighing 195 pounds and valued at $43,534, was taken out Nov. 22, 1854. The story—another time-worn veteran of the mining country—is that a man called Hance, chasing a stray mule in the vicinity, discovered the mine when he saw an outcropping of quartz in which yellow metal gleamed; with a rock he knocked off a chunk of gold weighing 14 pounds. When Hance sold his claim to Col. Alfred Morgan and five associates, the fight over a rich prize began; miners said that Morgan and his partners had each exceeded the limits of land one man could claim. A hoodlum named Billy Mulligan, backed by a tough bunch recruited from the San Francisco "Hounds," stepped in, seized part of the claim, and held it for a time. After several years of violence, the courts put Morgan in possession, but litigation continued until the entire property had come into the hands of another man, James G. Fair, of Comstock Lode fame.

MELONES (Sp., melons), 63.5 *m.* (700 alt., 75 pop.), in the days when it boasted a population of 5,000, was one of the toughest camps. Melones took its name from a nearby camp, where Mexican miners found coarse gold in the shape of melon seeds. Earlier it was called Slumgullion, for the thick, sticky mud along the river banks; and before that, Robinson's Ferry, for the man who ferried travelers across the river. Robinson sold the ferry in 1856 to Harvey Wood, who acquired a county franchise to operate it for 50 years. Within six weeks after the Morgan mine was opened, the ferry made $10,000 for him, and as time went on, it continued to earn so much that he could spend $40,000 on the toll roads approaching it.

State 49 winds up a ravine to a junction with a paved road at 65.6 *m.*

Left here up JACKASS HILL, where the men who packed supplies in to the miners used to stop overnight, tethering their donkeys. Mark Twain, who spent 5 months here in 1864-5, wrote: ". . . a flourishing city of two or three thousand population had occupied this grassy dead solitude during the flush times of twelve or fifteen years before, and where our cabin stood had once been the heart of the teeming hive . . ." On the summit is MARK TWAIN'S CABIN, 1 *m.*, restored except for the chimney and fireplace; a monument of quartz rock commemorates Twain's stay here as a guest of the Gillis brothers, at a time when he had to flee San Francisco because of debts. He used to sit under the oak before the door and smoke his pipe. It was here that he met the original of Dick Baker in *Roughing It*, Dick Stoker, of whom he wrote: "One of my comrades there—another of those victims of eighteen years of unrequited toil and blighted hopes—was one of the gentlest spirits that ever bore its patient cross in a weary exile: grave and simple Dick Baker, pocket miner of Dead-Horse Gulch."

In MORMON GULCH, where Mormon miners once pitched camp, stands TUTTLETOWN, 66.6 *m.* (1,500 alt., 164 pop.), which became a trade center and pack-mule stop on the old Slumgullion road, after Judge A. A. H. Tuttle built his log cabin here in August 1848. Mark Twain used to come down Jackass Hill to trade at the SWERER STORE (L), a stone structure erected in 1852. In the same year was built the right wing of the old frame TUTTLETOWN HOTEL (L), whose drinking trough is now a goldfish pond.

At 67.8 *m.* is a junction with a paved road.

Right on this road to the RAWHIDE MINE, 2.5 *m.*, where $6,000,000 has been taken from deep quartz veins. Rawhide Flat at this point gives a good view of TABLE MOUNTAIN (L), celebrated in Bret Harte's tales. This flat-topped volcanic mountain, a half-moon stretching for 60 miles, and the region contiguous to the Stanislaus River constitute the true Bret Harte country. As a young man, late in 1855, Harte passed through the region hunting for a camp that would hire him as a teacher. Here he gained the impressions that he wove into the sentimental tales that impressed stay-at-home Easterners of the *Atlantic Monthly* circle and made him famous.

At 70.7 *m.* on State 49 is a junction with a paved road.

Right on this road to SHAWS FLAT, 1 *m.* (2,100 alt., 15 pop.), where Mandeville Shaw planted an orchard in 1849 and where Tarleton Caldwell later planted a garden and black walnut trees. Here in 1855 were discovered the gold deposits of an ancient river channel, so rich that the yield of Caldwell's claim alone was estimated at $250,000. Tunnels were sunk far into Table Mountain; such men as James G. Fair and John B. Stetson got their start here. The camp was called Whimtown because of the many whims (windlasses) used in hoisting ore from the shafts. The MISSISSIPPI HOUSE (R), at the crossroads, was once a hotel, store, and post office. Still in service are the old bar and the patched bar chairs. From the ceiling, covered with stained muslin, hang kerosene lights; on the walls are guns, sconces, horn spoons, and other mining relics.

At 71.1 *m.* is a junction with a paved road.

Left on this road is COLUMBIA, 1.8 *m.* (2,200 alt., 200 pop.), a ghost of what was once the "Gem of the Southern Mines," the richest, noisiest, fastest growing, most spectacularly wicked camp in the Mother Lode. Roundabout lie 300 acres of weirdly shaped, brush-mantled crags, laid bare when the top soil was sluiced away to uncover the rich gravel beneath. From these acres have come $87,000,000 in gold. A party of Mexican miners, driven from their claims by gringos, found new diggings here in March, 1850; with backbreaking labor they carried ore in sacks to the streams and there pounded it in mortars and washed it. In the same month Dr. Thaddeus Hildreth, his brother, and three others, camping here overnight, were drenched by a sudden downpour. As they waited for their blankets to dry out the next morning, March 27, one of the party, John Walker, tried his luck at prospecting. He struck it rich, and within the first half week the Yankees were taking out 15 pounds of gold a day. By mid-April, Hildreth's Diggings had 6,000 residents, the advance guard of an army that was to swell to 15,000. In the meantime, however, the settlement had a serious setback to overcome, for the imposition of a $20 tax on foreign-born miners and the drying up of the streams in summer combined to drive away all but one of the 6,000 inhabitants. Recovering speedily from this handicap, it forged ahead to become a full-fledged metropolis, with 143 faro games, 30 saloons, 4 banks, 27 produce stores, 3 express offices—and an arena for bull-and-bear fights, which, described by Horace Greeley in the New York *Tribune,* is said to have given Wall Street its best-known phrases.

Columbia, one of the best preserved of the ghost towns, has more ancient and fewer modern buildings than any other spot in the Mother Lode. On Kennebec Hill at the southern outskirts, among cypresses, rises the square brick tower of ST. ANN'S CHURCH, built in 1856, which has altar murals painted by James Fallon. Main Street, following the contour of what was Matelot (Fr., sailor) Gulch, has wide-branching shade trees, brick and stone facades, old iron doors and shutters, fancy wrought iron railings, and shade-covered sidewalk canopies. At its southern end in FALLON'S HOTEL (R), where artist James Fallon's father did the honors in the 1860's and 1870's. The old red brick WELLS FARGO OFFICE (*adm. 25¢*) is now a museum; it contains old account books showing what prices once were; sugar $3 a pound, molasses $5 a gallon, flour $1.50 a pound, onions $1 a pound, sardines and lobsters $4 a can, candles 50¢ apiece, and special miners' knives $30 each. The onetime saloon, the STAGE DRIVERS' RETREAT (*adm. free*), Main and Fulton Sts. (L), is now the Golden Nugget Club of old-timers and a museum; the bar remains, and the old piano, brought around the Horn. Across the street (R) is the KNAPP GROCERY STORE, with heavy iron doors barred, which was saved from fire in 1857 when two barrels of vinegar were thrown on the flames. In the FIREHOUSE (R) are two old fire engines and an old fire hose of riveted buffalo hide; Papeets, the older of the two, was built for King Kamehameha of the Sandwich Islands, brought from New York to San Francisco, and sold to Columbia in 1859. The PIONEER SALOON (R), Main and Jackson Sts., built in 1858, housed a saloon and gambling hall on the ground floor and a fandango hall in the cellar. Beyond is the ruined CHINA STORE, half-hidden behind ailanthus trees. The PRESBYTERIAN CHURCH (1864), Jackson and Gold Sts., replacing a church of 1853, is at the edge of the former plaza from which the bell now hanging in the church tower used to summon miners to fires, mass meetings, and hangings. On the top of the hill at the northern outskirts is the two-story red-brown schoolhouse, opéned for its first term April 14, 1862. Beside it is a graveyard with marble headstones bearing old-fashioned epitaphs.

SONORA, 73.5 *m.* (1,850 alt., 2,278 pop.), seat of Tuolumne County, is on seven small hills. Though it had little room to spread between the wooded hillsides of its canyon, it has long since outstripped its old-time rival, Columbia, and boasts of churches, schools, and like civic improvements. In 1848 this was Sonorian Camp, settled by Mexicans from the state of Sonora. By November of that year half of the population was rotting with scurvy. A town government was organized to establish a hospital, which treated the victims with raw potatoes at $1.50 a pound and lime juice at $5 a bottle. During 1849 men of several nations arrived, until, on Saturday nights, the narrow streets were packed with as many as 5,000 miners. In June 1850, the new "gringo" government, unappreciative of Sonora's pioneers, imposed a $20 tax on foreign-born miners. Alarmed at the Yankee treachery, Mexicans, Chileans, and others gathered for discussion. Fearing an attack, the Americans organized a mass meeting under the American flag, and headed by fife and drum, with banners waving and guns popping, they marched in a mob on the camp. The Mexicans, however, also fearing an attack, were pulling down their tents and fleeing to hunt new diggings. When the excitement subsided, Sonora found itself with but a fifth of its former population.

Not Yankees but Chileans in 1851 discovered the richest pocket mine in the Mother Lode, the BIG BONANZA (prosperity) on PIETY HILL (R). Yankees, however, garnered its greatest riches, when three partners, who had acquired the mine at little cost in the 1870's, hit a deposit of almost pure gold after working it for some years. In one day they took out $160,000 and within a week, $500,000. The Big Bonanza still produces.

The acquisitive instincts of Sonora's settlers were perhaps best shown by a certain Judge Sullivan. In the first case tried before him he collected three ounces of gold from the defendant, a Mexican, for stealing a certain Mr. Smith's leggings, and one ounce from the plaintiff himself for bothering the judge with so trivial a complaint as the loss of the leggings. Again, when a wealthy citizen haled a penniless man into court for stealing a mule, Judge Sullivan decreed that the wealthy man should pay both fine and costs, since "the court could not be expected to sit without remuneration."

On the narrow side streets are adobe facades with overhanging balconies, mellowing frame houses in old gardens, and heavy, ivy-clad stone walls. ST. JAMES CHURCH (R), built in 1860, rears a cross-tipped spire above cypress trees and lilac bushes. The one-story, red-brick BAUMAN BREWERY on Washington Street opposite the high school, once supplied beer to 40 saloons. The two-story GUNN ADOBE (R), at the southern edge of town, was built by Mexican laborers for

Dr. Lewis C. Gunn in 1850. With new wings and balcony, it is now the Hotel Italia. The hotel parlor was Gunn's office as first county recorder and his print shop, where on July 4, 1850, he started the first newspaper published in the mining region, the Sonora *Herald*.

At Sonora is a junction (L) with State 108 (*see TOUR 6b*), which here unites with State 49.

State 49-108 winds into JAMESTOWN, 77.4 *m.* (1,500 alt., 814 pop.), which has retained some of its old facades, balconies, and sidewalk roofs. Called Jimtown by the miners, it was named for Col. George F. James, a San Francisco lawyer who tried his luck at mining here in 1848 but fought with other miners and left. Its prosperity sprang partly from the rich mines of TABLE MOUNTAIN— where the HUMBUG yielded $4,000,000 in its day, some of it in nuggets the size of hens' eggs.

The WOODS' CROSSING, 78.4 *m.*, marked by a monument of gold quartz, was a busy camp in 1848 and 1849, after the Reverend James Woods and his party discovered gold in the creek.

CHINESE CAMP, 84.3 *m.* (1,400 alt., 237 pop.), which Bret Harte wrote about as "Salvado," is only a handful of brick and adobe buildings. No trace is left of the 5,000 Chinese who mined for gold here in the 1850's. Their very origin is a mystery; some say that a ship's captain left his vessel in San Francisco Bay and brought his Chinese crew here to mine, others, that they were employed by English prospectors. Only 2 miles west, on a plain at the foot of Table Mountain, was fought the first tong war in California. On Sept. 26, 1856, armed with pikes, shovels, pitchforks, daggers, clubs, and a few muskets, 900 men of the Yan Wo Tong and 1200 of the Sam Tu Tong battled. After several hours of yelling and clashing, both sides withdrew. Since the warriors had never before used muskets, the total casualties were four killed and four wounded. At Chinese Camp is a junction with State 120 (*see TOUR 3b*), which unites westward with State 49.

In WOOD'S CREEK CANYON, 87.4 *m.*, are the hoists, dumps, and stamp mill of the EAGLE SHAWMUT MINE, producer of $5,000,000 in gold.

JACKSONVILLE, 88.7 *m.* (900 alt., 63 pop.), honors Col. Alden Jackson who discovered gold here in June 1849. Fire has destroyed all of the old buildings except the JACKSONVILLE HOTEL (L), built in the 1850's.

At 91.2 *m.* is the western junction with State 120 (*see TOUR 3b*).

From the MOCCASIN CREEK POWER HOUSE (L), 93.9 *m.*, with workers' bungalows on green lawns, State 49 climbs the steep sides of Moccasin Creek ravine, skirting views of range after range of mountains, green in the foreground, blue in the distance.

COULTERVILLE, 104.7 *m.* (1,675 alt., 380 pop.), is among almost treeless mountains covered with chaparral and sagebrush. Fortunes came out of these bare-looking slopes during the wild years when 3,000 Yankees and more than 1,000 Chinese tramped the streets of

Coulterville, then called Banderita, for the small red bandannas used by the first Mexican settlers. Little traffic passes through now; once in a while a stray cow wanders through the street, or a pack mule loaded with prospector's trappings; men dressed in blue jeans and work shirts stroll about, unhurried. In the plaza, fringed by old stone and adobe edifices, is an oak from which many a bad man, according to cherished local legend, dangled at the end of a rope. Along the main street, catalpa and umbrella trees shade brick and stone buildings, some roofless and crumbling. In front of the JEFFERY HOTEL (L), which has catered to several generations, at almost any time of day or evening, sit a squad of grizzled old-timers with stubbly chins, locally called the "Grand Jury."

South of Coulterville, State 49 climbs steep grades up mountain slopes that drop abruptly hundreds of feet by the roadside.

BAGBY, 115.9 *m.* (1,000 alt., 36 pop.), formerly Benton Mills, is now little more than a store, a couple of frame houses, and a station on the Yosemite Valley Railway. The foundations of FRÉMONT'S MILL AND DAM are by the river near the bridge. John C. Frémont, in the early 1850's, claimed this land as a part of his Mariposa grant and spent thousands of dollars on mills and mining equipment.

Crossing Merced River the highway ascends the steep slopes of HELL HOLLOW, a climb affording spectacular views. At the PACIFIC MINE, 118.7 *m.,* gold is being taken from a quartz vein. A turnout at 120.1 *m.* offers an unusual view. The river twists and turns a thousand feet below; to the north and west a seemingly endless procession of ranges melts into haze.

Now almost deserted, BEAR VALLEY, 121.6 *m.* (2,100 alt.), was built by Frémont as headquarters for his rich Mariposa mines. A jagged stone ruin (R), a tree growing within its walls, is FRÉMONT'S COMPANY STORE opened in 1851. Across the street are the FOUNDATIONS OF THE FRÉMONT HOUSE, where Frémont and his wife, Jessie, lived for a short time. Frémont's 44,000-acre Rancho de las Mariposas (ranch of the butterflies) was in the San Joaquin Valley when he bought it for $3,000 in 1847. Discovery of gold the year after made the gold-bearing foothills eastward so much more desirable that Frémont "floated" his lands in that direction—and the United States courts confirmed him in his ownership here, though the place was 50 miles east of the original claim. The move put Frémont in line to become a rich man for there seemed to be wealth hidden in the quartz ledges here. From a place within pistol shot of Bear Valley's main street, $200,000 was taken within four months in 1851. Frémont, however, had many troubles. First were the miners who swarmed the new diggings with the assertion that Mexican grants covered only agricultural and grazing rights, not minerals. A small war, with the aid of militia sent by a compliant governor, was required to oust them. Then followed lengthy litigation in the face of hostile public sentiment, piling up court costs and lawyers' fees; on top of that was a ruinous outlay for stamp mills, tunnels, and shafts; and finally, ore did not persist below the surface. Later Frémont said, "When I came to California I hadn't a cent. Now I owe two million dollars!"

Beside the road at 126.1 *m.* are the ruined walls of flat rocks and adobe of a TRABUCCO STORE (R), trading post of the early 1850's for old MOUNT OPHIR, 126.2 *m.* An obscure trail leads through the brush to the ruined mint, where hexagonal gold slugs worth $50 each were coined in the early 1850's.

MOUNT BULLION, 128.2 *m.* (2,100 alt., 16 pop.), was Princeton, until a more picturesque name was suggested by the nearby mountain, which was named for Frémont's father-in-law, Senator Thomas Hart Benton—nicknamed Old Bullion because of his many political battles about currency. Here more than 2,000 miners used to call for their mail. The low, iron-shuttered adobe (L) is the MARRE STORE, which supplied the miners in the 1860's. Just south of Mount Bullion is the old PRINCETON MINE; first owned by Frémont, the Princeton produced millions in gold.

Right from Mount Bullion on a graveled road to HORNITOS (Sp., little ovens), 13 *m.* (1,000 alt., 62 pop.), which got its name from the appellation given the tombs of its early Mexican settlers; two of them, shaped like square bake ovens, lie in ruins on the hillside below the weather-beaten Roman Catholic Church. The camp here in 1849 was known for its fiestas, fandango halls, gambling, and shooting frays. In the ruined GHIRARDELLI STORE, the "chocolate king" of later days began building his fortune as a merchant. Facing the plaza is (R) the old FANDANGO HALL in which the miners sported when they came in flush from the "diggin's." The two-story HORNITOS HOTEL, on an upper street, was built in 1860. The jail, built of stone with a strong iron door and one little window near the ceiling, was the scene of an early tragedy. A Chinese, after having been constantly annoyed by an American miner, lost his patience and shot his tormentor. He was lodged here and when attempts to lynch him failed, a man handed the prisoner some tobacco through the window; as the Chinese stretched out his hand, several of the miners seized it, pulled him against the window, fastened a rope around him, and tore him to pieces.

MARIPOSA (*see TOUR 3b*), 133.4 *m.,* is at a junction with State 140 (*see TOUR 3b*).

Tour 5

Junction with US 99—Bartle—McArthur Memorial (Burney Falls) State Park—Lassen Volcanic National Park—Quincy—Truckee; 277.7 *m.,* State 89.

Roadbed paved between US 99 and US 299, Manzanita Lake and Lake Almanor, and Quincy and Blairsden; elsewhere dirt or gravel. Accommodations at convenient intervals: lakeside hotels, resorts, camps.

State 89 cuts southeastward across northeastern California, seeming to seek out high and inaccessible splendors. It plunges through the Cascade Range, comes to a chaotic region, where lava has made no man's lands of the forests, and emerges between ridges of the Sierra Nevada, whose granite crags rise sheer from steel-blue lakes. The mark of man is plain along the route: forests thinned by lumbermen, carved mountainsides and piles of tailings left by miners, lakes created in hydroelectric developments. The road flows smoothly through the Feather River region, passes old mining towns, mountain stockfarms where cowboys ride herd, and reaches lakes and meadows where emigrant parties fought the Sierra snows—now a playground of summer and winter sports.

Section a. JUNCTION WITH US 99 *to* MORGAN SPRINGS; *139 m., State 89.*

State 89 branches east from the junction with US 99 (*see TOUR 8a*), 0 *m.,* 2 miles south of Mount Shasta City.

SNOWMAN HILL, 5.2 *m.,* rises (R) within 200 yards of the highway from Shasta's lower slopes. Glistening with snow from December to March, the hill is popular with winter sports enthusiasts, who gather for ski tournaments, snow frolics, and tobogganing.

McCLOUD, 10.6 *m.* (3,254 alt., 1,000 pop.), is a typical lumber town, loud with the whine of the great buzz saws in its mills, where huge logs become sweet-smelling yellow lumber. The town preserves, under altered spelling, the name of the Scot, Alexander Roderick McLeod, who in 1827 led southward the first band of Hudson's Bay Company trappers to penetrate northern California. They narrowly escaped starvation and death when severe weather forced them to cache their furs and traps and seek a warmer climate.

Left from McCloud is a road leading through the once heavily timbered McCloud Flat country, built up of glacial silt from Mount Shasta.
MUD CREEK, 3.4 *m.,* is in the area devastated by the mud flow from Konwakiton Glacier in August, 1924. Breaking loose from the creek banks, the avalanche of water and sediment spread over the country, leaving it a desolate waste. The glacial sediment, deposited in many places to a depth of 15 feet, overflowed into the McCloud River and was carried southward for several hundred miles.
At 9.6 *m.* is the junction with a dirt road; R. here 0.5 *m.,* to the Mc-CLOUD ICE CAVES. Entrance is by a 12-foot ladder through a cave-in. The caverns extend east and west for nearly three-tenths of a mile. In the west cave the glittering wall of ice remains until midsummer.

BARTLE, 32 *m.* (3,970 alt., 10 pop.), is a station on the McCloud Logging Railroad (a common carrier if passengers are willing to ride in the caboose). Guns and other paraphernalia unearthed here in 1874 were believed to be part of the McLeod party's cache. Headwaters of the McCloud River rise in this vicinity.

At Bartle is the junction with the dirt Lava Beds National Monument Rd. (*see TOUR 8A*).

CAYTON, 48 *m*. (3,300 alt., 26 pop.), and, CLARK CREEK, 52 *m*. (3,000 alt., 12 pop.), lie in a valley meadow between FORT MOUNTAIN and SOLDIER ,MOUNTAIN (L) and RED MOUNTAIN (R).

At 54 *m*. State 89 enters McARTHUR MEMORIAL (BURNEY FALLS) STATE PARK, a 335-acre recreational area (*60 improved camp sites; showers, cooking and laundering facilities*), surrounding BURNEY FALLS, where Lost River rushes from its underground channel to plunge in a double cataract—divided by a rocky island—128 feet into the gorge. Pine needles cushion the trail that winds down the eastern slope of the canyon. As the steady roar of the falls grows louder, a fine, cool mist, heady and invigorating, bathes the pine-scented air. The trail leads to the edge of the wide, dark-watered pool at the base of the falls, seen streaming in twin ribbons of white foam against purple rock and blue sky. From the steep, moss-covered banks on the far side of the gorge grow giant pines, green and straight. Many smaller waterfalls spring from the massed lava, bathing the walls with thin streams of transparent silver. At the foot of the falls, Lost River dashes along its boulder-strewn course to LAKE BRITTON, a mile distant, where a dam impounds its waters and those of the Pit River. The lake, kept stocked with bass, is a favorite with sportsmen. There is excellent trout fishing in Burney Creek, a mile above the falls.

At 61 *m*. is the junction with US 299 (*see TOUR 8a*).

The road, striking into Hat Creek Canyon, follows the winding course of this stream southward past HAT CREEK POST OFFICE (L), 83 *m*. (3,300 alt.).

SUBWAY CAVE (L), 81 *m*. (*flashlights required for exploration*), extends through an old lava flow for several hundred feet, with a flat, level floor and a ceiling 6 to 25 feet high.

The road crosses the northeastern boundary of LASSEN VOLCANIC NATIONAL PARK at 99 *m.,* within Lassen National Forest. The forest, a 1,306,727-acre reserve of rugged mountains, high plateaus, forests, and lakes at the northern end of the Sierra Nevada and the southern tip of the Cascade Range, was set aside in 1906. The park, a 163-square-mile mountainous expanse surrounding the dormant volcano, Lassen Peak, was created in 1916. Blacktail and mule deer abound, and sometimes a black bear appears; the chipmunks, which are especially numerous, are so tame they beg for food. Fishing is good here. During winter months, the Lassen Ski Club stages tournaments.

The weird, lava-devastated acres of the park are full of evidence of historic and prehistoric volcanic upheavals—sheer, jagged cliffs; great irregularly shaped rocks; fumaroles; boiling lakes, and mud pots that bubble and steam angrily; and wide ejecta-strewn areas where the countryside was laid waste by hot blasts, smothering lava, and mud flows. In sharp contrast with the olive greens, yellows, reds, and clay-whites of the volcanic phenomena are the fresh greens of the forests and grasses that are slowly reclaiming the devastation created by the volcano. In winter, when the park is a rolling blanket of snow, the gas and steam vents present a paradoxical picture of boiling coldness.

Just within the park, at 99.7 *m.*, State 89 joins with State 44.

> Right on State 44 (*stage service to Lassen Volcanic National Park four times weekly*) is VIOLA, 7 *m.* (4,390 alt., 65 pop.). The road drops gradually to SHINGLETOWN, 18 *m.* (2,700 alt., 320 pop.) and then precipitously to MILLVILLE, 37 *m.* (512 alt., 65 pop.), so named because the first grist mill in the county was opened there.
>
> REDDING (*see TOUR 3a*), 49.5 *m.*, is as the junction with US 99 (*see TOUR 3a*).

State 89 becomes the Lassen Peak Loop, and passes between pine fringed MANZANITA LAKE (R) and REFLECTION LAKE (L)—popular for fishing, swimming, and boating—which mirror in their placid surfaces the towering heights of Lassen Peak and Chaos Crags (*see below*).

At the eastern end of Manzanita Lake is the settlement of MANZANITA LAKE (*post office, campgrounds, lodge, cabins, store*), 100.5 *m.* (5,845 alt.), an all-year resort. At EDUCATIONAL HEADQUARTERS here are presented lectures on the park's flora and fauna, geology, and natural history. The MAY LOOMIS MEMORIAL MUSEUM specializes in the history of the region, with exhibits of lava specimens gathered during Lassen's eruptive period, and photographs of the volcano in action.

The CHAOS JUMBLES, 102.2 *m.*, covering a wide stretch on both sides of the highway, are the tops of the Chaos Crags which broke off and tumbled down.

The road swings northward in a hairpin curve which carries it briefly outside the park's boundaries and then southward. It climbs through a pass between the sloping sides (R) of RAKER CREEK (7,466 alt.), and the domes (L) of CHAOS CRAGS (8,458 alt.), old lava plugs, forced up about 200 years ago. Chaos Crags are aptly named, for nowhere in the park is there a scene of wilder confusion. It is hard to express the feeling of wonder—of being transported into some older world—engendered by their gigantic disarray. The pinkish lava domes are magnificent piles of angular pointed blocks heaped in almost inconceivable disorder among projecting pinnacles. Encircling them are enormous banks of pointed talus, some 1,000 feet high. The crags were formed in three stages of volcanic activity—first, the piling up of a series of cinder cones by explosive eruptions; then the pushing up of steepsided domes of viscous lava; and finally, the tearing down of the domes by new explosions that hurled vast masses of lava fragments over the vicinity. The remnant of a cinder cone formed in the first stage, its crater 600 feet wide and 60 feet deep, still appears on the southern slope of the crags.

HOT ROCK (R), 107.2 *m.*, a large, black boulder of lava, is said to have retained its warmth for a week after it had been blasted from the volcano.

Through EMIGRANT PASS, 109 *m.*, an old trail once ran along the west fork of Hat Creek.

The DEVASTATED AREA, 109.7 *m.*, is a great V-shaped section, starting where the lava and mud flowed down the northeast slope of Lassen Peak, and widened as it swept toward the park boundary. The mud, lava, and heat of the 1915 eruptions denuded the region of all vegetation. Volcanic ash and ejecta, either carried by the mud and lava flows or tossed by terrific blasts, blanket the entire area. Stripped of foliage, the trunks of some large trees reach polelike toward the sky. Nature is slowly reforesting; small trees have taken root in the bleakness.

At SUMMIT LAKE RANGER STATION, 111.9 *m.* (R), a ranger is glad to supply information and advice on almost any subject concerning Lassen Park—from how to build a campfire to the hibernating habits of bear.

SUMMIT LAKE, 112.2 *m.* (R), is a good camping spot (*two campgrounds; fishing, hiking*). Trails radiate to the CHAIN-OF-LAKES district in the eastern section of the park.

As the highway continues south, WHITE MOUNTAIN (R), a dome volcano of the same type as Lassen Peak, named for the color of its soil and rock, rises close to the road.

At KINGS CREEK MEADOWS, 117.2 *m.* (7,400 alt.), are public campgrounds (*campfire programs nightly during season*).

Right from this point on a foot trail to KINGS CREEK FALLS, 1.3 *m.*

At 121.8 *m.* is the summit (8,512 alt.) of the Lassen Peak Loop (*parking space*).

Right from the summit on a foot trail 2.5 *m.* to LASSEN PEAK (10,453 alt.) (*round trip 3 hours*), the only volcano recently active in the United States. One of a long succession of volcanoes—Mount Rainier, Mount Hood, Mount Shasta, and ancient Mount Mazama—Lassen Peak, standing at the point where a southerly spur of the Cascade Range joins the Sierra Nevada, is the only one not yet extinct.

The peak was named San José by the Spanish soldiers under Capt. Luís Argüello, who sighted it in 1820. It was renamed for Peter Lassen, Danish pioneer who in 1848 led an immigrant band off the Overland Trail in a supposed short-cut to the Sacramento Valley. The travelers suffered such hardships in crossing the craggy region around the peak that their route was dubbed "Lassen's Folly."

The great cone, a good example of the rather rare dome type of volcano, was formed by stiff, viscous lava thrust up through the vent in a bulging domelike form around the crater of an older, gently sloping volcano of the shield type. As the dome rose, a rock mantle (talus) of broken-off fragments sheathed its slopes. Unlike most dome volcanoes, Lassen has a funnel-shaped crater formed by escaping gases, so violent that at times they still shoot forth volcanic "ash." Once an oval-shaped bowl 1,000 feet across and 360 feet deep, it is now nearly choked up with rough lava.

For two centuries Lassen had slumbered, wrapped in a snowy mantle; suddenly on May 30, 1914, it began blasting forth cold lava, cinders, and smoke. The first eruption opened a new vent in the old crater, in which melting snow, trickling down, was converted into steam. For a year mild explosions—more than 150 in all—continued, throwing out chunks of cold lava that were not warm enough to melt snow and clouds of dust that were carried by the winds as far as 15 miles southward. Not until May, 1915, did the first glowing lava appear, streaming from a notch in the crater's rim down the northeastern slope in a 1,000-foot-long tongue. As the snow melted, mud flows swept 20-ton boulders 5 to 6 miles into Hat Creek and Lost Creek valleys. Three days later, a scorching blast felled trees 3 miles away, while smoke and volcanic ash spiraled into the sky 5 miles above the crater. The volcano's force was virtually spent by the end of 1915, although it occasionally spewed forth steam and ash during the next 2 years. After a final series of violent outbursts in May and June, 1917, it subsided into its former peace, having erupted about 300 times in all. Although not yet extinct, it is not expected to erupt again for many years.

LAKE HELEN (8,000 alt.), 122.5 m. (R), named for Helen Tanner Brodt, first white woman to climb Lassen Peak, lies within the serrated crater rim of ancestral Mount Tehama, once the dominating volcano of the region. The giant crater at the peak of its sloping cone, which had ceased erupting before the Ice Age, was destroyed by violent explosions, which left behind a great bowl, or caldera, encircled by remnant peaks—Brokeoff Mountain, Mount Diller, and Black Butte.

At 122.6 m. is the junction with a foot trail.

Left here 1.3 m. to BUMPASS HELL (*round trip about 2½ hours*), a small inferno of mud springs, geysers, boiling pools, steam and hot gas vents (fumaroles). The sulphurous gases of the steam vents, which send up clouds of vapor in the cool air of morning and evening, change the lavas into yellow, olive green, or red earthy materials, or into white clay-like substances.

LAKE EMERALD (*fishing prohibited*), 123 m. (R), reflects in its crystal-clear waters the jagged relics of the ancient crater rim. The trout gleaming in its clear depths snap at morsels of food tossed by visitors.

The SULPHUR WORKS, 127.7 m., visible from the road, is an area of steam vents, boilers, and mud pots which show that the lava beneath the surface has not entirely cooled. Below the roadway (R) are natural cauldrons of bubbling hot mud. A wooden platform allows good views, but the slippery footing makes closer exploration dangerous. Above the road (L) are smaller pools filled by scalding sulphur springs, whose chemical content is apparent both from the odor and from the yellows, greens, and reds of the rock and soil over which the waters spill. A shady creek, ice cold, tumbles over its rocky bed only a few yards from the steaming pools.

Lassen Peak Loop twists downward, skirting the lower slopes (R) of Eagle Peak (9,211 alt.), Mount Diller (9,086 alt.), Diamond Peak (7,969 alt.), Brokeoff Mountain (9,232 alt.), and (L) of Black Butte (8,208 alt.)—all remnants of ancient Mount Tehama's crater rim. The highest, Brokeoff Mountain, has one side jaggedly split away. On Diamond Peak, steam vents in the old crater wall are visible.

At 129.1 m. is the SULPHUR WORKS CHECKING STATION (*open 6 a.m.-10 p.m.*), and at 131 m. the road crosses the southern boundary of Lassen Volcanic National Park through a stone gateway erected in honor of Rep. John E. Raker, who fathered the establishment and development of the park.

At 134 *m.* the route turns L. to MORGAN SPRINGS (*see TOUR 6A*), 139 *m.* at the junction with State 36 (*see Tour 6A*); R. here. State 89 and State 36 are united for 19 miles (*see TOUR 6A*).

Section b.   JUNCTION WITH STATE 36 to TRUCKEE; 119.1 m.   State 89.

State 89 branches southward from its junction with State 36 (*see TOUR 6A*), 0 *m.*, 3 miles southwest of Chester (*see TOUR 6A*).

LAKE ALMANOR (L), 2.4 *m.*, an island-studded sheet of water 45 square miles in extent, is one of California's largest reservoirs used for hydroelectric development.   The name, despite its Spanish sound, was coined from syllables of the names Alice, Martha, and Elinore—daughters of the pioneer Earl family, whose father was president of the Great Western Power Company.   Peter Lassen's trail passed through the site of Lake Almanor, then called Big Meadows.   About midway of its length, at 30.8 *m.*, is the ALMANOR INN (*boating; bathing; fishing*).   Lake Almanor is noted for the size and abundance of its trout.

At LAKE ALMANOR DAM, 14.4 *m.*, the highway crosses the North Fork of the Feather River, and climbs to a point from which there is a view of the Sacramento Valley, 50 miles to the west.

Circling eastward again, State 89 enters historic country—the district of the Northern Mines, where gold rush immigrants found the precious metal in its original quartz veins, not scattered over hillsides by glaciers and carried to river bars by the streams' action, as in so many other mining regions.   Profitable up to the present time have been some of these mines, accounting for part of the prosperity of GREEN-VILLE, 24.4 *m.* (3,500 alt., 520 pop.), and CRESCENT MILLS, 29.4 *m.* (3,500 alt., 160 pop.).   Here fertile agricultural lands reach into the mountains.

There is a gentle climb to INDIAN FALLS, 32.7 *m.* (4,000 alt., 45 pop.).

At 35.7 *m.* is the junction with State 24 (*see TOUR 6B*), which unites with State 89 for 33 miles; L. here on State 24-89 (*see TOUR 6B*).

State 89 branches southward from its junction with State 24 at BLAIRSDEN (*see TOUR 6B*), 68.7 *m.*

At 73.1 *m.* is CLIO (4,581 alt., 45 pop.), a hamlet that could not at first decide what to call itself.   Several names, all unsatisfactory, had been suggested, when the keeper of the general store became aware of the name of the heating stove at which he was looking.   "Clio!" he cried.   "There's a name for our town."   And Clio it became.

CALPINE, 84.1 *m.* (5,000 alt., 600 pop.), lies in the agricultural area of Sierra Valley, one of the few level regions in the county.   It is a fruitful valley, a mile high.

At 87.7 *m.* is the junction with State 49 (*see TOUR 4a*), which unites with State 89 for 5 miles.   Left here on State 89-49.

State 89 branches southward from its junction with State 49 at
SIERRAVILLE (*see TOUR 4a*), 92.7 *m.*

At Little Truckee River, 102.8 *m.,* is a junction with an improved
road.

> Right here, 7 *m.,* over an early route, to WEBER LAKE (6,769 alt.),
> which mirrors in one square mile the beauty of the forested mountains that
> encompass it.

At 106.8 *m.* on State 89 is a junction with an improved mountain
road.

> Right here 2.9 *m.* to INDEPENDENCE LAKE (7,000 alt.), 3 miles long
> and very deep, from which flows one of the main branches of the Little
> Truckee River. It was named by the international charmer, Lola Montez
> —for whom lofty MOUNT LOLA (9,167 alt.), to the north is named—on
> July 4, 1853, when she came from Grass Valley (*see TOUR 4a*) with a
> picnic party.

A typical lumber camp is HOBART MILLS, 112.1 *m.* (5,925 alt.,
516 pop.), with its immense sawmills, surrounded by miles of logged-
over country.

At the confluence of ALDER and PROSSER CREEKS, 114.6 *m.,*
the California Emigrant Trail came in from the Northeast. Somewhere in this region the families of George and Jacob Donner in their
slow-moving wagons (*see TOUR 9a*), lagging behind the rest of the
party because of a broken axle, were halted by falling snow at the end
of October 1846. Encamped in crude huts of canvas and boughs banked
with snow, cut off by 5 miles of drifts from their fellow travelers at
Donner Lake, they tried to hold off starvation. Here the body of
George Donner was buried by Gen. Stephen W. Kearny's men in June
1847.

TRUCKEE, 119.1 *m.* (5,818 alt., 1,000 pop.) (*see TOUR 9a*), is
at the junction with US 40 (*see TOUR 9*).

Tour 6

(Lakeview, Ore.)—Alturas—Susanville—(Reno, Nev.)—Bridgeport
—Bishop—Independence—Randsburg—San Bernardino—San Diego;
US 395.
Oregon Line to San Diego, 824.9 *m.*

Paved roadbed throughout; open all seasons; snow during winter in northern
section. Southern Pacific R.R. parallels route between Oregon Line and Raven-

dale; Western Pacific R.R. between Litchfield and Susanville and between Doyle and Nevada Line; Southern Pacific R.R. between Nevada Line and Inyokern.
Accommodations limited except in larger towns.

Though running so far inland behind the Sierra Nevada that it dips for some distance through Nevada, US 395 is nonetheless the shortest route between southern California and the Pacific Northwest.

Section a. OREGON LINE TO NEVADA LINE; 213.2 m. US 395.

This section of US 395 runs through northeastern California across the level sagebrush carpeted floors of a chain of upland valleys, walled by tumbled mountain sides. Contrasting sharply with the flat sweep of brushland are sawtoothed mountain ranges. This is a dry, desolate land with harsh beauty of coloring—the yellow-gray, dun, and gray green of brush and plains; the brownish green of pine and juniper; the red brown of crags.

Here civilization seems remote. On the isolated fields and pastures, which the first log-cabin settlers guarded with shotguns from hostile Indians, the wilderness of sagebrush still encroaches. Something of the early West still appears in the spurred cowboys in 10-gallon hats, who herd their steers off the highway to make room for motorists, and in such relics as the creaking pump by the well in the yard and the rail fences.

US 395 crosses the Oregon Line 14 miles south of Lakeview, Ore., at PINE CREEK, 0 m. (4,900 alt.), where along rutted dirt streets sagging frame houses sprawl among willows and cottonwoods.

US 395 skirts the base (L) of the WARNER MOUNTAINS (5,000-10,000 alt.) for 60 miles. The higher peaks of the range are snow-clad the year round. In monotonous succession their undulating, brush-grown slopes, bristling near the peaks with scrubby juniper and crags, overshadow the highway. Goose Lake Valley (R) sweeps into the distance. A tawny fringe of pastures and hayfields slopes down to the blackish mud flats of dry GOOSE LAKE, once 10 miles wide and 28 to 40 miles long. The lake was dry in 1849 when immigrants drove their oxcarts across its bed; but the heavy rains of following years refilled it, and later settlers moved freight across it in boats. When it again went dry in 1924, the old road over the lake bottom appeared, with traces of campfires and abandoned wagons.

At 9.5 m. is the junction with a dirt road.

Left on this road to BUCK CREEK RANGER STATION, at the entrance to MODOC NATIONAL FOREST, 0.6 m., 1,500,594 acres. Here, amid every type of mountain country—from 10,000-foot peaks to level pine-clad plateaus—streams and lakes abound in trout, and the forests in game fowl and Rocky Mountain mule deer. Throughout the Warner Mountain sector, the Forest Service maintains a string of public camps.
The road emerges from pine woods at 2.7 m. to wind over the rock-strewn sagebrush wastes of Fandango Valley and up the craggy, juniper-wooded slopes of FANDANGO MOUNTAIN (L), to the summit of FAN-

DANGO PASS (6,100 alt.), 7.8 *m.* Through the pass from the desert
country eastward, in the early 1850's, came an immigrant wagon train.
Passing the summit, the travelers looked down upon the little valley and
the shining waters of Goose Lake. Finding game, grass and sweet water,
they camped. In their joy at what they thought was safe arrival at the
end of their journey, the company began to dance a hilarious fandango;
suddenly, Indian warriors, watching from the forest, swooped down without warning and massacred them.
    From the summit of Fandango Pass appears 65-mile-long Surprise
Valley, with a chain of three dry lakes: Upper, Middle, and Lower. The
valley owes its name to the surprise of a party of Nevadans, who came
upon it unexpectedly while pursuing Indians in 1861.
    At 11.5 *m.* is the junction with a rough, graveled road; 1. L. here
5.3 *m.* across the fields and pastures of the valley to FORT BIDWELL,
16.8 *m.* (4,740 alt., 462 pop.), overshadowed by the Warner Mountains
and the great barren Bidwell Mountains. Here, in 1866, was established a
fort, named for John Bidwell, where cavalrymen were stationed to hold
the Indians in check. Abandoned as a military post in 1892, it became a
Government school for descendants of once hostile tribesmen. In 1930
the barracks were torn down. The Indians remain, housed in neat white
cottages clustered round the schoolhouse and hospital on the western edge
of town.
    2. Right from the junction along dry Upper Lake 21 *m.* to CEDAR-
VILLE (*see below*).

Along the line of US 395 creaking prairie schooners rolled in the
late 1840's. Here ran the Applegate Cut-off. In June and July 1846,
Jesse and Lindsey Applegate, with the help of 13 others, opened the
route that bears their name, and that autumn piloted about 100 wagons
over it from Fort Hall, Idaho, into Oregon. The Applegate Cut-off
passed between Middle and Upper Lakes, along the western edge of
Surprise Valley, through Fandango Pass, down into Goose Lake Valley,
and southward along the lakeshore. From Goose Lake's southern end,
it struck northwestward across the lava beds past Tule and Clear Lakes
into the Klamath country of southern Oregon.
    Crossing Lassen Creek, US 395 climbs the burned-over slopes of
towering Sugar Hill. As it rounds a bend at 14.3 *m.,* the whole stretch
of Goose Lake springs suddenly into view. The highway descends to
the valley floor. Among fields with scattered barns and corrals are
orchards where excellent apples grow.
    DAVIS CREEK, 22 *m.* (4,995 alt., 84 pop.), amid pastures spotted
with clumps of willows, is a mere handful of ramshackle houses and
abandoned store buildings.
    The highway leaves Goose Lake Valley at 28.4 *m.,* and winds up
over a rocky waste of sagebrush and juniper to dip into the canyon of
the PIT RIVER (R), 31.4 *m.,* a creek winding over brush-grown
bottoms through craggy slopes. Along the canyon bed, like a half-
ruined wall of crumbling stone winding in and out around the edge of
the hilltops, rise the rocky palisades that fringe the vast plateau lying
to the west. Over this tableland, known as the Devil's Garden, grows
one of the largest unbroken stands of western juniper, a tract of 300,000
acres.
    At 37.1 *m.* is the junction with a paved road.

Left on this road, over a desolate mesa, to the cottonwood bordered canyon of THOMAS CREEK, 6 *m.*, along which the road climbs to BONNER GRADE, 8.3 *m.,* named for John H. Bonner, who built this road over the Warner Mountains in 1869.

Deep among pine and fir is the Forest Service CEDAR PASS PUBLIC CAMP, 9.6 *m.* Beyond a bend at 10.3 *m.,* great beetling crags, blackish and tinged with rose, jut pinnaclelike; for one mile these rocky masses overhang the highway.

CEDAR PASS SUMMIT (6,350 alt.), 11.2 *m.,* affords a view of tumbled peaks and ridges wooded with bristling conifers. In graceful curves the road winds downward along Cedar Creek. As pines give way to junipers at lower levels, far stretching Surprise Valley appears ahead, and beyond is the dim blue line of mountains in Nevada.

CEDARVILLE, 17.9 *m.* (4,768 alt., 400 pop.), is an old-fashioned village with wide, tree-lined dirt streets, along which stand old white clapboarded houses. One block R. of Main St., in a grove of tall cottonwoods stands the CRESSLER AND BONNER TRADING POST, a tiny cabin of hand-hewn logs with a shake roof, worn and weathered. Its builder, one Townsend, was killed by Indians soon after he built it in 1865; his widow sold it to William T. Cressler and John H. Bonner, who set up the first store in Modoc County, a trading post that carried on a thriving business with immigrants and later with the settlers of Surprise Valley.

The highway winds on over rolling country, across willow-fringed Pit River and into the level valley of the South Fork of the Pit.

At 42.8 *m.* is the junction with US 299 (*see TOUR 8a*) which, between this point and Alturas, is united with US 395.

ALTURAS, 43.5 *m.* (4,446 alt., 2,338 pop.) (*see TOUR 8a*), is at the junction with US 299 (*see TOUR 8a*).

South of Alturas are pastures and scattered farmhouses. Farther southward is a rolling, dreary waste of sagebrush.

At 60.1 *m.* is the junction with a dirt road.

Right on this road 1.7 *m.* to a junction with a dirt road; R. here and through a wooden gate 0.3 *m.* to a fork in the road; L. here, through another wooden gate, 1.6 *m.* to a farmhouse at the base of the hills. Here a wagon track, impassable except on foot, leads (L) through the barnyard and across swampy fields 1 *m.* to the mouth of CROOK'S CANYON, where tiny Hilton Creek gurgles among boulders overgrown with sagebrush and juniper.

Beyond, at the base of a rock-crowned hill, is the INFERNAL CAVERNS BATTLE-GROUND. Over the pleasant valley meadows six white marble headstones mark the graves of six of the men killed here September 26, 1867: two sergeants and four privates of the Twenty-third Infantry and the First Cavalry. The battle occurred when a band of about 100 Shoshones, Paiutes, and Pits who had terrorized the country round about were cornered by Gen. George Crook and a force of 65 soldiers. In a seemingly impregnable fortress of caves and rocks the Indians took their stand. After two days of fighting, they were forced out, but only after eight of Crook's men had been killed and 14 wounded.

After passing LIKELY, 63.1 *m.* (4,500 alt., 75 pop.), in the midst of wide-spreading pastures, US 395 climbs to a low pass between rugged South Fork Mountain (R) and Tule Mountain (7,136 alt.) (L), to twist over South Fork Mountain's lower slopes and wind along the shores of Tule Lake Reservoir (L), then descend again to valley plains.

MADELINE, 76.6 *m.* (5,300 alt., 92 pop.), stands at the upper end of a dreary sagebrush waste. About the railroad station huddle a bleak tavern, gas stations, and a handful of shanties.

Across the vast plain the highway continues southward to RAVEN-DALE, 98.1 *m.* (5,300 alt., 19 pop.), a group of cattle corrals and old houses with peeling paint. Then it enters a rolling, juniper-dotted wilderness and, at 107.2 *m.,* cuts into a wild region of rocky ridges, broken and jagged. Along the edge of the low tableland (R) stands a rocky embankment like a breastwork of stone piled by hand.

Green and fresh, Secret Valley appears suddenly like an oasis far below beyond the crags; but its meadows soon give way to another sagebrush waste.

As US 395 winds down from the pass, 128.2 *m.,* Honey Lake Valley, walled by the lofty peaks of the Sierra Nevada (R), appears in a widening panorama of fields and pastures, clumps of trees and rooftops. A valley 40 miles long and 20 miles wide, it was long the only settled section of Lassen County. Its first dwellers named it for the honeydew on trees and shrubs, from which the Indians made a sort of molasses. Here lived two Indian tribes; along the base of the Sierra, the poverty-stricken Washo, numbering only 900 in 1859; over the rest of the valley, the Pah Ute, 6,000 or 7,000 in number. The Pah Ute proved friendly to white men, visiting their houses and trading furs. Their chief, Old Winnemucca, in 1856 signed a treaty with the whites that provided for punishment to Indians for thieving and to white men for molesting squaws.

Across the sluggish, tule-bordered Susan River, deep among willows, the highway cuts into lush fields, past farmhouses and windmills in clumps of bushy cottonwoods. Here sprawls old-fashioned STAND-ISH, 138.7 *m.* (4,000 alt., 115 pop.), with a steepled church and belfry-topped schoolhouse, and a string of ancient stores and houses.

At 147.6 *m.* is the junction with State 36 (*see TOUR 6A*).

JOHNSTONVILLE, 148.1 *m.* (4,100 alt., 13 pop.), where tree-shaded houses gather about a schoolhouse, was the home of pioneer Robert Johnston. It once bore the name Toadtown because toads covered the ground during heavy rainstorms.

US 395 here swings sharply southeast. Overshadowed by the rugged, forested Sierra is JANESVILLE, 155.1 *m.* (4,236 alt., 200 pop.). Along the highway for a mile in forest clearings, straggle red, sagging frame houses, abandoned stores, and a little white schoolhouse with the ever-present belfry. Here in 1857 Malcolm Bankhead raised his two-story house of logs and a blacksmith shop. The town was named for his wife, when the post office was opened in 1864.

A few widely scattered houses, a store, and gas station are all that remain of BUNTINGVILLE, 157.2 *m.,* named for A. J. Bunting who opened a store here in 1878.

South of Buntingville, beyond the strip of farmland and pasture glimpsed between black oaks and pines (L) appears the vast, blackish bottom of dry HONEY LAKE.

MILFORD, 167.3 *m.* (4,180 alt., 69 pop.), is a few old buildings, on the edge of the orchards and pastures.

DOYLE, 185.7 *m.* (4,260 alt., 68 pop.), amid sagebrush, is hemmed in by desolate slopes. The route continues southeastward between mountain walls, on one side rock ribbed and barren, forested with green on the other.

STOY JUNCTION, 205.4 *m.,* marks the junction with State 24 (*see TOUR 6B*).

More and more rugged grow the rocky walls of the Sierra, as the highway runs through an arid expanse to reach the glistening white sheet of dry ALKALINE LAKE and the NEVADA LINE, 213.2 *m.,* at a point 15.6 miles west of Reno, Nev., and 83.2 miles north of a second crossing of the California Line.

Section b. NEVADA LINE to BISHOP; 131.5 m. US 395.

Skirting the eastern slopes of the Sierra Nevada, this section of US 395 winds through rugged, thinly settled country, warm and leafy in summer, bitterly cold and often piled with impenetrable snowdrifts in winter. Geologically, this region is young. The great cinder cones of Mono Craters—some reaching an elevation of 9,000 feet—and numerous bubbling hot springs are evidences of a great igneous field not yet burned out; it is estimated that volcanic activity may have taken place here as recently as 500 years ago. Sheep and cattle graze in the valleys, but the rugged back country is seldom penetrated save by sportsmen who come to hunt deer and to fish in the numerous high, cold lakes.

US 395 crosses the Nevada Line, 0 *m.,* 76 miles south of Reno (*see NEVADA GUIDE*). TOPAZ LAKE (L), on the line, a tranquil body of water encompassed by pinon-strewn hills, was formed in 1920-21 when the course of Walker River changed and inundated about 1,800 acres of a flourishing ranch.

After skirting Topaz Lake, US 395 passes between SLINKARD'S CANYON, 3.5 *m.,* and its broad residual delta (L), and traverses Antelope Valley.

WALKER RIVER, 4.2 *m.,* is the valley's principal source of water. In 1827 Jedediah Smith, traveling what was to become the Sonora Trail over the Sierra in the first crossing of that range by a white man, trod the banks of this stream on his eastward trek to Salt Lake City. In 1833-34 the trapping and exploring party of Capt. Joseph Walker reached the river, followed it to its source, and then battled through the defiles of the Sierra for 23 days before entering the central plains of California. This was the first westward passage of the mountains. In 1841 the Bidwell-Bartleson party, first of the overland settlers, followed this same river, and a decade later the trail had become a well-defined road leading into the central gold fields.

COLEVILLE, 9.4 *m.* (5,750 alt., 50 pop.), a tourist and farm trading hamlet, lines both sides of the highway beneath scattered shade trees.

WALKER CANYON, 15 *m.,* cut by the willow-lined river, is at the lower end of Antelope Valley.

A boundary of MONO NATIONAL FOREST is crossed at 16 *m.* Giant pines lean over Walker River, and cottonwoods and willows lend greenery to the jagged, crumbling walls of granite that tower above the road.

SHINGLE MILL PUBLIC CAMP, 20.3 *m.,* is a pine-sheltered clearing beside the river.

CHRIS FLATS PUBLIC CAMP (*stoves and tables*), 24.2 *m.,* lies on a sandy bar of the riverbank beneath cottonwoods and pines.

At 28.4 *m.* is the junction with State 108, paved.

Right on State 108, which ascends the Sierra Nevada, crossing it through SONORA PASS (9,642 alt.), 15.2 *m.* Hordes of fortune hunters swarmed over the route after the Sonora-Mono road to the Nevada silver mining country was cleared in the 1860's. The road descends past a string of outing camps to DARDANELLE (*cabins*), 31.2 *m.* (5,775 alt., 10 pop.), lying near the base of the striking serrated mountain ridge (R) for which it is named.

The TUOLUMNE COUNTY PUBLIC CAMP (L) is at 32.5 *m.*

The way leads down the crest of the narrow ridge between the Stanislaus River (R) and the beautiful North Fork of the Tuolumne (L).

COW CREEK RANGER STATION, 49.5 *m.* (5,750 alt.), consists of a few tree-shaded buildings.

At the mountain resort of STRAWBERRY, 53.5 *m.* (5,240 alt.), is the junction with a dirt road; L. here 2 *m.* to PINECREST, a mountain camp on the southern shore of STRAWBERRY LAKE, near ELEANOR LAKE. The lakes are guarded by granite cliffs surmounted by tier upon tier of somber, dark green pines.

LONGBARN (*hotel*), 63.9 *m.* (5,000 alt., 25 pop.), is in a summer and winter sports area. The snow-blanketed slopes round-about are thronged in season with skiers and tobogganers. Close by is the 1,800-foot toboggan slide of the Tuolumne Club.

CONFIDENCE, 69.7 *m.* (4,250 alt., 63 pop.), trading village of the surrounding mining and lumbering area, was named for the nearby Confidence Mine, that justified its name by producing $4,250,000 in gold.

At 75.7 *m.* is the junction with a dirt road; L. here 1 *m.* to SOULSBY-VILLE, (3,000 alt., 320 pop.), a mining town dating back to 1856.

At 80.7 *m.* is the junction with a dirt road; L. on this road 7 *m.* is TUOLUMNE (2,600 alt., 2,000 pop.), a mill center of sugar pine lumbering, lying in a circular basin on Turnback Creek.

SONORA, 83.2 *m.* (1,925 alt., 2,278 pop.), (*see TOUR 4b*), is at the junction with State 49 (*see TOUR 4b*).

FALES HOT SPRINGS, 31.8 *m.,* were discovered in 1867 by Archibald Samuel Fales, who crossed the plains in 1851. Fales had been a prospector, and a driver and guard on the Bodie-Sacramento Stage Line; but rheumatism necessitated his settling in the mud. Around his mud bath there sprang up a saloon, a freight depot, sheep pens, and accompanying evidences of civilization. The present establishment is a rustic collection of buildings around a concrete pool whose waters, laden with sodium, calcium, and magnesium, have a temperature of 180 degrees.

US 395 continues its ascent through hills that begin to lose their rotundity and rise in spires of crumbling rock.

DEVIL'S GATE, 33.1 *m.* (7,549 alt.), a great perpendicular mass of cracked green rock, rises sheer above both sides of the highway.

HUNTOON PUBLIC CAMP, (*stoves*) 40.5 *m.,* is (L) beside a small mountain stream, a tributary of Walker River.

Forsaking the course of the creek, the route crosses the southern boundary of MONO NATIONAL FOREST, 42.1 *m.,* and approaches secluded Bridgeport Valley, where small bands of cattle graze.

BRIDGEPORT, 45.7 *m.* (6,473 alt., 200 pop.), is in a valley ringed by the snowy peaks of the Sierra and low, pinon-covered hills. Dilapidated, partly crushed houses, long since abandoned, evidence the weight of winter snows. Bridgeport owes its existence to a geographical misunderstanding on the part of the early inhabitants of Mono County, who, in 1864, were amazed to learn that their county seat, Aurora, was in Nevada. Hurriedly the county papers were transferred from Aurora to a tiny roadside camp that later became Bridgeport. The town grew prosperous in the days when gold was plentiful, and built its gingerbread courthouse. Today, with gold scarce, it subsists upon what mining activity remains, upon the surrounding farm trade, and tourist patronage.

The ornate MONO COUNTY COURTHOUSE, a two-story, white structure (L) ornamented with red-trimmed windows, has appeared frequently in motion pictures. A cannon on its lawn is celebrated locally as having been a repository for "hooch" during prohibition days.

South of Bridgeport US 395 again climbs into the mountains. Green foliage covers the bottoms of the canyons; snow-capped peaks glisten in the distance; pinon and pines give verdant ornamentation to mountainsides scarred with green and black rock formations of increasing prominence.

At 53.1 *m.* is the junction with a dirt road.

Left on this road to a junction with a dirt road, 4.1 *m.;* L. on this road is BODIE, 13.7 *m.* (8,374 alt., 125 pop.). From 1876 to 1880 a mining town with 12,000 inhabitants, Bodie is today an aggregation of shacks clustered below the great mill and mine (R) on the mountain. Gold was first discovered in the Mono region in 1852; the Mono Trail was blazed from Big Oak Flat through the present Yosemite Park, and in 1859 W. S. Body found gold here. But in 1864 the Sonora Pass wagon road was opened, removing much of the Mono Trail traffic, in 1870 the Aurora mine failed, and it was not until 1876 that fortune again smiled with the unexpected development of the Bodie Mine, a wildcat venture. Population figures leaped. Saloons and gambling halls prospered; drunken miners threw 20-dollar gold pieces in the streets for small boys to spike with their tops. Occasionally guns blazed in the streets; the phrase, "Bad man from Bodie," became popular. By 1883 all the mines but two had closed, and in 1887 even they were consolidated. Finally, on June 24, 1932, fire destroyed most of what remained. The ROSECLIP MINE on the hill above (R) reopened in October, 1936.

Ascending the long grade, US 395 winds through hills clothed with meager bunch grass, desert sage, and needle grass.

The SITE OF DOGTOWN (L), 53.7 *m.,* several hundred yards from the highway, is marked by a few remnants of the stores and houses of the early mining town, probably the earliest settlement in the entire region. Its life was short, for in 1859 the population, lured by more attractive prospects, moved en masse to neighboring Monoville.

VIRGINIA LAKE JUNCTION, 59.7 *m.* (8,138 alt.), at the summit of the grade, is a gas station, store, and a group of tourist cabins.

MONO LAKE, 69 *m.,* though it appears fresh and inviting, is actually a briny deep, in which nothing but one small species of salt-water shrimp and the larvae of one tiny black fly can live. Its waters are so impregnated with soluble alkaline materials that storms, often violent in this region, sometimes pile the shores with' a soapy foam several feet thick. In the 87 square miles of water of the lake more than 19 different chemicals are held in solution. Rising above volcanic PAOHA ISLAND in the lake's center, there is visible on clear, still days a misty vapor from the island's hot spring. Another extinct crater, NEGIT ISLAND, also juts above the blue surface of the lake. Above it occasionally soar terns, locally called "Mono pigeons," and sea-gulls that have flown inland from the Pacific. The lake has achieved a certain measure of fame in literature and legend. Mark Twain tells in *Roughing It* of a dog that attained a running speed of 250 miles an hour after taking a swim in the lake. A more modern tale is of a long-haired dog that emerged from a swim with nothing left but its bark. But the water that feeds Mono Lake will not go to waste much longer, for, soon purified, it will go into the new Mono Basin Aqueduct and help to slake the thirst of metropolitan Los Angeles. The drainage from five streams, the Mill, Rush, Walker, Leevining, and Parker, is to be diverted by conduits leading to Grants Lake, six miles south of Mono Lake, where it will be impounded. From this Grants Lake Dam another conduit will lead the water to a 12-mile tunnel emerging near a tributary of the Owens River, whence it will flow down to the Los Angeles Aqueduct at Aberdeen.

MONOVILLE, 69.1 *m.* (6,419 alt., 20 pop.), a resort settlement on the shore of Mono Lake, is a summer supply center for campers and miners. Monoville thrived in the wild boom days but, unlike most mining towns, history records no bloodcurdling deeds of its early period; it was always, apparently, as peaceful as it is today. It was still fighting to be the county seat in 1864, and served for 50 years as the starting point for those seeking for "the lost cement mines." According to local legend, these mines were discovered by three German brothers on their way to California in the 1850's and were near the headwaters of the Owens River. In the vein of cement they found "lumps of gold set like raisins in a pudding"; but a bitter winter drove the brothers from their find, killing two and leaving the third insane. It was his babbled story of treasure that started the prolonged treasure hunt.

LEEVINING, 71.8 *m.* (7,000 alt., 80 pop.), derives its name from nearby Leevining Canyon, named for Lee Vining, who in 1852 led a party of prospectors to the first gold strike there.

At 72.1 *m.* is the junction with State 120, the Tioga Pass route (*see YOSEMITE TOUR 3*).

South of Leevining is a view (L) of a group of the MONO CRATERS, 73.1 *m.* Four of them, resembling gigantic ash heaps, are immediately and easily discernible. Actually there are 20, forming a crescent-shaped range, along the base of which US 395 proceeds for 10 miles through Pumice Valley, covered with fine silt pumice of past volcanic eruptions.

The AEOLIAN BUTTES (L), 78.1 *m.,* scarred and crumbled steps of red rock, are the oldest volcanic formations on Mono Basin.

At 99.7 *m.* is the junction with a dirt road.

Right on this road is MAMMOTH POST OFFICE, 4 *m.,* a few small houses and stores. At 4.2 *m.* is the junction with a dirt road; R. here 3.5 *m.* to an EARTHQUAKE FAULT (R), and to the DEVIL'S POST PILE NATIONAL MONUMENT, 11.5 *m.,* a rectangular area 2.5 miles long and 0.5 miles wide, extending along both sides of the Middle Fork of the San Joaquin River and containing clear evidence of recent volcanic activity. The 40-foot cliff of columnar basalt rearing above the turbulent San Joaquin is composed of columns that are nearly perfect prisms. Two feet in diameter and almost vertical, they fit together like the cells of a honeycomb. Most of the prisms are pentagonal, though there are some with four or six sides. Littering the base of the cliff are fragments of these prisms shaken down by some long-past earthquake.

Ten miles north are BANNER PEAK (12,953 alt.) and MOUNT RITTER (13,153 alt.); just south of the latter are the MINARETS, pinnacles of dark granite.

South of the Devil's Post Pile are the RAINBOW FALLS. Here the San Joaquin makes a 140-foot perpendicular drop into a box canyon, creating a scene of mist-sprayed grandeur.

At 8 *m.* on the main side road is the junction with a dirt road; R. or L. here into the vast region of lakes and resorts known collectively as MAMMOTH LAKES (8,931 alt.). These lakes, the joy of fishermen and vacationists, were once the scene of one of California's feverish gold rushes. In the summer of 1878 the town of Mammoth had a population of 125; in 1879 it had 2,500. A string of settlements had sprung up in the canyon and two semi-weekly newspapers flourished. But the exceptionally bitter winter of 1879-80 caused most of the miners to abandon their claims, and of those who remained three were frozen to death. Although Mammoth had a brief return of prosperity in 1880, the mines were nearly exhausted, and the next year saw the final decline.

At 103.1 *m.* is the junction with a dirt road.

Right on this road to CONVICT LAKE, 2.5 *m.* (7,583 alt.), a pellucid sheet of blue, fronted by a rustic resort for fishermen and backed by the imposing height of Mount Morrison (12,245 alt.). On September 17, 1871, 29 convicts escaped from the Nevada State Penitentiary and made their way to this lake, where they attempted to winter. Six of the desperadoes started south, and on their way met and murdered William Poor, a mail carrier. Outraged citizens in Aurora and Benton organized a posse, which set out for the convict stronghold. The posse reached the lake on September 24, and engaged in a gun battle in which Robert Morrison (for whom the distant peak is named) was killed. Several of the convicts escaped, but were later captured; two were hanged at Bishop; another was returned to the penitentiary.

The semiarid undulations of Long Valley stretch away (L), and in the far background rise the WHITE MOUNTAINS (14,242 alt.).

The ascent of SHERWIN GRADE is begun at 119.1 *m.* Over bare hills the highway climbs to the summit, 119.7 *m.* (6,430 alt.), from which is a view, ahead and below, of vast Owens Valley and the silver line of Owens River. From the summit the road descends in tortuous hairpin curves, frequently flanked (R) by sheer drops.

US 395, flanked (R) by the dull hues of the TUNGSTEN HILLS, traverses greener country and proceeds over the floor of Owens Valley between rows of poplars and oaks. Occasionally hayfields and cornfields border the road.

BISHOP, 131.5 *m.* (4,147 alt., 1,159 pop.), is the largest town in Owens Valley, and the chief business center of the area. It is a supply point for stockraising and mining interests. (Much tungsten is mined in the vicinity.) Sportsmen know it as a gateway and outfitting point for camping, fishing, and packing trips into the Sierra Nevada, which rise (R) more than 10,000 feet above the town.

Bishop was named for Bishop Creek, which in turn was named for Samuel A. Bishop, a Fort Tejon stockman, who drove the first herd of cattle into Owens Valley in 1861. He built two rough pine cabins on his St. Francis Ranch that were besieged by Paiutes during the Indian uprisings of the 1860's, and several times thereafter until Fort Independence (*see below*) was established in 1862. By 1863 settlers had come into Owens Valley in increasing numbers, and the village sprang up 3 miles northeast of Bishop's ranch.

At the northern end of Bishop is the junction with US 6 (*see TOUR 7a*), which unites with US 395 for 123 miles.

Right from Bishop on State 139 along Bishop Creek to the junction with South Fork Rd., 11 *m.;* L. 7.5 *m.* to SOUTH LAKE (9,750 alt.), source of the South Fork of Bishop Creek and popular for trout fishing. The main stream of Bishop Creek, which runs from the Lake Sabrina region in the high Sierra to Owens River at Bishop, is 14 miles in length. Its North, Middle, and South Forks penetrate a mountain area of more than 200 lakes. Dropping an average of 400 feet per mile, the main stream is equipped with seven power stations, the highest at an elevation of 8,000 feet. Its waters are also used for irrigation.

The Paiute inhabited this region before the arrival of white men. Among the most primitive of American Indians—neither planting, tilling, nor cultivating the soil—none the less they used the waters of this creek to aid the growth of their wild food plants. They watered the plots of wild seed, shrubs, and tubers in the spring by damming the creek and running a ditch to each field. In the fall the dam was destroyed and the waters allowed to return to the main channel.

On State 139 is LAKE SABRINA, 15 *m.* (9,150 alt.), headwaters of the Middle Fork of Bishop Creek, and noted for its rainbow and golden trout. From the lake five peaks towering 13,000 feet are visible.

Section c.   BISHOP to BROWN 124.7 m.   US 395-US 6.

This section of US 395 penetrates a land of contrasts—cool crests and burning lowlands, fertile agricultural regions and untamed deserts.

It is a land where Indians made a last stand against the invading white man, where bandits sought refuge from early vigilante retribution; a land of fortunes—past and present—in gold, silver, tungsten, marble, soda, and borax; and a land esteemed by sportsmen because of scores of lakes and streams abounding with trout and forests alive with game. The highway follows the irregular eastern base of the towering Sierra Nevada, past the highest peak in any of the States—Mount Whitney— at the western approach to Death Valley, the Nation's lowest, and hottest, area.

South of Bishop, 0 *m.*, US 6-395 traverses the length of flat Owens Valley, an 85-mile trough. Although little rain falls here, the land has great fertility. The Owens River, receiving the waters of swift tributaries, supplies unlimited amounts of irrigation water. Much of the farm land, however, has been acquired by the city of Los Angeles as watershed adjuncts to the Los Angeles Aqueduct, which taps Owens River.

BIG PINE, 16.5 *m.* (4,002 alt., 200 pop.), is a quiet village whose wooden sidewalks are shaded by great oaks and maples. Catering to motorists and the outfitting of fishing, packing, and hiking parties bound for the high Sierra constitute its chief sources of income.

>Right from Big Pine on Big Pine Creek Rd. to GLACIER LODGE (*rates reasonable*), 12 *m.*, and to a hiking trail at 14 *m.;* straight ahead on this trail to PALISADES GLACIER, 20 *m.*

TINEMAHA RESERVOIR (L), 24 *m.,* is a collecting basin of the Los Angeles Aqueduct System.

US 395 cuts through POVERTY HILLS, 24.3 *m.,* between scattered masses of volcanic outcroppings. Lava deposits appear with increasing frequency, and at 30.3 *m.* (L) is an extensive lava bed.

ABERDEEN, 31.6 *m.* (3,814 alt., 25 pop.), is the starting point of the LOS ANGELES AQUEDUCT, which is 233 miles long. It took five years to build (1908-1913), and cost $23,000,000. More than 40 miles of tunnel were bored through solid rock, the longest section measuring 26,780 feet. The completed aqueduct includes 142 separate tunnels aggregating almost 52 miles in length, 12 miles of steel siphons about 10 feet in diameter, 24 miles of open, unlined conduit, 39 miles of open cement-lined conduit, and 98 miles of covered conduit. The gravity system is used throughout.

At 42.5 *m.* is the junction with a paved road and with a dirt road.

>1. Right on paved road to MOUNT WHITNEY STATE FISH HATCHERY (*open 9-5 weekdays*), 1.4 *m.* whose red stone buildings occupy a parklike tract. Between two and one-half and three and one-half million trout fry are distributed annually from the hatchery.

>2. Left on dirt road 0.1 *m.* to the RUINS OF FORT INDEPENDENCE. A decaying, one-story log cabin, once the officers' quarters, is all that remains of the military camp that played a part in quelling the Inyo County Indian uprisings in the 1860's. The fort was established July 4, 1862, and maintained until 1877.

INDEPENDENCE, 45.8 *m.* (3,925 alt., 408 pop.), seat of Inyo County, is an outfitting point for pack trips into the Sierra by way of Kearsarge Pass and a shipping point for farm products.

The EASTERN CALIFORNIA MUSEUM (*open 9-6 weekdays*), in the basement of the INYO COUNTY COURTHOUSE, houses a collection of antiquated firearms used in the Indian wars, old sidesaddles, candle and bullet molds, files of newspapers and historical documents, Indian relics of California and Nevada, flora and minerals of the region, and a collection of photographs of Indian pictographs.

On the crest of the INYO MOUNTAINS (L) is an inaccessible monolith of weather-worn and storm-beaten granite known as the PAIUTE MONUMENT. Although 80 feet high, of a roughly conical shape, it appears from Independence as a slender, heaven-pointing finger.

By MANZANAR (Sp., apple orchard), 51.9 *m.* (3,872 alt., 153 pop.), is the JOHN SHEPHERD RANCH HOUSE (R), built in 1873 of materials brought by wagon from San Pedro, 250 miles away.

The ALABAMA HILLS (R), 56 *m.,* riven by glacial pressure in the Triassic period and rent by earth movements in subsequent ages, rise beside the highway. At the foot of the hills and paralleling the highway runs an EARTHQUAKE FAULT, along which the land dropped from 4 to 12 feet in the temblor of 1872, which took 26 lives.

LONE PINE, 61.6 *m.* (3,728 alt., 360 pop.), dating from the early 1850's, caters to tourists and outfits for trips to Mount Whitney. Within packing distance are more than 1,000 mountain lakes stocked with trout.

Right from Lone Pine on State 190, through HUNTERS FLAT (*hunting in season*), 10 *m.,* abounding with deer, bear, sage hen, grouse, and quail, to WHITNEY PORTAL, 14 *m.,* a pack station, marking the end of the motor road.

Straight ahead on a pack trail to OUTPOST CAMP, 18 *m.* (10,300 alt.), which lies just below the timber line in a setting of towering cliffs and green meadows. Lone Pine Creek tumbles over a series of falls (L) as the trail ascends past MIRROR LAKE, 19 *m.* Above stand the last stunted trees, outposts of the timber line. The trail now enters an area of mighty granite walls and boulder-strewn basins where, strangely, some of the loveliest of Alpine wild flowers grow. Upward the trail winds through fields of perpetual snow to the summit of MOUNT WHITNEY (14,495 alt.), 24 *m.* The mighty peak was named by the noted geologist, Clarence King (1842-1901), in honor of Prof. J. D. Whitney, leader of the California Geologic Survey party which in 1864 ascertained that this mountain was the loftiest peak in the United States, exclusive of Alaska. The first attempt to scale Mount Whitney was made by King in 1871, but, confused by storm clouds, he climbed Mount Langley by mistake. Unaware of his error, he published an account claiming first ascent of Mount Whitney. In 1873 W. A. Goodyear climbed Mount Langley, discovered King's marker, and published news of the mistake. King hurried west from New York and on September 19, 1873, climbed the true Mount Whitney. But others had deprived him by one month of the honor of making the first ascent. On August 18, 1873, A. H. Johnson, C. D. Begole, and John Lucas had reached the summit and given the mountain the name Fisherman's Peak, which for a time threatened to supersede the earlier name. The summit is a nearly level area of 3 to 4 acres, sloping slightly westward.

At 63.6 *m.* is the southern junction with State 190.

> Left on State 190 to a MARBLE QUARRY, 8 *m.* (L), whose product is noted for its coloring and quality. KEELER, 13 *m.* (3,610 alt., 300 pop.), a desert settlement, has been for many years the headquarters of a plant engaged in extracting soda-ash from Owens Lake.

> Left from Keeler on a dirt road 6 *m.* to CERRO GORDO (9,217 alt.), producing silver, lead, and zinc.

> At 30.4 *m.* on State 190 is the junction with a dirt road; R. here 6.2 *m.* to DARWIN (4,479 alt., 80 pop.), an old mining town whose population at one time numbered 1,500. The town bears the name of Dr. Darwin French, who in 1860, while searching for the fabulous lost Gunsight Mine, discovered silver and lead ledges in the COSO RANGE, 12 miles south.
> State 190 crosses Panamint Valley and ascends the Panamint Range to the western boundary of DEATH VALLEY NATIONAL MONUMENT, 63 *m.* (*see DEATH VALLEY TOUR 1*).

BARTLETT, 70.6 *m.* (3,690 alt., 70 pop.), center of operations of one of the largest borax mining companies in the United States, is by OWENS LAKE, 17 miles long and 10 miles wide which was named for Richard Owen, a member of John C. Frémont's 1845 expedition. Into it from the north flows Owens River. The level of the lake was once much higher; well-defined shore lines mark the continued recession of the waters. Originally it was an inland sea, created in the Ice Age by slow-moving glaciers; as the ice cap slowly receded melting torrents roared into the lower areas and formed inland seas, filled with salts, sodas, and other chemicals leached from the rocks. Through the centuries the waters, no longer replenished by melting ice streams, evaporated and left great arid beds—the dry lakes of today's desert.

CARTAGO, 82.7 *m.* (3,680 alt., 30 pop.), is a railroad village at the southern end of Owens Lake. An employees' town (L), once considered a model housing project, has been virtually abandoned since the lime, soda, and borax plant closed several years ago.

OLANCHA, 85.6 *m.* (3,649 alt., 75 pop.), is named for the Olancha tribe which formerly inhabited the region. In the background (R) is OLANCHA PEAK (12,135 alt.).

UPPER HAIWEE RESERVOIR, 91.4 *m.,* connects one mile south with LOWER HAIWEE RESERVOIR, the two forming one of the largest collecting basins in the Los Angeles aqueduct system.

US 395 crosses lava masses past foothill slopes (R) scarred by great misshapen boulders of volcanic substance.

LITTLE LAKE, 111.5 *m.* (3,172 alt., 23 pop.), is a tourist settlement named for a 10-acre, privately owned lake that gleams beside the road.

At 123.8 *m.* US 6 (*see TOUR 7b*) swings R.; the route turns sharply L. on US 395.

BROWN, 124.7 *m.* (2,400 alt., 51 pop.), is a railroad town on the Southern Pacific-Randsburg Line.

Section d. BROWN *to* JUNCTION US 66; 107.5 m. US 395

This section of US 395 continues through desert country tapped by gold and silver mines.

South of BROWN, 0 m., is INYOKERN, 9.6 m. (2,442 alt., 25 pop.), which in summer swelters in the heat of flat Indian Wells Valley. On the lone hotel, a weather-beaten frame structure, is a sign reading: "This is the hotel, believe it or not." At Inyokern is the junction with the Trona Road (*see DEATH VALLEY NATIONAL MONUMENT*).

The Rand Mountains, dark, rounded elevations, loom up straight ahead; the highway begins its ascent of the long grade up the range.

At 34.3 m. is the junction with an asphalt paved road.

Right on this road is RANDSBURG, 1 m. (3,523 alt., 443 pop.), a mining camp in the Rand Quadrangle, long a very productive mining district, named for the Rand gold-mining district in the Transvaal, South Africa. The town's unpainted weather-worn cabins sprawl over the rocky slopes on the northern flank of Rand Mountain, like those of a typical movie-set mining town. The single street divides a collection of ancient frame houses scattered about at random. On the slopes are the tin and galvanized iron structures of the mines, each complemented by a pile of tailings. Gold was first discovered in Goler Wash, nine miles northwest of Randsburg, in 1893, and dry-washing camps soon sprang up in Last Chance and Red Rock Canyons and at Summit Diggings. The richest mine was the Yellow Aster, on the side of Rand Mountain, which by 1925 had yielded about $10,000,-000 in gold. The ore in the Yellow Aster Mine, which is now a "glory hole," 1,200 feet deep, contains enough tungsten to pay all operating expenses, leaving the gold as clear profit. (A glory hole is an open excavation without shafts or tunnels, enabling its operators to recover a large quantity of ore at minimum expense.) The ore taken from this pit is crushed in the stamp mill and its minute particles of gold are recovered by a complex chemical process known as cyaniding.

From JOHANNESBURG, 35.2 m. (3,536 alt., 106 pop.), named for the chief city in the Transvaal, most of the glory of mining days has vanished, though a few miners still hopefully work old properties.

At RED MOUNTAIN, 37 m. (3,530 alt., 200 pop.), prospector Hamp Williams is said to have stumbled on California's richest silver mine by accident. Overtaken by a snowstorm one day in the winter of 1919, he sought shelter in a pit dug years before by another gold seeker. While crouching there he picked up a fragment of rock that appeared to contain metal; an assay subsequently showed it to be "horn silver," rich in value. Williams staked out a claim, later developed into the Big Kelly Mine and now known as the Rand Silver Mine. Today Red Mountain is cutting in on the social life of Johannesburg and Randsburg with its honky-tonks, dance halls, and drinking places, where miners of the Rand and men from Trona come to spend their leisure hours. As in a movie set of a rough-and-tumble border town, its buildings perch above the road level, the raucous jangle of mechanical pianos coming through the swinging doors of the saloons.

ATOLIA, 40.4 m. (3,600 alt., 150 pop.), is a far cr from the booming town that supplied the Allies in the World War with tungsten from the Atolia Tungsten Mine ever since new discoveries in China pushed the price of tungsten too low to justify operation at a profit.

US 395 sweeps across the vast Mojave Desert. No settlement, not even a gasoline station, marks the route until it approaches KRAMER JUNCTION, 64.2 m. (2,482 alt.), a filling station and auto camp. The road winds upgrade through the low Kramer Hills and levels out again across the Mojave. It passes through a region of great silence, of sagebrush and creosote bush stretching interminably. Near the southern end of the straightaway, occasional green, irrigated tracts break the tawny monotone of sand.

ADELANTO, 95.7 m. (2,900 alt., 300 pop.), is the center of an alfalfa-growing and poultry-raising district, reclaimed by the Mojave River.

The highway mounts steadily to the level sandy plateau of Baldy Mesa and sweeps across it toward the bulwark of the San Bernardino Mountains.

At 107.5 m. is the junction with US 66 (see TOUR 12b), which unites with US 395 to San Bernardino (see TOUR 12b).

Section e. SAN BERNARDINO to SAN DIEGO; 134.8 m. US 395.

Between a high inland plateau at the mouth of Cajon Pass and the coast, US 395 runs due southward through the oldest citrus producing area in southern California and across low, barren ranges to the coast.

SAN BERNARDINO, 0 m. (1,077 alt., 37,481 pop.) (see TOUR 12b), is at the junction with US 66 (see TOUR 12b).

At 3 m. US 99 (see TOUR 3d) unites westward with US 395 to COLTON (978 alt., 8,014 pop.) (see TOUR 3d), where US 395 branches L.

HIGHGROVE, 5 m. (500 pop.), is a trading post for the surrounding citrus ranches.

In RIVERSIDE, 10.2 m. (851 alt., 29,696 pop.) (see TOUR 13b), is a junction with US 60 (see TOUR 13b), which unites with US 395 southeastward to a junction at 14.7 m., where US 60 turns R.

BOX SPRINGS, 13.5 m., is a filling station and garage.

At 17.1 m. is a junction with a paved road.

Left on this road to MARCH FIELD, 2 m., an Army flying field (*open daylight hours*), with a 3,550-foot runway outlined with green lights, a paved landing mat of 450,000 square feet, 200 permanent buildings on the field, and eight miles of paved roads. The field was established in 1917 as a training school, named for Peyton C. March, Jr., son of the Chief of Staff and a victim of the World War. Since transfer of training activities to Texas in 1931, March Field has been occupied by tactical units of the Army Air Corps. It is now headquarters for the First Wing, Seventeenth Attack Group, and Nineteenth Bombardment Group of the U. S. Army. In addition to three attack squadrons and two bombing squadrons, there are two service squadrons, a station complement, a photo section, and ordnance, quartermaster, medical, finance, and wing headquarters detachments.

PERRIS, 26.1 *m.* (1,456 alt., 763 pop.), platted in 1885-1886 and incorporated in 1911, succeeded an older settlement, Pinecate (Sp., stink bug), 1.5 miles south on the Sante Fe Railway. The 12 rich gold mines in the vicinity have been worked out, but since the rise in the price of gold in 1933, the tailings have been reworked and some claims developed on a small scale.

Left from Perris on State 74 through acres of peach and apricot orchards, to HEMET, 16.2 *m.* (1,600 alt., 2,235 pop.), in the center of the Indian country where artists of ancient races have left rock paintings and carvings on boulders in the canyons.

1. Right from Hemet on State Street 2 *m.* to the RAMONA BOWL, a natural amphitheater where the Ramona Pageant, an adaptation of Helen Hunt Jackson's novel *Ramona* is presented yearly in April and May. Scores of metates, or corn-grinding holes, in the vicinity of the bowl, remain to mark the SITE OF THE PAHSITNAH VILLAGE, once the largest in the area. The road southward continues over St. John grade to a junction with State 79 (*see TOUR 6C*) at 24 *m.*

2. Left from Hemet 2.5 *m.* on San Jacinto Ave. to SAN JACINTO (1,550 alt., 1,346 pop.), at the base of the Lakeview Mountains and MOUNT RUDOLPH (2,629 alt.). San Jacinto, which occupies the site of Jusispah Village, one of the seven Indian rancherias of the San Jacinto Valley, was founded by Procco Akimo, a Russian exiled from his native land during the Tsarist terrors of the 1870's. The second non-stop transpolar flight from Russia to the United States terminated safely in a cow pasture 3 miles west of San Jacinto on July 8, 1937, when the fliers missed their goal, March Field.

GILMAN HOT SPRINGS, 7 *m.* (1,600 alt.), in the San Jacinto Mountains, is a resort with Indian lodges, bungalows, bath house, swimming pool, and recreation pavilion.

East of Hemet on State 74 is a junction with a dirt road, 21.8 *m.*

Left on this road 0.4 *m.* to a junction with another dirt road; L. here to SOBOBA HOT SPRINGS and the SOBOBA INDIAN RESERVATION, 4.9 *m.* (1,725 alt.), where about 125 Indians live in neat homes around a large hospital. One of the oldest Indian legends of this region relates that Tuchaipai, the Great Spirit, gave the people their choice of living forever, of dying temporarily, or of dying forever. They argued and deliberated for days while the smoke of their council fires rose high from the hills. Then they called in the Fly, who was growing very tired of hearing them talk. So he said to them: "Oh, you men, what are you talking so much about? Just tell the Great Spirit that you want to die forever and never come back again." And this is what the simple Indians told Tuchaipai, so that now when they die they can never come back again. But the Fly was sorry he had told them such a foolish thing, and ever since he has rubbed his hands together in apology.

At 34.9 *m.* on State 74 is a junction with a paved road.

Left on this road 4 *m.* to IDYLLWILD (5,300 alt., 376 pop.), (*rates reasonable*), a mountain resort with a large rustic lodge and cabins (*guides available*). The mountain slopes heavily covered with pines and big-cone spruce, rise northward to SAN JACINTO PEAK (10,300 alt.). The Indians say that a powerful demon, called Tahquitz, lives atop San Jacinto. Sometimes when he grows restless and angry with people, he stalks through the canyons wailing and howling through the night for victims—and this is what makes bad weather.

At 32 *m.* the Idyllwild Rd. meets US 60-70-99 (*see TOUR 13b*). State 74 continues to KEEN CAMP POST OFFICE, 35.9 *m.* (4,936 alt.), in a region of Jeffrey pines, with occasional sugar pines, firs, and yellow pines.

At 69.9 *m.* State 74 meets State 111 (*see TOUR 13b*).

GOOD HOPE MINE (R), 31 *m.*, the most productive gold mine in the district, has an electrically operated mill with daily capacity of 100 tons.

ELSINORE, 38 *m.* (1,286 alt., 1,350 pop.), is a resort on the northern shores of LAKE ELSINORE, a land-locked basin with no outlet whose waters, fed by subterranean springs, have been receding in recent years; in dry seasons it becomes little more than a smelly pond.

According to one of the two stories of the town's naming, it was named for Elsinore in Shakespeare's *Hamlet.* According to the other, corroborated by local tradition, two thirsty travelers, a Yankee and a Spaniard, came upon the lake after a dusty trek. The impetuous Spaniard rushed eagerly into the water up to his armpits and drank greedily. The cautious Yankee inquired, "How does it taste, senor?" The Spaniard, having by this time become aware of the strong mineral content of the water, replied in disgust, "Like 'ell, senor!" In the Elsinore Valley, rich in ores, an 11-pound nugget, largest ever found in southern California, was picked up. Airplanes land at Elsinore's landing field; amphibians and seaplanes, in the lake. Water sports, boating, and speedboat regattas are popular the year round and duck hunting in season.

Right from Elsinore on State 71 to a junction with State 74, 2.4 *m.;* L. on State 74 to the OLYMPIC FIELDS NUDIST COLONY, 7 *m.* (*inquire at gate for conditions of adm.*), the West's pioneer nudist colony, founded "on the proposition that the desire for release from clothing is inherent and normal, and that a periodic release from the too-insistent and destructive pressure of our high-speed social order is beneficial mentally, emotionally, and physically."

South of Elsinore, the route skirts Lake Elsinore and passes into the fertile Temecula Valley, once the wheatfield of Mission San Luis Rey. It now produces beef cattle and dairy products; hay, grain, and alfalfa; olives and walnuts.

At 51 *m.* is a junction with Hawthorne St., a paved road.

Left here to MURRIETA HOT SPRINGS, 3 *m.* (1,309 alt., 153 pop.), a resort (*all accommodations; rates reasonable*).

TEMECULA (Ind., the rising sun), 56.3 *m.* (1,003 alt., 255 pop.), a trading post for the residents of Temecula Valley, is a dwindling handful of wind-worn, dusty buildings—fewer today than in 1882 when the town was founded on the railroad connecting San Bernardino with San Diego. The tracks were washed out by torrential rains in 1892 and never replaced.

The inhabitants claim for Temecula the dubious distinction that the wind blows every afternoon. Some old timers insist that the natives are so accustomed to this strong wind that they will not come out of doors on the rare windless days.

Joe Winkel of Temecula, frequently mentioned in Herriman's cartoon, "Krazy Kat," is a real person, who settled here in 1902 and opened a bar that attracted newspaper men from coast cities. The saloon, still standing opposite the bank, was in old days the mecca for booted and spurred cowhands who brought great droves of beef stock to the railroad. Since the advent of truck and trailer transportation, the cowpuncher has abandoned his chaps for mechanic's overalls—but not his visits to Winkel's bar.

At 58.1 *m.* is a junction with State 79 (*see TOUR 6C*).

At 58.4 *m.* is a junction with a dirt road.

Left here, through PECHANGA CANYON, to PALA (Ind., water), 9 *m.* (411 alt., 260 pop.), trading center for the PALA INDIAN RESERVA-TION. Pala grew up around LA ASISTENCIA DE SAN ANTONIO DE PALA, established by Fr. Antonio Peyri for the Mission San Luis Rey. The restored chapel (*small adm. fee*) is (L) near the northern boundary of the reservation. Of particular interest are the detached bell tower, some vivid Indian murals, and a statue of St. Anthony carved in wood more than a century ago by a Mexican. Erected in 1816, Pala was deserted by its padres in 1829; its buildings, already in ruins before 1836, were almost demolished by flood in 1916. The Pala Reservation has a small village of portable wooden shelters. At the annual celebrations are included the Corpus Christi Fiesta, the San Antonio Fiesta, and a fiesta held on August 25th, which features a rodeo. American music and gambling have largely replaced tribal customs.
Left from Pala, 1 *m.*, to a KUNZITE MINE. This rare stone has been found only here and on the island of Madagascar.
RINCON, 17.8 *m.*, on the main side road, is an Indian trading post; the route continues L. here. Right 1.8 *m.* from Rincon, across SAN LUIS REY RIVER, is the RINCON INDIAN RESERVATION (800 alt., 170 pop.). A 3-day fiesta is held annually on August 24.
At 23.1 *m.* is a junction of the main side road with the paved Highway to the Stars; L. on this road 6.9 *m.* to CRESTLINE (55 pop.), a camp-ground. Left from Crestline 3.2 *m.* on a dirt road to PALOMAR STATE PARK (*campgrounds*).
North of Crestline the Highway to the Stars begins the steep ascent to PALOMAR OBSERVATORY, 34.7 *m.*, which occupies a 720-acre plateau on PALOMAR MOUNTAIN (6,126 alt.). It was erected for the Carnegie Institution and the California Institute of Technology by the Rockefeller Foundation, and is best known as the home of the 200-inch telescope with a 16-ton mirror. The observatory is 128 feet high; its dome is 135 feet in diameter. The 18-inch Schmidt telescope occupies its own observatory. Other buildings include cottages for the astronomers and scientists, and a dormitory for the staff workers.
On the Rincon Rd. at 38.9 *m.* is the junction with State 79 (*see Tour 6C*).

RAINBOW, 63 *m.* (1,051 alt., 56 pop.), on US 395 is in a tiny upland valley. From this point the route climbs the winding, chaparral lined Red Mountain Grade through rugged country.

At 66 *m.* is a junction with an oiled road.

Left on this road to LIVE OAK PARK, 3 *m.*, a natural wooded area set aside for public recreation (*picnic ground; open-air dance hall; play-ground*).

FALLBROOK, 70.5 *m.* (700 alt., 887 pop.), was settled in the 1880's. Because of the soil and climatic advantages, this is an ideal citrus-growing region. In late years avocado orchards have been planted and poultry farms established.

> Right from Fallbrook is DE LUZ, 9.9 *m.* (146 alt., 180 pop.), a mountain community in an area noted for deer hunting; quail, doves, and rabbits are also plentiful.

BONSALL, 78 *m.* (172 alt., 213 pop.), is a small trading center in a dairying and farming area.

At OCEANSIDE JUNCTION, 80.5 *m.*, is a junction with Mission Road (*see TOUR 2d*).

US 395 traverses rolling hills, for the most part planted with avocado, citrus, and other fruit trees on small ranches.

A post office and store were established at VISTA, 85.1 *m.* (330 alt., 544 pop.), in 1890 when the Oceanside-Escondido branch of the Santa Fe Railway was completed. Development of the town began in 1926, when water was brought to the district from Lake Henshaw. Vista has one of the oldest wineries in southern California.

At 85.1 *m.* is a junction with State 78.

> Right on State 78 to a junction with an oiled highway, 0.1 *m.*; R. here to the old COUTS ADOBE HOUSE of the RANCHO GUAJOME (Ind., home of the frog), built by Lt. Cave J. Couts in 1853. Four wings surround a large central patio; the roofs are still covered with the original dull red tiles. Cave J. Couts, Jr., who inherited the property, maintains it in the style of a Mexican hacienda, employing Indian servants. Helen Hunt Jackson described this rancho in *Ramona*.

SAN MARCOS, 91.5 *m.* (570 alt., 105 pop.), at the confluence of three valleys, is on the former Rancho Los Vallecitos de San Marcos.

At the MULBERRY GROVE AND SILK FACTORY (L), 85.1 *m.*, established in the late 1920's, an attempt is being made to establish silkworm culture in southern California. To date the attempts have been unsuccessful.

ESCONDIDO (*hidden valley*), 97.9 *m.* (650 alt., 3,421 pop.), lies in the midst of the former Wolfskill Ranch, comprising about 13,000 acres of the Rancho Rincon del Diablo. Purchased in 1885 by a syndicate, the ranch was subdivided and the town laid out. Though the surrounding lands raise a diversity of farm, orchard, and dairy produce, the staple product is grapes, of which more than 4,000 acres are under cultivation.

The outstanding social event of the year in Escondido is the Grape Day celebration (*September*). During the carnival, several tons of grapes are distributed to visitors, politicians orate in the public park, bands play, and at night, church meetings and dances end the festival. This holiday originated in 1905, to celebrate the final liquidation of irrigation district bonds which had been oppressive to the farmers for 20 years. When the bondholders agreed, in 1904, to accept 50 per cent of the face value of the securities, the indebtedness was paid. On September 9, 1905, a gala mass meeting was held and the redeemed bonds were ceremoniously burned before a crowd of 2,000 cheering farmers.

Left from Escondido on State 78 through the farming and poultry regions of Santa Maria Valley.

A monument marks the SAN PASQUAL BATTLEFIELD, 7.3 *m.*, where, in December 1846, Brig. Gen. Stephen W. Kearny attacked the Californian army under General Andrés Pico. The Californians escaped from the conflict with only a few slightly wounded, but 19 of Kearny's men were killed and 17 wounded. It is said that Kearny lost the battle through carelessness, and that there was little excuse for his unprepared attack.

State 78 passes through San Pasqual Valley and ascends San Pasqual Grade.

RAMONA, 18.5 *m.* (1,440 alt., 400 pop.), founded in 1886, is in a region of poultry farms; turkeys are the specialty.

WITCH CREEK, 30.9 *m.*, is a trading post for a small farming district. East of Witch Creek, State 78 traverses Santa Maria Valley.

At SANTA ISABEL, 34.1 *m.*, State 78 unites eastward with State 79 for 7.9 *m.* to JULIAN (*see TOUR 6C*).

BANNER, 49.1 *m.*, once a boom town, is now a camp and picnic ground (*adm. 25¢ and 50¢*) at the foot of Banner Grade. The region was filled with gold-mad miners soon after gold was discovered in Julian in 1870. The most important mines at Banner were the Redman and the Golden Chariot.

SCISSORS CROSSING, 54.1 *m.*, in the San Felipe Valley, was so named because of a pattern made by converging roads. Pedro Fages, who camped in this valley and gave it its present name, visited Indian villages here in 1782. Scissors Crossing is at the junction with a dirt road (*see TOUR 14b*).

BOREGO (Sp., *borrego,* yearling lamb) STATE PARK, 54.5 *m.* (452 alt., 12 pop.), covers some 200,000 acres of desert and mountain country. Within its borders are palm canyon, rugged mountains, and mesas covered with ocotillo and other desert growth. The park is part of the proposed Anza State Park, which will include three distinct desert areas and extend from the northern boundary of San Diego County to within a few miles of the Mexican border.

SENTENAC CANYON BRIDGE and GRAPEVINE MOUNTAIN are at 58.7 *m.* At 60.3 *m.* is the junction with Borego Valley Rd.

Left on this road to the BOREGO POST OFFICE, 8.1 *m.*, a filling station and trading post in the Borego Valley, a bowl-shaped desert basin. Farms and ranches of this productive valley are irrigated by water from wells.

In PALM CANYON PLAYGROUND, 15.7 *m.*, are many specimens of the Washingtonia palm tree, California's only native palm tree. Botanists say that this tree is "a residual remnant of the days of the saber-toothed tiger, ancestral horse, camel and ground sloth, whose fossils have been found here." Perhaps 500,000 years ago, this canyon was a palm-lined shore of the Gulf of California. The first grove of palms is an hour's hike (L) up Palm Canyon from the campground.

On State 78 at 78.3 *m.* is a junction with a dirt road.

Left on this road 3.7 *m.* to a GYPSUM MINE in the FISH CREEK MOUNTAINS. At the mine a trail leads several hundred yards through an unnamed canyon to an area covered with FOSSIL FOOTPRINTS, by a prehistoric watering hole where mastodons came to drink.

At 91.3 *m.* is the junction with US 99 (*see TOUR 3e*).

LAKE HODGES, 103 *m.*, is crossed on a concrete bridge. (*Boats rented, 35¢ an hour; bass, trout, crappie, perch.*)

BIG STONE PARK, 111.9 *m.* (*picnic grounds; adm. 25¢ per car*), is in a region of giant boulders. It was a favorite Indian camp ground, and for 50 miles around, rock paintings are found. The road winds to the CREST OF POWAY GRADE, at 113.9 *m.* (525 alt.), along chaparral covered slopes. (*Caution: limited visibility on curves.*)

At 126 *m.* is a junction with a dirt road.

Left on this road to MISIÓN SAN DIEGO DE ALCALA (*adm. 25¢*), 0.5 *m.*, which stands on a small knoll overlooking Mission Valley. Junípero Serra, on July 16, 1769, erected a crude hut on Presidio Hill in San Diego, which was the first of the 21 missions built by the Franciscans in California. In 1774, the mission was transferred to this place, where, on the night of November 5, 1775, an Indian attack destroyed the structure and caused the death of Fr. Luís Jaumé. The garrison, stationed at Presidio Hill, slept through the engagement. Jaumé is buried under the altar of the church.

The mission was rebuilt and dedicated in 1780. Prosperous years followed. Barracks were erected for soldiers, and grain houses, corrals, and dormitories for the Indian converts. A dam, built 5 miles up the river, was 220 feet long, with a gateway 12 feet high in the center.

An earthquake in 1803 destroyed the church, but by 1813 the buildings had been restored and enlarged. Though Mission San Diego was not one of the wealthiest, it owned, in 1830, more than 8,000 head of cattle, 1,000 horses and mules, 16,000 sheep, and controlled 1,506 Indians. With the passage of the Bill of Secularization in 1834, which returned mission property to public use, the mission declined. Richard Henry Dana visited the mission in 1835 and described it in his *Two Years Before the Mast*.

The U. S. Land Commission returned 22 acres of the mission grounds to the Church, that area on which the church stands; but neglect and weathering soon reduced the structure to ruin. The present building, a restoration, was erected in 1931. A parochial school is conducted in the modern buildings beside the mission. In the museum are many relics, among them old baptismal, marriage, and death records, the first pages in the handwriting of Junípero Serra.

The SAN DIEGO RIVER, 126.3 *m.*, like many southern California streams, is dry the greater part of the year. Occasionally, however, heavy rains cause it to flood the floor of Mission Valley.

At 128.6 *m.* is a junction with US 80, El Cajon Blvd. (*see TOUR 14b*).

SAN DIEGO, 134.8 *m.* (0-500 alt., 147,995 pop.) (*see SAN DIEGO*), is at the junction with US 101 (*see TOUR 2d*).

Tour 6A

Junction with US 395—Susanville—Chester—Mineral—Red Bluff; 112.3 *m.* State 36.

Roadbed paved. Daily bus service between Reno, Nev., and Redding. Accommodations only in larger towns.

This route climbs the rugged gorge of the Susan River, deep among pines, to cross the Sierra Nevada through Fredonyer Pass. It leads through the forested uplands around Lake Almanor, where power houses and lumber mills tap the water and timber resources of the mountains. From Mineral, southern gateway to Lassen Volcanic National Park, it descends through corridors of luxuriant fir and pine to the Central Valley's hot, grassy stretches.

State 36 branches west from its junction with US 395 (*see TOUR 6a*), 0 *m.,* at the northern edge of Johnstonville and crosses level stretches, where willow-fringed creeks meander over lush, haystack-dotted fields. Along this route, paralleling the sluggish, tule-bordered Susan River (L), ran one of the most traveled trails into California, the Noble Emigrant Route, surveyed through Noble's Pass across the Sierra in 1852. By 1855 most of the northern California immigration was following it. From the Humboldt River route through Nevada, it entered California around Honey Lake (*see TOUR 6a*), followed the north bank of the Susan River, and then diverged to continue around the north side of Lassen Peak (*see TOUR 5a*) through Noble's Pass to Shasta (*see TOUR 8b*), whose merchants had put up $2,000 for a wagon road. At Isaac Roop's trading post in Susanville a register was kept; in the period from August 2 to October 4, 1857, it recorded 99 trains passing through the valley, with 306 wagons and carriages, 665 horses and mules, 16,937 cattle, 835 men, 254 women, and 390 children.

SUSANVILLE, 4.7 *m.* (4,195 alt., 1,358 pop.), from a bench above the Susan River commands a view of far-stretching Honey Lake Valley (*see TOUR 6a*). The valley lies in the shadow of low, timbered hills (R) and the lofty, pine-forested ridges of the Sierra (L). Main Street, a broad boulevard sweeping up a slight rise into the heart of town, has a brisk, traffic-thronged air of modernity despite the booted men in wide-brimmed hats who lounge about and the pastures that reach to the very edge of the business district. Susanville's busy air is accentuated by the smokestacks and water towers of the great box factory and lumber mills at its edge. Lumber, cattle, and hay are the town's stock in trade. Above the downtown section and the straggling houses in the hollows around the mills rise the locust- and cottonwood-bordered streets of Susanville's west end, which takes to the heights.

To the site of Susanville in the spring of 1853, alone and penniless, came Isaac N. Roop on horseback from Shasta. He staked out a claim and built a cabin. In June of the year following, came Peter Lassen and a handful of prospectors; they dug a ditch and struck gold. By the end of 1857, besides log cabins with shake roofs and fireplaces, the settlement had one house of boards and at least one cook stove. There was little law, less Gospel; horse thieves made their rendezvous here and shooting scrapes became frequent. For amusement there was gambling everywhere, much whisky drinking, and once in a while a dance.

Susanville's past lives in the names of its streets, which honor its pioneers. Its oldest building, FORT DEFIANCE, stands on Weatherlow St., facing over the valley. This was the cabin that Roop built in July

1854. Here he stored his merchandise and supplies, and to it he brought water from Piute Creek in a half-mile ditch. In its day the cabin even had the honor of serving as capitol of a territory, which its founders called Nataqua (Ind., woman). Nataqua's boundaries hemmed in 50,000 square miles, from the northeast corner of California to 25 miles south of Lake Tahoe. So far away were California on one hand and the Utah Mormon settlements on the other that the valley's settlers determined to set up their own government. On April 26, 1856, they created Nataqua—and while they were at it, the town of Susanville—meeting at Roop House and electing Isaac Roop recorder and Peter Lassen surveyor. But Nataqua was short-lived. A year later the Honey Lake men were joining with settlers to the east in a demand for the establishment of the Territory of Nevada. In the same month, August 1857, California asserted jurisdiction when Plumas County created Honey Lake Township. Grumbling, some of the settlers paid their taxes, but not the 40 or 50 pioneers who had endured the early hardships and the Indian fights. In rebellion they set up a local government in 1858, and the year after helped elect Isaac Roop Provisional Governor of what became, in 1861, Nevada Territory, with Honey Lake Valley included as Roop County.

When California stuck to its claims, the stage was set for the Sagebrush War; and Roop House acquired its new name of Fort Defiance. When Probate Judge John S. Ward and Sheriff William Hill Naileigh, of Roop County, refused to refrain from exercising authority, as the Plumas County Court ordered, Sheriff E. H. Pierce, of Plumas County, arrested Naileigh. He sent Deputy Byers to arrest Ward too, but Isaac Roop and seven mounted men blocked the way with shotguns. Forced to give up Naileigh, because snow in the mountains prevented taking him back to Plumas County, Sheriff Pierce crossed the mountains alone. With a posse of 90 men he returned February 13, 1863, to find an armed force of from 75 to 100 fortified in Roop's cabin. Negotiations proved fruitless. On February 15 Pierce and his men occupied and fortified a barn 200 yards away. When one of them, who went out to bring in timber, was fired on and wounded, the battle began; and for five hours both parties blazed away at each other. An armistice followed. Assured by the men in the fort that they would burn down the town around him unless he surrendered, Sheriff Pierce agreed to stop on condition that each party disband and all officers cease functioning. News of the compromise reached a party of reinforcements from Quincy, seat of Plumas County, who were dragging a small cannon over the mountains through the snow. They turned about and dragged it back. The boundary dispute was settled when the California-Nevada Line was run northward from Lake Tahoe, east of Honey Lake Valley; but hard feelings persisted until the California Legislature, on April 1, 1864, created Lassen County with its seat at Susanville.

Left from Susanville on Weatherlow St. to a fork at 3.1 *m.;* L. here to another fork at 4.2 *m.;* R. here through bristling pines and across peaceful

Elysian Valley where Peter Lassen arrived in June 1855, with a party of prospectors, and found gold. Going back in October 1855, he brought tools, plows and farm implements, cows, oxen, and horses. With his friend, Isadore Meyerwitz, he settled on a 1-mile tract and built a long low cabin on the south side of Lassen Creek.

At 5.9 *m.* is a turnstile (L), the entrance to the grove of pines that shade LASSEN'S GRAVE. Two monuments overlook the pleasant pastures. The old one, erected by the Masons, June 24, 1862, a column of gray stone, fissured and crumbled, topped with an urn, bears the inscription: "In Memory of Peter Lassen, the Pioneer, who was killed by the Indians, April 26, 1859. Aged 66 years." On the modern granite obelisk beside it is the same inscription, and the words: "Erected in Honor of Peter Lassen by the people of the Northern Counties of the State of California."

State 36 winds up the jagged, pine-fringed gorge of the Susan River. At 12.7 *m.* it climbs away from the river, scaling the Sierra to the summit of FREDONYER PASS (5,750 alt.), 18.6 *m.*, and descends the long western slope.

At 27.4 *m.* is the junction with a paved road.

Left on this road is WESTWOOD, 1.2 *m.* (5,082 alt., 3,500 pop.), a company town huddled around the giant mills of the Red River Lumber Company. In July 1938 Westwood was the scene of a bitter labor dispute. When 600 members of the C.I.O. union, the International Woodworkers of America, called a strike in protest against a 17½ percent wage reduction, the lumber company closed its mills, throwing out of work an equal number of "company union" men—members of the Industrial Employees Union. The strike led to a struggle between the two groups of employees, with the C.I.O. men picketing the plant. On July 14 the I.E.U. members, aided by Westwood residents, came to blows with the C.I.O. workers. While some 2,000 men fought with fists, picks, axes, and rifles, deputy sheriffs turned high-pressure fire hose on the pickets. The C.I.O. men were defeated, and a "kangaroo" court drove them and their families out of town. The plant opened the next day. About a week later 300 C.I.O. men voted to return to work when the Red River Company promised to restore their seniority rights.

CHESTER, 40.9 *m.* (4,280 alt., 200 pop.), is a lumber town on the northwestern shore of Lake Almanor (*see TOUR 5b*), where power company employees make their homes.

Right from Chester on a dirt road 0.5 *m.* to the junction with a dirt road.
1. Right on this road 11 *m.* to JUNIPER LAKE CAMPGROUND (*undeveloped*), on the western shore of Juniper Lake, in the southeastern part of Lassen Volcanic National Park (*see TOUR 5a*). JUNIPER LAKE RESORT (*tents and cabins, saddle and pack horses, rowboats and motorboats; 25¢ charge per car for parking and $1 per car for passing over privately owned land to Horseshoe Lake*), 12 *m.*, is the starting point for trips into the lake-dotted lava wastes of eastern Lassen Volcanic National Park. Through this region extends the Chain-of-Lakes; Juniper Lake at the base of the ancient volcano, Mount Harkness; Horseshoe Lake, whose waters flow partly into the Feather and partly into the Pit River; sandy-edged Snag Lake, whose clear depths reveal the remains of trees growing at the south end before it was dammed by lava; and Butte Lake, edged by rugged lava shores, near the eastern base of Prospect Peak. Among others are Twin, Echo, Swan, Rainbow, and Chester Lakes.

2. Left from the junction on a dirt road into Warner Valley. LEE CAMP (*hotel, store, gasoline; saddle and pack horses; guide service*), is

at 12 *m.* and KELLY CAMP (*hotel, store, gasoline; saddle and pack horses; guide service*) at 14 *m.* The road crosses the southern boundary of Lassen Volcanic National Park (*see TOUR 5a*) at 14.4 *m.* A RANGER STATION (*information and maps*) is at 15.6 *m.*

DRAKESBAD RESORT (*tents and cabins; saddle horses and mounted guide service; 25¢ charge for non-patrons to visit any of Drakesbad property*), 18.1 *m.*, on Hot Springs Creek below Flatiron Ridge, is a center for exploration of the remote southeastern sector of Lassen Volcanic National Park. Just southward is BOILING SPRINGS LAKE, a bubbling cauldron of volcanic origin encircled by steaming mud pots. To the west, the solfataras of the DEVIL'S KITCHEN hiss in the lava-walled "Canyon of a Thousand Smokes," through which flows a tiny stream called the Little Styx. The lava-scarred region northeast is studded with volcanic peaks, accessible by trail.

At 43.9 *m.* is the junction with State 89 (*see TOUR 5a*), which unites with State 36 between this point and Morgan Springs.

The road climbs through fine stands of fir and pine to DEER CREEK PASS (5,000 alt.), 46.8 *m.*, and descends to MORGAN SPRINGS (*campground*), 63.5 *m.* (4,786 alt.).

Morgan Springs is at the junction with State 89 (*see TOUR 5a*).

In MINERAL (*cabins, lodge, golf course, garage*), 72.5 *m.* (4,800 alt., 50 pop.), a small vacation town on the edge of a wide mountain meadow fringed with dense stands of pine and fir, are the ADMINISTRATIVE HEADQUARTERS of Lassen Volcanic National Park (*see TOUR 5a*).

LASSEN CAMP (*cabins, saddle and pack horses, guide service*) is at 79.5 *m.*

The road winds through wooded gorges, where here and there a mountain stream flashes silver, skirting the base of an occasional cliff. Called in this section Ponderosa Way, it plunges through the deep shade of ponderosa pines. The sky is a narrow slit of blue above the treetops. Between the tree trunks, thickly covered with green moss on the north side, the sun falls in bright shafts. Moss-covered logs, felled when the road was cut through, lie along the way.

On either side at 97 *m.* rise great cliffs. As the road descends into the lower foothills, fields are strewn with masses of broken dark gray volcanic rock. Huge purplish-hued buttes rise in the distance. The flat-topped craters of several extinct volcanoes appear.

The road winds down from the foothills and strikes southward along the course of the Sacramento River to its junction with US 99E (*see TOUR 3B*) 109.5 *m.*; R. here. From this point State 36 and US 99E are united to RED BLUFF (*see TOUR 3a*), 112.3 *m.*, at the junction with US 99 (*see TOUR 3a*).

Tour 6B

Junction with US 395—Portola—Blairsden—Quincy—Rich Bar—Oroville—Marysville—Knights Landing—Woodland; 203.1 *m.*   State 24.

Paved roadbed throughout; open at all seasons.
Route paralleled by Western Pacific R.R. between Portola and Marysville.
Accommodations plentiful in large towns, mountain resorts open about May 1 to October 1.

State 24 climbs over the Sierra Nevada through Beckwourth Pass, lowest crossing in central and northern California, into the mountain-walled farmlands of Sierra Valley, largest in the Sierra. It winds between thick-forested slopes along the spectacular canyon of the Feather River, dashing over its turbulent course down the range's long western decline through the heart of one of the State's oldest placer mining regions. From the orange grove belt below the foothills, it levels out across the Sacramento Valley, paralleling the Feather River southward through far-reaching peach orchards and beet fields.

State 24 branches west from its junction with US 395 (*see TOUR 6a*), 0 *m.,* 11 miles north of the Nevada Line, into the barren brown foothills of the Sierra's eastern slope.

The road climbs easily to BECKWOURTH PASS, 2.2 *m.* (5,220 alt.), the lowest entrance to the State north of the desert gateways in southern California. Its discovery in the spring of 1850 was the outstanding achievement of the remarkable adventurer and trapper, James P. Beckwourth, son of a Revolutionary War officer and a slave mother. Born in Charlottesville, Virginia, in 1798, Beckwourth tired early of an apprenticeship to a Missouri blacksmith and went westward. His rovings had already carried him into the Rockies with Gen. W. H. Ashley's fur trading expedition of 1824 and had kept him some years among the Crows. Later in Florida he served in the U. S. Army and in New Mexico traded in furs, before he came to California to share in the revolution of 1846. After further exploits in New Mexico, he returned to California and discovered this pass.

"This, I saw at once"—he told his admiring biographer, T. D. Bonner,—"would afford the best wagon-road into the American Valley approaching from the eastward, and I imparted my news to three of my companions. . . . They thought highly of the discovery, and even proposed to associate with me in opening the road . . . I made known my discovery to a Mr. Turner, proprietor of the American Ranch, who entered enthusiastically into my views: it was a thing, he said, he had never dreamed of before. If I could but carry out my plans, and divert travel into that road he thought I should be a made man for life.

Therefore he drew up a subscription list, setting forth the merits of the project and showing how the road could be made practicable to Bidwell's Bar, and thence to Marysville. . . ."

Over the wagon road, opened in 1851, Beckwourth guided wagon trains through the pass. A dark-skinned man, dressed in leather coat and moccasins, who wore his hair in two long braids twisted with colored cloth, riding without a saddle, he made a vivid impression on a traveler in one train, 11-year-old Ina Coolbrith (later California's first poet laureate), in whose honor massive, evergreen-girdled MOUNT INA COOLBRITH (8,311 alt.), south of the pass, is named.

"In the spring of 1852," he told Bonner, "I established myself in Beckwourth Valley. . . . My house is considered the emigrant's landing place, as it is the first ranch he arrives at in the golden state." Here he dedicated to Bonner the autobiography on which his reputation as a liar is based, meanwhile consuming great quantities of rum. The more the two cronies drank, the more Indians Jim would remember having killed single-handed. When he was thoroughly "likkered up"—so the story goes—he would shout, "Paint her up, Bonner! Paint her up!" But fame was short for Beckwourth. His very name was distorted to Beckwith on early maps. Only recently has the correct spelling been restored.

State 24 descends from Beckwourth Pass to CHILCOTT, 6 m. (4,995 alt., 85 pop.), a shipping point for Sierra Valley, where farming and stock raising are carried on almost a mile above sea level.

At 7.1 m. is the junction with State 49 (see TOUR 4a). BECKWOURTH 17 m. (4,874 alt., 105 pop.), was once trade center of a lumbering area. State 24 now follows closely the Middle Fork of the FEATHER RIVER, past BECKWOURTH PEAK (7,248 alt.).

PORTOLA, 23 m. (4,834 alt., 1,400 pop.), a lumber and railroad center, the largest community in this Plumas Mountain region, is a new and somewhat raw looking town, named for the Portola Fiesta in San Francisco in 1909, commemorating Gaspar de Portola, California's first Spanish governor.

East of Portola State 24 follows Castle Canyon, hemmed in closely by rugged buttes. Those on the south, BECKWITH BUTTES, bear Jim Beckwourth's name incorrectly spelled.

BLAIRSDEN, 34 m. (4,500 alt., 262 pop.), is a center for winter sports in the upper Feather River recreation area. Here is a junction with State 89 (see TOUR 5b), which unites northwest with State 24 for 33 miles.

> Left from Blairsden on a dirt road to MOHAWK, 1.4 m., where there are sulphur springs (hotel open all year).

State 24-89 continues northwest from Blairsden, following the Middle Fork of the Feather River, here a dashing stream which swells to river-like proportions only in winter spate. El Rio de las Plumas (the river of the feathers) was the name that Capt. Luis Arguello and his band of Spanish explorers gave it when they came upon its lower regions in 1820 and found them strewn with wildfowl feathers or—according to another surmise—feathery willow pollen.

At 35 *m.* the FEATHER RIVER INN (*American plan; open June 1 to Oct. 1*) nestles among the pines. At SLOAT, 42.5 *m.* (4,115 alt.), a ranch house is open all year. SPRING GARDEN, 46 *m.* (3,965 alt., 125 pop.), is a summer resort.

At 55 *m.* is a junction with a dirt road.

Left on this road up steep grades to ONION VALLEY PASS (*trout fishing*), 17.2 *m.* (6,500 alt.). In its descent the road follows ridges between the Feather and Yuba drainage systems. At 30.1 *m.* is LA PORTE (5,000 alt.), an old mining town (*meals and lodging*). Between here and Strawberry Valley there is fine hunting for deer and quail and good trout fishing—particularly for those prepared to pack into the backcountry off this road. At 43.1 *m.* (3,650 alt.) is STRAWBERRY VALLEY (*meals and lodging*), once a rich mining area. West of RACKERBY, 57.3 *m.* (250 pop.), another old mining camp, near the upper waters of South Honcut Creek, the roadbed is paved; it rejoins State 24 at 78.3 *m.*

QUINCY, 59 *m.* (3,407 alt., 1,000 pop.), seat of Plumas County, is pleasantly situated in the American Valley; its white houses, seen against green meadows and pine clad slopes, give it the look of a Vermont village. The town was established in 1854 by H. J. Bradley, who, wanting to make it the county seat, erected a frame building in the rear of his hotel and offered it free for county use. There are both mining and farming in the vicinity and winter sports in season.

Left from Quincy a paved road leads up Spanish Creek 8 *m.* to MEADOW VALLEY (*cabins and meals May 1 to Nov. 1*) at the base of SPANISH PEAK, and 17 *m.* to BUCKS (*same accommodations*) on BUCKS LAKE (5,071 alt.).

At 65 *m.* on State 24 is KEDDIE (3,223 alt., 150 pop.), a junction on the Indian Valley Railroad and a shipping point for the surrounding fertile mountain valley.

At 67 *m.* is the northern junction with State 89 (*see TOUR 5b*); L. here, through the deep canyon of the North Fork of the Feather, down the long reaches of the Sierra's western slope. Arrow-straight pines and firs mantle the canyon walls.

PAXTON, 69 *m.* (3,080 alt., 30 pop.), formerly called Soda Bar because of its mineral springs, was an early placer mining town.

At TWAIN, 73 *m.* (2,909 alt., 145 pop.), is a mountain tavern on the far side of the river (L).

The highway serpentines down the narrow canyon to RICH BAR, 82 *m.* (2,502 alt., 52 pop.). Rich Bar—the Barra Rica of early Mexican placer miners—quite lived up to its name. Single pans of "dirt" produced from $100 to $1500, and altogether more than $3,000,000 in gold dust were sifted from its gravel.

At BELDEN, 87 *m.* (2,306 alt., 110 pop.), is a junction with a dirt road.

Right on this steep and winding road 14.4 *m.* to LONGVILLE (*meals and lodging*), on YELLOW CREEK (4,609 alt.). This and several other tributary streams that meet the Feather River below Belden afford fine fishing; there is also good grouse, deer, and bear hunting here.

Southwest of Belden the road, the railroad, and the river weave in and out down the canyon's twisting course. The canyon, green with somber pines, widens in places to a yawning gulf, narrows in others to a narrow cleft. The railroad climbs up the steep walls to the heights above and dips again to the river bed. Over its jagged, boulder-piled channel the river spills in snowy, foaming rapids.

East (L) of WORKMAN'S BAR (2,128 alt.), a number of peaks rise about 7,000 feet. At TOBIN, 94.5 m. (2,006 alt., 16 pop.), the highway makes one of its many crossings of the river over a concrete bridge. Opposite MERLIN, 99 m. (1,756 alt.), State 24 winds along the granite sides of GRIZZLY PEAK. In two places the road passes through tunnels bored through the solid rock of the bluff.

At PULGA (Sp., flea), 108 m. (1,380 alt., 20 pop.), the highway crosses the river on a graceful arch span 350 feet long, high above the railroad bridge, and 170 feet above the churning water. Pulga, at the mouth of Flea Valley, was formerly a populous gold mining camp called Big Bar before the railroad humbled it with a new name.

South of Pulga State 24 leaves the river canyon for the forested hills of Jarboe Pass and meets the river again at LAS PLUMAS, 120 m. (562 alt., 80 pop.). The water for the power plant at Las Plumas comes through a tunnel from Intake, a station 5 miles north, thus avoiding the big bend in the river. The highway once again crosses the Feather River at 130.8 m., then leaves it to traverse rolling hills covered with oaks and digger pines.

OROVILLE, 136 m. (205 alt., 3,698 pop.), a quiet, tree-shaded town at the base of the Sierra foothills, sprang up in the winter of 1849-50 as Ophir City, a tent town, when gold was discovered here. Discoveries elsewhere depopulated the place in 1852, but it boomed again when a canal brought water in 1856 to dry diggings nearby. Oroville in that year became the seat of Butte County, a city of 4,000, fifth largest in California, boasting horse races, two theaters, 65 saloons, and brothels and gambling houses at every other door. There was great excitement on February 26, 1857, when the steamer *Gazelle* arrived at the levee; but Oroville's river traffic was short lived; within three months, boats ceased to operate above rival Marysville. In the 1870's gold lured thousands of Chinese and Oroville's Chinatown was California's largest in 1872. Special trains brought them until there were 7,000 in the mines and 3,000 hangers-on. But here, as elsewhere, the Chinese were heavily taxed, robbed—even murdered—and not more than 50 remain.

California dredging began on the Feather River here in 1898, with the floating of the first successful bucket elevator dredge, built by W. P. Hammon and Thomas Couch. The dredges, as many as 44 operating at one time, extracted nearly $30,000,000 in gold within 20 years. One company offered to move and rebuild Oroville if permitted to wash out the gold-bearing gravel below it.

When mining died down, it was discovered that Oroville stood in a thermal belt suitable for growing semitropical fruits. Surrounded by olive groves and citrus and deciduous fruit orchards, it has fruit-packing houses and an olive-oil refinery. Mrs. Ehman of Oroville developed a commercial process for pickling ripe olives, and as a result of her efforts the city now has one of the largest ripe olive canning plants in the world.

The BUTTE COUNTY PIONEER MEMORIAL MUSEUM (*open Tues. 2-5*), in a little edifice of rough stone, houses relics of the gold days and early settlers.

1. Left from Oroville on Berry Creek Road 5.9 *m.* to the junction with a paved road; R. here 15.7 *m.* is FORBESTOWN (2,800 alt., 12 pop.), a lively mining center for four decades after B. F. Forbes founded it in 1850, now deserted in its mountain cove, a ghost town of heaped debris, old foundations and crumbling structures with fallen roofs.

At 9.4 *m.* on Berry Creek Rd., a stone monument (L), near the South Fork of the Feather River, marks BIDWELL'S BAR, where a camp sprang up soon after John Bidwell found gold there July 4, 1848. By 1853 it had 2,000 inhabitants. Digging went on everywhere—in the streets and under houses. Here the river, lifted from its bed and carried in a flume for miles, yielded rich gold-bearing gravel. Fluming operations reached their height in 1856-57. Meanwhile the diggings were being exhausted, and the whole population stampeded to Oroville, where a new boom was on. Across the river gorge hangs the first suspension bridge erected in California, its 407-foot cables fastened to anchors embedded in rock. The cables were brought around the Horn and the bridge was opened in 1856. Opposite the old red-brick toll house at its southern end is the OLD MOTHER ORANGE TREE, planted by Judge Joseph Lewis in 1856. Its seeds, which brought $1 an ounce, were planted in northern California's first citrus belt. Along the southern sandy shore (L) is BIDWELL'S BAR PARK (*swimming; picnic tables*).

2. Right from Oroville on a paved road crossing the Feather River 1 *m.* to a junction with a paved road; L. here 1 *m.* to THERMALITO (194 alt., 32 pop.), where northern California's first important orange grove was planted in 1886. In the surrounding "thermal belt," oranges ripen even earlier than in southern California.

The main side route turns R. over wooded slopes to TABLE MOUNTAIN, 6.6 *m.*, a mesalike eminence edged with deeply furrowed palisades. In the 1850's its sides were pierced with 35 tunnels by gold miners. Across the top, bright with wild flowers in spring, the road winds over wastelands scarred with patches of blackish rubble.

CHEROKEE, 11 *m.* (1,400 alt., 243 pop.), is a ramshackle hamlet sprawling beyond stone walls and picket fences, in a crag-strewn, pine-wooded hollow. Its name comes from the Cherokee Indians who settled here in 1853. They were driven from their lands in Georgia when white land grabbers discovered gold there; later they left their second home in Arkansas to follow the trappers' route that came to be known as the Cherokee Trail west to California. A mining center in the 1860's, Cherokee gained brief fame with the discovery of a few diamonds in the placer diggings. To the south rises a spur of Table Mountain with deeply scarred sides, site of the abandoned hydraulic SPRING VALLEY GOLD MINE; 100 miles of ditches and pipe lines built about 1870 carried Feather River water here. The mine's operations, spreading layers of sand over valley farm lands below, stirred bitter opposition among the farmers.

State 24 traverses a flat fertile valley, paralleling the Feather River (R).

At 147.7 *m.* is the junction with a paved road (*see TOUR 3B*).

MARYSVILLE (*see TOUR 3B*), 165 *m.,* is at the junction with US 99E (*see TOUR 3B*) with which State 24 is united to YUBA CITY, 166 *m.* (*see TOUR 3B*) ; L. at Yuba City.

State 24 runs southward through acres of peach orchards.

At 168 *m.* is the junction with a paved road.

> Left here, through low-lying fertile orchards, to NICOLAUS, 19.7 *m.* (33 alt., 89 pop.), an old river town.

On State 24 is TUDOR, 174 *m.* (44 alt., 38 pop.), in the heart of one of the State's largest clingstone peach areas; the Phillip cling peach was originated here.

> Left from Tudor on a paved road 1.2 *m.* to the junction with the Garden Highway; R. here 1.6 *m.* to the SITE OF HOCK FARM. By the roadside (L) stands the front wall, of rusty iron plates riveted together, of the old fort, which in 1842 stood with the farm on the banks of the Feather River. Named for an Indian village on the Feather, Hock Farm was John Augustus Sutter's chief stock ranch and the first white settlement in Sutter County. After the loss of Sutter's Fort (*see SACRAMENTO*) and most of his fortune, he retired here. From 1850 to 1868, he kept open house in a handsome mansion among gardens, orchard, and vineyard.

At 178 *m.* State 24 crosses the SUTTER BY-PASS, part of a drainage system built to control the Sacramento River in flood season.

ROBBINS, 186.3 *m.* (49 alt., 200 pop.), is a fruit shipping town.

At 194 *m.* the highway crosses the SACRAMENTO RIVER.

> Right from the northern end of the bridge on an improved road to KIRKVILLE, 9.4 *m.* (13 alt., 20 pop.) and COLES LANDING, 14.3 *m.* (17 alt.), busy shipping towns in early steamboat days.

At the southern end of the bridge is KNIGHTS LANDING, 195.3 *m.* (48 alt., 600 pop.), an early shipping point that still retains some of the river town atmosphere of the 1860's. Moldering false-front frame stores, a little askew, with wooden awnings over the boardwalks, stretch for two blocks along the river. Dr. William Knight was granted land here through marriage with a Mexican wife. In 1843, two years after he immigrated from New Mexico with the Workman-Howland party, he built a dwelling on Indian "Yoday" Mound: a rude hut of willow poles bound with rawhide, covered with walls of river tules plastered with mud. In the dense woods roundabout roamed grizzly bears. Laid out in 1849 as Baltimore, the place came to be known by Knight's name because of the ferry he had established.

State 24 cuts through extensive sugar-beet fields to a junction at 200.5 *m.* with an improved road.

> Left on this road 0.8 *m.* to the SPRECKELS SUGAR FACTORY (*open to visitors 9-9 workdays*). In the whirring, light-flooded interior of the factory, pervaded with a syrupy sweet smell of sugar, sugar beets are fed by conveyor belt to a complex apparatus of washers, scales, slicers, diffusion tanks, purifiers, filter presses, evaporators, vacuum pans, centrifugal machines, and driers; built at a cost of $2,500,000, the plant was opened in

August 1937. The founder of the company, German immigrant Claus Spreckels, who came to California in the 1850's, started the State's sugar beet industry when he built a plant in 1888 at Watsonville.

WOODLAND (see *TOUR 3a*), 203.1 *m.* (63 alt., 5,542 pop.), is at the junction with US 99W (see *TOUR 3a*).

Tour 6C

Junction with US 395—Warner Hot Springs—Santa Ysabel—Julian— Junction with US 80; 81.7 *m.*   State 79.

Limited accommodations.
Roadbed oiled or paved throughout.

From Temecula Valley this route climbs southeast through a mountain pass to a broad mountain basin in the highland area, and swings south through a fertile mountain valley to a famous gold mining district of pioneer days.

State 79 branches west from US 395, 0 *m.*, through lands formerly belonging to Mission San Luis Rey (see *TOUR 2c*).   On the south bank of the Temecula River, which parallels the road, is PECHANGA CEMETERY, an old Indian burial ground in which the prototype of Alessandro, Indian hero of Helen Hunt Jackson's *Ramona,* is buried. This Indian, Juan Diego, was shot by an American in 1877 because of a supposed horse theft.

The old WOLFE TRADING POST (R), 1.9 *m.* (*apply at office of Pauba ranch superintendent for adm.*), once a trading post and tavern kept by Louis Wolfe, is now a storeroom and sleeping quarters for the ranch laborers.   Mrs. Wolfe furnished many stories of the Temecula Indian evictions (see *below*) to Helen Hunt Jackson.

At 15.5 *m.* is a junction with a dirt road.

Right on this road to the RUINS OF THE AGUANGA STAGE STATION, 0.3 *m.*, a wooden building that served the Butterfield Overland Stage route.   The first stage reached Aguanga in October 1858, and stopped twice a week thereafter until 1861 (see *TOUR 14a*).

In the small cemetery (L), 15.5 *m.* Jacob Bergman and members of his family are buried.   Bergman drove the first Butterfield Stage through the valley.   His grandson, who lives near the Aguanga post office, has a collection of relics and mementos of the stage line.

AGUANGA, 17.3 *m.*, a post office, store, and service station, was a junction of the old trails, one of which, the San Bernardino-Sonora Road, went northeast to the San Gorgonio Pass and through the San

Bernardino Valley; the other, known as the Colorado Road, went north-west through Temecula.

At 17.4 *m.* is a junction with the Hemet Rd. (*see TOUR 6e*).

The OAK GROVE STAGE STATION, 23.4 *m.*, a well-preserved adobe building, is now a tavern. Oak Grove Valley has some of the finest oaks in southern California. OAK GROVE PUBLIC CAMP GROUND, 23.8 *m.* (*tables and ovens*), is in CLEVELAND NATIONAL FOREST. Opposite the camp is a ranger station.

At the entrance to the 44,000-acre WARNER'S RANCH, 29.4 *m.*, is a hollow (L), known as DEADMAN'S HOLE, named by a Butterfield stage driver who found a dead man beside the spring. Old timers in the San Diego back country have many tales of murders at this spot.

The ranch land was a pivotal center for three Indian peoples, the Luiseno and Cahuilla, of the Shoshonean linguistic stock, and the Diegueno of Yuman origin. The particular group that inhabited this area were the Cupeno, a Yuman tribe. (Their name is a Spanish corruption of the name of their village, Kupa.) To the west were the Luiseno, and to the north and east, extending far into the Colorado Desert, were the Cahuilla. When the Spanish padres made their first trip into the valley, on an expedition from Mission San Diego, they named it Valle de San José. They found 10 villages scattered about the valley, the largest of which was Kupa, at the hot springs, later called Agua Caliente (hot water). The valley was used jointly by the Mission San Luís Rey and the Mission San Diego. In 1836, after secularization, Silvestre de la Portilla received the valley as a grant, but abandoned his interests, and in 1844, Juan José Warner, a Connecticut Yankee born Jonathan Trumbull, was granted the entire Valle de San José. He had come to California in 1831 with the Jackson party and had taken Mexican citizenship papers. After the secularization of the missions the Indians drifted back to their ancestral lands and shifted for themselves. The Cupeno continued to live by the hot springs, where they often lay in the waters and muds throughout cold nights. During Warner's ownership, they were allowed to remain at their long-established ranchería because he needed their labor, though he often complained of their raids upon his stock. Paid three dollars a month, the usual wage at that time for Indians, they were occasionally stimulated with applications of the lash, an established custom.

Warner's Ranch was the first civilized stop west of the perilous Colorado Desert. Kearny and his army rested here on their way from Fort Leavenworth, Kansas, to join Commodore Stockton at San Diego, in 1846. Warner moved to Los Angeles after an Indian uprising in 1851, and by 1861 he had lost his interest in the ranch. In 1880, John G. Downey, a former governor of California, owned the property. The Indians' rights to occupy the land became a matter of controversy. A suit was taken to the Supreme Court of California, which decided against the Indians. In the meantime, the Sequoya League, aided by the reports of Helen Hunt Jackson, succeeded in having the Government investigate their plight. A commision bought 3,438 acres in the Pala

Valley, near the Pala Mission Chapel, for a reservation, and in 1903 the Indians were forcibly removed to it. They have lived peacefully in this new territory, though they are placed among Indians of a different linguistic stock. Warner's Valley is now the property of the San Diego Water Company and the western section of the old rancho has been covered by Lake Henshaw (*see below*). Much of the area is leased to private cattle raisers.

WARNER HOT SPRINGS, 38.3 *m.*, is a mineral springs resort (*cabins, campgrounds, hotel*). Its Spanish-type buildings are among elms and locust trees.

At 41.9 *m.* on State 79 is a junction with a dirt road.

Left here to the HEADQUARTERS OF WARNER'S RANCH, 1 *m.*, and to a well-preserved BUTTERFIELD STAGE STATION, 2 *m.*

MORETTIS, 46.3 *m.*, is a service station.

Right from Morettis to LAKE HENSHAW, 4 *m.*, a reservoir of the San Diego water system, built in 1922.

At 50.5 *m.* in Santa Ysabel Valley, is a junction with a dirt road.

Left on this road to the VOLCAN INDIAN SCHOOL, 0.5 *m.*, on the SANTA YSABEL INDIAN RESERVATION.

At 51.8 *m.* on State 79 is a junction with a dirt road.

Right here to the MESA GRANDE INDIAN RESERVATION, 7 *m.*

SANTA YSABEL CHAPEL (L), 52.2 *m.*, a concrete building, was built in 1924 on the site of an adobe *asistencia* (chapel) erected in 1822 by the padres of Mission San Diego. This branch of the mission never equaled the importance of Pala Chapel, but a mission report of 1822 mentioned a granary, several houses, a cemetery, and 540 baptized Indians. After secularization, Santa Ysabel fell into ruin, though some Indians still continued to attend services. Even after the chapel was completely obliterated, the bells continued to be rung from a framework of logs on which they had been mounted; later they mysteriously disappeared. No Indians live here because the acquisitive whites have pushed them farther into the rough back country.

The SANTA YSABEL CAMPO SANTO (cemetery), 52.3 *m.*, has been used since the 1820's. Nearby are the *enramadas* (arbors) made of green boughs brought from the surrounding hills, where the Indians gather twice a year for traditional festivals.

SANTA YSABEL, 53.8 *m.* (2,983 alt.), is a small trading center (*all accommodations*) at a junction with State 78 (*see TOUR 6e*), with which State 79 unites briefly.

WYNOLA, 56.8 *m.*, is a filling station and an elementary school.

At 60.8 *m.* is a junction with a paved road.

Right on this road to PINE HILLS RESORT, 2.5 *m.* (*lodge and cabin accommodations*). Nearby is CAMP MARSTON, a Y.M.C.A. camp for boys, named in honor of the donor of the tract, George W. Marston.

JULIAN, 61.4 *m.* (4,129 alt.), a boom town during the 1870's, is now a farmers' trade center, surrounded by pine-wooded resort areas. The town was established by the Bailey brothers and their cousins, the Julian brothers, who moved into the region in 1869, shortly after placer gold was discovered near the site of the present town.

In 1870 13-year-old Billy Gorman, who had arrived in Julian with his family from Texas, found a piece of white rock flecked with yellow. He took the quartz to his father, who opened a mine that was to become the George Washington, commemorating the date of the discovery— Washington's Birthday. As news of the strike spread, gold-seekers, gamblers, and their women flocked in, and for a decade the place was enlivened by quarrels, pistol shootings, and stabbings. Twenty-mule teams and wagons were used to haul ore to San Diego. About 1880, when gold had already become scarce in Julian, the big strike at Tombstone, Ariz., was made, and most Julian residents deserted the town. It has been estimated that more than $15,000,000 in gold were taken from the district.

At 61.7 *m.* is the junction with State 78 (*see TOUR 6e*).

At 66.7 *m.* is a junction with a county road.

Right on this road to the 840-acre INAJA (Ind., my springs) INDIAN RESERVATION, 7 *m.* (33 pop.), and the 80-acre COSMIT RESERVATION, 7.7 *m.* (unpopulated). This land, remarkable for its unspoiled beauty, is used mainly for grazing.

CUYAMACA (Ind., rain above) STATE PARK, 69.7 *m.,* is a resort area around CUYAMACA LAKE, part of San Diego's water supply system. In pioneer days it was known at La Laguna Que Se Seca (the lake that dries up).

At 81.7 *m.* is a junction with US 80 (*see TOUR 14b*), at a point 3 miles east of Descanso.

Tour 7

(Tonopah, Nev.)—Bishop—Brown—Mojave—Los Angeles—Wilmington—Long Beach; US 6.
Nevada Line to Long Beach, 355.2 *m.*

Paved roadbed throughout.
Southern Pacific Line parallels route between Nevada Line and Bishop.
Accommodations limited between Nevada Line and Bishop.

In 1937 US 6 was extended westward to form a single numbered route between Cape Cod and southern California. The sections in Nevada and Utah are being improved (1939).

Section a. NEVADA LINE to BISHOP; 41.5 m. US 6.

South of the Nevada Line US 6 sweeps through Benton Valley, a basin lying between three sections of Inyo National Forest, in the shadow of the 13,000-foot White Mountain Range. Crossing the range, the route emerges into Chalfant Valley, once the stronghold of the Paiute, and still one of the most primitive regions in California. At many points the faces of cliffs and granite mountain walls still bear the marks of aborigines in the form of petroglyphs (stone carvings) and pictographs (picture writings). The area is sparsely settled.

US 6 crosses the Nevada Line, 0 *m.,* 71 miles west of Tonopah, Nev., cuts southeastward across the valley, and aims directly for a towering granite spur which seemingly bars the way straight ahead. The highway rounds this cliff and swings due south through an opening between the mountains.

BENTON STATION, 7.5 *m.* (5,393 alt., 15 pop.), is a railroad shipping center and an outfitting point for fishing and pack trips into INYO NATIONAL FOREST, just south of the town. The jagged crest of MOUNT DUBOIS (13,545 alt.) rears conspicuously (L) above the mass of the White Mountains, a range nearly as high and fully as precipitous as the main mass of the Sierra Nevada, which bulks straight ahead. The White Mountain district of Inyo National Forest contains rugged areas equaling those in certain sections of the high Sierra and regions white men have not penetrated.

The bordering ranges move in toward highway and railroad in a wide pass at 10 *m.*

At 17 *m.* is the junction with a dirt road.

> Right on this road 0.3 *m.* to the INDIAN TRACK CARVINGS, accessible by a short climb up the steep bluff (L). The carvings consist of hundreds of tracks, the origin of which living Indians are unable to explain. They extend for 100 yards along the crest of a broken ridge. Prominent among them are the tracks of an infant's feet and the heavy marks of bears, dogs, coyotes, and cats. About 1888 the Paiute went on a rampage and destroyed many of the markings, which were made, they said, by "evil little men who crept from the rocks at night."

At 25 *m.* is the junction with a dirt road.

> Right on this road through Chidalgo Canyon to the INDIAN PICTURE CARVING LABYRINTH, 1 *m.,* a maze of rock carvings made in the remote past. Some of them are geometrical designs and some are of human figures, but most are crude renderings of animals: deer, bear, bighorn sheep, lizards, snakes, and a dragonfly.

As the mountain ranges again draw apart, the highway enters Chalfant Valley. The CHALFANT GROUP OF INDIAN WRITINGS (R), 27 *m.,* visible from the road, extend high on an almost unscalable wall for a half mile. The group consists of both petroglyphs and pictographs, some representing individual figures and others, large connected groups.

At 34.5 *m.* is the junction with a dirt road.

Right on this steep road, which winds to the top of a volcanic tableland, to the PAIUTE INDIAN RESERVATION, 5 *m.*, where dwell the remnants of the Indian tribes that once ranged over the region. At 5.5 *m.* are large INDIAN PETROGLYPHS. The most conspicuous unit is about 5.5 feet in diameter; others, linked with the largest unit by almost indistinguishable lines, constitute a series some 20 feet long. There is also an "inscriptive wall"—a projecting rock carved with designs described variously as a sun dial, a flood gage, and a calendar. The projection, extending 8 feet beyond the rock wall, is accessible only by ladder.

LAWS, 37 *m.* (4,200 alt., 84 pop.), is a railroad water stop; its inhabitants are chiefly railroad workers.

The highway crosses the OWENS RIVER, 37.4 *m.,* whose swift current flows through a deep gorge in the volcanic tableland.

At BISHOP, 41.5 *m.* (4,147 alt., 1,159 pop.) (*see TOUR 6b*), is the junction with US 395 (*see TOUR 6c*). South of Bishop US 6 and US 395 are united for 123.5 miles (*see TOUR 6b*).

Section b.   BROWN to LONG BEACH; 190.2 m.   US 6.

This section of US 6 sweeps southward across the flat basin of the Mojave Desert toward the distant San Gabriel Mountains in an almost level course. The arid desert is relieved at intervals by the green, irrigated farming districts of lower Antelope Valley. It crosses the San Gabriel, winds through Mint Canyon, and descends into San Fernando Valley. Through straggling metropolitan outskirts, it continues into Los Angeles and southward across the almost flat coastal plain.

South of its junction with US 395 (*see TOUR 6b*), 0 *m.,* on the western outskirts of Brown, US 6 skims along the western edge of broad, arid Indian Wells Valley through typical Mojave Desert country sparsely grown with creosote and wolfbush. Distantly (L) the ARGUS MOUNTAINS rise from the sandy plain—dun gray in the shadows, brilliant lavender where the sun's rays strike. To the west (R) rise the majestic ridges of the High Sierra. OWENS PEAK, (8,475 alt.), 1 *m.,* highest of the east slope Sierra pinnacles in this region, is conspicuous among sister peaks.

Unbroken desert landscape unrolls as US 6 moves across the heat-blistered valley. Paradoxically, a hundred yards from the road (R), winds the water-filled open concrete channel of the LOS ANGELES AQUEDUCT, which redeemed San Fernando Valley from a desert as arid as this.

At 20.6 *m.* is the junction with Hartz Rd.

Left on this road through LAST CHANCE CANYON to ROARING RIDGE PETRIFIED FOREST, 7 *m.* (*adm. 50¢, children free*), where tree sections of a petrified forest are scattered over hills that once teemed with animal life, as fossil discoveries—including tusks of a rhinoceros and an elephant—have proved. A series of dugouts in the canyon wall at 11 *m.* is a reminder of the gold-mining activity that once flourished in this gorge. In the dugouts, now fitted with doors and windows, dwell a strange community of miners who search for nuggets and "dust" in the surrounding hills.

RICARDO, 30.2 *m.* (2,443 alt.), with gas station, garage, and refreshment stand, is hemmed in by the EL PASO MOUNTAINS (L) and the foothills (R) of the PAIUTE MOUNTAINS.

From the desert US 6 now winds through a deep lateral gorge of RED ROCK CANYON, whose towering cliffs are of reddish-brown sandstone, carved by wind and weather into fantastic shapes, and into the desert again.

At 37.6 *m.* is the junction with graveled Jawbone Canyon Rd.

Right on this road through Jawbone Canyon to the HILL OF BLUE-GREEN STONE, 5 *m.,* a rock mass of bright and bizarre colors.

At 5.5 *m.* on the main side road is the junction with a dirt road; L. here 2.6 *m.* to a mountain of stone, white as snow. Known as "vitrox," this formation is used in the manufacture of dishes, vitrified tile, and enamel for bathroom fixtures.

CINCO (*gas station*), 40 *m.* (2,612 alt.), a construction camp when the Los Angeles Aqueduct (*see TOUR 6c*), was being built, lies at the base of brilliantly colored RED HILL.

The highway at 53 *m.* is bordered by an elfin forest of greasewood, where 10-foot yucca trees lift distorted trunks. The leaves of the greasewood bush give off a strong, acrid, yet rather pleasant odor when crushed. In the spring the bush is covered with yellow blossoms.

At 57 *m.* is the junction with US 466-91 (*see TOUR 11b*).

In MOJAVE, 58.3 *m.* (2,751 alt., 638 pop.), J. W. S. Perry built 10 huge wagons in 1883 to haul borax out of Death Valley, and for five following years these conveyances, drawn by 20-mule teams, plied between Death Valley and Mojave (*see DEATH VALLEY NATIONAL MONUMENT*). Today Mojave, a supply center for desert gold prospectors, is the heart of a rapidly widening agricultural district.

South of Mojave, the peaks of the High Sierra, which have towered close to the highway throughout, recede to merge with the lower TEHACHAPI MOUNTAINS. The intervening area—partly flat, sandy desert, partly rolling foothills and occasional low peaks—constitutes the Mojave mining district, where greatest activity centers about SOLEDAD MOUNTAIN, 62 *m.* (4,183 alt.), a dark gray rounded mass.

At 62.1 *m.* is the junction with a dirt road.

Right on this road to a lone, one-story frame building housing a filling station and lunchroom and grandiosely styling itself GOLDTOWN, 1 *m.* (2,600 alt., 4 pop.).

GOLDEN QUEEN MINE, 2 *m.,* with its extensive galvanized iron sheds, spidery loading shoots and great ore dumps, disfigures the slope of Soledad Mountain. This mine startlingly revived dwindling activity in the once fabulously rich district when discovered in 1935 by George Holmes, a prospector. He sold his find for $3,500,000.

ROSAMOND, 71.9 *m.* (2,310 alt., 204 pop.), is a supply center for ranching and mining interests. The hotel, built of quartz, has a fireplace studded with gold ore. White, desolate ROSAMOND DRY LAKE glitters (L) in the sun across 5 miles of desert.

US 6 crosses ANTELOPE VALLEY, 75 miles long. About a third of the narrow valley is under cultivation, producing alfalfa, pears, barley, wheat, and oats under dry farming methods. An experimental crop of 800 acres of sugar beets in the Lancaster-Palmdale region (*see below*) in 1936 led to a 4,000-acre crop in 1937.

In LANCASTER, 84.6 *m.* (2,356 alt., 1,550 pop.), branches of Los Angeles County administrative departments are maintained.

PALMDALE, 92.6 *m.* (2,669 alt., 1,224 pop.), is the business center of southern Antelope Valley, a fruit and alfalfa growing district, where 4,000 tons of Bartlett pears are shipped annually.

PALMDALE RESERVOIR (R), 95.4 *m.,* is one of several storage basins supplied from deep wells.

US 6 ascends the grade leading to MINT CANYON over foothills sparsely covered with chaparral and mountain juniper.

At 104.3 *m.* is the junction with Crown Valley Rd.

> Right on this unpaved road to GOVERNOR MINE, 1 *m.,* formerly the Old New York Mine. The mine was opened about 1889 and was worked sporadically until the early 1920's. An increase in the price of gold resulted in its reopening in 1932. The main tunnel penetrates 600 feet.

Mounting steadily between forested slopes, US 6 achieves the summit of MINT CANYON GRADE, (3,429 alt.), 107.5 *m.,* then descends into SIERRA PELONA VALLEY.

At 124.4 *m.* is the junction with Soledad Canyon Rd.

> Left on this paved road to SOLEDAD GORGE, 6.3 *m.,* a deep, rocky gash between cliffs 500 to 800 feet high.
> At 8.3 *m.* is the junction with Agua Dulce Canyon Rd.; L. here 2.5 *m.* through a geological wonderland of tilted rock formations, to a junction with a private dirt road; R. here to VASQUEZ CAVES, 3.5 *m.* (*adm. 25¢*), reputed hideout of the bandit, Tiburcio Vásquez, who in the 1860's terrorized coastal California. The caves are a series of small caverns gouged by wind and rain in the sandstone cliffs of ESCONDIDO CANYON. The VASQUEZ ROCKS, 5.3 *m.* (*adm. 50¢*), are a grotesque jumble. They, too, perpetuate the memory of the bandit chief, for tradition asserts Vásquez and his highwaymen led pursuing posses many a merry chase through this maze, invariably losing them before they had penetrated to his hideout in the caves.

The SANTA CLARA RIVER, 125.6 *m.,* usually a tiny trickle of water down a graveled bed, is a roaring, destructive torrent during the rainy season.

HILL RANCH (L), 129 *m.,* formerly the property of cowboy actor Hoot Gibson, is the scene of annual rodeos (*time and adm. vary*).

SAUGUS, 130.6 *m.* (1,171 alt., 151 pop.), is a Southern Pacific R.R. division point.

At 132.7 *m.* is the junction with Placeritas (Sp., little gold diggings) Canyon Rd.

> Left on this road to MONOGRAM VILLAGE (L), 0.5 *m.,* an outdoor location set of Monogram Pictures, Inc., of Hollywood, and to the OAK OF GOLDEN LEGEND (L), 3.6 *m.* Under this spreading oak the first gold dis-

covery in California was made in 1842 by Don Francisco López. Noting bright particles clinging to the roots of wild onions he had dug for his lunch, he had a test made, which revealed particles of gold. The discovery caused widespread excitement and brought prospectors from as far away as Mexico. In November 1842, the first California gold was shipped from the Placeritas mines to the U. S. Mint in Philadelphia.

At 133.4 *m.* is the junction with a dirt road.

Right on this road to the junction with a private dirt road, 0.2 *m.;* L. here to the NEWHALL REFINERY, 0.4 *m.,* California's first, built in 1876. The old stills, retorts, and petroleum vats have been carefully restored.

NEWHALL, 133.6 *m.* (1,273 alt., 1,104 pop.), now a trade center for ranchers, farmers, and oil producers, was the point from which oil exploitation in southern California began. Since discovery of oil in the district in 1861, the fields have produced steadily. Overlooking the town from a hill (R) is the ESTATE OF WILLIAM S. HART, former star of the Western motion pictures.

US 6 moves up the NEWHALL GRADE and through NEWHALL PASS, where paths of the eighteenth- and nineteenth-century trail blazers converged. NEWHALL TUNNELL (*use lights; drive slowly*), 136.1 *m.,* is a narrow bore through the ridge.

BOULDER MONUMENT (L), 136.4 *m.,* marks the entrance to a narrow canyon known as OLD FREMONT PASS, because this way in January, 1847, came Capt. John Charles Frémont on his way from Santa Barbara to Los Angeles. Later the pass was operated as a toll road, the owner exacting a stiff fee from hapless travelers. So steep was the grade (29%) that the tollmaster kept horses ready to pull wagons over the crest. At the top the wagons—and even early automobiles —had their wheels chained fast for the downward slide.

At 137.7 *m.* is the junction with US 99 (*see TOUR 3c*), which unites with US 6 between this point and Los Angeles.

LOS ANGELES, 164.9 *m.* (286 alt., 1,238,048 pop.), (*see LOS ANGELES*).

Los Angeles is at the junction with US 66 (*see TOUR 12c*), US 99 (*see TOUR 3c*), and US 60-70 (*see TOUR 13b*).

US 6 follows Figueroa St. south through city outskirts into nondescript rural sections with many tracts of unused land.

The narrow SHOESTRING STRIP, 176.8 *m.,* is a neck of Los Angeles City property that runs 8 miles through county territory to link the city with its harbor (*see TOUR 2B*); it was incorporated as Los Angeles territory in the city's movement to annex the harbor district and the seaport towns of Wilmington and San Pedro. The maneuver met frantic opposition from subdivision developers and civic independence supporters in the little municipalities whose territory lay in the way. Once the strategic strip was joined to Los Angeles, the city was ready to annex the towns of Wilmington and San Pedro and their harbors, which it did in 1909.

The tall steel and wood derricks of the ATHENS AND ROSE-CRANS OIL FIELDS, 177.2 *m.,* opened in 1923, rise from low hills on either side of the highway. The northern wells are "stripping" wells—which draw the last remaining oil from the field—and the southern ones are "flowing" wells—which produce oil without pumping.

At 179.2 *m.* is the junction with One Hundred Sixty-First St.

> Right on this asphalt-paved road is GARDENA, 1 *m.* (45 alt., 4,560 pop.). In and about its community center are substantial brick and concrete business and civic buildings of the Spanish-California type. The town is gradually filling with small manufacturing plants and businesses and with the stucco homes of those who like rural living near a large metropolitan center, although poultry raising and truck farming are still among its important assets.

At 180.8 *m.,* the highway forks; US 6 turns L. on Main Street past occasional marshy, reed-grown ponds where coots and killdeer come to feed. As roadside stands, small farms, and dwellings increase in number, big aluminum-painted oil-storage tanks, pumping plants and oil derricks appear·among fields and pastures.

WILMINGTON, 184.6 *m.* (0-38 alt., 14,907 pop.), (*see TOUR 2B*) is at the junction with US 101 Alt. (*see TOUR 2B*), which unites with US 6 to Long Beach.

The forests of oil derricks thicken as the highway passes great refineries and tank farms. Multiple-armed steel towers carrying high-tension power lines cross the road.

LONG BEACH, 190.2 *m.* (0-47 alt., 142,032 pop.), (*see LONG BEACH*).

Tour 8

Alturas—Burney—Redding—Weaverville—Jct. US 101; 290.3 *m.,* US 299.

Paved roadbed throughout, open all season; during periods of heavy snow, obtain road information at Alturas and Redding.

West of Alturas, in the northeastern corner of California, US 299 cuts diagonally across harsh lava country and the Cascade Range, paralleling the Pit River. West of Redding, in the northern end of the Sacramento Valley, it follows the Trinity River across the Coast Range through hydraulically scarred mountainsides and deserted mining camps.

Section a. ALTURAS to REDDING; 143.5 m. US 299.

ALTURAS, 0 *m.* (4,446 alt., 2,338 pop.), seat of Modoc County, at a junction with US 395 (*see TOUR 6a*), is the center of a region whose history is one of violent and bloody Indian warfare (*see TOUR 8A*). Alturas is principally a commercial center for ranchers who raise stock, potatoes, and alfalfa hay. The short residential streets are really wide, unpaved country lanes, their poplar-shaded lengths branching from the main thoroughfare. The town until 1874 was called Dorris Bridge, for its first permanent white settler, James Dorris, who in 1869 built a crude wooden bridge across the narrow creek at the east end of town and erected a house that became a shelter for travelers.

The creation of Modoc County was in the nature of a secession from the mother county, Siskiyou. The citizens of Dorris Bridge, angered by the refusal of county supervisors to build a road over the mountains between that settlement and Cedarville (*see TOUR 6a*), not only constructed the desired road themselves, but elected a representative to the legislature pledged to the creation of a new and separate county. Enemies of the bill succeeded in changing the name of the proposed county from Canby to Modoc, and rather than lose it entirely, they accepted the hated name of the local Indians, called Moa Docks (near southerners) by the Klamaths to the north.

At Modoc National Forest Headquarters, on Main St., information on camping, hunting, and fishing in the forest is available. The forest, extending northward is the home of mule-tail deer which weigh up to 350 pounds, dressed. Ducks, quail, geese, and sage hens are abundant. The 1,500,000-acre Modoc Forest is a range for about 94,000 head of sheep and more than 30,000 head of cattle and horses.

The huge barn (L) on Main St., which for many years has housed the Alturas Trading Post, looks today much as it did in the early 1870's when it was the Alturas Livery Stable. The town's most imposing structure, the stately gray stone building at the edge of town (L), constructed at a cost of $60,000 as headquarters of a narrow-gage railway line, has been deserted for years.

The long, low-roofed buildings occupying an extensive tract at 1.4 *m.,* are the $1,000,000 Pickering Lumber Mills, built before the business depression and never operated. The region waits hopefully for lumber prices to warrant the opening of the mill.

Crossing Rattlesnake Creek at 5 *m.,* the highway meets the Pit River, so called because the local Indians formerly dug conical pits in which to trap game and hostile tribesmen. The small openings to the pits were hidden by brush, and sharp stakes were placed in the bottoms to impale the victims.

West of here the broad expanse traversed is broken at intervals by small cultivated areas; tall windmills dominate tiny clusters of tree-sheltered farm buildings.

At KELLEY HOT SPRINGS (L), 16.2 *m., (cabins)* the mineral waters bubble from the ground in clouds of white steam and flow into a stream whose bed is colored vividly by the action of the minerals, its bright greens, red, and yellows softened by deposits of dusty gray and blue at the water's edge.

CANBY, 18.2 *m.* (4,351 alt., 75 pop.), named for Gen. Edward S. Canby of Modoc War fame (*see TOUR 8A*), lies among fields of alfalfa and timothy hay.

At 18.7 *m.* is a junction with a paved highway (*see TOUR 8A*).

US 299 follows Pit River, winding through a region of small farms and yellow pastureland. A hilly spur of the Warner Range looms larger now, roughly paralleling the highway. US 299 swings abruptly south across the west-bound river to CANBY BRIDGE (FOREST SERVICE) PUBLIC CAMPGROUND and leaves its south bank to wind up the Adin Mountains through hemlocks and pines. Small lumber camps reveal their positions in the hills by clouds of blue smoke that drift above distant treetops.

From the RONEY FLAT CAMPGROUND (R) at ADIN PASS SUMMIT, 28.2 *m.* (5,196 alt.), US 299 descends past INDIAN SPRINGS (*fuel, camping accommodations*), 33 *m.,* winding along sparkling Rush Creek through thinning woods to the farms of Big Valley. Harvest time finds these smooth reaches dotted by great stacks of yellow hay.

In ADIN, 39.9 *m.* (4,271 alt., 220 pop.), a small lumbering and farming community, is the BIG VALLEY RANGER STATION (R). Tall poplars line the roadway in front of scattered weather-beaten frame buildings and a tiny, white-steepled wooden church.

US 299 swings over a plateau covered with brush to BASSET HOT SPRINGS, 50.1 *m.,* in another of the small cultivated areas that break the monotony of the semiarid expanse, where mineral waters are piped into pools and tubs.

BIEBER, 52.2 *m.* (4,169 alt., 150 pop.), where the erratic Pit River is again crossed by the highway, was founded in 1877 by its first merchant and journalist, Nathan Bieber; it had been called Chalk Ford because of the numerous chalk deposits in the vicinity. ODD FELLOWS' HALL (1879), a two-story frame building on Main St., with its old-fashioned board walk and ancient iron pump, is a sharp contrast to its nearest neighbor, a modern building of gleaming white stucco.

NUBIEBER, 55 *m.* (4,169 alt., 200 pop.), is a small railroad and lumbering community which helped itself to its older neighbor's name.

The highway gradually ascends the foothills of the Bieber Mountains, passing the débris from logging activities: large piles of brush and dead wood which are gathered in spring and summer, when fire hazards are high, to be burned in winter. Rounding a sudden curve at 60.8 *m.,* the road swings high above a scene of rare grandeur. Behind are the treetops of the Bieber Ridge; in the distance ahead, the Pit River winds silver blue toward snow-capped Mount Shasta; and to the left the jagged bulks of Lassen Peak and Mount Burney rise above a vast checkerboard of green and gold—the neat farmlands of the Fall River Canyon.

McARTHUR, 70.2 *m.* (3,342 alt., 100 pop.), is within the SHASTA NATIONAL FOREST (*see GENERAL INFORMATION*).

FALL RIVER MILLS, 74 *m.* (3,307 alt., 200 pop.), a small lumbering community, is at the junction of the Pit and Fall Rivers, where the daily flow of water exceeds one billion gallons—more than enough to supply all the cities of the San Francisco Bay area for a year. Here from a 500-foot-long diversion dam on Fall River, an intake canal carries the water 1,000 feet to the base of the nearby hills, where a two-mile tunnel conveys it through an intervening hill to a point on the Pit River Canyon above the site of the Pit Power House No. 1 (*see below*).

Below this point the descent of the Pit becomes more precipitous. Subterranean waters, common in volcanic regions, are the chief sources of its tributaries.

US 299 here traverses the McCloud-Pit River mining region. The snow-white substance that frequently replaces the familiar rock and clay on roadside banks is diatomite or diatomaceous earth. The extensive deposits in this vicinity occur both in a solid form, which can be sawed into blocks, and as a white powder; but thus far it has been little exploited, although its commercial uses are many and varied. It is used for filtration, insulation, the making of sound records, dental pastes and powders, fingernail polish, building and refractory bricks, and as an ingredient of polish for metals, glasses, and lacquered surfaces.

At 78.2 *m.* is a junction with a narrow dirt road.

Left on this road 1 *m.* to the PIT POWER HOUSE NO. 1 of the Pacific Gas and Electric Company. A sudden turn in the winding road discloses red-roofed structures, like doll houses, in the canyon below; these are the homes of employees. At the far end of the valley is the gray-walled power house from which double transmission lines, supported by a series of twin towers, carry power more than 200 miles to a substation near Vacaville, from which it is delivered to Bay area consumers. From the Fall River tunnel (*see above*) the water is dropped 454 feet through vertical steel turbines, 14 feet in diameter. During construction of the power project, lack of transportation necessitated laying a 33.5-mile railroad between McCloud and Bartle. Construction of the Fall River tunnel was completed Sept. 30, 1922.

At 83.4 *m.* on US 299 is a junction with a dirt road.

Left on this road, crossing Hat Creek, to CASSEL (*post office, store, museum*), 3.7 *m.* (2,850 alt.), a settlement with a white population of 25 in a vicinity where between 50 and 60 families of the Hat Creek tribe live. The women are skillful basket-makers; their products are on sale at the store, which was built in 1876 by H. E. Williams. Ancient muskets, arrowheads, and arrows are on display here, as are scores of the Indian photographs for which Williams was known nationally.

Southwest of the junction, US 299 cuts through a thick stand of grass pine between banks of rich red clay to a junction with an oiled road, State 89 (*see TOUR 5a*), 89.5 *m.*

Burney, 90 *m.* (3,159 alt., 50 pop.), is a trading center for a lumbering, farming, and stock-raising district. Wheat, potatoes, and hay are Burney Valley's principal products. The town is named for Samuel Burney, an early English settler killed in an Indian raid in 1857.

West of Burney, US 299 begins the slow ascent of the Hatchet Mountains to the HATCHET MOUNTAIN LOOKOUT, 96 *m.,* commanding a splendid view of a vast forested area, near the summit (4,368 alt.), 97.8 *m.*

Beyond the rustic APPLE SHANTY, 106.9 *m.* (*mountain apples and cider for sale*), the forest climbs the foothills of the Snow Mountains (R).

South of MONTGOMERY CREEK, 109.3 *m.* (2,200 alt., 200 pop.), the road widens, following a downward grade through a less thickly wooded region. The tall pine forests give way to scattered oak, and sheep and cattle graze in wide green pastures beside the highway. At ROUND MOUNTAIN, 113 *m.* (2,200 alt., 100 pop.), US 299 enters COW CREEK CANYON, roughly paralleling the stream for which the district is named.

Beside the road in INGOT, 123 *m.* (2,000 alt., 100 pop.), on terraces (L) above Seaman's Gulch, are the deserted mine and smelter of the Afterthought Mining Company, built about 1922. After vain attempts to extract copper from the Copper Hill lode, the million-dollar plant, tramway system, and colony of company houses on the 1650-acre holdings were finally abandoned. In 1925 the California Zinc Company resumed operations, using the 300-ton selective flotation plant and the reverberating smelter, but with no more success than its predecessor, as the zinc and copper sulphides could not be cleaned separately. In a final desperate attempt to make the mine pay, the zinc company transported ore to their Bully Hill smelter over an 8.5-mile tramway system. Gaunt reminders of a more speculative era are the corroded tin roofs sagging above crumbling brick and stone foundations, the huge blast furnaces, and the rusted tram tracks that skirt the mountainside. The vertical workings are more than 800 feet deep. One main working runs east for 600 feet, then continues as a drift for 500 feet on the Afterthought lode and 400 feet northwest on the Copper Hill lode.

West of Ingot, US 299 traverses a level stretch of countryside, passing occasional small farmhouses, whose comfortable front porches are half hidden by honeysuckle vines.

At 141.5 *m.* is a junction with US 99 (*see TOUR 3a*), which unites with US 299 to REDDING, 143.5 *m.* (537 alt., 4,188 pop.), (*see TOUR 3a*).

Section b.   REDDING to JUNCTION with US 101;
146.8 m., US 299.

West of REDDING, 0 *m.,* US 299 climbs into the foothills of the TRINITY MOUNTAINS, roughly following the path blazed by Indians which trappers and miners of the 1840's beat into the well-traveled Trinity Trail. To and from the mining camps of the mountainous hinterland, mail and bullion were carried on horseback. In the late 1850's horse and mule pack trains gave way to stagecoaches, as the Buckhorn-Grass Valley Creek toll road was built from Redding to Weaverville. The entrance of the first coach into remote, mountain-hemmed Weaverville was such a gala occasion that, according to a contemporary report: "Trinity County citizens went out in buggies and on horseback, led by the German brass band, to greet and escort it into town."

SHASTA, 6 *m.* (990 alt., 150 pop.), onetime seat of Shasta County, was known until 1850 as Reading Spring, in honor of Maj. Pierson Reading (*see TOUR 8a*). In 1849 Reading Spring was a tent city of several hundred inhabitants—a lively trading post serving a mining region. By November of that year one Milton Magee attained local distinction as the only owner of a log cabin; and by 1852 Shasta had grown so rapidly that two frame hotels, the St. Charles and the Trinity House, were erected. The town was soon called the head of "Whoa Navigation" by the Shasta *Courier;* at one time more than 2,000 pack mules carried supplies to the northern mines, and as many as 100 freight teams were housed at Shasta in a single night. At the height of its prosperity, local merchants were sending out $100,000 in gold dust each week.

Frequent Indian outbreaks added to the general turbulence of the town's early days. On many occasions during the 1850's, bands of painted braves in fighting regalia staged war dances on Main Street. The *Courier* of March 2, 1853, reported it "unsafe to travel over any exposed portion of the country unarmed. The . . . Indians . . . are infesting the Sacramento River trail in such numbers and with such determined fierceness as to render it almost certain death to pass over that road." But later the constant threat of Indian hostilities was overshadowed by a more immediate catastrophe, for on June 14 the entire business district was wiped out by fire in a brief half hour. Flimsy pine buildings, lined with cotton cloth, were quickly reduced to ashes; but before the ashes cooled lumber had been ordered to rebuild the town. In 1855 the *Courier* announced: "There are 28 brick buildings in Shasta at a cash value of $225,000."

With a decline of mining Shasta lost its importance. Then, when the California-Oregon railroad was planned, it was decided that Shasta lay 3 miles too far west, with 400 feet too much altitude, to be included in the route, and today the brick buildings of which the *Courier* boasted stand deserted and crumbling. Only two are in use; one is the MASONIC HALL, the first in the State, in whose vaults repose the first charter of Western Star Lodge, No. 2, brought from Missouri by Peter Lassen in the early 1850's by ox train; the other is the LITSCH STORE (L), built in 1853. This old-fashioned general store, in addition to serving as post office, houses "Litsch's Free Museum of Historic Pioneer Relics." Here are firearms; paper cuffs and collars; gold dust pokes; scales that have weighed millions of dollars worth of "dust" since 1853; crude handmade wooden stirrups, brought across the plains in 1843; and one of the State's first music boxes. There are also relics of an unfortunate pioneer group, the Chinese: a hand-carved opium pipe said to be 150 years old and an iron pitchfork used in the tong war at Weaverville (*see below*).   On sale at the store is a gruesome postcard of the Ruggles brothers, John and Charles, captured and hanged by a vigilante group in 1892, after they had held up a stage and killed a messenger.

Near the highway (L) stands a roofless courthouse whose corroding cells once confined "Shorty" Hayes and "Sheet Iron" Jack; a contemporary lists the latter among the "many noted criminals" housed in the old jail.   From the town's first log jail Joaquin Miller once escaped; he was then living among Indians who were notorious horse thieves, and had joined them in their depredations.   At this period the young runaway from Oregon had an Indian wife and a half-Indian daughter named Cali-Shasta.

At 6.2 *m.* is a junction with a narrow dirt road.

> Left here to the RUINS OF THE SHURTLEFF RESIDENCE, 0.2 *m.,* on Shurtleff Hill, overlooking the town.   For 25 years Dr. Ben Shurtleff was Shasta's physician; in 1849 he was the camp's first mayor.   His home, partly constructed of materials brought around the Horn, was for many years a showplace.

West of Shasta, US 299 ascends by easy grades to the summit of SHASTA DIVIDE, 8 *m.* (1,390 alt.), which separates the watersheds of the Sacramento and Trinity Rivers.   The view extends over miles of treetops to massive mountain barriers.

Descending, US 299 enters WHISKEY TOWN, 10.8 *m.* (1,091 alt., 90 pop.), settled by miners near Whiskey Creek on the trail to Oregon.   The creek was christened when a barrel of whisky was lost by an unruly pack mule.   Postal authorities, disdaining the town's name, have called it Blair, Stella, and Schilling; but it continues to be known as Whiskey Town.   Three events are remembered in the history of the community.   In 1852 the first white woman "took up her residence" here; in the following year a bartender was lynched for shooting a fellow citizen to avenge an insult; and in the late 1850's, a certain Bon Mix erected a "commodious hotel."

TOWER HOUSE, 17 *m.* (1,247 alt., 5 pop.), dating from 1852, was a stage station on the toll road built from Shasta in the late 1850's and a point of departure for pack and bullock trains bound for the northern mines and for Oregon.

> Right from Tower House on an oiled road to FRENCH GULCH, 3 *m.* (1,346 alt., 618 pop.), depot on the Shasta-Yreka Turnpike, where the first mining is said to have been done here by a party of Frenchmen in 1849 or 1850.   The discovery of the Washington Quartz Mining Company claim prompted the Shasta *Courier* to report in March 1852 that "such rich diggings have been struck that miners are tearing down their houses to pursue the leads which extend under them."

West of Tower House US 299 follows the route of the old Buckhorn Toll Road, winding sharply into the thickly forested Trinity Mountains along the high rims of canyons.   From Buckhorn Mountain, 25.5 *m.* (3,212 alt.), it descends to BUCKHORN (*auto camp*) 29.6 m. (2,500 alt., 3 pop.), among the small farms of lovely Grass Valley.

The trading center of DOUGLAS CITY, 41.9 *m.* (1,700 alt., 110 pop.), lies beside the Trinity River near the mouth of Reading's Creek, where Pierson B. Reading made the first discovery of gold in Trinity County in the summer of 1848. As Reading later told the story: "My party consisted of three white men, one Delaware, one Chinook, and about sixty Indians from the Sacramento Valley. . . . I had one hundred and twenty head of cattle with an abundant supply of other provisions. After about six weeks work, parties came in from Oregon, who at once protested against my Indian labor." Having already taken out $80,000 in gold, Reading abandoned his diggings.

The Trinity River was so named by Reading on an earlier trapping expedition in 1845, under the delusion that it led into Trinidad Bay, which he had noted on old Spanish charts. Actually, the Trinity swings north to join the Klamath River. From 1849 until the outbreak of the World War, when machinery and labor costs became prohibitive, Trinity River and its tributaries were the scenes of various types of mining operations, from the simplest forms of placering to gigantic hydraulic operations. In 1933, when the price of gold rose, miners' shacks and equipment reappeared. The river banks, paralleling US 299 westward for 65 miles, are piled high at intervals with mounds of gravel left from placer mining and nearby hillsides are deeply scarred by hydraulic operations.

> Left from Douglas City on an oiled road climbing steadily 19 *m.* to a junction with a narrow dirt road; L. here 6.2 *m.* through green meadows to a picnic ground (*free*), from which a footpath leads between white moss-covered boulders to a gray-white limestone NATURAL BRIDGE, spanning a narrow gulch, SITE OF THE BRIDGE GULCH MASSACRE. In March 1852, following the killing of a man named Anderson by Wentoon Indians, miners from Weaverville (*see below*) overtook and killed about 100 Indians encamped here, pursued the handful of women and children huddled beneath the bridge and knifed them to death. A contemporary reported that a young miner who sickened of the slaughter, saved one Indian girl, took her to Weaverville and entrusted her to a "motherly" woman acquaintance—who promptly sold her to a teamster from Shasta for $45.

WEAVERVILLE, 47.7 *m.* (2,407 alt., 650 pop.), seat of Trinity County, has lost nothing of the charm of the old, "easy" West, though the vine-covered frame cottages along the locust-bordered main street now have lawns protected by white picket fences. Over the tree-shaded sidewalks of the business section project broad, second-story galleries, reached by outside circular stairways, which give upper-story tenants private entrances. Only the occasional boisterous activity of the early mining town is absent. John Martin's livery stable has become Miller's Garage with little outward change; but today's automobile turns in the wide street without the shouts that attended the maneuvering of the three-wagon freight train, drawn by ten or twelve horses controlled with a deft jerk rein and an astonishing profanity.

Weaverville's social gatherings are no longer punctuated with the roar of "six-shooters," nor is its justice the simple hearty violence once encountered by an unfortunate miner named Seymour. The latter was accused of stealing the money of a visitor from Klamath who had drunk too freely and fallen asleep in a convenient pigsty. According to an early writer, Seymour "was taken up by the authorities, then rescued by the people, then left to his own fate, and then, finally . . . the money was found in the pigsty, where the drunken curse had sought shelter and company." More deserved was the treatment of one John Fehly in 1857; Fehly, drunk in front of the Diana Saloon and threatening darkly that his partner had "better look out," drew his revolver and shot into the crowd, killing Dennis Murray. Led to the gallows, Fehly struggled violently, but was forced to submit by the "Infant," a youth of 16, 6 feet 6 inches tall. In a contemporary account the Infant is described as "well known in Weaverville . . . and supposed to be a descendant of him whose blindness was so fearfully avenged at Gaza upon the Philistines." Overcome, Fehly remarked, "Since I've got to go, give me a coal on my pipe," and went to the scaffold smoking.

Despite several early fires, many old buildings remain, among them the WEEKLY TRINITY JOURNAL OFFICE (the *Journal,* first published in 1856, is one of the four oldest newspapers in the State). MEMORIAL HALL (L), a museum (*open daily; free*), displays relics of '49—ore specimens from well-known mines, a wide variety of old firearms, and an Indian scalp.

Possibly a dozen Chinese remain in Weaverville today to care for the old CHINESE JOSS HOUSE (*open*); but in 1852 half of the town's population of 3,000 was Chinese. In the dim, candle-lit interior of the tiny building, fine, hand-painted tapestries hang beside an altar 3,000 years old. A gully (R), Five-Cent Gulch, is the SITE OF THE CHINA WAR; here, in 1852, members of two rival tongs, encouraged by amusement-seeking white miners, met in a battle. Cheered on by the miners, 300 Ah Yous were badly routed by 500 Young Wos. Soon only two warriors remained on the field; for fifteen minutes they stood, calmly stabbing each other with their crude iron forks, until one fell dead. The other man died after two weeks of suffering. No other serious casualty was reported. (The use of firearms was forbidden to orientals by the whites.)

> Right from Weaverville on a dirt road 15 *m.* to TRINITY ALPS CAMP (*cabins, dining room, horses, and guide service*), a resort in the Trinity Mountains. A few miles north of the resort is the SALMON-TRINITY ALPS PRIMITIVE REGION, a part of Trinity National Forest (*see GENERAL INFORMATION*), accessible only by foot and pack trip. Tallest of the jumble of mountains within the area is THOMPSON (SAWTOOTH) PEAK (8,936 alt.), on which are several glaciers.

US 299 ascends OREGON GULCH MOUNTAIN, where the old Baron La Grange Mine, opened in 1851—for years the largest operating hydraulic mine in the world—once blasted away the mountainside.

JUNCTION CITY, 57.1 *m.* (1,471 alt., 300 pop.), on Canyon Creek, is a trading center of ranchers and miners.

At about 61 *m.* (L) on Trinity River is the SITE OF ARKANSAS DAM, one of the earliest "wing" dams, constructed by some 60 miners in 1850 and twice rebuilt after being washed away by floods. "Wing damming" was a system of mining utilized at low water, whereby the top rock and sand of the river bed were removed down to the pay gravel.

BIG BAR, 74 *m.* (1,248 alt., 73 pop.), was settled, according to an early historian, "by one Jones in 1849, who got rich, left the locality, and is no more with the memory of his fellows . . . Big Bar was the first place in Trinity County where the first white woman ever made the first johnny cake or dumpling and there lived and dwelt, and this woman's name was Mrs. Walton, who, with her husband, settled here in 1850 . . ." Still another resident of Big Bar, in 1855, was "Commodore" Ligne, who, "in a spirit of acquisitiveness, used to sell claims to Chinamen and others, and upon payment being duly received, would in the most harmless way 'practicable' drive them away. It seems that some obstinate occupants were foolish enough to remonstrate . . . but the Commodore . . . put an end to this by a dexterous display of shotgun . . . and became a terror to the locality." After an unsuccessful attack on a miner, Ligne "prudently retreated to the woods and did not reappear before the County . . . sent a deputation . . . and invited him to headquarters." Eventually, the activities of the Commodore were confined to San Quentin.

DEL LOMA (Sp., of the mountain), 78.8 *m.* (*tourist cabins*), once an active mining camp known as Taylor's Flat, is in the vicinity of French, Little French, and Canadian Creek, supposedly named for a band of French Canadian trappers who left Oregon at the news of Reading's strike on the Trinity.

US 299 continues past the HAYDEN FOREST SERVICE CAMPGROUND (*improved*), 79.8 *m.*, to the settlement of BURNT RANCH, 91.1 *m.* (2,000 alt., 30 pop.), where farmhouses were destroyed by fire in an Indian raid of 1853. From SALYER, 100.5 *m.* (553 alt., 59 pop.), site of another FOREST SERVICE CAMPGROUND, it descends to less rugged country where trees shade the road.

At 106 *m.* is a junction with State 96 (*see TOUR 3a*).

US 299 again enters a rugged region of forest and canyon, passing BOISE CREEK PUBLIC CAMPGROUND, 107.7 *m.* (R), and EAST FORK PUBLIC CAMPGROUND, 112.2 *m.* (L), both maintained by the Forest Service.

The highway leaves the confines of a narrow mountain gorge to command a wide vista of valley grazing lands edged by rolling yellow hills to the south; beyond it climbs low hills and descends to canyons where ferns grow tall and green by small, deep streams.

At 139.6 *m.* is a junction with an oiled road.

Left here 2.5 *m.* to the OLD ARROW TREE. When this dead redwood was young and strong, peace was made in its immediate vicinity between two warring tribes, who thereafter considered it the boundary between their

domains. When a member of the tribes passed the spot, he shot an arrow
into the bark as a token of peace. As the original meaning fell into
obscurity, it became an altar for worship and a place of prayer. Passers
thrust sharpened sticks into the bark and prayed for luck. Squaws, after
striking their legs with redwood sprigs, threw them against the tree and
cried, "I leave you with all my sickness."

BLUE LAKE, 139.7 m. (40 alt., 555 pop.), is the trade center of
a farming and dairying area, distinguished by neat picket fences, tall
windmills and silos.

At 146.8 m. is a junction with US 101 (see TOUR 2a), at a
point 2 miles north of Arcata.

Tour 8A

Canby—Lava Beds National Monument—Medicine Lake—Bartle;
118.8 m.

Roadbed paved for first 25.7 miles. Elsewhere dirt and gravel, deeply rutted,
covered with powdered pumice and sharp lava fragments in places; travel
advised from May to October only. At least one extra tire should be carried.
Accommodations only at Canby and Medicine Lake; Forest Service camps at
Lava Beds National Monument and Medicine Lake.

The rough and inhospitable waste of lava beds, underground caverns,
and cinder cones through which this route leads is a part of a 250,000-
square mile volcanic region. The pioneers knew it as the "Dark and
Bloody Battleground of the Pacific," where the last and bloodiest of
California's Indian Wars was fought. It is now part of Modoc
National Forest.

The route branches northwest from its junction with US 299
(see TOUR 8a), 0 m., 0.5 miles west of Canby, and runs into a lonely,
almost unsettled region. The Forest Service HOWARD'S GULCH CAMP
GROUND, 7 m., lies at the edge of pleasant meadows. At 25.7 m. is a
junction with a dirt road; L. here on the dirt road, now the main route.

The entrance to MAMMOTH CAVE (R), 31.2 m.—50 yards from
the road—is marked by massed lava rocks. The cave stretches for
hundreds of yards underground.

At 32.2 m. is the junction with an unpaved road; L. here; then R.
at 36.2 m., crossing a boundary of the LAVA BEDS NATIONAL
MONUMENT, 38.6 m., a rectangular area about 10 miles long and
8 miles wide, set aside in 1925. The region is geologically young; its
last lava flow is estimated to have taken place only 5,000 years ago.
Seen from a distance, the lava beds are a dark, comparatively level

terrain, broken only by crater-pitted cinder cones. On closer inspection, they are revealed as a rugged labyrinth of caves and chasms, where the molten lava has congealed in innumerable strange shapes—fumaroles (chimneys) of gas-inflated lava, smoothly arched bridges, fantastically sculptured shapes, some of them resembling animals. The caves, of which more than a hundred have been explored, are found in the type of billowing lava known as pahoehoe; they were formed when the surface of the lava hardened and the still molten core drained away. In many of these underground galleries, delicate lace-like tracings and Indian pictographs in red, green, or yellow ochre decorate ceilings and walls; in some of the deeper ones, frost crystals, frozen waterfalls, or rivers of ice appear.

When white immigrants were settling northern California, the lava beds were the stronghold of the warlike Modoc. The Nation's costliest Indian conflict, the Modoc War of 1872-73, was required to subdue them. For 5 months a band of Modoc warriors, never numbering more than 60, held off some 1,200 soldiers. The cost of subduing them was more than half a million dollars and the lives of 83 whites.

The trouble began in 1869, when the Modocs were moved to the reservation in Oregon of their hereditary enemies, the Klamaths. When they got no satisfaction from the Indian Agent after their complaints against the persecution by Klamath, a small band led by young Kientpoos—usually called Captain Jack—and his sister, "Queen Mary," left the reservation and returned to their old hunting ground, the Lost River country, just across the line in California. Over the protests of Brig. Gen. E. R. S. Canby, Department Commander, cavalry from Fort Klamath was sent by demand of the Indian Agent to bring the Modoc back to the reservation—"peaceably if you can, forcibly, if you must."

After a fight in which several were killed and wounded on both sides, the Indians entrenched themselves in an almost impregnable position among caves and crevices here, while the soldiers settled down nearby to wait for reinforcements. On January 17, 1873, when the military force had grown to about 400 men, Colonel Wheaton, the commander, launched an attack against the Indians' main position, Captain Jack's stronghold. At the end of the day, the soldiers had worn themselves out chasing the elusive Modoc without ever having seen an Indian, and 39 whites had been killed.

Backed by more reinforcements, General Canby attempted to arrange a settlement of the dispute. On April 11, 1873, he met Captain Jack and several of his chiefs under a flag of truce. Suddenly, in the midst of the parley, he was shot down and killed by Captain Jack; another peace commissioner, Dr. Eleazer Thomas, was slain by "Boston Charley." The other three members of the commission escaped. The Indians had lost two of their staunchest champions.

The troops rallied for a methodical advance, occupying successive positions until they had surrounded the Modocs and cut off their water supply. On April 17 they assaulted the Indian stronghold and drove the defenders out. Four days later the Indians, now completely surrounded, separated into two groups for an attempt to escape. As soon as they tried to fight in the open, they found the odds against them; nonetheless, they cut Capt. Evan Thomas' detachment to pieces before they were finally rounded up. Captain Jack himself eluded capture until June 1. On October 4, he was hanged at Fort Klamath, with three of his aides, for the murder of the commissioners. The rest of the band was moved to a reservation in Kansas.

INDIAN WELL, 42.1 *m.* (*information available from ranger during summer*), campground and administrative headquarters for the monument, is a center for exploration. (*Gasoline lanterns for use in caves available; in larger caves, guide line of strong twine should be fastened at entrance and unwound as exploration progresses. Stout hiking boots essential; ordinary clothing suffices.*)

> Right from Indian Well on a dirt road 0.4 *m.* to the junction with a dirt road; R. here 0.3 *m.* to the junction with another dirt road; L. on this road 0.6 *m.* to Post Office Cave and Dragon's Head Cave.

Opposite the ranger station, at the entrance to the Labyrinth (L), a 2-mile maze of tunnels, is the Devil's Mush Pot, a huge kettle of rock from which molten lava once flowed. Inside the labyrinth are Jupiter's Thunderbolt, a smooth formation extending from wall to wall, and the Menagerie, a collection of animal likenesses formed by lava.

> Left from the labyrinth on a narrow graveled road, past Frog, Sunshine, Jupiter, and Sentinel Caves, to Catacomb Cavern (R), 0.6 *m.,* whose smooth-floored lava passages wind for nearly 1.5 miles, adorned with wall niches resembling the burial places of early Christians in Rome. In some sections are traceries like delicate lace on walls and ceiling.
> Opposite the entrance to the Catacombs is Crystal Cave. From the red lava walls of its "jewel chambers" frost crystals flash, diamond-like.

At 43.6 *m.* is the junction with an unpaved road; R. here on a narrow, winding route, now the main route, pitted with sharp lava fragments, which loops around the monument (*travel advised only for experienced drivers, with tires in good condition*). At 45 *m.* is the junction with a narrow unpaved road.

> Left here 0.6 *m.* to Big Painted Cave (L) and Little Painted Cave (L), on whose walls are many Indian pictographs.

Skull Cave (L), 45.2 *m.,* was so named because numerous skulls of pronghorn antelope and bighorn sheep were found in it; both animals are now extinct in this region. The domed roof of Skull Cave's main level is 75 feet high. In the third, and lowest, cavern, in a river of ice, are the bones of many animals. A short distance west of Skull Cave are (R) Ship Cavern and White Lace Cave. On the walls of the latter are natural, white, lace-like patterns.

The ice in Frozen River Cave, 46.3 *m.,* rarely melts; the depth of its frozen river is unknown.

A high LAVA BRIDGE is crossed near the entrance to CAPTAIN JACK'S ICE CAVE (R), 46.7 *m.,* one of the Indian leader's retreats during the Modoc War.

The road continues northward through lava wastes to FERN CAVE (R), 52.7 *m.* (4,114 alt.), which derives its name from the luxuriant masses of ferns that grow just within its entrance, kept green the year round in a natural hot bed formed in the rich soil by many steam vents. On cold winter days clouds of steam obscure the entrance to the cave. The walls here also bear Indian pictographs.

Behind the natural fortification of HOSPITAL ROCK (R), 54.6 *m.* (4,051 alt.), wounded soldiers were sheltered. The cavalry camped nearby in 1873.

The road crosses the northern monument boundary at Hospital Rock, then parallels its irregular line for about 8 miles. Around CAPTAIN JACK'S STRONGHOLD (L), 57.1 *m.,* centered much of the Modoc War activities. The caves, the lava trenches, and the natural rock fortifications look today as they did in 1873.

CANBY CROSS (L), 60.6 *m.,* erected by his soldiers, marks the spot where General Canby was murdered (*see above*).

At 62 *m.* is the junction with a dirt road; L. here, again crossing the northern boundary, 62.3 *m.* Nearby is the site of the Army headquarters during the Modoc War. In GILLEM'S GRAVEYARD (R), 62.6 *m.,* about 100 white soldiers were buried.

The route follows the base (R) of GILLEM BLUFF (4,500-4,700 alt.) for nearly 4 miles. Two large groups of fumaroles (L) are passed at about 67.6 *m.* These "chimneys" of gas-inflated lava are similar to the fire fountains of the Hawaiian volcano, Kilauea. About 0.5 miles east of the chimneys (*no trail*) is the place where the force led by Captain Thomas was badly defeated; two-thirds of the command and four (of five) officers were killed or wounded.

SCHONCHIN BUTTE (L), 70.1 *m.* (5,293 alt.), is the largest of the 11 cones of scoriaceous cinder in the southern part of the monument; it was named for a Modoc chief.

At 71.1 *m.* is the junction with a dirt road.

Right on this road 1.5 *m.* to BEARPAW CAVE (R), whose frozen waterfall and river of ice never melt.

At the junction (L) at 71.2 *m.* the loop road completes its rough circle; straight ahead (south) here, to a junction with a dirt road at 71.6 *m.;* R. here passing HIPPO BUTTE (R), 72.1 *m.* (5,488 alt.), and crossing the southern boundary of the Monument, 74.3 *m.,* at the base of 400-foot deep MAMMOTH CRATER (R). At 74.8 *m.* is the junction with a dirt road; the route turns R. here, and L. at 77.8 *m.*

The deep blue waters of MEDICINE LAKE (*private lodge and public camp*), 85.8 *m.,* fill a crater that was once the center of local volcanic activity. The lake is well stocked with game fish. Its sandy beaches are fringed with tall lodgepole pines.

Five miles northeast is GLASS MOUNTAIN (7,649 alt.), whose

bulk of jet black obsidian gleams when struck by the sun. Steam issuing from a 30-foot vent west of the top-most peak bears evidence of the underground fires still smouldering within. The pumice surface nearby is too hot to be touched. So light in weight are the volcanic rock fragments strewing the slopes of Glass Mountain that a man can toss a piece the size of a horse.

At Medicine Lake is the junction with an unpaved road; here the main route turns R., then L. at 91.8 *m.*

BARTLE (*see TOUR 5a*), 118.8 *m.* is at the junction with State 89 (*see TOUR 5a*).

<hr>

Tour 9

(Reno, Nev.)—Truckee—Auburn—Roseville—Sacramento—Vallejo—San Francisco; US 40.
Nevada Line to San Francisco, 219.9 *m.*

Paved roadbed throughout, with easy grades in mountains; usually free from snow.
Route paralleled by Southern Pacific R.R. between Nevada Line and Sacramento and at intervals between Sacramento and Carquinez Bridge. Accommodations plentiful; many resorts and camps in mountains.

US 40, most traveled artery between the East and central California, hurdles the sheer, rocky wall of the Sierra Nevada into the valley that stretches to the Golden Gate. From the Great American Basin it climbs to the granite heights of Donner Pass, traverses the boulder-piled Yuba River bottoms, coasts toboggan-like through forests and along river gorges offering hazy vistas of mountain ranges. It passes the half-ruined mining camps of the gold country and the titanic upheavals of the hydraulic workings. In the foothills where orchards appear in forest clearings, it wriggles between rolling evergreen knolls, then strikes across the great Sacramento Valley, and crosses the low Coast Range to San Francisco.

Section a, NEVADA LINE to SACRAMENTO, 124.9 m. US 40.

The mountain heights were a forbidding barrier to the pioneers. With prodigious labor they forced their lumbering ox-drawn schooners over tortuous trails and through brush-choked canyons, over knifelike ridges, between gaping chasms. Often, when a sheer cliff blocked the way, oxen had to be unyoked so the ponderous wagons could be lifted or lowered with ropes. The devious California Trail through

Architecture

Bertram Goodhue, Architect

PUBLIC LIBRARY, LOS ANGELES

PALACE OF FINE ARTS, SAN FRANCISCO

CARSON HOUSE, EUREKA

Frank Lloyd Wright, Architect

COURT HOLLYHOCK, BARNSDALL PARK, LOS ANGELES

HEALTH HOUSE, LOS ANGELES

Richard J. Neutra, Architect.

INTERIOR, MISSION SAN MIGUEL ARCANGEL

MISSION SAN CARLOS BORROMEO, NEAR CARMEL

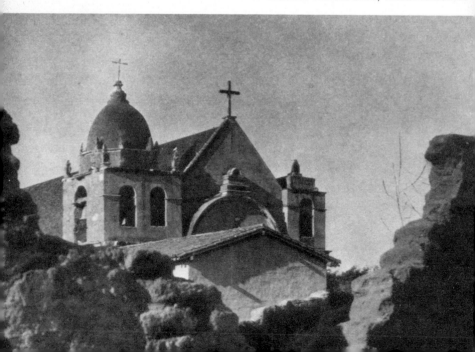

MISSION SANTA BARBARA

LOS ANGELES COUNTY HOSPITAL

TOWER OF CALIFORNIA BUILDING, BALBOA PARK, SAN DIEGO

Timothy Phlueger, Architect

450 SUTTER STREET, SAN FRANCISCO

Truckee Pass ran a few miles distant from what is now US 40, crossed it near Donner Lake, and recrossed it at Emigrant Gap. Over this trail in the autumn of 1844, 81-year-old Caleb Greenwood, mountaineer and trapper, led the 12 wagons of the Stevens-Murphy Party, first caravan on wheels to cross the Sierra. Others followed with terrible hardship in the autumn of the next year—the Swazey-Todd Party of horsemen; trappers on foot; the Grigsby-Ide Party of more than 100 men, women, and children led by Greenwood; and John C. Frémont on his third exploring expedition. In October 1846 the Donner Party, acting on vague advice, made the Salt Desert crossing and, arriving too late to scale the terrible pass that now bears their name, were caught by the snows.

A saga of transportation fully as exciting followed in 1864-66 when gangs of Chinese coolies swarmed the mountain, laying the rails of the Central Pacific eastward in a race with the Union Pacific, pushing westward from Omaha, that culminated in the completion of the first transcontinental railroad in Utah (1869). In June 1864 the "Big Four," Stanford, Hopkins, Huntington, and Crocker, had opened the Dutch Flat and Donner Lake Wagon Road. A road had reached Colfax, head of "wagon navigation," as early as 1849 and Dutch Flat a few years later; now the way lay open to the Comstock Lode mines in Nevada. For a brief interval stagecoaches raced over it, bearing passengers and freight; but as the Central Pacific was pushed forward —reaching Clipper Gap in June 1865 and Colfax in September—it killed all competition.

US 40 crosses the State Line, 0 m., 15 miles southwest of Reno, Nev., following the Truckee River, which is bordered by steep, craggy slopes. Frémont, camping at its mouth in January 1844 with his second expedition to the Far West, named it the Salmon Trout River because of the fine fish the Indians brought him. Later in the same year, the Stevens-Murphy Party gave it the name it now bears—that of the Paiute chief who guided them out of the burning alkali desert to the river's banks and pointed out the pass into California. His answer to all questions was "truckee," his equivalent for "okeh."

The boundary of TAHOE NATIONAL FOREST is crossed at 0.5 m.; the road runs for more than 50 miles through the forest. A reserve of more than 1,000,000 acres, it embraces an ever changing panorama of Sierra grandeur.

At 6.1 m. is a junction with a dirt road.

> Left on this road is FLORISTON, 0.5 m. (5,200 alt., 384 pop.), where rise the jumbled brick walls and smokestacks of a paper pulp mill—once the greatest producer in California. Red-roofed white frame cottages cling to the precipitous slopes.

From the winding canyon, US 40 climbs to a high, wide tableland, rimmed by mountains.

At 11.9 m. is a junction with a dirt road.

> Right on this road, crossing the river, to BOCA (mouth), 0.5 m. (5,535 alt., 25 pop.), once a lumbering town, now merely a handful of ramshackle

shanties around a bleak railroad station at the mouth of the Little Truckee River.

TRUCKEE, 19.8 *m.* (5,820 alt., 1,525 pop.) at the junction (R) with State 89 (*see TOUR 5b*), straggles along the banks of the river. Roundabout, pine forests cover the slopes with deep green, but Truckee itself, once a lumbering camp, now a railroad and stock-raising supply center, lacks even a sprig of green. Its ramshackle frame houses and weather-stained brick buildings sprawl over rocky slopes. On Saturday nights the cheap saloons and gambling halls overflow with lumberjacks, cow-punchers, and shepherds. In winter, when great glistening drifts fill the streets, the nearby snow-clad slopes resound with the shouts of skiers. The first California ski club was organized here in 1913. There are a variety of slides, a 1,000-foot toboggan slide with a power pull-back, and an ice rink illuminated for night skating. During the season are the weekly ski-jumping programs and the annual Sierra dog derbies. Often during the winter film companies work here.

At 20.8 *m.* is the western junction with State 89 (*see TOUR 10a*).

South of Truckee, US 40 plunges into a shadowy corridor of nut pines. A stone monument (L), 21.5 *m.,* faces north toward the low pass through which came the California Trail. About 90 yards south is the SITE OF THE GRAVES CABIN, erected by part of the Donner Party in 1846. At 22 *m.* another stone monument indicates the point where the emigrant trail turned south again, up Cold Creek Canyon, on its way to the summit. Here the Donner Party lost the trail.

The DONNER STATE MONUMENT (L), 22.3 *m.,* is an 11-acre tract set apart as a memorial to the Donner Party. At the end of October 1846, the vanguard of the train arrived at this point. Storm clouds were already gathering as they struggled up the rocky canyon of the Truckee; they made haste, but men and animals were footsore and exhausted; George Donner, the leader, had injured a leg. On October 28, a month earlier than usual, snow began to fall, burying the faint trail. They tried to go on, but could not, and turning back, pitched camp. Winter broke; November ended in four days and nights of continuous snow; December began with furious wind, sleet, and rain.

Led by well-to-do George and Jacob Donner and James F. Reed, the party had set out from Illinois in April. At Fort Bridger, on the strength of an open letter sent to travelers by the dare-devil mountaineer Lansford W. Hastings, who did not meet them as his letter had promised, they had taken the fatal step of breaking off from their companions of the trail to follow the unknown route later called the Hastings Cut-off. Even when they were compelled to break their way a few feet at a time through the thicket-choked canyons of the Wasatch Mountains in Utah, they had stubbornly refused to admit their mistake and turn back. By the time they had struggled for days and nights without water across the deserts beyond the Great Salt Lake, it was too late to correct the error. Utterly exhausted, their animals dying, they had rested for several days in the green meadows along the Truckee on the site of Reno; this final delay was their undoing.

In the camps at Alder Creek and Donner Lake, the snow became 20 feet deep. Starvation faced them, for their cattle had wandered off, and were buried in the drifts. By December 10, Jacob Donner and three others in the Donner huts on Alder Creek were dead. Soon the immigrants were living on the few mice they could catch, and on bark and twigs. In a desperate effort to escape, 10 men and 5 women, known as the "Forlorn Hope," started west on foot with provisions enough for 6 days, scaled the summit, and followed the ridge north of the North Fork of the Yuba River. Within a week one man had died; by Christmas Day, after 4 days without food, they could go no farther. A terrific storm had burst upon them, and for a whole week they were snowbound, huddling in terrible misery about their campfire. When the storm lifted, four more men had died; the starving survivors devoured their bodies. Another man died; he, too, was eaten—and so were the two Indian guides, killed when they began to falter. Struggling on, these survivors ate their moccasins, the strings of their snowshoes, a pair of old boots. Thirty-two days after they had set out, the 5 women and 2 remaining men reached an Indian village and were dragged on to the Johnson Ranch at Wheatland, leaving a trail of bloody footprints.

Relief parties set out from the Sacramento Valley. The first, seven men on foot, reached the camp at Donner Lake February 19, to find it buried under snowdrifts; the survivors, with nothing left to eat but hides, were in a torpor. With 21, mostly children, three of whom died on the way out, the rescuers started back, meeting on the way the second relief expedition, which reached the camp March 1. Seventeen more started back with it, only to be trapped by another blizzard, which held them in the snow for a week. Their feet and hands froze; three more died, and their bodies were eaten by the survivors. The third relief party found nine still alive at the camp, three of them too near death to travel; they, too, had been driven to eat the bodies of the dead. With five of these survivors, the relief party started back, but Tamsen Donner, renouncing her last chance to escape, said goodbye to her two little daughters and struggled back over the five miles of drifts to the camp at Alder Lake to nurse her dying husband. She had died, and her body had vanished, when the fourth relief party, seeking whatever of value remained at the camp for plunder, arrived to find one man still living in hideous squalor among the bones of his fellow travelers. Of the 81 who had pitched camp here in November 1846, only 45 crossed the mountains.

Left from the entrance to the PIONEER MONUMENT, 0.1 *m.*, a great stone block bearing the heroic bronze figures of a man, woman, and child. Here is the SITE OF THE SCHALLENBERGER CABIN, built by members of the Stevens-Murphy Party in November 1844, where young Moses Schallenberger, ill and unable to scale the pass, spent the winter alone, guarding the goods until he was rescued in March of the next year. When the vanguard of the Donner Party camped here November 1, 1846, the Breen family—only one to escape without losing at least one member—moved in.

Right from the end of the road on a foot trail, through a grove of nut pines, 0.3 *m.* to the huge granite boulder marking the SITE OF THE MURPHY

CABIN, in which lived Grandmother Murphy, her family, and others. The crude lean-to was built against the great smooth-faced rock, which served as the fireplace wall. Under the Murphy cabin in June 1847 Gen. Stephen W. Kearny's band buried the bones found in the vicinity.

US 40 curves around the edge of gleaming blue DONNER LAKE, 22.7 *m.* On August 25, 1846, Edwin Bryant, with eight companions, found the going so boggy here in many places that the mules sank to their bellies in the mire. The arresting outlines of CASTLE PEAK (9,139 alt.), rise (R) at the head of a long draw. Bryant, in the journal of his California trip, marveled at its "cyclopean magnitude, the . . . apparently regular and perfect . . . construction of its walls, turrets, and bastions."

In long curves US 40 begins to scale the all but perpendicular wall of granite that lifts ahead beneath the rock-ribbed crowns of DONNER PEAK (8,315 alt.) and LINCOLN PEAK (8,403 alt.). Blasted through solid rocks, the road twists in and out between overhanging ledges. Up the sheer precipice wriggles the long black caterpillar of the railroad snowsheds, worming at intervals through granite tunnels.

To young adventurers like Edwin Bryant and his companions, these heights offered a challenge; but they dismayed those who faced the passage with cumbersome, ox-drawn wagons loaded with belongings and women and children. Old Caleb Greenwood, however, guiding the Stevens-Murphy Party over the mountains in November 1844, exercised rare judgment and skill. They struggled upward until a rise of 10 or 12 feet blocked the way. Greenwood discovered a narrow crevice; through it the oxen were half pushed, half dragged, with men below and ropes above; the household goods were carried up piece by piece. Then, with the use of levers, log chains, and six or eight ox teams, the wagons were lifted over the face of the cliff. With inconceivable labor, several other barriers scarcely less difficult were conquered in the same way.

The highway climbs to the summit of DONNER PASS (7,135 alt.), 28.9 *m.* Here on an exposed point, where the wind seldom stops blowing, a UNITED STATES WEATHER BUREAU OBSERVATORY makes records of wind direction and velocity for the aid of air navigators.

In Summit Valley is LAKE VAN NORDEN (L), an artificial reservoir dotted with decaying stumps, and the winter resort of NORDEN (*hotel*), 30.2 *m.* (6,880 alt.), an ideal locale for winter sports because of its heavy snowfall, long season, and open slopes. SODA SPRINGS, 31.7 *m.* (6,784 alt.), is a handful of rustic resort cabins around a hotel.

Left from Soda Springs on a dirt road, through a mountain wilderness, to a junction with a dirt road, 8 *m.;* L. here 2 *m.* to SODA SPRINGS (5,975 alt.), long known as Hopkins's Springs, the resort that Mark Hopkins and Leland Stanford opened in the 1870's. A trail leads upstream about 1 *m.* to PAINTED ROCK, on the south side of the river, which shows prehistoric Indian pictographs.

At 18.2 *m.* is a junction with a dirt road; R. from this junction 5 *m.* to LAST CHANCE (4,500 alt.). A group of prospectors pushed their way to this place in 1850 and lingered on, greedy for the rich gold deposits, until their provisions were exhausted. Staking all on a last chance, one of the men went into the forest and, as luck would have it, shot a large buck. The camp survived. By 1852 it had grown into a real town, and by 1859 it had three lodge halls. Remnants of its short-lived glory appear in the old hotel and the scattered cabins that still shelter a handful of miners in this isolated wilderness.

US 40 runs through the canyon of the South Fork of the Yuba River, past a string of vacation camps, inns, and public camp grounds. The stream cascades down broken granite slopes; deep among the bordering conifers are piles of gray-white granite, ground from the mountain flanks by ancient glaciers. Here and there tiny meadows, bright with alpine flowers, soften the austerity.

At 44.8 *m.* is a junction with State 20.

Right on State 20, which drops down gently between long lanes of fir and cedar to BEAR RIVER, 4.5 *m.*, flowing through a narrow meadow at the upper end of Bear Valley (4,500 alt.) among high mountains. In these rich grasslands trains of weary, half-starved immigrants paused to refresh their gaunt livestock. The valley is the summer range for cattle from the dry foothill country and the scene of the annual "stampede" of the Flying J Ranch.

At Bear River is a junction with a dirt road; R. here 0.2 *m.* to a junction with a second dirt road; R. again to LAKE SPAULDING, 1.2 *m.* impounded by a stone and concrete dam built in 1912. In a huge cave blasted from the canyon wall stands the power house. A tunnel bored through rock carries the lake water to the electric turbine and back to Drum Canal, where it flows down Bear Canyon to the foothill orchards about Auburn. North of Lake Spaulding are a string of man-made lakes that drain into Lake Spaulding. Since the gold days these reservoirs have been turned to many uses: sluice mining in the 1850's, large-scale hydraulic mining in the 1860's and 1870's, irrigation of farms and orchards from the 1850's on, and generation of electric power since the turn of the century.

Westward, US 40 passes between the high earth embankments of YUBA PASS CUT, and coasts down the crest of the ridge into the meadows of Wilson Valley. On both sides the slopes fall away, R. into Bear River Valley 600 feet below, L. into the wooded canyon of the North Fork of the American River. Through this notch in the ridge, EMIGRANT GAP, the North Fork once spilled into the Yuba, but the upheaval of the Sierra Range lifted up the giant causeway between them; over this the highway now runs.

At 49.1 *m.* is a junction with an improved road.

Left on this road to EMIGRANT GAP (*cabins, hotel*), 0.5 *m.* (5,250 alt., 164 pop.). Up the steep canyon sides from the railroad track are mill buildings, lumber yards, and shanties. At the western edge of Tahoe National Forest, the village is a popular fishing and hunting center.

Emigrant Gap marks the boundary between the High Sierra and the gold-veined foothills. For 40 miles southward the highway rides the crest of the long, tapering ridge, affording magnificent panoramas of steep wooded canyons and gorges. Files of conifers appear on the receding crests.

At 58.4 *m.* is the junction with a graded road.

Right on this road is ALTA, 1.7 *m.* (3,602 alt., 113 pop.), a railroad station, where old-fashioned white cottages stand among apple orchards near a tiny lake. The road passes between broken picket fences, behind which are old houses surrounded in spring by bowers of blossoming fruit trees, purple lilac, and scarlet quince. On the heights above the village, summer visitors have built houses.

DUTCH FLAT, 3.5 *m.* (3,399 alt., 90 pop.), played a vivid part in the history of the northern mines. Settled in 1851 by German miners, Joseph Doranbach and his companions—"Dutchmen" in miners' parlance—it was soon crowded with thousands who flocked in to the placer deposits. It was a Dutch Flat man, Daniel W. Strong, who pointed out Donner Pass to Theodore Dehone Judah, young Central Pacific engineer, and Dutch Flat subscribed money generously for the railroad. After 1863, when the railroad "Big Four" opened their Dutch Flat and Donner Lake Wagon Road, Concord coaches and teamsters stopped at hostelries here. Dutch Flat had lost its importance as a stage center by the fall of the next year, when the railroad stretched 20 miles beyond to Cisco; but the spectacular hydraulic operations of the next decade, when one company worked as many as 32 claims at once on a gigantic scale, kept millions of dollars in gold passing over its counters.

CHINA STORE (L), a massive, fortresslike structure with tiny porthole windows, half stone and adobe and half wood, is all that remains of a Chinatown that housed 1,000 coolies of the railroad construction days.

Right from Dutch Flat a road winds through the DUTCH FLAT HYDRAULIC DIGGINGS, a waste of rugged, man-made ravines choked with rocks and rubble. In these many-hued stony acres, hexagonal crystals, fossils, and even at times a gold nugget, are found.

Crossing Bear River, the road climbs a steep canyon wall to LITTLE ROCK, 2.8 *m.* (2,900 alt.), once a mining town, YOU BET, 6 *m.* (3,000 alt.), and RED DOG, 7.7 *m.* (2,850 alt.), around which 2,000 miners dug for gold in the 1870's.

Descending from the dense forest between banks of reddish earth and crumbling rock, the highway, at 61.7 *m.,* cuts into a deep gash along the face of bluffs tinged with vivid hues of russet, buff, and rose red. Over the canyon bottoms (L) sprawl mounds of reddish earth and gravel, half overgrown with scrub pines; beyond rise crumbling pinnacles and blasted palisades. From the river channels of this region, where streams of the Tertiary era deposited a bed of auriferous gravel, 250 feet deep, 2 miles long, and a half mile wide, was washed out more than $15,000,000 worth of gold during the titanic hydraulic operations of the 1870's and 1880's.

In the midst of rose-streaked debris is GOLD RUN, 63.1 *m.* (3,224 alt., 114 pop.), active in the 1860's and 1870's. The log cabin on stilts beside the highway (L) at 63.7 *m.,* is the GOLD RUN TRADING POST, now a museum for pioneer relics.

US 40 runs through narrow defiles, where interlacing branches hide the sun. The forest of pine and cedar begins to thin out, making way for spreading black oaks, with tattered, yellow-green foliage, and for bushy gray-green manzanita.

COLFAX, 73.2 *m.* (2,422 alt., 912 pop.), is strung out along railroad sidings where boxcars wait by warehouses. On the hillsides are old-fashioned cottages. Nearby are orchards of Bartlett pears and Hungarian prunes, and vineyards of Tokay grapes. Called Alden

Grove by its settlers of 1849, the place was renamed Illinoistown in the early 1850's, and Colfax about 1869. During those turbulent years it was a head of "wagon navigation" to the gold mines; here goods were transferred to muleback for the journey to remote camps.

At 73.8 *m.* is a junction with a dirt road.

> Left on this road, down an easy grade, to MINERAL BAR, 5 *m.* (1,200 alt.), on the North Fork of the American River, where Judas trees grow in moist gullies of the steep canyon walls. The river rushes past abandoned diggings. When summer dries the river to a low-water level, a few miners still wash out a little yellow dust where scores once made their "piles."
>
> Steep and narrow, the way leads up the canyon wall to IOWA HILL, 10 *m.* (3,200 alt., 100 pop.), high on the neck of a ridge. Only one of the old brick buildings on the main street has survived the ravages of fire, and only a handful of white frame cottages remain to look primly out from lilac trees and hollyhocks. Over the grassy slopes above the village spread the remnants of deserted gardens and orchards; at the top of the hill, delicate manzanita bells fall softly on moss-grown headstones in the old cemetery. All about are signs of the treasure-trove which, first discovered in 1853, had yielded an estimated $20,000,000 by 1880. Long ago the rich conglomerate of the Blue Lead Channel, which ran under the town, was drifted out; tremendous hydraulic onslaughts all but washed the townsite away.

US 40 traverses an area of tiny orchards in forest clearings; the pears and apples grown here have unusually fine flavor and texture. The old type of diversified farming, which has all but disappeared from much of the State, lingers here in the small holdings given over to orchards, vineyards, and pastures for dairy cattle.

AUBURN, 90.5 *m.* (1,360 alt., 2,661 pop.) (*see TOUR 4a*) is at a junction with State 49 (*see TOUR 4a*).

At 91.8 *m.* is a junction with an oiled road.

> Right on this road is OPHIR, 1.5 *m.* (850 alt., 250 pop.), which began life as Spanish Corral, but exchanged it for the name of King Solomon's treasure trove. In 1852 the most populous town in Placer County, Ophir is still the trade center of its chief quartz-mining district. Among the nearby orchards and vineyards are the scars of old diggings, abandoned mining pits, dumps, and stamp mill foundations.

Diving into a long tunnel US 40 runs under NEWCASTLE, 94.6 *m.* (970 alt., 750 pop.), a hilltop town. Newcastle was the only one of the many camps at the head of Secret Ravine to survive. As orchards replaced the spent placer mines in the 1870's and 1880's, it became a fruit-packing and shipping center.

At 97.3 *m.* is a junction with a paved road.

> Right on this road is PENRYN, 0.2 *m.* (635 alt., 300 pop.), which wears (under slightly altered spelling) the name of the Welsh town, Penrhyn, from which came Griffith Griffith, who opened a granite quarry here in 1864. Penryn is today a fruit-shipping center.

LOOMIS, 99.9 *m.* (400 alt., 319 pop.), is the successor of Pine, which took its name from Pine Grove in nearby Secret Ravine, where mining began in 1850. Along the highway are strung squat business buildings, and along the railroad, the great fruit warehouses.

As the last orchard-mantled slopes of the Sierra foothills taper off, US 40 strikes over a level straightaway across the edges of the Sacramento Valley. Ahead lies open country, spotted with clumps of cottonwoods and willows. Into the distance sweep grassy knolls, dappled with groves of immense spreading oaks. This parklike oak-covered country, California's most characteristic landscape, encircles the great Central Valley and spreads over much of the Coast Range.

A large percentage of the population of ROCKLIN, 102.8 *m.* (248 alt., 724 pop.), is foreign-born—predominantly Finnish. The Finns maintain their own library and choral society, and work in the granite quarries from which Rocklin takes its name.

ROSEVILLE, 106.7 *m.* (163 alt., 6,425 pop.), at the junction with US 99E (*see TOUR 3B*), is a freight-clearing center clustering about the extensive Southern Pacific shops and yards. Its shady side streets of frame dwellings are lined by olive, maple, and fig trees. Heart of an area that grows plums, berries, almonds, and grapes, it ships large quantities of table fruits to Eastern markets.

NORTH SACRAMENTO, 124.9 *m.* (34 alt., 2,097 pop.), sprawls along the highway, a string of one-story shops and gas stations, typical city outskirts.

US 40 continues southward, and at 125.7 *m.* spans the tree-lined American River, on whose south fork James W. Marshall discovered gold in 1848.

SACRAMENTO, 124.9 *m.* (34 alt., 93,750 pop.) (*see SACRAMENTO*). Sacramento is at junctions with US 99 (*see TOUR 3a*) and State 24 (*see TOUR 9A*).

Section b.   SACRAMENTO to SAN FRANCISCO, 95 m. US 40.

Southwest of the State capital, the Victory Highway crosses the broad farmlands of the Sacramento Valley, passes through the low, orchard-covered foothills of the Coast Range, and follows the shores of San Pablo and San Francisco Bays into San Francisco. The first Yankee immigrants found much of the land already claimed by Mexican dons, but this did not hinder their attempts to possess it. After gold seekers swarmed in from coast to foothills in the 1850's, roads, railroads, and river boat lines were developed; later the land was divided into farms, pastures, and orchard plots. Along winding side roads in the quiet back country appear the crumbling adobes of the dons and the later frame mansions of the Yankee invaders; but the main highway runs through a countryside embellished with signboards, gas stations, and soda pop stands, through vast corporation-controlled farms, and through bleak company towns at factory gates.

At the western end of SACRAMENTO, 0 *m.*, is the 737-foot-long TOWER BRIDGE, a vertical lift span over the broad Sacramento River. Excavation for the bridge abutment on the city side brought to light, 20 feet underground, the tracks of the Central Pacific, first transcontinental railroad. The Sacramento, California's largest river, served for decades as the main artery of travel between the early San Francisco and this valley. The great flat-bottomed, paddle wheel river boats of rival lines raced each other from port to port, sometimes tying down safety valves until steam pressure rose to the explosion point. The Combination Line's *Pearl,* with 93 aboard, was racing the Citizens' Line's *Enterprise* on January 27, 1855, when her boilers exploded near Sacramento, killing 56 persons. Similar disasters on the *Washoe,* the *Yosemite,* and the *Belle* finally dampened the competitive spirit. In the end, the railroad put most of the river steamers out of business: today only one line operates between San Francisco and Sacramento.

At 2.1 *m.* is a junction with a paved road.

> Right on this road is BRODERICK, 0.5 *m.* (550 pop.), which was the seat of Yolo County for two brief periods (1851-57 and 1861-62), but lost the honor under stress of fire, flood, and political storm. Chief point of activity today is the waterfront, with launches and fishing craft tied up near boathouses and cabins on the riverbank; here old river steamboats, the *Red Bluff* and the *Dover,* lie beached. A weatherbeaten GREEK ORTHO-DOX CHURCH testifies to the many Russians who settled here. Along the river bank are the huts and shanties of squatters, and hobo "jungles."

Through the roadside clutter of city outskirts—billboards, auto camps, gas stations, fruit and vegetable stands, truck garden plots, and ranchers' shanties—US 40 strikes out across the level floor of the Sacramento Valley.

Yolo Bypass, 5.5 *m.,* is a 3-mile causeway over desolate, tule-grown marshlands—in springtime carpeted with yellow baeria, in autumn the haunt of wild geese. The deeply rutted road that formerly meandered over these swampy acres was impassable in spring when the swollen Sacramento flooded it with a muddy torrent. So yielding was the terrain that the railroad, paralleling the highway on a high embank-ment, used to sag until the tracks looked like a sway-backed horse. Unnumbered tons of rock had to be dumped into the swamp before the engineers won their fight. Today, when the river threatens to break its levees, flood gates are thrown open and this whole region is inundated.

The Sacramento Valley, level as the Midwest prairies, stretches ahead, an irregular checkerboard of tomato patches, strips of blue-green alfalfa, immense tracts of sugar beets, fields green in spring with waving grain and tawny with stubble in autumn. Scattered farm buildings huddle among trees.

By 1856, at DAVIS, 14.8 *m.* (54 alt., 1,243 pop.), Jerome C. Davis had 400 acres in wheat and barley, great herds of livestock, and orchards and vineyards.

The drooping feathery branches of gray-green tamarisks hide the fields and orchards of the University of California's DAVIS BRANCH OF THE COLLEGE OF AGRICULTURE. From the entrance (L), 15.4 *m.,* a driveway leads to a cluster of 40 classrooms and dormitories, athletic facilities, a model dairy, and pedigreed-livestock and poultry pens. The

1,076-acre farm includes 150 acres of orchard with more than 1,000 varieties of fruit, 27 acres of experimental vineyards, 250 acres planted with forage crops, 130 acres of pasture, and a 10-acre poultry plant.

At 16.2 *m.* is a junction with US 99 (*see TOUR 8a*).

DIXON, 26.3 *m.* (67 alt., 1,000 pop.), is a farming and dairying center, named for its founder, Thomas Dickson, whose name it soon forgot how to spell. The town grew up soon after the advent of the first transcontinental railroad, superseding the village of Silveyville, on the stage road to the gold mines.

Swinging southwest toward low tumbled hills, US 40 is skirted by neatly trimmed fields, orchards and pastures.

At 36.7 *m.* is a junction with a paved road.

Right on this road is VACAVILLE, 0.7 *m.* (166 alt., 1,556 pop.), on gentle knolls, where orchards adjoin rear gardens or look down on housetops. The warm, frostless slopes of hill-sheltered Vaca, Pleasants, and Laguna Valleys, each spring produce early cherries, apricots, peaches, plums and pears for the eastern market. Before 1850, when Vacaville was founded, the land roundabout was the range for the great cattle herds of Rancho de los Putos. As Yankee settlers began to arrive the lands were broken up into small farms and orchards. In this region are laid the opening scenes of Charles G. Norris' novel, *Brass.* On Merchant St. stands (L) the old frame PENA HOUSE; in the yard gnarled and blackened fig trees mingle with oleanders and aged pear, walnut, and poplar trees. Vacaville's Chinatown is a survival of the 1880's and 1890's, when Chinese workers flocked in to work in the fruit industry.

US 40 winds up into the smooth Vaca hills. Along the sheltered valley bottoms are apricot orchards, fragrant with delicate blossoms in spring, heavily laden with ripening fruit in summer. With the coming of the first winter rains, the parched hillsides are mantled with tall grass—lush grazing for sheep and cattle.

In this region, the poet, Edwin Markham, best known for his "The Man with the Hoe," spent his boyhood and early youth (1861-1870) as sheepherder and vaquero on his mother's cattle ranges. Here he plowed "the little valleys between the ridges for wheat and barley," and followed the "threshing machine in the time of harvesting." Somewhere in the vicinity, he shared in the "exhilarating spectacle" of the rodeo held yearly by the cattle king of the region.

The PENA ADOBE (L), 40.1 *m.,* sits in a garden under the shade of the fig and walnut trees, the pomegranate, the mission grape, and the Castilian rose cherished by early Spanish settlers. The old structure is now under a board siding.

US 40 descends and crosses level Suisun Valley, FAIRFIELD, 46.6 *m.* (12 alt., 1,131 pop.), seat of Solano County, is the trade center of farmers and orchardists. It spills over part of an old rancho acquired by two sea captains, Robert H. Waterman and Archibald A. Ritchie, who founded the town in 1859, and induced the transfer of the county seat from Benicia by their donation of land for a townsite.

Left from Fairfield on Union Ave. to SUISUN CITY, 0.8 *m.* (12 alt., 905 pop.), once connected with Fairfield by a mile-long plank road over a swamp, today divided from it only by the railroad tracks. All the way to this inland point, up winding Suisun Slough through the great salt-water marshes north of Suisun Bay, watercraft sailed in the 1850's to the landing place for Mexican ranchos. The old landing (L), near the Plaza, is still owned by a grandson of Capt. Josiah Wing, who began running watercraft here in 1850, erected a warehouse two years later, and in 1854 laid out the town. The clapboarded WING HOUSE, built in 1858, stands on a narrow street. Today canneries and packing plants, taking advantage of shipment both by water and rail, cluster here. The salt-water marshes, owned by sportsmen's clubs, offer excellent duck shooting and bass fishing.

Where today's wide roadbed runs westward past trim white farm-houses, the earliest travelers across Suisun Valley followed a dim trail through wild oats so tall that riders on horseback were hidden by them. Sometimes wild Spanish cattle attacked the wayfarer, or antelope and elk broke into a wild stampede.

The bronze STATUE OF FRANCISCO SOLANO is on a low knoll (R), 51.1 m. Solano was overlord of all the Indian tribes north of Suisun and San Pablo Bays. Born Sem Yoto, chief of the Suisune, he was baptized with a Spanish name by the fathers of Misión San Francisco de Solano at Sonoma, from whom he learned many of the arts of the white men. At the time Lieut. Mariano G. Vallejo conquered the Suscol in 1835, he won the friendship of Chief Solano, who aided him in the peace deliberations. On Rancho Suisun, granted to him by the Spaniards, Solano built a large adobe for himself and smaller ones for his people; the Yankees who passed this way in 1846 and 1847 found it occupied by the Indian, Jesús Molino, and surrounded by fields of peas, wheat, and other crops. His alliance with Chief Solano, who could muster a force of 1,000 plumed and painted warriors, was Vallejo's chief protection for the struggling new outposts of Spanish civilization against the depredations of the natives. When Solano County was organized in 1850, it was named at Vallejo's request for his Indian ally, whom he admired and trusted as a friend. "A splendid figure of a man" (he was 6 feet 7 inches tall), as Vallejo described him, Solano was "a keen, clearheaded thinker, readily grasped new ideas, learned to speak Spanish with ease and precision, and was so ready to debate, that few cared to engage with him in a contest of wits." The bronze likeness represents him as an Indian of magnificent physique, with one hand upraised in a gesture of peace—somewhat riddled by the potshots of latter-day hunters.

At 51.9 m. is a junction with a paved road.

> Right on this road is ROCKVILLE, 1.6 m. with a country store. Nearby, a substantial stone METHODIST EPISCOPAL CHURCH, erected in 1856, stands among flowering shrubs and trees in a graveyard.
> Left from Rockville, 0.5 m., to the great stone MARTIN HOUSE (R), with peaked roof and gables, projecting eaves, and deep window sills, in the style of an English manor-house. In 1850 Samuel Martin arrived, having crossed the plains from Pennsylvania with his family in a covered wagon, with men on horseback driving his herds. He gradually acquired land until he owned an estate of 11,000 acres. In the year Martin's party arrived, the last of the Suisune, whose chief village stood here, were

retreating into the mountains, carrying sacks of grain on their heads. On a wooded knoll back of the mansion are great, deeply embedded boulders that reveal mortar holes worn smooth during the grinding of grass seeds and acorns. The Suisune were an independent and self-reliant people, as the Spanish soldier, Gabriel Moraga, sent to subdue them in 1810, discovered. Many of them, retreating after a bloody encounter set fire to their huts and perished in the flames. Again, when José Sanchez led a second attempt at subjugation in 1817, they followed their chief, Malaca, in a resistance that was defeated only by the superior weapons of the Spanish. In a field (L) opposite the Martin House was a Suisune Burial Ground; a buckeye tree marks the GRAVE OF FRANCISCO SOLANO, who succeeded Malaca.

At 53.2 *m.* is a junction with State 12 (*see TOUR 2A*).

Climbing out of Suisun Valley, US 40 winds into AMERICAN CANYON, a shallow cleft through low, rounded hills dappled with clumps of oak and bay. Grass-covered in spring, these hill slopes give pasture to herds of sheep and cattle, which leave them close-cropped and bare throughout the summer and fall. As the highway leaves the hills, the tang of salt air greets the nostrils. Beyond is a panorama of Vallejo's city blocks (*see TOUR 2A*), topped by the steel masts of the Naval Radio Station, the silver Napa River, and Mount Tamalpais beyond San Pablo Bay.

At 62.3 *m.* is a junction with an oiled road (*see TOUR 2A*).

At 63.1 *m.* US 40 meets a paved road.

Left on this road to SOUTHAMPTON BAY, 3.7 *m.*, where the James Corbett-Joe Choynski prize fight was staged June 5, 1889, on a barge. The encounter was not quite an engagement with bare fists, for Corbett's hands were encased in 3-ounce mitts, Choynski's in driving gloves. Although Corbett broke both hands early in the fight, he went on pummeling Choynski until he knocked him out in the twenty-eighth round. Both had to be carried from the barge. Corbett's seconds were Thomas Williams and Porter Ashe; Choynski's were Nat Goodwin, Eddie Graney, and Jack Dempsey, the "Nonpareil."

BENICIA, 5.5 *m.* (2,913 pop.), along the northern shore of Carquinez Strait, at the base of low hills that slope down gently to the water's edge, is a monument to Gen. Mariano Vallejo's town-founding passion. It rose on his Rancho Suscol, which he deeded in 1846 to Dr. Robert Semple, editor of the *Californian,* and Thomas O. Larkin, only United States consul to Alta California (1844-46). Named Santa Francisca in honor of Vallejo's wife, the town dreamed for a brief interval of becoming the metropolis of San Francisco Bay; but when the citizens of Yerba Buena appropriated the name of the bay, Vallejo and his associates fell back on Señora Vallejo's second name, Benicia. In 1849, Benicia was a thriving waypoint on a main traveled road to the mines; in 1853-54 it was important enough to be the State capital. An army post, established here in 1849, and later an arsenal, made it a military headquarters of the Far West. When the Pacific Mail Steamship Company built wharves and shops along the deep-water harbor, it became a coaling and repair stop for river boats. As miners drifted back after the gold rush and settled in the valleys, Benicia became a quiet, orderly town, proud of its schools and churches.

Today its citizens preserve the landmarks of its past. Each year, during the Old Timers' Festival, a marker is placed to commemorate some feature of early days. California's OLDEST MASONIC HALL (1851) stands (R) on West J St. near 1st St.; it housed the State Legislature on its ground

floor in 1853 when Benicia was State capital. St. Paul's Episcopal
Church (1885), corner of 1st and J Sts., stands on the site of the first
Episcopal cathedral (1860) of the Diocese of Northern California. On I St.
near 1st St. is the Site of the Benicia Young Ladies' Seminary, founded
in 1852; in the 1860's it was bought by Dr. and Mrs. Cyrus Mills who
changed the name to Mills Seminary, and moved it to Oakland, where
later it became Mills College (*see OAKLAND*).

One of the first hotels in California, was the California House (1847),
on H St. (R) near 1st St., built for Maj. Stephen Cooper, whose daughter
was married here to Dr. Robert Semple in the town's first wedding. Remodeled into a brewery in 1854 and since rebuilt, it retains part of the
adobe wall. The red-brick Capitol, G and 1st Sts., housed the State
Legislature from December 1853 to April 1854, was the Solano County
Courthouse in 1854-59, and the town school in 1859-1882; today it is the
city hall, library, and museum.

Typical of California's early inns is the Solano Hotel (R), corner of
1st and E Sts., stopping place for famous men and women of the 1850's
and scene of gay social events. The Von Pfister Adobe Store (R), near
1st and D Sts., was built in 1847; here, where a certain Mr. Von Pfister
set up shop in 1848 with merchandise brought from Honolulu, Charles
Bennett announced James Marshall's discovery of gold.

At the foot of M St. is the United States Arsenal (1851), whose oldest
extant building (1869) is a sandstone edifice with a square clock tower.
Beyond waterfront shacks and fishing craft lies the abandoned *Solano,* one
of the twin Southern Pacific ferries which carried whole trains between
Benicia and Port Costa (1879-1930). In a barge anchored off Carquinez
Point, Jack London made a sojourn (1882-83), described in *John Barleycorn.*

The Municipal Park, 1st St. between K and L Sts., is on the site of
California's first Presbyterian Church, organized April 1849. California's
first convent school was St. Catherine's Seminary, L St. near 1st St., established at Monterey in 1851 by Dominican sisters and moved to Benicia in
1854. Bishop Wingfield's House, M and 2nd Sts., at the end of a tree-
lined drive was one of the buildings of St. Augustine Episcopal College,
instituted in 1867 on a site where a boys' academy had been since 1852.
The organization of St. Dominic's Church, I and 5th Sts., was organized
in 1854 by Father Villarosa, Dominican priest, and his community of
brothers; members of the order still use the priory quadrangle.

Left from 5th and M Sts. in Benicia on State 21 to St. Dominic's Ceme-
tery, 0.5 *m.,* where Doña María Concepción Argüello, who taught in St.
Catherine's Seminary from 1854 until her death in August 1857, lies buried.
Doña Concepción, immortalized in poetry by Bret Harte and in the novel
Rezanov by Gertrude Atherton, was not quite 16 when handsome Russian
Count Rezanov came to visit her father, Don Luís, comandante of the San
Francisco Presidio; Rezanov's mission was to secure food, potatoes especially, for the Russian settlement at Sitka, Alaska. He fell in love with
Doña María Concepción and she with him; but Rezanov said the Tsar's
consent to the marriage had to be obtained and he set off on the long
journey across the Pacific and over Siberia to St. Petersburg. Years passed
without word from him, but the girl waited. Giving up hope, she had
joined the Dominican Sisterhood before word came back that Rezanov
had died on the way home.

The Benicia Barracks (R), 0.8 *m.* now in the Army reservation that
includes the United States Arsenal stands on a site chosen by Gen. Persifer
Smith in 1849. Established in April of that year as State Army headquarters under command of Commodore Robert Stockton, they served the
post until 1908.

At 64.5 *m.* is a junction with State 29 (*see TOUR 2A*).
At 65.2 *m.* is the tollhouse of Carquinez Bridge (*45¢ a car, 5¢*

a passenger), completed in 1927. This $8,000,000 bridge, with a roadbed 4,482 feet long borne by towers rising 325 feet above water, was conceived by Avon Hanford and Oscar Klatt, who knew nothing of bridge building, and paid no attention to the warnings of wiseacres that the strait's swift-running tides would prevent the laying of piers. A million dollars of his own and his friends' money had been risked when Hanford died in 1926, but he lived to see the central pier foundations successfully laid. Klatt found capitalists ready to finance the rest of the construction. The foundations alone cost more than $2,500,000.

Through narrow Carquinez Strait, 8 miles long and 1 mile wide at its narrowest point, pour the waters from the Central Valley's two great rivers, the Sacramento and the San Joaquin. Bayard Taylor, visiting California in the gold days, compared the strait to the Bosporus, but said it had a greater natural beauty with its "bold shores" and its "varying succession of bays and headlands on either side." Through it passed the immense river traffic to the gold mines; today it carries products of the orchards, dairies, and grain farms of the hinterland.

Beyond the southern end of Carquinez Bridge rise the Contra Costa hills, bearing the name which the Spanish gave to the whole region lying across San Francisco Bay.

At 66.1 *m.* is a junction with a paved road.

> Left on this road is CROCKETT, 0.5 *m.* (0-100 alt., 3,885 pop.), spreading over a ravine and up the hillsides from the shore. A company town, Crockett huddles about the concrete CALIFORNIA-HAWAIIAN SUGAR REFINING CORPORATION PLANT (*visiting hours 10-1*). One of the fleet of great sea-going freighters, which bring 500,000 tons of raw cane sugar annually from the Hawaiian Islands, usually lies unloading at the dock. On the shellmound left behind by prehistoric aborigines, who hunted shellfish in a sheltered cove here, the first American settler, Thomas Edwards, built in 1867 the first house, a rough board and batten structure, on his 1800-acre ranch. The town was laid out with the advent of the railroad in 1877 and christened with the name of a one-time California Supreme Court Justice. In 1882 a foundry was built, and two years later the Starr flour mill, largest on the Pacific Coast at the time. This, superseded by a beet sugar refinery in 1898, became in 1906 the first unit of the C-H sugar refinery.

At Crockett is a junction with State 4 (*see TOUR 9A*).

A parkway (R), 66.4 *m.,* looks out over the cool gray waters of San Pablo Bay. At the foot of the bluffs, beyond the small wharves that jut out from shore, the tiny craft of bass fishermen bob in the swift tide. Pleasant as the scene is, Capt. Pedro Fages and Father Juan Crespi, the first Europeans to see it, March 30, 1772, gazed northward in dismay, for the stretch of water blocked their search for a land route to Point Reyes (*see TOUR 1a*). Both they and the men led by Capt. Juan Bautista de Anza, who arrived here April 2, 1776, watched with interest the Indian fishermen crossing the bay in rafts from their fishing coves on the southern shore to their villages on the opposite side.

Following the contours of receding highlands, US 40 runs now in a southwesterly direction through the succession of factory towns that string in a continuous chain along the shores of San Pablo Bay, where Mexican vaqueros once herded cattle.

At 67.7 *m.* is a junction with a paved road.

> Right on this road is SELBY, 0.2 *m.* (0-100 alt., 141 pop.), owned and operated by the American Smelting and Refining Company. Since 1885 the Selby smelter has produced $60,000,000 worth of gold, silver, lead, and antimony. Although lead is its main product, gold from California's Mother Lode and silver from Nevada's Comstock Lode have also been smelted here for many years.

OLEUM, 68 *m.* (0-100 alt., 217 pop.), a Union Oil Company town, huddles about a great refinery in the midst of gigantic oil tanks, at night lit up by great floodlights. Long trains of tank cars show black against the silver sheen of the bay. On the waterfront, oil cargoes are loaded and discharged at five modern piers. There are 900 tanks and the plant can refine 35,000 barrels of petroleum products daily.

RODEO, 69 *m.* (12 alt., 1,299 pop.), preserves in its name the days of Spanish dominion when ranchers held their yearly cattle rodeos in nearby Rodeo Valley. The town of Rodeo sprang up when two Irishmen, John and Patrick Tormey, started a meat-packing plant here on a 9,000-acre cattle ranch.

At 72 *m.* is a junction with an improved road.

> Right on this road is HERCULES, 0.3 *m.* (8 alt., 392 pop.), overlooking San Pablo Bay from parklike hilltops. In the ravines, which run down to the water's edge, stand the powder mills, acid house, mixing and packing house, and magazine of the Hercules Powder Works, each stationed in a separate gully as a result of a safety campaign occasioned by disastrous explosions. Established here in 1869 to manufacture dynamite for the mines, the plant covers 3,000 acres. At peak capacity it manufactures a quarter of a million pounds of explosives each month.

PINOLE, 72.4 *m.* (11 alt., 781 pop.), is on the former Rancho el Pinole, christened according to legend with the name that a little group of half-starved Spanish soldiers, who struggled out of the Cañada del Hombre to the bayshore, bestowed on the meal made out of acorns and grass seeds that friendly Indian squaws gave them to eat. Ignacio Martínez, comandante of the San Francisco Presidio 1822-32, had occupied these lands by 1829, long before they were officially granted to him in 1842; and he continued his aggressive cattle-raising activities under the American flag. A young Englishman, Dr. Samuel J. Tennant, physician to the king of the Hawaiian Islands, landed at Don Ignacio's embarcadero on one of his gold-prospecting voyages to the interior in 1849. Tennant was so captivated by the beauty of young Señorita Rafaela that he gave up both Hawaii and gold to marry her here Sept. 8, 1849. After Don Ignacio's death, when the Rancho el Pinole was divided among his children, Tennant, through his wife, came into control of a vast part of it, and later laid out the town of Pinole.

South of Pinole, US 40 strikes through open rolling country dotted with the giant oil tanks of a huge Standard Oil Company tank farm. Although it produces no oil, this region is one of the world's important oil storage centers. From fields, the nearest of them 250 miles away, oil is brought by pipe line, tankcars, and tankers. At 74.8 *m.* is a junction with a paved road.

Right on this road is GIANT, 1 *m.* (10-30 alt., 90 pop.), the company-owned town of the Giant Powder Company, on a peninsula jutting into San Pablo Bay. Half-hidden by the eucalyptus groves of Giant Park are the mills and warehouses. The Giant Powder Company, incorporated in 1867, was the first company in California to manufacture dynamite; for a number of years it held exclusive American rights to the manufacture under Nobel patents.

When De Anza and his expedition passed San Pablo Creek, 77 *m.*, on April 1, 1776, they found an Indian village on its banks, deep among liveoaks and sycamores. The friendly inhabitants turned out to gape at the strange procession. Behind the group's chaplain, in his brown Franciscan habit, chanting the *Alabado* (a Spanish hymn in praise of the sacrament), followed De Anza at the head of a cavalcade of soldiers on horseback, muleteers driving beasts of burden, and Indian servants. In exchange for gifts of glass beads, the Indians offered a feast of roasted cacomites, a species of wild iris.

SAN PABLO, 77.5 *m.* (35 alt., 489 pop.), oldest white settlement in this region, lies on tableland between San Pablo and Wildcat creeks. Here, before 1820, Misión San Francisco de Asís pastured great herds of cattle and sheep and built an adobe ranchhouse for the overseer. The whole region roundabout was part of the Rancho San Pablo of Francisco María Castro. Castro, who died in 1831, three years before the grant was confirmed, left half the estate to his wife and half to his 11 children, precipitating one of the most notable of the involved controversies that tangled California land titles.

The CASTRO ADOBE, built about 1838 by Don Francisco's son, Antonio, stands at the northwest corner of US 40 and Church St. Here, from 1849 until his death in 1882, lived Juan Bautista Alvarado, Mexican governor of Alta California (1836-1842), husband of Martina Castro. The little house, now a storeroom, has 30-inch walls that have been hidden by a wooden superstructure. The old garden is overgrown with weeds, and the wooden gateway is broken. The rear is a remnant of the orchard that Alvarado planted; it still sends forth a shower of pear and apple blossoms in the spring.

For a mile and a half east of RICHMOND, 79.5 *m.* (12 alt., 20,093 pop.), are auto camps, gas stations, and barbecue stands. The heart of town stretches westward over a headland jutting into San Francisco Bay. An industrial city on a deep-water harbor, Richmond is Contra Costa's outlet for farm and factory produce. It was established in 1899, when the Santa Fe Railway purchased a right-of-way to the bayshore here, and grew up around branch plants of such industrial corporations as the Standard Oil Company and the Ford Motor

Company. The more than 60 industrial plants within the city represent 20 major industries and many smaller ones. Richmond's workers are nearly all enrolled in industrial unions.

Richmond's Inner Harbor Channel, at the foot of 10th St., where George Ellis, schooner-operator, opened Ellis Landing in 1859, has been developed since 1917 by dredging and filling. Nearby is the $5,000,000 FORD MOTOR ASSEMBLING PLANT (*open 9-3 weekdays; guides*).

Separated from the downtown area by a thinly settled, industrial section reaching southward, is POINT RICHMOND. It is a water-front district, its air heavy with the odor of crude oil. From here RICHMOND POINT juts into the Outer Harbor with a 6-mile deep-water frontage sheltered by a sea wall. Standard Ave. leads north from Point Richmond to the STANDARD OIL REFINERY (*adm. by pass only*), one of the largest of its kind. Beyond the refinery, at the foot of Standard Ave., is the SAN RAFAEL-RICHMOND FERRY SLIP (*10¢ per person; auto and driver, 70¢; auto and 4 passengers, 80¢*).

EL CERRITO (the little hill), 80.6 *m.* (10-500 alt., 3,870 pop.), straggles along the highway for more than two miles. Beyond a pro-cession of gaudy signboards, gas stations, and roadstands, are scattered suburban bungalows; in nearby vacant lots, family goats feed on yellow buttercups in the spring. At the El Cerrito embarcadero, in early days, travelers landed from Don Victor Castro's whaleboat ferry, first to connect San Francisco with Contra Costa; Don Victor acquired it in exchange for his vegetable crop. Travelers were entertained in the 14-room CASTRO ADOBE, which stands in a eucalyptus grove on San Pablo Ave. Its older part, the low south wing, is said to have been built by Don Francisco himself before 1831. In the 1850's his son Victor built the two-story, balconied central section. Walls four feet thick guard a fountain, a winding staircase, and a tiny chapel, where mission fathers sometimes said mass (now altered beyond recognition).

El Cerrito Creek, 82.3 *m.*, forms the boundary between Contra Costa and Alameda Counties and between the cities of El Cerrito and Albany. On Aug. 16, 1820, Sgt. Luís Peralta, his sons, Domingo and Antonio, his friend, Lieut. Ignacio Martínez, and two or three soldiers, arrived here on horseback. "Unto this point, Señor, I wish possession," said Peralta to Martínez, the Governor's representative. Thus the Arroyo del Cerrito de San Antonio (Sp., gulch of the little hill of St. Anthony) was decreed the boundary between Rancho San Pablo (*see above*) and Peralta's 48,000-acre Rancho San Antonio, within whose boundaries lie today the cities of Albany, Berkeley, Emeryville, Piedmont, Oakland, Alameda, and San Leandro.

ALBANY, 83 *m.* (0-300 alt., 8,569 pop.), incorporated in 1908 as Ocean View, one year later took the name of its popular mayor's New York birthplace.

BERKELEY, 84.6 *m.* (0-1,300 alt., 82,109 pop.) (*see BERKE-LEY*).

South of Berkeley, US 40 follows a high-speed roadbed laid across the brackish mudflats of the bayshore, where the stagnant odor of decay wafts inland.   The grayish waters lap half-rotted pilings and sway small dories.

EMERYVILLE, 86.5 *m.* (0-60 alt., 2,336 pop.), has one industry to every 38 inhabitants.   Even before the advent of the Spanish, a populous settlement lay near here, as shown by the Indian shellmound. This mound, largest of the 425 in the San Francisco Bay region, yielded many artifacts when it was leveled for factory sites in 1924.   Where generations of Indians plundered the great beds of shellfish at the mouth of Temescal Creek, Vincente Peralta before 1836 had built an embarcadero for Rancho San Antonio.   In the late 1840's Yankees began to settle here on the Peralta acres; in later years the place became a popular racing center, the home of the California Jockey Club Track.

OAKLAND, 87.3 *m.* (0-1,550 alt., 284;063 pop.) (*see OAK-LAND*).

A turn here leads (R), through labyrinthine overpasses and underpasses, to a junction with US 50 (*see TOUR 10b*) at the entrance to the San Francisco-Oakland Bay Bridge (*see ARCHITECTURE*). From the plaza (*toll 50¢ an auto*), 88.6 *m.,* US 40 follows the great series of spans across San Francisco Bay, midway crossing Yerba Buena Island, through an unusually high double decker tunnel.

SAN FRANCISCO, 95 *m.* (18 alt., 634,394 pop.) (*see SAN FRANCISCO*).

Tour 9A

Sacramento—Rio Vista—Antioch — Pittsburg — Concord — Oakland; 118.4 *m.* State 24.

Roadbed paved.
Southern Pacific R. R. roughly parallels route between Antioch Toll Bridge and Walnut Creek.
Accommodations only in larger towns.

State 24 cuts across the southern end of the Sacramento Valley, following the top of the levee which hems in the Sacramento River's slow-moving waters.   On one side, it overlooks the river's busy traffic; on the other, the rich farmlands of the reclaimed delta region—a crazy-quilt of "islands" encompassed by meandering sloughs and sheltered by dikes as in the low country of the Netherlands.   It strikes through the industrial towns clustering at the confluence of the Sacramento and the San Joaquin Rivers and follows the windings of quiet, orchard-shaded valleys.

State 24 strikes southward from US 40 (*see TOUR 9*) in SAC-

RAMENTO, 0 *m.*, across level farmlands to FREEPORT, 9.3 *m.*
(30 alt., 120 pop.), a village on the eastern bank of the Sacramento;
then hugs the river's edge, traveling the crest of the levee.

The first known white men to see the Sacramento River were in
the Pedro Fages expedition, whose explorations of the eastern shore
of San Francisco Bay in 1772 carried them as far as the confluence of
the Sacramento and San Joaquin Rivers, where "from a point of
vantage," they saw the river's winding lower reaches.   The first recorded navigation of the river was in 1811, when Jose Antonio Sanchez
proceeded a little way upstream from the mouth in a small boat.   The
development of the great waterway into an important artery of travel
and trade was left to the Argonauts of 1848, who pressed up from
San Francisco on their way to the "diggin's" in vessels of every description—from tiny sail-craft to lumbering stern-wheelers.   The ambitious realtors of the day, quick to capitalize on the growing stream
of travelers, optimistically laid out a series of river towns at steamboat
landings—all but a few of which scarcely outlived the flush years of
the gold rush.

HOOD, 17.5 *m.* (25 alt., 150 pop.), is a shipping point on the
Sacramento River for fruits and vegetables.   COURTLAND, 21.7 *m.*
(14 alt., 750 pop.), among pear orchards and truck farms, is a canning,
packing and shipping center.

At 29.5 *m.* is the junction with a paved road.

> Left on this road, across the river, to WALNUT GROVE, 0.2 *m.* (9 alt.,
> 631 pop.), clustering under the levee.   Walnut Grove's ramshackle CHINA-
> TOWN is a reminder of the days when the Chinese were reclaiming the
> Sacramento delta region.   Today Japanese comprise the majority of the
> population.

The rich delta region lying southward is crisscrossed with dikes
that hem in winding sloughs, sheltering the lush black-loam farmlands,
often far below water level, from floods.   It was settled in the early
1850's by disappointed gold seekers who squatted here to raise their
own food.   In the 1870's, the Chinese coolies who had built the Central
Pacific Railroad were put to work reclaiming the delta region at low
wages.   With wheelbarrows they built up the first levees.   Gradually
the whole 425,000-acre region of tule marshes was reclaimed by an
elaborate system of levees, drainage canals, and pumping plants.   Today
the incalculably fertile black peat soil is irrigated by flood gates from
the levees.   Asparagus, pears, hops, beans, onions, celery, potatoes and
grains are farmed in enormous holdings.

RYDE, 32.1 *m.* (8 alt., 150 pop.), clusters at the river's edge on
Grand Island, largest of the delta "islands," encompassed by the Sacramento on one side and Steamboat Slough on the other.   It is a port
of call for river boats carrying agricultural products.

The broad, placid Sacramento is thronged with a motley parade of
water craft—the tiny, light-draught boats of the so-called "mosquito
fleet," slow-moving barges laden with sacks of grain, chugging stern-
wheelers, motorboats, launches, and houseboats.

The highway bridges the river to ISLETON, 39 *m.* (14 alt., 2,090 pop.), a prosperous farm trading and canning town that calls itself "the Asparagus Center of the World." In the green pastures of the surrounding dairy farms, herds of sleek Guernseys and Holsteins browse on alfalfa.

From the Sacramento delta region comes nearly one-half of the United States asparagus crop and about 90 per cent of the world's canned asparagus. In the level, far stretching fields Filipino field hands, decked in veils to keep the region's swarming gnats out of their eyes, cut the white and tender asparagus stalks as soon as they appear above ground. They thrust their long-handled knives into the earth to slice off the plants underground. The work starts at the break of dawn. The asparagus stalks are left in neat little piles along the furrows by the hands working with feverish haste lest the tender stalks wilt in the sun. In the old days, the piles of asparagus were picked up by small wagons drawn by horses shod with wide plates like snow-shoes; now tractors are used, outfitted with tires wide enough to keep them from sinking into the soft earth. The asparagus is rushed to nearby canneries, where it is cleaned, canned, cooked, and sealed—all within a few hours from the time it is cut.

At 43.6 *m.* is the junction with State 12, paved.

> Right on State 12, crossing the river to RIO VISTA, 1 *m.* (11 alt., 1,309 pop.), in the center of a huge reclamation project. It is a river shipping point for fruits and vegetables. The tule-fringed sloughs and marshlands of the vicinity are a mecca, in season, for hunters and fisher-men. During the migration season the marshes abound with ducks—chiefly mallard, green-winged teal, and sprig. The Wilson snipe, called hereabout the Jacksnipe, is abundant; and the spoonbill, red-head widgeon, and canvas-back are also found. Every year in October Rio Vista decks itself out in flags to receive visitors on its Bass Derby Day, when it awards a prize to the angler who lands the largest bass. Here, by the river's edge in the fall of 1857, Col. N. H. Davis laid out the settlement of Brazos del Rio (arms of the river) and in the following year built a wharf. A thriving town grew up—renamed in 1860 Rio Vista—only to be washed down the river, house by house, in the January floods of 1862, as the shivering inhabitants looked on from the hillsides. The settlers retreated to the Montezuma Hills, farther back from the waterfront, to rebuild.

State 24 diverges from the river at about 50.5 *m.* and strikes south-ward across Sherman Island to the ANTIOCH TOLL BRIDGE, 54.6 *m.* (*toll 60¢ for car and driver; 10¢ a passenger*) over the San Joaquin River. It parallels the San Joaquin westward for a short distance.

At 56.2 *m.* is the junction with State 4, paved.

> Left on State 4 is BRENTWOOD, 7.9 *m.* (77 alt., 340 pop.), among large fruit and nut orchards. Its chief industries are packing and shipping agricultural products. Right from Brentwood on a paved road, 5.3 *m.* to the junction with paved Marsh Creek Road; R. here 4 *m.* to the STONE HOUSE, in the midst of wide fields, built by "Doctor" John Marsh in 1856. Marsh, a Massachusetts immigrant, was granted a license to practice medicine by the Los Angeles *ayuntamiento* (council) when he displayed his Harvard diploma. He bought Rancho los Medanos (the sandhills) and settled in the shadow of Mount Diablo in 1837. The Indians of the region,

in return for his kindness in healing their sick and teaching them to trap
bear and otter, helped him to build a crude, thatch-roofed, floorless adobe
of four rooms and attic with a tule-roofed portico; plow a field and sow it
with wheat; and plant an orchard of figs, pears, and olives, and a vineyard
of grape cuttings brought from Mission San Jose. With his vaqueros,
who acted as his bodyguard, Marsh lived in solitary state, prizing his little
store of books and reading them—stretched out before the fireplace—until
he knew them by heart.

Toward everyone but his Indian neighbors, Marsh was sharp, even
niggardly. When the Bidwell-Bartleson Party, first to cross the Sierra into
California, came to his place in 1841, he charged them a good fee for his
hospitality. For his services as a doctor—he was the first and for several
years the only one in the San Joaquin Valley—he was paid in cattle, the
number of cows expected as a fee depending on the number of miles he
had to travel. A shrewd business man, he bargained on California's future
by sending regular letters East, chiefly to Missouri newspapers, to induce
immigration.

The "Stone House" was built for Marsh's bride, Abbie Tuck of Massachusetts, whom he married in 1851; but she died before it was finished.
It was built of local cream-colored freestone, quarried nearby, in "the old
English domestic style of architecture—a pleasing and appropriate union
of Manor House and Castle"—according to the San Francisco *Daily*
Evening Bulletin of July 1856. "The arched windows, the peaked roofs
and gables, the projecting eaves, the central tower sixty-five feet in height
. . . must be acknowledged a most felicitous deviation from the prevailing
style of rural architecture. . . . The building . . . is three stories in height,
with three gabled windows in the attic looking east, west, and south. On
three sides of the building is a piazza . . . supported by beautiful octagon
pillars; over this is a walk on a level with the second floor, enclosed by
an elaborately finished balustrade. . . ."

Marsh himself scarcely outlived the completion of his house. On September 24, 1856, he was murdered on the road to Martinez by four of his
Mexican neighbors, reputedly in revenge for his stingy and scornful
attitude.

On State 4 at 12.8 *m.* is the junction with paved Byron Rd.; R. (straight
ahead) is BYRON, 14.1 *m.* (30 alt., 400 pop.), shipping center for large
apricot orchards, where an Apricot Festival is celebrated each spring.

At 16.1 *m.* on Byron Rd. is the junction with a dirt road; R. here 0.8 *m.*
to BYRON HOT SPRINGS (*hotel, cottages; golf*), known to Yankee
settlers since 1849. The springs are of three types—a "hot Salt Spring"
(122°), a "Liver and Kidney Spring" (58°), and a "White Sulphur
Spring" (70°).

At 29.2 *m.* is the junction of Byron Rd. with US 50 (*see TOUR 10b*).

On State 24 is ANTIOCH, 60.2 *m.* (42 alt., 3,563 pop.), on the
San Joaquin's southern bank in rich silt deposited by the two great
rivers, a shipping point for industrial and agricultural products.
Antioch's first settlers were twin brothers, Joseph H. and W. W.
Smith, both carpenters and ordained ministers, who arrived here from
Boston with their families on the schooner *Rialto* in July 1849 and
took up quarter-sections of land. In September 1850 W. W. Smith
induced a shipload of New England families arriving from Maine on
the *California Packet* to settle here; he gave each family a lot on which
to build a home. At a Fourth of July picnic in 1851 the question of
naming the town arose. Smith suggested a Biblical name in honor
of his brother, who had meanwhile died; the name of Antioch (Syria),
where Christ's followers were first called Christians, was unanimously

adopted. Antioch's first house, the GEORGE W. KIMBALL HOUSE, still standing on Third Street next door to Scout's Hall, was the home of the captain of the *California Packet*. He built it in 1851 of Oregon pine with the proceeds of a crop of barley that he raised and hauled to San Francisco.

PITTSBURG, 64.8 *m.* (21 alt., 9,610 pop.), is a steel city, one of California's best small-scale versions of its Pennsylvania namesake. Here is the COLUMBIA STEEL COMPANY PLANT (*open by arrangement at firm's Russ Building offices, San Francisco*), whose giant rolling mills press red-hot ingots from the open-hearth furnaces into thin metal strips 100 feet long. Interesting to watch are the pouring of molten steel and the intricate processes in the manufacture of tin plate, corrugated iron, wire mesh, nails, and wire.

The new Yankee owners of part of Rancho los Medanos persuaded William Tecumseh Sherman of later Civil War fame to lay out a city here in 1849. With a small crew, Sherman sailed up the river from San Francisco, making soundings to chart the best channel through Suisun Bay to the confluence of the rivers. The city he platted was so large in area that one of the owners, Col. Jonathan D. Stevenson, who brought the First Regiment of New York Volunteers to California in March 1847, named it New York of the Pacific. Stevenson hoped it would grow into a prosperous seaport, but to globe trotter Bayard Taylor it was still in 1850 only a "three-house city."

For three decades after discovery of coal in the 1850's on the slopes of Mount Diablo, the town was a busy coal shipping port, renamed in 1863 Black Diamond for the best known of the mines. A railroad was built to the coal towns that grew up around the mines, settled by immigrants from the coal fields of England and Wales. The coal was of such poor grade, however, that the industry went into a slump after 1880, strangled by competition and too-lavish outlays of capital. Until 1909, when the town's industrial possibilities were recognized—and its name was correspondingly changed to Pittsburg—the population supported itself by salmon fishing. The quiet waters at the mouth of the Sacramento and San Joaquin are still thronged with the lateen-sailed boats of Italian and Greek fishermen who fish for shad, bass, and salmon. Their nets sometimes stretch halfway across the channel. In some of Jack London's *Tales of the Fish Patrol,* the lives of these fishermen are described.

State 24 rounds the northern slopes of the Mount Diablo Range and turns southwestward down broad, fertile Concord Valley, following the route blazed in the spring of 1772 by the first white men in the region, the Pedro Fages expedition, accompanied by Fray Juan Crespi, 12 soldiers, a muleteer, and an Indian servant. In search of a land route to Point Reyes, they had followed the eastern shore of San Francisco and the southern shore of San Pablo Bay, always finding their passage to the north blocked by water. On March 30, they entered Concord Valley. Climbing one of the hills of the Mount Diablo Range, they looked out over a vast expanse never before seen by any European—

the Sacramento Valley. That night they camped and, early the next morning, turned back toward Monterey, giving up their search.

CONCORD, 94.6 *m.* (65 alt., 1,125 pop.), shipping the farm produce of the surrounding valley, stands on the site of Rancho del Diablo (devil's ranch), granted to Salvio Pacheco in 1834. His descendants occupy the thick-walled adobe PACHECO HOUSE, standing in the shade of pepper trees at Concord and Salvio Avenues, which he built about a decade later. With its balconies, shuttered windows, and deep casements, it is well preserved within its protective wooden sheath. American squatters had begun settling on Pacheco's land by 1852; but his title was secured the next year by the United States Government. The patent date, 1853, is on the stone boundary posts in front of the house.

Right from Concord on a paved road is the old country village of PACHECO, 1.8 *m.* (35 alt., 200 pop.). The home of its first settler, the G. L. WALLRATH HOUSE, a redwood-timbered structure with ornamented eaves, built in 1853, stands amid trees and shrubbery on a hill on the northern edge of town. The town was laid out in 1857 around a warehouse and a flour mill by Dr. J. H. Carothers. It was largely swept away by flood in 1862, twice ravaged by fire in the next 6 years, and almost leveled by earthquake in 1868; but it survived all three disasters.

Right from Pacheco on State 21 to MARTINEZ, 6.9 *m.* (12 alt., 6,569 pop.), seat of Contra Costa County since 1850, facing broad Suisun Bay from the mouth of Alhambra Valley. Its quiet, rural air, enhanced by the spreading trees that shade its streets, belies its importance as an oil refinery, canning, and fishing center. It bears the name of Ignacio Martinez, comandante at the San Francisco Presidio 1828-31, who settled on neighboring Rancho El Pinole about 1836. The agent for the Martinez family, Col. William M. Smith, laid out the town in 1849.

Left from Martinez on Alhambra Ave., which becomes Franklin Canyon Road (State 4), 2 *m.* to the JOHN MUIR RANCH, where a large old-fashioned ranch house, the home of John Muir, overlooks orchards from a knoll in a wooded valley. Muir, who came to the United States from Scotland in 1849 at the age of 11, spent most of his life studying the mountains, valleys, glaciers, and wild life of California and Alaska, discovering and naming many of the peaks and glaciers along the Pacific Coast. One of the foremost advocates of National parks, he publicised the region's natural beauties in his books, best-known of which was probably *The Mountains of California* (1894).

West of Martinez State 21 follows the southern slope of Carquinez Strait (*see TOUR 9b*) to PORT COSTA, 12.9 *m.* (11 alt., 593 pop.), today almost abandoned, but once, in the days when California was one of the Nation's greatest grain-producing States, a port from whose wharves grain was shipped direct to Europe in ocean-going vessels.

At 14.3 *m.* on State 21 is CROCKETT (*see TOUR 9b*), at the junction with US 40 (*see TOUR 9b*).

WALNUT CREEK, 101.3 *m.* (147 alt., 1,014 pop.), is a country town in the midst of great walnut groves. Besides being a shipping center for soft-shell walnuts, this town supplies facilities for orchards and chicken ranches.

Left from Walnut Creek on State 21, paved, through the orchard-shaded acres of San Ramon Valley, once part of Rancho San Ramon, granted to Jose Maria Amador in 1833.

ALAMO (poplar), 3.2 *m.* (356 alt., 69 pop.), where poplars once grew thickly, is shaded today by the giant maples that line its main street. In 1848 or 1849 the first adobe was built here; and in 1854, two stores that drew their trade from the neighborhood's Spanish population. The sturdy FOSTER HOUSE (R), on the main street, was built by James Foster, who opened a wheelwright shop here in 1857.

DANVILLE, 6.3 *m.* (370 alt., 600 pop.), stands on land once owned by Daniel Inman, who first visited the site in 1852 and took up wheat farming in 1858.

Left from Danville on a paved road 3.4 *m.* to the south entrance to MOUNT DIABLO STATE PARK (*25¢ adm.; firewood sold at gate; picnicking facilities*). The road winds upward past the jumbled rocks of the DEVIL'S SLIDE and through the animal-like rock formations of the GARDEN OF THE JUNGLE GODS—including La Rana (the frog), La Ballena (the whale), and El Perro (the dog)—to PARK HEADQUARTERS, 8.5 *m.*

At 10.5 *m.* is the junction with a paved road; L. here 8 *m.* to the junction with a paved road; L. on this road 1.5 *m.* to the junction with another paved road; L. on this road 2.1 *m.* to Walnut Creek.

The main side route goes R. from the junction with the Walnut Creek road to the summit of MOUNT DIABLO (3,849 alt.), 15.1 *m.*, a rugged peak rising alone from a level plain to dominate the countryside for great distances in every direction. From the earliest days, explorers and pioneers set their course by its conical, volcano-like outline. Its summit was chosen in 1851 as the base point for United States surveys in California; the positions of all lands of the State, outside southern California and the Humboldt region, are still determined by reference to this point. Of the view from the crest, William Henry Brewer, who in 1862 climbed the mountain with the Whitney geological survey party, wrote: "Probably but few views in North America are more extensive—certainly nothing in Europe. . . . I made an estimate . . . that the extent of land and sea embraced between the extreme limits of vision amounted to eighty thousand square miles." A powerful revolving beacon light on the summit today guides aviators.

The mountain's ruggedly fantastic grandeur—with its two cones divided by a gap through which, wrote Brewer, "the wind roared with a violence almost terrific at times . . . and at intervals the clouds rushed through like a torrent"—gave rise to legends of its being haunted by a demon. Gen. Mariano G. Vallejo reported to the Legislature in 1850 that a battle between soldiers from San Francisco led by Gabriel Moraga and the Bolgones Indians, in 1806, was about to be decided in favor of the Indians, when "an unknown personage, decorated with the most extraordinary plumage and making divers movements, suddenly appeared. . . . The Indians were victorious. . . . The defeated soldiers, on ascertaining that the spirit went through the same ceremony daily and at all hours, named the mount 'Diablo.' . . . In the aboriginal tongue 'Puy' signifies 'Evil Spirit'; in Spanish it means 'Diablo,' and doubtless it signifies 'Devil' in the Anglo-American language." Whether or not the Puy may have been a medicine man impersonating the spirit of the mountain, he failed to prevail against the Spanish, who subdued the Bolgones in a second campaign the same year.

State 21 continues southward from Danville to SAN RAMON, 9.5 *m.* (470 alt., 200 pop.), where John White put up the first house in 1852, originally named Lynchville and nicknamed Limerick, because most of the settlers roundabout were Irish.

DUBLIN (*see TOUR 10b*), 15.4 *m.*, is at the junction with US 50 (*see TOUR 10b*).

State 24 turns westward from Walnut Creek into low hills.
The site of LAFAYETTE, 106.6 *m.* (280 alt., 750 pop.), at the

eastern edge of a small fertile valley, was chosen for a home in February 1848 by Elam Brown, a year and a half after his arrival in California as captain of a 16-wagon immigrant company. To save carrying his grain by ox team to the flour mill at San Jose, Brown in 1849 set up a horsepower mill near his house.

State 24 winds between rolling grazing lands to the BROADWAY TUNNEL, a low, level, double-bore tunnel, four lanes wide, 1.8 miles long, completed in 1937 at a cost of $4,500,000.

In OAKLAND (*see OAKLAND*), 118.4 *m.*, is the junction with US 50 (*see TOUR 10b*).

Tour 10

(Carson City, Nev.)—Lakeside—Placerville—Sacramento—Stockton —Tracy—San Francisco; US 50.
Nevada Line to San Francisco, 239.5 *m.*

Route paralleled by Southern Pacific R. R. between Placerville and Oakland, by Western Pacific R. R. between Sacramento and Stockton.
Accommodations plentiful.
Paved roadbed throughout, open all seasons except for brief periods during winter snowstorms at higher altitudes; excellent route for trailers.

Between the Nevada Line and Placerville, US 50 (the Lincoln Highway) climbs the crest of the forested Sierra Nevada Mountains, skirts the shores of popular Lake Tahoe, and runs through the heart of the El Dorado National Forest. West of Placerville the road winds down through foothills covered with oak and scrub pine to the level expanse of the great Sacramento Valley. From here the highway runs, straight and level, between the valley's farmlands and grazing fields, until, east of Stockton, it twists through the bald hills of the Mount Diablo Range and comes out on the eastern shore-line of San Francisco Bay.

Section a. NEVADA LINE to SACRAMENTO; 110 m., US 50.

For more than a decade this section of US 50 was part of an important overland route into California. Centuries before the gold rush it was an Indian trail. In the period 1850-1857 it was an immigrant course, rough, rocky, and almost unmarked. In 1858 the first crude wagon track was built over the mountains by public funds. In that same year, George Chorpenning carried the first overland mail over this thoroughfare from Salt Lake City across the Sierra to Placerville. When the rich Comstock Silver Lode was discovered in Washoe Valley,

Nev., in 1859, it brought boom times to the Placerville Road. As many as 3,000 freight wagons, with 25,000 animals, used it at one time, according to contemporary accounts. The cumbrous wagons carried loads of from three to eight tons, drawn by teams of six to ten horses or mules. Hay for the animals cost four to six cents a pound, and barley in proportion. Private companies got franchises on sections of the route from the State; grades were made easier, bridges built, and the road widened. In some places the profit from tolls during a single year was twice the original investment. In 1862 one section of the road, assessed at $14,000, collected $75,000 in tolls. Total toll charges for a 6-mule team and wagon over the whole length were from $32 to $36.

In April 1860, the first Pony Express rider galloped over this track. The riders kept up their record-making runs from St. Joe, Mo., to Sacramento until November 1861, when the overland telegraph spanned the continent with copper wire. The tremendous flow of traffic on the Placerville Road ceased when the transcontinental railway was completed through Donner Pass in 1869. With the opening of the automobile age, it again became one of the main cross country arteries.

LAKESIDE, 0 *m.* (6,225 alt., 4 pop.), on the Nevada line, 27 miles south of Carson City, Nev., is one of the long chain of summer resorts along the shore of LAKE TAHOE (R). In 1864 there was already a large log hotel here, entertaining many visitors from California and Nevada.

Lake Tahoe, by the crest of the Sierra Nevada, is of glacial origin, 21.6 miles long and 12 miles wide, with a surface area of 193 square miles. Meadow land and forested valley sweep from its blue waters to the summits of MONUMENT PEAK (10,085 alt.), MOUNT FREEL (10,900 alt.), and JOB'S SISTER (10,820 alt.). In *Roughing It,* Mark Twain wrote of Lake Tahoe: "We plodded on, and at last the lake burst upon us, a noble sheet of blue water . . . walled in by a rim of snow-clad peaks that towered aloft full 3,000 feet higher still. As it lay there with the shadows of the mountains brilliantly photographed upon its still surface, I thought it must surely be the fairest picture the whole earth affords. . . . Down through . . . these great depths, the water was not merely transparent, but dazzling, brilliantly so; we could see trout by the thousands winging about in the emptiness under us."

An old Washoe Indian legend said that a giant bird, the Ong, with a body like an eagle's and wings "larger than the tallest pine" lived in a nest at the bottom of the lake. From its nest gushed the waters that filled the lake. The Ong lived on human flesh and terrified the Indians. Finally an Indian brave fought it to death to rescue his sweetheart, and after that the Indians could paddle their canoes on the lake without danger of being torn by its terrible beak.

The first white men to report seeing Lake Tahoe were John C. Frémont and his topographer, Charles Preuss, on February 14, 1844, who discovered it from the heights of STEVEN'S PEAK (10,100 alt.). Frémont first called it "Mountain Lake," but on the map that he made of his first passage of the Sierra Nevada, it appears as "Lake Bonplan" (for the French botanist and traveling companion of Alexander von Humboldt). On the first official map of California this body of water was called "Lake Bigler," for the third governor of California. In 1862 William Henry Knight, map maker of the U. S. Department of the Interior, restored the Indian name of Tahoe, and subsequent maps have retained it, in spite of the fact that the legislative act of 1870 legalizing the name of Lake Bigler has never been repealed.

BIJOU (jewel), 1.6 m. (6,225 alt., 10 pop.), a former lumber camp, named by appreciative French lumberjacks 50 or 60 years ago, is now a summer resort. The long wharf at which lumber schooners docked while loading pine and fir logs to be freighted to the mills at Glenbrook, Nev., has been replaced by a pier for pleasure craft. Most of the great pine and fir forests about Lake Tahoe were cut over between 1860 and 1900. Their timbers built Virginia City, Nev., and its neighbor camps, and lined the shafts and tunnels of the Comstock Lode and other Nevada mines.

EL DORADO COUNTY PUBLIC PARK (*sanitary conveniences*), 2.1 m., is one of several public lake resorts.

AL TAHOE, 2.3 m. (6,225 alt., 150 pop.), a resort, known as Rowland's before 1912, is typical of the many recreation centers strung along the west side of the lake.

At 4.9 m. is a junction with State 89, a paved road.

Right on State 89 along the shore of the lake through an almost continuous line of resorts, to CASCADE LAKE (L), 5.2 m., one of the many small glacial lakes in the DESOLATION VALLEY PRIMITIVE AREA, a glacially eroded region of thick forests and granite crags.
BAY VIEW PUBLIC CAMP and INSPIRATION POINT (*camping and trailer accommodations*), 7.7 m., offer a fine view of EMERALD BAY. RUBICON POINT STATE PARK, 12 m., a promontory of the lake, is kept in its natural beauty by the State. MEEKS BAY (*hotel, cabin, camps*), 16.5 m., has an excellent sandy beach, regarded as one of the best swimming spots on the lake. Launches and speedboats leave from here for trips around the lake.
The road continues through TAHOE NATIONAL FOREST (L) of 576,227 acres.
TAHOE CITY (*all accommodations*), 27.5 m. (150 pop.), centers the resort area at the upper end of the lake. Many wealthy families have summer estates near here. The more modest cabins of people of moderate means are strung along the shore, almost as close together as bungalows in a suburban town.
TRUCKEE (*see TOUR 9a*), 41.5 m., is at the junction with US 40 (*see TOUR 9a*), also with another section of State 89 (*see TOUR 5b*).

South of Lake Tahoe, US 50 goes over the ridges of the glacial moraine that dams up the lower end of the lake.

At MEYERS, 9.4 m. (6,400 alt., 50 pop.), the old-fashioned inn is reminiscent of stagecoach and freighting days. At the MEYERS RANGER STATION (R) free maps and information regarding the El Dorado National Forest are available. Just north of the inn is the SITE OF YANK'S HOTEL, one of the many stage stations of the old Placerville Road.

Here, too, is the usual PONY EXPRESS MONUMENT with a bronze bas-relief of a rider. The story of how these daredevil riders united East and West was described by Mark Twain in *Roughing It:* "Saint Joe to Sacramento, 1900 miles in eight days! The pony-rider was usually a little man. He rode fifty miles without stopping, by daylight, moonlight, starlight, or through the blackness of darkness—just as it happened. He rode a splendid horse, born from a racer, and fed and lodged like a gentleman; kept him at his utmost speed for ten miles, and then, as he came crashing to the station where stood two men holding fast a fresh, impatient steed, the transfer of rider and mail bag was made in the twinkling of an eye, and away flew the eager pair, and were out of sight before the spectator could get hardly the ghost of a look. Both rider and horse went 'flying light.' The rider's dress was thin and fitted close; he wore a 'roundabout' and a skull-cap, and tucked his pantaloons into his boot tops like a race-rider. He carried no arms— he carried nothing that was not absolutely necessary, for even the postage on his literary freight was worth five dollars a letter. He got but little frivolous correspondence to carry—his bag had business letters mostly. His horse was stripped of all unnecessary weight, too. He wore light shoes, or none at all. The little flat mail-pockets strapped under the rider's thighs would each hold about the bulk of a child's primer. They held many and many an important business chapter and newspaper letter, but they were written on paper as airy and thin as gold-leaf, nearly, and thus bulk and weight were economized. The stagecoach traveled about a hundred to a hundred and twenty miles a day (twenty-four hours), the pony-rider about two hundred and fifty. There were about eighty pony-riders in the saddle all the time, night and day, stretching a long, scattering procession from Missouri to California, forty flying eastward, and forty toward the west, and among them making four hundred gallant horses earn a stirring livelihood and see a deal of scenery every single day in the year."

At ECHO CREEK, 10.6 *m.,* is the junction with a paved road, State 89.

Left on State 89 through LUTHER PASS, 9 *m.* (7,800 alt.), to a junction with State 8, 11.5 *m.;* L. on State 8-89, 6.5 *m.* to WOODFORDS (5,634 alt.), a small resort; R. from Woodfords on State 89, 6.6 *m.* to the junction with State 4 (*see TOUR 4*).

The main side route goes R. from the State 8-89 junction at the eastern end of Luther Pass on State 8, which rises to cross the main range of the Sierra Nevada through CARSON PASS (8,600 alt.), 19.8 *m.* Capt. John Frémont and "Kit" Carson found this pass in the winter of 1843-44 while looking for a direct route to California from the East; it was used by thousands of gold seekers. State 8 descends through a forested region, past several small mountain resorts and the sites of once active mining camps.

PINE GROVE, 74.6 *m.* (2,100 alt., 126 pop.), is at the junction with a dirt road; R. 3 *m.* on this to VOLCANO (2,150 alt., 150 pop.), in a crater-like hollow, rimmed by fir-covered hills. Once one of the richest and most populous towns of the Mother Lode, the dust of its main street is now rarely disturbed. Occasionally an old-timer shuffles along on his way to buy something at the store. Only the wind in the fir trees or the tinkle of cowbells, as the cows come home at sunset, breaks the stillness. In the spring of 1848 Gen. John A. Sutter mined on the creek that bears his name, and the next year men from Stevenson's regiment of New York Volunteers found rich deposits in SOLDIERS' GULCH, where in later years hydraulic washing left weird outcroppings of limestone. By 1850 Volcano was going full blast. Besides the saloons and fandango halls that every camp boasted, it had a Thespian Society and a Miners' Library Association. Opened in 1862 and still doing business is the dignified ST. GEORGE HOTEL (R); its lobby has been modernized, but the bar is the original, and here are kept a collection of miners' relics, among them a Swiss music box that still tinkles plaintively. At the end of the main street are the iron-shuttered ADAMS EXPRESS BUILDING (R) and the ODD FELLOWS AND MASONIC LODGE BUILDING. Here Angelo Rossi, Mayor of San Francisco (1939), was born. He sometimes visits his birthplace in a big car such as miners never dreamed of, escorted by motorcycle police with their sirens wailing.

JACKSON, 83.2 m. (see TOUR 4), is at a junction with State 49 (see TOUR 4).

US 50 begins its climb up through the pines to ECHO SUMMIT, 12.7 m. (7,365 alt.), at the top of JOHNSON'S PASS. From Summit Lodge is a magnificent view.

At 12.9 m. is a junction with a paved road.

> Right on this road to ECHO LAKE, 1 m. There are many camps in this section from which foot trails lead into the DESOLATION VALLEY PRIMITIVE AREA, a region preserved in its natural state. The tract of 41,380 acres at the headwaters of the Rubicon River is a picturesque region of granite peaks and blue alpine lakes.

The highway sweeps down the long western slope of the Sierra Nevada through luxuriant groves of pine, fir, and cedar with many free Forest Service camps and summer home tracts. At other choice places are privately owned homes and resorts.

The entrance to AUDRAIN LAKE CAMP (R) is passed at 13.3 m. LAKE AUDRAIN is a main source of the South Fork of the American River, down the canyon of which the highway passes. The old Hawley Grade into Lake Valley, used from 1859 to 1861, began at this point.

Audrain's station once stood on the site of the present DARRINGTON'S STORE (R), 14.3 m., on the edge of HAY PRESS MEADOWS, where an old-fashioned hay press baled the tall wild grasses that were cut here for sale at $90 to $100 a ton at Virginia City, Nev.

Another alpine meadow marks the site of the onetime stage station of PHILLIP'S (R), 15.4 m. (7,000 alt.), now a summer resort. Nearby is the ASPEN CREEK TRACT for summer homes, within a forest of fir.

TOLL HOUSE FLAT, 17.3 m., is the SITE OF SWAN'S UPPER TOLL HOUSE, where long lines of cumbersome wagons once waited to pay tolls.

The bold, granite ridge that bulwarks the canyon of the South Fork on the north forms the southern extension of Desolation Valley. A U-shaped, rocky gorge here comes down precipitously from the Desolation Valley Primitive Area, leaps the long, white cascades of HORSE TAIL FALLS (R), and follows the glacier-polished basin of Pyramid

Creek to the South Fork. High in the northwest is the austere, grey summit of PYRAMID PEAK (10,020 alt.).

To the south, LOVER'S LEAP (6,985 alt.) rises (L) a sheer 1,285 feet above the river. There is the usual legend of the Indian girl who plunged from that height because her love was unrequited. At the base of the cliff was the SLIPPERY FORD HOUSE. In 1863, Brewer, in *Up and Down California,* wrote: "Clouds of dust arose, filling the air, as we met long trains of ponderous wagons, loaded with merchandise, hay, grain—in fact everything that man or beast uses. We stopped at the Slippery Ford House. Twenty wagons stopped there, driving over a hundred horses or mules—heavy wagons, enormous loads, scarcely any less than three tons. The harness is heavy, often with a steel boy over the hames, in the form of an arch over each horse, and supporting four or five bells, whose chimes can be heard at all hours of the day. The wagons drew up on some small level place, the animals were chained to the tongue of the wagon, neighing or braying for their grain. They are well fed although hay costs four to five cents a pound, and barley accordingly—no oats are raised in this State, barley is fed instead.

"We are at an altitude of over six thousand feet, the nights are cold, and the dirty dusty teamsters sit about the fire in the barroom and tell tales—of how this man carried so many hundredweight with so many horses, a story which the rest disbelieve—tell stories of marvelous mules, and bad roads, and dull drivers, of fights at this bad place, where someone would not turn out, etc., until nine o'clock, when they crawl under their wagons with their blankets and sleep to be up at early dawn to attend to their teams."

A good ski course is at TWIN BRIDGES (R), 19.5 *m.*

At 21.2 *m.* is a junction with a graveled road.

> Left on this road to the STRAWBERRY HOUSE, 0.3 *m.,* a stopping place on the later Placerville Road and now a summer resort. The simple dignity of the old house, the commodious barns, and hay lofts nearby are vivid reminders of stagecoach days. They stand at the edge of a well-watered meadow, with the granite walls of the canyon close at hand.

PYRAMID RANGER STATION (R) and PYRAMID PUBLIC CAMP (L) are passed at 23.7 *m.*

For several miles US 50 follows the north bank of the river in long graceful curves; but the old stage road, bits of which can still be traced up and down the mountainside, was hewn from the canyonsides.

Passing the SITE OF LEON'S STATION (R), 28 *m.,* often known as Mother Weltie's in the old days, US 50 enters KYBURZ, 30.2 *m.* (4,700 alt., 10 pop.). Where DICK YARNOLD'S TOLL HOUSE once reaped a remunerative harvest, a store, hotel, and post office now serve tourists and summer campers. Southward, along the Silver Fork of the Truckee River, trails lead into the beautiful SILVER LAKE region (7,250 alt.).

In the shadow of SUGAR LOAF ROCK (R), 31 *m.,* the SUGAR LOAF HOUSE once stood, and the SITE OF PERRIN'S TOLL HOUSE is passed at 31.7 *m.* Ruins of an Old Bridge (L) across the river at 35.6 *m.* mark the eastern end of Oglesby Grade, one of four or five rival detours over which traffic to Virginia City sought easier and quicker routes in the sixties.

The fast rigs of Baker's stage line changed to horses at RIVERTON, 39.6 *m.* (3,300 alt.), formerly Moore's Station. The old hotel stands at the river's edge surrounded by poplar and locust trees.

Between 1859 and 1864, stages used the Brockliss Grade (R), the beginning of which is passed at 43.7 *m.* There is an old orchard and green meadow at the PACIFIC HOUSE, 43.8 *m.* (3,375 alt., 20 pop.).

At BULLION BEND, 47.6 *m.,* a stone monument (R) marks the spot where two stages were held up and robbed on the night of June 30, 1864. The road was then a narrow grade; six men leaped out from a clump of trees, covered Blair, driver of the first stage, with pistols and shotguns, seized his lead team, and ordered him to halt. When they called, "Throw down your treasure box!" Blair said he had none. Then they demanded the stage's cargo of bullion. "Come and get it," Blair answered. Two of the road agents covered him with their guns, and two others took out the bullion. Blair asked them not to rob the passengers, and the men replied, "We don't intend to. All we want is the treasure."

Just then the second stage came around the bend, driven by a man named Watson, from whom the robbers took three sacks of bullion and a small treasure box. The leader of the band, before they galloped off, wrote the following receipt: "This is to certify that I have received from Wells, Fargo & Co., the sum of $—— cash for the purpose of outfitting recruits enlisted in California for the Confederate States army. R. Henry Ingrim, Captain Commd'g Co. C. S. A. June, 1864."

Two of the highwaymen were arrested next morning in the THIR-TEEN MILE HOUSE, 49.2 *m.,* where they had overslept, and were taken to Placerville and jailed. When officers surprised others at Somerset House, 12 miles south, the cornered men unlimbered their pistols, killed the sheriff, wounded a constable, robbed them, and escaped. Thomas Poole, most notorious of the band, was captured later and executed.

SPORTSMAN'S HALL, which stood where the SNOW LINE AUTO CAMP (L), 51.2 *m.,* now is, was a stage and freight station with stable room for 500 horses.

Orchards climb the slopes above CAMINO, 54.7 *m.* (3,200 alt., 516 pop.), a busy town with mills and extensive lumberyards fragrant with stores of yellow pine.

SMITH'S FLAT (R), 59.4 *m.* (2,200 alt., 150 pop.), was a rich mining camp of the 1850's.

PLACERVILLE, 62.3 *m.* (1,848 alt., 2,322 pop.) (*see TOUR 4a*), is at a junction with State 49 (*TOUR 4a*), which unites with US 50 between this point and EL DORADO, 69.2 *m.* (1,610 alt., 417 pop.) (*see TOUR 4a*).

Between El Dorado and Sacramento, US 50 follows the old Carson Emigrant Trail, over which many of the forty-niners came into California. The trail was blazed by members of the Mormon Battalion on their way to Salt Lake City in the summer of 1848.

At SHINGLE SPRINGS, 74.4 *m.* (1,425 alt., 119 pop.), site of a shingle mill in 1849, many travel-worn gold seekers stopped for rest and refreshment. The gulches about the springs were filled with miners' cabins in 1850. The Shingle Spring House, now LOCUST TREE INN (L), 74.7 *m.,* was built in 1850 of lumber brought around the Horn.

The ruins of CLARKSVILLE, 82.5 *m.* (L) (600 alt., 25 pop.), are overgrown with ailanthus trees. Here and there, old iron doors still hang to broken stone walls. Roofs and windows are gone. Beyond the village signs of abandoned placer diggings are seen in the fields. From here, the broad, treeless hills slope gently westward to the great Sacramento Valley.

WHITE ROCK, 85.7 *m.,* once a stage stopping place known as the White Rock House, is now merely a railroad flag station. From here the original Placerville Road continued to Sacramento in a westerly direction instead of turning northwest as the present highway does.

The eastern end of a ten-mile gold-dredging area is at 90 *m.* Gigantic piles of smooth round stones line both sides of the highway, stones torn from the bed of an ancient river channel by the huge dredgers, which float on artificial ponds. Operations have been going on since 1880. Since 1922 dredging in Sacramento County has yielded $1,300,-000 in gold.

At FOLSOM, 91.8 *m.* (200 alt., 1,000 pop.), a row of brick stores, erected in the late 1850's and early 1860's, line the highway. Negro miners in 1849 dug for gold at this spot on the American River, and their camp was called Negro Bar. The camp, laid out on the Mexican rancho, Río de los Americanos, on the Coloma Road, was granted to William A. Leidesdorff, U. S. vice-consul, Oct. 8, 1844. A mere trail in 1847, when traced by Captain Sutter from his fort (*see SACRAMENTO*) to his sawmill on the South Fork of the American River, Coloma Road became the first route to the gold fields after Marshall's discovery in 1848 (*see TOUR 4*).

After the death of Leidesdorff in 1848, Capt. Joseph L. Folsom, assistant quartermaster of Stevenson's New York Volunteers, traveled to the West Indies to purchase the 35,000-acre estate on the American River from Leidesdorff's heirs. Its acquisition, together with other properties in San Francisco, made Folsom one of California's wealthiest men. In 1855 a town was surveyed by Theodore D. Judah, tireless advocate of a transcontinental railroad. In 1856 it became the temporary terminus of the Sacramento Valley Railroad, the first in California. In 1857 construction of the California Central Railroad between Folsom and Marysville was begun. From 1856 to 1864 Folsom prospered as a point of departure to the mining area. It was also an important freight depot, connected with the Placerville Road by a branch road to White Rock—the route followed by the present highway.

On April 4, 1860, Harry Roff, a curly haired lad of fifteen, galloped

through Folsom on the initial run of the Pony Express. The run between Sacramento and Placerville, a distance of 55 miles, was made in
2 hours and 59 minutes.

> Right from Folsom on a graveled road to FOLSOM STATE PENITENTIARY,
> 2 *m.,* a fortress-like, unwalled structure built on the south bank of the
> American River in 1880. Among its prisoners are J. B. McNamara, con-
> victed of the Los Angeles *Times* bombing, and Warren K. Billings, of the
> famed Mooney-Billings case. The site was selected because of its prox-
> imity to a granite quarry, a cheap water and power supply, and adjacent
> fertile fields. The first electric power plant in central California was
> constructed on the American River above the penitentiary, and the first
> power was transmitted from Folsom to Sacramento, July 13, 1895. The
> construction of the dam was begun in 1866 by the Natoma Water and
> Mining Company.

West of Folsom the landscape is dominated by artificial rock hills
thrown up during more than fifty years of dredging activity.

NATOMA, 93.5 *m.* (143 alt., 106 pop.), has been a mining center
since 1880, the amount of gold taken out by its dredges totaling more
than $40,000,000.

At ROUTIER, 103.1 *m.* (10 pop.), a long shed in front of an old
wayside station once protected horses and drivers from the heat of the
sun or the pouring rain. Leidesdorff's adobe ranchhouse stood on the
bank of the American River (R). Orchards and vineyards now cover
the acres of the former Rancho Río de los Americanos.

Hopfields appear at 106.1 *m.,* their green vines spread out over
acres of trellises that look like an immense summerhouse. The barnlike
buildings with round cupolas are hopkilns.

PERKINS, 107.9 *m.* (48 alt., 200 pop.), with its fruit-packing
sheds, is a center of diversified horticulture and viticulture.

The Brighton gristmill was erected on the south bank of the American River in 1847 by Mormons in the employ of Captain Sutter. The
news of gold called the millers away, but in 1849 a group of speculators
laid out a town at the site and called it BRIGHTON, 109.2 *m.* The
first site of Brighton, by the river, was abandoned in 1852, and the
present tract by the railroad was opened up in 1861.

SACRAMENTO, 110 *m.* (30 alt., 93,750 pop.) (*see SACRA-
MENTO*).

In Sacramento are junctions with US 99 (*see TOUR 3a*), US 99E
(*see TOUR 3b*), and US 40 (*see TOUR 9a*).

Between Sacramento and Stockton US 50 and US 99 are united
(*see TOUR 3b*).

Section b. STOCKTON to SAN FRANCISCO; 86.5 m., US 50.

STOCKTON, 0 *m.* (23 alt., 47,963 pop.) (*see STOCKTON*),
is at the junction with US 99 (*see TOUR 3b*), which continues southward. US 50 also continues southward, a few miles west of US 99.

At 5.2 *m.* is a junction with a paved road.

Left on this road is FRENCH CAMP, 0.5 *m.* (15 alt., 248 pop.), named for the Hudson's Bay Company trappers, many of them French-Canadians, who camped in this vicinity and hunted beaver and other fur-bearing animals along the river and its sloughs from 1830 to 1845.

For several miles US 50 passes through what was once the Rancho Campo de los Franceses, covering some hundred square miles of land between the Calaveras and San Joaquin Rivers. This estate was granted Jan. 13, 1844, to Wiliam Gulnac, a New Yorker, who had married a Mexican girl and become a Mexican citizen. Gulnac had hoped to colonize his land, but hostile Indians, a smallpox epidemic, and primitive conditions discouraged settlement. In 1845 he sold his entire estate to Capt. Charles M. Weber for $60, the amount of a grocery bill he owed to Weber. Weber induced settlement on his rancho only by practically giving the land away.

Across the ancient ford at the SAN JOAQUIN RIVER, 13.2 *m.* (*fishing and boating resort*), now bridged by railroad and highway, passed the Spanish cavalcade of Gabriel Moraga and Father Viader in 1810, and succeeding expeditions, following the well-worn Indian trail through the Tulares (place of tules) in search of mission sites. On these journeys, the Spanish saw Indians fishing and named the ford El Paso del Pescadero (the passage of the fishing place). The main trail from the Sierra Nevada to the coast valleys of California came to the ford as early as 1844. In seasons of high water, Indians ferried travelers across in *tule balsas* (Sp., rafts). After 1848 John Doak and Jacob Bonsell transported miners across the river in a yawl. When traffic to the mines became heavy, a substantial ferryboat was constructed, and high carrying rates—$8 for a team and wagon. $3 each for horsemen, and $1 each for pedestrians—netted the partners enormous profits from 1849 to 1852.

TRACY, 21 *m.* (49 alt., 3,829 pop.), was a stopping place of travelers from the time it was laid out on the Southern Pacific Railroad in the early 1870's. Its main street, lined with restaurants, cafés, and soft drink stands, is a popular stopping place for the truck drivers who pilot big loads through Altamont Pass.

At 25 *m.* is the junction with the paved Byron road (*see TOUR 9A*).

On the site of the MOUNTAIN HOUSE, 29.7 *m.* (193 alt., 20 pop.), a blue tent was pitched in 1849 to supply refreshments to miners on their way to the gold fields.

ALTAMONT, 35.1 *m.* (740 alt., 64 pop.), at the summit of ALTAMONT PASS, was settled in 1868, when the Southern Pacific Railroad was built. Ranch cattle feed on the smooth hills.

At 35.7 *m.* is a junction with an unimproved road.

Right on this road, through two gates (*please close*), to a farmhouse, 3 *m.* (*arrange here to enter a third gate; 25¢ a car*) at the base of BRUSHY PEAK (1,675 alt.), in the early 19th century called La Loma Alta de las Cuevas (high hill of the caves). The crest is grown with clumps of scrub oak, and on the lower eastern slope is an unusual group of water-worn sandstone caves. Like many another rocky outcropping in

California's remote highlands, these caves are said to have been a hide-out for Joaquin Murrieta and his robber band in the early 1850's. MURRIETA'S POST OFFICE is pointed out as the place where the bandit left messages for his gang. The post office is also a tomb; the body of a pioneer of the region was buried in the rocky crypt at his own request.

At 42 m. is a junction with a paved road.

Left on this road is LIVERMORE, 1 m. (487 alt., 3,119 pop.), since 1868 the principal center of trade and shipping for the farmers and manufacturers of the valley. One of California's largest rodeos is held here annually in June.

PLEASANTON, 6.2 m. (352 alt., 1,237 pop.), founded in 1868 celebrates La Fiesta del Vino when the grapes are purple in its vineyards.

THE LIVERMORE MONUMENT (R), 43.7 m., commemorates Robert Livermore, the first English-speaking settler in the valley. The young Britisher deserted from the ship *Colonel Young* in 1822, married Josefa Higuera, and wandered into the pleasant Valley of San José in 1835. In 1838, he and his partner, José Noriega, were granted the 8,880 acres of land which comprised the Rancho las Positas—named for the perennial springs or pools of water from which the creek flowed. Livermore's ranch house was noted for its hospitality to early immigrants. Nathaniel Greene Patterson, in March 1850, leased it for a hotel. Livermore erected a frame dwelling for himself in 1851; the timbers, shipped around the Horn, were used by his son in the present LIVERMORE HOUSE, erected on the same site in the 1880's, just north of the monument.

At 48.9 m. is a junction with a paved road.

Right on this road 7 m. to the rolling hills and pastures of TASSAJARA (Sp., a place where jerked beef is hung) VALLEY. Bret Harte came here in the autumn of 1856. An old-time religious camp meeting was in progress, which was later described in Harte's short story, *An Apostle of the Tules,* the scene of which was Tassajara Valley.

DUBLIN, 52.7 m. (367 alt., 200 pop.), is in a valley visited in 1811 by José María Amador, a young private in the San Francisco Company. Later, while major-domo at Mission San José, he drove the mission flocks and herds onto it. In 1834, in recompense for his military services, he was granted 16,517 acres. For a decade, Amador's adobe served as an inn on the Hayward-Stockton road to the mines, becoming the nucleus of a village. It is said that the village was christened Dublin by James Witt Dougherty, who bought the Amador house in 1852. Asked by a stranger what the place was called, he replied that the post office had been designated Dougherty's Station, but since there were so many Irish there, the settlement might as well be called Dublin. The name stuck.

Dublin is at the junction with State 21 (*see TOUR 9A*).

Left from Dublin on State 21, along the base of the Sierra de San José at the western edge of Livermore Valley, to ST. RAYMOND'S CHURCH, 0.1 m., dating from 1859. The JEREMIAH FALLON HOUSE (L), 1 m., was erected in 1850 of timbers cut from the San Antonio redwoods and of lumber brought around the Horn.   Beneath a giant oak tree (L), 3 *m.*, is the ALVISO ADOBE, built in 1845 by Francisco Alviso, major-domo of Rancho Santa Rita.   The well-preserved BERNAL ADOBE (R), 3.5 *m.*, was constructed in 1852 by Augustin Bernal, one of the grantees of Rancho el Valle de San José.

SUNOL, 8.5 *m.* (300 alt., 600 pop.), is among the hills at the edge of Sunol Valley's walnut groves.   In the 1840's the adobe ranch house of Antonio Sunol stood amid alders and sycamores near where the San Francisco water system's Grecian-style WATER TEMPLE now stands—south of the main road at the end of an avenue in a luxuriant garden.

The way leads westward into Niles Canyon, a winding gorge cut deep by Alameda Creek, whose "very deep pools . . . many sycamores, cottonwoods, and some live oaks and other trees" were noted by Padre Pedro Font of the Juan Bautista de Anza expedition in 1776.

NILES (*see below*), 15.9 *m.*, is at the junction with Foothill Boulevard (*see below*).

West of Dublin, US 50 crosses the wooded San Jose Range through HAYWARD PASS.   A thick growth of live oak, buckeye, bay, and other native trees cover the southern slopes.

At 60.6 *m.* is the junction with a paved road.

Left on this road is HAYWARD, 1.9 *m.* (116 alt., 5,530 pop.), which is one of the largest poultry centers in the country and has the largest pigeon lofts; it celebrates its chief industry with a yearly poultry and pigeon show.   Here in 1852, when Guillermo Castro owned the surrounding acres of Rancho San Lorenzo, William Hayward pitched his tent, having been visited at a previous site by Castro and informed that he was trespassing. The two came to an agreement, however; and when Castro laid out the town in 1854, he named it for his American friend.

Left from Hayward on Foothill Boulevard.

NILES, 11.3 *m.* (77 alt., 1,525 pop.), known as Vallejo Mills in the 1850's, grew up around a flour mill on José de Jesús Vallejo's Rancho Arroyo de la Alameda (ravine of the tree-lined road).   The stone foundations remain east of the railroad tracks and north of Niles Canyon Road, which is paralleled a mile up the canyon by the mill's stone aqueduct. The VALLEJO ADOBE, one of the Vallejo ranch houses, stands in the CALIFORNIA NURSERY, founded in 1865, where trees and shrubs cover hundreds of acres.

MISSION SAN JOSÉ, 15.8 *m.* (48 alt., 525 pop.), clusters around La Misión del Gloriosísimo Patriarcha Señor San José (the mission of the most glorious patriarch, St. Joseph), the fourteenth mission in order of time and one of the most prosperous, founded June 11, 1797, by Padre Fermín Francisco Lasuen.   The mission structures were first built of timber roofed with grass and later rebuilt of adobe.   The German explorer Georg Heinrich von Langsdorff, visiting here in May 1806, wrote: "The quantity of corn in the granaries far exceeded my expectations . . . and a proportionate quantity of maize, barley, pease, beans, and other grains. The kitchen garden is extremely well laid out, and kept in very good order . . ."

Strategically situated, Mission San José was a starting point for exploration of the interior and for punitive expeditions against the Indians; travelers often stopped here.   One of them, the praying Methodist trapper Jedediah Strong Smith, got a cold reception when he appealed in May 1827 for food and clothing to continue his journey.   Father Durán, unimpressed by a letter signed ". . . your strange, but real friend and Christian brother, J. S. Smith," put him in the guardhouse.   For two weeks he was a prisoner, until the Governor sent a guard to escort him to Monterey. Returning on November 24, he and his men spent two weeks at the mission repairing their guns, drying meat, baling goods, and rounding up horses before departure. Smith made a note in his journal about the music at the Mission services, which "consisted of 12 or 15 violins, 5 base vials and one flute."

The last mission but one to be secularized, San José was so neglected that by 1846, when Governor Pío Pico ordered it sold, its value had fallen to $12,000. Subsequently it was returned to the Church, passing into the keeping of the Sisters of St. Dominic. Of the original structures, only a section of the living quarters remains, a vine-clad adobe building partly restored in 1916. In the belfry of the modern, steepled parish chapel on the site of the old church hang two of the old bells, one dated 1815 and the other, 1826; inside are old vestments, silver relics, and a font of hammered copper. The ungainly three-story brick CONVENT OF THE DOMINICAN SISTERS stands in the rear. The mission gardens, with their statue of St. Dominic, have orange, lemon, fig, apricot, almond, and olive trees, some of them planted by the mission Indians for the padres.

Right from Mission San José on a paved road 1 *m.* to the OLHONE BURIAL GROUND, where a granite monument on a grassy knoll stands over the spot in which are buried about 4,000 Olhone who helped build Mission San José. Foothill Boulevard continues southward to WARM SPRINGS (*see below*), 19.5 *m.*, at the junction with State 17 (*see below*).

US 50 continues to SAN LEANDRO, 65.3 *m.* (48 alt., 11,555 pop.), seat of Alameda County from 1855 to 1872, which long called itself "Cherry City of California," celebrating the wealth of its surrounding cherry orchards at a yearly Cherry Festival. The town was settled in the early 1850's by squatters who tried to drive José Joaquín Estudillo and his family off their Rancho San Leandro by attacks on the white cattle that were Estudillo's chief pride. Although the Estudillos lived for a while in fear of their lives, in the long run they forced the squatters to pay for their land, and laid out a town for the county seat.

Around San Leandro live most of Alameda County's 25,000 Portuguese, chiefly dairy farmers, producing much of the area's milk. One of the most spectacular of their religious festivals celebrates the discovery of the Azores (from which came two-thirds of San Leandro's population). The peak of the celebration is a parade, with church dignitaries in full regalia. The largest of the elaborate floats represents Lusitania, the poetical figure symbolizing Portugal. Following the parade, thousands of visitors join the festivities, which feature a barbecue presided over by a queen of the festival, elected by popular ballot at one cent a vote.

Left from San Leandro on State 17 is SAN LORENZO, 3.4 *m.* (500 pop.), a suburb of San Leandro on the banks of San Leandro Creek, which was first known as Squattersville in 1851, when the squatters who overran Estudillo's land settled here.

At MOUNT EDEN, 7.2 *m.* (25 alt., 500 pop.), is the junction with a paved road; R. here 3 *m.* to the SAN MATEO-HAYWARD BAY BRIDGE across San Francisco Bay, with an over-all length of 12 miles and a length over water of 7.1 miles. All the cement that went into its construction was manufactured from oyster shells dredged from the bottom of the bay. At 15.8 *m.* is the junction with Bayshore Highway (US 101-Alt.) (*see TOUR 2b*).

State 17 continues to ALVARADO, 10.2 *m.* (11 alt., 1,850 pop.), site of an early beet sugar factory and of the CALIFORNIA SALT COMPANY WORKS

Here in the spring of 1853 were not one but three ambitious cities—J. M. Horner's Union City, founded in 1850; Henry C. Smith's New Haven, founded in 1851; and Alvarado, named for Mexican Gov. Juan Bautista Alvarado, founded in 1852-3—all rivaling one another and attempting to rival San Francisco. The name of the third survived for all three. The H. G. SMITH HOUSE, at the head of Vallejo Street, built in 1852, was the home of the founder of the first.

In the midst of vegetable gardens and orange groves is CENTERVILLE, 13.6 *m.* (1,700 pop.), a farm community on the site of one of the 425 Indian shell mounds discovered around San Francisco Bay.

IRVINGTON, 16.8 *m.* (72 alt., 1,000 pop.), was "Washington Corners" in the 1870's and 1880's, when Washington College, one of the State's pioneers in industrial education, was in operation.

At the junction with Foothill Boulevard (*see above*) is WARM SPRINGS, 20.3 *m.* (48 alt., 75 pop.), where the Spanish-Californian women of the neighborhood used to come to do their washing at hot springs. A resort opened here in 1850 was a gay watering place until the earthquake of 1868 destroyed it.

At 21.2 the junction with a private dirt road; L. here 1 *m.* to the HIGUERA ADOBE HOUSES, erected by José Higuera, owner of Rancho los Tularcitos. The older one, built about 1822, is a roofless fire-blackened ruin with crumbling walls, doorways, partitions, and hearth. The second, and larger, building, erected about 1831, is protected by an earthquake-warped wooden superstructure.

In MILPITAS (Sp., little maize patches), 24.8 *m.* (13 alt., 460 pop.), the residents of Pueblo San José used to hold harvest-time merry-makings in their corn, pepper, and squash patches along Penitencia Creek. The claimant of Rancho Milpitas, Nicolas Beryessa, suffered one misfortune after another: Frémont's battalion plundered his cattle and killed his brother, José de Reyes; squatters seized his land; and finally the Land Commission confirmed the rancho to a rival claimant, José María Alviso. He died insane in 1863.

1. Left from Milpitas on paved Calaveras Road, 1.5 *m.* to the ALVISO ADOBE, only remaining one of the four adobe ranch buildings that Alviso built about a century ago. The house, painted white with gay trimmings, stands in a flower garden amid orchards; its second story is encased in modern weather-boarding.

2. Right from Milpitas 4 *m.* on State 9, paved, is ALVISO (8 alt., 381 pop.), a shipping port at the head of Alviso Slough and a starting point for duck hunts in the sloughs and marshes of the vicinity. El Embarcadero de Santa Clara at this point was a port of call for Yankee hide traders from 1835 to 1850, serving the missions and ranchos of the Bay region. Richard Henry Dana wrote in *Two Years Before the Mast:* "Large boats, or launches, manned by Indians . . . are attached to the missions, and sent to the vessels with hides, to bring away goods in return." Here in 1840 settled Ignacio Alviso, mayordomo at Mission Santa Clara, who gave his name to the place. As trade increased with the gold rush, a steamer line from San Francisco was established—fare one way, $35 (and $10 additional for the stage trip to San Jose). After 1865 the railroads began to divert trade, and Alviso dwindled. Today its cove shelters transportation boats and the yachts of the South Bay Yacht Club.

At 8.3 *m.* is the junction of State 9 with US 101-Alt., the Bayshore Highway (*see TOUR 2b*).

SUNNYVALE (*see TOUR 2b*), 10.3 *m.,* is at the junction of State 9 with US 101 (*see TOUR 2b*).

The main side route (State 17) continues southward to SAN JOSE (*see SAN JOSE*), 32.3 *m.,* at the junction with US 101 (*see TOUR 2b*).

OAKLAND, 67 *m.* (0-1,550 alt., 284,063 pop.) (*see OAK-LAND*).

Left from 6th and Harrison Sts. in Oakland, through the POSEY TUBE (*see OAKLAND*), 0.6 *m.* to ALAMEDA (25 alt., 35,033 pop.), with tall old houses set among quiet gardens, modern apartment buildings, and industrial establishments. Built on a low, flat island separated from Oakland and the mainland by an estuary that is connected by a canal with San Leandro Bay, Alameda shares with Oakland its deep-water harbor and, on its southern and western shores, faces San Francisco Bay. On part of the former Rancho San Antonio, Alameda was settled in the early fifties largely by Yankees. The absence of heavy fogs attracted home builders. The town's position on the bay has stimulated shipbuilding, the fishing industry, and waterborne shipping. But Alameda remains principally a residential community and the majority of its working population is employed in other bay cities and towns.

Extending along Alameda's southwestern shore are several beach resorts and amusement parks; largest—and northernmost—is 125-acre NEPTUNE BEACH (*swimming, dancing, playground, amusement concessions*), at the foot of Webster St. The resort has an outdoor salt water plunge 300 feet long and 75 feet wide. Adjacent to the resorts are many fine residences and the small homes of retired seafarers. In LINCOLN PARK, at the foot of Santa Clara Ave., is a stone monument erected 1000 feet east of a place where an Indian shell mound, 400 feet long, 150 feet wide, 14 feet high, was excavated in 1908. The remains of 450 Indians, with stone implements and shell ornaments, were found there.

Occupying a tract equal to more than 50 city blocks between Webster St. and the estuary, with an entrance one block south of the Posey Tube's Alameda portal, is the SAN FRANCISCO BAY AIRDROME, home port for between 50 and 60 ships—charter and private. On Main St., at the western end of the island, is BENTON FIELD, where a large naval air base is under construction (1939). West of Benton Field, near the end of Alameda Pier, is ALAMEDA AIRPORT, western terminus for Pan-American Airways' clipper ships. From here in 1936 the China Clipper took off on its initial flight, inaugurating regular mail, express and passenger service to the Orient.

In Alameda's industrial zone is the BETHLEHEM SHIPBUILDING CORPORATION PLANT, on the Inner Harbor east of Webster St., one of the largest on the Pacific Coast. The plant made a world's record for speed in construction when it built the 12,000-ton *Invincible* in 24 days, July 1918. The ALASKA PACKERS' ASSOCIATION WINTER QUARTERS, at Fortmann Basin on the Estuary, harbor the concern's Alaska salmon fishing fleet, its shipyards and shops. At the west end of Alameda, facing the Bay, is the PACIFIC COAST BORAX COMPANY PLANT, which refines the crude borax brought from Death Valley.

The eastern approach to the SAN FRANCISCO-OAKLAND BAY BRIDGE (*toll 50¢ a car*) is at 78.1 *m.,* at the junction with US 40 (*see TOUR 9b*), which unites with US 50 westward.

SAN FRANCISCO, 86.5 *m.* (18 alt., 634,394 pop.) (*see SAN FRANCISCO*).

ᗕᗕᗕ

Tour 11

(Las Vegas, Nev.)—Baker—Barstow—Mojave—Tehachapi—Atascadero—Morro Bay; US 91-466.
Nevada Line to Morro Bay, 381.4 *m.*

Paved roadbed, open all seasons; extremely hot in summer.
Union Pacific R.R. parallels route between Midway and Yermo; Santa Fe R.R. between Barstow and Wasco.
Accommodations limited; extra supplies advisable in desert.

Section a. *NEVADA LINE to BARSTOW ; 117.2 m.* *US 466.*

South of the Nevada Line and the sere, cracked mud flats of Ivanpah Lake, this section of US 91-466 stretches over the wind-eroded mountains and the vast, torrid valleys of the Mojave Desert. It roughly parallels the route taken by the Mormon pioneers, who, traveling from Salt Lake City to the founding of San Bernardino, toiled in the heat with their cumbersome, crawling oxcarts. The land is still as they found it: inhospitable, ovenlike, feral, bleak, and deceptively lifeless, yet filled with the beauties of its far vistas and its variegated, ever-changing colors.

Great, quadrangular Mojave Desert, ranging from 2,000 to 5,000 feet in altitude—50 blistering valleys and scarred by worn-down mountains—is a land neither as old nor as cadaverous as it appears. Covered at least twice in ancient geologic times by an encroaching blanket of ocean, the region later raised itself to a precipitous land of sheer, needle-like volcanic crags and inconceivable chasms. Volcanic ash, mud, lava, and the effects of erosion at last filled the land's gorges; then great chains of warm lakes, linked by the now trickling Mojave River, supported a life of tropical verdure and roaming prehistoric animals. Slowly, with the rising of encompassing mountain ranges, the Mojave became a cooped-in desert. At the time when Columbus discovered America the last great vestiges of today's bone dry lakes were probably still in existence. Nor is the land dead, for there are innumerable insects, birds, reptiles, and mammals.

The route cuts across the parched bottom of Soda Lake, follows the dry Mojave River for long stretches, passes numerous small desert towns—many of them no more than filling stations with a scattering of desert shacks—rises several times over high and low mountain chains, all studded with the weirdly gesturing Joshua trees.

US 91-466 crosses the Nevada Line, 0 *m.,* 42 miles west of Las Vegas, Nev. Stretching far out on every side is a land yellow, cracked, glittering—a wide expanse of dry clay deposits washed by sudden, though infrequent, rains from the mountains into the shallow basin of dry and torrid IVANPAH LAKE. In the distance saw-toothed, desolate mountains meet the sky. Across the dry lake bed the road runs straight as a die, and then ascends the long upgrade, covered with tumbleweed, to the mountains.

LAKEVIEW STATION, 10.8 *m.*, is a solitary gasoline station sweltering by the roadside.

WHEATON SPRINGS, 12.1 *m.*, in hills dotted with green clumps of Spanish-bayonet, consists of little more than a service station and a cluster of cabins.

The Spanish-bayonet abounding on the nearby hillsides was extremely useful to the desert Indians. Soap was made from the roots, cordage from fibers in the leaves, and the flowers and fruit were considered a great delicacy.

Still ascending, US 466 skirts mountain washes, from the rocky beds of which mesquite trees—the water-searching marvels of the desert—raise their slender, delicately green, and tortuously gnarled shapes. These trees oftentimes send their roots hundreds of feet into the earth in search of moisture. On their delicate limbs grow the mesquite bean, once another food staple of the desert Indians.

MOUNTAIN PASS (*fuel, cabins*), 16.1 *m.* (4,700 alt.), snuggling between yellow hills and black crags, marks the summit of the pass between CLARK MOUNTAIN and the MESCAL RANGE. Clark Mountain, immense in the distance (R), yielded the bearded Mormon pioneer miners immense quantities of gold before the deposits were exhausted.

At CLARK MOUNTAIN STATION, 19.1 *m.*, the customary frame building housing a gas station and general store, backed by cabins, looks across the highway at a squat, barnlike structure with a corrugated metal roof—the gathering place of Death Valley Post 2884, Veterans of Foreign Wars. Every two weeks the building is noisy with the meeting of a group that has boasted as many as 150 members, many of whom ride from such distant points as Death Valley and San Bernardino.

US 466 slopes gently into the wide and arid wastes of a valley dotted with the pearly whiteness of saltbrush and pearlweed, and the olive green of creosote brush—that imperishable shrub which no hot sun can kill and which lends a deceptive appearance of verdancy to the desert floor.

WINDMILL STATION, 24.9 *m.*, is decorated, as its name implies, with a dusty windmill. Around the barren stand of buildings, the yucca, most fantastic of all the desert's growths, begins to make its appearance.

PASO ALTO (high pass), 31.7 *m.* (4,200 alt.) (*accommodations limited*), walled by jagged, crumbling spurs of volcanic rock, is at the summit of a pass; westward the road undulates through the hills in a gentle descent.

YUCCA GROVE, 32.9 *m.* (4,000 alt.) (*restaurant*), is amid a grove of yucca trees. In the daytime the fantastic posturing of yucca limbs seems to mock the traveler.   At night the dusky shadows of the contorted arms, backed by the star-crowded Mojave skies and the looming black bulks of hills, lend an air of deeper mystery to the desert.

The yucca, protected by law from destruction, was called the Joshua tree by Mormon pioneers.   Its reproduction is accomplished by a tiny white moth that lives only in its blossoms.

SODA LAKE, the great dry sink of dying Mojave River, lies far below in clear view, immense and glistening white, ringed with faint blue mountains.

BAKER, 50.7 *m.* (921 alt., 109 pop.), a sweltering desert hamlet, once a busy mining town, is at a junction with the Tonopah and Tidewater Line to Death Valley.

Before the advent of the railroad, Baker was on the line of march of the carriers of borax from Death Valley—the "20-mule" borax teams.

> Right from Baker on State 127 through brush-studded desert (*gas and oil at 8 m.; not again till Shoshone*).
> The Armagosa River, here a tiny stream, is crossed at 32 *m.*   The dark hills on the western horizon are clearer now; they are the rugged mountains of southern Death Valley.
> SHOSHONE (*hotel*), 57 *m.*, consists of a few scattered buildings; willows and low bushes indicate the presence of springs.   The highway enters increasingly mountainous country.
> At DEATH VALLEY JUNCTION, 83 *m.* (2,000 alt., 200 pop.), is the junction with State 190; L. on this route which ascends an easy grade to a low mountain pass, then descends to the eastern entrance of Death Valley National Monument, 100 *m.* (*see DEATH VALLEY Tour 1*).

West of Baker the most significant feature of the typical expanse of desert valley is still the glittering, dry surface of Soda Lake.   Here, in 1860, on this hard playa of baked sediment from the mountains, Indians and dragoons of the U. S. Army battled.   Under the command of Lieutenant Carr, a small body of men rode into the mesquite ambushes in search of Indians who had been waylaying desert travelers. In the ensuing battle three braves were killed, one seriously wounded, and a squaw was taken prisoner.   The Army maintained a camp on the floor of the dry lake until 1866.

BEACON STATION, 63.7 *m.* (*accommodations limited*), is named for the red airplane beacon half a mile away (L).

Visible straight ahead is one of the desert's fantastic formations— CAT MOUNTAIN.   This mass, resembling a great sleeping cat, is one of a number of rain-fissured hills in the Mojave which, through the years, have assumed the shapes of animals.   Below Cat Mountain are the flat and placid CRONISE LAKES, often mistaken for mirages. Frequently dry in summer, the lakes nevertheless made human habitation possible here long before the days of railroads.   Not visible from the highway are small farms, kept alive by judicious husbanding of the lake waters and by a thin trickle from deep-sunk wells; they produce a single crop—watermelons.

CRONISE STATION, 68.5 *m.*, is a straggling collection of frame houses.

The route descends into an immense and narrow valley, where the dry Mojave River parallels the highway. Weather-worn pearl-pink hills are passed; green mounds give way to black, crumbling ones atop residual slopes of yellow.

MIDWAY, 81.3 *m.,* is a scattering of buildings in a widening of the valley.

The CALIFORNIA STATE AGRICULTURAL QUARANTINE STATION and the DIVISION OF REGISTRATION OF MOTOR VEHICLES (*see GENERAL INFORMATION*) is at 102.7 *m.*

In YERMO, 103.6 *m.* (1,935 alt., 195 pop.), are dusty houses around a station and roundhouse of the Union Pacific R. R.

> Right from Yermo to CALICO, 4.1 *m.,* a ghost town perched high in the riotously colored CALICO MOUNTAINS. It was a large silver-mining settlement in the late 1880's; the decline in silver prices closed the mines.
> Left from Calico 0.5 *m.* through ODESSA CANYON to the SITE OF BISMARCK, a mining camp contemporaneous with Calico. Here lived Dorsey, a dog trained to carry the mail to and from Calico. In this section were found the first deposits of the volcanic clays with a crystalline borate of lime content, named colemanite for their discoverer, W. T. Coleman. They were extensively mined for production of borax until purer deposits were found elsewhere.

The CACTUS GARDENS, 111.2 *m.,* on a barren knoll adjoining the road, maintained by the State, contain a representative collection of all the varieties of the region's cacti, which are protected by law.

Pallid mountains loom in the distance; sycamores and alders spring into view; and clusters of houses become visible.

At 116 *m.* is the junction with US 66 (*see TOUR 12a*) which unites with US 91-466 into BARSTOW, 117.2 *m.* (*see TOUR 12a*).

Section b. BARSTOW to MORRO BAY; 264.2 m. US 466.

This section of US 466 strikes westward across a parched and monotonous plateau to the desert metropolis of Mojave, then winds over the Tehachapi Range, to the great fertile expanse of the San Joaquin Valley. West of Bakersfield US 466 runs directly westward through fertile ranches to a barren land studded with oil derricks. The highway traverses mountain valleys, and crosses the Santa Lucia Range to the Pacific Coast.

West of BARSTOW, 0 *m.,* US 466 winds in and out of low, rugged hills toward flat plains, which extend monotonously for miles ahead, relieved only by stunted sagebrush, creosotebush, and saltweed.

HAWES, 21.5 *m.* (2,495 alt., 30 pop.), is a railroad station surrounded by a few dusty houses.

KRAMER, 34.2 *m.* (2,482 alt., 100 pop.), is the sunburned home of the main plant of a large borax company. The one small hotel and a few gas stations are concessions to the tourist trade.

At 37.7 *m.* is the junction with a dirt road.

> Right on this road to the PACIFIC COAST BORAX WORKS, 3.1 *m.* In these dust-filmed buildings, the borax is separated from clay mined at a depth

of about 150 feet in the surrounding country. The separation is achieved by an ingenious system of blowers, the steady roar of which shatters the desert silence for miles around. The crystals are transported to Wilmington for refining. Borax, prized as a cleansing agent, has long been of commercial importance; for many years it was imported into the United States from Tibet, where it was obtained from saline lakes, then the only known deposit in the world. About a century ago, the chemical was discovered in the hot springs of Tuscany, Italy, recovered by evaporation, and sold to all parts of the world. It was not until 1856 that borax was discovered in California. The deposits at Kramer were discovered in 1912, when a homesteader drilling for water brought up white crystals. In 1925 it was learned that vast deposits of pure borax and sodium borate were concealed under the layer of desert sand. This compound, rasorite, has not been found elsewhere.

MUROC DRY LAKE, (L) 48.7 *m.,* is a barren, hard-packed, playa. The perfectly flat and saucerlike depression has been found ideal for automobile speed tests, and is used frequently for experimentation, both by racing car owners and manufacturers of stock models. The mud formed in the lake bed during the rainy seasons has been found peculiarly adaptable to the needs of oilwell drillers, and thousands of tons of the substance, known as rotary mud, are shipped annually to southern California drillers. On the east shore of the dry bed is the U. S. ARMY BOMBING RANGE, practice ground for aerial dreadnoughts.

West of MOJAVE, 67.5 *m.* (2,755 alt., 750 pop.) (*see TOUR 7b*), at a junction with US 6 (*see TOUR 7b*), US 466 plunges into more desert. Ahead loom the towering TEHACHAPI (Ind., land of plenty of acorns and good water) MOUNTAINS, purple, black, and rust-colored in the sunlight.

The LOS ANGELES AQUEDUCT, 75 *m.,* lies like an immense snake along the base of the mountains. US 466 traverses a canyon of the Tehachapis. A forest of yucca grows thicker as the canyon walls narrow, only to disappear as the walls reach vertiginous heights.

CAMERON, 79 *m.* (3,789 alt., 25 pop.), is a railroad shipping station for fruit.

Through TEHACHAPI PASS, 80.5 *m.* (3,793 alt.), thousands of early travelers forged their way. The gorge is beautiful, with black escarpments of mountain rock and the coloring contrast of trees.

As the pass grows wider, the highway nears the blue, tree-girt expanse of PROCTOR LAKE, (L), 84 *m.,* whose waters are highly saline. During the summer salt is frequently shoveled from the dry lake bottom by the wagonload and sold commercially.

MONOLITH, 85 *m.* (3,928 alt., 261 pop.), clusters around the giant MONOLITH CEMENT MILLS (L), which provided all the cement used in the construction of the Los Angeles Aqueduct.

US 466, still ascending, passes through land walled by mountains, but beginning to show evidences of the fruit growing made possible by the drilling of deep artesian wells. The region is noted for its prize-winning apples and pears.

TEHACHAPI, 88 *m.* (3,966 alt., 736 pop.), is the business and social center of a surrounding fruit area. Gold in the China Hill placers in 1854 drew the first settlers to Tehachapi—then 3 miles east; in 1876, when the railroad passed Tehachapi by, the town, Mohammed-like, went to the railroad.

At 91.4 *m.* is the junction with a paved road.

Left on this road to the CALIFORNIA INSTITUTE FOR WOMEN, 6 *m.* (*visiting hours of inmates, 9-3 daily*), a pleasing array of Normandy architecture rising in Cummings Valley. Around the penitentiary are no high walls; only a wire fence and one lone guard are required for approximately 175 women prisoners and 1,600 acres of ground. There is little of a penal atmosphere. Cottages resembling châteaus each accommodate about 40 women and one matron; inmates wear no uniforms and are permitted to decorate their rooms as they like. Opened in 1932, the institution is one of the most successful experiments in penology.

US 466 leaves Tehachapi Valley, and winds perilously into mountains clothed with gnarled and ancient oak trees.

The LOOP, 98.9 *m.*, high on a mountainside (R), is a shining thread of railroad tracks swinging in a huge circle, rapidly descending; 78 feet from the top it disappears into the mouth of a tunnel. A complete circle, 3,795 feet in circumference, has been completed.

WOODFORD, 100.6 *m.* (2,710 alt., 164 pop.), is a railroad point for scattered fruit farms.

The Tehachapi grade ends at 111.8 *m.;* the mountains are behind, imposing, verdant, dulled with purple; ahead is the flat and monotonous plain of the San Joaquin Valley. The tops of grimy oilwell derricks loom in the distance; as the road continues westward, their numbers increase, dotting the checkerboard of tilled fields like black-headed pins on a field map.

EDISON, 125.8 *m.* (572 alt., 50 pop.), is in one of the thickest forests of oilwell derricks in the district.

BAKERSFIELD, 133.5 *m.* (420 alt., 26,015 pop.) (*see TOUR 3b*), is at the junction with US 99 (*see TOUR 3b*), with which US 466 unites at FAMOSO, 145.8 *m.* (330 alt., 140 pop.).

West of Famoso US 466 cuts through tilled lands producing grapes, grain, and cotton; a few isolated homes and trees break the flatness.

WASCO, 152.3 *m.* (335 alt., 2,000 pop.), with its sun-bleached array of frame houses, serves as the community center for the nearby ranchers.

The land gradually changes its aspect, although not its contours. Divergent roads become fewer; tilled fields give way to grazing lands. The derricks of oilwells point upward from the fields in the distance.

LOST HILLS, 173.8 *m.* (300 alt., 200 pop.), is a community of oilfield workers and farmers.

ANTELOPE PLAIN stretches dismally ahead; dust devils, little whirlwinds swirling the cloying dust about briefly, are plentiful. Inflexibly straight, US 466 stretches ahead to the hazy bulk of the TEMBLOR RANGE. Rising gradually, the highway at last abandons its straight path to follow the curves of POLONIO PASS, 206.3 *m.* (1,850 alt.).

CHOLAME, 210.9 *m.* (1,200 alt., 571 pop.), in a high valley, is a supply center for ranchers.

SHANDON, 217.6 *m.* (1,035 alt., 112 pop.), by the San Juan River, consists of a business street several blocks long.

Zigzagging southwestward across the valley, past orchards, corn-fields, and cattle ranges, US 466 again rises into hills. Occasionally visible are white, red-topped farm buildings. Winding and dipping, the highway at last emerges from the rich irregularity of the hills into Creston Valley, 232.3 *m.*

US 466 passes the rambling Spanish type buildings of a resort, 236 *m.* (*luxury class*), and then turns abruptly (L) into the SANTA LUCIA RANGE.

ATASCADERO (Sp., deep miry place), 246.2 *m.* (853 alt., 2,042 pop.) (*see TOUR 2b*), is at the junction with US 101 (*see TOUR 2b*).

In a twisting ascent of the Santa Lucia Range US 466 reaches the summit, 251.5 *m.* Below and far distant is the sheen of the Pacific, meeting the sky in a blue-white haze. Nearer are the tumbled, rain-eroded slopes down which the highway twists, paralleling the course of the jagged cut named MORRO CREEK. Gradually, the land softens, and the road approaches the ocean on a high, level plateau.

US 466 reaches its terminus at a junction with State 1, 264.2 *m.* (*see TOUR 1c*), 1.2 miles north of Morro Bay.

Tour 12

(Kingman, Ariz.)—Needles—Barstow—San Bernardino—Los Angeles—Santa Monica; US 66.
Arizona Line to Santa Monica, 314.8 *m.*

Atchison, Topeka & Santa Fe Ry. parallels route between Needles and Victorville.
Accommodations scanty in desert sections; gas, oil, water, and food available at desert hamlets, but extra supplies should be carried; sleeping accommodations limited to tourist camps, except in larger towns.
Paved roadbed; extreme high temperatures between Kingman and San Bernardino in midsummer, occasional heavy windstorms in March and April.

West of the green banks of the Colorado River, US 66 traverses the arid Mojave Desert, a bleak plateau furrowed by scores of untillable valleys, shimmering in the fierce sunlight. The road mounts and dips in and out of these sinks, unrelieved in their desolation except after rare rains, when a thorny mantle of delicate-hued vegetation blazes into flower.   Ahead rises the blue bulk of the San Gabriel Mountains.   The highway runs steadily toward them, between hills of jumbled beauty, passing through widely spaced "towns"—mere groups of tourist cabins about gas stations and lunch rooms—to the desert city of Barstow.

Section a.   ARIZONA LINE to BARSTOW ; 167 m.   US 66.

US 66 crosses the Arizona Line, 0 *m.*, 54 miles west of Kingman, Ariz., on Topock (Ind., bridge) Bridge, which spans the deceptive Colorado (ruddy) River—here a lazy-looking stream that periodically goes on a bridge-smashing rampage—and drops US 66 onto California soil. The route follows the mesa edging the river with its fringe of green willows and sycamores.

At 1 *m.* is the junction with a dirt road.

> Left on this road to ROCK MAZE, 0.5 *m.*, above the river on a high bluff. Resembling at a distance a plowed field, this work of prehistoric aborigines is believed to have been a place for funeral rites. Rows of brownish pebbles, paralleling one another several feet apart in intersecting, roughly concentric patterns, extend over several acres. A local legend relates that the spirits of the dead, floating down the Colorado, entered the maze and shook off the evil spirits chasing them by losing them in the tangled pathways.

At 9.6 *m.* is the junction with a dirt road.

> Left on this road to NEEDLES MUNICIPAL AIRPORT, 0.8 *m.*

NEEDLES, 15.5 *m.* (481 alt., 3,144 pop.), spreading over a flood plain, is an oasis approached through a lane of tamarind and pepper trees. Founded as a way station after the Santa Fe tracks were laid in 1883, it was named for an isolated group of needle-like spires visible 15 miles southeastward in Arizona.

The railroad yards provide Needle's chief occupation. The mines that honeycomb the mountains roundabout yield gold, nonmetallic ores, and semiprecious stones, such as agates, moonstones and turquoise. In the fertile bottom lands, where Mojave Indians till many of the ranches, date palms lift waving fronds beside green truck gardens and citrus orchards.

A sub-tropical city, Needles seeks shelter from the sweltering heat in the shade of the palms, cottonwoods, tamarisks, and pepper trees that border its streets. A miscellany of business buildings surrounds the park that fronts the grayish stucco railroad station. In this torrid square, where temperatures often are 112° at midnight, regal Washingtonia palms, pepper trees, and alders border the grass. Couples stroll here, children play around the ornamental cannon, and swarthy Mojaves, garbed in gaudy scarlets, blues, and yellows, loiter about.

US 66 climbs the low bleached hills back of Needles and plunges westward into the MOJAVE DESERT (*see TOUR 11a, also NATURAL SETTING*), a region of fantastic formations, once swamped under ocean waters, then upheaved to bold heights, and finally buried under lava, mud, and ashes. The unevenly sloping, valley-furrowed desert floor is ringed with mountain chains whose changing hues—sepia, gray, lavender—fuse in the distance into a dull blue. Their bristling outlines and the glistening salt flats of occasional dry lakes provide the only variation to the parched, monotonous wastes. Cacti rear their rigid, spiny leaves in profusion. Here and there jut the stark branches of the Spanish bayonet and Joshua tree. After the heavy rains which come at infrequent intervals, the desert blazes with colorful flowers.

JAVA, 22 m. (936 alt.), a knot of dull reddish frame buildings bordering the tracks, is a desert railroad stop.

The cacti now become more conspicuous. Most widespread is the commonest western variety, the cholla. In times of great drought the cholla is eaten by cattle; a single spark of fire will ignite the whole plant, burn off the spines, and leave juicy green fodder. Interspersed are barrel cacti, stout cylinders sometimes six feet high. These contain a fibrous pulp, which, after the top is cut off, can be pounded to yield a liquid that assuages thirst; the Indians cooked their meat in the liquid with the aid of hot stones placed in the open barrels.

SOUTH PASS, 33 m. (2,700 alt.), is a cluster of adobe buildings offering tourist accommodations with a sign, "Water Free With Purchases Only."

From the slope west of the pass, the flat desert floor seems to be a fertile plain because of the deceptive greenery of the creosote bush. At intervals appear the tall towers of the Boulder Dam Power Line, webbed with glinting strands of cables, and at 37.3 m., the trim, red-roofed stucco bungalows (L) of the section workers on the line.

US 66 gradually climbs a craggy pass through the PAIUTE RANGE.

MOUNTAIN SPRINGS, 43 m. (2,720 alt., 5 pop.), at the summit, is a collection of neat little buildings—gas station, lunch room, and tourist cabins—near an irrelevant cross (L) on the hilltop, erected solely to induce passing tourists to stop and ask questions.

As the highway rounds the hump of the pass, snow-crowned MOUNT ANTONIO (Old Baldy) appears, towering in the far distance above the nearer mountain ranges.

At 55.5 m. is a junction with a dirt road.

> Right on this road 22.3 m. to MITCHELL'S CAVERNS (*guide service; adm. $1, children 50¢; campground with free wood and water*). The chilly, cavernous chambers, hollowed out of carboniferous limestone, form an underground labyrinth requiring three hours to traverse. More than 20 entrances have been discovered. Within, the ashes of aboriginal cave dwellers' campfires cover the floors. The caverns are frescoed, pillared, and ornamented with stalagmites and stalactites.

The area around ESSEX, 56 m. (1,700 alt., 30 pop.), sparsely vegetated though it appears, pastures herds of cattle with its grease-wood and bunch-grass.

US 66 continues over a vast plain, sparsely studded with the desert brush—a dull-toned land of mystic hues and vistas—between bright-colored CLIPPER MOUNTAINS (R), a jumble of volcanic rock turned yellow and brown by oxidation, and the OLD WOMAN MOUNTAINS (L), where the almost extinct Nelson mountain sheep clamber over the crags.

DANBY, 65 *m.* (1,353 alt.), a cluster of tourist cabins about a service station, is at the foot of a gradual ascent over bleak, unchanging terrain. SUMMIT, 73.5 *m.*, and CHAMBLESS, 76.5 *m.* (800 alt.), mere dots on the desert's face, provide gas pumps, tourist camps, cafés.

Far out on the desert (L), at 84.5 *m.,* wisps of smoke are seen rising from the stacks of the CALIFORNIA SALT WORKS, which mine pure salt in 40-foot shafts. Eastward, like a ruined castle, rises an abandoned GYPSUM MILL. Nearby (L) are the yellowish, salt-incrusted flats of BRISTOL DRY LAKE, its dry parts covered by puffy, powder-like "self-rising" soil in which a man would sink knee-deep. The lake's spectacular mirages, often create the illusion of a sheet of shimmering water, sometimes of cathedrals, cities, and mountain peaks floating through the sky.

AMBOY, 87 *m.* (614 alt., 95 pop.), is another typical highway stop, blistered by temperatures that often soar above 120° in mid-summer.

At 87 *m.* is the junction with a dirt road.

> Left on this road to the base of AMBOY CRATER, 1.5 *m.,* where a footpath leads up the side of the cone of dark gray pumice and lava, rising 200 feet above craggy lava beds.

On the vast desert, here and there, lies an abandoned auto, some-times on its back like an upturned turtle, or an occasional little pile of rocks, marking the boundary claims of some hopeful prospector or, topped with a weathered cross, the resting place of some luckless wanderer.

BAGDAD (*accommodations*), 95.5 *m.* (787 alt., 20 pop.), is merely a shell of the rip roaring camp that thrived here when the War Eagle and Orange Blossom gold mines to the north were active. The few old buildings that escaped destruction by fire in 1918 are threatened by fierce desert winds, as a huge oil tank with its sides blown in attests. Except for one other spot, Bagdad has less rain than any other place in or near the Mojave Desert—a mean annual average of but 2.3 inches; in four out of 20 years it has had no rainfall at all.

For 20 miles westward US 66 covers a desolate terrain almost as primitive as it was thousands of years ago. The railroad tracks are dotted with lonely stops without accommodations, which bear such curiously incongruous names as Siberia and Klondike.

In comparison with neighboring "towns," LUDLOW, 115.5 *m.* (1,782 alt., 150 pop.), is a metropolis. Here two narrow-gage rail-roads of the Tonopah & Tidewater connect with the Santa Fe.

The SLEEPING BEAUTY, a formation resembling a dormant, smiling human face is outlined by the crest of the CADY MOUN-

TAINS, northwestward. Directly north appears the yellowish blotch of LUDLOW DRY LAKE, where experiments have been made in processing the lake bed's fine "flour" gold.

The landscape at 129.5 m. suddenly losing its vegetation, darkens from gray to coal black. Above a 6-mile-wide lava field looms MOUNT PISGAH (L), an extinct volcano with a deep crater in the summit of its symmetrical 250-foot cone.

MOJAVE WATER CAMP, 136.6 m. and GUYMAN, 137 m., each has its small knot of sun-bleached buildings. Northwest of Guyman lies the glittering, salt-crusted bed of TROY DRY LAKE.

In a dry-farming region is NEWBERRY, 146.5 m. (1,631 alt., 175 pop.), once named simply Water. At the spring that flows beneath the overhanging black precipices of the NEWBERRY MOUN-TAINS, early travelers quenched their thirst. Newberry is a refreshing green oasis of alders, willows, and cottonwoods clustering about that desert rarity—a swimming pool. Water is a prized commodity. Trains of eighteen and twenty 10,000-gallon tank cars haul it daily as far as Bagdad for use in locomotive boilers. Melons, alfalfa, and apricots are shipped from here.

DAGGETT, 158 m. (2,006 alt., 102 pop.), a gay camp when gold and silver mines in this region were working at capacity is virtually deserted, though still a shipping point for the mines.

Along the tree-lined dry wash of the Mojave River, US 66 travels to BARSTOW, 167 m. (2,106 alt., 2,549 pop.), once a desert junction for overland wagon trains and later an outfitting point for Death Valley expeditions. It has now cast off its frontier-town aspect. Five-and-ten-cent stores and beauty parlors, auto agencies, and cocktail bars line the principal avenue. Barstow was the center for gold and silver mining in the 1890's when the present ghost town of Calico, in the Calico Mountains, was in its heyday. The town is now a division point of the Santa Fe Ry., whose shops employ 85 percent of its workmen. On surrounding farms, irrigated from wells, alfalfa is the principal crop.

Barstow is at the junction with US 466—91 (see TOUR 11).

Section b. BARSTOW to SAN BERNARDINO; 77.1 m. US 66.

This section of US 66 traverses barren and burning expanses of desert and crosses the heaped masses of the San Bernardino Mountains.

South of BARSTOW, 0 m., US 66 runs through billowing desert country; only the cottonwoods and willows on the banks of the Mojave River (R) relieve the tedium of rolling sandscape.

LENWOOD, 5.2 m. (2,229 alt., 200 pop.), is encircled by slate-colored elevations blanketed with desert growths. In the surrounding country are a few sprawling alfalfa fields and an occasional chicken ranch.

HODGE, 11.7 m. (2,150 alt., 102 pop.), is a supply center. Its brick grammar school, perched on a slight rise (L) serves the far-flung desert district between Barstow and Oro Grande (see below).

The Mojave River nears the highway in Hodge. Screwbean mesquite and green desert willows grow abundantly along its banks. Distantly, the harsh, jagged mass of IRON MOUNTAIN protrudes (R) islandlike from the sand and gravel wastes.

HELENDALE, 21.8 *m.* (2,424 alt., 150 pop.), is encompassed, oasis-like, by waving alfalfa and corn.

Beyond the cultivated circle of the Helendale district, the tawny desert spreads away. SHADOW MOUNTAIN, holding turquoise-bearing porphyry deposits that were worked by desert-dwelling Indians —predecessors of the Mojave—looms indistinctly on the western horizon (R) of HELENDALE MESA.

In the shade of wide-spreading sycamores and spirelike poplars, ORO GRANDE, 31.7 *m.* (2,648 alt., 600 est. pop.), sprawls along the highway, dreaming of the prosperous gold-boom days of the 1880's. Its population skyrocketed to 2,000 when in 1878 gold was discovered in the OLD SILVER MOUNTAINS and the GRANITE MOUNTAINS (L). After 1885 gold production diminished until in 1928 the last of the mines closed.

Crossing the Mojave River, here a turgid, muddy stream with a year-round flow, US 66 sweeps south through alfalfa fields and cattle ranges rich with foot-high bunch grass. As the highway mounts a long, easy grade, the fantastic yucca trees appear. The countryside soon takes on a verdant, cultivated appearance. The Mojave River becomes a stream of respectable size, serpentining between broad acres of farm land, fruit groves, and chicken and turkey ranches.

VICTORVILLE, 35.7 *m.* (2,716 alt., 2,500 pop.), is a curious blend of the present and the past—a past carefully preserved. This was Mormon Crossing from 1878 to 1885, until the river camp, by then grown to a roaring mining town, was named Victor—later Victorville. Mining here had dwindled to insignificant proportions by 1900, but the characteristic false front frontier buildings remained, attracting, a decade and a half later, the attention of the young motion-picture industry. From 1914 to 1937 the town and its "wild West" back country were used as the locale for more than 200 films. The first picture made here was a William S. Hart "quickie" in 1914. From 1916 to 1924 Hart made an average of two pictures a year in the vicinity, among them *Wild Bill Hickok, O'Malley of the Mounted,* and *Tumbleweed.* When the resemblance of D Street to the popular conception of Main Street in a "roaring" western town attracted other film producers such western stars as Harry Carey, Tom Mix and Hoot Gibson began performing in "horse operas" here. Will Rogers, too, was a frequent and popular visitor. The town's first talking picture, *In Old Arizona,* starred Warner Baxter. A Boulder Dam high-tension power line was used as a "prop" in *Slim,* starring Pat O'Brien and Henry Fonda as linesmen. Victorville admits its attempts to recapture its waning movie trade. The atmosphere of OLD TOWN across the railroad tracks (L) is zealously preserved. Even when new ranch houses, corrals, and stables are built in the cattle range back country, they are constructed in the old style to meet the demands of location scouts.   Meanwhile, Victorville pursues a more prosaic destiny as the trade center for irrigated farming and poultry and cattle ranches, and as headquarters for quarrying and mining interests.

In the heart of town is (L) the ARENA OF THE VICTORVILLE NON-PROFESSIONAL RODEO (*two days each Oct.; adm. $1*), sponsored by 50 Hollywood writers and actors.   Only cowboys working on the ranges of the Southwest are permitted to compete.

US 66 crosses rolling desert country again toward immense blue ranges.

MILLERS CORNER, 47.7 *m.* (3,050 alt.), has a gas station and a few cabins for motorists.

US 66 now sweeps across BALDY MESA (3,000 alt.), a vast, sun-scorched expanse of mesquite and scattered yucca trees.

At 49.6 *m.* is a junction with US 395 (*see TOUR 6d*), which unites with US 66 for about 30 miles southward.

As the desert surrenders to chaparral-covered foothills, US 66 crosses at 53 *m.* a boundary of the SAN BERNARDINO NA-TIONAL FOREST, a preserve of 804,045 acres, containing more than a billion board feet of merchantable timber—sugar and Jeffrey pine, big cone spruce, incense cedar and tamarack, among other species. It is maintained principally for watershed protection.   A number of streams and lakes in the high country furnish water for hydroelectric power and irrigation, and afford excellent trout fishing.

The mountains draw together to form the mouth of CAJON (Sp., box) PASS, through the Sierra Madre Mountains, for nearly a century the southeastern gateway for overland travel to the coast, since William Wolfskill blazed the Spanish Trail from Santa Fe to Los Angeles through it in 1831.   From the summit, 54 *m.* (4,301 alt.), is an inspiring view over mountains, deserts, orchards, and vineyards.   US 66 makes its descent in a series of twisting slopes.

At 59 *m.* is a junction with State 2.

1. Left here to LAKE ARROWHEAD, 24.3 *m.* (*see below*).
2. Right on State 2 through a region of grotesque sandstone formations, tooled by centuries of wind and weather into freak shapes, pockmarked with windholes and caves.
At 1.4 *m.* is a junction with a dirt road.
Left here to LONE PINE CANYON, 2 *m.* The main course of the SAN ANDREAS RIFT, one of the two geologic faults in the forest, runs up this canyon. Hundreds of thousands of years ago a rolling, uneven plain spread out where the San Gabriel Mountains now rise. This ancient plain represented the eroded remnants of a range dating from a still more remote period. A mighty underground earth movement began which obliterated the remaining traces of the earlier range and eventually thrust upward a vast, jagged mass. The upward thrust came between two faults whose courses are still clearly defined. The north fault, San Andreas Rift, extends from Cajon Pass through Lone Pine Canyon. Characterized as a "live" or "active" fault, it extends two-thirds the length of California, for an unknown distance northwest under the Pacific Ocean, and

across Mexico into the Caribbean Sea. It has caused many California earthquakes, including the San Francisco disturbance in 1906.

Stunted yuccas appear in the sagebrush fields away from the highway toward the base of the range. The road here parallels the route of the Mormons, who in 1851 came through the mountains to settle San Bernardino Valley. Attempting to follow the trail blazed through Cajon Pass in 1847 by an earlier detachment of the Mormon Battalion, the party could not maneuver its heavy wagons through "The Narrows" and was compelled to seek this route farther west.

At 8.3 *m.* the main route turns L. from State 138 on Wildhorse Canyon Rd.

WRIGHTWOOD, 13.5 *m.* (6,000 alt., 50 pop.), in Swartout Valley is a conifer sheltered year-round resort (*all accommodations*). From 500 to 600 persons vacation here during the height of the seasons.

BIG PINES CIVIC CENTER, 16.9 *m.* (6,864 alt.), is the heart of the recreational and administrative activities of BIG PINES RECREATION PARK (*all types of accommodations and recreational facilities*), supervised by the Los Angeles County Department of Playgrounds and Recreation. It consists of two divisions: Big Pines (2,700 acres) and Prairie Fork (1,620 acres) with 17 public campgrounds (*25¢ a day; $2.50 for calendar year*).

A NATURE THEATER, in a natural, pine-rimmed bowl (L) near the Civic Center, is used for group meetings, free lectures, campfire programs, and picnics.

Left from Civic Center 12 *m.* on the left fork of Blue Ridge Rd. to PRAIRIE FORK COUNTY PARK (*no accommodations*).

At 17 *m.* on the main road is a junction with Table Mountain Rd.

Right on this road 1.5 *m.* ascending through conifer forests to the SMITHSONIAN INSTITUTION SOLAR OBSERVATORY, the primary purpose of which is the recording of sunspots (*open 1:30-5 Thurs.*).

A well-equipped public campground, 18.8 *m.*, lies (R) in a parklike grove of giant pines and incense cedars.

JACKSON LAKE, 19.6 *m.*, in a steep-sided gulch (L) rimmed with tall conifers, is the water-sports center of the area.

CAMP MANZANITA, 20 *m.*, is fragrant with the sweetish aroma of the manzanita tree.

West of the WEST GATE RANGER STATION, 20.1 *m.* (6,150 alt.), at the Big Pines Recreation Park, the road goes down SHOEMAKER CANYON. As the 2,000-foot line is passed, hot desert air is felt.

At 28 *m.* is a junction with a paved road.

Left on this road 0.7 *m.* through BIG ROCK CREEK CANYON to a junction with a foot trail; R. on this trail 0.5 *m.* to DEVIL'S PUNCH BOWL, a region of vast, jumbled masses of sandstone. At some places marine fossils are embedded in the boulders of the creek bed.

At 2.2 *m.* on the paved road is one of a string of Forest Service camps.

VALYERMO (*cabins*) 28.2 *m.* (3,920 alt., 65 pop.), is a settlement in a bend of alder-grown Big Rock Creek.

VALYERMO CAMP FOR UNDERPRIVILEGED CHILDREN, (L), 29.2 *m.*, is maintained by the Los Angeles Police Department. Officers of the Crime Prevention Division of the Police Department, detailed to the camp, serve as cooks, waiters, gardeners, and handy men.

PALMDALE, 52.2 *m.* (2,669 alt., 1,224 pop.), is at the junction with US 6 (*see TOUR 7b*).

US 66, roughly following (R) alder-grown CAJON CREEK, rolls smoothly downgrade to DEVORE, 67.1 *m.* (2,025 alt., 153 pop.). MOUNT SAN GORGONIO (11,485 alt.), looms into view.

The ARROWHEAD, a natural phenomenon on the face of Arrowhead Peak, is visible at 75.2 *m.*

At 75.3 *m.* US 66 broad and palm-lined, turns R., dividing the business district (L) of SAN BERNARDINO, 77.1 *m.* (1,073 alt., 37,486 pop.), seat of San Bernardino County. The name San Bernardino was given by a party of missionaries, soldiers, and Indians from the San Gabriel Mission (*see below*) under Padre Francisco Dumetz, who entered the valley on May 20, 1810, the feast day of San Bernardino of Siena. In 1851, Capt. Jefferson Hunt arrived in the valley with a party of 500 Mormons from Salt Lake, who bought Rancho San Bernardino for $77,000 in 1852, and laid out a city along the broad, spacious lines of Salt Lake City. The Mormons remained dominant here until 1857, when Brigham Young, anxious to center his flock in Utah, issued a recall. San Bernardino is today a railroad and fruit-packing center.

The mammoth NATIONAL ORANGE SHOW BUILDING, E and Mill Sts., is the setting for the city's leading event (*held annually for 11 days beginning third Thurs. in Feb.; adm. 50¢*). The show presents numerous structures built with columns of citrus fruits; frequently a million oranges, lemons, and grapefruit are employed to achieve the desired effects.

The SAN BERNARDINO COUNTY COURTHOUSE, on Arrowhead Ave. between Third and Fourth Sts., is on the site of a fort that was the first structure erected by the Salt Lake pioneers. The fort was a large walled enclosure, holding numerous buildings, including a school and meetinghouse, storehouses, and the colony offices.

In PIONEER PARK, Sixth and E Sts., are the Memorial Auditorium, commemorating World War participants; a Sailors' and Soldiers' Monument, dedicated to heroes of the Mexican, Civil, and Spanish-American Wars; and a PIONEER CABIN (*open 9-5*), housing a collection of early Mormon relics.

San Bernardino is at a junction with US 395 (*see TOUR 6e*).

Left from San Bernardino on Third St. to Sierra Way (State 18); L. here in a serpentine ascent of WATERMAN CANYON in SAN BERNARDINO NATIONAL FOREST, 5.6 *m.*

At 7.9 *m.* is a junction with a private road; R. here 1 *m.* to a hot springs resort (rates reasonable), commanding a view of San Bernardino, Pomona, and San Gabriel Valleys from a 1,800-acre park. Dominating the region is the natural phenomenon from which the springs take their name—the huge arrowhead on the slope of ARROWHEAD PEAK, behind and above the spa. The arrowhead consists of outcroppings of quartz and gray granite, grown over with whitish weeds and grass; it covers an area of seven-and-a-half acres.

An Indian legend relates that the Great White Father sent an "arrow of fire" to guide the Cahuilla westward after they had been driven from their homes by aggressive neighbors. The arrowhead finally rested on a mountainside with its point toward a fertile valley (San Bernardino) and boiling hot springs. A legend of Mormon origin is to the effect that Brigham Young had a vision in which he saw a mountain with a strange device upon it. When he learned of the discovery of the arrowhead by the Mormon Battalion in 1851, he knew it to be the mountain of his dream and ordered the establishment of a Mormon settlement in the valley below.

State 18 continues to a junction with the old Mormon Road, 16.7 *m.*, marked (R) by the WAGON WHEEL MONUMENT. The 11-mile roadway was built in 1851 to facilitate transportation of timber for building homes in the valley; its terminus was a sawmill that the Mormons had established near the present Camp Seeley.

The route leaves the chaparral of the lower slopes and enters the big timber country of pine, spruce, and oak.

At 17 *m.* State 18 becomes Rim of the World Drive and curves steadily eastward, 8,000 feet above sea level.

At 17.1 *m.* is a junction with Crestline Rd.

Left on this road 3 *m.* to CAMP SEELEY, a year-round playground maintained by the city of Los Angeles. The lodge (*rates reasonable*) is the social and musical center.

From ARROWHEAD HIGHLAND SUMMIT, 19.9 *m.* (5,174 alt.), slopes billow down to green valleys far below. A few yards from the road (R) is SPHINX ROCK, a corroded formation, 50 feet high, in the shape of a human head.

At 20 *m.* is a junction with an unpaved road.

Left on this winding road to CRESTLINE VILLAGE, 3 *m.* (4,850 alt., 500 pop.), shopping center for nearby resorts. Lying in a forest of evergreens and pines, the village has a view of desert, valley, and mountains. CRESTLINE BOWL is frequently the setting for plays, pageants, and dramas. Nearby are two ski tracks, a quarter-mile toboggan slide, and three ashcan slides.

The route continues upward on the well-banked highway. (*Drinking fountains every 2 miles.*)

BAYLIS PARK PICNIC GROUNDS is at 20.8 *m.* (*free; tables grilles, water, sanitary conveniences*).

RIM OF THE WORLD MONUMENT, 21.6 *m.* (6,150 alt.), is a crude boulder pile, dedicated by John Steven McGroarty, poet laureate of California, in 1932 in delayed commemoration of the highway's completion.

From CREST SUMMIT, 23.7 *m.* (5,756 alt.), is a comprehensive view southward. The drive drops gradually, circling buttes and plunging through parallel walls of dense forests. Here and there, through openings in the pines, the roofs of distant lodges and resorts appear.

At 24.5 *m.* is a junction with Arrowhead Lake Rd.

Left on this well-paved road 2 *m.* through a narrow, heavily timbered canyon to ARROWHEAD VILLAGE (5,109 alt., 510 pop.), on the south shore of LAKE ARROWHEAD, made up of shops, hotels, theaters, cafés, and dance halls, largely in the Norman style. Roads and footpaths radiate to the innumerable resorts on the forested rim of the lake, from auto camps to luxury hotels.

Right from Arrowhead Village 3 *m.* on Lake Rd. to ARROWHEAD DAM. Before the dam was built in 1901 to impound spring and drainage waters, the present lake region was a tree-studded, dry basin.

SKY FOREST POST OFFICE, (L), 25.6 *m.,* on the main road, serves a few scattered mountain homes (*garage and fueling accommodations*).

At 33.6 *m.* is a junction with an unpaved road.

Right on this road 0.7 *m.* to tiny ARROWBEAR LAKE, on the shores of which is the VILLAGE OF ARROWBEAR (7,800 alt., 75 pop.), with a post office and general store. Scattered along the lake front are numerous camps (*cabins; low rates*).

Rim of the World Drive rolls eastward in a succession of curves along the crest of the San Bernardino Range.

At 34.8 *m.* is a junction with Green Valley Rd.

Left on this paved road 4.5 *m.* to GREEN VALLEY LAKE, a tiny body of water in the verdant depths of Green Valley. Hundreds of privately owned lodges cling to the steeply sloping mountainsides beneath the tall cone-bearing pines and spruce.

At 37.6 *m.* is a junction with a hiking trail.

Right 3 *m.* on this trail up forested slopes to a lookout station on KELLER PEAK (7,863 alt.).

Rim of the World Drive drops gradually, for about 6 miles, and at
45.6 *m.* crosses the top of BIG BEAR DAM. There was a small natural
lake here in 1845, when Benjamin Davis Wilson, for whom Mount Wilson
was named, and a party of men searched the region for Indians who had
been stealing cattle from ranchers. They shot 22 bears on the trip; from
this incident the valley received its name. Gold was discovered here in
1860, and in the subsequent brief gold rush roads were built and scores
of small shacks sprang up. By 1880 the district was almost deserted. The
first dam was built in 1884 to provide San Bernardino Valley cities with
water. The present dam, 6,750 feet high, was completed in 1911. The
reservoir, BIG BEAR LAKE, seven miles long, has become the center of a
very popular year-round playground thronged with resorts.

From PINE KNOT VILLAGE, 50.1 *m.* (6,750 alt., 750 pop.), commercial
center of the Big Bear resort district, radiate a network of roads and
trails.

Rim of the World Drive roughly follows the contour of Big Bear Lake
to BIG BEAR CITY, 54.9 *m.* (6,860 alt., 500 pop.), on part of the former
27,000-acre Baldwin estate.

BALDWIN LAKE, 58.6 *m.* (6,674 alt.), a natural catch basin for mountain water, is normally about one-fifth the size of Big Bear Lake, but,
unlike the latter, has attracted few visitors.

Section c. SAN BERNARDINO *to* SANTA MONICA; 71.1 *m.* US 66.

West of San Bernardino US 66 runs along the base of the Sierra
Madre Mountains through the heart of a picture post card landscape—
orange groves overlooked by snowcapped peaks. The tile-roofed stucco
towns among the orchards along the way are starting points for roads
and trails into the forested mountains.

West of SAN BERNARDINO, 0 *m.*, is RIALTO, 3 *m.* (1,203
alt., 1,642 pop.), with several orange-packing plants. From here US
66 runs through billowing foothills past miles of citrus groves and
vineyards.

The boulevard skirts the northern edge of FONTANA, 5.2 *m.*
(1,242 alt., 6,120 pop.), in a section of small citrus, grape, walnut,
poultry, and rabbit farms.

West of Fontana vineyards cover the foothills, dotted with wineries.

CUCAMONGA, 14.5 *m.* (1,220 alt., 2,040 pop.), named for
CUCAMONGA PEAK (8,911 alt.), the shopping center of a grape-
and olive-growing district, has several wineries.

UPLAND, 17 *m.* (1,210 alt., 4,713 pop.), is a citrus-packing
community with nine fruit-packing plants, surrounded by 6,000 acres
of oranges and lemons.

CLAREMONT, 19.4 *m.* (1,155 alt., 2,719 pop.), in the midst
of citrus groves and vineyards, is a city of tree-lined streets and attractive residences. It has a citrus-packing plant and a number of small
factories, but is essentially a college town.

POMONA COLLEGE was founded in Pomona in 1887 by the Reverend
Charles B. Sumner, a New England Congregational minister. The
following January the Santa Fe Railway gave 500 acres of land for a
campus here; an unfinished hotel, now Sumner Hall, was the first

college building. In 1894 the enrollment was 47; in 1937 it was 900. The buildings, of various architectural styles, are scattered over 24 tree-shaded city blocks. In 1927 Pomona became the sponsor of a plan for a group of affiliated colleges, Claremont Colleges, Inc., of which Pomona (co-educational) was the first unit and Scripps College, the second.

The 50-acre campus of SCRIPPS COLLEGE FOR WOMEN is cut by city streets. Scripps became a unit of Claremont Colleges, Inc., through a gift of Miss Ellen Scripps. The enrollment (200) is limited by rigid scholastic requirements. The buildings are of modified Spanish design.

LA VERNE, 21.4 m. (1,050 alt., 2,860 pop.), is a citrus-packing center. Retail stores depend heavily on the patronage of LA VERNE COLLEGE students. La Verne originated as Lordsburg during the 1890 land boom. When the bubble burst, the promoters found themselves burdened with a $75,000 three-story hotel. In 1891 the Santa Fe Railway induced new settlers to come to the region, among them a group of Dunkards who later bought the hotel and founded Lordsburg College. In 1916, when the town changed its name to La Verne, the college did likewise. It is a co-educational institution with an enrollment of 250.

At 23.3 m. is a junction with San Dimas Canyon Rd.

Right on this road to SAN DIMAS CANYON PARK, 0.5 m., 110 acres of naturally wooded land (*picknicking facilities*) at the foot of the San Gabriel Mountains. Hiking trails lead into the mountains. The motor road winds up the canyon to WOLFSKILL FALLS, 11 m.

GLENDORA, 25.9 m. (776 alt., 2,761 pop.) another citrus-packing community, was founded in 1887 by George Whitcomb, a Chicago manufacturer, who coined the name from the word "glen" and his wife's name, "Ledora." The first commercial orange grove here, planted by John Cook in 1866, is still productive.

AZUSA, 27.6 m. (611 alt., 4,808 pop.), dating from the boom year of 1887, is yet another citrus-shipping center. The name is derived from *Asuksag-na,* name of an Indian village here.

The name of DUARTE, 31.9 m. (600 alt., 1,326 pop.), center of an old orange-growing district, commemorates Andreas Duarte, grantee of a 4,000-acre tract on the site, who constructed a ditch to bring water from San Gabriel Canyon for irrigation purposes.

MONROVIA, 34.3 m. (560 alt., 10,090 pop.), was laid out in 1886 by W. N. Monroe, when lots today worth many thousands of dollars were sold for $100. Monrovia is surrounded by orange, lemon, and avocado groves and other orchards. Poultry raising and small gardening are important in the vicinity. The town is noted for a wide variety of trees and shrubs; in the northern part of town, is a papaya plantation.

ARCADIA, 35.9 m. (479 alt., 5,216 pop.), is largely peopled by Los Angeles commuters. Poultry and rabbit raising is carried on here.

The Lyon Pony Express Museum, (L) 36.4 *m*. (*8-6; adm.
25¢, children 10¢*), where the highway widens triangularly to meet
converging Huntington Drive, houses the privately owned exhibit of
W. Parker Lyon, former mayor of Fresno, California. The frame
buildings achieve a deliberately ramshackle effect, purportedly resembling a ghost city, with a "pioneer" attendant guarding the entrance.
Inside is an 1849 bullet-scarred bar, an old gold scale, a vigilante bell,
several stagecoaches, and a collection of Indian mementos and curios
of the 1840's and 1850's—but little to justify the name "Pony Express."
At 36.4 *m*. is a junction with Huntington Drive.

Left here to the main entrance (R) of Santa Anita Race Track, 0.5 *m*.
(*racing 1:30 p.m. weekdays, except Mon., during 2-month winter season
beginning about New Year's Day; adm. $1.10, parking 25¢*), named for the
"Lucky" Baldwin rancho, which it adjoins (R). It is the $1,000,000 home
of midwinter racing events that include a $100,000 handicap. Blue build-
ings with white roofs spread along one side of the 1-mile oval track,
backed by the lofty peaks of the San Gabriel Range. The grandstand seats
30,000; the stables can hold 1,500 horses. During the racing season the
500-acre scene is one of excitement and holiday bustle, thronged with
notables, among them Hollywood celebrities. The season's wagers amount
to more than $25,000,000.

SAN MARINO, 4.6 *m*. (557 alt., 3,730 pop.), has numerous attractive
bungalows and palatial mansions on the flat basin of San Gabriel Valley
and in the surrounding foothills. The city, named by the railroad magnate
and patron of arts, Henry E. Huntington, bans all structures except one-
family residences and supervises even the cost and architectural design of
proposed buildings.

At 4.7 *m*. is a junction with Monterey Rd.; R. here 0.5 *m*. to the Huntington Library and Art Gallery (*open 1:15-4:30 p.m. weekdays, except
Mondays, and first and third Sundays each month; adm. free, but by special
advance card only*). Massive wrought-iron gates (L) give access to the
207-acre landscaped park that surrounds the two white marble buildings.
Founded by Collis P. Huntington, the institution was established with a
self-perpetuating board of trustees in 1919 to house a valuable collection
of paintings and art objects assembled by Huntington over a period of
years. It has three principal divisions: the Library, the Art Gallery, and
the Botanical Gardens. The latter contain Japanese, rose, and cactus
gardens and a spacious sloping lawn planted with sub-tropical trees and
shrubs. The library contains 200,000 printed books, 4,000 manuscripts,
and more than 800,000 letters and documents, confined to English and
American literature, history and incunabula. Of special interest are the
Gutenberg Bible of the year 1455; the Ellesmere Chaucer on vellum; the
manuscripts of Milton's *Comus*, Tennyson's *Idylls of the King*, Stevenson's
A Child's Garden of Verses, Ruskin's *Seven Lamps of Architecture*, Kipling's *Recessional*, Mark Twain's *The Prince and the Pauper*, and Benjamin
Franklin's *Autobiography*. Among letters and documents are a large col-
lection of Lincolniana, a collection of Washington's letters, and Christopher
Columbus' letter announcing the discovery of America. The Art Gallery,
housed in what was once Huntington's mansion, contains a world-famous
collection of 18th century British paintings, including a large group of
Gainsboroughs, among them *The Blue Boy*, Sir Joshua Reynolds' *The
Tragic Muse, Pinkie* by Sir Thomas Lawrence, and canvases by such
painters as Raeburn, Romney, Hoppner, Turner, Cotes, Constable; and the
Americans, Copley, and West. Flemish and Italian paintings of the 15th
and 16th centuries, and a distinguished collection of porcelains and tapestries are in the west wing of the library.

SIERRA MADRE, 36.9 *m.* (835 alt., 3,550 pop.), is a foothill town surrounded by the deep green of orange groves. A trellised wistaria on the FENNEL ESTATE (*adm. 10¢*), Carter St. and Hermos Ave., planted in 1894, extends over an acre of ground, and its blooming season—March 10 to April 1—is occasion for the Sierra Madre Wistaria Fête, held annually since 1921.

At 40.2 *m.* is a junction with San Gabriel Blvd. (State 19).

Left on San Gabriel Blvd. to Mission Dr. 4 *m.;* R. on Mission Dr. to SAN GABRIEL, 5.1 *m.* (426 alt., 7,224 pop.), a town populated largely by Los Angeles commuters. San Gabriel's chief business is serving tourists. It was from San Gabriel that the Spanish governor, Felipe de Neve, marched with 44 soldiers, Indians, and Mexican colonists in September 1781 to found the pueblo of Nuestra Señora la Reina de Los Angeles.

MISSION SAN GABRIEL ARCANGEL, 314 Mission Dr. (*open 8-6; adm. 25¢*), now a parish church, was founded in 1771 by order of Fray Junípero Serra. The small band of monks sent from San Diego to establish San Gabriel were met upon arrival by a large band of painted savages who swooped down upon them. Resourcefully, the priests unfurled their banner on which was a painting of the Madonna, whereupon—so the story goes—the warriors threw down their weapons, made submission, and brought gifts. With energy the priests constructed their mission and founded a prosperous community. Their chief troubles were due to the turbulence of the Spanish soldiers stationed with them. When one of them stole an Indian's wife and beheaded the husband for objecting, "it was only," remarks a commentator, "by miraculous power that the missionaries were able to keep the Indians in hand." The original building, swept by river floods, was replaced by the present church in 1800-1806, and partly rebuilt after the 1812 earthquake. The church, rectangular in plan, is without the customary front towers. The exterior is relieved only by slender buttresses that line the long side walls and rise above the roof, forming pointed finials. The façade is unadorned except for religious figures set in arched niches high in the face of the two front buttresses. The gable end has a simple classic pediment. At the rear is a part of the patio, with one wing of the mission house and a vine-covered gable belfry. The main altar of the church is the most decorative feature of the mission. Its ornate retablo and reredos antedate the church and were probably brought from Mexico. The painted and gilded figures of the Saints, the elaborate scrolls and other ornaments were executed by Indians. Other notable features include the dado and curious dado crestings, painted on the walls.

The MISSION PLAYHOUSE, 320 Mission Dr., today a motion-picture theater, is the former home of California's epic, *The Mission Play,* by John Steven McGroarty. Next door is the GRAPEVINE ADOBE, advertised as the birthplace of Ramona. In a walled patio is a grapevine with a spread of 100 feet, bearing the date of 1771; it was actually planted in 1861.

Among San Gabriel's remaining Adobes of early days are the PURCELL ADOBE, 308 Mission Dr., which was built in 1768 to house the Spanish comandante and the padres while the mission was being erected; the MAY PLACE, 725 Carmelita St., built in 1851 by J. R. Evertson, Los Angeles' first census taker; the VIGARE ADOBE, 616 Ramona St., built by a soldier of the mission guard; and LA CASA VIEJA DE LÓPEZ (the old house of López), 330 N. Santa Anita St., believed to be one of the mission buildings.

West of its junction with San Gabriel Blvd., US 66 runs along Colorado Ave. through charming residential outskirts to the business center of Pasadena.

PASADENA, 43.2 *m.* (855 alt., 70,096 pop.) (*see PASADENA*).

Right from Colorado Ave. in Pasadena on Linda Vista Ave., which becomes La Cañada Rd., to Michigan Ave.; L. on Michigan Ave., which becomes Foothill Blvd., to Haskell Ave.; R. on Haskell Ave. to Angeles Crest Highway; L. on Angeles Crest Highway, which at this point enters the San Gabriel Mountains.

The highway follows a ledge over winding ARROYO SECO (Sp., dry creek). It proceeds upward toward the chaparral-covered slopes through spruce, oak, and bay trees, and rocky stretches partly covered with yucca. As the ascent continues gorges become deeper, canyon sides steeper, and the contorted strata of the early part of the route yield to the vast granite core of the San Gabriel Mountains.

NINO CANYON LOOKOUT STATION, 8.8 m., provides an excellent view (R) of BROWN MOUNTAIN (4,485 alt.), named for two sons of John Brown, the anti-slavery revolutionist, who settled in one of its remote glens after the Civil War.

WOODWARDIA CANYON, 11.4 m. (2,700 alt.), is an idyllic, fern-strewn gorge, named for the *Woodwardia radicans*.

At 11.9 m. is the junction with Dark Canyon trail.

Left on this trail 1.5 m. through GRIZZLY BEAR FLATS to BIG TUJUNGA CANYON, a wild region abounding in summer with rattlesnakes.

GEORGE'S GAP, 15.6 m. (3,750 alt.), provides a view westward. The name is a tribute to the culinary achievements of a cook stationed at an early ranger camp here. Across the canyon rises the gray granite peak of MOUNT JOSEPHINE (5,520 alt.). Beyond in the distance is CONDOR PEAK (5,430 alt.), named for the rare California condor, which rivals in size the great vulture-like Andean condor.

LADYBUG CANYON, 18 m. (3,650 alt.), is so-called because it is a State-maintained hibernation refuge for the red and black beetle used in combating scale and other citrus pests.

RED BOX DIVIDE, 20.3 m. (4,666 alt.), is the crest of the ridge dividing the drainage areas of the San Gabriel and Arroyo Seco Rivers. The divide was named for a large red box, a landmark for many years, in which early forest rangers kept fire-fighting equipment. The steep, rocky headlands of Mount Wilson in the distance are seen from this place; below lies the jumbled maze of torrent-cut canyons wrought by the two forks of the twisting San Gabriel River. Far beyond is MOUNT BALDY (10,080 alt.), snowcapped half the year, and behind it a saw-toothed sky line.

1. Right from Red Box Divide 2 m. on a trail to a secondary trail; L. here to the SUMMIT of MOUNT SAN GABRIEL, 5.5 m.

2. Right from Red Box Divide on a paved road is OPID'S RESORT, 1.5 m. (*rates reasonable*), in picturesque West Fork Canyon of the San Gabriel River.

Right from Angeles Crest Highway at Red Box Divide on Mount Wilson Rd. around sharp, blind curves.

The SADDLE, 22.7 m. (5,116 alt.), is a narrow ledge of rock bridging Mounts San Gabriel and Wilson; R. from the Saddle 2.9 m. on a trail to MOUNT LOWE.

CREST LOOKOUT, 24.1 m. (5,622 alt.), offers a sweeping view on three sides of jagged peaks and deep canyons; R. from Crest Lookout 1.2 m. on a hiking trail to MOUNT HARVARD. In 1889 a telescope was mounted on this peak by observers from Harvard University. The site was abandoned after one year because of the number of rattlesnakes.

MOUNT WILSON, 25.7 m. (5,710 alt.) (*adm. to grounds 50¢ a car, 25¢ a pedestrian—refunded to overnight guests; hotel rates reasonable*), is topped by a 1,050-acre, much eroded plateau in Angeles National Forest that is owned by the Mount Wilson Hotel Company, which has leased the land occupied by the Mount Wilson Observatory (*see below*) to the

Carnegie Institution for 100 years at a nominal sum. Benjamin Davis Wilson, for whom the peak is named, blazed a trail in 1864 to the summit, where he found two abandoned cabins on the plateau. Wilson's trail, early popular with hikers and riders, was used until the Mount Wilson Toll Road Company built the paved toll road. The hotel is a low, rustic building of stucco, with a wide veranda looking out over the vast valley.

MOUNT WILSON OBSERVATORY, whose white buildings, towers, and domes are scattered among the trees, is operated by the Carnegie Institution. The first telescope was set up in 1904. Originally planned primarily for solar research, "the necessity for seeking, among the stars and nebulae, for evidence as to the past and future stages of solar and stellar life" soon became evident, early resulting in a broadening of the scope of the observatory. Today eight telescopes are in use. There is a technical library of 13,000 volumes and 10,000 pamphlets. The institution maintains a large laboratory and optical shop in Pasadena.

The 100-INCH TELESCOPE (*shown daily from 1:30-2:30*) with a huge reflecting mirror, is housed in a large white dome northeast of the hotel. This telescope has helped to push the boundaries of the known universe out to about 100,000,000 light years. It admits 250,000 times more light than the unaided human eye and 2,500 times as much light as did the telescope with which Galileo began the modern era of astronomy in 1610. Images seen by the giant eye are recorded on photographic plates.

The 60-INCH TELESCOPE (*open for cosmic observation Fri. at 7:30-8:30 p.m.; adm. passes obtained by mail from the Carnegie Institution, Pasadena, two weeks in advance*) also has a reflecting mirror. Its dome is near the 100-inch telescope.

The 12-INCH TELESCOPE (*open for cosmic observation with accompanying lecture daily, except Mon., at 7:30 p.m.*) is in the museum. It is principally used to demonstrate the public lectures.

The SUN TELESCOPE (*not open*) is housed in a 150-foot tower that rises above the pine trees near a cluster of low, snub-nosed domes. This instrument, which produces an image of the sun 16 inches in diameter, is elevated to prevent reflected heat from interfering with the accurate operation of the delicate mirrors. To increase the steadiness of the lenses and mirrors at so great a height, an inner tower supports the instruments, an outer tower the dome.

The MUSEUM (*open 1:30-2 p.m.*), adjacent to the 100-inch telescope dome, shows transparencies of the more spectacular photographs made with the giant telescope.

LOS ANGELES, 54.2 *m.* (250 alt., 1,283,859 pop.) (*see LOS ANGELES*).

Los Angeles is at junctions with US 60-70-99 (*see TOUR 13b*) and US 101 (*see TOUR 2c*).

Right from Figueroa St. on Sunset Blvd. to a junction with Santa Monica Blvd.; L. on Santa Monica Blvd. to HOLLYWOOD, 57.6 *m.* (400 alt., 185,847 pop.) (*see HOLLYWOOD*).

BEVERLY HILLS, 62.2 *m.* (260 to 325 alt., 17,429 pop.), is the home of many luminaries of the cinema world. Standing like a small island almost surrounded by the irregular boundaries of Los Angeles, it is an independent city laid out in 1907 by a former resident of Beverly, Mass. Many of the earlier motion picture stars built homes here because the then undeveloped rolling foothills offered ample space for large estates near Hollywood studios and ocean beaches. Today it has become almost traditional for the principal screen stars to be represented in the community by large homes, partly because of their publicity value; and Beverly Hills residential architecture has achieved a new note of splendor. Most of the mansions are in the foothills; in the level lowland area south of Sunset Blvd. are smaller bungalows, bungalow courts, apartment houses, and hotels. Many privately owned concerns conduct tours through the city, and up-to-date guide books listing the names and the constantly changing addresses of the well-known residents are available (*see also HOLLYWOOD: Homes of Movie Stars*).

SANTA MONICA, 71.1 *m.* (140 alt., 37,146 pop.) (*see TOUR 2B*), is at the junction with US 101 Alt. (*see TOUR 2B*).

⋘⋘⋘⋘⋘⋘⋘⋘⋘⋘⋘⋙⋙⋙⋙⋙⋙⋙⋙⋙⋙⋙⋙⋙

Tour 13

(Quartzsite, Ariz.) — Blythe — Indio — Beaumont — Riverside — Los Angeles; US 60-70.
Arizona line to Los Angeles, 231.7 *m.*

Paved roadbed throughout; open all seasons.
Route paralleled by Southern Pacific R.R. between Indio and Los Angeles.
Accommodations adequate; service stations at infrequent intervals between Blythe and Indio; good auto courts.
Caution: For side trips on desert roads, carry good tires and extra food, gasoline and water. After cloudbursts, when water fills highway dips (indicated by pairs of stakes marked with two black bands), wait for water to run off, a matter of only a few minutes.

The west-bound traveler's introduction to US 60-70 is somewhat misleading. On the shelf bordering the west bank of the Colorado, all is green and cool; but as the route climbs its western margin, it encounters desert. The highway crosses a changing waste, now lumped into derby-shaped hills, now swept into sand piles that are often leveled smooth by the wind. On both sides, thorny vegetation stretches gray and dusty green to the flanking ranges. In the daytime, little animal life appears beyond an occasional mouse flashing across the asphalt with the urgency of a practised jaywalker. (*See FLORA AND FAUNA and TOUR 11a.*) At Indio, as the mountain barrier, for so many miles a hazy bulk running across the windshield, comes in to closer focus, the highway strikes boldly northwest tow rd the San Bernardino and San Jacinto ranges. From San Gorgonio Pass, it coasts down the long slope through pasture-lands, groves of fruit trees and walnuts, and wide green expanses of vineyards. The towns grow larger and noiser and the rural sections more urban as the road runs between gaudy palisades of billboards, gas stations, and clapboard eating houses into far-flung Los Angeles.

The Natural Setting

YOSEMITE FALLS, YOSEMITE NATIONAL PARK

MT. SHASTA

OWENS LAKE FROM CERRO GORDO

SAND DUNES

SIERRAS FROM OWENS VALLEY

PEDRO POINT, GULF OF FARRALON

MT. WHITNEY, FROM WHITNEY PORTAL

DONNER LAKE, FROM DONNER PASS

DANTE'S VIEW, DEATH VALLEY

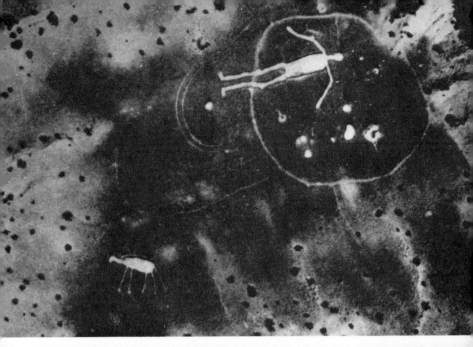

INDIAN PICTOGRAPH IN CALIFORNIA DESERT

ALONG THE MERCED RIVER, YOSEMITE VALLEY

DEER, SEQUOIA NATIONAL PARK

LUMBERING. A REDWOOD 18 FEET IN DIAMETER

The route was opened in 1862, when a stage line began carrying prospectors from California to the newly-discovered gold fields in western Arizona. The first stage, a 6-horse Concord of the type familiar to devotees of Western films, traveled from Los Angeles to La Paz in 12 days, carrying passengers for $40 apiece. Its drivers were murdered by a bandit whom they had attempted to hang; he later pleaded self-defense and was acquitted. Another party of travelers on the route was massacred by Indians. The stage line was operated until the railroad put it out of business in 1877. Over this road, in 1908, was run the first Los Angeles-to-Phoenix auto race, which the Los Angeles *Times* of that day hailed as "the most hazardous race ever undertaken." The victor, a steam-driven car, negotiated the 455 miles in 30 hours. The sparse population along the route engages chiefly in catering to travelers, occasionally in farming, mining, or health-seekers.

Section a. ARIZONA LINE *to* EASTERN JUNCTION US 99; *101 m. US 60-70.*

Between the Colorado River and Indio US 60-70 sweeps across the desert between distant mountain ranges, for long stretches in a virtually straight line.

The Arizona line, 0 *m.,* marked by the COLORADO (*ruddy*) RIVER, is crossed 19 miles west of Quartzsite, Ariz. The Colorado River was called Ahan Yava Kothickwa (all the water there is) by the Indians.

At **2.8** *m.* is a junction with State 195.

Right on State 195 to a series of spectacular INDIAN INTAGLIOS, 18 *m.* On the mesa extending westward from the bluffs of the river lie three sets of colossal figures of men and animals, cut into the white rock substratum by Indians in the remote past. The great size of these figures —the largest man is 167 feet long and has an arm spread of 164 feet— prevented their character from being recognized until they were first photographed from the air in 1932. The human figures are well proportioned, but the animals excite conjecture: they resemble horses, antelopes, or deer, but their identification is complicated by long buffalo tails. These figures are centuries old; beyond that little is known of their history or meaning.

BLYTHE, **4.5** *m.* (1,020 pop.), is a new town. Until 1910, all the settlers in the region were clustered on the Arizona bank of the river. In 1877 Thomas Blythe, an Englishman, filed claims on 40,000 acres along the river under the Swamp and Overflow Act, believing that this area could be turned into a new Nile Valley; but before he could develop it, he died of a paralytic stroke. His estate, in litigation for 21 years, was finally sold to the syndicate that platted the town in 1910. The farmers who were drawn to Blythe by the lure of rich overflow land soon had to contend with the source of the land's fertility. The powerful Colorado went on a yearly spree, cutting through the levees. Blythe residents fought the river, sank $4,500,000 in the battle, and in time lost 90 percent of their property to the State because of inability to liquidate the immense debt the river had forced upon them. The building of Boulder Dam ended the unequal struggle.

Blythe presents the first California superlative on this route; the fields lining the highway and running southward into the Palo Verde Valley grow long staple cotton, modestly proclaimed to be the best in the world. The highway traverses a plain checkered with snowy white patches and rich green alfalfa fields, and runs between flanking feathery green tamarisks.

Over a low ridge suddenly appears the COLORADO DESERT. This low sink was formed ages ago when the Coast Range—then twice its present height—cracked, the rear slope falling flat at the base of the western half, which remained erect. In time the scouring of wind and rain will wear down the ranges and plane off the region until it has the drab monotony of the older deserts. In the meantime—a two-million-year meantime—travelers may enjoy the cruel beauties of a desert in its youth, the pale pastels of its encircling mountains blending with the delicate grays and dusty tans of its rolling floor.

At 36.5 *m.* is a junction with a dirt road.

> Left on this road, which strikes off through the brush toward the CHUCKWALLA MOUNTAINS to CORN SPRINGS, 8 *m.*, an ancient Indian campsite, still strewn with shards and artifacts. Indians lived on the desert at unknown periods, spacing their camps over a long arc that curves to the northwest, apparently adhering to the course of a dried-up river.

DESERT CENTER, 49 *m.* (905 alt., 125 pop.), is a way station (*all accommodations*) where travelers mail, over a 70-day period, an average of 18,000 post cards purchased on the spot.

The COLORADO RIVER AQUEDUCT, 49.4 *m.,* veers toward the highway. Although at that point it runs underground and can be detected only by the long scar it has left on the plain, it lies within view, a great silver snake ascending the backbone of a ridge (Eagle Mountain Pumps Lift) to the northwest. Constructed at a cost of $220,000,000, the aqueduct carries water to 13 southern California cities; five pumping stations lift the water 1,000 feet, the highest point being the Hayfield Lift (R), 62.2 *m.,* and syphons draw it down the western slope to its original level. The pipe keeps pace with the highway, running for 17 miles under the COACHELLA MOUNTAINS until it cuts across the road 2 miles east of Cabazon and dives through the towering San Jacintos.

The highway passes between the OROCOPIA (abundance of gold) MOUNTAINS and the EAGLE RANGE, named for a rumored colony of eagles.

At 101 *m.* is the junction with US 99 (*see TOUR 3e*).

Section b. JUNCTION US 99 *to* LOS ANGELES; *130.7 m.* US 60-70-99.

Northwest of Indio US 60-70 traverses sand plains, rises through San Gorgonio Pass and descends into the fertile valleys and populous areas of the coast.

US 99 (*see TOUR 3e*) unites northward with US 60-70, 0 *m.*, 2 miles south of Indio.

INDIO, 2 *m.* (−22 alt., 3,500 pop.), named for the large number of Indians who comprised the settlement when it was a railroad construction camp, is primarily a highway service town. The main street is lined with rows of gas stations and garages. Although the town was established in 1876 as a distribution point for railroad freight, 50 years of rail service brought more vagrants to it than settlers. It was not until the highways drew traffic that the town began to grow. Then the areas around the town began to fill, and Indio now serves as a shopping center for producers of dates, cotton, and alfalfa. Twenty-ton Diesel trucks rumble through the streets the clock around. Tourist travel has modified the town's spirit somewhat; once known as a tough spot, it now has such urban amenities as a circulating library, a theater, stores with windows dressed in city style, venetian blinds, and similar frills.

Left from Indio on State 111—the Palm Springs Highway—which crosses Coachella Valley through date orchards and orange groves. The desert is encircled by mountains that are snow-covered during the winter and spring months. Long rows of date palms flank the roadway west of Indio. Far to the west the San Jacinto (Sp., St. Hyacinth) Mountains fall away into foothills and disappear.

SAN JACINTO PEAK (10,987 alt.) is visible for a hundred miles.

The highway is bordered by tamarisk trees (also known as athel trees), and by subtropical date palms looking like planted pompons, mingling their fronds high overhead. Just under the green density of the natural ceiling, the heavy date clusters hang, encased in paper or burlap cones during the early fall months when the fruit is ripening. The cones themselves, transparent in the filtered sunlight, resemble great bell-like blossoms, suspended above the long, still alleys of the groves. In spring bloom, the trees display whitish, candelabra-like spikes under the dome of the over-hanging foliage. Principally of the Deglet Noor variety, these trees were imported and set out in this region in 1904. They require unusual care, their natural thirst necessitating heavy irrigation at least twice a month. Dates can be purchased from the many roadside stands—along this route disguised as pyramids, Bedouin tents, or Persian shrines.

INDIAN WELLS, 8 *m.*, are fresh-water springs.

Tamarisks, tall cottonwoods, hung with bright green clusters of mistletoe in winter, border the highway at intervals. Many small irrigation canals, with water brought from deep wells, weave back and forth under the road. Gaudy signboards invite a visitor to the ranches, to sample the fruit, and to view the exhibits of date culture.

At 13 *m.* is the junction with State 74 (*see TOUR 6e*). West of this junction the whole 35-mile range of the Little San Bernardino Mountains is visible (L). Running close under the shadow of the San Jacinto Mountains (R), the highway is in darkness during late afternoon and at such times offers an excellent place from which to observe the shifting colors upon the desert and mountain walls as the sun nears the horizon.

The ANCIENT BEACH LINE is plainly visible (R) along mountain slopes and canyon walls (*see TOUR 3e*). Along the beach line, fossils and other evidence of former life are found.

CATHEDRAL CITY, 20.3 *m.* (*motor courts*), is a small trading center at the mouth of Cathedral Canyon.

At 25.6 *m* is the junction with a poor dirt road; L. on it 2.3 *m.* through great groves of palms, to the mouth of ANDREAS CANYON (R), and past MURRAY CANYON (R), 2.7 *m.*, to PALM CANYON NATIONAL MONUMENT, 5 *m.* At the head of Palm Canyon is a grove of 5,000 California fan palms, the only palm native to the western United States, ranging in age from seedlings to trees thousands of years old. Many of the giant palms show traces of fire on their lower trunks. Legend has it that the Cahuillas, who picked the clusters of berries from the palms for food, always burned the trees that belonged to a single family when the head of the family died, to enable the deceased person to carry his berry clusters with him on his journey.

At 12 *m.* is the junction with a canyon road; L. 0.5 *m.* on this road, which winds under the shadow of TAHQUITZ PEAK (8,826 alt.) to a parking space, from which a trail leads into TAHQUITZ CANYON. At the entrance to the canyon is TAHQUITZ BOWL, an outdoor amphitheater in which a play is given each summer. This canyon, like Palm, Murray, and Andreas Canyons, is in the Agua Caliente Reservation and the Indians exact minor tariffs from the tourists.

A creek flows down through deep rock gorges and splashes over an 80-foot drop into a pool, creating, during summer storms, a windy roar that the Indians called the voice of Tahquitz—a spirit who feeds on human flesh. There are many excellent trails ascending the canyon sides and affording good views.

PALM SPRINGS, 27.2 *m.* (430 alt., pop. subject to seasonal changes), one of the newest playgrounds of rich America, has been successively the domain of Cahuilla Indians, a stagecoach stop, and a desert home for the convalescent and tubercular. Today this ultrasmart winter resort for movie stars and for people who like and can afford to live where and as movie stars live, gleams as brightly as a new toy village. Its buildings are uniformly of California pseudo-Spanish architecture: the white, lemon, or buff-colored dwellings, entered by doors painted bright red, blue, or yellow, are surmounted by red tile roofs and enclosed by wooden fences, bordered by rows of pink and white oleanders or the green feathery plumage of tamarisk trees. Here are branches of the most expensive New York and Los Angeles shops; golf courses and hotels that range from the palatial to the modestly magnificent; private and public schools and no lack of masseurs and masseuses; dude cowhands for atmosphere and branch brokerage offices for the bigger businessmen.

First known as Agua Caliente (hot water)—so named by De Anza in 1774 because of its hot springs—the settlement dates from 1876, when the Southern Pacific first laid down its tracks through Coachella Valley. Until 1913 Palm Springs remained a sleepy little hamlet with a single store and a roadside inn on a poor desert road. A nearby gold mine, the Virginia Dale, offered the only attraction to people in search of a living, and the warm dry climate (average noontime temperature, 81°; average evening temperature, 4·°) made it an excellent but little known health resort. Then Hollywood, early in the 1930's, discovered the climatic and topographical charm of the little village resting on a shelf of the San Jacinto Mountain base at the edge of the desert. A new highway was cut through, Los Angeles and New York promoters got to work, and the modern town sprang up almost with the speed of a movie set.

Here one finds the desert safely pushed to the borders of a transplanted section of Hollywood Blvd. Guests sprint about town on bicycles, sip cocktails, play table tennis, explore the nearby desert on horseback, or, relaxing in some hotel garden, enjoy the lengthening shadow of the San

Jacinto and the quiet of the land stretching out to the eastern hills. After dark they visit the night clubs, casinos, and movies.

The town's SULPHUR SPRINGS lie just east of the business district on the AGUA CALIENTE RESERVATION; here the Indians who own the property maintain a bathhouse on the spot where their forefathers camped for hundreds of years. The commercial competition of the Indians has aroused the bitter antagonism of the townspeople.

Each year La Fiésta de los Monos (the feast of the images) is held on the reservation—now in a somewhat corrupt form owing to the presence of prosperous strangers who want quaint entertainment. This ancient Cahuilla rite is designed to aid the spirit in departing from this earth after death. When the number of deaths in a family reaches eight, the survivors gather to dance, wail, and chant. They make effigies of the deceased on wooden frames five feet high; dressing, painting, and decorating them is an elaborate ceremony lasting several days, during which the family is obliged to entertain a great crowd of tribal visitors. When the images have been completed, the tribe has an all-night dance; money is distributed among the guests. At dawn, when Lucero, the morning star, reaches a certain height, the images are burned in a pit, and their released spirits depart to the upper regions.

Directly west of Palm Springs is TACHEVAN (dry rock) CANYON; a short walk leads to a mountain stream trickling among brightly painted rocks—an ideal picnic site.

Right 0.5 m. from Palm Springs on a county road to the PALM SPRINGS AIRPORT.

North of Palm Springs small white stucco and plaster buildings, housing the offices of Los Angeles realtors and promoters, border State 111 more frequently than the date palms. Mesquite-covered desert land stretches northwest to the brown foothills of the Little San Bernardino Mountains.

At 37.7 m. is the junction with US 60-70-99 (see below).

Northwest of Indio US 60-70-99 runs over gradually rising sand plains past whitish billows of mesquite-spotted sand dunes to WHITE-WATER, 30.1 m. (1,130 alt., 100 pop.), a service stop under a grove of cottonwoods.

At 33.6 m. is a junction with State 111 (see above).

Near the road just north of this junction point is the OLIVER POWER GENERATOR, a curious funnel-shaped tube looking like the barrel of a giant blunderbuss, tiger-striped with an orange-lettered advertisement. It was designed to harness the wind that rushes down the pass and to transform it into electric power by means of propellers. The device worked, but promoters oversold the stock and discredited the scheme.

The highway rises westward through low SAN GORGONIO PASS, between the peaks of SAN JACINTO and SAN GOR-GONIO, both of which are usually snowcapped. Indians had used the pass for their winter trek to lower levels, but hostile tribes at top and bottom did much to discourage white travel. In 1862 the stage route to Ehrenberg started down the grade, but later shifted its terminus to Yuma and selected another route that took the stages through more miles of mountainous territory before dropping them to the hot floor of the desert. Passengers had protested at the frequency with which they had to clamber out and help the stages out of the sand.

Through this pass winds blow ceaselessly from the ocean to the desert. East winds seldom occur, but when they do Los Angeles wilts under blistering "Santa Anas," dry wind storms. These reversals usually occur on the rare occasions when rain strikes the desert. Foggy days on the coast intensify the rush of air toward the east, causing the harsh desert winds of April and May.

Along the highway long freight trains are frequently seen, two engines herding them slowly and powerfully up the grade. The Southern Pacific laid its tracks through here in 1875, after first winning the friendliness of the Cahuilla by promising them free rides.

CABAZON, 40.1 m. (1,791 alt., 100 pop.), is a Southern Pacific R.R. town with a roundhouse for the auxiliary engines that help push passenger and freight trains over the pass. The name, a corruption of the Spanish word *cabezón* (big head), was given by Spaniards, according to legend, for a local Indian chief with a very large head. The almost continuous winds from the pass have given the town a sandblasted appearance.

Upward through country increasingly green as the summit (2,559 alt.) is approached, the highway climbs into BANNING, 46.1 m. (2,350 alt., 2,750 pop.), laid out in 1883 by Phineas Banning, stage-coach operator. Banning is in a fruit-producing area.

Within recent years a camel frisked about the neighborhood of Banning, finally making such a nuisance of himself that he was hunted down by a posse and shot. This was undoubtedly an aged survivor of the government caravans that crossed the desert prior to the Civil War. For various reasons—the camels terrified horses, their feet were cut by stones, and the officers in charge hated the slow bad-tempered beasts —the experiment was closed; but the participating animals remained a problem for many years afterward. Some wild camels were sighted on the desert as late as 1890, and even now newcomers are solemnly assured they can expect to run into them at any moment.

1. Right from Banning on a dirt road to the MORONGO INDIAN RESERVATION, 5.5 m. (*appointments to visit reservation should be made with Indian Agent at Banning*). On this reservation, named for "Captain John" Morongo, a great Indian leader, live 294 Indians of the Cahuilla tribe and Serrano clan.

2. Right from Banning on a good dirt road through Banning Canyon, where desert and mountain meet in vivid contrast, to HIGHLAND SPRINGS, 2 m., a resort among mountains, streams, canyons, and pine forests. On the hotel grounds is an INDIAN GRINDING STONE, left by prehistoric tribes.

At INTERNATIONAL PARK, 2.5 m., another resort area, a Japanese cherry blossom festival is held each spring.

BOGART BOWL, a natural amphitheater adjacent to International Park, draws picnickers and receives wide notice as the focal point of an ambitious international peace program and as the setting of an annual Easter sunrise service.

BEAUMONT, 52.1 m. (2,559 alt., 1,331 pop.), spreads over a plain at the summit of the pass. The region was opened to Yankees in 1853 by a herd of straying cattle. Fast in pursuit, Dr. I. W. Smith, a Mormon, followed the errant beeves from San Bernardino to their final stopping point, directly north of the townsite. Smith at once began to pioneer in the region, beating off grizzlies and fleeing from Indians, until the area became somewhat sophisticated by the addition of a stage station and later a hotel (1884). Beaumont, called San Gorgonio from 1884 to 1887, did not grow with the customary California speed until a development company shifted the townsite and publicized the regional potentialities for fruit-growing. Apples were planted in vain; but cherries and almonds prospered; each spring thousands drive to see the cherry blossoms that cover the region with a sea of white billows.

At Beaumont is the junction where US 99-70 swings R. (*see TOUR 3d*), forming an alternate route between Beaumont and Ontario (*see TOUR 3d*). US 60 continued westward.

At the western margin of Beaumont the stately eucalyptus tree appears. These trees, imported from Australia in the belief that they could be exploited for their oil and hardwood, were set out in great tracts all over the State. But the trees proved practically valueless and they are now merely graceful additions to the coastal scenery. They grow with extreme rapidity, sometimes reaching a height of 175 feet in 25 years. The highway begins a winding passage through the MORENO BADLANDS, a country that hardly deserves the name. Through gullies and canyons appear foothills green with live-oaks. In spring these hills are gay with blue lupin, yellow wild mustard, and golden California poppies. US 60 next traverses a broad expanse of open land; great tracts of the reddish soil are used for the growing of grain, principally wheat, oats, and barley.

At 71 *m*. is a junction with US 395 (*see TOUR 6e*); which unites briefly westward with US 60.

RIVERSIDE, 76.5 *m*. (851 alt., 29,696 pop.), with wide streets bordered with palm trees and roses, has street lights shaped like the Indian rain cross—one light is at the top of the tall pole, two others are suspended from the crossarm. The first white man to tramp this soil came from over the Sierra. In 1774 Captain Juan de Anza, on his way from Arizona to Monterey, built a bridge across the flowing Santa Ana River here. The area was part of the Jurupa Rancho of Don Juan Bandini, mentioned by Dana in his *Two Years Before the Mast*. The discovery of gold brought in the Yankees, who soon elbowed the Mexicans out of their holdings. A flood in 1862, followed by two years of drought, decimated the herds and forced intensive development of water resources and agriculture. In 1870 the Southern California Colony Association purchased the ranchos and surveyed the Riverside townsite. Soon the hacienda gave way to the cottage.

The city's showplace is the block-square, privately owned GLEN-WOOD MISSION INN, bounded by Sixth, Seventh, Main, and Orange Sts. Its Patio Dining Court, Spanish Cloisters, and Courts of the Birds and the Bells are proudly displayed to visitors. Within the inn are collections of art objects and of pioneer relics.

Riverside is the trade center of the citrus ranches. Here in the broad valley of the Santa Ana River, the popular navel orange was developed. In 1873 a Riverside woman obtained from the Department of Agriculture at Washington two cuttings of a "sport" variety of orange, imported from Brazil. This orange had suddenly appeared on one tree in Bahia, secreting more juice and abandoning its ancient custom of reproducing by seed. It was the first seedless orange. Abetted in its waywardness by orchardists, it has been widely propagated. When the first trees were set out the shoots were so much in demand that a price of $1 a dozen was set upon them. Thieves stole so many shoots that it became necessary to surround the trees with a high barbed wire fence. The surviving PARENT NAVEL ORANGE TREE stands at the corner of Magnolia and Arlington Aves.

When John W. North, founder of Riverside, inaugurated a tree-planting program in 1876, he first proposed to line Magnolia Avenue with magnolia trees. He changed his mind, however, when he learned that magnolias cost $2 each, whereas eucalypti and peppers cost only 5¢ each; he planted the latter but kept the name.

The CITRUS EXPERIMENT STATION (*open weekdays*), at the northeastern end of the city, is operated by the University of California.

In Riverside is the western junction with US 395 (*see TOUR 6e*).

> Left from Riverside on Magnolia Ave. (State 18) to the SHERMAN INDIAN INSTITUTE, (L) 5.2 *m.*, a large resident, co-educational school for Indian children more than 14 years old; it occupies a 40-acre tract. Academic instruction is given to the twelfth grade, with special emphasis on vocational training.
> CORONA, 13.9 *m.* (700 alt., 8,100 pop.), formerly called South Riverside, has a circular boulevard. In 1913, when the automobile was still new, Ralph De Palma, Barney Oldfield, and Earl Cooper participated in a 300-mile, free-for-all race on the boulevard; Cooper, the winner, averaged a breath-taking 75 miles per hour.
> Corona stands on the former Rancho El Temescal. Both the ranch and the canyon southwest of the city were so named because of the many sweathouses in the region; these were around hot springs, which were popular with the red men, who practiced hydrotherapy.

West of Riverside, US 60 passes under a graystone archway, above which green terraces (L) circle the lower slopes of MOUNT RUBIDOUX (1,337 alt.). According to tradition, this hill was once the altar of Cahuilla and Serrano sun worship. Pagan influence has been obliterated by the erection of an immense cross on the peak, honoring Fra Junipero Serra, founder of the California missions. The cross, visible across the valleys, is the focal point of Easter sunrise services attended by thousands. On the side of the mountain stands the WORLD PEACE TOWER, dedicated by the people of Riverside to Frank A. Millar, proprietor of the Mission Inn, active in the promotion of international peace. At the foot of the mountain is the ST. FRANCIS SHRINE, with a fountain for birds.

The highway runs between a long lane of pepper trees with finely cut drooping leaves and clusters of red berries.

MIRA LOMA (lookout hill), 86 *m.* (787 alt., 250 pop.), is a little settlement surrounded by acres of vineyards. Grapes thrive in the sandy, irrigated soil.

At 95.7 *m.* is the junction with Central Ave.

Left on Central Ave. to CHINO (713 alt., 3,118 pop.), 3 *m.*, the trade center of a citrus and beet-sugar growing area. It was founded in 1887 when Richard Gird subdivided half of his 47,000-acre Rancho Del Chino into 10-acre farms and laid out a mile square townsite in the center.

The CALIFORNIA STATE PRISON FOR FIRST OFFENDERS occupies a tract between Edison, Central, Euclid, and N. Robles Aves. The capacity, when completed in 1939, will be 2,100 inmates. In the $4,000,000 prison will be a psychiatric hospital for the care of prisoners who have pleaded "not guilty by reason of insanity."

POMONA, 100.2 *m.* (861 alt., 20,804 pop.), was named for the Roman goddess of fruits at its founding in 1875. It is now the chief shipping point of a large citrus-growing region. The sheep of Mission San Gabriel, tended by Indian herdsmen, grazed here at the close of the eighteenth century, when Rancho San José was part of the mission's holdings. In 1830 the rancho's 2 square leagues were granted to Ygnacio Palomares and Ricardo Vejar, but there were few settlers here until after the rails of the Southern Pacific had been laid. The boom that attended the city's inception was followed by a 2-year drought, which left nothing but a cluster of houses amid sheep ranges. Only in 1882, with the formation of the Pomona Land and Water Company, did steady growth begin.

The PALOMARES ADOBE, 1569 N. Park Ave., back from the street among oleanders, jasmines, roses, and peach and orange trees, was built soon after 1837. Its low roof projects over a broad *corredor* and its outside stairway climbs through vines and creepers. Nearby, at 1475 N. Park Ave., hidden among flowers and fruit trees is the ALVARADO ADOBE, once the residence of Palomares' close friend, Ygnacio Alvarado, who had a private chapel in his home. Not far away, at 548 S. Kenoak Dr., is the CHRISTIAN OAK, under which, on Nov. 18, 1873, Father Zalvidea of Mission San Gabriel conducted a dedicatory mass for Rancho San José, and pronounced benediction on the Palomares and Vejar families.

GANESHA PARK, between Walnut and Val Vista Sts., named for a Hindu god, and planted to resemble a natural woodland, holds a large open-air GREEK THEATER and sport facilities. LOOKOUT POINT commands a fine panorama.

Adjoining Ganesha Park on the northwest are the 175-acre LOS ANGELES COUNTY FAIR GROUNDS, since 1922 the scene of what the exposition's literature calls "the biggest county fair in America." Half-a-million visitors flock in annually in September to see agricultural, horticultural, livestock, domestic arts, educational, machinery, and arts and crafts exhibits, as well as poultry, rabbits, and dairy produce. Thousands of entries compete for prizes against a carnival background. On the half-mile track, with its huge grandstand, is pari-mutuel racing.

Pomona is at the junction with US 99-70 (*see TOUR 3d*), which unites westward with US 60.

Left from Pomona on Hamilton Ave. to a junction with Valley Blvd. at 2.3 *m.*; R to SPADRA, 3.5 *m.* (711 alt., 275 pop.), named for his native home in Arkansas, Spadra Bluffs, by William Rubottom, first Yankee settler in Pomona Valley, who conducted a tavern.

On the DIAMOND BAR RANCH (L) 4.5 *m.*, against the rugged lower slopes of the Rocky Hills, is the two-story VEJAR ADOBE, second ranch house of Ricardo Vejar. Built in 1850, just two years before Yankee business methods reduced Vejar to poverty, the ranch house is one of the best examples of the adobe mansion in southern California, its broad corridores and handmade doors unmarred by the passage of time.

At 103.8 *m.* is an asphalt paved road.

Left on this road to the grounds of the W. K. KELLOGG INSTITUTE OF ANIMAL HUSBANDRY, 1 *m.* (*open daily except Mon.; adm. free*), sweeping down from the hilltops into lush green hollows, with scattered stucco buildings, embowered against the slopes. In the tile-roofed stables are spacious stalls grouped about a plot of green turf, in which are quartered more than 75 registered Arabian horses, many of them well known through their motion picture appearances. In the rear is a ring with grandstands where a horse show is presented at 2:00 and 3:30 p.m. on Sundays. The 750-acre farm, founded in 1925 by the corn flake king, was in 1932 presented to the University of California, together with a cash endowment of $600,000, as a foundation for a teaching and research institution of animal husbandry.

The highway runs through the far-spreading groves of the valley floor after an easy descent from the gently sloping SAN JOSE HILLS. At 108.5 *m.* is a junction with Citrus Ave.

Right on Citrus Ave. is COVINA, 1.2 *m.* (555 alt., 2,774 pop.), a typical San Gabriel Valley community centering about the 12 packing houses where oranges, lemons, grapefruit, and tangerines are wrapped and boxed for shipment. Here, white-walled, red-tiled homes, schools, and churches stand among thick-leaved citrus trees, clumps of ragged eucalypti, and lacy pepper trees.

US 60-70-99 strikes westward through a region of truck gardens and scattered shacks, and thence through alternating walnut and orange groves. Under the low-spreading branches of the walnuts a foamy yellow-green ocean of wild mustard rolls away. In blossomtime, the orange trees send out a sweet, heavy scent.

At 116.1 *m.* is a junction with Valley Blvd.

Right on Valley Blvd. to GAY'S LION FARM, 0.6 *m.* (*open daily except Mon., 10-5; adm. 50¢*), blazoned on signboards as the "Internationally Famous Gay's Lion Farm—the Farm Extraordinary." Here a plaster lion crouches before a background of log stockades, palm-thatched roofs, banana plants, and bamboo. Among the 5 acres of flowers and shrubs are nine lion houses occupied by more than 200 African lions (many of them credited with appearances before moving picture cameras) which the farm raises for sale. Chief attractions are the cubs, fed from nursing bottles.

MONTEREY PARK, 121.9 *m.* (475 alt., 6,406 pop.), incorporated in 1916, is in the low, rolling Monterey hills. The community is proud of its many old trees, which include the pepper, the California live-oak, pink-flowering white ironbark, Australian beech, Torrey pine, various types of palm, and several kinds of cork oak.

West of Monterey Park, US 60-70-99 runs between gas stations, real estate offices, and roadstands (offering for sale anything from eggs and puppies to firewood and chile con carne).

LOS ANGELES, 130.7 *m.* (*see LOS ANGELES*).

$$\mathrm{\textbf{<<<<<<<<<<<<<<<<<<<<<<<<<<<<<<<<<<<<<<<<<<<<<>>>>>>>>>>>>>>>>>>>>>>>>>>>>>>>>>>}}$$

Tour 14

(Yuma, Ariz.)—El Centro—Jacumba—La Mesa—San Diego, US 80. Arizona Line to San Diego, 177.6 *m.*

Caution: For side trips on sandy desert roads, car and equipment should be checked carefully. Extra food, fuel, and water should be carried, also gunny sacks to provide traction in loose sand.
San Diego & Arizona Eastern R.R. roughly parallels route.
Accommodations adequate except on side roads.
Paved roadbed throughout, open all seasons. Excellent route for trailers.

US 80 runs westward across the thinly populated southernmost section of California. In altitude the route varies from below sea level to an elevation of 4,050 feet. Spanish explorers first called this road the Jornada de la Muerte (journey of death) and El Camino del Diablo (devil's highway).

The first Butterfield stage, carrying mail from St. Louis to San Francisco, used this route in 1858. Twice a week after this until 1861 the long trip was made, the only scheduled service from East to West and one of the longest stage routes in history. The Butterfield line used 100 Troy and Concord coaches, 1,000 horses, 500 mules and 800 men. The eastern part of the route was menaced by Comanche, the middle part by Apache and the western section by Yuma and Mojave. Because road agents regarded the stages as legitimate prey, the coaches became traveling forts. Advertisements of the line in the East read, "Fare $200 in gold. Passengers are advised to provide themselves with a Sharp's rifle and one hundred rounds of ammunition. Through service from St. Louis to San Francisco by the quickest route. Twenty-four days travel in our luxurious stages and you will arrive in 'The Land of Gold'!" The outbreak of the Civil War ended the Southern control of Congress, which had forced the use of this hard and round-about route.

West of the Colorado River lies the great Colorado Desert, the dark brown Chocolate Mountains flanking its northern and eastern rims; a great series of shifting sand dunes lies diagonally across it, intersecting the highway between Yuma and Holtville. The Imperial Valley area, much of which is below sea level, lies in the heart of the desert—irrigated land in the white waste.

West of the desert, the highway climbs the forested mountains of the Peninsular Range; as the road winds down the western slope to the Pacific Coast, orange, lemon, and grapefruit groves, vineyards, and avocado orchards appear.

Section a. ARIZONA LINE *to* EL CENTRO; *56.6 m. US 80.*

The COLORADO (Sp., ruddy) RIVER, 0 *m.,* separates Arizona and California. It is crossed by a steel bridge, one end of whose span is in Yuma, Arizona.

The Colorado River was discovered, supposedly, by Hernando de Alarcón in August 1540; he named it Río Grande de Buena Esperanza (great river of good hope). For 15 days Alarcón and his party explored the river in small boats. Two land expeditions, commanded by Francisco Vásquez de Coronado, explored this territory in 1540 and 1541. Melchior Díaz, chief of one of the parties, named the river Río del Tizón (river of the firebrand) for the sticks of burning wood carried by the native Indians. Father Kino, the Jesuit priest, called it Río de los Martires (river of the martyrs), when he crossed the desert in 1701. The present name was given it by Governor Juan de Oñate of New Mexico in 1905 and was suggested by the reddish color imparted by silt suspended in the water.

When bridges were built across the Colorado in the 1870's and 1880's, an adventurous period of river history ended. Early explorers and adventurers crossed the river by fording or swimming their horses. In 1849, when men were crossing the continent to California by every possible route, two ferries were in operation. One was run by Indians using a boat abandoned by Gen. Alex Anderson of Tennessee; the other was operated by a Dr. Lincoln, in partnership with an outlaw, John Glanton. To quell competition, Glanton had his men kill Lincoln and wreck the Indians' boat. The Indians in turn wiped out Glanton and his gang and had the river to themselves until 1850. In that year L. J. (Don Diego) Iaeger led a group across the desert from San Diego. The men nearly died of thirst and heat before reaching the banks of the Colorado on July 10, 1850. Work on a ferryboat was started as soon as they recovered. Beams were hewed from cottonwoods, and fastened with wooden pegs.

West of the bridge the road traverses small Yuma or Bard Valley. The derivation of "Yuma" is uncertain, but was first mentioned by Father Kino. It may come from the word Yahmayo (Ind., sons of the captain, or, sons of the river).

The YUMA INDIAN SCHOOL and INDIAN AGENCY, 0.1 *m.,* on a hill (R), is on the site of the old Fort Yuma. A STATUE OF FATHER GARCÉS stands in front of the chapel. In 1781 the Mission Puríssima Concepción, which had been built on this spot, was destroyed by Indians who objected to the serflike conditions the fathers imposed. In 1880 an Indian school was opened on Don Diego's farm, somewhat northwest, but in 1890 the Catholic Church established this school on a

Government subsidy. The Indians are still reluctant to send their children to the white man's school.

The YUMA INDIAN MISSION (R), 0.2 *m.,* is on the Fort Yuma Indian Reservation.

At 0.3 *m.* is the junction with a graveled road.

Right on this road through the FORT YUMA INDIAN RESERVA-TION, covering 8,350 acres, where the dwindling members of the Yuman tribe have been living and farming since the 1880's. Scattered on each side of the road are the small adobe huts of the Indians with thatched roofs and ramadas (arbors) where the owners rest after work and hang their vegetables, skins, and utensils. Although the reservation is irrigated by a canal from Laguna Dam, the smaller farms are not well kept and look parched. It is noticeable that white inhabitants of the reservation outnumber the Indians.

ROSS CORNER, 5 *m.,* is a small trading center; L. here 19 *m.* on a sand road to the old PICACHO (summit) MINES. Gold was found here in 1860 by an Indian. Twenty years later Mexican prospectors struck a rich lode, and the town of PICACHO, 21.5 *m.,* sprang up. The gold brought gay times in its wake. Bull fights, fandangos, and fiestas were frequent. Enterprising Yankees built a stamp mill and a small railroad. The "bankroll" period ended when the mines were exhausted early in the twentieth century.

On the main side road is the UNITED STATES EXPERIMENTAL FARM (L), 6.5 *m.,* under the direction of the Division of Plant Introduction in Washington. The station, in operation for 13 years, has developed a disease-resistant alfalfa, now widely used.

BARD, 7 *m.* (87 alt., 550 pop.), is a settlement of the Bard Irrigation District.

POT HOLES, 10 *m.,* named for the pot holes in the river at this point, is little more than a group of houses occupied by the caretakers of the Laguna Dam.

The LAGUNA DAM, 12 *m.,* formerly called the Yuma Dam, is a diversion dam for irrigation purposes, the first undertaken by the United States Reclamation Service in California. The weir was completed in 1909, and the water turned into the canals the following year.

IMPERIAL DAM, 17.5 *m.,* is the headquarters for the All-American Canal (*see below*), part of the Boulder Dam Project, authorized by Congress in 1928. The dam, of the floating, or Indian weir type, has raised the surface of the Colorado River 22 feet.

WINTERHAVEN, 0.9 *m.* (85 alt., 1,100 pop.), a bustling, businesslike spot, was headquarters for the All-American Canal construction work.

ARAZ STAGE STATION, 5.8 *m.,* once a way-station for freight wagons, now provides gas and food for motorists.

The ALL-AMERICAN CANAL is crossed at 6.3 *m.* This irrigation canal is 80 miles long, 200 feet wide, and 22 feet deep at the water level. "Walking dredges," with booms 185 feet long and buckets that raised 14 cubic yards of sand at a scoop, were used to cut through the sand dunes. The canal can deliver 15,000 cubic feet of water per second to the Imperial Valley.

PILOT KNOB (1,000 alt.) is visible (L) along this stretch of the highway. It is a single, dark butte, composed of granite overlaid by volcanic rock and lava flows, and stands just north of the Mexican border.

At 9.1 *m.* is the junction with a dirt road.

Right on this road is OGILBY, 3.9 *m.* (365 alt., 60 pop.), once a booming mining town and now only a station on the Southern Pacific R.R. Gold was mined from 1879 to 1918 in the CARGO MUCHACHO (errand boy) MOUNTAINS, whose twin cones (2,000 alt.) rise 5 miles northeast of the town.

TUMCO, 10.5 *m.*, named for the initials of the United Mine Company, is another ghost of a mining camp. Early in the 1900's, Tumco had a population of 3,000, four saloons along Stingaree Gulch, and an occasional gunfight. The Tumco gold deposits were discovered by a Swedish track-walker, who apparently deviated from his line of duty.

Desert sand hills are visible on both sides of the highway at 14.2 *m.* Formed by the wind, the shifting dunes, some 200 feet high, sometimes bury the road. It was through such land that De Anza and his party struggled—the first white men known to have crossed the Colorado Desert. Juan Bautísta de Anza was captain of cavalry of the Royal Presidio of Tubac, Sonora, Mexico. Determined to find an overland route to the Pacific, he assembled his first expedition at Mission San Xavier del Bac, Mexico, and began his journey in 1774. He set up his first camp near the present Yuma. Wtih him were Father Garcés and Capt. Juan Valdéz, who has been called the Spanish "Kit Carson." Hostile Apaches stole many of his best horses, but a chief of another tribe helped the party immeasurably with food and guides. In 1775 De Anza organized a second expedition larger and better equipped, which crossed the desert and took colonists to San Francisco.

Vestiges of the Old Plank Road (L), parallel the highway at 14.6 *m.* This was built in 1914 and followed the contours of the sand hills across the desert; the present highway skirts their tops. Constant shifting of the sand made this narrow plank road expensive and difficult to maintain.

LITTLE VALLEY, 17 *m.*, a small valley amid shifting dunes, is one of Hollywood's favorite desert locations. Many a sheik picture and epic of the Foreign Legion has been shot here.

GRAY'S WELL, 20.4 *m.* (*restaurant, gasoline, cabins*), was named for Newt Gray of Holtville, who worked hardest for the extension of the desert road to Yuma.

West of Gray's Well is an arid country, part of the SALTON SINK (*see TOUR 3e*), typical of Imperial Valley before it was reclaimed by irrigation.

MIDWAY WELL, 29.6 *m.* (*service station and cafe*), is on the edge of the Imperial Valley.

At 40.6 *m.* parts of the ANCIENT BEACH LINE of Lake Cahuilla are visible. The beach line is a hard, elliptic ridge of sand around the Imperial Valley.

US 80 crosses the EAST HIGHLAND CANAL, 41.1 *m.*, which extends along the rim of the valley to a point north of Niland, and, with the Main Central Canal and the West Side Main Canal supplies water to the valley. The highway drops gradually here.

DATE CITY, 42.5 *m.* (15 alt.), is headquarters of a date-growing district. Fresh dates are on sale at stands lining the road.

HOLTVILLE, 48.7 m. (— 10 alt., 1,758 pop.), is the chief trading point for eastern Imperial Valley. It has a large Swiss colony and its major interest is dairying. The town was named for W. F. Holt, who bought large blocks of stock in the Imperial Water Companies from the California Development Company. The town has a strategic position next to a 40-foot drop in the Alamo River, where it was possible to build a hydroelectric plant and generate power.

The Alamo River was greatly enlarged by the flood of 1905, which cut a channel 50 feet deep in the sandy soil in places. It flows into the Salton Sea and is fed mostly by waste ditches at the present time (1939).

At MELOLAND, 52.7 m. (21 alt., 460 pop.), is the EXPERIMENTAL STATION (open to qualified persons) of the University of California's College of Agriculture. Here experiments are made in the application of scientific principles to the cultivation of land, especially in the production of field crops. Meloland is also a packing and shipping point.

EL CENTRO, 56.6 m. (— 52 alt., 8,480 pop.), is one of the chief trade, storage and shipping centers of Imperial Valley. It is also the seat of Imperial County, and second largest town below sea level in the United States. The town is in the heart of the most arid area in the country—reclaimed from the desert by irrigation.

The little city, with its shaded patios and carefully tended flower gardens, is a kind of miracle to those who knew the barren waste before irrigation waters arrived. It is a typical southern California town with a difference, having accepted its role as a tropical city. Here as in the cities much nearer the equator the stores have arcaded fronts over the sidewalks and many of the houses have air chambers under their roofs.

The valley has already become the scene of literature; the first novel celebrating it was Harold Bell Wright's *Winning of Barbara Worth;* Jefferson Worth's prototype was W. F. Holt, the town's founder. Its first sheriff, Mobley Meadows, who had an uncanny ability in tracking down horse-thieves, has been memorialized, indirectly, in THE PLAINSMAN, a statue for which he posed; it stands in the courthouse square.

A government scientist in 1853 saw the agricultural possibilities of the 600 square mile depression, which was called "the hollow of God's hand" by the Indians, but little attempt was made to irrigate it until 1900 when a private corporation began construction of a canal from the Colorado River. The first settlers appeared in the valley in 1901 in spite of the imperfect workings of the canal system. Then in 1904 and 1905 the Colorado, with its spring flood (see *TOUR 3e*), overflowed into the basin.

El Centro had been laid out in 1905 by Holt, but the population did not reach 5,000 until 1920. In the meantime extensive pressure was being put on Congress to take over the problem of irrigating this natural hotbed; the Boulder Dam project, of which the Imperial Valley project is a part, was authorized in 1928. This started a boom in land values, which had been anticipated by certain large corporations. In 1935 almost a third of the total farm acreage was in ranches containing more than 500 acres, 31 of them more than 1,000 acres. In 1934, 74 individuals and companies controlled approximately 47,700 acres of crop land. The first water from the All-American Canal is expected in 1940. Among the largest crops of the valley are melons, alfalfa, grapefruit, strawberries, grapes, lettuce, barley, and dates. Dairying also plays an important role.

The labor problem has been especially acute here. The Yankee field hand shied away from an area where a summer temperature of 125° was not unusual. The Mexicans who came in were accustomed to the peonage system and had a very low standard of living; at first they were glad to get any kind of work for almost any rate of pay and expected nothing in the way of living accommodations. They camped along the irrigation ditches, and cooked with and drank the mud-laden irrigation waters. After the war they were joined by Filipinos, Hindus, Japanese, and Negroes. The great Middle Western drought caused an influx of dust-bowl farmers, turned nomads with their families; they had been blown out of the only jobs they knew how to do and had turned to the new agricultural El Dorado. But there were no farms for them here and they became day laborers on the factory-farms. And they were less tractable than the older class of Imperial Valley migrants. Before long the labor unrest that was sweeping the country went below sea level and even the non-English speaking peoples were infected. Heat, non-resident ownership, the economic depression, labor organizers, and money-obligations contracted in pre-depression days, went into the brew that was soon bubbling madly. Practically everyone in the valley was personally concerned in agricultural production—bankers, town officials, store-keepers. The demands for better housing, for sanitary facilities, for better pay, made in 1930 when the first strike was called, came at a time when the farm owners were least able to meet them. The farm-corporation directors, far from the scene of the conflict, formed the backbone of the defense against any concessions. In 1934, 8,000 lettuce pickers struck; when the police attempted to break up picket-lines, the resultant melee in which blood was shed made headlines from coast to coast. State and Federal conciliators, including Brig. Gen. Pelham D. Glassford, were sent in to the valley and succeeded after much difficulty in gaining some concessions for the field laborers.

El Centro is at the junction with US 99 (see *TOUR 3e*).

Section b. EL CENTRO *to* SAN DIEGO; *121 m. US 80.*

Westward, this route traverses typical desert, then climbs out of Imperial Valley and penetrates the dry, brush-covered mountains that separate the depressed interior basin of southern California from the coastal slope. The verdure of parts of this mountain area is a refreshing contrast to the glaring white and monotonous brown of the desert.

The route is attractive at night, when the lights of villages are visible for unbelievable distances, and the many weird rock and sand formations so strikingly resemble box cars that the stranger thinks he is intoxicated. In the summer, the night drive—when the temperature has dropped far below the peak of the afternoon—is advisable.

West of EL CENTRO, 0 *m.,* US 80 passes many cabins, mostly uninhabited.

SEELEY, 8.1 *m.* (26 alt., 158 pop.), supplies farmers with necessities. It was founded in 1911, near the site of Silsbee, a town destroyed by the 1905-07 flood.

The channel of NEW RIVER, 8.5 *m.,* was eroded by swollen floodwaters of the Colorado. This was one of the few watering spots on the old desert trail between Fort Yuma and San Diego. Small humps of earth by the road, sculptured by the flood of 1905, look like the homes of cave dwellers.

DIXIELAND, 13.1 *m.* (sea level, 34 pop.), is a town waiting for the coming of water. It was established in 1909 in anticipation of a new high-line canal west of the present ones.

South of Dixieland, stretching into Mexico, is the YUHA PLAIN, a bleak and desolate land of modified sand hills and outcroppings of mica. De Anza crossed this bare stretch in 1774 and found a watering place which he called Pozo de Santa Rosa de las Lajas (wells of St. Rose of the flat stones), now called Yuha Wells. The YUHA BADLANDS are a three-mile strip along the Mexican border. In them are fossil beds of oyster shells, fish and reptile casts, and shapes resembling great sea bass—all deposited when this region was part of the sea.

The summit of SIGNAL MOUNTAIN (2,262 alt.), a knob (L) of old granite and schist in Mexico, is topped by an aviation beacon.

SUPERSTITION MOUNTAIN (750 alt.), 17.3 *m.,* rises (R) from the desert floor. It is probably an old volcano; the Indians say it is inhabited by evil spirits whose voices used to make weird rumblings.

At 17.8 *m.* is the junction with a desert road.

Right on this road, called the Butterfield Trail, is CARRIZO (reed grass), 19 *m.,* a small water hole fed by Carrizo Creek, which is usually dry. The SITE OF A BUTTERFIELD STAGE STATION is marked here by a pile of weathered timber and crumbling adobe. Eighty yards west is the grave of an alleged cattle rustler. A headstone reads, "Frank Fox. Killed 1882." He was shot while bathing in the creek and thus died with his boots off.

VALLECITO (little valley), 38 *m.* (*water and campsite*). The adobe BUTTERFIELD STAGE STATION here was rebuilt in 1934. Two men killed each other on this spot, according to the San Diego *Star* of Nov. 2, 1870, which wrote: "Two immigrants had an altercation on Monday last at Vallecito, resulting in the death of both . . . they took two shots apiece, both of the first shots missing and both of the second shots taking effect . . . one in the breast and the other in the abdomen . . . they were brothers-in-law and their families were present at the time of the difficulty."

At 57 *m.* is the junction with State 78 (*see TOUR 6e*).

PLASTER CITY, 21.1 *m.* (786 lat., 80 pop.), is the settlement and loading point of a company making plaster of paris from gypsum extracted 25 miles north, in Fish Creek Canyon.

At 25.1 *m.* is the junction with a desert road.

> Right on this road to the PAINTED GORGE, 7 *m.*, a cleft in the COYOTE MOUNTAINS, with highly colored walls in reds, pinks, delicate greens and hybrid hues. Coral deposits and beds of fossil oystershells are at the upper end.

COYOTE WELLS, 26.1 *m.* (*service station and cafe*), was for many years a watering place for desert travelers. The well was hidden in a mesquite clump and so named because the coyote can smell out water around the roots of the mesquite.

Dry washes and gullies in this area are signs of the infrequent but heavy summer rains that batter down the vegetation and erode the sandy cliffs. As the road gains altitude, such desert flora as the ocotillo, ironwood, cactus, and creosotebush give way to the juniper, the yucca, manzanita, and oak.

At SHEPARD'S BRIDGE, 31.6 *m.* (2,784 alt.), the highway begins the ascent of the Mountain Springs Grade through INCOPAH GORGE, a rocky gap at the southern rim of Imperial Valley. The grade which takes the jump from the desert floor to the uplands was regarded as an engineering triumph when it was finished in April 1913. It eliminates the hazards of the old Devil's Canyon route.

Near MOUNTAIN SPRINGS GAS STATION, 37.5 *m.* (2,886 alt.), some fine gems have been found in the essonite garnet deposits. They are sold as "California hyacinth." These hills also contain deposits of marble, feldspar, magnesia, and silica.

BOULDER PARK, 39.2 *m.,* the summit of Mountain Springs Grade, offers a far view of Imperial Valley and the desert.

JACUMBA (Ind., hut by the water), 48 *m.* (2,800 alt., 400 pop.), is a resort spa, 200 yards from the Mexican border, with mineral springs and baths. Chief patrons of this resort are residents of Imperial Valley, who have summer cabins on the mountain slopes. Jacumba was first a mail station on the Yuma route, established by James McCoy in 1852. McCoy built a fort and at one time held off an attack by 500 Indians.

About 3 miles north of Jacumba is the mouth of the 11-mile Carrizo Gorge, one of the most spectacular valleys of the region. The light-colored granite walls have been gullied and worn into deep lateral crevices and contain odd formations. High up on the precipitous slopes is a narrow contorted shelf bearing the tracks of a branch of the Southern Pacific Railroad.

ECKENER PASS HAMLET, 55.3 *m.,* was named for Dr. Hugo Eckener, who passed over this point in his Zeppelin flight across America, Aug. 26, 1929.

West of EL RICO, 59.2 *m.* (3,008 alt.), the highway traverses the CLEVELAND NATIONAL FOREST.

At LA POSTA, 65.6 *m.* (3,119 alt.), a service station, is a junction with a dirt road.

Right on this road to LA POSTA INDIAN RESERVATION, 0.8 *m.*, an area of 3,879 acres peopled by only three Indians.

BUCKMAN SPRINGS, 71.1 *m.* (3,225 alt.), was named for Col. Amos Buckman, who hunted for gold in this region in the 1860's.

Left from Buckman Springs on a dirt road to MORENA LAKE and MORENA RESORT, 8.5 *m.* (*boats and tackle for hire*). The lake is part of the San Diego water system. Its dam, 171 feet high, is of the rock-fill type, cheaper than concrete construction and more resistant to earthquake. A professional rainmaker, C. M. Hatfield, used this site for his precipitation plant in 1915, to try to bring rain after several dry seasons. Disastrous floods followed his experiments, washed away a dam, and filled Morena Lake to within 18 inches of capacity. Hatfield threatened to sue the city of San Diego for payment. The city answered with a threat to sue him for the damage done by the floodwaters. Both suits were dropped.

At LAGUNA JUNCTION, 73.9 *m.* (4,050 alt.), is a service station and restaurant.

Right from Laguna Junction on an oiled road to the LAGUNA MOUN-TAINS in Cleveland National Forest (*cabins, public campgrounds*), one of the best recreational districts in the region. The forest covers 815,000 acres, and is a game refuge. It takes in two parallel ranges of mountains, many lakes, and peaks. The road winds over mountains topped with chaparral and through valleys thick with pines. There are many varieties of pine and oak, incense cedar, big cone willow, and alder. The watershed brush cover is mainly chemical, redshank, lilac, and scrub oak, with some chinquapin, sumac, California laurel, toyon, wild cherry, and mountain mahogany.
At 8.8 *m.* is a junction with a dirt road; R. here 1 *m.* to the CUYA-PAIPE INDIAN RESERVATION. Once many Indians ran away from the white men to this region, but today this reservation, covering 5,000 acres, harbors only five Indians and these intermittently.
On the main side road is LAGUNA POST OFFICE, 10 *m.*, headquarters for the resort area.
At the FOREST RANGER STATION, 10.4 *m.* information is available on the forest. The road skirts rocky slopes on the edge of the desert, with the wilderness spread out like a relief map almost a mile below. At 12.4 *m.* is a junction with a footpath; R. on this path 1.5 *m.* to MONUMENT PEAK (6,321 alt.).

PINE VALLEY, 74.4 *m.* (4,016 alt.), is a resort (*hotel, cabins, trails*). Maj. William H. Emory who settled here in 1869 is said to have bought the land from an old Indian for a saddle horse and a pack horse.
GUATAY (Ind., large house), 77.1 *m.* (*gasoline, restaurant*), was named for GUATAY MOUNTAIN (5,300 alt.); this peak (L) looked like an enormous wigwam.
CUYAMACA (Ind., rain above) JUNCTION, 78.7 *m.,* is at the junction with State 79 (*see TOUR 6C*).
The VIEJAS INDIAN RESERVATION (R), 81.7 *m.,* is in a small valley named El Valle de Las Viejas (the valley of the old women) by the Spanish, because the Indian men ran away to the hills and left the women and children. About 80 Indians live here now on modern farms. Before the reservation was set aside, the valley was used for breeding and pasturing race horses.

ALPINE, 90.4 *m.* (1,860 alt., 350 pop.), is a resort (*modern accommodations*). Above the coastal fog belt, its crisp mountain air attracts people with bronchial trouble.

The road leaves the rough, mountainous district, and descends rapidly into a farming and horticultural region in El Cajon Valley. Wine and table grapes, oranges and lemons grow well in the fertile soil of this valley, where Spaniards pastured their stock.

FLINN SPRINGS, 97 *m.* (1,300 alt.), a resort (*camping and picnic grounds*), is just east of the old Rancho La Cañada de los Coches (colloq. Sp., valley of the hogs ranch), the smallest grant in California. In mission days the padres had a hog ranch here, and, until recently, it was quite common to see hogs running wild.

EL CAJON, 104.1 *m.* (450 alt., 1,050 pop.), occupies part of the land of the old El Cajon Rancho, opened for settlement in 1869.

At 106.7 *m.* is the junction with an oiled road.

Left on this road to MOUNT HELIX (Lat., spiral), 1 *m.* (1,380 alt.), topped by a cross 30 feet high. Sunrise services are held on Easter morning in the amphitheater. The name was suggested by the corkscrew road that winds to the summit, where there is a view of San Diego and the Pacific Ocean.

LA MESA, 108.3 *m.* (538 alt., 2,513 pop.), is a city of homes. In the surrounding foothills are fine estates. In the 1870's this section, called Allison's Springs, was used for grazing sheep. Wild game was so plentiful that a woman who ran a boarding house in the vicinity was able to supply her table with venison, rabbits, duck, and quail killed on her daily ramble near the house. La Mesa has an annual fall flower festival.

At La Mesa the highway enters the level coastal plain.

At 108.5 *m.* is the junction with a paved road.

Right on this road to MURRAY DAM AND LAKE, 1 *m.* For some time after the flood of 1916 this reservoir provided San Diego's sole water supply. Outboard motor and motorboat races are often held here.

At 112.3 *m.* is the junction with College Ave.

Right on College Ave. to SAN DIEGO STATE COLLEGE, 1.1 *m.* The buildings, of modified Moorish design, with creamy white walls and red tile roofs, are built around a square. In one corner of the quadrangle against the vine-covered arches of the buildings is *The Aztec,* a crouching figure cut from native diorite by Donal Hord, of the Federal Art Project. The AZTEC BOWL (L) is a football stadium. East of the campus is BLACK MOUNTAIN (1,590 alt.), and with a giant "S" on its side.

SAN DIEGO, 120.5 *m.* (0-500 alt., 170,000 pop.) (*see SAN DIEGO*), is at the junction with US 101 (*see TOUR 2d*).

Death Valley National Monument

Season: October to May; a few main roads open all year.
Administrative Offices: National Park Service Headquarters, Death Valley, California.
Admission: No fee; registration of license number of automobile, address of owner, number of passengers, required.
Transportation: From E. (*see TOUR 11a*), also by road branching from Nevada 5 at Beatty; by Tonopah and Tidewater R.R. (connecting with Union Pacific) to Death Valley Jct.; with stage fare between Death Valley and Death Valley Jct., approx. $5; from W. (*see TOUR 6c*).
Saddle horses at Furnace Creek Camp, $2.50 per half day.
Tanner all-expense motor tours: From Los Angeles to Death Valley and return, 200 miles within Death Valley; 2 passengers minimum, approx. $65 a person.
Airplane Service: Trips between Grand Central Airport, Glendale, Calif., and Death Valley Airport, Death Valley (inquire at Death Valley Hotel Co., Los Angeles). Emergency landing fields near Stove Pipe Wells Hotel and in Panamint Valley (unsafe when wet). On call service between Death Valley and Las Vegas, Boulder Dam, Nev. (Boulder Dam Tours, Inc., Las Vegas, Nev.)
Private Guide Service: Approx. $2 an hour and *private motor tours* (approx. $4 an hour) available at Furnace Creek Camp and Inn.
Accommodations: Furnace Creek Camp (*Sept. 1 to May 1; emergency accommodations in summer*), sleeping and housekeeping cabins, $2 a day and up; restaurant, store, service station. Furnace Creek Inn (*Nov. 1 to May 1*), American plan, $9.75 a day and up. Stove Pipe Wells Hotel (*Nov. 20 to May 1; emergency lodging and service station in summer*), European plan, $2 and up a day. Meals slightly more expensive than in cities.
Climate, Clothing, Equipment: Fall and spring, days warm to hot, nights cool; winter, days cool, nights chilly to cold; summer extremely hot, days 110° to 130°, nights 80° to 100°, low humidity at all times. Both cool and warm clothing in spring and fall, warm clothing in winter; stout shoes for walking. Field glasses desirable. Campers must bring own wood.
Medical Service: Physician at Furnace Creek Inn two days weekly. Consult park headquarters in emergency.

Warnings and Regulations: 45-mile speed limit. Register at ranger stations; travel only on roads that are open and patrolled, or make inquiries of rangers or at park headquarters. Carry abundant water for drinking purposes and radiator. Check gas and oil before all trips and carry additional supplies if long itinerary does not include service stations. Do not attempt to walk in valley during summer.

Recreational Facilities: Nine-hole golf course at Furnace Creek Ranch (*greens fee 50¢*); free Park Service lectures several evenings a week at Furnace Creek Ranch, at Furnace Creek Camp, and at Stove Pipe Wells Hotel. Swimming pool and tennis courts at Furnace Creek Inn.

Death Valley National Monument, established in 1933, covers 2,981 square miles, 500 of which are below sea level. The narrow trough of the valley curves for 140 miles between steep mountains of naked rock that are striped and patched with barbaric colors. The Panamint Range, rising 6,000 to 11,000 feet above sea level, gives Death Valley its western wall, and the Grapevine, the Funeral, and the Black Mountains, rising 4,000 to 8,000 feet, form its eastern wall. The heavy rains that sometimes fall on the mountains run swiftly off the steep barren slopes and cascade into the valley, where the water quickly vanishes. The valley floor, once the bed of an ancient lake, is streaked with white salt, gray clay, and yellow sand; in the glimmering salt beds is the lowest spot in North America. From June to September, while the days are a blaze of light and the rocks radiate stored heat at night, Death Valley is one of the hottest places in the world. The Indian name for the valley was Tomesha—ground afire. In the winter, snow lies lightly on the ranges, except on Telescope Peak, which is white until May, and sunny days in the valley are delightful. The great charm of the area lies in its magnificent range of color, which varies from hour to hour.

In contrast with a verdant land Death Valley seems completely barren, but it has a varied vegetation. In a wet year, when from two to five inches of rain fall, canyons, washes, and even the valley floor are tinted with gray desert holly and green creosote-bush, with cigarette plant, paperbag-bush, ephedras, sprucebush, saltbush, brittle-bush, and wetleaf. Two varieties of mesquite, cottonwoods, and willows are found. High on the Panamints and Grapevines are piñon, juniper, mountain mahogany, Rocky Mountain maple, and bristlecone and limber pine.

The animals include the Nelson bighorn sheep in the mountains, the desert coyote and kit fox, and the wild burro. The bushy-tailed antelope, ground squirrel, and the trade and wood rat are often encountered. Among the birds that live in the valley the year round are big black ravens, road runners, prairie falcons, the beautiful Le Conte thrasher and busy rock wrens. There are several varieties of lizards: whip-tailed, gridiron, horned toads, and chuckwallas. Rattlesnakes are rare. An inch-long killifish, found at Salt Creek and Saratoga Springs, is a leftover from the days when Death Valley was occupied by a lake.

Death Valley contains rock of all the great divisions of geologic time; without exaggeration it can be called the geologists' paradise. At one time this was probably a region of low mountains and wide valleys

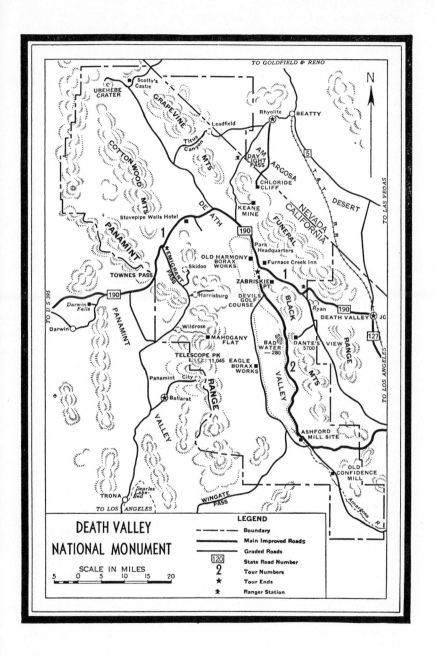

TO GOLDFIELD & RENO

N

Scotty's
Castle
UBEHEBE
CRATER
Leadfield
Rhyolite
BEATTY
GRAPEVINE
Titus
Canyon
MTS
COTTONWOOD MTS
DAY
LIGHT
PASS
ARGOSA
AMARGOSA
5
T. & T. R.R.
NEVADA DESERT
CHLORIDE
CLIFF
CALIFORNIA
TO LAS VEGAS
Stovepipe Wells Hotel
DEATH
KEANE
MINE
190
PANAMINT
1
Park
Headquarters
FUNERAL
EMIGRANT PASS
OLD HARMONY
BORAX
WORKS
Furnace Creek Inn
Skidoo
TO U.S. 395
TOWNES PASS
ZABRISKIE
PT.
1
Darwin
Falls
190
Harrisburg
DEVILS
GOLF
COURSE
BLACK
Ryan
DEATH VALLEY
190
JC
Darwin
PANAMINT
Wildrose
MAHOGANY
FLAT
BAD
WATER
-280
DANTE'S
5700
VIEW
127
TELESCOPE PK
11,045
RANGE
MTS
TO LOS ANGELES
EAGLE
BORAX
WORKS
2
Panamint
City
Ballarat
RANGE
VALLEY
VALLEY
ASHFORD
MILL SITE
OLD
CONFIDENCE
MILL
TRONA
Searles
Lake
Bed
WINGATE
PASS
Amargosa R.
TO LOS ANGELES

LEGEND

DEATH VALLEY
NATIONAL MONUMENT

SCALE IN MILES
5   0   5   10   15   20

- - - -	Boundary
————	Main Improved Roads
	Graded Roads
120	State Road Number
2	Tour Numbers
★	Tour Ends
⚑	Ranger Station

with streams and lakes. Then followed a period of great earth disturbance accompanied by volcanic actions; Death Valley was formed by faulting. At the end of the glacial period the valley was a lake, but the waters gradually evaporated, and the land became a desert.

The barrenness and furnace heat of this gash in the earth's crust took grim toll of life from prospectors and immigrants seeking shortcuts into California in pioneer days. The valley got its name when an immigrant train turned off the Los Angeles-Salt Lake Trail in 1849 into the sandy wastes. As they went on, the train broke up into two companies, each struggling for its life. The first, a party composed chiefly of unmarried men who called themselves the Jayhawkers, went ahead, leaving the men with women and children to struggle along as best they could. As they toiled across the valley, they too broke up into smaller groups. Some Jayhawkers died in the valley, one in the Mojave Desert; the majority survived.

A clergyman named Brier, his wife, and their three small children, who traveled with the Jayhawkers at intervals, struggled safely out of the area after harrowing hardships. As Mrs. Brier afterward told the story: "One valley ended in a canyon with great walls rising up almost as high as we could see. There seemed no way out, for it ended almost in a straight wall . . . In the morning the men returned with the same story: 'No water.' Even the stoutest heart sank then, for nothing but sagebrush and dagger trees greeted the eye. My husband tied little Kirk to his back and staggered ahead. The child would murmur occasionally, 'Oh, father, where's the water?' . . . I staggered and struggled wearily behind with our other two boys and the oxen. The little fellows bore up bravely and hardly complained, though they could barely talk, so dry and swollen were their lips and tongues . . . Every step I expected to sink down and die. I could hardly see."

In late December 1849, the 15 men and women and 7 children left behind by the Jayhawkers, known as the Bennett-Arcane Party, camped at Furnace Creek—too weary, hungry, and thirsty to go on. William Lewis Manly and John Rogers, volunteering to go ahead for aid and provisions, got across the valley and the bare mountains beyond to San Fernando. Returning with some pack animals, they passed a member of the party, lying dead beside his empty canteen. At the camp, they saw no sign of life. Manly fired his gun. A man climbed from under a wagon. In Manly's words, ". . . he threw up his arms high over his head and shouted—'The boys have come, the boys have come!' . . . The great suspense was over and our hearts were first in our mouths, and then the blood all went away and left us almost fainting . . . Bennett and Arcane caught us in their arms and embraced us with all their strength, and Mrs. Bennett . . . fell down on her knees and clung to me like a maniac in the great emotion that came to her, and not a word was spoken." Escaping from the valley, the party arrived finally at San Fernando March 7, 1850.

A few years later much search was made for a silver mine one of these immigrants had reported; it became known as the Lost Gunsight.

DEATH VALLEY NATIONAL MONUMENT 649

The French and George parties, who explored the valley in 1860 in an unsuccessful search for the mine, bestowed many of its present place names. Later prospectors also failed to find the Gunsight, but discovered deposits of gold, silver, copper, and other minerals. A few large deposits were found, and lusty towns flared briefly. A building or two, bottles, adobe walls, and a clutter of worthless debris mark their sites. Borax, however, provided the foundation for an industry that thrived for a number of years and was responsible for the development of the region.

PARK TOUR 1

Western Entrance at Towne's Pass to Eastern Entrance in Furnace Creek Wash; 56 *m.,* State 190.

Oiled roadbed.

State 190 descends the steep eastern face of the Panamints to the pale, brush-dotted floor of Death Valley, runs south for about 25 miles between high bordering ranges fantastically streaked with vivid colors, then continues east through the low pass of Furnace Creek Wash.

East of the monument boundary, at the summit of Towne's Pass (5,500 alt.), 0 *m. (see TOUR 6c),* State 190 crosses the rolling summits of the tawny Panamint Range and descends Emigrant Wash. The rocky wash, speckled with desert shrubs, was named for the Jayhawkers, who climbed it in their escape from Death Valley.

A RANGER STATION, 7.7 *m.* (1,542 alt.), which registers incoming cars, is at the junction with Emigrant Canyon Rd.

Right on Emigrant Canyon Rd., traversing Emigrant Canyon, 1.8 *m.,* a sandy wash between rounded hills, to EMIGRANT SPRING (R), 4.8 *m.* (4,045 alt.), which flows from a little cove above the road. For many years prospectors camped below the green thicket and pastured their burros on scanty growth in the wash. Drinking water for Stove Pipe Wells Hotel comes from this spring.

The road winds up the canyon to emerge on HARRISBURG FLATS, 9.5 *m.* (4,500 alt.); the cone-shaped mountain directly ahead is Telescope Peak.

At 10.3 *m.* is the junction with a road; L. here 8 *m.* to the SITE OF SKIDOO (5,500 alt.), a camp that grew up after a discovery of 1906 and produced more than $3,000,000 in gold. At its peak, 500 persons lived here, and it had a telephone line across Death Valley to Rhyolite.

At 11.7 *m.* is the junction with a road; L. here 6 *m.* to AUGUERRE-BERRY POINT (6,000 alt.; *view best in afternoon).* Below is Death Valley, cradled in colored, wrinkled mountains; eastward, beyond tawny and brown desert ranges is Charleston Peak (11,910 alt.), 80 miles away in Nevada.

The main side route continues across the brushy Panamints and descends through a narrow winding defile into WILD ROSE CANYON, to the junction with a dirt road 20.4 *m.;* L. here to SUMMER PARK HEADQUARTERS, 0.3 *m.* The road *(impassable when snow-covered)* continues to the stone CHARCOAL KILNS, 7.3 *m.,* built in the 1870's by George Hearst. MAHOGANY FLATS, 8.5 *m.* (8,133 alt.), on a saddle of the wooded Panamints, is at the end of the automobile road. A foot trail (R) leads 6 *m.* to TELESCOPE PEAK (11,045 alt.), so named because of the magnificent widespreading view it affords.

WILD ROSE SPRINGS, 21.7 *m.* (3,617 alt.), on the main side route was named for the roses the George party found here in 1860.

South of WILD ROSE STATION, 22.3 *m.* (*service station, lunch-room, grocery store*), the road descends a narrow canyon, and passes the park boundary at 25.1 *m.* The road continues to TRONA, 60 *m.*, and INYOKERN, 93 *m.*, on US 395 (*see TOUR 6d*).

Northeast of the ranger station State 190 descends steadily. On the eastern side of the white valley the Grapevine Mountains, banded in red and black, rise above huge gravel fans, deposits of alluvial débris swept from canyon mouths high above the valley floor.

At 16.8 *m.* is the junction with a road.

Right to MOSAIC CANYON, 3 *m.*, whose floor of vari-colored pebbles embedded in gray conglomerate has been worn to a mosaic-like surface.

STOVE PIPE WELLS HOTEL (sea level), 17 *m.*, is a simple resort. The OLD WAGON (L) was abandoned in the rough, sandy country 25 miles north by employees of the borax company in 1889.

South of the hotel, some 25 square miles of yellow SAND DUNES (L) rise in sharply sculptured lines. The mesquite, creosote, and four-winged saltbrush around the dunes are havens for small animal life. The road curves east across the SALT MARSHES and passes the DEVIL'S CORNFIELD, where the arrowweed resembles shocks of tied corn. This is the only definitely known Death Valley camp of the Jayhawkers in 1849.

At 25 *m.* is the junction with the oil-surfaced Ubehebe Crater Rd.

Right on this road 2.8 *m.* to the junction with a dirt road; L. here 0.4 *m.* to STOVEPIPE WELLS (— 49 alt.), now a rock well. The water holes in this sandy waste saved many lives. Drifting sand often filled the holes, so the spot was marked by a stovepipe, now at Stove Pipe Wells Hotel.

The Ubehebe Crater Rd. parallels the Grapevines and climbs gradually; at about 24 *m.* the brush-grown alluvial slopes of the Grapevines and Panamints merge.

At 33.5 *m.* is the junction with a dirt road; R. here, through Grapevine Canyon, 3 *m.*, to SCOTTY'S CASTLE (*open 8-6, adm. $1.00*), entered by a bridge. The handsome Provincial Spanish style buildings are believed to have cost Scotty and his wealthy partner, Albert M. Johnson, $2,000,000. The two main houses, separated by a patio, are flanked by a clock tower (L) and a guest house (R). The excavation in front of the main house is an unfinished swimming pool. Death Valley Scotty has lived in Death Valley for more than 30 years. His spectacular 45-hour trip from Los Angeles to Chicago in 1905, and his spending sprees in Los Angeles—where he was lavish with $100 bills, despite the fact that he was without known resources—have made him a much-publicized figure.

At 35.8 *m.* on the main road is the junction with a short one-way loop road; L. here through low mud cliffs and up cinder hills to the lip of UBEHEBE CRATER (2,900 alt.). The east wall of the 800-foot deep crater is spectacularly striped in brilliant red and orange.

The highway crosses a low range of hills. The Funeral Mountains (L) and the Panamint Range (R) hem in the valley. Snowcapped Telescope Peak (11,045 alt.) is the highest mountain in the area. The valley is stony and sparsely covered with brush.

At 31 *m.* is the junction with the Daylight Pass Rd.

Right on the Daylight Pass Rd., over oddly colored hills, 6 *m.* to the junction with a rough dirt road; R. here 5.3 *m.* to ruins of the property of the KEANE WONDER MINE (3,000 alt.), built after gold was found here in 1903. The mine was up the canyon.

HELL'S GATE, 10.5 *m.* (2,263 alt.), on the Daylight Pass Rd., was named by teamsters in 1905; when they left the protecting walls of the canyon, the tender noses of their horses were scorched by the burning summer winds of Death Valley. Toward the south are the white Salt Beds; bright colored mountains rise steeply on either side.

East of Hell's Gate, Boundary Canyon—between the Grapevine and Funeral Mountains—is narrow and steep. CORKSCREW PEAK (5,000 alt.) is circled by broad bands of gray and red.

A RANGER STATION, 17 *m.,* at the summit (4,317 alt.) of Daylight Pass, checks incoming cars. The monument boundary, 17.5 *m.,* is at the California-Nevada Line, 10 miles from the ghost town of Rhyolite, Nev.

At 38.7 *m.* on State 190 is the junction with an oiled road.

Left 0.6 *m.* to the DEATH VALLEY NATIONAL MONUMENT HEADQUARTERS (*information and maps*).

At 39.6 *m.* is the junction with a dirt road.

Left 0.2 *m.* to a parking station, from which a short footpath descends to the GNOME'S WORKSHOP; here, in the midst of acres of odd alkaline formation, is a tiny bitter-tasting stream forming miniature waterfalls.

The RUINS OF THE HARMONY BORAX WORKS are visible on a low bluff (R) at 40.5 *m.* Of this first borax works in Death Valley only some rusty machinery and a few adobe walls remain. Borax was discovered here by Aaron Winters, a prospector, who sold his claims in 1882 to W. T. Coleman and F. M. "Borax" Smith. The refined borax was hauled by the famous mule teams through Wingate Pass to Mojave, 160 miles away. Each outfit consisted of a lead wagon and a trailer carrying 20 tons of borax, which were drawn by teams of twelve to twenty mules, guided by a check line 125 feet long. The works were closed in 1887 when the price of borax fell, but the picturesque mule teams had become identified with the product. In 1890 colemanite, another form of borax, was discovered near Furnace Creek, and the industry again boomed. The largest mine at Ryan was operated until 1927, when a new type of borax that could be produced more economically was discovered on the Mojave Desert.

The green oasis of FURNACE CREEK RANCH (R), 42 *m.,* is irrigated by water from springs in Furnace Creek Wash. In early days alfalfa and hay for the borax teams were grown here, and date palms and long rows of tamarisk were planted to break the hot desert winds. Today, dates from these palm trees are sold (*50¢ a lb.*). Bellerin Teck, the first white man to settle in Death Valley, began farming here in 1870. Opposite the ranch is DEATH VALLEY AIRPORT (*hangar for rent; gas and service at Furnace Creek Camp*).

FURNACE CREEK CAMP, 42.2 *m.,* is in the southeast corner of the ranch. Beside the road are a borax wagon, trailer, and steam tractor used here in the eighties.

Right from Furnace Creek Camp to the INDIAN VILLAGE, 0.7 *m.*, where adobes have been built for about 30 Shoshone who live in the park. Before the whites came, the Indians wandered over the country in search of food. Although their culture was primitive, the women made very good baskets from materials found here.

At 42.5 *m.* is the junction with a road.

Left here 0.5 *m.* to TEXAS SPRINGS PUBLIC CAMPGROUND (*water, stone fireplaces, sanitary facilities*), on a bench above the valley.

Near Furnace Creek Jc., 43.3 *m.*, the meeting place with oiled East Highway (*see PARK TOUR 2*), is FURNACE CREEK INN (sea level), 43.4 *m.*, with its garage, service station, and small store. This is a luxury resort.

At 46.5 *m.* is the junction with an oiled road.

Right here 0.3 *m.* to Zabriskie Point, which reveals a far-reaching panorama of stark peaks and ridges. MANLY BEACON, a sharply pointed hill, is surrounded by eroded yellow clay hills.

At 47.8 *m.* is the exit of a one-way road (*see below*). Westward is an impressive view of Death Valley and the rugged mountains. The road continues east between cleanly sculptured brown and yellow hills.

At 50.6 *m.* is the junction with a one-way looping road.

Right here through TWENTY-MULE TEAM CANYON. The road dips and winds between low clay hills, scarred from mining ventures. The road rejoins State 190 at 4.4 *m.*

State 190 continues eastward, past the hot tan and rosy brown Funeral Mountains, banded with somber gray; striped PYRAMID PEAK (6,725 alt.) raises its blunt tip at the eastern end of the range. The Black Mountains (R) receive their name from the lava cap that crowns them.

At 54.5 *m.* is the junction with the Dante's View Rd.

Right on this road up a canyon wash where the flanks of the Black Mountains appear brilliantly streaked with rose, fawn, and milky green, 2.6 *m.*, to the junction with an oiled road; L. 2 *m.* to RYAN (2,500 alt.), a model company town while the Pacific Coast Borax Co. operated mines here from 1914 to 1928. Sightseeing trains (*fare $1*) run to borax mines, 7 miles distant.
The road continues up GREENWATER VALLEY (4,000 alt.), a shallow depression in the mountains; here is a junction with a dirt road 7.9 *m.*; L. here 3.8 *m.* to a junction with a dirt road; R. 1.9 *m.* to the SITE OF GREENWATER, a ghost town marked by widely scattered debris. Greenwater boomed in 1905 when copper was discovered; but deposits were scanty, and its saloons, its banks, and newspaper soon had no community to serve.
The main side route continues R. from the junction to DANTE'S VIEW (*light effects best in morning*), 13.9 *m.* (5,220 alt.), overlooking Death Valley from the summit of the Black Mountains. The two extremes of altitude in the 48 States are visible from this point. More than a mile below is Badwater (— 279.6 alt.), and westward over the Panamints in the snowy Sierra Nevada is Mt. Whitney (14,495 alt.). Snow-capped Telescope Peak just opposite in the Panamints towers more than two miles above the bottom of Death Valley and a mile above this spot. White salt

areas in the valley are sharply outlined against the gravel slopes. Mesquite thickets make green patches at Mesquite and Bennett Wells (L) and Furnace Creek Ranch (R). The steep, rugged mountain walls that baffled the Death Valley party of 1849 stretch north and south, and the Avawatz and Owlshead Mountains block the valley southward. Eastward, beyond the twisted slopes of the Black Mountains, are the barren desert ranges of southern Nevada.

A RANGER STATION, 55 *m.*, registers incoming cars. The boundary of the monument (2,000 alt.) is crossed at 56 *m.* (*see TOUR 12a*).

PARK TOUR 2

Furnace Creek Jct.—Badwater—Ashford Jct.—Saratoga Springs Jct.; 63 *m.*, East Highway.

Oiled roadbed between Furnace Creek Jct. and Ashford Jct.; remainder graded dirt road.

The East Highway explores the eastern side and extreme southern end of Death Valley, passing the Salt Beds and the lowest point in North America. The West Highway is an alternate of this road.

Branching south from State 190 at FURNACE CREEK JUNCTION, 0 *m.* (*see PARK TOUR 1*) the East Highway curves along the base of the Black Mountains.

MUSHROOM ROCK, 4.6 *m.*, is an oddly shaped formation carved by wind and sand.

At 5 *m.* is the junction with an unpaved one-way road, looping back to the main road.

Left on this road 0.2 *m.* to VOLCANIC DRIVE, which winds upward through hills tinted with rose, pale green, ocher, and sienna. At the summit brilliantly colored strata tilt skyward. Descending through yellow walls, the road turns sharply at 3.3 *m.*, becoming Artist's Drive, and climbs again. At the second summit it turns south, passes brightly tinted hills, and reaches a point overlooking Death Valley, whose floor is seen streaked with white, soft purple, and brown. The route rejoins the East Highway at 9 *m.*

The DEVIL'S GOLF COURSE lies below the highway, opposite the entrance to Volcanic Drive. The Salt Beds here are covered with ridges and pinnacles of salt, crystallized into a hard substance that breaks with a ringing sound.

At 6.3 *m.* is the junction with the graded West Highway.

Right here, across the Salt Beds, 13 *m.* to the GRAVES OF SHORTY HARRIS AND JIM DAYTON. Harris, a well-known Death Valley prospector, asked to be buried beside Jim Dayton, a borax company employee who died here in 1898 and was buried on the spot.

At 13.5 *m.* is the junction with a dirt road; L. here 0.2 *m.* to the EAGLE BORAX WORKS, the earliest borax extraction plant in Death Valley, of which nothing remains but a boiling pan which was hauled 140 miles over the desert.

At 17 *m.* on the West Highway is the junction with a road; L. here 0.3 *m.* to BENNETT'S WELL, a watering station on the early borax route.

The Bennett-Arcane party camped within a few miles of this spot in 1849-50.

At ASHFORD JUNCTION, 39 *m.*, the West Highway rejoins the East Highway (*see below*).

BADWATER, 16.8 *m.* (— 279.6 alt.), is the lowest point in North America; a marker on the mountain (L) indicates sea level. The salty pools (R) are fed by the Amargosa River, a small stream that flows south in Nevada and California, rounds the Black Mountains, and flows north in Death Valley.

ASHFORD JUNCTION, 45 *m.*, received its name from a mill built nearby in 1914 by the Ashford brothers. Here is the junction with the West Highway (*see above*). The route continues southeastward over gently rounded mesas and a dry lake bed, or playa.

SARATOGA SPRINGS JUNCTION is at 63 *m.*

> Left on a rough road 2 *m.* to SARATOGA SPRINGS; in the swampy marshes are a few pools, the home of the Tiny Death Valley fish. Migrant waterfowl rest here during the winter.

The East Highway continues beyond the monument 27 miles to a junction with State 127 (*see TOUR 11a*).

Sequoia and General Grant National Parks

Season: Both parks open all year. Sequoia's western entrance at Ash Mountain open all year; East Fork and Lost Grove entrances frequently closed by winter snows. General Grant's south entrance open all year.

Administrative Offices: Sequoia headquarters inside W. entrance; information office at Giant Forest, Sequoia National Park. Sequoia and General Grant National Parks Co., Giant Forest. Earl McKee, guide and packer, Giant Forest in summer, Three Rivers in winter. General Grant headquarters, the Plaza, General Grant National Park.

Admission: Free; yearly automobile permit covering both parks $1 except at Sequoia East Fork entrance, which is free. Ash Mountain and Lost Grove entrance to Sequoia open 9-5 except Saturdays and days preceding holidays, when they close at 11 p.m. South entrance to General Grant always open.

Transportation: Between June 10 and Sept. 10 busses leave Fresno at 8 a.m. daily for Giant Forest by way of Visalia and return at 1:45 p.m. daily through General Grant National Park; for service from Sept. 10 to June 9 (between Visalia and Giant Forest only) make advance reservation with Sequoia and General Grant National Parks Co., Giant Forest; no service to General Grant during this period.

Saddle horses at Giant Forest and near Plaza. Rates for short trips: two hrs., $1.50; half day, $3; day, $5. Daily rates for long trips: horses, $1.50; guides and packers, $5; cooks, $6. Food, supplies, and equipment furnished by guests.

Accommodations: Sequoia—Giant Forest Lodge, Camp Kaweah, and Pinewood Shelter Camp, open May 25 to Sept. 7; European, American, or housekeeping plan. Hospital Rock Camp, open all year; European plan and housekeeping. Giant Forest Winter Camp, open Sept. 7 to May 25; American plan and housekeeping; partly equipped housekeeping cabins, $1.50 a day for two persons, 50¢ a day for each additional person; fully equipped housekeeping cabins, $3 a day for two persons; American plan cabins from $5 a day each for two persons (without bath) to $8 a day for one person (private bath). Meals: breakfast, 75¢; luncheon and dinner, $1, and $1.25. Bearpaw Meadow Camp, on High Sierra Trail, overnight tents, $1.50 a person; meals, $1. More than

600 free campsites for automobile travelers, with water, stone fireplace, sanitary conveniences. Largest campgrounds at Giant Forest, Lodgepole, and Dorst Creek. General Grant—Grant Park and Meadow Shelter Camps, open May 2! to Sept. 25; European or housekeeping plan. Informal winter accommodations. Rates as at Sequoia. Many free campsites, equipped as at Sequoia.

Climate: Summers warm and dry, moderately cool nights. Rain seldom falls between May and Sept. Thunder showers frequent and nights cooler in high mountains.

Medical Service: Physician and small hospital at Giant Forest in summer.

Post Offices: Sequoia mail forwarded to Giant Forest Lodge and Camp Kaweah; otherwise must be called for at Giant Forest post office. General Grant mail forwarded to Grant Park Camp and Hume Lake (north of park); otherwise must be called for at the Plaza post office.

Naturalist Service: Park naturalists at Giant Forest Administration Building and the Plaza in charge of guide service. Lectures daily and campfire programs nightly in summer at Sequoia. Lectures and campfire programs two or three times weekly and concerts three times weekly in summer at General Grant.

Warnings and Regulations: Camping, smoking, and building of fires permitted only in designated areas. Do not harm or frighten animals. Do not feed bears or leave food within their reach or where they can break into containers.

Fishing: Rainbow, Loch Leven, eastern brook, German brown, and golden trout. Persons over 18 must procure license; available at Giant Forest. Fee for residents, $2; for non-residents, $3; for aliens, $5. Tackle available at Giant Forest. Bulletins containing regulations for current year supplied by rangers. Fishing permitted in all waters of parks unless prohibited by sign.

Bathing: Pools at Lodgepole Camp, Bridge Camp, Hospital Rock Camp, and Heather Lake, Sequoia. Swimming in Sequoia Lake near southwestern boundary of General Grant. Bathing permitted only in designated areas.

Sequoia and General Grant National Parks cover the wildest country on the western slopes of the Sierra Nevada. Sequoia stretches from the headwaters of the Kings River on the north to the headwaters of the Tule River on the south. The tallest peaks of the High Sierra— barely dominated by Mount Whitney (14,495 alt.), highest point in the 48 States—bound it on the east and the foothills of the Sierra on the west. Bisecting the park from north to south is a jagged granite ridge, the Great Western Divide. West of the divide are the park's major accommodations and most popular attractions, its motor roads, and shorter trails. Here, in the 4,000- to 8,000-feet elevations, are the groves and forests of California big trees (*Sequoia gigantea*) for which Sequoia is best known. Paralleling the divide for 25 miles, about half-way between it and the crest of the Sierra, are the 3,000-foot walls of the Kern River Canyon (*see TOUR 3b*). In the eastern section of Sequoia are high mountain lakes—of glacial origin, as are the mountainsides of exposed rock and the great, irregular granite ridges, cleared of their earth and vegetation by ice thousands of years ago. The Sierra —as a distinct range—dates from the latter part of the Jurassic period, when it began to rise from the receding Logan Sea; it is approximately 120,000,000 years old (*see NATURAL SETTING*).

When Hale D. Tharp, a farmer from Three Rivers, visited Sequoia in 1856 in search of pastures and a ranch site, he was met by peaceful Yokut. "The Indians liked me," Tharp said later, "because .. was good to them. I liked the Indians, too, for they were honest and

kind to each other. I never knew of a theft or murder among them."
In 1858 Tharp discovered Giant Forest and first saw the big trees, one
of which already had been described to him by the Indians as being so
large that it took 25 men, with hands clasped together, to encircle it.

The settlers who followed Tharp to the Three Rivers region were
less popular with the Yokut; by 1862 their increasing numbers were
forcing the Indians to retreat into the canyons of the lower ranges. At
this time they contracted their first white man's diseases—smallpox,
measles, and scarlet fever—and perished by the hundreds, crawling, unless restrained by force, into their sweat houses to die. Very simply
one of their leaders, Chief Chappo, had Tharp ask the white men to go
away. When told by his friend that the settlers refused to leave, Tharp
said that the chief and his braves "sat down and cried." By 1865 the
last of the tribe had retreated into the mountains.

An abortive gold strike in the fifties opened the area's first trails,
across the southern panhandle to the Kern River. The first official
exploration took place in the north, in the Kings River country, in 1861;
it was led by William H. Brewer of the U. S. Geological Survey.
Three years later Clarence King, who accompanied Brewer, crossed the
Kings-Kern Divide and climbed Mount Tyndal. In 1873 Mount
Whitney was climbed for the first time by A. H. Johnson, C. D. Begole,
and John Lucas. Eager miners again crossed the southern panhandle—
this time to found the noisy, fantastic settlement of Beulah on the advice
of a spiritualist "control" (*see TOUR 3b*). The town was short-lived,
but it left the park with its first wagon road. The next decade passed
quietly. Cattlemen, sheepherders, and hog drovers wandered over the
mountains in summer, trappers followed their lines in winter, and the
Indians dwindled away.

Then, in 1885, a stunned registrar in Visalia reported to Washington the application in one day of 55 claims of 160 acres each to timber
lands above the Marble Fork of the Kaweah. Applicants were members of a socialistic group who planned a Utopia in the wilderness (*see
TOUR 3b*). Immediately after filing, they organized the Tulare
Valley and Giant Forest Railroad Company and laid plans for the development of the land and the lumbering of sugar and yellow pine.
They visited Giant Forest, vowed solemnly never to cut the giant
Sequoias, and named the outstanding big trees after the heroes of the
Paris Commune and of American socialism. When the government
suspended the entire district from entry pending investigation, the colonists launched a series of litigations to secure title to their land. In the
following year they reorganized their company and formed the Kaweah
Co-operative Commonwealth Colony. A sawmill in the mountains was
to cut fir and pine lumber which would be hauled out over a community
built road and later a railroad. The road was started, and in the face of
incredible difficulties—the inexperience of the workers, the lack of equipment, the refractory nature of the terrain, and the political confusion
which developed in the administration of the colony—was built as far as
Colony Mill in less than four years. A small sawmill was installed.

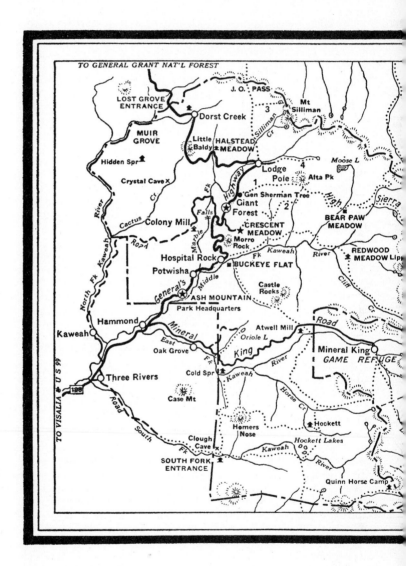

TO GENERAL GRANT NAT'L FOREST

J. O. PASS

LOST GROVE
ENTRANCE

Dorst Creek

3

Mt
Silliman

MUIR
GROVE

Little
Baldy

HALSTEAD
MEADOW

Moose L

Hidden Spr

Crystal Cave X

Lodge
Pole

4

Alta Pk

1

Gen Sherman Tree

Giant
Forest

2

High

Sierra

Falls

Colony Mill

Cactus

Road

CRESCENT
MEADOW

BEAR PAW
MEADOW

Morro
Rock

Hospital Rock

Potwisha

Fk

Kaweah

River

REDWOOD
MEADOW Lip

BUCKEYE FLAT

Clift

General's

Middle

Castle
Rocks

North Fk Kaweah River

Road

ASH MOUNTAIN

Park Headquarters

Hammond

Kaweah

Oak Grove

Mineral

East

Fk

Atwell Mill

Oriole L

King

Road

Mineral King
GAME REFUGE

Cold Spr

Kaweah

River

TO VISALIA ☆ U S 99

198

Three Rivers

Horse Cr.

Road

South

Fk

Case Mt

Homers
Nose

Hockett

Clough
Cave

Kaweah

Hockett Lakes

SOUTH FORK
ENTRANCE

River

Quinn Horse Camp

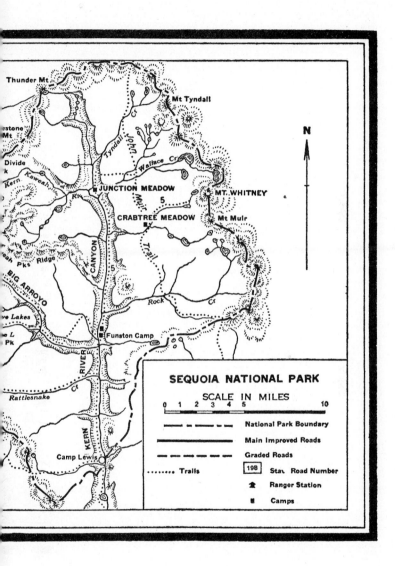

SEQUOIA NATIONAL PARK

SCALE IN MILES

0 1 2 3 4 5   10

— · — · — ·   National Park Boundary

━━━━━━   Main Improved Roads

— — — —   Graded Roads

········· Trails   198   Stat Road Number

🛆   Ranger Station

▮   Camps

There were commotions and feuds in the Kaweah Valley, dissension within the colony, debates in the State Legislature, articles in the newspapers all over the State, and finally over the country. Then, in September 1890, Sequoia National Park was created by Congress and troops were sent to expel the colonists and administer the new park. The colonists retreated with what grace they could muster, but their vocabulary was adopted by their neighbors. The Act of Congress was completely unexpected by the settlers in the vicinity, who for 30 years had hunted and grazed over the area at will. The local papers blossomed with phrases like "Cossack Terrorism" and the soldiers were booed in the streets of the villages and shot at from ambuscades in the forests.

Captain Dorst, the first military administrator of Sequoia and General Grant National Parks, created in 1890, found himself faced with a formidable array of problems. The sheep and cattlemen, who had come to look on the high country as their own, did not take kindly to the invitation of Congress to give up their privileges, yet no penalties had been provided for infractions of the rules. Just as an efficient administration was being developed the Spanish-American War broke out and the troops left. Sheep and cattle roamed at will, deer were slaughtered by hundreds. The First Utah Volunteer Company was sent to restore order, which they did by killing game with considerably more system and efficiency than the civilians. After a month they were withdrawn and replaced by regular troops.

The next 15 years were a period of gradual development. The hard-worked administrators built roads and improved services with the limited funds at their disposal. Slowly the park began to take on its present appearance. Outstanding among the military administrators were Lt. Hugh S. Johnson and Capt. Charles Young, commander of a troop of Negro cavalry known as the "Black Battalion." The natives still tell of the handsome black cavalrymen dressed in dark blue and mounted on coal black horses. On their first trip through Visalia, bound for the park, they were refused food at the local restaurants. When the troop was recalled and passed through the town again, Visalia's terrified restaurateurs left for the week end, and Captain Young and his soldiers were entertained by the community.

In 1914 a civilian administration replaced the military, and Walter Fry, who had been reared in the vicinity and had worked in and around the park since his youth, was appointed Superintendent. Fry inaugurated the policies that have kept Sequoia comparatively unspoiled. In 1920 he was appointed U. S. Commissioner for Sequoia and General Grant National Parks and his place was filled by Col. John R. White. White has endeavored to make Sequoia a model recreational and conservation area. In 1926 the Mt. Whitney-Kern River district was added to the park and the area increased from 252 to 604 square miles.

The park's outstanding attraction—the big tree—was present millions of years ago, when the present coal deposits were marshes crowded with dense and luxuriant vegetation. In time the Sequoia came to be one of the dominating trees of the northern hemisphere. Then, because of the Ice Age and changes in topography, its range became more and more restricted. The first known white men to discover it were the Joseph R. Walker party in 1839. After considerable controversy, it was named *Sequoia gigantea,* to distinguish it from the related coast species, the *Sequoia sempervirens.*

The size of the big tree has often been exaggerated. The greatest height measured is about 330 feet. Heights of 350 feet or more are theoretically possible, but almost all the largest trees have been broken off at the top by lightning. The extreme diameter above the root swellings averages about 27 feet. Similarly exaggerated stories of the great age of the trees are common. Most of the largest living specimens are probably from 1,500 to 3,000 years old. The big tree is scale-leafed and somewhat resembles the incense cedar, but its sprays are rounded rather than flattened, a light green in color. In youth the branches are slender, the tree is pyramidal in form, and the leaves are needle-like and of a bluish cast. After about 200 years the lower branches begin to drop off, the leaves flatten to scales and change in color, and the bark begins to split into ridges and turn from a purple grey to a cinnamon red. On mature trees the bark is from one to two feet thick, separated into long parallel ridges that make the trunk seem like an immense fluted Doric column; the few remaining branches, of enormous size, gnarled and twisted, add to the impression of massive power. The 32 big tree groves within the park stand at the edge of the Transition Zone (*see FLORA AND FAUNA*). The display of flowers, particularly in June and early July is profuse and brilliant.

General Grant Park was set aside principally to preserve the giant Sequoia for which it is named, which stands in one of its two splendid big tree groves. The park lies lower on the slopes of the Sierra than does Sequoia, at an average altitude of 6,500 feet. Its eastern boundary is the "hogback," Grant Park Ridge (7,350-7,750 alt.).

SEQUOIA PARK TOUR

Ash Mountain Entrance—Hospital Rock—Giant Forest Village—Lost Grove Entrance—General Grant South Entrance Station; 45.8 *m.,* Generals Highway.

Oil-surfaced roadbed throughout.

The Generals Highway, a continuation of State 198 (*see TOUR 3b*) crosses the boundary of Sequoia National Park, 0 *m.,* and continues to ASH MOUNTAIN PARK HEADQUARTERS, 1 *m.,* where incoming travelers are registered and automobile fees collected.

Northeast of Ash Mountain the highway climbs steadily, winding above the KAWEAH RIVER. Western sycamores grow along the canyon floor, and in early summer the grass is full of yellow blazing stars, crimson godetia, and wild hyacinth.

Before 1865 CAMP POTWISHA, 2.8 *m.,* a CCC camp in 1938, was the principal village of the Pot-wi-sha tribe of the Yokut. The mortar holes in which they ground their meal of acorns or buckeyes are still visible in the flat rocks below the road, and several well preserved pictographs are on the cliffs above. The Yokut, who had no knowledge of the tribes that left the prehistoric paintings, asked Hale Tharp to explain them.

East of Potwisha the road follows the twisting course of the Middle Fork of the Kaweah. The nearby mountains are characterized by unusual rock formations. Long, jagged granite scars cut the sides of some; others are walled by smooth, almost polished surfaces.

HOSPITAL ROCK CAMP (2,600 alt.), 5.2 m. (*all-year cabins; campsites*), is popular in winter with those who prefer to sleep in a warmer climate and drive to snow for the day. Opposite the camp is HOSPITAL ROCK. In the cave beneath this huge boulder (*reached by a short path*) the Indians stored their food, held pow-wows, and ministered to the sick and injured. Castle Rocks (R) and Moro Rock (L) tower 4,000 feet above, Hospital Rock like an altar before them. The place was a religious sanctuary for several tribes; numerous pictographs, their exact significance unknown, attest to the importance of the place in the lives of Indians.

Right from Hospital Rock on a narrow dirt road to BUCKEYE FLAT CAMP-GROUND, 0.5 m., and MORO CREEK, 2 m.

North of Hospital Rock the Generals Highway begins the long climb up the ridge between the Marble and Middle Forks of the Kaweah in a series of hairpin curves. The Yucca give way to buckeyes, which soon dominate the chaparral. The road cuts again and again through limestone, honeycombed with caves (*not safely accessible*). As the road continues to climb the limestone rocks are replaced by schists, the tightly pressed, metamorphosed stone that lies along the surface of the Sierra.

AMPHITHEATER POINT (4,450 alt.), 10 m. (*parking space*), overlooks the canyons below and the distant San Joaquin Valley.

At 13.4 m. is the junction with Colony Mill Rd.

Left on this rough dirt road, which the Kaweah Colonists (*see above*) were four years constructing, to the SITE OF THE KAWEAH COLONY SAWMILL, 6 m., on the Marble Fork. A RANGER STATION is here today.

The buildings of GIANT FOREST VILLAGE, 16.6 m. (6,412 alt.), residential and recreational center, stretch for a half mile along the highway. Trails radiate from the village into the eastern section of the park. Giant Forest Lodge, Camp Kaweah, Pinewood Camp, and several campgrounds are in the immediate vicinity.

The ADMINISTRATION BUILDING (*open 8-12, 1-5*) at the eastern end of the village (L) houses an administrative office, a TULARE COUNTY LIBRARY (*open 1-4:30 summer season*), and a MUSEUM. In the museum are a few Indian artifacts and a large relief map of the park showing all major roads and trails.

In front of the building is a SECTION OF A SEQUOIA, 9 feet 8 inches in diameter, that is estimated to have been about 1,705 years old at the time of its death.   Markers on some of the annual rings indicate events that occurred during the life of the tree, beginning with the invasion of Rome by the Goths in the year 250 and ending with the start of the World War in 1914.

Opposite the Administration Building is the CHURCH OF THE SEQUOIAS on a gently sloping clearing; here, in the shadow of giant Sequoias, are the log benches and stump pulpit used for outdoor religious services.

1. Left from Giant Forest Village on a footpath to BEETLE ROCK, 0.2 *m.,* a huge, smooth-topped granite promontory resembling the back of a beetle, high above Marble Canyon and overlooking the distant San Joaquin Valley.

2. Right from Giant Forest Village on an oil-surfaced road to the junction with a paved road, 0.1 *m.;* L. here 0.4 to BEAR HILL (*bears fed daily at 2:30 p.m.; ranger naturalist talk at 3*), a large enclosed area in which are the park incinerator and bear-feeding platform.

At 0.8 *m.* on the main side road is the AUTO LOG (L), a huge fallen big tree with a flattened top onto which an automobile may be driven.

At TRINITY CORNER, 1.2 *m.,* the main route goes R.   MORO ROCK, 1.6 *m.* (6,719 alt.), is climbed by a winding rock and concrete stairway. The view from its summit is magnificent, particularly at sunset.   A sheer 4,000 feet below is the Kaweah River, a shining thread.   In the east the pale moon rises above the slowly darkening, irregular ridges of the Great Western Divide.   Westward miles of hilltops reach toward the San Joaquin Valley, and in the far distance the red sun sinks behind the Coast Range.

At 2.1 *m.* is the junction with a paved road; R. here, past the PARKER GROUP, 2.2 *m.,* a small grove of giant Sequoias.

The main side road ends in a parking area at the southern end of CRESCENT MEADOW, 3.4 *m.,* filled with flowers and rich grass and surrounded by Sequoias.   This is one of the finest meadows of the middle altitudes in the entire Sierra.

a. Right from Crescent Meadow at a point a few yards north of the parking area on a trail 0.6 *m.* to THARP'S CABIN, a large, hollow big tree log that was converted into living quarters by Hale Tharp, who pastured his cattle in the nearby meadow.   The log house is preserved in its early state, and the carven "Hale Tharp, 1858" is protected by glass.   John Muir spent several nights here in 1875 and wrote enthusiastically of the "noble den."

b. Right from the parking area on the High Sierra Trail (here a pedestrian path; stock should leave from corral and join trail 4 miles east). This requires an average of 14 days as a round trip hike, and leads through wild, spectacular country, through deep canyons, past mountain lakes and meadows, to the Sierra's highest peaks.   Overnight camps are maintained in summer at approximate 10-mile intervals.

BEARPAW MEADOW (7,900 alt.), 12 *m.,* overlooks the Kaweah River Valley.   Beautiful HAMILTON LAKE (9,500 alt.) is at 16 *m.,* and the suspension bridge over HAMILTON GORGE in the Great Western Divide at 18 *m.*   KAWEAH GAP (10,800 alt.), 20 *m.,* offers sweeping views of the Kaweah Peaks Ridge and the main crest of the Sierra Nevada.   East of MORAINE LAKE (9,450 alt.), 30 *m.,* is the KERN RIVER CANYON at FUNSTON MEADOWS (6,700 alt.), 34.5 *m.*   The trail follows the canyon northward from Funston Meadows, past KERN HOT SPRINGS (6,900 alt.), 37 *m.,* to JUNCTION MEADOW (8,200 alt.).   From here it swings east for about 3.5 miles, then southward to CRABTREE MEADOW,

54.5 *m.*, Mount Whitney base camp. The summit of MOUNT WHITNEY (14,495 alt.) is at 62 *m.* Right from the summit on a trail 13 *m.* down the eastern slope to the junction with an automobile road (*see TOUR 6c*).

3. Left from Giant Forest on the Alta Trail (for pedestrians and equestrians). The KEYHOLE (L), 1.3 *m.*, is a big tree, fire-hollowed at the base, in whose sides have been burned openings resembling giant "keyholes."
At 1.6 *m.* at the junction with the Rim Rock Trail (L) stands the LINCOLN TREE (R), a rugged Sequoia 259 feet high with a diameter of 31 feet.
At 1.8 *m.* is the junction with a short trail; R. here 0.1 *m.* to CIRCLE MEADOW, on whose northern rim are the FOUNDERS GROVE, the CONGRESS GROUP, and the 250-foot PRESIDENT TREE.
At 2.3 *m.* on the Alta Trail is the junction with the Wolverton Corral Trail; R. here 4 *m.* to a junction with the High Sierra Trail (*see above*).
The Alta Trail continues northeastward, past lovely MEHRTEN MEADOW (*shelter cabin*) (9,000 alt.), on Mehrten Creek. ALTA MEADOWS (*good camping and pasture*), 7 *m.*, lies at the southern base of ALTA PEAK, 9.2 *m.* (11,211 alt.). The peak is the nearest point to Giant Forest from which Mount Whitney is visible. The view is exceptional.

The Generals Highway continues eastward to a junction with a graveled road, 17.1 *m.*

Right 0.1 *m.* to the LOWER CORRAL, one of the park's two stables (*horses available*). The HAZELWOOD PICNIC AREA is at 0.3 *m.*

At 17.5 *m.* on the highway is the junction with a trail.

1. Left on this trail through SUNSET ROCK CAMPGROUND, 0.5 *m.*, to SUNSET ROCK, 0.6 *m.*, a huge granite boulder offering the same view as Beetle Rock (*see above*). It is popular for sunset picnics.

2. Right 0.9 *m.* on Rim Rock Trail, along a granite ridge, to the junction with the Alta Trail (*see above*).

At 18.7 *m.* is the junction with an oil-surfaced road.

Right to a large parking area, 0.2 *m.* Opposite the area, in a park-like clearing (L), is the GENERAL SHERMAN TREE, the largest living thing. It was called the Karl Marx Tree by the Kaweah Colonists. The name was changed after James Wolverton, trapper and hunter, asserted he had discovered it in 1879, several years before the advent of the colonists. The height of the Sherman Tree, above the mean base, is 272.4 feet; its base circumference is 101.6 feet. Its age is estimated at between 3,000 and 4,000 years.
At 1 *m.* on the side road is a junction with an oil-surfaced road; L. 0.9 *m.* to a junction with a graded road; L. here 0.1 *m.* to the GOVERNMENT CORRAL (*horses*), called the upper corral.

At 20.9 *m.* on Generals Highway is the junction with a graded road.

Right here into LODGEPOLE CAMPGROUND (*swimming pool*), 0.2 *m.*, on the Marble Fork of the Kaweah. The special campsites for trailers are at 0.3 *m.*

1. Right 2.5 *m.* from Lodgepole Camp on a trail (for pedestrians or equestrians) to TOKOPAH FALLS. The trail ascends the canyon of the

Marble Fork of the Kaweah River through forests and meadows. The river gorge narrows between precipitous slopes, offering an example of the U-shaped glaciated valley of the Yosemite type.

2. Left 5 *m.* from Lodgepole Camp on Twin Lakes Trail (for pedestrians or equestrians) to CLOVER CREEK. TWIN LAKES (*fine trout fishing*), 7 *m.* (9,750 alt.), are at the base of SILLIMAN SHOULDER (10,500 alt.), which offers a fine mountain panorama.

At 27.4 *m.* on the Generals Highway is an attractive PICNIC AREA at the edge of HALSTEAD MEADOW.

DORST CREEK CAMPGROUND (L), 31.7 *m.*, one of the most pleasant of Sequoia's camping areas, occupies a thick forest of fir along the banks of Dorst Creek.

LOST GROVE RANGER STATION, 32.3 *m.*, marks the northwestern boundary of Sequoia National Park.

The Generals Highway continues northwestward, sweeping around one of the lateral ridges (6,500 average alt.) of the Sierra Nevada in long, easy curves. (*Road frequently closed by winter snows.*) The views of the San Joaquin Valley are numerous and impressive, and the road is lined with a mixed coniferous forest of great splendor. White fir, incense cedar, sugar pine, and western yellow pine predominate, and there are occasional Sequoias. The western dogwood, with large white blooms, is common beneath the larger trees and the steep slopes that fall away to the San Joaquin Valley are densely clothed with wild cherry, ceanothus, and other flowering shrubs.

At 45.8 *m.* is the southern boundary of General Grant National Park.

GENERAL GRANT PARK TOUR

South Entrance Station—Northern Junction with State 180; 2.5 *m.* Generals Highway.

The Generals Highway crosses the boundary of General Grant National Park, 0 *m.*, at the SOUTH ENTRANCE RANGER STATION.

At 0.2 *m.* is the junction with State 180 (*see TOUR 3b*).

At the PLAZA, 1 *m.*, near the center of the park, are Grant's ADMINISTRATIVE HEADQUARTERS. In the immediate vicinity are cabins, campgrounds, a store, the CORRAL, and the CHURCH OF THE SEQUOIAS, where outdoor religious services are held.

Right from the Plaza on oiled Rocking Rock Rd., 2.5 *m.* to ROCKING ROCK, a 48-ton granite slab balanced on the edge of PARK RIDGE. About 100 yards east is PANORAMIC POINT (7,500 alt.). Both vantages offer impressive views of KINGS RIVER CANYON, 20 miles north.

At 1.2 *m.* on Generals Highway is the junction with an oiled road.

Left on this road 0.1 *m.* to the junction with an oiled road; R. here 0.9 *m.* to the GRANT GROVE of big trees, largest of which is the GENERAL GRANT TREE, under which services are held at high noon each Christmas Day. The ancient tree is 267 feet high with a maximum base diameter of 40.3 feet and a diameter of 12 feet 200 feet above the ground.

The park's second outstanding group of Sequoias, NORTH GROVE (R), is passed at 1.5 *m.* From here the route swings sharply southward to the eastern shore of SEQUOIA LAKE (*trout and bass fishing*), 4 *m.* (5,300 alt.), 0.2 miles outside the park's western boundary. The 100-acre body of water is owned by the Y.M.C.A., which maintains several boys' camps on its shores.

The Generals Highway continues northward from the Plaza and crosses the park's northern boundary, 2.5 *m.,* where it becomes the Kings River Canyon Highway—State 180 (*see TOUR 3b*).

Yosemite National Park

Season: Summer season May 1 to Oct. 1; winter sports Dec. 15 to late April.
Administrative Offices: Headquarters at Government Center in park; regional headquarters, Sheldon Bldg., 461 Market St., San Francisco. Yosemite Park and Curry Co.: Government Center, Yosemite National Park; 39 Geary St., San Francisco; 612 S. Olive St., Los Angeles.
Admission: Free; yearly automobile permit $2, issued any entrance station. Entrance stations on All-Year Highway at Arch Rock (*open 5 a.m.-12 p.m.*); on Wawona Rd. (*open all year except during periods of heavy snow*) at South Entrance Gate (*open 6 a.m.-12 p.m. May 30 to Aug. 31, 6 a.m.-9:30 p.m. Sept. 1 to May 29*); on Big Oak Flat Rd. (*open about May 1 to Oct. 15*) at Tuolumne Grove Entrance Station and Gentry Checking Station (*one-way control: inbound 7-7:25 a.m. and at odd hours thereafter until 9-9:25 p.m.; out-bound 6-6:25 a.m. and at even hours thereafter until 8-8:25 p.m.*); on Tioga Rd. (*open about July 1 to Oct. 1*) at Aspen Valley (*open 6 a.m.-9:30 p.m.*) and Tioga Pass (*open 6 a.m.-9:30 p.m.*); and on road to O'Shaughnessy Dam at Mather Entrance Station (*open 6 a.m.-9:30 p.m.*).
Transportation: Yosemite Valley Railroad daily from Merced.
Highways from E. on State 120 (*TOUR 3b*) and State 140 (*TOUR 3b*); from S. on State 41 (*TOUR 3b*); from W. on State 120 (*TOUR 6b*).
Busses daily from Merced to Yosemite Valley; daily from Fresno in summer. Daily summer service within park from Yosemite Valley to Mirror Lake, Glacier Point, Tuolomne Meadows, Mariposa Grove, and Hetch Hetchy Dam. Marked trails 700 m. Saddle horses available near Happy Isles; rates, $3 half day, $5 full day; guides (necessary for long trips only), $3.50 half day, $6 full day. All-expense trips to High Sierra 3 days, $23 a person; 6 days, $46 a person. (*See TRAIL TOURS.*)
Accommodations: Five hotels (Yosemite Valley, Glacier Point, Mariposa Grove); three cabin groups (Yosemite Valley, Tuolomne Meadows; housekeeping tents and cabins (Yosemite Valley, Tuolomne Meadows); five High Sierra camps, open July and Aug. (Merced Lake, Vogelsang, Tuolomne Meadows, Glen Aulin, May Lake). Daily rates: hotels, $1.50 to $5 European plan, $5 to $12 American plan; cabins, $1.25 to $5.00 European plan, $3.75 to $8 American plan; meals, $1. Housekeeping tents and cabins (one day) from $1.50 for one or two persons to $7 for one or two persons; reduced rates

for longer stays. High Sierra camps for saddle and hiking parties; basic rates $1 a night, $1 a meal.

Six free public campgrounds (*sanitary conveniences*) in valley; others at Glacier Point, Mariposa Grove, Tuolomne Meadows, and along main roads. Camping permitted in spring, summer, and fall.

Winter Accommodations: Yosemite Lodge and Ahwahnee Hotel. Badger Pass Ski House in skiing area (refreshments).

Clothing and Equipment: Special clothing and equipment can be rented or purchased at general store in Old Village.

Medical Service: Medical, surgical, and dental services at Lewis Memorial Hospital, Yosemite Valley, all year; X-ray and emergency ambulance.

Postal Service: Post offices at Government Center and Wawona all year; address Yosemite National Park, Calif. Branch offices in summer at Camp Curry, Yosemite Lodge, Tuolomne Meadows.

Communication and Express Service: Telephone and telegraph service at Administration Building (Government Center), Ahwahnee Hotel, Yosemite Lodge, Camp Curry (Yosemite Valley). Money transfers handled at Administration Building. Express service at general store in Old Village; address "Care of Yosemite National Park, Calif., via El Portal."

Special Regulations: Dogs, cats, and firearms not allowed in Park overnight. Speed limit 35 m. Drive slowly at night, when bear and deer often cross roads. Do not feed bears or leave food within their reach; put food in very strong, locked containers or suspend 10 feet above ground in box between two trees. Fawns must be left alone; does will attack if young are disturbed. *Hunting and trapping prohibited.* Campers must register at camp entrance, keep camps clean, and put refuse in containers. (Get detailed information in park.)

Fishing: Licenses required. State laws apply (full rules at park). Closed waters so posted.

Entertainment: Regular summer schedule of entertainment, lectures, and expeditions; programs posted on bulletin boards. During summer ranger naturalists conduct daily nature walks (except Sundays); special bird walks at 8 a.m. each Wednesday; daily auto caravans to points of interest on valley floor at 9:30 a.m. and 2 p.m. (except Sunday); all-day hikes to Glacier Point, Vernal and Nevada Falls, and Tenaya Canyon several times weekly; 7-day hiking trips through the spectacular High Country regions. Brief educational talks morning and afternoon at museum; campfire programs in evenings at camps and lodges. Bears fed under spotlights at 8 p.m. (*see YOSEMITE TOUR 1*). Firefall nightly at 9 from tip of Glacier Point (best seen from meadows E. of Government Center or at Camp Curry). Dancing weekday evenings at Camp Curry. Skiing, skating, tobogganing, sleigh and dog sled riding, ski festivals and sports carnivals.

Yosemite National Park, a spectacular mountain region, lies on the western slope of the Sierra Nevada. Its eastern boundary, 40 miles from the Nevada State line, is on the crest of the Sierra; its western edge is in the dry foothills where the mountains merge with San Joaquin Valley. The park has 752,744 acres of mountains and forests, 429 lakes, a chain of mountain peaks averaging 10,000 feet and more, granite domes and monoliths, many trout streams, glaciers, and high mountain meadows. Five great waterfalls and many lesser ones drop over perpendicular cliffs as high as 1,612 feet.

Two main canyons bisect the park from east to west: Yosemite Valley to the south and the Grand Canyon of the Tuolumne to the north—both gouged down thousands of feet into solid rock by streams and glaciers.

Yosemite Valley (3,985 alt.), with waterfalls, Mirror Lake, Half

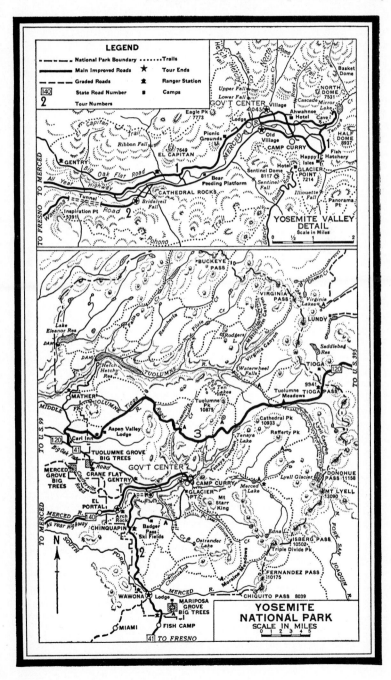

LEGEND

National Park Boundary ···· Trails
Main Improved Roads ★ Tour Ends
Graded Roads 🏠 Ranger Station
State Road Number ▪ Camps
Tour Numbers

YOSEMITE VALLEY
DETAIL
Scale in Miles

YOSEMITE
NATIONAL PARK
SCALE IN MILES

Dome, Glacier Point, and El Capitán, was the first area opened to travel; most of the public campgrounds and the main hotels and lodges are here. The population of the valley during the summer season is often 15,000. This single valley is so well known through books, paintings, photographs, motion pictures, and calendar illustrations that many consider it the whole of Yosemite National Park. It is only a small part—less than one-hundredth—of the total area.

Yosemite Valley is a U-shaped trough, 7 miles long with an average width of one mile, sunk 3,000 feet below the rim of the park and carved out of the granite slab of the Sierra by stream erosion and massive glacial action. The floor is level and parklike, with the Merced River meandering through its meadows and forests, dominated by immense domes and rock masses, which form a sheer wall around it. Dr. Bunnell, the man who named Yosemite, was so moved by the valley that he wrote years afterward, "As I looked at the grandeur of the scene a peculiar exalted sensation seemed to fill my whole being, and I found my eyes in tears with emotion."

Varieties of birds, mammals, trees, and flowers cover a wide range in the park, occupying five life zones, each with its distinct types of flora and fauna (see FLORA AND FAUNA). Over 230 varieties of birds have been catalogued, about 100 mammals, about 25 reptiles, and 12 amphibians. Tree squirrels and chipmunks scamper about camps looking for food; bear and deer wander over the valley unafraid of man. The Big Trees (Sequoia gigantea) of the Mariposa Grove, giants left over from the Age of Reptiles, are the park's outstanding trees. The valley floors, the mountain slopes, the ravines, and gorges are grown with luxuriant stands of pine, fir, hemlock, cedar, oak, maple, western yellow pine, Jeffrey pine, and California black oak. The 1,200 kinds of flowering plants and ferns are at their best in spring and early summer, when meadows are alive with Indian paintbrush, lupin, buttercups, wild geranium, leopard lilies, camas, and shooting stars.

During the Ice Age glaciers jammed Yosemite Valley, cut the river gorge from 500 to 1,500 feet deeper. Great rivers of ice, 2,000 feet thick, advanced through the Little Yosemite Valley and Tenaya Canyon to form a trunk glacier at the head of the valley 3,000 feet thick that filled the chasm with a slowly grinding mass of ice reaching to El Portal. Only the tops of the highest peaks stuck above the glaciers. When the Ice Age ended about 20,000 years ago, the glaciers melted and left a deep, 5-mile lake in Yosemite Valley, dammed by a terminal moraine near El Capitán. Streams and melting glaciers above soon filled it with débris and sand, forming the present valley floor.

For centuries before white men arrived, Indians lived in the valley, where they had at one time 40 villages. They belonged to the Miwok tribe, superior to most California Indians and especially skilled in basket making. Their name for the valley was Ahwahnee (deep grassy valley). "Yosemite" came from the Miwok word, Uzumati (grizzly bear), one of the tribal divisions or totems.

The first Americans to see the Yosemite region were members of

Joseph Walker's California expedition of 1833, who failed to impress its wonders on the world, although they told of "many small streams, which would shoot out from under high snow banks, and after running a short distance in deep chasms, precipitate themselves from one lofty precipice to another." The discovery of Yosemite Valley was accidental. Major James D. Savage and Dr. L. H. Bunnell, leading the "Mariposa Battalion" in an expedition to track down the warlike Miwok Indians and force them to sign a treaty, stumbled out of the forest on March 25, 1851, at Inspiration Point, where Yosemite Valley lay spread out before them. Bunnell was so impressed that he forgot the Indians. At the campfire on the bank of the Merced River that night, he suggested the name Yosemite. Afterward he spread the fame of the valley in his book, *Discovery of the Yosemite.*

In 1864 Congress granted Yosemite Valley and Mariposa Grove to California as a State park; in 1890 it established Yosemite National Park and in 1906 Yosemite State Park was incorporated in it. The park was guarded in summer by Federal troops and in winter by civilian rangers until the creation of the National Park Service in 1916.

YOSEMITE TOUR 1

Arch Rock Entrance Station—Yosemite Lodge—Government Center— Indian Caves—Happy Isles—Old Village; 17.2 *m.,* All-Year Highway, El Capitán Rd.

Oil-treated macadam roadbed throughout.

The All-Year Highway continues northeast from State 140 (*see TOUR 3b*) from the ARCH ROCK ENTRANCE STATION, 0 *m.* (2,855 alt.).

ARCH ROCK, 0.1 *m.,* at the western end of forest-choked Merced Canyon, is formed by two great granite boulders. The cliff-bound route runs through yellow pines, incense cedars, and Douglas firs. Across riotous Merced River (R), innumerable waterfalls tumble down the canyonside in a series of cascades. CASCADE FALLS, visible (L) at 3.1 *m.,* shoot from the rim of the canyon 594 feet above the road. INSPIRATION POINT (5,391 alt.) juts from the rim of the gorge high above granite PULPIT ROCK (4,195 alt.) across the river (R) at 4.8 *m.* At 5.8 *m.* is the junction with Pohono Rd.

Right on Pohono Rd., crossing the Merced River, 0.2 *m.* to FERN SPRINGS (R), bubbling cold and clear into a small stream where a unique species of salamander is found.

The road winds through the grassy reaches of pine- and oak-dotted BRIDAL VEIL MEADOWS. On the far side (L) at 0.6 *m.* a plaque in a grove of trees marks the GRAVES OF ROSE AND SHURBORN, prospectors from Coarse Gold Gulch ambushed here by Yosemite Indians May 26, 1852. The United States Cavalry expedition that buried their bodies shot five warriors in revenge and chased the rest southwestward into the Mono Lake region.

BRIDAL VEIL FALL (R), 1.5 *m.,* drops 620 feet from the cliff above in a delicate lacy pattern clouded with fine, rain-like spray. The mist that hangs in the air roundabout is tinged by the sun in late afternoon—the best time to see the fall—with changing rainbows of rich reds, blues, purples, and yellows, which the observer can reach out and touch.

The twin shafts of CATHEDRAL ROCKS (R), 2.4 *m.*, towering 2,154 feet above the valley floor, challenged mountain climbers until 1935, when youthful members of the Sierra Club inched up them with ropes and spikes like human flies under the lenses of motion picture cameras.

A concourse of shaggy brown or black Yosemite bears—and sometimes an uninvited coyote or skunk—usually gather at the concrete troughs of the BEAR FEEDING PITS (L), 3.3 *m.* (*feeding time 8 p.m.*) in the glare of floodlights when garbage is brought in from hotels and lodges. The bears, whose sense of smell is keener than their eyesight, come tracking down the scent of sugar or honey, set out to attract them. Mother bears sometimes bring their cubs and chase them up a tree for safety while they investigate the evening menu. The bears will eat almost everything but grapefruit rinds.

The route continues along the southern rim of the valley, past a meadow (R), 4.3 *m.*, starting point for the 4-mile trail to Glacier Point (*see Trail 3*), to OLD VILLAGE, 5.1 *m.* (*see below*).

East of the junction with Pohono Rd. the route continues as El Capitán Rd. through the Gates of the Valley, formed by the sheer precipices of El Capitán (L) and Cathedral Rocks (R). Beyond these towering granite portals lie the peaceful forest-fringed green meadows of the valley floor beneath the colossal upthrust of cliffs. High up on the north wall of the canyon (L), the slim stream of 1,602-foot RIBBON FALLS, highest in Yosemite, appears when snows are melting. Across the meadows, behind the projecting cliff of Glacier Point (R), bald granite Half Dome soars aloft. The stony peak in the distance is CLOUDS' REST, highest point on Yosemite's walls.

At EL CAPITAN CONTROL STATION, 7.2 *m.*, is the junction with Big Oak Flat Rd. (*see YOSEMITE TOUR 3*).

EL CAPITAN (L), 7.8 *m.*, bulking above the valley floor 3,604 feet, is the world's largest monolith of exposed granite. In volume it equals four Gibraltars; in height, three Empire State Buildings.

At ROCKY POINT (L), 9.9 *m.*, the road winds beside rough boulders that fell from the cliff above in February 1923, during one of the biggest rock slides in the valley's recent history. Just above the tree line, the face of the cliff bears evidence of glacial polish and rock striations that give it the appearance of rough concrete. Higher than Rocky Point are the THREE BROTHERS, three peaks looking like steps as they rise one above the other.

In the trim, Government-supplied modern cottages of the NEW INDIAN VILLAGE (L), 10.1 *m.* (*visitors welcome*), live about 60 Indians, descendants of the original Yosemite, Paiute, Mono, and other Indian peoples. The Indians sell baskets, beadwork, and other articles; they are given work preference in the valley.

YOSEMITE LODGE is at 10.6 *m.* (*cottages, cabins, swimming pool, lounge*).

At 10.7 *m.* is the junction with a paved road.

Left on this road 0.2 *m.* for the best view of YOSEMITE FALLS, which plummet downward in two separate falls—Upper and Lower Yosemite—in a ponderous 2,425 foot drop from the rim of the canyon wall to the floor. The Upper Yosemite Fall, highest free leaping waterfall in the world, drops 1,430 feet—nine times as far as Niagara. The 910-foot plunge of Middle Cascade carries it to 310-foot Lower Yosemite Fall.

From the end of the road, Lost Arrow Trail winds through black oaks, goldencup oaks, and California laurels to the foot of the lower fall, 0.7 *m.*

The route continues through a fine grove of glossy-leaved California black oaks to GOVERNMENT CENTER, 11.2 *m.* (4,045 alt.), administrative headquarters of Yosemite National Park. The YOSEMITE MUSEUM (*open daily 9-12, 1-5*) houses a library and exhibits devoted to all the park's major aspects; geology, flora and fauna, Indians, and history. A special feature is the relief scale models of Yosemite—with all trails, roads, falls, peaks, and glaciers marked—where riding and hiking trips can be planned in detail. Behind the museum are two Indian bark huts, a *temescal* (Ind., sweat house), and two grain storage stacks; the local Indians here demonstrate how their ancestors pounded acorns, harvested wild seeds, made baskets, and built huts. At the eastern edge of Government Center is modern LEWIS MEMORIAL HOSPITAL.

At the entrance (L) to the $1,000,000 AHWANEE HOTEL, 11.7 *m.,* Yosemite's luxury hostelry, built in rustic style of concrete blocks and rough timber in a forested nook of the valley, the route turns R. to a junction at 12 *m.* and then L. across two bridges over the Merced River.

The flat face of HALF DOME (8,927 alt.) towers straight ahead nearly a mile above the valley floor. Above the meadows (R) rises GLACIER POINT (7,214 alt.) (*see YOSEMITE TOUR 2*). The ROYAL ARCHES appear (L) at 12.6 *m.* on the perpendicular valley wall—the main arch measuring 1,000 feet in height and 1,800 feet in width—and behind them, the granite mass of NORTH DOME (7,531 alt.). The WASHINGTON COLUMN (5,912 alt.) lifts its top almost half a mile above the road right of the Royal Arches.

INDIAN CAVES (L), 13.1 *m.,* is the site of the old Indian village Lah-koo-hah (come out). Great granite boulders, knocked off by slides and glaciers, lie in a jumble at the foot of the cliff, forming several big caves and many small ones. Indians used these caves for storage, for shelter from storms, and sometimes for hide-outs. In front of the caves on a large flat rock are some bark huts where the Indians dance and chant in summer for the benefit of tourists.

At 13.2 *m.* is the junction with a paved road.

Left on this road through TENAYA CANYON to MIRROR LAKE, 0.5 *m.,* a favorite subject of painters and photographers. The lake is best before 9 a.m., when its glassy surface reflects Half Dome and CLOUDS REST (9,924 alt.) on the south side of Tenaya Canyon, and MOUNT WATKINS (8,600 alt.) and BASKET DOME (7,602 alt.) on the north side. Mirror Lake was formed by a rockslide from the walls of Tenaya Canyon which dammed up Tenaya Creek. Now the creek is slowly filling the lake bottom with silt.

At 13.5 *m.* is a junction; the route continues L. here, to cut through boulder-piled MEDIAL MORAINE, formed by glaciers during the Ice Age.

Around the rocky HAPPY ISLES, 14.1 *m.* (*parking space, picnicking, hiking*), foams the Merced River, shooting down from Vernal and Nevada Falls, with an unceasing roar. The STATE FISH HATCHERY (*open 8-12; 1-5*) has an annual output of nearly a million and a half Loch Levan and eastern brook trout. Long troughs inside the building are filled with growing fish that will stock park streams. The Concrete Footbridge (L) is the starting point for many short trail trips and long hikes.

CAMP 14 (R), 14.8 *m.*, is one of the largest of the park's free campgrounds.

The OLD APPLE ORCHARD (L), 14.9 *m.*, was planted by James Lamon, first homesteader in the valley, in the early 1860's.

CAMP CURRY, 15.1 *m.* (*lodge, cabins, tent houses*), is open during summer only, but in winter operates a skating rink, ashcan slide, and beginners' ski slopes.

JOSEPH LECONTE MEMORIAL LODGE (L), 15.5 *m.*, is a stone building erected by the Sierra Club and friends to the memory of the geologist who loved Yosemite so much. "Joe" Le Conte—as his students called him—was a professor at the University of California. Inside the lodge are a lounge, a library on Yosemite and the Sierra, and a collection of photographs.

In the OLD VILLAGE, 16.2 *m.* (*general stores, café*), formerly park headquarters, is CEDAR COTTAGE (L), built in 1859 of handsawn boards and shakes split from local pine. Back of the building is the BIG TREE ROOM, built around a large incense cedar that grows up through the roof.

YOSEMITE PARK TOUR 2

South Entrance Gate—Mariposa Big Tree Grove—Wawona—Glacier Point—Wawona Tunnel—Jct. with Pohono Bridge Rd.; 25.4 *m.*

At the SOUTH ENTRANCE GATE, 0 *m.* (*see TOUR 3b*), is the junction with a paved road.

Right on this road to the MARIPOSA GROVE OF BIG TREES, 2 *m.* (*lodge, museum, campground*), a 2-mile tract in which grow 617 giant Sequoias—some 200 of them measuring 10 feet or more in diameter at breast height. The grove was discovered in May 1857 by Galen Clark, whose cabin, built soon after the discovery, is reproduced in the BIG TREE GROVE MUSEUM.

The oldest tree in the grove is the gnarled GRIZZLY GIANT, estimated to be 3,800 years of age, which has a girth of 96.5 feet and a height of 209 feet. The fallen MASSACHUSETTS TREE near the museum, 280 feet long and 28 feet in diameter, which broke into sections when it was blown over in 1927, affords an opportunity to study the growth rings of the Sequoia. The FALLEN MONARCH, nearly 300 feet long and 26 feet in diameter, is of such size that a six-horse stage, a row of automobiles—and even a troop of United States cavalry—have been photographed on its trunk at various times. The TELESCOPE, 175 feet high and 18 feet in diameter, is still bearing cones, although its heart was burned out by fire. The road through the grove goes through a tunnel 8 feet high and 11 feet wide, cut through the base of the 231-foot WAWONA TREE in 1881.

WAWONA POINT (6,980 alt.), at the end of the loop road through the grove, overlooks the panoramic expanses of Wawona Basin and South Fork Canyon.

WAWONA (4,096 alt.), 4 m. (*hotel, store, campground, garage; tennis courts, golf course, and swimming pools; saddle and pack animals*), stands in a wide mountain meadow, fringed with a forest of pine and fir. The surrounding country, known as the Wawona Basin, was added to the park in 1932.

At CHINQUAPIN JUNCTION (6,050 alt.), 16 m. (*gas pump and lunch counter*), is a ranger station (*information*).

Right from Chinquapin Junction on Glacier Point Rd. 5.2 m. to BADGER PASS SKI HOUSE (*fireplace, restaurant, ski rental rooms*). The skiing here, comparing favorably with that at St. Moritz, ranges from easy practice slopes for beginners to steep, 11-mile downhill runs for experts. An "up-ski," or lift, tows skiers to the Ski Top (7,950 alt.), starting point of seven downhill runs.

GLACIER POINT (7,214 alt.), 16.1 m. (*hotel, restaurant*), commands the climax of all Yosemite views. From the top of the cliff beside OVERHANGING ROCK (L), Yosemite Valley lies, 3,254 feet below. The Merced River winds in a thin silver course through the deep green of the meadows and forests, which startlingly resemble a well-kept park in the midst of wild crags and mountains. Automobiles look like crawling beetles, and human beings are hardly visible. From the rim of the valley the High Sierra stretches out and up with all the domes, snowy peaks, waterfalls, cascades, and gorges distinct in the clear mountain air. Half Dome dominates the landscape. Vernal and Nevada Falls are visible (R).

At 23.2 m. the Wawona Road enters WAWONA TUNNEL, drilled and blasted through solid granite to avoid scarring the outside of the cliff. The tunnel was finished in 1933 at a cost of $837,000. It is 4,230 feet long, 28 feet wide, and 19 feet high. It includes the latest types of automatic ventilating and safety devices.

At 24 m. is the EAST PORTAL (4,408 alt.) of Wawona Tunnel. A wide parking area commands a sweeping panorama of Yosemite Valley, with massive El Capitán (L) and Half Dome looming in the distance. Right are the THREE GRACES and Bridal Veil Fall. A photograph near the granite curb gives the names and altitudes of the peaks and falls visible from this point.

At 25.4 m. is the junction with Pohono Rd. (*see YOSEMITE TOUR 1*).

YOSEMITE PARK TOUR 3

Junction with Big Oak Flat Rd.—Aspen Valley Entrance Station— Tenaya Camp—Tuolumne Meadows—Tioga Pass Entrance Station— Jct. with US 395; 66.4 m., State 120.

Oil-treated macadam roadbed between junction with Big Oak Flat Road and Aspen Valley Entrance Station, elsewhere partly dirt and partly paved; open from about July 1 to October 1.

. The Tioga Pass road follows the divide between the Merced and Tuolumne Rivers, passing chasms truly startling in size and reached so abruptly that the traveler is totally unprepared for their appearance; below, the rivers shine and glint in their gorges. Along this divide between the two rivers Captain Joseph Reddeford Walker, the first white man in the Yosemite region, led an exploring party in November 1833, coming through from the east. This route penetrates the heart of the High Sierra near the headwaters of the Tuolumne River in the northern sector of Yosemite National Park. This formerly little-known region includes, as John Muir wrote, "snowy mountains soaring into the sky twelve and thirteen thousand feet . . . separated by tremendous canyons and amphitheaters; gardens on their sunny brows, avalanches thundering down their long white slopes, cataracts roaring gray and foaming in the crooked, rugged gorges, and glaciers in their shadowy recesses . . ."

At 0 *m.* is the junction of State 120 (*see TOUR 3b*) with oil-surfaced Big Oak Flat Rd.

> Right on Big Oak Flat Rd. 0.3 *m.* to CARL INN (*fuel and refreshments*).
> The TUOLUMNE GROVE ENTRANCE STATION, 5.3 *m.* (*open 6-9*) is in the TUOLUMNE GROVE OF BIG TREES, near the headwaters of Crane Creek. The grove contains many of the best specimens left standing of the *Sequoia gigantea*, or Big Tree. The DEAD GIANT is one of the grove's "tunnel trees," originally 120 feet and still more than 100 feet in circumference, although several times damaged by forest fires. Through it passes a full-sized road. Also in this grove are two trees that have become united about 20 feet from the ground, named the SIAMESE TWINS. A little below the Dead Giant in a small ravine are the remains of what once was a titanic tree, estimated to be perhaps 4,000 years old.
> Big Oak Flat Rd. skirts sweeping vistas of Yosemite Valley as it passes through fine stands of fir and sugar pine. East of the GENTRY RANGER STATION, 15.3 *m.* (*telephone, information*), the road is under one-way control (*in-bound on odd hours only, out-bound on even hours only*).

At 23.3 *m.* is the junction with El Capitán Rd. in Yosemite Valley (*see YOSEMITE TOUR 1*).

At 2.1 *m.* on State 120 is the junction with an oiled road.

> Left here 6 *m.* to the MATHER ENTRANCE STATION (*open 6-9:30*) to Yosemite.
> The highway runs along the rim of Poopenaut Valley to the great concrete expanse of O'SHAUGHNESSY DAM, 12.2 *m.,* 20 years in the building, which blocks the mouth of Hetch Hetchy Valley, impounding a reservoir that supplies water and power to San Francisco. It is about 3 miles long and from a quarter to three-quarters of a mile wide, carved out by a huge glacier. For 2,000 feet the sheer granite walls of the canyon rise almost perpendicularly; the crests of pinnacles and domes in the range surrounding it rise twice that high above the lake. HETCH HETCHY FALLS, or the Wapama, on the north side below North Dome, form a cascade, not quite perpendicular. The varied battlements of rock resemble those of Yosemite Valley, although less impressive because smaller in size. A hunter by the name of Joseph Screech discovered this valley in 1850. The spelling of the name customarily used at the time was Hatchatchie, an Indian word for a kind of grass used for food.

At 8 *m.* is the ASPEN VALLEY ENTRANCE STATION (*open 6-9:30*) to Yosemite National Park.

From Aspen Valley, populous with silvery aspens, the Tioga Pass Road leads eastward across the Sierra highlands through magnificent stands of fir and pine. It traverses Long Gulch to YOSEMITE CREEK CAMPGROUND, on the upper waters of the torrent which plunges 5 miles downstream into Yosemite Valley.

Along the base (L) of MOUNT HOFFMAN (10,836 alt.) it proceeds, crossing Porcupine and Snow Flats, to TENAYA LAKE, 28 m. Indians called it Pyweack (Lake of the Shining Rocks) because of the glacier-burnished granite in the depths of the lake and on the shores. Here old Chief Tenaya and his band of Yosemites were chased down and captured in May 1851.

The road continues northeast, running along the base of Polly Dome, huge and massive, devoid of vegetation except for a great juniper tree perched jauntily high on its side. It passes Fairview Dome, another typical cupola of granite, and runs on into TUOLUMNE MEADOWS (8,594 alt.), 45.1 m. (gas station, garage, store, post office, lodge, free campground), in the basin of an ancient lake, a grassy floor of shining green in summer. Before the basin held a lake it was filled by a glacier from which poured streams of melting ice through Tuolumne, Hetch Hetchy, and Tenaya Canyons. In the northern section of the meadows is SODA SPRINGS, an especially popular spot for camping. The story is that biscuits made with the spring water have no equal for lightness; the carbon dioxide in the water raises them as baking-powder.

Tuolumne Meadows is a starting place for trips by foot or horseback down the Tuolumne River Gorge by way of Glen Aulin High Sierra Camp to Waterwheel Falls, where the river, John Muir wrote, "is one wild, exulting, onrushing mass of snowy purple bloom . . . gliding in magnificent silver plumes, dashing and foaming against huge boulder dams, leaping high in the air in wheel-like whirls. . . ." Farther down the canyon of the Tuolumne are half-mile-deep Muir Gorge and meadowed Pate Valley with its overhanging rocky walls where are Indian pictographs. Other trails from Tuolumne Meadows lead to Mount Conness and to glacier-shrouded, 13,090-foot Mount Lyell, dominating the upper Tuolumne Region from the east.

The road continues northeastward from Tuolumne Meadows. MOUNT CONNESS (12,560 alt.) rises ahead, named for the Senator who in 1864 secured legislation making the Yosemite region a public reserve.

TIOGA PASS (9,941 alt.), 52.1 m., the highest elevation of the route, marks the crest of the Sierra. Here the road leaves Yosemite National Park at the TIOGA PASS ENTRANCE STATION (open 6-9:30).

The rugged snow-mottled flanks of red MOUNT DANA (13,055 alt.), named for James Dwight Dana, American mineralogist and geologist, tower high to the southeast. On its slope lies TIOGA LAKE (R). Northeast of the lake is the old Tioga Mine, whose owners hired Chinese laborers to build the Tioga Road in the early '80's. ELLERY LAKE (R) lies at the head of Leevining Canyon, through which the road swoops downward in breath-taking curves. The descent is abrupt, twisting on narrow ledges carved on the edge of mountain slopes—and even from bare granite cliffs.

At 66.4 *m.* is the junction with US 395 (*see TOUR 6b*).

YOSEMITE PARK TRAILS

(Information on trails, fishing, and camping, and park maps available at Government Center and ranger stations. Hikers should avoid short cuts from designated trails, should start early on long hikes and return before dark, should register at chief ranger's office before starting on trips to isolated sections. Taxi service at 25¢ a person available to and from start of trails in upper half of valley; telephones available at base of all trails. Inquire at hotels or stables about daily saddle trips to trail points)

TRAIL 1: Happy Isles—Sierra Point—Vernal Fall—Nevada Fall; 3.5 *m.* (*Horses not allowed off valley floor without guide.*) The easiest of the trails off the valley floor, wide and paved, affording fine views of trees, rocks and waterfalls. From the footbridge in HAPPY ISLES, 0 *m.,* the trail winds along the cascading Merced River.

At 0.3 *m.* is the junction with a trail.

> Left here 0.5 *m.* over a series of switchbacks on the flank of Grizzly Peak to SIERRA POINT, where five great waterfalls—Upper and Lower Yosemite, Vernal, Nevada, and Illilouette—can be seen at one time.

As the main trail rounds the base of GRIZZLY PEAK, the mouth of ILLILOUETTE CANYON and 370-foot ILLILOUETTE FALL appear at its head (R).

VERNAL BRIDGE, 1.5 *m.,* offers a good view of Vernal Fall (*see below*).

At 1.7 *m.* is the junction with a horse trail, an alternate route.

> Right here 2.4 *m.,* to NEVADA FALL, GLACIER POINT, 7.3 *m.,* and MERCED LAKE, 12.9 *m.*

The main route, known for a short distance as the Mist Trail, where a fine rain descends from Vernal Fall, continues up the right side of the canyon in a series of steps across the steep cliffs and across the face of a perpendicular cliff on a narrow ledge (*iron handrails*).

The waters of 317-foot VERNAL FALL, 2.3 *m.,* one of the great falls of Yosemite, thunder from the top of the granite cliff in a wide sheet.

From Vernal Fall the trail sometimes zigzags up rocky slopes and then plunges into cool pine woods.

At 2.5 *m.* is the junction with a horse trail; the route continues L., crosses the river at DIAMOND CASCADES, climbs to SNOW FLAT, below LIBERTY CAP (7,072 alt.), and continues its ascent (L) another 500 feet, by the NEVADA FALL ZIGZAGS.

NEVADA FALL, 3.5 *m.* (5,910 alt.), drops 594 feet with a curious twist, breaking off at the edges to separate in what are known as spray rockets.

TRAIL 2: Happy Isles—Nevada Fall—Panorama Cliff—Glacier Point (7,214 alt.); 8.3 m. One of the easiest of the longer hikes, requiring about 6 hours.

TRAIL 3: Bridal Veil Rd.—Union Point—Glacier Point; 4.6 m. One of the most popular Yosemite trails, rewarding the climber with superb views; it rises rapidly in switchbacks up the valley rim through forests of Douglas fir and sugar pine.

TRAIL 4: Happy Isles—Vernal Fall—Nevada Fall—Half Dome (8,852 alt.); 8.3 m. A difficult climb, safe but requiring caution; canteens should be carried. Half Dome Summit, 4,892 feet above the valley floor, affords a view of the San Joaquin Valley and the Coast Range on clear days.

TRAIL 5: Happy Isles—Vernal Fall—Nevada Fall—Little Yosemite Valley—Clouds Rest; 10.5 m. A one-day climb to and from Clouds Rest (9,930 alt.), highest of the peaks enclosing Yosemite Valley.

TRAIL 6: Yosemite Valley—Columbia Point—Yosemite Point and Falls; 3.16 m. John Muir, a man "almost beside himself with the glory of the Sierras," described the view from Yosemite Point as one of the most impressive phenomena in the area.

TRAIL 7: Mirror Lake to North Dome, 8 m. This trail is very steep, and an early start should be made. Splendid views from North Dome, especially west to the Gates of the Valley and to the east where the colossal bulk of Half Dome dominates the scene.

TRAIL 8: Yosemite Valley—Happy Isles—Merced Lake—Vogelsang Pass and Camp—Tuolumne Meadows—Glen Aulin—Waterwheel Falls—May Lake—Mirror Lake; 70 m. This hike, led by a ranger naturalist every Monday morning during July and August (*reservations at Yosemite Museum; no charge*), covers the route in easy stages with a stop each night at a High Sierra camp (*cots and bedding $1; meals $1*). Provision is made for fishing, swimming, and walks to scenic point of interest along the route.

Golden Gate International Exposition

Season: February 18, 1939 to December 2, 1939, 288 days; open daily from 10 a.m.

Transportation: By Key System ferries from San Francisco and Oakland, one-way fare 10¢. By automobile from San Francisco: take upper deck of San Francisco-Oakland Bay Bridge to east end of Yerba Buena Island Tunnel and turn R. on Treasure Island Road; returning, follow extreme right lanes on causeway from island and turn R. on bridge. By automobile from East Bay points: take upper deck of San Francisco-Oakland Bay Bridge to west end of Yerba Buena Island Tunnel and turn R. on Treasure Island Road; returning, follow causeway, and turn L. on ramp over bridge, and R. on bridge. Bridge toll from San Francisco and Oakland: 50¢ round-trip for car and five occupants, 5¢ for each additional passenger; round-trip tolls collected at toll plaza on Yerba Buena Island from motorists from San Francisco; at main toll plaza near east end of bridge, from motorists from East Bay points. Parking space (cars parked by attendants) for 14,000 vehicles on Treasure Island.

Admission to Exposition Grounds: 50¢ for adults, 25¢ for children.

Accommodations: Transportation on island by motor caravan, rickshaw, and wheel-chair, small charge; nursery for children, small charge; restaurants, all prices.

Special Events: Among the special events scheduled for most of the Exposition's 288 days are celebrations in commemoration of the holidays of the United States and foreign nations, of visiting organizations and conventions, of cities, counties, and States. Scheduled events include the All-World Beef Cattle Show, Feb. 18-28; Japanese Doll Festival, March 3; Army Day, Apr. 6; Pan-American Day, Apr. 14; San Francisco Day, Apr. 18; Northern California Friendly Indian Pow-Wow, Apr. 22; Wild West Show and Rodeo, May 13-22; British Empire Day, May 27; Night Horse Show, June 30-July 9; Bastille Day, July 14; American Kennel Club All-Breed Dog Show, July 15-16; Alaska Day, Aug. 17; Welsh Eisteddfod, Sept. 2-3; Admission Day, Sept. 9; Central American Day, Sept. 15; China Day, Oct. 10; National Dairy Show, Oct. 21-30; Navy Day, Oct. 27; California Night Horse Show, Nov. 25-Dec. 2.

THE GOLDEN GATE INTERNATIONAL EXPOSITION, situated on man-made Treasure Island, north of Yerba Buena Island in San Francisco Bay, is America's official World's Fair of the West— "A Pageant of the Pacific." With eleven western States as its sponsors and the San Francisco Bay cities as its host communities, the exposition includes exhibits of 30 foreign nations and more than 350 industries. It is, in essence, a "travel fair," assembling the vast recreational resources of the Pacific Basin and displaying them as spectacular background for industrial progress.

The exposition is the third held in the San Francisco Bay region. The California Mid-Winter Exposition of 1894 was staged in Golden Gate Park; the Panama-Pacific Exposition of 1915, in San Francisco's Marina district, celebrated the opening of the Panama Canal; the 1939 exposition commemorates completion of the Golden Gate and San Francisco-Oakland Bay Bridges.

The exposition's island site rises from the solid foundation of rocky shoals, once a menace to mariners, that stretch north of Yerba Buena Island 26 feet under water. The first step in reclaiming this watery waste was to build great embankments out of 287,000 tons of quarried rock, outlining the island's boundaries. A fleet of dredgers next went to work dredging 20,000,000 cubic yards of mud and sand from the bottom of the Bay and piling it within the embankments to a height 13 feet above sea level. Over the mud and sand, "unsalted" by a leaching process, was spread a top dressing of loam brought by barges from the mainland. When the island-builders had finished their work, a 400-acre island appeared in the Bay, a mile long and two-thirds of a mile wide. A 900-foot paved causeway joined it to Yerba Buena Island and the San Francisco-Oakland Bay Bridge. Ferry slips and landings for small craft and flying boats were constructed at the island's edges. A 3,000,000-gallon reservoir was blasted in the rock of Yerba Buena Island and water piped to it from San Francisco over the bridge.

From the island, silhouetted against the Bay, rises the temporary $50,000,000 city built to house the exposition. Its ground plan and the architecture of its buildings are the work of an architects' commission consisting of Arthur Brown, Jr., Lewis P. Hobart, William G. Merchant, E. Weihe, and Timothy L. Pflueger. The exposition plan is compact and highly centralized, with broad avenues branching from a great circular Court of Honor near the southwest corner of the island. The architectural theme, based on an ancient walled city of the East, is a blend of traditional Oriental forms, employing the long horizontal lines, set-back pyramids, and exotic finials characteristic of Malayan, Incan, and Cambodian architecture.

The illusion of magnitude and splendor planned by the exposition's designers is heightened by the use of flaming banners, huge cylindrical lanterns, translucent glass fabric pillars, pylons with torchieres streaming flames of vapor. The buildings are finished in cement stucco mixed with vermiculite, a mica-like substance which, when applied to the wet stucco, gives the wall surfaces a radiant color, antique in texture, yet sparkling with a new brilliance. The colors used throughout are soft. An effective system of indirect lighting with thousands of floodlights accentuates the stepped set-backs and sculptures of the exhibition buildings, creating the illusion at night of a "magic city" in amber white and pastel shades of shimmering light, floating in the Bay. By daylight the grounds are colorful with green lawns, flowering bulbs and plants, lush tropical foliage bordering the fountains, radial walks, and broad avenues. Most colorful of all is the 25-acre "Persian Prayer Rug" of 1,500,000 cuttings of ice plant (*mesembryanthemum*) in pink, red, yellow, and orange shades laid out along the western waterfront.

The main entrance to the exposition is through the Portals of the Pacific, flanked by pyramidal entrance towers rising to the height of 12-story buildings and crowned with the colossal elephant heads which are a dominant decorative form.

The entrance leads into the central Court of Honor, where the 400-foot Tower of the Sun lifts its pinnacled spire, topped with a golden phoenix (O. C. Malmquist, sculptor) symbolizing the rise of San Francisco after the fire of 1906. From the Court of Honor radiate formally landscaped concourses, bordered by the main exhibit pavilions.

Northward an avenue flanked (R) by the Vacationland pavilion and (L) by the Hall of Electricity and Communication and the Hall of Science, leads to the Court of Pacifica. Facing the court on the north is the Recreation Building with its theater, exhibit rooms, play areas, and adjoining athletic stadium. On one side (L) is the entrance to the exposition from the San Francisco ferry slips and on the other (R), the entrance to the exposition's 40-acre amusement zone, the Gayway. Among the Gayway's features are a three-quarter-mile miniature railroad; the open-air pageantry of the Cavalcade of the Golden West; reproductions of Hollywood Boulevard, Barbary Coast, and Streets of the World; and a Chinese City with temples, tea gardens, huts and pagodas, markets, shops, and theaters.

Southward from the Court of Honor an avenue flanked (R) by the Hall of Mines, Metals, and Machinery and (L) by the Hall of Homes and Gardens leads into the Court of the Moon. At its south end is the Port of the Trade Winds between Treasure and Yerba Buena Islands, where junks, squarereriggers, yachts, and flying clippers anchor. On one side (R) is the horseshoe-shaped Administration Building. An avenue leading (L) from the Court of the Moon is bordered by the Palace of Fine and Liberal Arts and the Hall of Air Transportation. The Palace of Fine and Liberal Arts houses outstanding collections of modern American paintings and ancient masterpieces loaned by foreign governments, including Raphael's *Madonna of the Chair* and Botticelli's *Birth of Venus*.

The avenue leading eastward from the central Court of Honor is bordered (R) by the International Exhibits and California Agriculture pavilions and (L) by the Foods and Beverages pavilion. It leads into the Court of Flowers and beyond, into the Court of Reflections, which surrounds a great lagoon, the Lake of All Nations. Bordering the lagoon on the south are the California Building Group, housing exhibits of the State and counties of California; on the east, the United States Government Building and State exhibit pavilions; and on the north, the Pacific House and the various structures of the Pacific Nations Exhibit Area, displaying the industries, arts, foods, and entertainments of foreign nations.

The courts and buildings of the major group are adorned with sculpture and mural paintings executed by some of the most noted Western artists. Among these is Ralph Stackpole's colossal statue *Pacifica,* symbolizing the unity of the Pacific nations, standing 80 feet high in the Court of the same name. Other notable sculptures include Ettore Cadorin's *Evening Star,* a figure of Venus in the Court of the Moon; a bold relief mural, *The Peacemakers,* by Margaret, Helen, and Esther Bruton, crowning the entrance towers of the Portals of the Pacific; the balancing bas-reliefs, finished in gold, *Dance of Life* by Jacques Schnier, and *Path of Darkness* by Lulu Hawkins Braghetta; the winged figures surmounting the pylons in the Court of the Seven Seas representing the *Spirit of Adventure,* by P. O. Tognelli; the fountain groups in the Court of Pacifica, by Jacques Schnier, Brents Carlton, Adeline Kent, Sargent Johnson, Carl George, Ruth Wakefield, Cecilia Graham, and Helen Phillips. Another group in this court is Haig Patigian's *Creation.* In each of the four main exhibit buildings are sculptures by Raymond Puccinelli, Ettore Cadorin, and Carlo Taliabue. In the towers flanking the South Gardens are symbolic murals by Helen Forbes, Franz Bergmaun, and Nelson Poole; in the Pacific Building are eight great relief maps by Miguel Covarubias; and on the walls fronting the Court of the Flowers are six murals by Millard Sheets.

Treasure Island, once the exposition has closed and its temporary structures have been removed, will serve as a terminal for trans-Pacific flying clipper ships, which will take off and land in the sheltered lagoon between its southern edge and Yerba Buena Island. The three permanent structures built with Federal aid—the $800,000 administration building and the two $400,000 steel and concrete hangars, each 335 feet long and 78 feet high—will remain to serve the airport.

PART IV
Appendices

Chronology

1533   Pilot Fortuno Ximenes discovers an "island" (Lower California) west of Mexico. Killed while trying to land.

1535   May 5. Cortés lands where Ximenes was killed. Calls place Santa Cruz (possibly the later La Paz). Names the country *California*.

1539   Francisco de Ulloa surveys both shores of "Sea of Cortés" (later Gulf of California); misses mouth of Colorado River, but discovers that Baja (Lower) California is a peninsula.

1540   Hernando de Alarcón ascends gulf; discovers Colorado River. To contact him, Melchor Diaz traverses Arizona, and crosses Colorado River, near Yuma. He, or de Alarcón, first white man to set foot in Alta (Upper) California.

1542   Sept. 28. Juan Rodríguez Cabrillo sails into San Diego Bay, which he names "San Miguel."

1579   June 15. Francis Drake enters Drake's Bay; holds California's first Christian service, and claims "Nova Albion" in the name of Her Majesty, Queen Elizabeth.

1602   Nov. 10. Sebastián Vizcáino enters San Miguel Bay; renames it San Diego de Alcala. On Dec. 16 he anchors in Monterey Bay.

1697   Jesuits, under Father Juan María Salvatierra, begin mission at Loreta—first permanent colony in Baja California.

1701   Nov. 21. Father Eusebio Francisco Kino, Jesuit missionary, crosses southeastern corner of California, working among Indians of Pimeria Alta.

1767   Carlos III, of Spain, issues decree banishing Jesuits from all Spanish colonies.

1768   Father Junipero Serra, "patron saint of California," arrives at Loredo, with 16 Franciscan monks. Jesuit missions in Lower California surrendered.

1769   April. Two vessels arrive San Diego Bay, with supplies, to equip colony.

       May-June. Settlers and soldiers under Gov. Gaspar de Portolá, Capt. Fernando de Rivera y Moncada and Father Junipero Serra come overland from Lower California, with cattle.

       July 16. Father Serra blesses site of Misión San Diego de Alcala, first of 21 missions established in California within 54 years.

       Aug. 2. Portolá camps at site of Los Angeles; continues northward in search of Monterey Bay, but, unaware, passes it, Oct. 2. José Artego, of advance guard, sights San Francisco Bay (Nov. 2), but expedition turns back, reaching San Diego Jan. 24, 1770.

1770   June 3. Father Serra founds Misión San Carlos de Monterey (renamed San Carlos Borromeo de Carmelo in 1771, when removed). Governor Portolá establishes Monterey presidio (fort) and takes formal possession of country, in name of Carlos III.

1771   Two missions founded: San Antonio de Padua and San Gabriel Arcangel.

1772   March 20. Captain Pedro Fages leads expedition from Monterey to explore San Francisco Bay. First white men to see San Joaquin and Sacramento Valleys.
Sept. 1. Father Serra founds Misión San Luis Obispo de Tolosa.

1773   Aug. 19. Thirty miles S. of present Mexican border, Father Francisco Palóu sets cross to mark Baja and Alta California boundary.

1774   March 22. Juan Bautista de Anza reaches San Gabriel Mission from Sonora by overland route.

1775   Aug. 1. First white man to enter San Francisco Bay: Juan Manuel de Ayala, in ship *San Carlos*.
Aug. 16. By royal decree Monterey becomes capital of California.
Nov. 4. 800 Indians attack San Diego mission, kill Father Luis Jaume and burn buildings.
Dec. 24. Woman of Anza's party of colonists, en route from Sonora to San Francisco, gives birth to son, Salvator Ignacio Linares, first white child born in California.

1776   March 28. Anza, with 247 colonists, reaches site of San Francisco. The presidio of San Francisco founded Sept. 17. Two missions, San Francisco de Asis (Dolores) and San Juan Capistrano, founded.

1777   Jan. 12. Misión Santa Clara founded.
Nov. 29. San José de Guadalupe, first pueblo in California, founded.

1779   June 1. Governor Felipe de Neve drafts regulations for government of California.

1781   Sept. 4. Los Angeles founded.

1782   March 31. Misión San Buenaventura founded.

1784   Aug. 28. Father Serra dies and is buried at San Carlos Borromeo Mission.

1786   Sept. 14. Jean François Galaup de la Pérouse brings French scientific expedition into Monterey. Severely condemns mission system.

1786–91   Father Fermin Francisco de Lasuen, who succeeds Serra, founds four missions: Santa Barbara, La Purisma Concepcion, Santa Cruz, and La Soledad.

1791   Sept. 13. John Groeham (Graham), first American in California, reaches Monterey, ill; dies same day.

1792   Nov. 14. Captain George Vancouver, in British sloop *Discovery,* reaches San Francisco—first of his three visits to California.

1793   Pueblo of Branciforte founded on site of Santa Cruz.

1796   Oct. 29. Yankee skipper, Ebenezer Dorr, brings his ship, the *Otter,* into Monterey Bay—first American ship in California waters.

1797–98   Five missions founded: San Jose, San Juan Bautista, San Miguel Arcangel, San Fernándo Rey de Espana, and San Luis Rey de Francia.

1803   June 26.   Father de Lasuen dies at Misión San Carlos.

1804   Baja and Alta California separated.   Monterey is made capital of Alta California.   Santa Ines (Ynez) Mission founded.

1806   April 5.   Nikolai Petrovich Rezanof comes to San Francisco to buy supplies for Russian trading post at Sitka.   Presidio commander reluctantly permits sale.

1810   Mexicans revolt against Spain.

1811   Oct. 15.   San Joaquin and Sacramento rivers explored for first time by water.

1812   Fort Ross, Russian trading post, is built less than 100 miles north of San Francisco.

1816   Jan. 15.   Thomas Doak lands from *Albatross*, near Santa Barbara; becomes California's first American settler.

1817   Dec. 14.   Misión San Rafael Arcangel founded.

1818   Nov. 20.   Hippolyte de Bouchard brings two ships of war into Monterey Bay.   Captures city Nov. 22, sacks it; later attacks other coast towns, is resisted at San Diego; sails away.

1820   Population of Upper California 3,270.   Neophyte (Indian slave) population of missions 20,500.

1821   Feb.   Augustin Iturbide leads rebel army into Mexico City.   Becomes ruler.
       Oct.   Luis Arguello makes first extensive exploration of Sacramento Valley.

1822   April.   Monterey and other California garrisons lower Spanish flag; recognize Iturbide regency.
       Sept. 26.   California formally proclaimed province of Empire of Mexico.
       Nov. 9.   First provincial legislature elected; meets in Monterey.
       Nov. 22.   Luis Antonio Arguello, first native-born California governor, elected.

1823   July 4.   San Francisco Solano, 21st and last of Alta California missions, founded.

1824   Jan. 7.   News of abdication of Emperor and of establishment of the Republic of Mexico is received in Monterey.

1825   March 26.   California formally becomes a territory of the Mexican Republic.

1826   Nov. 6.   Captain Frederick William Beechey, of British Navy, maps San Francisco Bay.
       Nov. 27.   Jedediah S. Smith, with trappers, arrives at Misión San Gabriel; first Americans to make overland trip to California.

1830   Population of California 4,256.

1831   Nov. 29.   Pio Pico, Juan Bandini, and José Antonio Carrillo lead revolt against Governor Manuel Victoria, forcing his resignation.

1833   Aug. 17.   Mexican Congress decrees secularization of missions. (Completed in 1837.)

1834   Sept. 1.   Two hundred Mexican colonists arrive at San Diego from San Blas.

1835   May 23. Los Angeles is raised from pueblo to city status.

June 24. Algerez Mariano G. Vallejo founds presidio and pueblo at Misión San Francisco Solano. Names settlement *Sonoma*.

United States offers to buy California.

1836   Nov. 3. Don Juan Bautista Alvarado and José Castro lead revolt. Castro becomes governor.

Nov. 8. California *diputacion* issues declaration of independence. California remains free State for eight months.

1839   July 1. John Augustus Sutter, Swiss, lands in San Francisco. In 1840 acquires 11 sq. leagues of land, comprising New Helvetia, and builds Sutter's Fort. In 1841 acquires Russian property, Fort Ross, ending Russian encroachment in California.

1840   March 10. First Supreme Court of California, *Tribunal de Justicia,* is formed.

April 7. Arrest of Isaac Graham, American trapper settled in California, is followed by imprisonment of all "foreigners" (47) not married to California women. Graham acquitted of treason and released June 1841.

1841   Aug. 14. Wilkes expedition (first U. S. scientific expedition) arrives in San Francisco. James A. Dana, of party, writes of gold found in American River, confirming earlier reports.

Nov. 4. First overland immigrant train (Bidwell-Bartleson party), from midwestern U. S., arrives in California.

1842   March 9. Francisco Lopez, sheep-herder, discovers placer gold in Santa Feliciana (Placercita) Canyon. Twenty ounces of gold dust sent (Nov. 22) to Philadelphia mint, by Abel Stearns and Alfred Robinson, is first gold sent out of California.

Oct. 19. Believing U. S. and Mexico are at war, Commodore Thomas Catesby Jones, U. S. N., seizes Monterey and raises American flag. Two days later he apologizes and departs.

1843   May 1. Thomas Larkin, first and only U. S. consul to California (1843-46), appointed.

1844   March 8. Capt. John Charles Frémont, U. S. Army, arrives at Sutter's Fort.

Nov. 14. Californians start revolt which forces Governor Micheltorena's abdication.

Dec. 13. First wagon train over Truckee and Donner Lake route reaches Sutter's Fort.

1845   July 10. Further immigration of Americans to California forbidden by Mexican Government.

First wedding of Americans in California: Mary Peterson and James Williams, both from Missouri.

1846   March 6. Frémont raises American flag on Gabilan Peak, near Monterey. Ordered to leave California, he retreats on third night to Sutter's Fort.

May 13. War between U. S. and Mexico declared.

June 3. Col. Stephen W. Kearny is ordered to march to California from Santa Fé and take command of U. S. forces there.

June 14. The Bear Flag of "California Republic" is raised at Sonoma. Frémont takes command of Bear Flag revolt on July 5, declaring California's independence.

July 7. Commander John D. Sloat raises American flag at Monterey; California formally declared a possession of U. S.

July 9. American flag replaces Bear Flag at Sonoma.

Aug. 15. *Californian,* first California newspaper, is published in Monterey.

Sept. 23. American garrison at Los Angeles attacked by rebellious Californians. General uprising, led by Captain José María Flores, follows. In first battle, at Chino Rancho, Americans are routed.

Oct. 31. Donner party of immigrants halted by heavy snows at Donner Lake. Before rescue party arrives 39 of 87 members die.

1847 Jan. 9. At La Mesa last battle of rebellion won by U. S. forces; articles of capitulation signed at Rancho Cahuenga 4 days later.

Jan. 19. John C. Frémont becomes first American Governor of California, appointed by Com. Robert F. Stockton. Forty days later he is removed by Kearny; in August, is arrested at Fort Leavenworth, Kans., court-martialed and sentenced to dismissal from Army. Sentence later remitted but Frémont declines clemency and resigns.

1848 Jan. 24. James Wilson Marshall, building sawmill for Sutter on the American River, discovers the gold which starts California "gold-rush."

Feb. 2. Treaty of Guadalupe Hidalgo, ending war with Mexico, is signed. United States acquires California, New Mexico, Nevada, Utah, most of Arizona and part of Colorado.

Oct. 14. Town of Sacramento is founded by Sutter's son.

Nov. 9. First U. S. post office in California opened in San Francisco. White population of California about 15,000.

1849 Feb. 28. *California,* first steamer to bring "Gold Rush" passengers, comes into San Francisco with 365 passengers.

Aug. 17. Regular service between San Francisco and Sacramento begun, with *George Washington.*

Sept. 1. Forty-eight delegates convene in Colton Hall, Monterey, to draft State Constitution (adopted Oct. 10, signed Oct. 13, ratified Nov. 13).

Oct. 25. Democratic Party organized. Peter H. Burnett nominated for Governor; elected Nov. 13.

Dec. 24. San Francisco's first great fire destroys 50 houses.

1850 Feb. 4. Jayhawkers, an immigrant party, reach San Francisquito Ranch, after great suffering in Death Valley.

Feb. 18. Legislature creates original 27 counties.

April 22. Legislature passes law to protect rights of Indians.

Aug. 14. Armed squatters riot in Sacramento in dispute over validity of Sutter's grant.

Sept. 9. President Fillmore signs act of Congress admitting California as a State into the Union.

Population 92,597 (U. S. Census).

1851   March 3. Land commission appointed.

March 25. Chasing band of raiding Indians, Major James D. Savage discovers Yosemite Valley.

June 9. Vigilantes organize in San Francisco under Sam Brannan.

Aug. 31. *Flying Cloud,* famous Yankee clipper, arrives in San Francisco 81 days, 21 hours, after leaving New York.

1853   March 3. Congress authorizes survey of railroad route from Mississippi River to Pacific.

1854   Feb. 25. Sacramento made capital of State.

April 3. United States opens branch mint at San Francisco ending private coinage of gold.

1855   Feb. 22. Run on bank of Page, Bacon and Co. begins panic. Stringency becomes State-wide and lasts for two years.

Aug. 7. "Know Nothing" or "American" party hold State convention in Sacramento.

1856   Feb. 22. California's first railroad, Sacramento to Folsom, opened.

May 15. San Francisco Vigilantes reorganize on day after James King, crusading newspaper editor, is murdered by James Casey, politician; they hang Casey and drive corrupt city officials from office.

Aug. 23. First wagon road across Sierra Nevada is opened.

1857   Aug. 31. First overland stage reaches San Diego from San Antonio.

1859   Sept. 13. Senator David C. Broderick and Judge David S. Terry fight duel. Broderick is killed.

1860   April 14. San Franciscans get their first Pony Express mail. Postage $5 a half ounce.

1861   April 1. Vines of 1,400 different varieties, shipped from Europe, become nucleus of State's vineyards.

May 17. News of Fort Sumter's surrender received; California pledges its loyalty to the Union.

June 28. Central Pacific R.R. Co. of California is organized.

Oct. 24. First transcontinental telegraph line completed, ending need for Pony Express.

1867   May 13. San Francisco workers demand eight-hour day. Established for skilled labor in 1868.

1868   March 23. University of California is founded.

1869   May 10. First transcontinental railroad system, the Central Pacific and Union Pacific, completed; final spike, connecting the two railroads, is driven at Promontory, Utah.

1871   Oct. 24. "Chinese Massacre" in Los Angeles. Results in Chinese exclusion act of 1882.

1873   Jan. to June. Modoc War, California's last Indian trouble.

1877   Sept. 12. Workingmen's Party of California organized under Dennis Kearney.

1880   University of Southern California founded.

1885   Oct. 24. Orange Growers Protective Union of Southern California organized.

1886   Feb. 14. First trainload of oranges leave Los Angeles for the East.

1891   Oct. 1. Leland Stanford Jr. University opened, David Starr Jordan president.

1892   Dec. 31. Transmission of hydroelectric power from San Antonio Canyon to Pomona, 14 miles.

1896   Jan. 10. First water shipment of crude oil from Ventura to Rodeo.

1900   April 3. Work on reclamation of Imperial Valley by irrigation begins.

1903   Feb. 16. The golden poppy (*Eschscholtzia*) becomes official State flower.

1906   April 18. Great Fire, resulting from earthquake, of San Francisco.

1909   March 24. Direct Primary Law.

1910   Oct. 1. Los Angeles *Times* building dynamited. Later, two labor leaders, J. B. and J. J. McNamara, are convicted.

1911   Jan. 3. Hiram W. Johnson becomes Governor; serves two terms. (U. S. Senator for four successive terms from 1917.)
April 3. Initiative, Referendum and Recall Act is approved.
April 8. Workmen's Compensation Act passed.
Nov. 14. First woman voter in California appears at polls in Stockton.

1913   May 19. California Land Act prohibiting Japanese ownership of agricultural land is signed.

1914   Aug. 15. Panama Canal opened.

1915   Panama-California Exposition at San Diego and Panama-Pacific International Exposition at San Francisco.

1916   July 22. Bomb kills spectators of Preparedness Day parade in San Francisco. Warren K. Billings and Thomas Mooney are convicted. (Mooney is pardoned by Governor Olson on January 7, 1939.)

1926   Oct. 25. Site of University of California at Los Angeles is dedicated.

1929   Herbert Clark Hoover, of Palo Alto, Secretary of Commerce under Harding and Coolidge, becomes 31st President of the United States.

1930   Population 5,677,251.

1932   July. Tenth Olympiad opened at Los Angeles with athletes of 37 nations.

1933   Feb. 11. President Herbert Hoover, by proclamation, sets aside 1,601,800 acres in Inyo County, as Death Valley National Monument.
June. California adopts 21st Amendment to U. S. Constitution, repealing Prohibition amendment.

1934   Dec. 16. Work on All-American Canal, from Colorado River to W. of Calexico, begun.

1935   Feb. 1. Storage of Colorado River water, for California use, begun by closing gates at Boulder Dam.

1936   Nov. San Francisco-Oakland Bay Bridge opened.

1937   May. Golden Gate Bridge opened.

1938   Nov. 8. Culbert J. Olson (Democrat) elected Governor, succeeding Frank P. Merriam (Republican).

1939   Feb. 18. Golden Gate International Exposition on San Francisco Bay is opened.

A Select Reading List of California Books

Asbury, Herbert. *The Barbary Coast.* New York, 1933.

Atherton, Gertrude. *Adventures of a Novelist.* New York, 1932.

——— *California, an Intimate History.* New York, 1914 (rev. ed. 1927).

Audubon, John Woodhouse. *Audubon's Western Journal: 1849–1850.* Cleveland, 1906.

Austin, Mary. *The Land of Little Rain.* Boston, 1903. Describes the Mojave desert and adjoining regions.

Bancroft, Hubert Howe. *History of California.* 7 vols. San Francisco, 1884–90.

——— *Popular Tribunals.* San Francisco, 1890. Describes the vigilance committees of early California.

Banning, Capt. William, and George H. *Six Horses.* New York, 1930. Describes a coaching trip.

Bell, Major Horace. *On the Old West Coast.* New York, 1930.

——— *Reminiscences of a Ranger.* Los Angeles, 1881 (later ed. 1935, indexed).

Bolton, Herbert Eugene. *Anza's California Expeditions.* 5 vols. Berkeley, 1930.

——— *Spanish Exploration in the Southwest, 1542–1706.* New York, 1925.

Burbank, Luther, with Wilbur Hall. *The Harvest of the Years.* Boston, 1927. Burbank's own account of his experiments in plant breeding.

California. Works Progress Administration. Federal Writers' Project. *Death Valley.* New York, 1939.

——— *Los Angeles.* New York (1939).

——— *San Diego, a California City.* San Diego, 1937.

——— *San Francisco and the Bay Area.* New York (1939).

Carr, Harry. *Los Angeles, City of Dreams.* New York, 1935.

Chalfant, Willie A. *The Story of Inyo.* Chicago, 1922 (rev. ed. 1933). A record of Death Valley days.

Chapman, Charles E. *A History of California: the Spanish Period.* New York, 1921 (rev. ed. 1928).

Chase, J. Smeaton. *California Desert Trails.* Boston, 1919.

Chittenden, Hiram Martin. *The American Fur Trade of the Far West.* 3 vols. New York, 1902 (later ed. 1935).

Cleland, Robert Glass. *A History of California: the American Period.* New York, 1922.

Cleland, Robert Glass, and Osgood Hardy. *March of Industry.* Los Angeles, 1929.

Clemens, Samuel L. (Mark Twain). *Autobiography.* 2 vols. New York, 1924.

———— *Roughing It.* New York, 1872 (later ed. 1934). Describes a journey from St. Louis across the plains through Nevada, Utah, and California in the early 1860's.

Coblentz, Stanton A. *Villains and Vigilantes.* New York, 1936.

Colton, Walter. *Three Years in California.* New York, 1850.

Coolidge, Mary Roberts. *Chinese Immigration.* New York, 1909.

Cowan, Robert Ernest. *Forgotten Characters of Old San Francisco.* Los Angeles, 1938.

Cowan, Robert Ernest, and Robert Granniss Cowan. *A Bibliography of the History of California.* 3 vols. San Francisco, 1933.

Coyner, David H. *The Lost Trappers.* New York, 1892. Purports to be a description of adventures in the western country in the early 19th century.

Cross, Ira. B. *A History of the Labor Movement in California.* Berkeley, 1935.

Dana, Julian. *Sutter.* New York, 1934.

Dana, Richard Henry. *Two Years Before the Mast.* Boston, 1840 (later ed. 1936).

Davis, William Heath. *Seventy-five Years in California.* San Francisco, 1929.

Dawson, William Leon. *The Birds of California.* Los Angeles, 1921 (later ed. in 4 vols. 1923).

Denis, Alberta Johnston. *Spanish Alta California.* New York, 1927.

Derby, George H. *Phoenixiana.* San Francisco, 1856 (later ed. 1937).

Dobie, Charles Caldwell. *San Francisco, a Pageant.* New York, 1933.

Drake, Sir Francis, and others. *The World Encompassed.* A history of Sir Francis Drake's voyage by his nephew of the same name. London, 1628 (later ed. 1926).

Drury, Aubrey. *California, an Intimate Guide.* New York, 1935.

Eakle, Arthur Starr. *Minerals of California.* Sacramento, 1923.

Eldredge, Zoeth Skinner, ed. *History of California.* 5 vols. New York, 1915.

Englehardt, Fr. Zephyrin. *The Missions and Missionaries of California.* 4 vols. and index. San Francisco, 1908–16 (2d ed. in 2 vols. 1929–30).

Ferrier, William Warren. *Ninety Years of Education in California, 1846–1936.* Berkeley, 1937.

Forbes, Alexander. *A History of Upper and Lower California.* London, 1839 (later ed. San Francisco, 1937).

Forbes, Mrs. Harrie R. Piper. *California Missions and Landmarks.* Los Angeles, 1903 (8th ed. 1925).

Frémont, Mrs. Jessie Benton. *The Story of the Guard: a Chronicle of the War.* Boston, 1863.

Frémont, John Charles. *Memoirs of My Life.* Chicago, 1887.

Garrison, Myrtle. *Romance and History of California.* San Francisco, 1933.

Genthe, Arnold. *As I Remember.* New York, 1936.

Graves, Jackson A. *My Seventy Years in California, 1857–1927.* Los Angeles, 1927.

Gray, A. A. *History of California from 1542.* Boston, 1934.

Greenhow, Robert. *History of Oregon and California.* Boston, 1844 (4th ed. 1847).

Grinnell, Joseph, Joseph S. Dixon, and Jean M. Linsdale. *Fur-bearing Mammals of California.* 2 vols. Berkeley, 1937.

Gudde, Erwin G. *Sutter's Own Story.* New York, 1936.

Hampton, Benjamin Bowles. *A History of the Movies.* New York, 1928.

Hanna, Phil Townsend. *California through Four Centuries.* New York, 1935.

—— *Libros Californianos, or, Five Feet of California Books.* Los Angeles, 1931.

Hannaford, Donald R. *Spanish Colonial or Adobe Architecture of California, 1800–1850.* New York, 1931.

Harlan, Jacob Wright. *California '46 to '48.* San Francisco, 1888 (later ed. 1896). The writer crossed the plains in 1846, part of the way with the Donner party.

Harte, Bret. *The Letters of Bret Harte.* Boston, 1926.

Hittell, Theodore H. *History of California.* 4 vols. San Francisco, 1885-97.

Holder, Charles Frederick. *Life in the Open; Sport with Rod, Gun, Horse, and Hound in Southern California.* New York, 1906.

Hoover, Mildred Brooke. *Historic Spots in California.* Vol. III: *Counties of the Coast Range.* Stanford University, 1937.

Hopkins, Ernest Jerome. *What Happened in the Mooney Case.* New York, 1932.

Hunt, Rockwell D., and Nellie van de Grift Sanchez. *A Short History of California.* New York, 1929.

Irwin, Will. *Herbert Hoover.* New York, 1928.

Jackson, Mrs. Helen Hunt. *A Century of Dishonor; a Sketch of the United States Government's Dealings with Some of the Indian Tribes.* Boston, 1881 (later ed. 1905).

Jaeger, Edmund Carroll. *The California Deserts.* Stanford University, 1933.

James, George Wharton. *In and out of the Old Missions of California.* Boston, 1905 (rev. ed. 1927).

Jepson, Willis Linn. *A Manual of the Flowering Plants of California.* Berkeley, 1925.

—— *The Trees of California.* San Francisco, 1909 (2d ed. 1923).

Jordan, David Starr, and Vernon L. Kellogg. *The Scientific Aspects of Luther Burbank's Work.* San Francisco, 1909.

Kemble, Edward C. *A History of California Newspapers.* New York, 1927.

Kroeber, Alfred L. *Handbook of the Indians of California.* Washington, D. C., 1925. (Bureau of American Ethnology. Bulletin No. 78.)

Lewis, Oscar. *The Big Four*. New York, 1938. Describes Huntington, Stanford, Hopkins, and Crocker, and the building of the Central Pacific Railroad.

London, Mrs. Charmian. *The Book of Jack London*. 2 vols. New York, 1921.

Lyman, George D. *Ralston's Ring; California Plunders the Comstock Lode*. New York, 1937.

Manly, William Lewis. *Death Valley in '49*. San Jose, 1894 (rev. ed. 1929).

Mayo, Morrow. *Los Angeles*. New York, 1933.

Mitchell, Sydney B. *Gardening in California*. Garden City, N. Y., 1923.

Morley, Prof. S. Griswold. *The Covered Bridges of California*. Berkeley, 1928.

Muir, John. *John of the Mountains; the Unpublished Journals of John Muir*. Boston, 1938.

—— *The Mountains of California*. New York, 1894 (later ed. 1911).

—— *The Yosemite*. New York, 1912.

Neville, Amelia. *The Fantastic City San Francisco*. Boston, 1932.

Nevins, Allan. *Frémont, the World's Greatest Adventurer*. New York, 1928.

Newmark, Harris. *Sixty Years in Southern California, 1853–1913*. New York, 1916 (3d ed. 1930).

Older, Fremont. *My Own Story*. New York, 1919 (3d ed. 1926). The author was editor of the San Francisco *Call-Bulletin*.

Paine, Albert Bigelow. *Mark Twain, a Biography*. 3 vols. New York, 1912.

Palou, Francisco. *Historical Memoirs of New California*. 4 vols. Berkeley, 1926. First printed in 1857 in the *Diario oficial* of Mexico.

—— *Life and Apostolic Labors of the Venerable Father Junipero Serra, Founder of the Franciscan Missions of California*. Pasadena, 1913. First printed in 1787 in Mexico.

Parsons, Mary Elizabeth. *The Wild Flowers of California*. San Francisco, 1902 (later ed. 1914).

Pattie, James O. *Personal Narrative*. Cincinnati, 1831 (later ed. 1930). Purports to be an account of six years' hazardous travel from St. Louis to the Pacific Ocean and back through Mexico.

Powell, L. C. *An Introduction to Robinson Jeffers*. Dijon, France, 1932.

Reed, Ralph Daniel. *Geology of California*. Tulsa, Okla., 1933.

Rensch, H. E., E. G. Rensch, and Mildred Brooke Hoover. *Historic Spots in California*. Vol. I: *The Southern Counties*. Vol. II: *Valley and Sierra Counties*. Stanford University, 1932 and 1933.

Richman, Irving Berdine. *California under Spain and Mexico, 1535–1847*. Boston, 1911.

Rider, Fremont, ed. *Rider's California; a Guidebook for Travelers*. New York, 1925.

Ritchie, Robert Welles. *The Hell-roarin' Forty-niners*. New York, 1928.

Robinson, Alfred. *Life in California before the Conquest*. New York, 1846 (later ed. 1925).

Rourke, Constance M. *Troupers of the Gold Coast; or, The Rise of Lotta Crabtree.* New York, 1928.

Royce, Josiah. *California from the Conquest in 1846 to the Second Vigilance Committee in San Francisco (1856).* Boston, 1886 (later ed. 1892).

Sanchez, Nellie van de Grift. *Spanish and Indian Place Names of California, Their Meaning and Their Romance.* San Francisco, 1914.

Saunders, Charles Francis. *Finding the Worth While in California.* New York, 1916 (5th ed. 1937).

Scherer, James A. B. *The Japanese Crisis.* New York, 1916.

Shinn, C. H. *Mining-camps. A Study in American Frontier Government.* New York, 1885.

Sinclair, Upton. *American Outpost; a Book of Reminiscences.* New York, 1932.

———— *The EPIC Plan for California.* New York, 1934. EPIC stands for "End Poverty in California."

Soulé, Frank, John H. Gihon, and James Nisbet. *The Annals of San Francisco.* New York, 1855.

Starrett, Vincent. *Ambrose Bierce.* Chicago, 1920.

Stewart, George Rippey. *Ordeal by Hunger; the Story of the Donner Party.* New York, 1936.

———— *Bret Harte, Argonaut and Exile.* Boston, 1931.

Stewart, J. A. *Robert Louis Stevenson, His Work and His Personality.* 2 vols. New York, 1924.

Stoddard, Charles Warren. *In the Footprints of the Padres.* San Francisco, 1902 (rev. ed. 1912).

Stone, Irving. *Sailor on Horseback: the Biography of Jack London.* Boston, 1938.

Talbot, Clare. *Historic California in Book-plates.* Los Angeles, 1936.

Taylor, Bayard. *Eldorado; or, Adventures in the Path of Empire.* New York, 1850 (rev. ed. 1882).

Thomas, William H. *On Land and Sea; or, California in the Years 1843, '44, and '45.* Chicago, 1892.

Vancouver, George. *A Voyage of Discovery to the North Pacific Ocean, and Round the World . . . in the Years 1790-95.* 3 vols. London, 1798.

Walker, Franklin. *Frank Norris.* Garden City, N. Y., 1932.

White, Stewart Edward. *The Forty-niners; a Chronicle of the California Trail and El Dorado.* New Haven, 1918.

———— *The Story of California.* Garden City, N. Y., 1932 (later ed. 1937).

Woon, Basil. *Incredible Land: a Jaunty Baedeker to Hollywood and the Great Southwest.* New York, 1933.

———— *San Francisco and the Golden Empire.* New York, 1935.

Young, John P. *History of San Francisco.* 2 vols. Chicago, 1913.

———— *Journalism in California.* San Francisco, 1915.

Index

(Where more than one page number is given, the first number is the principal reference.)

La Brea Pits, 19-20, 225
La Habra, 399
La Honda, 330
La Jolla, 408
La Mesa, 644
La Panza, 390
La Porte, 53
La Verne, 619
Labor, 95-108; McNamara case, 100-1,
  63; Westwood strike, 531; Working-
  men's Party, 58-9, 97-8, 273, 447 (see
  also Migratory Workers)
Ladybug Canyon, 622
Lafayette, 586-7
Laguna Beach, 423
Laguna Junction, 643
Laguna Post Office, 643
Lakeport, 410
Lakeside, 588
Lakes: Almanor, 506; Arrowbear, 617;
  Arrowhead, 617; Blue, 410; Bristol
  Dry, 611; Britton, 502; Castaic, 451;
  Castle, 434; Clear, 410; Convict,
  516; Gold, 475; Henshaw, 541;
  Huntington, 445; Ivanpah, 603; Lit-
  tle, 520; Ludlow Dry, 612; Malibu,
  397; Mammouth, 516; Manzanita,
  503; Mirror, 673; Muroc Dry, 606;
  Reflection, 503; Sabrina, 517; Sher-
  wood, 396; South, 517; Tahoe, 16,
  588; Tenaya, 677; Troy Dry, 612;
  Weber, 507; Yosemite, 444
Lakeview Station, 603
Lancaster, 546
Las Cruces, 393
Las Flores, 405
Las Plumas, 536
Lassen Camp, 532
Lassen Peak, 504-5
Lassen, Peter, 465, 504, 529; grave of,
  531
Last Chance, 566-7
Lawndale, 369
Laws (P.O.), 544
Laytonville, 357
Lea, Homer, 377
Lebec, 451
Leevining, 515
Leland Stanford Junior Museum, 376
Lemoore, 446
Lenwood, 612
Lick Observatory, 381
Likely, 510
Lincoln, 469
Lincoln Mine, 488-9
Lindsay, 448
Little Rock, 568
Live Oak, 467
Livermore, 597
Livingston, 443

Lodi, 441
Loleta, 354
Lompoc, 347
Lompoc Valley, 347
London, Jack, 147, 242, 274, 361, 584
Lone Pine, 519
Longbarn, 513
Long Beach, 201-5
Longville, 535
Lookout Point, 351
Loomis, 569-70
Los Alamos, 392
Los Altos, 378
Los Angeles, 206-29; 13; Airport, 418;
  Harbor, 420
Los Angeles Aqueduct, 452, 518, 544,
  606
Los Angeles County Fair Grounds, 633
Los Gatos, 382
Los Molinos, 465
Los Nietos, 398
Lost Hills, 607
Lower Lake, 411
Loyalton, 475
Lucia, 345
Ludlow, 611
Lugo House, 215
Lyon Pony Express Museum, 620

McArthur, 550
McCloud, 501
McCloud Ice Caves, 501
Macdoel, 463
McFarland, 448
McPherson, Aimee Semple, 213
Madeline, 511
Madera, 444
Madrone, 383
Mahogany Flats, 649
Malaga, 445
Malibu, 415
Mammoth Cave, 558
Mammoth Post Office, 516
Manchester, 321
Manhattan Beach, 419
Manteca, 441
Manzanar, 519
Marble Mountain Primitive Area, 428
March Field, 522-3
Mare Island Navy Yard, 414
Maricopa, 471
Marine Stadium, 205
Mariposa, 444
Markham, Edwin, 302
Markleville, 494
Marsh, John, 582-3
Marshall, James W., 484-5, 53-4, 251,
  270, 472, 481
Martel, 489
Martin, Samuel, 573-4

Martinez, 585
Marysville, 467
Maxwell, 439
May Loomis Memorial Museum, 503
Meadow Valley, 535
Mecca, 458
Meloland, 639
Melones, 494-5
Mendocino, 319
Menlo Park, 374-5
Merced, 444
Merced River, 443
Meyers, 589-90
Micheltorena, Manuel, 49
Michigan Bluff, 484
Middletown, 411
Midway, 605
Migratory Workers, 69, 358, 441, 461-2, 640
Milford, 512
Millbrae, 369
Miller, Henry, 383-4
Miller, Joaquin, 144, 243
Millers Corner, 614
Mills House, Darius Ogden, 369-70
Mill Valley, 366
Millville, 503
Milpitas, 600
Mineral, 532
Mineral Bar, 569
Mineral King, 447
Mining towns, 474
Mira Loma, 632
Miranda, 356
Mission Beach, 408
Missions: 45, 69, 79, 131, 155; architecture, 167-8; Dolores, 291-2, 270; Indian resentment against, 37; Nuestra Senora de la Soledad, 388; Purisima Concepcion, 347-8; 636-7; Royal Presidio Chapel (Monterey), 233; San Antonio de Padua, 388-9; San Buenaventura, 394; San Carlos, 343; San Carlos de Monterey, 232; San Diego de Alcala, 528, 44; San Emigdio, 451; San Fernando Rey de Espana, 453; San Francisco de Asis, 362; San Francisco de Solano, 363, 362; San Gabriel Arcangel, 621, 398, 457; San Jose, 598-9; San Juan Bautista, 384; San Juan Capistrano, 404; San Luis Obispo De Tolosa, 391; San Luis Rey, 406; San Miguel Arcangel, 389; San Rafael Arcangel, 365, 362; Santa Barbara, 308-9; Santa Clara de Asis, 380-1; Santa Ynez, 392; secularization, 37-8, 46-7; Yuma Indian, 637
Mission San José (town), 598-9

Mitchell's Caverns, 610
Modesto, 443
Modoc War, 559-60
Moffett Field, 369
Mohawk, 534
Mojave, 545
Mojave Desert, 602, 11, 19, 609-10
Mojave Water Camp, 612
Mokelumne Hill, 490
Mono Craters, 516
Mono Lake, 515
Monogram Village, 546
Monolith, 606
Monoville, 515
Monrovia, 619
Montalvo, 396
Montara, 332
Montebello, 398
Monteciot, 393
Monterey, 230-36; capture of, 338-9; climate of, 13; Presidio of, 231
Monterey Park, 634
Monte Rio, 361
Montez, Lola, 482, 161, 477, 507
Montezuma Mine, 487
Montgomery Creek, 552
Mooney, Thomas, 102-3, 63, 115, 274, 276
Morena Resort, 643
Moreno Badlands, 631
Morettis, 541
Morgan, 616-17, 270, 595, 602, 615
Morgan Hill, 383
Morgan Mine, 494
Morgan Springs, 532
Morro, 346
Morro Rock, 346
Morrow Cove, 414
Mosaic Canyon, 650
Moss Beach, 332
Moss Brae Falls, 434
Moss Landing, 339
Mother Lode, 473-74, 484
Motion Picture Studios, 198
Mountain House, 596
Mountain Theater, 367
Mountain View, 378
Mount Bullion, 500
Mount Ecclesia, 406
Mount Eden, 599
Mount Hermon, 379
Mount Ophir, 500
Mount Shasta, 432
Mount Shasta City, 432
Mount Tamalpais, 366
Mount Wilson, 623
Mount Wilson Observatory, 623
Mountain Springs, 610
Mountain Springs Gas Station, 642
Movies, 120-30; on location, 613

Pomona, 618-9; Redlands, 456; San Diego, 644; San Francisco (College), 291; San Francisco College for Women, 290; San Francisco University, 290-1; San Jose, 301-2; Santa Ana, 403; Santa Barbara, 308; Santa Clara, 380; Scripps, 619; Southern California, 228; Stanford, Hopkins Marine Station, 340-1; Whittier, 399
Upland, 618
Upper Lake, 410

Vacaville, 572
Valdez, Capt. Juan, 638
Vallecito, 641
Vallejo, 413-4
Vallejo, Casa Grande, 364-5
Vallejo Casa Materna, 338
Vallejo Home State Monument, 364
Vallejo Home (Sonama), 363
Vallejo, Mariano, 413-4, 49, 131, 324, 362, 363, 364, 573, 574
Valley Ford, 325
Vallicito, 493
Valyermo, 615
Vasquez Caves, 546
Vasquez, Tiburcio, 385, 235
Venice, 417-8
Ventura, 394
Veterans' Administration Facility, 453
Vichy Springs, 358
Victorville, 613-4
Vigilantes, 55, 107, 112-3, 271-2, 356
Vina, 465
Virginia Lake Junction, 515
Visalia, 447
Vista, 526
Vizcaino, Sebastian, 305-6, 4, 43, 231, 260, 343
Volcano, 590-1

Walker, Joseph, 450, 512, 661, 670-1, 676
Walker Pass, 450
Walnut Creek, 585
Walnut Grove, 581
Warm Springs, 600
Warner Bros. Studios, 453
Warner Hot Springs, 541
Warner Valley, 531
Warner's Ranch, 540
Wasco, 607
Watchorn Lincoln Memorial, 457
Watsonville, 337-8
Wawona, 675
Wawona Point, 675

Wawona Tunnel, 675
Weather Bureau Observatory, 566
Weaverville, 555-6
Weber, Charles M., 312
Weberville, 487
Weed, 432
Weitchpec, 429
Welton Stanford Art Gallery, 376
Weott, 356
Westmoreland, 461
Westport, 318
Westwood, 199-200, 531
Whaling Station, Monterey, 235
Wheatland, 468-9
Wheaton Springs, 603
Whiskey Town, 554
White Rock, 594
White, Stewart Edward, 275
White Water, 629
Whitney, Mount, 519
Whittier, 399
Wild Rose Springs, 650
Wild Rose Station, 650
Williams, 439
Willits, 357
Willows, 439
Wilmington, 421
Winchester Mystery House, 382
Windmill Station, 603
Winebarrel Church, 359
Winterhaven, 637
Witch Creek, 527
Wolfskill, William, 614
Woodford, 607
Woodfords, 590
Woodland, 440
Woodside Store, 330
Workingmen's Association (see Labor)
Workman's Bar, 536
World's Tallest Tree, 355
Wrightwood, 615
Wrigley, William, Jr., 424
Wynola, 541

Yankee Jim's, 483
Yerba Buena Island, 278
Yermo, 605
Yolo, 440
Yolo Bypass, 571
Yosemite Falls, 672-3
Yosemite Museum, 673
You Bet, 568
Yountville, 412
Yreka, 430
Yuba City, 467
Yuba Pass, 475
Yuha Badlands, 641
Yucca Grove, 603-4

ABOUT THE AUTHORS

The Federal Writers' Project was established in 1935 as part of Federal #1, a project to provide work relief for artists and professionals under the Works Progress Administration. In the next four years, the Project produced works on local history, folkways, and culture, in addition to the magisterial American Guide Series.

Gwendolyn Wright, author of *Building the Dream: A Social History of Housing in America* and *Moralism and the Model Home*, received her Master's and Ph.D. in architecture from the University of California, Berkeley. She has taught at Berkeley, U.C.L.A., and Stanford, and is now teaching at Columbia University.